BARR W9-DIT-318

C◯MPACT GUIDE TO C◯LLEGES

12TH EDITION

*SKIDMORE
MUHLNBERG
WILLIAMS*

Compiled and Edited by the
College Division
Barron's Educational Series, Inc.

BARRON'S

All inquiries should be addressed to:
Barron's Educational Series, Inc.
250 Wireless Boulevard
Hauppauge, New York 11788
http://www.barronseduc.com

Library of Congress Catalog Card No. 87-640101
International Standard Book No. 0-7641-1320-8
International Standard Serial No. 1065-5018

PRINTED IN THE UNITED STATES OF AMERICA

9 8 7 6 5 4 3 2

CONTENTS

PREFACE

The twelfth edition of Barron's *Compact Guide to Colleges* offers an abridged version of our very popular Barron's *Profiles of American Colleges.* Now in its twenty-fourth edition, *Profiles* presents extensive descriptions of all regionally accredited four-year colleges and universities in the United States as well as colleges in Canada and abroad. As the number of colleges has grown, so has this collection of profiles; today, the book has information on more than 1670 schools.

We realize that many students are only interested in highly competitive colleges. For this reason we have attempted to present, in this compact volume, those schools that have Selector Ratings of Most Competitive, Highly Competitive, and Very Competitive. We have also included some schools that are rated Special, usually because of art or music programs or because they have unique academic programs. Finally, we have included those institutions with the largest undergraduate enrollments. Their Selector Ratings range from Most Competitive to Noncompetitive, according to Barron's College Admission Selector and represent all levels of admissions competitiveness. (For a complete description of the Selector, see the latter part of the section An Explanation of the College Entries.) Omission of a school does not mean that the college is in any way inferior to those included.

For each of the colleges included in this book, we present a capsule of basic information—most notably, enrollment and tuition data, along with the Selector Rating of admission competitiveness—and sections that describe the environment surrounding the college, student life (including housing and sports), the programs of study offered, admissions information and procedures, financial aid and computer facilities and availability. For in-depth descriptions of the colleges presented here and other colleges, we refer you to Barron's *Profiles of American Colleges,* available at your local bookseller.

As with all our college directories, we are grateful to the college admissions officers who supplied the data. We also are grateful to the many students, parents, and high school advisers who send us their comments and suggestions.

FINDING THE RIGHT COLLEGE

When you begin to think about college, you are embarking on a major research project. You have many choices available to you in order to get the best possible education for which you are qualified. Most readers of these profiles are high school seniors or recent high school graduates planning to enroll full time in four-year colleges or universities.

Let us help make the book work for you!

THE BUYERS' MARKET

When your parents graduated from high school in the 1970s, colleges were crowded with the baby boom generation. Since then, the teenaged population has been decreasing, whereas the number and variety of colleges has continued to expand. The law of supply and demand is on your side.

Today there are about 1650 four-year colleges and universities, of which 130 are specialized institutions, such as music and art colleges or theological seminaries. Most existing institutions have grown larger, and many have expanded their programs, offering master's and doctoral degrees as well as bachelor's.

Total graduate and undergraduate students has also grown, from under 4 million in 1960 to more than 14.3 million today. Almost half are part-time students, including many working adults; their numbers have been increasing since the 1960s and 1970s. Part-time enrollments are mostly concentrated in the two-year colleges, which enroll about a third of all students.

You Are In Demand

Four-year colleges and universities doubled their enrollments in the 1960s and 1970s, and they still need to fill their classrooms and dormitories with full-time students between 18 and 22 years of age. Such students are getting harder to find. The number of high school seniors hit an all-time high of 3.1 million in 1977. Based on current projections, graduating classes will fall to 2.3 million in the 21st century. That's why institutions are recruiting so vigorously, sending you mailings, visiting your high schools, and setting up displays at college fairs. They need you as much as you need them.

MAKING A SHORT LIST

You have probably already started a list of colleges you know about from friends or relatives who have attended them, from recommendations by teachers, or by their academic or athletic reputations. This list will grow as you read the profiles, receive college mailings, and attend college fairs. If you are interested in preparing for a very specific career, such as engineering, agriculture, health care, or architecture, you should add only institutions that offer that program. If you want to study business, teacher education, or the arts and sciences, almost every college can provide a suitable major. Either way, your list will soon include dozens of institutions. Most students apply to between two and five colleges. In order to narrow your list, you should follow a three-step process:

- **Check your realistic options,** eliminating colleges at which you would not qualify for admission and those that are beyond your family's financial means.
- **Screen the list** according to your preferences, such as institutional size, type, and location.
- **Evaluate the institutions,** using published information and campus visits to make judgments about which colleges can give you the best quality and value.

The following sections will guide you through each of these steps.

REALISTIC OPTIONS

Admissions Competitiveness

The first question most students ask about a college is, "How hard is it to get in?" It should certainly not be the last question. Admissions competitiveness is not the only, or even the most important, measurement of institutional quality. It makes sense to avoid wasting time, money, and useless disappointment applying to institutions for which you clearly are not qualified. Nevertheless, there are many colleges for which you are qualified, and you can make a good choice from among them. The buyer's market has not necessarily forced admission standards down everywhere. The most prestigious institutions are rarely affected by market conditions. Some of the better known public colleges and universities have raised their admission standards in recent years, as their lower prices have attracted larger numbers of applicants. But there remain hundreds of fine public and private colleges, with good local reputations, that will welcome your application.

Use the College Admissions Selector to compare your qualifications to the admissions competitiveness of the institutions of your list. Make sure you read the descriptions of standards very carefully. Even if you meet the stated qualifications for *Most Competitive* or *Highly Competitive* institutions, you cannot assume that you will be offered admission. These colleges receive applications from many more students than they can enroll and reject far more than they accept. When considering colleges rated *Very Competitive* or *Competitive*, remember that the median test scores identify the middle of the most recent freshman class; half of the admitted students had scores lower than the median, and half were above. If your high school grades and class rank are within the stated range, and your SAT I and ACT scores are even a little below the stated median, your chances of acceptance are very good. Students in the top quarter of their high school classes who score above 1200 on the SAT I or 26 on the ACT qualify for acceptance at the *Very Competitive* colleges and universities.

Students of average ability are admissible to most of the colleges and universities rated as *Competitive* and to virtually all of those rated as *Less Competitive*. They would need high school grades of C+ or better and SAT I total scores of about 1000 or ACT composite scores above 21.

Cost

The cost of the most expensive colleges and universities is approaching $30,000 a year. This is widely publicized and very frightening, especially to your parents. But you don't have to spend that much for a good education. Most private colleges charge between $15,000 and $19,000 a year for tuition and room and board. Public institutions generally cost between $7000 and $10,000 a year for in-state residents. Because many states have been cutting budgets in recent years, tuition at public institutions is now rising faster than at private ones. If you can commute to school from home, you can save about $3500 to $4500 in room and board, but should add the cost of transportation. The least expensive option is to attend a local community college for two years, at about $1000 a year, and then transfer to a four-year institution to complete your bachelor's degree. Depending on what you may qualify for in financial aid, and what your family is willing to sacrifice, you may have more choices than you think.

SCREEN BY PREFERENCE

The self-knowledge tests should indicate whether you are more likely to be comfortable far from or near to home, at an urban or rural campus, coed or single sex, or small or large college. It is best, however, not to eliminate any options without at least visiting a few campuses of different types to judge their feeling and style firsthand. Choosing the proper institutional size and whether to live on campus or commute from home are more complicated questions.

Large Universities and Small Colleges

Only one-fifth of American colleges and universities have enrollments of 5000 or more, but they account for more than half the 7 million plus students who are pursuing bachelor's degrees. The rest are spread out among more than 1000 smaller schools. There are advantages and disadvantages that go with size.

At a college of 5000 or fewer students, you will get to know the campus quickly. You will not have to compete with many other students for the use of the library or when registering for courses. You can get to know your professors personally and become familiar with most of your fellow students. On the other hand, you may have little privacy and a limited choice of activities. Students at small schools often feel pressure to conform to prevailing customs.

As colleges and universities enroll more students, they offer a greater variety of courses, professors, facilities, and activities. Within a large campus community, you can probably find others who share your special interests and form a circle of good friends. But you may also find the libraries more crowded, many classes closed out, and competition very stiff for athletic teams or musical groups.

Many of the largest institutions are universities offering Ph.Ds., medicine, law, or other doctoral programs as well as bachelor's and master's degrees. Many colleges that do not offer these programs call themselves universities; and a few universities, Dartmouth among them, continue to call themselves colleges. Don't go by the name, but by the academic program. Universities emphasize research. University faculty need specialized laboratory equipment, computers, library material, and technical assistance for their research.

Because this is very expensive, universities usually charge higher tuition than colleges, even to their undergraduate students. Tuition at public universities can run 25 to 100 percent more than at public colleges in the same state. Private universities generally charge about 50 percent more than similarly located private colleges. In effect, undergraduates at universities subsidize the high cost of graduate programs. Freshmen and sophomores usually receive some instruction from graduate student assistants and fellows, who are paid to be apprentice faculty members.

However, most private universities and many public ones have extensive reputations. They have larger and more up-to-date libraries, laboratories, computers, and other special resources than colleges. They attract students from many states and countries and provide a rich social and cultural environment.

Living On and Off Campus

Deciding whether you will stay in a dormitory or at home is more than a matter of finances or how close to the college you live. You should be aware that students who live on campus, especially during the freshman year, are more likely to pass their courses and graduate than students who commute from home. Campus residents spend more time with faculty members, have more opportunity to use the library and laboratories, and are linked to other students who help one another with their studies. Residence hall life usually helps students mature faster as they participate in social and organizational activities.

About 25 percent of college freshmen live with their parents. If you commute to school, you can get maximum benefits from your college experience by spending time on campus between and after classes. If you need a part-time job, get employment in the college library, offices, or dining halls. Use the library to do homework in an environment that may be less distracting than at home. If possible, have some dinners on campus, to make friends with other students and participate in evening social and cultural events. Get involved in campus activities, participating in athletics, working on the newspaper, attending a meeting, or rehearsing a play.

If you will be living on campus, you may be able to choose among different types of residence buildings. Small dormitories are two to four stories high and house 250 or fewer students. They foster more quiet and privacy than larger buildings. High-rise units can house 1000 or more. They usually offer dining halls, snack bars, game rooms, and laundries all under one roof. Most older halls provide single or double rooms, with shared bathrooms on each floor. Newer halls frequently offer suites, in which a common living/study area and bathroom are shared by eight to twelve students occupying single or double bedrooms. Some students enjoy a larger "family" group; others prefer having only one roommate.

Campus food is usually wholesome, bland, and laden with carbohydrates to meet the high energy demands of active young people. You may have a choice of food plans—perhaps 10 to 21 meals a week. Other plans allow you to prepay a fixed dollar amount and purchase food by the item rather than by the meal. Food services make most of their profits on meals that are paid for but never eaten. Choose a meal plan that fits your own eating habits. Meal plans can usually be supplemented or increased, but they rarely can be reduced or refunded. Many colleges today offer a wide variety of food including vegetarian and kosher diets as well as more salads and pasta.

Many students live off campus after their freshman or sophomore year, either by choice or because the school does not have room for them on campus. Schools try to provide listings of available off-campus rooms and apartments that meet good standards for safety and cleanliness. Many colleges also offer health care and food services to students who live off campus.

It is usually more expensive to live in an apartment than in a dormitory, especially if you plan to prepare your own meals. Great care must be taken in choosing apartment mates. In addition to the usual problems that may arise through personality conflicts, others may develop because apartment mates share payments for rent and utilities and responsibilities for cleaning, shopping, and cooking. It is much harder to find new people to share an apartment in mid-lease than it is to change roommates on campus.

GETTING THE MOST FROM YOUR CAMPUS VISIT

To learn everything important about a college, you need more than the standard presentation and tour given to visiting students and parents. Plan your visit for a weekday during the school term. This will let you see how classes are taught and how students live. It also is the best time to meet faculty and staff members, or to go to a dean's office for information. If the college does not schedule group presentations or tours at the time you want, call the office of admissions to arrange for an individual tour and interview. At the same time, ask the admissions office to make appointments with people you want to meet.

To find out about a specific academic program, ask to meet the department chairperson. If you are interested in athletics, religion, or music, meet the coach, the chaplain, or the conductor of the orchestra. Your parents will also want to talk to a financial aid counselor about scholarships, grants, and loans. The office of academic affairs can help with your questions about courses or the faculty. The office of student affairs is in charge of residence halls, health services, and extracurricular activities. Each of these areas has a dean or vice president and a number of assistants, so you should be able to get your questions answered even if you go in without an appointment.

Take advantage of a group presentation and tour if one is scheduled on the day of your visit. Much of what you learn may be familiar, but other students and parents will ask about some of the same things you want to know. Student tour guides are also good sources of information. They love to talk about their own courses, professors, and campus experiences.

Finally, explore the campus on your own. Visit the library and computer facilities, to see whether they are adequate for all the students using them. Check the condition of the buildings and the grounds. If they appear well maintained, the college probably has good overall management. If they look run-down, the college may have financial problems that also make it scrimp on the book budget or laboratory supplies. Visit a service office, such as the registrar, career planning, or academic advising. Observe whether they treat students courteously and seem genuinely interested in helping them.

Talk to some of the students who are already enrolled at the college. They will usually speak frankly about weekend activities, whether they find it easy to talk to professors out of class, and how much drinking or drug abuse there is on campus. Most importantly, meeting other students will help you discover how friendly the campus is and whether the college will suit you socially and intellectually.

More than buildings and courses of study, a college is a community of people. Only during a campus visit can you experience the human environment in which you will live and work during four critical years.

CHECKLIST QUESTIONS

The following questions form a checklist to evaluate each college or university you are considering. Use the Profiles, literature from the colleges, and your own inquiries and observations to get the answers.

I. Identify good possibilities. Only colleges for which all five answers are "Yes" should go on your final list.
   1. Is the college accredited by its regional association?
   2. Does the college offer the program I want to study?
   3. Do I have a good chance to be admitted?
   4. Can my family manage the costs?
   5. Is the location at an acceptable distance from home?

II. Compare colleges for quality and value. The more questions you answer "Yes," the better that college is for you.
A. Academics
   1. Does a majority of the faculty have doctoral degrees?
   2. Do the best research professors teach undergraduate courses?
   3. Do class sizes meet the standards described in this article?
   4. Do regular faculty members teach at least 80 percent of courses?
   5. Does the major program have enough full-time faculty members?
   6. Does the major program offer its courses on a regular schedule?
B. Support Services
   1. Is the library collection adequate for the college programs?
   2. Does the library offer good services and accessible hours?
   3. Are student computer facilities readily available?
   4. Do the people in the admissions, financial aid, and other service offices seem attentive and genuinely interested in helping students?

C. Campus Environment
1. Will I be comfortable with the size and setting of the campus?
2. Will I find activities that meet my interests?
3. Will I find the other students compatible?
4. Will I find the housing and food services suitable?
5. Does the campus seem well maintained and managed?

Sheldon Halpern
Barbara Aronson

AN EXPLANATION OF THE COLLEGE ENTRIES

The descriptions of the schools are presented in alphabetical order. For each school, the following information is presented. Bear in mind that, occasionally, certain data are not available or are not applicable. Also be aware that certain types of information, such as tuition, change continually.

THE HEADING

Name of the College
City, State, Zip Code

Phone and Fax Numbers

THE CAPSULE

The capsule of each profile provides basic information about the college at a glance. Wherever "n/av" is used in the capsule, it means the information was not available.

COMPLETE NAME OF SCHOOL **MAP CODE**
(Former Name, if any)
City, State, Zip Code **Fax and Phone Numbers**
(Accreditation Status, if a candidate)

Full-time: Full-time undergraduate enrollment
Part-time: Part-time undergraduate enrollment
Graduate: Graduate enrollment
Year: Semesters, quarters, summer sessions
Application Deadline: Fall admission deadline
Freshman Class: Number of students who applied, number accepted, number enrolled
SAT I: Median Verbal, Median Math
ACT: Median composite ACT
Faculty: Number of full-time faculty; AAUP category of school, salary-level symbol
Ph.D.s: Percentage of faculty holding Ph.D.
Student/Faculty: Full-time student/full-time faculty ratio
Tuition: Yearly tuition and fees (out-of-state if different)
Room & Board: Yearly room-and-board costs

ADMISSIONS SELECTOR RATING

Full-time, Part-time, Graduate

Enrollment figures are the clearest indication of the size of a college, and show whether or not it is coeducational and what the male-female ratio is. Graduate enrollment is presented to give a better idea of the size of the entire student body; some schools have far more graduate students enrolled than undergraduates.

Year

Some of the more innovative college calendars include the 4-1-4, 3-2-3, 3-3-1, and 1-3-1-4-3 terms. College administrators sometimes utilize various intersessions or interims—special short terms—for projects, independent study, short courses, or travel programs. The early semester calendar, which allows students to finish spring semesters earlier than those of the traditional semester calendar, gives students a head start on finding summer jobs. A modified semester (4-1-4) system provides a January or winter term, approximately four weeks long, for special projects that usually earn the same credit as one semester-long course. The trimester calendar divides the year into three equal parts; students may attend college during all three but generally take a vacation during any one. The quarter calendar divides the year into four equal parts; students usually attend for three quarters each year. The term calendar is essentially the same as the quarter calendar without the summer quarter; it has three sessions between September and June. The capsule also indicates schools that offer a summer session.

Application Deadline

Indicated here is the deadline for applications for admission to the fall semester. If there are no specific deadlines, it will say "open." Application deadlines for admission to other semesters are, where available, given in the admissions section of the profile.

Faculty

The first number given refers to the number of full-time faculty members at the college or university.

The Roman numeral and symbol that follow represent the salary level of faculty at the school as compared with faculty salaries nationally. This information is based on the salary report* published by the American Association of University Professors (AAUP). The Roman numeral refers to the AAUP category to which the particular college or university is assigned. (This allows for comparison of faculty salaries at the same types of schools.) Category I includes "institutions that offer the doctorate degree, and that conferred in the most recent three years an annual average of fifteen or more earned doctorates covering a minimum of three nonrelated disciplines." Category IIA includes "institutions awarding degrees above the baccalaureate, but not included in Category I." Category IIB includes "institutions awarding only the baccalaureate or equivalent degree." Category III includes "institutions with academic

*Source: Annual Report on the Economic Status of the Profession published in the March-April 1999 issue of *Academe:* Bulletin of the AAUP, 1012 Fourteenth St. N.W., Suite 500, Washington, D.C. 20005.

ranks, mostly two-year institutions." Category IV includes "institutions without academic ranks." (With the exception of a few liberal arts colleges, this category includes mostly two-year institutions.)

The symbol that follows the Roman numeral indicates into which percentile range the average salary of professors, associate professors, assistant professors, and instructors at the school falls, as compared with other schools in the same AAUP category. The symbols used in this book represent the following:

++$	95th percentile
+$	80th percentile
av$	60th percentile
–$	40th percentile
––$	20th percentile and below

If the school is not a member of AAUP, nothing will appear.

Ph.D.s

The figure here indicates the percentage of full-time faculty who have Ph.D.s or the highest terminal degree.

Student/Faculty

Student/faculty ratios may be deceptive because the faculties of many large universities include scholars and scientists who do little or no teaching. Nearly every college has some large lecture classes, usually in required or popular subjects, and many small classes in advanced or specialized fields. Here, the ratio reflects full-time students and full-time faculty, and some colleges utilize the services of a large part-time faculty. In general, a student/faculty ratio of 10 to 1 is very good.

If the faculty and student body are both mostly part-time, the entry will say "n/app."

Tuition

It is important to remember that tuition costs change continually and that in many cases, these changes are substantial. Particularly heavy increases have occurred recently and will continue to occur. On the other hand, some smaller colleges are being encouraged to lower tuitions, in order to make higher education more affordable. Students are therefore urged to contact individual colleges for the most current tuition figures.

The figure given here includes tuition and student fees for the school's standard academic year. If costs differ for state residents and out-of-state residents, the figure for nonresidents is given in parentheses. Where tuition costs are listed per credit hour (p/c), per course (p/course), or per unit (p/unit), student fees are not included. In some university systems, tuition is the same for all schools. However, student fees, and therefore the total tuition figure, may vary from school to school.

Room and Board

It is suggested that students check with individual schools for the most current room-and-board figures because, like tuition figures, they increase continually. The room-and-board figures given here represent the annual cost of a double room and all meals. The word "none" indicates that the college does not charge for room and board; "n/app" indicates that room and board are not provided.

Freshman Class
The numbers apply to the number of students who applied, were accepted, and enrolled in the 1999–2000 freshman class or in a recent class.

SAT I, ACT
Whenever available, the median SAT I scores—both Verbal and Mathematics—and the median ACT composite score for the 1999–2000 freshman class are given. If the school has not reported median SAT I or ACT scores, the capsule indicates whether the SAT I or ACT is required. NOTE: Test scores are reported for mainstream students.

Admissions Selector Rating
The College Admissions Selector Rating indicates the degree of competitiveness of admission to the college.

THE GENERAL DESCRIPTION

The Introductory Paragraph

This paragraph indicates, in general, what types of programs the college offers, when it was founded, whether it is public or private, and its religious affiliation. Baccalaureate program accreditation and information on the size of the school's library collection are also provided. Special facilities such as a museum and radio or TV station are also described in this paragraph.

Programs of Study

Listed here are the bachelor's degrees granted, strongest and most popular majors, and whether associate, master's, and doctoral degrees are awarded. Major areas of study have been included under broader general areas (shown in capital letters in the profiles) for quicker reference; however, the general areas do not necessarily correspond to the academic divisions of the college or university but are more career-oriented.

Special
Special programs are described here. Students at almost every college now have the opportunity to study abroad, either through their college or through other institutions. Internships with businesses, schools, hospitals, and public agencies permit students to gain work experience as they learn. The pass/fail grading option, now quite prevalent, allows students to take courses in unfamiliar areas without threatening their academic average. Many schools offer students the opportunity to earn a combined B.A.-B.S. degree, pursue a general studies (no major)

degree, or design their own major. Frequently students may take advantage of a cooperative program offered by two or more universities. Such a program might be referred to, for instance, as a 3-2 engineering program; a student in this program would spend three years at one institution and two at another. The number of national honor societies represented on campus is included. Schools also may conduct honors programs for qualified students, either university-wide or in specific major fields, and these also are listed.

Admissions

The admissions section gives detailed information on standards so you can evaluate your chances for acceptance. Where the SAT I or ACT scores of the 1999–2000 freshman class are broken down, you may compare your own scores. Because the role of standardized tests in the admissions process has been subject to criticism, more colleges are considering other factors such as recommendations from high school officials, leadership record, special talents, extracurricular activities, and advanced placement or honors courses completed. A few schools may consider education of parents, ability to pay for college, and relationship to alumni. Some give preference to state residents; others seek a geographically diverse student body.

Requirements
This subsection specifies the minimum high school class rank and GPA, if any, required by the college for freshman applicants. It indicates what standardized tests (if any) are required, whether an essay, interview, or audition is necessary, and if AP*/CLEP credit is given. If a college accepts applications on computer disk or on-line, those facts are so noted and described. Other factors used by the school in the admissions decision are also listed.

Procedure
This subsection indicates when you should take entrance exams, the application deadlines for various sessions, the application fee, and when students are notified of the admissions decision. Some schools note that their application deadlines are open; this can mean either that they will consider applications until a class is filled, or that applications are considered right up until registration for the term in which the student wishes to enroll. If a waiting list is an active part of the admissions procedure, the college may indicate what percentage of applicants are placed on that list and the number of wait-listed applicants accepted.

Financial Aid

This paragraph in each profile describes the availability of financial aid. It includes the percentage of freshmen and continuing students who

---

* Advanced Placement and AP are registered trademarks owned by the College Entrance Examination Board.
No endorsement of this product is implied or given.

receive aid, the average scholarship, loan, and work contract aid to freshmen, the average amount of need-based scholarships from all sources and the types and sources of aid available, such as scholarships, grants, loans, and work-study. It indicates if there is a formal appeal process for obtaining more money for the second semester. Aid application deadlines and required forms are also given.

Computers

This section details the make and model of the mainframe and the scope of computerized facilities that are available for academic use. Limitations (if any) on student use of computer facilities are outlined. It also gives information on the required or recommended ownership of a personal computer.

THE COLLEGE ADMISSION SELECTOR

The College Admissions *Selector Rating* groups the colleges and universities listed in *Profiles of American Colleges* according to degree of admissions competitiveness. The *Selector* is not a rating of colleges by academic standards or quality of education; it is rather an attempt to describe, in general terms, the situation a prospective student will meet when applying for admission. It includes seven categories: Most Competitive, Highly Competitive, Very Competitive, Competitive, Less Competitive, Noncompetitive, and Special. Most of the institutions in this book are in one of the top three categories.

The factors used in determining the category for each college are median entrance examination scores for the 1999–2000 freshman class (the SAT I score is derived by averaging the median verbal reasoning and the median mathematics reasoning scores; the ACT score is the median composite score); percentages of 1999–2000 freshmen scoring 500 and above and 600 and above on both the mathematical and verbal sections of the SAT I; percentages of 1999–2000 freshmen scoring 21 and above and 27 and above on the ACT; percentage of 1999–2000 freshmen who ranked in the upper fifth of their high school class and percentage who ranked in the upper two fifths; minimum class rank and grade point average (GPA) required for admission; and percentage of applicants to the 1999–2000 freshman class who were accepted. The *Selector* cannot and does not take into account all the other factors that each college considers when making admissions decisions. Colleges place varying degrees of emphasis on the factors within each of these categories.

State-supported institutions have been classified according to the requirements for state residents, but standards for admission of out-of-state students are usually higher. Colleges that are experimenting with the admission of students of high potential but lower achievement may appear in a less competitive category because of this fact.

A word of caution: The *Selector* is intended primarily for preliminary screening, to eliminate the majority of colleges that are not suitable for a particular student. Be sure to examine the admissions policies spelled out in the Admissions section of each profile. And remember that many colleges have to reject *qualified* students; the *Selector* will tell you what your chances are, not which colleges will accept you.

The following descriptions spell out the requirements for each category, but only in a general sense. A school that has very high test scores, for example, may also have low class rank and GPA requirements, which may place that school in a category lower than the scores would indicate.

Most Competitive

Even superior students will encounter a great deal of competition for admission to the colleges in this category. In general, these colleges require high school rank in the top 10% to 20% and grade averages of A to B+. Median freshman test scores at these categories are generally between 655 and 800 on the SAT I and 29 and above on the ACT. In addition, many of these colleges admit only a small percentage of those who apply—usually fewer than one third.

Highly Competitive

Colleges in this group look for students with grade averages of B+ to B and accept most of their students from the top 20% to 35% of the high school class. Median freshman test scores at these colleges range from 620 to 654 on the SAT I and 27 to 28 on the ACT. These schools generally accept between one third and one half of their applicants.

To provide for finer distinctions within this admissions category, a plus (+) symbol has been placed before some entries. These are colleges with median freshman scores of 645 or more on the SAT I or 28 or above on the ACT (depending on which test the college prefers), and colleges that accept fewer than one quarter of their applicants.

Very Competitive

The colleges in this category admit students whose averages are no less that B– and who rank in the top 35% to 50% of their graduating class. They report median freshman test scores in the 573 to 619 range on the SAT I and from 24 to 26 on the ACT. The schools in this category generally accept between one half and three quarters of their applicants.

The plus (+) has been placed before colleges with median freshman scores of 610 or above on the SAT I or 26 or above on the ACT (depending on which test the colleges prefers), and colleges that accept fewer than one third of their applicants.

Competitive

This category is a very broad one, covering colleges that generally have median freshman test scores between 500 and 572 on the SAT I and between 21 and 23 on the ACT. Most of these colleges require that students have high school averages in the C range. Generally, these colleges prefer students in the top 50% to 65% of the graduating class and accept between 75% and 85% of their applicants.

Colleges with a plus (+) are those with median SAT I scores of 563 or more or median ACT scores of 24 or above (depending on which test the college prefers), and those that admit fewer that half of their applicants.

Less Competitive

Included in this category are colleges with median freshman test scores below 500 on the SAT I and below 21 on the ACT; some colleges that require entrance examinations but do not report median scores; and colleges that admit students with averages below C who rank in the top 65% of the graduating class. These colleges usually admit 85% or more of their applicants.

Noncompetitive

The colleges in this category generally only require evidence of graduation from an accredited high school (although they may also require the completion of a certain number of high school units) or an equivalency degree. Some require that entrance examinations be taken for placement purposes only, or only by graduates of unaccredited high schools or only by out-of-state students. In some cases, insufficient capacity may compel a college in this category to limit the number of students that are accepted; generally, however, if a college accepts 98% or more of its applicants, or all of its in-state applicants, it automatically falls in this category.

Special

Listed here are colleges whose programs of study are specialized; professional schools of nursing, art, music, and other disciplines, or those oriented toward working adults. In general, the admissions requirements are not based primarily on academic criteria, but on evidence of talent or special interest in the field. Many other colleges and universities offer special-interest programs *in addition to* regular academic curricula, but such institutions have been given a regular competitive rating based on academic criteria.

KEY TO ABBREVIATIONS

DEGREES

A.A.—Associate of Arts
A.A.S.—Associate of Applied Science
A.B. or B.A.—Bachelor of Arts
A.B.J.—Bachelor of Arts in Journalism
A.S.—Associate of Science

B.A.—Bachelor of Arts
B.A.A.—Bachelor of Applied Arts
B.A.A.S. or B.Applied A.S.—Bachelor of Applied Arts and Sciences
B.Ac. or B.Acc.—Bachelor of Accountancy
B.A.C.—Bachelor of Science in Air Commerce
B.A.C.V.I.—Bachelor of Arts in Computer and Video Imaging
B.A.E. or B.A.Ed.—Bachelor of Arts in Education
B.A.G.E.—Bachelor of Arts in General Education
B.Agri.—Bachelor of Agriculture
B.A.G.S.—Bachelor of Arts in General Studies
B.A.J.S.—Bachelor of Arts in Judaic Studies
B.A.M.—Bachelor of Arts in Music
B.Applied Sc.—Bachelor of Applied Science
B.A.R.—Bachelor of Religion

B.Arch.—Bachelor of Architecture
B.Arch.Hist.—Bachelor of Architectural History
B.Arch.Tech.—Bachelor of Architectural Technology
B.Ar.Sc.—Baccalaurium Artium et Scientiae (honors college degree) (Bachelor of Arts & Sciences)
B.Art.Ed.—Bachelor of Art Education
B.A.S.—Bachelor of Applied Science
B.A.S.—Bachelor of Arts and Sciences
B.A.Sec.Ed.—Bachelor of Arts in Secondary Ed.
B.A.S.W.—B.A. in Social Work
B.A.T.—Bachelor of Arts in Teaching
B.B. or B.Bus.—Bachelor of Business
B.B.A.—Bachelor of Business Administration
B.B.E.—Bachelor of Business Education
B.C. or B.Com. or B.Comm.—Bachelor of Commerce
B.C.A.—Bachelor of Creative Arts
B.C.E.—Bachelor of Civil Engineering
B.C.E.—Bachelor of Computer Engineering
B.Ch. or B.Chem.—Bachelor of Chemistry
B.Ch.E.—Bachelor of Chemical Engineering
B.C.J.—Bachelor of Criminal Justice
B.C.M.—Bachelor of Christian Ministries
B.Church Mus.—Bachelor of Church Music
B.C.S.—Bachelor of College Studies
B.E.—Bachelor of English
B.E. or B.Ed.—Bachelor of Education
B.E.—Bachelor of Engineering
B.E.D.—Bachelor of Environmental Design
B.E.E.—Bachelor of Electrical Engineering
B.En. or B.Eng.—Bachelor of Engineering
B.E.S. or B.Eng.Sc.—Bachelor of Engineering Science
B.E.T.—Bachelor of Engineering Technology
B.F.A.—Bachelor of Fine Arts
B.G.S.—Bachelor of General Studies
B.G.S.—Bachelor of Geological Sciences
B.H.E.—Bachelor of Health Education
B.H.P.E.—Bachelor of Health and Physical Education
B.H.S.—Bachelor of Health Science
B.I.D.—Bachelor of Industrial Design
B.I.M.—Bachelor of Industrial Management
B.Ind.Tech.—Bachelor of Industrial Technology
B.Int.Arch.—Bachelor of Interior Architecture
B.Int.Design—Bachelor of Interior Design
B.I.S.—Bachelor of Industrial Safety
B.I.S.—Bachelor of Interdisciplinary Studies
B.J.—Bachelor of Journalism
B.J.S.—Bachelor of Judaic Studies
B.L.A. or B.Lib.Arts—Bachelor of Liberal Arts
B.L.A. or B.Land.Arch.—Bachelor in Landscape Architecture
B.L.I.—Bachelor of Literary Interpretation
B.L.S.—Bachelor of Liberal Studies
B.M. or B.Mus. or Mus.Bac.—Bachelor of Music
B.M.E.—Bachelor of Mechanical Engineering
B.M.E. or B.M.Ed. or B.Mus.Ed.—Bachelor of Music Education
B.Med.Lab.Sc.—Bachelor of Medical Laboratory Science
B.Min—Bachelor of Ministry
B.M.P. or B.Mu.—Bachelor of Music in Performance
B.Mus.A.—Bachelor of Applied Music
B.M.T.—Bachelor of Music Therapy
B.O.T.—Bachelor of Occupational Therapy

B.P.A.—Bachelor of Public Administration
B.P.E.—Bachelor of Physical Education
B.Perf.Arts—Bachelor of Performing Arts
B.Ph.—Bachelor of Philosophy
B.Pharm.—Bachelor of Pharmacy
B.Phys.Hlth.Ed.—Bachelor of Physical Health Education
B.P.S.—Bachelor of Professional Studies
B.P.T.—Bachelor of Physical Therapy
B.R.E.—Bachelor of Religious Education
B.R.T.—Bachelor of Respiratory Therapy
B.S. or B.Sc. or S.B.—Bachelor of Science
B.S.A. or B.S.Ag. or B.S.Agr.—Bachelor of Science in Agriculture
B.Sacred Mus.—Bachelor of Sacred Music
B.Sacred Theol.—Bachelor of Sacred Theology
B.S.A.E.—Bachelor of Science in Agricultural Engineering
B.S.A.E. or B.S.Art Ed.—Bachelor of Science in Art Education
B.S.Ag.E.—Bachelor of Science in Agricultural Engineering
B.S.A.S.—Bachelor of Science in Administrative Sciences
B.S.A.T.—Bachelor of Science in Athletic Training
B.S.B.—Bachelor of Science (business)
B.S.B.A. or B.S.Bus. Adm.—Bachelor of Science in Business Administration
B.S.Bus.—Bachelor of Science in Business
B.S.Bus.Ed.—Bachelor of Science in Business Education
B.S.C.—Bachelor of Science in Commerce
B.S.C.E. or B.S.C.I.E.—Bachelor of Science in Civil Engineering
B.S.C.E.T—B.S. in Computer Engineering Technology
B.S.Ch. or B.S.Chem. or B.S. in Ch.—Bachelor of Science in Chemistry
B.S.C.H.—Bachelor of Science in Community Health
B.S.Ch.E.—Bachelor of Science in Chemical Engineering
B.S.C.I.S.—Bachelor of Science in Computer Information Sciences
B.S.C.J.—Bachelor of Science in Criminal Justice
B.S.C.L.S.—Bachelor of Science in Clinical Laboratory Science
B.S.Comp.Eng.—Bachelor of Science in Computer Engineering
B.S.Comp.Sci. or B.S.C.S.—Bachelor of Science in Computer Science
B.S.Comp.Soft—Bachelor of Science in Computer Software
B.S.Comp.Tech.—Bachelor of Science in Computer Technology
B.Sc.(P.T.)—Bachelor of Science in Physical Therapy
B.S.C.S.T.—Bachelor of Science in Computer Science Technology
B.S.D.H.—Bachelor of Science in Dental Hygiene
B.S.Die—Bachelor of Science in Dietetics
B.S.E. or B.S.Ed. or B.S.Educ.—Bachelor of Science in Education
B.S.E. or B.S. in E. or B.S. in Eng.—Bachelor of Science in Engineering
B.S.E.E.—Bachelor of Science in Electrical Engineering
B.S.E.E.T.—Bachelor of Science in Electrical Engineering Technology
B.S.E.H.—Bachelor of Science in Environmental Health
B.S.Elect.T.—Bachelor of Science in Electronics Technology
B.S.El.Ed. or B.S. in Elem. Ed.—Bachelor of Science in Elementary Education
B.S.E.P.H.—Bachelor of Science in Environmental and Public Health
B.S.E.S.—Bachelor of Science in Engineering Science
B.S.E.S.—Bachelor of Science in Environmental Studies
B.S.E.T.—Bachelor of Science in Engineering Technology
B.S.F.—Bachelor of Science in Forestry
B.S.F.R.—Bachelor of Science in Forestry Resources
B.S.F.W.—Bachelor of Science in Fisheries and Wildlife
B.S.G.—Bachelor of Science in Geology
B.S.G.—Bachelor of Science in Gerontology
B.S.G.E.—Bachelor of Science in Geological Engineering
B.S.G.S.—Bachelor of Science in General Studies
B.S.H.C.A.—Bachelor of Science in Health Care Administration
B.S.H.E.—Bachelor of Science in Home Economics

B.S.H.F.—Bachelor of Science in Health Fitness
B.S.H.M.S.—Bachelor of Science in Health Management Systems
B.S.H.S.—Bachelor of Science in Health Sciences
B.S.H.S.—Bachelor of Science in Human Services
B.S.I.A.—Bachelor of Science in Industrial Arts
B.S.I.E.—Bachelor of Science in Industrial Engineering
B.S.I.M.—Bachelor of Science in Industrial Management
B.S. in Biomed.Eng.—Bachelor of Science in Biomedical Engineering
B.S. in C.D.—Bachelor of Science in Communication Disorders
B.S.Ind.Ed.—Bachelor of Science in Industrial Education
B.S.Ind.Tech.—Bachelor of Science in Industrial Technology
B.S. in Sec.Ed.—Bachelor of Science in Secondary Education
B.S.I.S.—Bachelor of Science in Interdisciplinary Studies
B.S.I.T.—Bachelor of Science in Industrial Technology
B.S.J.—Bachelor of Science in Journalism
B.S.L.E.—Bachelor of Science in Law Enforcement
B.S.M.—Bachelor of Science in Management
B.S.M.—Bachelor of Science in Music
B.S.M.E.—Bachelor of Science in Mechanical Engineering
B.S.Med.Tech. or B.S.M.T.—Bachelor of Science in Medical Technology
B.S.Met.E.—Bachelor of Science in Metallurgical Engineering
B.S.M.R.A.—Bachelor of Science in Medical Records Administration
B.S.M.T.—Bachelor of Science in Medical Technology
B.S.M.T.—Bachelor of Science in Music Therapy
B.S.Mt.E.—Bachelor of Science in Materials Engineering
B.S.Mus.Ed.—Bachelor of Science in Music Education
B.S.N.—Bachelor of Science in Nursing
B.S.Nuc.T.—Bachelor of Science in Nuclear Technology
B.S.O.A.—Bachelor of Science in Office Administration
B.S.O.E.—Bachelor of Science in Occupational Education
B.S.O.T.—Bachelor of Science in Occupational Therapy
B.S.P. or B.S.Pharm—Bachelor of Science in Pharmacy
B.S.P.A.—Bachelor of Science in Public Administration
B.S.Pcs.—Bachelor of Science in Physics
B.S.P.E.—Bachelor of Science in Physical Education
B.S.P.T.—Bachelor of Science in Physical Therapy
B.S.Rad.Tech.—Bachelor of Science in Radiation Technology
B.S.R.C.—Bachelor of Science in Respiratory Care
B.S.R.S.—Bachelor of Science in Radiological Science
B.S.R.T.T.—Bachelor of Science in Radiation Therapy Technology
B.S.S.—Bachelor of Science in Surveying
B.S.S.—Bachelor of Special Studies
B.S.S.A.—Bachelor of Science in Systems Analysis
B.S.Soc. Work or B.S.S.W.—Bachelor of Science in Social Work
B.S.Sp.—Bachelor of Science in Speech
B.S.S.T.—Bachelor of Science in Surveying and Topography
B.S.T. or B.S.Tech.—Bachelor of Science in Technology
B.S.S.W.E.—Bachelor of Science in Software Engineering
B.S.V.T.E.—Bachelor of Science in Vocational Technical Education
B.S.W.—Bachelor of Social Work
B.T. or B.Tech.—Bachelor of Technology
B.Th.—Bachelor of Theology
B.T.S.—Bachelor of Technical Studies
B.U.S.—Bachelor of Urban Studies
B.V.M.—Bachelor of Veterinarian Medicine
B.Voc.Arts or B.V.A.—Bachelor of Vocational Arts
B.V.E.D. or B.Voc.Ed.—Bachelor of Vocational Education

D.D.S.—Doctor of Dental Surgery

Ed.S.—Education Specialist

J.D.—Doctor of Jurisprudence

LL.B.—Bachelor of Laws

M.A.—Master of Arts
M.A.Ed.—Master of Arts in Education
M.A.T.—Master of Arts in Teaching
M.B.A.—Master of Business Administration
M.D.—Doctor of Medicine
M.F.A.—Master of Fine Arts
M.P.A.—Master of Public Administration
M.S.—Master of Science
Mus.B. or Mus.Bac.—Bachelor of Music

Ph.D.—Doctor of Philosophy

R.N.—Registered Nurse

S.B. or B.S. or B.Sc.—Bachelor of Science

REGIONAL ACCREDITING GROUPS
MSACS—Middle States Association of Colleges and Schools
NEASC—New England Association of Schools and Colleges
NCACS—North Central Association of Colleges and Schools
NASC—Northwest Association of Schools and Colleges
SACS—Southern Association of Colleges and Schools
WASC—Western Association of Schools and Colleges

INDEX BY STATE

19

20

Salisbury State University, **463**
Towson University, **534**
United States Naval Academy, **552**
University of Maryland/Baltimore
County, **600**
University of Maryland/College
Park, **601**
Washington College, **699**
Western Maryland College, **713**

MASSACHUSETTS
Amherst College, **37**
Art Institute of Boston at Lesley
College, **42**
Babson College, **48**
Bentley College, **65**
Berklee College of Music, **68**
Boston Architectural Center, **75**
Boston College, **76**
Boston University, **78**
Brandeis University, **83**
Clark University, **123**
College of the Holy Cross, **139**
Emerson College, **199**
Fisher College, **206**
Gordon College, **234**
Hampshire College, **245**
Harvard University/Harvard
College, **250**
Massachusetts College of Art, **331**
Massachusetts Institute of
Technology, **332**
Merrimack College, **338**
Mount Holyoke College, **360**
New England Conservatory of
Music, **369**
Northeastern University, **378**
Simmons College, **481**
Simon's Rock College of Bard, **483**
Smith College, **487**
Stonehill College, **516**
Tufts University, **542**
University of Massachusetts
Amherst, **604**
University of Massachusetts
Boston, **606**
Wellesley College, **707**
Wheaton College, **724**
Williams College, **729**
Worcester Polytechnic Institute, **735**

MICHIGAN
Albion College, **29**
Alma College, **34**
Center for Creative Studies/College
of Art and Design, **113**
Hillsdale College, **255**
Hope College, **261**
Kalamazoo College, **284**

Kendall College of Art and
Design, **286**
Kettering University, **289**
Michigan State University, **343**
Michigan Technological
University, **344**
University of Michigan/Ann
Arbor, **609**
University of Michigan/Dearborn, **612**
Wayne State University, **703**
Western Michigan University, **715**

MINNESOTA
Bethel College, **72**
Carleton College, **105**
College of Saint Benedict, **136**
Concordia College/Moorhead, **155**
Gustavus Adolphus College, **242**
Macalester College, **315**
Minneapolis College of Art and
Design, **354**
Saint John's University, **452**
Saint Olaf College, **461**
University of Minnesota/Morris, **613**
University of Minnesota/Twin
Cities, **615**
University of Saint Thomas, **645**

MISSISSIPPI
Belhaven College, **60**
Millsaps College, **350**
Mississippi State University, **355**
University of Mississippi, **617**

MISSOURI
College of the Ozarks, **140**
Drury University, **184**
Kansas City Art Institute, **285**
Saint Louis University, **457**
Stephens College, **512**
Truman State University, **540**
University of Missouri/Columbia, **618**
University of Missouri/Kansas
City, **620**
University of Missouri/Rolla, **622**
Washington University in St.
Louis, **701**
Webster University, **706**

NEBRASKA
Creighton University, **165**

NEW HAMPSHIRE
Dartmouth College, **168**

NEW JERSEY
College of New Jersey, The, **134**
Drew University/College of Liberal
Arts, **181**
Princeton University, **413**
Ramapo College of New Jersey, **418**

North Carolina State University, **375**
University of North Carolina at Asheville, **623**
University of North Carolina at Chapel Hill, **625**
Wake Forest University, **691**
Warren Wilson College, **693**

OHIO
Baldwin-Wallace College, **50**
Case Western Reserve University, **108**
Cedarville College, **111**
Cleveland Institute of Art, **128**
College of Wooster, **143**
Columbus College of Art and Design, **154**
Denison University, **173**
Hiram College, **257**
Kenyon College, **287**
Miami University, **341**
Oberlin College, **382**
Ohio State University, **385**
University of Cincinnati, **571**
University of Dayton, **578**
Wittenberg University, **732**

OKLAHOMA
Oklahoma Baptist University, **387**
Oklahoma City University, **388**
Oklahoma State University, **390**
University of Oklahoma, **631**
University of Tulsa, **664**

OREGON
Art Institute of Portland, **43**
George Fox University, **223**
Lewis and Clark College, **304**
Oregon State University, **393**
Pacific University, **400**
Reed College, **421**
Southern Oregon University, **491**
University of Portland, **637**
Willamette University, **727**

PENNSYLVANIA
Allegheny College, **32**
Beaver College, **58**
Bryn Mawr College, **91**
Bucknell University, **93**
Carnegie Mellon University, **106**
Dickinson College, **178**
Drexel University, **183**
Duquesne University, **188**
Elizabethtown College, **194**
Franklin and Marshall College, **217**
Geneva College, **221**
Gettysburg College, **231**
Grove City College, **239**
Haverford College, **252**

Juniata College, **282**
La Salle University, **292**
Lafayette College, **293**
Lebanon Valley College of Pennsylvania, **298**
Lehigh University, **301**
Messiah College, **339**
Moravian College, **358**
Muhlenberg College, **363**
Penn State University/University Park Campus, **403**
Saint Joseph's University, **454**
Susquehanna University, **517**
Swarthmore College, **519**
University of Pennsylvania, **633**
University of Pittsburgh at Pittsburgh, **635**
University of the Arts, **659**
University of the Sciences in Philadelphia, **662**
Ursinus College, **677**
Villanova University, **684**
Washington and Jefferson College, **696**
York College of Pennsylvania, **738**

RHODE ISLAND
Brown University, **87**
Bryant College, **90**
Providence College, **415**
Rhode Island School of Design, **426**

SOUTH CAROLINA
Clemson University, **127**
Converse College, **158**
Erskine College, **202**
Furman University, **220**
Presbyterian College, **412**
University of South Carolina at Columbia, **651**
Wofford College, **733**

SOUTH DAKOTA
Augustana College, **45**

TENNESSEE
Belmont University, **61**
Bryan College, **89**
Christian Brothers University, **118**
David Lipscomb University, **170**
Freed-Hardeman University, **218**
Lee University, **300**
Maryville College, **330**
Milligan College, **347**
Rhodes College, **427**
University of Tennessee at Knoxville, **654**
Vanderbilt University, **680**

AGNES SCOTT COLLEGE
Atlanta-Decatur, GA 30030

(404) 471-6285
(800) 868-8602; Fax: (404) 471-6414

Full-time: 838 women	**Faculty:** 75; IIB, ++$
Part-time: 1 man, 40 women	**Ph.D.s:** 100%
Graduate: 1 man, 7 women	**Student/Faculty:** 11 to 1
Year: semesters	**Tuition:** $16,025
Application Deadline: March 1	**Room & Board:** $6660
Freshman Class: 688 applied, 531 accepted, 241 enrolled	
SAT I or ACT: required	**VERY COMPETITIVE**

Agnes Scott College, founded in 1889, is an independent women's college affiliated with the Presbyterian Church (U.S.A.). It offers programs in liberal arts and sciences and teacher preparation. There is 1 graduate school. The library contains 208,283 volumes, 30,917 microform items, and 9800 audiovisual forms/CDs, and subscribes to 896 periodicals. Computerized library services include the card catalog, interlibrary loans, and database searching. Special learning facilities include a learning resource center, art gallery, planetarium, interactive learning center, and multimedia classroom. The 100-acre campus is in an urban area 6 miles from downtown Atlanta. Including residence halls, there are 24 buildings.

Programs of Study: Agnes Scott confers the B.A. degree. Master's degrees are also awarded. Bachelor's degrees are awarded in BIOLOGICAL SCIENCE (biochemistry and biology/biological science), COMMUNICATIONS AND THE ARTS (classical languages, classics, creative writing, dramatic arts, English, fine arts, French, German, music, and Spanish), COMPUTER AND PHYSICAL SCIENCE (astrophysics, chemistry, mathematics, and physics), SOCIAL SCIENCE (anthropology, classical/ancient civilization, economics, history, international relations, philosophy, political science/government, psychology, sociology, and women's studies). Biology, English, and psychology are the largest.

Special: There is cross-registration through ARCHE (a 19-member consortium), and more than 300 credit and noncredit internships are available. There is a 3-2 engineering program with the Georgia Institute of Technology, and the college offers dual, student-designed, and interdisciplinary majors, including anthropology/sociology, creative writing/English literature, math/economics, math/physics, astrophysics, women's studies, and international relations. Pass/fail options are also available. Opportunities for study abroad include exchange programs, a Global Awareness program, which combines fall and spring semester class work with a January travel experience, and Global Connections, a component added to a regular course offering that includes a 2- to 3-week travel and intercultural experience. Also offered are a Washington semester, an Atlanta semester, the PLEN Public Policy Semester, the Mills College Exchange, and a 3-4 architecture degree with Washington University. Teacher certification and Language Across the Curriculum programs are offered. B.A. degree requirements may be completed in 3 years. There are 9 national honor societies, including Phi Beta Kappa.

Admissions: 77% of the 1999-2000 applicants were accepted. The SAT I scores for the 1999-2000 freshman class were: Verbal--3% below 500, 31% between 500 and 599, 48% between 600 and 700, and 18% above 700. The ACT scores were 6% below 21, 17% between 21 and 23, 30% between 24 and 26, 20% between 27 and 28, and 27% above 28. 76% of the current freshmen were in the top fifth of their class; 89% were in the top two fifths. 4 freshmen graduated first in their class.

Requirements: The SAT I or ACT is required. Applicants (except early admission) must graduate from an accredited secondary school or have a GED. A total of 16 academic credits is recommended, including 4 years of English, 3 of math, and 2 each of a foreign language, science, and social studies. An essay is required, and an interview is recommended. An audition is required for those seeking a music scholarship. Applications are accepted on-line via CollegeLink, Apply, Common Application, Petersons, and ExPAN. AP credits are accepted. Important factors in the admissions decision are advanced placement or honor courses, recommendations by school officials, and leadership record.

Procedure: Freshmen are admitted fall and spring. Entrance exams should be taken late in the junior year or by January of the senior year. There are early decision, early admissions, and deferred admissions plans. Early decision applications should be filed by November 15; regular applications, by March 1 for fall entry and November 1 for spring entry, along with a $35 fee. Notification of early decision is sent December 15. 21 early decision candidates were accepted for the 1999-2000 class. A waiting list is an active part of the admissions procedure.

Financial Aid: In 1999-2000, 99% of all freshmen and 91% of continuing students received some form of financial aid. 71% of freshmen and 54% of continuing students received need-based aid. The average freshman award was $17,410. Of that total, scholarships or need-based grants averaged $12,448; loans averaged $2491 ($2625 maximum); and work contracts averaged $969 ($1600 maximum). 50% of undergraduates work part time. Average annual earnings from campus work are $1600. The average financial indebtedness of the 1999 graduate was $14,580. Agnes Scott is a member of CSS. The FAFSA, and the college's own financial statement are required. The CSS/Profile is required for early decision financial aid applicants. The fall application deadline is March 1.

Computers: The mainframe is an IBM RS/6000. There are more than 120 computers on the campus for student use, with more than 60 PCs located in 4 computer centers and 3 satellite centers in the residence halls, and 8 Macs located in the fine arts building and 5 in the language lab. All computers on campus are a part of the campus network, which provides Internet access to all students. Residence hall rooms have 1 port per student. All students may access the system. There are no time limits and no fees.

ALBERT A. LIST COLLEGE OF JEWISH STUDIES
(Formerly Jewish Theological Seminary)
New York, NY 10027-4649   (212) 678-8832; Fax: (212) 678-8947

Full-time: 69 men, 129 women	**Faculty:** 40
Part-time: none	**Ph.D.s:** 98%
Graduate: none	**Student/Faculty:** 5 to 1
Year: semesters, summer session	**Tuition:** $8620
Application Deadline: February 15	**Room & Board:** $8000
Freshman Class: 138 applied, 87 accepted, 48 enrolled	
SAT I Verbal/Math: 661/650	**ACT:** 28 **HIGHLY COMPETITIVE+**

Albert A. List College of Jewish Studies, the undergraduate division of the Jewish Theological Seminary, founded in 1886, is a private institution affiliated with the Conservative branch of the Jewish faith. List College offers programs in all aspects of Judaism, including Bible, rabbinics, literature, history, philosophy, education, and communal service. There is also a combined liberal arts program with Columbia University and Barnard College. The 3 libraries contain 320,000 volumes and 3500 microform items, and subscribe to 750 periodicals. Computerized library services include the card catalog, interlibrary loans, and database searching. Special learning facilities include a learning resource center, art gallery, a music center, a Jewish education research center, and the Jewish Museum Archives Center. The 1-acre campus is in an urban area on the upper west side of Manhattan. Including residence halls, there are 6 buildings.

Programs of Study: List College confers the B.A. degree. Bachelor's degrees are awarded in SOCIAL SCIENCE (biblical studies and Judaic studies).

Special: There is a joint program with Columbia University and a double-degree program with Barnard College, which enable students to earn 2 B.A. degrees in 4 to 4 1/2 years. Study abroad is available in Israel, England, France, and Spain. Student-designed majors, credit by exam, and nondegree study are also offered. There is a chapter of Phi Beta Kappa and a freshman honors program.

Admissions: 63% of the 1999-2000 applicants were accepted. The SAT I scores for the 1999-2000 freshman class were: Verbal--2% below 500, 20% between 500 and 599, 52% between 600 and 700, and 26% above 700, Math--4% below 500, 22% between 500 and 599, 70% between 600 and 700, and 4% above 700. The ACT scores were 10% between 21 and 23, 20% between 24 and 26, 40% between 27 and 28, and 30% above 28.

Requirements: The SAT I is required, as are SAT II: Subject tests. Applicants must be graduates of an accredited secondary school or have the GED. An essay and 2 recommendations are required; an interview is strongly recommended. Students can print on-line applications and submit them by mail. AP credits are accepted. Important factors in the admissions decision are advanced placement or honor courses, extracurricular activities record, and personality/intangible qualities.

Procedure: Freshmen are admitted fall and spring. Entrance exams should be taken in the spring of the junior year. There are early decision, early admissions, and deferred admissions plans. Early decision applications should be filed by November 15; regular applications, by February 15 for fall entry and November 1 for spring entry, along with a $60 fee. Notification of early decision is sent December 15; regular decision, April 15. 14 early decision candidates were accepted for the 1999-2000 class.

Financial Aid: 15% of undergraduates work part time. List College is a member of CSS. The CSS/Profile, the college's own financial statement, and 1040 tax forms are required. The fall application deadline is March 1.

Computers: All dorms have Internet connections. All students may access the system. There are no time limits and no fees.

ALBERTSON COLLEGE OF IDAHO
Caldwell, ID 83605-4432   (208) 459-5310
                                    (800) AC-IDAHO; Fax: (208) 459-5757

Full-time: 321 men, 412 women	**Faculty:** 60; IIB, av$
Part-time: 10 men, 20 women	**Ph.D.s:** 94%
Graduate: none	**Student/Faculty:** 12 to 1
Year: 4-1-4	**Tuition:** $16,310
Application Deadline: June 1	**Room & Board:** $4200
Freshman Class: 886 applied, 734 accepted, 290 enrolled	
SAT I Verbal/Math: 560/550	**ACT:** 24 **VERY COMPETITIVE**

Albertson College of Idaho, founded in 1891 as Albertson College, is a private institution offering degree programs in liberal arts education and the sciences. The college runs on a 12-6-12 calendar, with a 6-week intercession. In addition to regional accreditation, ACI has baccalaureate program accreditation with

NASDTEC. The 2 libraries contain 178,885 volumes, 27,850 microform items, and 1476 audiovisual forms/CDs, and subscribe to 820 periodicals. Computerized library services include the card catalog, interlibrary loans, and database searching. Special learning facilities include an art gallery, natural history museum, planetarium, and rock and mineral collection. The 43-acre campus is in a small town 25 miles west of Boise. Including residence halls, there are 21 buildings.

Programs of Study: ACI confers B.A. and B.S. degrees. Bachelor's degrees are awarded in BIOLOGICAL SCIENCE (biology/biological science), BUSINESS (accounting, business administration and management, international business management, and sports management), COMMUNICATIONS AND THE ARTS (art, creative writing, dramatic arts, English, music, and Spanish), COMPUTER AND PHYSICAL SCIENCE (chemistry, computer mathematics, mathematics, and physics), EDUCATION (English), SOCIAL SCIENCE (anthropology, economics, history, philosophy, political science/government, psychology, and religion). Biology, history, and philosophy are the strongest academically. Business, biology, and education are the largest.

Special: ACI offers several cooperative programs and a 3-2 engineering degree with 4 universities, as well as cross-registration with Northwest Nazarene University. Internships with major corporations, work-study programs on campus, a Washington semester, study abroad, pass/fail options, phys ed credit for military experience, an accelerated degree in business, and nondegree study are also available. The Gipson Scholar Program allows freshmen with superior records to design their own majors. There is 1 national honor society, and a freshman honors program. Most departments have honors programs.

Admissions: 83% of the 1999-2000 applicants were accepted. The SAT I scores for the 1999-2000 freshman class were: Verbal--23% below 500, 40% between 500 and 599, 26% between 600 and 700, and 11% above 700; Math--27% below 500, 37% between 500 and 599, 29% between 600 and 700, and 7% above 700. The ACT scores were 15% below 21, 27% between 21 and 23, 24% between 24 and 26, 15% between 27 and 28, and 19% above 28. 52% of the current freshmen were in the top fifth of their class; 75% were in the top two fifths. There were 10 National Merit finalists and 1 semifinalist. 27 freshmen graduated first in their class.

Requirements: The SAT I or ACT is required. Applicants must be high school graduates or present a GED certificate. ACI recommends that students have 4 years of English, 3 each of math, history, and social studies, and 2 of science. An essay and a teacher or guidance counselor recommendation are required. AP and CLEP credits are accepted. Important factors in the admissions decision are extracurricular activities record, leadership record, and recommendations by school officials.

Procedure: Freshmen are admitted to all sessions. Entrance exams should be taken by the fall of the senior year. There are early decision and deferred admissions plans. Early decision applications should be filed by November 15; regular applications, by June 1 for fall entry, along with a $25 fee. Notification of early decision is sent December 15; regular decision, on a rolling basis. 132 early decision candidates were accepted for the 1999-2000 class.

Financial Aid: In 1999-2000, 97% of all freshmen and 87% of continuing students received some form of financial aid. 84% of freshmen and 80% of continuing students received need-based aid. The average freshman award was $12,321. Of that total, scholarships or need-based grants averaged $5320 ($16,000 maximum); loans averaged $3605 ($10,500 maximum); work contracts averaged $1170 ($2200 maximum), and athletic and performance scholarships averaged $8100 ($24,200 maximum). 49% of undergraduates work part time. Average annual earnings from campus work are $1192. The average financial indebtedness

28

of the 1999 graduate was $15,400. ACI is a member of CSS. The FAFSA and the college's own financial statement are required. The fall application priority date is Februrary 15.

Computers: The mainframe is an HP 9000. There are 8 computer lab clusters with 120 PCs, all with access to the Internet. There are also mini labs in residence halls, and every room is wired to provide access to the Internet and other campus computer offerings. All students may access the system at designated times in computer labs; 24 hours in residence halls. There are no time limits and no fees.

ALBION COLLEGE
Albion, MI 49224

(517) 629-0600
(800) 858-6770; Fax: (517) 629-0569

Full-time: 680 men, 826 women	**Faculty:** 110
Part-time: 7 men, 13 women	**Ph.D.s:** 94%
Graduate: none	**Student/Faculty:** 14 to 1
Year: semesters, summer session	**Tuition:** $18,234
Application Deadline: open	**Room & Board:** $5220
Freshman Class: 1421 applied, 1206 accepted, 412 enrolled	
SAT I Verbal/Math: 579/589	**ACT:** 25 **VERY COMPETITIVE**

Albion College, established in 1835, is a private institution affiliated with the United Methodist Church and offering undergraduate degrees in liberal arts curricula. In addition to regional accreditation, Albion has baccalaureate program accreditation with NASM. The library contains 316,335 volumes, 22,819 microform items, and 5381 audiovisual forms/CDs, and subscribes to 986 periodicals. Computerized library services include the card catalog, interlibrary loans, and database searching. Special learning facilities include a learning resource center, art gallery, radio station, nature center, women's center, observatory, and honors program center. The 225-acre campus is in a small town 90 miles west of Detroit and 175 miles east of Chicago. Including residence halls, there are 30 buildings.

Programs of Study: Albion confers B.A. and B.F.A. degrees. Bachelor's degrees are awarded in BIOLOGICAL SCIENCE (biology/biological science), COMMUNICATIONS AND THE ARTS (English, fine arts, French, German, music, Spanish, speech/debate/rhetoric, and visual and performing arts), COMPUTER AND PHYSICAL SCIENCE (chemistry, computer science, geoscience, mathematics, and physics), EDUCATION (music and physical), SOCIAL SCIENCE (American studies, anthropology, economics, history, international studies, philosophy, political science/government, psychology, religion, and sociology). English, economics, and biology are the strongest academically and have the largest enrollments.

Special: Albion offers work-study and internship programs, study abroad in 17 countries, a Washington semester, and study in New York City, Philadelphia, Oak Ridge, Chicago, and the Virgin Islands. Students may earn a 3-2 engineering degree in conjunction with Columbia, Case Western Reserve, or Michigan Technological Universities, the University of Michigan, or Washington University in St. Louis. Student-designed majors, dual and interdisciplinary majors, including computational math, speech communication and theater, math/physics, and math/economics, and pass/fail grading are possible. There are 4 national honor societies, including Phi Beta Kappa, a freshman honors program, and 18 departmental honors programs.

Admissions: 85% of the 1999-2000 applicants were accepted. The SAT I scores for the 1999-2000 freshman class were: Verbal--15% below 500, 40% between 500 and 599, 31% between 600 and 700, and 13% above 700; Math--12% below

500, 42% between 500 and 599, 36% between 600 and 700, and 10% above 700. The ACT scores were 13% below 21, 25% between 21 and 23, 28% between 24 and 26, 14% between 27 and 28, and 20% above 28. 64% of the current freshmen were in the top fifth of their class; 95% were in the top two fifths. There were 7 National Merit finalists and 5 semifinalists. 21 freshmen graduated first in their class.

Requirements: The SAT I or ACT is required. Albion requires applicants to be in the upper 50% of their class. Applicants must graduate from an accredited secondary school or earn a GED. Completion of 15 Carnegie credits is required. A strong background in English, math, and the lab and social sciences is recommended. Applications are accepted on-line at the Albion web site via CollegeNet. AP and CLEP credits are accepted. Important factors in the admissions decision are advanced placement or honor courses, extracurricular activities record, and personality/intangible qualities.

Procedure: Freshmen are admitted fall and spring. Entrance exams should be taken in April or June of the junior year. There are early decision, early admissions, and deferred admissions plans. Application deadlines are open, and there is a $40 application fee. Notification of early decision is sent December 1; regular decision December 15 and on a rolling basis after January 1.

Financial Aid: In 1999-2000, 94% of all freshmen and 85% of continuing students received some form of financial aid. 70% of freshmen and 65% of continuing students received need-based aid. The average freshman award was $14,785. Of that total, scholarships or need-based grants averaged $11,679 ($20,050 maximum); loans averaged $3545 ($4625 maximum); and work contracts averaged $1352 ($1500 maximum). 57% of undergraduates work part time. Average annual earnings from campus work are $1023. The average financial indebtedness of a recent graduate was $14,337. Albion is a member of CSS. The FAFSA is required. The fall application deadline is March 1.

Computers: The mainframe is a DEC ALPHA 2100/400. Suites of Macs and PCs are available in locations across campus. They operate as on-line terminals and are connected to the campus network. All students may access the system most days and evening hours. There are no time limits and no fees. It is recommended that all students have personal computers.

ALFRED UNIVERSITY
Alfred, NY 14802-1205

(607) 871-2115
(800) 541-9229; Fax: (607) 871-2198

Full-time: 1017 men, 1018 women	**Faculty:** 172; IIA, av$
Part-time: 38 men, 39 women	**Ph.D.s:** 83%
Graduate: 138 men, 185 women	**Student/Faculty:** 12 to 1
Year: semesters, summer session	**Tuition:** $19,074
Application Deadline: February 1	**Room & Board:** $7174
Freshman Class: 1954 applied, 1592 accepted, 556 enrolled	
SAT I Verbal/Math: 550/550	**ACT:** 24 **VERY COMPETITIVE**

Alfred University, founded in 1836, is a private institution offering programs in business administration, liberal arts and sciences, engineering, and professional studies, and in art and design and ceramic engineering through the New York State College of Ceramics. The above tuition figures are for incoming freshmen. Contact the school for tuition rates at other academic levels. There are 5 undergraduate and 7 graduate schools. In addition to regional accreditation, Alfred has baccalaureate program accreditation with AACSB, ABET, and NASAD. The 2 libraries contain 287,734 volumes, 119,461 microform items, and 162,938 audiovisual forms/CDs, and subscribe to 10,508 periodicals. Computerized library services include the card catalog, interlibrary loans, and database searching. Special learning facilities include a learning resource center, art gallery, radio station, TV station, and observatory. The 232-acre campus is in a rural area 70 miles south of Rochester. Including residence halls, there are 54 buildings.

Programs of Study: Alfred confers B.A.,B.S., and B.F.A. degrees. Master's and doctoral degrees are also awarded. Bachelor's degrees are awarded in BIOLOGICAL SCIENCE (biology/biological science), BUSINESS (accounting, banking and finance, business administration and management, business economics, management science, and marketing/retailing/merchandising), COMMUNICATIONS AND THE ARTS (ceramic art and design, communications, dramatic arts, English, fine arts, French, German, glass, performing arts, and Spanish), COMPUTER AND PHYSICAL SCIENCE (chemistry, computer science, geology, mathematics, physics, and science), EDUCATION (art, athletic training, business, elementary, English, foreign languages, mathematics, science, secondary, and social studies), ENGINEERING AND ENVIRONMENTAL DESIGN (ceramic engineering, electrical/electronics engineering, environmental science, materials engineering, and mechanical engineering), HEALTH PROFESSIONS (health care administration), SOCIAL SCIENCE (criminal justice, crosscultural studies, economics, gerontology, history, interdisciplinary studies, philosophy, political science/government, psychology, public administration, and sociology). Ceramic engineering, electrical engineering, and business are the strongest academically. Ceramic engineering, accounting, and psychology are the largest.

Special: There are cooperative programs in engineering and business with Duke, Clarkson, and Columbia universities and SUNY/Brockport. There is cross-registration with the SUNY College of Technology and a 5-year program in environmental management/forestry with Duke. Alfred offers internships in all programs, extensive study abroad, Washington and Albany semesters, work-study, accelerated-degree programs, a general studies degree, student-designed majors, dual majors, credit by examination, and pass/fail options. A special feature is the New York State College of Ceramics, which offers programs and facilities in ceramic engineering and science as well as in art and design. There are 12 national honor societies, a freshman honors program, and 42 departmental honors programs.

Admissions: 81% of the 1999-2000 applicants were accepted. The SAT I scores for the 1999-2000 freshman class were: Verbal--20% below 500, 42% between 500 and 599, 30% between 600 and 700, and 8% above 700; Math--20% below 500, 44% between 500 and 599, 30% between 600 and 700, and 6% above 700. The ACT scores were 27% below 21, 25% between 22 and 24, 23% between 25 and 27, 16% between 28 and 30, and 9% above 31. 47% of the current freshmen were in the top fifth of their class; 76% were in the top two fifths. There were 15 National Merit finalists. 11 freshmen graduated first in their class.

Requirements: The SAT I or ACT is required. A GED is accepted. A minimum of 16 Carnegie units is required, including 4 years of English, 2 to 3 years each of math, history/social studies, and science. The remaining units may be either in a foreign language or any of the previously mentioned fields. An essay is required, and applicants to B.F.A. programs must submit a portfolio. Interviews are encouraged. Applications are accepted on-line at the school's web site. AP credits are accepted. Important factors in the admissions decision are advanced placement or honor courses, personality/intangible qualities, and extracurricular activities record.

Procedure: Freshmen are admitted fall and spring. Entrance exams should be taken in the junior year. There are early decision, early admissions, and deferred admissions plans. Early decision applications should be filed by December 1;

regular applications, by February 1 for fall entry and December 1 for spring entry, along with a $40 fee. Notification of early decision is sent December 15; regular decision, March 15. 56 early decision candidates were accepted for the 1999-2000 class.

Financial Aid: In a recent year, 93% of all freshmen and 85% of continuing students received some form of financial aid. 50% of undergraduates work part time. Average annual earnings from campus work are $1000. Alfred is a member of CSS. The CSS/Profile and the college's own financial statement are required. The fall application deadline is May 1.

Computers: The mainframes are 2 DEC VAX 11/785s, a VAX 8530, and 2 VAX 3100 systems. All buildings are connected to the campus network. There are numerous high-speed laser and color printers. More than 400 terminals are located across campus for student use. All students may access the system 24 hours a day, 7 days a week. There are no time limits and no fees.

ALLEGHENY COLLEGE
Meadville, PA 16335

(814) 332-4351
(800) 521-5293; Fax: (814) 337-0431

Full-time: 875 men, 977 women	**Faculty:** 131
Part-time: 10 men, 24 women	**Ph.D.s:** 92%
Graduate: none	**Student/Faculty:** 14 to 1
Year: semesters	**Tuition:** $20,690
Application Deadline: February 15	**Room & Board:** $4970
Freshman Class: 3014 applied, 2251 accepted, 564 enrolled	
SAT I Verbal/Math: 600/600	**ACT:** 25 **VERY COMPETITIVE**

Allegheny College, founded in 1815, is an independent liberal arts institution affiliated with the United Methodist Church. The library contains 722,290 volumes, 431,621 microform items, and 4986 audiovisual forms/CDs, and subscribes to 1311 periodicals. Computerized library services include the card catalog, interlibrary loans, and database searching. Special learning facilities include a learning resource center, art gallery, planetarium, radio station, TV studio, observatory, 283-acre experimental forest, and art studio. The 254-acre campus is in a small town 90 miles north of Pittsburgh and east of Cleveland. Including residence halls, there are 38 buildings.

Programs of Study: Allegheny confers B.A. and B.S. degrees. Bachelor's degrees are awarded in AGRICULTURE (natural resource management), BIOLOGICAL SCIENCE (biology/biological science and neurosciences), COMMUNICATIONS AND THE ARTS (art history and appreciation, communications, dramatic arts, English, French, German, multimedia, music, Spanish, and studio art), COMPUTER AND PHYSICAL SCIENCE (chemistry, computer science, geology, mathematics, and physics), ENGINEERING AND ENVIRONMENTAL DESIGN (computer graphics and environmental science), SOCIAL SCIENCE (economics, history, international studies, philosophy, political science/government, psychology, religion, and women's studies). Physical and biological sciences, and English are the strongest academically. Psychology, biology, and political science are the largest.

Special: Allegheny offers cross-registration in education with Chatham College, a Washington semester, internships, dual majors, student-designed majors, study abroad in 15 countries, nondegree study, and pass/fail options. A 3-2 engineering degree is available with Case Western Reserve, Columbia, Duke, Pittsburgh, and Washington Universities. There also are cooperative arrangements in medical technology and nursing with Rochester and Case Western Reserve Universities.

There are 13 national honor societies, including Phi Beta Kappa, and 17 departmental honors programs.

Admissions: 75% of the 1999-2000 applicants were accepted. The SAT I scores for the 1999-2000 freshman class were: Verbal--6% below 500, 42% between 500 and 599, 43% between 600 and 700, and 9% above 700; Math--7% below 500, 38% between 500 and 599, 47% between 600 and 700, and 8% above 700. The ACT scores were 11% below 21, 23% between 21 and 23, 35% between 24 and 26, 15% between 27 and 28, and 16% above 28. 65% of the current freshmen were in the top fifth of their class; 89% were in the top two fifths. There was 1 National Merit finalist and 2 semifinalists. 24 freshmen graduated first in their class.

Requirements: The SAT I or ACT is required. SAT II: Subject tests are recommended in writing and in the student's expected major. Graduation from an accredited secondary school is required for admission. Students must have 16 Carnegie units, including 4 years of English, 3 years each of math, science, and social studies, and 2 years of a foreign language. An essay is required, and an interview is recommended. Applications are accepted on computer disk and online through Embark, Apply!, and other services. AP and CLEP credits are accepted. Important factors in the admissions decision are advanced placement or honor courses, personality/intangible qualities, and leadership record.

Procedure: Freshmen are admitted fall and spring. Entrance exams should be taken by December of the senior year. There are early decision, early admissions, and deferred admissions plans. Early decision applications should be filed by January 15; regular applications, by February 15 for fall entry and November 1 for spring entry, along with a $30 fee. Notification of early decision is sent on a rolling basis from October 15; regular decision, April 1. 118 early decision candidates were accepted for the 1999-2000 class. 4% of all applicants are on a waiting list.

Financial Aid: In 1999-2000, 96% of all freshmen and 95% of continuing students received some form of financial aid. 77% of freshmen and 76% of continuing students received need-based aid. The average freshman award was $17,372. Of that total, scholarships or need-based grants averaged $12,426 ($26,635 maximum); loans averaged $4476 ($9325 maximum); and work contracts averaged $1240 ($1500 maximum). 71% of undergraduates work part time. Average annual earnings from campus work are $1398. The average financial indebtedness of the 1999 graduate was $17,375. The FAFSA and IRS 1040 for verification are required. The fall application deadline is February 15.

Computers: The mainframes are a TCP/IP network of 14 UNIX servers and 6 NT servers. 240 PCs are networked and available to students in the library and all academic buildings. All students may access the system 24 hours per day. There are no time limits and no fees. It is strongly recommended that all students have computers. A PC with an Intel proccessor and Windows software is preferred.

ALMA COLLEGE
Alma, MI 48801

(517) 463-7139
(800) 321-ALMA; Fax: (517) 463-7057

Full-time: 566 men, 771 women	**Faculty:** 90; IIB, ++$
Part-time: 23 men, 23 women	**Ph.D.s:** 81%
Graduate: none	**Student/Faculty:** 15 to 1
Year: 4-4-1	**Tuition:** $15,142
Application Deadline: open	**Room & Board:** $5460
Freshman Class: 1366 applied, 1133 accepted, 339 enrolled	
ACT: 25	**VERY COMPETITIVE**

Alma College, established in 1886, is a private, liberal arts institution affiliated with the Presbyterian Church (U.S.A.). In addition to regional accreditation, Alma has baccalaureate program accreditation with NASM. The library contains 230,398 volumes, 239,757 microform items, and 5619 audiovisual forms/CDs, and subscribes to 1223 periodicals. Computerized library services include the card catalog, interlibrary loans, and database searching. Special learning facilities include a learning resource center, art gallery, planetarium, radio station, audio-visual center, and a language lab. The 100-acre campus is in a small town 50 miles north of Lansing. Including residence halls, there are 24 buildings.

Programs of Study: Alma confers B.A., B.S., B.M., and B.F.A. degrees. Bachelor's degrees are awarded in BIOLOGICAL SCIENCE (biochemistry and biology/biological science), BUSINESS (business administration and management and international business management), COMMUNICATIONS AND THE ARTS (communications, dance, design, dramatic arts, English, French, German, music, and Spanish), COMPUTER AND PHYSICAL SCIENCE (chemistry, computer science, information sciences and systems, mathematics, and physics), EDUCATION (elementary and secondary), HEALTH PROFESSIONS (health science), SOCIAL SCIENCE (economics, history, philosophy, political science/government, psychology, religion, and sociology). Biology, business administration, and education are the strongest academically are the largest.

Special: Alma offers internships in many fields, study abroad in 12 countries, and a Washington semester at American University. There are work-study programs, dual majors, B.A.-B.S. degrees, and student-designed majors in a wide variety of subjects. The college confers 3-2 engineering degrees in conjunction with the University of Michigan, Michigan Technological University, and Washington University in St. Louis. Nondegree study may be pursued, and students have a pass/fail grading option. A 4-week spring term provides intensive study in 1 course, often combined with travel. There are 4 national honor societies, including Phi Beta Kappa, a freshman honors program, and 16 departmental honors programs.

Admissions: 83% of the 1999-2000 applicants were accepted. The ACT scores for the 1999-2000 freshman class were: 14% below 21, 22% between 21 and 23, 31% between 24 and 26, 19% between 27 and 28, and 16% above 28. 67% of the current freshmen were in the top fifth of their class; 90% were in the top two fifths. There were 4 National Merit finalists. 24 freshmen graduated first in their class.

Requirements: The SAT I or ACT is required. A GPA of 3.0 is required. The ACT is preferred. Applicants must have graduated from an accredited secondary school and have earned 16 Carnegie units, including 4 years of English and 3 each of math, science, and social studies, with 2 of a foreign language required. Alma prefers applicants in the upper 25% of their class. An essay is recommended, and a portfolio and audition are required for performing arts scholarships. Application forms are available on-line. AP and CLEP credits are accepted. Important factors in the admissions decision are advanced placement or honor courses, leadership record, and recommendations by school officials.

Procedure: Freshmen are admitted fall, winter, and spring. Entrance exams should be taken in the spring of the junior year or as late as the winter of the senior year. There are early decision, early admissions, and deferred admissions plans. Early decision applications should be filed by November 1; regular applications are open for fall entry. There is a $20 application fee. Notification of early decision is sent November 15; regular decision, on a rolling basis. 197 early decision candidates were accepted for the 1999-2000 class.

Financial Aid: In 1999-2000, 95% of all students received some form of financial aid. 69% of freshmen and 76% of continuing students received need-based aid. The average freshman award was $14,188. Of that total, scholarships or need-based grants averaged $11,233 ($18,500 maximum); loans averaged $2292 ($4125 maximum); work contracts averaged $500 ($1500 maximum); and external and restricted awards plus employee dependent tuition grants averaged $479. 42% of undergraduates work part time. Average annual earnings from campus work are $1500. The average financial indebtedness of the 1999 graduate was $9600. Alma is a member of CSS. The FAFSA is required. The fall application deadline is March 1.

Computers: The mainframes are 2 DEC Alpha 2100 4/275, and 1 DEC Alpha 200. The on-campus VAX network links 600 terminals, printers, and PCs across campus. Macs are available in 6 residence halls, department labs, the Colina Library classroom, and the Academic Center. All residence halls are wired for Internet access for a user fee. All students may access the system all hours. There are no time limits. It is recommended that all students have personal computers.

AMERICAN UNIVERSITY
Washington, DC 20016-8001

(202) 885-6053
Fax: (202) 885-1103

Full-time: 1838 men, 2923 women
Part-time: 351 men, 421 women
Graduate: 1655 men, 2393 women
Year: semesters, summer session
Application Deadline: February 1
Freshman Class: 7554 applied, 5603 accepted, 1203 enrolled
SAT I Verbal/Math: 604/582

Faculty: 452; I, av$
Ph.D.s: 92%
Student/Faculty: 11 to 1
Tuition: $20,373
Room & Board: $7982

ACT: 26   **VERY COMPETITIVE**

American University, founded in 1893, is an independent liberal arts institution affiliated with the Methodist Church. Some of the information in this profile is approximate. There are 5 undergraduate and 6 graduate schools. In addition to regional accreditation, AU has baccalaureate program accreditation with AACSB, ACEJMC, and NCATE. The 2 libraries contain 618,000 volumes, 790,000 microform items, and 10,880 audiovisual forms/CDs, and subscribe to 3500 periodicals. Computerized library services include the card catalog, interlibrary loans, and database searching. Special learning facilities include a learning resource center, an art gallery, a radio station, a TV station, a langauage resource center, a media center, a computing center, and a national center for health fitness. The 78-acre campus is in a suburban area 5 miles northwest of downtown Washington, D.C. Including residence halls, there are 37 buildings.

Programs of Study: AU confers B.A., B.S., B.F.A., and B.S.B.A. degrees. Master's and doctoral degrees are also awarded. Bachelor's degrees are awarded in BIOLOGICAL SCIENCE (biology/biological science), BUSINESS (accounting, banking and finance, business administration and management, international business management, management information systems, and marketing/retailing/merchandising), COMMUNICATIONS AND THE ARTS (art history and appreciation, audio technology, communications, design, dramatic arts, English, film arts, fine arts, French, German, journalism, languages, music, Russian, Spanish, and studio art), COMPUTER AND PHYSICAL SCIENCE (chemistry, computer science, information sciences and systems, mathematics, physics, and statistics), EDUCATION (elementary), SOCIAL SCIENCE (American studies, anthropology, criminal justice, economics, history, international studies, Judaic studies, philosophy, political science/government, psychology, religion, and sociology). Political science, international studies, and communications are the strongest academically. International studies and political science are the largest.

Special: AU offers co-op programs and internships in all majors, study abroad in 12 countries, and a Washington semester program. Work-study is available on campus and with local community service agencies. Dual majors, a liberal studies degree, an interdisciplinary program in environmental studies, student-designed majors, 3-2 engineering degrees, and B.A.-B.S. degrees are also available. Cross-registration may be arranged through the Consortium of Universities of the Washington Metropolitan Area. Credit for life experience, nondegree study, and pass/fail options are available. There are 20 national honor societies, including Phi Beta Kappa, and a freshman honors program.

Admissions: 74% of the 1999-2000 applicants were accepted. The SAT I Math scores for the 1999-2000 freshman class were 10% below 500, 48% between 500 and 599, 35% between 600 and 700, and 7% above 700. The ACT scores were 34% between 21 and 23, 63% between 24 and 26, and 3% above 28. 85% of the current freshmen were in the top quarter of their class; 92% were in the top half.

Requirements: The SAT I or ACT is required. A GPA of 2.0 is required. Students must have graduated from an accredited secondary school or have satisfactory scores on the GED. 16 Carnegie units are required, and high school courses must include 4 years of English, 3 years each of math, science, and academic electives, 2 years each of history and foreign language, and 1 year of social studies. Students must submit an essay. On-line applications are accepted through ExPAN, CollegeLink, and MacApply. AP and CLEP credits are accepted. Important factors in the admissions decision are advanced placement or honor courses, leadership record, and recommendations by school officials.

Procedure: Freshmen are admitted to all sessions. Entrance exams should be taken in the spring of the junior year or the fall of senior year. There are early decision, early admissions, and deferred admissions plans. Early decision applications should be filed by November 15; regular applications, by February 1 for fall entry, December 1 for spring entry, and April 15 for summer entry, along with a $45 fee. Notification of early decision is sent December 15; regular decision, March 30. 290 early decision candidates were accepted for a recent class. 2% of all applicants are on a waiting list.

Financial Aid: In 1999-2000, 47% of all freshmen and 44% of continuing students received some form of financial aid. 86% of freshmen and 81% of continuing students received need-based aid. The average freshman award was $18,480. 60% of undergraduates work part time. Average annual earnings from campus work are $1500. The average financial indebtedness of the 1999 graduate was $16,308. The FAFSA and the college's own financial statement are required. The fall application deadline is March 1.

Computers: The mainframe is an IBM 3090. More than 200 IBM, Macintosh, and other PCs are available for student use in various campus locations. All residence hall rooms are fully networked. All students may access the system. There are no time limits and no fees.

AMHERST COLLEGE
Amherst, MA 01002-5000   **(413) 542-2328; Fax: (413) 542-2040**

Full-time: 863 men, 801 women	**Faculty:** 179; IIB, ++$
Part-time: none	**Ph.D.s:** 94%
Graduate: none	**Student/Faculty:** 9 to 1
Year: semesters	**Tuition:** $25,259
Application Deadline: December 31	**Room & Board:** $6560
Freshman Class: 5194 applied, 997 accepted, 424 enrolled	
SAT I Verbal/Math: 700/697	**ACT:** 30 **MOST COMPETITIVE**

Amherst College, founded in 1821, is a private liberal arts institution. The 5 libraries contain 889,989 volumes, 478,944 microform items, and 55,121 audiovisual forms/CDs, and subscribe to 5343 periodicals. Computerized library services include the card catalog, interlibrary loans, and database searching. Special learning facilities include an art gallery, natural history museum, planetarium, radio station, observatory, the Emily Dickinson Homestead, and the Amherst Center for Russian Culture. The 964-acre campus is in a small town 90 miles west of Boston. Including residence halls, there are 67 buildings.

Programs of Study: Amherst confers the B.A. degree. Bachelor's degrees are awarded in BIOLOGICAL SCIENCE (biology/biological science and neurosciences), COMMUNICATIONS AND THE ARTS (classics, dance, dramatic arts, English, fine arts, French, German, Greek, Latin, music, Russian, and Spanish), COMPUTER AND PHYSICAL SCIENCE (astronomy, chemistry, computer science, geology, mathematics, and physics), SOCIAL SCIENCE (African American studies, American studies, anthropology, Asian/Oriental studies, economics, European studies, history, interdisciplinary studies, law, philosophy, political science/government, psychology, religion, sociology, and women's studies). English, political science, and economics are the largest.

Special: Students may cross-register through the Five College Consortium, the other members of which are all within 10 miles of Amherst, or through the Twelve College Exchange Program. A number of interterm and summer internships are available, as are 275 approved study-abroad options. Dual majors, student-designed interdisciplinary majors based on independent study as of junior or senior year, and work-study programs are possible. There are limited pass/fail options. There are 2 national honor societies, including Phi Beta Kappa, and all departments have honors programs.

Admissions: 19% of the 1999-2000 applicants were accepted. The SAT I scores for the 1999-2000 freshman class were: Verbal--6% between 500 and 599, 39% between 600 and 700, and 55% above 700; Math--6% between 500 and 599, 40% between 600 and 700, and 54% above 700. The ACT scores were 2% below 21, 2% between 21 and 23, 12% between 24 and 26, 17% between 27 and 28, and 68% above 28. 98% of the current freshmen were in the top fifth of their class; all were in the top two fifths. There were 84 National Merit semifinalists. 25% of freshmen who reported a class rank graduated first in their class.

Requirements: The SAT I or ACT is required, as well as 3 SAT II: Subject tests, preferably including the writing test. Applicants should be high school graduates or have earned the GED. Amherst strongly recommends that applicants take 4 years of English, math through precalculus, 3 or 4 years of a foreign language, 2 years of history and social science, and at least 2 years of natural science, including a lab science. 2 essays are required. Students may apply on-line through the school's web site or through the Common Application Consortium. Important factors in the admissions decision are advanced placement or honor courses, recommendations by school officials, and evidence of special talent.

Procedure: Freshmen are admitted in the fall. Entrance exams should be taken no later than December of the senior year. There are early decision and deferred admissions plans. Early decision applications should be filed by November 15; regular applications, by December 31 for fall entry, along with a $55 fee. Notification of early decision is sent December 15; regular decision, early April. 127 early decision candidates were accepted for the 1999-2000 class. 15% of all applicants are on a waiting list; 2 were accepted in 1999.

Financial Aid: In 1999-2000, 43% of all students received some form of financial aid. 41% of all students received need-based aid. The average freshman award was $23,605. Of that total, scholarships or need-based grants averaged $19,538 ($29,750 maximum); loans averaged $2624 ($4050 maximum); and work contracts averaged $1443 ($1600 maximum). 51% of undergraduates work part time. Average annual earnings from campus work are $944. The average financial indebtedness of the 1999 graduate was $11,908. Amherst is a member of CSS. The CSS/Profile and FAFSA are required. The fall application deadline is February 15.

Computers: The mainframes are a DEC VMS and a DEC UNIX. There are more than 160 PCs around campus. Most are located in the computer center, library, campus center, and labs. In addition, each student has a hard-wired point of access from each dorm room with Ethernet, Internet, and E-mail accounts. All students may access the system 24 hours a day. There are no time limits and no fees.

ARIZONA STATE UNIVERSITY-MAIN
Tempe, AZ 85287-0112   (480) 965-7789

Full-time: 12,451 men, 13,952 women	**Faculty:** 1248; I, -$
Part-time: 3665 men, 3890 women	**Ph.D.s:** 85%
Graduate: 4865 men, 5402 women	**Student/Faculty:** 21 to 1
Year: semesters, summer session	**Tuition:** $2261 ($9413)
Application Deadline: open	**Room & Board:** $5010
Freshman Class: 17,082 applied, 13,620 accepted, 5868 enrolled	
SAT I Verbal/Math: 548/559	**ACT:** 24 **VERY COMPETITIVE**

Arizona State University-Main, founded in 1885, is a publicly funded institution offering undergraduate programs in the arts and sciences, business, education, engineering, nursing, public programs, architecture and environmental design, social work, and fine arts. There are 10 undergraduate and 10 graduate schools. In addition to regional accreditation, ASU-Main has baccalaureate program accreditation with AACSB, ABET, ACCE, ACEJMC, ADA, CSAB, CSWE, FIDER, NAAB, NASM, NCATE, NLN, and NRPA. The 5 libraries contain 2,989,011 volumes, 5,246,784 microform items, and 52,061 audiovisual forms/CDs, and subscribe to 32,853 periodicals. Computerized library services include the card catalog, interlibrary loans, and database searching. Special learning facilities include an art gallery, planetarium, radio station, and TV station. The 716-acre campus is in a suburban area 10 miles east of Phoenix.

Programs of Study: ASU-Main confers B.A., B.S., B.A.E., B.F.A., B.I.S., B. Mus., B.S.D., B.S.E., B.S.L.A., B.S.N., B.S.P., and B.S.W. degrees. Master's and doctoral degrees are also awarded. Bachelor's degrees are awarded in AGRICULTURE (natural resource management and plant science), BIOLOGICAL SCIENCE (biochemistry, biology/biological science, environmental biology, microbiology, molecular biology, and wildlife biology), BUSINESS (accounting, banking and finance, management science, marketing/retailing/merchandising, purchasing/inventory management, real estate, recreation and leisure services, tourism, and transportation management), COMMUNICATIONS AND THE ARTS (art, art history and appreciation, broadcasting, ceramic art and design,

Chinese, communications, dance, dramatic arts, drawing, English, French, German, graphic design, industrial design, Italian, Japanese, journalism, media arts, metal/jewelry, music, music performance, music theory and composition, painting, photography, printmaking, Russian, sculpture, and Spanish), COMPUTER AND PHYSICAL SCIENCE (chemistry, computer science, geology, information sciences and systems, mathematics, and physics), EDUCATION (early childhood, elementary, music, secondary, and special), ENGINEERING AND ENVIRONMENTAL DESIGN (aeronautical engineering, architecture, bioengineering, chemical engineering, civil engineering, computer engineering, construction engineering, electrical/electronics engineering, engineering, industrial engineering, interior design, landscape architecture/design, materials science, mechanical engineering, urban design, and urban planning technology), HEALTH PROFESSIONS (clinical science, music therapy, nursing, and speech pathology/audiology), SOCIAL SCIENCE (African American studies, anthropology, criminal justice, economics, family/consumer resource management, geography, Hispanic American studies, history, humanities, interdisciplinary studies, parks and recreation management, philosophy, physical fitness/movement, political science/government, psychology, religion, social work, sociology, and women's studies). Engineering, architecture, and computer science are the strongest academically. Business, psychology, and elementary education are the largest.

Special: ASU-Main offers internships in many disciplines, study abroad in 10 countries, and a variety of interdisciplinary undergraduate programs. Students may participate in educational programs supported by several institutes and centers, such as the National Center for Electron Microscopy, the American Indian Institute, and the Center for Medieval and Renaissance Studies. Also available are continuing education programs and a summer math and science program for high school students. There are 26 national honor societies, including Phi Beta Kappa, and a freshman honors program.

Admissions: 80% of the 1999-2000 applicants were accepted. The SAT I scores for the 1999-2000 freshman class were: Verbal--28% below 500, 43% between 500 and 599, 22% between 600 and 700, and 6% above 700; Math--26% below 500, 40% between 500 and 599, 27% between 600 and 700, and 8% above 700. The ACT scores were 24% below 21, 27% between 21 and 23, 25% between 24 and 26, 12% between 27 and 28, and 13% above 28. 49% of the current freshmen were in the top fifth of their class; 76% were in the top two fifths. There were 136 National Merit finalists.

Requirements: The SAT I or ACT is required. The minimum composite score on the ACT is 22 for in-state students, 24 for out-of-state students; on the SAT I, 1040 for in-state students, 1110 for out-of-state students. ASU-Main requires applicants to be in the upper 25% of their class. A GPA of 3.0 is required. Graduation from an accredited secondary school must include 4 years each of English and math, 3 years of lab science, 2 years each of social science (including American history) and the same foreign language, and 1 year of fine arts. The GED, minimum score 50, is also accepted. AP and CLEP credits are accepted.

Procedure: Freshmen are admitted to all sessions. Entrance exams should be taken late in the junior year. Application deadlines are open; there is a $40 fee. Notification of early decision is sent December 1; regular decision, on a rolling basis.

Financial Aid: In 1998-99, 38% of all freshmen received some form of financial aid. 33% of freshmen received need-based aid. The average freshman award was $6135. The average financial indebtedness of the 1998 graduate was $17,385. ASU-Main is a member of CSS. The CSS/Profile, FAFSA, FFS or SFS is required. The fall application deadline is March 1.

Computers: There are IBM RS/6000/390s and 590s and an SGI Power Challenge as computer servers, HP 9000/735s as statistical servers, an IBM RS/6000 and HP 9000/735 as file servers, Sun SPARC20s, Sun SPARC10s, HP 9000/712s, and IBM RS/6000/250s as translators, an HP T500 and HP K200 for development as transaction servers, and Sun SPARC20s and Sun SPARC10s as miscellaneous servers. Also available are 770 Rycom, MAG, HAL, Zenith, and Mac PCs in 7 areas on campus. All students may access the system; 1 site is open 24 hours per day. There are no time limits and no fees.

ART CENTER COLLEGE OF DESIGN
Pasadena, CA 91103   (626) 396-2373; Fax: (626) 795-0578

Full-time: 806 men, 537 women	**Faculty:** 56
Part-time: none	**Ph.D.s:** 10%
Graduate: 49 men, 34 women	**Student/Faculty:** 24 to 1
Year: trimesters, summer session	**Tuition:** $18,050
Application Deadline: open	**Room & Board:** n/app
Freshman Class: 1148 applied, 741 accepted, 543 enrolled	
SAT I or ACT: required	**SPECIAL**

Art Center College of Design, founded in 1930, is a private, nonprofit institution offering programs in fine arts and design. There is 1 graduate school. In addition to regional accreditation, Art Center has baccalaureate program accreditation with NASAD. The library contains 64,000 volumes, 60,000 microform items, and 4000 audiovisual forms/CDs, and subscribes to 400 periodicals. Computerized library services include the card catalog and database searching. Special learning facilities include an art gallery. The 175-acre campus is in a suburban area 10 miles northwest of Los Angeles. There is 1 building.

Programs of Study: Art Center confers B.F.A. and B.S. degrees. Master's degrees are also awarded. Bachelor's degrees are awarded in COMMUNICATIONS AND THE ARTS (advertising, design, film arts, fine arts, graphic design, illustration, industrial design, and photography), ENGINEERING AND ENVIRONMENTAL DESIGN (environmental design). Illustration, graphic design, and industrial design are the largest.

Special: The college offers cross-registration with Occidental College and the California Institute of Technology, internships, and nondegree study.

Admissions: 65% of the 1999-2000 applicants were accepted.

Requirements: The SAT I or ACT is required. A GPA of 2.5 is required. In addition, applicants must be graduates of an accredited secondary school or have a GED. Official transcripts and a portfolio must be submitted. An interview is recommended. No applications accepted on computer disk or on-line. AP credits are accepted. Important factors in the admissions decision are evidence of special talent, advanced placement or honor courses, and extracurricular activities record.

Procedure: Freshmen are admitted to all sessions. Entrance exams should be taken in the senior year. Application deadlines are open, along with a $45 fee. Notification is sent on a rolling basis.

Financial Aid: 40% of undergraduates work part time. Average annual earnings from campus work are $1070. Art Center is a member of CSS. The FAFSA and the college's own financial statement are required. The fall application deadline is March 1.

Computers: Many personal and graphics computers are available. There are no time limits and no fees. It is strongly recommended that all students have personal Mac computers.

ART INSTITUTE OF ATLANTA
Atlanta, GA 30328

(770) 394-8300
(800) 275-4242; Fax: (770) 394-0008

Full-time: 922 men, 754 women
Part-time: 126 men, 137 women
Graduate: none
Year: quarters, summer session
Application Deadline: September 1
Freshman Class: n/av
SAT I or ACT: not required

Faculty: 49
Ph.D.s: 17%
Student/Faculty: 34 to 1
Tuition: $12,624
Room: $4539

SPECIAL

The Art Institute of Atlanta, founded in 1949, seeks to educate creative professionals. Some of the information in this profile is approximate. The Institute offers bachelor's degree programs in computer animation, graphic design, interior design, multimedia, and photographic imaging, and associate degree programs in culinary arts, graphic design, multimedia and web design, photographic imaging, and video production. In addition to regional accreditation, the Art Institute has baccalaureate program accreditation with FIDER. The library contains 30,460 volumes and 2428 audiovisual forms/CDs, and subscribes to 159 periodicals. Computerized library services include the card catalog, interlibrary loans, and database searching. Special learning facilities include a learning resource center and art gallery. The 2-acre campus is in a suburban area in the Metro-Atlanta community of Dunwoody, approximately 5 miles north of the city limits. There is 1 buildings.

Programs of Study: The Art Institute confers the B.F.A. degree. Associate degrees are also awarded. Bachelor's degrees are awarded in COMMUNICATIONS AND THE ARTS (graphic design, multimedia, and photography), ENGINEERING AND ENVIRONMENTAL DESIGN (computer graphics and interior design). Culinary arts, computer animation, and graphic design are the largest.

Special: There is cross-registration with English Language Centers. Internships and study abroad in 2 countries are possible.

Requirements: Students must submit SAT I, ACT, ASSET, or COMPASS test scores. (COMPASS testing is offered free at the college to any applicant needing it.) Preference is given to applicants with GPAs of 3.0 or above; a minimum GPA of 2.5 for bachelor's degree applicants is highly recommended. An official transcript showing high school GPA is required; the GED is accepted. An essay and an interview are required. Applications are accepted on-line at the school's web site. AP and CLEP credits are accepted.

Procedure: Freshmen are admitted to all sessions. Entrance exams should be taken prior to the application closing date. There are early admissions and deferred admissions plans. Early decision applications should be filed by September 1, along with a $50 fee. Notification is sent on a rolling basis.

Financial Aid: 86% of undergraduates work part time. Average annual earnings from campus work are $3690. The average financial indebtedness of the 1999 graduate was $6375. The FAFSA is required.

Computers: Students are allowed full Internet access in each of the college's 12 computer labs. There are 200 PCs for student use. All students may access the system. There are no time limits and no fees.

ART INSTITUTE OF BOSTON AT LESLEY COLLEGE
Boston, MA 02215

(617) 585-6700
(800) 773-0494; Fax: (617) 437-1226

Full-time: 243 men, 217 women	**Faculty:** 22
Part-time: 24 men, 50 women	**Ph.D.s:** 95%
Graduate: none	**Student/Faculty:** 21 to 1
Year: semesters, summer session	**Tuition:** $13,220
Application Deadline: see profile	**Room & Board:** $8200
Freshman Class: n/av	
SAT I Verbal/Math: 513/489	

The Art Institute of Boston at Lesley College (formerly, Art Institute of Boston), founded in 1912, is a private institution offering undergraduate visual art programs leading to baccalaureate degree, 3-year diplomas, and Advanced Professional Certificates. Some of the information in this profile is approximate. In addition to regional accreditation, AIB has baccalaureate program accreditation with NASAD. The library contains 9000 volumes and 450 audiovisual forms/CDs, and subscribes to 80 periodicals. Computerized library services include interlibrary loans and database searching. Special learning facilities include an art gallery. The campus is in an urban area in the Kenmore Square area of Boston. Including residence halls, there are 2 buildings.

Programs of Study: AIB confers the B.F.A. degree. Bachelor's degrees are awarded in COMMUNICATIONS AND THE ARTS (design, fine arts, illustration, and photography).

Special: There is cross-registration with Boston Architectural Center and Lesley College. Internships are required for design majors and encouraged for all other majors. Accelerated degree programs in all majors, study abroad in Italy, and dual majors in fine art/illustration, design/illustration, and illustration/animation are offered. There is a freshman honors program, and 1 departmental honors program.

Admissions: 86% of the 1999-2000 applicants were accepted.

Requirements: The SAT I or ACT is required. Applicants must submit official high school transcripts; a portfolio review is required. Letters of recommendation and a campus tour are encouraged. AP and CLEP credits are accepted. Important factors in the admissions decision are evidence of special talent, advanced placement or honor courses, and leadership record.

Procedure: Freshmen are admitted to all sessions. There is a deferred admissions plan. Application deadlines are open, but February 20 is preferred for fall entry. Notification is sent on a rolling basis. A waiting list is an active part of the admissions procedure.

Financial Aid: In a recent year, 75% of all freshmen and 74% of continuing students received some form of financial aid. 44% of freshmen and 49% of continuing students received need-based aid. The average freshman award was $8678. Of that total, scholarships or need-based grants averaged $2058 ($2500 maximum); loans averaged $5185 ($23,070 maximum); and work contracts averaged $1435 ($2000 maximum). 8% of undergraduates work part time. Average annual earnings from campus work were $1709. The average financial indebtedness of a recent graduate was $17,125. AIB is a member of CSS. The FAFSA and the college's own financial statement are required. The fall application deadline is March 15.

Computers: Computers are available for digital imaging, desktop publishing, animation, scanning, word processing, and Internet access. There are 3 labs of 50

Macs, and satellite computers are distributed in groups throughout the college for specialized uses. All students may access the system. There are no time limits and no fees.

ART INSTITUTE OF PORTLAND
Portland, OR 97201

(503) 228-6528
(888) 228-6528; Fax: (503) 228-4227

Full-time: 175 men, 187 women	**Faculty:** 15; III, --$
Part-time: 16 men, 65 women	**Ph.D.s:** 35%
Graduate: none	**Student/Faculty:** 24 to 1
Year: quarters, summer session	**Tuition:** $12,060
Application Deadline: open	**Room & Board:** n/app
Freshman Class: n/av	
SAT I or ACT: not required	**SPECIAL**

The Art Institute of Portland (formerly Bassist College), founded in 1963, is a private institution offering undergraduate programs in interior, graphic, and apparel design; computer animation; and multimedia and web design. The library contains 19,174 volumes and 400 audiovisual forms/CDs, and subscribes to 200 periodicals. Computerized library services include the card catalog, interlibrary loans, and database searching. Special learning facilities include a learning resource center. The 1-acre campus is in an urban area in downtown Portland. There are 2 buildings.

Programs of Study: AIPD confers the B.S. degree. Associate degrees are also awarded. Bachelor's degrees are awarded in COMMUNICATIONS AND THE ARTS (apparel design, graphic design, and multimedia), ENGINEERING AND ENVIRONMENTAL DESIGN (computer graphics and interior design). Interior design is the strongest academically. Computer animation is the largest.

Special: Field trips to Seattle are available. Internships are required for most bachelor's degree programs.

Requirements: A high school diploma is required. An interview with an admissions officer and an essay are required. AP and CLEP credits are accepted.

Procedure: Freshmen are admitted to all sessions. Application deadlines are open. There is a $50 fee. Notification is sent on a rolling basis.

Financial Aid: In 1999-2000, 80% of all freshmen and 76% of continuing students received some form of financial aid. 73% of freshmen and 62% of continuing students received need-based aid. The average freshman award was $9340. Of that total, scholarships or need-based grants averaged $1124 ($3125 maximum); loans averaged $7853 ($17,625 maximum); and outside scholarships, vocational rehabilitation, alternative loan programs, and tuition reimbursement averaged $861 ($11655 maximum). 6% of undergraduates work part time. Average annual earnings from campus work are $1500. The average financial indebtedness of the 1999 graduate was $10,490. AIPD is a member of CSS. The FAFSA and the college's own financial statement are required. The fall application deadline is rolling.

Computers: There are 3 IBM PCs and 15 CAD machines available. Students who have been trained in its use may access the system weekdays during lab hours. There are no time limits. The fee is $5 per quarter. It is strongly recommended that all students have personal computers.

AUGUSTANA COLLEGE

Rock Island, IL 61201-2296   **(309) 794-7341**
(800) 798-8100, ext. 7341; Fax: (309) 794-7422

Full-time: 895 men, 1287 women	**Faculty:** 144; IIB, av$
Part-time: 13 men, 14 women	**Ph.D.s:** 89%
Graduate: none	**Student/Faculty:** 15 to 1
Year: quarters, summer session	**Tuition:** $17,187
Application Deadline: open	**Room & Board:** $5037
Freshman Class: 2288 applied, 1835 accepted, 565 enrolled	
ACT: 26	**VERY COMPETITIVE+**

Augustana College, founded in 1860, is a private liberal arts institution affiliated with the Evangelical Lutheran Church in America. In addition to regional accreditation, Augustana has baccalaureate program accreditation with NASM and NCATE. The 3 libraries contain 260,131 volumes, 114,596 microform items, and 2639 audiovisual forms/CDs, and subscribe to 1870 periodicals. Computerized library services include the card catalog, interlibrary loans, and database searching. Special learning facilities include a learning resource center, art gallery, planetarium, radio station, a preschool, a center for communicative disorders, a geology museum, an observatory, a map library, a Swedish immigration research center, 2 outdoor environmental labs, and an educational technology building. The 115-acre campus is in a suburban area 165 miles west of Chicago. Including residence halls, there are 46 buildings.

Programs of Study: Augustana confers the B.A. degree. Bachelor's degrees are awarded in BIOLOGICAL SCIENCE (biology/biological science), BUSINESS (accounting and business administration and management), COMMUNICATIONS AND THE ARTS (art history and appreciation, classics, dramatic arts, English, French, German, music, Scandinavian languages, Spanish, speech/debate/rhetoric, and studio art), COMPUTER AND PHYSICAL SCIENCE (chemistry, computer science, earth science, geology, mathematics, and physics), EDUCATION (art, elementary, music, physical, and secondary), ENGINEERING AND ENVIRONMENTAL DESIGN (engineering physics, environmental science, landscape architecture/design, and preengineering), HEALTH PROFESSIONS (cytotechnology, occupational therapy, premedicine, and speech pathology/audiology), SOCIAL SCIENCE (Asian/Oriental studies, economics, geography, history, philosophy, political science/government, psychology, public administration, religion, and sociology). Business administration, biology, and education are the largest.

Special: Coordinated degree programs are offered in engineering, environmental management, forestry, landscape architecture, and occupational therapy with Duke, Iowa State, Northwestern, Purdue, and Washington (St. Louis) Universities and University of Illinois (Urbana-Champaign). Domestic and international internships are offered. Study abroad is possible in 17 countries, including China, Peru, Sweden, Germany, and France, as well as fall term study in East Asia, Europe, and Latin America. Interdisciplinary majors are offered in earth science, teaching, Asian studies, and public administration. A B.A.-B.S. degree in occupational therapy is offered, as well as 3-2 engineering programs with the University of Illinois, Purdue, Washington (St. Louis), and Iowa State Universities. Work-study programs, double majors, phys ed credits, and pass/fail options are available. There are 13 national honor societies, including Phi Beta Kappa, a freshman honors program, and 12 departmental honors programs.

Admissions: 80% of the 1999-2000 applicants were accepted. The ACT scores for the 1999-2000 freshman class were: 6% below 21, 22% between 21 and 23,

35% between 24 and 26, 18% between 27 and 28, and 19% above 28. 61% of the current freshmen were in the top fifth of their class; 88% were in the top two fifths.

Requirements: The SAT I or ACT is required. Applicants should be graduates of an accredited secondary school with 16 academic credits, including 4 in English, 3 in math, 2 each in science and social studies, and 1 in foreign language, and other science and math courses for appropriate majors. An audition for music majors and an interview are recommended. The GED is accepted. Augustana accepts the Common App on disk. Applications are accepted on-line at www.collegenet.com. AP credits are accepted. Important factors in the admissions decision are advanced placement or honor courses, evidence of special talent, and recommendations by school officials.

Procedure: Freshmen are admitted fall, winter, and spring. Entrance exams should be taken by fall of the senior year. There is a deferred admissions plan. Application deadlines are open. There is a $25 fee. Notification is sent on a rolling basis. 4% of all applicants are on a waiting list.

Financial Aid: In a recent year, 96% of all freshmen and 91% of continuing students received some form of financial aid. 66% of freshmen and 67% of continuing students received need-based aid. The average freshman award was $13,266. Of that total, scholarships or need-based grants averaged $9095 ($15,195 maximum); loans averaged $3150 ($4625 maximum); and work contracts averaged $1253 ($1350 maximum). 80% of undergraduates work part time. Average annual earnings from campus work are $810. The average financial indebtedness of a recent year's graduate was $16,230. Augustana is a member of CSS. The FAFSA and the college's own financial statement are required. The fall application deadline is April 5.

Computers: The mainframes are a DEC ALPHA 3000 and a DEC ALPHA 800. More than 750 college-owned PCs and 650 student-owned PCs are included in a comprehensive network linking academic and administrative buildings and residence halls. Access to the Internet and supercomputers at the University of Illinois is provided. An educational technology building provides extensive facilities for general and multimedia computing. Residence hall rooms have network jacks for student-owned computers. All students may access the system. There are no time limits and no fees. It is strongly recommended that all students have personal computers.

AUGUSTANA COLLEGE
Sioux Falls, SD 57197

(605) 336-5516
(800) 727-2844; Fax: (605) 336-5518

Full-time: 549 men, 1038 women	**Faculty:** 118; IIB, -$
Part-time: 62 men, 79 women	**Ph.D.s:** 90%
Graduate: 15 men, 31 women	**Student/Faculty:** 13 to 1
Year: 4-1-4, summer session	**Tuition:** $14,114
Application Deadline: open	**Room & Board:** $4058
Freshman Class: 1445 applied, 1242 accepted, 469 enrolled	
SAT I Verbal/Math: 570/580	**ACT:** 24 **VERY COMPETITIVE**

Augustana College, founded in 1860, is a private liberal arts institution affiliated with the Evangelical Lutheran Church in America. In addition to regional accreditation, Augustana has baccalaureate program accreditation with CSWE, NASM, NCATE, and NLN. The library contains 236,376 volumes, 86,124 microform items, and 5180 audiovisual forms/CDs, and subscribes to 1043 periodicals. Computerized library services include the card catalog, interlibrary loans, and database searching. Special learning facilities include an art gallery, natural history museum, and radio station. The 100-acre campus is in a suburban area 150 miles north of Omaha, Nebraska. Including residence halls, there are 17 buildings.

Programs of Study: Augustana confers the B.A. degree. Master's degrees are also awarded. Bachelor's degrees are awarded in BIOLOGICAL SCIENCE (biology/biological science), BUSINESS (accounting, business administration and management, and management information systems), COMMUNICATIONS AND THE ARTS (art, communications, dramatic arts, English, French, German, journalism, modern language, music, and Spanish), COMPUTER AND PHYSICAL SCIENCE (chemistry, computer science, mathematics, and physics), EDUCATION (athletic training, drama, education of the deaf and hearing impaired, elementary, health, music, secondary, social studies, and special), ENGINEERING AND ENVIRONMENTAL DESIGN (engineering physics), HEALTH PROFESSIONS (health, health science, medical technology, nursing, and speech pathology/audiology), SOCIAL SCIENCE (economics, history, international relations, international studies, philosophy, physical fitness/movement, political science/government, psychology, religion, social work, and sociology). Biology, chemistry, and government are the strongest academically. Education, biology, and business are the largest.

Special: Internships, study abroad in 40 countries, and a 3-2 engineering degree with Columbia University, Washington University in St. Louis, or University of Minnesota are offered. A Washington semester with Lutheran College Washington Consortium or American University is offered. Credit for life experience is possible. There are 17 national honor societies, and 4 departmental honors programs.

Admissions: 86% of the 1999-2000 applicants were accepted. The SAT I scores for the 1999-2000 freshman class were: Verbal--10% below 500, 54% between 500 and 599, 24% between 600 and 700, and 12% above 700; Math--14% below 500, 38% between 500 and 599, 36% between 600 and 700, and 12% above 700. The ACT scores were 16% below 21, 28% between 21 and 23, 26% between 24 and 26, 17% between 27 and 28, and 14% above 28. 50% of the current freshmen were in the top fifth of their class; 79% were in the top two fifths. There were 4 National Merit finalists. 38 freshmen graduated first in their class.

Requirements: The SAT I or ACT is required. Augustana requires applicants to be in the upper 50% of their class. A GPA of 2.5 is required. In addition, graduation from an accredited secondary school is preferred; however, a GED will be accepted. Applicants should have completed 4 years of high school English, 3 each of math and science, and 2 each of a foreign language and history. An interview is recommended. AP and CLEP credits are accepted. Important factors in the admissions decision are advanced placement or honor courses, leadership record, and parents or siblings attending the school.

Procedure: Freshmen are admitted fall, spring, and summer. Entrance exams should be taken in the spring of the junior year or early fall of the senior year. There are early admissions and deferred admissions plans. Application deadlines are open. There is a $25 fee. Notification is sent on a rolling basis.

Financial Aid: In 1999-2000, 96% of all freshmen and 91% of continuing students received some form of financial aid. 77% of freshmen and 76% of continuing students received need-based aid. The average freshman award was $11,000. Of that total, scholarships or need-based grants averaged $5200; loans averaged $4650; and work contracts averaged $1300. 94% of undergraduates work part time. Average annual earnings from campus work are $1225. The average financial indebtedness of the 1999 graduate was $17,561. Augustana is a member of CSS. The FAFSA is required. The fall application deadline is March 1.

Computers: The mainframe is an IBM RS/6000. More than 360 computers, mostly Pentium models, are available to students, with 125 available 24 hours per day. Each residence hall has a computer lab. All students may access the system. There are no time limits. A fee is charged for students using the system from residence hall rooms.

AUSTIN COLLEGE
Sherman, TX 75090-4440

(903) 813-3000
(800) 442-5363; Fax: (903) 813-3198

Full-time: 561 men, 658 women	**Faculty:** 79; IIB, ++$
Part-time: 6 men, 8 women	**Ph.D.s:** 96%
Graduate: 3 men, 21 women	**Student/Faculty:** 15 to 1
Year: 4-1-4, summer session	**Tuition:** $15,427
Application Deadline: March 1	**Room & Board:** $5891
Freshman Class: 1003 applied, 782 accepted, 324 enrolled	
SAT I Verbal/Math: 600/600	**ACT:** 27 **VERY COMPETITIVE**

Austin College, founded in 1849, is a private liberal arts institution affiliated with the Presbyterian Church (U.S.A.), offering programs in business, liberal arts, and health. There is 1 graduate school. The library contains 156,755 volumes, 99,029 microform items, and 6178 audiovisual forms/CDs, and subscribes to 12,568 periodicals. Computerized library services include the card catalog, interlibrary loans, and database searching. Special learning facilities include a learning resource center, social science lab, television studios for media instruction, environmental research areas near Lake Texoma, and a facility for advanced computing and 3-D graphics. The 60-acre campus is in a suburban area 60 miles north of Dallas. Including residence halls, there are 28 buildings.

Programs of Study: AC confers the B.A. degree. Master's degrees are also awarded. Bachelor's degrees are awarded in BIOLOGICAL SCIENCE (biology/biological science), BUSINESS (business administration and management), COMMUNICATIONS AND THE ARTS (classics, communications, English, fine arts, French, German, Latin, music, and Spanish), COMPUTER AND PHYSICAL SCIENCE (chemistry, mathematics, and physics), EDUCATION (physical), SOCIAL SCIENCE (American studies, economics, history, interdisciplinary studies, international studies, Latin American studies, philosophy, political science/government, psychology, religion, and sociology). Chemistry, biology, and international studies, are the strongest academically. Business administration, psychology, and biology are the largest.

Special: AC offers co-op programs with Central College and the Institute for European Studies, internships during the January and summer terms, study abroad in 10 countries, and a Washington summer seminar. Work-study, accelerated degree programs in all majors, and dual and student-designed majors are available. There is a 3-2 engineering degree program in conjunction with the University of Texas at Dallas, Columbia University, Washington University in St. Louis, and Texas A&M University. Nondegree study, pass/fail options, preprofessional teacher education programs, and a January term with experimental and off-campus opportunities are offered. There are 11 national honor societies.

Admissions: 78% of the 1999-2000 applicants were accepted. The SAT I scores for the 1999-2000 freshman class were: Verbal--6% below 500, 36% between 500 and 599, 42% between 600 and 700, and 16% above 700; Math--9% below 500, 38% between 500 and 599, 40% between 600 and 700, and 13% above 700. The ACT scores were 4% below 21, 16% between 21 and 23, 27% between 24 and 26, 16% between 27 and 28, and 37% above 28. 69% of the current freshmen

were in the top fifth of their class; 89% were in the top two fifths. There were 6 National Merit finalists. 18 freshmen graduated first in their class.

Requirements: The SAT I or ACT is required. AC requires applicants to be in the upper 50% of their class. Applicants must be graduates of an accredited secondary school or have a GED. The minimum recommended academic requirements are 4 credits in English, 3 each in math and science, 2 each in social studies and foreign language, and 1 in art/music/theater. An essay is required, and an interview is recommended. Applications are accepted on-line. AP and CLEP credits are accepted. Important factors in the admissions decision are advanced placement or honor courses, leadership record, and evidence of special talent.

Procedure: Freshmen are admitted fall, spring, and summer. Entrance exams should be taken in the junior year or the fall of the senior year. There are early decision, early admissions, and deferred admissions plans. Early decision applications should be filed by December 1; priority applications, by March 1 for fall entry, along with a $35 fee. Notification of early decision is sent beginning January 1; regular decision, on April 15. 30 early decision candidates were accepted for the 1999-2000 class.

Financial Aid: In 1999-2000, 96% of all freshmen and 93% of continuing students received some form of financial aid. 69% of freshmen and 62% of continuing students received need-based aid. The average freshman award was $15,963. Of that total, scholarships or need-based grants averaged $10,490 ($14,785 maximum); loans averaged $3016 ($8000 maximum); work contracts averaged $1522 ($1600 maximum); and non-need-based loans, including CAL, PLUS, and Unsubsidized Stafford, averaged $6108 ($21,425 maximum). 40% of undergraduates work part time. Average annual earnings from campus work are $1500. The average financial indebtedness of the 1999 graduate was $21,550. AC is a member of CSS. The FAFSA and the college's own financial statement are required. The fall application deadline is April 1.

Computers: The mainframe is a DEC ALPHA 4100. Students have access to 25 Dell Pentiums, 15 Mac Power PCs, 15 HP 712 workstations, and an SGI Indigo Extreme from the main computer labs. Each residence hall also has a computer cluster with PCs and Macs. The college provides free laser printing for students and access to the campus network and the Internet, including a full array of software, from residence hall rooms. All students may access the system 10 hours daily (24 hours in some locations). There are no time limits and no fees.

BABSON COLLEGE
Babson Park, MA 02457

(781) 239-5522
(800) 488-3696; Fax: (781) 239-4135

Full-time: 1096 men, 605 women	**Faculty:** 143; IIB, ++$
Part-time: none	**Ph.D.s:** 91%
Graduate: 1187 men, 543 women	**Student/Faculty:** 12 to 1
Year: semesters, summer session	**Tuition:** $21,072
Application Deadline: February 1	**Room & Board:** $8392
Freshman Class: 2582 applied, 1170 accepted, 414 enrolled	
SAT I or ACT: required	**HIGHLY COMPETITIVE**

Babson College, founded in 1919, is a private institution offering programs in business. There is 1 graduate school. In addition to regional accreditation, Babson has baccalaureate program accreditation with AACSB. The library contains 131, 330 volumes, 346,579 microform items, and 4129 audiovisual forms CDs, and subscribes to 1545 periodicals. Computerized library services include the card catalog, interlibrary loans, and database searching. Special learning facilities include a learning resource center, art gallery, radio station, performing arts theater, center for entrepreneurial studies, management center, and language and culture center. The 380-acre campus is in a suburban area 14 miles west of Boston. Including residence halls, there are 65 buildings.

Programs of Study: Babson confers the B.S.M. degree. Master's degrees are also awarded. Bachelor's degrees are awarded in BUSINESS (business administration and management).

Special: There is cross-registration with Brandeis University and Pine Manor, Wellesley, and Regis Colleges. Internships and study abroad in 20 countries are available. All concentrations are self-designed. There are 7 national honor societies, a freshman honors program, and 1 departmental honors program.

Admissions: 45% of the 1999-2000 applicants were accepted. The SAT I scores for the 1999-2000 freshman class were: Verbal--8% below 500, 49% between 500 and 599, 40% between 600 and 700, and 3% above 700; Math--2% below 500, 27% between 500 and 599, 56% between 600 and 700, and 15% above 700. 57% of the current freshmen were in the top fifth of their class; 85% were in the top two fifths.

Requirements: The SAT I or ACT is required. SAT II: Subject tests in writing and mathematics are required. applicants must be graduates of an accredited secondary school or have a GED. 16 academic courses are required, including 4 credits of English, 3 of math, 2 of social studies, and 1 of science. A fourth year of math is strongly recommended. Essays are required. An interview is recommended. Applications are accepted on computer disk and on-line via CollegeLink, ExPAN, CollegeView, and College Edge. AP and CLEP credits are accepted. Important factors in the admissions decision are advanced placement or honor courses, evidence of special talent, and leadership record.

Procedure: Freshmen are admitted fall and spring. Entrance exams should be taken prior to application (SAT I or ACT). SAT II: Subject tests should be taken by June of the senior year. There are early decision, early admissions, and deferred admissions plans. Early decision applications should be filed by December 1 or January 1; regular applications, by February 1 for fall entry and November 1 for spring entry, along with a $50 fee ($100 international). Notification of early decision is sent January 1 or February 1; regular decision, April 1. 36 early decision candidates were accepted for the 1999-2000 class. 7% of all applicants are on a waiting list.

Financial Aid: In 1999-2000, 47% of all freshmen and 44% of continuing students received some form of financial aid. 41% of freshmen and 40% of continuing students received need-based aid. The average freshman award was $17,150. Of that total, scholarships or need-based grants averaged $13,094 ($24,000 maximum); loans averaged $2867 ($4625 maximum); and work contracts averaged $1189 ($1800 maximum). 25% of undergraduates work part time. Average annual earnings from campus work are $1000. The average financial indebtedness of the 1999 graduate was $18,000. Babson is a member of CSS. The CSS/Profile or FAFSA and tax returns are required. The fall application deadline is February 15.

Computers: Residence hall rooms have access to GlobeNet through a 10-Base-T Ethernet connection. Access to the Internet, including Netscape for browsing the World Wide Web, and E-mail are also provided. All students may access the system. There are no time limits and no fees. The college strongly recommends that students have PCs or IBM Thinkpad 570. Dell Latitude CPf is recommended.

BALDWIN-WALLACE COLLEGE
Berea, OH 44017-2088   (440) 826-2222; Fax: (440) 826-3830

Full-time: 1216 men, 1748 women	**Faculty:** 159; IIB, ++$
Part-time: 332 men, 706 women	**Ph.D:s:** 78%
Graduate: 258 men, 386 women	**Student/Faculty:** 19 to 1
Year: semesters, summer session	**Tuition:** $14,640
Application Deadline: May 1	**Room & Board:** $5260
Freshman Class: 2115 applied, 1721 accepted, 715 enrolled	
SAT I Verbal/Math: 550/560	**ACT:** 24 **VERY COMPETITIVE**

Baldwin-Wallace College, established in 1845, is a private liberal arts institution affiliated with the United Methodist Church. There are 2 graduate schools. In addition to regional accreditation, B-W has baccalaureate program accreditation with NASM and NCATE. The 3 libraries contain 250,000 volumes, 103,000 microform items, and 18,500 audiovisual forms/CDs, and subscribe to 1000 periodicals. Computerized library services include the card catalog, interlibrary loans, and database searching. Special learning facilities include a learning resource center, art gallery, and radio station. The 56-acre campus is in a suburban area 14 miles southwest of Cleveland. Including residence halls, there are 57 buildings.

Programs of Study: B-W confers B.A., B.S., B.M., B.M.E, and B.S.Ed. degrees. Master's degrees are also awarded. Bachelor's degrees are awarded in BIOLOGICAL SCIENCE (biology/biological science), BUSINESS (accounting, banking and finance, business administration and management, marketing/retailing/merchandising, personnel management, and sports management), COMMUNICATIONS AND THE ARTS (broadcasting, communications, dance, dramatic arts, English, fine arts, French, German, music business management, music performance, Spanish, and speech/debate/rhetoric), COMPUTER AND PHYSICAL SCIENCE (chemistry, computer science, earth science, geology, mathematics, and physics), EDUCATION (art, elementary, foreign languages, health, home economics, music, science, secondary, social studies, and special), ENGINEERING AND ENVIRONMENTAL DESIGN (engineering), HEALTH PROFESSIONS (medical laboratory technology, music therapy, predentistry, premedicine, speech pathology/audiology, and sports medicine), SOCIAL SCIENCE (community services, criminal justice, economics, history, international relations, philosophy, physical fitness/movement, political science/government, prelaw, psychology, religion, and sociology). Business, music, and education are the largest.

Special: Special academic programs include internships that can qualify for credit, work-study programs, student teaching in England, and study abroad in Europe, India, Japan, Central America, and the Middle East. There is cross-registration within the Cleveland Commission on Higher Education, as well as 3-2 programs in social work and biology with Case Western Reserve University, in forestry with Duke University, and in engineering with Columbia, Washington, and Case Western Reserve universities; a 2-2 co-op allied health program is offered with local community colleges. B-W also offers the Consortium for Music Therapy, accelerated degree programs, a general studies degree, a B.A.-B.S. degree, dual and student-designed majors, credit for life, military, and work experience, and pass/fail options. The Continuing Education Program offers degrees through evening and weekend colleges. There are 5 national honor societies, a freshman honors program, and 11 departmental honors programs.

Admissions: 81% of the 1999-2000 applicants were accepted. The SAT I scores for the 1999-2000 freshman class were: Verbal--24% below 500, 39% between 500 and 599, 33% between 600 and 700, and 4% above 700; Math--20% below

500, 42% between 500 and 599, 31% between 600 and 700, and 7% above 700. The ACT scores were 21% below 21, 28% between 21 and 23, 29% between 24 and 26, 13% between 27 and 28, and 9% above 28. 54% of the current freshmen were in the top fifth of their class; 81% were in the top two fifths. 31 freshmen graduated first in their class.

Requirements: The SAT I or ACT is required. B-W requires applicants to be in the upper 50% of their class. A GPA of 2.5 is required. The recommended minimum score for the ACT is 20; for the SAT I, a composite score of 900 (450 each in verbal and math). The scores are used to support data from the high school record; alternative scores are considered. Applicants must be graduates of an accredited secondary school or have earned a GED. 16 academic credits are required, including 4 in English, 3 each in math, natural science, and social science, and 2 in a foreign language; alternative distributions are considered. A teacher's recommendation is required. AP and CLEP credits are accepted. Important factors in the admissions decision are leadership record, extracurricular activities record, and recommendations by school officials.

Procedure: Freshmen are admitted to all sessions. Entrance exams should be taken late in the junior year or early in the senior year. There is a deferred admissions plan. Applications should be filed by May 1 for fall entry, March 15 for spring entry, and June 15 for summer entry, along with a $15 fee. Notification is sent on a rolling basis.

Financial Aid: In a recent year 75% of freshmen and 60% of continuing students received need-based aid. The average freshman award was $10,000. Of that total, scholarships or need-based grants averaged $8038 ($18,156 maximum); loans averaged $2855 ($4425 maximum); and work contracts averaged $1600 ($2000 maximum). 80% of undergraduates work part time. Average annual earnings from campus work are $1436. B-W is a member of CSS. The FAFSA and the college's own financial statement are required. The fall application deadline is May 1.

Computers: The mainframe is an IBM RISC 6000 Model 350. The RISC 6000 is networked with approximately 50 PCs in the math and computer science building. The machine may also be accessed via modem. More than 300 PCs are available for student use throughout the campus. All students may access the system 24 hours a day. There are no time limits and no fees.

BARD COLLEGE
Annandale-on-Hudson, NY 12504
(914) 758-7472
Fax: (914) 758-5208

Full-time: 506 men, 699 women	**Faculty:** 106; IIB, ++$
Part-time: 18 men, 38 women	**Ph.D.s:** 97%
Graduate: 67 men, 123 women	**Student/Faculty:** 11 to 1
Year: 4-1-4	**Tuition:** $24,000
Application Deadline: January 31	**Room & Board:** $7220
Freshman Class: 2508 applied, 1177 accepted, 349 enrolled	
SAT I Verbal/Math: 660/610	**HIGHLY COMPETITIVE**

Bard College, founded in 1860, is an independent liberal arts and sciences institution affiliated historically with the Association of Episcopal Colleges. Discussion-oriented seminars and independent study are encouraged, tutorials are on a one-to-one basis, and most classes are kept small, with fewer than 20 students. There are 4 graduate schools. The library contains 260,000 volumes, 5670 microform items, and 5600 audiovisual forms/CDs, and subscribes to 850 periodicals. Computerized library services include the card catalog, interlibrary loans, and database searching. Special learning facilities include a learning resource center, art gallery, radio station, ecology field station, the Jerome Levy International Economics Institute, the Institute for Writing and Thinking, the International Academy for Scholarship and the Arts, the Center for Curatorial Studies and Art in Contemporary Culture, and an archeological field school. The 600-acre campus is in a rural area 100 miles north of New York City. Including residence halls, there are 70 buildings.

Programs of Study: Bard confers B.A. and B.S. degrees. Master's and doctoral degrees are also awarded. Bachelor's degrees are awarded in BIOLOGICAL SCIENCE (biochemistry, biology/biological science, cell biology, ecology, microbiology, and molecular biology), COMMUNICATIONS AND THE ARTS (American literature, art history and appreciation, Chinese, classical languages, classics, creative writing, dance, dramatic arts, drawing, English, English literature, film arts, French, German, Germanic languages and literature, Italian, music history and appreciation, music performance, music theory and composition, painting, photography, Russian, sculpture, and Spanish), COMPUTER AND PHYSICAL SCIENCE (chemistry, mathematics, natural sciences, and physics), ENGINEERING AND ENVIRONMENTAL DESIGN (drafting and design and environmental science), HEALTH PROFESSIONS (predentistry and premedicine), SOCIAL SCIENCE (African studies, American studies, anthropology, archeology, area studies, Asian/Oriental studies, British studies, Celtic studies, clinical psychology, developmental psychology, Eastern European studies, economics, European studies, French studies, history, history of philosophy, history of science, human development, interdisciplinary studies, Italian studies, Judaic studies, Latin American studies, medieval studies, philosophy, political science/government, prelaw, religion, Russian and Slavic studies, social psychology, social science, sociology, and Spanish studies). Social studies, languages and literature, and the arts are the largest.

Special: Bard offers opportunities for study abroad, internships (no academic credit), a Washington semester, dual majors, student-designed majors, accelerated degree programs, and pass/fail options. Cross-registration is available with Vassar College and SUNY/New Paltz. A 3-2 engineering degree is available with the Columbia University School of Engineering. Other 3-2 degrees are available in forestry and environmental studies, social work, architecture, city and regional planning, public health, and business administration. There are also opportunities for independent study; multicultural and ethnic studies; community, regional, and environmental studies; area studies; and the International Honors Program.

Admissions: 47% of the 1999-2000 applicants were accepted. The SAT I scores for the 1999-2000 freshman class were: Verbal--2% below 500, 18% between 500 and 599, 51% between 600 and 700, and 29% above 700; Math--3% below 500, 34% between 500 and 599, 48% between 600 and 700, and 15% above 700. 80% of the current freshmen were in the top fifth of their class; 98% were in the top two fifths. There were 2 National Merit finalists and 16 semifinalists. 20 freshmen graduated first in their class.

Requirements: Bard requires applicants to be in the upper 50% of their class. A GPA of 3.0 is required. Bard places strong emphasis on the academic background and intellectual curiosity of applicants, as well as indications of the student's commitment to social and environmental concerns, independent research, volunteer work, and other important extracurricular activities. Students applying for admission are expected to have graduated from an accredited secondary school (the GED is accepted) and must submit written essays with the application. The high school record should include a full complement of college-preparatory courses. Honors and advanced placement courses are also considered. An interview is recommended. Students may apply on-line with Common Application or

Peterson's. AP credits are accepted. Important factors in the admissions decision are advanced placement or honor courses, evidence of special talent, and extracurricular activities record.

Procedure: Freshmen are admitted fall and spring. There are early decision, early admissions, and deferred admissions plans. Early decision applications should be filed by December 1; regular applications, by January 31 for fall entry and December 1 for spring entry, along with a $40 fee. Notification of early decision is sent January 1; regular decision, April 1. 245 early decision candidates were accepted for the 1999-2000 class. 8% of all applicants are on a waiting list.

Financial Aid: In 1999-2000, 63% of all freshmen and 66% of continuing students received some form of financial aid. 58% of freshmen and 61% of continuing students received need-based aid. The average freshman award was $19,180. Of that total, scholarships or need-based grants averaged $15,055 ($20,000 maximum); loans averaged $2625 ($4125 maximum); and work contracts averaged $1500 (maximum). 50% of undergraduates work part time. Average annual earnings from campus work are $1200. The average financial indebtedness of the 1999 graduate was $16,000. Bard is a member of CSS. The CSS/Profile or FAFSA is required. The fall application deadline is February 15.

Computers: The computer center houses more than 90 networked IBM and Mac PCs. There are more than 400 additional terminals and PCs located in the library, academic departments, and throughout the campus. All students may access the system. There are no time limits and no fees.

BARNARD COLLEGE/COLUMBIA UNIVERSITY

New York, NY 10027-6598   (212) 854-2014; Fax: (212) 854-6220

Full-time: 2250 women	**Faculty:** 178; IIB, ++$
Part-time: 68 women	**Ph.D.s:** 93%
Graduate: none	**Student/Faculty:** 13 to 1
Year: semesters	**Tuition:** $22,316
Application Deadline: January 15	**Room & Board:** $9084
Freshman Class: 3883 applied, 1443 accepted, 558 enrolled	
SAT I Verbal/Math: 670/660	**ACT:** 28 **MOST COMPETITIVE**

Barnard College, founded in 1889, is an independent affiliate of Columbia University. It is an undergraduate women's liberal arts college. The library contains 205,751 volumes, 16,886 microform items, and 13,819 audiovisual forms/CDs, and subscribes to 555 periodicals. Computerized library services include the card catalog, interlibrary loans, and database searching. Special learning facilities include a learning resource center, art gallery, radio station, TV station (with Columbia University), greenhouse, history of physics lab, child development research and study center, dance studio, modern theater, women's research archives within a women's center, and multimedia labs and classrooms. The 4-acre campus is in an urban area occupying 4 city blocks of Manhattan's Upper West Side. Including residence halls, there are 15 buildings.

Programs of Study: The college confers the B.A. degree. Bachelor's degrees are awarded in BIOLOGICAL SCIENCE (biochemistry and biology/biological science), COMMUNICATIONS AND THE ARTS (art history and appreciation, classics, comparative literature, dance, dramatic arts, English, French, German, Greek, Italian, Latin, linguistics, music, Russian, and Spanish), COMPUTER AND PHYSICAL SCIENCE (astronomy, chemistry, computer science, mathematics, physics, and statistics), ENGINEERING AND ENVIRONMENTAL DESIGN (architecture and environmental science), SOCIAL SCIENCE (American studies, anthropology, biopsychology, classical/ancient civilization, East Asian studies, economics, European studies, history, international studies, medieval studies, Middle Eastern studies, philosophy, political science/government, psychology, religion, sociology, urban studies, and women's studies). English, biology, and psychology are the strongest academically. Psychology, English, and economics are the largest.

Special: Barnard offers cross-registration with Columbia University, more than 2500 internships with New York City firms and institutions, and study abroad worldwide. A 3-2 engineering program with the Columbia School of Engineering and double-degree programs with the Columbia University Schools of International and Public Affairs, Law, and Dentistry, the Juilliard School, and the Jewish Theological Seminary are possible. The college offers dual and student-designed majors and multidisciplinary majors, including economic history. There is 1 national honor society, Phi Beta Kappa.

Admissions: 37% of the 1999-2000 applicants were accepted. The SAT I scores for the 1999-2000 freshman class were: Verbal--11% between 500 and 599, 56% between 600 and 700, and 33% above 700; Math--13% between 500 and 599, 66% between 600 and 700, and 21% above 700. The ACT scores were 6% between 21 and 23, 20% between 24 and 26, 25% between 27 and 28, and 49% above 28. 95% of the current freshmen were in the top fifth of their class; 100% were in the top two fifths. There were 2 National Merit finalists.

Requirements: The SAT I or ACT is required. If taking the SAT I, an applicant must also take 3 SAT II: Subject tests, one of which must be in writing or literature. A GED is accepted. Applicants should prepare with 4 years of English, 3 of math, 3 or 4 of a foreign language, 2 of a lab science, and 1 of history. An interview is recommended. Applications are accepted on-line via Apply or the school's web site. AP credits are accepted. Important factors in the admissions decision are advanced placement or honor courses, evidence of special talent, and extracurricular activities record.

Procedure: Freshmen are admitted fall and spring. Entrance exams should be taken by January of the senior year. There are early decision, early admissions, and deferred admissions plans. Early decision applications should be filed by November 15; regular applications, by January 15 for fall entry, along with a $45 fee. Notification of early decision is sent December 15; regular decision, April 1. 134 early decision candidates were accepted for a recent class. 18% of all applicants are on a waiting list.

Financial Aid: In 1999-2000, 54% of all freshmen and 57% of continuing students received some form of financial aid. 42% of freshmen and 44% of continuing students received need-based aid. The average freshman award was $22,750. Of that total, scholarships or need-based grants averaged $280 ($32,224 maximum); loans averaged $2600 (maximum); and work contracts averaged $1700 (maximum). 37% of undergraduates work part time. The average financial indebtedness of the 1999 graduate was $13,430. the college is a member of CSS. The CSS/Profile or FAFSA, the college's own financial statement, parent and student federal tax returns, and the business/farm supplement and/or noncustodial parent statement, if applicable, are required. The fall application deadline is February 1.

Computers: The mainframe is an IBM RS/6000. All students have access to 3 academic computer labs that provide networked access to software, bibliographic searching, and Columbia University mainframe links. Several academic departments maintain computer labs for student use. All dormitories are also wired and connected to the network. All students may access the system. There are no time limits and no fees. The college recommends that all students have PCs.

BATES COLLEGE
Lewiston, ME 04240

(207) 786-6000; Fax: (207) 786-6025

Full-time: 835 men, 871 women	**Faculty:** 165; IIB, ++$
Part-time: none	**Ph.D.s:** 95%
Graduate: none	**Student/Faculty:** 10 to 1
Year: 4-4-1 (5-week spring short term)	**Tuition:** see profile
Application Deadline: January 15	**Room & Board:** see profile
Freshman Class: 3860 applied, 1266 accepted, 479 enrolled	
SAT I Verbal/Math: 660/660	**MOST COMPETITIVE**

Bates College, founded in 1855, is a private liberal arts institution. A comprehensive fee of $31,400 includes tuition and room and board. The library contains 635,422 volumes, 293,905 microform items, and 46,493 audiovisual forms/CDs, and subscribes to 1950 periodicals. Computerized library services include the card catalog, interlibrary loans, and database searching. Special learning facilities include a learning resource center, art gallery, planetarium, radio station, tv station, a 654-acre mountain conservation area, the Muskie archives, an observatory, and a language resource center. The 109-acre campus is in a suburban area 140 miles north of Boston. Including residence halls, there are 70 buildings.

Programs of Study: Bates confers B.A. and B.S. degrees. Bachelor's degrees are awarded in BIOLOGICAL SCIENCE (biochemistry, biology/biological science, and neurosciences), COMMUNICATIONS AND THE ARTS (art, Chinese, dramatic arts, East Asian languages and literature, English, French, German, Japanese, music, Russian, Spanish, and speech/debate/rhetoric), COMPUTER AND PHYSICAL SCIENCE (chemistry, geology, mathematics, and physics), ENGINEERING AND ENVIRONMENTAL DESIGN (environmental science), SOCIAL SCIENCE (African American studies, American studies, anthropology, classical/ancient civilization, economics, history, philosophy, political science/government, psychology, religion, sociology, and women's studies). Biology, psychology, and English are the largest.

Special: Internships, research apprenticeships, study abroad, and a Washington semester are possible. Dual, student-designed, and interdisciplinary majors, including classical and medieval studies, and a 3-2 engineering degree with Columbia University, Dartmouth College, Case Western Reserve University, Rensselaer Polytechnic Institute, and Washington University in St. Louis are available. Students in any major may graduate in 3 years, and a B.A.-B.S. is possible in all majors. Students may also participate in the Williams-Mystic Seaport program in marine biology and maritime history, and exchanges with Spelman College, Morehouse College, Washington and Lee University, and McGill University are possible. There are 2 national honor societies, including Phi Beta Kappa, and 29 departmental honors programs.

Admissions: 33% of the 1999-2000 applicants were accepted. The SAT I scores for the 1999-2000 freshman class were: Verbal--1% below 500, 9% between 500 and 599, 60% between 600 and 700, and 30% above 700; Math--1% below 500, 7% between 500 and 599, 63% between 600 and 700, and 29% above 700. 88% of the current freshmen were in the top fifth of their class; 99% were in the top two fifths.

Requirements: Candidates for admission should have completed 4 years of English, 3 each of math and history or social studies, and 2 each of science and foreign language. Essays are required and an interview on or off campus is strongly recommended. The submission of test scores is optional. Bates accepts applications electronically via Embark.com and Common Application. AP credits are accepted. Important factors in the admissions decision are advanced placement or honor courses, evidence of special talent, and leadership record.

Procedure: Freshmen are admitted fall and winter. There are early decision, early admissions, and deferred admissions plans. Early decision applications should be filed by November 15 (Round I) or January 1 (Round II); regular applications, by January 15 for fall entry and November 1 for winter entry, along with a $50 fee. Notification of early decision is sent December 16 (Round I) and January 24 (Round II); regular decision, by March 31. 166 early decision candidates were accepted for the 1999-2000 class. 7% of all applicants are on a waiting list.

Financial Aid: In 1999-2000, 49% of all freshmen and 44% of continuing students received some form of financial aid. 46% of freshmen and 40% of continuing students received need-based aid. The average freshman award was $21,717. Of that total, scholarships or need-based grants averaged $18,732; loans averaged $1585; and work contracts averaged $1400. 50% of undergraduates work part time. Average annual earnings from campus work are $1400. Bates is a member of CSS. The CSS/Profile or FAFSA is required. Parent and student tax returns and W-2 forms are also required. The fall application deadline is January 15.

Computers: The mainframes are a DEC ALPHA 2100, a Dual Processor RISC, and a DEC 1000 RISC. All students are assigned a user ID, which provides access to academic software, E-mail, and the Internet. There are 785 college desktop computers and workstations. More than 1300 computers were recently hooked up to the system in dorm rooms. All students may access the system. There are no time limits and no fees.

BAYLOR UNIVERSITY
Waco, TX 76798   (254) 710-3435; (800) BAYLOR-U

Full-time: 4629 men, 6405 women	**Faculty:** 650; I, -$
Part-time: 196 men, 242 women	**Ph.D.s:** 78%
Graduate: 1011 men, 851 women	**Student/Faculty:** 17 to 1
Year: semesters, summer session	**Tuition:** $11,082
Application Deadline: open	**Room & Board:** $4580
Freshman Class: 7212 applied, 6262 accepted, 2772 enrolled	
SAT I Verbal/Math: 570/590	**ACT:** 24 **VERY COMPETITIVE**

Baylor University, founded in 1845, is an independent institution offering undergraduate programs in liberal arts and sciences, business, computer science, education, engineering, music, and nursing. There are 7 undergraduate and 10 graduate schools. In addition to regional accreditation, Baylor has baccalaureate program accreditation with AACSB, AALE, ABET, ACEJMC, ADA, AHEA, APTA, CAHEA, CSWE, NASM, NCATE, and NLN. The 9 libraries contain 2,163,456 volumes, 2,075,595 microform items, and 66,854 audiovisual forms/CDs, and subscribe to 8307 periodicals. Computerized library services include the card catalog, interlibrary loans, and database searching. Special learning facilities include a learning resource center, art gallery, natural history museum, radio station, and tv station. The 432-acre campus is in an urban area 100 miles south of Dallas/Fort Worth. Including residence halls, there are 65 buildings.

Programs of Study: Baylor confers B.A., B.S., B.B.A., B.F.A., B.M., B.M.E., B.S.Av.Sc., B.S.C.S., B.S.E., B.S.Ed., B.S.F.C.S., B.S.I., and B.S.N. degrees. Master's and doctoral degrees are also awarded. Bachelor's degrees are awarded in AGRICULTURE (forestry and related sciences and soil science), BIOLOGICAL SCIENCE (biochemistry, biology/biological science, life science, neurosciences, and nutrition), BUSINESS (accounting, banking and finance, business administration and management, business economics, business statistics, business systems analysis, entrepreneurial studies, fashion merchandising, human resources, insurance, international business management, management information systems, marketing/retailing/merchandising, personnel management, and real estate), COMMUNICATIONS AND THE ARTS (applied music, art, art history and appreciation, broadcasting, classics, communications, creative writing, dramatic arts, English, French, German, Greek (classical), journalism, languages, Latin, music, music history and appreciation, music performance, music theory and composition, performing arts, Russian, Spanish, speech/debate/rhetoric, studio art, telecommunications, and theater design), COMPUTER AND PHYSICAL SCIENCE (applied mathematics, chemistry, computer science, earth science, geology, geophysics and seismology, information sciences and systems, mathematics, and physics), EDUCATION (art, business, computer, drama, elementary, English, foreign languages, health, home economics, journalism, mathematics, museum studies, music, physical, reading, recreation, science, secondary, social science, social studies, and special), ENGINEERING AND ENVIRONMENTAL DESIGN (airline piloting and navigation, architecture, engineering, environmental science, interior design, and mechanical engineering), HEALTH PROFESSIONS (community health work, health science, medical laboratory technology, nursing, optometry, predentistry, premedicine, speech pathology/audiology, and speech therapy), SOCIAL SCIENCE (American studies, anthropology, archeology, Asian/Oriental studies, biblical languages, child care/child and family studies, dietetics, economics, family/consumer studies, fashion design and technology, forensic studies, geography, history, interdisciplinary studies, international public service, Latin American studies, law, philosophy, physical fitness/movement, political science/government, prelaw, psychology, public administration, religion, religious education, religious music, Russian and Slavic studies, social work, sociology, and urban studies). Biology, business, and education are the largest.

Special: Baylor offers cooperative programs in architecture, business, dentistry, medicine, and optometry, internships in each school, study abroad and student exchange in more than 30 countries, and pass/fail options. There are also honors and university scholars programs and faculty exchange with 4 schools in China, 1 in Japan, 1 in Thailand, and 1 in Russia. There are 35 national honor societies, including Phi Beta Kappa, and a freshman honors program.

Admissions: 87% of the 1999-2000 applicants were accepted. The SAT I scores for the 1999-2000 freshman class were: Verbal--13% below 500, 48% between 500 and 599, 30% between 600 and 700, and 9% above 700; Math--11% below 500, 43% between 500 and 599, 37% between 600 and 700, and 9% above 700. The ACT scores were 12% below 21, 35% between 21 and 23, 28% between 24 and 26, 13% between 27 and 28, and 13% above 28. 59% of the current freshmen were in the top fifth of their class; 84% were in the top two fifths. There were 51 National Merit finalists.

Requirements: The SAT I or ACT is required, with a recommended minimum composite score of 1100 on the SAT I or 24 on the ACT. Baylor requires applicants to be in the upper 50% of their claass. Applicants must be graduates of an accredited secondary school. An interview is recommended. Applications are accepted on-line at www.baylor.edu/~admissions/apply.html. AP and CLEP credits are accepted. Important factors in the admissions decision are advanced placement or honor courses, leadership record, and parents or siblings attending the school.

Procedure: Freshmen are admitted to all sessions. Entrance exams should be taken in spring of the junior year or fall of the senior year. There is an early admissions plan. Application deadlines are open; there is a $35 fee. Notification is sent on a rolling basis beginning September 15.

Financial Aid: In 1999-2000, 83% of all freshmen and 71% of continuing students received some form of financial aid. 47% of freshmen and 49% of continuing students received need-based aid. The average freshman award was $8751. Of that total, scholarships or need-based grants averaged $3485 ($16,245 maximum); loans averaged $4251 ($15,550 maximum); and work contracts averaged $1015 ($2650 maximum). 27% of undergraduates work part time. Average annual earnings from campus work are $2141. Baylor is a member of CSS. The FAFSA is required. The fall application deadline is May 1.

Computers: The mainframes include DEC VAX 6510, DEC ALPHA 2100, and IBM 2003 computers. There are 750 Macs and 450 PCs available in student labs, dormitories, and other computing areas on campus; all are networked with E-mail and Internet access. Most systems are accessible 24 hours a day, 7 days per week. There are no time limits and no fees.

BEAVER COLLEGE
Glenside, PA 19038

(215) 572-2910
(888) BEAVER-3; Fax: (215) 572-4049

Full-time: 331 men, 931 women	**Faculty:** 92; IIA, av$
Part-time: 95 men, 285 women	**Ph.D.s:** 85%
Graduate: 281 men, 848 women	**Student/Faculty:** 14 to 1
Year: semesters, summer session	**Tuition:** $17,160
Application Deadline: open	**Room & Board:** $7310
Freshman Class: 1776 applied, 1124 accepted, 434 enrolled	
SAT I Verbal/Math: 540/510	**VERY COMPETITIVE**

Beaver College, founded in 1853, is a private institution, affiliated with the Presbyterian Church (U.S.A), offering undergraduate and graduate programs in the fine arts, the sciences, business, education, and preprofessional fields. There is 1 graduate school. In addition to regional accreditation, Beaver has baccalaureate program accreditation with APTA and NASAD. The library contains 129,008 volumes, 43,900 microform items, and 2625 audiovisual forms CDs, and subscribes to 795 periodicals. Computerized library services include interlibrary loans. Special learning facilities include a learning resource center, art gallery, radio station, observatory, theater, computer graphics and communication labs, and multimedia classrooms. The 55-acre campus is in a suburban area 10 miles north of Philadelphia. Including residence halls, there are 17 buildings.

Programs of Study: Beaver confers B.A., B.S., and B.F.A. degrees. Master's and doctoral degrees are also awarded. Bachelor's degrees are awarded in BIOLOGICAL SCIENCE (biology/biological science), BUSINESS (accounting, banking and finance, business administration and management, marketing/retailing/merchandising, and personnel management), COMMUNICATIONS AND THE ARTS (communications, dramatic arts, English, fine arts, graphic design, illustration, photography, and theater design), COMPUTER AND PHYSICAL SCIENCE (chemistry, computer science, mathematics, and science), EDUCATION (art, early childhood, elementary, secondary, and special), ENGINEERING AND ENVIRONMENTAL DESIGN (engineering, environmental science, and interior design), HEALTH PROFESSIONS (art therapy, health care administration, predentistry, premedicine, preoptometry, and preveterinary science), SOCIAL SCIENCE (history, liberal arts/general studies, philosophy, political science/government, prelaw, psychobiology, psychology, and sociology). Education, psychology, and chemistry are the strongest academically. Fine arts, business, and biology are the largest.

Special: Internships are encouraged in all majors. There are study-abroad programs in 9 countries and co-op programs in business, computer science, chemistry, actuarial science, and accounting. There is a 3-2 engineering program with Columbia University and a 3-4 optometry program with the Pennsylvania College of Optometry. Beaver also offers a Washington semester, work-study, student-designed majors, a dual major in chemistry and business, interdisciplinary majors in artificial intelligence and scientific illustration, credit by exam and for life/military/work experience, and nondegree study. There are 3 national honor societies, including Phi Beta Kappa, and a freshman honors program.

Admissions: 63% of the 1999-2000 applicants were accepted. The SAT I scores for the 1999-2000 freshman class were: Verbal--32% below 500, 44% between 500 and 599, 21% between 600 and 700, and 3% above 700; Math--36% below 500, 43% between 500 and 599, 20% between 600 and 700, and 1% above 700. 51% of the current freshmen were in the top fifth of their class; 78% were in the top two fifths.

Requirements: The SAT I is required and the ACT is recommended. Applicants must be graduates of an accredited secondary school or have a GED. A total of 16 academic credits is required, including 4 years of English, 3 each of math and social studies, and 2 each of a foreign language and science. An essay is required. All art and illustration majors (except art education) must submit a portfolio. Beaver accepts electronically transmitted applications. Applications are accepted on-line via the college's web site at www.beaver.edu. AP and CLEP credits are accepted. Important factors in the admissions decision are advanced placement or honor courses, recommendations by school officials, and leadership record.

Procedure: Freshmen are admitted fall and spring. There are early decision, early admissions, and deferred admissions plans. Application deadlines are open; the fee is $30. Notification of early decision is sent December 1; regular decision, on a rolling basis. 12 early decision candidates were accepted for the 1999-2000 class.

Financial Aid: In a recent year, 95% of all freshmen and 92% of continuing students received some form of financial aid. 90% of freshmen and 87% of continuing students received need-based aid. The average freshman award was $15,214. Of that total, scholarships or need-based grants averaged $9810 ($11,000 maximum); loans averaged $4492 ($10,625 maximum); and work contracts averaged $795 ($1500 maximum). 60% of undergraduates work part time. Average annual earnings from campus work are $756. The average financial indebtedness of a recent graduate was $17,125. Beaver is a member of CSS. The FAFSA, the college's own financial statement, the PHEAA, and parent and student tax returns are required. The fall application deadline is March 15.

Computers: The mainframes are a DEC ALPHA 3000 and a DEC ALPHA 2100. PCs and Macs are available in 8 computer labs across campus. Residence halls, offices, and classrooms are networked, and all have access to the Internet and the Web. All students may access the system. There are no time limits and no fees.

BELHAVEN COLLEGE
Jackson, MS 39202

(601) 968-5940
(800) 960-5940; Fax: (601) 968-8946

Full-time: 450 men, 717 women
Part-time: 56 men, 94 women
Graduate: 26 men, 72 women
Year: semesters, summer session
Application Deadline: open
Freshman Class: 518 applied, 333 accepted, 155 enrolled
SAT I Verbal/Math: 590/570

Faculty: 52
Ph.D.s: 84%
Student/Faculty: 22 to 1
Tuition: $10,340
Room & Board: $3850

ACT: 24   **VERY COMPETITIVE**

Belhaven College, founded in 1883, is a private liberal arts institution with a Presbyterian heritage. There is 1 graduate school. In addition to regional accreditation, Belhaven has baccalaureate program accreditation with NASAD and NASM. The library contains 99,264 volumes, 7619 microform items, and 2776 audiovisual forms/CDs, and subscribes to 494 periodicals. Computerized library services include the card catalog, interlibrary loans, and database searching. Special learning facilities include an art gallery. The 42-acre campus is in an urban area in Jacson. Including residence halls, there are 13 buildings.

Programs of Study: Belhaven confers B.A., B.S., B.A.A., B.B.A., and B.F.A. degrees. Associate and master's degrees are also awarded. Bachelor's degrees are awarded in BIOLOGICAL SCIENCE (biology/biological science), BUSINESS (accounting, business administration and management, and sports management), COMMUNICATIONS AND THE ARTS (art, ballet, communications, dance, dramatic arts, English, and music), COMPUTER AND PHYSICAL SCIENCE (chemistry, computer science, information sciences and systems, and mathematics), EDUCATION (elementary), HEALTH PROFESSIONS (sports medicine), SOCIAL SCIENCE (biblical studies, history, humanities, philosophy, and psychology). Biology, and business are the strongest academically. Business and education are the largest.

Special: Students may participate in various internships, including one in Washington, D.C., or in 6 countries through the study-travel program. Belhaven also offers dual majors, nondegree study, pass/fail options, a 3-2 engineering degree with Mississippi State University, and work-study. 2 1-month summer sessions and 2 2-week minisessions offer additional opportunities for credit. There are 4 national honor societies, a freshman honors program, and 1 departmental honors program.

Admissions: 64% of the 1999-2000 applicants were accepted. The SAT I scores for the 1999-2000 freshman class were: Verbal--7% below 500, 55% between 500 and 599, 15% between 600 and 700, and 23% above 700; Math--15% below 500, 51% between 500 and 599, 26% between 600 and 700, and 8% above 700. The ACT scores were 21% below 21, 29% between 21 and 23, 24% between 24 and 26, 17% between 27 and 28, and 9% above 28. 32% of the current freshmen were in the top fifth of their class; 63% were in the top two fifths. There was 1 National Merit finalist. 4 freshmen graduated first in their class,

Requirements: The SAT I or ACT is required; the ACT is preferred. A GPA of 2.0 is required. Applicants should be graduates of an accredited secondary school, with 16 academic units, including 4 of English, 2 of math, 1 each of history and natural science, a recommended 2 of a foreign language, and 6 of electives. A personal recommendation is also required. AP and CLEP credits are accepted. Important factors in the admissions decision are advanced placement or honor courses, and extracurricular activities record.

Procedure: Freshmen are admitted to all sessions. Entrance exams should be taken in the junior year. There is an early admissions plan. Application deadlines are open. There is a $25 application fee. Notification is sent on a rolling basis.

Financial Aid: In 1999-2000, 90% of all freshmen and 92% of continuing students received some form of financial aid. 86% of all students received need-based aid. The average freshman award was $8853. Of that total, scholarships or need-based grants averaged $4253 (maximum); loans averaged $2000 (maximum); work contracts averaged $1545; and state grants averaged $1055 (maximum). 12% of undergraduates work part time. Average annual earnings from campus work are $1545. The average financial indebtedness of the 1999 graduate was $16,000. The FAFSA and the college's own financial statement are required. The fall application deadline is April 1.

Computers: More than 30 PCs are available for academic use in the library and computer lab. All are wired to the campus fiber-optic network, the Internet, and the World Wide Web. All students may access the system. There are no time limits and no fees.

BELMONT UNIVERSITY
Nashville, TN 37212-3757

(615) 460-6785
(800) 56E-NROL; Fax: (615) 460-5434

Full-time: 838 men, 1292 women	**Faculty:** 195; IIA, --$
Part-time: 141 men, 250 women	**Ph.D.s:** 68%
Graduate: 203 men, 299 women	**Student/Faculty:** 11 to 1
Year: semesters, summer session	**Tuition:** $11,550
Application Deadline: August 1	**Room & Board:** $5000
Freshman Class: 1130 applied, 884 accepted, 427 enrolled	
SAT I Verbal/Math: 570/560	**ACT:** 24 **VERY COMPETITIVE**

Belmont University, founded in 1951, is a private, Christian liberal arts university affiliated with the Tennessee Baptist Convention. There are 6 undergraduate and 4 graduate schools. In addition to regional accreditation, Belmont has baccalaureate program accreditation with CSWE, NASM, NCATE, and NLN. The library contains 173,086 volumes, 16,658 microform items, and 22,247 audiovisual forms/CDs, and subscribes to 1381 periodicals. Computerized library services include the card catalog, interlibrary loans, and database searching. Special learning facilities include a learning resource center, art gallery, radio station, and TV station. The 55-acre campus is in an urban area in Nashville. Including residence halls, there are 22 buildings.

Programs of Study: Belmont confers B.A., B.S., B.B.A., B.F.A., B.M., and B.S.N. degrees. Master's degrees are also awarded. Bachelor's degrees are awarded in BIOLOGICAL SCIENCE (biology/biological science), BUSINESS (accounting, business administration and management, hotel/motel and restaurant management, management science, and marketing/retailing/merchandising), COMMUNICATIONS AND THE ARTS (communications, English, French, music, and music performance), COMPUTER AND PHYSICAL SCIENCE (chemistry, computer science, mathematics, and physics), EDUCATION (elementary, physical, and science), HEALTH PROFESSIONS (nursing), SOCIAL SCIENCE (economics, history, philosophy, political science/government, psychology, religion, and social work). Music, business, and humanities are the strongest academically. Business, music, and nursing are the largest.

Special: Dual degree programs are available with Auburn University and the University of Tennessee at Knoxville. Programs require 3 years of study at Belmont followed by 2 years at the other institution. There are 11 national honor societies, a freshman honors program, and 3 departmental honors programs.

Admissions: 78% of the 1999-2000 applicants were accepted. The SAT I scores for the 1999-2000 freshman class were: Verbal--18% below 500, 47% between 500 and 599, 32% between 600 and 700, and 3% above 700; Math--20% below 500, 48% between 500 and 599, 28% between 600 and 700, and 4% above 700. The ACT scores were 13% below 21, 27% between 21 and 23, 29% between 24 and 26, 15% between 27 and 28, and 15% above 28. 56% of the current freshmen were in the top fifth of their class; 77% were in the top two fifths. 18 freshmen graduated first in their class.

Requirements: The SAT I is required and the ACT is recommended. Belmont requires applicants to be in the upper 50% of their class. A GPA of 3.0 is required. The college expects a composite score of at least 21 on the ACT and 1000 on the SAT I. Applicants should be high school graduates or hold the GED. Secondary preparation should include 4 units of English, 3 of math, and 2 each of a foreign language, history, science, and social studies. Potential music majors must audition. Applications are accepted on computer disk and on-line via CollegeView and ExPAN. AP and CLEP credits are accepted. Important factors in the admissions decision are advanced placement or honor courses, recommendations by school officials, and evidence of special talent.

Procedure: Freshmen are admitted fall, spring, and summer. Entrance exams should be taken during the junior or senior year. There is an early admissions plan. Applications should be filed by August 1 for fall entry and December 1 for spring entry, along with a $35 fee. Notification is sent on a rolling basis.

Financial Aid: In 1999-2000, 65% of all freshmen and 45% of continuing students received some form of financial aid. 47% of freshmen and 42% of continuing students received need-based aid. The average freshman award was $6779. Of that total, scholarships or need-based grants averaged $3684 ($15,616 maximum); loans averaged $4657 ($14,625 maximum); and work contracts averaged $1500. 9% of undergraduates work part time. Average annual earnings from campus work are $1500. The average financial indebtedness of the 1999 graduate was $20,469. Belmont is a member of CSS. The FAFSA is required. The fall application deadline is March 1.

Computers: The mainframe is a Sun 3500 server. 5 computer labs across campus provide students with access to the campus network, applications, and the Internet. Residence halls are wired for computer access with student-provided computers. All students may access the system. There are no time limits and no fees.

BELOIT COLLEGE
Beloit, WI 53511

(608) 363-2500
(800) 356-0751; Fax: (608) 363-2075

Full-time: 500 men, 670 women	**Faculty:** 91; IIB, ++$
Part-time: 10 men, 43 women	**Ph.D.s:** 98%
Graduate: none	**Student/Faculty:** 13 to 1
Year: semesters	**Tuition:** $20,440
Application Deadline: March 15	**Room & Board:** $4628
Freshman Class: 1495 applied, 1001 accepted, 305 enrolled	
SAT I Verbal/Math: 640/610	**ACT:** 27 **HIGHLY COMPETITIVE**

Beloit College, founded in 1846, is an independent liberal arts institution. The library contains 235,435 volumes, 159,173 microform items, and 15,590 audiovisual forms/Ds, and subscribes to 940 periodicals. Computerized library services include the card catalog, interlibrary loans, and database searching. Special learning facilities include a learning resource center, art gallery, natural history museum, planetarium, radio station, TV station, comprehensive language lab, observatory, and theater complex. The 40-acre campus is in a small town 70 miles west of Milwaukee, 90 miles northwest of Chicago, and 50 miles south of Madison Including residence halls, there are 50 buildings.

Programs of Study: Beloit confers B.A. and B.S. degrees. Bachelor's degrees are awarded in BIOLOGICAL SCIENCE (biochemistry and biology/biological science), BUSINESS (business administration and management), COMMUNICATIONS AND THE ARTS (art history and appreciation, creative writing, English, French, German, music, Russian, Spanish, and studio art), COMPUTER AND PHYSICAL SCIENCE (chemistry, computer science, geology, mathematics, and physics), EDUCATION (art), SOCIAL SCIENCE (anthropology, economics, history, international relations, philosophy, political science/government, psychology, religion, and sociology). Anthropology, English, and geology are the strongest academically. Anthropology, biology, and English are the largest.

Special: Beloit offers cross-registration with the University of Wisconsin/ Madison, internships, study abroad in 29 countries, and a Washington semester. Dual majors, student-designed and interdisciplinary majors, and nondegree study are available. Students may take a 2-2 nursing program and a 3-2 medical technology program with Rush University. A 3-2 engineering degree is offered with 9 institutions, and co-op programs are available in social services, forestry and environmental management, engineering, nursing, medical technology, and business administration. An intensive summer language program is offered in Chinese, Japanese, Hungarian, and Russian. There are 6 national honor societies, including Phi Beta Kappa.

Admissions: 67% of the 1999-2000 applicants were accepted. The SAT I scores for the 1999-2000 freshman class were: Verbal--10% below 500, 25% between 500 and 599, 45% between 600 and 700, and 20% above 700; Math--11% below 500, 29% between 500 and 599, 49% between 600 and 700, and 11% above 700. The ACT scores were 8% below 21, 16% between 21 and 23, 26% between 24 and 26, 19% between 27 and 28, and 31% above 28. 60% of the current freshmen were in the top fifth of their class; 85% were in the top two fifths. There were 11 National Merit semifinalists. 11 freshmen graduated first in their class.

Requirements: The SAT I or ACT is required, and SAT II: Subject tests are recommended. In addition, applicants must be graduates of an accredited secondary school, with 4 years of English, 3 years each of math and science, and 2 years each of foreign language and social studies. The GED is accepted. An essay is required, and an interview is recommended. Applications are accepted on-line and on computer disk via Common Application (Windows version), CollegeLink, and Apply software systems. AP and CLEP credits are accepted. Important factors in the admissions decision are extracurricular activities record, leadership record, and personality/intangible qualities.

Procedure: Freshmen are admitted fall and spring. Entrance exams should be taken before Christmas of the senior year. There are early decision, early admissions, and deferred admissions plans. For priority consideration, early decision applications should be filed by December 1; regular applications, by March 15 for fall entry, along with a $25 fee. Notification of early decision is sent December 15; regular decision, on a rolling basis. 35 early decision candidates were accepted for the 1999-2000 class. A waiting list is an active part of the admissions procedure.

Financial Aid: In 1999-2000, 91% of all freshmen and 87% of continuing students received some form of financial aid. 73% of freshmen and 71% of continuing students received need-based aid. Scholarships or need-based grants averaged $12,977 ($20,220 maximum); loans averaged $3162 ($5550 maximum); and work contracts averaged $1293 ($1500 maximum). 89% of undergraduates work part time. Average annual earnings from campus work are $1200. The average financial indebtedness of the 1999 graduate was $12,896. Beloit is a member of CSS. The FAFSA and the college's own financial statement are required. The fall application deadline is April 15.

Computers: The mainframes are IBM RISC/6000 Models H340 and H320. Students can use the networked computers for E-mail and for class programming using Logic, FORTRAN, Pascal, Java, C, statistical packages, and specific departmental programs. The networks can be accessed via more than 27 terminal servers and PCs throughout the campus; there are numerous computer labs. A new fiber-optic network allows access from all residential rooms, classrooms, and off-campus sites. All students may access the system at any time. There are no time limits and no fees.

BENNINGTON COLLEGE
Bennington, VT 05201

(802) 442-6349
(800) 833-6845; Fax: (802) 440-4320

Full-time: 134 men, 313 women	**Faculty:** 58
Part-time: none	**Ph.D.s:** 81%
Graduate: 33 men, 91 women	**Student/Faculty:** 8 to 1
Year: 4-1-4	**Tuition:** $22,500
Application Deadline: January 1	**Room & Board:** $5650
Freshman Class: 632 applied, 487 accepted, 170 enrolled	
SAT I Verbal/Math: 623/543	**VERY COMPETITIVE**

Bennington College, founded in 1932, is a private liberal arts institution where students design their own programs in consultation with faculty, who are active practitioners of the disciplines they teach. The 2 libraries contain 120,000 volumes, 6740 microform items, and 1174 audiovisual form/CDs, and subscribe to 488 periodicals. Computerized library services include the card catalog, interlibrary loans, and database searching. Special learning facilities include a learning resource center, art gallery, radio station, observatory, dance archives, script library, photography darkrooms, electronic music studio and music practice rooms, several theaters and dance studios, ceramics studio and kilns, greenhouse, working community farm, pond for biological studies, and early childhood center. The 550-acre campus is in a small town 45 miles east of Albany. Including residence halls, there are 59 buildings.

Programs of Study: Bennington confers the B.A. degree. Master's degrees are also awarded. Bachelor's degrees are awarded in BIOLOGICAL SCIENCE (biology/biological science), COMMUNICATIONS AND THE ARTS (Chinese, creative writing, dance, dramatic arts, English, fine arts, French, German, languages, literature, music, photography, and Spanish), COMPUTER AND PHYSICAL SCIENCE (chemistry, computer science, mathematics, and physics), EDUCATION (early childhood), ENGINEERING AND ENVIRONMENTAL DESIGN (architecture), SOCIAL SCIENCE (anthropology, history, philosophy, political science/government, and psychology). Interdisciplinary studies, literature, and languages are the largest.

Special: 8-week work/internships are required all 4 years (during January and February). Cross-registration with Southern Vermont and Williams Colleges is possible. A cooperative program with the Bank Street College of Education in New York City offers a joint advanced degree in education. In addition, study abroad in England, Germany, and other countries, an individually arranged Washington semester, and dual and student-designed majors are offered. Grading is pass/fail with an extensive written evaluation.

Admissions: 77% of the 1999-2000 applicants were accepted. The SAT I scores for the 1999-2000 freshman class were: Verbal--2% below 500, 32% between

500 and 599, 56% between 600 and 700, and 10% above 700; Math--20% below 500, 9% between 500 and 599, 27% between 600 and 700, and 4% above 700. 58% of the current freshmen were in the top fifth of their class; 90% were in the top two fifths.

Requirements: The SAT I or ACT is required. Applicants should have 16 credits, including 4 units in English, 3 each in math, science, and social studies, 2 or 3 in foreign language, and 2 in history; art and music courses are highly recommended. Essays and an interview are required, and a portfolio is recommended for certain majors. The GED is accepted. Applications may be downloaded from the college website. Important factors in the admissions decision are evidence of special talent, extracurricular activities record, and personality/intangible qualities.

Procedure: Freshmen are admitted fall and spring. Entrance exams should be taken during the spring of the junior year or the fall of the senior year. There are early decision, early admissions, and deferred admissions plans. Early decision applications should be filed by November 15; regular applications, by January 1 for fall entry and January 1 for spring entry, along with a $50 fee. Notification of early decision is sent December 1; regular decision, April 1. 19 early decision candidates were accepted for the 1999-2000 class. A waiting list is an active part of the admissions procedure.

Financial Aid: In 1999-2000, 84% of all freshmen and 87% of continuing students received some form of financial aid. 68% of freshmen and 78% of continuing students received need-based aid. The average freshman award was $17,125. Of that total, scholarships or need-based grants averaged $13,617. The average financial indebtedness of the 1999 graduate was $19,300. Bennington is a member of CSS. The FAFSA, the college's own financial statement, and student and parent tax returns are required. The fall application deadline is March 1.

Computers: PCs are available in the media and language and culture centers. All students may access the system. There are no time limits and no fees. It is recommended that all students have personal computers, specifically a Mac.

BENTLEY COLLEGE
Waltham, MA 02452-4705

(781) 891-2244
(800) 523-2354; Fax: (781) 891-3414

Full-time: 2039 men, 1413 women	**Faculty:** 224; IIA, ++$
Part-time: 378 men, 379 women	**Ph.D.s:** 82%
Graduate: 826 men, 674 women	**Student/Faculty:** 15 to 1
Year: semesters, summer session	**Tuition:** $17,840
Application Deadline: February 15	**Room & Board:** $8260
Freshman Class: 4600 applied, 2622 accepted, 900 enrolled	
SAT I Verbal/Math: 541/574	**VERY COMPETITIVE**

Bentley College is a private institution that integrates information technology with a broad business and arts and scienes curriculum, to provide students with the most advanced business education possible. There is 1 graduate school. In addition to regional accreditation, Bentley has baccalaureate program accreditation with AACSB. The library contains 212,113 volumes, 221,398 microform items, and 4931 audiovisual forms/CDs, and subscribes to 8017 periodicals. Computerized library services include the card catalog, interlibrary loans, database searching, and web access. Special learning facilities include a learning resource center, art gallery, planetarium, and radio station; the Financial Trading Room, offering real-time data on global financial markets; the Accounting Center for Electronic Learning and Business Management, providing hands-on experience with systems and software used in accounting, auditing, and assurance service functions; the Marketing Technologies Showcase, featuring the latest technological tools for marketing products and services; the Design and Usability Testing Center for creating and testing prototypes of user interfaces, on-line information systems, and other tools in the field of information design; and academic learning centers for help in economics-finance, writing, math, and modern languages. The 143-acre campus is in a suburban area in Waltham, 10 miles west of Boston. Including residence halls, there are 43 buildings.

Programs of Study: Bentley confers B.A. and B.S. degrees. Associate and master's degrees are also awarded. Bachelor's degrees are awarded in BUSINESS (accounting, banking and finance, business economics, management science, and marketing/retailing/merchandising), COMMUNICATIONS AND THE ARTS (English and technical and business writing), COMPUTER AND PHYSICAL SCIENCE (information sciences and systems and mathematics), SOCIAL SCIENCE (economics, history, international studies, liberal arts/general studies, paralegal studies, and philosophy). Accountancy, finance, and management are the largest.

Special: There is cross-registration with Regis College and Brandeis University, and internships are available in all departments. The college offers study abroad in 11 countries, a Washington semester, work-study programs, accelerated degree programs, student-designed majors, credit by exam, and nondegree study. There is also a minor concentration program through which business majors can broaden their exposure to the arts and sciences, and arts and science majors can minor in business or interdisciplinary topics. There is 1 national honor society, and 3 departmental honors programs.

Admissions: 57% of the 1999-2000 applicants were accepted. The SAT I scores for the 1999-2000 freshman class were: Verbal--28% below 500, 53% between 500 and 599, 18% between 600 and 700, and 1% above 700; Math--14% below 500, 52% between 500 and 599, 30% between 600 and 700, and 4% above 700. 46% of the current freshmen were in the top fifth of their class; 81% were in the top two fifths.

Requirements: The SAT I is required. Applicants must be graduates of an accredited high school or have a GED. Recommended high school preparation is 4 units each in English and math, including algebra I and II and geometry; 3 units in lab science; 2 to 3 units in a foreign language; 2 units in social science; and 2 additional units in English, math, social science or lab science, foreign langauage, speech, or advanced accounting. Applications are accepted on-line at the school's web site. AP and CLEP credits are accepted. Important factors in the admissions decision are advanced placement or honor courses and recommendations by school officials.

Procedure: Freshmen are admitted fall and spring. Entrance exams should be taken before the January test date. There are early decision, early admissions, and deferred admissions plans. Early decision applications should be filed by December 1; regular applications, by February 15 for fall entry and November 15 for spring entry, along with a $35 fee. Notification of early decision is sent December 28; regular decision, April 1. 62 early decision candidates were accepted for the 1999-2000 class. A waiting list is an active part of the admissions procedure.

Financial Aid: In 1999-2000, 66% of all freshmen and 60% of continuing students received some form of financial aid. 52% of freshmen and 51% of continuing students received need-based aid. The average freshman award was $16,579. Of that total, scholarships or need-based grants averaged $10,864 ($17,730 maximum); loans averaged $3292 ($4925 maximum); and work contracts averaged $1755 ($2000 maximum). 26% of undergraduates work part time. Average annual earnings from campus work are $1330. The average financial indebtedness of the 1999 graduate was $17,438. Bentley is a member of CSS. The CSS/Profile or FAFSA is required. The fall application deadline is February 1.

Computers: The mainframes are a DEC VAX 6620 and a DEC VAX 6510. With one "port-per-pillow" in residence halls, students have individual access from their dorm room to the campus computing system and the Internet. A growing number of Bentley classrooms feature port-per-seat network connections as well. The college also provides more than 100 PCs and Macs in centralized labs. All have network access. All students may access the system during lab hours, 7 days a week. There are no time limits and no fees. All undergraduate students are required to have laptop computers. The IBM ThinkPad 390E. is recommended.

BEREA COLLEGE
Berea, KY 40404

(606) 986-9341, ext. 5083
(800) 326-5948; Fax: (606) 986-4506

Full-time: 645 men, 847 women	**Faculty:** 122; IIB, +$
Part-time: 10 men, 20 women	**Ph.D.s:** 91%
Graduate: none	**Student/Faculty:** 12 to 1
Year: 4-1-4, summer session	**Tuition:** see profile
Application Deadline: open	**Room & Board:** n/app
Freshman Class: 1751 applied, 595 accepted, 423 enrolled	
SAT I Verbal/Math: 550/540	**ACT:** 23 **VERY COMPETITIVE**

Berea College, founded in 1855, is a private liberal arts institution. As part of the educational program, each student is expected to perform some of the labor required in maintaining the institution while carrying a normal academic load. For participation in the student labor programs, each student is credited with a labor grant of $2800 toward the $15,700 cost of education. Any portion of the $15,700 cost not covered by federal or state grants will be covered by a college scholarship. Fees are $199. In addition to regional accreditation, Berea has baccalaureate program accreditation with ADA, NCATE, and NLN. The library contains 329, 902 volumes, 113,623 microform items, and 4267 audiovisual forms/CDs, and subscribes to 1530 periodicals. Computerized library services include the card catalog, interlibrary loans, and database searching. Special learning facilities include a learning resource center, art gallery, planetarium, and a geology museum. The 140-acre campus is in a small town 40 miles south of Lexington. Including residence halls, there are 58 buildings.

Programs of Study: Berea confers B.A. and B.S. degrees. Bachelor's degrees are awarded in AGRICULTURE (agriculture), BIOLOGICAL SCIENCE (biology/biological science), BUSINESS (business administration and management), COMMUNICATIONS AND THE ARTS (art, classical languages, dramatic arts, English, French, German, industrial design, music, and Spanish), COMPUTER AND PHYSICAL SCIENCE (chemistry, mathematics, and physics), EDUCATION (art, elementary, foreign languages, home economics, middle school, music, physical, and secondary), ENGINEERING AND ENVIRONMENTAL DESIGN (industrial engineering technology), HEALTH PROFESSIONS (nursing), SOCIAL SCIENCE (child care/child and family studies, dietetics, economics, history, philosophy, political science/government, psychology, religion, and sociology). Business administration is the largest.

Special: Students may study abroad in Italy, Austria, Spain, France, Germany, and Japan. Internships, work-study programs, and independent, dual, and student-designed majors are available. A 3-2 engineering degree is offered with Washington University and University of Kentucky. All students participate in an on-campus work program 10 to 15 hours per week. There are 17 national honor societies.

Admissions: 34% of the 1999-2000 applicants were accepted. The SAT I scores for the 1999-2000 freshman class were: Verbal--29% below 500, 42% between 500 and 599, 27% between 600 and 700, and 2% above 700; Math--34% below 500, 44% between 500 and 599, 20% between 600 and 700, and 2% above 700. The ACT scores were 22% below 21, 33% between 21 and 23, 27% between 24 and 26, 15% between 27 and 28, and 5% above 28. 58% of the current freshmen were in the top fifth of their class; 85% were in the top two fifths. 11 freshmen graduated first in their class.

Requirements: The SAT I or ACT is required. Berea requires applicants to be in the upper 40% of their class. Applicants should be graduates of an accredited secondary school. The GED is accepted. Home-schooled students are also encouraged to apply. Financial need is a requirement for admission. Berea recommends that applicants present as part of their high school record 4 units in English, 3 in math, and 2 each in science and social studies. Work in a foreign language is highly desirable. AP and CLEP credits are accepted. Important factors in the admissions decision are ability to finance college education, geographic diversity, and advanced placement or honor courses.

Procedure: Freshmen are admitted fall and summer. Entrance exams should be taken late in the junior year or early in the senior year. There is an early admissions plan. Application deadlines are open, but early review begins November 30. Notification is sent on a rolling basis.

Financial Aid: In 1999-2000, all students received some form of need-based financial aid. The average freshman award was $19,454. Of that total, scholarships or need-based grants averaged $18,551; loans averaged $441; and work contracts averaged $882. All undergraduates work part time. Average annual earnings from campus work are $1175. The FAFSA is required. The fall application deadline is April 1.

Computers: The mainframe is an HP 9000. Approximately 190 networked PCs for student use are located in the computer center lab, residence halls, library, and departmental labs. All students may access the system 24 hours a day, 7 days a week. There are no time limits and no fees.

BERKLEE COLLEGE OF MUSIC
Boston, MA 02215-3693

(617) 266-1400, ext. 2222
(800) 421-0084; Fax: (617) 747-2047

Full-time and Part-time: 2316 men, 699 women	**Faculty:** 156; IIB, +$
	Ph.D.s: 9%
Graduate: none	**Student/Faculty:** n/av
Year: semesters, summer session	**Tuition:** $15,800
Application Deadline: rolling	**Room & Board:** $8090
Freshman Class: 2300 applied, 1859 accepted, 858 enrolled	
SAT I or ACT: required	**SPECIAL**

Berklee College of Music, founded in 1945, is a private institution offering programs in all areas of contemporary music production and engineering, film scoring, music business/management, composition, music synthesis, music education, music therapy, performance, contemporary writing and production, jazz composition, songwriting, and professional music. The library contains 28,176 volumes and 17,681 audiovisual forms/CDs. Computerized library services include the card catalog. Special learning facilities include a learning resource center and 10 recording studios, 5 performance venues, and film scoring, music synthesis, and songwriting labs. The campus is in an urban area in the Fenway Cultural District, Back Bay, Boston. Including residence halls, there are 14 buildings.

Programs of Study: Berklee confers the B.M. degree. Master's degrees are also awarded. Bachelor's degrees are awarded in COMMUNICATIONS AND THE ARTS (audio technology, film arts, jazz, music, music business management, music performance, and music theory and composition), EDUCATION (music), HEALTH PROFESSIONS (music therapy). Performance, professional music, and music production and engineering are the largest.

Special: Berklee offers cross-registration with the Pro-Arts Consortium, study abroad in the Netherlands, internships in music education and music production and engineering, 5-year dual majors, and a 4-year professional (nondegree) diploma program. Work-study programs, an accelerated degree program, student-designed majors, and credit by exam are available.

Admissions: 81% of the 1999-2000 applicants were accepted.

Requirements: The SAT I or ACT is required. A GPA of 2.0 is required. Applicants must be graduates of an accredited secondary school that has a college preparatory program or have their GED. An audition and interview are recommended. Applicants must also submit a detailed reference letter regarding their training and experience in music, a letter from a private instructor, school music director, or professional musician. AP credits are accepted. Important factors in the admissions decision are evidence of special talent, extracurricular activities record, and recommendations by alumni.

Procedure: Freshmen are admitted to all sessions. Entrance exams should be taken in the fall of the senior year of high school. There are early decision and deferred admissions plans. Applications are accepted on a rolling basis. The fee is $65. Notification is sent on a rolling basis.

Financial Aid: 13% of undergraduates work part time. The CSS/Profile, FFS, and the college's own financial statement are required. Check with the school for current deadlines.

Computers: The mainframe is an IBM RS/6000 operating under AIX Version 4.32. There are more than 45 networked Macs in the learning center. All students may access the system. There are no time limits and no fees.

BETHANY COLLEGE
Bethany, WV 26032

(304) 829-7611
(800) 922-7611; Fax: (304) 829-7142

Full-time: 318 men, 331 women	**Faculty:** 57; IIB, av$
Part-time: 4 men, 2 women	**Ph.D.s:** 76%
Graduate: none	**Student/Faculty:** 11 to 1
Year: semesters, 2-week January term	**Tuition:** $18,574
Application Deadline: open	**Room & Board:** $6122
Freshman Class: 690 applied, 513 accepted, 170 enrolled	
SAT I Verbal/Math: 510/506	**ACT:** 23 **VERY COMPETITIVE**

Bethany College, founded in 1840, is a liberal arts institution affiliated with the Christian Church (Disciples of Christ). In addition to regional accreditation, Bethany has baccalaureate program accreditation with CSWE and NCATE. The library contains 201,930 volumes, 3600 microform items, and 4293 audiovisual forms/CDs, and subscribes to 585 periodicals. Computerized library services include the card catalog, interlibrary loans, and database searching. Special learning facilities include a learning resource center, radio station, and TV station. The 300-acre campus is in a small town 14 miles north of Wheeling and 39 miles southwest of Pittsburgh. Including residence halls, there are 33 buildings.

Programs of Study: Bethany confers B.A. and B.S. degrees. Bachelor's degrees are awarded in BIOLOGICAL SCIENCE (biochemistry and biology/biological science), BUSINESS (accounting and business economics), COMMUNICA-TIONS AND THE ARTS (communications, English, fine arts, French, German, journalism, languages, and Spanish), COMPUTER AND PHYSICAL SCIENCE (chemistry, computer science, mathematics, and physics), EDUCATION (early childhood, elementary, English, foreign languages, physical, science, secondary, and special), HEALTH PROFESSIONS (predentistry and premedicine), SO-CIAL SCIENCE (economics, history, international studies, philosophy, political science/government, prelaw, psychology, religion, and social work). Communication, economics, and political science are the strongest academically. Communication, economics, and education are the largest.

Special: Bethany offers a 3-2 engineering degree with Columbia, Washington, and Case Western Reserve Universities, internships (required with many majors), study abroad in France, Spain, England, Germany, Canada, Japan, Puerto Rico, Argentina, and Sweden, a Washington semester, and work-study programs. B.A.-B.S. degrees and dual majors in all majors, a general studies degree, student-designed majors in interdisciplinary studies, and pass/fail options in nonmajor courses also are offered. There is also a voluntary January term. There are 15 national honor societies and a freshman honors program.

Admissions: 74% of the 1999-2000 applicants were accepted. The SAT I scores for the 1999-2000 freshman class were: Math--46% below 500, 41% between 500 and 599, and 16% between 600 and 700. 51% of the current freshmen were in the top fifth of their class; 65% were in the top two fifths. 4 freshmen graduated first in their class.

Requirements: The SAT I or ACT is required. A GPA of 2.5 is required. Applicants must have 15 Carnegie units, which should include 4 years of English, 3 each in math and science, and 2 each in foreign language, history, and social studies. An essay, an interview, a portfolio, and an audition are recommended, depending on the major. The GED is accepted. Students may apply on-line via Bethany's web site. AP and CLEP credits are accepted. Important factors in the admissions decision are advanced placement or honor courses, extracurricular activities record, and recommendations by school officials.

Procedure: Freshmen are admitted fall and spring. Entrance exams should be taken during the junior year. There is a deferred admissions plan. Application deadlines are open. There is a $25 fee. Notification is sent on a rolling basis.

Financial Aid: In 1999-2000, 95% of all freshmen and 92% of continuing students received some form of financial aid. 65% of freshmen and 70% of continuing students received need-based aid. The average freshman award was $17,000. Of that total, scholarships or need-based grants averaged $11,300 ($18,230 maximum); loans averaged $2650 ($5100 maximum); and work contracts averaged $1000 ($1500 maximum). 79% of undergraduates work part time. Average annual earnings from campus work are $820. The average financial indebtedness of the 1999 graduate was $18,000. The FAFSA and the college's own financial statement are required. The fall application deadline is May 1.

Computers: The mainframe is a Hewlett-Packard. The system is for administrative use only. There are 20 terminals for the mainframe in the computer center. There is also a Mac computer center with 8 student labs. In addition, there are computer labs for English, economics, communications, biology, chemistry, education, and social sciences, with about 200 PCs available. Students may access the system 24 hours daily. There are no time limits and no fees.

BETHEL COLLEGE
North Newton, KS 67117

(316) 283-2500
(800) 522-1887; Fax: (316) 284-5286

Full-time: 212 men, 215 women	**Faculty:** 39; IIB, --$
Part-time: 20 men, 30 women	**Ph.D.s:** 95%
Graduate: none	**Student/Faculty:** 11 to 1
Year: 4-1-4, summer session	**Tuition:** $11,800
Application Deadline: open	**Room & Board:** $4700
Freshman Class: 303 applied, 255 accepted, 160 enrolled	
ACT: 24	**VERY COMPETITIVE**

Bethel College, established in 1887, is a private liberal arts institution affiliated with the General Conference Mennonite Church. In addition to regional accreditation, Bethel has baccalaureate program accreditation with CSWE and NLN. The 2 libraries contain 127,300 volumes, 6063 microform items, and 154,354 audiovisual forms/CDs, and subscribe to 787 periodicals. Computerized library services include interlibrary loans and database searching. Special learning facilities include a learning resource center, art gallery, natural history museum, and radio station. The 60-acre campus is in a suburban area 25 miles north of Wichita. Including residence halls, there are 13 buildings.

Programs of Study: Bethel confers B.A., B.S., and B.S.N. degrees. Bachelor's degrees are awarded in BIOLOGICAL SCIENCE (biology/biological science), BUSINESS (accounting and business administration and management), COMMUNICATIONS AND THE ARTS (art, communications, English, German, music, and Spanish), COMPUTER AND PHYSICAL SCIENCE (chemistry, mathematics, natural sciences, and physics), EDUCATION (elementary), HEALTH PROFESSIONS (nursing), SOCIAL SCIENCE (history, human ecology, peace studies, psychology, religion, social science, and social work). Nursing, business, and visual and performing arts are the largest.

Special: Students may cross-register with Associated Colleges of Central Kansas (ACCK) institutions and Hesston College. Internships are required in many majors. Work-study programs, study abroad in 9 countries, dual majors, student-designed majors, and pass/fail options are also available. The college offers a 3-2 engineering degree with Washington University, University of Kansas, and Kansas State University. 2 departments have honors programs.

Admissions: 84% of the 1999-2000 applicants were accepted. The ACT scores for the 1999-2000 freshman class were: 23% below 21, 26% between 21 and 23, 20% between 24 and 26, 18% between 27 and 28, and 13% above 28. 8 freshmen graduated first in their class.

Requirements: The SAT I or ACT is required. A GPA of 2.5 is required. Applicants should present a minimum ACT composite of 25 or SAT I total of 890 with a minimum GPA of 2.5. The GED is accepted. Auditions are required of candidates applying for some scholarships, and interviews are recommended for all applicants. Specific departmental requirements may vary. CLEP, AP, and International Baccalaureate credit may be awarded. Important factors in the admissions decision are evidence of special talent, recommendations by alumni, and parents or siblings attending the school.

Procedure: Freshmen are admitted to all sessions. Entrance exams should be taken by the fall of the senior year. There is an early admissions plan. Application deadlines are open. The application fee is $20. Notification is sent on a rolling basis.

Financial Aid: In 1999-2000, 99% of all freshmen and 93% of continuing students received some form of financial aid. 83% of freshmen and 73% of continu-

ing students received need-based aid. The average freshman award was $12,704. Of that total, scholarships or need-based grants averaged $4954 ($11,350 maximum); loans averaged $2749 ($9500 maximum); and work contracts averaged $1000 ($1500 maximum). 58% of undergraduates work part time. Average annual earnings from campus work are $765. The average financial indebtedness of the 1999 graduate was $13,610. Bethel is a member of CSS. The FAFSA is required. The fall application deadline is March 15.

Computers: The mainframe is an IBM PC server with NT software. 30 IBM and Mac PCs with printers are available in the campus computer center, library, and music and nursing labs. All students may access the system 18 hours a day. There are no time limits. The fee is $20 per semester.

BETHEL COLLEGE
St. Paul, MN 55112
(651) 638-6242
(800) 255-8706; Fax: (651) 638-1490

Full-time: 933 men, 1584 women	**Faculty:** 134; IIB, av$
Part-time: 62 men, 142 women	**Ph.D.s:** 72%
Graduate: 70 men, 192 women	**Student/Faculty:** 19 to 1
Year: 4-1-4, summer session	**Tuition:** $15,300
Application Deadline: April 1	**Room & Board:** $5410
Freshman Class: 1465 applied, 1185 accepted, 589 enrolled	
SAT I Verbal/Math: 576/590	**ACT:** 24 **VERY COMPETITIVE**

Bethel College, established in 1871, is a private liberal arts college affiliated with the Baptist General Conference. In addition to regional accreditation, Bethel has baccalaureate program accreditation with CSWE, NCATE, and NLN. The library contains 150,203 volumes, 116,405 microform items, and 6270 audiovisual forms/CDs, and subscribes to 842 periodicals. Computerized library services include the card catalog, interlibrary loans, and database searching. Special learning facilities include a learning resource center, art gallery, and radio station. The 231-acre campus is in a suburban area 10 miles north of Minneapolis/St. Paul.

Programs of Study: Bethel confers B.A., B.S., B.Mus., and B.Mus.Ed. degrees. Associate and master's degrees are also awarded. Bachelor's degrees are awarded in BIOLOGICAL SCIENCE (biochemistry and biology/biological science), BUSINESS (accounting, banking and finance, business administration and management, and marketing/retailing/merchandising), COMMUNICATIONS AND THE ARTS (communications, dramatic arts, English, fine arts, multimedia, music, Spanish, and speech/debate/rhetoric), COMPUTER AND PHYSICAL SCIENCE (chemistry, computer science, mathematics, and physics), EDUCATION (art, athletic training, business, early childhood, elementary, foreign languages, health, mathematics, music, physical, science, and secondary), ENGINEERING AND ENVIRONMENTAL DESIGN (engineering and applied science and environmental science), HEALTH PROFESSIONS (nursing), SOCIAL SCIENCE (economics, ethnic studies, history, international relations, philosophy, political science/government, psychology, religion, social work, and youth ministry). Physical sciences, life sciences, and computer science are the strongest academically. Education, business, and biology are the largest.

Special: Students may arrange internships, study abroad in various countries, participate in a Washington semester with the Christian College Coalition, and select various work-study programs. Dual majors in cross-cultural studies are available. Students may design their own majors, earn a 3-2 engineering degree, and select limited pass/fail options. An adult degree completion program is offered. There is a freshman honors program.

Admissions: 81% of the 1999-2000 applicants were accepted. The SAT I scores for the 1999-2000 freshman class were: Verbal--19% below 500, 37% between 500 and 599, 38% between 600 and 700, and 6% above 700; Math--21% below 500, 40% between 500 and 599, 31% between 600 and 700, and 8% above 700. There were 3 National Merit semifinalists.

Requirements: The SAT I or ACT is required. Bethel requires applicants to be in the upper 50% of their class. The PSAT is accepted. In addition, applicants must be graduates of an accredited secondary school or have a GED. An interview is recommended. AP and CLEP credits are accepted. Important factors in the admissions decision are advanced placement or honor courses, extracurricular activities record, and personality/intangible qualities.

Procedure: Freshmen are admitted to all sessions. There is an early admissions plan. Applications should be filed by April 1 for fall entry and January 15 for spring entry, along with a $25 fee. Notification is sent on a rolling basis. A waiting list is an active part of the admissions procedure.

Financial Aid: In a recent year, 90% of all freshmen and continuing students received some form of financial aid. 70% of all students received need-based aid. The average freshman award was $11,400. 45% of undergraduates work part time. Average annual earnings from campus work are $900. Bethel is a member of CSS. The FAFSA, the college's own financial statement, and students' and parents' most recent federal tax returns are required. The fall application deadline is April 15.

Computers: The mainframes are a Dell system PC and an 850 workgroup server for Macs. The computer labs have more than 125 Macs and IBM PCs; the on-campus housing options are fully wired, allowing for 2 mainframe connections per room. All students may access the system 24 hours a day. There are no time limits and no fees.

BIOLA UNIVERSITY
La Mirada, CA 90639-0001

(562) 903-4752
(800) OK-BIOLA; Fax: (562) 903-4709

Full-time: 861 men, 1490 women	**Faculty:** 95; IIA, --$
Part-time: 99 men, 114 women	**Ph.D.s:** 68%
Graduate: 788 men, 520 women	**Student/Faculty:** 25 to 1
Year: 4-1-4, summer session	**Tuition:** $15,914
Application Deadline: June 1	**Room & Board:** $5139
Freshman Class: 1501 applied, 1263 accepted, 567 enrolled	
SAT I Verbal/Math: 551/546	**ACT:** 23 **VERY COMPETITIVE**

Biola University, founded in 1908, is a private, interdenominational Christian institution offering undergraduate and graduate degrees in arts and sciences, psychology, theology, intercultural studies, and business. There are 6 undergraduate and 5 graduate schools. In addition to regional accreditation, Biola has baccalaureate program accreditation with ACBSP, NASAD, NASM, and NLN. The library contains 251,000 volumes, 446,277 microform items, and 10,343 audiovisual forms/CDs, and subscribes to 1188 periodicals. Computerized library services include the card catalog, interlibrary loans, and database searching. Special learning facilities include a learning resource center, art gallery, radio station, TV and film studio and 3-D art facility. The 95-acre campus is in a suburban area 22 miles southeast of Los Angeles. Including residence halls, there are 39 buildings.

Programs of Study: Biola confers B.A., B.S., and B.M. degrees. Master's and doctoral degrees are also awarded. Bachelor's degrees are awarded in BIOLOGI-

CAL SCIENCE (biochemistry and biology/biological science), BUSINESS (business administration and management), COMMUNICATIONS AND THE ARTS (broadcasting, communications, English, film arts, music, music business management, radio/television technology, and Spanish), COMPUTER AND PHYSICAL SCIENCE (computer science, mathematics, and physical sciences), EDUCATION (art, Christian, elementary, and physical), HEALTH PROFESSIONS (nursing and speech pathology/audiology), SOCIAL SCIENCE (biblical studies, Christian studies, crosscultural studies, history, humanities, liberal arts/general studies, philosophy, psychology, social science, and sociology). Biblical studies, liberal studies, and radio/television/film are the strongest academically. Business, communications, and psychology are the largest.

Special: Cross-registration with the Au Sable Institute of Environmental Studies is possible. Biola offers internships, summer travel tours, study abroad, and an American studies program in Washington D.C., sponsored by the Christian College Coalition. Special programs include L.A. Film Studies, a semester in Hollywood working in the film industry; Biola Baja, a three week program at Vermillion Sea Field Station; family studies course at Focus on the Family Institute in Colorado Springs; a China studies program at Fudan University in Shanghai, China; and a development theory studies program in Honduras. Also available are on- and off-campus work-study programs, a B.A.- B.S. degree, a 3-2 engineering degree with the University of Southern California, dual and student-designed majors, and nondegree study. There are 3 national honor societies and 2 departmental honors programs.

Admissions: 84% of the 1999-2000 applicants were accepted. The SAT I scores for the 1999-2000 freshman class were: Verbal--20% below 500, 43% between 500 and 599, 31% between 600 and 700, and 6% above 700; Math--25% below 500, 43% between 500 and 599, 27% between 600 and 700, and 5% above 700. The ACT scores were 22% below 21, 26% between 21 and 23, 28% between 24 and 26, 9% between 27 and 28, and 14% above 28. 44 freshmen graduated first in their class.

Requirements: The SAT I or ACT is required. A GPA of 2.8 is required. Applicants need not be graduates of an accredited secondary school. The GED is accepted. Students should have completed 15 academic credits, including 4 years each of English and foreign language, 3 of math, and 2 each of social studies and science. All students must be evangelical Christians who can demonstrate Christian character, leadership ability, and the aptitude for possible success in college. Applicants must submit 2 personal references: 1 from their pastor or someone on the pastoral staff, and 1 from the school last attended, or from an employer if they have been out of school for a year and have been working. An essay and interview are required. Applications are accepted on-line. AP and CLEP credits are accepted. Important factors in the admissions decision are personality/intangible qualities, recommendations by school officials, and leadership record.

Procedure: Freshmen are admitted to all sessions. Entrance exams should be taken before February 1. There are early decision, early admissions, and deferred admissions plans. Early decision applications should be filed by February 1; regular applications, by June 1 for fall entry and January 1 for spring entry, along with a $45 fee. Notification is sent on a rolling basis.

Financial Aid: In 1999-2000, 85% of all students received some form of financial aid. 65% of freshmen and 68% of continuing students received need-based aid. The average freshman award was $12,300. Of that total, scholarships or need-based grants averaged $8384 ($24,000 maximum); loans averaged $3000 ($4500 maximum); and work contracts averaged $2000 ($2500 maximum). 32% of undergraduates work part time. Average annual earnings from campus work are $3000. The average financial indebtedness of the 1999 graduate was $14,000.

The FAFSA and the university's own financial statement are required. California residents should submit the Cal Grant GPA verification form. The fall application deadline is March 2.

Computers: The mainframes are an HP 9000/Series 300, a DEC VAX 3100, and a DEC VAX 2100. There is 1 main computer center for the HP and VAX terminals. In addition, Mac and IBM PC labs are located throughout the campus. All residence hall rooms have Internet access. All students may access the system every day. There are no time limits and no fees.

BOSTON ARCHITECTURAL CENTER
Boston, MA 02115   **(617) 262-5000; Fax: (617) 585-0121**

Full-time: 310 men, 112 women	**Faculty:** n/av
Part-time: 55 men, 13 women	**Ph.D.s:** 80%
Graduate: 106 men, 77 women	**Student/Faculty:** n/av
Year: semesters, summer session	**Tuition:** $6405
Application Deadline: open	**Room & Board:** n/app
Freshman Class: 368 applied, 281 accepted, 183 enrolled	
SAT I or ACT: not required	**SPECIAL**

Boston Architectural Center, founded in 1889 as the Boston Architectural Club, is an independent, commuter institution offering professional programs in architecture and interior design. Students work in architectural and interior design offices during the day and attend classes at night. There are 2 undergraduate and 2 graduate schools. In addition to regional accreditation, BAC has baccalaureate program accreditation with NAAB. The library contains 25,000 volumes, and subscribes to 140 periodicals. Computerized library services include the card catalog and database searching. Special learning facilities include an art gallery. The campus is in an urban area in Boston. There are 2 buildings.

Programs of Study: BAC confers B.Arch. and B.Int.Design degrees. Master's degrees are also awarded. Bachelor's degrees are awarded in ENGINEERING AND ENVIRONMENTAL DESIGN (architecture and interior design).

Special: BAC offers study abroad and cross-registration with schools in the Professional Arts Consortium in Boston and with the Art Institute of Boston for studio and professional courses. The participating schools are BAC, Berklee College of Music, Boston Conservation, Emerson College, Massachusetts College of Art and School of the MFA.

Admissions: 76% of the 1999-2000 applicants were accepted.

Requirements: All applicants who have graduated from high school or have a college degree are admitted on a first-come, first-served basis. Official transcripts from previously attended secondary schools and colleges must be submitted to determine qualification for admission and advanced placement. Applications are accepted on-line at BAC's web site. AP credits are accepted.

Procedure: Freshmen are admitted fall and spring. There is a deferred admissions plan. Application deadlines are open, along with a $50 fee. The college accepts all applicants. Notification is sent on a rolling basis.

Financial Aid: In 1999-2000, 37% of all freshmen and 63% of continuing students received some form of financial aid. 38% of freshmen and 62% of continuing students received need-based aid. The average freshman award was $6457. Of that total, scholarships or need-based grants averaged $1440 ($3125 maximum); and federal loans averaged $5830 ($6625 maximum). The average financial indebtedness of the 1999 graduate was $40,000. BAC is a member of CSS. The FAFSA and the college's own financial statement are required. The fall application deadline is March 31.

Computers: There are 50 Macs and IBM PCs available for student use, all with Internet access. All students may access the system. There are no time limits. There is a $75 lab fee for certain courses.

BOSTON COLLEGE
Chestnut Hill, MA 02467 (617) 552-3100
(800) 360-2522; Fax: (617) 552-0798

Full-time: 4339 men, 4851 women	**Faculty:** 631; I, ++$
Part-time: none	**Ph.D.s:** 98%
Graduate: 1972 men, 2691 women	**Student/Faculty:** 15 to 1
Year: semesters, summer session	**Tuition:** $22,256
Application Deadline: January 1	**Room & Board:** $8250
Freshman Class: 19,946 applied, 6976 accepted, 2284 enrolled	
SAT I or ACT: required	**MOST COMPETITIVE**

Boston College, founded in 1863, is an independent institution affiliated with the Roman Catholic Church and the Jesuit Order. It offers undergraduate programs in the arts and sciences, business, nursing, and education, and graduate and professional programs. There are 4 undergraduate and 7 graduate schools. In addition to regional accreditation, BC has baccalaureate program accreditation with AACSB, CSWE, NCATE, and NLN. The 6 libraries contain 1,737,880 volumes, 3,249,601 microform items, and 118,054 audiovisual forms/CDs, and subscribe to 20,910 periodicals. Computerized library services include the card catalog, interlibrary loans, and database searching. Special learning facilities include a learning resource center, art gallery, radio station, and TV station. The 240-acre campus is in a suburban area 6 miles west of Boston. Including residence halls, there are 90 buildings.

Programs of Study: BC confers B.A. and B.S. degrees. Master's and doctoral degrees are also awarded. Bachelor's degrees are awarded in BIOLOGICAL SCIENCE (biochemistry and biology/biological science), BUSINESS (accounting, banking and finance, business administration and management, business economics, human resources, management science, marketing/retailing/merchandising, and operations research), COMMUNICATIONS AND THE ARTS (art history and appreciation, classics, communications, dramatic arts, English, film arts, French, Italian, linguistics, music, romance languages and literature, and studio art), COMPUTER AND PHYSICAL SCIENCE (chemistry, computer science, geology, geophysics and seismology, information sciences and systems, mathematics, and physics), EDUCATION (early childhood, elementary, secondary, and special), ENGINEERING AND ENVIRONMENTAL DESIGN (environmental science), HEALTH PROFESSIONS (nursing), SOCIAL SCIENCE (classical/ancient civilization, economics, German area studies, Hispanic American studies, history, human development, philosophy, political science/government, psychology, Russian and Slavic studies, sociology, and theological studies). Humanities and social sciences are the strongest academically. English, finance, psychology, and communication are the largest.

Special: There are internship programs in arts and sciences. Students may cross-register with Boston University, Brandeis University, Hebrew College, Pine Manor College, Regis College, and Tufts University. BC also offers a Washington semester with American University, work-study programs with nonprofit agencies, study abroad, dual and student-designed majors, credit by exam, and pass/fail options. Students may pursue a 3-2 engineering program with Boston University and accelerated programs in business, social work, and education. There are also special programs in social work and philosophy/theology, in language immersion, capstone courses, and in exploring fundamental questions of faith, peace, and justice. There are 12 national honor societies, including Phi Beta Kappa, a freshman honors program, and 8 departmental honors programs.

Admissions: 35% of the 1999-2000 applicants were accepted. The SAT I scores for the 1999-2000 freshman class were: Verbal--5% below 500, 24% between 500 and 599, 57% between 600 and 700, and 15% above 700; Math--3% below 500, 18% between 500 and 599, 60% between 600 and 700, and 19% above 700. 86% of the current freshmen were in the top fifth of their class; 97% were in the top two fifths. There were 7 National Merit finalists.

Requirements: The SAT I or ACT is required. Students must also take SAT II: Subject tests in writing, mathematics level I or II, and any third test. Applicants must be graduates of an accredited high school completing 4 units each of English, foreign language, and math, and 3 units of science. Those students applying to the School of Nursing must complete at least 2 years of a lab science, including 1 year of chemistry. Applicants to the School of Management are strongly encouraged to take 4 years of math. An essay is required. Electronic application materials are available through SNAP technologies at www.collegedge.com, www.nassp.org, and www.apply.embark.com/ugrad/bc. AP credits are accepted. Important factors in the admissions decision are evidence of special talent, leadership record, and advanced placement or honor courses.

Procedure: Freshmen are admitted fall and spring. Entrance exams should be taken no later than January of the senior year. There are early admissions and deferred admissions plans. Early decision applications should be filed by October 15; regular applications, by January 1 for fall entry and November 1 for spring entry, along with a $55 fee. Notification of early decision is sent December 15; regular decision, April 15. A waiting list is an active part of the admissions procedure.

Financial Aid: In 1998-1999, 49% of all freshmen and 48% of continuing students received some form of financial aid. 47% of freshmen and 46% of continuing students received need-based aid. The average freshman award was $18,793. Of that total, scholarships or need-based grants averaged $13,934 ($21,760 maximum); loans averaged $3459; and work contracts averaged $1400 ($1500 maximum). 19% of undergraduates work part time. Average annual earnings from campus work are $1500. The average financial indebtedness of the 1998 graduate was $16,417. BC is a member of CSS. The CSS/Profile or FAFSA and the federal IRS income tax form, W-2's, Divorced/Separated Statement (when applicable) are required. The fall application deadline is February 1.

Computers: The mainframes are an IBM 3270 and DEC VAX 11/785 and 8700 units. More than 200 PCs are available, providing database searches, optical disk references, and on-line access to catalog services. Software includes word processing, programming languages, statistical analysis, graphics production, and database management packages. Printers include high-speed line printers, high-resolution dot-matrix printers, and laser printers. Professionals and students assist students with aspects of computing. Project AGORA brings voice, data, and video to every student through a campus computing center that manages the phone system and includes cable access, satellite and video conferencing, cable casting of university events, and video program production and training. All students may access the system at all times. There are no time limits and no fees.

BOSTON UNIVERSITY
Boston, MA 02215   (617) 353-2300; Fax: (617) 353-9695

Full-time: 6376 men, 9497 women	**Faculty:** 1209
Part-time: 1143 men, 1002 women	**Ph.D.s:** 80%
Graduate: 4968 men, 5501 women	**Student/Faculty:** 13 to 1
Year: semesters, summer session	**Tuition:** $24,100
Application Deadline: January 1	**Room & Board:** $8130
Freshman Class: 28,090 applied, 15,561 accepted, 4225 enrolled	
SAT I Verbal/Math: 630/640	**ACT:** 28 **HIGHLY COMPETITIVE**

Boston University, founded in 1839, is a private institution offering undergraduate and graduate programs in basic studies, liberal arts, communication, hotel and food administration, allied health education management, and fine arts. There are 10 undergraduate and 16 graduate schools. In addition to regional accreditation, BU has baccalaureate program accreditation with AACSB, ABET, NASM, and NCATE. The 23 libraries contain 1.7 million volumes, 2.6 million microform items, and 50,788 audiovisual forms/CDs, and subscribe to 20,129 periodicals. Computerized library services include the card catalog, interlibrary loans, and database searching. Special learning facilities include a learning resource center, art gallery, planetarium, radio station, TV station, astronomy observatory, 20th century archives, theater and theater company in residence, scientific computing and visualization lab, the Geddes language lab, a speech, language, and hearing clinic, hotel/food administration culinary center, performance center, multimedia center, center for photonics research, center for remote sensing, and the Metcalf Center for Science and Engineering. The 133-acre campus is in an urban area on the Charles River in Boston's Back Bay. Including residence halls, there are 337 buildings.

Programs of Study: BU confers B.A., B.S., B.F.A., B.Mus., B.S.B.A. degrees. Master's and doctoral degrees are also awarded. Bachelor's degrees are awarded in BIOLOGICAL SCIENCE (biochemistry, biology/biological science, ecology, marine biology, neurosciences, nutrition, and physiology), BUSINESS (accounting, banking and finance, business administration and management, hotel/motel and restaurant management, international business management, management information systems, marketing/retailing/merchandising, operations research, and organizational behavior), COMMUNICATIONS AND THE ARTS (advertising, art history and appreciation, broadcasting, classics, communications, dramatic arts, English, film arts, French, German, graphic design, Greek (classical), Greek (modern), Italian, journalism, Latin, linguistics, music, music history and appreciation, music performance, music theory and composition, painting, public relations, Russian, sculpture, Spanish, theater design, and theater management), COMPUTER AND PHYSICAL SCIENCE (applied mathematics, astronomy, astrophysics, chemistry, computer science, earth science, information sciences and systems, mathematics, physics, and planetary space science), EDUCATION (art, athletic training, bilingual/bicultural, drama, early childhood, education of the deaf and hearing impaired, elementary, English, foreign languages, mathematics, music, physical, science, social studies, and special), ENGINEERING AND ENVIRONMENTAL DESIGN (aeronautical engineering, biomedical engineering, computer engineering, electrical/electronics engineering, engineering, environmental science, industrial engineering, manufacturing engineering, and mechanical engineering), HEALTH PROFESSIONS (exercise science, health science, occupational therapy, physical therapy, predentistry, premedicine, rehabilitation therapy, and speech pathology/audiology), SOCIAL SCIENCE (American studies, anthropology, archeology, classical/ancient civilization, East Asian studies, economics, geography, history, interdisciplinary studies, international relations, Latin American studies, philosophy, physical fitness/movement, political science/government, psychology, religion, Russian and Slavic studies, sociology, and urban studies). The University Professors Program, accelerated medical and dental programs, and the management honors program are the strongest academically. Communication/journalism, business administration and management, and engineering are the largest.

Special: Cross-registration is permitted with Brandeis University, Tufts University, Boston College, and Hebrew College in Massachusetts. Opportunities are provided for internships, co-op programs in engineering, a Washington semester, on- and off-campus work-study, accelerated degrees in medicine and dentistry, B.A.-B.S. degrees, dual majors, student-designed majors, credit by exam, nondegree studies, pass/fail options, and study abroad in 14 countries. A 3-2 engineering degree is offered with 16 schools, and 2-2 engineering agreements with 6 schools, plus 107 other 2-2 agreements. The University Professors Program offers a creative cross-disciplinary approach, and the College of Basic Studies offers team teaching. There are 12 national honor societies, including Phi Beta Kappa, and a freshman honors program.

Admissions: 55% of the 1999-2000 applicants were accepted. The SAT I scores for the 1999-2000 freshman class were: Verbal--1% below 500, 27% between 500 and 599, 53% between 600 and 700, and 19% above 700; Math--1% below 500, 25% between 500 and 599, 55% between 600 and 700, and 20% above 700. The ACT scores were 6% between 18 and 23, 67% between 24 and 29, and 26% above 30. 82% of the current freshmen were in the top fifth of their class; 98% were in the top two fifths. There were 49 National Merit finalists. 139 freshmen graduated first in their class.

Requirements: The SAT I or ACT is required. applicants are evaluated on an individual basis. Evidence of strong academic performance in a college prep curriculum, including 4 years of English, math, science, and social studies/history with at least 3 years of a foreign language, will be the most important aspect of a student's application review. SAT II: Subject tests are required for the accelerated medical and dental programs and recommended for the College of Communication, The University Professors, and the College of Arts and Sciences. Candidates for the School for the Arts must present a portfolio or participate in an audition. Applications are accepted on-line via CollegeView, ExPAN, and at the school's web site. AP and CLEP credits are accepted.

Procedure: Freshmen are admitted fall and spring. Entrance exams should be taken in the junior year or early in the senior year. There are early decision, early admissions, and deferred admissions plans. Early decision applications should be filed by November 1; regular applications, by January 1 for fall entry and November 1 for spring entry, along with a $50 fee. Notification of early decision is sent in mid-December; regular decision, in mid-March. 123 early decision candidates were accepted for the 1999-2000 class. 5% of all applicants are on a waiting list.

Financial Aid: In 1999-2000, 71% of all freshmen and 64% of continuing students received some form of financial aid. 55% of freshmen and 50% of continuing students received need-based aid. The average freshman award was $21,214. Of that total, scholarships or need-based grants averaged $15,000 ($32,000 maximum); loans averaged $3231 ($5625 maximum); and work contracts averaged $1954 ($2000 maximum). 79% of undergraduates work part time. Average annual earnings from campus work are $1747. The average financial indebtedness of the 1999 graduate was $18,702. BU is a member of CSS. The CSS/Profile or FAFSA is required. The fall application deadline is February 15.

Computers: The mainframe is an IBM RS/6000 cluster. The campus network provides the entire university community with high-speed access to E-mail, the Internet, the World Wide Web, and other resources. Facilities include a supercomputer cluster of SGI/Cray Origin 2000 systems, an SGI Power Challenge Array , several SGI workstations, and a computer graphics lab. All students may access the system 24 hours a day. There are no time limits and no fees.

BOWDOIN COLLEGE
Brunswick, ME 04011 (207) 725-3100; Fax: (207) 725-3101

Full-time: 777 men, 831 women	**Faculty:** 120; IIB, ++$
Part-time: 2 men, 7 women	**Ph.D.s:** 94%
Graduate: none	**Student/Faculty:** 13 to 1
Year: semesters	**Tuition:** $24,955
Application Deadline: January 1	**Room & Board:** $6520

Freshman Class: 3942 applied, 1263 accepted, 464 enrolled
SAT I Verbal/Math: 680/680   **MOST COMPETITIVE**

Bowdoin College, established in 1794, is a private liberal arts institution. The 5 libraries contain 901,589 volumes and 17,455 audiovisual forms/CDs, and subscribe to 2137 periodicals. Computerized library services include the card catalog, interlibrary loans, and database searching. Special learning facilities include a learning resource center, art gallery, radio station, tv station, museum of art, arctic museum, language media center, women's resource center, electronic classroom, coastal studies center, the John Brown Russwurm African American Center, and the Craft Barn, a ceramics studio and photography darkroom. The Bowdoin Scientific Station, located in the Bay of Fundy, New Brunswick, Canada, is a 200-acre island for scientific study by Bowdoin students. The 110-acre campus is in a small town 25 miles northeast of Portland. Including residence halls, there are 92 buildings.

Programs of Study: Bowdoin confers A.B. and B.A. degrees. Bachelor's degrees are awarded in BIOLOGICAL SCIENCE (biochemistry, biology/biological science, and neurosciences), COMMUNICATIONS AND THE ARTS (art history and appreciation, classics, English, French, German, music, romance languages and literature, Russian, Spanish, studio art, and visual and performing arts), COMPUTER AND PHYSICAL SCIENCE (chemistry, computer science, geology, mathematics, and physics), ENGINEERING AND ENVIRONMENTAL DESIGN (environmental science), SOCIAL SCIENCE (African studies, anthropology, archeology, Asian/Oriental studies, classical/ancient civilization, economics, history, philosophy, political science/government, psychology, religion, sociology, and women's studies). Biology, economics, and English are the strongest academically. Biology, government and legal studies, and history are the largest.

Special: Students may take advantage of about 100 approved programs all over the world, including Intercollegiate Center for Classical Studies in Rome, Intercollegiate Sri Lanka Education (ISLE), South India Term Abroad (SITA), The Swedish Program, Semester in Environmental Science at the Marine Biological Laboratory, Woods Hole, and the Twelve College Exchange (including Williams College-Mystic Seaport and National Theater Institute). Dual majors in any combination, interdisciplinary majors, student-designed majors, and pass/fail options are available. The college offers a 3-2 engineering degree with the California Institute of Technology and Columbia University and a 3-3 legal studies degree with Columbia University Law School. There is a chapter of Phi Beta Kappa.

Admissions: 32% of the 1999-2000 applicants were accepted. The SAT I scores for the 1999-2000 freshman class were: Verbal--1% below 500, 7% between 500 and 599, 48% between 600 and 700, and 44% above 700; Math--9% between 500 and 599, 53% between 600 and 700, and 38% above 700.

Requirements: There are no specific academic requirements, but typical applicants for admission will have 4 years each of English, social studies, foreign language, and math, 3 1/2 years of science, and 1 course each in art, music, and history. A high school record, 2 teacher recommendations, and an essay are required. AP credits are accepted. Important factors in the admissions decision are advanced placement or honor courses, recommendations by school officials, and evidence of special talent.

Procedure: Freshmen are admitted in the fall. Entrance exams are required for counseling and placement only and should be submitted by the late summer before the freshman year. There are early decision and deferred admissions plans. Early decision applications should be filed by November 15; regular applications, by January 1 for fall entry, along with a $55 fee. Notification of early decision is sent December 15; regular decision, April 15. 182 early decision candidates were accepted for the 1999-2000 class. 1% of all applicants are on a waiting list.

Financial Aid: In 1999-2000, 36% of all freshmen and 37% of continuing students received some form of financial aid, including need-based aid. The average freshman award was $20,321. Of that total, scholarships or need-based grants averaged $17,030 ($29,500 maximum); loans averaged $3529 ($4100 maximum); and work contracts averaged $895 ($900 maximum). 55% of undergraduates work part time. Average annual earnings from campus work are $1062. The average financial indebtedness of the 1999 graduate was $15,820. Bowdoin is a member of CSS. The CSS/Profile, FAFSA, and the college's own financial statement are required. The fall application deadline is February 15.

Computers: The mainframes are 2 DEC ALPHA 1000 servers, 2 ALPHA server 1200s, and 1 Compaq DS 20. Students access servers from 165 public PCs and terminals. More than 1000 students access the network from their dorm rooms, including the Internet and Web. Almost all students use E-mail. All students may access the system 24 hours a day. There are no time limits and no fees. It is strongly recommended that all students have personal computers.

BRADLEY UNIVERSITY
Peoria, IL 61625

(309) 677-1000
(800) 447-6460; Fax: (309) 677-2797

Full-time: 2074 men, 2409 women	**Faculty:** 321; IIA, av$
Part-time: 211 men, 267 women	**Ph.D.s:** 86%
Graduate: 514 men, 362 women	**Student/Faculty:** 14 to 1
Year: semesters, summer session	**Tuition:** $13,960
Application Deadline: open	**Room & Board:** $5300
Freshman Class: 4545 applied, 3699 accepted, 1079 enrolled	
SAT I Verbal/Math: 580/610	**ACT:** 25 **VERY COMPETITIVE**

Bradley University is an independent, privately endowed institution. The University offers a full range of baccalaureate and graduate-level programs, as well as personal attention, from a faculty dedicated to student learning. There are 5 undergraduate schools and 1 graduate school. In addition to regional accreditation, Bradley has baccalaureate program accreditation with AACSB, ABET, ACCE, ADA, NASAD, NASM, NCATE, and NLN. The library contains 508,000 volumes, 784,000 microform items, and 23,400 audiovisual forms/CDs, and subscribes to 1975 periodicals. Computerized library services include the card catalog, interlibrary loans, and database searching. Special learning facilities include a learning resource center, art gallery, radio station, and TV station. The 75-acre campus is in an urban area 160 miles southwest of Chicago. Including residence halls, there are 41 buildings.

Programs of Study: Bradley confers B.A., B.S., B.F.A., B.M., B.S.C., B.S.C.E., B.S.E.E., B.S.I.E., B.S.M.E., B.S.M.F.E., B.S.M.F.E.T., B.S.N., and B.S.P.T. degrees. Master's degrees are also awarded. Bachelor's degrees are awarded in BIOLOGICAL SCIENCE (biochemistry, biology/biological science, and molecular biology), BUSINESS (accounting, banking and finance, business administration and management, insurance and risk management, international business management, management information systems, and marketing/retailing/merchandising), COMMUNICATIONS AND THE ARTS (art history and appreciation, communications, dramatic arts, English, French, German, graphic design, music, music performance, music theory and composition, photography, printmaking, sculpture, Spanish, and studio art), COMPUTER AND PHYSICAL SCIENCE (actuarial science, chemistry, computer science, geoscience, information sciences and systems, mathematics, and physics), EDUCATION (early childhood, elementary, foreign languages, home economics, music, secondary, and special), ENGINEERING AND ENVIRONMENTAL DESIGN (civil engineering, construction engineering, electrical/electronics engineering, engineering physics, environmental science, industrial engineering, manufacturing engineering, manufacturing technology, and mechanical engineering), HEALTH PROFESSIONS (medical laboratory technology, nursing, and physical therapy), SOCIAL SCIENCE (criminal justice, economics, family/consumer studies, history, international studies, philosophy, political science/government, psychology, religion, social work, and sociology). Business, engineering, and natural sciences are the strongest academically. Business, engineering, and communication are the largest.

Special: Special academic programs include an honors program, co-op programs, internships, a Washington semester, work-study programs, study abroad in 12 countries, B.A.-B.S. degrees in most majors, dual majors, and leadership fellowships. There are 31 national honor societies, and a freshman honors program.

Admissions: 81% of the 1999-2000 applicants were accepted. The SAT I scores for the 1999-2000 freshman class were: Verbal--12% below 500, 44% between 500 and 599, 34% between 600 and 700, and 10% above 700; Math--10% below 500, 34% between 500 and 599, 44% between 600 and 700, and 12% above 700. The ACT scores were 10% below 21, 21% between 21 and 23, 32% between 24 and 26, 18% between 27 and 28, and 19% above 28. 54% of the current freshmen were in the top fifth of their class; 80% were in the top two fifths. There were 17 National Merit finalists. 52 freshmen graduated first in their class.

Requirements: The SAT I or ACT is required. A GPA of 2.5 is required. Applications are accepted on-line. AP and CLEP credits are accepted. Important factors in the admissions decision are evidence of special talent, extracurricular activities record, and advanced placement or honor courses.

Procedure: Freshmen are admitted to all sessions. Entrance exams should be taken in the spring of the junior year or the fall of the senior year. There is an early admissions plan. Application deadlines are open. There is a $35 fee. Notification is sent on a rolling basis. 3% of all applicants are on a waiting list.

Financial Aid: In 1999-2000, 91% of all freshmen and 82% of continuing students received some form of financial aid. 60% of freshmen and 55% of continuing students received need-based aid. The average freshman award was $11,213. Of that total, scholarships or need-based grants averaged $5300 ($13,840 maximum); loans averaged $2500 ($4125 maximum); and work contracts averaged $1200 ($1800 maximum). 26% of undergraduates work part time. Average annual earnings from campus work are $950. The average financial indebtedness of the 1999 graduate was $15,500. Bradley is a member of CSS. The FAFSA is required. The fall application deadline is March 1.

Computers: The mainframe is a Control Data CYBER 930. There are about 2000 AT&T, Zenith, IBM, and Mac PCs available throughout the campus. All students may access the system 24 hours a day. There are no time limits and no fees.

BRANDEIS UNIVERSITY
Waltham, MA 02454

(781) 736-3500
(800) 622-0622; Fax: (781) 736-3536

Full-time: 1348 men, 1730 women	**Faculty:** 316; I, av$
Part-time: 13 men, 21 women	**Ph.D.s:** 95%
Graduate: 725 men, 690 women	**Student/Faculty:** 10 to 1
Year: semesters, summer session	**Tuition:** $25,174
Application Deadline: January 31	**Room & Board:** $7040
Freshman Class: 5792 applied, 2989 accepted, 794 enrolled	
SAT I Verbal/Math: 660/660	**HIGHLY COMPETITIVE+**

Brandeis University, founded in 1948, is a private liberal arts institution. There are 3 graduate schools. The 3 libraries contain 834,376 volumes, 877,131 microform items, and 23,165 audiovisual forms/CDs, and subscribe to 16,119 periodicals. Computerized library services include the card catalog, interlibrary loans, and database searching. Special learning facilities include a learning resource center, art gallery, radio station, an astronomical observatory, a cultural center, a treasure hall, an art museum, and an audiovisual center. The 235-acre campus is in a suburban area 10 miles west of Boston. Including residence halls, there are 98 buildings.

Programs of Study: Brandeis confers B.A. and B.S. degrees. Master's and doctoral degrees are also awarded. Bachelor's degrees are awarded in BIOLOGICAL SCIENCE (biochemistry, biology/biological science, and neurosciences), COMMUNICATIONS AND THE ARTS (American literature, art history and appreciation, classics, comparative literature, dramatic arts, English, English literature, fine arts, French, German, linguistics, music, performing arts, Russian, and Spanish), COMPUTER AND PHYSICAL SCIENCE (chemistry, computer science, mathematics, physics, and science), SOCIAL SCIENCE (African American studies, African studies, American studies, anthropology, economics, European studies, history, Islamic studies, Judaic studies, Latin American studies, Middle Eastern studies, Near Eastern studies, philosophy, political science/government, psychology, and sociology). Sciences, history, and English are the strongest academically. Psychology, economics, and biology are the largest.

Special: Students may pursue interdepartmental programs in 18 different fields. Students may cross-register with Boston College, Boston University, Tufts University, Wellesley College, Babson College, and Bentley College. Study abroad is possible in 48 countries. Internships are available in virtually every field, and a work-study program is also provided. Dual and student-designed majors can be arranged. The university also offers credit by exam, nondegree study, and pass/fail options. Opportunities for early acceptance to area medical schools are offered to Brandeis students. There are 4 national honor societies, including Phi Beta Kappa, and a freshman honors program. All departments have honors programs.

Admissions: 52% of the 1999-2000 applicants were accepted. The SAT I scores for the 1999-2000 freshman class were: Verbal--1% below 500, 15% between 500 and 599, 54% between 600 and 700, and 30% above 700; Math--2% below

500, 15% between 500 and 599, 50% between 600 and 700, and 33% above 700. 86% of the current freshmen were in the top fifth of their class; 99% were in the top two fifths.

Requirements: The SAT I or ACT is required. Students submitting the SAT I score must also take 3 SAT II: Subject tests, including writing. The ACT may be submitted instead of the SAT I and II. Applicants should prepare with 4 years of high school English, 3 each of foreign language and math, and at least 1 each of science and social studies. An essay is required, and an interview is recommended. Brandeis accepts applications on-line and on computer disk via Common Application, CollegeLink, Apply, and their web site. AP credits are accepted. Important factors in the admissions decision are advanced placement or honor courses, recommendations by school officials, and extracurricular activities record.

Procedure: Freshmen are admitted fall and spring. Entrance exams should be taken by the fall of the senior year. There are early decision and deferred admissions plans. Early decision applications should be filed by January 1; regular applications, by January 31 for fall entry and December 1 for spring entry, along with a $50 fee. Notification of early decision is sent 4 weeks after application completion; regular decision, by April 15. 149 early decision candidates were accepted for the 1999-2000 class. 9% of all applicants are on a waiting list.

Financial Aid: In 1999-2000, 50% of all students received some form of financial aid. 50% of freshmen and 48% of continuing students received need-based aid. The average freshman award was $17,956. Of that total, scholarships or need-based grants averaged $13,454; and loans averaged $3686. 64% of undergraduates work part time. Average annual earnings from campus work are $805. Brandeis is a member of CSS. The CSS/Profile, FAFSA, and copies of student and parent income tax returns for matriculating students are required. The fall application deadline is January 31.

Computers: The mainframe is a DEC VAX cluster for undergraduate network services. There are three clusters located throughout the campus containing more than 100 Mac and IBM computers and printers for both. All Macs and some IBMs are connected to the campus network via an Ethernet gateway, giving students access to Student Network Services accounts. Access to the mainframe is also available from students' rooms. All students may access the system. There are no time limits and no fees.

BRIGHAM YOUNG UNIVERSITY
Provo, UT 84602   (801) 378-2537; Fax: (801) 378-4264

Full-time: 12,254 men, 14,219 women	**Faculty:** 1395; I, -$
Part-time: 1728 men, 1718 women	**Ph.D.s:** 82%
Graduate: 1725 men, 1087 women	**Student/Faculty:** 19 to 1
Year: 4-4-2-2, summer session	**Tuition:** $2830 ($4250)
Application Deadline: February 15	**Room & Board:** $4454
Freshman Class: 8078 applied, 5181 accepted, 4197 enrolled	
ACT: 27	**HIGHLY COMPETITIVE**

Brigham Young University, founded in 1875, is a private university affiliated with the Church of Jesus Christ of Latter-day Saints. There are 10 undergraduate and 11 graduate schools. In addition to regional accreditation, Brigham Young or BYU has baccalaureate program accreditation with AACSB, ABET, ACCE, ACEJMC, ADA, ASLA, CSAB, CSWE, NASAD, NASDTEC, NASM, NCATE, and NLN. The 3 libraries contain 2,539,726 volumes, 2,450,309 microform items, and 52,905 audiovisual forms/CDs, and subscribe to 16,218 periodicals.

Computerized library services include the card catalog, interlibrary loans, and database searching. Special learning facilities include a learning resource center, art gallery, natural history museum, planetarium, radio station, TV station, an archaeological museum, an earth science museum, reading and writing labs, and math, language, and computer labs. The 638-acre campus is in a suburban area 45 miles south of Salt Lake City. Including residence halls, there are 354 buildings.

Programs of Study: BYU confers B.A., B.S., B.F.A., B.Mus., and B. Independent Studies. degrees. Associate, master's, and doctoral degrees are also awarded. Bachelor's degrees are awarded in AGRICULTURE (agronomy, animal science, horticulture, and wildlife management), BIOLOGICAL SCIENCE (biochemistry, biology/biological science, botany, microbiology, nutrition, and zoology), BUSINESS (accounting, banking and finance, business administration and management, fashion merchandising, management information systems, and tourism), COMMUNICATIONS AND THE ARTS (advertising, art history and appreciation, broadcasting, Chinese, communications, comparative literature, dance, design, dramatic arts, English, film arts, French, German, graphic design, Greek, illustration, industrial design, Italian, Japanese, journalism, Korean, Latin, linguistics, music, painting, photography, Portuguese, printmaking, public relations, Russian, sculpture, and Spanish), COMPUTER AND PHYSICAL SCIENCE (chemistry, computer science, geology, mathematics, physics, and statistics), EDUCATION (art, business, early childhood, elementary, foreign languages, home economics, industrial arts, middle school, music, physical, science, secondary, special, and teaching English as a second/foreign language (TESOL/TEFOL)), ENGINEERING AND ENVIRONMENTAL DESIGN (chemical engineering, civil engineering, computer engineering, construction management, electrical/electronics engineering, electrical/electronics engineering technology, geological engineering, interior design, manufacturing technology, and mechanical engineering), HEALTH PROFESSIONS (health science, nursing, and speech pathology/audiology), SOCIAL SCIENCE (American studies, anthropology, Asian/Oriental studies, Canadian studies, clothing and textiles management/production/services, dietetics, economics, European studies, family/consumer studies, fashion design and technology, food science, geography, history, human development, humanities, international relations, Latin American studies, Near Eastern studies, philosophy, political science/government, psychology, public affairs, social work, and sociology). Engineering, accounting, and business are the strongest academically. Business, education, and communications are the largest.

Special: Brigham Young offers cooperative programs, internships, study abroad in 12 countries, a Washington semester, dual majors, nondegree study, and credit for life and work experience. There is a freshman honors program, and 28 departmental honors programs.

Admissions: 64% of the 1999-2000 applicants were accepted. The ACT scores for the 1999-2000 freshman class were: 3% below 21, 10% between 21 and 23, 29% between 24 and 26, 24% between 27 and 28, and 35% above 28. 81% of the current freshmen were in the top fifth of their class; 96% were in the top two fifths. There were 133 National Merit finalists. 438 freshmen graduated first in their class in a recent year.

Requirements: The ACT is required. Applicants must be graduates of an accredited secondary school. The GED is accepted. The school recommends that applicants complete 4 years of English, 2 years of math beyond algebra, and courses in foreign language, science, history, and social studies. Essays and letters of recommendation are required with application. Biographical, geographical, accomplishments, and essays, as well as the scholarship application may be completed on-line, although additional information is also required. Contact http://ar.byu.

edu/admissions/apply_electronically/. AP and CLEP credits are accepted. Important factors in the admissions decision are advanced placement or honor courses, recommendations by school officials, and evidence of special talent.

Procedure: Freshmen are admitted to all sessions. Entrance exams should be taken by December of the senior year. There are early admissions and deferred admissions plans. Applications should be filed by February 15 for fall entry, October 1 for winter entry, February 15 for spring entry, and February 15 for summer entry, along with a $25 fee. Notification is sent on a rolling basis.

Financial Aid: Brigham Young is a member of CSS. The FFS is required. The fall application deadline is April 15.

Computers: PCs are available in departments and computer labs throughout the campus. All students may access the system anytime. There are no time limits and no fees. It is recommended that students in accounting, the Business School, and the Law School have personal computers.

BRIGHAM YOUNG UNIVERSITY/HAWAII
Laie, HI 96762 (808) 293-3738; Fax: (808) 293-3741

Full-time: 852 men, 1305 women	**Faculty:** 110
Part-time: 50 men, 88 women	**Ph.D.s:** 66%
Graduate: none	**Student/Faculty:** 20 to 1
Year: 4-4-2-2, summer session	**Tuition:** see profile
Application Deadline: February 15	**Room & Board:** $5125
Freshman Class: 1100 applied, 507 accepted, 425 enrolled	
ACT: 22	**VERY COMPETITIVE**

Brigham Young University/Hawaii, founded in 1955 by the Church of Latter-day Saints, is a private institution offering programs in liberal arts, business, and education. Admissions priority is given to members of the Church of Latter-day Saints (LDS). Tuition is $2875 for LDS students and $4325 for non-LDS students. There are 3 undergraduate schools. The library contains 19,500 volumes, 900,000 microform items, and 4800 audiovisual forms/CDs, and subscribes to 1100 periodicals. Computerized library services include the card catalog, interlibrary loans, and database searching. Special learning facilities include a learning resource center, art gallery, and natural history museum. The nearby Polynesian Cultural Center houses an art collection and an artifact collection and provides valuable research opportunities for students in related programs. The 200-acre campus is in a small town 38 miles from Honolulu. Including residence halls, there are 42 buildings.

Programs of Study: BYUH confers B.A., B.S., B.F.A., and B.S.W. degrees. Associate degrees are also awarded. Bachelor's degrees are awarded in BIOLOGICAL SCIENCE (biology/biological science), BUSINESS (accounting, hospitality management services, international business management, and tourism), COMMUNICATIONS AND THE ARTS (art, English, fine arts, and music), COMPUTER AND PHYSICAL SCIENCE (chemistry, computer programming, computer science, information sciences and systems, and mathematics), EDUCATION (art, business, elementary, English, mathematics, science, secondary, social science, special, and teaching English as a second/foreign language (TESOL/TEFOL)), HEALTH PROFESSIONS (predentistry and premedicine), SOCIAL SCIENCE (Hawaiian studies, history, interdisciplinary studies, international studies, Pacific area studies, physical fitness/movement, political science/government, psychology, social work, and sociology). Biological science, information systems, and education are the strongest academically. International business management, information systems, and biology sciences are the largest.

Special: BYUH offers work-study programs with the Polynesian Cultural Center, cooperative programs in most majors, nondegree study, student-designed majors in interdisciplinary studies, dual majors in elementary education and special education, and pass/fail options. There are 5 national honor societies, and a freshman honors program.

Admissions: 46% of the 1999-2000 applicants were accepted. The ACT scores for the 1999-2000 freshman class were: 27% below 21, 32% between 21 and 23, 29% between 24 and 26, 9% between 27 and 28, and 3% above 28.

Requirements: The ACT is required and the SAT I is recommended. A GPA of 3.0 is required. The applicant should be a high school graduate. Home-schooled and other nontraditional students should call for more information. AP and CLEP credits are accepted. Important factors in the admissions decision are geographic diversity, evidence of special talent, and personality/intangible qualities.

Procedure: Freshmen are admitted to all sessions. Entrance exams should be taken prior to the application deadline. There are early admissions and deferred admissions plans. Applications should be filed by February 15 for fall entry, October 31 for winter entry, February 15 for spring entry, and February 15 for summer entry, along with a $25 fee. Notification is sent April 1. 10% of all applicants are on a waiting list.

Financial Aid: In 1999-2000, 60% of all freshmen and 82% of continuing students received some form of financial aid. 12% of freshmen and 26% of continuing students received need-based aid. 50% of undergraduates work part time. Average annual earnings from campus work are $6000. BYUH is a member of CSS. The FAFSA is required. The fall application deadline is February 15.

Computers: The mainframe is an IBM RS/6000. Students can use the mainframe via the Web for registration and access to student information. Students can also log in to network servers to access their E-mail and the Internet from any computer on campus. There are approximately 300 computers available to students in campus labs. All students may access the system 18 hours per day. There are no time limits. The fee is $25.

BROWN UNIVERSITY
Providence, RI 02912

(401) 863-2378; Fax: (401) 863-9300

Full-time: 2738 men, 3039 women	**Faculty:** 547; I, ++$
Part-time: 150 men, 181 women	**Ph.D.s:** 98%
Graduate: 899 men, 751 women	**Student/Faculty:** 11 to 1
Year: semesters, summer session	**Tuition:** $25,372
Application Deadline: January 1	**Room & Board:** $7094
Freshman Class: 14,756 applied, 2509 accepted, 1414 enrolled	
SAT I Verbal/Math: 700/700	**ACT:** 30 **MOST COMPETITIVE**

Brown University, founded in 1764, is a liberal arts institution and one of the Ivy League schools. There is 1 graduate school. In addition to regional accreditation, Brown has baccalaureate program accreditation with ABET. The 6 libraries contain 3 million volumes, 1 million microform items, and 26,342 audiovisual forms/CDs, and subscribe to 15,090 periodicals. Computerized library services include the card catalog, interlibrary loans, and database searching. Special learning facilities include a learning resource center, art gallery, planetarium, radio station, TV station, and anthropology museum. The 140-acre campus is in an urban area 45 miles south of Boston. Including residence halls, there are 243 buildings.

Programs of Study: Brown confers A.B. and Sc.B. degrees. Master's and doctoral degrees are also awarded. Bachelor's degrees are awarded in BIOLOGICAL SCIENCE (biochemistry, biology/biological science, biophysics, and neurosciences), BUSINESS (organizational behavior), COMMUNICATIONS AND THE ARTS (American literature, art history and appreciation, classics, comparative literature, English, French, German, Italian, linguistics, music, performing arts, and Slavic languages), COMPUTER AND PHYSICAL SCIENCE (applied mathematics, chemistry, computer science, geology, mathematics, and physics), EDUCATION (education), ENGINEERING AND ENVIRONMENTAL DESIGN (architectural technology, engineering, and environmental science), HEALTH PROFESSIONS (biomedical science), SOCIAL SCIENCE (African American studies, anthropology, cognitive science, East Asian studies, economics, Hispanic American studies, history, international relations, Judaic studies, Latin American studies, medieval studies, philosophy, political science/ government, psychology, Russian and Slavic studies, sociology, South Asian studies, urban studies, and women's studies). Biological sciences, English and American literature, and history are the largest.

Special: Students may cross-register with Rhode Island School of Design, or study abroad in any of 57 programs in 18 countries. A combined A.B.-S.C.B. degree is possible in any major field with 5 years of study. Dual and student-designed majors, community internships, and pass/fail options are available. Students may pursue 5-year programs in the arts or sciences, or the 8-year program in the liberal medical education continuum. There is a chapter of Phi Beta Kappa and several departmental honors programs.

Admissions: 17% of the 1999-2000 applicants were accepted. The SAT I scores for the 1999-2000 freshman class were: Verbal--2% below 500, 12% between 500 and 599, 32% between 600 and 700, and 54% above 700; Math--1% below 500, 7% between 500 and 599, 38% between 600 and 700, and 54% above 700. The ACT scores were 7% between 18 and 23, 43% between 24 and 29, and 51% between 30 and 36. 96% of the current freshmen were in the top fifth of their class; All were in the top two fifths. 159 freshmen graduated first in their class.

Requirements: The SAT I or ACT is required, along with any 3 SAT II: Subject tests. The ACT may be substituted for both the SAT I and II. Applications must be graduates of accredited high schools. Secondary preparation is expected to include courses in English, foreign language, math, lab science, the arts (music or art), and history. A personal essay is required. The high school transcript is a most important criterion for admission. AP credits are accepted. Important factors in the admissions decision are advanced placement or honor courses, evidence of special talent, and recommendations by school officials.

Procedure: Freshmen are admitted fall and spring. Entrance exams should be taken in the junior or senior year. There are early action, early admissions, and deferred admissions plans. Early action applications should be filed by November 1; regular applications, by January 1 for fall entry, along with a $55 fee. Notification of early action is sent December 15; regular decision, April 1. 720 early decision candidates were accepted for the 1999-2000 class. 3% of all applicants are on a waiting list.

Financial Aid: In 1999-2000, 41% of all freshmen and 40% of continuing students received some form of financial aid, including need based aid. The average freshman award was $20,726. Of that total, scholarships or need-based grants averaged $17,205 ($33,335 maximum); loans averaged $3066 ($4350 maximum); and work contracts averaged $2000 (maximum). 34% of undergraduates work part time. Average annual earnings from campus work are $1334. The average financial indebtedness of the 1999 graduate was $22,240. Brown is a member of CSS. The CSS/Profile, FAFSA, and some state forms are required. The fall application deadline is January 1.

Computers: There are more than 400 workstations in several campus locations equipped with Macs and IBM PCs. Students may access the mainframe from dormitory rooms. The main computer center is open 18 hours a day and around the clock during exam periods. All students may access the system at any time. There are no time limits and no fees.

BRYAN COLLEGE
Dayton, TN 37321-7000

(423) 775-7204
(800) 277-9522; Fax: (423) 775-7199

Full-time: 197 men, 285 women	**Faculty:** 30; IIB, --$
Part-time: 9 men, 11 women	**Ph.D.s:** 90%
Graduate: none	**Student/Faculty:** 16 to 1
Year: semesters, summer session	**Tuition:** $11,800
Application Deadline: open	**Room & Board:** $3950
Freshman Class: 582 applied, 414 accepted, 177 enrolled	
ACT: 24 (mean)	**VERY COMPETITIVE**

Bryan College, founded in 1930, is a private, nonprofit, Christian institution that is evangelical and interdenominational. Its emphases are on the liberal arts, business, health science, fine arts, Bible and religious studies, music, and teacher preparation. The library contains 90,000 volumes, 13,489 microform items, and 3015 audiovisual forms/CDs, and subscribes to 700 periodicals. Computerized library services include interlibrary loans and database searching. Special learning facilities include a learning resource center and a museum of natural science. The 130-acre campus is in a small town 40 miles north of Chattanooga. Including residence halls, there are 28 buildings.

Programs of Study: Bryan confers B.A. and B.S. degrees. Associate degrees are also awarded. Bachelor's degrees are awarded in BIOLOGICAL SCIENCE (biology/biological science), BUSINESS (accounting and business administration and management), COMMUNICATIONS AND THE ARTS (communications, English, and music), COMPUTER AND PHYSICAL SCIENCE (mathematics), EDUCATION (athletic training, elementary, physical, and science), HEALTH PROFESSIONS (exercise science), SOCIAL SCIENCE (Christian studies, history, liberal arts/general studies, psychology, and religion). Elementary education and biology are the strongest academically. Liberal arts and elementary licensure, business, and psychology are the largest.

Special: Special academic programs include practicums in business and psychology, and psychology internships. An American Studies Program in Washington and a study-abroad Latin American Studies Program are offered through the Christian College coalition. A dual major in Christian education and church music is available. 4 hours of phys ed credits may be granted for basic training in the military. There is a freshman honors program.

Admissions: 71% of the 1999-2000 applicants were accepted. In a recent year, 4 freshmen graduated first in their class.

Requirements: The SAT I or ACT is required, with the ACT preferred. Clear admission is granted to applicants who have graduated from an approved high school and who have a minimum GPA of 2.5 with a minimum composite score of 18 on the ACT or 860 on the SAT I; clear admission is also granted to applicants with a minimum GPA of 2.0 and a composite score of 20 on the ACT or 920 on the SAT I. The high school record should include a minimum of 18 academic credits with a recommended distribution of 4 units of English, 3 each of math, science, and social science/humanities, and 2 of a foreign language. The GED is also accepted. References are required and an interview is recommended. Applications are accepted on-line. AP and CLEP credits are accepted. Important factors in the admissions decision are parents or siblings attending the school, recommendations by alumni, and recommendations by school officials.

Procedure: Freshmen are admitted fall and spring. Entrance exams should be taken before the fall of the senior year. There are early admissions and deferred admissions plans. Application deadlines are open. There is a $20 fee. Notification is sent on a rolling basis.

Financial Aid: In a recent year, 85% of all freshmen and 90% of continuing students received some form of financial aid. 71% of freshmen and 88% of continuing students received need-based aid. 80% of undergraduates work part time. The average financial indebtedness of a recent graduate was $17,500. Bryan is a member of CSS. The FAFSA is required. The fall application deadline is May 1.

Computers: There are 46 PCs available in 5 computer labs in both residence halls and academic areas. Residence hall rooms have campus network hookups available. All students may access the system at all times. There are no time limits. The fee is $125 per semester.

BRYANT COLLEGE
Smithfield, RI 02917-1284

(401) 232-6100
(800) 622-7001; Fax: (401) 232-6741

Full-time: 1515 men, 972 women	**Faculty:** 119; IIB, ++$
Part-time: 156 men, 221 women	**Ph.D.s:** 79%
Graduate: 295 men, 196 women	**Student/Faculty:** 21 to 1
Year: semesters, summer session	**Tuition:** $16,350
Application Deadline: open	**Room & Board:** $6950
Freshman Class: 2953 applied, 2099 accepted, 647 enrolled	
SAT I Verbal/Math: 520/540	**ACT:** 24 **VERY COMPETITIVE**

Bryant College, founded in 1863, is a private, primarily residential institution that offers degrees in both business and liberal arts. There is 1 graduate school. In addition to regional accreditation, Bryant has baccalaureate program accreditation with AACSB. The library contains 124,497 volumes, 13,000 microform items, and 808 audiovisual forms/CDs, and subscribes to 3000 periodicals. Computerized library services include the card catalog, interlibrary loans, and database searching. Special learning facilities include a learning resource center, radio station, and a technology center, a learning/language lab, a writing center, an academic center, a discovery lab, a paperless classroom, and a center for international business. The 387-acre campus is in a suburban area 12 miles northwest of Providence. Including residence halls, there are 43 buildings.

Programs of Study: Bryant confers B.A.B.S., B.S.B.A., and B.A.L.S. degrees. Associate and master's degrees are also awarded. Bachelor's degrees are awarded in BUSINESS (accounting, banking and finance, business administration and management, and marketing/retailing/merchandising), COMMUNICATIONS AND THE ARTS (communications and English), COMPUTER AND PHYSICAL SCIENCE (actuarial science and information sciences and systems), SOCIAL SCIENCE (economics, history, and international studies). Accounting, finance, and financial services are the strongest academically. Marketing, accounting, and management are the largest.

Special: Bryant offers internships, study abroad in 21 countries, on-campus work-study programs, dual concentrations, credit for military experience, and nondegree study. There are 3 national honor societies, a freshman honors program, and 8 departmental honors programs.

Admissions: 71% of the 1999-2000 applicants were accepted. The SAT I scores for the 1999-2000 freshman class were: Verbal--36% below 500, 50% between 500 and 599, 12% between 600 and 700, and 2% above 700; Math--23% below

500, 50% between 500 and 599, 24% between 600 and 700, and 3% above 700. The ACT scores were 19% below 21, 19% between 21 and 23, 42% between 24 and 26, 12% between 27 and 28, and 8% above 28. 32% of the current freshmen were in the top fifth of their class; 72% were in the top two fifths. 6 freshmen graduated first in their class.

Requirements: The SAT I or ACT is required. A GPA of 2.5 is required. Applicants must be graduates of an accredited secondary school or have a GED certificate. A total of 16 Carnegie units is required, including 4 years of English, 3 years of math (minimum algebra I and II), and 2 years of social studies, and 1 year of lab science. An essay is required. An interview is highly recommended. Applicants may apply on-line via CollegeLink, APPLY!, Next Stop College, Universal Application, Common Application on-line, or through Bryant's Internet address: www.bryant.edu. AP and CLEP credits are accepted. Important factors in the admissions decision are advanced placement or honor courses, recommendations by school officials, and leadership record.

Procedure: Freshmen are admitted fall and spring. Entrance exams should be taken before January of the senior year. There are early admissions and deferred admissions plans. There is a $50 fee. Notification is sent on a rolling basis beginning November 1. 10% of all applicants are on a waiting list.

Financial Aid: In 1999-2000, 89% of all freshmen and 87% of continuing students received some form of financial aid. 42% of all students received need-based aid. The average freshman award was $13,070. Of that total, scholarships or need-based grants averaged $6564 ($16,350 maximum); loans averaged $4125 ($4500 maximum); and work contracts averaged $1570 ($3335 maximum). 18% of undergraduates work part time. Average annual earnings from campus work are $1570. The average financial indebtedness of the 1999 graduate was $19,995. Bryant is a member of CSS. The CSS/Profile or FAFSA and the college's own financial statement are required. The fall application deadline is February 15.

Computers: The mainframe is an SGI ORIGIN 200. More than 140 Pentium computers in the technology center, and another 207 in various classrooms, give students access to application software, E-mail, and the Web. Dormitories are wired for access to the campus network. All students may access the system 24 hours per day. There are no time limits and no fees. It is strongly recommended that all students have personal computers.

BRYN MAWR COLLEGE
Bryn Mawr, PA 19010-2899

(610) 526-5152
(800) 262-1885; Fax: (610) 526-7471

Full-time: 1197 women	**Faculty:** 126; IIA, ++$
Part-time: 4 men, 55 women	**Ph.D.s:** 99%
Graduate: 79 men, 384 women	**Student/Faculty:** 10 to 1
Year: semesters, summer session	**Tuition:** $23,360
Application Deadline: January 15	**Room & Board:** $8100
Freshman Class: 1596 applied, 944 accepted, 321 enrolled	
SAT I Verbal/Math: 670/640	**HIGHLY COMPETITIVE+**

Bryn Mawr College, founded in 1885, is an independent, liberal arts institution, primarily for women. The undergraduate college is for women only. The two graduate schools and postbaccalaureate program are coeducational. There is 1 undergraduate school and 2 graduate schools. The 4 libraries contain 1,062,594 volumes, 145,876 microform items, and 1458 audiovisual forms/CDs, and subscribe to 1800 periodicals. Computerized library services include the card catalog, interlibrary loans, and database searching. Special learning facilities include a learning resource center, art gallery, radio station, an archeological museum, and a language learning center with audio, video, and computer technology. The 135-acre campus is in a suburban area 11 miles west of Philadelphia. Including residence halls, there are 57 buildings.

Programs of Study: Bryn Mawr confers the A.B. degree. Master's and doctoral degrees are also awarded. Bachelor's degrees are awarded in BIOLOGICAL SCIENCE (biochemistry and biology/biological science), COMMUNICATIONS AND THE ARTS (art history and appreciation, Chinese, classical languages, classics, comparative literature, English, fine arts, French, German, Greek, Italian, Latin, music, romance languages and literature, Russian, and Spanish), COMPUTER AND PHYSICAL SCIENCE (applied mathematics, astronomy, chemistry, geology, mathematics, and physics), SOCIAL SCIENCE (American studies, anthropology, archeology, Asian/Oriental studies, behavioral science, East Asian studies, economics, history, philosophy, political science/government, psychology, religion, sociology, and urban studies). Biology, English, and history are the largest.

Special: Students may cross-register with Haverford and Swarthmore Colleges and the University of Pennsylvania. Bryn Mawr sponsors and cosponsers study abroad in 27 countries, student-designed and dual majors, pass/fail options, work-study programs, an accelerated degree program, and a 3-2 engineering degree with the University of Pennsylvania. 32 departments have honors programs.

Admissions: 59% of the 1999-2000 applicants were accepted. The SAT I scores for the 1999-2000 freshman class were: Verbal--2% below 500, 12% between 500 and 599, 46% between 600 and 700, and 39% above 700; Math--3% below 500, 20% between 500 and 599, 60% between 600 and 700, and 18% above 700. The ACT scores were 4% between 21 and 23, 16% between 24 and 26, 35% between 27 and 28, and 40% above 28. 85% of the current freshmen were in the top fifth of their class. There were 11 National Merit finalists. 20 freshmen graduated first in their class.

Requirements: The SAT is required, but the ACT may be substituted. SAT II: Subject tests in writing and 2 other areas are required. Applicants must be graduates of an accredited secondary school. The GED is accepted. Applicants should complete 4 years of English, at least 3 years of foreign language, 3 years of math, and 1 year each of science and history. An essay is required. An interview is strongly recommended. AP credits are accepted. Important factors in the admissions decision are advanced placement or honor courses, evidence of special talent, and extracurricular activities record.

Procedure: Freshmen are admitted in the fall. Entrance exams should be taken in the spring of the junior year or fall of the senior year. There are early decision, early admissions, and deferred admissions plans. Early decision applications should be filed by November 15; regular applications, by January 15 for fall entry, along with a $50 fee. Notification of early decision is sent December 15; regular decision, April 1. 81 early decision candidates were accepted for the 1999-2000 class. 10% of all applicants are on a waiting list.

Financial Aid: In 1999-2000, 56% of all freshmen and 54% of continuing students received some form of financial aid. 54% of freshmen and 56% of continuing students received need-based aid. The average freshman award was $19,982. Of that total, scholarships or need-based grants averaged $16,226; loans averaged $1294; and work contracts averaged $2462. 75% of undergraduates work part time. Average annual earnings from campus work are $1442. The average financial indebtedness of the 1999 graduate was $13,300. Bryn Mawr is a member of CSS. The CSS/Profile or FAFSA and the college's own financial statement are required. The fall application deadline is January 15.

Computers: The mainframes are an HP, Sun, and UNIX systems. The computing center, libraries, the Language Learning Center and research labs throughout the humanities, social sciences, and natural sciences, the research center, and some classrooms are equipped with desktop computers. E-mail accounts and Internet access are available to all students and in more than 98% of the dormitory rooms. All students may access the system every day. There are no time limits and no fees.

BUCKNELL UNIVERSITY
Lewisburg, PA 17837　　　　(570) 577-1101; Fax: (570) 577-3760

Full-time: 1738 men, 1619 women	**Faculty:** 280; IIA, ++$
Part-time: 15 men, 31 women	**Ph.D.s:** 94%
Graduate: 69 men, 88 women	**Student/Faculty:** 12 to 1
Year: semesters, summer session	**Tuition:** $22,881
Application Deadline: January 1	**Room & Board:** $5469
Freshman Class: 7011 applied, 3072 accepted, 889 enrolled	
SAT I: required	**HIGHLY COMPETITIVE**

Bucknell University, established in 1846, is an independent institution offering undergraduate and graduate programs in arts, music, education, humanities, management, engineering, sciences, and social sciences. There are 2 undergraduate schools and 1 graduate school. In addition to regional accreditation, Bucknell has baccalaureate program accreditation with ABET, CSAB, and NASM. The library contains 670,000 volumes, 760,345 microform items, and 8217 audiovisual forms/CDs, and subscribes to 3543 periodicals. Computerized library services include the card catalog, interlibrary loans, and database searching. Special learning facilities include an art gallery, radio station, outdoor natural area, greenhouse, primate facility, observatory, photography lab, art gallery, women's resource center, library resources training lab, electronic classroom, multimedia lab, conference center, performing arts center, and multicultural, writing, craft, and poetry centers. The 393-acre campus is in a small town 75 miles north of Harrisburg. Including residence halls, there are 110 buildings.

Programs of Study: Bucknell confers B.A., B.S., B.C.S.E., B.Mus., B.S.B.A., B.S.C.E., B.S.Ch.E., B.S.Ed., B.S.E.E., and B.S.M.E. degrees. Master's degrees are also awarded. Bachelor's degrees are awarded in BIOLOGICAL SCIENCE (biochemistry, biology/biological science, and cell biology), BUSINESS (accounting and business administration and management), COMMUNICATIONS AND THE ARTS (art, art history and appreciation, classics, dramatic arts, English, fine arts, French, German, music, music history and appreciation, music performance, music theory and composition, Russian, and Spanish), COMPUTER AND PHYSICAL SCIENCE (chemistry, computer science, geology, mathematics, and physics), EDUCATION (early childhood, education, educational statistics and research, elementary, music, and secondary), ENGINEERING AND ENVIRONMENTAL DESIGN (chemical engineering, civil engineering, computer engineering, electrical/electronics engineering, engineering, environmental science, and mechanical engineering), SOCIAL SCIENCE (anthropology, East Asian studies, economics, geography, history, interdisciplinary studies, international relations, Latin American studies, philosophy, political science/government, psychology, religion, sociology, and women's studies). Humanities, biology, and English are the strongest academically. English, biology, and management are the largest.

Special: Bucknell offers internships, study abroad in more than 60 countries, a Washington semester, a 5-year B.A.-B.S. degree in arts and engineering, a 3-2 engineering degree, and dual and student-designed majors. An interdisciplinary major in animal behavior is offered through the biology and psychology departments. Nondegree study is possible and a pass/fail grading option is offered in some courses. The Residential College program offers opportunities for an academic-residential mix and faculty-student collaborative learning. Undergraduate research opportunities are available in the humanities/social sciences and the sciences and engineering. There are 23 national honor societies, including Phi Beta Kappa and a freshman honors program. All departments have honors programs as well.

Admissions: 44% of the 1999-2000 applicants were accepted. The SAT I scores for the 1999-2000 freshman class were: Verbal--4% below 500, 33% between 500 and 599, 53% between 600 and 700, and 10% above 700; Math--2% below 500, 23% between 500 and 599, 57% between 600 and 700, and 18% above 700. 78% of the current freshmen were in the top fifth of their class; 96% were in the top two fifths.

Requirements: The SAT I is required. A GPA of 2.5 is required. Applicants must graduate from an accredited secondary school or have a GED. 16 units must be earned, including 4 in English, 3 in math, 2 each in history, science, social studies, and a foreign language. An essay is required, and an interview is recommended. Music applicants are required to audition. A portfolio is recommended for art applicants. Applications are accepted on disk and on-line at http://www.applyweb.com/aw?buckn. AP credits are accepted. Important factors in the admissions decision are advanced placement or honor courses, recommendations by school officials, and evidence of special talent.

Procedure: Freshmen are admitted in the fall. Entrance exams should be taken before January 1. There are early decision, early admissions, and deferred admissions plans. Early decision applications should be filed by November 15; regular applications, by January 1 for fall entry and December 1 for spring entry, along with a $50 fee. Notification of early decision is sent December 15; regular decision, by April 1. 346 early decision candidates were accepted for the 1999-2000 class. 32% of all applicants are on a waiting list.

Financial Aid: In 1999-2000, 60% of all students received some form of financial aid. 50% of freshmen and 51% of continuing students received need-based aid. The average freshman award was $17,494. Of that total, scholarships or need-based grants averaged $16,857 ($29,500 maximum); loans averaged $3073 ($4000 maximum); and work contracts averaged $580 ($1500 maximum). 40% of undergraduates work part time. Average annual earnings from campus work are $1500. The average financial indebtedness of the 1999 graduate was $15,500. Bucknell is a member of CSS. The CSS/Profile or FAFSA and noncustodial parent's statement, and business/farm supplement are required. The fall application deadline is January 1.

Computers: More than 400 PCs with network access are available in labs, classrooms, the library, lounges, collaborative work spaces, and student housing. All students have free unlimited access to network resources and the Internet. All students may access the system 24 hours per day, 7 days per week. There are no time limits and no fees. The university strongly recommends that all students have PCs.

BUTLER UNIVERSITY
Indianapolis, IN 46208

(317) 940-8100
(888) 940-8100; Fax: (317) 940-8124

Full-time: 1252 men, 2048 women	**Faculty:** 228; IIA, av$
Part-time: 43 men, 69 women	**Ph.D.s:** 79%
Graduate: 356 men, 379 women	**Student/Faculty:** 15 to 1
Year: semesters, summer session	**Tuition:** $17,360
Application Deadline: open	**Room & Board:** $5850
Freshman Class: 3116 applied, 2682 accepted, 861 enrolled	
SAT I Verbal/Math: 560/510	**ACT:** 25 **VERY COMPETITIVE**

Butler University, founded in 1855, is an independent institution offering programs in liberal arts and sciences, business administration, fine arts, pharmacy, and health sciences. There are 5 undergraduate and 5 graduate schools. In addition to regional accreditation, Butler has baccalaureate program accreditation with AACSB, ACPE, CAAHEP, NASM, and NCATE. The 2 libraries contain 299,843 volumes, 185,122 microform items, and 16,641 audiovisual forms/ CDs, and subscribe to 2359 periodicals. Computerized library services include the card catalog, interlibrary loans, and database searching. Special learning facilities include a learning resource center, TV station, and observatory with planetarium. The 290-acre campus is in a suburban area 5 miles from downtown Indianapolis. Including residence halls, there are 19 buildings.

Programs of Study: Butler confers B.A., B.S., B.F.A., B.M., B.S.H.S., and B. S.P. degrees. Master's and doctoral degrees are also awarded. Bachelor's degrees are awarded in BIOLOGICAL SCIENCE (biology/biological science), BUSINESS (accounting, banking and finance, international business management, and marketing/retailing/merchandising), COMMUNICATIONS AND THE ARTS (arts administration/management, communications, dance, dramatic arts, English, French, German, Greek, journalism, Latin, music, music business management, music performance, music theory and composition, performing arts, Spanish, speech/debate/rhetoric, and telecommunications), COMPUTER AND PHYSICAL SCIENCE (actuarial science, chemistry, computer science, mathematics, and physics), EDUCATION (elementary, music, and secondary), HEALTH PROFESSIONS (pharmacy, physician's assistant, and speech pathology/audiology), SOCIAL SCIENCE (anthropology, criminal justice, economics, history, international studies, philosophy, political science/government, psychology, religion, and sociology). Pharmacy, chemistry, and biology are the strongest academically. Business, education, and pharmacy are the largest.

Special: Butler offers cross-registration with the 4 other members of the Consortium for Urban Education, co-op programs in business administration, and internships in pharmacy, arts administration, and business programs. A 3-2 degree program in engineering with Purdue University and in forestry with Duke University, extensive study-abroad programs, and work-study programs are available. There are dual majors including French, German, and Spanish combined with business studies, student-designed majors, a general studies degree, pass/fail options, and nondegree study. There are 5 national honor societies and a freshman honors program.

Admissions: 86% of the 1999-2000 applicants were accepted. The SAT I scores for the 1999-2000 freshman class were: Verbal--17% below 500, 43% between 500 and 599, 33% between 600 and 700, and 7% above 700; Math--13% below 500, 41% between 500 and 599, 38% between 600 and 700, and 8% above 700. The ACT scores were 10% below 21, 23% between 21 and 23, 30% between 24 and 26, 17% between 27 and 28, and 20% above 28. 62% of the current freshmen

were in the top fifth of their class; 87% were in the top two fifths. There were 4 National Merit finalists and 5 semifinalists. 49 freshmen graduated first in their class.

Requirements: The SAT I or ACT is required. Butler requires applicants to be in the upper 50% of their class. A GPA of 2.0 is required. Applicants should be graduates of an accredited secondary school, but Butler will consider talented or gifted students without a diploma. Students should have earned at least 17 academic units, based on 4 years of English, 3 each of math and lab science, 2 each of a foreign language and history/social science, and the rest of electives. An audition is required for dance, music, and theater majors, and an interview is required for radio/TV majors. Butler accepts applications on computer disk or online. AP and CLEP credits are accepted.

Procedure: Freshmen are admitted to all sessions. Entrance exams should be taken during the junior year. There are early admissions and deferred admissions plans. Application deadlines are open; there is a $25 fee. Notification is sent on a rolling basis. 2% of all applicants are on a waiting list; 55 were accepted in 1999.

Financial Aid: In 1999-2000, 90% of all freshmen and 89% of continuing students received some form of financial aid. 43% of freshmen and 45% of continuing students received need-based aid. The average freshman award was $10,485. Of that total, scholarships or need-based grants averaged $7377 ($17,180 maximum); and loans averaged $3108 ($20,625 maximum). 40% of undergraduates work part time. Average annual earnings from campus work are $1200. The average financial indebtedness of the 1999 graduate was $10,000. Butler is a member of CSS. The FAFSA and the college's own financial statement are required. The fall application deadline is March 1.

Computers: The mainframe is a DEC VAX 6610. Ethernet fiber-optic technology connects all Mac and MS/DOS PCs (150 in labs for students) to the mainframe. All students may access the system 24 hours a day. There are no time limits and no fees. It is recommended that all students have personal computers.

CALIFORNIA COLLEGE OF ARTS AND CRAFTS
San Francisco, CA 94107 (415) 703-9535
(800) 447-1ART; Fax: (415) 703-9539

Full-time: 379 men, 549 women	**Faculty:** 35
Part-time: 30 men, 59 women	**Ph.D.s:** 60%
Graduate: 24 men, 46 women	**Student/Faculty:** 27 to 1
Year: semesters, summer session	**Tuition:** $18,368
Application Deadline: March 1	**Room & Board:** $5858
Freshman Class: 363 applied, 264 accepted, 102 enrolled	
SAT I Verbal/Math: 530/500	**ACT:** 20 SPECIAL

California College of Arts and Crafts, established in 1907, is a private professional arts institution offering programs in fine arts, design, and architecture studies. There are 4 undergraduate and 4 graduate schools. In addition to regional accreditation, CCAC has baccalaureate program accreditation with FIDER, NAAB, and NASAD. The 2 libraries contain 50,000 volumes, 40 microform items, and 710 audiovisual forms/CDs, and subscribe to 250 periodicals. Computerized library services include the card catalog, interlibrary loans, and database searching. Special learning facilities include a learning resource center and art gallery. The campus, 4 acres and 2 city blocks, are in an urban area. Including residence halls, there are 15 buildings.

Programs of Study: CCAC confers B.Arch. and B.F.A. degrees. Master's degrees are also awarded. Bachelor's degrees are awarded in COMMUNICATIONS AND THE ARTS (ceramic art and design, film arts, glass, graphic design, illustration, industrial design, metal/jewelry, painting, photography, printmaking, and sculpture), ENGINEERING AND ENVIRONMENTAL DESIGN (architecture, furniture design, and interior design), SOCIAL SCIENCE (fashion design and technology and textiles and clothing). Design, architecture, and painting/drawing are the largest.

Special: Cross-registration is permitted with Mills and Holy Names colleges in Oakland and with the University of San Francisco. Opportunities are provided for internships, study abroad, student-designed majors, and nondegree study.

Admissions: 73% of the 1999-2000 applicants were accepted. The SAT I scores for the 1999-2000 freshman class were: Verbal--37% below 500, 22% between 500 and 599, 38% between 600 and 700, and 2% above 700; Math--47% below 500, 36% between 500 and 599, and 18% between 600 and 700. The ACT scores were 50% below 21, 7% between 21 and 23, 36% between 24 and 26, and 7% between 27 and 28.

Requirements: The SAT I or ACT is recommended. A GPA of 2.0 is required. Graduation from an accredited secondary school is required; a GED will be accepted. An essay, portfolio, and letters of recommendation are required. An interview is strongly recommended. AP credits are accepted. Important factors in the admissions decision are evidence of special talent, advanced placement or honor courses, and leadership record.

Procedure: Freshmen are admitted fall and spring. For priority consideration, applications should be filed by March 1 for fall entry, along with a $30 fee. Notification is sent on a rolling basis.

Financial Aid: In 1999-2000, 80% of all freshmen and 60% of continuing students received some form of financial aid. 70% of freshmen and 60% of continuing students received need-based aid. The average freshman award was $18,261. Of that total, scholarships or need-based grants averaged $9069 ($17,420 maximum); loans averaged $2655 ($5000 maximum); and work contracts averaged $2000 ($2500 maximum). All undergraduates work part time. Average annual earnings from campus work are $1168. The average financial indebtedness of the 1999 graduate was $22,500. CCAC is a member of CSS. The FAFSA and the college's own financial statement are required. The fall application deadline is March 1.

Computers: The mainframe is an HP 3000. Mulitmedia computer labs house Mac Power PCs and Quadras, scanners, printers, removable media drives, CD recorders, and Quick Cam cameras. Various software is available. The labs are networked to the Internet. All students may access the system. There are no time limits and no fees.

Pasadena, CA 91125

(626) 395-6341
(800) 568-8324; Fax: (626) 683-3026

Full-time: 635 men, 272 women	**Faculty:** 432; I, ++$
Part-time: none	**Ph.D.s:** 100%
Graduate: 755 men, 227 women	**Student/Faculty:** 2 to 1
Year: quarters	**Tuition:** $19,476
Application Deadline: January 1	**Room & Board:** $6000
Freshman Class: 2894 applied, 520 accepted, 234 enrolled	
SAT I Verbal/Math: 740/790	**MOST COMPETITIVE**

California Institute of Technology, founded in 1891, is a private institution offering programs in engineering, science, and math. Some of the information in this profile is approximate. There are 6 graduate schools. In addition to regional accreditation, Caltech has baccalaureate program accreditation with ABET. The 16 libraries contain 559,595 volumes, 821 microform items, and 824 audiovisual forms/CDs, and subscribe to 4500 periodicals. Computerized library services include the card catalog, interlibrary loans, and database searching. Special learning facilities include a learning resource center. The 124-acre campus is in a suburban area 12 miles northeast of Los Angeles. Including residence halls, there are 103 buildings.

Programs of Study: Caltech confers the B.S. degree. Master's and doctoral degrees are also awarded. Bachelor's degrees are awarded in BIOLOGICAL SCIENCE (biology/biological science), COMMUNICATIONS AND THE ARTS (literature), COMPUTER AND PHYSICAL SCIENCE (astronomy, chemistry, geochemistry, geology, geophysics and seismology, mathematics, physics, and planetary and space science), ENGINEERING AND ENVIRONMENTAL DESIGN (aeronautical engineering, chemical engineering, civil engineering, electrical/electronics engineering, engineering, engineering and applied science, and mechanical engineering), SOCIAL SCIENCE (economics, history, political science/government, and social science). Engineering, applied science, and electrical engineering are the largest.

Special: Caltech offers cross-registration with Scripps College, Occidental College, and Art Center College of Design, various work-study programs, including those with NASA's Jet Propulsion Laboratory, dual majors in any major, and independent studies degrees with faculty-approved student-designed majors are possible. A 3-2 engineering degree is possible with Bowdoin, Grinnell, Occidental, Pomona, Reed, and Whitman Colleges, and Ohio Wesleyan and Wesleyan Universities. Pass/fail options are available for freshmen. A summer undergraduate research fellowship program is offered.

Admissions: 18% of the 1999-2000 applicants were accepted. The SAT I scores for the 1999-2000 freshman class were: Verbal--2% between 500 and 599, 22% between 600 and 700, and 76% above 700; Math--3% between 600 and 700 and 97% above 700. 100% of the current freshmen were in the top fifth of their class. There were 35 National Merit finalists. 80 freshmen graduated first in their class.

Requirements: The SAT I is required. SAT II: Subject tests in writing, math level II, and one in physics, biology, or chemistry are also required. Applicants should have completed 4 years of high school math, 3 of English, 1 each of chemistry and history, and 5 units from other concentrations. Important factors in the admissions decision are advanced placement or honor courses, recommendations by school officials, and evidence of special talent.

Procedure: Freshmen are admitted in the fall. Entrance exams should be taken through December of the senior year. There are early decision, early admissions, and deferred admissions plans. Early decision applications should be filed by November 1; regular applications, by January 1 for fall entry, along with a $40 fee. Notification of early decision is sent December 31; regular decision, April 1. 131 early decision candidates were accepted in a recent class. 2% of all applicants are on a waiting list.

Financial Aid: In 1998-1999, 58% of all freshmen and 67% of continuing students received some form of financial aid. 56% of freshmen and 57% of continuing students received need-based aid. The average freshman award was $16,905. The average financial indebtedness of a recent graduate was $12,648. Caltech is a member of CSS. The CSS/Profile or FAFSA is required. The fall application deadline is January 15.

Computers: The mainframe is a SUN/UNIX cluster. Terminals are located in all buildings, including student housing. The mainframe computer can also be accessed from student-owned PCs. All students may access the system anytime. There are no time limits and no fees.

CALIFORNIA INSTITUTE OF THE ARTS
Valencia, CA 91355

(805) 253-7863
(800) 545-ARTS; Fax: (805) 254-8352

Full-time: 433 men, 363 women	**Faculty:** 88
Part-time: 4 men, 3 women	**Ph.D.s:** n/av
Graduate: 210 men, 205 women	**Student/Faculty:** 9 to 1
Year: semesters	**Tuition:** $20,010
Application Deadline: January 15	**Room & Board:** $6000
Freshman Class: 1271 applied, 503 accepted, 128 enrolled	
SAT I or ACT: not required	**SPECIAL**

California Institute of the Arts, founded in 1961, is a private, nonprofit institution offering undergraduate and graduate programs in art, dance, film and video, music, and theater, and graduate majors in directing, integrated media, and writing. There are 6 undergraduate and 6 graduate schools. In addition to regional accreditation, Cal Arts has baccalaureate program accreditation with NASAD and NASM. The library contains 96,306 volumes, 5320 microform items, and 17,718 audiovisual forms/CDs, and subscribes to 382 periodicals. Computerized library services include the card catalog, interlibrary loans, and database searching. Special learning facilities include an art gallery, radio station, TV station, movie theater, sound stages, and scenery construction shops. The 60-acre campus is in a suburban area 30 miles north of Los Angeles. Including residence halls, there are 3 buildings.

Programs of Study: Cal Arts confers the B.F.A. degree. Master's degrees are also awarded. Bachelor's degrees are awarded in COMMUNICATIONS AND THE ARTS (dance, dramatic arts, film arts, fine arts, and music). Art is the strongest academically. Film and video, and art are the largest.

Special: The university offers internships with local and national companies, student-designed majors, interdisciplinary studies, study abroad in 6 countries, and a cooperative education program.

Admissions: 40% of the 1999-2000 applicants were accepted.

Requirements: Applicants must be graduates of an accredited secondary school or have a GED certificate. They must submit an official transcript and an essay. Portfolios and auditions are required and an interview is recommended. AP credits are accepted. Important factors in the admissions decision are personality/intangible qualities, evidence of special talent, and advanced placement or honor courses.

Procedure: Freshmen are admitted fall and spring. There is a deferred admissions plan. Applications should be filed by January 15 for fall entry and November 15 for spring entry, along with a $60 fee. Notification is sent on a rolling basis. 1% of all applicants are on a waiting list.

Financial Aid: In 1999-2000, 60% of all freshmen and 64% of continuing students received some form of financial aid. 52% of freshmen and 60% of continuing students received need-based aid. The average freshman award was $15,072. Of that total, scholarships or need-based grants averaged $7300; loans averaged $8300. The average financial indebtedness of the 1999 graduate was $24,873. Cal Arts is a member of CSS. The FAFSA is required. The fall application deadline is March 1.

Computers: In addition to the library's computer center, the graphic design school has a Mac computer-imaging, text, and visual motion lab. The film and video school offers computer animation labs and editing equipment. The theater and dance schools feature computerized lighting facilities, and the music school has computerized composition and digital synthesis systems. All students may access the system. There are no time limits and no fees.

CALIFORNIA STATE UNIVERSITY, FULLERTON
Fullerton, CA 92634 (714) 278-2370

Full-time: 6452 men, 9357 women	**Faculty:** 628; IIA, ++$
Part-time: 2961 men, 3679 women	**Ph.D.s:** 87%
Graduate: 1677 men, 3041 women	**Student/Faculty:** 25 to 1
Year: semesters, summer session	**Tuition:** $1809 ($7713)
Application Deadline: open	**Room & Board:** $3672
Freshman Class: 23,111 applied, 15,442 accepted, 8412 enrolled	
SAT I Verbal/Math: 457/483	**COMPETITIVE**

California State University/Fullerton, founded in 1957, is part of the California State University system. The school offers programs in the arts, business and economics, communications, engineering and computer science, human development and community services, humanities and social science, and natural science and math. There are 7 undergraduate and 7 graduate schools. In addition to regional accreditation, Cal State Fullerton has baccalaureate program accreditation with AACSB, ABET, ACEJMC, NASAD, NASM, NCATE, and NLN. The library contains 654,790 volumes, 964,344 microform items, and 15,786 audiovisual forms/CDs, and subscribes to 2500 periodicals. Computerized library services include the card catalog, interlibrary loans, and database searching. Special learning facilities include a learning resource center, art gallery, arboretum, herbarium, a center for economic education, a developmental research center, a foreign language lab, an institute for economic and environmental studies, an institute for molecular biology and nutrition, a phonetic research lab, a social science research center, and a sport and movement institute. The 225-acre campus is in a suburban area 30 miles east of Los Angeles. Including residence halls, there are 22 buildings.

Programs of Study: Cal State Fullerton confers B.A., B.S., B.F.A., and B.M. degrees. Master's degrees are also awarded. Bachelor's degrees are awarded in BIOLOGICAL SCIENCE (biochemistry, biology/biological science, ecology, marine biology, microbiology, and zoology), BUSINESS (accounting, banking and finance, business administration and management, business economics, international business management, management information systems, management science, and marketing/retailing/merchandising), COMMUNICATIONS AND THE

ARTS (advertising, art, broadcasting, communications, comparative literature, dance, design, dramatic arts, English, film arts, fine arts, French, German, Japanese, journalism, linguistics, music, photography, Spanish, and speech/debate/rhetoric), COMPUTER AND PHYSICAL SCIENCE (chemistry, computer science, geology, mathematics, physics, and statistics), EDUCATION (art, early childhood, music, and physical), ENGINEERING AND ENVIRONMENTAL DESIGN (civil engineering, electrical/electronics engineering, engineering and applied science, and mechanical engineering), HEALTH PROFESSIONS (nursing and speech pathology/audiology), SOCIAL SCIENCE (African American studies, American studies, anthropology, child psychology/development, criminal justice, economics, geography, history, human services, Latin American studies, liberal arts/general studies, Mexican-American/Chicano studies, philosophy, political science/government, psychology, religion, Russian and Slavic studies, and sociology). Business administration, communications, and psychology are the largest.

Special: The university offers cross-registration with other schools in the California State University system, the University of California, and California Community colleges, internships and co-op programs in 45 academic areas, study abroad in 18 countries, and work-study programs both on and off campus. A B.A.-B.S. degree in chemistry, dual and student-designed majors, and pass/fail options are also available. There are 16 national honor societies, a freshman honors program, and 13 departmental honors programs.

Admissions: 67% of the 1999-2000 applicants were accepted. The SAT I scores for the 1999-2000 freshman class were: Verbal--66% below 500, 26% between 500 and 599, 7% between 600 and 700, and 1% above 700; Math--56% below 500, 31% between 500 and 599, 12% between 600 and 700, and 1% above 700.

Requirements: The SAT I or ACT is required. A GPA of 2.0 is required. Applicants must be graduates of an accredited secondary school or have a GED certificate. Secondary school courses must include 4 years of English, 3 years each of approved electives and math, 2 years of a foreign language, and 1 year each of science, history, and visual or performing arts. Admission is based on the Qualifiable Eligibility Index, a combination of the high school GPA and either the SAT or ACT score. Auditions are required for music majors. Applications are accepted on-line. AP and CLEP credits are accepted.

Procedure: Freshmen are admitted fall and spring. Entrance exams should be taken during the senior year of high school. There is an early admissions plan. Application deadlines are open; the fee is $55. Notification is sent on a rolling basis.

Financial Aid: Cal State Fullerton is a member of CSS. The FAFSA and SAAC (Student Aid Application for California) are required. The fall application deadline is March 2.

Computers: The mainframes are a DEC VAX 8550 and an IBM 3090/150E. Students may access the mainframe via school-based and computer center labs. All students may access the system 24 hours a day. There are no time limits and no fees.

CALIFORNIA STATE UNIVERSITY, LONG BEACH

Long Beach, CA 90840-0106

(310) 985-4141
Fax: (310) 985-4973

Full-time: 7451 men, 10,908 women	**Faculty:** 903; IIA, ++$
Part-time: 2660 men, 3090 women	**Ph.D.s:** 85%
Graduate: 2246 men, 3656 women	**Student/Faculty:** 20 to 1
Year: semesters, summer session	**Tuition:** $1768 ($9868)
Application Deadline: November 30	**Room & Board:** $5200
Freshman Class: 12,591 applied, 10,233 accepted, 3482 enrolled	
SAT I Verbal/Math: 470/490	**COMPETITIVE**

California State University/Long Beach, founded in 1949, is a nonprofit institution that is part of the California State University system. The commuter university offers undergraduate programs through the colleges of health and human services, liberal arts, natural sciences and math, business administration, engineering, the arts, and education. There are 7 undergraduate and 7 graduate schools. In addition to regional accreditation, CSULB has baccalaureate program accreditation with AACSB, ABET, ACEJMC, AHEA, APTA, CSWE, FIDER, NASAD, NASM, NLN, and NRPA. The 2 libraries contain 1,118,719 volumes, 1,577,689 microform items, and 38,033 audiovisual forms CDs, and subscribe to 3573 periodicals. Computerized library services include the card catalog and database searching. Special learning facilities include a learning resource center, art gallery, radio station, and TV station. The 322-acre campus is in a suburban area 25 miles southeast of Los Angeles. Including residence halls, there are 84 buildings.

Programs of Study: CSULB confers B.A., B.S., B.F.A., B.M., and B.Voc.Ed. degrees. Master's degrees are also awarded. Bachelor's degrees are awarded in BIOLOGICAL SCIENCE (biochemistry, biology/biological science, botany, marine biology, microbiology, and zoology), BUSINESS (accounting, banking and finance, business administration and management, business data processing, marketing/retailing/merchandising, and personnel management), COMMUNICATIONS AND THE ARTS (art, broadcasting, comparative literature, dance, design, dramatic arts, English, film arts, French, Japanese, journalism, music, photography, Spanish, and speech/debate/rhetoric), COMPUTER AND PHYSICAL SCIENCE (chemistry, computer science, earth science, geology, mathematics, and physics), EDUCATION (vocational), ENGINEERING AND ENVIRONMENTAL DESIGN (aerospace studies, chemical engineering, civil engineering, computer engineering, electrical/electronics engineering, engineering, engineering technology, and mechanical engineering), HEALTH PROFESSIONS (health care administration, health science, nursing, and speech pathology/audiology), SOCIAL SCIENCE (African American studies, American studies, anthropology, Asian/Oriental studies, criminal justice, dietetics, economics, geography, Hispanic American studies, history, interdisciplinary studies, international studies, parks and recreation management, philosophy, political science/government, psychology, religion, social work, sociology, and women's studies). Art, biological sciences, and music are the strongest academically. Business administration, psychology, and liberal studies are the largest.

Special: The university offers cross-registration with California State University/Dominguez Hills for courses not offered at CSULB. Internships, study abroad in 22 countries, dual majors in engineering, a 3-2 engineering degree, student-designed majors, and pass/fail options are also available. There are 23 national honor societies, including Phi Beta Kappa, and a freshman honors program.

Admissions: 81% of the 1999-2000 applicants were accepted. The SAT I scores for the 1999-2000 freshman class were: Verbal--60% below 500, 31% between 500 and 599, 8% between 600 and 700, and 1% above 700; Math--52% below 500, 36% between 500 and 599, 10% between 600 and 700, and 2% above 700. There were 13 National Merit finalists and 2 semifinalists. 53 freshmen graduated first in their class.

Requirements: The SAT I or ACT is recommended. CSULB requires applicants to be in the upper 33% of their class. A GPA of 2.0 is required. Applicants must be graduates of an accredited secondary school and have completed 4 years of English, 3 years each of math and electives, 2 years of foreign language, and 1 year each of lab science, U.S. history or U.S. history and government, and 1 visual and performing arts. Students are admitted on the basis of the Eligibility Index, which is computed from the secondary school GPA and the SAT I or ACT scores. California residents with a minimum 3.0 GPA are automatically admissible. A portfolio is required for art and design students. An audition is required for dance, music, and theater students. The university accepts applications on computer disk and on-line. AP and CLEP credits are accepted.

Procedure: Freshmen are admitted fall and spring. Entrance exams should be taken during the fall semester of the senior year. Applications should be filed by November 30 for fall entry and August 31 for spring entry, along with a $55 fee. Notification is sent on a rolling basis.

Financial Aid: In 1999-2000, 48% of all freshmen and 40% of continuing students received some form of financial aid. 42% of freshmen and 36% of continuing students received need-based aid. The average freshman award was $5461. Of that total, scholarships or need-based grants averaged $3417 ($6000 maximum); loans averaged $2000 ($4125 maximum); and work contracts averaged $1125 ($2000 maximum). 74% of undergraduates work part time. Average annual earnings from campus work are $1900. The average financial indebtedness of the 1999 graduate was $6400. CSULB is a member of CSS. The FAFSA is required. The fall application deadline is March 2.

Computers: Students use network/server-based systems rather than a mainframe. Four main labs with a total of approximately 550 PC or Mac systems, plus 54 college-based labs with a total of between 550 and 1100 PC/Mac systems, are open for student use 5 or more days a week. Internet and Web access are automatically available on most of the available systems. All students may access the system during open lab hours, which vary across campus. There are no time limits and no fees.

CALIFORNIA STATE UNIVERSITY, NORTHRIDGE
Northridge, CA 91328   (818) 677-3700; Fax: (818) 677-3766

Full-time: 6696 men, 9385 women	**Faculty:** 830; IIA, ++$
Part-time: 2416 men, 3063 women	**Ph.D.s:** 83%
Graduate: 2006 men, 4381 women	**Student/Faculty:** 19 to 1
Year: semesters, summer session	**Tuition:** $1916 ($9790)
Application Deadline: November 30	**Room & Board:** $5865
Freshman Class: 9227 applied, 7350 accepted, 2625 enrolled	
SAT I Verbal/Math: 466/450	**COMPETITIVE**

California State University, Northridge, founded in 1958, is part of the state-supported university system and offers degree programs in the liberal arts and sciences, business administration, education, engineering, music, health fields, and fine arts. There are 8 undergraduate schools and 1 graduate school. In addition to regional accreditation, CSUN has baccalaureate program accreditation with AACSB, ABET, ACEJMC, AHEA, APTA, CAHEA, CSAB, NASM, NCATE, and NRPA. The 3 libraries contain 1,207,345 volumes and 3,043,380 microform items, and subscribe to 2754 periodicals. Computerized library services include the card catalog, interlibrary loans, and database searching. Special learning facilities include a learning resource center, art gallery, planetarium, radio station, TV station, observatory, anthropological museum, botanical gardens, urban archives center, Natural Center on Deafness, and Center for the Study of Cancer and Development Biology. The 353-acre campus is in a suburban area 25 miles north of Los Angeles. Including residence halls, there are 47 buildings.

Programs of Study: CSUN confers B.A., B.S., and B.M. degrees. Master's degrees are also awarded. Bachelor's degrees are awarded in BIOLOGICAL SCIENCE (biochemistry, biology/biological science, cell biology, environmental biology, and microbiology), BUSINESS (accounting, banking and finance, business administration and management, management information systems, marketing/retailing/merchandising, real estate, and recreation and leisure services), COMMUNICATIONS AND THE ARTS (art history and appreciation, broadcasting, dance, design, dramatic arts, English, film arts, French, German, journalism, linguistics, music, Spanish, and speech/debate/rhetoric), COMPUTER AND PHYSICAL SCIENCE (astrophysics, chemistry, computer science, earth science, geology, mathematics, physics, and radiological technology), EDUCATION (business, home economics, and physical), ENGINEERING AND ENVIRONMENTAL DESIGN (engineering), HEALTH PROFESSIONS (health, health care administration, medical laboratory technology, nursing, physical therapy, recreation therapy, and speech pathology/audiology), SOCIAL SCIENCE (African American studies, anthropology, child psychology/development, criminology, dietetics, economics, geography, history, liberal arts/general studies, Mexican-American/Chicano studies, philosophy, political science/government, psychology, social work, sociology, and urban studies). Liberal studies is the strongest academically. Business administration and economics, psychology, and liberal studies are the largest.

Special: Cross-registration is offered through the Intra System Visitor Program. Study abroad in 16 countries, internships, university work-study programs, dual majors, student-designed majors, credit for military experience, and pass/fail options for elective courses are offered. There are 4 national honor societies, a freshman honors program, and 8 departmental honors programs.

Admissions: 80% of the 1999-2000 applicants were accepted. The SAT I scores for the 1999-2000 freshman class were: Verbal--68% below 500, 25% between 500 and 599, 6% between 600 and 700, and 1% above 700; Math--64% below 500, 26% between 500 and 599, 9% between 600 and 700, and 1% above 700.

Requirements: CSUN requires applicants to be in the upper 33% of their class. A GPA of 2.0 is required. The SAT I or ACT is required for students with a GPA below 3.0 (3.6 for nonresidents). Applicants should have completed 4 years of high school English, 3 each of math and academic electives, 2 of foreign language, and 1 each of lab science, U.S. history/government, and visual/performing arts. Applications are accepted on-line through CSU-Mentor. AP and CLEP credits are accepted. Important factors in the admissions decision are recommendations by school officials, evidence of special talent, and leadership record.

Procedure: Freshmen are admitted fall and spring. Entrance exams should be taken by December of the senior year. There is an early decision plan. Applications should be filed by November 30 for fall entry and August 31 for spring entry, along with a $55 fee. Notification is sent on a rolling basis.

Financial Aid: In 1999-2000, scholarships or need-based grants averaged $1435; loans averaged $3873; and work contracts averaged $1403. The average financial indebtedness of the 1999 graduate was $12,000. CSUN is a member of CSS. The SAAC financial statement is required. The fall application deadline is March 2.

Computers: The mainframe is an IBM 4381. There are 1700 PCs on campus; 300 are networked by DOS and UNIX. The computers are located in some labs and classrooms, libraries, and student housing. All students may access the system 24 hours a day, 7 days a week. There are no time limits and no fees.

CARLETON COLLEGE
Northfield, MN 55057

(507) 646-4190
(800) 995-CARL; Fax: (507) 646-4526

Full-time: 882 men, 993 women	**Faculty:** 178; IIB, ++$
Part-time: none	**Ph.D.s:** 95%
Graduate: none	**Student/Faculty:** 11 to 1
Year: trimesters	**Tuition:** $23,469
Application Deadline: January 15	**Room & Board:** $4761
Freshman Class: 3457 applied, 1606 accepted, 510 enrolled	
SAT I or ACT: required	**MOST COMPETITIVE**

Carleton College, founded in 1866, is a private liberal arts college. The library contains 706,950 volumes, 118,532 microform items, and 790 audiovisual forms/CDs, and subscribes to 1674 periodicals. Computerized library services include the card catalog, interlibrary loans, and database searching. Special learning facilities include a learning resource center, art gallery, radio station, observatory, and 850-acre arboretum. The 945-acre campus is in a small town 35 miles south of Minneapolis-St. Paul. Including residence halls, there are 29 buildings.

Programs of Study: Carleton confers the B.A degree. Bachelor's degrees are awarded in BIOLOGICAL SCIENCE (biology/biological science), COMMUNICATIONS AND THE ARTS (art history and appreciation, classics, English, French, German, Greek, Latin, music, romance languages and literature, Russian, Spanish, and studio art), COMPUTER AND PHYSICAL SCIENCE (chemistry, computer science, geology, mathematics, and physics), SOCIAL SCIENCE (African American studies, African studies, American studies, anthropology, Asian/Oriental studies, classical/ancient civilization, economics, history, international relations, Latin American studies, philosophy, political science/government, psychology, religion, sociology, and women's studies). Biology, English, and political science are the largest.

Special: Students may cross-register with Saint Olaf College and pursue a variety of internships. The college offers study abroad in 46 countries. Dual majors in all areas and student-designed majors are available. Students may earn a 3-2 engineering degree with Washington or Columbia University, a 3-2 degree in nursing, and a 3-3 degree in law. Pass/fail options are offered. There is a chapter of Phi Beta Kappa.

Admissions: 46% of the 1999-2000 applicants were accepted. The SAT I scores for the 1999-2000 freshman class were: Verbal--1% below 500, 7% between 500 and 599, 41% between 600 and 699, and 51% between 700 and 800; Math--1% below 500, 10% between 500 and 599, 49% between 600 and 699, and 41% between 700 and 800. The ACT scores were 1% between 18 and 23, 46% between 24 and 29, and 54% between 30 and 36. 89% of the current freshmen were in the top quarter of their class; 99% were in the top half. There were 85 National Merit finalists. 45 freshmen graduated first in their class.

Requirements: The SAT I or ACT is required. There are no secondary school requirements, but it is recommended that applicants have completed 4 years of English, 3 years each of math and a foreign language, 2 years each of history and science, and 1 year of social studies. An essay and 2 teacher recommendations are required. Applications are accepted on-line via CollegeLink and Apply. AP credits are accepted. Important factors in the admissions decision are advanced placement or honor courses, personality/intangible qualities, and evidence of special talent.

Procedure: Freshmen are admitted in the fall. Entrance exams should be taken before March 1. There are early decision and deferred admissions plans. Early decision applications should be filed by November 15; regular applications, by January 15 for fall entry, along with a $30 fee. Notification of early decision is sent December 15; regular decision, by April 15. 179 early decision candidates were accepted for the 1999-2000 class. A waiting list is an active part of the admissions procedure.

Financial Aid: In 1999-2000, 48% of all freshmen and 70% of continuing students received some form of financial aid. The average freshman award was $18,346. Of that total, scholarships or need-based grants averaged $14,101; and loans averaged $3237. 77% of undergraduates work part time. Average annual earnings from campus work are $1690. The average financial indebtedness of the 1999 graduate was $14,720. Carleton is a member of CSS. The CSS/Profile or FAFSA is required. The fall application deadline is February 15.

Computers: All students may access the system 24 hours a day. There are no time limits and no fees.

CARNEGIE MELLON UNIVERSITY
Pittsburgh, PA 15213 (412) 268-2082; Fax: (412) 268-7838

Full-time: 3241 men, 1806 women	**Faculty:** 1042; I, ++$
Part-time: 61 men, 28 women	**Ph.D.s:** 96%
Graduate: 2230 men, 944 women	**Student/Faculty:** 5 to 1
Year: semesters, summer session	**Tuition:** $21,300
Application Deadline: January 1	**Room & Board:** $6810
Freshman Class: 14,130 applied, 5358 accepted, 1254 enrolled	
SAT I Verbal/Math: 651/710	**MOST COMPETITIVE**

Carnegie Mellon University, established in 1900, is a private nonsectarian institution offering undergraduate programs in liberal arts and science and professional technology. There are 6 undergraduate and 7 graduate schools. In addition to regional AACSB accreditation, Carnegie Mellon has baccalaureate program accreditation with AACSB, ABET, NAAB, NASAD, and NASM. The 3 libraries contain 935,888 volumes, 885,422 microform items, and 50,465 audiovisual forms/CDs, and subscribe to 3209 periodicals. Computerized library services include the card catalog, interlibrary loans, and database searching. Special learning facilities include a learning resource center, art gallery, and radio station. The 103-acre campus is in a suburban area 4 miles from downtown Pittsburgh. Including residence halls, there are 80 buildings.

Programs of Study: Carnegie Mellon confers B.A., B.S., B.A.H., B.Arch., B.F.A., and B.S.A. degrees. Master's and doctoral degrees are also awarded. Bachelor's degrees are awarded in BIOLOGICAL SCIENCE (biology/biological science), BUSINESS (business administration and management, business economics, and marketing/retailing/merchandising), COMMUNICATIONS AND THE ARTS (communications, design, dramatic arts, English, fine arts, French, German, journalism, languages, music, and Spanish), COMPUTER AND PHYSICAL SCIENCE (chemistry, computer programming, computer science, information sciences and systems, mathematics, physics, and statistics), EDUCATION (music), ENGINEERING AND ENVIRONMENTAL DESIGN (chemical engineering, civil engineering, computer engineering, electrical/electronics engineering, engineering, and mechanical engineering), SOCIAL SCIENCE (economics, history, philosophy, political science/government, psychology, public administration, social science, and urban studies). Computer Science, engineering, and business administration are the strongest academically. Engineering is the largest.

Special: Students may cross-register with other Pittsburgh Council of Higher Education institutions. Also available are internships, work-study programs, study abroad in Germany, Switzerland, and Japan, a Washington semester, accelerated degrees, B.A.-B.S. degrees, co-op programs, dual majors, and limited student-designed majors. There are 10 national honor societies, including Phi Beta Kappa, and a freshman honors program.

Admissions: 38% of the 1999-2000 applicants were accepted. The SAT I scores for the 1999-2000 freshman class were: Verbal--4% below 500, 19% between 500 and 599, 48% between 600 and 700, and 29% above 700; Math--1% below 500, 9% between 500 and 599, 33% between 600 and 700, and 57% above 700. 87% of the current freshmen were in the top fifth of their class; 97% were in the top two fifths. 84 freshmen graduated first in their class.

Requirements: The SAT I or ACT is required. SAT II: Subject tests in writing and math are required for all applicants. Engineering applicants must take the chemistry or physics test. Science applicants may take either of these or the biology test. Business and liberal arts applicants must take a third test of their choice. Applicants must graduate from an accredited secondary school or have a GED. They must earn 16 Carnegie units. All applicants must have completed 4 years of English. Applicants to the Carnegie Institute of Technology and the Mellon College of Science must take 4 years of math and 1 year each of biology, chemistry, and physics. Essays are required, and interviews are recommended. Art and design applicants must submit a portfolio. Drama and music applicants must audition. Applications are accepted on-line at the school's web site. AP credits are accepted. Important factors in the admissions decision are advanced placement or honor courses, leadership record, and evidence of special talent.

Procedure: Freshmen are admitted in the fall. Entrance exams should be received by February 15. There are early decision, early admissions, and deferred admissions plans. Early decision applications should be filed by November 15; regular applications, by January 1 for fall entry, along with a $50 fee. Notification of early decision is sent January 15; regular decision, April 15. 95 early decision candidates were accepted for the 1999-2000 class. A waiting list is an active part of the admissions procedure.

Financial Aid: In 1999-2000, 76% of all freshmen received some form of financial aid. 56% of freshmen and 48% of continuing students received need-based aid. The average freshman award was $15,710. Of that total, scholarships or need-based grants averaged $12,887; loans averaged $3886; and work contracts averaged $1902. 70% of undergraduates work part time. Average annual earnings from campus work are $1902. The average financial indebtedness of the 1999 graduate was $17,880. Carnegie Mellon is a member of CSS. The FAFSA, the college's own financial statement and the parent and student federal tax returns and W-2 forms are required. The fall application deadline is February 15.

Computers: The mainframes are a DEC VAX 6320, 6330, and 11/780 models and a Sun 3280. The campuswide computer network extends to every office and dormitory room, connecting hundreds of PCs and advanced workstations. All students may access the system 24 hours per day. There are no time limits and no fees.

CASE WESTERN RESERVE UNIVERSITY
Cleveland, OH 44106
(216) 368-4450; Fax: (216) 368-5111

Full-time: 1858 men, 1199 women	**Faculty:** 463; I, +$
Part-time: 169 men, 154 women	**Ph.D.s:** 95%
Graduate: 3156 men, 2764 women	**Student/Faculty:** 7 to 1
Year: semesters, summer session	**Tuition:** $19,354
Application Deadline: February 1	**Room & Board:** $5470
Freshman Class: 4307 applied, 3135 accepted, 766 enrolled	
SAT I or ACT: required	**HIGHLY COMPETITIVE+**

Case Western Reserve University, founded in 1826, is a private institution offering undergraduate, graduate, and professional programs in arts and sciences, dentistry, engineering, law, management, medicine, nursing, and social work. There are 4 undergraduate and 7 graduate schools. In addition to regional accreditation, CWRU has baccalaureate program accreditation with AACSB, ABET, ADA, CAHEA, CSWE, NASM, and NLN. The 7 libraries contain 2 million volumes, 2.3 million microform items, and 114,750 audiovisual forms/CDs, and subscribe to 14,520 periodicals. Computerized library services include the card catalog, interlibrary loans, and database searching. Special learning facilities include a learning resource center, art gallery, natural history museum, and radio station. The 152-acre campus is in an urban area 4 miles east of downtown Cleveland. Including residence halls, there are 87 buildings.

Programs of Study: CWRU confers B.A., B.S., B.S.E., and B.S.N. degrees. Master's and doctoral degrees are also awarded. Bachelor's degrees are awarded in BIOLOGICAL SCIENCE (biochemistry, biology/biological science, and nutrition), BUSINESS (accounting and business administration and management), COMMUNICATIONS AND THE ARTS (art history and appreciation, classics, communications, comparative literature, dramatic arts, English, French, German, music, and Spanish), COMPUTER AND PHYSICAL SCIENCE (applied mathematics, astronomy, chemistry, computer science, fluid and thermal science, geology, mathematics, natural sciences, physics, polymer science, and statistics), EDUCATION (art and music), ENGINEERING AND ENVIRONMENTAL DESIGN (aeronautical engineering, biomedical engineering, chemical engineering, civil engineering, computer engineering, electrical/electronics engineering, engineering, engineering physics, environmental science, materials science, mechanical engineering, and systems engineering), HEALTH PROFESSIONS (nursing), SOCIAL SCIENCE (American studies, anthropology, Asian/Oriental studies, economics, French studies, German area studies, gerontology, history, history of science, international studies, Japanese studies, philosophy, political science/government, psychology, religion, and sociology). Engineering, accounting, and biology are the strongest academically. Engineering, biology, and psychology are the largest.

Special: CWRU offers co-op programs with more than 160 employers; students may alternate classroom study with full-time employment. Cross-registration with 13 institutions in the Cleveland area is available, as well as internships in government, corporations, and nonprofit agencies. Students may participate in study abroad, a Washington semester, work-study programs, and accelerated-degree programs. B.A.-B.S. degrees, dual and student-designed majors, 3-2 engineering degrees, nondegree study, independent study, and pass/fail options are possible. There are extensive opportunities for undergraduates to work with faculty on research projects. Preprofesional Scholars Programs in medicine, dentistry, and law are available. Interdisciplinary majors, such as environmental geology and a double major in pre-architecture, and intradisciplinary majors, such as nutritional biochemistry and metabolism, are available. There are 3 national honor societies, including Phi Beta Kappa.

Admissions: 73% of the 1999-2000 applicants were accepted. The SAT I scores for the 1999-2000 freshman class were: Verbal--7% below 500, 18% between 500 and 599, 48% between 600 and 700, and 27% above 700; Math--3% below 500, 13% between 500 and 599, 45% between 600 and 700, and 39% above 700. The ACT scores were 3% below 21, 7% between 21 and 23, 16% between 24 and 26, 18% between 27 and 28, and 56% above 28. 86% of the current freshmen were in the top fifth of their class.

Requirements: The SAT I or ACT is required. SAT II: Subject tests in writing plus 2 others of the student's choice are strongly recommended for students who take the SAT I. Applicants must be graduates of an accredited secondary school. The GED is accepted. 16 high school academic credits are required, including 4 years of English, 3 of math, (4 for science, math, and engineering majors), and 1 of lab science (2 for science and math majors and premedical students). 2 to 4 years of foreign language are strongly recommended. Engineering, math, and science students should take the SAT II: Subject tests in math I/IC or IIC and physics and/or chemistry. A writing sample of the student's choice is required, and an interview is recommended. CWRU accepts applications on-line and on computer disk via CollegeView/Hobsons AppZap, CollegeLink, Embark.com, Apply!, and CWRU's own CD-Rom application. AP credits are accepted. Important factors in the admissions decision are advanced placement or honor courses, leadership record, and recommendations by school officials.

Procedure: Freshmen are admitted to all sessions. Entrance exams should be taken by the fall of the senior year; CWRU recommends also taking the test during the spring of the junior year. There are early decision, early admissions, and deferred admissions plans. Early decision applications should be filed by January 1; regular applications, by February 1 for fall entry. Notification is sent April 1. A waiting list is an active part of the admissions procedure.

Financial Aid: In 1999-2000, 92% of all freshmen and 91% of continuing students received some form of financial aid. 64% of freshmen and 57% of continuing students received need-based aid. The average freshman award was $18,843. 70% of undergraduates work part time. Average annual earnings from campus work are $2900. The average financial indebtedness of the 1999 graduate was $19,375. CWRU is a member of CSS. The CSS/Profile or FAFSA is required. The fall application deadline is February 1.

Computers: The mainframe is an IBM 9672R22. CWRUnet, the university's high-speed fiber-optic network, connects every residence-hall room with academic departments, libraries, and labs on campus, giving students desktop access to the Internet, a software library, CD-ROM databases, and other electronic resources. Many students purchase networkable PCs through special university purchase arrangements. There are also a number of open-access computer labs at various locations on campus with PCs for student use. All students may access the system 24 hours a day. There are no time limits and no fees.

CATHOLIC UNIVERSITY OF AMERICA
Washington, DC 20064

(202) 319-5305
(800) 673-2772; Fax: (202) 319-6533

Full-time: 1087 men, 1248 women	**Faculty:** 291; I, -$
Part-time: 94 men, 128 women	**Ph.D.s:** 97%
Graduate: 1496 men, 1544 women	**Student/Faculty:** 8 to 1
Year: semesters, summer session	**Tuition:** $18,972
Application Deadline: February 15	**Room & Board:** $7765
Freshman Class: 2604 applied, 2295 accepted, 797 enrolled	
SAT I or ACT: required	**VERY COMPETITIVE**

Catholic University of America, founded in 1887 and affiliated with the Roman Catholic Church, offers undergraduate programs through the schools of arts and sciences, engineering, architecture, nursing, philosophy, the Benjamin T. Rome School of Music, and the Metropolitan College. There are 7 undergraduate and 10 graduate schools. In addition to regional accreditation, CUA has baccalaureate program accreditation with ABET, ACPE, CSWE, NAAB, NASDTEC, NASM, NCATE, and NLN. The 8 libraries contain 1,450,190 volumes, 1,473,449 microform items, and 35,080 audiovisual forms/CDs, and subscribe to 10,925 periodicals. Computerized library services include the card catalog, interlibrary loans, and database searching. Special learning facilities include a learning resource center, art gallery, radio station, archeology lab, rare book collection, and electronic/computer classrooms. The 144-acre campus is in an urban area in Washington, D.C. Including residence halls, there are 50 buildings.

Programs of Study: CUA confers B.A., B.S., B.A.G.S., B.B.E., B.C.E., B.E.E., B.M., B.M.E., B.Ph., B.S.C.S., B.S.N., B.Arch, and B.S.Arch degrees. Master's and doctoral degrees are also awarded. Bachelor's degrees are awarded in BIOLOGICAL SCIENCE (biochemistry and biology/biological science), BUSINESS (accounting, banking and finance, business administration and management, human resources, international economics, and management science), COMMUNICATIONS AND THE ARTS (art, art history and appreciation, classics, communications, dramatic arts, English, French, German, Latin, music, music history and appreciation, music performance, music theory and composition, musical theater, painting, piano/organ, sculpture, Spanish, and voice), COMPUTER AND PHYSICAL SCIENCE (chemistry, computer science, elementary particle physics, mathematics, and physics), EDUCATION (art, drama, early childhood, education, elementary, English, mathematics, music, and secondary), ENGINEERING AND ENVIRONMENTAL DESIGN (architecture, biomedical engineering, civil engineering, electrical/electronics engineering, engineering, environmental science, and mechanical engineering), HEALTH PROFESSIONS (medical laboratory technology and nursing), SOCIAL SCIENCE (anthropology, economics, history, liberal arts/general studies, medieval studies, philosophy, political science/government, psychology, religion, social work, and sociology). Politics is the strongest academically. Architecture is the largest.

Special: Cross-registration is available with the Consortium of Universities of the Washington Metropolitan Area. Opportunities are also provided for internships, accelerated degree programs, dual majors, pass/fail options, and study abroad in 10 countries. There are 14 national honor societies, including Phi Beta Kappa, and a freshman honors program.

Admissions: 88% of the 1999-2000 applicants were accepted. The SAT I scores for the 1999-2000 freshman class were: Verbal--12% below 500, 41% between 500 and 599, 34% between 600 and 700, and 10% above 700; Math--16% below 500, 43% between 500 and 599, 32% between 600 and 700, and 7% above 700.

The ACT scores were 20% below 21, 17% between 21 and 23, 30% between 24 and 26, 11% between 27 and 28, and 22% above 28. 47% of the current freshmen were in the top fifth of their class; 79% were in the top two fifths.

Requirements: The SAT I or ACT is required. The SAT II: Writing test is required for placement, and the SAT II: Foreign Language test is recommended. Applicants must be graduates of an accredited secondary school. The GED is accepted. Students should present 17 academic credits, including 4 each in English, and social studies, 3 each in math and science, 2 in foreign languages, and 1 in fine arts or humanities. An essay is required. An audition is required for music applicants and a portfolio for architecture applicants is recommended. Applications are accepted on-line at Apply.cua.edu. AP and CLEP credits are accepted. Important factors in the admissions decision are extracurricular activities record, leadership record, and advanced placement or honor courses.

Procedure: Freshmen are admitted fall and spring. Entrance exams should be taken by February of the senior year of high school. There are early admissions and deferred admissions plans. Applications should be filed by February 15 for fall entry November 15 for early action, and December 1 for spring entry, along with a $50 fee. Notification of early decision is sent December 15; regular decision, April 1.

Financial Aid: In 1999-2000, 92% of all freshmen and 84% of continuing students received some form of financial aid. 67% of freshmen and 59% of continuing students received need-based aid. The average freshman award was $14,000. Of that total, scholarships or need-based grants averaged $10,986 ($16,638 maximum); loans averaged $3982 ($20,000 maximum); and work contracts averaged $1500 ($2000 maximum). 45% of undergraduates work part time. Average annual earnings from campus work are $1500. CUA is a member of CSS. The CSS/Profile or FAFSA is required. The fall application deadline is February 15.

Computers: The mainframes are a Sun E4500, Sun E450, DEC ALPHA 4100 and 2100, and a Compaq 1850. There are 400 networked PCs spread across the campus for student use. All dorms are wired and students have access to the Internet and Web. All students may access the system 24 hours a day. There are no time limits and no fees.

CEDARVILLE COLLEGE
Cedarville, OH 45314-0601

(937) 766-2211
(800) CEDARVILLE; Fax: (937) 766-2760

Full-time: 1194 men, 1451 women	**Faculty:** 158
Part-time: 59 men, 58 women	**Ph.D.s:** 63%
Graduate: none	**Student/Faculty:** 17 to 1
Year: quarters, summer session	**Tuition:** $10,746
Application Deadline: open	**Room & Board:** $4788
Freshman Class: 1814 applied, 1340 accepted, 729 enrolled	
SAT I Verbal/Math: 590/580	**ACT:** 25 **VERY COMPETITIVE**

Cedarville College, founded in 1887, is an independent Baptist college of arts and sciences offering programs in engineering, nursing, accounting, computer information systems, and education. The school is known for its religious commitment, conservative values, and community outreach programs. In addition to regional accreditation, the 'Ville has baccalaureate program accreditation with ABET and NLN. The library contains 158,942 volumes, 24,408 microform items, and 5372 audiovisual forms/CDs, and subscribes to 962 periodicals. Computerized library services include the card catalog, interlibrary loans, and database searching. Special learning facilities include a radio station, media resource center, and observatory. The 400-acre campus is in a small town 12 miles south of Springfield. Including residence halls, there are 36 buildings.

Programs of Study: The 'Ville confers B.A., B.S., B.M.E., B.S.E.E., B.S.M.E., and B.S.N. degrees. Associate degrees are also awarded. Bachelor's degrees are awarded in BIOLOGICAL SCIENCE (biology/biological science), BUSINESS (accounting, banking and finance, business administration and management, management information systems, and marketing/retailing/merchandising), COMMUNICATIONS AND THE ARTS (broadcasting, communications, dramatic arts, English, multimedia, music, Spanish, and technical and business writing), COMPUTER AND PHYSICAL SCIENCE (chemistry, computer science, information sciences and systems, mathematics, and physics), EDUCATION (athletic training, Christian, early childhood, elementary, foreign languages, mathematics, middle school, music, physical, science, social studies, and special), ENGINEERING AND ENVIRONMENTAL DESIGN (electrical/electronics engineering and mechanical engineering), HEALTH PROFESSIONS (nursing), SOCIAL SCIENCE (American studies, biblical studies, criminal justice, history, international studies, missions, pastoral studies, philosophy, political science/government, prelaw, psychology, public administration, religious music, social science, social work, and sociology). Business, education, and math are the largest.

Special: Internships, study abroad, a Washington semester, dual majors, B.A.-B.S. degrees in biology and math, work-study programs with the college, and pass/fail options are available. There is a freshman honors program.

Admissions: 74% of the 1999-2000 applicants were accepted. The SAT I scores for the 1999-2000 freshman class were: Verbal--11% below 500, 40% between 500 and 599, 39% between 600 and 700, and 10% above 700; Math--13% below 500, 43% between 500 and 599, 35% between 600 and 700, and 9% above 700. The ACT scores were 6% below 21, 26% between 21 and 23, 31% between 24 and 26, 17% between 27 and 28, and 20% above 28. 59% of the current freshmen were in the top fifth of their class; 84% were in the top two fifths. There were 14 National Merit finalists and semifinalists. 70 freshmen graduated first in their class.

Requirements: The SAT I or ACT is required. the 'Ville requires applicants to be in the upper 50% of their class. A GPA of 3.0 is required. The SAT I or ACT (preferred) is required, with scores above the national average preferred. The college recommends that applicants have 4 years of English and 3 each of social studies, math, science, and a foreign language. The GED is accepted. Recommendations from a local pastor and a high school counselor are required. An interview is recommended. AP and CLEP credits are accepted. Important factors in the admissions decision are personality/intangible qualities, recommendations by school officials, and advanced placement or honor courses.

Procedure: Freshmen are admitted to all sessions. Entrance exams should be taken by December of the senior year. There are early admissions and deferred admissions plans. Application deadlines are open. There is a $30 application fee. Notification is sent on a rolling basis. A waiting list is an active part of the admissions procedure.

Financial Aid: In 1999-2000, 90% of all freshmen and 75% of continuing students received some form of financial aid. 70% of freshmen and 61% of continuing students received need-based aid. The average freshman award was $8490. Of that total, scholarships or need-based grants averaged $4022 ($13,600 maximum); loans averaged $2904 ($8125 maximum); and work contracts averaged $824 ($2600 maximum). 38% of undergraduates work part time. Average annual earnings from campus work are $1300. The average financial indebtedness of the

1999 graduate was $15,510. The FAFSA and the college's own financial statement are required. The fall application deadline is March 1.

Computers: The mainframe is an HP 9000/800, model G60. A network connects 4 public computer labs with more than 100 PCs and about 1000 residence hall rooms, which are equipped with PCs and printers. The network provides access to more than 150 software packages, library resources, E-mail, and the Internet. All students may access the system 24 hours a day from dorm rooms or up to 93 hours a week in the labs. There are no time limits and no fees.

CENTER FOR CREATIVE STUDIES/COLLEGE OF ART AND DESIGN
Detroit, MI 48202
(313) 664-7425
(800) 952-ARTS; Fax: (313) 872-2739

Full-time: 531 men, 361 women	**Faculty:** 45; IIB, -$
Part-time: 70 men, 63 women	**Ph.D.s:** 30%
Graduate: none	**Student/Faculty:** 20 to 1
Year: semesters, summer session	**Tuition:** $15,551
Application Deadline: March 1	**Room & Board:** $3100
Freshman Class: 652 applied, 457 accepted, 280 enrolled	
SAT I Verbal/Math: 521/526	**ACT:** 20 SPECIAL

The Center for Creative Studies/College of Art and Design, established in 1926, is a private, independent institution offering comprehensive 4-year B.F.A programs in animation and digital media, crafts, fine arts, communication design, industrial design, interior design, and photography. In addition to regional accreditation, CCS-CAD has baccalaureate program accreditation with NASAD. The library contains 21,000 volumes and subscribes to 100 periodicals. Special learning facilities include a learning resource center and art gallery. The 11-acre campus is in an urban area 3 miles from downtown Detroit in the University Cultural Center, which includes the Detroit Institute of Art. Including residence halls, there are 6 buildings.

Programs of Study: CCS-CAD confers the B.F.A degree. Bachelor's degrees are awarded in COMMUNICATIONS AND THE ARTS (advertising, animation, ceramic art and design, fine arts, glass, graphic design, illustration, industrial design, metal/jewelry, painting, photography, printmaking, and sculpture), ENGINEERING AND ENVIRONMENTAL DESIGN (interior design), SOCIAL SCIENCE (textiles and clothing). Communication design is the largest.

Special: Internships are available within the student's departmental major. Credit for internships is available.

Admissions: 70% of the 1999-2000 applicants were accepted.

Requirements: The SAT I or ACT is required. A GPA of 2.5 is required. Applicants must graduate from an accredited secondary school or earn a GED. A portfolio of representative work and an essay are required. Applications are accepted on-line at the school's web site. AP and CLEP credits are accepted. Important factors in the admissions decision are evidence of special talent and advanced placement or honor courses.

Procedure: Freshmen are admitted fall and winter. There is a deferred admissions plan. Applications should be filed by March 1 for fall entry and December 1 for spring entry, along with a $35 fee. Notification is sent on a rolling basis.

Financial Aid: In 1999-2000, 99% of all freshmen and 93% of continuing students received some form of financial aid. 14% of undergraduates work part time. Average annual earnings from campus work are $1200. The average financial indebtedness of the 1999 graduate was $20,850. The FAFSA is required. The fall application deadline is February 21.

Computers: All students may access the system. There are no time limits and no fees. It is strongly recommended that all students have personal computers.

CENTRE COLLEGE
Danville, KY 40422

(606) 238-5350
(800) 423-6236; Fax: (606) 238-5373

Full-time: 499 men, 517 women	**Faculty:** 91; IIB, +$
Part-time: 3 men, 4 women	**Ph.D.s:** 91%
Graduate: none	**Student/Faculty:** 11 to 1
Year: 4-2-4	**Tuition:** $16,050
Application Deadline: February 1	**Room & Board:** $5300
Freshman Class: 1142 applied, 977 accepted, 253 enrolled	
SAT I Verbal/Math: 620/630	**ACT:** 27 **VERY COMPETITIVE+**

Centre College, founded in 1819 by the Presbyterian Church (U.S.A.), is an independent liberal arts and sciences institution. The library contains 156,667 volumes, 3946 microform items, and 3500 audiovisual forms CDs, and subscribes to 2076 periodicals. Computerized library services include the card catalog, interlibrary loans, and database searching. Special learning facilities include an art gallery and a performing arts center. The 100-acre campus is in a small town 35 miles southwest of Lexington and 80 miles southeast of Louisville. Including residence halls, there are 54 buildings.

Programs of Study: Centre confers B.A. and B.S. degrees. Bachelor's degrees are awarded in BIOLOGICAL SCIENCE (biochemistry, biology/biological science, and molecular biology), COMMUNICATIONS AND THE ARTS (dramatic arts, English, fine arts, French, German, music, and Spanish), COMPUTER AND PHYSICAL SCIENCE (chemistry, computer science, mathematics, physical chemistry, and physics), EDUCATION (elementary), SOCIAL SCIENCE (anthropology, classical/ancient civilization, economics, history, international relations, philosophy, political science/government, psychobiology, psychology, religion, and sociology). English, economics, and biology are the strongest academically.

Special: Centre offers internships, study abroad in 9 countries, work-study, and a 3-2 engineering degree with Vanderbilt University, Washington University at St. Louis, Columbia University, and the University of Kentucky. Student-designed majors, interdisciplinary majors including chemical physics, secondary education certification, prelaw and premedicine programs, and pass/fail options also are available. There are 8 national honor societies, including Phi Beta Kappa.

Admissions: 86% of the 1999-2000 applicants were accepted. The SAT I scores for the 1999-2000 freshman class were: Verbal--2% below 500, 33% between 500 and 599, 44% between 600 and 700, and 21% above 700; Math--4% below 500, 30% between 500 and 599, 47% between 600 and 700, and 18% above 700. The ACT scores were 9% between 21 and 23, 34% between 24 and 26, 18% between 27 and 28, and 39% above 28. 75% of the current freshmen were in the top fifth of their class; 95% were in the top two fifths.

Requirements: The SAT I or ACT is required. No minimum test scores are required. Students should have completed a minimum of 15 academic credits, including 4 years each in English and math, 3 years each in science and social studies, 2 years in foreign language, and 1 year in an art- or music-related course. An essay is required and an interview is strongly recommended. Applications are accepted on computer disk and on-line. AP and CLEP credits are accepted. Important factors in the admissions decision are advanced placement or honor courses, recommendations by school officials, and personality/intangible qualities.

Procedure: Freshmen are admitted in the fall. Entrance exams should be taken by November of the senior year. There are early decision, early admissions, and deferred admissions plans. Early decision applications should be filed by November 15; regular applications, by February 1 for fall entry, along with a $30 fee. Notification of early decision is sent December 15; regular decision, March 1. 52 early decision candidates were accepted for the 1999-2000 class. 5% of all applicants are on a waiting list.

Financial Aid: In 1999-2000, 90% of all students received some form of financial aid. 67% of freshmen and 54% of continuing students received need-based aid. The average freshman award was $15,120. 49% of undergraduates work part time. Average annual earnings from campus work are $1312. The average financial indebtedness of the 1999 graduate was $13,000. Centre is a member of CSS. The FAFSA and the college's own financial statement are required. The fall application deadline is March 1.

Computers: There are 150 PCs available for network use in the residence halls, various classroom buildings, and the library. Residence hall rooms are connected to the network. All students may access the system. There are no time limits and no fees.

CHAPMAN UNIVERSITY
Orange, CA 92866

(714) 997-6711
(888) CUAPPLY; Fax: (714) 997-6713

Full-time: 1116 men, 1388 women	**Faculty:** 160; IIA, ++$
Part-time: 85 men, 133 women	**Ph.D.s:** 77%
Graduate: 532 men, 854 women	**Student/Faculty:** 16 to 1
Year: 4-1-4, summer session	**Tuition:** $20,496
Application Deadline: January 31	**Room & Board:** $7928
Freshman Class: 2345 applied, 1387 accepted, 540 enrolled	
SAT I Verbal/Math: 573/568	**ACT:** 24 **VERY COMPETITIVE**

Chapman University, founded in 1861, is an independent institution affiliated with the Disciples of Christ Christian Church, offering degree programs in liberal and fine arts, business, education, and the health sciences. There are 7 undergraduate and 8 graduate schools. In addition to regional accreditation, Chapman has baccalaureate program accreditation with AACSB, APTA, and NASM. The library contains 198,638 volumes, 156 microform items, and 2710 audiovisual forms/CDs, and subscribes to 1914 periodicals. Computerized library services include the card catalog, interlibrary loans, and database searching. Special learning facilities include a learning resource center, art gallery, radio station, and a food science sensory lab. The 60-acre campus is in a suburban area 35 miles southeast of Los Angeles. Including residence halls, there are 25 buildings.

Programs of Study: Chapman confers B.A., B.S., B.F.A., B.M., and B.S.B.A. degrees. Master's and doctoral degrees are also awarded. Bachelor's degrees are awarded in BIOLOGICAL SCIENCE (biology/biological science), BUSINESS (accounting, business administration and management, and organizational behavior), COMMUNICATIONS AND THE ARTS (art, communications, dramatic arts, English, film arts, French, music, and Spanish), COMPUTER AND PHYSICAL SCIENCE (chemistry, computer science, information sciences and systems, and mathematics), ENGINEERING AND ENVIRONMENTAL DESIGN (environmental science), HEALTH PROFESSIONS (health science and music therapy), SOCIAL SCIENCE (economics, food science, history, law, liberal arts/ general studies, peace studies, philosophy, physical fitness/movement, political science/government, psychology, religion, social science, and sociology). Business, communications, and liberal studies are the largest.

Special: Cooperative and internship programs are available. Students may study abroad for a semester or spend a semester in Washington, D.C. Dual and student-designed majors are possible. A general studies degree, B.A.-B.S. degrees, non-degree study options, and pass/fail options are also permitted. There is 1 national honor society, Phi Beta Kappa, and a freshman honors program.

Admissions: 59% of the 1999-2000 applicants were accepted. The SAT I scores for the 1999-2000 freshman class were: Verbal--17% below 500, 51% between 500 and 599, 29% between 600 and 700, and 3% above 700; Math--13% below 500, 52% between 500 and 599, 31% between 600 and 700, and 4% above 700. The ACT scores were 17% below 21, 30% between 21 and 23, 35% between 24 and 26, 13% between 27 and 28, and 5% above 28. 41% of the current freshmen were in the top fifth of their class; 81% were in the top two fifths. 7 freshmen graduated first in their class.

Requirements: The SAT I or ACT is required. A GPA of 2.8 is required. Applicants should be graduates of accredited high schools or have earned the GED. Secondary preparation should include 3 years of social science or electives, and 2 each of composition and/or literature, science, a foreign language, and math, including algebra II. Prospective art or music majors should show some preparation in those fields. A personal essay is required. An on-campus interview is recommended. Applications are accepted on-line, and may be submitted at the university's web site, www.chapman.edu. AP and CLEP credits are accepted. Important factors in the admissions decision are advanced placement or honor courses, evidence of special talent, and leadership record.

Procedure: Freshmen are admitted fall and spring. Entrance exams should be taken by fall of the senior year. There is an early admissions plan. Applications should be filed by January 31 for fall entry, November 15 for spring entry, and June 1 for summer entry, along with a $30 fee. Notification is sent on a rolling basis. 5% of all applicants are on a waiting list.

Financial Aid: In 1999-2000, 88% of all freshmen and 80% of continuing students received some form of financial aid. 56% of freshmen and 60% of continuing students received need-based aid. The average freshman award was $17,500. Of that total, scholarships or need-based grants averaged $11,075; loans averaged $3200; and work contracts averaged $1900. 95% of undergraduates work part time. Average annual earnings from campus work are $2200. The average financial indebtedness of the 1999 graduate was $17,700. The FAFSA is required. The fall application deadline is March 2.

Computers: The mainframe is an HP 3000/957. There are 46 Mac II SI's and SE's, 50 IBM, Dell, and other PCs, 3 DEC MicroVAX II UNIX-based minicomputers, 2 DEC workstations that are networked and have access to the Internet, 25 Power Mac 6100/60s, 1 DEC ALPHA, and 1 SGT. All students may access the system 8 a.m. to 11 p.m. There are no time limits and no fees.

CHRISTENDOM COLLEGE
Front Royal, VA 22630

(540) 636-2900
(800) 877-5456; Fax: (540) 636-1655

Full-time: 120 men, 132 women	**Faculty:** 21
Part-time: 1 man, 6 women	**Ph.D.s:** 81%
Graduate: 44 men, 41 women	**Student/Faculty:** 12 to 1
Year: semesters	**Tuition:** $11,530
Application Deadline: April 1	**Room & Board:** $3950
Freshman Class: 162 applied, 138 accepted, 74 enrolled	
SAT I Verbal/Math: 641/584	**ACT:** 25 **VERY COMPETITIVE+**

Christendom College, founded in 1977, is a liberal arts institution affiliated with the Roman Catholic Church. There is 1 graduate school. The library contains 49, 254 volumes, 816 microform items, and 1076 audiovisual forms/CDs, and subscribes to 219 periodicals. Computerized library services include the card catalog, interlibrary loans, and database searching. Special learning facilities include a learning resource center, art gallery, and writing center. The 100-acre campus is in a rural area 65 miles west of Washington, D.C. Including residence halls, there are 19 buildings.

Programs of Study: Christendom confers the B.A. degree. Associate and master's degrees are also awarded. Bachelor's degrees are awarded in COMMUNICATIONS AND THE ARTS (classics, English, and French), SOCIAL SCIENCE (history, philosophy, political science/government, and theological studies). Philosophy is the strongest academically. History is the largest.

Special: Christendom offers summer internships in Washington, D.C., for political science students, and also sponsors summer programs in Rome, Dublin, and Spain. Students may pursue dual majors. There is a work-study program with the college. 5 departments have honors programs.

Admissions: 85% of the 1999-2000 applicants were accepted. The SAT I scores for the 1999-2000 freshman class were: Verbal--2% below 500, 35% between 500 and 599, 33% between 600 and 700, and 30% above 700; Math--16% below 500, 36% between 500 and 599, 36% between 600 and 700, and 12% above 700. The ACT scores were 16% below 21, 5% between 21 and 23, 33% between 24 and 26, 27% between 27 and 28, and 19% above 28. 50% of the current freshmen were in the top fifth of their class; 75% were in the top two fifths. 1 freshman graduated first in the class.

Requirements: The SAT I or ACT is required; the SAT I is preferred. A minimum composite score of 1000 on the SAT I or 21 on the ACT is required. Christendom requires applicants to be in the upper 50% of their class. A GPA of 3.0 is required. Applicants need not be graduates of an accredited secondary school. GED certificates are accepted. Students should have completed 4 years of English, 2 each of foreign language, math, history, and science, and 1 of social studies. Essays and letters of recommendation are required. Interviews are recommended. AP credits are accepted. Important factors in the admissions decision are advanced placement or honor courses, leadership record, and evidence of special talent.

Procedure: Freshmen are admitted fall and spring. There are early action and early admissions plans. Early action applications should be filed by December 1; regular applications, by April 1 for fall entry and December 15 for spring entry, along with a $25 fee. Notification of early action is sent December 15; regular decision, on a rolling basis. 3% of all applicants are on a waiting list; 6 were accepted in 1999.

Financial Aid: In 1999-2000, 73% of all freshmen and 63% of continuing students received some form of financial aid. 57% of freshmen and 54% of continuing students received need-based aid. The average freshman award was $8180. Of that total, scholarships or need-based grants averaged $4500 ($11,300 maximum); loans averaged $3100 ($6700 maximum); and work contracts averaged $1620 (maximum). 50% of undergraduates work part time. Average annual earnings from campus work are $1620. The average financial indebtedness of the 1999 graduate was $8980. Christendom is a member of CSS. The college's own financial statement is required. The fall application deadline is April 1.

Computers: There is a computer lab network of 16 PCs for student use, offering word processsing and E-mail, and 3 PCs for Internet access in the library. All students may access the system. There are no time limits and no fees.

CHRISTIAN BROTHERS UNIVERSITY
Memphis, TN 38104-5581

(901) 321-3205
(800) 288-7576; Fax: (901) 321-3202

Full-time: 639 men, 694 women	**Faculty:** 82; IIB, -$
Part-time: 72 men, 92 women	**Ph.D.s:** 79%
Graduate: 167 men, 222 women	**Student/Faculty:** 16 to 1
Year: semesters, summer session	**Tuition:** $13,490
Application Deadline: July 15	**Room & Board:** $4080
Freshman Class: 268 enrolled	
ACT: 24	**VERY COMPETITIVE**

Christian Brothers University, founded in 1871, is a private, nonprofit institution affiliated with the Roman Catholic Church. Its programs emphasize the liberal arts and sciences, business, engineering and engineering management, health science, telecommunications management, and teacher preparation. There are 4 undergraduate and 3 graduate schools. In addition to regional accreditation, CBU has baccalaureate program accreditation with ABET. The library contains 100,000 volumes, 4000 microform items, and 300 audiovisual forms/CDs, and subscribes to 560 periodicals. Computerized library services include the card catalog, interlibrary loans, and database searching. Special learning facilities include a learning resource center and art gallery. The 70-acre campus is in an urban area in Memphis. Including residence halls, there are 18 buildings.

Programs of Study: CBU confers B.A. and B.S. degrees. Master's degrees are also awarded. Bachelor's degrees are awarded in BIOLOGICAL SCIENCE (biology/biological science), BUSINESS (accounting, business administration and management, business economics, management science, and marketing/retailing/merchandising), COMMUNICATIONS AND THE ARTS (English and technical and business writing), COMPUTER AND PHYSICAL SCIENCE (chemistry, computer science, information sciences and systems, mathematics, natural sciences, and physics), EDUCATION (elementary), ENGINEERING AND ENVIRONMENTAL DESIGN (chemical engineering, civil engineering, electrical/electronics engineering, engineering physics, and mechanical engineering), HEALTH PROFESSIONS (premedicine and prepharmacy), SOCIAL SCIENCE (history, human development, liberal arts/general studies, prelaw, psychology, and religion). Engineering, accounting, and psychology are the strongest academically. Psychology, biology, and electrical engineering are the largest.

Special: Special academic programs include on-campus work-study and internships for all juniors and seniors. There is cross-registration with Memphis College of Art, Memphis Theological Seminary, and LeMoyne-Owen College. An accelerated degree program is available to all business and psychology majors through the evening program, and a general studies degree is offered. Up to 36 hours of nondegree study is possible, as are dual majors and pass/fail options. There are 3 national honor societies and a freshman honors program.

Admissions: The ACT scores for the 1999-2000 freshman class were: 12% below 21, 30% between 21 and 23, 28% between 24 and 26, 13% between 27 and 28, and 18% above 28. 51% of the current freshmen were in the top fifth of their class; 71% were in the top two fifths.

Requirements: The SAT I or ACT is required. The SAT I score should be 830, 415 verbal and 415 math; the ACT score should be 20. CBU requires applicants to be in the upper 67% of their class. A GPA of 3.0 is required. Other admissions requirements include graduation from an accredited secondary school, with a college-preparatory curriculum recommended. The GED is accepted. An interview is advised. AP and CLEP credits are accepted. Important factors in the admissions decision are advanced placement or honor courses, leadership record, and recommendations by school officials.

Procedure: Freshmen are admitted to all sessions. Entrance exams should be taken by the end of the junior year. There is a deferred admissions plan. Applications should be filed by July 15 for fall entry, January 1 for spring entry, and May 15 for summer entry, along with a $25 fee. Notification is sent on a rolling basis.

Financial Aid: 95% of undergraduates work part time. Average annual earnings from campus work are $750. The average financial indebtedness of the recent graduate was $10,900. The FAFSA is required.

Computers: The mainframe is a DEC VAX 6000-410. There are also 190 PCs and terminals available for student use in computer centers and academic buildings. There is a campuswide fiber-optic-based LAN and software for word processing, spreadsheets, databases, engineering, accounting, calculus, math, writing, chemistry, physics, and biology. Students with their own PCs may also access the Internet from dorm rooms. All students may access the system during the 91 hours per week of computer center operation; 24-hour dial-in phone access is available. There are no time limits and no fees.

CITY UNIVERSITY OF NEW YORK/BARUCH COLLEGE

New York, NY 10010-5585   **(212) 802-2300; Fax: (212) 802-2310**

Full-time: 3721 men, 4504 women	**Faculty:** 455
Part-time: 1745 men, 2628 women	**Ph.D.s:** 87%
Graduate: 1372 men, 1284 women	**Student/Faculty:** 17 to 1
Year: semesters, summer session	**Tuition:** $3275 ($6875)
Application Deadline: May 1	**Room & Board:** n/app
Freshman Class: 14,688 applied, 2653 accepted, 1170 enrolled	
SAT I Verbal/Math: 500/540	**VERY COMPETITIVE**

Baruch College was founded in 1919 and became a separate unit of the City University of New York in 1968. some of the information in this profile is approximate. It offers undergraduate programs in business and public administration, liberal arts and sciences, and education. There are 2 undergraduate and 3 graduate schools. In addition to regional accreditation, Baruch has baccalaureate program accreditation with AACSB. The library contains 270,000 volumes, 1,600,000 microform items, and 500 audiovisual forms/CDs, and subscribes to 2100 periodicals. Computerized library services include the card catalog, interlibrary loans, and database searching. Special learning facilities include a learning resource center, art gallery, and radio station. The campus is in an urban area. There are 6 buildings.

Programs of Study: Baruch confers B.A. and B.B.A. degrees. Master's and doctoral degrees are also awarded. Bachelor's degrees are awarded in BUSINESS (accounting, investments and securities, management science, marketing management, marketing/retailing/merchandising, operations research, and personnel management), COMMUNICATIONS AND THE ARTS (advertising, communications, English, journalism, music, and Spanish), COMPUTER AND PHYSICAL SCIENCE (actuarial science, computer management, mathematics, and statistics), EDUCATION (early childhood and elementary), SOCIAL SCIENCE (economics, history, industrial and organizational psychology, philosophy, political science/government, psychology, public administration, and sociology). Economics, English, and math are the strongest academically. Accounting is the largest.

Special: The college offers internships and study abroad in Great Britain, France, Germany, Mexico, and Israel. Students may design their own liberal arts major. A federal work-study program is available, and pass/fail options are permitted for liberal arts majors. There is 1 national honor society.

Admissions: 18% of the 1999-2000 applicants were accepted. The SAT I scores for the 1999-2000 freshman class were: Verbal--46% below 500, 41% between 500 and 599, 12% between 600 and 700, and 1% above 700; Math--29% below 500, 44% between 500 and 599, 24% between 600 and 700, and 4% above 700.

Requirements: The SAT I is required. A GPA of 80.0 is required. with a minimum composite score of 1100. Applicants must present an official high school transcript (a GED will be accepted) indicating a minimum average grade of 80% in academic subjects. AP and CLEP credits are accepted.

Procedure: Freshmen are admitted fall and spring. There is an early admissions plan. Applications should be filed by May 1 for fall entry and November 5 for spring entry, along with a $40 fee. Notification is sent in March.

Financial Aid: In 1999-2000, 89% of all freshmen and 68% of continuing students received some form of financial aid. 67% of freshmen and 59% of continuing students received need-based aid. The average freshman award was $2060. Of that total, scholarships or need-based grants averaged $5400; loans averaged $1500; and work contracts averaged $900. 5% of undergraduates work part time. Average annual earnings from campus work are $2500. The average financial indebtedness of the 1999 graduate was $9660. The FAFSA is required. The fall application deadline is May 1.

Computers: There are 469 PCs available in the computer center, media center, resource center, library, computer labs, and classrooms. All students may access the system. There are no fees.

CITY UNIVERSITY OF NEW YORK/QUEENS COLLEGE

Flushing, NY 11367-1597   (718) 997-5608; Fax: (718) 997-5617

Full-time: 2795 men, 4382 women	**Faculty:** 536
Part-time: 1467 men, 2922 women	**Ph.D.s:** 95%
Graduate: 1180 men, 2940 women	**Student/Faculty:** 15 to 1
Year: semesters, summer session	**Tuition:** $3403 ($7003)
Application Deadline: January 1	**Room & Board:** n/app
Freshman Class: 4632 applied, 2686 accepted, 1037 enrolled	
SAT I Verbal/Math: 538/548	**VERY COMPETITIVE**

Queens College, founded in 1937, is a public commuter institution within the City University of New York system. Some of the information in this profile is approximate. The 2 libraries contain 710,000 volumes, 765,000 microform items, and 27,000 audiovisual forms/CDs, and subscribe to 3200 periodicals. Computerized library services include the card catalog, interlibrary loans, and database searching. Special learning facilities include a learning resource center, art gallery, a center for the performing arts, and a center for environmental teaching and research located on Long Island. The 76-acre campus is in an urban area 10 miles from Manhattan. There are 20 buildings.

Programs of Study: Queens confers B.A., B.S., B.F.A., and B.Mus. degrees. Master's degrees are also awarded. Bachelor's degrees are awarded in BIOLOGICAL SCIENCE (biology/biological science), BUSINESS (accounting and labor studies), COMMUNICATIONS AND THE ARTS (art, art history and appreciation, communications, comparative literature, dance, dramatic arts, English, English as a second/foreign language, film arts, French, German, Greek, Hebrew, Italian, Latin, linguistics, music, Russian, Spanish, and studio art), COMPUTER AND PHYSICAL SCIENCE (chemistry, computer science, geology, mathematics, and physics), EDUCATION (art, early childhood, elementary, foreign languages, health, home economics, mathematics, music, physical, science, secondary, and social studies), HEALTH PROFESSIONS (predentistry, premedicine, and speech pathology/audiology), SOCIAL SCIENCE (anthropology, East Asian studies, economics, history, home economics, interdisciplinary studies, Judaic studies, Latin American studies, philosophy, political science/government, pre-law, psychology, religion, sociology, urban studies, and women's studies). Anthropology, biology, and chemistry are the strongest academically. Accounting, elementary education, and computer science are the largest.

Special: Queens offers cooperative programs in all majors, study abroad, independent study, interdisciplinary and dual majors, internships in business and liberal arts fields and journalism, a 3-2 engineering degree with Columbia University or CCNY/CUNY, pass/fail options, work-study, and nondegree study. The SEEK program provides financial and educational resources for underprepared freshmen. There are 15 national honor societies, including Phi Beta Kappa, and a freshman honors program.

Admissions: 58% of the 1999-2000 applicants were accepted. The SAT I scores for the 1999-2000 freshman class were: Verbal--30% below 500, 42% between 500 and 599, 20% between 600 and 700, and 8% above 700; Math--24% below 500, 44% between 500 and 599, 24% between 600 and 700, and 8% above 700. 52% of the current freshmen were in the top fifth of their class; 89% were in the top two fifths.

Requirements: The SAT I is required. A GPA of 2.5 is required. High school preparation should include 4 years each of English and social studies, 3 each of math and foreign language, and 2 of lab science. AP and CLEP credits are accepted.

Procedure: Freshmen are admitted fall and spring. Entrance exams should be taken in the spring of the junior year or the fall of the senior year. There is an early admissions plan. Applications should be filed by January 1 for fall entry and October 15 for spring entry, along with a $40 fee. Notification is sent on a rolling basis.

Financial Aid: In 1999-2000, 50% of all freshmen and 13% of continuing students received some form of financial aid. 26% of freshmen and 28% of continuing students received need-based aid. The average freshman award was $3500. The average financial indebtedness of the 1999 graduate was $12,000. The FAFSA is required. The fall application deadline is May 1.

Computers: The mainframe is a Hitachi Data Systems Model 8023. A computer center has DEC VAX and IBM systems. Extensive PC facilities are also provided throughout the campus, and there are a variety of support services for PC users.

Those students enrolled in computer science courses may access the system during day and evening hours. There are no fees.

CLAREMONT MCKENNA COLLEGE
Claremont, CA 91711-6425   **(909) 621-8088; Fax: (909) 621-8516**

Full-time: 564 men, 453 women	**Faculty:** 107; IIB, ++$
Part-time: none	**Ph.D.s:** 100%
Graduate: none	**Student/Faculty:** 10 to 1
Year: semesters	**Tuition:** $20,760
Application Deadline: January 15	**Room & Board:** $7060
Freshman Class: 2827 applied, 785 accepted, 253 enrolled	
SAT I Verbal/Math: 690/690	**ACT:** 29 **MOST COMPETITIVE**

Claremont McKenna College, founded in 1946, is a highly selective liberal arts college with a curricular emphasis on economics, government, international relations, and public affairs. The 4 libraries contain 2 million volumes, and subscribe to 6065 periodicals. Computerized library services include the card catalog, interlibrary loans, and database searching. Special learning facilities include a learning resource center, art gallery, radio station, and 9 research institutes. The 50-acre campus is in a small town 35 miles east of downtown Los Angeles. Including residence halls, there are 29 buildings.

Programs of Study: CMC confers the B.A. degree. Bachelor's degrees are awarded in BIOLOGICAL SCIENCE (biochemistry and biology/biological science), BUSINESS (accounting, business economics, and management engineering), COMMUNICATIONS AND THE ARTS (Chinese, classics, dramatic arts, English literature, film arts, fine arts, French, German, literature, music, Russian, and Spanish), COMPUTER AND PHYSICAL SCIENCE (chemistry, geology, information sciences and systems, mathematics, physics, science, and science and management), EDUCATION (education), ENGINEERING AND ENVIRONMENTAL DESIGN (environmental science), HEALTH PROFESSIONS (premedicine), SOCIAL SCIENCE (African American studies, American studies, anthropology, Asian/Oriental studies, economics, European studies, history, international relations, Mexican-American/Chicano studies, philosophy, political science/government, prelaw, psychobiology, psychology, religion, sociology, and women's studies). Economics, government, and international relations are the strongest academically. Economics, accounting, and government are the largest.

Special: CMC students may cross-register at any of the Claremont Colleges and may participate in exchange programs with Haverford, Spelman, or Colby Colleges. Students may study abroad in 32 countries or spend a semester in Washington, D.C. Part-time and full-time internships and dual and student-designed majors are available. There are 3-2 programs in management-engineering with Stanford University, Harvey Mudd College, and others, and a 3-3 program with Columbia Law School. A multidisciplinary program in leadership studies and an interdisciplinary program in legal studies are offered. There are limited pass/fail options. There are 5 national honor societies, including Phi Beta Kappa, and a freshman honors program.

Admissions: 28% of the 1999-2000 applicants were accepted. The SAT I scores for the 1999-2000 freshman class were: Verbal--12% between 500 and 599, 44% between 600 and 700, and 44% above 700; Math--11% between 500 and 599, 42% between 600 and 700, and 47% above 700. The ACT scores were 3% between 21 and 23, 17% between 24 and 26, 30% between 27 and 28, and 50% above 28. 93% of the current freshmen were in the top fifth of their class; 99% were in the top two fifths. There were 22 National Merit finalists and 33 semifinalists. 32 freshmen graduated first in their class.

Requirements: The SAT I is required. Applicants must be graduates of an accredited high school or have earned the GED. Secondary preparation must include 4 years of English, 3 years (preferably 4) of math, at least 2 years of a foreign language and science, and 1 year of history. A personal essay is required, and an interview is recommended. The application is available on computer disk. Applications are accepted on-line. AP credits are accepted. Important factors in the admissions decision are advanced placement or honor courses, leadership record, and recommendations by school officials.

Procedure: Freshmen are admitted fall and spring. Entrance exams should be taken during the junior year or between October and January of the senior year. There are early decisions, early admissions, and deferred admissions plans. Early decision applications should be filed by November 15; regular applications by January 15 for fall entry and November 1 for spring entry, along with a $50 fee. Notification of early decision is sent December 15; regular decision, April 1. 35 early decision candidates were accepted for the 1999-2000 class. 17% of all applicants are on a waiting list.

Financial Aid: The average freshman award was $21,039. Of that total, scholarships or need-based grants averaged $16,700; loans averaged $2750; and work contracts averaged $1250. 51% of undergraduates work part time. Average annual earnings from campus work are $1012. The average financial indebtedness of the 1999 graduate was $12,000. CMC is a member of CSS. The CSS/Profile or FAFSA is required. The fall application deadline is February 1.

Computers: The mainframe is 2 DEC VAXs. Students have access to the VAXs through lab terminals. In addition, Mac and IBM PCs, with an extensive software library, are available. All students may access the system. There are no time limits and no fees.

CLARK UNIVERSITY
Worcester, MA 01610-1477

(508) 793-7431
(800) 462-5275; Fax: (508) 793-8821

Full-time: 792 men, 1157 women	**Faculty:** 165; IIA, +$
Part-time: 87 men, 146 women	**Ph.D.s:** 99%
Graduate: 390 men, 431 women	**Student/Faculty:** 12 to 1
Year: semesters, summer session	**Tuition:** $22,620
Application Deadline: February 1	**Room & Board:** $4350
Freshman Class: 3236 applied, 2372 accepted, 487 enrolled	
SAT I Verbal/Math: 570/560	**ACT:** 22 **VERY COMPETITIVE**

Clark University, founded in 1887, is an independent liberal arts and research institution. There are 3 graduate schools. In addition to regional accreditation, Clark has baccalaureate program accreditation with AACSB and NASDTEC. The 4 libraries contain 560,836 volumes, 60,000 microform items, and 1000 audiovisual forms/CDs, and subscribe to 1650 periodicals. Computerized library services include the card catalog, interlibrary loans, and database searching. Special learning facilities include a learning resource center, art gallery, center for music with 2 studios for electronic music, 2 theaters, magnetic resonance imaging facility, arboretum, campus cable network, TV studio, and student radio station. The 50-acre campus is in an urban area 50 miles west of Boston. Including residence halls, there are 56 buildings.

Programs of Study: Clark confers the B.A. degree. Master's and doctoral degrees are also awarded. Bachelor's degrees are awarded in BIOLOGICAL SCIENCE (biochemistry and biology/biological science), BUSINESS (business administration and management), COMMUNICATIONS AND THE ARTS (art history and appreciation, comparative literature, dramatic arts, English, film arts, fine arts, French, German, languages, music, romance languages and literature, Spanish, studio art, and visual and performing arts), COMPUTER AND PHYSICAL SCIENCE (chemistry, computer science, mathematics, and physics), ENGINEERING AND ENVIRONMENTAL DESIGN (environmental science), HEALTH PROFESSIONS (predentistry and premedicine), SOCIAL SCIENCE (classical/ancient civilization, economics, geography, history, human ecology, international relations, philosophy, political science/government, prelaw, psychology, and sociology). Psychology, geography, and environmental studies are the strongest academically. Psychology and government and international relations are the largest.

Special: For-credit internships are available in all disciplines with private corporations and small businesses, medical centers, and government agencies. There is cross-registration with members of the Worcester Consortium, including Holy Cross and Worcester Polytechnic Institute. Clark also offers study abroad in 10 countries, a Washington semester with American University, work-study programs, dual and student-designed majors, pass/no record options, and a 3-2 engineering degree with Columbia University, Washington University, and Worcester Polytechnic Institute. A gerontology certificate is offered with the Worcester Consortium for Higher Education. Integrated undergraduate/graduate programs are available in environmental science and policy, international development and social change, management, biology, chemistry, communications, education, history, and physics. High-achieving, 4-year degree students at Clark are eligible for a tuition-free fifth year, to combine an undergraduate major with an advanced degree in 10 possible areas. There are 7 national honor societies, including Phi Beta Kappa.

Admissions: 73% of the 1999-2000 applicants were accepted. The SAT I scores for the 1999-2000 freshman class were: Verbal--18% below 500, 38% between 500 and 599, 37% between 600 and 700, and 7% above 700; Math--18% below 500, 48% between 500 and 599, 30% between 600 and 700, and 4% above 700. The ACT scores were 40% between 18 and 23, 51% between 24 and 29, and 9% between 30 and 36. 56% of the current freshmen were in the top fifth of their class; 81% were in the top two fifths. 8 freshmen graduated first in their class.

Requirements: The SAT I or ACT is required. A GPA of 3.27 is required. The SAT II: Writing test is also required. Applicants must graduate from an accredited secondary school or have a GED. 16 Carnegie units are required, including 4 years of English, 3 each of math and science, and 2 each of foreign language, history, and social studies. An interview is recommended. AP credits are accepted. Important factors in the admissions decision are advanced placement or honor courses, recommendations by alumni, and recommendations by school officials.

Procedure: Freshmen are admitted fall and spring. Entrance exams should be taken by November of the senior year. There are early decision, early admissions, and deferred admissions plans. Early decision applications should be filed by November 15; regular applications, by February 1 for fall entry and November 15 for spring entry, along with a $40 fee. Notification of early decision is sent in January ; regular decision, April 1. 45 early decision candidates were accepted for the 1999-2000 class. 1% of all applicants are on a waiting list.

Financial Aid: In 1999-2000, 81% of all freshmen and 79% of continuing students received some form of financial aid. 65% of freshmen and 62% of continuing students received need-based aid. The average freshman award was $15,982. Of that total, scholarships or need-based grants averaged $12,436 ($22,400 maximum); loans averaged $3831 ($4825 maximum); and work contracts averaged $1454 ($1500 maximum). 44% of undergraduates work part time. Average annual earnings from campus work are $1003. The average financial indebtedness of the 1999 graduate was $17,224. Clark is a member of CSS. The CSS/Profile or FAFSA is required. The fall application deadline is February 1.

Computers: The mainframes are a cluster including the DEC VAX 6420, and 6410 the VAX Station 3100/76, and the DEC ALPHA Systems 3000/400, 2000/233, 4000/710, and ALPHA Server 4000. There are networked departmental systems in various buildings throughout campus and PC and Mac computers in 2 public computer labs, plus campuswide access to the Internet. All students may access the system 7 days per week via direct connections from the campus network (including residence halls) and through modems. There are no time limits and no fees.

CLARKSON UNIVERSITY
Potsdam, NY 13699

(315) 268-6479
(800) 527-6577; Fax: (315) 268-7647

Full-time: 1862 men, 652 women	**Faculty:** 140; I, av$
Part-time: 30 men, 37 women	**Ph.D.s:** 93%
Graduate: 210 men, 111 women	**Student/Faculty:** 18 to 1
Year: semesters, summer session	**Tuition:** $20,205
Application Deadline: March 1	**Room & Board:** $7484
Freshman Class: 2568 applied, 2119 accepted, 707 enrolled	
SAT I Verbal/Math: 576/620	**VERY COMPETITIVE+**

Clarkson University, founded in 1896, is a private institution offering undergraduate programs in engineering, business, science, and the liberal arts, and graduate programs in engineering, businesss, science, and health sciences. There are 4 undergraduate and 4 graduate schools. In addition to regional accreditation, Clarkson has baccalaureate program accreditation with AACSB and ABET. The library contains 237,251 volumes, 276,552 microform items, and 1524 audiovisual forms/CDs, and subscribes to 1226 periodicals. Computerized library services include the card catalog, interlibrary loans, and database searching. Special learning facilities include a learning resource center, natural history museum, radio station, and TV station. The 640-acre campus is in a rural area 70 miles north of Watertown and 75 miles south of Ottawa, Canada. Including residence halls, there are 43 buildings.

Programs of Study: Clarkson confers B.S. and B.P.S. degrees. Master's and doctoral degrees are also awarded. Bachelor's degrees are awarded in BIOLOGICAL SCIENCE (biology/biological science), BUSINESS (accounting, banking and finance, management information systems, management science, and marketing/retailing/merchandising), COMMUNICATIONS AND THE ARTS (technical and business writing), COMPUTER AND PHYSICAL SCIENCE (chemistry, computer science, mathematics, and physics), ENGINEERING AND ENVIRONMENTAL DESIGN (aeronautical engineering, chemical engineering, civil engineering, computer engineering, electrical/electronics engineering, engineering management, industrial administration/management, and mechanical engineering), HEALTH PROFESSIONS (industrial hygiene), SOCIAL SCIENCE (economics, history, humanities, political science/government, psychology, social science, and sociology). Engineering, business, and sciences are the strongest academically. Mechanical, civil, and computer engineering are the largest.

Special: Clarkson offers cross-registration with the Associate Colleges of the St. Lawrence Valley: St. Lawrence University and Potsdam and Canton colleges. Co-op programs in all academic areas, dual majors in business and liberal arts, interdisciplinary majors in engineering, and management, and professional studies, internships, accelerated degree programs, student-designed majors in the

B.P.S. degree program, and study abroad in England, Sweden, Germany, Australia, and Canada are possible. There are 3-2 engineering programs with many institutions in the Northeast; students who participate take the first 3 years of the prescribed program at a 4-year liberal arts institution, and then transfer with junior standing into one of Clarkson's 4-year engineering curricula. There are 9 national honor societies, including Phi Beta Kappa, a freshman honors program, and 2 departmental honors programs.

Admissions: 83% of the 1999-2000 applicants were accepted. The SAT I scores for the 1999-2000 freshman class were: Verbal--13% below 500, 49% between 500 and 599, 32% between 600 and 700, and 7% above 700; Math--8% below 500, 34% between 500 and 599, 48% between 600 and 700, and 13% above 700. 67% of the current freshmen were in the top fifth of their class; 89% were in the top two fifths. There were 2 National Merit finalists. 22 freshmen graduated first in their class.

Requirements: The SAT I is required and the ACT is recommended. SAT II: Subject tests are also recommended. Applicants must have graduated from an accredited secondary school or have the GED. An essay and interview are also recommended. Applications are accepted on computer disk and on-line via the Internet. AP and CLEP credits are accepted. Important factors in the admissions decision are advanced placement or honor courses, recommendations by school officials, and extracurricular activities record.

Procedure: Freshmen are admitted fall and spring. There are early decision, early admissions, and deferred admissions plans. Early decision I applications should be filed by December 1; early decision II applications by January 15; regular applications, by March 1 for fall entry and December 1 for spring entry, along with a $30 fee. Notification of early decision I is sent January 1; early decision II, February 1; regular decision, February. 162 early decision candidates were accepted for the 1999-2000 class.

Financial Aid: In 1999-2000, 95% of all freshmen and 90% of continuing students received some form of financial aid. 85% of freshmen and 82% of continuing students received need-based aid. The average freshman award was $18,480. Of that total, scholarships or need-based grants averaged $11,240 ($27,202 maximum); loans averaged $5490 ($8625 maximum); work contracts averaged $1100 ($1200 maximum); and externally sponsored scholarships/awards averaged $650. 45% of undergraduates work part time. Average annual earnings from campus work are $900. The average financial indebtedness of the 1999 graduate was $18,110. Clarkson is a member of CSS. The FAFSA is required. The fall application deadline is February 15.

Computers: The mainframes are an IBM 4381 and an RS 6000. About 100 terminals are available in clusters throughout the campus. All students may access the system. There are no time limits and no fees. All students are required to have personal computers.

CLEMSON UNIVERSITY
Clemson, SC 29634-5124   (864) 656-2287; Fax: (864) 656-0622

Full-time: 6871 men, 5756 women	**Faculty:** 1076; I, -$
Part-time: 492 men, 343 women	**Ph.D.s:** 84%
Graduate: 1771 men, 1637 women	**Student/Faculty:** 12 to 1
Year: semesters, summer session	**Tuition:** $3470 ($9456)
Application Deadline: May 1	**Room & Board:** $4130

Freshman Class: 9501 applied, 6484 accepted, 2893 enrolled
SAT I Verbal/Math: 560/570   **ACT:** 25   **VERY COMPETITIVE**

Clemson University, founded in 1889, is a public institution with programs in agriculture, architecture, commerce and industry, education, engineering, forest and recreation resources, liberal arts, nursing, and sciences. There are 5 undergraduate and 1 graduate school. In addition to regional accreditation, Clemson has baccalaureate program accreditation with AACSB, ABET, CSAB, NAAB, NCATE, NLN, and NRPA. The library contains 906,625 volumes and 1,052,414 microform items, and subscribes to 11,574 periodicals. Computerized library services include the card catalog, interlibrary loans, and database searching. Special learning facilities include an art gallery, planetarium, and radio station. The 1400-acre campus is in a small town 32 miles west of Greenville. Including residence halls, there are 584 buildings.

Programs of Study: Clemson confers B.A., B.S., B.F.A, and B.L.A. degrees. Master's and doctoral degrees are also awarded. Bachelor's degrees are awarded in AGRICULTURE (agriculture, animal science, forestry and related sciences, forestry production and processing, horticulture, and soil science), BIOLOGICAL SCIENCE (biochemistry, biology/biological science, and microbiology), BUSINESS (accounting, banking and finance, business administration and management, management science, and marketing/retailing/merchandising), COMMUNICATIONS AND THE ARTS (communications, design, English, fine arts, French, German, modern language, and Spanish), COMPUTER AND PHYSICAL SCIENCE (chemistry, computer science, geology, information sciences and systems, mathematics, and physics), EDUCATION (agricultural, early childhood, elementary, industrial arts, secondary, and special), ENGINEERING AND ENVIRONMENTAL DESIGN (agricultural engineering, ceramic engineering, chemical engineering, civil engineering, computer engineering, construction management, electrical/electronics engineering, graphic arts technology, industrial administration/management, industrial engineering, landscape architecture/design, mechanical engineering, and textile technology), HEALTH PROFESSIONS (medical laboratory technology, nursing, predentistry, premedicine, prepharmacy, preveterinary science, and speech pathology/audiology), SOCIAL SCIENCE (economics, food science, history, parks and recreation management, philosophy, political science/government, prelaw, psychology, and sociology). Engineering and architecture are the strongest academically. Marketing is the largest.

Special: Co-op programs are available in all majors except nursing. Work-study programs and study abroad in 38 countries are offered. There are 22 national honor societies, a freshman honors program, and 40 departmental honors programs.

Admissions: 68% of the 1999-2000 applicants were accepted. The SAT I scores for the 1999-2000 freshman class were: Verbal--16% below 500, 51% between 500 and 599, 28% between 600 and 700, and 4% above 700; Math--11% below 500, 44% between 500 and 599, 36% between 600 and 700, and 7% above 700. The ACT scores were 9% below 21, 24% between 21 and 23, 35% between 24 and 26, 13% between 27 and 28, and 19% above 28. 56% of the current freshmen

were in the top fifth of their class; 88% were in the top two fifths. There were 22 National Merit finalists. 119 freshmen graduated first in their class.

Requirements: The SAT I or ACT is required. In addition, applicants should be graduates of an accredited secondary school. The GED is accepted. Clemson accepts applications on-line via ExPAN available on the university's Internet home page. AP and CLEP credits are accepted. Important factors in the admissions decision are advanced placement or honor courses, parents or siblings attending the school, and recommendations by school officials.

Procedure: Freshmen are admitted fall, spring, and summer. Entrance exams should be taken during spring of the junior year or fall of the senior year. There are early admissions and deferred admissions plans. Applications should be filed by May 1 for fall entry and December 15 for spring entry, along with a $40 fee. Notification is sent on a rolling basis. 5% of all applicants are on a waiting list.

Financial Aid: In a recent year, 62% of all freshmen and 57% of continuing students received some form of financial aid. 38% of freshmen and 35% of continuing students received need-based aid. The average freshman award was $5780. Of that total, scholarships or need-based grants averaged $4436 ($16,000 maximum); loans averaged $3008 ($7625 maximum); and work contracts averaged $1950 ($2000 maximum). 55% of undergraduates work part time. Average annual earnings from campus work are $1325. The average financial indebtedness of a recent graduate was $13,338. The CSS/Profile, FAFSA, FFS, or SFS is required. The fall application deadline is April 1.

Computers: The mainframe is an HDS AS/EX-80. There are also 600 PCs available. All students may access the system. There are no time limits and no fees.

CLEVELAND INSTITUTE OF ART
Cleveland, OH 44106

(216) 421-7427
(800) 223-4700; Fax: (216) 421-7438

Full-time: 260 men, 237 women	**Faculty:** 48
Part-time: 12 men, 16 women	**Ph.D.s:** 90%
Graduate: none	**Student/Faculty:** 10 to 1
Year: semesters	**Tuition:** $14,745
Application Deadline: July 1	**Room & Board:** $5076
Freshman Class: 460 applied, 415 accepted, 173 enrolled	
SAT I Verbal/Math: 558/534	**ACT:** 23 **SPECIAL**

Cleveland Institute of Art, founded in 1882, is an independent professional school of art offering a 5-year B.F.A. degree. Some of the information in this profile is approximate. In addition to regional accreditation, CIA has baccalaureate program accreditation with NASAD. The 3 libraries contain 40,000 volumes and 1600 audiovisual forms/CDs, and subscribe to 260 periodicals. Computerized library services include the card catalog, interlibrary loans, and database searching. Special learning facilities include an art gallery and natural history museum. The 500-acre campus is in an urban area 4 miles east of downtown Cleveland, sharing a campus with Case Western Reserve University. Including residence halls, there are 3 buildings.

Programs of Study: CIA confers the B.F.A. degree. Bachelor's degrees are awarded in COMMUNICATIONS AND THE ARTS (advertising, applied art, design, graphic design, industrial design, painting, photography, and studio art). Industrial design, painting, and metals are the strongest academically. Industrial design, graphic design, and painting are the largest.

Special: Cross-registration with Case Western Reserve University and the Cleveland Commission on Higher Education, internships for thrid-, fourth-, and fifth-year students with business and industry, and study abroad in 3 countries are available. There are joint programs with Case Western Reserve University in art education and medical illustration.

Admissions: 90% of the 1999-2000 applicants were accepted. The SAT I scores for the 1999-2000 freshman class were: Verbal--21% below 500, 47% between 500 and 599, 26% between 600 and 700, and 6% above 700; Math--31% below 500, 41% between 500 and 599, 26% between 600 and 700, and 2% above 700. The ACT scores were 31% below 21, 26% between 21 and 23, 25% between 24 and 26, 11% between 27 and 28, and 7% above 28. 29% of the current freshmen were in the top fifth of their class; 64% were in the top two fifths.

Requirements: The SAT I or ACT is required, with SAT I minimum scores of 350 verbal and 350 math or an ACT minimum composite score of 15. Applicants must be graduates of an accredited secondary school. The GED is accepted. Students should have completed 4 units each of art, English, and math, 2 each of history, science, and social studies, and 1 of a foreign language. An essay and a portfolio are required. An interview is strongly recommended. AP and CLEP credits are accepted. Important factors in the admissions decision are evidence of special talent, personality/intangible qualities, and leadership record.

Procedure: Freshmen are admitted fall and spring. Entrance exams should be taken during the junior year. There are early decision, early admissions, and deferred admissions plans. Applications should be filed by July 1 for fall entry, along with a $30 fee. Notification is sent on a rolling basis. 5% of all applicants are on a waiting list.

Financial Aid: In 1999-2000, 86% of all freshmen and 83% of continuing students received some form of financial aid. 73% of freshmen and 75% of continuing students received need-based aid. The average freshman award was $10,235. Average annual earnings from campus work are $2700. The average financial indebtedness of the 1999 graduate was $16,253. CIA is a member of CSS. The CSS/Profile, the college's own financial statement, and federal tax forms are required. The fall application deadline is March 15.

Computers: 20 Amiga PCs are available in the computer lab. There are 15 Macintosh PCs in the industrial design and interior design labs and 15 in the graphic design and illustration labs. Students may access the system for up to 2 hours. There are no fees.

COE COLLEGE
Cedar Rapids, IA 52402　　　　　　　　　　　　**(319) 399-8500**
(800) (877) CALL-COE; Fax: (319) 399-8816

Full-time: 515 men, 599 women	**Faculty:** 86; IIB, av$
Part-time: 58 men, 74 women	**Ph.D.s:** 92%
Graduate: 13 men, 45 women	**Student/Faculty:** 13 to 1
Year: 4-1-4, summer session	**Tuition:** $17,540
Application Deadline: March 1	**Room & Board:** $5020
Freshman Class: 1087 applied, 921 accepted, 323 enrolled	
SAT I Verbal/Math: 580/560	**ACT:** 25　**VERY COMPETITIVE**

Coe College, founded in 1851, is a private liberal arts institution affiliated with the Presbyterian Church (U.S.A.). There is 1 graduate school. In addition to regional accreditation, Coe has baccalaureate program accreditation with NASM and NLN. The 2 libraries contain 202,181 volumes, 9748 microform items, and 9278 audiovisual forms/CDs, and subscribe to 898 periodicals. Computerized library services include the card catalog, interlibrary loans, and database searching. Special learning facilities include a learning resource center, art gallery, planetarium, radio station, and ornithological wing. The 75-acre campus is in an urban area 225 miles west of Chicago. Including residence halls, there are 19 buildings.

Programs of Study: Coe confers B.A., B.Mus., and B.S.N. degrees. Master's degrees are also awarded. Bachelor's degrees are awarded in BIOLOGICAL SCIENCE (biochemistry, biology/biological science, and molecular biology), BUSINESS (accounting and business administration and management), COMMUNICATIONS AND THE ARTS (art, dramatic arts, English, French, German, literature, music, public relations, and Spanish), COMPUTER AND PHYSICAL SCIENCE (chemistry, computer science, mathematics, physics, and science), EDUCATION (athletic training, elementary, music, physical, and secondary), ENGINEERING AND ENVIRONMENTAL DESIGN (environmental science and preengineering), HEALTH PROFESSIONS (medical laboratory technology, nursing, physical therapy, predentistry, and premedicine), SOCIAL SCIENCE (African American studies, American studies, Asian/Oriental studies, classical/ancient civilization, economics, history, human services, interdisciplinary studies, philosophy, political science/government, prelaw, psychology, religion, sociology, and women's studies). Biology, psychology, and chemistry are the strongest academically. Economics, business administration, and psychology are the largest.

Special: Coe offers cross-registration with nearby Mount Mercy College and the University of Iowa; cooperative programs with Washington University in St. Louis in engineering (a 3-2 degree program), and in architecture (a 3-4 degree program), and with the University of Chicago in social services administration; Washington and New York semesters; and study abroad in 12 countries. Internships, nondegree study, and dual and student-designed majors also are possible. Core course instructors serve as students' mentors. There are 5 national honor societies, including Phi Beta Kappa, a freshman honors program, and honors programs in all departments.

Admissions: 85% of the 1999-2000 applicants were accepted. The SAT I scores for the 1999-2000 freshman class were: Verbal--16% below 500, 42% between 500 and 599, 38% between 600 and 700, and 4% above 700; Math--19% below 500, 54% between 500 and 599, and 27% between 600 and 700. The ACT scores were 18% below 21, 28% between 21 and 23, 24% between 24 and 26, 17% between 27 and 28, and 13% above 28. 52% of the current freshmen were in the top fifth of their class; 84% were in the top two fifths. 12 freshmen graduated first in their class.

Requirements: The SAT I or ACT is required. Coe requires applicants to be in the upper 40% of their class. A GPA of 2.8 is required. Coe recommends that applicants have 4 years in English, 3 each in math, history, science, and social studies, and 2 in foreign language. All students must submit an essay. In addition, fine arts students need a portfolio or audition. The GED is accepted. Coe accepts applications on-line via CollegeLink and Apply. AP and CLEP credits are accepted. Important factors in the admissions decision are advanced placement or honor courses, recommendations by school officials, and leadership record.

Procedure: Freshmen are admitted fall and spring. Entrance exams should be taken in the spring of the junior year or the fall of the senior year. There are early action, early admissions, and deferred admissions plans. Early action applications should be filed by December 15; regular applications, by March 1 for fall entry. Notification of early decision is sent January 15; regular decision, March 15.

Financial Aid: In 1999-2000, 94% of all freshmen and 92% of continuing students received some form of financial aid. 85% of freshmen and 82% of continuing students received need-based aid. The average freshman award was $17,064. Of that total, scholarships or need-based grants averaged $12,840 ($17,540 maximum); loans averaged $4325 ($5625 maximum); and work contracts averaged

$1200 ($1500 maximum). 48% of undergraduates work part time. Average annual earnings from campus work are $1200. The average financial indebtedness of the 1999 graduate was $15,375. The FAFSA is required. The fall application deadline is March 1.

Computers: The main computer system is a LAN operating under Novell netware. Students may access the campus network from approximately 189 PCs located in 7 labs on campus. All residence hall rooms are networked for student-owned machines. All students may access the system 24 hours a day. There are no time limits and no fees.

COLBY COLLEGE
Waterville, ME 04901

(207) 872-3168
(800) 723-3032; Fax: (207) 872-3474

Full-time: 853 men, 911 women	**Faculty:** 147; IIB, ++$
Part-time: none	**Ph.D.s:** 98%
Graduate: none	**Student/Faculty:** 12 to 1
Year: 4-1-4	**Tuition:** see profile
Application Deadline: January 15	**Room & Board:** see profile
Freshman Class: 4363 applied, 1425 accepted, 489 enrolled	
SAT I Verbal/Math: 660/660	**ACT:** 28 **MOST COMPETITIVE**

Colby College, founded in 1813, is a private liberal arts college. Students are charged a comprehensive fee of $31,580 annually, which includes tuition and room and board. The 3 libraries contain 924,900 volumes, 299,660 microform items, and 19,630 audiovisual forms CDs, and subscribe to 2550 periodicals. Computerized library services include the card catalog, interlibrary loans, and database searching. Special learning facilities include a learning resource center, art gallery, radio station, TV station, observatory, satellite dishes, arboretum, and state wildlife management area. The 714-acre campus is in a small town 75 miles north of Portland. Including residence halls, there are 58 buildings.

Programs of Study: Colby confers the A.B. degree. Bachelor's degrees are awarded in BIOLOGICAL SCIENCE (biochemistry, biology/biological science, and cell biology), COMMUNICATIONS AND THE ARTS (art, art history and appreciation, classics, English, German, music, performing arts, Russian, Spanish, and studio art), COMPUTER AND PHYSICAL SCIENCE (chemistry, computer science, earth science, geology, mathematics, and physics), ENGINEERING AND ENVIRONMENTAL DESIGN (environmental science), SOCIAL SCIENCE (African American studies, American studies, anthropology, classical/ancient civilization, East Asian studies, economics, French studies, history, international studies, Latin American studies, philosophy, political science/government, psychology, religion, sociology, and women's studies). Biology, chemistry, and physics are the strongest academically. Biology, English, and economics are the largest.

Special: Colby offers study abroad through various programs in numerous countries, Washington semester programs through American University and the Washington Center, on-campus work-study, exchange programs with various colleges and universities, a 3-2 engineering degree with Dartmouth College, the University of Rochester, and Case Western Reserve University, and maritime and oceanographic studies programs. Dual and student-designed majors are possible. There are 9 national honor societies, including Phi Beta Kappa, and 24 departmental honors programs.

Admissions: 33% of the 1999-2000 applicants were accepted. The SAT I scores for the 1999-2000 freshman class were: Verbal--1% below 500, 17% between

131

500 and 599, 59% between 600 and 700, and 22% above 700; Math--4% below 500, 13% between 500 and 599, 57% between 600 and 700, and 27% above 700. The ACT scores were 3% below 21, 3% between 21 and 23, 21% between 24 and 26, 25% between 27 and 28, and 48% above 28. 80% of the current freshmen were in the top fifth of their class; 95% were in the top two fifths. 9 freshmen graduated first in their class.

Requirements: The SAT I or ACT is required. Candidates should be high school graduates with a recommended academic program of 4 years of English, 3 each of foreign language and math, and 2 each of science (including lab work), social studies/history, and other college-preparatory courses. To obain Colby's application on disk, write or call the Admissions Office, or download from http://www.colby.edu/. Applications are also accepted on-line via Common App, Apply, and others. AP credits are accepted. Important factors in the admissions decision are advanced placement or honor courses, leadership record, and personality/intangible qualities.

Procedure: Freshmen are admitted fall and winter. Entrance exams should be taken by January of the senior year. There are early decision and deferred admissions plans. Early decision applications should be filed by November 15 or January 1. Regular applications should be filed by January 15 for fall entry, along with a $50 fee. Early decision notification is sent December 15 or February 1. Regular notification is sent April 1. 195 early decision candidates were accepted for the 1999-2000 class. 7% of all applicants are on a waiting list.

Financial Aid: 66% of all students received some form of financial aid. 42% of freshmen and 41% of continuing students received need-based aid. The average freshman award was $18,900. Of that total, scholarships or need-based grants averaged $16,800 ($27,980 maximum); loans averaged $2300 ($2950 maximum); and work contracts averaged $1000 ($1500 maximum). 66% of undergraduates work part time. Average annual earnings from campus work are $700. The average financial indebtedness of the 1999 graduate was $16,000. Colby is a member of CSS. The CSS/Profile, FAFSA, or the college's own financial statement is required. The fall application deadline is February 1.

Computers: The mainframes are three HP806/E25, an HP820/D280, an HP871/D270, an HP770/J210, and an HP867/G40. Access to the campus network, local resources, and the Internet is available in all classrooms, labs, offices, and library study areas, as well as from each residence hall, where there is a port for every student and additional ports in lounges. 280 computers are available for student use in open clusters, departmental clusters, and labs. Laser printers are available for student use in all clusters, and there are no fees for printing. There is no charge for access to the Internet, and students are provided with an E-mail account and storage space for personal web pages. All students may access the system 24 hours a day. There are no time limits and no fees. Colby strongly recommends that students have their own personal computer and further recommends the Mac or the Dell Optiplex/Latitude.

COLGATE UNIVERSITY
Hamilton, NY 13346   (315) 228-7401; Fax: (315) 228-7544

Full-time: 1355 men, 1449 women	**Faculty:** 217; IIB, ++$
Part-time: 29 men, 33 women	**Ph.D.s:** 99%
Graduate: 4 men, 4 women	**Student/Faculty:** 13 to 1
Year: semesters	**Tuition:** $24,750
Application Deadline: January 15	**Room & Board:** $6330
Freshman Class: 5589 applied, 2341 accepted, 750 enrolled	
SAT I Verbal/Math: 644/651	**ACT:** 29 **MOST COMPETITIVE**

Colgate University, founded in 1819, is a private liberal arts institution. There is 1 graduate school. The 2 libraries contain 615,940 volumes, 474,987 microform items, and 7877 audiovisual forms/CDs, and subscribe to 2299 periodicals. Computerized library services include the card catalog, interlibrary loans, and database searching. Special learning facilities include an art gallery, radio station, TV station, anthropology museum, and observatory. The 550-acre campus is in a rural area 45 miles southeast of Syracuse and 35 miles southwest of Utica. Including residence halls, there are 86 buildings.

Programs of Study: Colgate confers the B.A. degree. Master's degrees are also awarded. Bachelor's degrees are awarded in BIOLOGICAL SCIENCE (biochemistry, biology/biological science, molecular biology, and neurosciences), COMMUNICATIONS AND THE ARTS (art history and appreciation, classics, dramatic arts, English, French, German, Greek, Latin, music, Russian, Spanish, and studio art), COMPUTER AND PHYSICAL SCIENCE (astronomy, chemistry, computer science, geology, geophysics and seismology, mathematics, natural sciences, physical sciences, and physics), EDUCATION (education), ENGINEERING AND ENVIRONMENTAL DESIGN (environmental science), SOCIAL SCIENCE (African studies, anthropology, Asian/Oriental studies, economics, geography, history, humanities, international relations, Latin American studies, Native American studies, peace studies, philosophy, political science/government, psychology, religion, Russian and Slavic studies, social science, sociology, and women's studies). English, economics, and history are the largest.

Special: Colgate offers various internships, semester and summer research opportunities with faculty, work-study, study abroad in 16 countries, accelerated degree programs, dual majors, and student-designed majors. A 3-2 engineering degree with Columbia and Washington Universities and Rensselaer Polytechnic Institute, a 3-4 architecture degree with Washington University, credit by exam, and pass/fail options are available. There are 8 national honor societies, including Phi Beta Kappa, and a freshman honors program. All departments have honors programs.

Admissions: 42% of the 1999-2000 applicants were accepted. The SAT I scores for the 1999-2000 freshman class were: Verbal--2% below 500, 20% between 500 and 599, 59% between 600 and 700, and 19% above 700; Math--3% below 500, 15% between 500 and 599, 62% between 600 and 700, and 20% above 700. The ACT scores were 2% between 21 and 23, 11% between 24 and 26, 20% between 27 and 28, and 67% above 28. 85% of the current freshmen were in the top fifth of their class; 97% were in the top two fifths. 31 freshmen graduated first in their class.

Requirements: The SAT I or ACT is required. Students may submit the SAT I and SAT II: Subject tests in writing and 2 other disciplines, or the ACT. 2 teacher recommendations and a counselor's report are required. An interview, though not evaluated, is recommended. Students should present 16 or more Carnegie credits, based on 4 years each of English and math and at least 3 of lab science, social science, and a foreign language, with electives in the arts. Colgate accepts applications on computer disk or on-line, via Mac Apply, CollegeLink, ExPAN, and the Common Application. AP and CLEP credits are accepted. Important factors in the admissions decision are advanced placement or honor courses, recommendations by school officials, and leadership record.

Procedure: Freshmen are admitted in the fall. Entrance exams should be taken in time for score reports to reach the University by January 15. There are early decision, early admissions, and deferred admissions plans. Early decision applications should be filed by November 15 or January 15; regular applications, by January 15 for fall entry, along with a $50 fee. Notification of early decision is sent by December 15 oe after January 1; regular decision, April 1. 233 early decision candidates were accepted for the 1999-2000 class. 7% of all applicants are on a waiting list.

Financial Aid: In 1999-2000, 45% of all freshmen and 43% of continuing students received some form of financial aid. 40% of all students received need-based aid. The average freshman award was $22,175. Of that total, scholarships or need-based grants averaged $18,500 ($31,640 maximum); loans averaged $2625 (maximum); and work contracts averaged $1550 (maximum). 50% of undergraduates work part time. Average annual earnings from campus work are $890. The average financial indebtedness of the 1999 graduate was $12,750. Colgate is a member of CSS. The CSS/Profile and FAFSA are required. The fall application deadline is February 1.

Computers: The mainframe is a DEC VAX 11/780. There are 400 terminals on campus offering a wide variety of applications software. In addition, all residence halls are wired for networked computers. All students may access the system. There are no time limits and no fees. It is strongly recommended that all students have personal computers.

COLLEGE OF NEW JERSEY, THE
Ewing, NJ 08628-0718

(609) 771-2131
(800) 624-0967; Fax: (609) 637-5174

Full-time: 2237 men, 3302 women	**Faculty:** 322; IIA, +$
Part-time: 156 men, 235 women	**Ph.D.s:** 88%
Graduate: 135 men, 682 women	**Student/Faculty:** 17 to 1
Year: semesters, summer session	**Tuition:** $5685 ($9002)
Application Deadline: February 15	**Room & Board:** $6330
Freshman Class: 5755 applied, 3163 accepted, 1209 enrolled	
SAT I Verbal/Math: 620/640	**HIGHLY COMPETITIVE**

The College of New Jersey, founded in 1855, is a public institution offering programs in the liberal arts, sciences, business, engineering, nursing, and education. There are 5 undergraduate schools, and 1 graduate school. In addition to regional accreditation, TCNJ has baccalaureate program accreditation with AACSB, ABET, CSAB, NASDTEC, NASM, NCATE, and NLN. The library contains 500,000 volumes, 250,000 microform items, and 2483 audiovisual forms/CDs, and subscribes to 4697 periodicals. Computerized library services include the card catalog, interlibrary loans, and database searching. Special learning facilities include a learning resource center, art gallery, planetarium, radio station, TV station, and microscopy lab. The 289-acre campus is in a suburban area 6 miles northwest of Trenton in central New Jersey. Including residence halls, there are 37 buildings.

Programs of Study: TCNJ confers B.A., B.S., B.F.A., B.M., and B.S.N. degrees. Master's degrees are also awarded. Bachelor's degrees are awarded in BIOLOGI-

CAL SCIENCE (biology/biological science), BUSINESS (accounting, business administration and management, international business management, management science, and marketing/retailing/merchandising), COMMUNICATIONS AND THE ARTS (communications, English, fine arts, graphic design, journalism, music, and Spanish), COMPUTER AND PHYSICAL SCIENCE (chemistry, computer science, mathematics, physics, and statistics), EDUCATION (art, early childhood, education of the deaf and hearing impaired, elementary, English, health, music, physical, special, and technical), ENGINEERING AND ENVIRONMENTAL DESIGN (engineering and applied science), HEALTH PROFESSIONS (nursing), SOCIAL SCIENCE (criminal justice, economics, history, philosophy, political science/government, psychology, and sociology). Biology, English, and computer science are the strongest academically. Biology, elementary education, and psychology are the largest.

Special: TCNJ offers cross-registration with the New Jersey Marine Science Consortium, numerous internships in the public and private sectors, and study abroad in more than a dozen countries through the International Student Exchange program (ISEP). Pass/fail options are possible. Specially designed research courses allow students to participate in collaborative scholarly projects with members of the faculty. Combined advanced-degree professional programs are offered in law and justice, medicine, and optometry with other area schools. There are 9 national honor societies, a freshman honors program, and 17 departmental honors programs.

Admissions: 55% of the 1999-2000 applicants were accepted. The SAT I scores for the 1999-2000 freshman class were: Verbal--2% below 500, 38% between 500 and 599, 51% between 600 and 700, and 9% above 700; Math--1% below 500, 29% between 500 and 599, 58% between 600 and 700, and 12% above 700. 95% of the current freshmen were in the top fifth of their class; All were in the top two fifths. There was 1 National Merit finalist and 2 semifinalists. 41 freshmen graduated first in their class.

Requirements: The SAT I is required. Applicants must have earned 16 academic credits in high school, consisting of 4 in English, 2 each in math, science, and social studies, and 6 others distributed among math, science, social studies, and a foreign language. An essay is required. Art majors must submit a portfolio, and music majors must audition. The GED is accepted. The SAT II: Writing test is required for placement purposes. Applications are accepted on-line through an enrollment services system at www.embark.com. AP and CLEP credits are accepted. Important factors in the admissions decision are advanced placement or honor courses, leadership record, and evidence of special talent.

Procedure: Freshmen are admitted fall and spring. Entrance exams should be taken by the end of the junior year or early in the senior year. There are early decision and early admissions plans. Early decision applications should be filed by November 15; regular applications, by February 15 for fall entry, November 1 for spring entry, and May 1 for summer entry, along with a $50 fee. Notification of early decision is sent December 15; regular decision, April 1. 217 early decision candidates were accepted for the 1999-2000 class. 6% of all applicants are on a waiting list.

Financial Aid: In 1999-2000, 73% of all freshmen and 75% of continuing students received some form of financial aid. 50% of students received need-based aid. The average freshman award was $4600. Of that total, scholarships or need-based grants averaged $2600 ($10,500 maximum); loans averaged $3200 ($10,500 maximum); and work contracts averaged $1200 ($2000 maximum). 26% of undergraduates work part time. Average annual earnings from campus work are $1200. The average financial indebtedness of the 1999 graduate was $13,000.

TCNJ is a member of CSS. The FAFSA and copies of students' and parents' tax returns as applicable are required. The fall application deadline is May 1.

Computers: The mainframe is an IBM ES9000 9121-320. There are 400 networked PCs and workstations available in 23 academic computing labs throughout the campus, including 3 in residence halls. Students have access to the campuswide network from their residence hall rooms. In addition, 2370 student PCs are connected to the Internet. All students may access the system. There are no time limits and no fees. The college strongly recommends that all students have PCs.

COLLEGE OF SAINT BENEDICT
St. Joseph, MN 56374-2099

(320) 363-5308
(800) 544-1489; Fax: (320) 363-5010

Full-time: 1952 women	**Faculty:** 126
Part-time: 1 man, 47 women	**Ph.D.s:** 77%
Graduate: none	**Student/Faculty:** 15 to 1
Year: 4-1-4	**Tuition:** $16,441
Application Deadline: open	**Room & Board:** $5025
Freshman Class: 1119 applied, 1024 accepted, 515 enrolled	
SAT I Verbal/Math: 580/560	**ACT:** 24 **VERY COMPETITIVE**

The College of Saint Benedict, established in 1887, is a private, Benedictine Catholic institution offering undergraduate liberal arts study for women in conjunction with St. John's University, a Benedictine Catholic institution for men. The coordinate institutions share an academic calendar, academic curriculum, and most cocurriculum programs. In addition to regional accreditation, St. Benedict has baccalaureate program accreditation with ADA, CSWE, NASM, NCATE, and NLN. The 4 libraries contain 569,410 volumes, 114,851 microform items, and 19,589 audiovisual forms/ CDs, and subscribe to 1717 periodicals. Computerized library services include the card catalog, interlibrary loans, and database searching. Special learning facilities include a learning resource center, art gallery, natural history museum, radio station, and an arboretum at St. John's University. The 315-acre campus is in a small town 70 miles northwest of Minneapolis and 10 miles west of St. Cloud. Including residence halls, there are 33 buildings.

Programs of Study: St. Benedict confers B.A. and B.S.N. degrees. Bachelor's degrees are awarded in BIOLOGICAL SCIENCE (biology/biological science and nutrition), BUSINESS (accounting and management science), COMMUNICATIONS AND THE ARTS (art, classics, communications, dramatic arts, English, fine arts, French, German, music, and Spanish), COMPUTER AND PHYSICAL SCIENCE (chemistry, computer science, mathematics, natural sciences, and physics), EDUCATION (elementary), ENGINEERING AND ENVIRONMENTAL DESIGN (preengineering), HEALTH PROFESSIONS (medical laboratory technology, nursing, predentistry, premedicine, prepharmacy, and preveterinary science), SOCIAL SCIENCE (dietetics, economics, history, humanities, liberal arts/general studies, pastoral studies, peace studies, philosophy, political science/government, prelaw, psychology, social science, social work, sociology, and theological studies). Biology, chemistry, and math are the strongest academically. Elementary education, nursing, and premedicine are the largest.

Special: Students may cross-register with St. John's University. There are study-abroad programs in Ireland, Japan, China, South America, South Africa, Central America, Australia, Scandinavia, and 6 European cities. Internships, dual and student-designed majors in math/computer science and in preprofessional programs, and liberal studies degrees may be pursued. A 3-2 engineering program is offered through several universities. Nondegree study and a pass/fail grading option are also available. There is 1 national honor society, and a freshman honors program.

Admissions: 92% of the 1999-2000 applicants were accepted. The SAT I scores for the 1999-2000 freshman class were: Verbal--13% below 500, 45% between 500 and 599, 35% between 600 and 700, and 7% above 700; Math--19% below 500, 43% between 500 and 599, 35% between 600 and 700, and 3% above 700. The ACT scores were 9% below 21, 31% between 21 and 23, 33% between 24 and 26, 15% between 27 and 28, and 12% above 28. 61% of the current freshmen were in the top fifth of their class; 89% were in the top two fifths. 23 freshmen graduated first in their class.

Requirements: The SAT I or ACT is required. St. Benedict requires applicants to be in the upper 60% of their class. A GPA of 2.8 is required. Applicants must be graduates of an accredited secondary school. Academic preparation should include 17 units, including 4 of English, 3 of math, 2 each of a lab science and social studies, and 6 electives. A foreign language is recommended. An essay is required, and interviews are recommended. Applications are accepted on-line at the school's web site or on computer disk via Common Application, CollegeLink, and ExPAN. Details can be found at the on-line application site at http://www.csbsju.edu/admission/index.html. AP and CLEP credits are accepted. Important factors in the admissions decision are leadership record, evidence of special talent, and extracurricular activities record.

Procedure: Freshmen are admitted fall and spring. Entrance exams should be taken during the spring of the junior year or fall of the senior year. There is a deferred admissions plan. Application deadlines are open, and there is a $25 fee. Notification is sent on a rolling basis. A waiting list is an active part of the admissions procedure.

Financial Aid: In 1999-2000, 92% of all freshmen and 88% of continuing students received some form of financial aid. 73% of freshmen and 77% of continuing students received need-based aid. The average freshman award was $14,391. Of that total, scholarships or need-based grants averaged $8634 ($14,085 maximum); loans averaged $4147 ($5125 maximum); and work contracts averaged $1610 ($2075 maximum). 44% of undergraduates work part time. Average annual earnings from campus work are $1610. The average financial indebtedness of the 1999 graduate was $17,445. St. Benedict is a member of CSS. The FAFSA and the college's own financial statement are required. The fall application deadline is May 1.

Computers: The mainframe is a Windows NT network. Students have free, 24-hour access to computers in each college residence, in numerous departments, and in 4 public access areas. Most residence halls and apartments are computer-wired. All students may access the system 24 hours per day. There are no time limits and no fees.

COLLEGE OF THE ATLANTIC
Bar Harbor, ME 04609

(207) 288-5015
(800) 528-0025; Fax: (207) 288-4126

Full-time: 85 men, 177 women	**Faculty:** 19
Part-time: 7 men, 5 women	**Ph.D.s:** 95%
Graduate: 1 man, 4 women	**Student/Faculty:** 14 to 1
Year: terms	**Tuition:** $19,485
Application Deadline: March 1	**Room & Board:** $5400
Freshman Class: 234 applied, 171 accepted, 73 enrolled	
SAT I Verbal/Math: 633/588	**ACT:** 26 **HIGHLY COMPETITIVE**

College of the Atlantic, founded in 1969, is a private liberal arts college dedicated to the study of human ecology. There is 1 graduate school. The library contains 35,000 volumes, 65 microform items, and 410 audiovisual forms/CDs, and subscribes to 410 periodicals. Computerized library services include the card catalog, interlibrary loans, and database searching. Special learning facilities include a learning resource center, art gallery, natural history museum, writing center, taxidermy lab, photography lab, marine mammal research center, 2 greenhouses, an 80-acre organic farm, and 2 offshore research stations. The 29-acre campus is in a small town 45 miles southeast of Bangor, along the Atlantic Ocean shoreline. Including residence halls, there are 13 buildings.

Programs of Study: COA confers the B.A. degree. Master's degrees are also awarded. Bachelor's degrees are awarded in SOCIAL SCIENCE (human ecology).

Special: Teacher certification is offered in elementary and secondary science, English, and social studies education. Students may cross-register with the University of Maine. Study abroad is available in Uruguay, Mexico, and the Czech Republic. Students arrange internships with a broad range of employers. Pass/fail grading options are available.

Admissions: 73% of the 1999-2000 applicants were accepted. The SAT I scores for the 1999-2000 freshman class were: Verbal--29% between 500 and 599, 50% between 600 and 700, and 21% above 700; Math--10% below 500, 48% between 500 and 599, 34% between 600 and 700, and 8% above 700. The ACT scores were 33% between 21 and 23, 17% between 24 and 26, and 50% between 27 and 28. 63% of the current freshmen were in the top fifth of their class; 96% were in the top two fifths. There were 2 National Merit finalists and 7 semifinalists.

Requirements: The SAT I or ACT is recommended. Candidates for admission must be high school graduates who have completed 4 years of English, 3 to 4 of math, 2 to 3 of science, 2 of a foreign language, and 1 of history. Applications are accepted on computer disk and on-line at the school's web site. AP and CLEP credits are accepted. Important factors in the admissions decision are advanced placement or honor courses, leadership record, and personality/intangible qualities.

Procedure: Freshmen are admitted fall, winter, and spring. Entrance exams should be taken in the junior or senior year. There are early decision and deferred admissions plans. Early decision applications should be filed by December 1; regular applications, by March 1 for fall entry, November 15 for winter entry, and February 15 for spring entry, along with a $45 fee. Notification of early decision is sent December 15; regular decision, April 1. 23 early decision candidates were accepted for the 1999-2000 class. A waiting list is an active part of the admissions procedure.

Financial Aid: In 1999-2000, 78% of all freshmen and 74% of continuing students received some form of financial aid. 72% of freshmen and 70% of continu-

ing students received need-based aid. The average freshman award was $17,479. Of that total, scholarships or need-based grants averaged $10,895 ($16,500 maximum); loans averaged $3137 ($8125 maximum); and work contracts averaged $1917 ($2100 maximum). 86% of undergraduates work part time. Average annual earnings from campus work are $1000. The average financial indebtedness of the 1999 graduate was $17,125. COA is a member of CSS. The FAFSA and the college's own financial statement are required. The fall application deadline is February 15.

Computers: More than 40 PCs, including Dell System 220/325, IBM XTs and ATs, and Macs, are available in 2 computer centers and a science lab. The graphics lab contains 7 workstations and peripherals. There is Internet access in each dormitory room, with worldwide E-mail capability. All students may access the system 24 hours a day. There are no time limits and no fees. It is recommended that students have a network capable personal computer. A Mac, Dell, Gateway, Toshiba, or IBM is recommended.

COLLEGE OF THE HOLY CROSS
Worcester, MA 01610

(508) 793-2443
(800) 442-2421; Fax: (508) 793-3888

Full-time: 1320 men, 1458 women	**Faculty:** 221; IIB, ++$
Part-time: none	**Ph.D.s:** 94%
Graduate: none	**Student/Faculty:** 13 to 1
Year: semesters	**Tuition:** $22,910
Application Deadline: January 15	**Room & Board:** $7320
Freshman Class: 4836 applied, 2114 accepted, 724 enrolled	
SAT I Verbal/Math: 630/630	**MOST COMPETITIVE**

College of the Holy Cross, founded in 1843, is a private liberal arts college affiliated with the Roman Catholic Church and the Jesuit Order. The 3 libraries contain 565,800 volumes, 15,073 microform items, and 22,780 audiovisual forms/CDs, and subscribe to 1728 periodicals. Computerized library services include the card catalog, interlibrary loans, and database searching. Special learning facilities include an art gallery, radio station, greenhouses, facilities for aquatic research, and a multimedia resource center. The 174-acre campus is in a suburban area 45 miles west of Boston. Including residence halls, there are 27 buildings.

Programs of Study: Holy Cross confers the A.B. degree. Bachelor's degrees are awarded in BIOLOGICAL SCIENCE (biology/biological science), COMMUNICATIONS AND THE ARTS (art history and appreciation, classics, dramatic arts, English, French, German, Greek, Latin, music, Russian, Spanish, and studio art), COMPUTER AND PHYSICAL SCIENCE (chemistry, mathematics, and physics), SOCIAL SCIENCE (anthropology, economics, European studies, history, philosophy, political science/government, psychology, religion, and sociology). English, psychology, and economics are the largest.

Special: Local internships are available through the Center for Interdisciplinary and Special Studies in health and education, law and business, journalism, social service, state and local government, scientific research, and cultural affairs. Student-designed majors, dual majors including economics-accounting, a Washington semester, and study abroad are possible. There is a 3-2 engineering program with Columbia University, Dartmouth College, and Washington University in St. Louis, and premedicine and predentistry programs are available. Students may cross-register with other universities in the Colleges of Worcester Consortium. Nondegree study is possible. There are 12 national honor societies, including Phi Beta Kappa, and 5 departmental honors programs.

Admissions: 44% of the 1999-2000 applicants were accepted. The SAT I scores for the 1999-2000 freshman class were: Verbal--3% below 500, 26% between 500 and 599, 55% between 600 and 700, and 16% above 700; Math--2% below 500, 25% between 500 and 599, 56% between 600 and 700, and 17% above 700. 83% of the current freshmen were in the top fifth of their class; 97% were in the top two fifths. There were 11 National Merit finalists. 21 freshmen graduated first in their class.

Requirements: The SAT I or ACT is required. Applicants should be graduates of an accredited secondary school or hold the GED. Recommended preparatory courses include English, foreign language, history, math, and science. An essay and SAT II: Subject tests in writing and 2 other areas are required. An interview is recommended. AP credits are accepted. Important factors in the admissions decision are advanced placement or honor courses, recommendations by school officials, and extracurricular activities record.

Procedure: Freshmen are admitted in the fall. Entrance exams should be taken by January of the senior year. There are early decision, early admissions, and deferred admissions plans. Early decision applications should be filed by December 15; regular applications, by January 15 for fall entry, along with a $50 fee. Notification of early decision is sent on a rolling basis from December 10 to February 28; regular decision, April 1. 192 early decision candidates were accepted for the 1999-2000 class. 9% of all applicants are on a waiting list.

Financial Aid: In 1999-2000, 65% of all freshmen and 60% of continuing students received some form of financial aid. 60% of freshmen and 53% of continuing students received need-based aid. The average freshman award was $14,484. Of that total, scholarships or need-based grants averaged $12,420 ($22,500 maximum); loans averaged $4587 ($4725 maximum); work contracts averaged $1277 ($1500 maximum); and outside sources averaged $2771. 36% of undergraduates work part time. Average annual earnings from campus work are $1390. The average financial indebtedness of the 1999 graduate was $17,459. Holy Cross is a member of CSS. The CSS/Profile or FAFSA is required. The fall application deadline is February 1.

Computers: The mainframe is a DEC ALPHA 3100. There are 4 public labs and a dozen departmental labs on campus housing more than 200 Intel PCs and 50 Macs. Every residence hall room has access to the college computer network. All students may access the system 24 hours per day. There are no time limits and no fees.

COLLEGE OF THE OZARKS
Point Lookout, MO 65726

(417) 334-6411, ext. 4219
(800) 222-0525; Fax: (417) 335-2618

Full-time: 594 men, 667 women	**Faculty:** 89; IIB, av$
Part-time: 74 men, 94 women	**Ph.D.s:** 61%
Graduate: 3 women	**Student/Faculty:** 14 to 1
Year: semesters	**Tuition:** $150
Application Deadline: March 15	**Room & Board:** $2500
Freshman Class: 2752 applied, 495 accepted, 418 enrolled	
ACT: 21	**VERY COMPETITIVE+**

College of the Ozarks, founded in 1906, is a private liberal arts college affiliated with the Presbyterian Church (U.S.A.). Instead of paying tuition, students work a total of 560 hours in campus jobs and are responsible only for room and board, books, personal expenses, and an incidental fee of $150. Students may also elect to work in a summer program, which will cover their room and board costs as well. The 2 libraries contain 111,750 volumes, 28,350 microform items, and 4551 audiovisual forms/CDs, and subscribe to 736 periodicals. Computerized library services include interlibrary loans and database searching. Special learning facilities include a learning resource center, art gallery, planetarium, radio station, museum, grist mill, weaving studio, airport, firehouse, print shop, orchid greenhouses, fruitcake/jelly kitchens, day care center, and 3 farm operations. The 1000-acre campus is in a small town 40 miles south of Springfield, adjacent to the resort town of Branson. Including residence halls, there are 82 buildings.

Programs of Study: C of O confers B.A. and B.S. degrees. Bachelor's degrees are awarded in AGRICULTURE (agriculture), BIOLOGICAL SCIENCE (biology/biological science), BUSINESS (accounting, business administration and management, and hotel/motel and restaurant management), COMMUNICATIONS AND THE ARTS (art, communications, English, French, German, music, Spanish, and theater design), COMPUTER AND PHYSICAL SCIENCE (chemistry, computer science, information sciences and systems, and mathematics), EDUCATION (art, elementary, foreign languages, industrial arts, middle school, physical, secondary, technical, and vocational), ENGINEERING AND ENVIRONMENTAL DESIGN (aviation computer technology, graphic arts technology, and preengineering), HEALTH PROFESSIONS (medical technology, nursing, prepharmacy, preveterinary science, and speech pathology/audiology), SOCIAL SCIENCE (criminal justice, dietetics, family/consumer studies, history, home economics, interdisciplinary studies, philosophy, political science/government, psychology, religion, and sociology). Business administration, sciences, and history are the strongest academically. Business administration is the largest.

Special: The college offers co-op programs, study abroad in the Netherlands, internships through numerous departments, preprofessional programs in nursing, medical technology, and engineering, a 3-2 engineering degree program, student-designed interdisciplinary majors, and credit for military experience. Pass/fail grading is allowed for proficiency exams. There are 4 national honor societies and 4 departmental honors programs.

Admissions: 18% of the 1999-2000 applicants were accepted. The ACT scores for the 1999-2000 freshman class were: 42% below 21, 32% between 21 and 23, 17% between 24 and 26, 6% between 27 and 28, and 3% above 28. 10 freshmen graduated first in their class.

Requirements: The SAT I or ACT is required. C of O prefers that applicants be in the upper 50% of their class. A GPA of 2.0 is required. Applicants must be graduates of accredited secondary schools or have earned a GED or have an ACT score of 19 or better. A physical exam, financial aid application, 2 recommendations (preferably from school personnel), and an interview are required. Applications are accepted on-line at the school's web site. AP and CLEP credits are accepted. Important factors in the admissions decision are leadership record, extracurricular activities record, and recommendations by school officials.

Procedure: Freshmen are admitted fall and spring. Entrance exams should be taken in October or December of the senior year. There are early decision and early admissions plans. Early decision applications should be filed by February 15; regular applications, by March 15 for fall entry. Notification of early decision is sent February; regular decision, in March. 200 early decision candidates were accepted for the 1999-2000 class. 5% of all applicants are on a waiting list.

Financial Aid: In 1999-2000, all students received some form of financial aid. 90% of all students received need-based aid. The average freshman award was $9886. Of that total, scholarships or need-based grants averaged $5500 ($7002 maximum); and work contracts averaged $2884 (maximum). All of undergraduates work part time. Average annual earnings from campus work are $2884. The average financial indebtedness of a recent graduate was $2211. The FAFSA is required. The fall application deadline is open.

Computers: There are 136 PCs. Various other campus departments have computers for classroom instruction and use. All students may access the system from 8 a.m. to 11 p.m. There are no time limits and no fees.

COLLEGE OF WILLIAM AND MARY
Williamsburg, VA 23187-8795

(757) 221-4223
Fax: (757) 221-1242

Full-time: 2293 men, 3111 women	**Faculty:** 453; I, av$
Part-time: 61 men, 87 women	**Ph.D.s:** 92%
Graduate: 992 men, 1009 women	**Student/Faculty:** 12 to 1
Year: semesters, summer session	**Tuition:** $4610 ($16,434)
Application Deadline: January 5	**Room & Board:** $4897
Freshman Class: 6878 applied, 3090 accepted, 1301 enrolled	
SAT I Verbal/Math: 660/660	**ACT:** 31 **MOST COMPETITIVE**

College of William and Mary, founded in 1693, is the second-oldest college in the United States. The public institution offers undergraduate degrees in the Arts and Sciences. Graduate programs are offered in arts and sciences, law, business, education, and marine science. There are 2 undergraduate and 5 graduate schools. In addition to regional accreditation, William and Mary has baccalaureate program accreditation with AACSB and NCATE. The 9 libraries contain 1.4 million volumes, 2.2 million microform items, and 27,116 audiovisual forms/CDs, and subscribe to 11,556 periodicals. Computerized library services include the card catalog, interlibrary loans, and database searching. Special learning facilities include a learning resource center, art gallery, radio station, anthropology museum, and art studio. The 1200-acre campus is in a small town 50 miles southeast of Richmond. Including residence halls, there are 166 buildings.

Programs of Study: William and Mary confers B.A., B.S., A.B., and B.B.A. degrees. Master's and doctoral degrees are also awarded. Bachelor's degrees are awarded in BIOLOGICAL SCIENCE (biology/biological science), BUSINESS (business administration and management), COMMUNICATIONS AND THE ARTS (classics, English, fine arts, French, German, music, Spanish, and speech/debate/rhetoric), COMPUTER AND PHYSICAL SCIENCE (chemistry, computer science, geology, mathematics, and physics), SOCIAL SCIENCE (American studies, anthropology, economics, history, interdisciplinary studies, international relations, international studies, philosophy, political science/government, psychology, religion, and sociology). Business, English, and biology are the largest.

Special: William and Mary offers 3-2 programs with Rensselaer Polytechnic Institute, Columbia University, Case Western Reserve University, and Washington University in St. Louis, and a forestry/environmental science program with Duke University. Also available are departmental internships, study abroad in more than 12 countries, dual and student-designed majors, a Washington semester, nondegree study, and pass/fail options. There are 3 national honor societies, including Phi Beta Kappa, a freshman honors program, and 19 departmental honors programs.

Admissions: 45% of the 1999-2000 applicants were accepted. The SAT I scores for the 1999-2000 freshman class were: Verbal--1% below 500, 16% between 500 and 599, 49% between 600 and 700, and 34% above 700; Math--2% below 500, 17% between 500 and 599, 55% between 600 and 700, and 26% above 700. The ACT scores were 14% between 27 and 28 and 86% above 28. 95% of the current freshmen were in the top fifth of their class; 100% were in the top two fifths. There were 48 National Merit finalists and 27 semifinalists. 76 freshmen graduated first in their class.

Requirements: The SAT I or ACT is required. An essay and 3 SAT II: Subject tests, including the test in writing, are strongly recommended. AP credits are accepted. Important factors in the admissions decision are advanced placement or honor courses, evidence of special talent, and extracurricular activities record.

Procedure: Freshmen are admitted fall and spring. Entrance exams should be taken in spring of the junior year or fall of the senior year. There are early decision, early admissions, and deferred admissions plans. Early decision applications should be filed by November 1; regular applications, by January 5 for fall entry and November 1 for spring entry, along with a $40 fee. Notification of early decision is sent December 1; regular decision, April 1. 381 early decision candidates were accepted for the 1999-2000 class. 22% of all applicants are on a waiting list.

Financial Aid: In 1999-2000, 60% of all freshmen and 55% of continuing students received some form of financial aid. 30% of all students received need-based aid. The average freshman award was $7410. Of that total, scholarships or need-based grants averaged $5306 ($13,480 maximum); loans averaged $2652 ($3625 maximum); and work contracts averaged $944 ($1200 maximum). 40% of undergraduates work part time. Average annual earnings from campus work are $1000. William and Mary is a member of CSS. The FAFSA is required. The fall application deadline is February 15.

Computers: The mainframe is an IBM 4381 Model T24 HDS 6660. There are 300 PCs located in 16 locations around campus. All dormitories are wired for Internet connection. All students may access the system. There are no time limits and no fees.

COLLEGE OF WOOSTER
Wooster, OH 44691

(330) 263-2270
(800) 877-9905; Fax: (330) 263-2621

Full-time: 799 men, 886 women	**Faculty:** 134; IIB, ++$
Part-time: 8 men, 16 women	**Ph.D.s:** 96%
Graduate: none	**Student/Faculty:** 13 to 1
Year: semesters, summer session	**Tuition:** $20,530
Application Deadline: February 15	**Room & Board:** $5420
Freshman Class: 2195 applied, 1735 accepted, 517 enrolled	
ACT: 26	**VERY COMPETITIVE+**

The College of Wooster, founded in 1866, is a liberal arts college. In addition to regional accreditation, Wooster has baccalaureate program accreditation with NASM. The library contains 650,538 volumes, 258,478 microform items, and 6745 audiovisual forms/CDs, and subscribes to 1254 periodicals. Computerized library services include the card catalog, interlibrary loans, and database searching. Special learning facilities include a learning resource center, art gallery, and radio station. The 320-acre campus is in a suburban area 54 miles south of Cleveland. Including residence halls, there are 37 buildings.

Programs of Study: Wooster confers B.A., B.Mus., and B.Mus.Ed. degrees. Bachelor's degrees are awarded in BIOLOGICAL SCIENCE (biochemistry and biology/biological science), BUSINESS (business economics), COMMUNICATIONS AND THE ARTS (communications, comparative literature, dramatic arts, English, fine arts, French, German, Greek (classical), Latin, music, and Spanish), COMPUTER AND PHYSICAL SCIENCE (chemistry, computer science, geology, mathematics, and physics), SOCIAL SCIENCE (African American studies, anthropology, area studies, economics, history, international relations, philosophy, political science/government, psychology, religion, Russian and Slavic studies, sociology, urban studies, and women's studies). History, chemistry, and English are the strongest academically. History, English, and biology are the largest.

Special: A 3-2 engineering degree is offered in conjunction with Case Western Reserve and Washington Universities. A B.A.-B.S. degree is offered in music/music education. Cross-registration is possible with off-campus programs of the Great Lakes Colleges Association. Internships are available in American politics in Washington, D.C., the Ohio State Legislature, and the U.S. State Department, as well as in professional theater and economics. Student-designed majors, double majors, study abroad, a Washington semester, nondegree study, and pass/fail options for a limited number of courses are available. All seniors participate in a 2-term independent-study project in the major. The student chooses the topic and works on a one-to-one basis with a faculty mentor. A sophomore research program is available by application. There are 12 national honor societies, including Phi Beta Kappa.

Admissions: 79% of the 1999-2000 applicants were accepted. The SAT I scores for the 1999-2000 freshman class were: Verbal--9% below 500, 41% between 500 and 599, 37% between 600 and 700, and 13% above 700; Math--11% below 500, 39% between 500 and 599, 39% between 600 and 700, and 11% above 700. The ACT scores were 1% between 12 and 17, 21% between 18 and 23, 62% between 24 and 29, and 15% above 29. 64% of the current freshmen were in the top 10% of their class; 95% were in the top half. There were 7 National Merit finalists. 19 freshmen graduated first in their class.

Requirements: The SAT I or ACT is required, with an SAT I composite score of 990 or an ACT minimum composite score of 20. In addition, applicants should be graduates of an accredited secondary school. The GED is accepted. Students should have completed a minimum of 16 high school academic credits. The school also requires an essay and recommends an interview. Applications are accepted on computer disk through Common Application and CollegeLink. AP credits are accepted. Important factors in the admissions decision are advanced placement or honor courses, recommendations by school officials, and leadership record.

Procedure: Freshmen are admitted fall and winter. Entrance exams should be taken in the fall of the senior year. There are early decision, early admissions, and deferred admissions plans. Early decision applications should be filed by December 1; regular applications, by February 15 for fall entry, along with a $35 fee. Notification of early decision is sent December 15; regular decision, April 1. 72 early decision candidates were accepted for the 1999-2000 class. 3% of all applicants are on a waiting list.

Financial Aid: In 1999-2000, 97% of all freshmen and 65% of continuing students received some form of financial aid. 70% of freshmen and 51% of continuing students received need-based aid. The average freshman award was $14,854. Of that total, scholarships or need-based grants averaged $12,770 ($19,150 maximum); loans averaged $5737 ($20,410 maximum); and work contracts averaged $1455 ($2490 maximum). 50% of undergraduates work part time. Average annual earnings from campus work are $850. The average financial indebtedness of the 1999 graduate was $15,800. Wooster is a member of CSS. The CSS/Profile and the college's own financial statement are required. The fall application deadline is February 15.

Computers: The mainframe is a DEC VAX 4500. File servers, laser printers, and other minicomputers are available on campus for student use. More than 500 PCs have been linked to WoosterNet, the campuswide local area network that provides computing capabilities 24 hours a day. Luce Residence Hall has a desktop publishing lab. All students may access the system any time. There are no time limits and no fees.

COLORADO COLLEGE
Colorado Springs, CO 80903

(719) 389-6344
(800) 542-7214; Fax: (719) 389-6816

Full-time: 861 men, 1074 women	**Faculty:** 166; IIB, ++$
Part-time: 3 men, 3 women	**Ph.D.s:** 97%
Graduate: 5 men, 18 women	**Student/Faculty:** 12 to 1
Year: see profile	**Tuition:** $21,822
Application Deadline: January 15	**Room & Board:** $5568
Freshman Class: 3519 applied, 1709 accepted, 504 enrolled	
SAT I or ACT: required	**HIGHLY COMPETITIVE**

Colorado College, founded in 1874, is an independent liberal arts institution. The academic year is based on the Block Plan, under which students take only 1 course during each of the eight 3-1/2-week-long blocks of study; there is also a 9-week 3-block summer session. There is 1 graduate school. In addition to regional accreditation, CC has baccalaureate program accreditation with NASM. The library contains 685,000 volumes, 102,000 microform items, and 18,900 audiovisual forms/CDs, and subscribes to 1178 periodicals. Computerized library services include the card catalog, interlibrary loans, and database searching. Special learning facilities include a learning resource center, art gallery, radio station, electronic music studio, writer's workbench, telescope dome, and foreign language video lab. The 90-acre campus is in a suburban area 70 miles south of Denver. Including residence halls, there are 52 buildings.

Programs of Study: CC confers the B.A. degree. Master's degrees are also awarded. Bachelor's degrees are awarded in BIOLOGICAL SCIENCE (biochemistry, biology/biological science, and neurosciences), COMMUNICATIONS AND THE ARTS (art history and appreciation, classics, comparative literature, dance, dramatic arts, English, French, German, music, romance languages and literature, Russian, Spanish, and studio art), COMPUTER AND PHYSICAL SCIENCE (chemistry, computer mathematics, geology, mathematics, and physics), ENGINEERING AND ENVIRONMENTAL DESIGN (environmental science), SOCIAL SCIENCE (anthropology, Asian/Oriental studies, economics, history, history of philosophy, liberal arts/general studies, philosophy, political science/government, psychology, religion, sociology, Southwest American studies, and women's studies). English, biology, and psychology are the largest.

Special: In addition to its modular schedule, CC offers co-op programs with Rush University for nursing, Manchester University in England, the universities of Regensburg and Gottingen in Germany, and the Kansai Gaidai in Japan. Internships, study abroad in 25 countries, a Washington semester, student-designed majors, a general studies degree, and pass/fail options are offered. A 3-2 engineering degree is offered with Columbia University, Rensselaer Polytechnic Institute, Washington University, and the University of Southern California. There are 3 national honor societies, including Phi Beta Kappa.

Admissions: 49% of the 1999-2000 applicants were accepted. The ACT scores for the 1999-2000 freshman class were: 8% between 21 and 23, 21% between 24 and 26, 20% between 27 and 28, and 48% above 28. 70% of the current freshmen were in the top fifth of their class; 89% were in the top two fifths. 38 freshmen graduated first in their class.

Requirements: The SAT I or ACT is required. Applicants should have completed at least 16 (18 to 20 recommended) high school academic credits. The GED is

145

accepted. An essay is required. Applications are accepted on-line via Embark. com, Commonapp.org, or nextstopcollege.cbreston.org. AP credits are accepted. Important factors in the admissions decision are advanced placement or honor courses, extracurricular activities record, and personality/intangible qualities.

Procedure: Freshmen are admitted fall, spring, and summer. Entrance exams should be taken by the fall of the senior year. There are early admissions and deferred admissions plans. Early decision applications should be filed by November 15; regular applications, by January 15 for fall entry and November 1 for spring entry, along with a $40 fee. Notification of early decision is sent January 1; regular decision, April 15. 5% of all applicants are on a waiting list.

Financial Aid: In 1999-2000, 47% of all freshmen and 56% of continuing students received some form of financial aid. 38% of freshmen and 48% of continuing students received need-based aid. The average freshman award was $18,446. Of that total, scholarships or need-based grants averaged $14,759 ($28,070 maximum); loans averaged $2708 ($6625 maximum); and work contracts averaged $975 ($1375 maximum). 38% of undergraduates work part time. Average annual earnings from campus work are $850. The average financial indebtedness of the 1999 graduate was $13,418. CC is a member of CSS. The CSS/Profile or FAFSA is required. The fall application deadline is February 15.

Computers: The mainframes are a Data General 8520 and a 4605, used for administrative purposes. Academic computing is supported by a distributed network of PCs and Macs. There are 116 machines in public labs and 161 in departmental labs. The local area network is 10/100 Mb with a Gb backbone. All students may access the system. There are no time limits and no fees. It is strongly recommended that all students have personal computers.

COLORADO SCHOOL OF MINES
Golden, CO 80401-1842 (303) 273-3220
(800) 446-9488; Fax: (303) 273-3509

Full-time: 1821 men, 581 women	**Faculty:** 150; I, -$
Part-time: 54 men, 17 women	**Ph.D.s:** 86%
Graduate: 562 men, 167 women	**Student/Faculty:** 16 to 1
Year: semesters, summer session	**Tuition:** $5211 ($15,311)
Application Deadline: June 1	**Room & Board:** $4920
Freshman Class: 1886 applied, 1502 accepted, 566 enrolled	
SAT I Verbal/Math: 590/650	**ACT:** 28 **VERY COMPETITIVE**

The Colorado School of Mines, founded in 1874, is a public institution offering programs in science, economics, and engineering. There is 1 graduate school. In addition to regional accreditation, CSM has baccalaureate program accreditation with ABET. The library contains 356,000 volumes and 236,000 microform items, and subscribes to 2700 periodicals. Computerized library services include the card catalog, interlibrary loans, and database searching. Special learning facilities include a geology museum. The 373-acre campus is in a small town 15 miles west of Denver. Including residence halls, there are 35 buildings.

Programs of Study: CSM confers the B.S. degree. Master's and doctoral degrees are also awarded. Bachelor's degrees are awarded in COMPUTER AND PHYSICAL SCIENCE (chemistry, mathematics, and physics), ENGINEERING AND ENVIRONMENTAL DESIGN (chemical engineering, engineering, geological engineering, geophysical engineering, metallurgical engineering, mining and mineral engineering, and petroleum/natural gas engineering), SOCIAL SCIENCE (economics). Chemical engineering, geological engineering, and petroleum engineering are the strongest academically. General engineering, chemical engineering, and mathematical and computing sciences are the largest.

Special: Co-op programs, internships in the humanities, accelerated degree programs in all majors, dual majors, study abroad in 7 countries, and nondegree study are offered. There is 1 national honor society, a freshman honors program, and 3 departmental honors programs.

Admissions: 80% of the 1999-2000 applicants were accepted. The SAT I scores for the 1999-2000 freshman class were: Verbal--8% below 500, 36% between 500 and 599, 46% between 600 and 700, and 10% above 700; Math--1% below 500, 24% between 500 and 599, 50% between 600 and 700, and 25% above 700. The ACT scores were 1% below 21, 9% between 21 and 23, 19% between 24 and 26, 41% between 27 and 28, and 30% above 28. 82% of the current freshmen were in the top fifth of their class; all were in the top two fifths. 57 freshmen graduated first in their class.

Requirements: The SAT I or ACT is required. CSM requires applicants to be in the upper 33% of their class. Applicants must be graduates of an accredited secondary school. The GED is accepted. Students should have completed 16 high school academic credits, including 4 credits each of English and math, 3 of science, 2 of social studies, and 3 academic electives. Applications are accepted on computer disk via CollegeLink, Apply 2000, and Peterson's uniform application, and are accepted on-line via CSM's web site. AP credits are accepted. Important factors in the admissions decision are advanced placement or honor courses, leadership record, and recommendations by school officials.

Procedure: Freshmen are admitted to all sessions. Entrance exams should be taken late in the junior year or early in the senior year. There is a deferred admissions plan. Applications should be filed by June 1 for fall entry, December 1 for spring entry, and June 10 for summer entry, along with a $25 fee. Notification is sent on a rolling basis.

Financial Aid: In 1999-2000, 85% of all students received some form of financial aid. 70% of all students received need-based aid. The average freshman award was $9500. Of that total, scholarships or need-based grants averaged $4760 ($10,000 maximum); loans averaged $4970 ($6600 maximum); and work contracts averaged $750 ($1000 maximum). 70% of undergraduates work part time. Average annual earnings from campus work are $750. The average financial indebtedness of the 1999 graduate was $17,500. CSM is a member of CSS. The FAFSA and the college's own financial statement are required. The fall application deadline is March 1.

Computers: The mainframe is an IBM RS/6000 systems running AIX. Students can use all public computer systems managed by the CSM Computing Center. This includes central UNIX servers, UNIX workstations, PCs, terminals, and special devices. About 150 systems of various types are available in public (campus) access labs. In addition, many departments have computer labs for use by students in that department. Students can dial in to the campus system and the Internet to access many resources. All residence hall rooms are wired for direct access to the campus network. All students may access the system. Dial-in access and direct network connection is available any time. Computer labs are open 7 a.m. to midnight Monday to Thursday, 7 a.m. to 6 p.m. on Friday, 9 a.m. to 5:30 p.m. on Saturday, and 9 a.m. to midnight on Sunday. There are no time limits and no fees.

COLORADO STATE UNIVERSITY
Fort Collins, CO 80523-0015

(970) 491-6909
Fax: (970) 491-7799

Full-time: 8035 men, 8666 women	**Faculty:** 979; I, av$
Part-time: 1056 men, 1043 women	**Ph.D.s:** 92%
Graduate: 1898 men, 2084 women	**Student/Faculty:** 17 to 1
Year: semesters, summer session	**Tuition:** $3062 ($10,748)
Application Deadline: July 1	**Room & Board:** $5022
Freshman Class: 9844 applied, 8104 accepted, 3137 enrolled	
SAT I Verbal/Math: 560/550	**ACT:** 24 **VERY COMPETITIVE**

Colorado State University, founded in 1870 and part of the Colorado State University system, is a public, land-grant institution, offering 70 undergraduate majors. There are 8 undergraduate and 1 graduate school. In addition to regional accreditation, Colorado State has baccalaureate program accreditation with AACSB, ABET, ACCE, ACEJMC, ADA, ASLA, CSWE, FIDER, NASM, NCATE, NRPA, and SAF. The 4 libraries contain 1,803,493 volumes, 2,453,704 microform items, and 6935 audiovisual forms/CDs, and subscribe to 20,496 periodicals. Computerized library services include the card catalog, interlibrary loans, and database searching. Special learning facilities include a learning resource center, art gallery, radio station, TV station, enviornmental learning center, and plant environmental research center. The 666-acre campus is in a suburban area in Fort Collins, 65 miles north of Denver. Including residence halls, there are 100 buildings.

Programs of Study: Colorado State confers B.A., B.S., B.F.A., and B.M. degrees. Master's and doctoral degrees are also awarded. Bachelor's degrees are awarded in AGRICULTURE (agricultural business management, agricultural economics, agronomy, animal science, equine science, fishing and fisheries, forestry and related sciences, horticulture, natural resource management, and range/farm management), BIOLOGICAL SCIENCE (biochemistry, biology/biological science, botany, microbiology, nutrition, wildlife biology, and zoology), BUSINESS (accounting, apparel and accessories marketing, banking and finance, business administration and management, hotel/motel and restaurant management, marketing/retailing/merchandising, and recreational facilities management), COMMUNICATIONS AND THE ARTS (art, English, French, German, journalism, music, performing arts, Spanish, speech/debate/rhetoric, and technical and business writing), COMPUTER AND PHYSICAL SCIENCE (chemistry, computer science, geology, information sciences and systems, mathematics, physical sciences, physics, and statistics), EDUCATION (agricultural, home economics, and physical), ENGINEERING AND ENVIRONMENTAL DESIGN (agricultural engineering, chemical engineering, civil engineering, construction management, electrical/electronics engineering, engineering and applied science, industrial engineering technology, interior design, landscape architecture/design, and mechanical engineering), HEALTH PROFESSIONS (environmental health science and occupational therapy), SOCIAL SCIENCE (anthropology, economics, history, home economics, human development, liberal arts/general studies, philosophy, political science/government, psychology, social work, sociology, and water resources). Natural resources, biochemistry, and occupational therapy are the strongest academically. Psychology, biological sciences, and art are the largest.

Special: Colorado State offers co-op programs with Metropolitan State College and Universidad Autonoma in Mexico and participates in cross-registration with AIMS Community College. Study abroad in more than 30 countries, a semester at sea, work-study programs, internships, B.A.-B.S. degrees, and pass/fail options are available. Teaching certification students receive a bachelor's degree in their chosen subject and also complete a certification sequence through the School of Education. There are 43 national honor societies, including Phi Beta Kappa, a freshman honors program, and 1 departmental honors program. All departments have honors program.

Admissions: 82% of the 1999-2000 applicants were accepted. The SAT I scores for the 1999-2000 freshman class were: Verbal--24% below 500, 50% between 500 and 599, 23% between 600 and 700, and 4% above 700; Math--21% below 500, 46% between 500 and 599, 28% between 600 and 700, and 5% above 700. The ACT scores were 13% below 21, 31% between 21 and 23, 32% between 24 and 26, 14% between 27 and 28, and 11% above 28. 48% of the current freshmen were in the top fifth of their class; 82% were in the top two fifths. There were 14 National Merit finalists and 9 semifinalists. 103 freshmen graduated first in their class.

Requirements: The SAT I or ACT is required. The average freshman has a composite SAT I score of 1114 and an ACT composite of 24. Graduation from secondary school is required. The GED is accepted. Students should have completed 18 high school credits, 15 of which are academic credits, including 4 years of English, 3 of math algebra I, geometry;, algebra II, 2 of natural science, 2 of social science, and 1 additional year of natural or social science. An essay is recommended. Applications are accepted on-line through the World Wide Web. AP and CLEP credits are accepted. Important factors in the admissions decision are advanced placement or honor courses, leadership record, and recommendations by school officials.

Procedure: Freshmen are admitted to all sessions. Entrance exams should be taken during the junior year or early fall of the senior year. There is an early admissions plan. Applications should be filed by July 1 for fall entry and December 1 for spring entry, along with a $30 fee. Notification is sent on a rolling basis.

Financial Aid: In 1999-2000, 54% of all freshmen and 66% of continuing students received some form of financial aid. 38% of freshmen and 48% of continuing students received need-based aid. The average freshman award was $6200. Of that total, scholarships or need-based grants averaged $1000; loans averaged $3000; and work contracts averaged $2200. 24% of undergraduates work part time. Average annual earnings from campus work are $2200. The average financial indebtedness of the 1999 graduate was $16,253. The FAFSA is required. The fall application deadline is March 1.

Computers: The mainframes are an IBM 9672 Model R22, 4 IBM/6000 servers (production servers), and 4 additional network servers. There are numerous student computer labs on campus, including some in residence halls, dial-up modems, and access to the Internet. Every residence hall room has high-speed Internet access. All students may access the system 24 hours a day. There are no time limits and no fees.

COLUMBIA UNIVERSITY/COLUMBIA COLLEGE

New York, NY 10027   **(212) 854-2522; Fax: (212) 854-1209**

Full-time: 1908 men, 2005 women	**Faculty:** 632; I, ++$
Part-time: none	**Ph.D.s:** 100%
Graduate: none	**Student/Faculty:** 6 to 1
Year: semesters, summer session	**Tuition:** $24,974
Application Deadline: January 1	**Room & Board:** $7732
Freshman Class: 13,013 applied, 1767 accepted, 964 enrolled	
SAT I or ACT: required	**MOST COMPETITIVE**

Columbia College of Columbia University, founded in 1754, is a private college offering programs in the liberal arts. There are 2 undergraduate schools. The library subscribes to 66,000 periodicals. Computerized library services include the card catalog and interlibrary loans. Special learning facilities include an art gallery, planetarium, radio station, TV station, geological research center, and the Nevis Laboratory Center for study of high energy particle physics. The 36-acre campus is in an urban area in New York City. Including residence halls, there are 37 buildings.

Programs of Study: Columbia confers the A.B. degree. Bachelor's degrees are awarded in BIOLOGICAL SCIENCE (biochemistry, biology/biological science, biophysics, and neurosciences), COMMUNICATIONS AND THE ARTS (art history and appreciation, classics, comparative literature, dance, dramatic arts, English, film arts, French, German, Germanic languages and literature, Greek, Latin, music, Russian, Spanish, and visual and performing arts), COMPUTER AND PHYSICAL SCIENCE (astronomy, astrophysics, chemistry, computer science, earth science, geochemistry, geology, geophysics and seismology, mathematics, physics, and statistics), ENGINEERING AND ENVIRONMENTAL DESIGN (architecture and environmental science), SOCIAL SCIENCE (African American studies, anthropology, archeology, Asian/Oriental studies, classical/ancient civilization, East Asian studies, economics, Hispanic American studies, history, Italian studies, Latin American studies, medieval studies, Middle Eastern studies, philosophy, political science/government, psychology, religion, Russian and Slavic studies, sociology, urban studies, and women's studies). English, history, and political science are the largest.

Special: There is a co-op program with Oxford and Cambridge Universities in England and the Kyoto Center for Japanese Studies in Japan, and cross-registration with the Juilliard School and Barnard College. Combined B.A.-B.S. degrees are offered via 3-2 or 4-1 engineering programs. There is also a 5-year B.A./M.I.A. with Columbia's School of International and Public Affairs. The college offers study abroad in France, work-study, internships, credit by exam, pass/fail options, and dual, student-designed, and interdisciplinary majors including regional studies and ancient studies. There is a chapter of Phi Beta Kappa.

Admissions: 14% of the 1999-2000 applicants were accepted. 83% of the current freshmen were in the top tenth of their class; 93% were in the top fifth.

Requirements: The SAT I or ACT and 3 SAT II: Subject tests, one of which must be writing, are required. A GED is accepted. Students should prepare with 4 years of English and 3 or 4 years each of foreign language, history and social studies, math, and lab science. An essay is required, and an interview is recommended. 2 academic faculty recommendations and a written evaluation or recommendation from a school official are also required. AP credits are accepted. Important factors in the admissions decision are advanced placement or honor courses, recommendations by school officials, and leadership record.

Procedure: Freshmen are admitted in the fall. Entrance exams should be taken in the summer of the junior year or fall of the senior year. There are early decision, early admissions, and deferred admissions plans. Early decision applications should be filed by November 1; regular applications, by January 1 for fall entry, along with a $50 fee. Notification is sent March 31. 4% of all applicants are on a waiting list.

Financial Aid: Columbia awards assistance only to students who demonstrate financial need. In a recent year, 49% of all freshmen and 50% of continuing students received need-based aid. The average freshman award was $21,143. Of that total, scholarships or need-based grants averaged $15,834. Columbia is a member of CSS. The CSS/Profile or FAFSA, the college's own financial statement, federal tax returns, and the business/farm supplement and/or the divorced/separated parents statement if applicable are required. Check with the school for current deadlines.

Computers: The mainframes are comprised of 3 Sun 4/280s, a DEC VAX 8700, and an IBM 4341. There are computer labs and stand-alone terminals throughout the campus and computer clusters in residence halls. Every dorm room has an Ethernet connection. All students may access the system and extra time can be bought.

COLUMBIA UNIVERSITY/FU FOUNDATION SCHOOL OF ENGINEERING AND APPLIED SCIENCE
New York, NY 10027   (212) 854-2521; Fax: (212) 854-1209

Full-time: 910 men, 338 women	**Faculty:** 108; I, ++$
Part-time: none	**Ph.D.s:** 100%
Graduate: none	**Student/Faculty:** 12 to 1
Year: semesters	**Tuition:** $24,974
Application Deadline: January 1	**Room & Board:** $7732
Freshman Class: 2293 applied, 661 accepted, 319 enrolled	
SAT I or ACT: required	**MOST COMPETITIVE**

The Fu Foundation School of Engineering and Applied Science of Columbia University, founded in 1864, offers undergraduate and graduate degree programs in engineering. In addition to regional accreditation, Columbia Engineering has baccalaureate program accreditation with ABET. The library subscribes to 66,000 periodicals. Computerized library services include the card catalog, interlibrary loans, and database searching. Special learning facilities include an art gallery, planetarium, radio station, and TV station. The 32-acre campus is in an urban area in New York City.

Programs of Study: Columbia Engineering confers the B.S. degree. Master's and doctoral degrees are also awarded. Bachelor's degrees are awarded in BUSINESS (operations research), COMPUTER AND PHYSICAL SCIENCE (applied mathematics, applied physics, and computer science), ENGINEERING AND ENVIRONMENTAL DESIGN (biomedical engineering, chemical engineering, civil engineering, computer engineering, electrical/electronics engineering, engineering management, engineering mechanics, geological engineering, industrial engineering technology, materials science, mechanical engineering, metallurgical engineering, and mining and mineral engineering). Computer science, electrical engineering, and mechanical engineering are the largest.

Special: Students may study at Columbia College or any of more than 90 other liberal arts colleges throughout the country in a 5-year program leading to the combined B.A.-B.S. degree. There is cross-registration with Barnard College,

Teacher's College, and the Juilliard School. The school offers study abroad, internships, work-study, and pass/fail options. There is a chapter of Phi Beta Kappa.

Admissions: 29% of the 1999-2000 applicants were accepted. 84% of the current freshmen were in the top tenth of their class; 94% were in the top fifth.

Requirements: The SAT I or ACT is required, as are SAT II: Subject tests in mathematics I or II, chemistry or physics, and writing. Applicants must be graduates of an accredited secondary school with a recommended 4 years of English, 3 or 4 of history and social studies, 2 or 3 of a foreign language, 1 each of physics and chemistry, and math courses through calculus. Also required are a written evaluation or recommendation from a college adviser or guidance counselor and 2 recommendations from teachers of academic classroom subjects (1 from a teacher of math). An essay is required, and an interview is recommended. AP credits are accepted. Important factors in the admissions decision are advanced placement or honor courses, evidence of special talent, and extracurricular activities record.

Procedure: Freshmen are admitted in the fall. Entrance exams should be taken in the spring of the junior year and/or fall of the senior year. There are early decision and deferred admissions plans. Early decision applications should be filed by November 1; regular applications, by January 1 for fall entry, along with a $50 fee. Notification is sent March 31. A waiting list is an active part of the admissions procedure.

Financial Aid: Columbia awards assistance only to students who demonstrate financial need. In a recent year, 59% of all freshmen and 60% of continuing students received need-based aid. The average freshman award was $21,574. Of that total, scholarships or need-based grants averaged $16,127. Columbia Engineering is a member of CSS. The CSS/Profile or FAFSA and the school's own financial statement are required. Check with the school for current deadlines.

Computers: The mainframes are comprised of a Prime, 13 DEC VAX 11/750s, 3 AT&T 3B20s, 75 AT&T 3B2 supermicros, an HP 9050, a system of HP 9900s, 2 IRIS computers, and an IBM Interactive Graphics Lab. There are also PCs available in labs and classrooms. Academic buildings and residence halls are wired to the campus network. There is a high-speed modem pool for off-campus access. Every residence hall room has an Ethernet connection. All students may access the system 24 hours a day. There are no time limits and no fees.

COLUMBIA UNIVERSITY/SCHOOL OF GENERAL STUDIES
New York, NY 10027   (212) 854-2772; Fax: (212) 854-6316

Full-time: 260 men, 291 women	**Faculty:** n/av
Part-time: 252 men, 342 women	**Ph.D.s:** n/av
Graduate: n/av	**Student/Faculty:** n/av
Year: semesters, summer session	**Tuition:** $24,389
Application Deadline: July 1	**Room & Board:** $10,000
Freshman Class: 784 applied, 307 accepted, 239 enrolled	
SAT I or ACT: recommended	**VERY COMPETITIVE**

The School of General Studies of Columbia University, founded in 1947, offers liberal arts degree programs and postgraduate studies for adult men and women whose post-high school education has been interrupted or postponed by at least 1 year. The 22 Columbia Unioversity libraries contain more than 6 million volumes. Computerized library services include the card catalog, interlibrary loans, and database searching. Special learning facilities include a learning resource center, art gallery, and radio station. The campus is in an urban area on the upper west side of Manhattan in New York City.

Programs of Study: GS confers B.A. and B.S. degrees. Master's and doctoral degrees are also awarded. Bachelor's degrees are awarded in BIOLOGICAL SCIENCE (biology/biological science), COMMUNICATIONS AND THE ARTS (art history and appreciation, classics, comparative literature, dance, dramatic arts, English literature, film arts, French, German, Italian, literature, music, Slavic languages, Spanish, and visual and performing arts), COMPUTER AND PHYSICAL SCIENCE (applied mathematics, astronomy, chemistry, computer science, geoscience, mathematics, physics, and statistics), ENGINEERING AND ENVIRONMENTAL DESIGN (architecture and environmental science), SOCIAL SCIENCE (African American studies, anthropology, archeology, classical/ancient civilization, East Asian studies, economics, French studies, German area studies, Hispanic American studies, history, Italian studies, Latin American studies, Middle Eastern studies, philosophy, political science/government, psychology, religion, sociology, urban studies, and women's studies).

Special: Preprofessional studies in allied health and medical fields and interdisciplinary majors, minors, and concentrations are offered. Internships in New York City, work-study programs on campus, study abroad, a 3-2 engineering degree at Columbia University School of Engineering and Applied Science, B.A.-B.S. degrees, and dual majors are available. There is a chapter of Phi Beta Kappa.

Admissions: 39% of the 1999-2000 applicants were accepted.

Requirements: The SAT I or ACT is recommended. A GPA of 2.5 is required. SAT I, ACT, or Columbia's General Studies Admissions Exam scores should be submitted along with high school and all college transcripts. An autobiographical statement is required. An interview is encouraged. Applications are accepted online at the school's web site. AP credits are accepted. Important factors in the admissions decision are advanced placement or honor courses, personality/intangible qualities, and evidence of special talent.

Procedure: Freshmen are admitted to all sessions. Entrance exams should be taken as early as possible. Applications should be filed by July 1 for fall entry, November 15 for spring entry, and April 1 for summer entry, along with a $50 fee. Notification is sent on a rolling basis.

Financial Aid: In 1999-2000, 75% of all freshmen received some form of financial aid. 25% of freshmen and 30% of continuing students received need-based aid. The average freshman award was $2100. Of that total, scholarships or need-based grants averaged $4000 ($8500 maximum); and work contracts averaged $2500 ($5000 maximum). 75% of undergraduates work part time. Average annual earnings from campus work are $2500. The average financial indebtedness of the 1999 graduate was $30,000. GS is a member of CSS. The FAFSA and the college's own financial statement are required. The fall application deadline is May 30.

Computers: The mainframe is an IBM. Computer accounts allow access to the Internet, E-mail, commercial news wires, labs, and on-line services. All students may access the system. Students may access the system 1 hour. The school strongly recommends that students have their own personal computer.

COLUMBUS COLLEGE OF ART AND DESIGN
Columbus, OH 43215   (614) 224-9101; Fax: (614) 222-4040

Full-time: 699 men, 569 women	**Faculty:** 75
Part-time: 166 men, 263 women	**Ph.D.s:** 47%
Graduate: none	**Student/Faculty:** 17 to 1
Year: semesters, summer session	**Tuition:** $13,730
Application Deadline: open	**Room & Board:** $6000
Freshman Class: 665 applied, 482 accepted, 341 enrolled	
SAT I Verbal/Math: 540/510	**ACT:** 23 **SPECIAL**

Columbus College of Art & Design, founded in 1879, is a private institution offering undergraduate programs in art and fine arts. In addition to regional accreditation, CCAD has baccalaureate program accreditation with NASAD. The library contains 41,396 volumes and 13,475 microform items, and subscribes to 254 periodicals. Computerized library services include the card catalog and database searching. Special learning facilities include a learning resource center, and an art gallery. The 17-acre campus is in an urban area in Columbus. Including residence halls, there are 15 buildings.

Programs of Study: CCAD confers the B.F.A. degree. Bachelor's degrees are awarded in COMMUNICATIONS AND THE ARTS (advertising, fine arts, graphic design, illustration, industrial design, and media arts), ENGINEERING AND ENVIRONMENTAL DESIGN (interior design), SOCIAL SCIENCE (fashion design and technology). Illustration and advertising design are the largest.

Special: Cross-registration is offered with Franklin, Ohio State, and Capital Universities; Ohio Dominican, Otterbein, and Pontifical Colleges; and Columbus State Community College, Mount Carmel College of Nursing, and DeVry Institute of Technology. Internships are available, as are on-campus work-study, dual majors, and nondegree study.

Admissions: 72% of the 1999-2000 applicants were accepted. The SAT I scores for the 1999-2000 freshman class were: Verbal--38% below 500, 44% between 500 and 599, and 18% between 600 and 700; Math--55% below 500, 27% between 500 and 599, 17% between 600 and 700, and 1% above 700. The ACT scores were 48% below 21, 23% between 21 and 23, 19% between 24 and 26, 5% between 27 and 28, and 5% above 28.

Requirements: The SAT I or ACT is recommended. A GPA of 2.0 is required. Applicants should be graduates of an accredited secondary school or have the GED. A portfolio of artwork indicative of abilities must be submitted. An interview is advised. AP credits are accepted. Important factors in the admissions decision are evidence of special talent, recommendations by school officials, and recommendations by alumni.

Procedure: Freshmen are admitted fall and winter. Application deadlines are open. There is a $25 fee. Notification is sent on a rolling basis.

Financial Aid: In 1999-2000, 72% of all freshmen and 85% of continuing students received some form of financial aid. 60% of freshmen and 80% of continuing students received need-based aid. The average freshman award was $6105. Of that total, scholarships or need-based grants averaged $3000; loans averaged $2625; and work contracts averaged $1563. 53% of undergraduates work part time. Average annual earnings from campus work are $3126. The average financial indebtedness of the 1999 graduate was $21,730. CCAD is a member of CSS. The FAFSA and the college's own financial statement are required. The fall application deadline is April 3.

Computers: There are 115 computers available for student use. The 3 computer systems include Mac Desktop Publishing, Mac CADD, and SGIs. All students may access the system during scheduled lab hours and class time. There are no time limits. Fees vary.

CONCORDIA COLLEGE/MOORHEAD
Moorhead, MN 56562

(218) 299-3004 (collect)
(800) 699-9897; Fax: (218) 299-3947

Full-time: 1031 men, 1781 women	**Faculty:** 183
Part-time: 40 men, 66 women	**Ph.D.s:** 72%
Graduate: none	**Student/Faculty:** 15 to 1
Year: semesters, summer session	**Tuition:** $13,340
Application Deadline: open	**Room & Board:** $3760
Freshman Class: 2112 applied, 1854 accepted, 793 enrolled	
SAT I Verbal/Math: 580/580	**ACT:** 24 **VERY COMPETITIVE**

Concordia College, founded in 1891, is a private, liberal arts institution affiliated with the Evangelical Lutheran Church in America. In addition to regional accreditation, Concordia has baccalaureate program accreditation with ADA, CSWE, NASM, NCATE, and NLN. The library contains 300,000 volumes, 43,296 microform items, and 11,048 audiovisual forms/CDs, and subscribes to 1463 periodicals. Computerized library services include the card catalog, interlibrary loans, and database searching. Special learning facilities include a learning resource center, art gallery, radio station, TV station, and an observatory. The 120-acre campus is in an urban area 240 miles northwest of Minneapolis and St. Paul. Including residence halls, there are 36 buildings.

Programs of Study: Concordia confers B.A. and B.M. degrees. Bachelor's degrees are awarded in BIOLOGICAL SCIENCE (biology/biological science), BUSINESS (accounting, business administration and management, international business management, and office supervision and management), COMMUNICATIONS AND THE ARTS (advertising, apparel design, art history and appreciation, classical languages, communications, creative writing, dramatic arts, English, French, German, journalism, Latin, literature, music, music performance, public relations, Spanish, speech/debate/rhetoric, and studio art), COMPUTER AND PHYSICAL SCIENCE (chemistry, computer science, mathematics, and physics), EDUCATION (art, business, elementary, foreign languages, health, home economics, middle school, music, physical, science, secondary, and social studies), ENGINEERING AND ENVIRONMENTAL DESIGN (environmental science and preengineering), HEALTH PROFESSIONS (health, health care administration, medical laboratory technology, nursing, predentistry, premedicine, and preveterinary science), SOCIAL SCIENCE (dietetics, economics, family/consumer studies, history, humanities, international relations, ministries, philosophy, political science/government, prelaw, psychology, religion, Russian and Slavic studies, Scandinavian studies, social work, and sociology). Premedicine, prelaw, and math are the strongest academically. Business administration, communications, and biology are the largest.

Special: Cross-registration is offered through the Tri-College University Consortium. Co-op programs and internships are available in most majors, and accelerated degree programs and dual majors are available in all majors. There is a Washington semester and an urban studies semester in Chicago. Study abroad in more than 30 countries, on- and off-campus work-study, a B.A.-B.M. degree in music, and 3-2 and 2-2 engineering degrees with Washington and North Dakota State universities and the University of Minnesota are possible. Nondegree study for special students and pass/fail options are also available. There are 10 national honor societies, a freshman honors program, and 11 departmental honors programs.

Admissions: 88% of the 1999-2000 applicants were accepted. The SAT I scores for the 1999-2000 freshman class were: Verbal--17% below 500, 39% between 500 and 599, 38% between 600 and 700, and 7% above 700; Math--19% below 500, 38% between 500 and 599, 40% between 600 and 700, and 3% above 700. The ACT scores were 21% below 21, 26% between 21 and 23, 25% between 24 and 26, 16% between 27 and 28, and 12% above 28. 49% of the current freshmen were in the top fifth of their class; 78% were in the top two fifths. There were 5 National Merit finalists and 5 semifinalists.

Requirements: The SAT I or ACT is required. 2 character references are required, and an interview is recommended. The GED is accepted. Academic performance and preparation, as evidenced in a high school transcript, is the single most important factor in the admissions decision. Applications are accepted on disk or on-line via the college's home page on the web or through CollegeLink. AP and CLEP credits are accepted. Important factors in the admissions decision are recommendations by school officials, advanced placement or honor courses, and personality/intangible qualities.

Procedure: Freshmen are admitted to all sessions. Entrance exams should be taken by the first semester of the senior year. There are early admissions and deferred admissions plans. Application deadlines are open. The fee is $20. Notification is sent on a rolling basis. A waiting list is an active part of the admissions procedure.

Financial Aid: In 1999-2000, 85% of all freshmen and 87% of continuing students received some form of financial aid. 70% of all students received need-based aid. The average freshman award was $11,611. Of that total, scholarships or need-based grants averaged $6835 ($16,860 maximum); loans averaged $4903 ($18,500 maximum); and work contracts averaged $1136 ($3000 maximum). 52% of undergraduates work part time. Average annual earnings from campus work are $1058. The average financial indebtedness of the 1999 graduate was $18,135. Concordia is a member of CSS. The FAFSA and the college's own financial statement are required.

Computers: The mainframe is a Unisys A2400 Model 311. IBM and Mac PCs are available in 16 computer labs on campus and in each residence hall. All students are assigned an E-mail account and have access to about 265 computers, all of which have Internet access. All students may access the system 20 to 24 hours per day. There are no time limits and no fees.

CONNECTICUT COLLEGE
New London, CT 06320-4196

(860) 439-2200
Fax: (860) 439-4301

Full-time: 716 men, 934 women	**Faculty:** 161; IIB, ++$
Part-time: 41 men, 73 women	**Ph.D.s:** 97%
Graduate: 15 men, 41 women	**Student/Faculty:** 10 to 1
Year: semesters	**Tuition:** $30,595
Application Deadline: January 1	**Room & Board:** See Profile
Freshman Class: 3700 applied, 1454 accepted, 477 enrolled	
SAT I Verbal/Math: 640/630	**ACT:** 26 **HIGHLY COMPETITIVE**

Connecticut College, founded in 1911, is a private institution offering degree programs in the liberal arts and sciences. Tuition and room and board are combined in a comprehensive fee. The library contains 475,489 volumes, 279,453 microform items, and 18,700 audiovisual forms/CDs, and subscribes to 2467 periodicals. Computerized library services include the card catalog, interlibrary loans, and database searching. Special learning facilities include a radio station and an arboretum. The 702-acre campus is in a small town midway between Boston and New York City. Including residence halls, there are 51 buildings.

Programs of Study: Connecticut College confers the B.A. degree. Master's degrees are also awarded. Bachelor's degrees are awarded in BIOLOGICAL SCIENCE (biochemistry, biology/biological science, botany, and zoology), COMMUNICATIONS AND THE ARTS (art history and appreciation, Chinese, classics, dance, dramatic arts, English, French, German, Japanese, languages, music, and studio art), COMPUTER AND PHYSICAL SCIENCE (chemistry, mathematics, and physics), SOCIAL SCIENCE (anthropology, Asian/Oriental studies, child psychology/development, economics, Hispanic American studies, history, international relations, philosophy, political science/government, psychology, religion, sociology, and urban studies). Government, history, and psychology are the largest.

Special: Cross-registration with area colleges, internships in government, human services, and other fields, a Washington semester at American University, dual majors, student-designed majors, a 3-2 engineering degree with Washington University in St. Louis and Boston University, nondegree study, and satisfactory/unsatisfactory options are available. One third of the junior class studies abroad. An international studies certificate program is available, which combines competency in a foreign language, an internship, and study abroad. There are 3 national honor societies, including Phi Beta Kappa.

Admissions: 39% of the 1999-2000 applicants were accepted. The SAT I scores for the 1999-2000 freshman class were: Verbal--3% below 500, 24% between 500 and 599, 52% between 600 and 700, and 21% above 700; Math--4% below 500, 23% between 500 and 599, 56% between 600 and 700, and 17% above 700. The ACT scores were 19% between 21 and 23, 37% between 24 and 26, 18% between 27 and 28, and 26% above 28. 83% of the current freshmen were in the top fifth of their class; 99% were in the top two fifths. There were 2 National Merit semifinalists. 11 freshmen graduated first in their class.

Requirements: The SAT II: Subject tests or the ACT is required. In addition, applicants must be graduates of an accredited secondary school. An essay is required and an interview is recommended. AP credits are accepted. Important factors in the admissions decision are advanced placement or honor courses, leadership record, and evidence of special talent.

Procedure: Freshmen are admitted fall and spring. There are early decision and deferred admissions plans. Early decision applications should be filed by November 15; regular applications, by January 1 for fall entry and December 1 for spring entry, along with a $50 fee. Notification of early decision is sent December 15; regular decision, April 1. 173 early decision candidates were accepted for the 1999-2000 class. 25% of all applicants are on a waiting list.

Financial Aid: In 1999-2000, 48% of all freshmen and 50% of continuing students received some form of financial aid, inluding need-based aid. The average freshman award was $20,158. Of that total, scholarships or need-based grants averaged $18,056 ($32,965 maximum); loans averaged $3125 (maximum); and work contracts averaged $1000 (maximum). 63% of undergraduates work part time. Average annual earnings from campus work are $687. The average financial indebtedness of the 1999 graduate was $15,669. Connecticut College is a member of CSS. The CSS/Profile, FAFSA, and parent and student tax forms are required. The fall application deadline is January 15.

Computers: The mainframes are a DEC MicroVAX 3900, a DEC System 5500, and a DEC ALPHA Server. There are 3 public terminal rooms for the mainframe system. Macs and IBM PCs are available for student use in computer labs and individual departments. Laser printers, plotters, and scanners are also available. A campuswide network links computer clusters, classrooms, labs, dormitory rooms, and the library with voice data and video transmission capabilities. The Internet is also available. All students may access the system 24 hours a day. There are no time limits and no fees.

CONVERSE COLLEGE
Spartanburg, SC 29302

(864) 596-9041
(800) 766-1125; Fax: (864) 596-9225

Full-time: 661 women	**Faculty:** 71
Part-time: 94 women	**Ph.D.s:** 75%
Graduate: 106 men, 653 women	**Student/Faculty:** 11 to 1
Year: 4-1-4, summer session	**Tuition:** $15,230
Application Deadline: August 15	**Room & Board:** $4645
Freshman Class: 622 applied, 477 accepted, 144 enrolled	
SAT I Verbal/Math: 560/550	**ACT:** 22 **VERY COMPETITIVE**

Converse College, founded in 1889, is a private, women's liberal arts college. Some of the information in this profile is approximate. Men are admitted to the graduate programs. There are 2 undergraduate and 2 graduate schools. In addition to regional accreditation, Converse College has baccalaureate program accreditation with NASM. The library contains 150,000 volumes, 310 microform items, and 12,000 audiovisual forms/CDs, and subscribes to 700 periodicals. Computerized library services include the card catalog, interlibrary loans, and database searching. Special learning facilities include a learning resource center, art gallery, and natural history museum. The 72-acre campus is in an urban area 80 miles southwest of Charlotte. Including residence halls, there are 27 buildings.

Programs of Study: Converse College confers B.A., B.S., B.F.A., and B.Mus. degrees. Master's degrees are also awarded. Bachelor's degrees are awarded in BIOLOGICAL SCIENCE (biology/biological science), BUSINESS (accounting and business administration and management), COMMUNICATIONS AND THE ARTS (English, fine arts, French, languages, modern language, music, and Spanish), COMPUTER AND PHYSICAL SCIENCE (chemistry, computer science, and mathematics), EDUCATION (art, early childhood, elementary, foreign languages, music, science, and secondary), ENGINEERING AND ENVIRONMENTAL DESIGN (interior design), HEALTH PROFESSIONS (art therapy, predentistry, and premedicine), SOCIAL SCIENCE (economics, history, political science/government, prelaw, psychology, religion, and sociology). English, politics, and chemistry are the strongest academically. Education, business, and interior design are the largest.

Special: There are co-op programs and cross-registration with Wofford College. Internships, study abroad, a work-study program, accelerated degree programs, B.A.-B.S. degrees in business, biology, and chemistry, and dual majors are offered. There are 10 national honor societies, a freshman honors program, and 10 departmental honors programs.

Admissions: 77% of the 1999-2000 applicants were accepted. The SAT I scores for the 1999-2000 freshman class were: Verbal--12% below 500, 54% between 500 and 599, 28% between 600 and 700, and 6% above 700; Math--26% below 500, 51% between 500 and 599, 20% between 600 and 700, and 3% above 700. The ACT scores were 22% below 21, 35% between 21 and 23, 30% between 24 and 26, 10% between 27 and 28, and 3% above 28. 70% of the current freshmen were in the top fifth of their class; 82% were in the top two fifths.

Requirements: The SAT I or ACT is recommended. A GPA of 2.0 is required. Applicants should be graduates of an accredited secondary school, having completed 20 Carnegie units, including 4 years of English, 3 of math, 2 each of foreign language, science, and social studies, and 1 of history. The GED is accepted. An interview is recommended for all students and an audition is recommended for music students. Applications are accepted on computer disk through CollegeLink and on-line through the web site. AP and CLEP credits are accepted. Important factors in the admissions decision are advanced placement or honor courses, recommendations by school officials, and leadership record.

Procedure: Freshmen are admitted to all sessions. Entrance exams should be taken by the senior year of high school. There is an early decision plan. Early decision applications should be filed by November; regular applications, by August 15 for fall entry, along with a $35 fee. Notification of early decision is sent in November; regular decision, on a rolling basis.

Financial Aid: In 1999-2000, 69% of all freshmen and 70% of continuing students received some form of financial aid. 67% of freshmen and 70% of continuing students received need-based aid. The average freshman award was $15,333. The average financial indebtedness of the 1999 graduate was $13,770. Converse College is a member of CSS. The FAFSA is required. The fall application deadline is March 15.

Computers: The mainframe is an ALPHA. There are also 2 computer labs as well as PCs in the library and dormitories. All students may access the system. There are no time limits and no fees.

COOPER UNION FOR THE ADVANCEMENT OF SCIENCE AND ART
New York, NY 10003-7183 (212) 353-4120; Fax: (212) 353-4342

Full-time: 561 men, 296 women	**Faculty:** 53; IIB, ++$
Part-time: 7 men, 8 women	**Ph.D.s:** 82%
Graduate: 24 men, 8 women	**Student/Faculty:** 16 to 1
Year: semesters, summer session	**Tuition:** $500
Application Deadline: see profile	**Room & Board:** $6000
Freshman Class: 2216 applied, 290 accepted, 200 enrolled	
SAT I Verbal/Math: 670/700	**MOST COMPETITIVE**

The Cooper Union for the Advancement of Science and Art, founded in 1859, is a privately endowed institution. Students who are U.S. residents are admitted under full scholarship, which covers the tuition of $8300. There is an additional fee of $500. Cooper Union offers undergraduate degrees in architecture, art, and engineering, and graduate degrees in engineering. There are 3 undergraduate schools and 1 graduate school. In addition to regional accreditation, Cooper Union has baccalaureate program accreditation with ABET, NAAB, and NASAD. The library contains 100,000 volumes, 50,000 microform items, and 300 audiovisual forms/CDs, and subscribes to 350 periodicals. Computerized library services include the card catalog, interlibrary loans, and database searching. Special learning facilities include a learning resource center, art gallery, and a center for speaking and writing, an electronic resources center, and a visual resources center. The campus is in an urban area located in the heart of lower Manhattan. Including residence halls, there are 5 buildings.

Programs of Study: Cooper Union confers B.S., B.Arch., B.E., and B.F.A. degrees. Master's degrees are also awarded. Bachelor's degrees are awarded in COMMUNICATIONS AND THE ARTS (fine arts and graphic design), ENGINEERING AND ENVIRONMENTAL DESIGN (architecture, chemical engineering, civil engineering, electrical/electronics engineering, engineering, and mechanical engineering). Engineering is the largest.

Special: Cross-registration with New School University, internships, study abroad for art students in 8 countries, and for engineering students in 6 countries, and some pass/fail options are available. Nondegree study is possible. An accelerated degree in engineering is also available. There are 4 national honor societies, and 1 departmental honors program.

Admissions: 13% of the 1999-2000 applicants were accepted. The SAT I scores for the 1999-2000 freshman class were: Verbal--6% below 500, 17% between 500 and 599, 47% between 600 and 700, and 30% above 700; Math--6% below 500, 13% between 500 and 599, 26% between 600 and 700, and 55% above 700. All of the current freshmen were in the top fifth of their class.

Requirements: The SAT I is required. Engineering applicants must take SAT II: Subject tests in mathematics I or II and physics or chemistry. Graduation from an approved secondary school is required. Applicants should have completed 16 to 18 high school academic credits, depending on their major. An essay is part of the application process. Art students must submit a portfolio. Art and architecture applicants must complete a project called the hometest. AP credits are accepted. Important factors in the admissions decision are evidence of special talent, advanced placement or honor courses, and personality/intangible qualities.

Procedure: Freshmen are admitted in the fall. Entrance exams should be taken before February 1. There are early decision, early admissions, and deferred admissions plans. Early decision applications should be filed by December 1; regular applications, by January 1 for fall entry, January 1 for architecture; January 10 for art; and February 1 for engineering. Along with a $35 fee. Notification of early decision is sent December 20; regular decision, April 1. 51 early decision candidates were accepted for the 1999-2000 class. 1% of all applicants are on a waiting list.

Financial Aid: In 1999-2000, 43% of all freshmen and 34% of continuing students received some form of financial aid. 43% of freshmen and 34% of continuing students received need-based aid. The average freshman award was $3600. Of that total, scholarships or need-based grants averaged $2700 ($4000 maximum); loans averaged $2470 ($2625 maximum); and work contracts averaged $1000 ($2000 maximum). 27% of undergraduates work part time. Average annual earnings from campus work are $1545. The average financial indebtedness of the 1999 graduate was $10,080. Cooper Union is a member of CSS. The CSS/Profile or FAFSA is required. The fall application deadline is May 1.

Computers: The mainframe is a DEC VAX 11/780. The computer center, located in the Engineering Building, contains more than 100 workstations and PCs, all available for student use. All students have access to E-mail and the Internet. All students may access the system whenever the Engineering Building is open. There are no time limits and no fees.

CORCORAN SCHOOL OF ART AND DESIGN
Washington, DC 20006

(202) 639-1814
(888) CORCORAN; Fax: (202) 639-1830

Full-time: 106 men, 181 women	**Faculty:** 34
Part-time: 10 men, 15 women	**Ph.D.s:** 63%
Graduate: none	**Student/Faculty:** 8 to 1
Year: semesters, summer session	**Tuition:** $14,140
Application Deadline: open	**Room:** $4700
Freshman Class: 124 applied, 86 accepted, 42 enrolled	
SAT I Verbal: 525	**SPECIAL**

Established in 1890, the Corcoran college of Art and Design (formerly Corcoran School of Art) is a private professional art college offering undergraduate programs in fine art, design, and photography. In addition to regional accreditation, Corcoran has baccalaureate program accreditation with NASAD. The library contains 19,000 volumes and subscribes to 130 periodicals. Computerized library services include interlibrary loans. Special learning facilities include a learning resource center and art gallery. The 7-acre campus is in an urban area in Washington, D.C. There are 3 buildings.

Programs of Study: Corcoran confers the B.F.A. degree. Associate degrees are also awarded. Bachelor's degrees are awarded in COMMUNICATIONS AND THE ARTS (fine arts, graphic design, and photography). Fine arts is the largest.

Special: Cooperative programs are permitted with the ACE and AICA art college consortiums. Opportunities are provided for internships in graphic design and photography, credit by exam, work-study programs with the Corcoran Gallery of Art, and nondegree study.

Admissions: 69% of the 1999-2000 applicants were accepted. The SAT I scores for the 1999-2000 freshman class were: Verbal--36% below 500, 50% between 500 and 599, 11% between 600 and 700, and 3% above 700. 36% of the current freshmen were in the top fifth of their class; all were in the top two fifths.

Requirements: The SAT I or ACT is required. A GPA of 2.5 is required. Applicants must have graduated from an approved secondary school; a GED will be accepted. A portfolio is required, and an interview is recommended. AP credits are accepted. Important factors in the admissions decision are evidence of special talent, personality/intangible qualities, and advanced placement or honor courses.

Procedure: Freshmen are admitted fall and spring. Entrance exams should be taken prior to January 30 of the senior year. There is a deferred admissions plan. Application deadlines are open; there is a $30 fee. Notification is sent on a rolling basis.

Financial Aid: In 1999-2000, 83% of all freshmen and 69% of continuing students received some form of financial aid. 56% of freshmen and 55% of continuing students received need-based aid. The average freshman award was $12,891. Of that total, scholarships or need-based grants averaged $3976 ($4250 maximum); loans averaged $3550 ($4000 maximum); and credit-based loans averaged $8119 ($12,300 maximum). 12% of undergraduates work part time. Average annual earnings from campus work are $1849. The average financial indebtedness of the 1999 graduate was $35,000. Corcoran is a member of CSS. The CSS/Profile and the college's own financial statement are required. The fall application deadline is March 15.

Computers: In labs, the student lounge, and the library there are Macs, Power Macs, and PCs as well as workstations and servers. Internet access is available. Students in computer graphics may access the system during lab hours. There are no fees.

CORNELL COLLEGE
Mount Vernon, IA 52314-1098

(319) 895-4215
(800) 747-1112; Fax: (319) 895-4451

Full-time: 386 men, 559 women	**Faculty:** 75; IIB, ++$
Part-time: 10 men, 10 women	**Ph.D.s:** 89%
Graduate: none	**Student/Faculty:** 13 to 1
Year: see profile	**Tuition:** $18,995
Application Deadline: February 1	**Room & Board:** $5140
Freshman Class: 1104 applied, 892 accepted, 271 enrolled	
SAT I Verbal/Math: 580/580	**ACT:** 25 **VERY COMPETITIVE**

Cornell College, founded in 1853, is an independent institution affiliated with the United Methodist Church. Its emphases are on the liberal arts and on student service and leadership. Cornell has a 1-course-at-a-time calendar in which the year is divided into nine 3½-week terms. In addition to regional accreditation, Cornell has baccalaureate program accreditation with NASM. The library contains 128,800 volumes, 232,454 microform items, and 6727 audiovisual forms/CDs, and subscribes to 750 periodicals. Computerized library services include the card catalog, interlibrary loans, and database searching. Special learning facilities include a learning resource center, art gallery, natural history museum, and radio station. The 129-acre campus is in a small town 15 miles east of Cedar Rapids. Including residence halls, there are 41 buildings.

Programs of Study: Cornell confers B.A., B.Mus., B.Ph., and B.S.S. degrees. Bachelor's degrees are awarded in BIOLOGICAL SCIENCE (biology/biological science), BUSINESS (international business management), COMMUNICATIONS AND THE ARTS (dramatic arts, English, fine arts, French, German, languages, music, Russian, Spanish, and speech/debate/rhetoric), COMPUTER AND PHYSICAL SCIENCE (chemistry, computer science, geology, mathematics, and physics), EDUCATION (art, elementary, foreign languages, music, science, and secondary), ENGINEERING AND ENVIRONMENTAL DESIGN (environmental science), SOCIAL SCIENCE (anthropology, classical/ancient civilization, economics, history, international relations, Latin American studies, medieval studies, philosophy, political science/government, psychology, religion, Russian and Slavic studies, sociology, and women's studies). Biology, chemistry, and philosophy are the strongest academically. Psychology, education, and English are the largest.

Special: Special academic programs include 25 study-abroad opportunities and internships, including a Washington Center internship, cross-registration with Rush University; an accelerated degree program in all majors, as well as dual majors in all areas; student-designed majors toward a B.S.S. degree; and interdepartmental/interdisciplinary majors that include biochemistry and molecular biology and origins of behavior. There is a 3-2 engineering program, a 3-4 architecture program, and a 3-2 occupational therapy program with Washington University in St. Louis; a 3-2 social services program with the University of Chicago; a 3-2 forestry and environmental management program with Duke University; and a 3-2 natural resource management program with the University of Michigan. Nondegree study is possible, as are pass/fail options, with restrictions. There are 2 national honor societies, including Phi Beta Kappa.

Admissions: 81% of the 1999-2000 applicants were accepted. The SAT I scores for the 1999-2000 freshman class were: Verbal--13% below 500, 43% between 500 and 599, 37% between 600 and 700, and 7% above 700; Math--46% between 500 and 599, 38% between 600 and 700, and 5% above 700. The ACT scores were 10% below 21, 21% between 21 and 23, 32% between 24 and 26, 20% between 27 and 28, and 17% above 28. 52% of the current freshmen were in the top fifth of their class; 80% were in the top two fifths. There was 1 National Merit finalist. 12 freshmen graduated first in their class.

Requirements: The SAT I or ACT is required. Cornell requires applicants to be in the upper 50% of their class. A GPA of 2.5 is required. Applicants should be graduates of an accredited secondary school, with a recommended 4 years each of English and history/social studies, 3 each of math and science, 2 to 4 of a foreign language, and 1 each of art and music. The GED is accepted. An essay is required and an interview is advised. Applications are accepted on computer disk or via the college's web site. AP and CLEP credits are accepted. Important factors in the admissions decision are leadership record, evidence of special talent, and personality/intangible qualities.

Procedure: Freshmen are admitted to all sessions. Entrance exams should be taken in the spring of the junior year. There are early decision, early admissions, and deferred admissions plans. Early decision applications should be filed by November 15; regular applications, by February 1 for fall entry, along with a $25 fee. Notification of early decision is sent December 20; regular decision, on a rolling basis. 52 early decision candidates were accepted for the 1999-2000 class.

Financial Aid: In 1999-2000, 98% of all freshmen and 96% of continuing students received some form of financial aid. 70% of freshmen and 80% of continuing students received need-based aid. The average freshman award was $16,800. Of that total, scholarships or need-based grants averaged $12,780 ($15,000 maximum); loans averaged $3275 ($3625 maximum); and work contracts averaged $800 ($1200 maximum). 71% of undergraduates work part time. Average annual earnings from campus work are $1000. The average financial indebtedness of the 1999 graduate was $18,025. Cornell is a member of CSS. The FAFSA, the college's own financial statement, and student, and parent tax returns are required. The fall application deadline is March 1.

Computers: The mainframes are Intel server class machines. There are also 80 PCs in academic labs, the library, and the Commons. All academic computer facilities have access to the Internet system. Students may also access the system by modem. All students may access the system from 7 a.m. to 11 p.m. There are no time limits and no fees.

CORNELL UNIVERSITY
Ithaca, NY 14850 (607) 255-5241

Full-time: 7137 men, 6532 women	**Faculty:** 1461; I, ++$
Part-time: none	**Ph.D.s:** 97%
Graduate: 3156 men, 2196 women	**Student/Faculty:** 9 to 1
Year: semesters, summer session	**Tuition:** $10,330 - $23,848
Application Deadline: January 1	**Room & Board:** $7827
Freshman Class: 19,949 applied, 6561 accepted, 3134 enrolled	
SAT I Verbal/Math: 660/700	**MOST COMPETITIVE**

Cornell University was founded in 1865 as a land-grant institution. Privately supported undergraduate divisions include the College of Architecture, Art, and Planning; the College of Arts and Sciences; the College of Engineering; and the School of Hotel Administration. State-assisted undergraduate divisions include the College of Agriculture and Life Sciences, the College of Human Ecology, and the School of Industrial and Labor Relations. There are 7 undergraduate and 4 graduate schools. In addition to regional accreditation, Cornell has baccalaureate program accreditation with AACSB, ABET, ASLA, CSWE, and FIDER. The 17 libraries contain 6,448,496 volumes, 7,489,325 microform items, and 140,525 audiovisual forms/CDs, and subscribe to 62,076 periodicals. Computerized library services include the card catalog, interlibrary loans, and database searching. Special learning facilities include a learning resource center, art gallery, planetarium, radio station, bird sanctuary, 4 designated national resource centers, and 2 local optical observatories. The 745-acre campus is in a rural area 60 miles south of Syracuse. Including residence halls, there are 770 buildings.

Programs of Study: Cornell confers B.A., B.S., B.Arch., and B.F.A. degrees. Master's and doctoral degrees are also awarded. Bachelor's degrees are awarded in AGRICULTURE (agricultural business management, agricultural economics, agriculture, agronomy, animal science, horticulture, international agriculture, natural resource management, plant science, and soil science), BIOLOGICAL SCIENCE (biology/biological science, botany, entomology, evolutionary biology, genetics, microbiology, neurosciences, and nutrition), BUSINESS (business administration and management, hotel/motel and restaurant management, labor studies, and operations research), COMMUNICATIONS AND THE ARTS (art history and appreciation, classics, communications, comparative literature, dance, design, dramatic arts, English, fine arts, French, German, Greek, Italian, languages, Latin, linguistics, music, photography, Russian, and Spanish), COMPUTER AND PHYSICAL SCIENCE (astronomy, atmospheric sciences and meteorology, chemistry, computer science, geology, mathematics, physics, and statistics), EDUCATION (education), ENGINEERING AND ENVIRONMENTAL DESIGN (agricultural engineering, architecture, chemical engineering, city/community/regional planning, civil engineering, electrical/electronics engineering, engineering physics, environmental engineering technology, landscape architecture/design, materials science, and mechanical engineering), SOCIAL SCIENCE (African studies, American studies, anthropology, archeology, Asian/Oriental studies, classical/ancient civilization, economics, family/consumer studies, food production/management/services, food science, German area studies, history, human development, human services, Near Eastern studies, philosophy, political science/government, psychology, public affairs, religion, rural sociology, Russian and Slavic studies, social science, sociology, textiles and clothing, urban studies, and women's studies). Hotel administration, industrial and labor relations, and engineering are the largest.

Special: Co-op programs are offered in the College of Engineering and the School of Industrial and Labor Relations. Cross-registration is available with Ithaca College. Public-policy internships are available in Washington, D.C., Albany, and New York City. Cornell also offers study abroad in more than 50 countries, B.A.-B.S. and B.A.-B.F.A. degrees, interdisciplinary/intercollegiate options, student-designed and dual majors, work-study programs, accelerated degree programs, pass/fail options, and limited nondegree study. There are 3 national honor societies, including Phi Beta Kappa.

Admissions: 33% of the 1999-2000 applicants were accepted. The SAT I scores for the 1999-2000 freshman class were: Verbal--2% below 500, 15% between 500 and 599, 49% between 600 and 700, and 34% above 700; Math--1% below 500, 8% between 500 and 599, 37% between 600 and 700, and 54% above 700. 94% of the current freshmen were in the top fifth of their class; 100% were in the top two fifths.

Requirements: The SAT I or ACT is required. An essay is required as part of the application process. Other requirements vary by division or program, including specific SAT II: Subject tests and selection of courses within the minimum 16 secondary-school academic units needed. An interview and/or portfolio is required for specific majors. Applications are accepted on-line via ExPAN and Apply. AP credits are accepted. Important factors in the admissions decision are advanced placement or honor courses, evidence of special talent, and leadership record.

Procedure: Freshmen are admitted fall and spring. Entrance exams should be taken by December of the senior year. There are early decision and deferred admissions plans. Early decision applications should be filed by November 10; regular applications, by January 1 for fall entry and November 10 for spring entry, along with a $65 fee. Notification of early decision is sent mid-December; regular decision, mid-April. 976 early decision candidates were accepted for the 1999-2000 class. 7% of all applicants are on a waiting list.

Financial Aid: In 1999-2000, 63% of all freshmen and 55% of continuing students received some form of financial aid. 50% of freshmen and 46% of continuing students received need-based aid. The average freshman award was $18,600. Of that total, scholarships or need-based grants averaged $14,000 ($36,000 maximum); loans averaged $5300 ($6640 maximum); and work contracts averaged $1800 ($2400 maximum). The average financial indebtedness of the 1999 graduate was $16,000. Cornell is a member of CSS. The CSS/Profile and the IRS form after enrollment are required. The fall application deadline is February 15.

Computers: The mainframe includes 2 IBM 3090/600s. Students have access to 7 campuswide computer centers and more than 20 departmental facilities with more than 700 PCs/terminals, as well as networks in the residence halls. All students may access the system. There are no time limits and no fees. It is recommended that students in engineering have personal computers.

CREIGHTON UNIVERSITY
Omaha, NE 68178-0001

(402) 280-2703
(800) 282-5835; Fax: (402) 280-2685

Full-time: 1478 men, 2045 women	**Faculty:** 242; IIA, av$
Part-time: 182 men, 271 women	**Ph.D.s:** 92%
Graduate: 1164 men, 1185 women	**Student/Faculty:** 15 to 1
Year: semesters, summer session	**Tuition:** $14,132
Application Deadline: open	**Room & Board:** $5446
Freshman Class: 3112 applied, 2830 accepted, 855 enrolled	
SAT I Verbal/Math: 576/586	**ACT:** 26 **VERY COMPETITIVE+**

Creighton University, established in 1878, is a private Catholic institution conducted by the Jesuits and offering undergraduate programs in arts and sciences, business, and nursing. There are 4 undergraduate and 5 graduate schools. In addition to regional accreditation, Creighton has baccalaureate program accreditation with AACSB, ACPE, NCATE, and NLN. The 3 libraries contain 796,801 volumes, 287,561 microform items, and 17,517 audiovisual forms/CDs, and subscribe to 9859 periodicals. Computerized library services include the card catalog, interlibrary loans, and database searching. Special learning facilities include a learning resource center, art gallery, planetarium, radio station, and TV station. The 78-acre campus is in an urban area near downtown Omaha. Including residence halls, there are 46 buildings.

Programs of Study: Creighton confers B.A., B.S., B.F.A., B.S. Atmospheric Science, B.S.B.A., B.S.Chem., B.S. Computer Science, B.S. Environmental Science, B.S. Mathematics, B.S.N., B.S. Physics, B.S.Soc., and B.S.W. degrees. Associate, master's, and doctoral degrees are also awarded. Bachelor's degrees are awarded in BIOLOGICAL SCIENCE (biology/biological science), BUSINESS (accounting, banking and finance, business administration and management, international business management, management information systems, and marketing/retailing/merchandising), COMMUNICATIONS AND THE ARTS (art, communications, dramatic arts, English, fine arts, French, German, Greek, journalism, Latin, music, Spanish, and speech/debate/rhetoric), COMPUTER AND PHYSICAL SCIENCE (atmospheric sciences and meteorology, chemistry, computer science, mathematics, and physics), EDUCATION (elementary, secondary, and special), ENGINEERING AND ENVIRONMENTAL DESIGN (environmental science), HEALTH PROFESSIONS (emergency medical technologies, nursing, occupational therapy, and sports medicine), SOCIAL SCIENCE (American studies, classical/ancient civilization, economics, history, ministries, philosophy, political science/government, prelaw, psychology, social work, sociology, and theological studies). Nursing, biology, and finance are the largest.

Special: The university offers preengineering co-op programs with the University of Detroit and Washington University in St. Louis, study abroad in London, Cork, Tokyo, and Rome, a Washington semester, internships, and work-study programs. Nursing students may take an accelerated degree program, and B.A.-B.S. degrees are possible. Dual majors, nondegree study, pass/fail options, and credit for life, military, and work experience are available. There are 13 national honor societies, a freshman honors program, and 1 departmental honors program.

Admissions: 91% of the 1999-2000 applicants were accepted. The SAT I scores for the 1999-2000 freshman class were: Verbal--16% below 500, 43% between 500 and 599, 35% between 600 and 700, and 6% above 700; Math--16% below 500, 37% between 500 and 599, 38% between 600 and 700, and 9% above 700. The ACT scores were 10% below 21, 21% between 21 and 23, 28% between 24 and 26, 19% between 27 and 28, and 22% above 28. 61% of the current freshmen were in the top fifth of their class; 85% were in the top two fifths. 50 freshmen graduated first in their class.

Requirements: The SAT I or ACT is required. Creighton requires applicants to be in the upper 50% of their class. A GPA of 2.5 is required. In addition, applicants must be graduates of an accredited secondary school. The GED is accepted. Students should have completed 16 credits, including 4 credits in English, 3 each in math and electives, and 2 each in foreign language, science, and social studies. On-line applications may be submitted via Creighton's web site. Home-schooled students are welcome. AP and CLEP credits are accepted. Important factors in the admissions decision are recommendations by school officials, advanced placement or honor courses, and leadership record.

Procedure: Freshmen are admitted to all sessions. Entrance exams should be taken prior to May 1 of the senior year. Application deadlines are open; there is a $30 fee. Notification is sent on a rolling basis.

Financial Aid: In 1999-2000, 90% of all freshmen and 85% of continuing students received some form of financial aid. 59% of freshmen and 56% of continuing students received need-based aid. The average freshman award was $10,814. Of that total, scholarships or need-based grants averaged $5390 ($17,186 maximum); loans averaged $3994 ($4625 maximum); and work contracts averaged $1430 ($2000 maximum). 74% of undergraduates work part time. Average annual earnings from campus work are $1213. The average financial indebtedness of the 1999 graduate was $20,517. Creighton is a member of CSS. The FAFSA and the university's own financial statement are required. The fall application deadline is April 1.

Computers: The mainframe is a Unisys 220/400. There are also 250 Macs and AT&T PCs available throughout the campus and in computer labs. All students may access the system during computer center hours. There are no time limits and no fees.

D'YOUVILLE COLLEGE
Buffalo, NY 14201

(716) 881-7600
(800) 777-3921; Fax: (716) 881-7790

Full-time: 246 men, 654 women
Part-time: 44 men, 157 women
Graduate: 294 men, 788 women
Year: semesters, summer session
Application Deadline: see profile
Freshman Class: 720 applied, 519 accepted, 128 enrolled
SAT I Verbal/Math: 515/500

Faculty: 95
Ph.D.s: 73%
Student/Faculty: 9 to 1
Tuition: $10,900
Room & Board: $5380

ACT: 24　　**VERY COMPETITIVE**

D'Youville College, founded in 1908, is a private, nonsectarian liberal arts institution. In addition to regional accreditation, D'Youville has baccalaureate program accreditation with ADA, APTA, CAHEA, CSWE, and NLN. The library contains 91,524 volumes, 155,000 microform items, and 3116 audiovisual forms/CDs, and subscribes to 740 periodicals. Computerized library services include the card catalog and database searching. Special learning facilities include a learning resource center. The 7-acre campus is in an urban area 1 mile north of Buffalo. Including residence halls, there are 8 buildings.

Programs of Study: D'Youville confers B.A., B.S., B.S.N., and B.S.W. degrees. Master's degrees are also awarded. Bachelor's degrees are awarded in BIOLOGICAL SCIENCE (biology/biological science), BUSINESS (accounting, business administration and management, and marketing/retailing/merchandising), COMMUNICATIONS AND THE ARTS (English and literature), EDUCATION (business, elementary, secondary, and special), HEALTH PROFESSIONS (nursing, occupational therapy, physical therapy, and physician's assistant), SOCIAL SCIENCE (dietetics, history, philosophy, and sociology). Education and health professions are the strongest academically. Health professions, business, and nursing are the largest.

Special: D'Youville has cross-registration with member colleges of the Western New York Consortium. Internships, work-study programs, dual majors, and pass/fail options are available. Accelerated 5-year B.S.-M.S. programs in physical therapy, occupational therapy, international business, nursing, and dietetics are offered. For freshmen with undecided majors, the Career Discovery Program offers special courses, internships, and faculty advisers. There is 1 national honor society, and 6 departmental honors programs.

Admissions: 72% of the 1999-2000 applicants were accepted. The SAT I scores for the 1999-2000 freshman class were: Verbal--35% below 500, 58% between 500 and 599, 5% between 600 and 700, and 3% above 700; Math--39% below 500, 53% between 500 and 599, and 9% between 600 and 700. The ACT scores were 16% below 21, 28% between 21 and 23, 36% between 24 and 26, and 20% between 27 and 28. 49% of the current freshmen were in the top fifth of their class; 88% were in the top two fifths. There were 3 National Merit semifinalists.

Requirements: The SAT I or ACT is required. D'Youville requires applicants to be in the upper 40% of their class. A GPA of 2.0 is required. Applicants should have completed 16 Carnegie units, including 4 years of high school English, 3 of social studies, and 1 each of math and science; some majors require additional years of math and science. The GED is accepted. An interview is recommended. AP and CLEP credits are accepted. Important factors in the admissions decision are advanced placement or honor courses, evidence of special talent, and leadership record.

Procedure: Freshmen are admitted fall and spring. There is a deferred admissions plan. Check with the school for current application deadlines. The applicati8on fee is $25. Notification is sent on a rolling basis.

Financial Aid: In 1999-2000, 98% of all freshmen and 82% of continuing students received some form of financial aid. 85% of freshmen and 80% of continuing students received need-based aid. The average freshman award was $5844. Of that total, scholarships or need-based grants averaged $5000 ($10,000 maximum); loans averaged $3400 ($5125 maximum); and work contracts averaged $800. 26% of undergraduates work part time. Average annual earnings from campus work are $800. The average financial indebtedness of the 1999 graduate was $14,000. D'Youville is a member of CSS. The FAFSA and New York State TAP are required. The fall application deadline is April 15.

Computers: The mainframe is a Sun. There are 3 computer labs as well as computers located in the residence hall. Mac and DOS computers are networked. There is a fiber optic computer network with ports throughout the college, including the dorms. All students may access the system. There are no time limits and no fees.

DARTMOUTH COLLEGE
Hanover, NH 03755   (603) 646-2875; Fax: (603) 646-1216

Full-time: 2109 men, 1938 women	**Faculty:** 336; I, +$
Part-time: none	**Ph.D.s:** 99%
Graduate: none	**Student/Faculty:** 12 to 1
Year: see profile, summer session	**Tuition:** $24,884
Application Deadline: January 1	**Room & Board:** $7209
Freshman Class: 10,260 applied, 2131 accepted, 1059 enrolled	
SAT I Verbal/Math: 720/720	**MOST COMPETITIVE**

Dartmouth College, chartered in 1769, is a private, liberal arts institution offering a wide range of graduate and undergraduate programs. There is a year-round academic calendar of 4 10-week terms. There are 4 graduate schools. The 9 libraries contain 2 million volumes, 2.3 million microform items, and 344,000 audiovisual forms/CDs and subscribe to 20,000 periodicals. Computerized library services include the card catalog, interlibrary loans, and database searching. Special learning facilities include a learning resource center, art gallery, radio station, center for performing arts, life sciences lab, physical sciences center, and observatory. The 265-acre campus is in a rural area 140 miles northwest of Boston. Including residence halls, there are 100 buildings.

Programs of Study: Dartmouth confers B.A. and B.Eng. degrees. Master's and doctoral degrees are also awarded. Bachelor's degrees are awarded in BIOLOGICAL SCIENCE (biochemistry, biology/biological science, evolutionary biology, and genetics), COMMUNICATIONS AND THE ARTS (art history and appreciation, Chinese, classics, comparative literature, creative writing, dramatic arts, English, film arts, fine arts, French, German, Greek, Italian, languages, Latin, linguistics, literature, music, romance languages and literature, Russian, Spanish, studio art, and visual and performing arts), COMPUTER AND PHYSICAL SCIENCE (chemistry, computer science, earth science, geology, mathematics, and physics), EDUCATION (education), ENGINEERING AND ENVIRONMENTAL DESIGN (engineering and environmental science), SOCIAL SCIENCE (African American studies, African studies, anthropology, archeology, Asian/Oriental studies, Caribbean studies, cognitive science, economics, geography, history, Latin American studies, Native American studies, philosophy, political science/government, psychology, religion, Russian and Slavic studies, social science, sociology, and women's studies). Biology, government, and economics are the largest.

Special: Students may design programs using the college's unique Dartmouth Plan, which divides the academic calender into 4 10-week terms, based on the seasons. The plan permits greater flexibility for vacations and for the 45 study-abroad programs in 22 countries, including Italy, France, Scotland, Russia, and Brazil. Cross-registration is offered through the Twelve College Exchange Network, which includes Amherst and Mount Holyoke. Exchange programs also exist with the University of California at San Diego, McGill University in Montreal, selected German universities, Keio University in Tokyo, and Beijing Normal University in China. There are special academic programs in Washington, D.C., and Tucson, Arizona. Students may design their own interdisciplinary majors, involving multiple departments if desired, take dual majors in all fields, or satisfy a modified major involving 2 departments, with emphasis in 1. Hands-on computer science education, internships, combined B.A.-B.S. degrees, and work-study programs also are available. A 3-2 engineering degree is offered with Dartmouth's Thayer School of Engineering. There are 2 national honor societies, including Phi Beta Kappa. All departments have honors programs.

Admissions: 21% of the 1999-2000 applicants were accepted. The SAT I scores for the 1999-2000 freshman class were: Verbal--6% between 500 and 599, 29% between 600 and 700, and 65% above 700; Math--5% between 500 and 599, 29% between 600 and 700, and 66% above 700. 95% of the current freshmen were in the top fifth of their class; 99% were in the top two fifths. 168 freshmen graduated first in their class.

Requirements: The SAT I or ACT is required, as are 3 SAT II: Subject tests. Evidence of intellectual capacity, motivation, and personal integrity are prime considerations in the highly competitive admissions process, which also considers talent, accomplishment, and involvement in nonacademic areas. Course requirements are flexible, but students are urged to take English, foreign language, math, lab science, and history. The GED is accepted. AP credits are accepted.

Procedure: Freshmen are admitted in the fall. Entrance exams should be taken no later than January of the senior year. There are early decision and deferred admissions plans. Early decision applications should be filed by November 1; regular applications, by January 1 for fall entry, along with a $60 fee. Notification of early decision is sent December 15; regular decision, April 15. 395 early decision candidates were accepted for the 1999-2000 class. A waiting list is an active part of the admissions procedure.

Financial Aid: In 1999-2000, 60% of all freshmen received some form of financial aid. 42% of freshmen received need-based aid. The average freshman award was $19,154. Dartmouth is a member of CSS. The CSS/Profile or FAFSA and the college's own financial statement are required. The fall application deadline is February 1.

Computers: The mainframes are an IBM, a DEC, and a Honeywell. More than 7000 PCs are available for student use. The computer network links dormitory rooms, administrative and academic buildings, and mainframe computers on and off campus. Students can access scholarly databases, a collegewide E-mail system, and the Internet. All students may access the system 24 hours daily. There are no time limits and no fees. Most students use the Mac operating system.

DAVID LIPSCOMB UNIVERSITY
Nashville, TN 37204-3951

(615) 269-1776
(800) 333-4358; Fax: (615) 269-1804

Full-time: 872 men, 1112 women	**Faculty:** 89; IIB, av$
Part-time: 148 men, 185 women	**Ph.D.s:** 83%
Graduate: 114 men, 73 women	**Student/Faculty:** 22 to 1
Year: semesters, summer session	**Tuition:** $9689
Application Deadline: open	**Room & Board:** $4344
Freshman Class: 1615 applied, 1496 accepted, 598 enrolled	
SAT I Verbal/Math: 540/550	**ACT:** 23 **VERY COMPETITIVE**

David Lipscomb University, founded in 1891, is a private liberal arts institution affiliated with the Church of Christ. There are 5 undergraduate and 3 graduate schools. In addition to regional accreditation, DLU has baccalaureate program accreditation with ACBSP, ADA, CSWE, NASM, and NCATE. The library contains 150,512 volumes, 26,018 microform items, and 1240 audiovisual forms/CDs, and subscribes to 38,685 periodicals. Computerized library services include the card catalog, interlibrary loans, and database searching. Special learning facilities include a learning resource center, art gallery, radio station, and TV station. The 65-acre campus is in a suburban area 2 miles south of downtown Nashville. Including residence halls, there are 16 buildings.

Programs of Study: DLU confers B.A. and B.S. degrees. Master's degrees are also awarded. Bachelor's degrees are awarded in BIOLOGICAL SCIENCE (biochemistry and biology/biological science), BUSINESS (accounting, banking and finance, business administration and management, fashion merchandising, and marketing/retailing/merchandising), COMMUNICATIONS AND THE ARTS (communications, English, French, German, languages, music, public relations, and Spanish), COMPUTER AND PHYSICAL SCIENCE (chemistry, computer science, mathematics, and physics), EDUCATION (art, elementary, foreign languages, music, physical, and science), ENGINEERING AND ENVIRONMENTAL DESIGN (preengineering), HEALTH PROFESSIONS (predentistry, premedicine, and prepharmacy), SOCIAL SCIENCE (American studies, biblical languages, dietetics, food production/management/services, history, home economics, political science/government, prelaw, psychology, religion, social work, and urban studies). Chemistry, biology, and accounting are the strongest academically. Business, medicine, and education are the largest.

Special: DLU offers internships and 3-2 engineering degrees with University of Tennessee at Knoxville, and Auburn, Vanderbilt, and Tennessee Technological Universities. An adult credit and noncredit studies program and pass/fail options for phys ed activity courses are available. A 3-2 program with Vanderbilt University leads to a B.S. in prenursing from Lipscomb and a master of science in nursing from Vanderbilt. There is 1 national honor society, a freshman honors program, and 18 departmental honors programs.

Admissions: 93% of the 1999-2000 applicants were accepted. The SAT I scores for the 1999-2000 freshman class were: Verbal--25% below 500, 45% between 500 and 599, 25% between 600 and 700, and 5% above 700; Math--28% below 500, 37% between 500 and 599, 31% between 600 and 700, and 4% above 700. The ACT scores were 27% below 21, 26% between 21 and 23, 22% between 24 and 26, 12% between 27 and 28, and 13% above 28. 74% of the current freshmen were in the top fifth of their class; 97% were in the top two fifths. In a recent year, there were 2 National Merit finalists.

Requirements: The SAT I or ACT is required. A GPA of 2.25 is required. Candidates for admission should be graduates of accredited secondary schools. The

GED is accepted. 14 academic units are required, including 4 of English and 2 each of history, math, science, and additional academic studies; 2 of a foreign language are highly recommended. Applications are accepted on-line. AP and CLEP credits are accepted. Important factors in the admissions decision are advanced placement or honor courses, personality/intangible qualities, and leadership record.

Procedure: Freshmen are admitted to all sessions. There is an early decision plan. Application deadlines are open. There is a $50 fee. Notification is sent on a rolling basis. 8 early decision candidates were accepted for a recent class.

Financial Aid: In a recent year, 75% of all freshmen and 54% of continuing students received some form of financial aid. 36% of all students received need-based aid. The average freshman award was $3600. Of that total, scholarships or need-based grants averaged $1031 ($5000 maximum); and loans averaged $2500. 58% of undergraduates work part time. Average annual earnings from campus work are $800. The average financial indebtedness of a recent graduate was $12, 500. DLU is a member of CSS. The FAFSA is required. The fall application deadline is February 28.

Computers: The mainframes are 3 DEC ALPHA computers, 1 VAX 4100, and 1 VAX 4500. There are computer labs in every building on campus, including residence halls. There are computer hookups in every dorm room. All students may access the system 24 hours a day. There are no time limits and no fees.

DAVIDSON COLLEGE
Davidson, NC 28036

(704) 892-2230
(800) 768-0380; Fax: (704) 892-2016

Full-time: 827 men, 825 women	**Faculty:** 152; IIB, ++$
Part-time: none	**Ph.D.s:** 99%
Graduate: none	**Student/Faculty:** 11 to 1
Year: semesters	**Tuition:** $22,218
Application Deadline: January 2	**Room & Board:** $6340
Freshman Class: 2824 applied, 1080 accepted, 455 enrolled	
SAT I Verbal/Math: 670/670	**ACT:** 29 **MOST COMPETITIVE**

Davidson College, founded in 1837, is an independent liberal arts institution affiliated with the Presbyterian Church (U.S.A.). In addition to regional accreditation, Davidson has baccalaureate program accreditation with NCATE. The library contains 557,945 volumes, 448,985 microform items, and 3071 audiovisual forms/CDs, and subscribes to 2887 periodicals. Computerized library services include the card catalog, interlibrary loans, and database searching. Special learning facilities include a learning resource center, art gallery, radio station, and arboretum. The 450-acre campus is in a small town 19 miles north of Charlotte. Including residence halls, there are 75 buildings.

Programs of Study: Davidson confers A.B. and B.S. degrees. Bachelor's degrees are awarded in BIOLOGICAL SCIENCE (biology/biological science), COMMUNICATIONS AND THE ARTS (art, classics, dramatic arts, English, French, German, music, and Spanish), COMPUTER AND PHYSICAL SCIENCE (chemistry, mathematics, and physics), SOCIAL SCIENCE (anthropology, economics, history, interdisciplinary studies, philosophy, political science/government, psychology, religion, and sociology). Biology, English, and political science are the largest.

Special: Davidson offers interdisciplinary international and Asian studies programs and study abroad in 11 countries as well as through other schools study-abroad programs. A 3-2 engineering program may be arranged with Columbia,

Duke, Georgia Institute of Technology, North Carolina State, and Washington Universities. Students may design their own majors, cross-register with any college in the Charlotte Area Educational Consortium, enroll in a Washington, D.C., or Philadelphia semester or a semester or month-long environmental program at the School for Field Studies, or undertake independent study. There are 12 national honor societies, including Phi Beta Kappa, and 21 departmental honors programs.

Admissions: 38% of the 1999-2000 applicants were accepted. The SAT I scores for the 1999-2000 freshman class were: Verbal--2% below 500, 17% between 500 and 599, 45% between 600 and 700, and 35% above 700; Math--1% below 500, 16% between 500 and 599, 53% between 600 and 700, and 30% above 700. The ACT scores were 9% between 22 and 24, 26% between 25 and 27, 36% between 28 and 30, 26% between 31 and 33, and 3 % between 34 and 36. 94% of the current freshmen were in the top fifth of their class; all were in the top two fifths. 39 freshmen graduated in the top 1% of their class.

Requirements: The SAT I or ACT is required. SAT II: Subject tests in writing, mathematics level I or II, and 1 other subject are strongly recommended. At least 16 high school units are required, although 20 units are recommended. These should include 4 units of English, 3 units of math, 2 units of the same foreign language, 2 units of science, and 2 units of history/social studies. It is strongly recommended that high school students continue for the third and fourth years in science and in the same foreign language, continue math through calculus, and take additional courses in history. Applications are accepted on computer disk via Apply. AP credits are accepted. Important factors in the admissions decision are advanced placement or honor courses, recommendations by school officials, and leadership record.

Procedure: Freshmen are admitted in the fall. Entrance exams should be taken by January of the senior year. There are early decision, early admissions, and deferred admissions plans. Early decision applications should be filed by November 15; regular applications, by January 2 for fall entry, along with a $50 fee. Notification of early decision is sent December 15; regular decision, April 1. 195 early decision candidates were accepted for the 1999-2000 class. A waiting list is an active part of the admissions procedure.

Financial Aid: In 1999-2000, 53% of all freshmen and 57% of continuing students received some form of financial aid. 29% of all students received need-based aid. The average freshman award was $14,800. Of that total, scholarships or need-based grants averaged $13,100 ($27,200 maximum); loans averaged $3340 ($5500 maximum); and work contracts averaged $1440 ($1700 maximum). 40% of undergraduates work part time. Average annual earnings from campus work are $1250. The average financial indebtedness of the 1999 graduate was $14,270. Davidson is a member of CSS. The CSS/Profile or FAFSA and the college's own financial statement are required. The fall application deadline is February 15.

Computers: The mainframes are 32 servers, including an HP 9000 K360, Digital ALPHA Server 1200, and several Dell Poweredge 2300s and 6350s. Students may use the host computer and PC network for word processing, computation and graphics (Mathematica, Quattro), statistics (SAS, SPSS, Minitab), and e-mail and the Internet. Access is available from more than 130 networked PCs in academic buildings and the college library and connected to student PCs in residence hall rooms through Ethernet jacks. All students may access the system 24 hours per day. There are no time limits and no fees.

DENISON UNIVERSITY

Granville, OH 43023

(740) 587-6276
(800) DENISON; Fax: (740) 587-6306

Full-time: 940 men, 1137 women	**Faculty:** 167; IIB, ++$
Part-time: 5 men, 7 women	**Ph.D.s:** 98%
Graduate: none	**Student/Faculty:** 12 to 1
Year: semesters	**Tuition:** $21,690
Application Deadline: February 1	**Room & Board:** $5760
Freshman Class: 2991 applied, 2054 accepted, 587 enrolled	
SAT I Verbal/Math: 602/609	**ACT:** 27 **HIGHLY COMPETITIVE**

Denison University, founded in 1831, is a private independent institution of liberal arts and sciences. The library contains 347,624 volumes, 94,545 microform items, and 22,698 audiovisual forms/CDs, and subscribes to 1214 periodicals. Computerized library services include the card catalog, interlibrary loans, and database searching. Special learning facilities include a learning resource center, art gallery, planetarium, radio station, TV station, observatory, field research station in a 350-acre biological reserve, high resolution spectrometer, economics computer labs, and modern languages lab. The 1200-acre campus is in a suburban area 30 miles east of Columbus. Including residence halls, there are 60 buildings.

Programs of Study: Denison confers B.A., B.S., and B.F.A. degrees. Bachelor's degrees are awarded in BIOLOGICAL SCIENCE (biochemistry and biology/biological science), COMMUNICATIONS AND THE ARTS (communications, dance, dramatic arts, English, film arts, fine arts, French, German, languages, Latin, media arts, music, Spanish, and speech/debate/rhetoric), COMPUTER AND PHYSICAL SCIENCE (chemistry, computer science, geology, mathematics, and physics), EDUCATION (education and physical), ENGINEERING AND ENVIRONMENTAL DESIGN (environmental science), SOCIAL SCIENCE (African American studies, anthropology, classical/ancient civilization, East Asian studies, economics, history, Latin American studies, philosophy, political science/government, psychology, religion, and women's studies). Psychology, philosophy, and physics are the strongest academically. English, economics, and history are the largest.

Special: Work-study programs, a Washington semester, study-abroad programs in 35 countries, student-designed majors, a math/economics dual major, a dual major in education and various other majors, a philosophy, political science, and economics interdisciplinary major, and pass/fail options are available. A 3-2 engineering program is offered with Rensselaer Polytechnic Institute, and Case Western Reserve and Washington Universities. A May-term internship is available at 200 U.S. locations. A B.A.-B.S. degree, accelerated degree programs, and nondegree study are possible. There are 15 national honor societies, including Phi Beta Kappa, and a freshman honors program. All academic departments offer honors courses.

Admissions: 69% of the 1999-2000 applicants were accepted. The SAT I scores for the 1999-2000 freshman class were: Verbal--7% below 500, 42% between 500 and 599, 40% between 600 and 700, and 11% above 700; Math--4% below 500, 37% between 500 and 599, 47% between 600 and 700, and 12% above 700. The ACT scores were 3% below 21, 12% between 21 and 23, 24% between 24 and 26, 25% between 27 and 28, and 36% above 28. 73% of the current freshmen were in the top fifth of their class; 90% were in the top two fifths. There were 16 National Merit finalists and 8 semifinalists. 39 freshmen graduated first in their class.

Requirements: The SAT I or ACT is required. Applicants should have completed 16 Carnegie units, including 4 each in English, math, and science, 3 in foreign language, 2 in social studies, and 1 each in art, history, and academic electives. An essay is part of the application process. An interview is advised, and a portfolio or an audition is recommended for art or music majors, respectively. Applications can be downloaded from the school's web site. AP credits are accepted. Important factors in the admissions decision are geographic diversity, evidence of special talent, and advanced placement or honor courses.

Procedure: Freshmen are admitted in the fall. Entrance exams should be taken by December of the senior year. There are early decision, early admissions, and deferred admissions plans. Early decision applications should be filed by January 1; regular applications, by February 1 for fall entry, along with a $40 fee. Notification of early decision is sent January 1; regular decision, April 1. 81 early decision candidates were accepted for the 1999-2000 class. 16% of all applicants are on a waiting list.

Financial Aid: In 1999-2000, 99% of all freshmen and 97% of continuing students received some form of financial aid. 49% of freshmen and 47% of continuing students received need-based aid. The average freshman award was $21,325. Of that total, scholarships or need-based grants averaged $13,274 ($20,380 maximum); loans averaged $2380 ($4625 maximum); and work contracts averaged $1875 (maximum). 62% of undergraduates work part time. Average annual earnings from campus work are $1754. The average financial indebtedness of the 1999 graduate was $14,021. Denison is a member of CSS. The FAFSA and the college's own financial statement are required. The fall application deadline is April 1.

Computers: The mainframe is a DEC ALPHA 2200. More than 800 PCs are connected to the campus network. About 400 of those are available to students in public computer clusters and department labs. All residence halls have network services, including E-mail, the World Wide Web and the Internet, libraries, directory services, local events calendar, and personal web pages. All students may access the system 24 hours a day. There are no time limits and no fees.

DEPAUL UNIVERSITY
Chicago, IL 60604

(312) 362-8300
(800) 4-DEPAUL; Fax: (312) 362-5749

Full-time: 3291 men, 4493 women	**Faculty:** 519
Part-time: 1547 men, 2445 women	**Ph.D.s:** n/av
Graduate: 3955 men, 3818 women	**Student/Faculty:** 15 to 1
Year: quarters, summer session	**Tuition:** $14,700
Application Deadline: August 15	**Room & Board:** $6300
Freshman Class: 6050 applied, 4737 accepted, 1749 enrolled	
SAT I Verbal/Math: 570/557	**ACT:** 23 **VERY COMPETITIVE**

DePaul University, founded by the Vincentian Order in 1898, is a private Catholic institution with 2 main campuses: the Lincoln Park Campus houses undergraduate programs in liberal arts and sciences, education, theater, and music, and the Loop Campus offers programs in commerce, law, computer science, telecommunications, and information systems. There are 7 undergraduate and 8 graduate schools. In addition to regional accreditation, DePaul has baccalaureate program accreditation with AACSB, NASM, NCATE, and NLN. The 3 libraries contain 738,072 volumes, 309,701 microform items, and 25,000 audiovisual forms/CDs, and subscribe to 15,890 periodicals. Computerized library services include the card catalog, interlibrary loans, and database searching. Special learning facilities include an art gallery, radio station, a performing arts center, a recording studio, and a marketing research center. The 36-acre campus is in an urban area in Chicago. Including residence halls, there are 39 buildings.

Programs of Study: DePaul confers B.A., B.S., B.F.A, B.M., and B.S.C. degrees. Master's and doctoral degrees are also awarded. Bachelor's degrees are awarded in BIOLOGICAL SCIENCE (biology/biological science), BUSINESS (accounting, banking and finance, business administration and management, business economics, and marketing/retailing/merchandising), COMMUNICATIONS AND THE ARTS (applied music, art, communications, comparative literature, dramatic arts, English, fine arts, French, German, Italian, jazz, music, music business management, Spanish, and theater design), COMPUTER AND PHYSICAL SCIENCE (chemistry, computer science, information sciences and systems, mathematics, and physics), EDUCATION (early childhood, elementary, foreign languages, music, physical, and secondary), ENGINEERING AND ENVIRONMENTAL DESIGN (environmental science), HEALTH PROFESSIONS (medical laboratory technology), SOCIAL SCIENCE (American studies, economics, geography, history, international studies, Judaic studies, Latin American studies, philosophy, political science/government, psychology, religion, social science, social studies, sociology, urban studies, and women's studies). Computer science, preprofessional, and psychology are the strongest academically. Accountancy, finance, and management are the largest.

Special: A co-op program in Jewish studies is offered with Spertus College of Judaica. Numerous internships in communications, commerce, and social sciences are possible. Study abroad is offered in 11 countries, and in a West European Seminar in Comparative Business Practices. Accelerated degree programs, dual majors, a certificate program in acting and costume construction, pass/fail options, and concentrations within the theater major, including acting, costume design, general theater studies, lighting design, playwriting, production theater management, and theater technology, are available. The School for New Learning provides evening and weekend degree programs for adult learners, with credit given for life and work experience. There are 21 national honor societies, a freshman honors program, and 29 departmental honors programs.

Admissions: 78% of the 1999-2000 applicants were accepted. The SAT I scores for the 1999-2000 freshman class were: Verbal--18% below 500, 44% between 500 and 599, 31% between 600 and 700, and 7% above 700; Math--24% below 500, 41% between 500 and 599, 31% between 600 and 700, and 4% above 700. The ACT scores were 19% below 21, 32% between 21 and 23, 24% between 24 and 26, 14% between 27 and 28, and 11% above 28. 44% of the current freshmen were in the top fifth of their class; 77% were in the top two fifths. 17 freshmen graduated first in their class, in a recent year.

Requirements: The SAT I or ACT is required. DePaul requires applicants to be in the upper 50% of their class. A GPA of 2.5 is required. Applicants should have completed 16 Carnegie units or submit the GED. A portfolio is required for theater majors, and an audition for acting and music majors. AP and CLEP credits are accepted. Important factors in the admissions decision are advanced placement or honor courses, leadership record, and extracurricular activities record.

Procedure: Freshmen are admitted to all sessions. Entrance exams should be taken by the spring of the junior year. There are early decision, early admissions, and deferred admissions plans. Early decision applications should be filed by November 15; regular applications, by August 15 for fall entry, December 3 for winter entry, February 24 for spring entry, and June 12 for summer entry, along with a $25 fee. Notification of early decision is sent December 1; regular decision, on a rolling basis.

Financial Aid: 73% of undergraduates work part time. Average annual earnings from campus work are $2000. DePaul is a member of CSS. The CSS/Profile is required. The fall application deadline is April 1.

Computers: The mainframe is an IBM system/390 Multiprize 2000. There are also 200 mainframe terminals and more than 600 PCs available. All students may access the system 14 hours each day or 24 hours a day by modem. There are no time limits and no fees. It is strongly recommended that all students have personal computers.

DEPAUW UNIVERSITY
Greencastle, IN 46135

(765) 658-4006
(800) 447-2495; Fax: (765) 658-4007

Full-time: 951 men, 1223 women	**Faculty:** 188; IIB, ++$
Part-time: 17 men, 25 women	**Ph.D.s:** 93%
Graduate: none	**Student/Faculty:** 12 to 1
Year: 4-1-4	**Tuition:** $19,730
Application Deadline: February 15	**Room & Board:** $6080
Freshman Class: 2687 applied, 1813 accepted, 581 enrolled	
SAT I or ACT: required	**HIGHLY COMPETITIVE**

DePauw University, founded in 1837, is a private institution affiliated with the United Methodist Church, offering programs in the fields of liberal arts and music. There are 2 undergraduate schools. In addition to regional accreditation, De-Pauw has baccalaureate program accreditation with NASM and NCATE. The 4 libraries contain 254,806 volumes, 331,600 microform items, and 10,890 audiovisual forms/CDs, and subscribe to 1518 periodicals. Computerized library services include the card catalog, interlibrary loans, and database searching. Special learning facilities include a learning resource center, art gallery, natural history museum, radio station, TV station, observatory, and nature preserve. The 175-acre campus is in a small town 45 miles west of Indianapolis. Including residence halls, there are 55 buildings.

Programs of Study: DePauw confers B.A., B.M.A., B.M.E., and B.Mu. degrees. Bachelor's degrees are awarded in BIOLOGICAL SCIENCE (biology/biological science), COMMUNICATIONS AND THE ARTS (art history and appreciation, classical languages, communications, English, English literature, French, German, Greek, Latin, music, music business management, music performance, music theory and composition, romance languages and literature, Spanish, and studio art), COMPUTER AND PHYSICAL SCIENCE (chemistry, computer science, earth science, geology, mathematics, and physics), EDUCATION (elementary and music), ENGINEERING AND ENVIRONMENTAL DESIGN (pre-engineering), HEALTH PROFESSIONS (medical technology), SOCIAL SCIENCE (anthropology, classical/ancient civilization, East Asian studies, economics, geography, history, interdisciplinary studies, peace studies, philosophy, physical fitness/movement, political science/government, psychology, religion, Russian and Slavic studies, sociology, and women's studies). English, economics, and communications are the largest.

Special: DePauw offers dual majors in any 2 disciplines, student-designed majors, internships for honors programs and winter-term projects, unlimited study-abroad options through cooperative arrangements with other universities, a Washington semester, pass/fail options, and credit by departmental examination. Also available are 3-2 engineering degrees with Case Western Reserve, Columbia, and Washington universities, and a 3-2 nursing program with Rush University Hospital in Chicago. The Media Fellows, Management Fellows, and Science

Research Fellows programs offer majors in any discipline, plus a semester-long internship. There are 13 national honor societies, including Phi Beta Kappa, and a freshman honors program.

Admissions: 67% of the 1999-2000 applicants were accepted. The SAT I scores for the 1999-2000 freshman class were: Verbal--8% below 500, 46% between 500 and 599, 38% between 600 and 700, and 8% above 700; Math--7% below 500, 44% between 500 and 599, 41% between 600 and 700, and 8% above 700. The ACT scores were 7% below 21, 19% between 21 and 23, 34% between 24 and 26, 18% between 27 and 28, and 22% above 28. 80% of the current freshmen were in the top fifth of their class; all were in the top two fifths. There were 10 National Merit finalists. 28 freshmen graduated first in their class.

Requirements: The SAT I or ACT is required. Graduation from an accredited secondary school or a GED is required for admission. Course distribution must include 4 in English, 3 to 4 each in math, social studies, and science (2 or more with lab), and 2 to 4 in a foreign language. An essay is required, and an interview is strongly recommended. Applicants for the School of Music must audition. Applications are accepted on computer disk or on-line at the school's web site. AP and CLEP credits are accepted. Important factors in the admissions decision are advanced placement or honor courses, recommendations by school officials, and personality/intangible qualities.

Procedure: Freshmen are admitted fall and spring. Entrance exams should be taken as early as possible. There are early decision, early admissions, and deferred admissions plans. Early decision applications should be filed by December 1; regular applications, by February 15 for fall entry and December 1 for spring entry, along with a $40 fee. Notification of early decision is sent December 15; regular decision, April 1. 33 early decision candidates were accepted for the 1999-2000 class. A waiting list is an active part of the admissions procedure.

Financial Aid: In 1999-2000, 99% of all freshmen and 96% of continuing students received some form of financial aid. 55% of freshmen and 47% of continuing students received need-based aid. The average freshman award was $19,671. Of that total, scholarships or need-based grants averaged $15,624 ($21,485 maximum); loans averaged $2512 ($3825 maximum); and work contracts averaged $1535 ($1700 maximum). 39% of undergraduates work part time. Average annual earnings from campus work are $749. The average financial indebtedness of the 1999 graduate was $13,218. DePauw is a member of CSS. The CSS/Profile, FAFSA or the college's own financial statement are required. The fall application deadline is February 15.

Computers: The mainframe is a DEC ALPHA D520 cluster. 130 PCs are available for student use. Locations include the computer center, library, residence halls, fraternities, sororities, and all academic offices. All public PCs, student rooms, classrooms, and faculty/staff offices are wired for access to the campuswide network and the Internet. Seminars are taught regularly, and all students have a computer account. All students may access the system 24 hours a day. There are no time limits and no fees.

DICKINSON COLLEGE
Carlisle, PA 17013

(717) 245-1231
(800) 644-1773; Fax: (717) 245-1442

Full-time: 804 men, 1228 women	**Faculty:** 154; IIB, ++$
Part-time: 16 men, 19 women	**Ph.D:s:** 96%
Graduate: none	**Student/Faculty:** 13 to 1
Year: semesters, summer session	**Tuition:** $24,450
Application Deadline: February 1	**Room & Board:** $6450
Freshman Class: 3439 applied, 2183 accepted, 620 enrolled	
SAT I or ACT: recommended	**HIGHLY COMPETITIVE**

Dickinson College, founded in 1773, is a private institution offering a liberal arts curriculum including international education and science. The library contains 452,632 volumes, 190,922 microform items, and 13,139 audiovisual forms/CDs, and subscribes to 1772 periodicals. Computerized library services include the card catalog, interlibrary loans, and database searching. Special learning facilities include an art gallery, planetarium, radio station, fiber optic and satellite telecommunications networks, telescope observatory, and an archival collection. The 114-acre campus is in a suburban area about 20 miles west of Harrisburg and 2 hours from Washington, DC. Including residence halls, there are 109 buildings.

Programs of Study: Dickinson confers B.A. and B.S. degrees. Bachelor's degrees are awarded in BIOLOGICAL SCIENCE (biochemistry and biology/biological science), BUSINESS (international business management), COMMUNICATIONS AND THE ARTS (classical languages, dance, dramatic arts, English, fine arts, French, German, Greek, Latin, music, Russian, Spanish, and theater design), COMPUTER AND PHYSICAL SCIENCE (chemistry, computer science, geology, mathematics, and physics), ENGINEERING AND ENVIRONMENTAL DESIGN (environmental science), HEALTH PROFESSIONS (environmental health science), SOCIAL SCIENCE (American studies, anthropology, classical/ancient civilization, East Asian studies, economics, history, international studies, Italian studies, Judaic studies, medieval studies, philosophy, political science/government, psychology, public affairs, religion, Russian and Slavic studies, and sociology). International education/foreign languages, natural sciences, and preprofessional programs are the strongest academically. Foreign languages, political science, and English are the largest.

Special: Students may cross-register with Central Pennsylvania Consortium Colleges. Also available are internships, academic year or summer study abroad in 9 countries, a Washington semester, work-study programs, accelerated degree programs, dual majors, student-designed majors, nondegree study, pass/fail options, and a 3-3 law degree with the Dickinson School of Law of the Pennsylvania State University. There are 3-2 engineering degrees offered with Case Western Reserve University, Rensselaer Polytechnic Institute, and University of Pennsylvania. Instruction in 12 languages is available. There are certification programs in Latin American studies, secondary education, and women's studies. Linkage programs are available with 7 graduate programs in business, accounting, and public administration at various institutions. There are 15 national honor societies, including Phi Beta Kappa, and 35 departmental honors programs.

Admissions: 63% of the 1999-2000 applicants were accepted. The SAT I scores for the 1999-2000 freshman class were: Verbal--7% below 500, 39% between 500 and 599, 43% between 600 and 700, and 11% above 700; Math--8% below 500, 46% between 500 and 599, 40% between 600 and 700, and 6% above 700. 78% of the current freshmen were in the top fifth of their class; 98% were in the

top two fifths. There were 18 National Merit finalists. 19 freshmen graduated first in their class.

Requirements: The SAT I or ACT is recommended. The SAT I and SAT II: Subject tests are optional submissions. The GED is accepted. Applicants should have completed 16 academic credits, including 4 years of English, 3 each of math and science, 2 (preferably 3) of foreign language, 2 of social studies, and 2 additional courses drawn from the above areas. An essay is required and an interview is recommended. Applications are accepted on computer disk and on-line via Common App, CollegeView, CollegeLink, and others. AP credits are accepted. Important factors in the admissions decision are advanced placement or honor courses, extracurricular activities record, and recommendations by school officials.

Procedure: Freshmen are admitted in the fall. Entrance exams should be taken in the spring of the junior year or the fall of the senior year. There are early decision and deferred admissions plans. Early decision applications should be filed by January 15; regular applications, by February 1 for fall entry, along with a $40 fee. Notification of early decision is sent February 15; regular decision, March 31. 106 early decision candidates were accepted for the 1999-2000 class. 19% of all applicants are on a waiting list.

Financial Aid: In 1999-2000, 84% of all freshmen and 72% of continuing students received some form of financial aid. 71% of freshmen and 65% of continuing students received need-based aid. The average freshman award was $18,842. Of that total, scholarships or need-based grants averaged $14,725 ($23,200 maximum); loans averaged $1907 ($5625 maximum); work contracts averaged $691 ($1400 maximum); and federal, state, and outside aid averaged $1517 ($20,525 maximum). 39% of undergraduates work part time. Average annual earnings from campus work are $1531. The average financial indebtedness of the 1999 graduate was $17,752. Dickinson is a member of CSS. The CSS/Profile is required. The fall application deadline is February 1.

Computers: The mainframe is a DEC 4100 ALPHA AXP. A fiber-optic network enables students to have private personal computer hookup to the mainframe from their residence hall rooms. All students are assigned ALPHA accounts for E-mail and Internet communications. There are more than 400 PCs and Macs in public areas and instructional spaces. All students may access the system. There are no time limits and no fees.

DRAKE UNIVERSITY
Des Moines, IA 50311

(515) 271-3181
(800) 44-DRAKE; Fax: (515) 271-2831

Full-time: 1219 men, 1737 women	**Faculty:** 233; IIA, +$
Part-time: 98 men, 180 women	**Ph.D.s:** 96%
Graduate: 641 men, 771 women	**Student/Faculty:** 13 to 1
Year: semesters, summer session	**Tuition:** $16,580
Application Deadline: March 1	**Room & Board:** $4870
Freshman Class: 2388 applied, 2147 accepted, 782 enrolled	
SAT I Verbal/Math: 568/585	**ACT:** 25 **VERY COMPETITIVE**

Drake University, founded in 1881, is a private institution offering undergraduate and graduate programs in arts and sciences, business and public administration, pharmacy and health sciences, journalism and mass communication, education, and fine arts. Some of the information in this profile is approximate. There are 6 undergraduate and 2 graduate schools. In addition to regional accreditation, Drake has baccalaureate program accreditation with AACSB, ACEJMC, ACPE, NASAD, NASM, NCATE, and NLN. The 2 libraries contain 454,698 volumes,

754,980 microform items, and 6000 audiovisual forms/CDs, and subscribe to 2905 periodicals. Computerized library services include the card catalog, interlibrary loans, and database searching. Special learning facilities include a learning resource center, art gallery, radio station, TV station, observatory, and the Henry G. Harmon Fine Arts Center. The 120-acre campus is in a suburban area in Des Moines. Including residence halls, there are 48 buildings.

Programs of Study: Drake confers B.A., B.S., B.A.Journ. and Mass Comm., B. Art., B.Art Ed., B.F.A., B.Mus., B.Mus.Ed., B.S.B.A., B.S.Ed, B.S.N., and B.S. Pharm. degrees. Master's and doctoral degrees are also awarded. Bachelor's degrees are awarded in BIOLOGICAL SCIENCE (biology/biological science), BUSINESS (accounting, banking and finance, business administration and management, insurance, and marketing/retailing/merchandising), COMMUNICATIONS AND THE ARTS (advertising, art history and appreciation, broadcasting, communications, design, dramatic arts, English, fine arts, French, German, graphic design, journalism, languages, music, music business management, music theory and composition, public relations, Spanish, and speech/debate/rhetoric), COMPUTER AND PHYSICAL SCIENCE (actuarial science, chemistry, computer science, mathematics, and physics), EDUCATION (art, early childhood, elementary, English, foreign languages, journalism, mathematics, middle school, music, reading, science, secondary, social science, and social studies), ENGINEERING AND ENVIRONMENTAL DESIGN (environmental science, interior design, and military science), HEALTH PROFESSIONS (medical laboratory technology, nursing, pharmacy, predentistry, and premedicine), SOCIAL SCIENCE (economics, history, international relations, philosophy, political science/government, prelaw, psychology, religion, social science, and sociology). Actuarial science, pharmacy, and rhetoric and communication studies are the strongest academically. Natural sciences, social sciences, and business are the largest.

Special: Study abroad is available in 67 countries and at sea. The university offers cross-registration, internships, a Washington semester, a United Nations semester, and work-study programs. Dual majors, B.A.-B.S. degrees, a 3-2 engineering degree, student-designed majors, credit for military and work experience, and nondegree study are possible. Students may take a maximum of 12 hours of course work on a credit/no credit basis. Drake emphasizes the use of computer technology. All schools and colleges incorporate computers into their courses of study. There are 22 national honor societies, including Phi Beta Kappa, and a freshman honors program.

Admissions: 90% of the 1999-2000 applicants were accepted. The SAT I scores for the 1999-2000 freshman class were: Verbal--20% below 500, 41% between 500 and 599, 29% between 600 and 700, and 10% above 700; Math--17% below 500, 34% between 500 and 599, 40% between 600 and 700, and 9% above 700. The ACT scores were 9% below 21, 24% between 21 and 23, 28% between 24 and 26, 17% between 27 and 28, and 22% above 28. 53% of the current freshmen were in the top fifth of their class; 83% were in the top two fifths. There were 13 National Merit finalists in a recent year.

Requirements: The SAT I or ACT is required. Drake requires applicants to be in the upper 50% of their class. A GPA of 3.0 is required. Applicants must be graduates of an accredited secondary school. The GED is accepted. Students must have completed 4 years of English, 2 years of math, and 10 other units to be selected from English, foreign languages, social studies, math, lab sciences, and others. A portfolio is required for art majors and for those seeking scholarship consideration. An audition is necessary for admission to the music program. Tapes are accepted. Applications are accepted on-line and on computer disk via several programs. AP and CLEP credits are accepted. Important factors in the admissions decision are advanced placement or honor courses, extracurricular activities record, and leadership record.

Procedure: Freshmen are admitted to all sessions. Entrance exams should be taken during the spring of the junior year or early fall of the senior year. There are early admissions and deferred admissions plans. For priority consideration, applications should be filed by August 1; otherwise, applications should be filed by March 1 for fall entry and December 1 for spring entry, along with a $25 fee. Notification is sent on a rolling basis.

Financial Aid: In 1999-2000, 97% of all freshmen and 96% of continuing students received some form of financial aid. 60% of freshmen and 59% of continuing students received need-based aid. The average freshman award was $14,290. Of that total, scholarships or need-based grants averaged $7290; loans averaged $4745; and work contracts averaged $1600. 53% of undergraduates work part time. Average annual earnings from campus work are $1000. The average financial indebtedness of the 1999 graduate was $19,630. Drake is a member of CSS. The FAFSA is required. The fall application deadline is March 1.

Computers: The mainframes are 2 Digital 4000/600s, 1 Digital 4000/300, and 3 Digital ALPHA Server 2100s with quad processors. Every residence hall room is equipped with a Power Mac 7100 computer, printer, and software. A data network permits students to access a variety of services from their rooms, including the campuswide information system, the on-line library catalog, the Internet, and E-mail. Several additional computer labs are located across campus. All students may access the system. There are no time limits. The fee is $100 (for residence hall residents).

DREW UNIVERSITY/COLLEGE OF LIBERAL ARTS

Madison, NJ 07940   (973) 408-DREW; Fax: (973) 408-3068

Full-time: 607 men, 823 women	**Faculty:** 117; IIA, +$
Part-time: 22 men, 34 women	**Ph.D.s:** 93%
Graduate: 373 men, 338 women	**Student/Faculty:** 12 to 1
Year: semesters, summer session	**Tuition:** $23,008
Application Deadline: February 15	**Room & Board:** $6564
Freshman Class: 2400 applied, 1799 accepted, 405 enrolled	
SAT I Verbal/Math: 610/605	**VERY COMPETITIVE**

The College of Liberal Arts was added to Drew University in 1928 and is part of an educational complex that includes a theological school and a graduate school. Drew is a private, independent institution affiliated with the United Methodist Church. There are 2 graduate schools. The library contains 472,726 volumes and 358,583 microform items, and subscribes to 2612 periodicals. Computerized library services include the card catalog, interlibrary loans, and database searching. Special learning facilities include an art gallery, radio station, observatory, photography gallery, and TV satellite dish. The 186-acre campus is in a small town 30 miles west of New York City. Including residence halls, there are 57 buildings.

Programs of Study: Drew confers the B.A. degree. Master's and doctoral degrees are also awarded. Bachelor's degrees are awarded in BIOLOGICAL SCIENCE (biology/biological science and life science), COMMUNICATIONS AND THE ARTS (classics, dramatic arts, English, fine arts, French, German, music, Russian, Spanish, and visual and performing arts), COMPUTER AND PHYSICAL SCIENCE (chemistry, computer science, mathematics, physical sciences, and physics), SOCIAL SCIENCE (American studies, anthropology, behavioral science, economics, ethnic studies, history, philosophy, political science/government, psychobiology, psychology, religion, Russian and Slavic studies, social science, sociology, and theological studies). Biological and physical sciences are the strongest academically. Social sciences is the largest.

Special: Drew offers co-op programs with the University of Miami, the University of Hawaii, and Duke University, as well as cross-registration with the College of Saint Elizabeth and Fairleigh Dickinson University. There are also dual majors, study abroad, a Wall Street semester, a Washington semester, student-designed majors, internships, field work, 3-2 engineering programs with Washington University in St. Louis and the Stevens Institute of Technology, and a 7-year B.A.-M.D. program in Medicine with UMDNJ. There are 11 national honor societies, including Phi Beta Kappa, and 12 departmental honors programs.

Admissions: 75% of the 1999-2000 applicants were accepted. The SAT I scores for the 1999-2000 freshman class were: Verbal--8% below 500, 34% between 500 and 599, 39% between 600 and 699, and 18% above 699; Math--9% below 500, 39% between 500 and 599, 38% between 600 and 699, and 14% above 699. 70% of the current freshmen were in the top quarter of their class; 92% were in the top half.

Requirements: The SAT I or ACT is required; the SAT I is preferred. The university strongly recommends 18 academic credits or Carnegie units, including 4 in English, 3 in math, and 2 each in foreign language, science, social studies, and history, with the remaining 3 in additional academic courses. 3 SAT II: Subject tests are recommended, including 1 in writing. An essay is also required, and an interview is recommended. AP and CLEP credits are accepted. Important factors in the admissions decision are advanced placement or honor courses, leadership record, and extracurricular activities record.

Procedure: Freshmen are admitted fall and spring. Entrance exams should be taken by January of the senior year. There are early decision, early admissions, and deferred admissions plans. Early decision applications should be filed by December 1 or January 15; regular applications, by February 15 for fall entry and December 1 for spring entry, along with a $40 fee. Notification of early decision is sent December 24 or February 15; regular decision, March 15. 44 early decision candidates were accepted for the 1999-2000 class. A waiting list is an active part of the admissions procedure.

Financial Aid: In a recent year, 82% of all freshmen and 80% of continuing students received some form of financial aid. 56% of freshmen and 57% of continuing students received need-based aid. The average freshman award was $13,000. Of that total, scholarships or need-based grants averaged $11,428 ($20,866 maximum); loans averaged $2096 ($4600 maximum); and work contracts averaged $1594 ($1700 maximum). 80% of undergraduates work part time. Average annual earnings from campus work are $1300. The average financial indebtedness of the 1999 graduate was $12,880. The CSS/Profile or FFS is required. The fall application deadline is March 1.

Computers: All full-time students are provided with a free Pentium notebook computer, a printer, and accompanying software. An extensive software library and additional computers are located on campus. Students also have access to the Internet and E-mail, with connections in many of the residence halls. All students may access the system. There are no time limits and no fees.

DREXEL UNIVERSITY
Philadelphia, PA 19104

(215) 895-2400
(800) 2-DREXEL; Fax: (215) 895-5939

Full-time: 4728 men, 2855 women	**Faculty:** 461; I, -$
Part-time: 1265 men, 684 women	**Ph.D.s:** 96%
Graduate: 1496 men, 987 women	**Student/Faculty:** 16 to 1
Year: quarters, summer session	**Tuition:** $16,330
Application Deadline: March 1	**Room & Board:** $7950
Freshman Class: 9206 applied, 6176 accepted, 1882 enrolled	
SAT I Verbal/Math: 560/590	**VERY COMPETITIVE**

Drexel University, established in 1891, is a private institution with undergraduate programs in business and administration, engineering, information studies, design arts, and arts and sciences. There are 9 undergraduate and 8 graduate schools. In addition to regional accreditation, Drexel has baccalaureate program accreditation with AACSB, ABET, ADA, FIDER, NAAB, and NASAD. The library contains 290,000 volumes, 651,500 microform items, and 32,935 audiovisual forms/CDs, and subscribes to 9662 periodicals. Computerized library services include the card catalog, interlibrary loans, and database searching. Special learning facilities include a learning resource center, art gallery, radio station, and TV station. The 38-acre campus is in an urban area near the center of Philadelphia. Including residence halls, there are 34 buildings.

Programs of Study: Drexel confers B.S. and B.Arch. degrees. Master's and doctoral degrees are also awarded. Bachelor's degrees are awarded in BIOLOGICAL SCIENCE (biology/biological science and nutrition), BUSINESS (accounting, business administration and management, fashion merchandising, hotel/motel and restaurant management, international business management, management information systems, and marketing/retailing/merchandising), COMMUNICATIONS AND THE ARTS (communications, design, film arts, graphic design, literature, music, photography, and video), COMPUTER AND PHYSICAL SCIENCE (chemistry, computer science, mathematics, physics, and science), EDUCATION (education), ENGINEERING AND ENVIRONMENTAL DESIGN (architectural engineering, architecture, chemical engineering, civil engineering, computer engineering, construction management, electrical/electronics engineering, environmental engineering, environmental science, interior design, materials engineering, and mechanical engineering), HEALTH PROFESSIONS (predentistry and premedicine), SOCIAL SCIENCE (fashion design and technology, food production/management/services, history, international studies, political science/government, prelaw, psychology, and sociology). Engineering, business, and design arts are the strongest academically. Electrical and computer engineering, business, and architecture are the largest.

Special: The Drexel Plan of Cooperative Education enables students to alternate periods of full-time classroom studies and full-time employment with university-approved employers. Participation in cooperative education is mandatory, for most students. Cross-registration is available with Eastern Mennonite College, Indiana University of Pennsylvania, and Lincoln University. Drexel also offers study abroad, internships, accelerated degrees, 3-3 engineering degrees, dual majors, nondegree study, credit/no credit options, and a Sea Education Association semester. There is a freshman honors program.

Admissions: 67% of the 1999-2000 applicants were accepted. The SAT I scores for the 1999-2000 freshman class were: Verbal--16% below 500, 50% between 500 and 599, 31% between 600 and 700, and 3% above 700; Math--9% below 500, 43% between 500 and 599, 42% between 600 and 700, and 6% above 700.

183

47% of the current freshmen were in the top fifth of their class; 80% were in the top two fifths. There were 26 National Merit finalists in a recent year. 12 freshmen graduated first in their class.

Requirements: The SAT I or ACT is required. A GPA of 2.0 is required. Applicants must be graduates of an accredited secondary school. The GED is accepted. An interview is recommended. Applications may be submitted on-line to the university's Web page. AP and CLEP credits are accepted. Important factors in the admissions decision are advanced placement or honor courses, evidence of special talent, and recommendations by school officials.

Procedure: Freshmen are admitted to all sessions. Entrance exams should be taken by January 15 of the senior year. There are early admissions and deferred admissions plans. Applications should be filed by March 1 for fall entry, along with a $35 fee. Notification is sent on a rolling basis.

Financial Aid: In 1999-2000, 90% of all freshmen and 85% of continuing students received some form of financial aid. 67% of freshmen and 52% of continuing students received need-based aid. The average freshman award was $12,094. Of that total, scholarships or need-based grants averaged $6248; loans averaged $3212 ($8362 maximum); and work contracts averaged $609 ($1200 maximum). 16% of undergraduates work part time. Average annual earnings from campus work are $600. In sophomore and later years, co-op earnings average about $10,000 per year. Drexel is a member of CSS. The FAFSA is required. The fall application deadline is May 1.

Computers: The mainframes are an IBM 9121/320 and a Sun Server 670. Students may access the mainframe, the library, and the Internet through PCs in dormitories or residences. There are also 610 networked public computers available. All students may access the system 24 hours a day. There are no time limits and no fees. It is strongly recommended that all students have personal computers.

DRURY UNIVERSITY
Springfield, MO 65802

(417) 873-7205
(800) 922-2274; Fax: (417) 866-3873

Full-time: 669 men, 762 women	**Faculty:** 118; IIB, av$
Part-time: 11 men, 13 women	**Ph.D.s:** 90%
Graduate: 91 men, 196 women	**Student/Faculty:** 12 to 1
Year: semesters, summer session	**Tuition:** $10,795
Application Deadline: August 1	**Room & Board:** $4030
Freshman Class: 994 applied, 902 accepted, 378 enrolled	
ACT: 24	**VERY COMPETITIVE**

Drury University, formerly Drury College, founded in 1873, is a private university with degree programs emphasizing the liberal arts, architecture, business, communications, economics, education, and health sciences. There are 5 graduate schools. In addition to regional accreditation, Drury has baccalaureate program accreditation with ACBSP, NAAB, and NCATE. The library contains 250,758 volumes, 121,609 microform items, and 2356 audiovisual forms/CDs, and subscribes to 772 periodicals. Computerized library services include the card catalog, interlibrary loans, and database searching. Special learning facilities include an art gallery, radio station, TV station, teleconference facility, and an art and architecture slide collection. The 60-acre campus is in an urban area 200 miles southwest of St. Louis and 150 miles southeast of Kansas City. Including residence halls, there are 19 buildings.

Programs of Study: Drury confers B.A., B.Arch., B.M., and B.M.Ed. degrees. Master's degrees are also awarded. Bachelor's degrees are awarded in BIOLOGI-

CAL SCIENCE (biology/biological science), BUSINESS (accounting, business administration and management, and international business management), COMMUNICATIONS AND THE ARTS (advertising, art history and appreciation, broadcasting, communications, dramatic arts, English, fine arts, French, German, journalism, music, public relations, Spanish, and speech/debate/rhetoric), COMPUTER AND PHYSICAL SCIENCE (chemistry, information sciences and systems, mathematics, and physics), EDUCATION (elementary, music, physical, secondary, and special), ENGINEERING AND ENVIRONMENTAL DESIGN (architecture and environmental science), HEALTH PROFESSIONS (exercise science, nursing, predentistry, premedicine, and preveterinary science), SOCIAL SCIENCE (criminology, economics, history, philosophy, physical fitness/movement, political science/government, prelaw, psychology, and sociology). Premedicine, preprofessional programs, and architecture are the strongest academically. Business administration, biology, and communication are the largest.

Special: Drury offers cross-registration with Regents College in London, a cooperative program in international business, study abroad in 6 countries, internships, a Washington semester, credit by examination, nondegree study, dual majors in most majors, satisfactory/unsatisfactory options, and a 3-2 engineering degree in conjunction with the University of Missouri and Washington University in St. Louis, as well as a premedical arrangement with St. Louis University and the University of Missouri-Columbia. There are 12 national honor societies, and a freshman honors program. All departments have honors program.

Admissions: 91% of the 1999-2000 applicants were accepted. The ACT scores for the 1999-2000 freshman class were: 16% below 21, 28% between 21 and 23, 29% between 24 and 26, 10% between 27 and 28, and 17% above 28. 49% of the current freshmen were in the top fifth of their class; 76% were in the top two fifths. There was 1 National Merit finalist and 3 semifinalists. 20 freshmen graduated first in their class.

Requirements: The SAT I or ACT is required. Drury requires applicants to be in the upper 50% of their class. A GPA of 2.7 is required. In addition, applicants must be graduates of an accredited secondary school or have a GED certificate. Recommended high school credits include 4 units of English and at least 3 each of math through algebra II, natural science, and social studies. An essay and a reference from the high school counselor or principal are required. Applications are accepted on-line at the school's web site. AP and CLEP credits are accepted. Important factors in the admissions decision are advanced placement or honor courses, extracurricular activities record, and leadership record.

Procedure: Freshmen are admitted to all sessions. Entrance exams should be taken in the spring of the junior year or fall of the senior year. There are early admissions and deferred admissions plans. Applications should be filed by August 1 for fall entry and December 1 for spring entry, along with a $20 fee. Notification is sent on a rolling basis.

Financial Aid: In 1999-2000, 88% of all freshmen and 82% of continuing students received some form of financial aid. 77% of freshmen and 70% of continuing students received need-based aid. The average freshman award was $5937. Of that total, scholarships or need-based grants averaged $4050 ($10,450 maximum); loans averaged $1450 ($10,500 maximum); and work contracts averaged $1500 ($2000 maximum). 87% of undergraduates work part time. Average annual earnings from campus work are $1350. The average financial indebtedness of the 1999 graduate was $12,285. Drury is a member of CSS. The FAFSA and the college's own financial statement are required. The fall application deadline is April 1.

Computers: The mainframes are an IBM AS/400, available only to office employees. The technology center has more than 100 PCs available to all students for academic use, including teleconferencing and access to the Internet. All students may access the system 24 hours a day, 7 days a week in the technology center. There are no time limits and no fees.

DUKE UNIVERSITY
Durham, NC 27706
(919) 684-3214; Fax: (919) 681-8941

Full-time: 3287 men, 3035 women	**Faculty:** 717
Part-time: 25 men, 21 women	**Ph.D.s:** 97%
Graduate: 2928 men, 2515 women	**Student/Faculty:** 9 to 1
Year: semesters, summer session	**Tuition:** $24,751
Application Deadline: January 2	**Room & Board:** $7088
Freshman Class: 13,407 applied, 3779 accepted, 1630 enrolled	
SAT I Verbal/Math: 690/710	**MOST COMPETITIVE**

Duke University, founded in 1838, is a private institution affiliated with the United Methodist Church and offering undergraduate programs in arts and sciences and engineering. There are 2 undergraduate and 8 graduate schools. In addition to regional accreditation, Duke has baccalaureate program accreditation with AACSB, ABET, ACPE, AHEA, APTA, NCATE, NLN, and SAF. The 9 libraries contain 4.6 million volumes, 3.4 million microform items, and 191,430 audiovisual forms/CDs, and subscribe to 32,003 periodicals. Computerized library services include the card catalog, interlibrary loans, and database searching. Special learning facilities include a learning resource center, art gallery, radio station, TV station, marine lab at Beaufort, primate center, center for international studies, nuclear lab, free electron laser, science research center, and institutes of the arts, statistics and decision sciences, policy sciences and public affairs, centers for teaching and learning, community service, geometric computing, culture, and women. The 9350-acre campus is in a suburban area 285 miles southwest of Washington, D.C. Including residence halls, there are 230 buildings.

Programs of Study: Duke confers A.B., B.S., and B.S.E. degrees. Master's and doctoral degrees are also awarded. Bachelor's degrees are awarded in BIOLOGICAL SCIENCE (anatomy and biology/biological science), COMMUNICATIONS AND THE ARTS (African languages, art history and appreciation, classical languages, dramatic arts, English, Germanic languages and literature, linguistics, literature, music, Slavic languages, Spanish, and visual and performing arts), COMPUTER AND PHYSICAL SCIENCE (chemistry, computer science, geology, mathematics, and physics), ENGINEERING AND ENVIRONMENTAL DESIGN (biomedical engineering, civil engineering, electrical/electronics engineering, environmental science, materials science, and mechanical engineering), SOCIAL SCIENCE (African American studies, African studies, anthropology, area studies, Asian/Oriental studies, Canadian studies, classical/ancient civilization, economics, French studies, history, Italian studies, medieval studies, philosophy, political science/government, psychology, public affairs, religion, sociology, and women's studies). The sciences, public policy studies, and political science are the strongest academically. Biology, psychology, and history are the largest.

Special: Duke offers cross-registration with the University of North Carolina/Chapel Hill and North Carolina State and North Carolina Central Universities. Also available are internships through the Career Development Center, study abroad in 22 countries, and a Washington semester. An accelerated degree program is possible, achieving graduation in 3 years or combining the senior year with the first graduate year of the law, business, or environment schools. Several 3-2 and 4-1 medical technology programs (degree completed at Duke) are available. Project Calc, an innovative program in calculus, is also offered. Dual majors of any combination, student-designed majors, nondegree study, and pass/fail options are possible. There are 3 national honor societies, including Phi Beta Kappa.

Admissions: 28% of the 1999-2000 applicants were accepted. The SAT I scores for the 1999-2000 freshman class were: Verbal--2% below 500, 9% between 500 and 599, 40% between 600 and 700, and 49% above 700; Math--6% between 500 and 599, 31% between 600 and 700, and 62% above 700. 95% of the current freshmen were in the top fifth of their class; 99% were in the top two fifths.

Requirements: The SAT I or ACT is required. 3 SAT II: Subject tests, including writing, are required. Applicants must be graduates of an accredited secondary school and have completed 15 academic credits, with 4 in English and 3 each in math, science, and foreign language; an additional 2 in social studies or history are recommended. Engineering students must have 4 credit units in math and 1 in physics or chemistry. An essay is required and an interview is recommended. A portfolio or audition is advised in appropriate instances. AP credits are accepted. Important factors in the admissions decision are advanced placement or honor courses, recommendations by school officials, and extracurricular activities record.

Procedure: Freshmen are admitted fall and spring. Entrance exams should be taken in October of the junior year for early decision applicants and by January of the senior year for regular decision. There are early decision, early admissions, and deferred admissions plans. Early decision applications should be filed by November 1; regular applications, by January 2 for fall entry and October 15 for spring entry, along with a $60 fee. Notification of early decision is sent December 15; regular decision, April 15. 536 early decision candidates were accepted for the 1999-2000 class. A waiting list is an active part of the admissions procedure.

Financial Aid: In 1999-2000, 40% of all students received some form of financial aid. 36% of freshmen and 38% of continuing students received need-based aid. The average freshman award was $19,030. Of that total, scholarships or need-based grants averaged $16,565 ($32,770 maximum); loans averaged $2994 ($5520 maximum); and work contracts averaged $1088 ($2300 maximum). 30% of undergraduates work part time. Average annual earnings from campus work are $1400. The average financial indebtedness of the 1999 graduate was $16,098. Duke is a member of CSS. The CSS/Profile or FAFSA is required. The fall application deadline is February 1.

Computers: The mainframe is an IBM 9672. Students may access a number of computer clusters located throughout the campus, providing access to networked and nonnetworked PCs and to workstations. About 600 terminals/PCs are available for general student use. All students have access to E-mail and the Internet. All residential rooms have a 10 MB Ethernet connection to the Duke Network of Unix systems and to the Internet. All students may access the system 24 hours a day. There are no time limits and no fees. It is recommended that all students have personal computers.

DUQUESNE UNIVERSITY
Pittsburgh, PA 15282-0201

(412) 396-5000
(800) 456-0590; Fax: (412) 396-5644

Full-time: 2111 men, 2936 women	**Faculty:** 380; IIA, +$
Part-time: 213 men, 277 women	**Ph.D.s:** 92%
Graduate: 1825 men, 2380 women	**Student/Faculty:** 13 to 1
Year: semesters, summer session	**Tuition:** $14,378
Application Deadline: July 1	**Room & Board:** $6314
Freshman Class: 3783 applied, 3180 accepted, 1214 enrolled	
SAT I Verbal/Math: 540/543	**ACT:** 24 **VERY COMPETITIVE**

Duquesne University, founded in 1878, is a private institution affiliated with the Roman Catholic Church, offering programs in liberal arts, natural and environmental sciences, nursing, health sciences, pharmacy, business, music, teacher preparation, preprofessional training, and law. There are 9 undergraduate and 10 graduate schools, including Continuing Education. In addition to regional accreditation, Duquesne has baccalaureate program accreditation with AACSB, ACPE, APTA, NASM, NCATE, and NLN. The 2 libraries contain 629,145 volumes, 259,466 microform items, and 22,381 audiovisual forms/CDs, and subscribe to 3800 periodicals. Computerized library services include the card catalog, interlibrary loans, and database searching. Special learning facilities include a learning resource center, art gallery, radio station, TV station, and and 81 multimedia classrooms. The 43-acre campus is in an urban area on a private, self-contained campus in the center of Pittsburgh. Including residence halls, there are 30 buildings.

Programs of Study: Duquesne confers B.A., B.S., B.S.A.T., B.S.B.A., B.S.Ed., B.S.H.M.S., B.S.H.S., B.S.M., B.S.M.E., B.S.M.T., B.S.N., B.S.P.S., and B.S. P.T. degrees. Master's and doctoral degrees are also awarded. Bachelor's degrees are awarded in BIOLOGICAL SCIENCE (biochemistry, biology/biological science, and microbiology), BUSINESS (accounting, banking and finance, business administration and management, international business management, investments and securities, marketing and distribution, marketing/retailing/merchandising, and sports management), COMMUNICATIONS AND THE ARTS (audio technology, classical languages, communications, English, Greek, journalism, Latin, literature, media arts, music, music performance, Spanish, and studio art), COMPUTER AND PHYSICAL SCIENCE (chemistry, computer science, information sciences and systems, mathematics, and physics), EDUCATION (athletic training, early childhood, education of the deaf and hearing impaired, elementary, foreign languages, music, science, secondary, and special), HEALTH PROFESSIONS (health care administration, health science, music therapy, nursing, occupational therapy, pharmacy, physical therapy, physician's assistant, and speech pathology/audiology), SOCIAL SCIENCE (classical/ancient civilization, history, philosophy, political science/government, prelaw, psychology, sociology, and theological studies). Chemistry, biology, and environmental science are the strongest academically. Business, liberal arts, and health sciences are the largest.

Special: The university offers co-op programs in business, communications, nursing, and health sciences, cross-registration through the Pittsburgh Council on Higher Education, internships, study abroad in 12 to 13 countries, work-study programs at 100 sites, and a Washington semester. Also available are B.A.-B.S. degrees, Saturday College, a general studies degree, an accelerated degree program, dual and student-designed majors, a 3-2 engineering program with Case Western Reserve University and University of Pittsburgh, pass/fail options, and credit for life, military, and work experience. There are 4 national honor societies, a freshman honors program, and 24 departmental honors programs.

Admissions: 84% of the 1999-2000 applicants were accepted. The SAT I scores for the 1999-2000 freshman class were: Verbal--32% below 500, 46% between 500 and 599, 20% between 600 and 700, and 2% above 700; Math--31% below 500, 45% between 500 and 599, 22% between 600 and 700, and 2% above 700. The ACT scores were 22% below 21, 27% between 21 and 23, 26% between 24 and 26, 13% between 27 and 28, and 12% above 28. 46% of the current freshmen were in the top fifth of their class; 74% were in the top two fifths.

Requirements: The SAT I or ACT is required. A GPA of 2.8 is required. students should have either a high school diploma or the GED. Applicants are required to have 16 academic credits, including 4 each in English and academic electives, and 8 combined in social studies, language, math, or science. An audition is required for music majors. An essay is required and an interview is recommended. AP and CLEP credits are accepted. Important factors in the admissions decision are advanced placement or honor courses, geographic diversity, and ability to finance college education.

Procedure: Freshmen are admitted to all sessions. There are early decision, early admissions, and deferred admissions plans. Early decision applications should be filed by November 1; regular applications, by July 1 for fall entry, December 1 for spring entry, and April 1 for summer entry, along with a $50 fee. Notification of early decision is sent December 15; regular decision, after December 15. 227 early decision candidates were accepted for the 1999-2000 class.

Financial Aid: In 1999-2000, 89% of all freshmen and 76% of continuing students received some form of financial aid. 58% of freshmen and 46% of continuing students received need-based aid. The average freshman award was $9898. Of that total, scholarships or need-based grants averaged $6542 ($22,934 maximum); loans averaged $1895 ($4625 maximum); work contracts averaged $1178 ($2318 maximum); and outside grants and loans averaged $283 ($6000) maximum. 29% of undergraduates work part time. Average annual earnings from campus work are $1611. The average financial indebtedness of the 1999 graduate was $13,114. Duquesne is a member of CSS. The FAFSA and the college's own financial statement are required. The fall application deadline is May 1.

Computers: The mainframe is a DEC ALPHA. There are also 550 PCs available in labs throughout the campus. All students can use the entire system 24 hours from residence halls, campus, and home. There are 81 multimedia classrooms. Both the campus net and the Internet are used for E-mail, library access, research, and on-line courses. There are no time limits and no fees. It is strongly recommended that all students have personal computers.

EARLHAM COLLEGE
Richmond, IN 47374

(765) 983-1600
(800) 327-5426; Fax: (765) 983-1560

Full-time: 484 men, 619 women	**Faculty:** 88; IIB, +$
Part-time: 4 men, 16 women	**Ph.D.s:** 98%
Graduate: 23 men, 30 women	**Student/Faculty:** 13 to 1
Year: semesters plus May term	**Tuition:** $20,256
Application Deadline: February 15	**Room & Board:** $4810
Freshman Class: 1038 applied, 869 accepted, 296 enrolled	
SAT I Verbal/Math: 620/580	**ACT:** 26 **VERY COMPETITIVE**

Earlham College, established in 1847 by the Society of Friends, is a private liberal arts institution that emphasizes Quaker values. It offers undergraduate programs in humanities, fine arts, social sciences, languages, music, and natural sciences. There is 1 graduate school. The 2 libraries contain 381,739 volumes, 224,282 microform items, and 1972 audiovisual forms/ CDs, and subscribe to 1339 periodicals. Computerized library services include the card catalog, interlibrary loans, and database searching. Special learning facilities include a learning resource center, art gallery, natural history museum, planetarium, radio station, observatory, herbarium, and greenhouse. The 800-acre campus is in a small town 70 miles east of Indianapolis and 40 miles west of Dayton, Ohio. Including residence halls, there are 57 buildings.

Programs of Study: Earlham confers the B.A. degree. Master's degrees are also awarded. Bachelor's degrees are awarded in BIOLOGICAL SCIENCE (biology/biological science), BUSINESS (management science), COMMUNICATIONS AND THE ARTS (art, dramatic arts, English, French, German, music, and Spanish), COMPUTER AND PHYSICAL SCIENCE (chemistry, computer science, geology, mathematics, and physics), EDUCATION (education), ENGINEERING AND ENVIRONMENTAL DESIGN (environmental science), SOCIAL SCIENCE (African American studies, anthropology, classical/ancient civilization, economics, history, human development, international relations, international studies, Japanese studies, Latin American studies, peace studies, philosophy, political science/government, psychology, religion, sociology, and women's studies). Natural sciences, psychology, and English are the strongest academically. Biology, English, and psychology are the largest.

Special: Opportunities are provided for dual majors, co-op programs in education, nursing, business, and architecture, cross-registration with Indiana University, internships, work-study programs, accelerated degree programs, nondegree study, and student-designed majors. Study abroad is available through 27 foreign and domestic programs. Pre-professional and professional options are offered in law and medicine. There is a 3-2 engineering degree with Case Western Reserve University, Columbia University, University of Rochester, and Rensselaer Polytechnic Institute. There is 1 national honor society, Phi Beta Kappa.

Admissions: 84% of the 1999-2000 applicants were accepted. The SAT I scores for the 1999-2000 freshman class were: Verbal--6% below 500, 33% between 500 and 599, 43% between 600 and 700, and 18% above 700; Math--14% below 500, 42% between 500 and 599, 38% between 600 and 700, and 7% above 700. The ACT scores were 18% below 21, 24% between 21 and 23, 30% between 24 and 26, 21% between 27 and 28, and 6% above 28. 38% of the current freshmen were in the top fifth of their class; 70% were in the top two fifths. There were 3 National Merit finalists. 3 freshmen graduated first in their class.

Requirements: The SAT I is required. A GPA of 3.0 is required. In most cases, graduation from an accredited secondary school is required; a GED will be accepted. Home-schooled students are not required to take the GED or have a high school diploma. Students must have completed at least 15 academic credits, including 4 years of English, 3 of math, and 2 each of science, history or social studies, and a foreign language. Students are required to submit an essay and letters of recommendation from a teacher and guidance counselor. An interview is recommended. Applications are accepted on computer disk and on-line; Earlham is a member of the Common Application group. AP and CLEP credits are accepted. Important factors in the admissions decision are advanced placement or honor courses, evidence of special talent, and extracurricular activities record.

Procedure: Freshmen are admitted fall and spring. Entrance exams should be taken during the spring of the junior year or early fall of the senior year. There are early decision, early admissions, and deferred admissions plans. Early decision applications should be filed by December 1; regular applications, by February 15 for fall entry, and November 15 for winter or spring entry, along with a

$30 fee. Notification of early decision is sent December 15; regular decision, March 15. 27 early decision candidates were accepted for the 1999-2000 class.

Financial Aid: In 1999-2000, 80% of all freshmen and 67% of continuing students received some form of financial aid. 68% of freshmen and 61% of continuing students received need-based aid. The average freshman award was $19,982. Of that total, scholarships or need-based grants averaged $11,401 ($25,068 maximum); loans averaged $3687 ($5125 maximum); and work contracts averaged $1648 (maximum). 55% of undergraduates work part time. Average annual earnings from campus work are $790. The average financial indebtedness of the 1999 graduate was $10,366. Earlham is a member of CSS. The FAFSA and the college's own financial statement are required. The fall application deadline is March 1.

Computers: The mainframes are a DEC MicroVAX 3100-80, 2 DEC ALPHA 1000s, 2 Dell Power Edge 2100/200s, and Power Mac G3. There are 6 public computer labs containing a total of 120 machines. All lab machines give access to the Internet, the World Wide Web, and E-mail services. In addition, students who have their own computers can connect from dorm rooms to the campus LAN. All students may access the system 24 hours a day. There are no time limits and no fees.

EASTMAN SCHOOL OF MUSIC
Rochester, NY 14604

(716) 232-8601
(800) 388-9695; Fax: (716) 274-1088

Full-time: 215 men, 282 women	**Faculty:** 89
Part-time: 1 man, 3 women	**Ph.D.s:** 55%
Graduate: 152 men, 179 women	**Student/Faculty:** 6 to 1
Year: semesters	**Tuition:** $20,786
Application Deadline: January 1	**Room & Board:** $7512
Freshman Class: 1092 applied, 298 accepted, 158 enrolled	
SAT I or ACT: not required	**SPECIAL**

Eastman School of Music, founded in 1921, is a private professional school of music within the University of Rochester. In addition to regional accreditation, Eastman has baccalaureate program accreditation with NASM. The library contains 185,758 volumes, 15,868 microform items, and 66,564 audiovisual forms CDs, and subscribes to 620 periodicals. Computerized library services include the card catalog, interlibrary loans, and database searching. Special learning facilities include a learning resource center, art gallery, recording studios, a music library, a theater, and 3 recital halls. The 3-acre campus is in an urban area in downtown Rochester. Including residence halls, there are 5 buildings.

Programs of Study: Eastman confers the B.M. degree. Master's and doctoral degrees are also awarded. Bachelor's degrees are awarded in COMMUNICATIONS AND THE ARTS (jazz, music, music performance, and music theory and composition), EDUCATION (music). Performance is the largest.

Special: The school and the University of Rochester cooperatively offer the B.A. degree with a music concentration. All the facilities of the university are open to Eastman students. Cross-registration is also available with colleges in the Rochester Consortium. Dual majors are available in all areas of study. Internships and study abroad are also possible.

Admissions: 27% of the 1999-2000 applicants were accepted.

Requirements: Applicants should be graduates of an accredited secondary school with 16 academic credits, including 4 years of English. The GED is accepted. An audition and an interview are required, as are 3 letters of recommendation. Some majors have other specific requirements. Important factors in the admissions decision are evidence of special talent, recommendations by alumni, and personality/intangible qualities.

Procedure: Freshmen are admitted fall and spring. Applications should be filed by January 1 for fall entry and November 1 for spring entry, along with a $50 fee. Notification is sent on a rolling basis. 10% of all applicants are on a waiting list.

Financial Aid: In 1999-2000, 99% of all freshmen and 98% of continuing students received some form of financial aid. 73% of freshmen and 71% of continuing students received need-based aid. The average freshman award was $16,060. Of that total, scholarships or need-based grants averaged $10,970 ($14,500 maximum); loans averaged $2625 ($5125 maximum); work contracts averaged $750 ($1500 maximum); and external grants and awards averaged $1000 ($11,250 maximum). 70% of undergraduates work part time. Average annual earnings from campus work are $800. The average financial indebtedness of the 1999 graduate was $10,000. Eastman is a member of CSS. The CSS/Profile or FAFSA and the college's own financial statement are required. The fall application deadline is February 1.

Computers: The mainframe is an SGI origin 200 (UNIX). IBM PCs and Macs are located in residence halls, the library, and the main building. There is also a computer music center with Musical Instrument Digital Interface. Residence hall rooms are wired for Internet access. A new Internet Cafe is located in the main building and contains 8 Macs. All students may access the system. There are no time limits. The fee is $50.

ECKERD COLLEGE
St. Petersburg, FL 33711

(727) 864-8331
(800) 456-9009; Fax: (727) 866-2304

Full-time: 682 men, 831 women	**Faculty:** 96; IIB, +$
Part-time: 9 men, 8 women	**Ph.D.s:** 95%
Graduate: none	**Student/Faculty:** 16 to 1
Year: 4-1-4, summer session	**Tuition:** $17,975
Application Deadline: April 1	**Room & Board:** $4960
Freshman Class: 1783 applied, 1363 accepted, 405 enrolled	
SAT I Verbal/Math: 580/590	**ACT:** 25 **VERY COMPETITIVE**

Eckerd College, founded in 1958, is a private liberal arts institution affiliated with the Presbyterian Church (U.S.A.). Interdisciplinary programs are an important part of the school's curriculum. This is reflected in the organization of the faculty into collegia, rather than into traditional departments. The library contains 113,850 volumes, 14,606 microform items, and 1941 audiovisual forms/CDs, and subscribes to 3009 periodicals. Computerized library services include the card catalog, interlibrary loans, and database searching. Special learning facilities include an art gallery, radio station, tv station, and a sea mammal necropsy lab. The 267-acre campus is in a suburban area on 1 1/4 miles of waterfront, 5 miles south of St. Petersburg. Including residence halls, there are 67 buildings.

Programs of Study: Eckerd confers B.A. and B.S. degrees. Bachelor's degrees are awarded in BIOLOGICAL SCIENCE (biology/biological science and marine science), BUSINESS (international business management and management science), COMMUNICATIONS AND THE ARTS (comparative literature, creative writing, dramatic arts, English, French, German, music, Russian, Spanish, and visual and performing arts), COMPUTER AND PHYSICAL SCIENCE (chemistry, computer science, mathematics, and physics), ENGINEERING AND ENVI-

RONMENTAL DESIGN (environmental science), HEALTH PROFESSIONS (predentistry and premedicine), SOCIAL SCIENCE (American studies, anthropology, economics, history, human development, humanities, international relations, philosophy, political science/government, prelaw, psychology, religion, sociology, and women's studies). Marine science, international business, and management are the largest.

Special: Eckerd offers internships in management and human development. Work-study programs, dual majors in all subjects, interdisciplinary majors in international relations and environmental studies, student-designed majors, nondegree study, and pass/fail options are also available. Study-abroad programs are available in a number of countries. Students may earn B.A.-B.S. degrees in biology, chemistry, and marine science. A 3-2 engineering degree is offered with Auburn, Washington, and Columbia Universities and the University of Miami. The Program for Experienced Learners (students 25 and older) offers independent study, weekend courses, and credit for experiential learning. There are 7 national honor societies and a freshman honors program. All departments have honors programs.

Admissions: 76% of the 1999-2000 applicants were accepted. The SAT I scores for the 1999-2000 freshman class were: Verbal--18% below 500, 45% between 500 and 599, 30% between 600 and 700, and 7% above 700; Math--16% below 500, 42% between 500 and 599, 36% between 600 and 700, and 6% above 700. The ACT scores were 11% below 21, 29% between 21 and 23, 27% between 24 and 26, 17% between 27 and 28, and 16% above 28. 46% of the current freshmen were in the top fifth of their class; 73% were in the top two fifths. There were 2 National Merit finalists and 3 semifinalists. 8 freshmen graduated first in their class.

Requirements: The SAT I or ACT is required. A GPA of 2.0 is required. Graduation from an accredited secondary school or satisfactory scores on the GED are required. High school courses must include 4 years of English, 3 each of math and science, 2 each of a foreign language and social studies, and 1 of history. SAT II: Subject tests in writing, literature, and math are recommended. An essay is required and an interview is recommended. AP and CLEP credits are accepted. Important factors in the admissions decision are advanced placement or honor courses, leadership record, and personality/intangible qualities.

Procedure: Freshmen are admitted fall, winter, and spring. Entrance exams should be taken in October, November, or December. There are early admissions and deferred admissions plans. Applications should be filed by April 1 for fall entry, December 1 for winter entry, and December 1 for spring entry, along with a $25 fee. Notification is sent beginning in October. 13% of all applicants are on a waiting list.

Financial Aid: In 1999-2000, 89% of all freshmen and 88% of continuing students received some form of financial aid. 65% of freshmen and 64% of continuing students received need-based aid. The average freshman award was $14,750. Of that total, scholarships or need-based grants averaged $9800 ($22,000 maximum); loans averaged $3200 ($4500 maximum); and work contracts averaged $1500 ($2500 maximum). 75% of undergraduates work part time. Average annual earnings from campus work are $1100. The average financial indebtedness of the 1999 graduate was $17,000. Eckerd is a member of CSS. The FAFSA is required. The fall application deadline is March 15.

Computers: The mainframes are 2 Sun SPARC computers. There are 20 PCs in a Novell Network in the computer lab and 40 PCs in the science lab through which students may access the mainframe. Students with their own personal computers may access the mainframe through modems or Ethernet from their dormitory rooms. Each dormitory has a lab with 3 computers connected to the network.

All students may access the system at any time. There are no time limits and no fees.It is strongly recommended that all students have personal computers.

ELIZABETHTOWN COLLEGE
Elizabethtown, PA 17022   (717) 361-1400; Fax: (717) 361-1365

Full-time: 567 men, 1031 women	**Faculty:** 103; IIB, ++$
Part-time: 51 men, 129 women	**Ph.D.s:** 84%
Graduate: none	**Student/Faculty:** 16 to 1
Year: semesters, summer session	**Tuition:** $18,220
Application Deadline: see profile	**Room & Board:** $5380
Freshman Class: 2219 applied, 1724 accepted, 504 enrolled	
SAT I Verbal/Math: 560/560	**VERY COMPETITIVE**

Elizabethtown College, founded in 1899, is a private college founded by members of the Church of the Brethren and offering 40 undergraduate degrees in the arts, sciences, and humanities and professional programs. In addition to regional accreditation, E-town has baccalaureate program accreditation with ACBSP, CSWE, and NASM. The library contains 227,460 volumes, 14,294 microform items, and 14,178 audiovisual forms/CDs, and subscribes to 1082 periodicals. Computerized library services include the card catalog, interlibrary loans, and database searching. Special learning facilities include a learning resource center, art gallery, radio station, TV station, and meeting house for the study of Anabaptist and Pietist groups. The 185-acre campus is in a small town 20 miles southeast of Harrisburg. Including residence halls, there are 24 buildings.

Programs of Study: E-town confers B.A. and B.S. degrees. Bachelor's degrees are awarded in AGRICULTURE (forestry and related sciences), BIOLOGICAL SCIENCE (biochemistry, biology/biological science, and biotechnology), BUSINESS (accounting, business administration and management, and international business management), COMMUNICATIONS AND THE ARTS (art, communications, English, French, German, music, and Spanish), COMPUTER AND PHYSICAL SCIENCE (chemistry, computer science, mathematics, physics, and science), EDUCATION (early childhood, elementary, music, and secondary), ENGINEERING AND ENVIRONMENTAL DESIGN (computer engineering, engineering, engineering physics, environmental science, and industrial engineering), HEALTH PROFESSIONS (clinical science, music therapy, and occupational therapy), SOCIAL SCIENCE (economics, history, philosophy, political science/government, psychology, religion, social studies, social work, and sociology). Sciences, occupational therapy, and international business are the strongest academically. Business administration, communications, and elementary and early childhood education are the largest.

Special: Cross-registration with Brethren Colleges Abroad, work-study programs, internships, study abroad in 12 countries, a Washington semester, accelerated degrees, and dual majors, including sociology/anthropology, are available. A 3-2 engineering degree is offered with Pennsylvania State University; a 2-2 allied health degree and a 3-3 physical therapy degree with Thomas Jefferson University, Widener University, and the University of Maryland/Baltimore County; and a 3-2 forestry or environmental management degree with Duke University. There are 13 national honor societies, a freshman honors program, and 19 departmental honors programs.

Admissions: 78% of the 1999-2000 applicants were accepted. The SAT I scores for the 1999-2000 freshman class were: Verbal--20% below 500, 52% between 500 and 599, 25% between 600 and 700, and 3% above 700; Math--26% below 500, 41% between 500 and 599, 30% between 600 and 700, and 3% above 700. 50% of the current freshmen were in the top fifth of their class; 81% were in the

top two fifths. There were 3 National Merit semifinalists. 8 freshmen graduated first in their class.

Requirements: The SAT I or ACT is required. Recommended composite scores for the SAT I range from 1040 to 1190; for the ACT, 19 to 24. Applicants must be graduates of an accredited secondary school or have earned a GED. The college encourages completion of 18 academic credits, based on 4 years of English, 3 of math, 2 each of lab science, social studies, and consecutive foreign language, and 5 additional college preparatory units. An audition is required for music majors and an interview is required for occupational therapy majors. Applications are accepted on computer disk submitted by hard copy and on-line through CollegeLink and Apply. AP and CLEP credits are accepted. Important factors in the admissions decision are advanced placement or honor courses, recommendations by school officials, and extracurricular activities record.

Procedure: Freshmen are admitted to all sessions. Entrance exams should be taken in spring of the junior year or fall of the senior year. There are early admissions and deferred admissions plans. Application deadlines are December 15 for occupational therapy majors, March 1 for international business majors, and January 15 for the honors program. Others should apply before February of their senior year. There is a $20 fee. Notification is sent on a rolling basis.

Financial Aid: In 1999-2000, 94% of all freshmen and 91% of continuing students received some form of financial aid. 77% of freshmen and 73% of continuing students received need-based aid. The average freshman award was $14,117. Of that total, scholarships or need-based grants averaged $10,440 ($20,560 maximum); loans averaged $2679 ($3625 maximum); and work contracts averaged $1388 ($1500 maximum). 68% of undergraduates work part time. Average annual earnings from campus work are $768. The average financial indebtedness of the 1999 graduate was $15,633. E-town is a member of CSS. The FAFSA, the college's own financial statement, and family federal tax returns are required. The fall application deadline is March 15.

Computers: A 24-hour terminal room allows student access to E-mail and word processing. Several labs house a total of 40 Macs and 43 PCs, all connected to the Internet. All residence hall rooms also have Internet access. Approximately 75% of freshmen have their own computers. All students may access the system any time from residence hall rooms. There are no time limits and no fees.

ELMIRA COLLEGE
Elmira, NY 14901

(607) 735-1724
(800) 935-6472; Fax: (607) 735-1718

Full-time: 463 men, 695 women	**Faculty:** 78; IIB, -$
Part-time: none	**Ph.D.s:** 98%
Graduate: none	**Student/Faculty:** 15 to 1
Year: modified (4-4-1), summer session	**Tuition:** $21,330
Application Deadline: June 15	**Room & Board:** $7080
Freshman Class: 1520 applied, 1093 accepted, 308 enrolled	
SAT I Verbal/Math: 540/530	**ACT:** 25 **VERY COMPETITIVE**

Elmira College, founded in 1855, is a private liberal arts institution offering general and preprofessional programs. In addition to regional accreditation, Elmira has baccalaureate program accreditation with NLN. The library contains 389,000 volumes, 796,000 microform items, and 6261 audiovisual forms CDs, and subscribes to 855 periodicals. Computerized library services include the card catalog, interlibrary loans, and database searching. Special learning facilities include a learning resource center, art gallery, radio station, speech and hearing clinic, and

Mark Twain's study. The 42-acre campus is in a suburban area 90 miles south-west of Syracuse. Including residence halls, there are 25 buildings.

Programs of Study: Elmira confers B.A. and B.S. degrees. Bachelor's degrees are awarded in BIOLOGICAL SCIENCE (biochemistry and biology/biological science), BUSINESS (accounting, business administration and management, business economics, international business management, and marketing/retailing/merchandising), COMMUNICATIONS AND THE ARTS (art, classics, dramatic arts, English literature, fine arts, French, languages, music, and Spanish), COMPUTER AND PHYSICAL SCIENCE (chemistry and mathematics), EDUCATION (art, elementary, foreign languages, science, and secondary), ENGINEERING AND ENVIRONMENTAL DESIGN (environmental science), HEALTH PROFESSIONS (medical laboratory technology, nursing, predentistry, premedicine, and speech pathology/audiology), SOCIAL SCIENCE (American studies, anthropology, criminal justice, history, human services, international studies, philosophy, political science/government, prelaw, psychology, and sociology). History, theater, and premedicine are the strongest academically. Psychology, management, and education are the largest.

Special: The required field experience program provides a career-related internship as well as community service. A junior year abroad program, a Washington semester, an accelerated degree program, a general studies degree, student-designed majors, and pass/fail options are available. A 3-2 chemical engineering degree is offered with Clarkson University. B.A.-B.S. degrees are offered in biochemistry, biology, chemistry, economics, education, environmental studies, history, math, political science, and psychology. Elmira is a member of the Spring Term Consortium, enabling students to take 6-week courses at participating institutions. There are 10 national honor societies, including Phi Beta Kappa.

Admissions: 72% of the 1999-2000 applicants were accepted. The SAT I scores for the 1999-2000 freshman class were: Verbal--31% below 500, 41% between 500 and 599, 25% between 600 and 700, and 3% above 700; Math--31% below 500, 47% between 500 and 599, 19% between 600 and 700, and 3% above 700. The ACT scores were 25% below 21, 25% between 21 and 23, 14% between 24 and 26, 23% between 27 and 28, and 13% above 28. 48% of the current freshmen were in the top fifth of their class; 70% were in the top two fifths. There were 2 National Merit finalists and 6 semifinalists. 31 freshmen graduated first in their class.

Requirements: The SAT I or ACT is required. In addition, applicants should have completed 4 years of high school English, 3 of math, and 2 of science, or GED equivalent. An essay is part of the application process. An interview is strongly recommended. Applications are accepted on-line. AP and CLEP credits are accepted. Important factors in the admissions decision are advanced placement or honor courses, extracurricular activities record, and recommendations by school officials.

Procedure: Freshmen are admitted fall and winter. Entrance exams should be taken by January of the entry year. There are early decision, early admissions, and deferred admissions plans. Early decision applications should be filed by January 15; regular applications, by June 15 for fall entry and December 1 for winter entry, along with a $40 fee. Notification of early decision is sent January 31; regular decision, on a rolling basis. 56 early decision candidates were accepted for the 1999-2000 class. 6% of all applicants are on a waiting list.

Financial Aid: In 1999-2000, 90% of all students received some form of financial aid. 70% of all students received need-based aid. The average freshman award was $18,200. Of that total, scholarships or need-based grants averaged $12,000 ($20,930 maximum); loans averaged $4900 ($8125 maximum); work contracts averaged $750 ($1800 maximum); and federal and state grants averaged

$3,345 ($7,250 maximum). 50% of undergraduates work part time. Average annual earnings from campus work are $900. The average financial indebtedness of the 1999 graduate was $20,100. Elmira is a member of CSS. The CSS/Profile or FAFSA and state application are required. The priority date for fall entry is March 1; for winter entry, December 1.

Computers: The mainframe is a DEC VAX 4000-600 minicomputer. More than 75 PCs (Windows 95 and Mac) connected to the Internet and Windows NT file servers are available to students in the computer center and the library. All students may access the system weekdays 15 hours per day and weekends 8 to 10 hours per day. There are no time limits and no fees.

ELON COLLEGE
Elon College, NC 27244-2010
(336) 584-2772
(800) 334-8448; Fax: (336) 538-3986

Full-time: 1416 men, 2164 women	**Faculty:** 192; IIB, +$
Part-time: 59 men, 62 women	**Ph.D.s:** 83%
Graduate: 115 men, 145 women	**Student/Faculty:** 19 to 1
Year: 4-1-4, summer session	**Tuition:** $12,896
Application Deadline: February 1	**Room & Board:** $4551
Freshman Class: 5179 applied, 3166 accepted, 1000 enrolled	
SAT I Verbal/Math: 550/550	**VERY COMPETITIVE**

Elon College, founded in 1889 by the United Church of Christ, is a private comprehensive institution that offers programs in the liberal arts and sciences and career-oriented fields of study. There are 3 graduate schools. In addition to regional accreditation, Elon has baccalaureate program accreditation with CAHEA and NCATE. The library contains 212,261 volumes, 711,542 microform items, and 5084 audiovisual forms/CDs, and subscribes to 4858 periodicals. Computerized library services include the card catalog, interlibrary loans, and database searching. Special learning facilities include a learning resource center, art gallery, radio station, TV station, a writing center, a botanical preserve, and an observatory. The 502-acre campus is in a suburban area adjacent to Burlington and 17 miles east of Greensboro. Including residence halls, there are 104 buildings.

Programs of Study: Elon confers B.A., B.S., and B.F.A. degrees. Master's degrees are also awarded. Bachelor's degrees are awarded in BIOLOGICAL SCIENCE (biology/biological science), BUSINESS (accounting, business administration and management, and sports management), COMMUNICATIONS AND THE ARTS (art, broadcasting, communications, dramatic arts, English, film arts, French, journalism, music, music performance, musical theater, and Spanish), COMPUTER AND PHYSICAL SCIENCE (chemistry, computer science, mathematics, and physics), EDUCATION (elementary, foreign languages, health, mathematics, middle school, music, physical, science, secondary, social science, and special), ENGINEERING AND ENVIRONMENTAL DESIGN (environmental science, military science, and preengineering), HEALTH PROFESSIONS (medical technology and sports medicine), SOCIAL SCIENCE (economics, history, human services, international studies, philosophy, political science/government, psychology, public administration, religion, and sociology). Business, education, and music theater are the strongest academically. Business, education, and journalism and communication are the largest.

Special: Elon offers co-op programs in most majors, dual majors, student-designed majors, cross-registration with 7 other colleges and universities in North Carolina, paid and unpaid internships, study abroad in 25 countries, a Washington semester, work-study programs, pass/fail options, and a 3-2 dual engineering degree program with North Carolina State University. The 3-week January term includes extensive international study opportunites and courses with domestic travel components. There are 22 national honor societies, a freshman honors program, and 7 departmental honors programs.

Admissions: 61% of the 1999-2000 applicants were accepted. The SAT I scores for the 1999-2000 freshman class were: Verbal--19% below 500, 55% between 500 and 599, 24% between 600 and 700, and 2% above 700; Math--19% below 500, 55% between 500 and 599, 25% between 600 and 700, and 1% above 700. 40% of the current freshmen were in the top fifth of their class; 75% were in the top two fifths. There was 1 National Merit finalist. 11 freshmen graduated first in their class.

Requirements: The SAT I or ACT is required. A GPA of 2.3 is required. students must be graduates of an accredited secondary school or have a GED certificate. They should have completed 4 credits in English, 3 or more in math, 2 or more in a foreign language, 2 or more in science, including at least one lab science, and 2 or more in social studies, including U.S. history. AP and CLEP credits are accepted. Important factors in the admissions decision are advanced placement or honor courses, evidence of special talent, and leadership record.

Procedure: Freshmen are admitted to all sessions. Entrance exams should be taken in the spring of the junior year and the fall of the senior year. There are early decision and deferred admissions plans. Early decision applications should be filed by November 15; regular applications, by February 1 for fall entry and December 1 for spring entry, along with a $25 fee. Notification of early decision is sent on a rolling basis by December 15; regular decision, on a rolling basis after December 20. 205 early decision candidates were accepted for the 1999-2000 class. 17% of all applicants are on a waiting list.

Financial Aid: In 1999-2000, 72% of all freshmen and 64% of continuing students received some form of financial aid. 45% of freshmen and 38% of continuing students received need-based aid. The average freshman award was $8167. Of that total, scholarships or need-based grants averaged $4296 ($17,447 maximum); loans averaged $2167 ($9625 maximum); and work contracts averaged $1704 ($2500 maximum). 26% of undergraduates work part time. Average annual earnings from campus work are $1100. The average financial indebtedness of the 1999 graduate was $7356. Elon is a member of CSS. The CSS/Profile or FAFSA and the college's own financial statement are required. The fall application deadline is March 15.

Computers: The mainframe is an HP 9000/series 887. The computer labs have 500 PC workstations connected to the HP mainframe, to 3 Novell servers, to the library, and to the Internet. Macs and PCs are both available. All students may access the system 24 hours a day via modem. There are no time limits and no fees. It is recommended that all students have personal computers.

EMERSON COLLEGE
Boston, MA 02116　　　　　　(617) 824-8600; Fax: (617) 824-8609

Full-time: 1165 men, 1495 women	**Faculty:** 88; IIA, ++$
Part-time: 146 men, 329 women	**Ph.D.s:** 71%
Graduate: 257 men, 595 women	**Student/Faculty:** 30 to 1
Year: semesters, summer session	**Tuition:** $19,316
Application Deadline: February 1	**Room & Board:** $8734
Freshman Class: 2747 applied, 1791 accepted, 653 enrolled	
SAT I Verbal/Math: 600/560	**ACT:** 25　　**VERY COMPETITIVE**

Emerson College, founded in 1880, is a private, independent college devoted to the study of commmunication and performing arts. There are 3 undergraduate and 3 graduate schools. The library contains 193,000 volumes, 11,000 microform items, and 8352 audiovisual forms/CDs, and subscribes to 728 periodicals. Computerized library services include the card catalog, interlibrary loans, and database searching. Special learning facilities include a learning resource center, radio station, TV station, film production facilities, computerized newsroom, speech-language-hearing clinics, and proscenium stage theatre. The campus is in an urban area in the Back Bay and Theatre District of Boston. Including residence halls, there are 15 buildings.

Programs of Study: Emerson confers B.A., B.S., B.F.A., and B.S.Sp. degrees. Master's and doctoral degrees are also awarded. Bachelor's degrees are awarded in BUSINESS (marketing management), COMMUNICATIONS AND THE ARTS (advertising, broadcasting, communications, creative writing, dramatic arts, film arts, journalism, media arts, musical theater, performing arts, public relations, publishing, radio/television technology, speech/debate/rhetoric, theater design, and theater management), HEALTH PROFESSIONS (speech pathology/ audiology), SOCIAL SCIENCE (interdisciplinary studies and prelaw). Writing, literature, and publishing are the strongest academically as well as the largest.

Special: Student-designed, interdisciplinary, and dual majors are available. Cross-registration is offered with the Berklee College of Music, Boston Conservatory, Massachusetts College of Art, Museum of Fine Arts School, and other Boston area schools. 700 internships are possible in Boston and 250 in Los Angeles. Emerson has nondegree study and pass/fail options, as well as study abroad in the Netherlands and Czech Republic. There are 3 national honor societies, a freshman honors program, and 6 departmental honors programs.

Admissions: 65% of the 1999-2000 applicants were accepted. The SAT I scores for the 1999-2000 freshman class were: Verbal--4% below 500, 41% between 500 and 599, 42% between 600 and 700, and 12% above 700; Math--16% below 500, 53% between 500 and 599, 29% between 600 and 700, and 3% above 700. The ACT scores were 7% below 21, 23% between 21 and 23, 38% between 24 and 26, 20% between 27 and 28, and 12% above 28. 38% of the current freshmen were in the top fifth of their class; 76% were in the top two fifths. 5 freshmen graduated first in their class.

Requirements: The SAT I or ACT is required. In addition, candidates must be graduates of an accredited secondary school or hold a GED certificate. They must have completed 16 Carnegie units, including 4 in English and 3 each in science, social studies, foreign language, and math. An essay is required. Auditions and interviews are required for performing arts candidates. AP and CLEP credits are accepted. Important factors in the admissions decision are advanced placement or honor courses, evidence of special talent, and recommendations by school officials.

Procedure: Freshmen are admitted fall and spring. Entrance exams should be taken before January of the senior year. There are early decision, early admissions, and deferred admissions plans. Early decision applications should be filed by November 15; regular applications, by February 1 for fall entry and November 1 for spring entry, along with a $45 fee. Notification of early decision is sent December 15; regular decision, March 15. 213 early decision candidates were accepted for the 1999-2000 class. 13% of all applicants are on a waiting list.

Financial Aid: In 1999-2000, 76% of all freshmen and 65% of continuing students received some form of financial aid. 66% of freshmen and 74% of continuing students received need-based aid. The average freshman award was $14,900. Of that total, scholarships or need-based grants averaged $10,600 ($18,100 maximum); loans averaged $3200 ($4125 maximum); and work contracts averaged $1600 ($1700 maximum). 56% of undergraduates work part time. Average annual earnings from campus work are $1600. The average financial indebtedness of the 1999 graduate was $17,125. Emerson is a member of CSS. The CSS/Profile or FAFSA and the college's own financial statement are required. The fall application deadline is March 1.

Computers: The mainframe is a DEC VAX 4500. Many PCs are available in the academic computing center and new media center. All campus buildings, including residence halls, are networked and have direct access to the college server. All students may access the system 24 hours a day. There are no time limits and no fees. The school strongly recommends that students have their own personal computer.

EMORY UNIVERSITY
Atlanta, GA 30322
(800) 727-6036

Full-time: 2482 men, 2834 women	**Faculty:** 583; I, ++$
Part-time: none	**Ph.D.s:** 98%
Graduate: 2269 men, 2924 women	**Student/Faculty:** 9 to 1
Year: semesters, summer session	**Tuition:** $23,120
Application Deadline: January 15	**Room & Board:** $7750
Freshman Class: 9850 applied, 4196 accepted, 1244 enrolled	
SAT I Verbal/Math: 665/675	**MOST COMPETITIVE**

Emory University, founded in 1836, is a private institution affiliated with the United Methodist Church. There are 4 undergraduate and 7 graduate schools. The 7 libraries contain 2.7 million volumes, 240,000 microform items, and 3000 audiovisual forms/CDs, and subscribe to 18,842 periodicals. Computerized library services include the card catalog, interlibrary loans, and database searching. Special learning facilities include a learning resource center, art gallery, radio station, TV station, the Michael C. Carlos Museum, the Carter Center, and facilities for direct monitoring of Russian domestic television. The 674-acre campus is in a suburban area 5 miles northeast of downtown Atlanta. Including residence halls, there are 121 buildings.

Programs of Study: Emory confers B.A., B.S., B.B.A., and B.S.N. degrees. Associate, master's, and doctoral degrees are also awarded. Bachelor's degrees are awarded in BIOLOGICAL SCIENCE (biology/biological science and neurosciences), BUSINESS (accounting, banking and finance, business administration and management, business economics, and marketing/retailing/merchandising), COMMUNICATIONS AND THE ARTS (art history and appreciation, classics, creative writing, dance, dramatic arts, English, film arts, French, Greek, Latin, literature, modern language, music, and Spanish), COMPUTER AND PHYSICAL SCIENCE (chemistry, computer science, mathematics, and physics), EDUCATION (educational statistics and research), HEALTH PROFESSIONS (nursing),

SOCIAL SCIENCE (African studies, anthropology, Asian/Oriental studies, classical/ancient civilization, economics, European studies, French studies, German area studies, history, international studies, Judaic studies, Latin American studies, medieval studies, philosophy, political science/government, psychology, religion, Russian and Slavic studies, sociology, and women's studies). Sciences, English, and psychology are the strongest academically. Biology, English, and psychology are the largest.

Special: Special academic programs include cross-registration with Atlanta area colleges and universities, departmental internships, work-study programs, dual majors, 3-2 engineering degrees with Georgia Tech, and pass/fail options. There is a Washington semester, B.A.-B.S. degrees, and study abroad in many countries. There are accelerated degree programs offered in biology, chemistry, math, physics, English, history, philosophy, political science, sociology, and computer science. There are 25 national honor societies, including Phi Beta Kappa.

Admissions: 43% of the 1999-2000 applicants were accepted. The SAT I scores for the 1999-2000 freshman class were: Verbal--17% between 500 and 599, 60% between 600 and 700, and 23% above 700; Math--15% between 500 and 599, 59% between 600 and 700, and 26% above 700. The ACT scores were 1% between 21 and 23, 7% between 24 and 26, 60% between 27 and 28, and 32% above 28. 93% of the current freshmen were in the top fifth of their class; All were in the top two fifths. There were 56 National Merit finalists.

Requirements: The SAT I or ACT is required, and 1 SAT II: Subject test is recommended. The student must have acquired 16 academic credits in secondary school, including 4 years of English, 3 of math, and 2 each of history and science. The university requires the student to submit an essay. Applications are accepted on computer disk via CollegeLink and on-line. AP credits are accepted. Important factors in the admissions decision are advanced placement or honor courses, recommendations by school officials, and extracurricular activities record.

Procedure: Freshmen are admitted in the fall. Entrance exams should be taken prior to applying. There are early decision, early admissions, and deferred admissions plans. Early decision applications should be filed by November 1 for round I, January 1 for round II; regular applications, by January 15 for fall entry, along with a $40 fee. Notification of early decision is sent December 15; regular decision, April 1. 417 early decision candidates were accepted for the 1999-2000 class. 5% of all applicants are on a waiting list.

Financial Aid: In 1999-2000, 57% of all freshmen and 64% of continuing students received some form of financial aid. 36% of freshmen and 42% of continuing students received need-based aid. The average freshman award was $17,205. Of that total, scholarships or need-based grants averaged $12,980; loans averaged $2625; and work contracts averaged $1600. 70% of undergraduates work part time. Average annual earnings from campus work are $1500. The average financial indebtedness of the 1999 graduate was $16,578. Emory is a member of CSS. The CSS/Profile or FAFSA is required. The fall application deadline is February 15.

Computers: The mainframes are an IBM 9672-E01 and Sun SPARC 20J. There are about 600 PCs located in the library, dormitories, computing centers, and some academic departments. All students may access the system 24 hours a day. There are no time limits and no fees.

ERSKINE COLLEGE
Due West, SC 29639

(864) 379-8830
(800) 241-8721; Fax: (864) 379-2167

Full-time: 207 men, 299 women	**Faculty:** 41; IIB, -$
Part-time: 3 men, 1 woman	**Ph.Ds:** 85%
Graduate: none	**Student/Faculty:** 12 to 1
Year: 4-1-4, summer session	**Tuition:** $15,229
Application Deadline: open	**Room & Board:** $4844
Freshman Class: 616 applied, 498 accepted, 158 enrolled	
SAT I Verbal/Math: 556/547	**VERY COMPETITIVE**

Erskine College, founded in 1839, is a private liberal arts college affiliated with the Associate Reformed Presbyterian Church. There is 1 graduate school. The library contains 151,231 volumes, 28,549 microform items, and 916 audiovisual forms/CDs, and subscribes to 707 periodicals. Computerized library services include the card catalog, interlibrary loans, and database searching. Special learning facilities include an art gallery, radio station, and TV station. The 85-acre campus is in a rural area 90 miles west of Columbia. Including residence halls, there are 23 buildings.

Programs of Study: Erskine confers A.B. and B.S. degrees. Master's and doctoral degrees are also awarded. Bachelor's degrees are awarded in BIOLOGICAL SCIENCE (biology/biological science), BUSINESS (business administration and management and sports management), COMMUNICATIONS AND THE ARTS (English, music, and music business management), COMPUTER AND PHYSICAL SCIENCE (chemistry, mathematics, natural sciences, and physics), EDUCATION (athletic training, Christian, early childhood, elementary, foreign languages, music, physical, and special), HEALTH PROFESSIONS (health science, medical laboratory technology, predentistry, premedicine, and sports medicine), SOCIAL SCIENCE (American studies, behavioral science, history, psychology, religion, and social studies). Business administration and biology are the largest.

Special: Externships are available during the January term. Study abroad in 4 countries, a 3-2 engineering degree with Clemson University, and pass/fail options are offered. There are 5 national honor societies, and 7 departmental honors programs.

Admissions: 81% of the 1999-2000 applicants were accepted. The SAT I scores for the 1999-2000 freshman class were: Verbal--29% below 500, 36% between 500 and 599, 29% between 600 and 700, and 5% above 700; Math--31% below 500, 41% between 500 and 599, 22% between 600 and 700, and 6% above 700. 51% of the current freshmen were in the top fifth of their class; 83% were in the top two fifths. 7 freshmen graduated first in their class.

Requirements: The SAT I or ACT is required, but grades from college preparatory courses are weighed twice as heavily as the SAT I or ACT scores. Applicants must be graduates of an accredited secondary school. The GED is accepted. Applicants should have a minimum of 14 high school academic credits, including 4 credits of English and 2 credits each of math, science, and history. AP credits are accepted. Important factors in the admissions decision are advanced placement or honor courses, recommendations by school officials, and extracurricular activities record.

Procedure: Freshmen are admitted to all sessions. Entrance exams should be taken in the spring of the junior year or the fall of the senior year. Application deadlines are open; the fee is $15. Notification is sent on a rolling basis.

Financial Aid: In 1999-2000, 95% of all freshmen and 96% of continuing students received some form of financial aid. 80% of freshmen and 75% of continu-

ing students received need-based aid. The average freshman award was $13,459. Of that total, scholarships or need-based grants averaged $7176 ($17,579 maximum); loans averaged $2210 ($5500 maximum); and work contracts averaged $100 ($1000 maximum). 35% of undergraduates work part time. Average annual earnings from campus work are $795. The average financial indebtedness of the 1999 graduate was $5767. Erskine is a member of CSS. The FAFSA and the college's own financial statement are required. The fall application deadline is August 1.

Computers: The mainframe is a DEC ALPHA Server 800. Students may access the Internet via the LAN from their dorm rooms or use any of the 90 public computers on campus. All students may access the system from 7 a.m. to 1 a.m. Monday to Saturday, and from 1 p.m. to 1 a.m. Sunday. Dorm Internet access is unlimited. There are no time limits. The fee is $45 per year. It is strongly recommended that all students have personal computers.

EUGENE LANG COLLEGE OF NEW SCHOOL UNIVERSITY
(Formerly Eugene Lang College of the New School for Social Research)

New York, NY 10011   (212) 229-5665; Fax: (212) 229-5355

Full-time: 152 men, 306 women	**Faculty:** 14
Part-time: 15 men, 47 women	**Ph.D.s:** 100%
Graduate: none	**Student/Faculty:** 33 to 1
Year: semesters	**Tuition:** $19,915
Application Deadline: February 1	**Room & Board:** $9005
Freshman Class: 718 applied, 390 accepted, 120 enrolled	
SAT I Verbal/Math: 590/520	**VERY COMPETITIVE**

Eugene Lang College, established in 1978, is the liberal arts undergraduate division of New School University (formerly the New School for Social Research). There are 4 undergraduate and 6 graduate schools. The 4 libraries contain 142,000 volumes and 65,000 microform items, and subscribe to 750 periodicals. Computerized library services include the card catalog, interlibrary loans, and database searching. Special learning facilities include an art gallery and writing center. The 5-acre campus is in an urban area in the heart of Greenwich Village. Including residence halls, there are 14 buildings.

Programs of Study: Eugene Lang College confers the B.A. degree. Master's and doctoral degrees are also awarded. Bachelor's degrees are awarded in COMMUNICATIONS AND THE ARTS (creative writing, dramatic arts, and English), EDUCATION (education), SOCIAL SCIENCE (crosscultural studies, economics, history, political science/government, prelaw, psychology, social science, sociology, urban studies, and women's studies). Creative writing, history, urban studies, and education are the strongest academically. Writing and cultural studies are the largest.

Special: Lang College offers a concentration rather than a traditional major; there is no core curriculum and students are instructed in small seminars. Students may cross-register with other New School divisions. A large variety of internships for credit, study abroad, B.A./M.A. and B.A./M.S.T. options, a B.A./B.F.A. degree with Parsons School of Design and the New School's Jazz and Contemporary Music Program, student-designed majors, and nondegree study are available.

Admissions: 54% of the 1999-2000 applicants were accepted. The SAT I scores for the 1999-2000 freshman class were: Verbal--8% below 500, 48% between 500 and 599, 32% between 600 and 700, and 12% above 700; Math--41% below

500, 38% between 500 and 599, 19% between 600 and 700, and 2% above 700. 51% of the current freshmen were in the top fifth of their class; 84% were in the top two fifths. There were 4 National Merit finalists and 15 semifinalists. 4 freshmen graduated first in their class.

Requirements: The SAT I or ACT is required. 4 SAT II: Subject tests may be substituted for either test. Applicants must be enrolled in a strong college preparatory program. The GED is accepted. An essay and an interview are required. Art students must present a portfolio and complete a home exam. Jazz students are required to audition. AP credits are accepted. Important factors in the admissions decision are personality/intangible qualities, advanced placement or honor courses, and recommendations by school officials.

Procedure: Freshmen are admitted fall and spring. Entrance exams should be taken in May of the junior year or October of the senior year. There are early decision, early admissions, and deferred admissions plans. Early decision applications should be filed by November 15; regular applications, by February 1 for fall entry and November 15 for spring entry, along with a $30 fee. Notification of early decision is sent December 15; regular decision, April 1. 20 early decision candidates were accepted for the 1999-2000 class. 8% of all applicants are on a waiting list.

Financial Aid: In 1999-2000, 78% of all freshmen and 80% of continuing students received some form of financial aid. 75% of freshmen and 79% of continuing students received need-based aid. The average freshman award was $14,566. Of that total, scholarships or need-based grants averaged $10,906; and loans averaged $3125. 40% of undergraduates work part time. The average financial indebtedness of the 1999 graduate was $17,125. The FAFSA is required. The fall application deadline is March 1.

Computers: The mainframe is an HP. Macs and IBM PCs are available for student use in an academic computing center. Students can arrange for access for statistical course work and dissertation research. There are no time limits and no fees. It is strongly recommended that all students have personal computers.

FAIRFIELD UNIVERSITY
Fairfield, CT 06430-5195   **(203) 254-4100; Fax: (203) 254-4199**

Full-time: 1458 men, 1693 women	**Faculty:** 190; IIA, +$
Part-time: 468 men, 445 women	**Ph.D.s:** 92%
Graduate: 425 men, 638 women	**Student/Faculty:** 15 to 1
Year: semesters, summer session	**Tuition:** $20,435
Application Deadline: February 1	**Room & Board:** $7380
Freshman Class: 6457 applied, 3966 accepted, 837 enrolled	
SAT I Verbal/Math: 575/584	**VERY COMPETITIVE**

Fairfield University, founded by the Jesuits in 1942, is an independent, Roman Catholic Jesuit institution. There are 5 undergraduate and 5 graduate schools. In addition to regional accreditation, Fairfield has baccalaureate program accreditation with AACSB, ABET, and NLN. The library contains 206,849 volumes, 658, 184 microform items, and 11,045 audiovisual forms/CDs, and subscribes to 1881 periodicals. Computerized library services include the card catalog, interlibrary loans, and database searching. Special learning facilities include an art gallery, radio station, TV station, media center, a 750-seat concert hall/theater, and a rehearsal and improvisation theater. The 200-acre campus is in a suburban area 60 miles northeast of New York City. Including residence halls, there are 30 buildings.

Programs of Study: Fairfield confers B.S. and B.A. degrees. Master's degrees are also awarded. Bachelor's degrees are awarded in BIOLOGICAL SCIENCE (biology/biological science and neurosciences), BUSINESS (accounting, banking and finance, business administration and management, international business management, and marketing/retailing/merchandising), COMMUNICATIONS AND THE ARTS (communications, English, fine arts, French, German, Italian, and Spanish), COMPUTER AND PHYSICAL SCIENCE (chemistry, computer science, information sciences and systems, mathematics, and physics), HEALTH PROFESSIONS (nursing), SOCIAL SCIENCE (economics, history, philosophy, political science/government, psychology, religion, and sociology). Visual and performing arts, psychology, and international studies are the strongest academically. Biology, psychology, and communication are the largest.

Special: Fairfield participates in CIEE, offers study abroad in 5 countries, a Washington semester, a federal work-study program, B.A.-B.S. degrees in economics, international studies, and psychology, and dual majors in all subjects. A 3-2 engineering degree is offered with the University of Connecticut, Rensselaer Polytechnic Institute, Columbia University, and Steven Institute of Technology. A general studies degree and credit for life, military, and work experience are available through the School of Continuing Education. Internships, both credit and noncredit, are offered at area corporations, publications, banks, and other businesses. Minors include women's studies, marine science, black studies, environmental studies, jazz, classical studies, Russian and Eastern studies, biochemistry, and Judaic studies. There are 14 national honor societies, including Phi Beta Kappa, and a freshman honors program.

Admissions: 61% of the 1999-2000 applicants were accepted. The SAT I scores for the 1999-2000 freshman class were: Verbal--10% below 500, 54% between 500 and 599, 31% between 600 and 700, and 4% above 700; Math--8% below 500, 49% between 500 and 599, 38% between 600 and 700, and 5% above 700. 47% of the current freshmen were in the top fifth of their class; 81% were in the top two fifths. 15 freshmen graduated first in their class.

Requirements: The SAT I is required. Fairfield requires applicants to be in the upper 40% of their class. A GPA of 3.0 is required. Applicants must be graduates of an accredited secondary school. The GED is accepted. A B average is required. Students should have completed 15 academic credits, including 4 credits of English, 3 credits each of history and math, and 2 credits each of a foreign language and lab science. The school recommends SAT II: Subject tests in writing, literature, language, and math, and, for nursing and science majors, in the sciences. An interview is recommended. Application forms are available on-line. AP and CLEP credits are accepted. Important factors in the admissions decision are advanced placement or honor courses, leadership record, and evidence of special talent.

Procedure: Freshmen are admitted in the fall. Entrance exams should be taken in the spring of the junior year or fall of the senior year. There are early decision and deferred admissions plans. Early decision applications should be filed by November 15; regular applications, by February 1 for fall entry, along with a $50 fee. Notification of early decision is sent January 1; regular decision, April 1. 91 early decision candidates were accepted for the 1999-2000 class. 3% of all applicants are on a waiting list.

Financial Aid: In 1999-2000, 70% of all freshmen and 69% of continuing students received some form of financial aid. 56% of freshmen and 54% of continuing students received need-based aid. The average freshman award was $15,757. Of that total, scholarships or need-based grants averaged $10,632 ($30,615 maximum); loans averaged $3625 ($5625 maximum); and work contracts averaged $1500 (maximum). 39% of undergraduates work part time. Average annual earnings from campus work are $838. The average financial indebtedness of the 1999 graduate was $19,300. Fairfield is a member of CSS. The CSS/Profile, FAFSA, parent and student tax returns, and a verification statement from first-time applicants are required. The fall application deadline is December 1.

Computers: The mainframe is a VAX 6430. Staffed computer labs are maintained in all academic buildings. Macs and IBM PS/2 PCs are available. Terminals are networked throughout campus for access to Netscape and the mainframe. All students may access the system daily until midnight. There are no time limits. The fee is $45 for computer science courses. The university strongly recommends that all students have personal computers.

FISHER COLLEGE
Boston, MA 02116-1500   (617) 236-8818; (800) 446-1226

Full-time: 129 men, 356 women	**Faculty:** 19
Part-time: 3 men, 16 women	**Ph.D.s:** 39%
Graduate: none	**Student/Faculty:** 26 to 1
Year: semesters	**Tuition:** $13,900
Application Deadline: open	**Room & Board:** $7000
Freshman Class: 948 applied, 416 accepted, 314 enrolled	
SAT I: not required	**VERY COMPETITIVE**

Fisher College, founded in 1903, is an independent institution offering baccalaureate degrees in liberal arts and business. The 2 libraries contain 32,000 volumes and 1400 audiovisual forms/CDs, and subscribe to 210 periodicals. Computerized library services include the card catalog, interlibrary loans, and database searching. Special learning facilities include a learning resource center. The 1-acre campus is in an urban area in Boston. Including residence halls, there are 12 buildings.

Programs of Study: Fisher College confers the B.S. degree. Associate degrees are also awarded. Bachelor's degrees are awarded in BUSINESS (business administration and management).

Special: Internships and work-study are available, as are B.A.-B.S. degrees and dual majors. There is 1 national honor society, Phi Theta Kappa.

Admissions: 44% of the 1999-2000 applicants were accepted.

Requirements: Applications are accepted on-line at the college's web site. Important factors in the admissions decision are recommendations by school officials, advanced placement or honor courses, and leadership record.

Procedure: Freshmen are admitted fall and spring. Application deadlines are open. There is a $25 fee. Notification is sent on a rolling basis.

Financial Aid: In 1999-2000, 77% of all freshmen and 51% of continuing students received some form of financial aid. 75% of freshmen received need-based aid. The average freshman award was $10,611. Of that total, scholarships or need-based grants averaged $11,125 ($15,625 maximum); loans averaged $4625 ($8625 maximum); and work contracts averaged $1800 ($2500 maximum). 38% of undergraduates work part time. Average annual earnings from campus work are $479. The average financial indebtedness of the 1999 graduate was $14,125. The FAFSA is required.

Computers: All students may access the system. There are no time limits and no fees.

FLAGLER COLLEGE

St. Augustine, FL 32085-1027

(904) 829-6481
(800) 304-4208; Fax: (904) 826-0094

Full-time: 645 men, 1054 women	**Faculty:** 59
Part-time: 14 men, 23 women	**Ph.D.s:** 68%
Graduate: none	**Student/Faculty:** 29 to 1
Year: semesters, summer session	**Tuition:** $6130
Application Deadline: March 1	**Room & Board:** $3800
Freshman Class: 1575 applied, 486 accepted, 419 enrolled	
SAT I Verbal/Math: 560/540	**ACT:** 23 **VERY COMPETITIVE+**

Flagler College, founded in 1968, is an independent liberal arts college. The library contains 82,065 volumes, 67,491 microform items, and 2424 audiovisual forms/CDs, and subscribes to 456 periodicals. Computerized library services include the card catalog, interlibrary loans, and database searching. Special learning facilities include a learning resource center, art gallery, and radio station. The 35-acre campus is in a small town 35 miles south of Jacksonville and 45 miles north of Daytona Beach. Including residence halls, there are 13 buildings.

Programs of Study: Flagler confers the B.A. degree. Bachelor's degrees are awarded in BUSINESS (accounting, business administration and management, and sports management), COMMUNICATIONS AND THE ARTS (art, communications, dramatic arts, English, fine arts, graphic design, and Spanish), EDUCATION (art, education of the deaf and hearing impaired, elementary, and secondary), SOCIAL SCIENCE (history, Latin American studies, philosophy, psychology, religion, and social science). Business, education, and Latin American studies are the strongest academically. Business, education, and communications are the largest.

Special: The school offers internships, work-study, and dual majors. Students may participate in study-abroad programs in almost any country. Students majoring in deaf education can work directly with students at the Florida State School for the Deaf and Blind. Students in the fashion buying, merchandising, or design program participate in the visiting student program at the Fashion Institute of Technology in New York City. There are 4 national honor societies and 2 departmental honors programs.

Admissions: 31% of the 1999-2000 applicants were accepted. The SAT I scores for the 1999-2000 freshman class were: Verbal--17% below 500, 55% between 500 and 599, 24% between 600 and 700, and 4% above 700; Math--24% below 500, 56% between 500 and 599, 19% between 600 and 700, and 1% above 700. The ACT scores were 16% below 21, 42% between 21 and 23, 25% between 24 and 26, 11% between 27 and 28, and 6% above 28. 44% of the current freshmen were in the top fifth of their class; 82% were in the top two fifths. 7 freshmen graduated first in their class.

Requirements: The SAT I or ACT is required. Flagler requires applicants to be in the upper 50% of their class. A GPA of 2.8 is required. Graduation from an accredited secondary school, or a satisfactory score on the GED, is required for admission. Students must have a total of 19 academic credits. High school courses must include 4 credits of English, 3 credits each of math and science, and 2 credits of a foreign language. An essay is required, and an interview is recommended. AP and CLEP credits are accepted. Important factors in the admissions decision are advanced placement or honor courses, leadership record, and extracurricular activities record.

Procedure: Freshmen are admitted fall and spring. Entrance exams should be taken during the fall of the senior year at the latest. There are early decision and deferred admissions plans. Early decision applications should be filed by January 15; regular applications, by March 1 for fall entry and November 15 for winter entry, along with a $20 fee. Notification of early decision is sent February 1; regular decision, March 15. 376 early decision candidates were accepted for the 1999-2000 class. 16% of all applicants are on a waiting list.

Financial Aid: In 1999-2000, 85% of all freshmen and 83% of continuing students received some form of financial aid. 39% of freshmen and 41% of continuing students received need-based aid. The average freshman award was $6320. Of that total, scholarships or need-based grants averaged $3643 ($9930 maximum); loans averaged $2531 ($2625 maximum); and work contracts averaged $146 ($800 maximum). 63% of undergraduates work part time. Average annual earnings from campus work are $525. The average financial indebtedness of the 1999 graduate was $13,763. The FAFSA and the college's own financial statement are required. The fall application deadline is April 1.

Computers: The mainframe is a DEC PDP 11/34A. Students have no access to the mainframe. The college has a ratio of 1 computer to every 8 students. All have access to the Internet and the Web. All students may access the system during library hours. There are no time limits and no fees.

FLORIDA AGRICULTURAL AND MECHANICAL UNIVERSITY

Tallahassee, FL 32307-3200

(850) 599-3796
Fax: (850) 561-2428

Full-time: 3918 men, 5489 women	**Faculty:** 601; IIA, av$
Part-time: 737 men, 930 women	**Ph.D.s:** 53%
Graduate: 302 men, 599 women	**Student/Faculty:** 16 to 1
Year: semesters, summer session	**Tuition:** $2346 ($9334)
Application Deadline: May 15	**Room & Board:** $3600
Freshman Class: 5648 applied, 3969 accepted, 1974 enrolled	
SAT I or ACT: required	**VERY COMPETITIVE**

Florida Agricultural and Mechanical University, founded in 1887 and a public institution within the state university system of Florida, offers undergraduate programs in agriculture, allied health science, architecture, the arts and sciences, business and industry, education, engineering, journalism, pharmacy and pharmaceutical sciences, upper-level nursing, and technology. There are 11 undergraduate schools and 1 graduate school. In addition to regional accreditation, Florida A&M has baccalaureate program accreditation with AACSB, ABET, ACEJMC, ACPE, APTA, CSWE, NAAB, NCATE, and NLN. The 8 libraries contain 485,985 volumes, 82,000 microform items, and 62,610 audiovisual forms/CDs, and subscribe to 3639 periodicals. Computerized library services include the card catalog and database searching. Special learning facilities include a learning resource center, art gallery, radio station, black archives, and observatory. The 419-acre campus is in an urban area 169 miles east of Jacksonville. Including residence halls, there are 111 buildings.

Programs of Study: Florida A&M confers B.A., B.S., B.Arch., B.C.J., B.S. Arch. and Constr.E.T., B.S.Arch.Studies, B.S.Arch.E.T., B.S.C.E., B.S.C.E.T., B. S.Ch.E., B.S.Constr.E.T., B.S.E.E., B.S.Elect.E.T., B.S.H.C.M., B.S.I.E., B.S.J., B.S.M.E., B.S.M.R.A., B.S.N., B.S.Pharm., B.S.P.T., B.S.R.T., B.S.T., and B. S.W. degrees. Associate, master's, and doctoral degrees are also awarded. Bachelor's degrees are awarded in AGRICULTURE (animal science and horticulture), BIOLOGICAL SCIENCE (biology/biological science), BUSINESS (accounting, banking and finance, business administration and management, and business economics), COMMUNICATIONS AND THE ARTS (dramatic arts, English, fine arts, journalism, and music), COMPUTER AND PHYSICAL SCIENCE (actuarial science, chemistry, computer science, mathematics, and physics), EDUCATION (art, business, early childhood, elementary, industrial arts, music, and science), ENGINEERING AND ENVIRONMENTAL DESIGN (chemical engineering, civil engineering, electrical/electronics engineering, engineering technology, industrial engineering, and mechanical engineering), HEALTH PROFESSIONS (nursing, occupational therapy, pharmacy, physical therapy, predentistry, and premedicine), SOCIAL SCIENCE (criminal justice, economics, history, political science/government, psychology, public administration, social science, social work, and sociology). Business, engineering, and pharmacy are the strongest academically. Business, pharmacy, and arts and sciences are the largest.

Special: Cooperative programs and cross-registration are offered in conjunction with Florida State University. Internships are available either on or off campus. Florida A&M also offers a Washington semester for architecture majors, a B.A.-B.S. degree, credit for life experience, and pass/fail options. Nondegree study is possible. There are 10 national honor societies, and a freshman honors program.

Admissions: 70% of the 1999-2000 applicants were accepted.

Requirements: The SAT I or ACT is required, with a minimum composite score of 900 on the SAT I, or 450 on each part, or 19 on the ACT. A GPA of 3.2 is required. Applicants must be graduates of accredited secondary schools or have earned a GED. The university requires 19 academic credits, including 4 each in English and academic electives, 3 each in math, science, and social studies, and 2 in foreign language. AP and CLEP credits are accepted. Important factors in the admissions decision are recommendations by school officials, extracurricular activities record, and evidence of special talent.

Procedure: Freshmen are admitted to all sessions. Entrance exams should be taken by the fall of the senior year. There are early admissions and deferred admissions plans. Applications should be filed by May 15 for fall entry, November 15 for spring entry, and April 1 for summer entry, along with a $20 fee. Notification is sent on a rolling basis.

Financial Aid: The university prefers the FFS but will accept the CSS/Profile. The fall application deadline is April 1.

Computers: The mainframe is an IBM 4381 Model 13. The school provides more than 100 Apple, Mac, and IBM PCs for academic use. All students may access the system. There are no time limits and no fees.

FLORIDA INSTITUTE OF TECHNOLOGY
Melbourne, FL 32901-6975

(321) 674-8030
(800) 888-4348; Fax: (321) 723-9468

Full-time: 1246 men, 543 women	**Faculty:** 150
Part-time: 92 men, 52 women	**Ph.D.s:** 94%
Graduate: 1449 men, 796 women	**Student/Faculty:** 12 to 1
Year: semesters, summer session	**Tuition:** $17,300
Application Deadline: open	**Room & Board:** $5270
Freshman Class: 1939 applied, 1531 accepted, 397 enrolled	
SAT I Verbal/Math: 550/570	**ACT:** 25 **VERY COMPETITIVE**

Florida Institute of Technology, founded in 1958, offers undergraduate degrees in engineering and science, liberal arts, business, psychology, and aeronautics. There are 5 undergraduate schools and 1 graduate school. In addition to regional accreditation, Florida Tech has baccalaureate program accreditation with ABET and CSAB. The library contains 368,517 volumes, 291,883 microform items, and 7362 audiovisual forms/CDs, and subscribes to 3270 periodicals. Computerized library services include the card catalog, interlibrary loans, and database searching. Special learning facilities include a learning resource center, radio station, and tv station. The 130-acre campus is in a small town 70 miles east of Orlando. Including residence halls, there are 64 buildings.

Programs of Study: Florida Tech confers B.A., B.S., and B.S.B.A. degrees. Associate, master's, and doctoral degrees are also awarded. Bachelor's degrees are awarded in AGRICULTURE (fishing and fisheries), BIOLOGICAL SCIENCE (biochemistry, biology/biological science, marine biology, and marine science), BUSINESS (business administration and management), COMMUNICATIONS AND THE ARTS (communications), COMPUTER AND PHYSICAL SCIENCE (applied mathematics, astrophysics, atmospheric sciences and meteorology, chemistry, computer programming, computer science, information sciences and systems, oceanography, physics, and planetary and space science), EDUCATION (science), ENGINEERING AND ENVIRONMENTAL DESIGN (aeronautical engineering, aeronautical science, aerospace studies, aviation administration/ management, aviation computer technology, chemical engineering, civil engineering, computer engineering, electrical/electronics engineering, environmental science, mechanical engineering, and ocean engineering), HEALTH PROFESSIONS (predentistry and premedicine), SOCIAL SCIENCE (humanities, interdisciplinary studies, and psychology). Engineering, science, and aeronautics are the strongest academically. Computer engineering, marine biology, and aviation management are the largest.

Special: Florida Tech offers co-op programs in all majors and double programs in environmental and chemical engineering, physics and space science, and math and computer science. Internships are available in the senior year for various majors, including psychology and aeronautics. Study-abroad programs are available in 5 countries. There are 3 national honor societies.

Admissions: 79% of the 1999-2000 applicants were accepted. The SAT I scores for the 1999-2000 freshman class were: Verbal--21% below 500, 49% between 500 and 599, 26% between 600 and 700, and 4% above 700; Math--17% below 500, 44% between 500 and 599, 34% between 600 and 700, and 5% above 700. The ACT scores were 16% below 21, 24% between 21 and 23, 33% between 24 and 26, 14% between 27 and 28, and 13% above 28. 43% of the current freshmen were in the top fifth of their class; 77% were in the top two fifths. There were 2 National Merit finalists and 5 semifinalists. 5 freshmen graduated first in their class.

Requirements: The SAT I or ACT is required. A GPA of 2.5 is required. Applicants must be graduates of an accredited secondary school or have a GED certificate. At least 18 academic credits or Carnegie units are required, including 4 years each of English, math, and science. An essay is required and an interview is recommended. Applications are accepted on-line at www.fit.edu/prosstud/ undergrad/. AP and CLEP credits are accepted. Important factors in the admissions decision are advanced placement or honor courses, recommendations by school officials, and extracurricular activities record.

Procedure: Freshmen are admitted fall, spring, and summer. Entrance exams should be taken during the junior year or the beginning of the senior year of high school. There are early admissions and deferred admissions plans. Application deadlines are open; the fee is $35. Notification is sent on a rolling basis.

Financial Aid: 20% of undergraduates work part time. Average annual earnings from campus work are $1500. Florida Tech is a member of CSS. The FAFSA is required. The fall application deadline is March 15.

Computers: The mainframe is a Sun Enterprise 3000. Students may access the system through more than 250 workstations located in general public or department labs, and through dial-up lines. All students in residence on the central campus have direct network access in their rooms. Students have access internally to the Florida Tech Web-based intranet and externally to the Internet. All students may access the system 24 hours per day. There are no time limits and no fees.

FLORIDA INTERNATIONAL UNIVERSITY
Miami, FL 33199   (305) 348-2363; Fax: (305) 348-3648

Full-time: 6085 men, 7857 women	**Faculty:** 869; I, --$
Part-time: 5342 men, 6425 women	**Ph.D.s:** 96%
Graduate: 2228 men, 3359 women	**Student/Faculty:** 16 to 1
Year: semesters, summer session	**Tuition:** $2322 ($9311)
Application Deadline: open	**Room:** $4436
Freshman Class: 5391 applied, 3006 accepted, 1516 enrolled	
SAT I Verbal/Math: 560/553	**ACT:** 24 **VERY COMPETITIVE**

Florida International University, founded in 1965, is part of the State University System of Florida. Undergraduate degrees are offered through the Colleges of Arts and Sciences, Business Administration, Education, Engineering, Health Sciences, and Urban and Public Affairs and the Schools of Accounting, Computer Science, Architecture, Hospitality Management, Music, and Journalism and Mass Communication. The North and University Park campuses are in Miami, and there are 2 educational centers in Fort Lauderdale. There are 12 undergraduate and 12 graduate schools. In addition to regional accreditation, FIU has baccalaureate program accreditation with AACSB, ABET, ACCE, ACEJMC, ADA, APTA, ASLA, CSWE, NAAB, NASM, NCATE, and NLN. The 2 libraries contain 1,397,808 volumes, 3,236,347 microform items, and 115,550 audiovisual forms/CDs, and subscribe to 9910 periodicals. Computerized library services include the card catalog, interlibrary loans, and database searching. Special learning facilities include a learning resource center, radio station, and an art museum. The 573-acre campus is in an urban area 10 miles west of downtown Miami. Including residence halls, there are 24 buildings.

Programs of Study: FIU confers B.A., B.S., B.Ac., B.B.A., B.F.A., B.H.S.A., B.M., B.P.A., and B.S.N. degrees. Associate, master's, and doctoral degrees are also awarded. Bachelor's degrees are awarded in BIOLOGICAL SCIENCE (biology/biological science), BUSINESS (accounting, banking and finance, business administration and management, hospitality management services, international business management, management information systems, management science, marketing/retailing/merchandising, personnel management, real estate, and transportation management), COMMUNICATIONS AND THE ARTS (art, communications, dance, dramatic arts, English, French, German, music, Portuguese, and Spanish), COMPUTER AND PHYSICAL SCIENCE (applied mathematics, chemistry, computer science, geology, mathematics, physics, and statistics), EDUCATION (art, education of the emotionally handicapped, education of the mentally handicapped, elementary, English, foreign languages, health, home economics, mathematics, music, physical, science, social studies, special, specific learning disabilities, and vocational), ENGINEERING AND ENVIRONMENTAL DESIGN (architectural technology, chemical engineering, civil engineering, computer engineering, construction management, electrical/electronics engineering, environmental science, industrial engineering, interior design, and mechanical engineering), HEALTH PROFESSIONS (health care administration, medical laboratory technology, nursing, occupational therapy, and rehabilitation therapy), SOCIAL SCIENCE (criminal justice, dietetics, economics, history, humanities, international relations, Italian studies, liberal arts/general studies, parks and recreation management, philosophy, political science/government, psychology, public administration, religion, social work, sociology, urban studies, and women's studies). Accounting, engineering, and biology are the strongest academically. Accounting, hospitality management, and elementary education are the largest.

Special: FIU offers co-op and work-study programs, and study abroad in 6 countries. Accelerated degree programs, nondegree study, dual majors, and B.A.-B.S. degrees in chemistry, enviornmental studies, and geology may also be arranged. There are 25 national honor societies, a freshman honors program, and 18 departmental honors programs.

Admissions: 56% of the 1999-2000 applicants were accepted. The SAT I scores for the 1999-2000 freshman class were: Verbal--10% below 500, 57% between 500 and 599, 19% between 600 and 700, and 14% above 700; Math--13% below 500, 57% between 500 and 599, 17% between 600 and 700, and 13% above 700. The ACT scores were 6% below 21, 50% between 21 and 23, 35% between 24 and 26, 7% between 27 and 28, and 3% above 28. 9 freshmen graduated first in their class in a recent year.

Requirements: The SAT I or ACT is required. A GPA of 2.0 is required. Applicants must be graduates of an accredited secondary school or have a GED certificate. The required academic courses include 4 units in English, 3 each in math, natural science, and social studies, 2 in a foreign language, and 4 in academic electives. The university's placement tests must be taken the semester before attending. An interview may be required. Admissions diskettes are available upon request. A printable on-line application is available. AP and CLEP credits are accepted. Important factors in the admissions decision are advanced placement or honor courses, evidence of special talent, and recommendations by school officials.

Procedure: Freshmen are admitted to all sessions. Entrance exams should be taken during the spring of the junior year. There are early admissions and deferred admissions plans. Application deadlines are open. There is a $20 fee. Notification is sent on a rolling basis.

Financial Aid: In 1999-2000, 88% of all freshmen and 80% of continuing students received some form of financial aid. 72% of freshmen and 73% of continuing students received need-based aid. The average freshman award was $4191. Of that total, scholarships or need-based grants averaged $3521 ($7799 maximum); loans averaged $2636 ($10,500 maximum); and work contracts averaged $2451 ($2500 maximum). 6% of undergraduates work part time. Average annual earnings from campus work are $2000. The average financial indebtedness of the 1999 graduate was $4650. FIU is a member of CSS. The FAFSA is required. The fall application deadline is March 1.

Computers: The mainframes are a DEC VAX 8800 and a Sun 4/280. Students may access the campus Ethernet network through terminals and PCs and through dial-up access from home. All students may access the system 8 a.m. to 4 a.m. There are no time limits and no fees.

FLORIDA STATE UNIVERSITY
Tallahassee, FL 32306-2400

(850) 644-6200
Fax: (850) 644-0197

Full-time: 9984 men, 12,491 women	**Faculty:** 1029; I, -$
Part-time: 1647 men, 1953 women	**Ph.D.s:** 90%
Graduate: 3167 men, 4085 women	**Student/Faculty:** 22 to 1
Year: semesters, summer session	**Tuition:** $2195 ($9184)
Application Deadline: March 1	**Room & Board:** $4951
Freshman Class: 21,249 applied, 13,490 accepted, 5153 enrolled	
SAT I Verbal/Math: 580/583	**ACT:** 25 **HIGHLY COMPETITIVE**

Florida State University, a public institution founded in 1857, is 1 of 88 research universities nationwide to receive the Research I classification as designated by the Carnegie Foundation for the Advancement of Teaching. There are 15 undergraduate and 16 graduate schools. In addition to regional accreditation, FSU has baccalaureate program accreditation with AACSB, ABET, ADA, AHEA, ASLA, CSWE, FIDER, NASM, NCATE, NLN, and NRPA. The 6 libraries contain 2, 310,597 volumes, 4,802,657 microform items, and 42,298 audiovisual forms/CDs, and subscribe to 15,228 periodicals. Computerized library services include the card catalog, interlibrary loans, and database searching. Special learning facilities include a learning resource center, art gallery, planetarium, radio station, tv station, nuclear accelerator, x-ray emission lab, marine lab, supercomputers, the National High Magnetic Field Laboratory and the Oak Ridge National Laboratory. The 463-acre campus is in a suburban area 163 miles west of Jacksonville. Including residence halls, there are 213 buildings.

Programs of Study: FSU confers B.A., B.S., B.F.A, B.M., B.M.Ed., and B.S.N. degrees. Associate, master's, and doctoral degrees are also awarded. Bachelor's degrees are awarded in AGRICULTURE (plant science), BIOLOGICAL SCIENCE (biochemistry, biology/biological science, cell biology, ecology, evolutionary biology, genetics, marine biology, molecular biology, nutrition, physiology, and zoology), BUSINESS (accounting, banking and finance, business administration and management, entrepreneurial studies, fashion merchandising, hotel/motel and restaurant management, insurance and risk management, international business management, management information systems, marketing/retailing/merchandising, personnel management, real estate, recreation and leisure services, and small business management), COMMUNICATIONS AND THE ARTS (advertising, American literature, apparel design, art history and appreciation, broadcasting, classics, communications, crafts, creative writing, dance, dramatic arts, English, fiber/textiles/weaving, film arts, French, German, Greek, Italian, Latin, linguistics, music, music history and appreciation, music performance, music theory and composition, musical theater, piano/organ, public relations, Russian, Spanish, speech/debate/rhetoric, strings, studio art, voice, and winds), COMPUTER AND PHYSICAL SCIENCE (actuarial science, applied mathematics, atmospheric sciences and meteorology, chemistry, computer science, geology, mathematics, physical chemistry, physics, science, and statistics), EDUCATION (art, early childhood, education of the emotionally handicapped, education of the mentally handicapped, education of the visually handicapped, elementary, English, foreign languages, health, home economics, mathematics, music, physical, school psychology, science, social science, and specific learning disabilities), ENGINEERING AND ENVIRONMENTAL DESIGN (bioengineering, chemical engineering, civil engineering, electrical/electronics engineering, environmental engineering, environmental science, industrial engineering, interior design, materials engineering, and mechanical engineering),

HEALTH PROFESSIONS (community health work, music therapy, nursing, predentistry, premedicine, preoptometry, prepharmacy, preveterinary science, rehabilitation therapy, and speech pathology/audiology), SOCIAL SCIENCE (American studies, anthropology, Asian/Oriental studies, Caribbean studies, child care/child and family studies, classical/ancient civilization, clinical psychology, clothing and textiles management/production/services, criminology, dietetics, Eastern European studies, economics, experimental psychology, family/consumer studies, fashion design and technology, food science, geography, history, home economics, humanities, international relations, Latin American studies, philosophy, political science/government, prelaw, psychology, religion, Russian and Slavic studies, social science, social work, sociology, and women's studies). Computer science and natural science are the strongest academically. Business, communication, and biology are the largest.

Special: Cross-registration with Florida Agricultural and Mechanical University and Tallahassee Community College is possible, as is study at FSU centers in London or Florence and in programs in Costa Rica, France, Russia, Spain, Switzerland, and Vietnam, among other countries. FSU offers cooperative programs in engineering, computer science, business, and communication, work-study programs, and general studies and combined B.A.-B.S. degrees. Internships are required in criminology, human science, and social work. There are preprofessional programs in health and law. There are 49 national honor societies, including Phi Beta Kappa, a freshman honors program, and 54 departmental honors programs.

Admissions: 63% of the 1999-2000 applicants were accepted. The SAT I scores for the 1999-2000 freshman class were: Verbal--15% below 500, 51% between 500 and 599, 29% between 600 and 700, and 5% above 700; Math--14% below 500, 52% between 500 and 599, 30% between 600 and 700, and 4% above 700. The ACT scores were 9% below 21, 28% between 21 and 23, 29% between 24 and 26, 18% between 27 and 28, and 16% above 28. 78% of the current freshmen were in the top fifth of their class; 97% were in the top two fifths. There were 90 National Merit finalists and 2 semifinalists.

Requirements: The SAT I or ACT is required. It is recommended that in-state students have at least an A-/B+ weighted average and a minimum composite SAT I score of 1100, or 25 on the ACT. Out-of-state students must meet higher standards. Applicants should have the following high school units: 4 in English, 3 in math, natural science, and social science, and 2 in a foreign language. Other factors include the number of honors, AP, and IB classes, strength of academic curriculum, class rank, and others. Applications are accepted on-line at the school's web site. AP and CLEP credits are accepted. Important factors in the admissions decision are advanced placement or honor courses, evidence of special talent, and recommendations by school officials.

Procedure: Freshmen are admitted fall, spring, and summer. Entrance exams should be taken beginning in the second semester of the junior year. There is an early admissions plan. Applications should be filed by March 1 for fall or summer entry, and November 1 for spring entry, along with a $20 fee. Notification is sent on a rolling basis.

Financial Aid: In 1999-2000, 74% of all freshmen and 60% of continuing students received some form of financial aid. 27% of freshmen and 33% of continuing students received need-based aid. The average freshman award was $7957. Of that total, scholarships or need-based grants averaged $2541 ($3500 maximum); loans averaged $2682 ($3000 maximum); and work contracts averaged $1811 ($2990 maximum). 2% of undergraduates work part time. Average annual earnings from campus work are $1778. The average financial indebtedness of the 1999 graduate was $15,458. FSU is a member of CSS. The FAFSA and the college's own financial statement are required. The fall application deadline is March 1.

Computers: The mainframes are an IBM RS/6000 and a 9076 SP2, a Cray Y-MP and a CM-2, a CDC CYBER 850, and a DEC VAX 6210. There is also a supercomputer on campus. All students may access the system although use of some machines is restricted to particular majors or graduate students. There are no time limits and no fees. It is recommended that students in engineering programs have personal computers.

FORDHAM UNIVERSITY
Bronx, NY 10458

(718) 817-4000
(800) FORDHAM; Fax: (718) 367-3426

Full-time: 2376 men, 3312 women	**Faculty:** 447; I, +$
Part-time: 318 men, 572 women	**Ph.D.s:** 94%
Graduate: 2734 men, 4239 women	**Student/Faculty:** 13 to 1
Year: semesters, summer session	**Tuition:** $19,540
Application Deadline: February 1	**Room & Board:** $6485 - $9580
Freshman Class: 8600 applied, 5352 accepted, 1584 enrolled	
SAT I Verbal/Math: 590/570	**ACT:** 25 **VERY COMPETITIVE**

Fordham University, founded in 1841, is an independent institution offering an education based on the Jesuit tradition, with 2 campuses in New York City, 1 in the Bronx and the other in Manhattan near Lincoln Center. There are 4 undergraduate and 6 graduate schools. In addition to regional accreditation, Fordham University has baccalaureate program accreditation with AACSB and NCATE. The 2 libraries contain 1,749,713 volumes, 2,586,483 microform items, and 7784 audiovisual forms/CDs, and subscribe to 12,022 periodicals. Computerized library services include the card catalog, interlibrary loans, and database searching. Special learning facilities include a radio station, a seismic station, and an archeological org site on campus. The 85-acre campus is in an urban area adjacent to the Bronx Zoo and New York Botanical Garden. Including residence halls, there are 32 buildings at the 85-acre Bronx campus.

Programs of Study: Fordham University confers B.A., B.S., and B.F.A. degrees. Master's and doctoral degrees are also awarded. Bachelor's degrees are awarded in BIOLOGICAL SCIENCE (biology/biological science), BUSINESS (accounting, business administration and management, business economics, international business management, and marketing management), COMMUNICATIONS AND THE ARTS (art history and appreciation, broadcasting, classical languages, communications, comparative literature, creative writing, dance, dramatic arts, English, film arts, fine arts, French, German, Italian, journalism, music, performing arts, photography, Russian, Spanish, and visual and performing arts), COMPUTER AND PHYSICAL SCIENCE (chemistry, computer science, information sciences and systems, mathematics, physics, and science), EDUCATION (education and mathematics), ENGINEERING AND ENVIRONMENTAL DESIGN (preengineering), HEALTH PROFESSIONS (predentistry, premedicine, and preveterinary science), SOCIAL SCIENCE (African American studies, African studies, American studies, anthropology, classical/ancient civilization, criminal justice, economics, French studies, German area studies, history, international studies, Italian studies, Latin American studies, medieval studies, Middle Eastern studies, peace studies, philosophy, political science/government, prelaw, psychology, religion, Russian and Slavic studies, social science, social work, sociology, Spanish studies, theological studies, urban studies, and women's studies). Communications, social sciences, and English are the strongest academically. Business, psychology, and history are the largest.

215

Special: Fordham University offers career-oriented internships in communications and other majors during the junior or senior year with New York City companies and institutions. A combined 3-2 engineering program is available with Columbia University and Case Western University. Study abroad, a Washington semester, accelerated degree programs, dual and student-designed majors, and pass/fail options are available. There are 6 national honor societies, including Phi Beta Kappa, and a freshman honors program. Each of the full-time undergraduate colleges has an honors program.

Admissions: 62% of the 1999-2000 applicants were accepted. The SAT I scores for the 1999-2000 freshman class were: Verbal--7% below 500, 46% between 500 and 599, 38% between 600 and 700, and 9% above 700; Math--11% below 500, 51% between 500 and 599, 33% between 600 and 700, and 4% above 700. The ACT scores were 7% below 21, 21% between 21 and 23, 37% between 24 and 26, 18% between 27 and 28, and 17% above 28. 57% of the current freshmen were in the top fifth of their class; 85% were in the top two fifths. There were 9 National Merit semifinalists. 20 freshmen graduated first in their class.

Requirements: The SAT I or ACT is required. Fordham University requires applicants to be in the upper 40% of their class. A GPA of 3.0 is required. Applicants should have completed 4 years of high school English and 3 each of math, science, social studies, history, and foreign language. An essay is part of the application process. An interview is recommended. Auditions are required for theater and dance majors. Applications are accepted on-line via www.nymentor.org. AP and CLEP credits are accepted. Important factors in the admissions decision are parents or siblings attending the school, leadership record, and recommendations by school officials.

Procedure: Freshmen are admitted fall and spring. Entrance exams should be taken by December of the senior year. There are early decision, early admissions, and deferred admissions plans. Early decision applications should be filed by November 1; regular applications, by February 1 for fall entry and November 1 for spring entry, along with a $50 fee. Notification of early decision is sent December 15; regular decision, April 1. 76 early decision candidates were accepted for the 1999-2000 class. 7% of all applicants are on a waiting list.

Financial Aid: In 1999-2000, 73% of all freshmen and 69% of continuing students received some form of financial aid. 69% of freshmen and 59% of continuing students received need-based aid. The average freshman award was $16,570. Of that total, scholarships or need-based grants averaged $11,689; loans averaged $2820; and work contracts averaged $3471. 95% of undergraduates work part time. Average annual earnings from campus work are $1600. The average financial indebtedness of the 1999 graduate was $15,379. Fordham University is a member of CSS. The CSS/Profile or FAFSA is required. The fall application deadline is February 1.

Computers: The mainframe is a DEC VAX system. More than 900 PCs are available to students in labs throughout both campuses. Labs can be found in the libraries, academic buildings, and residence halls. Most are connected to the mainframe and have access to the World Wide Web. All residence halls are also wired for hookup to the university network and the Internet. All students may access the system. There are no time limits and no fees.

FRANKLIN AND MARSHALL COLLEGE

Lancaster, PA 17604-3003   (717) 291-3951; Fax: (717) 291-4389

Full-time: 907 men, 924 women	**Faculty:** 161; IIB, ++$
Part-time: 19 men, 14 women	**Ph.D.s:** 95%
Graduate: none	**Student/Faculty:** 11 to 1
Year: semesters, summer session	**Tuition:** $23,770
Application Deadline: February 1	**Room & Board:** $5730
Freshman Class: 3927 applied, 1956 accepted, 516 enrolled	
SAT I Verbal/Math: 631/638	**ACT:** 27 **HIGHLY COMPETITIVE**

Franklin and Marshall College, founded in 1787, is a private liberal arts institution. The 2 libraries contain 345,000 volumes, 250,000 microform items, and 8500 audiovisual forms/CDs, and subscribe to 1703 periodicals. Computerized library services include the card catalog, interlibrary loans, and database searching. Special learning facilities include a learning resource center, art gallery, natural history museum, planetarium, radio station, TV station, instructional media services, advanced language lab, a writing center, and student newspaper. The 125-acre campus is in a suburban area 60 miles west of Philadelphia. Including residence halls, there are 44 buildings.

Programs of Study: F & M confers the B.A. degree. Bachelor's degrees are awarded in BIOLOGICAL SCIENCE (biology/biological science), BUSINESS (accounting and business administration and management), COMMUNICATIONS AND THE ARTS (classics, dramatic arts, English, fine arts, French, German, Greek, Latin, music, and Spanish), COMPUTER AND PHYSICAL SCIENCE (chemistry, geology, mathematics, and physics), SOCIAL SCIENCE (African studies, American studies, anthropology, biopsychology, economics, history, philosophy, political science/government, psychology, religion, and sociology). Biology, neuroscience, and chemistry are the strongest academically. Government, business administration, and biology are the largest.

Special: There is a 3-2 degree program in forestry and environmental studies with Duke University as well as 3-2 degree programs in engineering with the University of Pennsylvania, Columbia University, Rensselaer Polytechnic Institute, Case Western Reserve, Georgia Institute of Technology, and Washington University at St. Louis. Cross-registration with the Central Pennsylvania Consortium allows students to study at nearby Dickinson College or Gettysburg College. Students may also study architecture and urban planning at Columbia University, studio art at the School of Visual Arts in New York City, theater in Connecticut, oceanography in Massachusetts, and American studies at American University. There are study-abroad programs in England, France, Germany, Greece, Italy, Denmark, India, Japan, and other countries. There are internships for credit, joint majors, student-designed majors, independent study, interdisciplinary studies, optional first-year seminars, collaborative projects, pass/fail options, and nondegree study. There are 12 national honor societies, including Phi Beta Kappa, and honors programs in all departments.

Admissions: 50% of the 1999-2000 applicants were accepted. The SAT I scores for the 1999-2000 freshman class were: Verbal--2% below 500, 31% between 500 and 599, 48% between 600 and 700, and 19% above 700; Math--1% below 500, 26% between 500 and 599, 52% between 600 and 700, and 21% above 700. 84% of the current freshmen were in the top fifth of their class; 97% were in the top two fifths. There were 5 National Merit finalists and 7 semifinalists. 32 freshmen graduated first in their class.

Requirements: The SAT I is required. Standardized tests are optional for students in the top 10% of their class. The SAT II: Writing test is required. Applicants

217

must be graduates of accredited secondary schools. Recommended college preparatory study includes 4 years each of English and math, 3 or 4 of foreign language, 3 each of lab science and history/social studies, and 1 or 2 courses in art or music. All students must also submit their high school transcripts, recommendations from a teacher and a counselor, and a personal essay. An interview is recommended. AP and CLEP credits are accepted. Important factors in the admissions decision are advanced placement or honor courses, recommendations by school officials, and extracurricular activities record.

Procedure: Freshmen are admitted in the fall. Entrance exams should be taken by December of the senior year. There are early decision, early admissions, and deferred admissions plans. Early decision applications should be filed by November 15 for round I, January 15 for round II; regular applications, by February 1 for fall entry, along with a $50 fee. Notification is sent April 1. 235 early decision candidates were accepted for the 1999-2000 class. 20% of all applicants are on a waiting list.

Financial Aid: In 1999-2000, 61% of all freshmen and 57% of continuing students received some form of financial aid. 45% of freshmen and 46% of continuing students received need-based aid. The average freshman award was $16,971. Of that total, scholarships or need-based grants averaged $13,778 ($29,250 maximum); loans averaged $2385 ($3625 maximum); and work contracts averaged $808 ($1550 maximum). 50% of undergraduates work part time. Average annual earnings from campus work are $1340. The average financial indebtedness of the 1999 graduate was $15,982. F & M is a member of CSS. The CSS/Profile or FAFSA is required. If applicable, the Business/Farm Supplement and Noncustodial Parents Statement must also be submitted. The fall application deadline is February 1.

Computers: The mainframe is a DEC MicroVAX 3800. A computer workroom houses 32 Macs, 6 Apple LaserWriter printers, 1 Color Apple printer, and 1 HP laser printer that is directly connected to the mainframe. All of the Macs are on the campuswide network for access to file servers and the academic VAX. A team of 25 student computing consultants is available for computing support and problem-solving assistance. All students may access the system 24 hours a day, 7 days a week. There are no time limits and no fees. The college strongly recommends that all students have Mac computers.

FREED-HARDEMAN UNIVERSITY
Henderson, TN 38340
(901) 989-6651
(800) 630-3480; Fax: (901) 989-6047

Full-time: 595 men, 715 women	**Faculty:** 89; IIA, --$
Part-time: 49 men, 61 women	**Ph.D.s:** 71%
Graduate: 145 men, 266 women	**Student/Faculty:** 15 to 1
Year: semesters, 2 summer sessions	**Tuition:** $8558
Application Deadline: September 1	**Room & Board:** $4230
Freshman Class: 874 applied, 632 accepted, 324 enrolled	
ACT: 23	**VERY COMPETITIVE**

Freed-Hardeman University, founded in 1869, is a private liberal arts institution associated with Churches of Christ. There are 6 undergraduate and 3 graduate schools. In addition to regional accreditation, FHU has baccalaureate program accreditation with ACBSP, CSWE, and NCATE. The library contains 135,091 volumes, 218,813 microform items, and 40,500 audiovisual forms/CDs, and subscribes to 1460 periodicals. Computerized library services include the card catalog, interlibrary loans, and database searching. Special learning facilities include a learning resource center, art gallery, radio station, TV station, and a Cancer Research Institute. The 120-acre campus is in a small town 85 miles east of Memphis and 13 miles south of Jackson. Including residence halls, there are 26 buildings.

Programs of Study: FHU confers B.A., B.S., B.B.A., and B.S.W. degrees. Master's degrees are also awarded. Bachelor's degrees are awarded in AGRICULTURE (agricultural business management), BIOLOGICAL SCIENCE (biology/biological science), BUSINESS (accounting, banking and finance, business administration and management, and marketing/retailing/merchandising), COMMUNICATIONS AND THE ARTS (art, broadcasting, communications, dramatic arts, English, fine arts, public relations, and speech/debate/rhetoric), COMPUTER AND PHYSICAL SCIENCE (chemistry, computer programming, computer science, information sciences and systems, mathematics, and physical sciences), EDUCATION (art, early childhood, elementary, health, middle school, music, physical, science, secondary, and special), ENGINEERING AND ENVIRONMENTAL DESIGN (preengineering), HEALTH PROFESSIONS (predentistry, premedicine, preoptometry, prepharmacy, and preveterinary science), SOCIAL SCIENCE (biblical studies, child care/child and family studies, family/consumer studies, history, ministries, psychology, and social work). Premedicine, preengineering, and business are the strongest academically. Business, Bible, and elementary education are the largest.

Special: FHU offers cross-registration with Lambuth and Union Universities, study abroad in Belgium and Austria, a B.A.-B.S. degree in Bible, biology, communication, and arts and humanities, co-op programs, field practicum opportunities in several majors, student-designed majors, 3-2 engineering degrees with 6 universities, and nondegree study. There are 4 national honor societies, a freshman honors program, and 13 departmental honors programs.

Admissions: 72% of the 1999-2000 applicants were accepted. The ACT scores for the 1999-2000 freshman class were: 33% below 21, 26% between 21 and 23, 17% between 24 and 26, 12% between 27 and 28, and 12% above 28.

Requirements: The ACT is required, with a minimum composite score of 19. A GPA of 2.25 is required. Candidates for admission should be graduates of an accredited secondary school. An interview is recommended. AP and CLEP credits are accepted. Important factors in the admissions decision are personality/intangible qualities, recommendations by school officials, and leadership record.

Procedure: Freshmen are admitted to all sessions. There is an early admissions plan. Applications should be filed by September 1 for fall entry and January 10 for spring entry. Notification is sent on a rolling basis.

Financial Aid: In 1999-2000, 85% of all freshmen and 87% of continuing students received some form of financial aid. 77% of freshmen and 74% of continuing students received need-based aid. The average freshman award was $4980. Of that total, scholarships or need-based grants averaged $1700 ($11,200 maximum); loans averaged $2200 ($6625 maximum); and work contracts averaged $1080 ($2000 maximum). 33% of undergraduates work part time. Average annual earnings from campus work are $1080. The average financial indebtedness of the 1999 graduate was $9220. FHU is a member of CSS. The FAFSA is required. The fall application deadline is April 1.

Computers: The mainframe is a DEC VAX 4500. Apple and Mac PCs are available in student labs and other locations, and each residence hall room has access. All students may access the system. There are no time limits. The fee is $100 per semester.

FURMAN UNIVERSITY

Greenville, SC 29613   (864) 294-2034; Fax: (864) 294-3127

Full-time: 1133 men, 1366 women	**Faculty:** 191; IIB, ++$
Part-time: 62 men, 70 women	**Ph.D.s:** 94%
Graduate: 97 men, 534 women	**Student/Faculty:** 13 to 1
Year: 3-2-3, summer session	**Tuition:** $18,266
Application Deadline: February 1	**Room & Board:** $4848
Freshman Class: 3317 applied, 2156 accepted, 684 enrolled	
SAT I Verbal/Math: 620/622	**ACT:** 27 **HIGHLY COMPETITIVE**

Founded in 1826, Furman University is an independent liberal arts institution. In addition to regional accreditation, Furman has baccalaureate program accreditation with NASDTEC and NASM. The library contains 498,500 volumes, 704,000 microform items, and 3850 audiovisual forms/CDs, and subscribes to 2464 periodicals. Computerized library services include the card catalog, interlibrary loans, and database searching. Special learning facilities include a learning resource center, art gallery, radio station, and observatory, and cable TV with on-campus broadcasting. The acaddemic calendar is 12 weeks-8 weeks-12 weeks. The 750-acre campus is in a suburban area 5 miles north of Greenville. Including residence halls, there are 41 buildings.

Programs of Study: Furman confers B.A., B.S., B.G.S., and B.M. degrees. Master's degrees are also awarded. Bachelor's degrees are awarded in BIOLOGICAL SCIENCE (biology/biological science), BUSINESS (accounting and business administration and management), COMMUNICATIONS AND THE ARTS (art, communications, dramatic arts, English, French, German, Greek, Latin, music, music performance, music theory and composition, piano/organ, and Spanish), COMPUTER AND PHYSICAL SCIENCE (chemistry, computer science, mathematics, and physics), EDUCATION (education, elementary, and music), ENGINEERING AND ENVIRONMENTAL DESIGN (environmental science and pre-engineering), HEALTH PROFESSIONS (health science), SOCIAL SCIENCE (Asian/Oriental studies, economics, history, philosophy, political science/government, psychology, religion, religious music, sociology, and urban studies). Sciences, music, and psychology are the strongest academically. Political science, biology, and business administration are the largest.

Special: A 3-2 engineering degree is offered with Georgia Institute of Technology, Clemson, North Carolina State, Auburn, and Washington University at St. Louis. Internships, study abroad in at least 15 countries, a Washington semester with an internship in a government agency or political organization, and work-study programs are offered. B.A.-B.S. degrees, dual majors, interdisciplinary majors such as computer science-math, math-economics, and computing-business, and student-designed majors are available. A bachelor of general studies degree is granted in the evening division. Nondegree study and pass/fail options are possible. Furman features student/faculty research programs. There are 20 national honor societies, including Phi Beta Kappa.

Admissions: 65% of the 1999-2000 applicants were accepted. The SAT I scores for the 1999-2000 freshman class were: Verbal--3% below 500, 35% between 500 and 599, 47% between 600 and 700, and 15% above 700; Math--6% below 500, 28% between 500 and 599, 52% between 600 and 700, and 14% above 700. The ACT scores were 4% below 21, 10% between 21 and 23, 34% between 24 and 26, 23% between 27 and 28, and 29% above 28. 83% of the current freshmen were in the top fifth of their class; 95% were in the top two fifths. There were 45 National Merit finalists. 50 freshmen graduated first in their class.

Requirements: The SAT I or ACT is required. Applicants must be high school graduates or hold a GED. Students should have earned at least 20 units in high school, including 4 of English, 3 each of history, math, and science, and 2 each of social studies and foreign language. 2 essays are required. A portfolio or an audition, where appropriate, is recommended. Furman accepts applications on computer disk through CollegeLink, ExPAN, Apply, and the Common Application. AP credits are accepted. Important factors in the admissions decision are advanced placement or honor courses, extracurricular activities record, and leadership record.

Procedure: Freshmen are admitted to all sessions. Entrance exams should be taken by the late junior or early senior year. There are early decision, early admissions, and deferred admissions plans. Early decision applications should be filed by December 1; regular applications, by February 1 for fall, spring, or summer entry, and December 1 for winter entry, along with a $40 fee. Notification of early decision is sent January 1; regular decision, March 15. 479 early decision candidates were accepted for the 1999-2000 class. 15% of all applicants are on a waiting list.

Financial Aid: In 1999-2000, 82% of all freshmen and 75% of continuing students received some form of financial aid. 44% of freshmen and 52% of continuing students received need-based aid. The average freshman award was $12,914. Of that total, scholarships or need-based grants averaged $9877 ($23,100 maximum); loans averaged $2764 ($5500 maximum); and work contracts averaged $537 ($1500 maximum). 56% of undergraduates work part time. Average annual earnings from campus work are $1500. The average financial indebtedness of the 1999 graduate was $11,750. Furman is a member of CSS. The FAFSA and the college's own financial statement are required. The fall application deadline is February 1.

Computers: The mainframe consists of a DEC ALPHA Server 4000 5/300 running Tru 64 UNIX. Departmental and general access labs accommodate approximately 300 desktop systems, which include PCs, Macs, Suns, X-terminals, and SGI stations. The campus is fully networked for E-mail, network sharing, Internet access, and web hosting. All residence halls are wired for student PCs with connections to the campus network. Network ports are available across campus for personal notebook systems. A full range of software, including programs specific to academic majors, is offered. All students may access the system 8 a.m. to midnight daily. There are no time limits and no fees.

GENEVA COLLEGE
Beaver Falls, PA 15010

(724) 847-6500
(800) 847-8255; Fax: (724) 847-6776

Full-time: 730 men, 878 women	**Faculty:** 74; IIB, av$
Part-time: 126 men, 143 women	**Ph.D.s:** 70%
Graduate: 99 men, 151 women	**Student/Faculty:** 22 to 1
Year: semesters, summer session	**Tuition:** $12,650
Application Deadline: open	**Room & Board:** $4952
Freshman Class: 1093 applied, 803 accepted, 350 enrolled	
SAT I Verbal/Math: 550/550	**ACT:** 24 **VERY COMPETITIVE**

Geneva College, founded in 1848, is a private institution affiliated with the Reformed Presbyterian Church of North America. The college offers undergraduate programs in the arts and sciences, business, education, health science, biblical and religious studies, engineering, and preprofessional training. In addition to regional accreditation, Geneva has baccalaureate program accreditation with ABET and ACBSP. The library contains 162,661 volumes, 171,375 microform items, and 23,758 audiovisual forms/CDs, and subscribes to 907 periodicals. Computerized library services include the card catalog, interlibrary loans, and database searching. Special learning facilities include a radio station, TV station, and observatory. The 50-acre campus is in a small town 35 miles northwest of Pittsburgh. Including residence halls, there are 30 buildings.

Programs of Study: Geneva confers B.A., B.S., B.S.B.A., B.S.Ed., and B.S.E. degrees. Associate and master's degrees are also awarded. Bachelor's degrees are awarded in BIOLOGICAL SCIENCE (biology/biological science), BUSINESS (accounting and business administration and management), COMMUNICATIONS AND THE ARTS (applied music, broadcasting, communications, creative writing, English, music, music business management, Spanish, and speech/debate/rhetoric), COMPUTER AND PHYSICAL SCIENCE (applied mathematics, chemistry, computer science, and physics), EDUCATION (elementary, mathematics, and music), ENGINEERING AND ENVIRONMENTAL DESIGN (aviation administration/management, chemical engineering, and engineering), HEALTH PROFESSIONS (speech pathology/audiology), SOCIAL SCIENCE (biblical studies, counseling/psychology, history, human services, interdisciplinary studies, ministries, philosophy, political science/government, psychology, and sociology). Engineering, business administration, and chemical engineering are the strongest academically. Elementary education, business administration, and engineering are the largest.

Special: Cross-registration is offered in conjunction with Pennsylvania State University/Beaver Campus and Community College of Beaver County. There is a 3-1 degree program in cardiovascular technology, and accelerated degree programs in human resources and community ministry. Off-campus study includes programs at the Philadelphia Center for Urban Theological Studies, a Washington semester, a summer program at Au Sable, Institute of Environmental Studies in Michigan, art studies in Pittsburgh, film studies in Los Angeles, and study abroad in Costa Rica, Egypt, China, England, Russia, and Israel. Geneva also offers internships, independent study, and credit by proficiency exam. Nondegree study is available through adult education programs. There are 2 national honor societies, a freshman honors program, and 1 departmental honors program.

Admissions: 73% of the 1999-2000 applicants were accepted. The SAT I scores for the 1999-2000 freshman class were: Verbal--24% below 500, 47% between 500 and 599, 25% between 600 and 700, and 4% above 700; Math--27% below 500, 40% between 500 and 599, 30% between 600 and 700, and 6% above 700. The ACT scores were 16% below 21, 33% between 21 and 23, 36% between 24 and 26, 10% between 27 and 28, and 5% above 28. 41% of the current freshmen were in the top fifth of their class; 68% were in the top two fifths.

Requirements: The SAT I or ACT is required. Geneva requires applicants to be in the upper 50% of their class. A GPA of 2.5 is required. Applicants must be graduates of an accredited secondary school or have earned a GED. Geneva requires 16 academic units, based on 4 each of English and electives, 3 of social studies, 2 each of math and foreign language, and 1 of science. An essay is required, and an interview is recommended. Applications are accepted on-line via Geneva's web site, CollegeLink, and Mac Apply. AP and CLEP credits are accepted. Important factors in the admissions decision are recommendations by school officials, advanced placement or honor courses, and leadership record.

Procedure: Freshmen are admitted to all sessions. Entrance exams should be taken during the junior or senior year. There are early admissions and deferred admissions plans. Application deadlines are open. There is a $25 fee. Notification is sent on a rolling basis.

Financial Aid: In a recent year, 93% of all freshmen and 90% of continuing students received some form of financial aid. 90% of freshmen and 85% of continuing students received need-based aid. The average freshman award was $7600. Of that total, scholarships or need-based grants averaged $4600 ($6000 maximum); loans averaged $2234 ($2625 maximum); and work contracts averaged $800 ($1000 maximum). 65% of undergraduates work part time. Average annual earnings from campus work are $1000. The average financial indebtedness of the 1999 graduate was $20,000. Geneva is a member of CSS. The FAFSA is required. The fall application deadline is April 15.

Computers: The mainframe is an IBM AS/400. Access to the campus network and to the Internet is provided to all students. There are more than 150 PCs throughout the campus that students can use. Some of these are in general-purpose labs and others are in discipline-specific labs. Many residence hall rooms are also wired for connection to the campus network. All students may access the system. There are no time limits. The fee is $100 per semester.

GEORGE FOX UNIVERSITY
Newberg, OR 97132

(503) 538-8383
(800) 765-4369; Fax: (503) 538-7234

Full-time: 523 men, 810 women	**Faculty:** 92; IIA, -$
Part-time: 145 men, 203 women	**Ph.D.s:** 72%
Graduate: 299 men, 453 women	**Student/Faculty:** 14 to 1
Year: semesters	**Tuition:** $16,890
Application Deadline: June 1	**Room & Board:** $5325
Freshman Class: 815 applied, 742 accepted, 305 enrolled	
SAT I Verbal/Math: 570/560	**VERY COMPETITIVE**

George Fox University, founded in 1891, is a private school of liberal arts and sciences operated by the Northwest Yearly Meeting of Friends (Quaker). There are 3 undergraduate and 4 graduate schools. In addition to regional accreditation, George Fox has baccalaureate program accreditation with NASM. The library contains 128,986 volumes, 203,740 microform items, and 4558 audiovisual forms/CDs, and subscribes to 1244 periodicals. Computerized library services include the card catalog, interlibrary loans, and database searching. Special learning facilities include a learning resource center, art gallery, radio station, television production studio, and a Quaker museum. The 75-acre campus is in a small town 23 miles southwest of Portland. Including residence halls, there are 60 buildings.

Programs of Study: George Fox confers B.A. and B.S. degrees. Master's and doctoral degrees are also awarded. Bachelor's degrees are awarded in BIOLOGICAL SCIENCE (biology/biological science), BUSINESS (business economics, human resources, and management science), COMMUNICATIONS AND THE ARTS (art, communications, literature, music, Spanish, and telecommunications), COMPUTER AND PHYSICAL SCIENCE (chemistry, computer science, information sciences and systems, and mathematics), EDUCATION (elementary, health, home economics, mathematics, middle school, music, physical, science, secondary, and social studies), ENGINEERING AND ENVIRONMENTAL DESIGN (preengineering), HEALTH PROFESSIONS (predentistry, premedicine, and preveterinary science), SOCIAL SCIENCE (biblical studies, economics, history, home economics, international studies, ministries, prelaw, psychology, religion, social work, and sociology). Natural sciences is the strongest academically. Business is the largest.

Special: There is a 3-2 engineering degree with the University of Portland, Oregon State University, and Washington University in St. Louis, and cross-registration through the Oregon Independent College Association. George Fox also offers internships with area companies, study abroad in Kenya, England, Costa Rica, Russia, Egypt, Spain, and China, and a Washington semester through the Christian College Coalition. Work-study programs with the college, B.A.-B.S. degrees in all majors, dual and student-designed interdisciplinary majors, and pass/fail options in upper-division courses outside of the major also are offered. There is a freshman honors program.

Admissions: 91% of the 1999-2000 applicants were accepted. The SAT I scores for the 1999-2000 freshman class were: Verbal--24% below 500, 35% between 500 and 599, 37% between 600 and 700, and 4% above 700; Math--27% below 500, 37% between 500 and 599, 32% between 600 and 700, and 4% above 700. 55% of the current freshmen were in the top fifth of their class; 83% were in the top two fifths. There was 1 National Merit finalist and 3 semifinalists. 24 freshmen graduated first in their class.

Requirements: The SAT I or ACT is required. Applicants need 16 academic credits or 14 Carnegie units, including a suggested 4 units of English and 2 units each of a foreign language, math, science, and social studies. An essay and 2 personal recommendations are required; a portfolio, audition, and interview are recommended in certain majors. Applications are acceptd on-line at www.apply.com. AP and CLEP credits are accepted. Important factors in the admissions decision are advanced placement or honor courses, recommendations by school officials, and recommendations by alumni.

Procedure: Freshmen are admitted fall and spring. Entrance exams should be taken in fall or winter. There are early admissions and deferred admissions plans. Applications should be filed by June 1 for fall entry and December 1 for spring entry, along with a $40 fee. Notification is sent on a rolling basis.

Financial Aid: In 1999-2000, 93% of all freshmen and 94% of continuing students received some form of financial aid. 77% of freshmen and 79% of continuing students received need-based aid. The average freshman award was $15,767. Of that total, scholarships or need-based grants averaged $9251 ($22,289 maximum); loans averaged $5385 ($23,335 maximum); and work contracts averaged $1131 ($2925 maximum). 63% of undergraduates work part time. Average annual earnings from campus work are $1285. The average financial indebtedness of the 1999 graduate was $14,163. George Fox is a member of CSS. The FAFSA is required. The fall application deadline is August 1.

Computers: The mainframe is a DEC Alpha 2000. Computers Across the Curriculum provides each entering freshman with a computer to use while a student and to keep after graduation. Students also have access to a full computer resource area, including color monitors and printers and a training center. There is a Mac lab with 21 computers and an IBM lab with 25 Pentium computers. Network and Internet access is provided in all residences and at other plug-in locations on campus. All students may access the system. There are no time limits and no fees.

GEORGE MASON UNIVERSITY

Fairfax, VA 22030-4444   (703) 993-2400; Fax: (703) 993-2392

Full-time: 4736 men, 5975 women	**Faculty:** 633; I, av$
Part-time: 2049 men, 2502 women	**Ph.D.s:** 84%
Graduate: 3795 men, 5123 women	**Student/Faculty:** 16 to 1
Year: semesters, summer session	**Tuition:** $3756 ($12,516)
Application Deadline: February 1	**Room & Board:** $5080
Freshman Class: 6506 applied, 3856 accepted, 2130 enrolled	
SAT I Verbal/Math: 520/530	**VERY COMPETITIVE**

George Mason University, founded in 1972, offers undergraduate and graduate degrees in arts and sciences, business, information technology and engineering, fine arts, computational sciences and informatics, conflict analysis, nursing and health science, and education. Some of the information in this profile is approximate. A second campus in Arlington houses a professional school, the School of Law, and the International Institute. There are 5 undergraduate and 10 graduate schools. In addition to regional accreditation, GMU has baccalaureate program accreditation with AACSB, ABET, CSWE, NCATE, and NLN. The 5 libraries contain 800,000 volumes, 900,000 microform items, and 16,000 audiovisual forms/CDs, and subscribe to 10,000 periodicals. Computerized library services include the card catalog, interlibrary loans, and database searching. Special learning facilities include an art gallery, radio station, and tv station. The 802-acre campus is in a suburban area 18 miles southwest of Washington, D.C., in the Greater Washington Metropolitan area. Including residence halls, there are 92 buildings.

Programs of Study: GMU confers B.A., B.S., B.A.T.S., B.F.A., B.I.S., B.M., B.S.E., B.S.E.D., and B.S.N. degrees. Master's and doctoral degrees are also awarded. Bachelor's degrees are awarded in BIOLOGICAL SCIENCE (biology/biological science), BUSINESS (accounting, banking and finance, business administration and management, management information systems, and marketing/retailing/merchandising), COMMUNICATIONS AND THE ARTS (art history and appreciation, classics, communications, dance, dramatic arts, English, fine arts, French, German, journalism, music, Spanish, speech/debate/rhetoric, and studio art), COMPUTER AND PHYSICAL SCIENCE (chemistry, computer science, earth science, geology, information sciences and systems, mathematics, and physics), EDUCATION (foreign languages, health, industrial arts, physical, and teaching English as a second/foreign language (TESOL/TEFOL)), ENGINEERING AND ENVIRONMENTAL DESIGN (electrical/electronics engineering, systems engineering, and urban planning technology), HEALTH PROFESSIONS (nursing, premedicine, preveterinary science, and public health), SOCIAL SCIENCE (American studies, anthropology, criminal justice, economics, geography, history, interdisciplinary studies, international relations, parks and recreation management, philosophy, political science/government, prelaw, psychology, public administration, Russian and Slavic studies, social work, and sociology). Economics, public affairs, and public policy are the strongest academically. Biology, public affairs, and communication are the largest.

Special: GMU offers co-op programs in all majors with Shenandoah University, Virginia Polytechnic Institute and State University, Old Dominion University, and the University of Virginia, cross-registration with the Washington Consortium of Universities, internships through academic departments, study abroad in 10 countries, and on-campus work-study programs. Also available are dual and student-designed majors, nondegree study, and pass/fail options. The Program for Alternative General Education (PAGE) offers interdisciplinary studies for freshmen and sophomores. New Century College is an integrated program of study that emphasizes collaboration, experimental learning, and self-reflection. There are 3 national honor societies, a freshman honors program, and 8 departmental honors programs.

Admissions: 59% of the 1999-2000 applicants were accepted. The SAT I scores for the 1999-2000 freshman class were: Verbal--35% below 500, 46% between 500 and 599, 15% between 600 and 700, and 4% above 700; Math--34% below 500, 44% between 500 and 599, 19% between 600 and 700, and 3% above 700. The ACT scores were 22% below 21, 59% between 21 and 23, and 19% between 24 and 26.

Requirements: The SAT I or ACT is required. Applicants must be graduates of an accredited secondary school or have a GED certificate. A minimum of 18 credits is required, including 4 years of English, 3 each of math, science, social studies, and electives, and 2 of foreign language. An essay is recommended. Applications are accepted on computer disk and on-line. AP and CLEP credits are accepted. Important factors in the admissions decision are advanced placement or honor courses, evidence of special talent, and recommendations by school officials.

Procedure: Freshmen are admitted fall and spring. Entrance exams should be taken during the spring of the junior year. There are early admissions and deferred admissions plans. Applications should be filed by February 1 for fall entry and November 1 for spring entry, along with a $30 fee. Notification of early decision is sent January 15; regular decision, April 1.

Financial Aid: In 1999-2000, 53% of all freshmen and 48% of continuing students received some form of financial aid. 39% of freshmen and 38% of continuing students received need-based aid. The average freshman award was $6393. The average financial indebtedness of the 1999 graduate was $13,826. GMU is a member of CSS. The FAFSA is required. The fall application deadline is March 1.

Computers: The mainframes are a DEC ALPHA 2100 and an IBM ES 9121/300. 510 terminals are located in public student labs, the libraries, dormitories, and academic departments. All students may access the system 24 hours per day. There are no time limits and no fees.

GEORGE WASHINGTON UNIVERSITY
Washington, DC 20052

(202) 994-6040
(800) 447-3765; Fax: (202) 994-0325

Full-time: 3165 men, 4262 women	**Faculty:** 567; I, ++$
Part-time: 666 men, 602 women	**Ph.D.s:** 92%
Graduate: 5810 men, 5841 women	**Student/Faculty:** 13 to 1
Year: semesters, summer session	**Tuition:** $23,960
Application Deadline: February 1	**Room & Board:** $8210
Freshman Class: 14,326 applied, 7087 accepted, 2120 enrolled	
SAT I Verbal/Math: 620/620	**ACT:** 26 **HIGHLY COMPETITIVE**

George Washington University, founded in 1821, is a private institution providing degree programs in arts and sciences, business, engineering, international affairs, health sciences, education, law, and public health. There are 6 undergraduate and 8 graduate schools. In addition to regional accreditation, GW has baccalaureate program accreditation with AACSB, ABET, CAHEA, CSAB, NASAD, NASM, and NCATE. The 3 libraries contain 1,841,842 volumes, 2,468,719 microform items, and 17,246 audiovisual forms/CDs, and subscribe to 14,729 periodicals. Computerized library services include the card catalog, interlibrary loans, and database searching. Special learning facilities include a learning resource center, art gallery, radio station, and TV station. The 37-acre campus is in an urban area 3 blocks west of the White House. Including residence halls, there are 123 buildings.

Programs of Study: GW confers B.A., B.S., B.Accy., B.B.A., B.Mus., B.S.C.E., B.S.C.Eng., B.S.C.S., B.S.E.E., B.S.H.S., B.S.M.E., and B.S.S.A. degrees. Associate, master's, and doctoral degrees are also awarded. Bachelor's degrees are awarded in BIOLOGICAL SCIENCE (biology/biological science), BUSINESS (accounting, banking and finance, business administration and management, business economics, human resources, international business management, marketing management, and tourism), COMMUNICATIONS AND THE ARTS (art history and appreciation, broadcasting, Chinese, classics, communications, dance, dramatic arts, English, fine arts, French, German, Japanese, journalism, literature, multimedia, music, music performance, public relations, Russian, and Spanish), COMPUTER AND PHYSICAL SCIENCE (applied mathematics, chemistry, computer science, geology, information sciences and systems, mathematics, physics, statistics, and systems analysis), ENGINEERING AND ENVIRON-MENTAL DESIGN (civil engineering, computer engineering, electrical/electronics engineering, engineering, environmental science, and mechanical engineering), HEALTH PROFESSIONS (clinical science, emergency medical technologies, medical laboratory technology, nuclear medical technology, physician's assistant, premedicine, radiological science, and speech pathology/audiology), SOCIAL SCIENCE (American studies, anthropology, archeology, criminal justice, East Asian studies, economics, European studies, geography, history, human services, humanities, interdisciplinary studies, international relations, Judaic studies, Latin American studies, liberal arts/general studies, Middle Eastern studies, philosophy, physical fitness/movement, political science/government, psychology, religion, and sociology). Political communication, international affairs, and biological sciences are the strongest academically. Psychology, political science, and international affairs. are the largest.

Special: Cross-registration is available through the Consortium of Colleges and Universities. There are co-op programs in education, business, engineering, arts and sciences, and international affairs, and internships throughout the Washington metropolitan area. Study abroad in locations throughout the world, work-study programs, dual majors, student-designed majors, and a 3-2 engineering degree program with 8 colleges are also available. Nondegree study, a general studies degree, credit by exam, and pass/fail options are possible. There are 12 national honor societies, including Phi Beta Kappa, a freshman honors program, and 21 departmental honors programs.

Admissions: 49% of the 1999-2000 applicants were accepted. The SAT I scores for the 1999-2000 freshman class were: Verbal--5% below 500, 32% between 500 and 599, 48% between 600 and 700, and 15% above 700; Math--3% below 500, 34% between 500 and 599, 51% between 600 and 700, and 12% above 700. The ACT scores were 4% below 21, 16% between 21 and 23, 31% between 24 and 26, 24% between 27 and 28, and 25% above 28. 75% of the current freshmen were in the top fifth of their class; 98% were in the top two fifths.

Requirements: The SAT I or ACT is required. Students must have successfully completed a strong academic program in high school. SAT II: Subject tests are strongly recommended. An essay, 1 teacher recommendation, and 1 counselor recommendation are required. An interview is encouraged. The Common application is accepted on disk and on-line, and applications may also be submitted on-line via CollegeLink. AP and CLEP credits are accepted. Important factors in the admissions decision are advanced placement or honor courses, recommendations by school officials, and leadership record.

Procedure: Freshmen are admitted to all sessions. Entrance exams should be taken in the junior year and the fall semester of the senior year. There are early decision, early admissions, and deferred admissions plans. Early decision applications should be filed by November 1; regular applications, by February 1 for fall entry, along with a $60 fee. Notification of early decision is sent December 15; regular decision, March 15. 403 early decision candidates were accepted for the 1999-2000 class. A waiting list is an active part of the admissions procedure.

Financial Aid: In 1998-99, 70% of all freshmen and 60% of continuing students received some form of financial aid. 48% of freshmen and 39% of continuing students received need-based aid. The average freshman award was $15,064. Of that total, scholarships or need-based grants averaged $10,954; loans averaged $6240; and work contracts averaged $824. The average financial indebtedness of the 1998 graduate was $18,953. GW is a member of CSS. The CSS/Profile or FAFSA and the university's own financial statement are required. The fall application deadline is February 1.

Computers: The mainframes are an IBM 4381/R14, a Sun SPARC Station 2000, and 7 Citrix servers. All residence halls have computer rooms, and the campus computer center and library lab are open 24 hours a day. In addition, 7 computer classrooms are available as walk-in labs when classes are not scheduled. Modems are available on the campus network. All dorm rooms are networked fiber-optically. All students may access the system any time. There are no time limits and no fees. The university strongly recommends that all students have PCs. An IBM, Dell, Compaq, or Mac is recommended.

GEORGETOWN UNIVERSITY
Washington, DC 20057   (202) 687-3600; Fax: (202) 687-5084

Full-time: 2797 men, 3288 women	**Faculty:** 647; I, ++$
Part-time: 104 men, 172 women	**Ph.D.s:** 96%
Graduate: 3140 men, 2997 women	**Student/Faculty:** 9 to 1
Year: semesters, summer session	**Tuition:** $23,295
Application Deadline: January 10	**Room & Board:** $8693
Freshman Class: 13,244 applied, 3024 accepted, 1479 enrolled	
SAT I or ACT: required	**MOST COMPETITIVE**

Georgetown University, founded in 1789, is a private institution affiliated with the Roman Catholic Church and offers programs in arts and sciences, business administration, foreign service, languages and linguistics, and nursing. There are 4 undergraduate and 3 graduate schools. In addition to regional accreditation, Georgetown has baccalaureate program accreditation with AACSB and NLN. The 6 libraries contain 2,363,799 volumes, 3,665,068 microform items, and 65, 248 audiovisual forms/CDs, and subscribe to 27,379 periodicals. Computerized library services include the card catalog, interlibrary loans, and database searching. Special learning facilities include a learning resource center, art gallery, planetarium, and radio station. The 110-acre campus is in an urban area 1.5 miles northwest of downtown Washington, D.C. Including residence halls, there are 60 buildings.

Programs of Study: Georgetown confers B.A.B., B.S., B.A.L.S., B.L.S., B.S. B.A., B.S.F.S., B.S.L.A., B.S.L.I., and B.S.N. degrees. Master's and doctoral degrees are also awarded. Bachelor's degrees are awarded in BIOLOGICAL SCIENCE (biochemistry and biology/biological science), BUSINESS (accounting, banking and finance, business administration and management, international business management, and marketing/retailing/merchandising), COMMUNICATIONS AND THE ARTS (Arabic, Chinese, classics, comparative literature, English, fine arts, French, German, Italian, Japanese, linguistics, Portuguese, Russian, and Spanish), COMPUTER AND PHYSICAL SCIENCE (chemistry, computer science, mathematics, and physics), HEALTH PROFESSIONS (health and nursing), SOCIAL SCIENCE (American studies, economics, history, interdisciplinary studies, international relations, philosophy, political science/government, psychology, religion, and sociology). International affairs, finance and government are the strongest academically. Government, finance, and international affairs are the largest.

Special: Cross-registration is available with a consortium of universities in the Washington metropolitian area. Opportunities are provided for internships, study abroad in 35 countries, work-study programs, student-designed majors, and dual majors. A general studies degree, B.A.-B.S. degrees, nondegree study, credit by examination, and pass/fail options are also offered. There are 16 national honor societies, including Phi Beta Kappa, a freshman honors program, and 8 departmental honors programs.

Admissions: 23% of the 1999-2000 applicants were accepted. The SAT I scores for the 1999-2000 freshman class were: Verbal--3% below 500, 12% between 500 and 599, 48% between 600 and 700, and 37% above 700; Math--2% below 500, 13% between 500 and 599, 51% between 600 and 700, and 34% above 700. The ACT scores were 3% below 21, 7% between 21 and 23, 14% between 24 and 26, 16% between 27 and 28, and 60% above 28. 90% of the current freshmen were in the top fifth of their class; 95% were in the top two fifths. 114 freshmen graduated first in their class.

Requirements: The SAT I or ACT is required. In addition, graduation from an accredited secondary school is required, including 4 years of English, a minimum of 2 each of a foreign language, math, and social studies, and 1 of natural science. An additional 2 years each of math and science is required for students intending to major in math, science, nursing, or business. SAT II: Subject tests are strongly recommended. Applicants to the Walsh School of Foreign Service and the Faculty of Languages and Linguistics are required to submit results of an SAT II: Subject test in a modern foreign language. A disk application is available from the Office of Undergraduate Admissions. MacApply may also be used, but the application must also be submitted in paper form. AP credits are accepted. Important factors in the admissions decision are academic record evidence of special talent, and leadership record.

Procedure: Freshmen are admitted in the fall. Entrance exams should be taken in the junior year and again at the beginning of the senior year. There is a deferred admissions plan. Early action applications should be filed by November 1; regular applications, by January 10 for fall entry, along with a $50 fee. Notification of early action is sent December 15; regular decision, April 1. 600 early decision candidates were accepted for the 1999-2000 class. 7% of all applicants are on a waiting list.

Financial Aid: In 1999-2000, 55% of all freshmen and 52% of continuing students received some form of financial aid. 47% of freshmen and 45% of continuing students received need-based aid. The average freshman award was $18,050. Of that total, scholarships or need-based grants averaged $14,900 ($27,000 maximum); loans averaged $2625 (maximum); and work contracts averaged $2400 (maximum). 55% of undergraduates work part time. Average annual earnings from campus work are $2500. The average financial indebtedness of the 1999 graduate was $17,000. Georgetown is a member of CSS. The CSS/Profile or FAFSA is required. The fall application deadline is February 1.

Computers: The mainframes are an IBM ES/9000-320 and a DEC VAX 4000-200, 4000-300, and 8700. In addition, there are about 360 terminals and PCs in the library, computer labs, and the School of Business. All students may access the system. There are no time limits and no fees.

GEORGIA INSTITUTE OF TECHNOLOGY
Atlanta, GA 30332 (404) 894-4154; Fax: (404) 894-9511

Full-time: 6678 men, 2791 women	**Faculty:** 709; I, ++$
Part-time: 588 men, 1999 women	**Ph.D.s:** 93%
Graduate: 2866 men, 953 women	**Student/Faculty:** 13 to 1
Year: semesters, summer session	**Tuition:** $3108 ($10,350)
Application Deadline: January 15	**Room & Board:** $4976
Freshman Class: 7602 applied, 5210 accepted, 2318 enrolled	
SAT I Verbal/Math: 630/670	**HIGHLY COMPETITIVE+**

Georgia Institute of Technology, founded in 1885, is a public technological institution offering programs in architecture; management, policy, and international affairs; engineering; computing; and science. There are 6 undergraduate and 6 graduate schools. In addition to regional accreditation, Georgia Tech has baccalaureate program accreditation with AACSB, ABET, CSAB, and NAAB. The 2 libraries contain 2,077,369 volumes, 2,765,393 microform items, and 113,525 audiovisual forms/CDs, and subscribe to 14,400 periodicals. Computerized library services include the card catalog, interlibrary loans, and database searching. Special learning facilities include a learning resource center, art gallery, and radio station. The 365-acre campus is in an urban area. Including residence halls, there are 165 buildings.

Programs of Study: Georgia Tech confers the B.S. and many specialized bachelor's degrees in science, engineering, and computing fields. Master's and doctoral degrees are also awarded. Bachelor's degrees are awarded in BIOLOGICAL SCIENCE (biology/biological science), BUSINESS (business administration and management and management science), COMMUNICATIONS AND THE ARTS (industrial design), COMPUTER AND PHYSICAL SCIENCE (applied mathematics, applied physics, chemistry, computer science, earth science, mathematics, physics, and polymer science), ENGINEERING AND ENVIRONMENTAL DESIGN (aeronautical engineering, architecture, chemical engineering, civil engineering, computer engineering, construction management, construction technology, electrical/electronics engineering, industrial engineering, materials engineering, materials science, mechanical engineering, nuclear engineering, technology and public affairs, and textile engineering), SOCIAL SCIENCE (economics, history, international relations, psychology, public affairs, and textiles and clothing). Engineering, computer science, and the sciences are the strongest academically. Computer science, and mechanical and industrial engineering are the largest.

Special: Extensive co-op programs, cross-registration with other Atlanta-area colleges, and internships are available. Study abroad in numerous countries is possible. An engineering transfer program is offered within the university system, and a liberal arts-engineering dual-degree program serves area colleges and institutions nationwide. Students have access to multidisciplinary and certificate programs outside their major field of study. The Georgia Tech Regional Engineering Program (GTREP) offers undergraduate and graduate degrees in collaboration with Armstrong Atlantic State University, Georgia Southern University, and Savannah State University. There are 11 national honor societies.

Admissions: 69% of the 1999-2000 applicants were accepted. The SAT I scores for the 1999-2000 freshman class were: Verbal--4% below 500, 28% between 500 and 599, 52% between 600 and 700, and 16% above 700; Math--1% below 500, 10% between 500 and 599, 55% between 600 and 700, and 34% above 700. 80% of the current freshmen were in the top fifth of their class; 96% were in the

top two fifths. There were 94 National Merit finalists. 84 freshmen graduated first in their class.

Requirements: The SAT I or ACT is required. Candidates for admission must have completed 4 years each of English and math, 3 of science, 2 each of history and a foreign language, and 1 of social studies. To apply on-line, applicants may contact the Office of Undergraduate Admissions or locate Georgia Tech on the World Wide Web at http://www.enrollment.gatech.edu. AP credits are accepted. Important factors in the admissions decision are leadership record, extracurricular activities record, and evidence of special talent.

Procedure: Freshmen are admitted fall and spring. Entrance exams should be taken by the end of the junior year. Applications should be filed by January 15 for fall entry, along with a $50 fee. Notification is sent March 15.

Financial Aid: In 1999-2000, 86% of all freshmen and 58% of continuing students received some form of financial aid. 68% of freshmen and 41% of continuing students received need-based aid. The average freshman award was $7081. Of that total, scholarships or need-based grants averaged $4057 ($10,000 maximum) and loans averaged $3026 ($5800 maximum). Average annual earnings from campus work are $1800. The average financial indebtedness of the 1999 graduate was $16,500. Georgia Tech is a member of CSS. The FAFSA and the college's own financial statement are required. The fall application deadline is March 1.

Computers: The mainframes are a CDC CYBER Model 990, a CRAY Y/MP-EL, a DEC ALPHA 3000/400, an IBM ES/9000-260, a Sun 4/490, a Sun SPARC Center 2000, a Sun SPARC 20, a SUN VitraEnterprise 4000, an SGI Origin 2000, and an SGI Origin 200. Students have access to 330 public seats in computer clusters at 9 locations on campus. Off campus, students may access one of more than 300 dial-in lines or use the service provided through MCI to access the computer network; on campus, students may use the Ethernet connection from any residence hall. All students may access the system. There are no time limits and no fees. Georgia Tech requires all students to have personal computers that feature, at minimum, a 28.8 modem, a CD-ROM, and a 15-inch color monitor.

GETTYSBURG COLLEGE
Gettysburg, PA 17325-1484

(717) 337-6100
(800) 431-0803; Fax: (717) 337-6145

Full-time: 1103 men, 1209 women	**Faculty:** 161; IIB, ++$
Part-time: 14 men, 22 women	**Ph.D.s:** 90%
Graduate: none	**Student/Faculty:** 14 to 1
Year: semesters	**Tuition:** $24,032
Application Deadline: February 15	**Room & Board:** $5644
Freshman Class: 3871 applied, 2624 accepted, 689 enrolled	
SAT I or ACT: required	**HIGHLY COMPETITIVE**

Gettysburg College, founded in 1832, is an independent residential college affiliated with the Lutheran Church. It offers programs in the liberal arts and sciences. The library contains 392,436 volumes, 22,762 microform items, and 18,456 audiovisual forms/CDs, and subscribes to 1579 periodicals. Computerized library services include the card catalog, interlibrary loans, and database searching. Special learning facilities include an art gallery, planetarium, radio station, TV station, electron microscopes, spectrometers, optics lab, plasma physics lab, greenhouse, observatory, child study lab, and fine and performing arts facilities. The 225-acre campus is in a small town 30 miles south of Harrisburg, 55 miles from

Baltimore, MD, and 80 miles from Washington DC. Including residence halls, there are 60 buildings.

Programs of Study: Gettysburg confers B.A., B.S., and B.S.M.E. degrees. Bachelor's degrees are awarded in BIOLOGICAL SCIENCE (biochemistry and biology/biological science), BUSINESS (business administration and management), COMMUNICATIONS AND THE ARTS (art history and appreciation, classics, dramatic arts, English, French, German, Greek, Latin, music, Spanish, and studio art), COMPUTER AND PHYSICAL SCIENCE (chemistry, computer science, mathematics, and physics), EDUCATION (elementary, foreign languages, music, science, and secondary), ENGINEERING AND ENVIRONMENTAL DESIGN (environmental science), HEALTH PROFESSIONS (health science, predentistry, and premedicine), SOCIAL SCIENCE (anthropology, economics, history, international relations, philosophy, political science/government, prelaw, psychology, religion, sociology, and women's studies). The natural sciences, political science, and psychology are the strongest academically. Management, political science, and psychology are the largest.

Special: The college offers an extensive study-abroad program and has special centers worldwide. There are summer internships and a Washington semester with American University. Cross-registration is possible with members of the Central Pennsylvania Consortium. There is a United Nations semester at Drew University, and a 3-2 engineering program with Columbia University, Rensselaer Polytechnic Institute, and Washington University in St. Louis. There are also joint programs in optometry with the Pennsylvania College of Optometry, and forestry and environmental studies with Duke University. The college also offers dual majors, student-designed majors, and B.A.-B.S. degrees in biology, math, chemistry, physics, biochemistry, and molecular biology. There are 19 national honor societies, including Phi Beta Kappa.

Admissions: 68% of the 1999-2000 applicants were accepted. The SAT I scores for the 1999-2000 freshman class were: Verbal--6% below 500, 51% between 500 and 599, 37% between 600 and 700, and 6% above 700; Math--5% below 500, 47% between 500 and 599, 42% between 600 and 700, and 6% above 700. 75% of the current freshmen were in the top fifth of their class; 99% were in the top two fifths. In a recent year, 17 freshmen graduated first in their class.

Requirements: The SAT I or ACT is required. Gettysburg requires applicants to be in the upper 40% of their class. A GPA of 3.0 is required. The GED is accepted. An essay is required. Art students must submit a portfolio, and music students must audition. An interview and SAT II: Subject tests are recommended. Students may apply on-line using the Common Application, CollegeLink, or www.gettysburg.edu. AP credits are accepted. Important factors in the admissions decision are advanced placement or honor courses, evidence of special talent, and recommendations by school officials.

Procedure: Freshmen are admitted fall and spring. Entrance exams should be taken by the January testing date of the senior year. There are early decision, early admissions, and deferred admissions plans. Early decision applications should be filed by February 1; regular applications, by February 15 for fall entry and December 1 for spring entry, along with a $40 fee. Notification is sent April 1. 106 early decision candidates were accepted for the 1999-2000 class. 5% of all applicants are on a waiting list.

Financial Aid: In 1999-2000, 56% of all freshmen and 55% of continuing students received some form of financial aid. 55% of all students received need-based aid. The average freshman award was $19,800. Of that total, scholarships or need-based grants averaged $15,300 ($23,900 maximum); loans averaged $3000 ($3600 maximum); and work contracts averaged $1400 ($1600 maximum). 38% of undergraduates work part time. Average annual earnings from campus work are $1400. The average financial indebtedness of the 1999 graduate was $13,200. Gettysburg is a member of CSS. The CSS/Profile or FAFSA is required. The fall application deadline is February 15.

Computers: The mainframes include multiple Sun Microsystems and UNIX-based servers. A campuswide network has connections to the Internet. PCs are available in labs and other locations throughout the campus. All students may access the system 24 hours a day. There are no time limits and no fees. The college strongly recommends that all studens have PCs.

GONZAGA UNIVERSITY
Spokane, WA 99258-0001

(509) 323-6572
(800) 322-2584; Fax: (509) 324-5780

Full-time: 1203 men, 1378 women	**Faculty:** 225; IIA, av$
Part-time: 63 men, 109 women	**Ph.D.s:** 86%
Graduate: 632 men, 951 women	**Student/Faculty:** 11 to 1
Year: semesters, summer session	**Tuition:** $16,760
Application Deadline: March 1	**Room & Board:** $4980
Freshman Class: 701 enrolled	
SAT I Verbal/Math: 576/577	**ACT:** 26 **VERY COMPETITIVE**

Gonzaga University, founded in 1887, is a private, liberal arts institution affiliated with the Roman Catholic Church and the Society of Jesus (Jesuits). The university offers undergraduate and graduate degrees in arts and sciences, business, education, engineering, and professional studies. There are 5 undergraduate and 5 graduate schools. In addition to regional accreditation, Gonzaga has baccalaureate program accreditation with AACSB, ABET, NCATE, and NLN. The 2 libraries contain 329,369 volumes, 539,579 microform items, and 2557 audiovisual forms/CDs, and subscribe to 2200 periodicals. Computerized library services include the card catalog, interlibrary loans, and database searching. Special learning facilities include a learning resource center, art gallery, radio station, and TV station. The 108-acre campus is in an urban area near downtown Spokane. Including residence halls, there are 94 buildings.

Programs of Study: Gonzaga confers B.A., B.S., B.B.A., B.E., B.G.S., and B.S.N. degrees. Master's and doctoral degrees are also awarded. Bachelor's degrees are awarded in BIOLOGICAL SCIENCE (biology/biological science), BUSINESS (accounting, business administration and management, and business economics), COMMUNICATIONS AND THE ARTS (art, broadcasting, dramatic arts, English, French, German, journalism, literature, music, public relations, Spanish, and speech/debate/rhetoric), COMPUTER AND PHYSICAL SCIENCE (chemistry, computer science, mathematics, and physics), EDUCATION (music, physical, and special), ENGINEERING AND ENVIRONMENTAL DESIGN (civil engineering, computer engineering, electrical/electronics engineering, and mechanical engineering), HEALTH PROFESSIONS (exercise science and nursing), SOCIAL SCIENCE (classical/ancient civilization, criminal justice, economics, history, interdisciplinary studies, international studies, Italian studies, liberal arts/general studies, philosophy, political science/government, psychology, religion, and sociology). Engineering and business administration are the strongest academically. Business, engineering, and history are the largest.

Special: Cross-registration with Whitworth College, internships, study abroad in 5 countries, a Washington semester, and on- and off-campus work-study programs are offered. High school juniors and seniors may take 6 credits per semester. There is a limited pass/fail option, and a general studies degree, student-designed majors, and dual majors are possible. There are 9 national honor societies, and a freshman honors program.

Admissions: The SAT I scores for the 1999-2000 freshman class were: Verbal--22% below 500, 43% between 500 and 599, 30% between 600 and 700, and 5% above 700; Math--20% below 500, 46% between 500 and 599, 30% between 600 and 700, and 4% above 700. The ACT scores were 12% below 21, 27% between 21 and 23, 32% between 24 and 26, 8% between 27 and 28, and 21% above 28. 44% of the current freshmen were in the top fifth of their class; 65% were in the top two fifths. There were 4 National Merit finalists and 12 semifinalists. 60 freshmen graduated first in their class.

Requirements: The SAT I or ACT is required. Applicants should be graduates of an accredited secondary school or hold a GED certificate. They must have completed 17 academic credits consisting of 4 years of English, 3 of math, 2 of a foreign language, 1 each of history and science, and 6 years of electives, 4 of which must be from the above subjects and the arts. An essay and letters of recommendation are required. An interview is recommended. Applications are accepted on computer disk and on-line via Apply, CollegeLink, CollegeView, ExPAN, and the school's web site. AP and CLEP credits are accepted. Important factors in the admissions decision are advanced placement or honor courses, leadership record, and extracurricular activities record.

Procedure: Freshmen are admitted to all sessions. Entrance exams should be taken by May of the junior year. There are early admissions and deferred admissions plans. Applications should be filed by March 1 for fall entry and December 1 for spring entry, along with a $40 fee. Notification is sent on a rolling basis. 4% of all applicants are on a waiting list.

Financial Aid: In 1999-2000, 90% of all freshmen and 89% of continuing students received some form of financial aid. 71% of freshmen and 67% of continuing students received need-based aid. The average freshman award was $15,407. Of that total, scholarships or need-based grants averaged $9903; loans averaged $6076; and work contracts averaged $1900. 34% of undergraduates work part time. Average annual earnings from campus work are $2244. The average financial indebtedness of the 1999 graduate was $32,928. Gonzaga is a member of CSS. The FAFSA is required. The fall application deadline is February 1.

Computers: The mainframe is an HP K220 running HOPX 10.20. The central academic system is available from more than 300 PCs spread throughout 11 computer labs. Students may also access the system from the residence hall Ethernet network, via the campus modem pool, or directly through the Internet. All students may access the system 24 hours per day. There are no time limits and no fees. It is recommended that all students have personal computers.

GORDON COLLEGE
Wenham, MA 01984

(978) 927-2300, ext.4217
(800) 343-1379; Fax: (978) 524-3704

Full-time: 521 men, 966 women	**Faculty:** 84; IIB, +$
Part-time: 18 men, 31 women	**Ph.D.s:** 97%
Graduate: 10 men, 31 women	**Student/Faculty:** 18 to 1
Year: semesters	**Tuition:** $16,420
Application Deadline: March 5	**Room & Board:** $5050
Freshman Class: 963 applied, 734 accepted, 385 enrolled	
SAT I Verbal/Math: 600/580	**ACT:** 26 **VERY COMPETITIVE**

Gordon College, founded in 1889, is an independent Christian college emphasizing a Christian approach to the liberal arts and sciences. There is 1 graduate school. In addition to regional accreditation, Gordon has baccalaureate program accreditation with CSWE and NASM. The library contains 173,753 volumes, 31,

318 microform items, and 8263 audiovisual forms/CDs, and subscribes to 552 periodicals. Computerized library services include the card catalog, interlibrary loans, and database searching. Special learning facilities include a learning resource center and art gallery. The 500-acre campus is in a small town 25 miles north of Boston. Including residence halls, there are 28 buildings.

Programs of Study: Gordon confers A.B., B.S., and B.Mu. degrees. Master's degrees are also awarded. Bachelor's degrees are awarded in BIOLOGICAL SCIENCE (biology/biological science), BUSINESS (accounting, business administration and management, and recreation and leisure services), COMMUNICATIONS AND THE ARTS (art, communications, English, French, German, languages, music, music performance, and Spanish), COMPUTER AND PHYSICAL SCIENCE (chemistry, computer science, mathematics, and physics), EDUCATION (early childhood, elementary, middle school, music, and special), SOCIAL SCIENCE (biblical studies, economics, history, international studies, philosophy, physical fitness/movement, political science/government, psychology, social work, sociology, and youth ministry). English, biology, and psychology are the strongest academically. English, psychology, and biblical studies are the largest.

Special: Gordon offers cooperative education, internships, and cross-registration with other institutions in the Northeast Consortium of Colleges and Universities in Massachusetts. There is a 3-2 engineering program with the University of Massachusetts at Lowell and a 2-2 program in allied health with the Thomas Jefferson College of Allied Health Science in Philadelphia. B.A.-B.S. degrees, dual majors, student-designed majors, nondegree study, and pass/fail options are all available. Off-campus study opportunities include a Washington semester, the Christian College Consortium Visitor Program, the LaVida Wilderness Expedition, the Nova Scotia Student Exchange Program, the Tropical Coastal Waters Program, and study abroad in Europe, the Middle East, China and Latin America. There are 2 national honor societies, and 11 departmental honors programs.

Admissions: 76% of the 1999-2000 applicants were accepted. The SAT I scores for the 1999-2000 freshman class were: Verbal--10% below 500, 38% between 500 and 599, 43% between 600 and 700, and 9% above 700; Math--11% below 500, 45% between 500 and 599, 39% between 600 and 700, and 5% above 700. The ACT scores were 18% below 21, 12% between 21 and 23, 50% between 24 and 26, 13% between 27 and 28, and 6% above 28. 48% of the current freshmen were in the top fifth of their class; 68% were in the top two fifths. There were 3 National Merit finalists. 10 freshmen graduated first in their class.

Requirements: The SAT I or ACT is required. Gordon requires applicants to be in the upper 50% of their class. A GPA of 2.8 is required. Applicants must graduate from an accredited secondary school or have a GED. A minimum of 17 Carnegie units is required, including 4 English courses and 2 courses each in math, science, and social studies. Foreign language is a recommended elective. An essay, a personal reference, and an interview are required. Music majors must audition. Applications are accepted on-line through CollegeLink. AP and CLEP credits are accepted. Important factors in the admissions decision are advanced placement or honor courses and leadership record.

Procedure: Freshmen are admitted to all sessions. Entrance exams should be taken in the spring of the junior year and the fall of the senior year. There are early decision, early admissions, and deferred admissions plans. Early decision applications should be filed by December 1; regular applications, by March 5 for fall entry and November 1 for spring entry, along with a $40 fee. Notification of early decision is sent January 15; regular decision, on a rolling basis. 1% of all applicants are on a waiting list.

Financial Aid: In 1999-2000, 77% of all freshmen and 87% of continuing students received some form of financial aid. 74% of freshmen and 69% of continuing students received need-based aid. The average freshman award was $14,030. Of that total, scholarships or need-based grants averaged $7929 ($10,000 maximum); loans averaged $2500 ($5500 maximum); and work contracts averaged $1500 ($1700 maximum). 90% of undergraduates work part time. Average annual earnings from campus work are $1200. The average financial indebtedness of the 1999 graduate was $13,185. Gordon is a member of CSS. The CSS/Profile or FAFSA is required. The fall application deadline is March 1.

Computers: The mainframe consists of 4 DEC/Compaq ALPHAs. There are also 75 Macs and IBM PCs available in student labs and the computer center. The campus network may be accessed from residence halls, and there is access to the Internet and the World Wide Web. All students may access the system at any time. There are no time limits and no fees.

GOUCHER COLLEGE
Baltimore, MD 21204

(410) 337-6100
(800) 468-2437; Fax: (410) 337-6354

Full-time: 299 men, 789 women	**Faculty:** 81; IIB, ++$
Part-time: 14 men, 29 women	**Ph.D.s:** 94%
Graduate: 130 men, 439 women	**Student/Faculty:** 13 to 1
Year: semesters	**Tuition:** $20,350
Application Deadline: February 1	**Room & Board:** $7380
Freshman Class: 2078 applied, 1763 accepted, 324 enrolled	
SAT I Verbal/Math: 610/570	**VERY COMPETITIVE**

Goucher College, founded in 1885, is a private liberal arts college. There are 5 graduate schools. In addition to regional accreditation, Goucher has baccalaureate program accreditation with NCATE. The library contains 299,568 volumes, 65,077 microform items, and 8572 audiovisual forms/CDs, and subscribes to 1138 periodicals. Computerized library services include the card catalog, interlibrary loans, and database searching. Special learning facilities include a learning resource center, art gallery, TV studio, theater, technology/learning center, international technology and media center, and centers for writing, math, and politics. The 287-acre campus is in a suburban area 8 miles north of Baltimore. Including residence halls, there are 18 buildings.

Programs of Study: Goucher confers the B.A. degree. Master's degrees are also awarded. Bachelor's degrees are awarded in BIOLOGICAL SCIENCE (biology/biological science), BUSINESS (management science), COMMUNICATIONS AND THE ARTS (art, communications, dance, dramatic arts, English, French, historic preservation, music, Russian, and Spanish), COMPUTER AND PHYSICAL SCIENCE (chemistry, computer science, and mathematics), EDUCATION (elementary and special), SOCIAL SCIENCE (American studies, economics, European studies, history, interdisciplinary studies, international relations, international studies, philosophy, political science/government, psychology, religion, sociology, and women's studies). Biology, chemistry, history education, and English are the strongest academically. English, management, and psychology are the largest.

Special: Goucher offers internships, study abroad in 11 countries, and other off-campus experiences. The college also collaborates with many of the 22 other colleges in the Baltimore Collegetown Network (www.colltown.org). Students may cross-register with Johns Hopkins University, Towson University, Loyola College, Morgan State University, College of Notre Dame, Baltimore Hebrew University, and Maryland Institute, College of Art. An advanced degree program with the Monterey Institute for International Studies, B.A.-B.S. degrees, and a 3-2 engineering degree with Johns Hopkins University are offered. Dual majors are an option, and student-designed majors and pass/no pass options are also available. There is 1 national honor society, Phi Beta Kappa, a freshman honors program, and 18 departmental honors programs.

Admissions: 85% of the 1999-2000 applicants were accepted. The SAT I scores for the 1999-2000 freshman class were: Verbal--14% below 500, 33% between 500 and 599, 43% between 600 and 700, and 10% above 700; Math--17% below 500, 4% between 500 and 599, 35% between 600 and 700, and 4% above 700. 49% of the current freshmen were in the top fifth of their class; 81% were in the top two fifths. 5 freshmen graduated first in their class.

Requirements: The SAT I or ACT is required. Applicants should be graduates of an accredited high school or have earned the GED. Secondary preparation should include at least 14 academic units, preferably 4 in English, 3 in math (algebra I and II and geometry), 2 each in the same foreign language and in lab science, and 2 or 3 in social studies. A personal essay is required and an interview is recommended. Prospective arts majors are urged to seek an audition or submit a portfolio. Applications are accepted on computer disk. AP credits are accepted. Important factors in the admissions decision are extracurricular activities record, recommendations by school officials, and advanced placement or honor courses.

Procedure: Freshmen are admitted fall and spring. Entrance exams should be taken in spring of the junior year or fall of the senior year. There are early decision, early admissions, and deferred admissions plans. Early decision applications should be filed by December 1; regular applications, by February 1 for fall entry and December 1 for spring entry, along with a $40 fee. Notification of early decision is sent January 15; regular decision, April 1. 6% of all applicants are on a waiting list.

Financial Aid: In 1999-2000, 79% of all freshmen and 85% of continuing students received some form of financial aid. 54% of freshmen and 43% of continuing students received need-based aid. The average freshman award was $13,500. Of that total, scholarships or need-based grants averaged $8500 ($20,200 maximum); loans averaged $3500 ($5500 maximum); and work contracts averaged $1050 ($1500 maximum). 46% of undergraduates work part time. Average annual earnings from campus work are $1200. The average financial indebtedness of the 1999 graduate was $13,000. Goucher is a member of CSS. The CSS/Profile, FAFSA, and the college's own financial statement are required. The fall application deadline is February 15.

Computers: The mainframe is an HP 9000, Series 800. PCs are available in academic labs, dorms, and the library. All dorm rooms are wired for direct access to the Internet and the Web. An intracampus network is in place. All students may access the system. Some facilities are available around the clock. There are no time limits and no fees.

GRINNELL COLLEGE
Grinnell, IA 50112

(515) 269-3600
(800) 247-0113; Fax: (515) 269-4800

Full-time: 582 men, 713 women	**Faculty:** 133; IIB, ++$
Part-time: 15 men, 25 women	**Ph.D.s:** 88%
Graduate: none	**Student/Faculty:** 10 to 1
Year: semesters	**Tuition:** $19,460
Application Deadline: February 1	**Room & Board:** $5600
Freshman Class: 1757 applied, 1175 accepted, 325 enrolled	
SAT I Verbal/Math: 680/660	**ACT:** 29 **HIGHLY COMPETITIVE+**

Grinnell College, founded in 1846, is a private institution that offers undergraduate degree programs in the arts and sciences. The 3 libraries contain 393,583 volumes, 76,641 microform items, and 17,191 audiovisual forms/CDs, and subscribe to 2781 periodicals. Computerized library services include the card catalog, interlibrary loans, and database searching. Special learning facilities include a learning resource center, art gallery, and observatory, physics museum, print and drawing gallery, and student-run radio station. The 95-acre campus is in a small town 55 miles east of Des Moines. Including residence halls, there are 64 buildings.

Programs of Study: Grinnell confers the B.A. degree. Bachelor's degrees are awarded in BIOLOGICAL SCIENCE (biology/biological science), COMMUNICATIONS AND THE ARTS (art, Chinese, classics, dramatic arts, English, French, German, music, Russian, and Spanish), COMPUTER AND PHYSICAL SCIENCE (chemistry, computer science, mathematics, physics, and science), SOCIAL SCIENCE (American studies, anthropology, economics, history, philosophy, political science/government, psychology, religion, and sociology). Math, history, and biology are the largest.

Special: Students may participate in more than 100 study-abroad programs in 33 countries or in off-campus study at selected locations in the United States. Grinnell offers cooperative programs in architecture with Washington University in St. Louis and a 3-2 engineering program with California Institute of Technology, Columbia University, and Rensselaer Polytechnic Institute. There is also an extensive internship program, a general studies degree in science, student-designed majors, and S/D/F grading options in selected courses. Grinnell's special "plus-2" option permits students to add 2 credits to a regular course through independent study. Students may pursue one of 10 interdisciplinary concentrations in addition to their major. Accelerated degree programs of 6 to 7 semesters may be approved on an individual basis. There are 2 national honor societies, including Phi Beta Kappa.

Admissions: 67% of the 1999-2000 applicants were accepted. The SAT I scores for the 1999-2000 freshman class were: Verbal--1% below 500, 14% between 500 and 599, 49% between 600 and 700, and 36% above 700; Math--1% below 500, 15% between 500 and 599, 58% between 600 and 700, and 26% above 700. The ACT scores were 1% below 21, 4% between 21 and 23, 13% between 24 and 26, 21% between 27 and 28, and 61% above 28. 80% of the current freshmen were in the top fifth of their class; 99% were in the top two fifths. There were 30 National Merit finalists. 33 freshmen graduated first in their class.

Requirements: The SAT I or ACT is required. Applicants must be graduates of accredited secondary schools. The college requires 16 Carnegie units, recommending 4 each in English and math, and 3 each in laboratory science, social studies, and a foreign language. An essay is required and an interview is recommended. AP credits are accepted. Important factors in the admissions decision are

238

advanced placement or honor courses, extracurricular activities record, and leadership record.

Procedure: Freshmen are admitted in the fall. Entrance exams should be taken during the second semester of the junior year or early in the fall semester of the senior year. There are early decision, early admissions, and deferred admissions plans. Early decision applications should be filed by December 1; regular applications, by February 1 for fall entry, along with a $30 fee. Notification of early decision is sent December 20; regular decision, April 1. 35 early decision candidates were accepted for the 1999-2000 class. 4% of all applicants are on a waiting list; none were accepted in 1999.

Financial Aid: In 1999-2000, 91% of all freshmen and 85% of continuing students received some form of financial aid. 57% of freshmen and 51% of continuing students received need-based aid. The average freshman award was $13,994. Of that total, scholarships or need-based grants averaged $11,726 ($23,560 maximum); loans averaged $3621 ($4875 maximum); and work contracts averaged $1370 ($1500 maximum). 62% of undergraduates work part time. Average annual earnings from campus work are $1000. The average financial indebtedness of the 1999 graduate was $8007. Grinnell is a member of CSS. The FAFSA and the college's own financial statement are required. The fall application deadline is February 1.

Computers: There are no mainframes. Central servers include two Proliant 6000s running Windows NT and a Compaq Alpha Server 4100 running UNIX. There are more than 250 networked computers on campus for the exclusive use of students. All college residences have network connections. All students may access the system 24 hours a day. There are no time limits and no fees.

GROVE CITY COLLEGE
Grove City, PA 16127-2104   (724) 458-2100; Fax: (724) 458-3395

Full-time: 1161 men, 1122 women	**Faculty:** 113
Part-time: 13 men, 17 women	**Ph.D.s:** 75%
Graduate: 4 men, 7 women	**Student/Faculty:** 20 to 1
Year: semesters	**Tuition:** $6976
Application Deadline: February 15	**Room & Board:** $4048
Freshman Class: 2163 applied, 957 accepted, 586 enrolled	
SAT I Verbal/Math: 628/630	**ACT:** 27 **HIGHLY COMPETITIVE**

Grove City College, founded in 1876, is a private, liberal arts and science college affiliated with the Presbyterian Church (U.S.A.). There is 1 graduate school. In addition to regional accreditation, Grove City has baccalaureate program accreditation with ABET. The library contains 158,000 volumes, 230,000 microform items, and 520 audiovisual forms/CDs, and subscribes to 1200 periodicals. Computerized library services include the card catalog, interlibrary loans, and database searching. Special learning facilities include an art gallery and radio station. The 150-acre campus is in a small town 60 miles north of Pittsburgh. Including residence halls, there are 27 buildings.

Programs of Study: Grove City confers B.A., B.S., B.Mus., B.S.E.E., and B.S. M.E. degrees. Master's degrees are also awarded. Bachelor's degrees are awarded in BIOLOGICAL SCIENCE (biochemistry and biology/biological science), BUSINESS (accounting, banking and finance, business administration and management, international business management, management information systems, and marketing/retailing/merchandising), COMMUNICATIONS AND THE ARTS (communications, English, French, music, music business management, music performance, and Spanish), COMPUTER AND PHYSICAL SCIENCE (chemistry, computer science, mathematics, and physics), EDUCATION (elementary, music, science, and secondary), ENGINEERING AND ENVIRONMENTAL DESIGN (electrical/electronics engineering, industrial administration/management, and mechanical engineering), HEALTH PROFESSIONS (predentistry and premedicine), SOCIAL SCIENCE (economics, history, philosophy, political science/government, prelaw, psychology, religion, and religious music). Business, engineering, and education are the strongest academically and have the largest enrollment.

Special: The college offers study abroad, summer internships, 3 accelerated degree programs, student-designed interdisciplinary majors, nondegree study for special students, and a Washington semester. There are 9 national honor societies, and 13 departmental honors programs.

Admissions: 44% of the 1999-2000 applicants were accepted. The SAT I scores for the 1999-2000 freshman class were: Verbal--4% below 500, 28% between 500 and 599, 50% between 600 and 700, and 18% above 700; Math--5% below 500, 22% between 500 and 599, 56% between 600 and 700, and 17% above 700. The ACT scores were 4% below 21, 12% between 21 and 23, 25% between 24 and 26, 27% between 27 and 28, and 32% above 28. 80% of the current freshmen were in the top fifth of their class; 95% were in the top two fifths. There are 12 National Merit finalists. 76 freshmen graduated first in their class.

Requirements: The SAT I or ACT is required. The academic or college preparatory course is highly recommended, including 4 units each of English, history, math, science, and a foreign language. An essay is required of all applicants, and an audition is required of music students. An interview is highly recommended. AP and CLEP credits are accepted. Important factors in the admissions decision are advanced placement or honor courses, evidence of special talent, and personality/intangible qualities.

Procedure: Freshmen are admitted fall and spring. Entrance exams should be taken in the spring of the junior year or the fall of the senior year. There are early decision, early admissions, and deferred admissions plans. Early decision applications should be filed by November 15; regular applications, by February 15 for fall entry and January 1 for spring entry, along with a $30 fee. Notification of early decision is sent December 15; regular decision, March 15. 318 early decision candidates were accepted for the 1999-2000 class. 40% of all applicants are on a waiting list.

Financial Aid: In 1999-2000, 57% of all freshmen and 51% of continuing students received some form of financial aid. 49% of freshmen and 37% of continuing students received need-based aid. The average freshman award was $6096. Of that total, scholarships or need-based grants averaged $4173 ($13,971 maximum); and loans averaged $5765 ($13,971 maximum). 28% of undergraduates work part time. Average annual earnings from campus work are $750. The average financial indebtedness of the 1999 graduate was $11,383. Grove City is a member of CSS. The college's own financial statement is required. The fall application deadline is April 15.

Computers: The mainframe is a DEC VAX 6250. The technological learning center houses 120 PCs and terminal stations. Every full-time student has a laptop computer and printer with the ability to connect to the Internet, intranet, and E-mail accounts. All students may access the system 8 a.m. to 11 p.m., Monday through Friday; 8 a.m. to 5 p.m., Saturday; and 2 p.m. to 11 p.m., Sunday. There are no time limits and no fees. It is strongly recommended that all students have personal computers. All freshmen receive a Compac color notebook computer.

GUILFORD COLLEGE

Greensboro, NC 27410

(336) 316-2100
(800) 992-7759; Fax: (336) 316-2954

Full-time: 513 men, 607 women	**Faculty:** 89; IIB, av$
Part-time: 55 men, 70 women	**Ph.D.s:** 89%
Graduate: none	**Student/Faculty:** 13 to 1
Year: semesters, summer session	**Tuition:** $16,150
Application Deadline: February 15	**Room & Board:** $5610
Freshman Class: 1227 applied, 938 accepted, 232 enrolled	
SAT I Verbal/Math: 600/570	**ACT:** 24 **VERY COMPETITIVE**

Guilford College, founded in 1837, by the Religious Society of Friends (Quakers), is a private liberal arts and sciences institution. In addition to regional accreditation, Guilford College has baccalaureate program accreditation with NCATE. The library contains 250,000 volumes, 19,455 microform items, and 9336 audiovisual forms/CDs, and subscribes to 942 periodicals. Computerized library services include the card catalog, interlibrary loans, and database searching. Special learning facilities include a learning resource center, art gallery, radio station, an observatory, and a multimedia learning center for cultures and languages. The 340-acre campus is in a suburban area on 340 wooded acres in northwest Greensboro. Including residence halls, there are 31 buildings.

Programs of Study: Guilford College confers A.B., B.S., B.A.S., and B.F.A. degrees. Bachelor's degrees are awarded in BIOLOGICAL SCIENCE (biology/biological science), BUSINESS (accounting, business administration and management, and sports management), COMMUNICATIONS AND THE ARTS (dramatic arts, English, fine arts, French, German, music, and Spanish), COMPUTER AND PHYSICAL SCIENCE (chemistry, geology, mathematics, and physics), EDUCATION (elementary, physical, and secondary), ENGINEERING AND ENVIRONMENTAL DESIGN (environmental science), HEALTH PROFESSIONS (sports medicine), SOCIAL SCIENCE (African American studies, criminal justice, economics, history, humanities, international studies, peace studies, philosophy, political science/government, psychology, religion, sociology, and women's studies). Psychology, natural sciences, and interdisciplinary studies are the strongest academically. Management, psychology, and English are the largest.

Special: There are 3-2 degree programs available in forestry and environmental studies with Duke University, and in physician assistant training with Bowman Gray School of Medicine at Wake Forest University. Guilford also offers many internships, a Washington semester, work-study programs, dual majors, the B.A.-B.S. degree, student-designed majors, study abroad in 8 countries, pass/fail options, and cross-registration with members of the Greater Greensboro Consortium (8 colleges/universities). There are 2 national honor societies, a freshman honors program, and 13 departmental honors programs.

Admissions: 76% of the 1999-2000 applicants were accepted. The SAT I scores for the 1999-2000 freshman class were: Verbal--11% below 500, 38% between 500 and 599, 34% between 600 and 700, and 17% above 700; Math--15% below 500, 48% between 500 and 599, 32% between 600 and 700, and 5% above 700. The ACT scores were 18% below 21, 18% between 21 and 23, 25% between 24 and 26, 22% between 27 and 28, and 17% above 28. 41% of the current freshmen were in the top fifth of their class; 87% were in the top two fifths. 8 freshmen graduated first in their class.

Requirements: The SAT I or ACT is required. A GPA of 2.0 is required. A minimum SAT I composite score of 1000 or ACT score of 22 is recommended. Applicants should have completed 20 Carnegie units, including 4 in English, 2 each in foreign language and science, and 1 each in history and social studies. The GED is accepted. An essay is required and an interview is recommended. Applications are accepted on-line at the Guilford web site. AP and CLEP credits are accepted. Important factors in the admissions decision are advanced placement or honor courses, recommendations by school officials, and evidence of special talent.

Procedure: Freshmen are admitted fall and spring. Entrance exams should be taken in spring of the junior year or fall of the senior year. There are early decision, early admissions, and deferred admissions plans. Early decision applications should be filed by November 15; regular applications, by February 15 for fall entry and December 1 for spring entry, along with a $25 fee. Notification of early decision is sent December 15; regular decision, April 1. 35 early decision candidates were accepted for the 1999-2000 class. A waiting list is an active part of the admissions procedure.

Financial Aid: In a recent year, 85% of all freshmen and 79% of continuing students received some form of financial aid. 67% of freshmen and 61% of continuing students received need-based aid. The average freshman award was $12,226. Of that total, scholarships or need-based grants averaged $10,789 ($14,180 maximum); loans averaged $4154 ($6625 maximum); and work contracts averaged $920 ($2000 maximum). 56% of undergraduates work part time. Average annual earnings from campus work are $825. The average financial indebtedness of a recent graduate was $11,197. Guilford College is a member of CSS. The FAFSA is required. The fall application deadline is March 1.

Computers: The mainframes are a DEC ALPHA 4000 and Compaq NT servers. There are also 250 terminals and PCs in the central lab and classroom building, with access from other buildings through the campus network. All students have E-mail and Internet access, and all residence hall rooms have network connections. All students may access the system 24 hours a day. There are no time limits and no fees.

GUSTAVUS ADOLPHUS COLLEGE
St. Peter, MN 56082-1498   (507) 933-7676
(800) GUSTAVU; Fax: (507) 933-6270

Full-time: 1105 men, 1387 women	**Faculty:** 170; IIB, +$
Part-time: 28 men, 23 women	**Ph.D.s:** 87%
Graduate: none	**Student/Faculty:** 15 to 1
Year: 4-1-4, summer session	**Tuition:** $17,480
Application Deadline: May 1	**Room & Board:** $4320
Freshman Class: 1993 applied, 1567 accepted, 659 enrolled	
SAT I Verbal/Math: 600/620	**ACT:** 26 **VERY COMPETITIVE+**

Gustavus Adolphus College, founded in 1862, is a private liberal arts college affiliated with the Lutheran Church. In addition to regional accreditation, Gustavus has baccalaureate program accreditation with NASM, NCATE, and NLN. The library contains 260,758 volumes, 31,385 microform items, and 13,839 audiovisual forms/CDs, and subscribes to 1221 periodicals. Computerized library services include the card catalog, interlibrary loans, and database searching. Special learning facilities include an art gallery, radio station, and arboretum. The 330-acre campus is in a small town 65 miles southwest of Minneapolis. Including residence halls, there are 55 buildings.

Programs of Study: Gustavus confers the B.A. degree. Bachelor's degrees are awarded in BIOLOGICAL SCIENCE (biochemistry and biology/biological science), **BUSINESS** (accounting, business administration and management, business economics, and international business management), **COMMUNICATIONS AND THE ARTS** (classics, communications, dance, dramatic arts, English, fine arts, French, German, music, Russian, Scandinavian languages, Spanish, and speech/debate/rhetoric), **COMPUTER AND PHYSICAL SCIENCE** (chemistry, computer science, geology, mathematics, and physics), **EDUCATION** (art, business, elementary, foreign languages, health, middle school, music, science, and secondary), **HEALTH PROFESSIONS** (nursing, physical therapy, predentistry, and premedicine), **SOCIAL SCIENCE** (anthropology, criminal justice, economics, geography, history, philosophy, political science/government, prelaw, psychology, religion, social science, and sociology). Physical science and social science are the strongest academically. Business, biology, and social science are the largest.

Special: Co-op programs in nursing with St. Olaf College and cross-registration with Minnesota State University are available. The college offers internships, a Washington semester, study abroad in 22 countries, student-designed majors, nondegree study, and pass/fail options for some courses. A 3-2 engineering degree program with Washington University and the University of Minnesota is offered. The Curriculum II core offers a 12-course interdisciplinary program. There are 16 national honor societies, including Phi Beta Kappa, and 12 departmental honors programs.

Admissions: 79% of the 1999-2000 applicants were accepted. The SAT I scores for the 1999-2000 freshman class were: Verbal--7% below 500, 41% between 500 and 599, 33% between 600 and 700, and 19% above 700; Math--6% below 500, 32% between 500 and 599, 48% between 600 and 700, and 14% above 700. The ACT scores were 9% below 21, 20% between 21 and 23, 30% between 24 and 26, 17% between 27 and 28, and 24% above 28. 59% of the current freshmen were in the top fifth of their class; 88% were in the top two fifths. There were 7 National Merit finalists and 8 semifinalists.

Requirements: The SAT I or ACT is required. In addition, applicants must have completed 4 years of English, 3 each of math and science, and 2 each of a foreign language, history, and social studies. Applications are accepted on-line via College Net or the school's own web site. AP credits are accepted. Important factors in the admissions decision are advanced placement or honor courses, evidence of special talent, and parents or siblings attending the school.

Procedure: Freshmen are admitted fall, winter, and spring. Entrance exams should be taken in the fall of the senior year. There are early decision, early admissions, and deferred admissions plans. Early decision applications should be filed by November 15; regular applications, by May 1 for fall entry, December 15 for winter entry, and January 15 for spring entry, along with a $25 fee. Notification of early decision is sent December 1; regular decision, on a rolling basis. 93 early decision candidates were accepted for the 1999-2000 class.

Financial Aid: In 1999-2000, 90% of all freshmen and 82% of continuing students received some form of financial aid. 65% of freshmen and 63% of continuing students received need-based aid. The average freshman award was $12,490. Of that total, scholarships or need-based grants averaged $7290; loans averaged $3500 ($4500 maximum); and work contracts averaged $1400 ($1600 maximum). 71% of undergraduates work part time. Average annual earnings from campus work are $1400. The average financial indebtedness of the 1999 graduate was $15,800. Gustavus is a member of CSS. The FAFSA and the college's own financial statement are required. The fall application deadline is April 1.

Computers: The mainframes are a DEC MicroVAX 3600 and a MicroVAX II. Students have access to 6 computer networks, some of which are connected with the Minnesota State University System. These include 55 Mac, 50 IBM, and 27

NeXT PCs located in the library and various academic buildings. There is also an electronic music lab. All students may access the system. There are no time limits and no fees. The college strongly recommends that all students have PCs.

HAMILTON COLLEGE
Clinton, NY 13323

(315) 859-4421
(800) 843-2655; Fax: (315) 859-4457

Full-time: 873 men, 836 women	**Faculty:** 187; IIB, +$
Part-time: 3 women	**Ph.D.s:** 83%
Graduate: none	**Student/Faculty:** 9 to 1
Year: semesters	**Tuition:** $25,000
Application Deadline: January 15	**Room & Board:** $6200
Freshman Class: 3909 applied, 1660 accepted, 500 enrolled	
SAT I or ACT: required	**HIGHLY COMPETITIVE**

Hamilton College, founded in 1793, is a private, nonsectarian, liberal arts school offering undergraduate programs in the arts and sciences. The 3 libraries contain 538,377 volumes, 419,461 microform items, and 52,051 audiovisual forms/CDs, and subscribe to 3585 periodicals. Computerized library services include the card catalog and database searching. Special learning facilities include an art gallery, radio station, and an observatory. The 1200-acre campus is in a rural area 9 miles southwest of Utica. Including residence halls, there are 51 buildings.

Programs of Study: Hamilton confers the B.A. degree. Bachelor's degrees are awarded in BIOLOGICAL SCIENCE (biochemistry, biology/biological science, and neurosciences), COMMUNICATIONS AND THE ARTS (art, art history and appreciation, classics, communications, comparative literature, creative writing, dance, dramatic arts, English, French, German, languages, music, Spanish, and studio art), COMPUTER AND PHYSICAL SCIENCE (chemistry, computer science, geology, mathematics, and physics), SOCIAL SCIENCE (African studies, American studies, anthropology, archeology, Asian/Oriental studies, classical/ ancient civilization, economics, history, international relations, philosophy, political science/government, psychobiology, psychology, public affairs, religion, Russian and Slavic studies, sociology, and women's studies). English, government, and history are the largest.

Special: Cross-registration is permitted with Colgate University and Utica College of Syracuse University. Opportunities are provided for internships, a cooperative program through the Williams College Mystic Seaport Program in Connecticut, and a Washington semester. Accelerated degree programs, dual majors, nondegree study, pass/fail options, student-designed majors, a program for early assurance of acceptance to medical school, and study abroad in many countries are available. 3-2 engineering degrees are offered with Washington University, Rensselaer Polytechnic Institute, and Columbia University. There are 4 national honor societies, including Phi Beta Kappa.

Admissions: 42% of the 1999-2000 applicants were accepted. The SAT I scores for a recent freshman class were: Verbal--5% below 500, 29% between 500 and 599, 47% between 600 and 700, and 19% above 700; Math--3% below 500, 28% between 500 and 599, 56% between 600 and 700, and 13% above 700. 79% of the current freshmen were in the top quarter of their class; 98% were in the top half.

Requirements: The SAT I or ACT is required. Although graduation from an accredited secondary school or a GED is desirable, and a full complement of college-preparatory courses is recommended, Hamilton will consider all highly recommended candidates who demonstrate an ability and desire to perform at intellectually demanding levels. An essay is required, and an interview is recommended. Applications may be submitted on-line at www.hamilton.edu/admission/application/download.html. AP credits are accepted. Important factors in the admissions decision are advanced placement or honor courses, recommendations by school officials, and parents or siblings attending the school.

Procedure: Freshmen are admitted in the fall. Entrance exams should be taken prior to February of the senior year. There are early decision, early admissions, and deferred admissions plans. Early decision applications should be filed by November 15; regular applications, by January 15 for fall entry, along with a $50 fee. Notification of early decision is sent December 15; regular decision, by April 15. 191 early decision candidates were accepted for the 1999-2000 class. 5% of all applicants are on a waiting list.

Financial Aid: In 1999-2000, 50% of all freshmen and 57% of continuing students received some form of financial aid. The average freshman award was $19,925. Of that total, scholarships or need-based grants averaged $17,054; loans averaged $1921; and work contracts averaged $2870. 48% of undergraduates work part time. Average annual earnings from campus work are $1400. The average financial indebtedness of the 1999 graduate was $16,776. Hamilton is a member of CSS. The CSS/Profile or FAFSA is required. The fall application deadline is February 1.

Computers: The mainframes are a DEC 5100, DEC 5000/25, and DEC 5500. There are 100 Macs and 50 PCs in public computer labs. Students have full access to the Internet, including in residence halls. All students may access the system more than 100 hours per week. There are no time limits and no fees.

HAMPSHIRE COLLEGE
Amherst, MA 01002   (413) 559-5471; Fax: (413) 559-5631

Full-time: 1172 men and women	**Faculty:** 84; IIB, ++$
Part-time: none	**Ph.D.s:** 91%
Graduate: none	**Student/Faculty:** 14 to 1
Year: 4-1-4	**Tuition:** $25,400
Application Deadline: February 1	**Room & Board:** $6622
Freshman Class: 1960 applied, 1079 accepted, 297 enrolled	
SAT I Verbal/Math: 660/600	**ACT:** 30 **HIGHLY COMPETITIVE**

Hampshire College, founded in 1965, is a private institution offering a liberal arts education with an emphasis on independent research, creative work, and multidisciplinary study. The library contains 111,000 volumes, 3822 microform items, and 35,657 audiovisual forms/CDs, and subscribes to 750 periodicals. Computerized library services include the card catalog, interlibrary loans, and database searching. Special learning facilities include an art gallery, TV station, multimedia center, farm center, music and dance studios, optics lab, electronics shop, integrated greenhouse and aquaculture facility, fabrication shop, and performing arts center. The 800-acre campus is in a rural area 20 miles north of Springfield. Including residence halls, there are 28 buildings.

Programs of Study: Hampshire confers the B.A. degree. Bachelor's degrees are awarded in AGRICULTURE (agriculture and animal science), BIOLOGICAL SCIENCE (biology/biological science, botany, ecology, marine biology, nutrition, and physiology), COMMUNICATIONS AND THE ARTS (art history and appreciation, communications, comparative literature, creative writing, dance, dramatic arts, film arts, fine arts, journalism, linguistics, literature, media arts, music, performing arts, photography, and video), COMPUTER AND PHYSICAL SCIENCE (chemistry, computer science, geology, mathematics, physics, and science), EDUCATION (education), ENGINEERING AND ENVIRON-MENTAL DESIGN (architecture, environmental design, and environmental science), HEALTH PROFESSIONS (health science and premedicine), SOCIAL SCIENCE (African American studies, African studies, American studies, anthropology, Asian/Oriental studies, cognitive science, crosscultural studies, economics, family/consumer studies, geography, history, humanities, international relations, international studies, Judaic studies, Latin American studies, law, Middle Eastern studies, peace studies, philosophy, political science/government, psychology, religion, sociology, urban studies, and women's studies). Film/photography/video is the strongest academically. Social sciences is the largest.

Special: Cross-registration is possible with other members of the Five-College Consortium (Amherst College, the University of Massachusetts, Smith College, and Mount Holyoke). Internships, multidisciplinary dual majors, and study abroad are offered. All majors are student-designed. Students may comlete their programs in fewer than 4 years.

Admissions: 55% of the 1999-2000 applicants were accepted. The SAT I scores for the 1999-2000 freshman class were: Verbal--3% below 500, 19% between 500 and 599, 49% between 600 and 700, and 29% above 700; Math--9% below 500, 41% between 500 and 599, 40% between 600 and 700, and 10% above 700. 49% of the current freshmen were in the top fifth of their class; 78% were in the top two fifths. There were 10 National Merit semifinalists. 2 freshmen graduated first in their class.

Requirements: Applicants must submit all transcripts from 9th grade on or GED/state equivalency exam results. Students are required to submit a personal statement and an analytic essay or academic paper. An interview is recommended. AP credits are accepted. Important factors in the admissions decision are personality/intangible qualities, evidence of special talent, and extracurricular activities record.

Procedure: Freshmen are admitted fall and spring. There are early decision, early admissions, and deferred admissions plans. Early decision applications should be filed by November 15; regular applications, by February 1 for fall entry and November 15 for spring entry, along with a $50 fee. Notification of early decision is sent December 15; regular decision, April 1. 32 early decision candidates were accepted for the 1999-2000 class. 11% of all applicants are on a waiting list.

Financial Aid: In 1999-2000, 56% of all freshmen and 55% of continuing students received some form of financial aid. 56% of freshmen and 54% of continuing students received need-based aid. The average freshman award was $19,925. Of that total, scholarships or need-based grants averaged $15,400 ($25,700 maximum); loans averaged $2625 (maximum); and work contracts averaged $1900 (maximum). 66% of undergraduates work part time. Average annual earnings from campus work are $2000. The average financial indebtedness of the 1999 graduate was $16,000. Hampshire is a member of CSS. The CSS/Profile, FAFSA, and the college's own financial statement are required. The fall application deadline is February 1.

Computers: The mainframe is a Sun SPARC Station 20 model 50. Hampshire uses a variety of computers as file servers. Several computing labs on campus allow students access to PCs and networked systems. In addition, all student rooms are networked and many students own PCs. All students may access the system 24 hours per day via their own PCs or at designated hours in the labs, generally 8 a.m. to midnight, but up to 24 hours at the end of each semester. There are no time limits and no fees.

HANOVER COLLEGE
Hanover, IN 47243

(812) 866-7022
(800) 213-2178; Fax: (812) 866-7098

Full-time: 520 men, 593 women	**Faculty:** 100; IIB, +$
Part-time: 4 men, 6 women	**Ph.D.s:** 82%
Graduate: none	**Student/Faculty:** 11 to 1
Year: 4-4-1	**Tuition:** $11,045
Application Deadline: March 1	**Room & Board:** $4655
Freshman Class: 1145 applied, 941 accepted, 340 enrolled	
SAT I Verbal/Math: 570/570	**ACT:** 25 **VERY COMPETITIVE**

Hanover College, founded in 1827 and the oldest private college in Indiana, is a liberal arts school affiliated with the United Presbyterian Church. In addition to regional accreditation, Hanover has baccalaureate program accreditation with NCATE. The library contains 451,028 volumes, 160,083 microform items, and 4783 audiovisual forms/CDs, and subscribes to 1231 periodicals. Computerized library services include the card catalog, interlibrary loans, and database searching. Special learning facilities include a learning resource center, art gallery, planetarium, TV station, and a geology museum. The 650-acre campus is in a rural area 45 miles north of Louisville, Kentucky. Including residence halls, there are 35 buildings.

Programs of Study: Hanover confers the B.A. degree. Bachelor's degrees are awarded in BIOLOGICAL SCIENCE (biology/biological science), BUSINESS (business administration and management), COMMUNICATIONS AND THE ARTS (art, art history and appreciation, classics, communications, dramatic arts, English, French, German, music, and Spanish), COMPUTER AND PHYSICAL SCIENCE (chemistry, computer science, geology, mathematics, and physics), EDUCATION (elementary and physical), SOCIAL SCIENCE (anthropology, economics, history, international studies, Latin American studies, medieval studies, philosophy, political science/government, psychology, sociology, and theological studies). Arts and sciences and interdisciplinary studies are the strongest academically. Business administration is the largest.

Special: The college offers a 3-2 engineering degree with Washington University in St. Louis, a B.A.-B.S. degree in engineering, internships, study abroad, a Washington semester, student-designed majors in international studies and Latin American studies, and a dual major in sociology/anthropology. In addition, there is cross-registration with the Spring Term Consortium, the University of Indianapolis, and Alma, Elmira, Northland, Transylvania, Wartburg, and William Woods Colleges. There are 4 national honor societies, and 4 departmental honors programs.

Admissions: 82% of the 1999-2000 applicants were accepted. The SAT I scores for the 1999-2000 freshman class were: Verbal--19% below 500, 46% between 500 and 599, 30% between 600 and 700, and 5% above 700; Math--13% below 500, 44% between 500 and 599, 38% between 600 and 700, and 5% above 700. The ACT scores were 9% below 21, 17% between 21 and 23, 36% between 24 and 26, 18% between 27 and 28, and 20% above 28. There were 2 National Merit finalists and 8 semifinalists. 22 freshmen graduated first in their class.

Requirements: The SAT I or ACT is required. Admission is competitive, based on the applicant pool. The college requires 16 academic credits, including 4 years of English and 2 each of a foreign language, math, science, and either history or social studies. The GED is accepted. The college also requires a foreign language achievement test as well as an essay; an interview is recommended. Applications may be submitted on computer disk. AP credits are accepted. Important factors

247

in the admissions decision are recommendations by school officials, advanced placement or honor courses, and extracurricular activities record.

Procedure: Freshmen are admitted in the fall. Entrance exams should be taken late in the spring of the junior year. There are early admissions and deferred admissions plans. Early decision applications should be filed by December 1; regular applications, by March 1 for fall entry, along with a $25 fee. Notification of early decision is sent in mid-December ; regular decision, on a rolling basis after January 20. 7% of all applicants are on a waiting list.

Financial Aid: In 1999-2000, 60% of all freshmen and 74% of continuing students received some form of financial aid. 60% of freshmen and 71% of continuing students received need-based aid. The average freshman award was $10,084. Of that total, scholarships or need-based grants averaged $5580 ($6500 maximum); and loans averaged $1836 ($2625 maximum). 27% of undergraduates work part time. Average annual earnings from campus work are $650. The average financial indebtedness of the 1999 graduate was $11,735. Hanover is a member of CSS. The CSS/Profile or FAFSA is required. The fall application deadline is March 1.

Computers: The mainframe is a DEC ALPHA Server 2100. Mac and PC networks are available. Students may access the system in computer labs and through ports located in every dormitory room. All students may access the system in the labs from 8 a.m. to 11 p.m. Monday through Thursday, 8 a.m. to 5 p.m. Friday, 8 a.m. to 5 p.m. Saturday, and 8 a.m. to 11 p.m. Sunday. There are no time limits and no fees.

HARDING UNIVERSITY
Searcy, AR 72149-0001

(501) 279-4407
(800) 477-4407; Fax: (501) 279-4076

Full-time: 1603 men, 1927 women	**Faculty:** 189
Part-time: 81 men, 141 women	**Ph.D.s:** 66%
Graduate: 89 men, 135 women	**Student/Faculty:** 19 to 1
Year: semesters, summer session	**Tuition:** $7955
Application Deadline: June 1	**Room & Board:** $4250
Freshman Class: 1614 applied, 1291 accepted, 940 enrolled	
SAT I Verbal/Math: 560/550	**ACT:** 24 **VERY COMPETITIVE**

Harding University, founded in 1924, is a private Christian institution composed of the Colleges of Arts and Sciences and Bible and Religion and the Schools of Business, Education, and Nursing. There are 5 undergraduate and 2 graduate schools. In addition to regional accreditation, Harding has baccalaureate program accreditation with ACBSP, CSWE, NASM, NCATE, and NLN. The library contains 438,520 volumes, 153,000 microform items, and 6750 audiovisual forms/CDs, and subscribes to 1341 periodicals. Computerized library services include the card catalog, interlibrary loans, and database searching. Special learning facilities include a learning resource center, art gallery, natural history museum, radio station, and TV station. The 200-acre campus is in a small town 50 miles northeast of Little Rock. Including residence halls, there are 50 buildings.

Programs of Study: Harding confers B.A., B.S., B.B.A., B.F.A., B.M.E., B. Mus., B.S.M.T., B.S.N., and B.S.W. degrees. Master's degrees are also awarded. Bachelor's degrees are awarded in BIOLOGICAL SCIENCE (biochemistry and biology/biological science), BUSINESS (accounting, business administration and management, business economics, human resources, international business management, marketing/retailing/merchandising, and sports management), COMMUNICATIONS AND THE ARTS (advertising, art, broadcasting, communications, design, dramatic arts, English, fine arts, French, graphic design, music, painting, and Spanish), COMPUTER AND PHYSICAL SCIENCE (chemistry, computer science, mathematics, and physics), EDUCATION (early childhood, elementary, foreign languages, music, and secondary), ENGINEERING AND ENVIRON-MENTAL DESIGN (interior design), HEALTH PROFESSIONS (medical technology, nursing, predentistry, premedicine, and speech pathology/audiology), SOCIAL SCIENCE (American studies, dietetics, economics, history, home economics, international studies, liberal arts/general studies, ministries, political science/government, psychology, public administration, religion, social science, social work, and sociology). Business, premedicine, and the sciences are the strongest academically. Business and education are the largest.

Special: The Harding campus in Florence, Italy, and programs in Greece, England, and Australia offer international studies. Internships are given in social work, teaching, nursing, and international missions. Co-op programs in all majors, work-study programs, dual majors, a general studies degree, nondegree study, and pass/fail options are available. A 3-2 engineering degree is offered with the University of Missouri, Georgia Institute of Technology, and the University of Southern California. There are 3 national honor societies, a freshman honors program, and 13 departmental honors programs.

Admissions: 80% of the 1999-2000 applicants were accepted. The SAT I scores for the 1999-2000 freshman class were: Verbal--15% below 500, 42% between 500 and 599, 37% between 600 and 700, and 6% above 700; Math--22% below 500, 41% between 500 and 599, 30% between 600 and 700, and 7% above 700. The ACT scores were 25% below 21, 24% between 21 and 23, 22% between 24 and 26, 11% between 27 and 28, and 18% above 28. There were 24 National Merit finalists and 20 semifinalists. 41 freshmen graduated first in their class.

Requirements: The SAT I or ACT is required. Harding requires applicants to be in the upper 50% of their class. A GPA of 3.0 is required. A lower GPA can be offset by higher test scores. Applicants should be graduates of an accredited secondary school and have completed 19 high school hours, including 4 each in English and math, 3 each in science and social studies, 3 in art, history, or music, and 2 in a foreign language. An interview is highly recommended. AP and CLEP credits are accepted. Important factors in the admissions decision are leadership record, recommendations by school officials, and advanced placement or honor courses.

Procedure: Freshmen are admitted to all sessions. Entrance exams should be taken in the junior year or early in the senior year. There are early admissions and deferred admissions plans. Applications should be filed by June 1 for fall entry and November 1 for spring entry, along with a $35 fee. Notification is sent on a rolling basis. 20% of all applicants are on a waiting list.

Financial Aid: In 1999-2000, 93% of all freshmen and 91% of continuing students received some form of financial aid. 52% of freshmen and 57% of continuing students received need-based aid. The average freshman award was $9173. Of that total, scholarships or need-based grants averaged $4046 ($12,305 maximum); loans averaged $6540 ($14,900 maximum); and work contracts averaged $1295 ($2884 maximum). 58% of undergraduates work part time. Average annual earnings from campus work are $866. The average financial indebtedness of the 1999 graduate was $19,711. Harding is a member of CSS. The CSS/Profile or FFS is required. The fall application deadline is May 1.

Computers: The mainframe is a DEC VAX 3600. There are numerous terminals for accessing the mainframe and 200 PCs available for student use. Many students have their own computers and it is strongly recommended that all students have personal computers. All students may access the system. The fee is $100.

HARVARD UNIVERSITY/HARVARD COLLEGE
Cambridge, MA 02138 (617) 495-1551

Full-time: 3596 men, 3096 women	**Faculty:** 837; I, ++$
Part-time: 7 men, 5 women	**Ph.D.s:** 99%
Graduate: 5894 men, 5077 women	**Student/Faculty:** 8 to 1
Year: semesters, summer session	**Tuition:** $24,407
Application Deadline: January 1	**Room & Board:** $7757
Freshman Class: 18,160 applied, 2055 accepted, 1652 enrolled	
SAT I or ACT: required	**MOST COMPETITIVE**

Harvard College (formerly Harvard and Radcliff Colleges), is the undergraduate college of Harvard University. Harvard College was founded in 1636. Harvard University also has 10 graduate schools. In addition to regional accreditation, Harvard has baccalaureate program accreditation with ABET. The 97 libraries contain 13 million volumes, and subscribe to 100,000 periodicals. Computerized library services include the card catalog, interlibrary loans, and database searching. Special learning facilities include a learning resource center, art gallery, natural history museum, planetarium, and radio station. The 380-acre campus is in an urban area across the Charles River from Boston. Including residence halls, there are 400 buildings.

Programs of Study: Harvard confers A.B. and S.B. degrees. Master's and doctoral degrees are also awarded. Bachelor's degrees are awarded in BIOLOGICAL SCIENCE (biochemistry, biology/biological science, and biophysics), COMMUNICATIONS AND THE ARTS (art history and appreciation, Chinese, classics, creative writing, English, fine arts, folklore and mythology, French, German, Greek, Hebrew, Italian, Japanese, Latin, linguistics, literature, music, Portuguese, Russian, and Spanish), COMPUTER AND PHYSICAL SCIENCE (applied mathematics, astronomy, chemistry, computer science, geology, geophysics and seismology, mathematics, physical sciences, physics, and statistics), ENGINEERING AND ENVIRONMENTAL DESIGN (engineering, environmental design, environmental science, and preengineering), SOCIAL SCIENCE (African American studies, American studies, anthropology, Asian/Oriental studies, economics, European studies, history, humanities, Middle Eastern studies, philosophy, political science/government, psychology, religion, Russian and Slavic studies, Sanskrit and Indian studies, social science, social studies, sociology, and women's studies). Economics, government, and biology are the largest.

Special: Students may cross-register with MIT and with other schools within the university, and may design their own concentrations or enroll for nondegree study. Internships and study abroad may be arranged. Accelerated degree programs, dual majors, a 3-2 engineering degree, and a combined A.B.-S.B. in engineering are offered. There are pass/fail options. There is a chapter of Phi Beta Kappa.

Admissions: 11% of the 1999-2000 applicants were accepted. 98% of the current freshmen were in the top fifth of their class; all were in the top two fifths.

Requirements: The SAT I or ACT is required, as well as 3 SAT II: Subject tests. Applicants need not be high school graduates but are expected to be well prepared academically. An essay and an interview are required, in addition to a transcript, counselor report, and 2 teacher recommendations from academic disciplines. AP credits are accepted. Important factors in the admissions decision are evidence of special talent, personality/intangible qualities, and recommendations by school officials.

Procedure: Freshmen are admitted in the fall. Entrance exams should be taken by January of the senior year. There are early admissions and deferred admissions plans. Applications should be filed by January 1 for fall entry, along with a $60 fee. Notification is sent April 3. A waiting list is an active part of the admissions procedure.

Financial Aid: In 1999-2000, 80% of all freshmen and 69% of continuing students received some form of financial aid. 48% of freshmen and 46% of continuing students received need-based aid. The average freshman award was $21,229. 70% of undergraduates work part time. Harvard is a member of CSS. The CSS/Profile, FAFSA, the college's own financial statement, and federal tax forms are required. The fall application deadline is February 15.

Computers: All residences have Internet access. There are also PCs available for use in the science center and all residence halls. All students may access the system 24 hours per day. There are no time limits and no fees.

HARVEY MUDD COLLEGE
Claremont, CA 91711   (909) 621-8011; Fax: (909) 607-7046

Full-time: 510 men, 183 women	**Faculty:** 75; IIB, ++$
Part-time: none	**Ph.D.s:** 100%
Graduate: 5 men, 1 woman	**Student/Faculty:** 9 to 1
Year: semesters	**Tuition:** $22,083
Application Deadline: January 15	**Room & Board:** $8017
Freshman Class: 1522 applied, 535 accepted, 170 enrolled	
SAT I Verbal/Math: 720/760	**MOST COMPETITIVE**

Harvey Mudd College, founded in 1955, is one of the Claremont Colleges. It is an independent college specializing in engineering and physical science education within a liberal arts tradition. There is 1 graduate school. In addition to regional accreditation, Harvey Mudd has baccalaureate program accreditation with ABET. The library contains 1.9 million volumes, and subscribes to 6800 periodicals. Computerized library services include the card catalog, interlibrary loans, and database searching. Special learning facilities include an art gallery, planetarium, and radio station. The 30-acre campus is in a suburban area 35 miles east of Los Angeles. Including residence halls, there are 18 buildings.

Programs of Study: Harvey Mudd confers the B.S. degree. Bachelor's degrees are awarded in BIOLOGICAL SCIENCE (biology/biological science), COMPUTER AND PHYSICAL SCIENCE (chemistry, computer science, mathematics, and physics), ENGINEERING AND ENVIRONMENTAL DESIGN (engineering). Engineering is the largest.

Special: Students may cross-register at any of the other Claremont Colleges. Internships are available for engineering and math majors. Study abroad, a Washington semester, work-study, a joint computer science/math major, and student-designed majors are available. A 3-2 engineering degree with Claremont McKenna College is possible, as is a 4-1 B.S./M.B.A. with Claremont Graduate University. Some courses may be audited. The first semester for freshmen is taken on a pass/fail basis; thereafter, only 1 noncore and nonmajor course per semester may be taken on that basis. There is 1 national honor society. All departments have honors programs.

Admissions: 35% of the 1999-2000 applicants were accepted. The SAT I scores for the 1999-2000 freshman class were: Verbal--3% between 500 and 599, 40% between 600 and 700, and 57% above 700; Math--6% between 600 and 700 and 94% above 700. 99% of the current freshmen were in the top fifth of their class. There were 50 National Merit finalists and 50 semifinalists. 31 freshmen graduated first in their class.

Requirements: The SAT I is required. Applicants must be graduates of an accredited secondary school and have completed 4 years each of English and math (including algebra, demonstrative and analytic geometry, trigonometry, and calculus) and 1 year each of physics and chemistry. The college strongly recommends that applicants take 2 years of a foreign language and 1 year each of history and biology. SAT II: Subject tests in math II, writing, and 1 other subject are required. Applicants must submit 2 personal essays and are encouraged to seek an interview. Applications are accepted on-line. AP credits are accepted. Important factors in the admissions decision are advanced placement or honor courses, recommendations by school officials, and leadership record.

Procedure: Freshmen are admitted in the fall. Entrance exams should be taken by January of the senior year. There are early decision and deferred admissions plans. Early decision applications should be filed by November 15; regular applications by January 15 for fall entry, along with a $50 fee. Notification of early decision is sent December 15; regular decision, April 1. 47 early decision candidates were accepted for the 1999-2000 class. 21% of all applicants are on a waiting list.

Financial Aid: In 1999-2000, 92% of all freshmen and 78% of continuing students received some form of financial aid. 62% of freshmen and 58% of continuing students received need-based aid. The average freshman award was $14,867. Of that total, scholarships or need-based grants averaged $10,374 ($23,426 maximum); loans averaged $3466 ($4000 maximum); and work contracts averaged $737 ($1720 maximum). 27% of undergraduates work part time. Average annual earnings from campus work are $649. The average financial indebtedness of the 1999 graduate was $17,544. Harvey Mudd is a member of CSS. The CSS/Profile or FAFSA is required. The fall application deadline is February 1.

Computers: The mainframes are a Sun Ultra Enterprise 2 and others. Students may access systems from dorm rooms, academic labs, and classrooms. 90% of students own PCs that are attached to the campus network via Ethernet. More than 150 systems ranging from Mac and Windows PCs to SGI, Sun, and HP UNIX workstations are available on the network for student use. All students may access the system 24 hours a day. There are no time limits and no fees. It is strongly recommended that all students have a personal computer.

HAVERFORD COLLEGE
Haverford, PA 19041-1392   (610) 896-1350; Fax: (610) 896-1338

Full-time: 528 men, 590 women	**Faculty:** 102; IIB, ++$
Part-time: none	**Ph.D.s:** 97%
Graduate: none	**Student/Faculty:** 11 to 1
Year: semesters	**Tuition:** $23,780
Application Deadline: January 15	**Room & Board:** $7620
Freshman Class: 2650 applied, 862 accepted, 302 enrolled	
SAT I or ACT: required	**MOST COMPETITIVE**

Haverford College, founded in 1833, is a private liberal arts college. The 5 libraries contain 513,444 volumes, 89,079 microform items, and 10,191 audiovisual forms CDs, and subscribe to 1961 periodicals, including electronic journals. Computerized library services include the card catalog, interlibrary loans, and database searching. Special learning facilities include an art gallery, radio station, observatory, and arboretum. The 200-acre campus is in a suburban area 10 miles west of Philadelphia. Including residence halls, there are 70 buildings.

Programs of Study: Haverford confers B.A. and B.S. degrees. Bachelor's degrees are awarded in BIOLOGICAL SCIENCE (biology/biological science), COMMUNICATIONS AND THE ARTS (art history and appreciation, classics, comparative literature, English, fine arts, French, German, Italian, music, romance languages and literature, Russian, and Spanish), COMPUTER AND PHYSICAL SCIENCE (astronomy, chemistry, geology, mathematics, and physics), SOCIAL SCIENCE (anthropology, archeology, East Asian studies, economics, history, philosophy, political science/government, psychology, religion, sociology, and urban studies). Natural and physical sciences, English, and history are the strongest academically. English, biology, and history are the largest.

Special: Haverford offers internship programs, cross-registration with Bryn Mawr College, Swarthmore College, and the University of Pennsylvania, study abroad in 33 countries, dual majors, student-designed majors, and a 3-2 engineering degree with the University of Pennsylvania. Pass/fail options are limited to 4 in 4 years. There is 1 national honor society, Phi Beta Kappa, and 28 departmental honors programs.

Admissions: 33% of the 1999-2000 applicants were accepted. The SAT I scores for the 1999-2000 freshman class were: Verbal--3% below 500, 12% between 500 and 599, 38% between 600 and 700, and 47% above 700; Math--3% below 500, 13% between 500 and 599, 45% between 600 and 700, and 39% above 700. 93% of the current freshmen were in the top fifth of their class; all were in the top two fifths.

Requirements: The SAT I or ACT is required. The SAT II: Writing test is required, plus 2 others. Candidates for admission must be graduates of an accredited secondary school and have taken 4 courses in English, 3 each in a foreign language and math, and 1 each in science and history. The GED is accepted. An essay is required and an interview is recommended. Haverford accepts applications on computer disk, and on-line via Embark.com and CollegeLink. AP credits are accepted. Important factors in the admissions decision are advanced placement or honor courses, leadership record, and recommendations by school officials.

Procedure: Freshmen are admitted in the fall. Entrance exams should be taken before January 15. There are early decision, early admissions, and deferred admissions plans. Early decision applications should be filed by November 15; regular applications, by January 15 for fall entry, along with a $50 fee. Notification of early decision is sent December 15; regular decision, by April 15. 86 early decision candidates were accepted for the 1999-2000 class. A waiting list is an active part of the admissions procedure.

Financial Aid: 38% of freshmen and 44% of continuing students received need-based aid. The average freshman award was $23,254. Of that total, scholarships or need-based grants averaged $17,230; loans averaged $2188; work contracts averaged $1434; Pell, SEOG, state grants, and outside scholarships averaged $2402. Haverford is a member of CSS. The CSS/Profile or FAFSA is required. The fall application deadline is January 31.

Computers: The mainframes are multiple Sun SPARC Stations as distributed servers. There are approximately 75 publicly accessible Macs and PCs available in 2 computer labs and in the library. There are special-purpose computing labs available to students in foreign language, physical sciences, biology, psychology, and math/computer science, which have an additional 70 machines. Every student has a UNIX account, which allows use of E-mail and personal web space. All rooms in the major dormitories and all publicly accessible computers are networked and have direct Internet access. All students may access the system. There are no time limits and no fees.

Conway, AR 72032

(501) 450-1362
(800) 277-9017; Fax: (501) 450-3843

Full-time: 522 men, 605 women	**Faculty:** 80; IIB, +$
Part-time: 1 man, 13 women	**Ph.D.s:** 100%
Graduate: 2 men, 2 women	**Student/Faculty:** 14 to 1
Year: trimesters	**Tuition:** $11,725
Application Deadline: open	**Room & Board:** $4415
Freshman Class: 962 applied, 832 accepted, 331 enrolled	
SAT I Verbal/Math: 641/617	**ACT:** 27 **VERY COMPETITIVE+**

Hendrix College, founded in 1876, is a private, liberal arts college affiliated with the United Methodist Church. There is 1 graduate school. In addition to regional accreditation, Hendrix has baccalaureate program accreditation with NASM and NCATE. The library contains 197,995 volumes, 161,657 microform items, and 3719 audiovisual forms/CDs, and subscribes to 704 periodicals. Computerized library services include the card catalog, interlibrary loans, and database searching. Special learning facilities include an art gallery, radio station, and a writing lab. The 65-acre campus is in a suburban area 25 miles northwest of Little Rock. Including residence halls, there are 37 buildings.

Programs of Study: Hendrix confers the B.A. degree. Master's degrees are also awarded. Bachelor's degrees are awarded in BIOLOGICAL SCIENCE (biology/biological science), BUSINESS (business economics), COMMUNICATIONS AND THE ARTS (art, dramatic arts, English, French, German, music, and Spanish), COMPUTER AND PHYSICAL SCIENCE (chemistry, computer science, mathematics, and physics), EDUCATION (physical), SOCIAL SCIENCE (anthropology, history, interdisciplinary studies, international relations, philosophy, political science/government, psychology, religion, and sociology). Chemistry, economics, and religion are the strongest academically. Psychology, history, and biology are the largest.

Special: Internships and work-study may be arranged in all fields. The college offers 3-2 engineering programs with Columbia, Vanderbilt, and Washington universities. Also available are a Washington semester, study abroad, dual majors, and student-designed interdisciplinary studies. Students can pursue minors in all academic departments, as well as gender studies and cultural anthropology. There are 4 national honor societies, including Phi Beta Kappa, and all departments have honors programs.

Admissions: 86% of the 1999-2000 applicants were accepted. The SAT I scores for the 1999-2000 freshman class were: Verbal--5% below 500, 25% between 500 and 599, 46% between 600 and 700, and 25% above 700; Math--8% below 500, 30% between 500 and 599, 43% between 600 and 700, and 19% above 700. The ACT scores were 4% below 21, 12% between 21 and 23, 26% between 24 and 26, 17% between 27 and 28, and 41% above 28. 70% of the current freshmen were in the top fifth of their class; 91% were in the top two fifths. There were 19 National Merit finalists and 24 semifinalists. 27 freshmen graduated first in their class.

Requirements: The SAT I or ACT is required. In addition, Hendrix recommends that applicants have completed 4 high school units in English, 3 to 4 each in math and social studies, 2 to 3 in science, and 2 in a foreign language. The GED is accepted. AP and CLEP credits are accepted. Important factors in the admissions decision are leadership record, advanced placement or honor courses, and extra-curricular activities record.

Procedure: Freshmen are admitted fall, winter, and spring. Entrance exams should be taken during the junior and senior years. There are early admissions and deferred admissions plans. Application deadlines are open, along with a $25 fee. Notification is sent on a rolling basis. 1% of all applicants are on a waiting list.

Financial Aid: In 1999-2000, 94% of all freshmen and 95% of continuing students received some form of financial aid. 59% of freshmen and 44% of continuing students received need-based aid. The average freshman award was $12,417. Of that total, scholarships or need-based grants averaged $8444 ($21,370 maximum); loans averaged $3191 ($18,650 maximum); work contracts averaged $561 ($1500 maximum); and Veterans benefits, faculty/staff-related grants, and ministerial-related grants averaged $221 ($11,400 maximum). 36% of undergraduates work part time. Average annual earnings from campus work are $1454. The average financial indebtedness of the 1999 graduate was $5877. Hendrix is a member of CSS. The FAFSA and the college's own financial statement are required. The fall application deadline is February 15.

Computers: The mainframe is a DEC ALPHA Server 1000 time-sharing system. There are computer labs utilizing 44 Macs and 31 PCs. In addition, all dormitory rooms are wired for computer hookup. All students may access the system 24 hours a day, 7 days a week. There are no time limits. The fee is $30.

HILLSDALE COLLEGE
Hillsdale, MI 49242   (517) 437-7341; Fax: (517) 437-0190

Full-time: 543 men, 566 women	**Faculty:** 89
Part-time: 10 men, 19 women	**Ph.D.s:** 85%
Graduate: none	**Student/Faculty:** 12 to 1
Year: semesters, summer session	**Tuition:** $13,460
Application Deadline: July 15	**Room & Board:** $5630
Freshman Class: 1008 applied, 849 accepted, 332 enrolled	
SAT I Verbal/Math: 620/600	**ACT:** 26 **VERY COMPETITIVE+**

Hillsdale College, founded in 1844, is a private liberal arts college emphasizing preprofessional, business, and education programs. The 3 libraries contain 175,000 volumes, 42,000 microform items, and 6500 audiovisual forms/CDs, and subscribe to 1494 periodicals. Computerized library services include the card catalog, interlibrary loans, and database searching. Special learning facilities include a learning resource center and a media center, an early childhood education lab, an arboretum, a 3000-book economics library, and a rare books room. The 250-acre campus is in a small town 120 miles southwest of Detroit. Including residence halls, there are 50 buildings.

Programs of Study: Hillsdale confers B.A. and B.S. degrees. Bachelor's degrees are awarded in BIOLOGICAL SCIENCE (biology/biological science), BUSINESS (accounting, banking and finance, business administration and management, international business management, and marketing/retailing/merchandising), COMMUNICATIONS AND THE ARTS (classics, comparative literature, dramatic arts, English, fine arts, French, German, music, Spanish, and speech/debate/rhetoric), COMPUTER AND PHYSICAL SCIENCE (chemistry, mathematics, and physics), EDUCATION (art, early childhood, elementary, foreign languages, middle school, music, physical, science, and secondary), HEALTH PROFESSIONS (predentistry, premedicine, and preveterinary science), SOCIAL SCIENCE (American studies, Christian studies, economics, European studies, history, political science/government, prelaw, psychology, religion, social science, and sociology). History, economics, and biology are the strongest academically. Business, history, and English. are the largest.

Special: Special academic programs include the Washington Journalism Internship at the National Journalism Center and the Washington-Hillsdale Intern Program (WHIP), which places students in congressional or government offices. Students may study abroad in France, Germany, or Spain, and qualified students are chosen to attend Oxford University for a year. A business internship is offered in London at Regents College. The college offers an accelerated degree; interdisciplinary majors, including political economy combining economics, history, and political science; 3-2 and 2-2 engineering degrees; and work-study programs at the city radio station WCSR and the city newspaper, the Hillsdale Daily News. There are 16 national honor societies, and a freshman honors program.

Admissions: 84% of the 1999-2000 applicants were accepted. The SAT I scores for the 1999-2000 freshman class were: Verbal--7% below 500, 30% between 500 and 599, 40% between 600 and 700, and 23% above 700; Math--9% below 500, 38% between 500 and 599, 41% between 600 and 700, and 12% above 700. The ACT scores were 7% below 21, 19% between 21 and 23, 34% between 24 and 26, 15% between 27 and 28, and 25% above 28. 63% of the current freshmen were in the top fifth of their class; 90% were in the top two fifths. There were 11 National Merit finalists and 45 semifinalists. 15 freshmen graduated first in their class.

Requirements: The SAT I or ACT is required. Hillsdale requires applicants to be in the upper 50% of their class. A GPA of 3.2 is required. In addition, the student must be a high school graduate or have earned a GED, and must have completed 4 years of English, 3 each of math and science, and 2 each of history, social studies, and foreign language. The college requires a letter of recommendation and an essay. An interview is also recommended. For music majors, an audition is required. The school recommends taking SAT II: Subject tests. Applications can be obtained on-line. AP and CLEP credits are accepted. Important factors in the admissions decision are advanced placement or honor courses, leadership record, and extracurricular activities record.

Procedure: Freshmen are admitted to all sessions. Entrance exams should be taken in the spring of the junior year and/or the fall of the senior year. There is an early admissions plan. Applications should be filed by July 15 for fall entry, December 15 for spring entry, and May 1 for summer entry, along with a $15 fee. Notification is sent on a rolling basis.

Financial Aid: In 1999-2000, 84% of all freshmen and 81% of continuing students received some form of financial aid. 70% of freshmen and 65% of continuing students received need-based aid. The average freshman award was $10,000. Of that total, scholarships or need-based grants averaged $6300 ($13,220 maximum); loans averaged $3300 ($7000 maximum); and work contracts averaged $1000. 65% of undergraduates work part time. Average annual earnings from campus work are $1250. The average financial indebtedness of the 1999 graduate was $10,000. Hillsdale is a member of CSS. The CSS/Profile or FAFSA and the college's own financial statement are required. The fall application deadline is April 15.

Computers: The mainframe is an IBM AS/400. The computer lab, located in the student center, has more than 100 PCs available for student use. Laser printers are also available, along with wordprocessing and software workshops, E-mail, Internet, and the World Wide Web. All students may access the system at any time. There are no time limits and no fees.

HIRAM COLLEGE
Hiram, OH 44234

(330) 569-5169
(800) 362-5280; Fax: (330) 569-5944

Full-time: 424 men, 456 women	**Faculty:** 68; IIB, +$
Part-time: 7 men, 8 women	**Ph.D.s:** 97%
Graduate: none	**Student/Faculty:** 13 to 1
Year: split semesters, summer session	**Tuition:** $17,935
Application Deadline: March 15	**Room & Board:** $5954
Freshman Class: 853 applied, 741 accepted, 279 enrolled	
SAT I Verbal/Math: 580/560	**ACT:** 24 **VERY COMPETITIVE**

Hiram College, founded in 1850, is a private, residential liberal arts and sciences institution. In addition to regional accreditation, Hiram has baccalaureate program accreditation with NASM. The library contains 178,776 volumes, 96,049 microform items, and 8795 audiovisual forms/CDs, and subscribes to 885 periodicals. Computerized library services include the card catalog, interlibrary loans, and database searching. Special learning facilities include a learning resource center, art gallery, planetarium, radio station, a 260-acre biological field station, and a field station in the Upper Peninsula of Michigan. The 110-acre campus is in a rural area 35 miles southeast of Cleveland. Including residence halls, there are 28 buildings.

Programs of Study: Hiram confers the B.A. degree. Bachelor's degrees are awarded in BIOLOGICAL SCIENCE (biology/biological science), BUSINESS (international economics and management science), COMMUNICATIONS AND THE ARTS (art, art history and appreciation, classics, communications, dramatic arts, English, French, German, language arts, music, and Spanish), COMPUTER AND PHYSICAL SCIENCE (applied physics, chemistry, computer science, and mathematics), EDUCATION (elementary), ENGINEERING AND ENVIRONMENTAL DESIGN (environmental science), SOCIAL SCIENCE (economics, history, philosophy, political science/government, psychobiology, psychology, religion, social studies, and sociology). Biology, computer science, and education are the strongest academically. Biology, education, and management are the largest.

Special: There is cross-registration through the Cleveland Commission on Higher Education and a 3-2 engineering program with Case Western Reserve and Washington Universities. There is a Washington semester and study abroad in many countries with courses taught by Hiram faculty. Double majors and individually arranged internships in all fields, student-designed majors, and pass/no credit options are possible. There are 8 national honor societies, including Phi Beta Kappa.

Admissions: 87% of the 1999-2000 applicants were accepted. The SAT I scores for the 1999-2000 freshman class were: Verbal--24% below 500, 34% between 500 and 599, 32% between 600 and 700, and 10% above 700; Math--27% below 500, 34% between 500 and 599, 31% between 600 and 700, and 8% above 700. The ACT scores were 23% below 21, 28% between 21 and 23, 23% between 24 and 26, 15% between 27 and 28, and 10% above 28. 52% of the current freshmen were in the top fifth of their class; 79% were in the top two fifths. 13 freshmen graduated first in their class.

Requirements: The SAT I or ACT is required. Applicants should have completed 16 academic units or the GED equivalent. An essay is required. A portfolio, audition, and interview are recommended. Applications are accepted on disk or online through CollegeLink, Common App, and Apply. AP and CLEP credits are accepted. Important factors in the admissions decision are advanced placement or honor courses, leadership record, and extracurricular activities record.

Procedure: Freshmen are admitted fall and spring. Entrance exams should be taken no later than the fall of the senior year. There are early admissions and deferred admissions plans. Applications should be filed by March 15 for fall entry and December 1 for spring entry, along with a $25 fee. Notification is sent on a rolling basis.

Financial Aid: In 1999-2000, 93% of all students received some form of financial aid. 82% of all students received need-based aid. The average freshman award was $17,827. Of that total, scholarships or need-based grants averaged $9656 ($16,590 maximum); loans averaged $2651 ($6625 maximum); and work contracts averaged $1216 ($1600 maximum). 71% of undergraduates work part time. Average annual earnings from campus work are $1202. The average financial indebtedness of the 1999 graduate was $18,925. Hiram is a member of CSS. The FAFSA is required. The fall application deadline is March 1.

Computers: The mainframe is a DEC ALPHA Server 2100 5/250. The college network may be accessed from student-owned PCs in residence halls and from PC labs throughout the campus. The network allows access to the Internet and the Web. Each residence hall has a lab with 5 to 8 PCs. More than 60 additional PCs are available in classrooms and other locations. All students may access the system 24 hours a day, 7 days per week. There are no time limits and no fees.

HOBART AND WILLIAM SMITH COLLEGES
Geneva, NY 14456-3397   H: (315) 781-3622; WS: (315) 781-3472
H: (800) 852-2256   WS: (800) 245-0100; Fax: (315) 781-3471

Full-time: 873 men, 954 women	**Faculty:** 145; IIB, ++$
Part-time: 1 man, 2 women	**Ph.D.s:** 98%
Graduate: none	**Student/Faculty:** 13 to 1
Year: semesters	**Tuition:** $24,342
Application Deadline: February 1	**Room & Board:** $6882
Freshman Class: 2634 applied, 1970 accepted, 501 enrolled	
SAT I or ACT: required	**VERY COMPETITIVE**

Hobart College, a men's college founded in 1822, shares campus, classes, and faculty with William Smith College, a women's college founded in 1908. Together, these coordinate colleges offer degree programs in the liberal arts. The library contains 345,661 volumes, 76,243 microform items, and 7422 audiovisual forms CDs, and subscribes to 2056 periodicals. Computerized library services include the card catalog, interlibrary loans, and database searching. Special learning facilities include a learning resource center, art gallery, radio station, 100-acre natural preserve, and 70-foot research vessel. The 170-acre campus is in a small town 50 miles west of Syracuse and 50 miles east of Rochester, on the north shore of Seneca Lake. Including residence halls, there are 75 buildings.

Programs of Study: HWS confers B.A. and B.S. degrees. Bachelor's degrees are awarded in BIOLOGICAL SCIENCE (biology/biological science), COMMUNICATIONS AND THE ARTS (Chinese, classics, dance, English, fine arts, French, Japanese, music, and Spanish), COMPUTER AND PHYSICAL SCIENCE (chemistry, computer science, geoscience, mathematics, and physics), ENGINEERING AND ENVIRONMENTAL DESIGN (architecture and environmental science), SOCIAL SCIENCE (American studies, anthropology, Asian/Oriental studies, economics, history, philosophy, political science/government, psychology, religion, Russian and Slavic studies, sociology, urban studies, and women's studies). Natural sciences, environmental studies, and creative writing are the strongest academically. English, economics, and political science are the largest.

Special: Students are encouraged to spend at least 1 term in a study-abroad program, offered in more than 29 countries and locales within the United States. Options include a United Nations term, a Washington semester, an urban semester, and prearchitecture semesters in New York, Paris, Florence, or Copenhagen. HWS offers dual and student-designed majors, credit for life/military/work experience, nondegree study, and pass/fail options. There are also advanced business degree programs with Clarkson University and Rochester Institute of Technology and 3-2 engineering degrees with Columbia University, Rensselaer Polytechnic Institute, and Dartmouth College. There are 9 national honor societies, including Phi Beta Kappa, and all departments have honors programs.

Admissions: 75% of the 1999-2000 applicants were accepted. The SAT I scores for the 1999-2000 freshman class were: Verbal--11% below 500, 54% between 500 and 599, 31% between 600 and 700, and 4% above 700; Math--12% below 500, 51% between 500 and 599, 34% between 600 and 700, and 3% above 700. 47% of the current freshmen were in the top fifth of their class; 82% were in the top two fifths.

Requirements: The SAT I or ACT is required. SAT II: Subject tests are not required but will be considered if taken. A GED is accepted. A total of 18 academic credits is required, including 4 years of English, 3 of math, and at least 2 each of lab science, foreign language, and history. An essay is required; an interview is recommended. Applications are accepted on-line. AP credits are accepted. Important factors in the admissions decision are advanced placement or honor courses, evidence of special talent, and leadership record.

Procedure: Freshmen are admitted in the fall. Entrance exams should be taken in the junior or senior year. There are early decision, early admissions, and deferred admissions plans. Early decision applications should be filed by January 1; regular applications, by February 1 for fall entry, along with a $45 fee. Notification of early decision is sent February 1; regular decision, April 1. 72 early decision candidates were accepted for the 1999-2000 class. 8% of all applicants are on a waiting list.

Financial Aid: In 1999-2000, 71% of all students received some form of financial aid. 69% of freshmen and 68% of continuing students received need-based aid. The average freshman award was $24,583. Of that total, scholarships or need-based grants averaged $18,457 ($23,750 maximum); loans averaged $2625 ($6625 maximum); and work contracts averaged $1200 ($1500 maximum). 70% of undergraduates work part time. Average annual earnings from campus work are $687. The average financial indebtedness of the 1999 graduate was $15,338. HWS is a member of CSS. The CSS/Profile or FAFSA is required. The fall application deadline is February 15.

Computers: The mainframes are a DEC ALPHA 2100 and a DEC VAX 6520. There are 122 PCs and 60 terminals directly connected to the mainframe, with 114 PCs networked. The 4 PC labs provide access to the on-line library catalog system, E-mail, and the Internet. All students have E-mail accounts, and computers in student rooms are directly connected to the mainframe. All students may access the system from 8 a.m. to 1 a.m., 7 days a week. There are no time limits and no fees.

HOOD COLLEGE
Frederick, MD 21701-8575
(301) 696-3400
(800) 922-1599; Fax: (301) 696-3819

Full-time: 28 men, 604 women	**Faculty:** 73; IIA, -$
Part-time: 71 men, 191 women	**Ph.D.s:** 96%
Graduate: 276 men, 606 women	**Student/Faculty:** 9 to 1
Year: semesters, summer session	**Tuition:** $17,600
Application Deadline: February 15	**Room & Board:** $6900
Freshman Class: 533 applied, 413 accepted, 169 enrolled	
SAT I Verbal/Math: 570/550	**VERY COMPETITIVE**

Hood College, founded in 1893, is an independent, comprehensive college, primarily for women, that offers an integration of the liberal arts and professional preparation, as well as undergraduate majors in the natural sciences. There is 1 graduate school. In addition to regional accreditation, Hood has baccalaureate program accreditation with ADA and CAHEA. The library contains 182,000 volumes, 671,765 microform items, and 3550 audiovisual forms/CDs, and subscribes to 930 periodicals. Computerized library services include the card catalog, interlibrary loans, and database searching. Special learning facilities include a learning resource center, art gallery, aquatic center, child development lab, observatory, and Whitaker Campus Center, a library and information technology center that forms the hub of the campuswide computing network. The 50-acre campus is in a suburban area 45 miles northwest of Washington, D.C., and 45 miles west of Baltimore. Including residence halls, there are 31 buildings.

Programs of Study: Hood confers B.A. and B.S. degrees. Master's degrees are also awarded. Bachelor's degrees are awarded in BIOLOGICAL SCIENCE (biochemistry and biology/biological science), BUSINESS (business administration and management and management science), COMMUNICATIONS AND THE ARTS (art, communications, English, French, German, and Spanish), COMPUTER AND PHYSICAL SCIENCE (chemistry, computer science, information sciences and systems, and mathematics), EDUCATION (early childhood, English, foreign languages, mathematics, science, secondary, and special), ENGINEERING AND ENVIRONMENTAL DESIGN (environmental science), SOCIAL SCIENCE (economics, history, Latin American studies, law, philosophy, political science/government, psychology, religion, social work, and sociology). Biology, chemistry, and math are the strongest academically. Management, biology, and education are the largest.

Special: The college offers a Washington semester with American University, dual majors, student-designed majors, credit for life experience, nondegree study, pass/fail options, and cross-registration with area colleges and the Duke University Marine Sciences Education Consortium. Internships of up to 15 credits are available in all majors at more than 600 sites throughout the United States and abroad. Students may study abroad in the Dominican Republic, Japan, Spain, France, and other countries. A 3-2 engineering degree is offered with George Washington University. There are 11 national honor societies and a freshman honors program.

Admissions: 77% of the 1999-2000 applicants were accepted. The SAT I scores for the 1999-2000 freshman class were: Verbal--16% below 500, 48% between 500 and 599, 27% between 600 and 700, and 9% above 700; Math--28% below 500, 48% between 500 and 599, 21% between 600 and 700, and 3% above 700. 58% of the current freshmen were in the top fifth of their class; 84% were in the top two fifths. In a recent year, there was 1 National Merit finalist. 10 freshmen graduated first in their class.

Requirements: The SAT I or ACT is required. Hood requires applicants to be in the upper 40% of their class. A GPA of 2.5 is required. In addition, applicants should be graduates of an accredited secondary school. The GED is accepted. Hood recommends the completion of at least 16 academic credits in high school, including courses in English, social sciences, natural sciences, foreign languages, and math. An essay is required and an interview is recommended. Hood accepts applications on disk via CollegeLink. AP and CLEP credits are accepted. Important factors in the admissions decision are advanced placement or honor courses, leadership record, and personality/intangible qualities.

Procedure: Freshmen are admitted fall and spring. Entrance exams should be taken in spring of the junior year or fall of the senior year. There are early admissions and deferred admissions plans. Applications should be filed by February 15 for fall entry and December 31 for spring entry, along with a $35 fee. Notification is sent March 15.

Financial Aid: In 1999-2000, 92% of all freshmen and 82% of continuing students received some form of financial aid. 70% of freshmen and 66% of continuing students received need-based aid. The average freshman award was $19,138. Of that total, scholarships or need-based grants averaged $13,478 ($20,725 maximum); loans averaged $4695 ($5265 maximum); and work contracts averaged $1800 (maximum). 51% of undergraduates work part time. Average annual earnings from campus work are $1800. The average financial indebtedness of the 1999 graduate was $12,000. Hood is a member of CSS. The FAFSA is required. The fall application deadline is March 1.

Computers: The mainframes comprises Compaq Alpha 800, 2100a, and 4000 servers. Students may use the 10 PCs in a 24-hour computing lab or dial in from off campus. There are 150 PCs in 6 student labs and 28 Macs in other labs, and 3 to 4 computers in each residence hall. All students may access the system 24 hours per day from a PC in the 24-hour computing lab, from a student's PC in a residence hall, or from the student's home if there is a modem. Otherwise, the system may be accessed weekdays 8:30 a.m. to midnight in the PC lab. There are no time limits and no fees. The school strongly recommends that student's have their own Celeron 400 with 64 MB RAM, 8 GB or more hard drive, and 8M VideoRam.

HOPE COLLEGE
Holland, MI 49423

(616) 395-7469
(800) 968-7850; Fax: (616) 395-7130

Full-time: 1110 men, 1665 women	**Faculty:** 204; IIB, ++$
Part-time: 74 men, 94 women	**Ph.D.s:** 80%
Graduate: none	**Student/Faculty:** 14 to 1
Year: semesters, summer session	**Tuition:** $16,024
Application Deadline: open	**Room & Board:** $5030
Freshman Class: 2089 applied, 1863 accepted, 728 enrolled	
SAT I Verbal/Math: 582/592	**ACT:** 25 **VERY COMPETITIVE**

Hope College, founded by Dutch pioneers in 1866, is a liberal arts institution affiliated with the Reformed Church in America. In addition to regional accreditation, Hope has baccalaureate program accreditation with CSWE, NASAD, NASM, NCATE, and NLN. The 2 libraries contain 308,245 volumes, 245,923 microform items, and 10,654 audiovisual forms/CDs, and subscribe to 1535 periodicals. Computerized library services include the card catalog, interlibrary loans, and database searching. Special learning facilities include a learning resource center, art gallery, radio station, tv station, academic support center, and modern and classical language lab. The 45-acre campus is in a suburban area 26 miles southwest of Grand Rapids and 5 miles east of Lake Michigan. Including residence halls, there are 105 buildings.

Programs of Study: Hope confers B.A., B.S., B.Mus., and B.S.N. degrees. Bachelor's degrees are awarded in BIOLOGICAL SCIENCE (biochemistry and biology/biological science), BUSINESS (accounting and business administration and management), COMMUNICATIONS AND THE ARTS (communications, dance, dramatic arts, English, fine arts, French, German, music, and Spanish), COMPUTER AND PHYSICAL SCIENCE (chemistry, computer science, geology, mathematics, and physics), EDUCATION (art, business, elementary, foreign languages, music, science, secondary, and special), ENGINEERING AND ENVIRONMENTAL DESIGN (engineering), HEALTH PROFESSIONS (nursing, predentistry, and premedicine), SOCIAL SCIENCE (economics, history, international relations, philosophy, physical fitness/movement, political science/government, prelaw, psychology, religion, social work, and sociology). Preprofessional, biological sciences, and psychology are the strongest academically. Business, biology, and English are the largest.

Special: The college offers internships in all academic areas as well as on-campus work-study programs, study abroad, and Washington, Chicago, New York, and Philadelphia semesters. Students may take dual majors or work toward a 3-2 engineering degree with Michigan, Case Western, and Washington universities, as well as others. There are 20 national honor societies, including Phi Beta Kappa.

Admissions: 89% of the 1999-2000 applicants were accepted. The SAT I scores for the 1999-2000 freshman class were: Verbal--16% below 500, 43% between 500 and 599, 31% between 600 and 700, and 10% above 700; Math--15% below 500, 38% between 500 and 599, 37% between 600 and 700, and 12% above 700. The ACT scores were 9% below 21, 42% between 21 and 25, 43% between 26 and 30, and 6% above 30. 58% of the current freshmen were in the top fifth of their class; 81% were in the top two fifths. There were 15 National Merit finalists. 54 freshmen graduated first in their class.

Requirements: The SAT I or ACT is required. The college requires a high school transcript, which must include 4 years of English, 2 each of math, a foreign language, and social science, and 1 year of a lab science, as well as 5 other academic courses. The college requires submission of an essay and recommends an interview. A portfolio or audition is required for certain majors. The GED is considered. AP and CLEP credits are accepted. Important factors in the admissions decision are advanced placement or honor courses, leadership record, and evidence of special talent.

Procedure: Freshmen are admitted fall, winter, and spring. Entrance exams should be taken during spring of the junior year or fall of the senior year. There is a deferred admissions plan. Application deadlines are open; the fee is $25. Notification is sent on a rolling basis.

Financial Aid: In 1999-2000, 89% of all students received some form of financial aid. 55% of freshmen and 51% of continuing students received need-based aid. The average freshman award was $11,834. Of that total, scholarships or need-based grants averaged $9034 ($21,054 maximum); loans averaged $3306 ($4924 maximum); and work contracts averaged $1500 maximum. 82% of undergraduates work part time. Average annual earnings from campus work are $1021. The average financial indebtedness of the 1999 graduate was $15,152. Hope is a member of CSS. The CSS/Profile or FAFSA is required. The fall application deadline is February 15.

Computers: The mainframe is a DEC VAX 4200. Terminals and PCs are located in most dormitories and academic buildings and in the library and the student center. All students may access the system 24 hours a day. There are no time limits and no fees.

HOUGHTON COLLEGE
Houghton, NY 14744

(716) 567-9353
(800) 777-2556; Fax: (716) 567-9522

Full-time: 484 men, 834 women	**Faculty:** 78; IIB, av$
Part-time: 26 men, 35 women	**Ph.D.s:** 82%
Graduate: none	**Student/Faculty:** 17 to 1
Year: 4-4-1	**Tuition:** $14,590
Application Deadline: open	**Room & Board:** $5160
Freshman Class: 1000 applied, 913 accepted, 293 enrolled	
SAT I Verbal/Math: 591/576	**ACT:** 26 **VERY COMPETITIVE**

Houghton College, founded in 1883, is a Christian liberal arts college with more than 40 majors and programs. In addition to regional accreditation, Houghton has baccalaureate program accreditation with NASM. The library contains 219,908 volumes, 25,595 microform items, and 5407 audiovisual forms/CDs, and subscribes to 3036 periodicals. Computerized library services include the card catalog, interlibrary loans, and database searching. Special learning facilities include an art gallery, radio station, and equestrian center. The 1300-acre campus is in a rural area 65 miles southeast of Buffalo, and 70 miles southwest of Rochester. Including residence halls, there are 17 buildings.

Programs of Study: Houghton confers B.A., B.S., and B.M. degrees. Associate degrees are also awarded. Bachelor's degrees are awarded in BIOLOGICAL SCIENCE (biology/biological science), BUSINESS (accounting, business administration and management, and recreation and leisure services), COMMUNICATIONS AND THE ARTS (art, communications, creative writing, English, French, music performance, music theory and composition, and Spanish), COMPUTER AND PHYSICAL SCIENCE (chemistry, computer science, mathematics, physics, and science), EDUCATION (elementary, music, physical, science, and vocational), ENGINEERING AND ENVIRONMENTAL DESIGN (environmental science), HEALTH PROFESSIONS (medical technology), SOCIAL SCIENCE (biblical studies, history, humanities, international studies, ministries, philosophy, political science/government, psychology, religion, and sociology). Biology, chemistry, and religion are the strongest academically. Elementary education, biology, and psychology are the largest.

Special: Students may cross-register with members of the Western New York Consortium. Internships are available in psychology, social work, business, graphic design, communication, athletic training, recreation, English, and Christian education. Study abroad in 25 countries, a Washington semester, dual majors, and a 3-2 engineering degree with Clarkson and Washington Universities. Credit for military experience and nondegree study are possible. There are 2 national honor societies, and a freshman honors program.

Admissions: 91% of the 1999-2000 applicants were accepted. The SAT I scores for the 1999-2000 freshman class were: Verbal--14% below 500, 40% between 500 and 599, 37% between 600 and 700, and 9% above 700; Math--16% below 500, 46% between 500 and 599, 31% between 600 and 700, and 7% above 700. The ACT scores were 13% below 21, 24% between 21 and 23, 30% between 24 and 26, 14% between 27 and 28, and 19% above 28. 53% of the current freshmen were in the top fifth of their class; 80% were in the top two fifths. There were 5 National Merit semifinalists. 16 freshmen graduated first in their class.

Requirements: The SAT I or ACT is required. Houghton requires applicants to be in the upper 50% of their class. A GPA of 2.5 is required. A minimum composite score of 900 on the SAT I or 20 on the ACT is recommended. Applicants must graduate from an accredited secondary school or have a GED. A total of 16 academic credits is recommended, including 4 of English, 3 of social studies, and 2 each of foreign language, math, and science. An essay is required. Music students must audition. An interview is recommended. On-line applications are accepted at, www.houghton.edu. AP and CLEP credits are accepted. Important factors in the admissions decision are personality/intangible qualities, recommendations by school officials, and advanced placement or honor courses.

Procedure: Freshmen are admitted fall and spring. Entrance exams should be taken in the spring of the junior year or fall of the senior year. There are early admissions and deferred admissions plans. Application deadlines are open. The application fee is $25. Notification of regular decision is sent January 1.

Financial Aid: In 1999-2000, 98% of all freshmen and 93% of continuing students received some form of financial aid. 76% of freshmen and 81% of continuing students received need-based aid. The average freshman award was $9907. Of that total, scholarships or need-based grants averaged $6885 ($19,590 maximum); loans averaged $3003 ($18,925 maximum); and work contracts averaged $1200 ($1500 maximum). 54% of undergraduates work part time. Average annual earnings from campus work are $658. Houghton is a member of CSS. The FAFSA and the college's own financial statement are required. The fall application deadline is March 15.

Computers: The mainframe is a DEC VAX 8200. For the 1999-2000 school year, laptops will be issued to all newly entering class of 2001, class of 2002, and class of 2003 students. All students have access to 2 computer labs (51 PCs total) from 6 a.m. to midnight 6 days per week and also to a smaller lab of 12 PCs available 24 hours a day, 7 days per week. All students may access the system. Those who have laptops or other compatible systems also have access 24 hours a day through network connections in each dorm room (1 port per pillow). There are no time limits and no fees. Students must have PCs. The required make and model may change from year to year.

HOWARD PAYNE UNIVERSITY
Brownwood, TX 76801-2794

(915) 649-8027
(800) 880-4478; Fax: (915) 649-8901

Full-time: 598 men, 568 women	**Faculty:** 78
Part-time: 150 men, 180 women	**Ph.D.s:** 55%
Graduate: none	**Student/Faculty:** 15 to 1
Year: semesters, summer session	**Tuition:** $9000
Application Deadline: August 15	**Room & Board:** $3960
Freshman Class: 499 enrolled	
SAT I Verbal/Math: 546/528	**ACT:** 24 **VERY COMPETITIVE**

Howard Payne University, founded in 1889 and affiliated with the Baptist General Convention of Texas, offers undergraduate programs in the arts and sciences, business administration, education, Christianity, music, and social sciences. There are 6 undergraduate schools. In addition to regional accreditation, HPU has baccalaureate program accreditation with CSWE and NASM. The library contains 111,000 volumes, 260,000 microform items, and 6800 audiovisual forms/CDs, and subscribes to 805 periodicals. Computerized library services include the card catalog, interlibrary loans, and database searching. Special learning facilities include a radio station, a children's literature center, an audio production facility, a TV production studio, and a video editing facility. The 29-acre campus is in a small town 120 miles southwest of Dallas/Fort Worth. Including residence halls, there are 23 buildings.

Programs of Study: HPU confers B.A., B.S., B.A.A.S, B.B.A., and B.M. degrees. Bachelor's degrees are awarded in BIOLOGICAL SCIENCE (biology/biological science), BUSINESS (accounting and business administration and management), COMMUNICATIONS AND THE ARTS (art, communications, dramatic arts, English, multimedia, music, and Spanish), COMPUTER AND PHYSICAL SCIENCE (chemistry, computer science, and mathematics), EDUCATION (art, athletic training, elementary, and secondary), ENGINEERING AND ENVIRONMENTAL DESIGN (environmental science and occupational safety and health), HEALTH PROFESSIONS (medical technology), SOCIAL SCIENCE (Christian studies, counseling/psychology, history, liberal arts/general studies, physical fitness/movement, political science/government, psychology, social work, and sociology). Biology, chemistry, and political science are the strongest academically. Business management, elementary education, and exercise and sports science are the largest.

Special: Cross-registration is offered with several hospitals, and internships are available in many fields. HPU offers credit for experience for B.A.A.S. candidates only, study abroad in Israel and England, pass/fail options, and work-study programs. Special programs include the Douglas MacArthur Academy of Freedom, an interdisciplinary honors program in the social sciences; a chemistry honors program; and a provisional program for underprepared students. There are 4 national honor societies, including Phi Beta Kappa, a freshman honors program, and 2 departmental honors programs.

Admissions: The SAT I scores for the 1999-2000 freshman class were: Verbal--25% below 500, 54% between 500 and 599, 20% between 600 and 700, and 1% above 700; Math--37% below 500, 48% between 500 and 599, 13% between 600 and 700, and 2% above 700. The ACT scores were 17% below 21, 34% between 21 and 23, 36% between 24 and 26, 8% between 27 and 28, and 5% above 28. 52% of the current freshmen were in the top fifth of their class; 84% were in the top two fifths. There was 1 National Merit finalist. 7 freshmen graduated first in their class.

Requirements: The SAT I or ACT is required. Applicants must be graduates of an accredited secondary school or have a GED and have completed 3 credits of English, 2 of science or math, 1 of social science, and the remaining from courses approved by the Texas Education Agency. Graduates of high schools or home study programs that are not accredited by a regional or state accrediting agency will have their work reviewed by the admissions committee on an individual basis. AP and CLEP credits are accepted. Important factors in the admissions decision are recommendations by school officials, leadership record, and personality/intangible qualities.

Procedure: Freshmen are admitted to all sessions. Entrance exams should be taken during the senior year. There is an early admissions plan. Applications should be filed by August 15 for fall entry and January 1 for spring entry, along with a $25 fee. Notification is sent on a rolling basis.

Financial Aid: In 1999-2000, 80% of all freshmen and 90% of continuing students received some form of financial aid. 55% of freshmen and 60% of continuing students received need-based aid. The average freshman award was $7225. Of that total, scholarships or need-based grants averaged $1500 ($3000 maximum); loans averaged $2625 ($7500 maximum); and work contracts averaged $1200 ($2000 maximum). 60% of undergraduates work part time. Average annual earnings from campus work are $2000. The average financial indebtedness of the 1999 graduate was $16,500. The FFS is required. The fall application deadline is March 1.

Computers: The mainframe is an IBM AS/400. 11 computer labs, with a total of approximately 225 computers, are available to all students. Also available are

35 computers on a 286 Novell Local Area Network. All students may access the system 24 hours a day in 3 labs in the dormitories and 8 a.m. to 10 p.m., Monday through Friday in the Instructional Building labs. There are no time limits and no fees.

HUNTINGDON COLLEGE
Montgomery, AL 36106-2148　　　　　　　　　　　　**(334) 833-4497**
(800) 763-0313; Fax: (334) 833-4347

Full-time: 240 men, 381 women	**Faculty:** 46; IIB, --$
Part-time: 25 men, 59 women	**Ph.D.s:** 80%
Graduate: none	**Student/Faculty:** 14 to 1
Year: 4-1-4, summer session	**Tuition:** $11,410
Application Deadline: open	**Room & Board:** $5200
Freshman Class: 691 applied, 542 accepted, 165 enrolled	
SAT I Verbal/Math: 560/580	**ACT:** 25　　**VERY COMPETITIVE**

Huntingdon College, founded in 1854, is a private liberal arts institution related to the United Methodist Church. In addition to regional accreditation, Huntingdon has baccalaureate program accreditation with NASM. The library contains 102,074 volumes, 47,443 microform items, and 1517 audiovisual forms/CDs, and subscribes to 391 periodicals. Computerized library services include interlibrary loans and database searching. Special learning facilities include a learning resource center, art gallery, recital hall, and theater. The 58-acre campus is in a suburban area 90 miles south of Birmingham. Including residence halls, there are 18 buildings.

Programs of Study: Huntingdon confers the B.A. degree. Associate degrees are also awarded. Bachelor's degrees are awarded in AGRICULTURE (soil science), BIOLOGICAL SCIENCE (biology/biological science), BUSINESS (accounting and business administration and management), COMMUNICATIONS AND THE ARTS (art, arts administration/management, communications, dance, dramatic arts, English, music, musical theater, and speech/debate/rhetoric), COMPUTER AND PHYSICAL SCIENCE (chemistry, computer science, and mathematics), EDUCATION (art, dance, early childhood, elementary, music, and physical), ENGINEERING AND ENVIRONMENTAL DESIGN (computer graphics), HEALTH PROFESSIONS (exercise science and prepharmacy), SOCIAL SCIENCE (American studies, European studies, history, international studies, political science/government, psychology, public administration, public affairs, religion, and religious education). Biology, chemistry, and psychology are the strongest academically. Biology, business, education are the largest.

Special: The Huntingdon plan includes an opportunity for travel/study experiences offered as part of regular educational costs, hands-on learning experiences in every program of study, dual majors, internships, and co-op programs in business and computer science. The public affairs tri-subject major combines politics with 2 other areas, including history, philosophy, psychology, and communications. Cross-registration is available with Auburn University Montgomery, Faulkner University, and the Marine Environmental Sciences Consortium in Dauphin Island. There are 14 national honor societies, and 13 departmental honors programs.

Admissions: 78% of the 1999-2000 applicants were accepted. The SAT I scores for the 1999-2000 freshman class were: Verbal--10% below 500, 54% between 500 and 599, 32% between 600 and 700, and 4% above 700; Math--21% below 500, 36% between 500 and 599, 39% between 600 and 700, and 4% above 700. The ACT scores were 5% below 21, 27% between 21 and 23, 38% between 24

and 26, 8% between 27 and 28, and 22% above 28. 64% of the current freshmen were in the top fifth of their class; 86% were in the top two fifths. 12 freshmen graduated first in their class.

Requirements: The SAT I or ACT is required. Huntingdon requires applicants to be in the upper 50% of their class. A GPA of 2.3 is required. Applicants should have completed 4 years of high school English, 3 credits each in math and history, and 2 credits each of science, foreign language, and humanities. An interview is recommended. A portfolio or audition may be required. Students can apply online via CollegeView and by using the Apply CD-ROM. AP and CLEP credits are accepted. Important factors in the admissions decision are evidence of special talent, leadership record, and advanced placement or honor courses.

Procedure: Freshmen are admitted fall and spring. Entrance exams should be taken in the spring of the junior year. There is an early admissions plan. Application deadlines are open, along with a $25 fee. Notification is sent on a rolling basis.

Financial Aid: In 1999-2000, 98% of all freshmen and 93% of continuing students received some form of financial aid. 61% of all students received need-based aid. The average freshman award was $9911. Of that total, scholarships or need-based grants averaged $6606 ($10,500 maximum); loans averaged $2348 ($6625 maximum); work contracts averaged $412 ($1236 maximum); and Alabama Student Grants averaged $545 ($768 maximum). 79% of undergraduates work part time. Average annual earnings from campus work are $850. The average financial indebtedness of the 1999 graduate was $15,262. Huntingdon is a member of CSS. The FAFSA and the college's own financial statement are required. The fall application deadline is April 15.

Computers: The mainframe is a network of powerful PCs. All freshmen are provided a Gateway 2000 computer, which they may keep upon graduation. The computers include Windows 98, Netscape Communicator, Corel WordPerfect Suite 8.0, Oxford Biblical Library, and other required software. All residence hall rooms, classrooms, and faculty and administrative offices have direct access to the Internet. Students living off campus have dial-up access to the network. The computer center has 16 PCs and 18 Power Macs, 2 laser printers, a high-resolution color printer, a color scanner, 2 computer-mounted digital cameras, 2 portable digital cameras, and 2 digital drawing tablets. Computers and ink-jet printers are also located in residence hall study rooms. All students may access the system 24 hours a day, 7 days a week. There are no time limits and no fees.

ILLINOIS INSTITUTE OF TECHNOLOGY
Chicago, IL 60616

(312) 567-3025
(800) 448-2329; Fax: (312) 567-6939

Full-time: 1045 men, 315 women	**Faculty:** 293; I, -$
Part-time: 405 men, 85 women	**Ph.D.s:** 99%
Graduate: 2820 men, 1440 women	**Student/Faculty:** 5 to 1
Year: semesters, summer session	**Tuition:** $16,660
Application Deadline: open	**Room & Board:** $5000
Freshman Class: n/av	
SAT I or ACT: required	**VERY COMPETITIVE**

Illinois Institute of Technology, founded in 1890, is a private institution offering undergraduate programs in architecture, engineering, applied mathematics, biology, chemistry, physics, computing, political science, and psychology. Figures given in the above capsule are approximate. There are 3 undergraduate and 7 graduate schools. In addition to regional accreditation, IIT has baccalaureate program accreditation with ABET. The library contains 538,166 volumes, 556,458 microform items, and 1555 audiovisual forms/CDs, and subscribes to 5811 periodicals. Computerized library services include the card catalog, interlibrary loans, and database searching. Special learning facilities include a learning resource center and radio station. The 120-acre campus is in an urban area 3 miles south of downtown Chicago. Including residence halls, there are 31 buildings.

Programs of Study: IIT confers B.S. and B.Arch. degrees. Master's and doctoral degrees are also awarded. Bachelor's degrees are awarded in BIOLOGICAL SCIENCE (biology/biological science and molecular biology), COMMUNICATIONS AND THE ARTS (technical and business writing), COMPUTER AND PHYSICAL SCIENCE (chemistry, computer science, information sciences and systems, mathematics, and physics), ENGINEERING AND ENVIRONMENTAL DESIGN (aeronautical engineering, architectural engineering, architecture, chemical engineering, civil engineering, computer engineering, electrical/electronics engineering, environmental engineering, mechanical engineering, and metallurgical engineering), SOCIAL SCIENCE (political science/government and psychology). All engineering programs are the strongest academically. Architecture and engineering are the largest.

Special: IIT offers numerous internships, co-op programs in engineering, and dual majors. Study abroad may be arranged in Mexico, People's Republic of China, and several European countries. A 3-2 engineering degree is offered with Saint Xavier College. Accelerated degree programs are available in prelaw. There are 3 national honor societies, and a freshman honors program.

Requirements: The SAT I or ACT is required. In addition, graduation from an accredited secondary school is required for admission. The school requires 16 academic credits, including 4 units each of English and math, 2 of science, and 1 of history. Applications are accepted on-line at the school's web site and via CollegeLink and numerous others. AP credits are accepted.

Procedure: Freshmen are admitted fall and spring. Entrance exams should be taken by December of the senior year. There is a deferred admissions plan. Application deadlines are open. There is a $30 fee. Notification is sent on a rolling basis.

Financial Aid: In a recent year, 90% of all freshmen and 80% of continuing students received some form of financial aid. 85% of freshmen and 80% of continuing students received need-based aid. The average freshman award was $23,407. Of that total, scholarships or need-based grants averaged $13,661 ($25,433 maximum); loans averaged $2625 ($12,000 maximum); and work contracts averaged $1500; and Pell, SEOG, and state grants averaged $4700 ($8950 maximum). 50% of undergraduates work part time. Average annual earnings from campus work are $1500. The average financial indebtedness of the 1999 graduate was $17,500. IIT is a member of CSS. The FAFSA is required. Check with the school for current deadlines.

Computers: The mainframes are a DEC VAX 3600 and an SGI Challenge. There are also many Macs and SGI UNIX workstations available in academic buildings. Dormitory rooms are linked to the university network, providing Internet and E-mail access. All students may access the system. There are no time limits and no fees. It is recommended that all students have personal computers, specifically computers using the MS/DOS operating system.

ILLINOIS WESLEYAN UNIVERSITY

Bloomington, IL 61702-2900
(309) 556-3031
(800) 332-2498; Fax: (309) 556-3411

Full-time: 908 men, 1169 women	**Faculty:** 171; IIB, ++$
Part-time: 4 men, 9 women	**Ph.D.s:** 95%
Graduate: none	**Student/Faculty:** 12 to 1
Year: 4-4-1	**Tuition:** $19,370
Application Deadline: March 1	**Room & Board:** $4980
Freshman Class: 2565 applied, 1644 accepted, 571 enrolled	
SAT I Verbal/Math: 610/630	**ACT:** 27 **HIGHLY COMPETITIVE**

Illinois Wesleyan University, founded in 1850, is a private institution offering programs in liberal arts, fine arts, and nursing. In addition to regional accreditation, Illinois Wesleyan has baccalaureate program accreditation with NASM and NLN. The 2 libraries contain 254,195 volumes, 13,919 microform items, and 18,500 audiovisual forms/CDs, and subscribe to 1045 periodicals. Computerized library services include the card catalog, interlibrary loans, and database searching. Special learning facilities include a learning resource center, art gallery, radio station, TV station, natural history preserve, observatory, multicultural center, and 20-acre tract of virgin timberland. The 72-acre campus is in a suburban area 130 miles from Chicago and 160 miles from St. Louis. Including residence halls, there are 70 buildings.

Programs of Study: Illinois Wesleyan confers B.A., B.S., B.F.A., B.Mus., B.Mus.Ed., and B.S.N. degrees. Bachelor's degrees are awarded in BIOLOGICAL SCIENCE (biology/biological science), BUSINESS (accounting, banking and finance, business administration and management, insurance and risk management, and international business management), COMMUNICATIONS AND THE ARTS (dramatic arts, English, fine arts, French, German, music, music theory and composition, musical theater, piano/organ, Russian, Spanish, and voice), COMPUTER AND PHYSICAL SCIENCE (chemistry, computer science, mathematics, natural sciences, and physics), EDUCATION (elementary), HEALTH PROFESSIONS (nursing), SOCIAL SCIENCE (economics, history, international studies, philosophy, political science/government, psychology, religion, and sociology). Business and economics, the fine arts, and the physical sciences are the strongest academically. The physical sciences, music, and business and economics are the largest.

Special: There are several co-op programs, including a 3-2 degree in forestry and environmental studies with Duke University, a 2-2 engineering degree with the University of Illinois, and 3-2 engineering programs with a number of universities. Students may study abroad in many locations throughout the world through the Institute for the International Education of Students (IES), Pembroke College, University of Oxford, Beaver College Center for Study Abroad, and many other programs. The university also offers work-study, internships in many areas, Washington and United Nations semesters, dual and student-designed majors, and pass/fail options. There are 23 national honor societies.

Admissions: 64% of the 1999-2000 applicants were accepted. The SAT I scores for the 1999-2000 freshman class were: Verbal--4% below 500, 38% between 500 and 599, 40% between 600 and 700, and 18% above 700; Math--2% below 500, 31% between 500 and 599, 46% between 600 and 700, and 21% above 700. The ACT scores were 10% between 21 and 23, 28% between 24 and 26, 26% between 27 and 28, and 36% above 28. 73% of the current freshmen were in the top fifth of their class; 96% were in the top two fifths. There were 18 National Merit finalists and 20 semifinalists. 46 freshmen graduated first in their class.

Requirements: The SAT I or ACT is required. Illinois Wesleyan requires applicants to be in the upper 30% of their class. A GPA of 3.0 is required. In addition, applicants should graduate from an accredited secondary school, though a GED may be accepted. 15 academic credits are required, including 4 units of English, 3 each of natural science, math, and a foreign language, and 2 of social science. An audition is required for drama and music majors. Applications are accepted on-line. AP and CLEP credits are accepted. Important factors in the admissions decision are advanced placement or honor courses, evidence of special talent, and leadership record.

Procedure: Freshmen are admitted fall and spring. Entrance exams should be taken in the spring of the junior year. There are early admissions and deferred admissions plans. Applications should be filed by March 1 for fall entry. Notification is sent on a rolling basis.

Financial Aid: In 1999-2000, 80% of all freshmen and 87% of continuing students received some form of financial aid. 65% of freshmen and 61% of continuing students received need-based aid. The average freshman award was $13,290. Of that total, scholarships or need-based grants averaged $10,786 ($19,340 maximum); loans averaged $3216 ($4320 maximum); and work contracts averaged $1636 ($1895 maximum). 51% of undergraduates work part time. Average annual earnings from campus work are $1743. The average financial indebtedness of the 1999 graduate was $16,258. Illinois Wesleyan is a member of CSS. The CSS/Profile or FAFSA and the college's own financial statement are required. The fall application deadline is March 1.

Computers: The mainframe is an IBM AS/400. There are more than 450 IBM, Mac, and other PC terminals available in various computer labs and dormitories. Access to the Internet and World Wide Web is available through the campus network. All students may access the system. There are no time limits and no fees.

INDIANA UNIVERSITY - PURDUE UNIVERSITY INDIANAPOLIS
Indianapolis, IN 46202-5143
(317) 274-4591
Fax: (317) 278-1862

Full-time: 4654 men, 6837 women	**Faculty:** 1676; IIA, +$
Part-time: 3473 men, 5100 women	**Ph.D.s:** 91%
Graduate: 1089 men, 1564 women	**Student/Faculty:** 7 to 1
Year: semesters, summer session	**Tuition:** $3713 ($10,961)
Application Deadline: open	**Room & Board:** $3450
Freshman Class: 5763 applied, 4956 accepted, 3455 enrolled	
SAT I Verbal/Math: 478/471	**ACT:** 19 **LESS COMPETITIVE**

The Indianapolis campus, founded in 1946, has offered undergraduate and graduate instruction under the auspices of both Purdue and Indiana universities since 1969. The state-controlled institution serves a primarily commuter student body and offers degree programs in the arts and sciences, business, education, engineering and technology, health science, religious studies, and professional training. There are 16 undergraduate and 5 graduate schools. In addition to regional accreditation, IUPUI has baccalaureate program accreditation with AACSB, ABET, ACCE, ACEJMC, ADA, APTA, CAHEA, CSWE, NASAD, NASM, NCATE, and NLN. The 4 libraries contain 1,283,015 volumes, 2,306,273 microform items, and 129,233 audiovisual forms/CDs, and subscribe to 16,865 periodicals. Computerized library services include the card catalog and database searching. Special learning facilities include an art gallery, 85-acre medical center, and electronic classroom. The 370-acre campus is in an urban area near downtown Indianapolis. Including residence halls, there are 58 buildings.

Programs of Study: IUPUI confers B.A., B.S., B.A.E., B.F.A., B.G.S., B.S.E., B.S.E.E., B.S.M.E., and B.S.W. degrees. Associate, master's, and doctoral degrees are also awarded. Bachelor's degrees are awarded in BIOLOGICAL SCIENCE (biology/biological science), BUSINESS (accounting, banking and finance, business administration and management, business economics, human resources, insurance, labor studies, marketing/retailing/merchandising, office supervision and management, real estate, and tourism), COMMUNICATIONS AND THE ARTS (American Sign Language, art history and appreciation, ceramic art and design, communications, English, fine arts, French, German, journalism, media arts, painting, photography, printmaking, sculpture, Spanish, and speech/debate/rhetoric), COMPUTER AND PHYSICAL SCIENCE (chemistry, computer science, geology, mathematics, and physics), EDUCATION (art, elementary, health, physical, secondary, and social studies), ENGINEERING AND ENVIRONMENTAL DESIGN (computer engineering, computer technology, construction technology, electrical/electronics engineering, electrical/electronics engineering technology, engineering, engineering technology, environmental science, manufacturing technology, mechanical engineering, mechanical engineering technology, and woodworking), HEALTH PROFESSIONS (cytotechnology, dental hygiene, environmental health science, health care administration, medical laboratory technology, medical technology, nuclear medical technology, nursing, occupational therapy, physical therapy, public health, radiation therapy, and respiratory therapy), SOCIAL SCIENCE (anthropology, criminal justice, economics, geography, history, liberal arts/general studies, philosophy, political science/government, psychology, public affairs, religion, social work, and sociology). Engineering and technology, nursing, and education are the largest.

Special: There is a metropolitan studies program for career work in the city and cross-registration with the Consortium for Urban Education. IUPUI also offers study abroad, combined B.A.-B.S. degree programs, internships, work-study programs, dual majors, student-designed majors, nondegree study, nontraditional programs for adult learners, and interdisciplinary majors such as business economics and public policy, health occupations education, and interdisciplinary engineering. There are 2 national honor societies, a freshman honors program, and 2 departmental honors programs.

Admissions: 86% of the 1999-2000 applicants were accepted. 22% of the current freshmen were in the top quarter of their class; 52% were in the top half.

Requirements: The SAT I or ACT is required for recent high school graduates. Applicants should be graduates of an accredited high school, rank in the upper half of their class, and have completed 14 Carnegie units, including 4 in English, 3 in math, 2 in social studies, and 1 in lab science. The university accepts applications on computer disk. AP and CLEP credits are accepted. Recommendations by school officials is an important factor in the admissions decision.

Procedure: Freshmen are admitted to all sessions. Entrance exams should be taken by the end of junior year or fall of the senior year. There are early admissions and deferred admissions plans. Application deadlines are open; the fee is $35. Notification is sent on a rolling basis.

Financial Aid: In a recent year, 58% of all freshmen and 54% of continuing students received some form of financial aid. 58% of freshmen and 54% of continuing students received need-based aid. The average freshman award was $1300. Of that total, scholarships or need-based grants averaged $935; loans averaged $2259; and work contracts averaged $2424. Average annual earnings from campus work are $500. IUPUI is a member of CSS. The FAFSA is required. For priority consideration, the fall application deadline is March 1.

Computers: The mainframe is an IBM 3090. PCs are available for all students. All students may access the system up to 24 hours a day in some clusters. There are no time limits. The fee is $161 per semester.

INDIANA UNIVERSITY AT BLOOMINGTON
Bloomington, IN 47405-1106

(812) 855-0661
Fax: (812) 855-5102

Full-time: 11,983 men, 14,156 women	**Faculty:** 1627; I, av$
Part-time: 669 men, 653 women	**Ph.D.s:** 87%
Graduate: 3161 men, 3304 women	**Student/Faculty:** 16 to 1
Year: semesters, summer session	**Tuition:** $4212 ($12,920)
Application Deadline: February 1	**Room & Board:** $5492
Freshman Class: 20,095 applied, 16,238 accepted, 6583 enrolled	
SAT I Verbal/Math: 545/553	**ACT:** 24 **VERY COMPETITIVE**

Indiana University Bloomington, founded in 1820, is a comprehensive institution that is part of the Indiana University system. The university offers undergraduate programs in arts and sciences, allied health sciences, business, dentistry, education, health, physical education, recreation, journalism, music, nursing, optometry, public and environmental affairs, social work, and informatics. There are 9 undergraduate and 9 graduate schools. In addition to regional accreditation, IU has baccalaureate program accreditation with AACSB, ACBSP, ACEJMC, ADA, APTA, ASLA, CAHEA, CSWE, FIDER, NASAD, NASM, NCATE, and NLN. The 22 libraries contain 6,042,532 volumes, 4,160,651 microform items, and 623,835 audiovisual forms/CDs, and subscribe to 42,293 periodicals. Computerized library services include the card catalog, interlibrary loans, and database searching. Special learning facilities include a learning resource center, art gallery, natural history museum, radio station, TV station, observatory, arboretum, museum of world cultures, garden and nature center, musical arts center, and more than 70 research centers. The 1878-acre campus is in a small town 50 miles southwest of Indianapolis. Including residence halls, there are 489 buildings.

Programs of Study: IU confers B.A., B.S., B.F.A., B.M., B.M.E., and B.S.G.S. degrees. Associate, master's, and doctoral degrees are also awarded. Bachelor's degrees are awarded in BIOLOGICAL SCIENCE (biochemistry, biology/biological science, microbiology, and nutrition), BUSINESS (accounting, apparel and accessories marketing, banking and finance, business administration and management, business economics, entrepreneurial studies, insurance, labor studies, management information systems, marketing/retailing/merchandising, real estate, recreation and leisure services, sports management, and tourism), COMMUNICATIONS AND THE ARTS (audio technology, ballet, classics, communications, comparative literature, dance, dramatic arts, East Asian languages and literature, English, fine arts, folklore and mythology, French, German, guitar, Italian, jazz, journalism, Latin, linguistics, music, music performance, music theory and composition, piano/organ, Portuguese, Russian, Spanish, speech/debate/rhetoric, studio art, telecommunications, visual and performing arts, and voice), COMPUTER AND PHYSICAL SCIENCE (astronomy, astrophysics, chemistry, computer science, earth science, geology, information sciences and systems, mathematics, physics, and science), EDUCATION (athletic training, early childhood, educational media, elementary, health, middle school, music, physical, school psychology, secondary, and special), ENGINEERING AND ENVIRONMENTAL DESIGN (aerospace studies, environmental science, interior design, and occupational safety and health), HEALTH PROFESSIONS (health science, optometry, public health, and speech pathology/audiology), SOCIAL SCIENCE (African American studies, anthropology, cognitive science, criminal justice, dietetics, East Asian studies, economics, family/consumer studies, gender studies, geography, history, human development, international studies, Judaic studies, liberal arts/general studies, Near Eastern studies, parks and recreation management, philosophy, physical fitness/movement, political science/government, psychology, public administration, public affairs, religion, Russian and Slavic studies, social studies, sociology, and women's studies). Sciences, music, and business are the strongest academically. Business, education, and arts and sciences are the largest.

Special: IU offers cooperative programs with universities in many countries, including the People's Republic of China, a variety of internships, and study abroad in more than 25 countries. A Washington semester, work-study programs, B.A.-B.S. degrees in the sciences and liberal arts, dual majors, and the general studies degree through the School of Continuing Studies are available. Student-designed majors through the Individualized Major Program, credit for military experience, nondegree study through the School of Continuing Studies, and pass/fail options are also available. There are 18 national honor societies, including Phi Beta Kappa, and a freshman honors program.

Admissions: 81% of the 1999-2000 applicants were accepted. 55% of the current freshmen were in the top quarter of their class; 93% were in the top half. There were 26 National Merit finalists. 121 freshmen graduated first in their class.

Requirements: The SAT I or ACT is required. Applicants must be graduates of an accredited secondary high school or have a GED certificate. SAT II: Subject tests are recommended for credit and placement. Auditions for music majors are required. An interview is recommended for information purposes. Applications may be submitted on-line via the World Wide Web. AP and CLEP credits are accepted. Important factors in the admissions decision are advanced placement or honor courses, parents or siblings attending the school, and recommendations by school officials.

Procedure: Freshmen are admitted to all sessions. Entrance exams should be taken in the late junior year or early senior year. There is a deferred admissions plan. For priority consideration, applications should be filed by February 1 for fall entry, November 1 for spring entry, and February 1 for summer entry, along with a $40 fee. Notification is sent on a rolling basis.

Financial Aid: In a recent year, 42% of freshmen and 39% of continuing students received need-based aid. The average freshman award was $5007. Of that total, scholarships or need-based grants averaged $3965; loans averaged $2703; and work contracts averaged $1407. 71% of undergraduates work part time. Average annual earnings from campus work are $1453. The average financial indebtedness of the 1999 graduate was $8303. IU is a member of CSS. The FAFSA is required. For priority consideration, the fall application deadline is March 1.

Computers: The mainframe is a DEC system. More than 1500 Macs and PCs are available in more than 55 computing labs across campus. All dormitories are wired to handle student PCs. All students may access the system 24 hours a day. There are no time limits. The fee is $200. It is recommended that all students have personal computers, and computer science students must have them.

IOWA STATE UNIVERSITY
Ames, IA 50011-2011

(515) 294-5836
(800) 262-3810; Fax: (515) 294-2592

Full-time: 10,829 men, 8776 women	**Faculty:** 1086; I, av$
Part-time: 1059 men, 839 women	**Ph.D.s:** 87%
Graduate: 2483 men, 1726 women	**Student/Faculty:** 14 to 1
Year: semesters, summer session	**Tuition:** $2906 ($9748)
Application Deadline: August 21	**Room & Board:** $4171
Freshman Class: 12,172 applied, 10,717 accepted, 4085 enrolled	
SAT I Verbal/Math: 590/620	**ACT:** 24 **VERY COMPETITIVE**

Iowa State University, established in 1858, is a public land-grant institution offering undergraduate and graduate programs in agriculture, business, design, education, engineering, family and consumer sciences, liberal arts and sciences, and veterinary medicine. There are 8 schools undergraduate and 1 graduate school. In addition to regional accreditation, Iowa State has baccalaureate program accreditation with AACSB, ABET, ACEJMC, ADA, AHEA, ASLA, CSAB, FIDER, NAAB, NASM, and SAF. The library contains 2,167,294 volumes, 3,015,078 microform items, and 901,338 audiovisual forms/CDs, and subscribes to 22,455 periodicals. Computerized library services include the card catalog, interlibrary loans, and database searching. Special learning facilities include a learning resource center, art gallery, natural history museum, planetarium, radio station, and TV station. The 1788-acre campus is in a suburban area 30 miles north of Des Moines. Including residence halls, there are 175 buildings.

Programs of Study: Iowa State confers B.A, B.S., B.Arch., B.B.A., B.F.A., B.L.A., B.L.S., and B.Mus. degrees. Master's and doctoral degrees are also awarded. Bachelor's degrees are awarded in AGRICULTURE (agricultural business management, agricultural mechanics, agriculture, agronomy, animal science, dairy science, fishing and fisheries, forestry and related sciences, horticulture, international agriculture, plant protection (pest management), and plant science), BIOLOGICAL SCIENCE (biochemistry, biology/biological science, biophysics, botany, entomology, genetics, microbiology, nutrition, plant pathology, wildlife biology, and zoology), BUSINESS (accounting, banking and finance, business administration and management, fashion merchandising, hotel/motel and restaurant management, international business management, management science, marketing/retailing/merchandising, and transportation management), COMMUNICATIONS AND THE ARTS (advertising, communications, design, English, fine arts, French, German, graphic design, illustration, journalism, linguistics, music, Russian, Spanish, and speech/debate/rhetoric), COMPUTER AND PHYSICAL SCIENCE (atmospheric sciences and meteorology, chemistry, computer science, earth science, geology, mathematics, physics, and statistics), EDUCATION (agricultural, art, early childhood, elementary, health, home economics, industrial arts, middle school, music, physical, science, and secondary), ENGINEERING AND ENVIRONMENTAL DESIGN (aeronautical engineering, agricultural engineering, architecture, ceramic engineering, chemical engineering, city/community/regional planning, civil engineering, computer engineering, construction engineering, electrical/electronics engineering, engineering, engineering technology, environmental science, food services technology, industrial engineering technology, interior design, landscape architecture/design, mechanical engineering, and metallurgical engineering), SOCIAL SCIENCE (anthropology, child care/child and family studies, child psychology/development, dietetics, economics, family and community services, family/consumer resource management, family/consumer studies, fashion design and technology, food production/management/

services, food science, history, international relations, liberal arts/general studies, philosophy, political science/government, psychology, religion, social work, sociology, and textiles and clothing). Engineering, agriculture, and statistics are the strongest academically. Engineering, business, and agriculture are the largest.

Special: Iowa State offers cooperative programs in engineering, forestry, agronomy, chemistry, computer science, economics, agricultural systems technology, business administration, industrial technology, and performing arts, and cross-registration with the Universities of Iowa and Northern Iowa. Internships, study abroad in more than 100 countries, dual majors, the B.A.-B.S. degree, student-designed majors, and accelerated degree programs are available. Interdisciplinary studies include agricultural biochemistry, agricultural systems technology, animal ecology, public service and administration in agriculture, and engineering operations. There are work-study programs, a Washington semester, nondegree study, and pass/no pass options. There are 15 national honor societies, including Phi Beta Kappa, a freshman honors program, and 7 departmental honors programs.

Admissions: 88% of the 1999-2000 applicants were accepted. The SAT I scores for the 1999-2000 freshman class were: Verbal--16% below 500, 33% between 500 and 599, 29% between 600 and 700, and 19% above 700; Math--12% below 500, 26% between 500 and 599, 37% between 600 and 700, and 23% above 700. The ACT scores were 3% between 12 and 17, 40% between 18 and 23, 46% between 24 and 29, and 11% above 29. 56% of the current freshmen were in the top fifth of their class; 91% were in the top two fifths. There were 111 National Merit finalists.

Requirements: The SAT I or ACT is required. Iowa State requires applicants to be in the upper 50% of their class. Applicants must graduate from an accredited secondary school. The GED is accepted. For admission to freshman standing, students must have completed 4 years of English, 3 each of math and science, and 2 to 3 of social studies. For the College of Liberal Arts and Sciences, 2 years of a single foreign language are also required. Applications are accepted on-line via ExPAN, Apply, CollegeView, and others and at the school's web site. AP and CLEP credits are accepted.

Procedure: Freshmen are admitted to all sessions. Entrance exams should be taken during the spring of the junior year or the fall of the senior year. There is a deferred admissions plan. Applications should be filed by August 21 for fall entry and January 10 for spring entry, along with a $20 fee. Notification is sent on a rolling basis.

Financial Aid: In 1999-2000, 63% of all freshmen and 55% of continuing students received some form of financial aid. 53% of freshmen and 49% of continuing students received need-based aid. The average freshman award was $6032. Of that total, scholarships or need-based grants averaged $2430 ($3061 maximum); loans averaged $2924 ($3817 maximum); and work contracts averaged $3086 ($3993 maximum). 26% of undergraduates work part time. Average annual earnings from campus work are $3300. The average financial indebtedness of the 1999 graduate was $16,836. Iowa State is a member of CSS. The FAFSA is required. The fall application deadline is March 1.

Computers: More than 125 instructional computing labs and classrooms are located in campus buildings and residence halls. These sites contain more than 2200 PCs, Macs, and workstations. Almost all machines are connected to the campus network and the Internet. All enrolled students qualify for a network account, which gives them access to E-mail, the Web, newsgroups, and other network services. Word processors, spreadsheets, statistical analysis, programming languages, and other microcomputer and UNIX workstation application software are available. All students may access the system. Residence hall labs, Computation Center labs, and a few other sites are open 24 hours a day. Access to labs in academic buildings is restricted to building hours. There are no time limits. The fee is $47 per semester. Engineering, MIS, and computer science students pay a higher fee.

ITHACA COLLEGE
Ithaca, NY 14850-7020

(607) 274-3124
(800) 429-4274; Fax: (607) 274-1900

Full-time: 2451 men, 3084 women	**Faculty:** 392; IIA, av$
Part-time: 65 men, 102 women	**Ph.D.s:** 92%
Graduate: 62 men, 196 women	**Student/Faculty:** 14 to 1
Year: semesters, summer session	**Tuition:** $18,410
Application Deadline: March 1	**Room & Board:** $7956
Freshman Class: 8302 applied, 6101 accepted, 1587 enrolled	
SAT I or ACT: required	**VERY COMPETITIVE**

Ithaca College, founded in 1892, is a private college offering undergraduate and graduate programs in business, communications, health science and human performance, humanities and sciences, and music. There are 5 undergraduate schools and 1 graduate school. In addition to regional accreditation, Ithaca has baccalaureate program accreditation with APTA, NASM, and NRPA. The library contains 365,772 volumes, 272,898 microform items, and 31,556 audiovisual forms/CDs, and subscribes to 2400 periodicals. Computerized library services include the card catalog, interlibrary loans, and database searching. Special learning facilities include an art gallery, radio station, TV station, digital audio and video labs, speech, hearing, wellness, and physical therapy clinics, a greenhouse, a financial "trading room", an observatory, and electroacoustic music studios. The 757-acre campus is in a small town 250 miles northwest of New York City. Including residence halls, there are 60 buildings.

Programs of Study: Ithaca confers B.A., B.S., B.F.A., and Mus.B. degrees. Master's degrees are also awarded. Bachelor's degrees are awarded in BIOLOGICAL SCIENCE (biochemistry and biology/biological science), BUSINESS (accounting, banking and finance, business administration and management, business economics, human resources, international business management, marketing management, marketing/retailing/merchandising, organizational behavior, personnel management, recreation and leisure services, and sports management), COMMUNICATIONS AND THE ARTS (art, art history and appreciation, broadcasting, communications, dramatic arts, English, film arts, fine arts, French, German, jazz, journalism, languages, media arts, modern language, music, music performance, music theory and composition, musical theater, performing arts, photography, public relations, Spanish, speech/debate/rhetoric, studio art, telecommunications, theater design, theater management, video, and visual and performing arts), COMPUTER AND PHYSICAL SCIENCE (chemistry, computer mathematics, computer science, information sciences and systems, mathematics, and physics), EDUCATION (athletic training, education, education of the deaf and hearing impaired, educational media, English, foreign languages, health, mathematics, middle school, music, physical, science, secondary, social studies, and speech correction), ENGINEERING AND ENVIRONMENTAL DESIGN (environmental science), HEALTH PROFESSIONS (allied health, clinical science, community health work, health, health care administration, health science, hospital administration, occupational therapy, physical therapy, predentistry, premedicine, public health, recreation therapy, rehabilitation therapy, speech pathology/audiology, speech therapy, and sports medicine), SOCIAL SCIENCE (anthropology, economics, history, industrial and organizational psychology, interdisciplinary studies, liberal arts/general studies, philosophy, physical fitness/

movement, political science/government, prelaw, psychology, social studies, and sociology). Physical therapy, theater, and music are the strongest academically. Television-radio, music, and physical therapy are the largest.

Special: Cross-registration is available with Cornell University and Wells College. Opportunities are also provided for internships, work-study programs, dual majors, accelerated degree programs, nondegree study, pass/fail options, student-designed majors, a 3-2 engineering degree with Cornell University, a B.A.-B.S. degree, credit for life experience, and study abroad in London, Valencia, and other foreign cities. A 4-1 advanced business degree program and a 3-1 optometry program are also available. There are 21 national honor societies, a freshman honors program, and 16 departmental honors programs.

Admissions: 73% of the 1999-2000 applicants were accepted. The SAT I scores for the 1999-2000 freshman class were: Verbal--13% below 500, 44% between 500 and 599, 38% between 600 and 700, and 5% above 700; Math--14% below 500, 47% between 500 and 599, 35% between 600 and 700, and 4% above 700. 51% of the current freshmen were in the top fifth of their class; 79% were in the top two fifths. There were 6 National Merit finalists. 26 freshmen graduated first in their class.

Requirements: The SAT I or ACT is required. Ithaca requires applicants to be in the upper 25% of their class. In addition, applicants should be graduates of an accredited secondary school with a minimum of 16 Carnegie units, including 4 years of English, 3 each of math, science, and social studies, 2 of foreign language, and other college-preparatory electives. The GED is accepted. An essay is required, as is an audition for music and theater students. In some majors, a portfolio and an interview are recommended. Applications are accepted on-line at the school's web site. AP and CLEP credits are accepted.

Procedure: Freshmen are admitted fall and spring. Entrance exams should be taken in spring of the junior year or fall of the senior year. There are early decision, early admissions, and deferred admissions plans. Early decision applications should be filed by November 1; regular applications, by March 1 for fall entry and December 1 for spring entry, along with a $45 fee. Notification of early decision is sent December 15; regular decision, on a rolling basis. 254 early decision candidates were accepted for the 1999-2000 class.

Financial Aid: In 1999-2000, 81% of all freshmen and 78% of continuing students received some form of financial aid. 64% of freshmen and 65% of continuing students received need-based aid. The average freshman award was $14,701. Of that total, scholarships or need-based grants averaged $10,187 ($28,166 maximum); loans averaged $2891 ($8625 maximum); work contracts averaged $1428 ($2300 maximum); and tuition remission and veterans' benefits averaged $196 (18,410 maximum). 42% of undergraduates work part time. Average annual earnings from campus work are $1600. Ithaca is a member of CSS. The FAFSA is required. The CSS/Profile is required for early decision applicants only. The fall application deadline is March 1.

Computers: The mainframes are a DEC VAX 11/750 and a DEC VAX 11/785. Students may access the VAX mainframes from approximately 430 PCs/terminals in the library, computer labs, and classrooms. All residence halls are fully networked and have access to the Internet and Web. All students may access the system 24 hours a day. There are no time limits and no fees.

Full-time: 5565 men, 7620 women	**Faculty:** 642; IIA, +$
Part-time: 272 men, 211 women	**Ph.D.s:** n/av
Graduate: 232 men, 448 women	**Student/Faculty:** 21 to 1
Year: semesters, summer session	**Tuition:** $3926 ($9532)
Application Deadline: January 15	**Room & Board:** $5182
Freshman Class: 12,980 applied, 8494 accepted, 3039 enrolled	
SAT I Verbal/Math: 580/590	**VERY COMPETITIVE**

James Madison University, founded in 1908, is a public institution with programs in science and math, business, education and psychology, arts and letters, and integrated science and technology. There are 5 undergraduate and 1 graduate school. In addition to regional accreditation, JMU has baccalaureate program accreditation with AACSB, ADA, CSWE, FIDER, NASAD, NASM, NCATE, and NLN. The 3 libraries contain 503,254 volumes, 987,505 microform items, and 27,300 audiovisual forms/CDs, and subscribe to 2406 periodicals. Computerized library services include the card catalog, interlibrary loans, and database searching. Special learning facilities include a learning resource center, art gallery, planetarium, radio station, arboretum, music library, and CISAT Library Services. The 472-acre campus is in a small town 123 miles southwest of Washington, D.C. Including residence halls, there are 95 buildings.

Programs of Study: JMU confers B.A., B.S., B.B.A., B.F.A., B.I.S., B.M., B.S.N., and B.S.W. degrees. Master's and doctoral degrees are also awarded. Bachelor's degrees are awarded in BIOLOGICAL SCIENCE (biology/biological science), BUSINESS (accounting, banking and finance, business administration and management, business economics, hospitality management services, international business management, management science, marketing/retailing/merchandising, recreation and leisure services, and tourism), COMMUNICATIONS AND THE ARTS (art, art history and appreciation, communications, communications technology, dance, design, dramatic arts, English, fine arts, media arts, modern language, music, and speech/debate/rhetoric), COMPUTER AND PHYSICAL SCIENCE (chemistry, computer management, computer science, geology, information sciences and systems, mathematics, physics, science technology, and statistics), EDUCATION (business), HEALTH PROFESSIONS (health science, nursing, and speech pathology/audiology), SOCIAL SCIENCE (anthropology, dietetics, economics, geography, history, international studies, philosophy, physical fitness/movement, political science/government, psychology, public administration, religion, social science, social work, and sociology). Biology, business, and communication are the strongest academically. Psychology, communications, and English are the largest.

Special: JMU offers internships, work-study programs, a Washington semester, and study abroad in London, Paris, Florence, Salamanca, and Martinique. An individualized study degree, nondegree study, pass/fail options, and credit for life, military, and work experience are available. There are 33 national honor societies, a freshman honors program, and 36 departmental honors programs.

Admissions: 65% of the 1999-2000 applicants were accepted. The SAT I scores for the 1999-2000 freshman class were: Verbal--11% below 500, 54% between 500 and 599, 32% between 600 and 700, and 3% above 700; Math--11% below 500, 47% between 500 and 599, 38% between 600 and 700, and 4% above 700. 81% of the current freshmen were in the top quarter of their class; 99% were in the top half. 22 freshmen graduated first in their class.

Requirements: The SAT I or ACT is required. JMU requires applicants to be in the upper 50% of their class. A GPA of 2.5 is required. Applicants must be graduates of an accredited secondary school. They must show solid achievement in 4 or more academic courses each year of high school. A personal statement is required. Art students must present a portfolio. Theater, dance, and music students must audition. Nursing students must apply to the nursing department in addition to applying for undergraduate admission. Applications are accepted on-line via Apply. AP credits are accepted. Important factors in the admissions decision are advanced placement or honor courses, extracurricular activities record, and evidence of special talent.

Procedure: Freshmen are admitted in the fall. Entrance exams should be taken in the spring of the junior year or fall of the senior year. There is an early admissions plan. Early decision applications should be filed by November 1; regular applications, by January 15 for fall entry, along with a $30 fee. Notification of early decision is sent mid-January; regular decision, in April. 17% of all applicants are on a waiting list.

Financial Aid: In 1999-2000, 54% of all freshmen and 61% of continuing students received some form of financial aid. 37% of freshmen and 39% of continuing students received need-based aid. The average freshman award was $4796. Of that total, scholarships or need-based grants averaged $3025 ($6700 maximum); loans averaged $2461 ($2625 maximum); and work contracts averaged $1190 ($1785 maximum). 28% of undergraduates work part time. Average annual earnings from campus work are $1190. The average financial indebtedness of the 1999 graduate was $11,000. The FAFSA is required. The fall application deadline is February 15.

Computers: The mainframe is a DEC 4100. Computers are located in classrooms, labs, residence halls, academic buildings, and the library. All students may access the system 23 hours a day. There are no time limits and no fees. It is recommended that all students have personal computers, and business students are required to have them. Contact the College of Business for the recommended hardware configuration.

JOHNS HOPKINS UNIVERSITY
Baltimore, MD 21218   (410) 516-8171; Fax: (410) 516-6025

Full-time: 2295 men, 1609 women	**Faculty:** 369; I, +$
Part-time: 15 men, 6 women	**Ph.D.s:** 99%
Graduate: 790 men, 536 women	**Student/Faculty:** 11 to 1
Year: 4-1-4, summer session	**Tuition:** $23,660
Application Deadline: January 1	**Room & Board:** $9300
Freshman Class: 9497 applied, 3158 accepted, 1012 enrolled	
SAT I Verbal/Math: 670/702	**ACT:** 30 **MOST COMPETITIVE**

The Johns Hopkins University, founded in 1876, is a private multicampus institution offering undergraduate degrees through the Schools of Arts and Sciences and Engineering, and graduate degrees through those and the Schools of International Studies, Nursing, Medicine, and Hygiene and Public Health, and the Peabody Institute (music). There are 4 undergraduate and 8 graduate schools. In addition to regional accreditation, Johns Hopkins has baccalaureate program accreditation with ABET. The 4 libraries contain 3,172,679 volumes, 3.7 million microform items, and 29,094 audiovisual forms/CDs, and subscribe to 20,390 periodicals. Computerized library services include the card catalog, interlibrary loans, and database searching. Special learning facilities include an art gallery, radio station, and TV station. The 140-acre campus is in an urban area 3 miles north of downtown Baltimore. Including residence halls, there are 36 buildings.

Programs of Study: Johns Hopkins confers B.A. and B.S. degrees. Master's and doctoral degrees are also awarded. Bachelor's degrees are awarded in BIOLOGICAL SCIENCE (biology/biological science, biophysics, and neurosciences), COMMUNICATIONS AND THE ARTS (art history and appreciation, classics, English, French, German, media arts, and music), COMPUTER AND PHYSICAL SCIENCE (chemistry, computer science, earth science, mathematics, and physics), ENGINEERING AND ENVIRONMENTAL DESIGN (biomedical engineering, chemical engineering, civil engineering, electrical/electronics engineering, engineering, engineering mechanics, environmental engineering, environmental science, materials engineering, and mechanical engineering), HEALTH PROFESSIONS (premedicine and public health), SOCIAL SCIENCE (anthropology, cognitive science, crosscultural studies, East Asian studies, economics, history, history of science, humanities, international studies, Latin American studies, Near Eastern studies, philosophy, political science/government, prelaw, psychology, sociology, and urban studies). The sciences, English, and history are the strongest academically. Biology, international studies, and biomedical engineering are the largest.

Special: Johns Hopkins offers an extensive array of special programs, including internships, dual majors in music and art, and sciences and engineering, cross-registration with all Baltimore-area colleges and all Johns Hopkins divisions, a cooperative 5-year civil engineering program, a student-designed semester in Washington, D.C., and various multidisciplinary programs. Students may enroll at Johns Hopkins in Bologna, Italy, or Nanjing, China, or arrange programs in Europe, South America, the Far East, or Australia. Accelerated degrees are available in 21 fields. Students may earn combined B.A.-B.S. degrees in biomedical, computer, or mathematical engineering or a combined B.A.-B.M. through the Peabody Institute. Pass/fail options are available in nonmajor courses. There are 7 national honor societies, including Phi Beta Kappa, and 25 departmental honors programs.

Admissions: 33% of the 1999-2000 applicants were accepted. The SAT I scores for the 1999-2000 freshman class were: Verbal--2% below 500, 13% between 500 and 599, 52% between 600 and 700, and 33% above 700; Math--8% between 500 and 599, 37% between 600 and 700, and 55% above 700. The ACT scores were 1% below 21, 5% between 21 and 23, 5% between 24 and 26, 14% between 27 and 28, and 75% above 28. 91% of the current freshmen were in the top fifth of their class; 99% were in the top two fifths. In a recent year,there were 72 National Merit finalists. In a recent year,87 freshmen graduated first in their class.

Requirements: The SAT I or ACT is required. Applicants should be graduates of an accredited secondary school or have the GED. The university recommends that secondary preparation include 4 years each of English and math, 2 or 3 of social science or history, at least 2, preferably 3, of laboratory science, and 2 of a foreign language. Applicants must submit SAT II: Subject tests in writing and literature and 2 others of their choice. 2 personal essays are required, and an interview is recommended. Common App, CollegeLink, and Mac Apply computer disk applications are accepted. Applications are also accepted on-line via the university's own service at apply.jhu.edu. AP credits are accepted. Important factors in the admissions decision are advanced placement or honor courses, leadership record, and evidence of special talent.

Procedure: Freshmen are admitted in the fall. Entrance exams should be taken by January for regular decision, or by November for early decision. There are early decision, early admissions, and deferred admissions plans. Early decision applications should be filed by November 15; regular applications, by January 1 for fall entry, along with a $55 fee. Notification of early decision is sent December 15; regular decision, by April 15. 276 early decision candidates were accepted for the 1999-2000 class. 10% of all applicants are on a waiting list.

Financial Aid: In a recent year, 50% of all freshmen and 58% of continuing students received some form of financial aid. 45% of freshmen and 55% of continuing students received need-based aid. The average freshman award was $21,240. Of that total, scholarships or need-based grants averaged $15,071 ($22,000 maximum); loans averaged $3500 ($4600 maximum); and work contracts averaged $1800 ($1900 maximum). 50% of undergraduates work part time. Average annual earnings from campus work are $1500. The average financial indebtedness of the 1999 graduate was $15,000. Johns Hopkins is a member of CSS. The FAFSA and the college's own financial statement are required. The fall application deadline is February 1.

Computers: The mainframes are an AT&T 3B4000, a DEC VAX 6410, an IBM 3081, and a UNIX O/S. PC labs are available for student use in academic buildings and in some residence halls, with one lab open 24 hours a day. Residence halls are Internet ready. All students may access the system 24 hours a day, 7 days a week. There are no time limits. The fee is $60.

JUILLIARD SCHOOL
New York, NY 10023-6588

(212) 799-5000, ext. 223
Fax: (212) 724-6420

Full-time: 238 men, 238 women	**Faculty:** 100
Part-time: 4 men, 2 women	**Ph.D.s:** n/av
Graduate: 144 men, 152 women	**Student/Faculty:** 5 to 1
Year: semesters	**Tuition:** $16,600
Application Deadline: see profile	**Room & Board:** $6850
Freshman Class: n/av	
SAT I or ACT: not required	**SPECIAL**

The Juilliard School, founded in 1905, is a private college of dance, music, and drama. There is 1 graduate school. The library contains 73,000 volumes, 1399 microform items, and 20,500 audiovisual forms/CDs, and subscribes to 205 periodicals. Computerized library services include the card catalog, interlibrary loans, and database searching. Special learning facilities include 200 practice rooms, 5 theaters, scenery and costume shops, and dance studios. The campus is in an urban area in New York City. Including residence halls, there are 2 buildings.

Programs of Study: Juilliard confers B.Mus. and B.F.A. degrees. Master's and doctoral degrees are also awarded. Bachelor's degrees are awarded in COMMUNICATIONS AND THE ARTS (dance, dramatic arts, music theory and composition, percussion, piano/organ, strings, voice, and winds). Piano, voice, and violin are the largest.

Special: A joint program with Columbia University and Barnard College allows students to obtain a 5-year B.A.-B.Mus. degree. Internships are available with cultural organizations in New York City. There is study abroad in music academies in England, Israel, and Russia. Work-study programs, accelerated degrees and dual majors in music, a combined B.Mus.-M.Mus. degree, nondegree study, and pass/fail options are available.

Requirements: A high school diploma or GED is required. Students are accepted primarily on the basis of personal auditions rather than tests. AP credits are accepted. Important factors in the admissions decision are evidence of special talent and personality/intangible qualities.

Procedure: Freshmen are admitted in the fall. Personal auditions should be completed in December for opera, February for drama and regionals in dance and mu-

281

sic, March for dance and music, and May for dance and music departments that remain open. The fee is $100. There is an early admissions plan. 5% of all applicants are on a waiting list.

Financial Aid: In 1999-2000, 91% of all freshmen and 86% of continuing students received some form of financial aid, including need-based aid. The average freshman award was $12,779. Of that total, scholarships or need-based grants averaged $9480 ($22,900 maximum); loans averaged $2428 ($2625 maximum); and work contracts averaged $1500. All of undergraduates work part time. Average annual earnings from campus work are $1500. The average financial indebtedness of the 1999 graduate was $12,000. Juilliard is a member of CSS. The FAFSA and the college's own financial statement are required. The fall application deadline is March 1.

Computers: All students may access the system. Students may access the system during lab hours. There are no fees.

JUNIATA COLLEGE
Huntingdon, PA 16652

(814) 641-3420
(877) JUNIATA; Fax: (814) 641-3100

Full-time: 549 men, 681 women	**Faculty:** 86; IIB, +$
Part-time: 11 men, 27 women	**Ph.D.s:** 92%
Graduate: none	**Student/Faculty:** 14 to 1
Year: semesters, summer session	**Tuition:** $18,450
Application Deadline: March 15	**Room & Board:** $5110
Freshman Class: 1133 applied, 964 accepted, 325 enrolled	
SAT I Verbal/Math: 570/573	**VERY COMPETITIVE**

Juniata College, founded in 1876, is an independent liberal arts college affiliated with the Church of the Brethren. In addition to regional accreditation, Juniata has baccalaureate program accreditation with CSWE. The library contains 208,000 volumes, 200 microform items, and 1300 audiovisual forms/CDs, and subscribes to 3500 periodicals. Computerized library services include the card catalog, interlibrary loans, and database searching. Special learning facilities include an art gallery, a radio station, an observatory, an environmental studies field station, a nature preserve, an early childhood education center, and a ceramics studio with an Anagama kiln. The 1167-acre campus is in a small town 31 miles south of State College, in the heart of rural Pennsylvania. Including residence halls, there are 33 buildings.

Programs of Study: Juniata confers B.A. and B.S. degrees. Bachelor's degrees are awarded in BIOLOGICAL SCIENCE (biochemistry, biology/biological science, botany, ecology, marine science, microbiology, molecular biology, and zoology), BUSINESS (accounting, business administration and management, international business management, management information systems, and marketing/retailing/merchandising), COMMUNICATIONS AND THE ARTS (art history and appreciation, communications, English, French, German, Russian, Spanish, and studio art), COMPUTER AND PHYSICAL SCIENCE (chemistry, computer science, geology, mathematics, natural sciences, and physics), EDUCATION (early childhood, elementary, English, foreign languages, health, mathematics, museum studies, science, secondary, social studies, and special), ENGINEERING AND ENVIRONMENTAL DESIGN (environmental science and preengineering), HEALTH PROFESSIONS (preallied health, predentistry, premedicine, and preveterinary science), SOCIAL SCIENCE (anthropology, criminal justice, economics, history, humanities, international studies, ministries, peace studies, political science/government, prelaw, psychology, public administration, social science, social work, and sociology). Prehealth programs, chemistry, and biology are the strongest academically. Biology, business, and education are the largest.

Special: Juniata offers cooperative programs in marine science, cytogenetics, cytotechnology, marine biology, biotechnology, nursing, medical technology, diagnostic imaging, occupational and physical therapy, dentistry, medicine, optometry, and podiatry. Internships, study abroad in 11 countries, Washington and Philadelphia semesters, and nondegree study are also offered. There are 3-2 engineering degrees with Columbia, Clarkson, Washington, and Pennsylvania State Universities, a 3-3 law program with Duquesne University, and various preprofessional programs, including optometry, medicine, dentistry, pharmacy, and podiatry. With the assistance of 2 faculty advisers, most students design their own program of emphasis to meet individual goals. There are 8 national honor societies, a freshman honors program, and 5 departmental honors programs.

Admissions: 85% of the 1999-2000 applicants were accepted. The SAT I scores for the 1999-2000 freshman class were: Verbal--17% below 500, 51% between 500 and 599, 27% between 600 and 700, and 5% above 700; Math--17% below 500, 44% between 500 and 599, 33% between 600 and 700, and 6% above 700. 64% of the current freshmen were in the top fifth of their class; 90% were in the top two fifths. There were 2 National Merit semifinalists. 10 freshmen graduated first in their class.

Requirements: The SAT I is required. A GPA of 2.8 is required. Candidates for admission should be graduates of an accredited secondary school and have completed 16 academic credits, including 4 in English, 2 in a foreign language, and a combination of 10 in math, social studies, and lab science. The GED is accepted, and home schoolers are encouraged to apply. An essay is required and an interview is recommended. Applications are accepted on computer disk and on-line via the Private School Consortium's Common App. AP credits are accepted. Important factors in the admissions decision are advanced placement or honor courses, leadership record, and recommendations by school officials.

Procedure: Freshmen are admitted fall and spring. Entrance exams should be taken in the junior or senior years. There are early decision, early admissions, and deferred admissions plans. Early decision applications should be filed by November 15; regular applications, by March 15 for fall entry and December 1 for spring entry, along with a $30 fee. Notification of early decision is sent December 31; regular decision, on a rolling basis.

Financial Aid: In 1999-2000, 93% of all freshmen and 87% of continuing students received some form of financial aid. 76% of freshmen and 79% of continuing students received need-based aid. In a recent year, the average freshman award was $15,501. Of that total, scholarships or need-based grants averaged $11,268 ($22,120 maximum); loans averaged $2761 ($4125 maximum); work contracts averaged $1169 ($1200 maximum); and other government-funded awards averaged $756 ($10,000 maximum). 55% of undergraduates work part time. Average annual earnings from campus work are $703. The average financial indebtedness of the 1999 graduate was $16,395. The CSS/Profile or FAFSA is required. The fall application deadline is March 1.

Computers: The mainframes are a DEC VAX 4000/500 and an HP 9000. All dorm rooms are equipped for full Internet and Intranet access. There are also numerous maintenance terminals, PCs, and Macs located throughout the campus. Students have access to all locations and are provided with a personal account. All students may access the system. There are no time limits and no fees. The college strongly recommends that students have Dell PCs.

KALAMAZOO COLLEGE
Kalamazoo, MI 49006-3295

(616) 337-7166
(800) 253-3602; Fax: (616) 337-7390

Full-time: 617 men, 763 women	**Faculty:** 90; IIB, +$
Part-time: none	**Ph.D.s:** 90%
Graduate: none	**Student/Faculty:** 15 to 1
Year: quarters	**Tuition:** $19,188
Application Deadline: February 15	**Room & Board:** $5787
Freshman Class: 1410 applied, 1087 accepted, 370 enrolled	
SAT I Verbal/Math: 640/622	**ACT:** 28 **HIGHLY COMPETITIVE+**

Kalamazoo College is a liberal arts and sciences institution founded in 1833. The library contains 300,978 volumes, 53,875 microform items, and 15,213 audiovisual forms/CDs, and subscribes to 1192 periodicals. Computerized library services include the card catalog, interlibrary loans, and database searching. Special learning facilities include a learning resource center, art gallery, and radio station. The 60-acre campus is in a suburban area 140 miles from Detroit and Chicago. Including residence halls, there are 30 buildings.

Programs of Study: Kalamazoo confers the B.A. degree. Bachelor's degrees are awarded in BIOLOGICAL SCIENCE (biology/biological science), BUSINESS (business economics), COMMUNICATIONS AND THE ARTS (art, art history and appreciation, dramatic arts, English, French, German, music, and Spanish), COMPUTER AND PHYSICAL SCIENCE (chemistry, computer science, mathematics, and physics), HEALTH PROFESSIONS (health science), SOCIAL SCIENCE (anthropology, classical/ancient civilization, history, human development, interdisciplinary studies, international relations, international studies, philosophy, political science/government, psychology, religion, and sociology). Foreign languages, international studies and commerce, and health sciences are the strongest academically. Economics, English, and political science are the largest.

Special: Students may study abroad and choose from among 900 career internships in the United States, Europe, Asia, and Africa. The school offers a Washington semester, allows dual and interdisciplinary majors, and has cross-registration with Western Michigan University. A 3-2 engineering degree is offered with Washington University and the University of Michigan. There are accelerated 3-year programs in predentistry, premedicine, and preveterinary medicine. There are 3 national honor societies, including Phi Beta Kappa.

Admissions: 77% of the 1999-2000 applicants were accepted. The SAT I scores for the 1999-2000 freshman class were: Verbal--7% below 500, 29% between 500 and 599, 47% between 600 and 700, and 17% above 700; Math--7% below 500, 34% between 500 and 599, 47% between 600 and 700, and 12% above 700. The ACT scores were 1% below 21, 7% between 21 and 23, 27% between 24 and 26, 28% between 27 and 28, and 37% above 28. 75% of the current freshmen were in the top fifth of their class; 95% were in the top two fifths. There were 10 National Merit finalists. 15 freshmen graduated first in their class.

Requirements: The SAT I or ACT is required. The college also requires a high school transcript, an essay, and teacher and counselor recommendations; an interview is recommended. Applications are accepted on computer disk. AP credits are accepted. Important factors in the admissions decision are advanced placement or honor courses, evidence of special talent, and leadership record.

Procedure: Freshmen are admitted fall and winter. Entrance exams should be taken by December of the senior year. There are early admissions and deferred admissions plans. Early decision applications should be filed by November 15; regular applications, by February 15 for fall entry, along with a $35 fee. Notification of early decision is sent December 1; regular decision, April 1. 19% of all applicants are on a waiting list.

Financial Aid: In 1999-2000, 98% of all freshmen and 96% of continuing students received some form of financial aid. 49% of freshmen and 50% of continuing students received need-based aid. The average freshman award was $11,720. Of that total, scholarships or need-based grants averaged $9745 ($18,000 maximum); loans averaged $3370 ($6625 maximum); work contracts averaged $1600 ($1845 maximum); and tuition remission programs averaged $6214 ($19,188 maximum). 40% of undergraduates work part time. Average annual earnings from campus work are $1045. The average financial indebtedness of the 1999 graduate was $17,100. Kalamazoo is a member of CSS. The CSS/Profile or FAFSA is required. The fall application deadline is February 15.

Computers: The mainframe is a Sun Ultra 2. There are 130 PCs available for student use, 10 of which are limited to physics students. All IBM/Mac computers are networked on the Internet. All rooms in the residence halls are wired for network access. All students may access the system. There are no time limits and no fees. It is strongly recommended that all students have personal computers.

KANSAS CITY ART INSTITUTE
Kansas City, MO 64111

(816) 474-5224
(800) 522-5224; Fax: (816) 802-3309

Full-time: 262 men, 283 women	**Faculty:** 41; IIB, av$
Part-time: 6 men, 8 women	**Ph.D.s:** 96%
Graduate: none	**Student/Faculty:** 13 to 1
Year: semesters, summer session	**Tuition:** $18,218
Application Deadline: April 15	**Room & Board:** $5500
Freshman Class: 386 applied, 312 accepted, 108 enrolled	
SAT I Verbal/Math: 563/541	**ACT:** 23 SPECIAL

The Kansas City Art Institute, founded in 1885, is an independent professional college of art and design. In addition to regional accreditation, KCAI has baccalaureate program accreditation with NASAD. The library contains 37,000 volumes, and subscribes to 120 periodicals. Computerized library services include the card catalog and database searching. Special learning facilities include a learning resource center and art gallery. The 17-acre campus is in an urban area. Including residence halls, there are 14 buildings.

Programs of Study: KCAI confers the B.F.A. degree. Bachelor's degrees are awarded in COMMUNICATIONS AND THE ARTS (art history and appreciation, ceramic art and design, creative writing, design, fiber/textiles/weaving, fine arts, painting, photography, printmaking, sculpture, and video).

Special: KCAI offers internships with major corporations such as Hallmark and Disney, independent study, work-study programs, study abroad, cross-registration, intermedia majors, an exchange program, and nondegree study.

Admissions: 81% of the 1999-2000 applicants were accepted. The SAT I scores for the 1999-2000 freshman class were: Verbal--17% below 500, 48% between 500 and 599, 25% between 600 and 700, and 10% above 700; Math--31% below 500, 37% between 500 and 599, 27% between 600 and 700, and 5% above 700. The ACT scores were 22% below 21, 36% between 21 and 23, 24% between 24 and 26, 8% between 27 and 28, and 10% above 28.

Requirements: The SAT I or ACT is required. A GPA of 2.5 is required. In addition, applicants must submit a portfolio consisting of 10 to 20 pieces of artwork, 2 letters of recommendation, and high school transcripts. The GED is accepted. A statement of purpose and an interview are required. AP and CLEP credits are accepted. Important factors in the admissions decision are evidence of special talent, advanced placement or honor courses, and recommendations by school officials.

Procedure: Freshmen are admitted fall and spring. Entrance exams should be taken in spring of the junior year or fall of the senior year. There are early admissions and deferred admissions plans. Early decision applications should be filed by January 15; regular applications, by April 15 for fall entry, along with a $25 fee. Notification is sent on a rolling basis.

Financial Aid: In a recent year, 90% of all freshmen and 80% of continuing students received some form of financial aid. 57% of freshmen and 66% of continuing students received need-based aid. The average freshman award was $12,814. Of that total, scholarships or need-based grants averaged $6638 ($9000 maximum); loans averaged $2625 ($3625 maximum); and work contracts averaged $1000. 65% of undergraduates work part time. Average annual earnings from campus work are $1000. The average financial indebtedness of the recent graduate was $17,125. KCAI is a member of CSS. The FAFSA and student and parent IRS tax forms, if requested. are required. The fall application deadline is February 15.

Computers: There is a computer graphics center with software for computer-generated art and design, including digital painting, image processing and composing, layout and illustration, and 3-D modeling and animation. All students may access the system. There are no time limits and no fees. It is recommended that design and illustration majors have PCs.

KENDALL COLLEGE OF ART AND DESIGN
Grand Rapids, MI 49503-3194   (616) 451-2787
(800) 676-2787; Fax: (616) 831-9689

Full-time: 475 men and women	**Faculty:** 33
Part-time: 178 men and women	**Ph.D.s:** 100%
Graduate: none	**Student/Faculty:** 14 to 1
Year: semesters, summer session	**Tuition:** $10,900
Application Deadline: open	**Room & Board:** n/app
Freshman Class: n/av	
SAT I or ACT: required	**SPECIAL**

The Kendall College of Art and Design, founded in 1928, is a school of design studies and the fine arts. In addition to regional accreditation, Kendall College has baccalaureate program accreditation with FIDER and NASAD. The library contains 23,000 volumes, 1000 microform items, and 3500 audiovisual forms/CDs, and subscribes to 150 periodicals. Computerized library services include the card catalog. Special learning facilities include a learning resource center, art gallery, a model/wood shop, a photography lab, a printmaking lab, fine art studios, and a student gallery. The 1-acre campus is in an urban area in downtown Grand Rapids. There are 2 buildings.

Programs of Study: Kendall College confers B.S. and B.F.A. degrees. Bachelor's degrees are awarded in COMMUNICATIONS AND THE ARTS (art history and appreciation, fine arts, illustration, industrial design, media arts, and multimedia), ENGINEERING AND ENVIRONMENTAL DESIGN (furniture design and interior design). Illustration and visual communications are the largest.

Special: Cross-registration is offered through a consortium of schools. Internships are available in all majors. Study abroad may be arranged by the student and approved by the college.

Requirements: The SAT I or ACT is required. Kendall College requires applicants to be in the upper 50% of their class. A GPA of 2.3 is required. A high school transcript is required. Scores from either the ACT or the SAT I are not required if the applicant has been out of high school for at least 3 years. The GED certificate is accepted. Students must submit an essay with their application. A portfolio and an interview are also recommended. Prospective students are encouraged to take courses in drawing, painting, and design in high school. AP and CLEP credits are accepted. Important factors in the admissions decision are leadership record, personality/intangible qualities, and evidence of special talent.

Procedure: Freshmen are admitted to all sessions. There are early decision, early admissions, and deferred admissions plans. Application deadlines are open. The application fee is $35. Notification is sent on a rolling basis.

Financial Aid: In 1999-2000, 86% of all freshmen and 81% of continuing students received some form of financial aid. 65% of freshmen and 68% of continuing students received need-based aid. The average freshman award was $7888. Of that total, scholarships or need-based grants averaged $4230; loans averaged $5420 ($15,189 maximum); work contracts averaged $2145 ($3465 maximum); and student-obtained outside awards averaged $1230 ($2500 maximum). 1% of undergraduates work part time. Average annual earnings from campus work are $2475. The average financial indebtedness of the 1999 graduate was $18,000. Kendall College is a member of CSS. The FAFSA is required. The fall application deadline is February 15.

Computers: The college provides Mac computers for student use in classroom work and design. Library computers provide Internet access. Students may use the computer labs from 8 a.m. to 12 p.m. The fee is $25 per semester.

KENYON COLLEGE
Gambier, OH 43022-9623

(740) 427-5776
(800) 848-2468; Fax: (740) 427-5770

Full-time: 696 men, 878 women	**Faculty:** 131; IIB, ++$
Part-time: 6 men, 9 women	**Ph.D.s:** 96%
Graduate: none	**Student/Faculty:** 12 to 1
Year: semesters	**Tuition:** $24,590
Application Deadline: February 1	**Room & Board:** $4160
Freshman Class: 2420 applied, 1644 accepted, 459 enrolled	
SAT I Verbal/Math: 670/640	**ACT:** 29 **HIGHLY COMPETITIVE+**

Kenyon College, founded in 1824, is a private liberal arts and sciences college affiliated with the Episcopal Church. The library contains 342,092 volumes, 130,751 microform items, and 9542 audiovisual forms/CDs, and subscribes to 1180 periodicals. Computerized library services include the card catalog, interlibrary loans, and database searching. Special learning facilities include a learning resource center, art gallery, radio station, TV station, and observatory. The 800-acre campus is in a small town 50 miles northeast of Columbus. Including residence halls, there are 52 buildings.

Programs of Study: Kenyon confers the B.A. degree. Bachelor's degrees are awarded in BIOLOGICAL SCIENCE (biochemistry, biology/biological science, molecular biology, and neurosciences), COMMUNICATIONS AND THE ARTS (art history and appreciation, classics, dance, dramatic arts, English, French, German, Greek (classical), Latin, modern language, music, Spanish, and studio art), COMPUTER AND PHYSICAL SCIENCE (chemistry, mathematics, and physics), SOCIAL SCIENCE (anthropology, economics, history, international studies, philosophy, political science/government, psychology, religion, and sociology). English, history, and political science are the largest.

Special: Students may study abroad in many countries. The college also offers dual and student-designed majors, pass/fail options, internships, a spring break externship program, a Washington semester consisting of apprenticeships in any of several U.S. programs, and a 3-2 engineering degree with Case Western Reserve, Washington University in St. Louis, and Rensselaer Polytechnic Institute, as well as a 3-2 nursing degree with Case Western Reserve and a 3-2 environmental studies program with Duke University. Kenyon's Interdisciplinary Program in Humane Studies offers a tutorial-based concentration on the human predicament. There are 3 national honor societies, including Phi Beta Kappa.

Admissions: 68% of the 1999-2000 applicants were accepted. The SAT I scores for the 1999-2000 freshman class were: Verbal--1% below 500, 18% between 500 and 599, 44% between 600 and 700, and 36% above 700; Math--4% below 500, 31% between 500 and 599, 44% between 600 and 700, and 21% above 700. The ACT scores were 1% below 21, 6% between 21 and 23, 17% between 24 and 26, 26% between 27 and 28, and 50% above 28. 74% of the current freshmen were in the top fifth of their class; 93% were in the top two fifths. There were 34 National Merit finalists and 37 semifinalists. 24 freshmen graduated first in their class.

Requirements: The SAT I or ACT is required. Applicants should be graduates of an accredited secondary school. Kenyon recommends 4 units each of English, foreign language, and math and 3 units each of science and social studies. Candidates are encouraged to exceed the minimum requirements, especially in math and science, and to take advanced placement or honors work in at least 2 subjects. An essay and interview are important criteria in the admissions decision. Talent in music, theater, art, writing, and athletics is given extra consideration. Students may apply using a computer disk provided a printout is sent with the disk. AP credits are accepted. Important factors in the admissions decision are advanced placement or honor courses, recommendations by school officials, and extracurricular activities record.

Procedure: Freshmen are admitted in the fall. Entrance exams should be taken in the fall of the senior year. There are early decision, early admissions, and deferred admissions plans. Early decision applications should be filed by December 1; regular applications, by February 1 for fall entry, along with a $45 fee. Notification of early decision is sent December 15; regular decision, April 1. 105 early decision candidates were accepted for the 1999-2000 class. 10% of all applicants are on a waiting list.

Financial Aid: In 1999-2000, 68% of all freshmen and 53% of continuing students received some form of financial aid. 41% of freshmen and 39% of continuing students received need-based aid. The average freshman award was $18,897. Of that total, scholarships or need-based grants averaged $13,273 ($25,000 maximum); loans averaged $3642 ($4625 maximum); work contracts averaged $962 ($1000 maximum), and federal and state/grants and outside awards averaged $1020. 64% of undergraduates work part time. Average annual earnings from campus work are $858. The average financial indebtedness of the 1999 graduate was $16,194. Kenyon is a member of CSS. The CSS/Profile or FAFSA is required. The fall application deadline is February 15.

Computers: The mainframes are a 2 DEC VAX 4500s, a DEC VAX 4600, a DEC VAX 4200, and a DEC MicroVAX 3100. Students may access the campus network via 145 terminals and 110 PCs connected to the campus local area network. Public access locations include residence halls, classrooms, labs, studios, the library, and public computing areas. For a small fee, students with PCs may have personal network connections from their residence rooms. All students may access the system 24 hours a day. There are no time limits and no fees.

KETTERING UNIVERSITY
(Formerly GMI Engineering & Management Institute)
Flint, MI 48504-4898 (810) 762-7865
(800) 955-4464; Fax: (810) 762-9837

Full-time: 2048 men, 505 women	**Faculty:** 139; IIB, ++$
Part-time: none	**Ph.D.s:** 84%
Graduate: 480 men, 133 women	**Student/Faculty:** 18 to 1
Year: alternating 12-wk terms, summer session	**Tuition:** $14,775
	Room & Board: $4020

Application Deadline: open
Freshman Class: 1813 applied, 1289 accepted, 586 enrolled
SAT I Verbal/Math: 590/630   **ACT:** 26   **HIGHLY COMPETITIVE**

Kettering University (formerly GMI Engineering & Management Institute) is an independent college founded in 1919. In the 5 year undergraduate program students alternate 12-week terms of full-time classes with 12-week terms of full-time paid professional cooperative education (co-op) work experience in industry. Students typically begin co-op during their freshman year and co-op in 43 states and several countries. There is 1 graduate school. In addition to regional accreditation, GMI/Kettering University has baccalaureate program accreditation with ABET and ACBSP. The library contains 94,738 volumes, 516 microform items, and 276 audiovisual forms/CDs, and subscribes to 540 periodicals. Computerized library services include the card catalog, interlibrary loans, and database searching. Special learning facilities include a learning resource center, art gallery, radio station, and Alumni Foundation Collection of Industrial History. The 51-acre campus is in a suburban area 60 miles north of Detroit. Including residence halls, there are 7 buildings.

Programs of Study: GMI/Kettering University confers B.S.A.M., B.S.A.P., B.S. C.E., B.S.C.S., B.S.E.C., B.S.E.E., B.S.I.E., B.S.M., B.S.M.E., and B.S.M.S.E. degrees. Master's degrees are also awarded. Bachelor's degrees are awarded in BUSINESS (business administration and management), COMPUTER AND PHYSICAL SCIENCE (applied mathematics, applied physics, and computer science), ENGINEERING AND ENVIRONMENTAL DESIGN (computer engineering, electrical/electronics engineering, environmental science, industrial engineering, manufacturing engineering, and mechanical engineering). Mechanical engineering and electrical engineering are the largest.

Special: All Kettering University/GMI undergraduate students participate in paid cooperative education work experience. Students may pursue a dual major in electrical and mechanical engineering, and student-designed majors can be arranged within the curriculum structure. An accelerated degree program in engineering is available, as well as study abroad in 5 countries. There are 7 national honor societies.

Admissions: 71% of the 1999-2000 applicants were accepted. The SAT I scores for the 1999-2000 freshman class were: Verbal--18% below 500, 40% between 500 and 599, 33% between 600 and 700, and 9% above 700; Math--30% between 500 and 599, 51% between 600 and 700, and 19% above 700. The ACT scores were 8% below 21, 17% between 21 and 23, 34% between 24 and 26, 23% between 27 and 28, and 18% above 28. 61% of the current freshmen were in the top fifth of their class; 90% were in the top two fifths. There were 4 National Merit finalists. 20 freshmen graduated first in their class.

Requirements: The SAT I or ACT is required. Applicants must graduate from an accredited secondary school with a minimum of 16 academic credits. Applicants must have completed 3 years of English, 3 1/2 years of math, including trigonometry, and 2 years of lab science, 1 of which must be chemistry or physics (both are strongly recommended). Applications can be submitted on-line through the university's web site. AP and CLEP credits are accepted. Important factors in the admissions decision are leadership record, advanced placement or honor courses, and extracurricular activities record.

Procedure: Freshmen are admitted fall and summer. Entrance exams should be taken during the spring of junior year and fall of senior year. There is a deferred admissions plan. Application deadlines are open, and there is a $25 application fee. Notification is sent on a rolling basis.

Financial Aid: In 1999-2000, 88% of all freshmen and 77% of continuing students received some form of financial aid. 88% of freshmen and 77% of continuing students received need-based aid. The average freshman award was $8168. Of that total, scholarships or need-based grants averaged $6273 ($14,760 maximum); loans averaged $2625 ($6625 maximum); and work contracts averaged $800 ($1600 maximum). All students participate in paid cooperative work experiences that typically begin in the freshman year. Average total income from co-op work over the 5-year program range from $40,000 to more than $65,000. The average financial indebtedness of the 1999 graduate was $30,000. GMI/Kettering University is a member of CSS. The FAFSA and the colege's own financial statement are required. The fall application deadline is February 14.

Computers: The mainframes are a Sun SPARC server and a VAX 11-785. All campus buildings and residence hall rooms are fully networked. Telephone and web access is available from off campus. There are more than 300 workstations, networked PCs, and CAD/CAE workstations for general student use. Standalone and dedicated PCs and microprocessors are available in most labs. All students may access the system 24 hours per day, 7 days per week. There are no time limits and no fees. It is recommended that all students have personal computers.

KNOX COLLEGE
Galesburg, IL 61401

(309) 341-7123
(800) 678-KNOX; Fax: (309) 341-7070

Full-time: 536 men, 653 women	**Faculty:** 99; IIB, +$
Part-time: 11 men, 20 women	**Ph.D.s:** 92%
Graduate: none	**Student/Faculty:** 12 to 1
Year: 3 10-week terms	**Tuition:** $19,836
Application Deadline: February 15	**Room & Board:** $5280
Freshman Class: 1360 applied, 1018 accepted, 300 enrolled	
SAT I Verbal/Math: 620/620	**ACT:** 27 **HIGHLY COMPETITIVE**

Knox College, founded in 1837, is an independent liberal arts college. The 3 libraries contain 285,007 volumes, 96,447 microform items, and 3100 audiovisual forms/CDs, and subscribe to 685 periodicals. Computerized library services include the card catalog, interlibrary loans, and database searching. Special learning facilities include a learning resource center, natural history museum, radio station, and a 760-acre biological field station near the campus. The 82-acre campus is in a small town 180 miles southwest of Chicago. Including residence halls, there are 42 buildings.

Programs of Study: Knox confers the B.A. degree. Bachelor's degrees are awarded in BIOLOGICAL SCIENCE (biochemistry and biology/biological science), COMMUNICATIONS AND THE ARTS (art history and appreciation, classics, creative writing, dramatic arts, English literature, French, German, modern language, music, Russian, Spanish, and studio art), COMPUTER AND PHYSICAL SCIENCE (chemistry, computer science, mathematics, and physics),

EDUCATION (elementary and secondary), ENGINEERING AND ENVIRON-MENTAL DESIGN (environmental science), SOCIAL SCIENCE (African American studies, American studies, anthropology, economics, German area studies, history, international relations, philosophy, political science/government, psychology, Russian and Slavic studies, sociology, and women's studies). Biology, chemistry, and English are the strongest academically. Economics, biology, and education are the largest.

Special: The normal academic load is 3 courses per term, with 3 terms per year. Cooperative programs are offered with Washington University in St. Louis in architecture and engineering; Columbia University in engineering and law; University of Illinois at Urbana-Champaign and Rensselaer Polytechnic Institute in engineering; Rush University in medicine, nursing, and medical technology; Duke University in forestry and environmental management; and University of Chicago in law and social work. Study abroad is available in 20 countries. Other programs include a Washington semester, an urban studies semester, science and library research programs, work-study programs, and numerous internships. Dual majors, student-designed majors, and pass/fail options are available. Early admission to Rush Medical College is possible. Nondegree study is possible. There are 7 national honor societies, including Phi Beta Kappa, and 5 departmental honors programs.

Admissions: 75% of the 1999-2000 applicants were accepted. The SAT I scores for the 1999-2000 freshman class were: Verbal--12% below 500, 29% between 500 and 599, 39% between 600 and 700, and 20% above 700; Math--11% below 500, 34% between 500 and 599, 41% between 600 and 700, and 14% above 700. The ACT scores were 6% below 21, 18% between 21 and 23, 25% between 24 and 26, 22% between 27 and 28, and 29% above 28. 66% of the current freshmen were in the top fifth of their class; 89% were in the top two fifths. There were 8 National Merit finalists. 10 freshmen graduated first in their class.

Requirements: The SAT I or ACT is required. In addition, applicants should be graduates of an accredited secondary school with 15 academic credits, including 4 in English, 3 each in math, science, and history and social studies, and 2 in foreign language. An essay is part of the application process. An interview is recommended. Applications are accepted on computer disk and on-line through Apply, CollegeLink, and other services. AP and CLEP credits are accepted. Important factors in the admissions decision are advanced placement or honor courses, recommendations by school officials, and extracurricular activities record.

Procedure: Freshmen are admitted to all sessions. Entrance exams should be taken by December 15. There are early admissions and deferred admissions plans. Early action applications should be filed by December 1; regular applications, by February 15 for fall entry, November 1 for winter entry, and February 1 for spring entry, along with a $35 fee. Notification of early action is sent December 31; regular decision, March 31.

Financial Aid: In 1999-2000, 93% of all freshmen and 90% of continuing students received some form of financial aid. 81% of freshmen and 77% of continuing students received need-based aid. The average freshman award was $17,074. Of that total, scholarships or need-based grants averaged $13,902 ($19,608 maximum); loans averaged $3433 ($4625 maximum); and work contracts averaged $1303 ($1545 maximum). 67% of undergraduates work part time. Average annual earnings from campus work are $1024. The average financial indebtedness of the 1999 graduate was $15,715. Knox is a member of CSS. The FAFSA, the college's own financial statement, and student and parent tax returns are required. The fall application deadline is March 1.

Computers: The mainframes are HP 9000 UNIX servers and NT servers. Virtually every campus building is linked via a fiber-optic Ethernet network. There are

5 public networked computer labs equipped with more than 200 Power Macs and Pentiums. Students may connect PCs from their rooms to the library, E-mail services, software applications, and the Internet. All students may access the system. A large student computer lab is open 24 hours. Others are open until midnight. There are no time limits and no fees.

LA SALLE UNIVERSITY
Philadelphia, PA 19141-1199 (215) 951-1500
(800) 328-1910; Fax: (215) 951-1656

Full-time: 1445 men, 1621 women	**Faculty:** 182; IIA, +$
Part-time: 260 men, 677 women	**Ph.D.s:** 87%
Graduate: 750 men, 902 women	**Student/Faculty:** 17 to 1
Year: semesters, summer session	**Tuition:** $17,260
Application Deadline: April 15	**Room & Board:** $7300
Freshman Class: 3088 applied, 2440 accepted, 808 enrolled	
SAT I Verbal/Math: 550/550	**VERY COMPETITIVE**

La Salle University, founded in 1863, is a private institution conducted under the auspices of the Christian Brothers of the Roman Catholic Church. The university offers undergraduate and graduate programs in the arts and sciences, business, education, fine arts, religious studies, and nursing. There are 3 undergraduate and 3 graduate schools. In addition to regional accreditation, La Salle has baccalaureate program accreditation with AACSB, CSWE, and NLN. The library contains 400,300 volumes, 276,600 microform items, and 18,753 audiovisual forms/CDs, and subscribes to 1635 periodicals. Computerized library services include the card catalog, interlibrary loans, and database searching. Special learning facilities include a learning resource center, art gallery, radio station, TV station, and a Japanese tea ceremony house. The 100-acre campus is in an urban area 8 miles northwest of the center of Philadelphia. Including residence halls, there are 56 buildings.

Programs of Study: La Salle confers B.A., B.S., B.S.W., and B.S.N. degrees. Associate, master's, and doctoral degrees are also awarded. Bachelor's degrees are awarded in BIOLOGICAL SCIENCE (biochemistry, biology/biological science, and nutrition), BUSINESS (accounting, banking and finance, business administration and management, international economics, management information systems, marketing/retailing/merchandising, and organizational behavior), COMMUNICATIONS AND THE ARTS (classical languages, communications, English, fine arts, French, German, Italian, multimedia, music, Russian, and Spanish), COMPUTER AND PHYSICAL SCIENCE (chemistry, computer science, geology, information sciences and systems, and mathematics), EDUCATION (elementary, foreign languages, science, secondary, social studies, and special), ENGINEERING AND ENVIRONMENTAL DESIGN (computer graphics and environmental science), HEALTH PROFESSIONS (nursing, preallied health, predentistry, premedicine, and speech pathology/audiology), SOCIAL SCIENCE (criminal justice, economics, history, philosophy, political science/government, prelaw, psychology, public administration, religion, social work, and sociology). Chemistry, English, and accounting are the strongest academically. Accounting, education, and communication are the largest.

Special: Cross-registration is offered in conjunction with Chestnut Hill College, and there is a 2-2 program in allied health with Thomas Jefferson University. La Salle also offers study abroad, co-op programs in business, work-study programs, internships in most majors, dual and majors, and pass/fail options. An E-Commerce Institute has been created to educate all students about this emerging business tool. There are 13 national honor societies and a freshman honors program.

Admissions: 79% of the 1999-2000 applicants were accepted. The SAT I scores for the 1999-2000 freshman class were: Verbal--17% below 500, 54% between 500 and 599, 24% between 600 and 700, and 5% above 700; Math--17% below 500, 52% between 500 and 599, 27% between 600 and 700, and 3% above 700. 45% of the current freshmen were in the top fifth of their class; 82% were in the top two fifths. In a recent year, 12 freshmen graduated first in their class.

Requirements: The SAT I or ACT is required. La Salle requires applicants to be in the upper 50% of their class. SAT II: Subject tests in writing and math are recommended. Applicants must be graduates of accredited secondary schools or have earned a GED. La Salle requires 16 academic units, based on 4 years of English, 3 of math, 2 of foreign language, and 1 of history, with the remaining 6 units in academic electives; science and math majors must have an additional one-half unit of math. An essay is required, and an interview is recommended. AP and CLEP credits are accepted. Important factors in the admissions decision are advanced placement or honor courses, leadership record, and recommendations by school officials.

Procedure: Freshmen are admitted fall and spring. Entrance exams should be taken before February of the senior year. There are early admissions and deferred admissions plans. Applications should be filed by April 15 for fall entry and December 15 for spring entry, along with a $35 fee. Notification is sent on a rolling basis.

Financial Aid: In 1999-2000, 85% of all students received some form of financial aid. 65% of freshmen and 58% of continuing students received need-based aid. The average freshman award was $15,770. Of that total, scholarships or need-based grants averaged $8000 ($17,260 maximum); loans averaged $4700; and work contracts averaged $1800. 22% of undergraduates work part time. Average annual earnings from campus work are $1600. The average financial indebtedness of the 1999 graduate was $13,000. La Salle is a member of CSS. The FAFSA is required. The fall application deadline is February 15.

Computers: The mainframe is a SUN ES-5000. The university provides 900 PCs. A LAN is available for student use. Dormitories are wired for network and Internet access. All students may access the system 8 a.m. to 11 p.m. weekdays, 9 a.m. to 7 p.m. Saturday, and noon to 11 p.m. Sunday. There are no time limits and no fees.

LAFAYETTE COLLEGE
Easton, PA 18042
(610) 330-5355

Full-time: 1092 men, 1070 women	**Faculty:** 183; IIB, +$
Part-time: 92 men, 29 women	**Ph.D.s:** 100%
Graduate: none	**Student/Faculty:** 12 to 1
Year: semesters, summer session	**Tuition:** $22,929
Application Deadline: January 1	**Room & Board:** $7106
Freshman Class: 4429 applied, 2135 accepted, 583 enrolled	
SAT I Verbal/Math: 605/645	**MOST COMPETITIVE**

Lafayette College, founded in 1826 and affiliated with the Presbyterian Church (U.S.A.) is a private, undergraduate institution emphasizing the liberal arts and engineering. In addition to regional accreditation, Lafayette has baccalaureate program accreditation with ABET. The 2 libraries contain 486,000 volumes and 105,949 microform items, and subscribe to 2309 periodicals. Computerized library services include the card catalog, interlibrary loans, and database searching.

Special learning facilities include a learning resource center, art gallery, radio station, geological museum, foreign languages lab, and calculus lab. The 112-acre campus is in a suburban area 70 miles west of New York City. Including residence halls, there are 65 buildings.

Programs of Study: Lafayette confers A.B., B.S., and B.S. Eng. degrees. Bachelor's degrees are awarded in BIOLOGICAL SCIENCE (biochemistry and biology/biological science), BUSINESS (business economics), COMMUNICATIONS AND THE ARTS (English, fine arts, French, German, music history and appreciation, music theory and composition, and Spanish), COMPUTER AND PHYSICAL SCIENCE (chemistry, computer science, geology, mathematics, and physics), ENGINEERING AND ENVIRONMENTAL DESIGN (chemical engineering, civil engineering, electrical/electronics engineering, and mechanical engineering), HEALTH PROFESSIONS (predentistry), SOCIAL SCIENCE (American studies, anthropology, economics, history, interdisciplinary studies, international relations, philosophy, political science/government, prelaw, psychology, religion, Russian and Slavic studies, and sociology). Engineering, psychology, and English are the strongest academically. Economics, business, and engineering are the largest.

Special: Cross-registration through the Lehigh Valley Association of Independent Colleges, internships in all academic departments, study abroad in 3 countries as well as through other individually arranged plans, a Washington semester at American University, and work-study programs with area employers are possible. An accelerated degree plan in all majors, dual and student-designed majors, 5-year dual-degree programs, and pass/fail options in any nonmajor subject also are available. There are 12 national honor societies, including Phi Beta Kappa, and 24 departmental honors programs.

Admissions: 48% of the 1999-2000 applicants were accepted. The SAT I scores for the 1999-2000 freshman class were: Verbal--10% below 500, 29% between 500 and 599, 50% between 600 and 700, and 11% above 700; Math--7% below 500, 18% between 500 and 599, 53% between 600 and 700, and 22% above 700. 90% of the current freshmen were in the top fifth of their class; 96% were in the top two fifths.

Requirements: The SAT I is required. Applicants need 4 years of English, 3 years of math (4 for science or engineering majors), 2 years each of foreign language and science (with physics and chemistry for science or engineering students), and an additional 5 to 8 units. An essay is required and an interview recommended. The GED is accepted. AP credits are accepted. Important factors in the admissions decision are advanced placement or honor courses, evidence of special talent, and personality/intangible qualities.

Procedure: Freshmen are admitted in the fall. Entrance exams should be taken by January of the senior year. There are early decision, early admissions, and deferred admissions plans. Early decision applications should be filed by January 15; regular applications, by January 1 for fall entry, along with a $50 fee. Notification of early decision is sent within 30 days; regular decision, mid-March. 142 early decision candidates were accepted for the 1999-2000 class. A waiting list is an active part of the admissions procedure.

Financial Aid: In 1999-2000, 59% of all freshmen and 66% of continuing students received some form of financial aid. 50% of freshmen and 48% of continuing students received need-based aid. The average freshman award was $16,113. Of that total, scholarships or need-based grants averaged $12,583 ($30,050 maximum); loans averaged $3158 ($6625 maximum); and work contracts averaged $1232 ($2000 maximum); and external grants averaged $2649 ($9000 maximum). 54% of undergraduates work part time. Average annual earnings from campus work are $850. The average financial indebtedness of the 1999 graduate was $10,537. Lafayette is a member of CSS. The CSS/Profile, FAFSA, the college's own financial statement, the Business/Farm supplement, and the Divorce/Separation parent statement (if applicable) are required. The fall application deadline is February 15.

Computers: The mainframes are a DEC VAX 6310, an ARIX, and an IBM 9375. Students have unlimited 24-hour access to the campus network, PCs, and multiuser systems. More than 200 computers are available for student use; all residence hall rooms are connected to the campus network. All students may access the system. There are no time limits and no fees.

LAKE FOREST COLLEGE
Lake Forest, IL 60045-2399

(847) 735-5000
(800) 828-4751; Fax: (847) 735-6271

Full-time: 515 men, 692 women	**Faculty:** 83; IIB, ++$
Part-time: 14 men, 20 women	**Ph.D.s:** 92%
Graduate: 3 men, 10 women	**Student/Faculty:** 15 to 1
Year: semesters, summer session	**Tuition:** $20,530
Application Deadline: March 1	**Room & Board:** $4820
Freshman Class: 1296 applied, 1004 accepted, 341 enrolled	
SAT I Verbal/Math: 570/560	**ACT:** 25 **VERY COMPETITIVE**

Lake Forest College, founded in 1857, is a liberal arts institution affiliated by heritage with the Presbyterian Church (U.S.A.). The 2 libraries contain 275,569 volumes, 101,709 microform items, and 11,047 audiovisual forms/CDs, and subscribe to 1170 periodicals. Computerized library services include the card catalog, interlibrary loans, and database searching. Special learning facilities include a learning resource center, art gallery, radio station, multimedia language lab, and an electronic music studio with practice rooms. The 107-acre campus is in a suburban area 30 miles north of Chicago. Including residence halls, there are 30 buildings.

Programs of Study: Lake Forest confers the B.A. degree. Master's degrees are also awarded. Bachelor's degrees are awarded in BIOLOGICAL SCIENCE (biology/biological science), BUSINESS (business economics), COMMUNICATIONS AND THE ARTS (art, communications, English, French, German, music, and Spanish), COMPUTER AND PHYSICAL SCIENCE (chemistry, computer science, mathematics, and physics), EDUCATION (education), ENGINEERING AND ENVIRONMENTAL DESIGN (environmental science), SOCIAL SCIENCE (American studies, anthropology, area studies, Asian/Oriental studies, economics, history, international relations, Latin American studies, philosophy, political science/government, psychology, and sociology). English, business, and education are the largest.

Special: Lake Forest offers cross-registration with Barat College and Associated Colleges of the Midwest, an extensive internship program, a student-designed Independent Scholar Program, and study abroad in 14 countries. Dual and interdisciplinary majors, including American studies, Asian studies, area studies, art (studio and art history), comparative literature, and environmental studies, are available. There is a Washington semester with American University and a work-study program. A 3-2 engineering degree with Washington University at St. Louis and a 3-2 extended degree program in social service with the University of Chicago School of Social Service Administration are offered. Several minors and a pass/fail option are available. There are 11 national honor societies, including Phi Beta Kappa, and a freshman honors program.

Admissions: 77% of the 1999-2000 applicants were accepted. The SAT I scores for the 1999-2000 freshman class were: Verbal--16% below 500, 47% between

500 and 599, 30% between 600 and 700, and 7% above 700; Math--19% below 500, 49% between 500 and 599, 29% between 600 and 700, and 3% above 700. The ACT scores were 9% below 21, 30% between 21 and 23, 31% between 24 and 26, 17% between 27 and 28, and 13% above 28. 46% of the current freshmen were in the top fifth of their class; 76% were in the top two fifths. There were 3 National Merit finalists and 12 semifinalists. 8 freshmen graduated first in their class.

Requirements: The SAT I or ACT is required. Applicants are advised to complete 16 academic credits, including 4 in English, 2 to 4 each in social and natural sciences, 3 in math, and study in 1 or more foreign languages. A GED is accepted. An interview is encouraged. Applications are accepted on computer disk and on-line via CollegeLink, the Common Application, ExPAN, and Mac Apply. AP credits are accepted. Important factors in the admissions decision are advanced placement or honor courses, evidence of special talent, and extracurricular activities record.

Procedure: Freshmen are admitted fall and winter. Entrance exams should be taken in the junior or senior year. There are early decision, early admissions, and deferred admissions plans. Early decision applications should be filed by January 1; regular applications, by March 1 for fall entry and December 15 for spring entry, along with a $35 fee. Notification of early decision is sent January 21; regular decision, March 21. 101 early decision candidates were accepted for the 1999-2000 class. 4% of all applicants are on a waiting list.

Financial Aid: In 1999-2000, 87% of all freshmen and 84% of continuing students received some form of financial aid. 79% of freshmen and 74% of continuing students received need-based aid. The average freshman award was $16,465. Of that total, scholarships or need-based grants averaged $12,462 ($23,000 maximum); loans averaged $2625; and work contracts averaged $1500. 86% of undergraduates work part time. Average annual earnings from campus work are $1575. The average financial indebtedness of the 1999 graduate was $14,708. Lake Forest is a member of CSS. The FAFSA is required. The fall application deadline is March 1.

Computers: There are 190 computers that access the mainframe, the majority of which are available for student use. There are also more than 100 PCs in 11 computer labs in residence halls and academic buildings available for student use. The residence hall PCs have word processing, database management, and spreadsheet software capabilities. Internet network hookups in residence hall rooms are possible at no charge. All students may access the system 24 hours a day, 7 days a week. There are no time limits and no fees.

LAWRENCE UNIVERSITY
Appleton, WI 54912

(920) 832-6500
(800) 227-0982; Fax: (920) 832-6782

Full-time: 537 men, 634 women	**Faculty:** 120; IIB, +$
Part-time: 33 men, 42 women	**Ph.D.s:** 96%
Graduate: none	**Student/Faculty:** 10 to 1
Year: terms	**Tuition:** $21,012
Application Deadline: January 15	**Room & Board:** $4851
Freshman Class: 1348 applied, 1096 accepted, 332 enrolled	
SAT I or ACT required	**HIGHLY COMPETITIVE**

Lawrence University, founded in 1847, is an independent liberal arts institution with a conservatory of music. In addition to regional accreditation, Lawrence has baccalaureate program accreditation with NASM. The library contains 361,382 volumes, 103,509 microform items, and 16,595 audiovisual forms/CDs, and subscribes to 1394 periodicals. Computerized library services include the card catalog, interlibrary loans, and database searching. Special learning facilities include a learning resource center, art gallery, natural history museum, and radio station. The 84-acre campus is in an urban area 100 miles north of Milwaukee. Including residence halls, there are 38 buildings.

Programs of Study: Lawrence confers B.A. and B.Mus. degrees. Bachelor's degrees are awarded in BIOLOGICAL SCIENCE (biology/biological science and neurosciences), COMMUNICATIONS AND THE ARTS (art history and appreciation, classics, dramatic arts, English, French, German, linguistics, music performance, music theory and composition, Russian, Spanish, and studio art), COMPUTER AND PHYSICAL SCIENCE (chemistry, computer science, geology, mathematics, and physics), EDUCATION (art, music, and secondary), ENGINEERING AND ENVIRONMENTAL DESIGN (environmental science), SOCIAL SCIENCE (anthropology, East Asian studies, economics, gender studies, history, international relations, philosophy, political science/government, psychology, and religion). Biology, music, and physics are the strongest academically. Biology, psychology, and music are the largest.

Special: Lawrence offers Chicago-based programs in urban studies, urban education, and the arts, a humanities program at the Newberry Library, and a science internship at Oak Ridge National Laboratory and a biological field station in Minnesota. There are study-abroad programs in 14 countries, a Washington semester, limited pass/fail options, student-designed majors, and nondegree study. Students may take a 3-2 engineering degree with Columbia or Washington Universities, Rensselaer Polytechnic Institute, or the University of Michigan. Also available are 3-2 programs in forestry and environmental studies with Duke University, in occupational therapy with Washington University in St. Louis and in allied health sciences (nursing/medical technology) with Rush-Presbyterian-St. Luke's Medical Center in Chicago. A 5-year B.A.-B.Mus. degree is offered. There are 8 national honor societies, including Phi Beta Kappa, and 21 departmental honors programs.

Admissions: 81% of the 1999-2000 applicants were accepted. The SAT I scores for the 1999-2000 freshman class were: Verbal--2% below 500, 18% between 500 and 599, 56% between 600 and 700, and 25% above 700; Math--6% below 500, 20% between 500 and 599, 51% between 600 and 700, and 23% above 700. The ACT scores were 1% below 21, 12% between 21 and 23, 25% between 24 and 26, 23% between 27 and 28, and 39% above 28. 72% of the current freshmen were in the top fifth of their class; 92% were in the top two fifths. There were 8 National Merit finalists and 18 semifinalists. 19 freshmen graduated first in their class.

Requirements: The SAT I or ACT is required. In addition, applicants should complete 16 high school academic credits. Lawrence requires an essay, reports from a teacher and counselor, and, for music majors, an audition. The school recommends the SAT II: Writing test, an interview, and, for art majors, a portfolio. Applications are accepted on computer disk, and on-line via CollegeLink, Common Application, Wisconsin Mentor, Apply, and CollegeNet. AP credits are accepted. Important factors in the admissions decision are advanced placement or honor courses, evidence of special talent, and extracurricular activities record.

Procedure: Freshmen are admitted in the fall. Entrance exams should be taken in the spring of the junior year or fall of the senior year. There are early decision, early admissions, and deferred admissions plans. Applications should be filed by January 15 for fall entry, along with a $30 fee. Notification of early decision is sent December 1; regular decision, April 1. 47 early decision candidates were accepted for the 1999-2000 class. 5% of all applicants are on a waiting list.

Financial Aid: In 1999-2000, 90% of all freshmen and 83% of continuing students received some form of financial aid. 65% of freshmen and 63% of continuing students received need-based aid. The average freshman award was $18,100. Of that total, scholarships or need-based grants averaged $12,100 ($24,150 maximum); loans averaged $4200 ($6600 maximum); and work contracts averaged $1800 ($2300 maximum). 70% of undergraduates work part time. Average annual earnings from campus work are $1500. The average financial indebtedness of the 1999 graduate was $16,595. Lawrence is a member of CSS. The FAFSA and the university's own financial statement are required. The fall application deadline is March 15.

Computers: The university has several midrange Compaq systems. Some model numbers in use are 1000A, 2100, and DS20. Internet access is available from nearly anywhere on campus, including student rooms. There are a number of computer labs located in the larger residence halls, in the library, and in major academic buildings. All students are provided with disk space for storing important documents and developing web pages. All students may access the system 24 hours a day. There are no time limits. It is strongly recommended that all students have PCs.

LEBANON VALLEY COLLEGE OF PENNSYLVANIA

Annville, PA 17003-0501

(717) 867-6180
(800) 445-6181; Fax: (717) 867-6026

Full-time: 744 men, 591 women	**Faculty:** 80; IIB, +$
Part-time: 147 men, 325 women	**Ph.D.s:** 82%
Graduate: 161 men, 96 women	**Student/Faculty:** 17 to 1
Year: semesters, summer session	**Tuition:** $17,260
Application Deadline: open	**Room & Board:** $5490
Freshman Class: 2385 applied, 1661 accepted, 445 enrolled	
SAT I Verbal/Math: 542/549	**ACT:** 23 **VERY COMPETITIVE**

Lebanon Valley College of Pennsylvania, founded in 1866, is a private institution affiliated with the United Methodist Church. The college offers undergraduate programs in the arts and sciences. In addition to regional accreditation, LVC has baccalaureate program accreditation with NASM. The library contains 161,642 volumes, 18,380 microform items, and 3246 audiovisual forms/CDs, and subscribes to 740 periodicals. Computerized library services include the card catalog, interlibrary loans, and database searching. Special learning facilities include a learning resource center, art gallery, and radio station. The 200-acre campus is in a small town 7 miles east of Hershey. Including residence halls, there are 33 buildings.

Programs of Study: LVC confers B.A., B.S., B.M., B.S.Ch., B.S.Med.Tech., and B.S.Ed. degrees. Associate and master's degrees are also awarded. Bachelor's degrees are awarded in BIOLOGICAL SCIENCE (biochemistry and biology/biological science), BUSINESS (accounting, hotel/motel and restaurant management, and international business management), COMMUNICATIONS AND THE ARTS (audio technology, English, French, German, music, music performance, and Spanish), COMPUTER AND PHYSICAL SCIENCE (actuarial science, chemistry, computer science, mathematics, and physics), EDUCATION (elementary, music, and secondary), ENGINEERING AND ENVIRONMENTAL DESIGN (engineering), HEALTH PROFESSIONS (medical laboratory technology, occupational therapy, physical therapy, predentistry, premedicine, prepharmacy, and preveterinary science), SOCIAL SCIENCE (American studies, economics, history, philosophy, political science/government, prelaw, psychobiology, psychology, religion, and sociology). Actuarial science, natural sciences, and education are the strongest academically. Education, business, and natural sciences are the largest.

Special: Study abroad is available in 6 countries through the college's affiliation with the International Student Exchange Program and the LVC College in Cologne Program. LVC is also affiliated with several colleges and universities in England, France, Spain, the Netherlands, and New Zealand. There are 3-2 degree programs in engineering with the University of Pennsylvania and Case Western Reserve and Widener Universities, in forestry with Duke University, and in medical technology with Hahnemann University. There is also a 2-2 degree program in allied health sciences with Thomas Jefferson University. LVC offers internships in a number of areas. There are 6 national honor societies and 11 departmental honors programs.

Admissions: 70% of the 1999-2000 applicants were accepted. The SAT I scores for the 1999-2000 freshman class were: Verbal--30% below 500, 44% between 500 and 599, 24% between 600 and 700, and 2% above 700; Math--30% below 500, 41% between 500 and 599, 27% between 600 and 700, and 2% above 700. The ACT scores were 31% below 21, 20% between 21 and 23, 17% between 24 and 26, 21% between 27 and 28, and 1% above 28. 56% of the current freshmen were in the top fifth of their class; 84% were in the top two fifths. There was 1 National Merit semifinalist. 2 freshmen graduated first in their class.

Requirements: The SAT I or ACT is required. Applicants must be graduates of accredited secondary schools or have earned a GED. LVC requires 16 academic units or 16 Carnegie units, including 4 in English, 2 each in math and foreign language, and 1 each in science and social studies. An interview is recommended. Students applying as music majors must also audition. Applications are accepted on-line at the school's web site. AP and CLEP credits are accepted. Important factors in the admissions decision are advanced placement or honor courses, leadership record, and personality/intangible qualities.

Procedure: Freshmen are admitted fall and spring. Entrance exams should be taken in the spring of the junior year. There is a deferred admissions plan. Application deadlines are open, but submissions by March 1 are given priority. The application fee is $25. Notification is sent on a rolling basis.

Financial Aid: In 1999-2000, 98% of all freshmen and 95% of continuing students received some form of financial aid. 78% of all students received need-based aid. The average freshman award was $13,924. Of that total, scholarships or need-based grants averaged $7918 ($9095 maximum); loans averaged $3565 ($4125 maximum); work contracts averaged $1029 ($1300 maximum); and outside scholarships averaged $1770 ($7745 maximum). 54% of undergraduates work part time. Average annual earnings from campus work are $625. The average financial indebtedness of the 1999 graduate was $17,462. LVC is a member of CSS. The FAFSA and the college's own financial statement are required. The fall application deadline is March 1.

Computers: The mainframes are a DEC ALPHA server a Compaq ProLiant server. Servers and other networked resources (including the Internet and Web) can be reached from 200 college-owned student computers located throughout the campus. Resident students may also connect their own PCs to the campus network via Ethernet and have access to the same resources. Approximately 600 resident student computers were connected in the fall of 1999. All students may access the system. There are no time limits.

LEE UNIVERSITY
Cleveland, TN 37311

(423) 614-8500
(800) 533-9930; Fax: (423) 614-8533

Full-time: 1262 men, 1658 women	**Faculty:** 131; IIB, --$
Part-time: 117 men, 118 women	**Ph.Ds:** 58%
Graduate: 41 men, 63 women	**Student/Faculty:** 22 to 1
Year: semesters, summer session	**Tuition:** $6358
Application Deadline: September 1	**Room & Board:** $3840

Freshman Class: 1175 applied, 1060 accepted, 699 enrolled
SAT I Verbal/Math: 528/558 **ACT:** 22 **VERY COMPETITIVE**

Lee University, founded in 1918, is a private, liberal arts institution affiliated with the Church of God. There are 4 undergraduate and 4 graduate schools. In addition to regional accreditation, Lee has baccalaureate program accreditation with NASM. The 2 libraries contain 153,424 volumes, 4984 microform items, and 12,881 audiovisual forms/CDs, and subscribe to 2000 periodicals. Computerized library services include the card catalog, interlibrary loans, and database searching. Special learning facilities include a learning resource center, natural history museum, and audiovisual center. The campus is in a suburban area 25 miles north of Chattanooga.

Programs of Study: Lee confers B.A., B.S., and B.M.E. degrees. Master's degrees are also awarded. Bachelor's degrees are awarded in BIOLOGICAL SCIENCE (biology/biological science), BUSINESS (accounting and business administration and management), COMMUNICATIONS AND THE ARTS (communications, English, French, German, music, and Spanish), COMPUTER AND PHYSICAL SCIENCE (chemistry, computer programming, mathematics, and science), EDUCATION (elementary, music, and physical), HEALTH PROFESSIONS (medical laboratory technology), SOCIAL SCIENCE (crosscultural studies, history, human development, psychology, religious education, social science, and sociology). English, sociology, Bible, and theology are the strongest academically. Business, human development, psychology, and biology are the largest.

Special: Lee offers internships, cross-registration with the Coalition for Christian Colleges and Universities, study abroad, a Washington semester, numerous work-study programs, dual and student-designed majors, nondegree study, and limited pass/fail options. Every student completes a minor in religion. There are 6 national honor societies, a freshman honors program, and 1 departmental honors program.

Admissions: 90% of the 1999-2000 applicants were accepted. The SAT I scores for the 1999-2000 freshman class were: Verbal--37% below 500, 39% between 500 and 599, 20% between 600 and 700, and 3% above 700; Math--44% below 500, 33% between 500 and 599, 20% between 600 and 700, and 2% above 700. 20% of the current freshmen were in the top fifth of their class; 64% were in the top two fifths. 18 freshmen graduated first in their class.

Requirements: The SAT I or ACT is required. A GPA of 2.0 is required, with a composite score of 860 on the SAT I or 17 on the ACT. Students must be graduates of accredited secondary schools. The GED is accepted. A portfolio is recommended. AP and CLEP credits are accepted. Important factors in the admissions decision are advanced placement or honor courses, leadership record, and recommendations by school officials.

Procedure: Freshmen are admitted fall and spring. Entrance exams should be taken prior to registration. Early decision applications should be filed by January

1; regular applications, by September 1 for fall entry, along with a $25 fee. Notification is sent on a rolling basis.

Financial Aid: In 1999-2000, 75% of all freshmen and 72% of continuing students received some form of financial aid. 70% of freshmen and 80% of continuing students received need-based aid. The average freshman award was $5589. Of that total, scholarships or need-based grants averaged $3057 ($10,030 maximum); loans averaged $2442 ($4625 maximum); work contracts averaged $1513 ($2637 maximum); and PLUS/SLS averaged $5425 ($10,300 maximum). 10% of undergraduates work part time. Average annual earnings from campus work are $1513. The average financial indebtedness of the 1999 graduate was $10,892. Lee is a member of CSS. The FAFSA and the college's own financial statement are required. The fall application deadline is April 15.

Computers: The mainframe is an IBM AS/400. There are PCs available for student use in the computer labs. All students may access the system. There are no time limits. The fee is $25 per semester.

LEHIGH UNIVERSITY
Bethlehem, PA 18015   (610) 758-3100; Fax: (610) 758-4361

Full-time: 2689 men, 1810 women	**Faculty:** 391; I, +$
Part-time: 65 men, 41 women	**Ph.D.s:** 99%
Graduate: 1009 men, 745 women	**Student/Faculty:** 12 to 1
Year: semesters, summer session	**Tuition:** $23,150
Application Deadline: January 1	**Room & Board:** $6630
Freshman Class: 8853 applied, 4228 accepted, 1079 enrolled	
SAT I Verbal/Math: 608/642	**MOST COMPETITIVE**

Lehigh University, founded in 1865, is a private university offering both undergraduate and graduate programs in liberal arts, science, engineering, and business, and graduate programs in education. There are 3 undergraduate and 4 graduate schools. In addition to regional accreditation, Lehigh has baccalaureate program accreditation with AACSB, ABET, and NCATE. The 2 libraries contain 1,354,100 volumes, 2,113,130 microform items, and 3915 audiovisual forms/CDs, and subscribe to 10,797 periodicals. Computerized library services include the card catalog, interlibrary loans, and database searching. Special learning facilities include a learning resource center, art gallery, radio station, TV station, Special Collections/Rare Book Reading Room, and International Multimedia Resource Center. The 1600-acre campus is in a suburban area 60 miles north of Philadelphia and 80 miles southwest of New York City. Including residence halls, there are 153 buildings.

Programs of Study: Lehigh confers B.A., B.S., B.S.B.A., and B.S.E. degrees. Master's and doctoral degrees are also awarded. Bachelor's degrees are awarded in BIOLOGICAL SCIENCE (biochemistry, biology/biological science, and molecular biology), BUSINESS (accounting, banking and finance, business administration and management, business economics, and marketing/retailing/merchandising), COMMUNICATIONS AND THE ARTS (art, classics, dramatic arts, English, French, German, journalism, music, and Spanish), COMPUTER AND PHYSICAL SCIENCE (chemistry, computer science, information sciences and systems, mathematics, natural sciences, physics, science technology, and statistics), EDUCATION (social foundations), ENGINEERING AND ENVIRONMENTAL DESIGN (architecture, chemical engineering, civil engineering, computer engineering, electrical/electronics engineering, engineering mechanics, engineering physics, environmental science, industrial engineering, materials engineering, and mechanical engineering), HEALTH PROFESSIONS (predentistry, premedicine, and preoptometry), SOCIAL SCIENCE (African studies, American studies, anthropology, Asian/Oriental studies, behavioral science, classical/ancient civilization, cognitive science, economics, history, international public service, international relations, philosophy, political science/government, psychology, religion, Russian and Slavic studies, sociology, and urban studies). Architecture, accounting, and mechanical engineering are the largest.

Special: The university offers co-op programs through the Colleges of Engineering and Applied Science and Business and Economics, cross-registration with the Lehigh Valley Association of Independent Colleges, study abroad in 40 countries, internships, a Washington semester, several work-study programs, accelerated degree programs in medicine, dentistry and optometry, student-designed majors, many combinations of dual majors, a B.A.-B.S. degree, a 3-2 engineering degree, and pass/fail options. A 6-year B.A.-M.D. degree with the Medical College of Pennsylvania and a 7-year B.A.-D.D.S. degree with Pennsylvania State University are possible. There are 18 national honor societies, including Phi Beta Kappa, and a freshman honors program.

Admissions: 48% of the 1999-2000 applicants were accepted. The SAT I scores for the 1999-2000 freshman class were: Verbal--6% below 500, 42% between 500 and 599, 44% between 600 and 700, and 8% above 700; Math--2% below 500, 24% between 500 and 599, 57% between 600 and 700, and 17% above 700. 80% of the current freshmen were in the top fifth of their class; 98% were in the top two fifths. There were 12 National Merit finalists. 80 freshmen graduated first in their class.

Requirements: The SAT I or ACT is required. Candidates for admission should have completed 4 years of English, and 2 years each of a foreign language, history, math, science, and social science. Most students present 4 years each of science, math, and English. An on-campus interview is recommended. AP credits are accepted. Important factors in the admissions decision are advanced placement or honor courses, evidence of special talent, and leadership record.

Procedure: Freshmen are admitted fall and spring. Entrance exams should be taken by the January test date. There is an early decision plan. Early decision applications should be filed by November 15; regular applications, by January 1 for fall entry and November 15 for spring entry, along with a $50 fee. Notification of early decision is sent December 15; regular decision, by April 1. 226 early decision candidates were accepted for the 1999-2000 class. 28% of all applicants are on a waiting list.

Financial Aid: In 1999-2000, 56% of all freshmen and 60% of continuing students received some form of financial aid. 49% of freshmen and 50% of continuing students received need-based aid. The average freshman award was $18,600. Of that total, scholarships or need-based grants averaged $13,900 ($28,000 maximum); loans averaged $3500 ($5500 maximum); and work contracts averaged $1200 ($1500 maximum). 27% of undergraduates work part time. Average annual earnings from campus work are $980. The average financial indebtedness of the 1999 graduate was $15,178. Lehigh is a member of CSS. The CSS/Profile or FAFSA and the college's own financial statement are required. The fall application deadline is January 15.

Computers: The mainframes are clusters of high-speed IBM RS/6000 computers, with more than 115 workstations in public sites. There are also more than 400 PCs available for student use in libraries, academic buildings, and computer centers. There are computer ports in all classrooms, dormitories, and offices. Many LANs and high-speed fiber-optic networks are available. All students may access the system 24 hours per day, 7 days per week. There are no time limits and no fees.

LETOURNEAU UNIVERSITY

Longview, TX 75607

(903) 233-3400
(800) 759-8811; Fax: (903) 233-3411

Full-time: 1267 men, 1105 women	**Faculty:** 58; IIB, -$
Part-time: 77 men, 80 women	**Ph.D.s:** 71%
Graduate: 162 men, 119 women	**Student/Faculty:** 40 to 1
Year: semesters, summer session	**Tuition:** $11,720
Application Deadline: August 15	**Room & Board:** $5068
Freshman Class: 956 applied, 807 accepted, 374 enrolled	
SAT I Verbal/Math: 582/596	**ACT:** 24 **VERY COMPETITIVE**

Le Tourneau University, founded in 1946, is a private, nondenominational Christian institution offering programs in aeronautical science, business administration, engineering, education, liberal arts, technology, computer science, natural and mathematical sciences, physical education, and others. There are 8 undergraduate schools and 1 graduate school. In addition to regional accreditation, Le-Tourneau has baccalaureate program accreditation with ABET. The library contains 89,116 volumes, 2146 microform items, and 2134 audiovisual forms/CDs, and subscribes to 599 periodicals. Computerized library services include the card catalog, interlibrary loans, and database searching. Special learning facilities include a learning resource center. The 162-acre campus is in an urban area 60 miles West of Shreveport, Louisiana. Including residence halls, there are 55 buildings.

Programs of Study: LeTourneau confers B.A., B.S., B.B.A., and B.B.M. degrees. Associate and master's degrees are also awarded. Bachelor's degrees are awarded in BIOLOGICAL SCIENCE (biology/biological science), BUSINESS (accounting, business administration and management, management information systems, marketing management, and marketing/retailing/merchandising), COMMUNICATIONS AND THE ARTS (English), COMPUTER AND PHYSICAL SCIENCE (chemistry, computer mathematics, computer science, and mathematics), EDUCATION (business, elementary, physical, science, and secondary), ENGINEERING AND ENVIRONMENTAL DESIGN (aeronautical science, aeronautical technology, computer engineering, computer technology, electrical/electronics engineering, engineering, engineering technology, industrial administration/management, mechanical engineering, and welding engineering), HEALTH PROFESSIONS (health, medical laboratory technology, premedicine, and preveterinary science), SOCIAL SCIENCE (biblical studies, history, interdisciplinary studies, prelaw, psychology, and public administration). Engineering, computer science, and math are the strongest academically. Engineering and aeronautical science are the largest.

Special: Le Tourneau offers co-op programs in engineering, business, accounting, computer science, biology, design technology, and others, internships through business and liberal arts programs, an American studies program with the Council for Christian Colleges and Universities, credit for experience, and international studies in England, Egypt, Russia, China, and Costa Rica. There is a freshman honors program and 1 departmental honors program.

Admissions: 84% of the 1999-2000 applicants were accepted. The SAT I scores for the 1999-2000 freshman class were: Verbal--16% below 500, 43% between 500 and 599, 28% between 600 and 700, and 13% above 700; Math--10% below 500, 37% between 500 and 599, 36% between 600 and 700, and 17% above 700. The ACT scores were 12% below 21, 29% between 21 and 23, 26% between 24 and 26, 13% between 27 and 28, and 20% above 28. 11 freshmen graduated first in their class.

Requirements: The SAT I or ACT is required, with a recommended minimum composite score of 950 on the SAT I or 20 on the ACT. LeTourneau requires applicants to be in the upper 50% of their class. A GPA of 2.5 is required. Applicants must be graduates of an accredited secondary school or have the GED. They should have completed 16 academic credits, including 4 in English and 3 each in math, social studies, natural science, and electives. An essay is required. Applications can be downloaded from the schools web site. AP and CLEP credits are accepted. Important factors in the admissions decision are advanced placement or honor courses, personality/intangible qualities, and extracurricular activities record.

Procedure: Freshmen are admitted to all sessions. Entrance exams should be taken by the fall of the senior year. There is an early admissions plan. Applications should be filed by August 15 for fall entry and January 5 for spring entry, along with a $25 fee. Notification is sent within days of receiving the completed application.

Financial Aid: In 1999-2000, 94% of all freshmen and 89% of continuing students received some form of financial aid. 45% of freshmen and 41% of continuing students received need-based aid. The average freshman award was $8568. Of that total, scholarships or need-based grants averaged $5323 ($13,175 maximum); loans averaged $2177 ($18,795 maximum); work contracts averaged $566 ($1500 maximum); and outside scholarships averaged $502 ($14,565 maximum) 43% of undergraduates work part time. Average annual earnings from campus work are $1236. The average financial indebtedness of the 1999 graduate was $16,858. LeTourneau is a member of CSS. The FAFSA is required. The preferred fall application deadline is February 15.

Computers: The mainframe is a MicroVAX. Every room on campus has 2 ports for access to the LeTNet and Web. The CAD lab has 25 computers, and there are 8 PCs in the library and 75 in computer labs. All students may access the system. There are no time limits and no fees.

LEWIS AND CLARK COLLEGE
Portland, OR 97219-7899
(503) 768-7040
(800) 444-4111; Fax: (503) 768-7055

Full-time: 694 men, 1010 women	**Faculty:** 118; IIB, ++$
Part-time: 19 men, 19 women	**Ph.D.s:** 93%
Graduate: 594 men, 867 women	**Student/Faculty:** 14 to 1
Year: semesters, summer session	**Tuition:** $20,326
Application Deadline: February 1	**Room & Board:** $6208
Freshman Class: 3013 applied, 2088 accepted, 521 enrolled	
SAT I or ACT: required	**VERY COMPETITIVE**

Lewis and Clark College, founded in 1867, is a private, independent liberal arts and sciences institution with a global reach. There are 2 graduate schools. In addition to regional accreditation, LC has baccalaureate program accreditation with NASM. The 2 libraries contain 703,706 volumes, 654,548 microform items, and 10,786 audiovisual forms/CDs, and subscribe to 6689 periodicals. Computerized library services include the card catalog, interlibrary loans, and database searching. Special learning facilities include a learning resource center, art gallery, radio station, TV station, telescope, research astronomical observatory, language lab, and greenhouse. The 115-acre campus is in a suburban area 6 miles south of downtown Portland. Including residence halls, there are 55 buildings.

Programs of Study: LC confers the B.A. degree. Master's degrees are also awarded. Bachelor's degrees are awarded in BIOLOGICAL SCIENCE (biochemistry and biology/biological science), BUSINESS (business economics), COMMUNICATIONS AND THE ARTS (art history and appreciation, communications, dramatic arts, English, fine arts, languages, music, and studio art), COMPUTER AND PHYSICAL SCIENCE (chemistry, computer science, mathematics, and physics), ENGINEERING AND ENVIRONMENTAL DESIGN (environmental science), SOCIAL SCIENCE (anthropology, East Asian studies, economics, French studies, German area studies, Hispanic American studies, history, interdisciplinary studies, international relations, philosophy, political science/government, psychology, religion, and sociology). Psychology, English, and biology are the strongest academically. Psychology, international affairs, and English are the largest.

Special: LC offers cross-registration with the Oregon Independent College Association, which includes Reed College and the University of Portland; internships; one of the oldest and largest study-abroad programs in the United States, encompassing 60 countries; semesters in Washington and New York City; and dual and student-designed majors. A 3-2 engineering program is available with Columbia and Washington universities, the University of Southern California, and the Oregon Graduate Institute. There are 5 national honor societies, including Phi Beta Kappa, and 22 departmental honors programs.

Admissions: 69% of the 1999-2000 applicants were accepted. The SAT I scores for the 1999-2000 freshman class were: Verbal--3% below 500, 29% between 500 and 599, 48% between 600 and 700, and 20% above 700; Math--5% below 500, 36% between 500 and 599, 47% between 600 and 700, and 12% above 700. The ACT scores were 5% below 21, 13% between 21 and 23, 23% between 24 and 26, 26% between 27 and 28, and 33% above 28. 64% of the current freshmen were in the top fifth of their class; 89% were in the top two fifths. There were 13 National Merit finalists. 20 freshmen graduated first in their class.

Requirements: The SAT I or ACT is required. A GPA of 2.0 is required. A GED may be accepted. It is recommended that applicants have 4 years each of English and math, 3 to 4 years of science, 3 years each of history/social studies and foreign language, and 1 year of fine arts. An essay is required and an interview recommended. The college also admits exceptional students through the Portfolio Path option. This allows students to create an academic portfolio of materials they feel best demonstrates the strengths of their program; 3 academic teacher recommendations are required and test scores are optional. Applications are accepted on computer disk and on-line via CollegeNet, CollegeLink, Apply, the CommonApp, or LC's web site. AP credits are accepted. Important factors in the admissions decision are advanced placement or honor courses, recommendations by school officials, and leadership record.

Procedure: Freshmen are admitted fall and spring. Entrance exams should be taken during the spring of the junior year and the fall of the senior year. There are early admissions and deferred admissions plans. Applications should be filed by February 1 for fall entry, December 1 for spring entry, and May 1 for summer entry, along with a $45 fee. Notification of early action is sent January 15; regular decision, April 1. 5% of all applicants are on a waiting list.

Financial Aid: In 1999-2000, 77% of all freshmen and 70% of continuing students received some form of financial aid. 60% of freshmen and 53% of continuing students received need-based aid. The average freshman award was $16,695. Of that total, scholarships or need-based grants averaged $11,720 ($20,136 maximum); loans averaged $2136 ($4625 maximum); and work contracts averaged $1300 ($2000 maximum). 72% of undergraduates work part time. Average annual earnings from campus work are $984. LC is a member of CSS. The FAFSA and the college's own financial statement are required. The fall application deadline is February 1.

Computers: The mainframes are a Sun DEC ALPHA Server 2100/A500 and an ALPHA Server 2000/400. The campus servers are networked with 6 UNIX workstations and 5 X-Windows terminals. They run the UNIX operating system and are interconnected through Ethernet on campus with the library, residence halls, and academic buildings. Mac and PC clusters are available 24 hours per day in the library and in residence halls. A T1 line connects the campus to the regional Internet. All students may access the system 24 hours a day. There are no time limits and no fees.

LOUISIANA STATE UNIVERSITY AND AGRICULTURAL AND MECHANICAL COLLEGE

Baton Rouge, LA 70803   (225) 388-1175; Fax: (225) 388-4433

Full-time: 10,905 men, 12,060 women	**Faculty:** 1294; I, --$
Part-time: 1308 men, 1649 women	**Ph.D.s:** 80%
Graduate: 2447 men, 2608 women	**Student/Faculty:** 18 to 1
Year: semesters, summer session	**Tuition:** $2881 ($7081)
Application Deadline: May 1	**Room & Board:** $4130
Freshman Class: 9382 applied, 7713 accepted, 4927 enrolled	
ACT: 24	**VERY COMPETITIVE**

Louisiana State University and Agricultural and Mechanical College, a public institution founded in 1860 and part of the Louisiana State University System, offers programs in agriculture, arts and sciences, basic sciences, business administration, design, education, engineering, music and dramatic arts, and mass communication. There are 12 undergraduate and 4 graduate schools. In addition to regional accreditation, LSU has baccalaureate program accreditation with AACSB, ABET, ACCE, ACEJMC, ADA, ASLA, CSWE, FIDER, NAAB, NASAD, NASM, NCATE, and SAF. The 2 libraries contain 3,054,740 volumes, 5,181,401 microform items, and 21,786 audiovisual forms/CDs, and subscribe to 21,990 periodicals. Computerized library services include the card catalog, interlibrary loans, and database searching. Special learning facilities include a learning resource center, art gallery, natural history museum, radio station, tv station, 3 herbariums, and museums of natural science, geoscience, rural life, and art. The 2000-acre campus is in an urban area. Including residence halls, there are 250 buildings.

Programs of Study: LSU confers B.A., B.S., B.A. in M.C., B.Arch., B.F.A., B.G.S., B.Int.Design, B.Land.Arch., B.M., B.M.Ed., B.S.B.E., B.S.C.E., B.S.Ch.E., B.S.Cons.M., B.S.E.E., B.S.Env.Engineering, B.S.F., B.S.I.E., B.S. in Geol., B.S. M.E., and B.S.P.E. degrees. Master's and doctoral degrees are also awarded. Bachelor's degrees are awarded in AGRICULTURE (agricultural business management, animal science, forestry and related sciences, natural resource management, and plant science), BIOLOGICAL SCIENCE (biochemistry, biology/biological science, botany, microbiology, nutrition, and wildlife biology), BUSINESS (accounting, banking and finance, business administration and management, business economics, international economics, management information systems, management science, and marketing/retailing/merchandising), COMMUNICATIONS AND THE ARTS (communications, dramatic arts, English, fine arts, French, German, Latin, music, Spanish, and speech/debate/rhetoric), COMPUTER AND PHYSICAL SCIENCE (chemistry, computer science, geology, mathematics, and physics), EDUCATION (elementary, music, secondary, and vocational), ENGINEERING AND ENVIRONMENTAL DESIGN (architecture, bioengineering, chemical engineering, civil engineering, computer engineering, construction management, electrical/electronics engineering, environmental engineering, industrial engineering, interior design, landscape architecture/design, mechanical engineering, and petroleum/natural gas engineering), HEALTH PROFESSIONS (speech pathology/audiology), SOCIAL SCIENCE (anthropology, dietetics, economics, family/consumer studies, food science, geography, history, international studies, liberal arts/general studies, philosophy, physical fitness/movement, political science/government, psychology, Russian and Slavic studies, sociology, and textiles and clothing). Biological sciences, chemical engineering, and chemistry are the strongest academically. Elementary grades education, general sciences, and mass communication are the largest.

Special: Co-op programs in numerous majors, cross-registration with Southern University, internships, study abroad, and work-study programs are offered. B.A. -B.S. degrees, dual majors, a general studies degree, nondegree study, an evening school, a program of study for adult learners, and pass/fail options are available. There are 38 national honor societies, including Phi Beta Kappa, a freshman honors program, and 17 departmental honors programs.

Admissions: 82% of the 1999-2000 applicants were accepted. The ACT scores for the 1999-2000 freshman class were: 21% below 21, 32% between 21 and 23, 24% between 24 and 26, 12% between 27 and 28, and 10% above 28. 46% of the current freshmen were in the top fifth of their class; 76% were in the top two fifths. There were 33 National Merit finalists and 33 semifinalists. 148 freshmen graduated first in their class.

Requirements: The SAT I or ACT is required. A GPA of 2.5 is required. Applicants must be graduates of an accredited secondary school. GED certificates may be accepted in unusual circumstances. Students must have completed 4 credits in English, 3 each in specific math, science, and social studies courses, 2 credits in a foreign language, 1/2 credit in computer skills, and 2 additional credits from the above categories or certain courses in the visual and performing arts. Applications may be submitted on-line at http://web.srr.lsu.edu/admissions. AP and CLEP credits are accepted. Important factors in the admissions decision are advanced placement or honor courses, evidence of special talent, and recommendations by school officials.

Procedure: Freshmen are admitted to all sessions. Entrance exams should be taken in the fall of the senior year. There is an early admissions plan. Applications should be filed by May 1 for summer or fall entry, and December 1 for spring entry, along with a $25 fee. Notification is sent on a rolling basis.

Financial Aid: In 1999-2000, 94% of all freshmen and 70% of continuing students received some form of financial aid. 27% of freshmen and 32% of continuing students received need-based aid. The average freshman award was $4834. Of that total, scholarships or need-based grants averaged $3000 ($6800 maximum); loans averaged $3500 ($11,600 maximum); and work contracts averaged $1400 ($7400 maximum). 25% of undergraduates work part time. Average annual earnings from campus work are $1900. The average financial indebtedness of the 1999 graduate was $17,093. The FAFSA is required. The fall application deadline is February 1.

Computers: The mainframes are an IBM 4672/RX3 and an IBM SP. Public labs contain more than 800 networked PCs. All students may access the system up to 16 hours per day, 7 days per week. There are no time limits and no fees. It is recommended that students in the College of Design have personal computers.

LOYOLA COLLEGE IN MARYLAND
Baltimore, MD 21210
(410) 617-5012
(800) 221-9107; Fax: (410) 617-2176

Full-time: 1473 men, 1834 women	**Faculty:** 234; IIA, +$
Part-time: 32 men, 38 women	**Ph.D.s:** 93%
Graduate: 1161 men, 1725 women	**Student/Faculty:** 14 to 1
Year: semesters, summer session	**Tuition:** $19,930
Application Deadline: January 15	**Room & Board:** $7200
Freshman Class: 6129 applied, 4036 accepted, 947 enrolled	
SAT I Verbal/Math: 602/603	**HIGHLY COMPETITIVE**

Loyola College, founded in 1852, is a private liberal arts college affiliated with the Roman Catholic Church and the Jesuit tradition. It offers degree programs in arts and sciences, and business and management. There are 2 undergraduate and 2 graduate schools. In addition to regional accreditation, Loyola has baccalaureate program accreditation with AACSB, ABET, CSAB, and NASDTEC. The library contains 349,238 volumes, 435,091 microform items, and 25,559 audiovisual forms/CDs, and subscribes to 2075 periodicals. Computerized library services include the card catalog, interlibrary loans, and database searching. Special learning facilities include an art gallery. The 89-acre campus is in an urban area 3 miles from downtown Baltimore. Including residence halls, there are 29 buildings.

Programs of Study: Loyola confers B.A., B.S., B.B.A., B.S.E.E., and B.S.E.S. degrees. Master's and doctoral degrees are also awarded. Bachelor's degrees are awarded in BIOLOGICAL SCIENCE (biology/biological science), BUSINESS (accounting and business administration and management), COMMUNICATIONS AND THE ARTS (communications, creative writing, English, fine arts, French, German, Latin, and Spanish), COMPUTER AND PHYSICAL SCIENCE (chemistry, computer science, mathematics, and physics), EDUCATION (elementary), ENGINEERING AND ENVIRONMENTAL DESIGN (electrical/electronics engineering and engineering), HEALTH PROFESSIONS (speech pathology/audiology), SOCIAL SCIENCE (classical/ancient civilization, economics, history, philosophy, political science/government, psychology, sociology, and theological studies). General business, psychology, and biology are the largest.

Special: Loyola offers cross-registration with Johns Hopkins, Towson State, and Morgan State universities, Goucher College, the College of Notre Dame, Maryland Art Institute, and Peabody Conservatory. Credit-bearing internships are available in most majors, and there are study-abroad programs in Thailand, Belgium, and England. Work-study programs and dual majors are also offered. There are 23 national honor societies, including Phi Beta Kappa, a freshman honors program, and 1 departmental honors program.

Admissions: 66% of the 1999-2000 applicants were accepted. The SAT I scores for the 1999-2000 freshman class were: Verbal--5% below 500, 44% between 500 and 599, 44% between 600 and 700, and 7% above 700; Math--6% below 500, 39% between 500 and 599, 50% between 600 and 700, and 5% above 700. 58% of the current freshmen were in the top fifth of their class; 89% were in the top two fifths. 10 freshmen graduated first in their class.

Requirements: The SAT I is required. Applicants should have graduated from an accredited secondary school or have earned the GED. Secondary preparation should include 4 years of English, 3 to 4 each of math, foreign language, natural science, and classical or modern foreign language, and 2 to 3 of history. A personal essay is required; an interview is recommended. AP and CLEP credits are accepted. Important factors in the admissions decision are advanced placement or honor courses, recommendations by school officials, and extracurricular activities record.

Procedure: Freshmen are admitted fall and spring. Entrance exams should be taken by December of the senior year. There are early admissions and deferred admissions plans. Applications should be filed by January 15 for fall entry and December 15 for spring entry, along with a $30 fee. Notification is sent April 15. 8% of all applicants are on a waiting list.

Financial Aid: In 1999-2000, 68% of all freshmen and 63% of continuing students received some form of financial aid. 57% of freshmen and 52% of continuing students received need-based aid. The average freshman award was $14,020. Of that total, scholarships or need-based grants averaged $9260 ($17,700 maximum); loans averaged $3010 ($3625 maximum); and work contracts averaged $1750 ($1750 maximum). 14% of undergraduates work part time. Average annual earnings from campus work are $1450. The average financial indebtedness of the 1999 graduate was $15,020. Loyola is a member of CSS. The CSS/Profile or FAFSA is required. The fall application deadline is February 1.

Computers: The mainframes are 2 DEC VAX 11/785 computers. There are also more than 200 PCs and Macs available. All students may access the system. There are no time limits and no fees.

LOYOLA MARYMOUNT UNIVERSITY
Los Angeles, CA 90045

(310) 338-2750
(800) LMU-INFO; Fax: (310) 338-2797

Full-time: 1847 men, 2486 women	**Faculty:** 161; IIA, ++$
Part-time: 191 men, 203 women	**Ph.D.s:** 83%
Graduate: 542 men, 692 women	**Student/Faculty:** 13 to 1
Year: semesters, summer session	**Tuition:** $18,411
Application Deadline: February 1	**Room & Board:** $7322
Freshman Class: 6341 applied, 3959 accepted, 1024 enrolled	
SAT I Verbal/Math: 575/575	**VERY COMPETITIVE**

Loyola Marymount University, a private institution founded in 1911 and affiliated with the Roman Catholic Church, offers programs in liberal arts, business administration, fine arts, science, and engineering. There are 4 undergraduate schools and 1 graduate school. In addition to regional accreditation, LMU has baccalaureate program accreditation with AACSB, ABET, and NCATE. The 2 libraries contain 764,711 volumes, 1,268,814 microform items, and 24,808 audiovisual forms/CDs. Computerized library services include the card catalog, interlibrary loans, and database searching. Special learning facilities include a learning resource center, art gallery, radio station, the Burns Fine Arts Center, and the Little Theatre. The 128-acre campus is in a suburban area 15 miles southwest of downtown Los Angeles on a mesa overlooking Marina del Rey. Including residence halls, there are 36 buildings.

Programs of Study: LMU confers B.A., B.S., B.B.A., B.S.A., and B.S.E. degrees. Master's degrees are also awarded. Bachelor's degrees are awarded in BIOLOGICAL SCIENCE (biochemistry and biology/biological science), BUSINESS (accounting and business administration and management), COMMUNICATIONS AND THE ARTS (art history and appreciation, classics, communications, dance, dramatic arts, English, French, Greek, Latin, media arts, music, Spanish, and studio art), COMPUTER AND PHYSICAL SCIENCE (chemistry, computer science, mathematics, natural sciences, and physics), ENGINEERING AND ENVIRONMENTAL DESIGN (civil engineering, computer graphics, electrical/electronics engineering, engineering physics, environmental science, and mechanical engineering), SOCIAL SCIENCE (African American studies, Asian/Oriental studies, classical/ancient civilization, economics, European studies, history, humanities, liberal arts/general studies, philosophy, political science/government, psychology, sociology, theological studies, and urban studies). Communication arts, political science, and engineering are the strongest academically. Psychology, sociology, and business administration are the largest.

Special: LMU offers internships and volunteer work experience with local firms, study abroad in Europe, Mexico, Japan, and China, a Washington semester, dual majors, work-study, student-designed and individualized studies majors, accelerated degree programs in all majors, a general studies degree, nondegree study, and pass/fail options for electives. There are 2 national honor societies, and a freshman honors program.

Admissions: 62% of the 1999-2000 applicants were accepted. The SAT I scores for the 1999-2000 freshman class were: Verbal--17% below 500, 53% between 500 and 599, 26% between 600 and 700, and 5% above 700; Math--18% below 500, 47% between 500 and 599, 31% between 600 and 700, and 5% above 700.

Requirements: The SAT I or ACT is required. A GPA of 2.9 is required. In addition, prospective students must be graduates of an accredited secondary school and have completed 4 years of English, 3 each of a foreign language, math, and social studies, 2 of science, and 1 of an academic elective. A recommendation from an official of a previous school and essays are required. An interview is recommended. Applications are accepted on computer disk (disks are available from LMU) and on-line at the school's web site. AP credits are accepted. Important factors in the admissions decision are advanced placement or honor courses, recommendations by school officials, and evidence of special talent.

Procedure: Freshmen are admitted fall and spring. Entrance exams should be taken during the spring of the junior year or fall of the senior year. There is a deferred admissions plan. Applications should be filed by February 1 for fall entry and December 1 for spring entry, along with a $40 fee. Notification is sent on a rolling basis. 5% of all applicants are on the 2000 waiting list.

Financial Aid: In 1999-2000, 72% of all freshmen and 71% of continuing students received some form of financial aid. 69% of freshmen and 66% of continuing students received need-based aid. The average freshman award was $16,180. Of that total, scholarships or need-based grants averaged $3957 ($17,932 maximum); loans averaged $2981 ($3500 maximum); and work contracts averaged $2610 ($7800 maximum). 37% of undergraduates work part time. Average annual earnings from campus work are $2600. The average financial indebtedness of the 1999 graduate was $18,542. LMU is a member of CSS. The CSS/Profile or FAFSA is required. The fall application deadline is February 15.

Computers: The mainframe is an IBM 4381. There are 40 PCs in a student lab networked with Internet access. The library houses 30 PCs with Internet access. Residence halls are wired for access to a campuswide network through students' personal computers. The system may be accessed through a 24-hour dial-in service. All students may access the system. Lab hours are Monday to Thursday 8 a.m. to 2 a.m., Friday 8 a.m. to 10 p.m., Saturday 9 a.m. to 6 p.m., and Sunday noon to 2 a.m. Students may access the system 2 hours for remote access. There are no fees. It is strongly recommended that students have a personal computer.

LOYOLA UNIVERSITY NEW ORLEANS

New Orleans, LA 70118

(504) 865-3240
(800) 4-LOYOLA; Fax: (504) 865-3383

Full-time: 1106 men, 1768 women	**Faculty:** 217; IIA, +$
Part-time: 211 men, 466 women	**Ph.D.s:** 88%
Graduate: 680 men, 877 women	**Student/Faculty:** 12 to 1
Year: semesters, summer session	**Tuition:** $14,582
Application Deadline: August 1	**Room & Board:** $5856
Freshman Class: 2190 applied, 1817 accepted, 808 enrolled	
SAT I Verbal/Math: 600/575	**ACT:** 26 **VERY COMPETITIVE+**

Loyola University New Orleans, founded in 1912, is a private institution operated by the Society of Jesus and affiliated with the Roman Catholic Church. There are 4 undergraduate schools and 1 graduate school. In addition to regional accreditation, Loyola has baccalaureate program accreditation with AACSB, NASM, and NLN. The 2 libraries contain 384,774 volumes, 1,233,074 microform items, and 13,829 audiovisual forms/CDs, and subscribe to 5111 periodicals. Computerized library services include the card catalog, interlibrary loans, and database searching. Special learning facilities include a learning resource center, art gallery, radio station, and TV station. The 20-acre campus is in an urban area 5 miles from downtown New Orleans. Including residence halls, there are 24 buildings.

Programs of Study: Loyola confers B.A., B.S., B.Acc., B.A.S., B.B.A., B.C.J., B.F.A., B.L.S., B.Mus., B.Mus.Ed., B.Mus. Therapy, and B.S.N. degrees. Master's degrees are also awarded. Bachelor's degrees are awarded in BIOLOGICAL SCIENCE (biology/biological science), BUSINESS (accounting, banking and finance, business administration and management, international business management, management science, marketing/retailing/merchandising, and organizational behavior), COMMUNICATIONS AND THE ARTS (communications, communications technology, creative writing, dramatic arts, English, fine arts, French, German, graphic design, jazz, music performance, music theory and composition, piano/organ, Russian, Spanish, studio art, and visual and performing arts), COMPUTER AND PHYSICAL SCIENCE (chemistry, computer science, information sciences and systems, mathematics, physics, and radiological technology), EDUCATION (elementary and music), HEALTH PROFESSIONS (music therapy and nursing), SOCIAL SCIENCE (classical/ancient civilization, criminal justice, economics, history, human development, philosophy, political science/government, psychology, religion, religious education, social science, and sociology). Biology, chemistry, and English are the strongest academically. Communications, psychology, and biology are the largest.

Special: Cross-registration is available with Xavier University, Notre Dame Seminary, the University of New Orleans, Tulane University, and Southern University of New Orleans. Internships with the New Orleans business community are available. Study abroad in 7 countries, work-study programs, dual and student-designed majors, nondegree studies, and a general studies program are offered. A Washington semester through American University and a 3-2 engineering degree with Tulane University are possible. There are 24 national honor societies, a freshman honors program, and 7 departmental honors programs.

Admissions: 83% of the 1999-2000 applicants were accepted. The SAT I scores for the 1999-2000 freshman class were: Verbal--9% below 500, 39% between 500 and 599, 42% between 600 and 700, and 10% above 700; Math--13% below 500, 45% between 500 and 599, 38% between 600 and 700, and 4% above 700. The ACT scores were 1% below 21, 28% between 21 and 23, 31% between 24

and 26, 19% between 27 and 28, and 20% above 28. 9 freshmen graduated first in their class.

Requirements: The SAT I or ACT is required. Candidates for admission must be graduates of an accredited secondary school or have a GED. They should have completed 4 units in high school English and 3 each in math, science, and social sciences, along with 4 academic electives; 2 units in a foreign language are recommended. A portfolio is required for fine arts students; an audition for music majors. An interview is recommended for scholarship consideration. Applications are accepted on-line via the school's web site or through Common App, ExPAN, CollegeLink, or other services. AP and CLEP credits are accepted. Important factors in the admissions decision are advanced placement or honor courses, recommendations by school officials, and evidence of special talent.

Procedure: Freshmen are admitted to all sessions. Entrance exams should be taken during the junior or senior year. There is a deferred admissions plan. Applications should be filed by August 1 for fall entry and January 1 for spring entry, along with a $20 fee. Notification is sent on a rolling basis.

Financial Aid: In 1999-2000, 58% of all freshmen and 57% of continuing students received some form of financial aid. 36% of freshmen and 40% of continuing students received need-based aid. The average freshman award was $13,633. Of that total, scholarships or need-based grants averaged $3039; and loans averaged $3759. The average financial indebtedness of the 1999 graduate was $15,887. Loyola is a member of CSS. The FAFSA is required. The fall application deadline is May 1.

Computers: The mainframes are an IBM SP/2, an IBM ES/9000, a DEC VAX 3100-80, and 2 DEC ALPHA 3000 Model 300s. Students may connect to the system via 2500 campuswide Internet ports, 48 modem lines, 75 public workstations, and Internet-ready residence hall rooms. All students may access the system at any time. There are no time limits. The fee is $50 per semester. It is recommended that all students have personal computers, preferably an IBM PC.

LOYOLA UNIVERSITY OF CHICAGO
Chicago, IL 60611　　　　　　　　　　　(312) 915-6500
　　　　　　　　　　　　(800) 262-2373; Fax: (312) 915-7216

Full-time: 1949 men, 3474 women	**Faculty:** 606; I, av$
Part-time: 780 men, 1393 women	**Ph.D.s:** 97%
Graduate: 2166 men, 3597 women	**Student/Faculty:** 9 to 1
Year: semesters, summer session	**Tuition:** $18,190
Application Deadline: April 1	**Room & Board:** $7006
Freshman Class: 5422 applied, 4467 accepted, 1067 enrolled	
SAT I Verbal/Math: 580/580	**ACT:** 25　　**VERY COMPETITIVE**

Loyola University of Chicago, founded in 1870, is a private Roman Catholic university offering undergraduate curricula in the arts and sciences, business, nursing, social work, and education. There are 5 undergraduate and 9 graduate schools. In addition to regional accreditation, Loyola has baccalaureate program accreditation with AACSB, CSWE, NCATE, and NLN. The 3 libraries contain 1.5 million volumes, 1 million microform items, and 9192 audiovisual forms/CDs, and subscribe to 10,229 periodicals. Computerized library services include the card catalog, interlibrary loans, and database searching. Special learning facilities include a learning resource center, art gallery, radio station, nursing resource center, theater, seismograph station, and electron microscope. The 105-acre campus is in an urban area in Chicago. Including residence halls, there are 130 buildings.

Programs of Study: Loyola confers B.A., B.S., B.A.Classics, B.B.A., B.S.Ed., and B.S.N. degrees. Master's and doctoral degrees are also awarded. Bachelor's degrees are awarded in BIOLOGICAL SCIENCE (biology/biological science), BUSINESS (accounting, banking and finance, business administration and management, business economics, marketing/retailing/merchandising, and personnel management), COMMUNICATIONS AND THE ARTS (communications, dramatic arts, English, fine arts, French, German, Greek, Italian, Latin, and Spanish), COMPUTER AND PHYSICAL SCIENCE (chemistry, computer science, mathematics, and physics), EDUCATION (elementary and special), HEALTH PROFESSIONS (nursing, predentistry, premedicine, and preveterinary science), SOCIAL SCIENCE (anthropology, classical/ancient civilization, criminal justice, economics, history, philosophy, political science/government, psychology, religion, social work, sociology, and theological studies). Biology, psychology, and nursing are the largest.

Special: Sophomores and juniors may study in Italy or Mexico. Dual majors, a Washington semester, nondegree study, and pass/fail options are available. The school also offers a B.A.-B.S. degree in chemistry and a 2-3 engineering degree with the University of Illinois at Urbana-Champaign. For working adults, Mundelein College offers fully accredited programs leading to baccalaureate degrees in arts and sciences, business and education. There is a chapter of Phi Beta Kappa and, a freshman honors program.

Admissions: 82% of the 1999-2000 applicants were accepted. The SAT I scores for the 1999-2000 freshman class were: Verbal--16% below 500, 47% between 500 and 599, 30% between 600 and 700, and 7% above 700; Math--22% below 500, 44% between 500 and 599, 28% between 600 and 700, and 6% above 700. The ACT scores were 18% below 21, 23% between 21 and 23, 27% between 24 and 26, 16% between 27 and 28, and 16% above 28. 54% of the current freshmen were in the top fifth of their class; 84% were in the top two fifths. 21 freshmen graduated first in their class.

Requirements: The SAT I or ACT is required. In addition, graduation from an accredited secondary school or satisfactory scores on the GED are required for admission. 15 academic credits are required. Secondary school courses should include 4 credits of English, 2 of math, and 1 each of science and social studies. An interview is recommended but an essay is not required. Applications are accepted on-line at the school's web site. AP and CLEP credits are accepted. Important factors in the admissions decision are advanced placement or honor courses, evidence of special talent, and leadership record.

Procedure: Freshmen are admitted to all sessions. Entrance exams should be taken as early as possible, normally in the spring of the junior year. Applications should be filed by April 1 for fall entry and December 1 for spring entry, along with a $25 fee. Notification is sent on a rolling basis.

Financial Aid: In 1999-2000, 84% of all freshmen and 80% of continuing students received some form of financial aid. 72% of freshmen and 65% of continuing students received need-based aid. The average freshman award was $17,876. Of that total, scholarships or need-based grants averaged $12,806 ($17,750 maximum); loans averaged $2860 ($5625 maximum); and work contracts averaged $2210 ($3000 maximum). 90% of undergraduates work part time. Average annual earnings from campus work are $2000. The average financial indebtedness of the 1999 graduate was $11,712. Loyola is a member of CSS. The FAFSA is required. The fall application deadline is March 1.

Computers: The mainframe is an IBM 3081K. More than 190 PCs, networked to commonly used software packages, are available for student use. More than 75 terminals access the mainframe computer for heavy-duty analytical packages.

All students may access the system whenever facilities are available. There are no time limits and no fees.

LYON COLLEGE
Batesville, AR 72503-2317

(870) 698-4250
(800) 423-2542; Fax: (870) 698-4622

Full-time: 180 men, 237 women	**Faculty:** 42; IIB, -$
Part-time: 14 men, 35 women	**Ph.D.s:** 93%
Graduate: none	**Student/Faculty:** 10 to 1
Year: semesters, summer session	**Tuition:** $10,622
Application Deadline: August 1	**Room & Board:** $4703
Freshman Class: 470 applied, 380 accepted, 141 enrolled	
SAT I Verbal/Math: 575/555	**ACT:** 26 **VERY COMPETITIVE+**

Lyon College, founded in 1872, is an independent liberal arts institution affiliated with the Presbyterian Church (U.S.A.). In addition to regional accreditation, Lyon has baccalaureate program accreditation with NCATE. The library contains 135,922 volumes, 2400 microform items, and 4899 audiovisual forms/CDs, and subscribes to 880 periodicals. Computerized library services include the card catalog, interlibrary loans, and database searching. Special learning facilities include a learning resource center, art gallery, a language lab, and experimental theater. The 136-acre campus is in a small town 90 miles north of Little Rock. Including residence halls, there are 28 buildings.

Programs of Study: Lyon confers B.A. and B.S. degrees. Bachelor's degrees are awarded in BIOLOGICAL SCIENCE (biology/biological science), BUSINESS (accounting and business administration and management), COMMUNICATIONS AND THE ARTS (art, dramatic arts, English, music, and Spanish), COMPUTER AND PHYSICAL SCIENCE (chemistry, computer science, and mathematics), SOCIAL SCIENCE (economics, history, political science/government, psychology, and religion). Chemistry and biology are the strongest academically. Biology, economics, and English are the largest.

Special: Internships and cross-registration with the University of Arkansas Community College at Batesville and Ozarka College. A 2-2 engineering program is offered with the University of Missouri in Rolla, and a 3-2 program is offered with the University of Arkansas at Fayetteville. Work-study courses, study abroad, dual majors, student-designed majors, pass/fail options, and credit for military experience are available. There are 7 national honor societies, and a freshman honors program.

Admissions: 81% of the 1999-2000 applicants were accepted. The SAT I scores for the 1999-2000 freshman class were: Verbal--38% below 500, 25% between 500 and 599, 31% between 600 and 700, and 6% above 700; Math--28% below 500, 34% between 500 and 599, 31% between 600 and 700, and 6% above 700. The ACT scores were 5% below 21, 25% between 21 and 23, 25% between 24 and 26, 23% between 27 and 28, and 22% above 28. 73% of the current freshmen were in the top fifth of their class; 93% were in the top two fifths. There was 1 National Merit finalist. 14 freshmen graduated first in their class.

Requirements: The SAT I or ACT is required. A GPA of 2.3 is required. Applicants should have completed a minimum of 16 high school units, including 4 in English, 3 to 4 each in science and math, 3 in social sciences, and 1 to 2 in a foreign language. A letter of recommendation and an admission interview are recommended. Applications are available on the college's Web site. AP credits are accepted. Important factors in the admissions decision are advanced placement or honor courses, leadership record, and evidence of special talent.

Procedure: Freshmen are admitted fall and spring. Entrance exams should be taken in the spring of junior year and the fall of senior year. There are early admissions and deferred admissions plans. Applications should be filed by August 1 for fall entry and January 5 for spring entry, along with a $25 fee. Notification is sent on a rolling basis.

Financial Aid: In 1999-2000, 100% of all freshmen and 97% of continuing students received some form of financial aid. 65% of freshmen and 59% of continuing students received need-based aid. The average freshman award was $11,606. Of that total, scholarships or need-based grants averaged $6137 ($14,975 maximum); loans averaged $2675 ($4000 maximum); and work contracts averaged $1398 ($1545 maximum). 40% of undergraduates work part time. Average annual earnings from campus work are $1367. The average financial indebtedness of the 1999 graduate was $13,610. Lyon is a member of CSS. The FAFSA is required. The fall application deadline is April 1.

Computers: The mainframes include an IBM RISC 6000, 1 DEC ALPHA, and several Intel-based NT servers. Students have access to campus information resources from 84 computers in classrooms, residence hall lounges, the Union, and the library. Students may also access these resources in residence hall rooms using their own PCs. Access to the Internet is available from any network access point with a user ID and password. All students may access the system. There are no time limits. The fee is $200.

MACALESTER COLLEGE
St. Paul, MN 55105

(651) 696-6357
(800) 231-7974; Fax: (651) 696-6724

Full-time: 743 men, 1030 women	**Faculty:** 147; IIB, ++$
Part-time: 25 men, 37 women	**Ph.D.s:** 93%
Graduate: none	**Student/Faculty:** 11 to 1
Year: semesters	**Tuition:** $20,688
Application Deadline: January 15	**Room & Board:** $5760
Freshman Class: 3161 applied, 1680 accepted, 460 enrolled	
SAT I Verbal/Math: 670/650	**ACT:** 29 HIGHLY COMPETITIVE+

Macalester College, founded in 1855, is a nonsectarian liberal arts institution affiliated with the United Presbyterian Church. In addition to regional accreditation, Macalester has baccalaureate program accreditation with NASM and NCATE. The library contains 398,989 volumes, 71,092 microform items, and 7558 audiovisual forms/CDs, and subscribes to 1747 periodicals. Computerized library services include the card catalog, interlibrary loans, and database searching. Special learning facilities include a learning resource center, art gallery, radio station, and a 280-acre natural history study area 25 miles from campus. The 53-acre campus is in an urban area midway between downtown St. Paul and Minneapolis. Including residence halls, there are 36 buildings.

Programs of Study: Macalester confers the B.A. degree. Bachelor's degrees are awarded in BIOLOGICAL SCIENCE (biology/biological science and neurosciences), COMMUNICATIONS AND THE ARTS (art, classics, communications, dramatic arts, English, French, linguistics, music, Russian, and Spanish), COMPUTER AND PHYSICAL SCIENCE (chemistry, computer science, geology, mathematics, and physics), ENGINEERING AND ENVIRONMENTAL DESIGN (environmental science), SOCIAL SCIENCE (anthropology, East Asian studies, economics, geography, German area studies, history, international relations, Japanese studies, Latin American studies, philosophy, political science/government, psychology, religion, Russian and Slavic studies, social science, sociology, urban studies, and women's studies). International studies, economics, and biology are the strongest academically. Math/ computer science, Spanish, and history are the largest.

Special: Cross-registration at Minneapolis College of Art and Design is offered; in addition, the college belongs to several consortiums, including the Associated Colleges of the Twin Cities. There also are cooperative programs in liberal arts and architecture with Washington University in St. Louis, engineering with the University of Minnesota, and nursing with Rush-Presbyterian-St Luke's Medical Center in Chicago. About half of Macalester students complete internships at more than 200 sites in Minneapolis and St. Paul. Students may study abroad in many countries. Credit by exam under supervision of individual instructors, non-degree study, student-designed majors, and pass/fail options for no more than 1 course per semester also are available. There are 15 national honor societies, including Phi Beta Kappa.

Admissions: 53% of the 1999-2000 applicants were accepted. The SAT I scores for the 1999-2000 freshman class were: Verbal--1% below 500, 13% between 500 and 599, 51% between 600 and 700, and 34% above 700; Math--2% below 500, 17% between 500 and 599, 62% between 600 and 700, and 19% above 700. The ACT scores were 5% between 21 and 23, 16% between 24 and 26, 22% between 27 and 28, and 58% above 28. 88% of the current freshmen were in the top fifth of their class; 99% were in the top two fifths. There were 42 National Merit finalists and 4 semifinalists. 58 freshmen graduated first in their class.

Requirements: The SAT I or ACT is required. Applicants should have earned at least 16 academic credits, including 4 years of English and 3 each in math, lab science, foreign language, and social studies/history. The college also expects applicants to have taken honors, AP, or IB courses where available. An essay is required, and an interview is recommended. Applications are accepted on disk and on-line. AP credits are accepted.

Procedure: Freshmen are admitted in the fall. Entrance exams should be taken in the fall of the senior year. There are early decision and deferred admissions plans. Early decision applications should be filed by November 15, and January 15; regular applications, by January 15 for fall entry, along with a $40 fee. Notification of early decision is sent December 15 and February 7; regular decision, April 1. 109 early decision candidates were accepted for the 1999-2000 class. 4% of all applicants are on a waiting list.

Financial Aid: In 1999-2000, 74% of all freshmen and 79% of continuing students received some form of financial aid. 68% of freshmen and 70% of continuing students received need-based aid. The average freshman award was $16,295. Of that total, scholarships or need-based grants averaged $13,141 ($20,500 maximum); loans averaged $1832 ($3500 maximum); and work contracts averaged $1322 ($1500 maximum). 66% of undergraduates work part time. Average annual earnings from campus work are $1240. The average financial indebtedness of the 1999 graduate was $14,200. Macalester is a member of CSS. The CSS/Profile, FAFSA, parent's W-2s and tax forms, and student tax forms are required. The fall application deadline is February 8.

Computers: The mainframe is a DEC ALPHA 2000 server. The central computer provides access to the Internet and to E-mail. There are approximately 300 PCs and Macs available for general student use. All students may access the system 24 hours a day. There are no time limits and no fees.

MAHARISHI UNIVERSITY OF MANAGEMENT
Fairfield, IA 52557   **(515) 472-1110; Fax: (515) 472-1179**

Full-time: 102 men, 108 women	**Faculty:** 71
Part-time: 407 men, 360 women	**Ph.D.s:** 66%
Graduate: 169 men, 145 women	**Student/Faculty:** 3 to 1
Year: n/app	**Tuition:** $15,430
Application Deadline: April 15	**Room & Board:** $5200
Freshman Class: 114 applied, 99 accepted, 90 enrolled	
SAT I Verbal/Math: 592/567	**ACT:** 23 **VERY COMPETITIVE**

Maharishi University of Management, established in 1971, is a private institution offering undergraduate and graduate programs in a broad range of disciplines. The University provides Consciousness-Based education and incorporates the group practice of the Maharishi Transcendental meditation technique into a traditional academic program. There is 1 graduate school. The 2 libraries contain 145,000 volumes, 59,900 microform items, and 13,276 audiovisual forms/CDs, and subscribe to 850 periodicals. Computerized library services include the card catalog, interlibrary loans, and database searching. Special learning facilities include a learning resource center, art gallery, radio station, psychophysiology, electronic engineering, visual technology, and physics labs, and a scanning electron microscope. The 94-acre campus is in a small town 114 miles southeast of Des Moines. Including residence halls, there are 94 buildings.

Programs of Study: Maharishi University of Management confers B.A., B.S., and B.F.A. degrees. Associate, master's, and doctoral degrees are also awarded. Bachelor's degrees are awarded in BIOLOGICAL SCIENCE (biochemistry and biology/biological science), BUSINESS (management science), COMMUNICATIONS AND THE ARTS (dramatic arts, fine arts, literature, and music), COMPUTER AND PHYSICAL SCIENCE (chemistry, computer science, mathematics, and physics), EDUCATION (education), ENGINEERING AND ENVIRONMENTAL DESIGN (electrical/electronics engineering, electrical/electronics engineering technology, and electromechanical technology), SOCIAL SCIENCE (cognitive science, political science/government, and psychology). Engineering, math, and computer science are the strongest academically. Fine arts and management are the largest.

Special: Opportunities are provided for internships, B.A.-B.S. degrees in biochemistry, biology, chemistry, computer science, and psychology, study abroad, and nondegree study. Systematic programs are offered in the science of creative intelligence, by which students apply knowledge to practical professional values. There are several 1-month blocks a year during which students may study art in Italy, literature in Switzerland, or business in Japan. There is a freshman honors program. The school is on a block system consisting of 5 blocks per semester, 4 weeks each block, and 4 credits per block.

Admissions: 87% of the 1999-2000 applicants were accepted. The SAT I scores for the 1999-2000 freshman class were: Verbal--15% below 500, 30% between 500 and 599, 40% between 600 and 700, and 15% above 700; Math--10% below 500, 60% between 500 and 599, 20% between 600 and 700, and 10% above 700. There was 1 National Merit finalist and 2 semifinalists.

Requirements: The SAT I or ACT is required. A GPA of 2.5 is required. Applicants must graduate from an accredited secondary school or have a GED. An essay and 2 personal recommendations are required. An interview is recommended. Applications are accepted on-line. AP and CLEP credits are accepted. Important factors in the admissions decision are personality/intangible qualities, recommendations by school officials, and leadership record.

Procedure: Freshmen are admitted fall and spring. Entrance exams should be taken in the fall of the senior year or spring of the junior year. Applications should be filed by April 15 for fall entry and January 1 for winter entry, along with a $25 fee. Notification is sent on a rolling basis.

Financial Aid: In 1999-2000, 97% of all freshmen and 98% of continuing students received some form of financial aid. 88% of freshmen and 93% of continuing students received need-based aid. The average freshman award was $16,746. Of that total, scholarships or need-based grants averaged $11,475 ($15,200 maximum); loans averaged $3917 ($10,500 maximum); and work contracts averaged $1354 ($1400 maximum). 75% of undergraduates work part time. Average annual earnings from campus work are $1400. The average financial indebtedness of the 1999 graduate was $16,500. Maharishi University of Management is a member of CSS. The FAFSA and the college's own financial statement are required.

Computers: About 130 IBM and Mac PCs are available throughout the campus. All students may access the system daytime and evenings. There are no time limits and no fees.

MAINE COLLEGE OF ART
Portland, ME 04101

(207) 775-3052
(800) 639-4808; Fax: (207) 772-5069

Full-time: 135 men, 185 women	**Faculty:** 36
Part-time: 26 men, 35 women	**Ph.D.s:** 70%
Graduate: 10 men, 16 women	**Student/Faculty:** 9 to 1
Year: semesters	**Tuition:** $16,710
Application Deadline: open	**Room & Board:** $6390
Freshman Class: 432 applied, 363 accepted, 151 enrolled	
SAT I Verbal/Math: 530/540	**ACT:** 21 SPECIAL

Maine College of Art, established in 1882, is a private, independent visual art college. There is 1 graduate school. In addition to regional accreditation, MECA has baccalaureate program accreditation with NASAD. The library contains 18,500 volumes and 150 audiovisual forms/CDs, and subscribes to 100 periodicals. Computerized library services include the card catalog, interlibrary loans, and database searching. Special learning facilities include an art gallery. The campus is in an urban area 100 miles north of Boston in downtown Portland. Including residence halls, there are 6 buildings.

Programs of Study: MECA confers the B.F.A. degree. Master's degrees are also awarded. Bachelor's degrees are awarded in COMMUNICATIONS AND THE ARTS (graphic design, metal/jewelry, painting, photography, printmaking, and sculpture), ENGINEERING AND ENVIRONMENTAL DESIGN (ceramic science). Graphic design is the largest.

Special: Cross-registration with Bowdoin College and the Greater Portland Alliance of Colleges and Universities is available, as are internships utilizing professional artists and design and photography studios. The continuing studies program provides for nondegree study. A minor in art history is also offered, as are dual and student-designed majors.

Admissions: 84% of the 1999-2000 applicants were accepted. The SAT I scores for the 1999-2000 freshman class were: Verbal--34% below 500, 42% between 500 and 599, 20% between 600 and 700, and 4% above 700; Math--56% below 500, 30% between 500 and 599, 12% between 600 and 700, and 2% above 700. The ACT scores were 20% below 21, 60% between 21 and 23, and 20% between 27 and 28. 21% of the current freshmen were in the top fifth of their class; 54% were in the top two fifths.

Requirements: The SAT I or ACT is required. It is recommended that candidates for admission complete 4 years of English, 3 years each of art and math, and 2 years each of foreign language, science, and social studies. Applications are accepted on computer disk. AP credits are accepted. Important factors in the admissions decision are evidence of special talent, recommendations by school officials, and advanced placement or honor courses.

Procedure: Freshmen are admitted fall and spring. Entrance exams should be taken in the fall of the senior year. There are early admissions and deferred admissions plans. Application deadlines are open; there is a $40 application fee. Notification is sent on a rolling basis.

Financial Aid: In 1999-2000, 86% of all students received some form of financial aid or need-based aid. The average freshman award was $12,873. Of that total, scholarships or need-based grants averaged $6541 ($10,668 maximum); loans averaged $6248 ($16,625 maximum); and work contracts averaged $85 ($1025 maximum). 21% of undergraduates work part time. Average annual earnings from campus work are $2025. The average financial indebtedness of the 1999 graduate was $23,000. MECA is a member of CSS. The FAFSA is required. The fall application deadline is March 1.

Computers: Technology allowing digital imaging, animation, web site design, and Internet access is available to students through the Imaging Center. General computer access is available in the student center. All students may access the system. Time is scheduled around classroom use. There are no time limits and no fees.

MANHATTAN COLLEGE
Riverdale, NY 10471

(718) 862-7200
(800) 622-9235; Fax: (718) 862-8019

Full-time: 1329 men, 1166 women	**Faculty:** 164; IIA, +$
Part-time: 137 men, 71 women	**Ph.D.s:** 92%
Graduate: 204 men, 180 women	**Student/Faculty:** 15 to 1
Year: semesters, summer session	**Tuition:** $16,050
Application Deadline: March 1	**Room & Board:** $7450
Freshman Class: 3767 applied, 2749 accepted, 645 enrolled	
SAT I Verbal/Math: 546/549	**VERY COMPETITIVE**

Manhattan College, founded in 1853, is a private institution affiliated with the Christian Brothers of the Catholic Church. It offers degree programs in the arts and sciences, education and human services, business, and engineering. There are 5 undergraduate and 3 graduate schools. In addition to regional accreditation, Manhattan has baccalaureate program accreditation with ABET, AHEA, and CAHEA. The 4 libraries contain 193,100 volumes, 383,480 microform items, and 3244 audiovisual forms/CDs, and subscribe to 1527 periodicals. Computerized library services include the card catalog, interlibrary loans, and database searching. Special learning facilities include a learning resource center, radio station, nuclear reactor lab, and media center. The 26-acre campus is in an urban area 10 miles north of midtown Manhattan. Including residence halls, there are 28 buildings.

Programs of Study: Manhattan confers B.A. and B.S. degrees. Master's degrees are also awarded. Bachelor's degrees are awarded in BIOLOGICAL SCIENCE (biochemistry and biology/biological science), BUSINESS (accounting, banking and finance, business economics, international business management, and marketing/retailing/merchandising), COMMUNICATIONS AND THE ARTS (communications, English, French, and Spanish), COMPUTER AND PHYSICAL SCIENCE (chemistry, computer science, information sciences and systems, mathematics, and physics), EDUCATION (early childhood, elementary, foreign languages, health, middle school, physical, science, secondary, and special), ENGINEERING AND ENVIRONMENTAL DESIGN (chemical engineering, civil engineering, electrical/electronics engineering, environmental engineering, and mechanical engineering), HEALTH PROFESSIONS (predentistry, premedicine, and radiological science), SOCIAL SCIENCE (economics, history, peace studies, philosophy, political science/government, prelaw, psychology, religion, sociology, and urban studies). Engineering and business are the strongest academically. Arts, business, and education are the largest.

Special: Manhattan offers co-op programs in 11 majors, cross-registration with the College of Mount St. Vincent, and off-campus internships in business, industry, government, and social or cultural organizations. Students may study abroad in 10 countries and enter work-study programs with major U.S. corporations, health services, or in the arts. A general studies degree, a 3-2 engineering degree, a dual major in international business, credit by exam, and nondegree study are also available. There are 22 national honor societies, including Phi Beta Kappa, a freshman honors program, and 28 departmental honors programs.

Admissions: 73% of the 1999-2000 applicants were accepted. The SAT I scores for the 1999-2000 freshman class were: Verbal--30% below 500, 47% between 500 and 599, 20% between 600 and 700, and 2% above 700; Math--31% below 500, 45% between 500 and 599, 21% between 600 and 700, and 2% above 700. There were 3 National Merit semifinalists. 12 freshmen graduated first in their class.

Requirements: The SAT I is required. A GPA of 3.0 is required. Applicants must graduate from an accredited secondary school or have earned a GED. 16 academic units are required, including 4 of English, 3 each of math and social studies, and 2 of foreign language, lab sciences, and electives. An essay is required and an interview is recommended. The college accepts applications on-line via Common App, ExPAN, CollegeView, and CollegeLink. AP and CLEP credits are accepted. Important factors in the admissions decision are advanced placement or honor courses, leadership record, and recommendations by school officials.

Procedure: Freshmen are admitted fall and spring. Entrance exams should be taken in the spring of the junior year or the fall of the senior year. There are early decision and deferred admissions plans. Early decision applications should be filed by November 15; regular applications, by March 1 for fall entry and December 1 for spring entry, along with a $35 fee. Notification of early decision is sent December 1; regular decision, on a rolling basis. 18 early decision candidates were accepted for the 1999-2000 class. 4% of all applicants are on a waiting list.

Financial Aid: In 1999-2000, 88% of all freshmen and continuing students received some form of financial aid. 66% of freshmen and 68% of continuing students received need-based aid. The average freshman award was $11,167. Of that total, scholarships or need-based grants averaged $5124 ($24,910 maximum); loans averaged $2420 ($2625 maximum); and work contracts averaged $800 ($1200 maximum). 15% of undergraduates work part time. Average annual earnings from campus work are $600. The average financial indebtedness of the 1999 graduate was $11,570. Manhattan is a member of CSS. The FAFSA and the college's own financial statement are required. The fall application deadline is February 1.

Computers: The mainframe is a DEC VAX 8350. Terminals and PCs are located in the computer center and in engineering labs. In addition, all residence halls are capable of providing Internet access to students who have their own computers. All students may access the system 13 hours a day in the labs and 24 hours a day in residence halls or by modem. There are no time limits and no fees.

MARIST COLLEGE
Poughkeepsie, NY 12601

(914) 575-3226
(800) 436-5483; Fax: (914) 575-3215

Full-time: 1637 men, 2164 women	**Faculty:** 162; IIA, -$
Part-time: 257 men, 370 women	**Ph.D.s:** 83%
Graduate: 288 men, 294 women	**Student/Faculty:** 24 to 1
Year: semesters, summer session	**Tuition:** $14,754
Application Deadline: March 1	**Room & Board:** $7418
Freshman Class: 6179 applied, 3449 accepted, 980 enrolled	
SAT I Verbal/Math: 549/558	**VERY COMPETITIVE**

Marist College, founded in 1946, is an independent liberal arts college with a Catholic tradition. There is 1 graduate school. The library contains 113,858 volumes, 207,512 microform items, and 5646 audiovisual forms/CDs, and subscribes to 4758 periodicals. Computerized library services include interlibrary loans and database searching. Special learning facilities include a learning resource center, art gallery, radio station, TV station, gallery of Lowell Thomas memorabilia, estuarine and environmental studies lab, public opinion institute, and economic research center. The 150-acre campus is in a suburban area 75 miles north of New York City on the Hudson River. Including residence halls, there are 46 buildings.

Programs of Study: Marist confers B.A., B.S., and B.P.S. degrees. Master's degrees are also awarded. Bachelor's degrees are awarded in BIOLOGICAL SCIENCE (biology/biological science), BUSINESS (accounting, business administration and management, and fashion merchandising), COMMUNICATIONS AND THE ARTS (communications, English, fine arts, French, Russian, and Spanish), COMPUTER AND PHYSICAL SCIENCE (chemistry, computer mathematics, computer science, information sciences and systems, and mathematics), EDUCATION (special), ENGINEERING AND ENVIRONMENTAL DESIGN (environmental science), HEALTH PROFESSIONS (medical technology), SOCIAL SCIENCE (American studies, child psychology/development, criminal justice, economics, fashion design and technology, history, interdisciplinary studies, political science/government, psychology, and social work). Computer science, computer information systems, and natural sciences are the strongest academically. Business administration, communications, and education are the largest.

Special: Marist offers cross-registration with schools in the mid-Hudson area and study abroad in Europe, Africa, Latin America, Central America, and the Far East. The school also offers a 3-year degree in social work, co-op programs in computer science and computer information systems, work-study programs, a B.A.-B.S. degree, and dual and student-designed majors. There are internships available with more than 250 organizations in the United States and abroad, including New York State Legislature and White House programs. There are 4 national honor societies and a freshman honors program.

Admissions: 56% of the 1999-2000 applicants were accepted. The SAT I scores for the 1999-2000 freshman class were: Verbal--18% below 500, 61% between 500 and 599, 18% between 600 and 700, and 3% above 700; Math--18% below 500, 57% between 500 and 599, 23% between 600 and 700, and 2% above 700. 43% of the current freshmen were in the top fifth of their class; 85% were in the top two fifths. There were 3 National Merit finalists and 16 semifinalists. 7 freshmen graduated first in their class.

Requirements: The SAT I or ACT is required. Marist requires applicants to be in the upper 50% of their class. A grade average of 83 is required. Applicants should have 16 high school units, including a recommended 4 in English, 3 in math, 2 each in science, language, and social studies, and 1 in U.S. history, art, and music. The GED is accepted. An essay and campus visit are recommended. Applications are accepted on-line via the Marist web page. AP and CLEP credits are accepted. Important factors in the admissions decision are leadership record, advanced placement or honor courses, and recommendations by school officials.

Procedure: Freshmen are admitted fall and spring. Entrance exams should be taken during the fall of the senior year. There are early decision, early admissions, and deferred admissions plans. Early decision applications should be filed by December 1; regular applications, by March 1 for fall entry and December 1 for spring entry, along with a $40 fee. Notification of early decision is sent January 15; regular decision, March 15. 539 early decision candidates were accepted for the 1999-2000 class. 8% of all applicants are on a waiting list.

Financial Aid: In 1999-2000, 81% of all freshmen and 72% of continuing students received some form of financial aid. 66% of freshmen and 64% of continuing students received need-based aid. The average freshman award was $10,880. Of that total, scholarships or need-based grants averaged $5100 ($10,000 maximum). 34% of undergraduates work part time. Average annual earnings from campus work are $1200. Marist is a member of CSS. The FAFSA is required. The fall application deadline is February 15.

Computers: The mainframe is an IBM 9672-RC4. The campus center has a drop-in lab available to all students from 8 a.m. to midnight during the week and longer on weekends. All dormitory rooms are equipped with data jacks allowing students to hook up PCs with the mainframe and to access library files. Overall, there are 12 areas on campus providing more than 300 terminals for student use, as well as 185 PCs and numerous printers. All students may access the system. There are no time limits and no fees.

MARLBORO COLLEGE
Marlboro, VT 05344

(802) 257-4333
(800) 343-0049; Fax: (802) 257-4154

Full-time: 114 men, 161 women	**Faculty:** 33
Part-time: 6 men, 9 women	**Ph.D.s:** 84%
Graduate: none	**Student/Faculty:** 8 to 1
Year: semesters	**Tuition:** $19,660
Application Deadline: March 1	**Room & Board:** $6750
Freshman Class: 308 applied, 247 accepted, 99 enrolled	
SAT I Verbal/Math: 610/580	**VERY COMPETITIVE**

Marlboro College, established in 1946, is a private institution offering degrees in the liberal and fine arts and humanities, and employing self-designed programs of study. There is 1 graduate school. The library contains 52,900 volumes, 5100 microform items, and 750 audiovisual forms/CDs, and subscribes to 171 periodicals. Computerized library services include the card catalog, interlibrary loans, and database searching. Special learning facilities include a learning resource center, art gallery, and planetarium. The 350-acre campus is in a rural area 9 miles west of Brattleboro, 2 1/2 hours from Boston. Including residence halls, there are 36 buildings.

Programs of Study: Marlboro confers B.A., B.S., B.A. in International Studies, and B.S. in International Studies degrees. Master's degrees are also awarded. Bachelor's degrees are awarded in BIOLOGICAL SCIENCE (biochemistry, biology/biological science, botany, and microbiology), COMMUNICATIONS AND THE ARTS (creative writing, dance, dramatic arts, English, fine arts, French,

German, Greek, Italian, Latin, linguistics, music, photography, Russian, and Spanish), COMPUTER AND PHYSICAL SCIENCE (chemistry, computer science, mathematics, physics, and statistics), HEALTH PROFESSIONS (premedicine), SOCIAL SCIENCE (anthropology, economics, history, interdisciplinary studies, international studies, philosophy, political science/government, prelaw, psychology, social science, and sociology). Sciences, humanities, and world studies are the strongest academically. Literature, biology, and sociology are the largest.

Special: Marlboro offers a variety of internships, cross-registration with Huron University in London, and study abroad in many countries. The World Studies Program combines liberal arts with international studies, including 6 months of internship work in another culture. Accelerated and B.A.-B.S. degree programs are available. Students may pursue dual majors. Majors reflect an integrated course of study designed by students and their faculty advisors during the junior year. .

Admissions: 80% of the 1999-2000 applicants were accepted. The SAT I scores for the 1999-2000 freshman class were: Verbal--5% below 500, 24% between 500 and 599, 47% between 600 and 700, and 24% above 700; Math--24% below 500, 39% between 500 and 599, 29% between 600 and 700, and 8% above 700. 33% of the current freshmen were in the top fifth of their class; 67% were in the top two fifths.

Requirements: The SAT I is required. Applicants must graduate from an accredited secondary school or have a GED. They must earn 16 Carnegie units and complete 4 years of English and 3 years each of math, science, history, and a foreign language. SAT II: Subject tests are recommended. Essays and interviews are required. Auditions and portfolios are recommended in appropriate cases. Applications are accepted on-line on Marlboro's web page. AP and CLEP credits are accepted. Important factors in the admissions decision are advanced placement or honor courses, evidence of special talent, and recommendations by school officials.

Procedure: Freshmen are admitted fall and spring. Entrance exams should be taken by October before entry. There are early decision, early admissions, and deferred admissions plans. Early decision applications should be filed by November 15; regular applications, by March 1 for fall entry and November 1 for spring entry, along with a $30 fee. Notification of early decision is sent December 15; regular decision, April 1. 15 early decision candidates were accepted for the 1999-2000 class.

Financial Aid: In 1999-2000, 85% of all freshmen and 78% of continuing students received some form of financial aid. 82% of freshmen and 71% of continuing students received need-based aid. The average freshman award was $20,907. Of that total, scholarships or need-based grants averaged $12,007 ($22,305 maximum); loans averaged $4190 ($6625 maximum); alternative loans exceeding need averaged $7283 ($24,480); and work contracts averaged $1866 ($1930 maximum). 68% of undergraduates work part time. Average annual earnings from campus work are $1118. The average financial indebtedness of the 1999 graduate was $15,531. Marlboro is a member of CSS. The CSS/Profile or FAFSA is required. The fall application deadline is March 1.

Computers: Macs are available in a computer lab, and all on campus dorm rooms are wired for Internet access. All students may access the system 24 hours a day. There are no time limits and no fees.

MARQUETTE UNIVERSITY
Milwaukee, WI 53201-1881

(414) 288-7302
(800) 222-6544; Fax: (414) 288-3764

Full-time: 3094 men, 3619 women	**Faculty:** I, -$
Part-time: 242 men, 283 women	**Ph.D.s:** n/av
Graduate: 1075 men, 835 women	**Student/Faculty:** n/av
Year: semesters, summer session	**Tuition:** $17,336
Application Deadline: open	**Room & Board:** $6086
Freshman Class: 6925 applied, 5795 accepted, 1723 enrolled	
SAT I Verbal/Math: 570/580	**ACT:** 25 **VERY COMPETITIVE**

Marquette University, established in 1881, is a private Roman Catholic Jesuit institution. There are 7 undergraduate and 4 graduate schools. In addition to regional accreditation, Marquette has baccalaureate program accreditation with AACSB, ABET, ACEJMC, ADA, APTA, ASLA, CSWE, NCATE, and NLN. The 3 libraries contain 719,906 volumes, 1,127,091 microform items, and 7296 audiovisual forms/CDs, and subscribe to 9157 periodicals. Computerized library services include the card catalog, interlibrary loans, and database searching. Special learning facilities include a learning resource center, art gallery, radio station, and TV station. The 80-acre campus is in an urban area 90 miles north of Chicago. Including residence halls, there are 48 buildings.

Programs of Study: Marquette confers B.A., B.S., and B.S.N. degrees. Associate, master's, and doctoral degrees are also awarded. Bachelor's degrees are awarded in BIOLOGICAL SCIENCE (biochemistry, biology/biological science, and molecular biology), BUSINESS (accounting, banking and finance, business administration and management, business economics, human resources, international business management, management information systems, and marketing/retailing/merchandising), COMMUNICATIONS AND THE ARTS (advertising, broadcasting, communications, dramatic arts, English, French, German, journalism, public relations, and Spanish), COMPUTER AND PHYSICAL SCIENCE (chemistry, computer science, information sciences and systems, mathematics, physics, and statistics), EDUCATION (secondary), ENGINEERING AND ENVIRONMENTAL DESIGN (biomedical engineering, civil engineering, computer engineering, electrical/electronics engineering, engineering, environmental engineering, industrial engineering technology, and mechanical engineering), HEALTH PROFESSIONS (clinical science, dental hygiene, medical laboratory technology, nursing, physical therapy, and speech pathology/audiology), SOCIAL SCIENCE (anthropology, criminal justice, criminology, economics, history, interdisciplinary studies, international relations, philosophy, political science/government, psychology, social science, social work, sociology, and theological studies). Physical therapy, biomedical engineering, and biology are the strongest academically. Nursing, psychology, and accounting are the largest.

Special: Marquette offers co-op programs in engineering, internships, study abroad, a Washington summer term, and work-study programs. Dual and student-designed majors, nondegree study, and pass/fail options are available. Cross-registration is possible with Milwaukee Institute of Art and Design, and there is a 2-2 engineering program with Waukesha County Technical College. The Freshman Frontier Program offers academic support for selected freshmen who do not meet regular admission requirements but show potential for success. The Educational Opportunity Program affords students from minority groups and low-income families the opportunity to attend the school. There are 13 national honor societies, including Phi Beta Kappa, and a freshman honors program.

Admissions: 84% of the 1999-2000 applicants were accepted. The SAT I scores for the 1999-2000 freshman class were: Verbal--14% below 500, 46% between 500 and 599, 33% between 600 and 700, and 7% above 700; Math--15% below 500, 41% between 500 and 599, 37% between 600 and 700, and 8% above 700. 68% of the current freshmen were in the top quarter of their class; 94% were in the top half. In a recent year, 75 freshmen graduated first in their class.

Requirements: The SAT I or ACT is required. Marquette requires applicants to be in the upper 50% of their class. Applicants must be graduates of an accredited secondary school with a recommended 18 credits, including 4 years of English, 3 each of social studies and math, 2 each of sciences and foreign language, and 4 of additional academic subjects. Most students rank in the upper quarter of their high school class. The GED is accepted, with a minimum score of 225. Applicants must demonstrate ability, preparation, and motivation. An interview is recommended. AP and CLEP credits are accepted. Important factors in the admissions decision are advanced placement or honor courses, recommendations by school officials, and leadership record.

Procedure: Freshmen are admitted to all sessions. Entrance exams should be taken in the junior year and repeated early in the senior year if necessary. There is an early admissions plan. Application deadlines are open; there is a $30 fee. Notification is sent on a rolling basis.

Financial Aid: In 1999-2000, 64% of freshmen and 60% of continuing students received need-based aid. The average freshman award was $15,777. Of that total, scholarships or need-based gifts averaged $9762; need-based loans averaged $4101; and need-based self-help averaged $5304. 78% of undergraduates work part time. The average financial indebtedness of the 1999 graduate was $20,721. The FAFSA and the university's own financial statement are required.

Computers: The mainframe is comprised of various DEC VAX models in a cluster configuration. There are more than 1000 time-sharing terminals and PCs in residence halls, libraries, and academic facilities. Students can also use word-processing facilities in the library, computing center, and various buildings. Residence halls are wired for Web and Internet access. All students may access the system 24 hours a day Sunday through Thursday and 10 a.m. to 10 p.m. weekends when classes are in session. There are no time limits and no fees.

MARY WASHINGTON COLLEGE
Fredericksburg, VA 22401-5358　　　　　　　　**(540) 654-2000**
(800) 468-5614; Fax: (540) 654-1857

Full-time: 1063 men, 2186 women	**Faculty:** 180; IIB, ++$
Part-time: 199 men, 459 women	**Ph.D.s:** 89%
Graduate: 10 men, 29 women	**Student/Faculty:** 18 to 1
Year: semesters, summer session	**Tuition:** $3204 ($9414)
Application Deadline: February 1	**Room & Board:** $5298
Freshman Class: 4405 applied, 2450 accepted, 841 enrolled	
SAT I Verbal/Math: 612/596	**HIGHLY COMPETITIVE**

Mary Washington College, founded in 1908, is a public liberal arts and sciences institution. There is 1 graduate school. In addition to regional accreditation, the college has baccalaureate program accreditation with NASM. The library contains 335,061 volumes, 521,056 microform items, and 2210 audiovisual forms/CDs, and subscribes to 1715 periodicals. Computerized library services include the card catalog, interlibrary loans, and database searching. Special learning facilities include an art gallery, radio station, and center for historic preservation. The 176-acre campus is in a small town 50 miles south of Washington, D.C., and 50 miles north of Richmond. Including residence halls, there are 40 buildings.

Programs of Study: The college confers B.A., B.S., B.L.S., and B.P.S. degrees. Master's degrees are also awarded. Bachelor's degrees are awarded in BIOLOGI-CAL SCIENCE (biology/biological science), BUSINESS (business administration and management), COMMUNICATIONS AND THE ARTS (art history and appreciation, classics, dramatic arts, English, French, German, historic preservation, languages, Latin, music, Spanish, and studio art), COMPUTER AND PHYSICAL SCIENCE (chemistry, computer science, geology, mathematics, and physics), ENGINEERING AND ENVIRONMENTAL DESIGN (environmental science), HEALTH PROFESSIONS (predentistry, premedicine, and preveterinary science), SOCIAL SCIENCE (American studies, economics, geography, history, international relations, philosophy, political science/government, prelaw, psychology, religion, and sociology). Business administration, psychology, and English are the largest.

Special: Study abroad in 41 countries, a Washington semester, and credit for off-campus work experience are available. The college offers cooperative programs in computer science, physics, and math, dual majors, work-study programs, student-designed majors, and pass/fail options. More than 500 internships for credit are also available. Teacher licensure preparation is offered for elementary and secondary education. There are 20 national honor societies, including Phi Beta Kappa, and 25 departmental honors programs.

Admissions: 56% of the 1999-2000 applicants were accepted. The SAT I scores for the 1999-2000 freshman class were: Verbal--37% below 500, 37% between 500 and 599, 50% between 600 and 700, and 10% above 700; Math--6% below 500, 43% between 500 and 599, 45% between 600 and 700, and 6% above 700. 77% of the current freshmen were in the top fifth of their class; 97% were in the top two fifths. There was 1 National Merit finalist and 7 semifinalists. 18 freshmen graduated first in their class.

Requirements: The SAT I or ACT is required. Applicants must be graduates of an accredited secondary school or hold the GED. Students should complete 16 high school academic credits, including 4 credits of English, 3 to 4 of foreign language, and 3 each of math, science, and social studies. An SAT II: Subject test is strongly recommended. Application essays are required. Applications are accepted on-line via ExPAN and CollegeLink, and can be downloaded from the college's web site. AP and CLEP credits are accepted. Important factors in the admissions decision are advanced placement or honor courses, evidence of special talent, and recommendations by school officials.

Procedure: Freshmen are admitted fall and spring. Entrance exams should be taken by January of the senior year. There are early decision and early admissions plans. Early decision applications should be filed by November 1; regular applications, by February 1 for fall entry and November 1 for spring entry, along with a $35 fee. Notification of early decision is sent December 15; regular decision, April 1. 158 early decision candidates were accepted for the 1999-2000 class. A waiting list is an active part of the admissions procedure.

Financial Aid: In a recent year, 55% of all freshmen and 60% of continuing students received some form of financial aid. 40% of freshmen and 45% of continuing students received need-based aid. The average freshman award was $4790. Of that total, scholarships or need-based grants averaged $1500 ($2000 maximum); loans averaged $2100 ($2625 maximum); and work contracts averaged $1250 ($1900 maximum). 20% of undergraduates work part time. Average annual earnings from campus work are $1400. The average financial indebtedness of a recent graduate was $11,000. the college is a member of CSS. The FAFSA is required. The fall application deadline is March 1.

Computers: The mainframe is an HP 3000/969. The college has a fiber-optic network. All students can access Netscape (Internet) and the web from residence hall rooms. Several 24-hour computer labs are available for student use. All students may access the system. There are no time limits and no fees.

MARYCREST INTERNATIONAL UNIVERSITY
Davenport, IA 52804
(319) 327-9609
(800) 728-9705; Fax: (319) 327-9620

Full-time: 129 men, 151 women	**Faculty:** 21; IIB, --$
Part-time: 33 men, 55 women	**Ph.D.s:** 52%
Graduate: 60 men, 335 women	**Student/Faculty:** 13 to 1
Year: semesters, summer session	**Tuition:** $12,700
Application Deadline: open	**Room & Board:** $4840
Freshman Class: 371 applied, 292 accepted, 134 enrolled	
ACT: 22	**VERY COMPETITIVE**

Marycrest International University, founded in 1939, is a private liberal arts school. There is 1 graduate school. In addition to regional accreditation, Marycrest has baccalaureate program accreditation with CSWE and NLN. The library contains 101,401 volumes, 25,356 microform items, and 5354 audiovisual forms/CDs, and subscribes to 129 periodicals. Computerized library services include the card catalog, interlibrary loans, and database searching. Special learning facilities include a learning resource center, art gallery, computer graphics lab, law library, and multimedia and journalism labs. The 30-acre campus is in an urban area 180 miles west of Chicago. Including residence halls, there are 12 buildings.

Programs of Study: Marycrest confers B.A., B.S., B.S.N., and B.S.W. degrees. Associate and master's degrees are also awarded. Bachelor's degrees are awarded in BIOLOGICAL SCIENCE (biology/biological science), BUSINESS (accounting and business administration and management), COMMUNICATIONS AND THE ARTS (communications and English), COMPUTER AND PHYSICAL SCIENCE (computer science and mathematics), EDUCATION (elementary), ENGINEERING AND ENVIRONMENTAL DESIGN (computer graphics and environmental science), HEALTH PROFESSIONS (nursing), SOCIAL SCIENCE (history, Native American studies, psychology, social science, and social work). Business, computer graphics, and education are the strongest academically. Education, computer graphics, and nursing are the largest.

Special: Within majors there are emphases in elementary education, business, and international relations, as well as prelaw, predentistry, premedicine, and preveterinary. Internships, practicums, and cooperative programs in communications, business, history, prelaw, computer science, and multimedia are available. Work-study on campus and study abroad in Japan, Germany, the Netherlands, England, and other countries are possible. B.A.-B.S. degrees in numerous subjects, dual majors, student-designed majors, nondegree study, and pass/fail options are also offered. Business majors participate in 2 8-week sessions per semester. There is 1 national honor society.

Admissions: 79% of the 1999-2000 applicants were accepted. The ACT scores for the 1999-2000 freshman class were: 14% below 21, 40% between 21 and 23, 41% between 24 and 26, 3% between 27 and 28, and 2% above 28.

Requirements: The ACT is required and the SAT I is recommended. Marycrest requires applicants to be in the upper 50% of their class. A GPA of 2.3 is required. Applicants must be graduates of an accredited secondary school and should have earned 16 academic credits, including 4 in English, 3 in foreign language, 2 each of math and social studies, and 1 in science. An interview is required. The GED is accepted. Applications are accepted on-line. AP and CLEP credits are accepted. Important factors in the admissions decision are leadership record, evidence of special talent, and extracurricular activities record.

Procedure: Freshmen are admitted to all sessions. There are early decision, early admissions, and deferred admissions plans. Application deadlines are open. The application fee is $25. Notification is sent on a rolling basis.

Financial Aid: In 1999-2000, 89% of all students received some form of financial aid. 84% of freshmen and 85% of continuing students received need-based aid. The average freshman award was $10,025. Of that total, scholarships or need-based grants averaged $3500 ($5000 maximum); loans averaged $2625 ($6625 maximum); and work contracts averaged $1000 ($2000 maximum). Pell, SEOG, and ITG grants were also awarded. 35% of undergraduates work part time. Average annual earnings from campus work are $1000. The average financial indebtedness of the 1999 graduate was $17,125. Marycrest is a member of CSS. The FAFSA is required. The fall application deadline is April 15.

Computers: The mainframes are a DEC VAX and an ALPHA 2000 VMS server. In addition, there are 85 PCs for general use and 2 computer-equipped classrooms next to the library. The computer graphics lab is open 24 hours a day. All students may access the system Monday through Friday 8 a.m. to 10 p.m., Saturdays 8 a.m. to 5 p.m., and Sundays 1 p.m. to 8 p.m. There are no time limits. The fee is $5 per credit hour. The university strongly recommends that all students have PCs.

MARYLAND INSTITUTE, COLLEGE OF ART
Baltimore, MD 21217   (410) 225-2222; Fax: (410) 225-2337

Full-time: 470 men, 621 women	**Faculty:** 78
Part-time: 9 men, 15 women	**Ph.D.s:** 87%
Graduate: 58 men, 81 women	**Student/Faculty:** 14 to 1
Year: semesters, summer session	**Tuition:** $18,460
Application Deadline: January 15	**Room & Board:** $6300
Freshman Class: 1496 applied, 776 accepted, 305 enrolled	
SAT I: required	**SPECIAL**

Maryland Institute, College of Art, founded in 1826, is a private accredited institution offering undergraduate and graduate degrees in the fine arts. There are 6 graduate schools. In addition to regional accreditation, MICA has baccalaureate program accreditation with FIDER and NASAD. The library contains 51,000 volumes and 4600 audiovisual forms/CDs, and subscribes to 300 periodicals. Computerized library services include the card catalog, interlibrary loans, and database searching. Special learning facilities include a learning resource center and 7 large art galleries, open to the public year-round, and featuring work by MICA faculty, students, and nationally and internationally known artists, and a slide library containing 200,000 slides. The 12-acre campus is in an urban area in the Mt. Royal cultural center of Baltimore. Including residence halls, there are 20 buildings.

Programs of Study: MICA confers the B.F.A. degree. Master's degrees are also awarded. Bachelor's degrees are awarded in COMMUNICATIONS AND THE ARTS (ceramic art and design, drawing, fiber/textiles/weaving, fine arts, graphic design, illustration, painting, photography, printmaking, and sculpture), ENGINEERING AND ENVIRONMENTAL DESIGN (interior design). Fine arts, painting, graphic design, and graphic design are the strongest academically. Fine arts, painting, and illustration are the largest.

Special: Exchange programs are offered with Goucher College, Loyola and Notre Dame colleges, Johns Hopkins University, the Peabody Conservatory of Music, and the University of Baltimore. Cross-registration is possible with any member schools in the Alliance of Independent Colleges of Art and the East Coast Art

Schools Consortium. A New York studio semester is available. Study abroad is possible in the junior year in any of 10 countries, including the Maryland Institute's Center for Advanced art and Culture in Aux-en-Provence, France. Student-designed majors are available, and there are work-study programs. Juniors and seniors who meet prerequisites are eligible for credit-earning internships locally and nationally.

Admissions: 52% of the 1999-2000 applicants were accepted. The SAT I scores for the 1999-2000 freshman class were: Verbal--15% below 500, 44% between 500 and 599, 33% between 600 and 700, and 8% above 700; Math--30% below 500, 44% between 500 and 599, 23% between 600 and 700, and 3% above 700. 38% of the current freshmen were in the top fifth of their class; 67% were in the top two fifths. There were 3 National Merit semifinalists. 5 freshmen graduated first in their class.

Requirements: The SAT I is required. Emphasis is primarily on the applicant's portfolio, which is reviewed as part of the admissions process. Applicants submit 12 to 20 pieces of their best current work in and out of school, including samples of drawings from observation. Academic history, including grades and course level, is also seriously considered. AP credits are accepted. Important factors in the admissions decision are evidence of special talent, advanced placement or honor courses, and personality/intangible qualities.

Procedure: Freshmen are admitted fall and spring. Entrance exams should be taken in the spring of the junior year. There are early decision, early admissions, and deferred admissions plans. Early decision applications should be filed by November 15; regular applications by January 15 for fall entry, and December 1 for spring entry, along with a $45 fee. Notification of early decision is sent December 15; regular decision, March 1. 25 early decision candidates were accepted for the 1999-2000 class.

Financial Aid: In 1999-2000, 76% of all freshmen and 74% of continuing students received some form of financial aid. 51% of freshmen and 68% of continuing students received need-based aid. The average freshman award was $8625. Of that total, scholarships or need-based grants averaged $4900 ($19,725 maximum); loans averaged $2625 ($4325 maximum); and work contracts averaged $1100 ($2000 maximum). 62% of undergraduates work part time. Average annual earnings from campus work are $1100. The average financial indebtedness of the 1999 graduate was $12,500. MICA is a member of CSS. The FAFSA and the college's own financial statement are required. The fall application deadline is March 1.

Computers: The mainframes are an IBM AS/400, an IBM Netfinity 7000, and an IBM Netfinity 5500 M10. There are 226 IBM PCs and Macs available for student use throughout the campus with Internet access. Every student has an E-mail address, and residence halls are wired for Internet access. Also available are high-end peripherals such as scanners, digital cameras, printers, digital video editing equipment, and state-of-the-art software for 2-D and 3-D applications. All students may access the system 24 hours a day. There are no time limits and no fees.

MARYVILLE COLLEGE
Maryville, TN 37804

(423) 981-8092
(800) 597-2687; Fax: (423) 981-8010

Full-time: 432 men, 540 women	**Faculty:** 63; IIB, av$
Part-time: 9 men, 20 women	**Ph.D.s:** 87%
Graduate: none	**Student/Faculty:** 15 to 1
Year: 4-1-4, summer session	**Tuition:** $16,025
Application Deadline: March 1	**Room & Board:** $5080
Freshman Class: 1744 applied, 1416 accepted, 313 enrolled	
SAT I Verbal/Math: 547/538	**ACT:** 24 **VERY COMPETITIVE**

Maryville College, founded in 1819, is a private liberal arts college affiliated with the Presbyterian Church (U.S.A.). In addition to regional accreditation, Maryville has baccalaureate program accreditation with NASM. The 2 libraries contain 118, 263 volumes, 5673 microform items, and 3340 audiovisual forms/CDs, and subscribe to 795 periodicals. Computerized library services include the card catalog, interlibrary loans, and database searching. Special learning facilities include an art gallery, greenhouse, and college woods. The 350-acre campus is in a suburban area 15 miles south of Knoxville. Including residence halls, there are 24 buildings.

Programs of Study: Maryville confers B.A. and B.Mus. degrees. Bachelor's degrees are awarded in BIOLOGICAL SCIENCE (biochemistry and biology/biological science), BUSINESS (business administration and management and recreation and leisure services), COMMUNICATIONS AND THE ARTS (art, creative writing, dramatic arts, English, fine arts, music, and Spanish), COMPUTER AND PHYSICAL SCIENCE (chemistry, computer science, mathematics, and physics), EDUCATION (art, elementary, music, science, and secondary), ENGINEERING AND ENVIRONMENTAL DESIGN (environmental science and preengineering), HEALTH PROFESSIONS (health science, nursing, predentistry, and premedicine), SOCIAL SCIENCE (economics, history, human services, international relations, interpreter for the deaf, political science/government, prelaw, psychology, religion, social science, and sociology). Biology, chemistry, and English are the strongest academically. Business, biology, and child development with teacher licensure are the largest.

Special: Maryville offers cross-registration with the University of Tennessee, internships, study abroad in 7 countries, a Washington semester, accelerated degree programs, a B.A.-B.S. degree, and dual and student-designed majors. There are 3-2 engineering degrees offered with regional universities. Nondegree study and pass/fail options are possible. There is a freshman honors program.

Admissions: 81% of the 1999-2000 applicants were accepted. The SAT I scores for the 1999-2000 freshman class were: Verbal--31% below 500, 37% between 500 and 599, 26% between 600 and 700, and 5% above 700; Math--36% below 500, 34% between 500 and 599, 30% between 600 and 700, and 1% above 700. The ACT scores were 33% below 21, 16% between 21 and 23, 22% between 24 and 26, 17% between 27 and 28, and 12% above 28. 47% of the current freshmen were in the top fifth of their class; 75% were in the top two fifths. 6 freshmen graduated first in their class.

Requirements: The SAT I or ACT is required. A GPA of 2.5 is required. The minimum composite score on the SAT I is 950; on the ACT, 20. Candidates should be graduates of accredited secondary schools or have the GED. They should also have 15 academic credits with 4 years of English, 3 each of math and science, 2 years of foreign language, and 2 of history or social studies. An essay, portfolio, audition, and interview are all recommended. Applications are accepted on-line. AP and CLEP credits are accepted. Important factors in the admissions decision are advanced placement or honor courses, recommendations by school officials, and leadership record.

Procedure: Freshmen are admitted fall, spring, and summer. Entrance exams should be taken in October of the senior year. There are early decision, early admissions, and deferred admissions plans. Early decision applications should be filed by November 15; regular applications, by March 1 for fall entry, November 1 for spring entry, and May 1 for summer entry, along with a $25 fee. Notification of early decision is sent December 1; regular decision, April 1.

Financial Aid: In 1999-2000, 99% of all freshmen and 97% of continuing students received some form of financial aid. 97% of all freshmen and continuing students received need-based aid. The average freshman award was $15,449. Of that total, scholarships or need-based grants averaged $10,350 ($14,200 maximum); loans averaged $4634 ($5625 maximum); and work contracts averaged $1200 (maximum). 45% of undergraduates work part time. Average annual earnings from campus work are $1200. The average financial indebtedness of the 1999 graduate was $15,625. Maryville is a member of CSS. The FAFSA is required. The fall application deadline is March 1.

Computers: There are 62 PCs on a local area network in staffed student labs with access to E-mail, the Internet, and the Web. All students may access the system 7 days a week, 16 hours a day. There are no time limits and no fees. It is recommended that all students have personal computers.

MASSACHUSETTS COLLEGE OF ART
Boston, MA 02115   (617) 232-1555, ext. 235; Fax: (617) 566-4034

Full-time: 514 men, 730 women	**Faculty:** 72
Part-time: 79 men, 188 women	**Ph.D.s:** 71%
Graduate: 49 men, 56 women	**Student/Faculty:** 17 to 1
Year: semesters, summer session	**Tuition:** $3808 ($10,668)
Application Deadline: March 1	**Room & Board:** $6922
Freshman Class: 1049 applied, 497 accepted, 252 enrolled	
SAT I Verbal/Math: 570/540	**SPECIAL**

Massachusetts College of Art, founded in 1873, is a public institution offering undergraduate and graduate programs in art, design, and education. There is 1 graduate school. In addition to regional accreditation, MassArt has baccalaureate program accreditation with NASAD. The library contains 232,900 volumes, 8700 microform items, and 125,000 audiovisual forms/CDs, and subscribes to 757 periodicals. Computerized library services include the card catalog and interlibrary loans. Special learning facilities include an art gallery, a computer arts center, performance spaces, and film viewing rooms. The 5-acre campus is in an urban area in Boston. Including residence halls, there are 6 buildings.

Programs of Study: MassArt confers the B.F.A. degree. Master's degrees are also awarded. Bachelor's degrees are awarded in COMMUNICATIONS AND THE ARTS (art history and appreciation, film arts, fine arts, graphic design, illustration, industrial design, photography, and studio art), EDUCATION (art), ENGINEERING AND ENVIRONMENTAL DESIGN (architecture), SOCIAL SCIENCE (fashion design and technology). Painting, illustration, and graphic design are the largest.

Special: MassArt offers cross-registration with several consortiums, internships for advanced students, on- and off-campus work-study programs, study-abroad and foreign-exchange programs, an open major for exceptional students, and dual majors in most combinations of concentrations.

Admissions: 47% of the 1999-2000 applicants were accepted. The SAT I scores for the 1999-2000 freshman class were: Verbal--18% below 500, 45% between 500 and 599, 32% between 600 and 700, and 5% above 700; Math--26% below 500, 54% between 500 and 599, 17% between 600 and 700, and 3% above 700. 45% of the current freshmen were in the top fifth of their class; 77% were in the top two fifths.

Requirements: The SAT I is required. A GPA of 2.9 is required. In addition, applicants should be graduates of an accredited secondary school or have earned the GED. College-preparatory studies should include as a minimum 4 years of English, 3 each of math and science, 2 each of social studies and a foreign language, plus 2 academic electives. A personal essay and portfolio are required, and an interview and letters of reference are recommended. AP and CLEP credits are accepted. Important factors in the admissions decision are evidence of special talent, recommendations by school officials, and personality/intangible qualities.

Procedure: Freshmen are admitted fall and spring. Entrance exams should be taken in the early fall of the senior year. There are early decision, early admissions, and deferred admissions plans. Early decision applications should be filed by December 1; regular applications, by March 1 for fall entry and November 1 for spring entry, along with a $25 fee. Notification of early decision is sent December 20; regular decision, on a rolling basis. 13 early decision candidates were accepted for the 1999-2000 class. 10% of all applicants are on a waiting list.

Financial Aid: In 1999-2000, 75% of all freshmen and 65% of continuing students received some form of financial aid. 54% of freshmen and 46% of continuing students received need-based aid. The average freshman award was $7356. Of that total, scholarships or need-based grants averaged $3200 ($10,700 maximum); loans averaged $2650 ($6235 maximum); and work contracts averaged $1300 ($2000 maximum). 84% of undergraduates work part time. Average annual earnings from campus work are $800. The average financial indebtedness of the 1999 graduate was $14,500. MassArt is a member of CSS. The CSS/Profile, FAFSA, FFS or SFS is required. The fall application deadline is May 1.

Computers: The mainframe is an IBM. MassArt provides Amiga, Mac, IBM, and NEC PCs for academic use. They are located in the computer center. All students may access the system. There are no time limits. The fee is $100 for students using the computer arts center who are not enrolled in a computer design course. There are computers available in the library for all students at no fee.

MASSACHUSETTS INSTITUTE OF TECHNOLOGY
Cambridge, MA 02139
(617) 253-4791; Fax: (617) 258-8304

Full-time: 2497 men, 1743 women	**Faculty:** 900; I, ++$
Part-time: 35 men, 25 women	**Ph.D.s:** 99%
Graduate: 4153 men, 1519 women	**Student/Faculty:** 5 to 1
Year: 4-1-4	**Tuition:** $25,636
Application Deadline: January 1	**Room & Board:** $6900
Freshman Class: 9136 applied, 1742 accepted, 1048 enrolled	
SAT I Verbal/Math: 710/760	**ACT:** 32 **MOST COMPETITIVE**

Massachusetts Institute of Technology, founded in 1861, is a private, independent, land-grant institution offering programs in architecture and planning, engineering, humanities and social science, science, health sciences, technology, and management. There are 6 undergraduate and 6 graduate schools. In addition to regional accreditation, MIT has baccalaureate program accreditation with AACSB, ABET, CSAB, and NAAB. The 11 libraries contain 2,579,814 volumes, 2,

298,263 microform items, and 25,055 audiovisual forms/CDs, and subscribe to 19,112 periodicals. Computerized library services include the card catalog, interlibrary loans, and database searching. Special learning facilities include an art gallery, radio station, and TV station. The 155-acre campus is in an urban area 1 mile north of Boston. Including residence halls, there are 158 buildings.

Programs of Study: MIT confers the S.B. degree. Master's and doctoral degrees are also awarded. Bachelor's degrees are awarded in BIOLOGICAL SCIENCE (biology/biological science), BUSINESS (management science), COMMUNICATIONS AND THE ARTS (art, creative writing, dramatic arts, German, literature, media arts, and music), COMPUTER AND PHYSICAL SCIENCE (chemistry, computer science, earth science, mathematics, and physics), ENGINEERING AND ENVIRONMENTAL DESIGN (aeronautical engineering, aerospace studies, chemical engineering, civil engineering, computer engineering, electrical/electronics engineering, environmental engineering, materials engineering, materials science, mechanical engineering, nuclear engineering, ocean engineering, and urban planning technology), SOCIAL SCIENCE (American studies, anthropology, archeology, cognitive science, East Asian studies, economics, history, Latin American studies, medieval studies, philosophy, political science/government, psychology, Russian and Slavic studies, and women's studies). Architecture, engineering, and management are the strongest academically. Engineering is the largest.

Special: MIT offers cross-registration with Wellesley and Harvard, cooperative programs, engineering internships, junior year abroad, work-study in on- and some off-campus research labs, accelerated degree programs and dual majors in all fields, and student-designed majors. A general studies degree, credit by examination, and pass/fail options are possible. Alternative programs are available to a limited number of freshmen, providing for smaller academic communities within MIT. There are 12 national honor societies, including Phi Beta Kappa, and 8 departmental honors programs.

Admissions: 19% of the 1999-2000 applicants were accepted. The SAT I scores for the 1999-2000 freshman class were: Verbal--1% below 500, 6% between 500 and 599, 35% between 600 and 700, and 58% above 700; Math--12% between 600 and 700 and 87% above 700. The ACT scores were 1% between 21 and 23, 5% between 24 and 26, 10% between 27 and 28, and 85% above 28. 99% of the current freshmen were in the top fifth of their class; 100% were in the top two fifths. 218 freshmen graduated first in their class.

Requirements: The SAT I or ACT is required. 3 SAT II: Subject tests, including math, science, and writing, literature, or history are required. 14 academic units are recommended, including 4 each of English and math, 3 of lab science, 2 of social studies, and 1 of foreign language. The GED is accepted. Essays, 2 teacher evaluations, and an interview are required. Applications may be submitted on computer disk and on-line via the school's web site, http://web.mit.edu. AP credits are accepted. Important factors in the admissions decision are recommendations by school officials, extracurricular activities record, and evidence of special talent.

Procedure: Freshmen are admitted in the fall. Entrance exams should be taken by the January test date. There are early admissions and deferred admissions plans. Early decision applications should be filed by November 1; regular applications, by January 1 for fall entry, along with a $55 fee. Notification of early decision is sent in late December; regular decision, April 1. 506 early decision candidates were accepted for the 1999-2000 class. 6% of all applicants are on a waiting list.

Financial Aid: In a recent year, 63% of freshmen and 60% of continuing students received need-based aid. The average freshman award was $19,094. 56%

of undergraduates work part time. Average annual earnings from campus work are $1449. The average financial indebtedness of a recent graduate was $22,625. MIT is a member of CSS. The CSS/Profile or FAFSA, the college's own financial statement, and tax returns are required. The fall application deadline is January 16.

Computers: The mainframe is an IBM ES/9000 Model 570. An Athena Computing Environment provides approximately 700 public workstations distributed across campus. Specialized departmental computing facilities are also available. Digital-network connections are provided to dorm rooms and living groups. All students may access the system at all times. There are no time limits and no fees.

MCKENDREE COLLEGE
Lebanon, IL 62254

(618) 537-6835
(800) BEARCAT; Fax: (618) 537-6496

Full-time: 602 men, 871 women	**Faculty:** 60; IIB, av$
Part-time: 167 men, 421 women	**Ph.D.s:** 83%
Graduate: none	**Student/Faculty:** 25 to 1
Year: semesters, summer session	**Tuition:** $11,250
Application Deadline: open	**Room & Board:** $4250
Freshman Class: 1049 applied, 766 accepted, 253 enrolled	
ACT: 24	**VERY COMPETITIVE**

McKendree College, founded in 1828, is the oldest college in Illinois. It is a private liberal arts institution affiliated with the United Methodist Church. In addition to regional accreditation, McKendree has baccalaureate program accreditation with NLN. The library contains 79,963 volumes, 25,375 microform items, and 3650 audiovisual forms/CDs, and subscribes to 501 periodicals. Computerized library services include the card catalog, interlibrary loans, and database searching. Special learning facilities include a learning resource center, a greenhouse, and archives. The 80-acre campus is in a small town 23 miles east of St. Louis. Including residence halls, there are 25 buildings.

Programs of Study: McKendree confers B.A., B.S., B.B.A., B.F.A., B.S.Ed., and B.S.N. degrees. Bachelor's degrees are awarded in BIOLOGICAL SCIENCE (biology/biological science), BUSINESS (accounting, banking and finance, business administration and management, and marketing/retailing/merchandising), COMMUNICATIONS AND THE ARTS (art, communications, English, fine arts, music, and speech/debate/rhetoric), COMPUTER AND PHYSICAL SCIENCE (chemistry, computer science, information sciences and systems, and mathematics), EDUCATION (art, athletic training, business, elementary, and physical), HEALTH PROFESSIONS (medical laboratory technology and nursing), SOCIAL SCIENCE (economics, history, international relations, philosophy, political science/government, psychology, religion, social science, and sociology). Biology and computer science are the strongest academically. Business, computer science, and nursing are the largest.

Special: McKendree offers internships, work-study programs, study abroad in England and Ireland, a Washington semester, dual and student-designed majors, and nondegree study, as well as a 3-2 program in occupational therapy with Washington University in St. Louis. There are 9 national honor societies, and a freshman honors program.

Admissions: 73% of the 1999-2000 applicants were accepted. The ACT scores for the 1999-2000 freshman class were: 26% below 21, 24% between 21 and 23, 32% between 24 and 26, 10% between 27 and 28, and 8% above 28. 63% of the current freshmen were in the top fifth of their class; 81% were in the top two fifths. There was 1 National Merit finalist. 16 freshmen graduated first in their class.

Requirements: The SAT I or ACT is recommended. McKendree requires applicants to be in the upper 50% of their class. A GPA of 2.5 is required. Students must be high school graduates or submit the GED certificate. Completion of at least 15 units of high school work is recommended. A recommendation from the secondary school counselor is required. Applications are accepted on-line via the school's web site. AP and CLEP credits are accepted. Important factors in the admissions decision are advanced placement or honor courses, leadership record, and recommendations by school officials.

Procedure: Freshmen are admitted to all sessions. Application deadlines are open. Notification is sent on a rolling basis.

Financial Aid: In 1999-2000, 88% of all freshmen and 50% of continuing students received some form of financial aid. 62% of freshmen and 36% of continuing students received need-based aid. The average freshman award was $9512. Of that total, scholarships or need-based grants averaged $6794 ($12,000 maximum); loans averaged $2214 ($6625 maximum); and work contracts averaged $1818 ($2472 maximum). 49% of undergraduates work part time. Average annual earnings from campus work are $501. The average financial indebtedness of the 1999 graduate was $11,434. McKendree is a member of CSS. The FAFSA is required.

Computers: The mainframe is a DEC ALPHA 4000. There are more than 325 terminals on campus and 270 in individual residence rooms. Students may use any of the PCs across 4 labs on campus, another 40 PCs in 2 labs at remote centers, or their own PC in their residence room. All students may access the system. There are no time limits and no fees. It is strongly recommended that all students have personal computers.

MERCER UNIVERSITY
Macon, GA 31207-0001

(912) 301-2650
(800) 637-2378; Fax: (912) 301-2828

Full-time: 1190 men, 2101 women	**Faculty:** 196; IIA, +$
Part-time: 251 men, 550 women	**Ph.D.s:** 93%
Graduate: 1090 men, 1563 women	**Student/Faculty:** 17 to 1
Year: semesters, summer session	**Tuition:** $16,290
Application Deadline: open	**Room & Board:** $5380
Freshman Class: 3227 applied, 2524 accepted, 628 enrolled	
SAT I Verbal/Math: 550/550	**ACT:** 23 **VERY COMPETITIVE**

Mercer University, founded in 1833, is a private institution affiliated with the Georgia Baptist Convention. The university offers degree programs in liberal arts, business and economics, education, engineering, and professional studies. Mercer also offers a Great Books program as an alternative to the traditional core curriculum. There are 4 undergraduate and 7 graduate schools. In addition to regional accreditation, Mercer has baccalaureate program accreditation with ABET and NASM. The 2 libraries contain 418,865 volumes, 3,055,812 microform items, and 57,166 audiovisual forms/CDs. Computerized library services include the card catalog, interlibrary loans, and database searching. Special learning facilities include a learning resource center. The 130-acre campus is in a suburban area 85 miles south of Atlanta. Including residence halls, there are 58 buildings.

Programs of Study: Mercer confers B.A., B.S., B.B.A., B.M., B.M.D., B.M.E., B.S.E., B.S.M., and B.S.P. degrees. Master's and doctoral degrees are also awarded. Bachelor's degrees are awarded in BIOLOGICAL SCIENCE (biology/

biological science), BUSINESS (accounting, banking and finance, business administration and management, and marketing/retailing/merchandising), COMMUNICATIONS AND THE ARTS (English, French, German, Greek, Latin, music, and Spanish), COMPUTER AND PHYSICAL SCIENCE (chemistry, computer science, mathematics, natural sciences, and physics), EDUCATION (early childhood, elementary, music, secondary, and special), ENGINEERING AND ENVIRONMENTAL DESIGN (biomedical engineering, electrical/electronics engineering, environmental engineering, industrial engineering, and mechanical engineering), HEALTH PROFESSIONS (predentistry, premedicine, and prepharmacy), SOCIAL SCIENCE (economics, history, philosophy, political science/government, prelaw, psychology, religion, social science, and sociology). Engineering, chemistry, and English are the strongest academically. Business, English, and engineering are the largest.

Special: Mercer offers co-op programs in all majors, cross-registration with Wesleyan College, B.A.-B.S. degrees in various science and math fields, internships, student-designed majors, work-study programs, and satisfactory-unsatisfactory options for elective courses. Students may study abroad in Spain, France, Great Britain, Australia, Hong Kong, and Morocco. There are 2 national honor societies, a freshman honors program, and 20 departmental honors programs.

Admissions: 78% of the 1999-2000 applicants were accepted. The SAT I scores for the 1999-2000 freshman class were: Verbal--25% below 500, 48% between 500 and 599, 23% between 600 and 700, and 4% above 700; Math--23% below 500, 48% between 500 and 599, 26% between 600 and 700, and 3% above 700. The ACT scores were 26% below 21, 28% between 21 and 23, 26% between 24 and 26, 9% between 27 and 28, and 11% above 28. 61% of the current freshmen were in the top fifth of their class; 84% were in the top two fifths.

Requirements: The SAT I or ACT is required. A GPA of 2.5 is required. Applicants must be graduates of an accredited secondary school and have completed 13 academic units. Students should submit their transcript and class rank, a recommendation from a guidance counselor, and a list of extracurricular activities, including employment. AP and CLEP credits are accepted. Important factors in the admissions decision are advanced placement or honor courses, extracurricular activities record, and evidence of special talent.

Procedure: Freshmen are admitted to all sessions. Entrance exams should be taken in the spring of the junior year or fall of the senior year. There are early admissions and deferred admissions plans. Application deadlines are open. There is a $25 fee. Notification is sent on a rolling basis.

Financial Aid: In a recent year, 94% of all freshmen and 90% of continuing students received some form of financial aid. 60% of freshmen and 51% of continuing students received need-based aid. The average freshman award was $14,567. Of that total, scholarships or need-based grants averaged $11,101 ($19,538 maximum); loans averaged $3778 ($15,000 maximum); and work contracts averaged $535 ($2000 maximum). 45% of undergraduates work part time. Average annual earnings from campus work are $1500. The average financial indebtedness of the 1999 graduate was $12,833. Mercer is a member of CSS. The FAFSA and the college's own financial statement are required. The priority fall application deadline is April 1.

Computers: The mainframes are DEC ALPHA 2100 and VAX 4000 models. Terminals are located in designated public and departmental student computer labs, and they can be accessed from off campus. All students may access the system 24 hours per day if the student has dial-in access. There are no time limits and no fees.

MERCY COLLEGE
Dobbs Ferry, NY 10522-1189　　　　　　　(914) 693-7600
　　　　　　　　　　　　　　　(800)MERCY NY; Fax: (914) 674-7382

Full-time: 1505 men, 34,230 women	**Faculty:** 125; IIA, +$
Part-time: 700 men, 2130 women	**Ph.D.s:** 63%
Graduate: 230 men, 1020 women	**Student/Faculty:** 39 to 1
Year: semesters, summer session	**Tuition:** $7875
Application Deadline: open	**Room & Board:** $8000
Freshman Class: n/av	
SAT I or ACT: not required	**LESS COMPETITIVE**

Mercy College, founded in 1950, is an independent institution offering programs in liberal arts, fine arts, business, and health science. There are 5 graduate schools. In addition to regional accreditation, Mercy has baccalaureate program accreditation with CSWE. The 10 libraries contain 600,000 volumes, and subscribe to 1170 periodicals. Computerized library services include the card catalog, interlibrary loans, and database searching. Special learning facilities include a learning resource center, art gallery, radio station, TV station, computer lab, and reference library. The 40-acre campus is in a suburban area 12 miles north of New York City. Including residence halls, there are 12 buildings.

Programs of Study: Mercy confers B.A. and B.S. degrees. Associate and master's degrees are also awarded. Bachelor's degrees are awarded in BIOLOGICAL SCIENCE (biology/biological science), BUSINESS (accounting and business administration and management), COMMUNICATIONS AND THE ARTS (English, journalism, music, and speech/debate/rhetoric), COMPUTER AND PHYSICAL SCIENCE (computer science, information science and systems, and mathematics), EDUCATION (education of the deaf and hearing impaired, elementary, special, and teaching English as a second/foreign language (TESOL/TEFOL)), HEALTH PROFESSIONS (medical laboratory technology, nursing, recreation therapy, and veterinary science), SOCIAL SCIENCE (behavioral science, criminal justice, history, interdisciplinary studies, paralegal studies, political science/government, psychology, social work, and sociology). The health professions programs is the strongest academically. Business is the largest.

Special: Mercy offers internships in each major, co-op programs in education, work-study programs through the Westchester Employee Association, study abroad, dual majors and degrees, credit for life experience, nondegree study, and pass/fail options. There are 14 national honor societies, including Phi Beta Kappa, a freshman honors program, and 14 departmental honors programs.

Requirements: Applicants must be graduates of an accredited secondary school or have a GED certificate. They should have completed at least 16 academic units. An interview is encouraged and a letter of recommendation from the high school counselor or principal is required. Art students must submit a portfolio; music students must audition. Applications are accepted on-line at www.merlin. mercynet.edu. AP and CLEP credits are accepted.

Procedure: Entrance exams should be taken between October and January of the senior year. There are early admissions and deferred admissions plans. Application deadlines are open. There is a $35 fee. Notification is sent on a rolling basis.

Financial Aid: Mercy is a member of CSS. The CSS/Profile is required.

Computers: The mainframe is an IBM 4381. There are also 250 IBM PCs and Macs, as well as graphics workstations with IBM XTs and Vectrix graphics boards. All students may access the system. There are no time limits. The fee is $35.

MERRIMACK COLLEGE

North Andover, MA 01845 (978) 837-5100; Fax: (978) 837-5133

Full-time: 1000 men, 1000 women	**Faculty:** 128; IIB, av$
Part-time: 300 men, 350 women	**Ph.D.s:** 75%
Graduate: none	**Student/Faculty:** 16 to 1
Year: semesters, summer session	**Tuition:** $15,710
Application Deadline: March 1	**Room & Board:** $7500
Freshman Class: 2710 applied, 1750 accepted, 560 enrolled	
SAT I Verbal/Math: 530/550	**VERY COMPETITIVE**

Merrimack College, founded in 1947 by the Augustinian clergy of the Roman Catholic Church, offers undergraduate programs in science, engineering, business administration, and liberal arts. In addition to regional accreditation, Merrimack has baccalaureate program accreditation with ABET. The library contains 133,000 volumes, 7200 microform items, and 1000 audiovisual forms/CDs, and subscribes to 900 periodicals. Computerized library services include the card catalog, interlibrary loans, and database searching. Special learning facilities include a learning resource center, art gallery, planetarium, TV station, the National Microscale Chemistry Center, and the Urban Resource Institute. The 220-acre campus is in a suburban area 25 miles north of Boston. Including residence halls, there are 33 buildings.

Programs of Study: Merrimack confers B.A. and B.S. degrees. Associate and master's degrees are also awarded. Bachelor's degrees are awarded in BIOLOGICAL SCIENCE (biochemistry and biology/biological science), BUSINESS (accounting, business administration and management, business economics, international business management, and marketing/retailing/merchandising), COMMUNICATIONS AND THE ARTS (communications, English, and modern language), COMPUTER AND PHYSICAL SCIENCE (chemistry, computer science, mathematics, and physics), EDUCATION (elementary and secondary), ENGINEERING AND ENVIRONMENTAL DESIGN (civil engineering, electrical/electronics engineering, and environmental science), HEALTH PROFESSIONS (allied health, predentistry, premedicine, and sports medicine), SOCIAL SCIENCE (economics, history, philosophy, political science/government, prelaw, psychology, religion, and sociology). Science, engineering, and business are the strongest academically. Business, psychology, and liberal arts are the largest.

Special: Merrimack offers cooperative programs in business, engineering, liberal arts, and computer science, cross-registration through the Northeast Consortium, internships in all arts and science programs, study abroad in 6 countries, and a Washington semester at American University. Work-study programs, a 5-year combined B.A.-B.S. degree in many major fields, and dual and self-designed majors are available. General studies, nondegree study, and pass/fail options are possible.

Admissions: 65% of the 1999-2000 applicants were accepted. The SAT I scores for the 1999-2000 freshman class were: Verbal--6% below 500, 67% between 500 and 599, 25% between 600 and 700, and 2% above 700; Math--7% below 500, 69% between 500 and 599, 19% between 600 and 700, and 5% above 700. The ACT scores were 2% below 21, 80% between 21 and 23, 15% between 24 and 26, and 3% between 27 and 28. 25% of the current freshmen were in the top fifth of their class; 65% were in the top two fifths. There was 1 National Merit finalist. 9 freshmen graduated first in their class.

Requirements: The SAT I or ACT is required. Merrimack requires applicants to be in the upper 50% of their class. A GPA of 2.5 is required. For business administration, humanities, and social science majors, Merrimack recommends that applicants complete 4 units of English, 3 each of math and science, and 2 of social studies. For other majors, an additional math course and 1 additional course in science are needed. An essay is required, and an interview is recommended. Applicants should have completed 16 Carnegie units. Applications are accepted online via Apply and CollegeLink. AP and CLEP credits are accepted. Important factors in the admissions decision are advanced placement or honor courses, recommendations by school officials, and leadership record.

Procedure: Freshmen are admitted fall and spring. Entrance exams should be taken during the spring of the junior year and the fall of the senior year. There are early decision, early admissions, and deferred admissions plans. Early decision applications should be filed by November 30; regular applications, by March 1 for fall entry and December 15 for spring entry, along with a $40 fee. Notification of early decision is sent December 15; regular decision, on a rolling basis. 30 early decision candidates were accepted for a recent class. 4% of all applicants are on a waiting list.

Financial Aid: In 1999-2000, 85% of all freshmen and 70% of continuing students received some form of financial aid. 70% of freshmen and 52% of continuing students received need-based aid. The average freshman award was $10,107. Of that total, scholarships or need-based grants averaged $7500 ($17,800 maximum); loans averaged $1500 ($4125 maximum); work contracts averaged $1000 ($2000 maximum); and donor-sponsored awards averaged $450 ($3600 maximum). 68% of undergraduates work part time. Average annual earnings from campus work are $1300. The average financial indebtedness of the 1999 graduate was $15,715. Merrimack is a member of CSS. The CSS/Profile or FAFSA is required. The fall application deadline is February 15.

Computers: The mainframe is a DEC VAX 11/785. PCs for academic use are available in the library, classrooms, and residence halls. All students may access the system. There are no time limits and no fees. It is strongly recommended that all students have an IBM or Gateway personal computer.

MESSIAH COLLEGE
Grantham, PA 17027

(717) 691-6000
(800) 233-4220; Fax: (717) 796-5374

Full-time: 1035 men, 1630 women	**Faculty:** 141; IIB, av$
Part-time: 14 men, 56 women	**Ph.D.s:** 77%
Graduate: none	**Student/Faculty:** 19 to 1
Year: semesters, summer session	**Tuition:** $13,880 ($15,000)
Application Deadline: open	**Room & Board:** $5500 ($5580)
Freshman Class: 2088 applied, 1681 accepted, 678 enrolled	
SAT I Verbal/Math: 590/585	**ACT:** 26 **VERY COMPETITIVE**

Messiah College, founded in 1909, is a Christian liberal arts college with an interdenominational Christian affiliation. In addition to regional accreditation, Messiah has baccalaureate program accreditation with ABET, ADA, CSWE, NASM, and NLN. The library contains 240,204 volumes, 103,579 microform items, and 11,997 audiovisual forms/CDs, and subscribes to 1316 periodicals. Computerized library services include the card catalog, interlibrary loans, and database searching. Special learning facilities include a learning resource center, art gallery, radio station, and a natural science museum. The 400-acre campus is in a small town 10 miles south of Harrisburg. Including residence halls, there are 46 buildings.

Programs of Study: Messiah confers B.A. and B.S. degrees. Bachelor's degrees are awarded in BIOLOGICAL SCIENCE (biochemistry and biology/biological science), BUSINESS (accounting, business administration and management, business systems analysis, international business management, marketing/retailing/merchandising, and personnel management), COMMUNICATIONS AND THE ARTS (art history and appreciation, broadcasting, communications, dramatic arts, English, fine arts, French, German, journalism, music, and Spanish), COMPUTER AND PHYSICAL SCIENCE (chemistry, computer science, mathematics, and physics), EDUCATION (art, early childhood, elementary, mathematics, music, physical, science, secondary, and social studies), ENGINEERING AND ENVIRONMENTAL DESIGN (civil engineering, engineering, and environmental science), HEALTH PROFESSIONS (nursing, recreation therapy, and sports medicine), SOCIAL SCIENCE (biblical studies, dietetics, economics, family/consumer studies, history, humanities, ministries, philosophy, physical fitness/movement, political science/government, psychology, religion, social work, and sociology). Language, and literature, nursing, and engineering are the strongest academically. Elementary education, nursing, and biology are the largest.

Special: Students may cross-register at Temple University in Philadephia. Off-campus study is available in Daystar University in Kenya, through Brethren Colleges Abroad, Jerusalem University College and in Latin American, Central American, Middle East, and Russian studies programs, among others. Off-campus options within the United States include the American Studies program, AuSable Institute of Environmental Studies, Los Angeles Film Studies, Oregon Extension, and others. Students may also spend a semester or year at any of 12 other Christian Consortium colleges in a student exchange program. Numerous internships, practical, and ministry opportunities are available. There are 2 national honor societies, a freshman honors program, and 6 departmental honors programs.

Admissions: 81% of the 1999-2000 applicants were accepted. The SAT I scores for the 1999-2000 freshman class were: Verbal--12% below 500, 42% between 500 and 599, 36% between 600 and 700, and 10% above 700; Math--16% below 500, 40% between 500 and 599, 35% between 600 and 700, and 9% above 700. The ACT scores were 12% below 21, 20% between 21 and 23, 27% between 24 and 26, 17% between 27 and 28, and 25% above 28. 59% of the current freshmen were in the top fifth of their class; 84% were in the top two fifths. There were 13 National Merit finalists. 43 freshmen graduated first in their class.

Requirements: The SAT I or ACT is required. Applicants must have graduated from an accredited high school or the equivalent. Secondary preparation of students who enroll usually includes 4 units in English, 3 or 4 in math, 3 each in natural science, social studies, and foreign languages, and 4 in academic electives. Students who enroll are usually in the top one third of their class and have a B average or better. A campus visit with interview/information session is recommended. Potential music majors must audition. Applications are accepted online via Messiah's Web page. AP and CLEP credits are accepted. Important factors in the admissions decision are leadership record, recommendations by school officials, and advanced placement or honor courses.

Procedure: Freshmen are admitted fall and spring. Entrance exams should be taken in the spring of the junior year. There are early admissions and deferred admissions plans. Application deadlines are open. There is a $30 fee. Notification is sent on a rolling basis. A waiting list is an active part of the admissions procedure.

Financial Aid: In 1999-2000, 97% of all freshmen and 93% of continuing students received some form of financial aid. 80% of freshmen and 78% of continuing students received need-based aid. The average freshman award was $12,237. Of that total, scholarships or need-based grants averaged $7397 ($15,000 maximum); loans averaged $3992 ($7625 maximum); and work contracts averaged $1656 ($1675 maximum). 48% of undergraduates work part time. Average annual earnings from campus work are $1802. The average financial indebtedness of the 1999 graduate was $17,000. Messiah is a member of CSS. The FAFSA is required. The fall priority application deadline is April 1.

Computers: The mainframe is an HP3000 model 959/KS200. There are 450 computers for student use located in the computer center, department labs, library, and residence halls. Dorm rooms are wired for network connection for PCs. E-mail and Internet access are available. All students may access the system 24 hours a day. There are no time limits and no fees.

MIAMI UNIVERSITY
Oxford, OH 45056   (513) 529-2531; Fax: (513) 529-1550

Full-time: 6440 men, 7942 women	**Faculty:** 773; I, -$
Part-time: 422 men, 484 women	**Ph.D.s:** 89%
Graduate: 538 men, 749 women	**Student/Faculty:** 19 to 1
Year: semesters, summer session	**Tuition:** $6112 ($12,766)
Application Deadline: January 31	**Room & Board:** $5330
Freshman Class: 11,993 applied, 9425 accepted, 3605 enrolled	
SAT I Verbal/Math: 580/593	**ACT:** 26 **VERY COMPETITIVE+**

Miami University, founded in 1809, is a public institution offering a variety of programs in the liberal arts and preprofessional-vocational training. There are 6 undergraduate schools and 1 graduate school. In addition to regional accreditation, Miami University has baccalaureate program accreditation with AACSB, ABET, ADA, AHEA, ASLA, NAAB, NASAD, NASM, NCATE, and NLN. The 4 libraries contain 2,190,506 volumes, 2,836,092 microform items, and 125,297 audiovisual forms/CDs, and subscribe to 11,862 periodicals. Computerized library services include the card catalog, interlibrary loans, and database searching. Special learning facilities include a learning resource center, art gallery, natural history museum, radio station, and TV station. The 1921-acre campus is in a small town 35 miles northwest of Cincinnati. Including residence halls, there are 162 buildings.

Programs of Study: Miami University confers B.A., B.S., B.E.D., B.F.A., B. Mus., and B.Phil. degrees. Master's and doctoral degrees are also awarded. Bachelor's degrees are awarded in BIOLOGICAL SCIENCE (biochemistry, biology/biological science, botany, microbiology, and zoology), BUSINESS (accounting, banking and finance, business administration and management, business economics, management information systems, marketing/retailing/merchandising, operations research, organizational behavior, personnel management, purchasing/inventory management, and sports management), COMMUNICATIONS AND THE ARTS (art, broadcasting, communications, dramatic arts, English, fine arts, French, German, Greek, Latin, linguistics, music, music performance, Russian, Spanish, speech/debate/rhetoric, and telecommunications), COMPUTER AND PHYSICAL SCIENCE (chemistry, computer science, geology, mathematics, physics, and statistics), EDUCATION (art, athletic training, early childhood, elementary, foreign languages, health, middle school, music, physical, science, secondary, and special), ENGINEERING AND ENVIRONMENTAL DESIGN (architecture, engineering, engineering management, engineering physics, engineering technology, environmental design, environmental science, interior design, manufacturing engineering, and paper and pulp science), HEALTH PROFESSIONS (exercise science, health, medical technology, nursing, premedicine, and speech pathology/audiology), SOCIAL SCIENCE (African American studies, American studies, anthropology, classical/ancient civilization, dietetics, economics, family/consumer studies, geography, history, interdisciplinary studies, international relations, international studies, philosophy, physical fitness/ movement, political science/government, prelaw, psychology, public administration, religion, social science, social work, sociology, and urban studies). Zoology, chemistry, and accountancy are the strongest academically. Accountancy, elementary education, and marketing are the largest.

Special: The university offers cross-registration with Cincinnati-area colleges, study abroad in 15 countries, co-op programs in the School of Applied Science, internships in health and sport studies and applied science, a 3-2 engineering degree with Case Western Reserve and Columbia Universities, and a 3-2 forestry degree with Duke University. Students may pursue student-designed majors through the School of Interdisciplinary Studies or interdisciplinary majors, including decision sciences and history of art and architecture. There are 30 national honor societies, including Phi Beta Kappa, and a freshman honors program.

Admissions: 79% of the 1999-2000 applicants were accepted. The SAT I scores for the 1999-2000 freshman class were: Verbal--9% below 500, 46% between 500 and 599, 38% between 600 and 700, and 7% above 700; Math--7% below 500, 36% between 500 and 599, 47% between 600 and 700, and 10% above 700. The ACT scores were 1% below 18, 23% between 18 and 23, 64% between 24 and 29, and 12% 30 and above. 70% of the current freshmen were in the top quarter of their class; 96% were in the top half.

Requirements: The SAT I or ACT is required. Candidates for admission must ordinarily be graduates of accredited secondary schools or hold the GED and should have completed 4 units of English, 3 each of math, science, and social studies/history, 2 of a foreign language, and 1 of fine arts. An audition, a portfolio, or an interview is required for direct admission to majors in the School of Fine Arts. Applications are accepted on-line via the university's web site. AP and CLEP credits are accepted. Important factors in the admissions decision are advanced placement or honor courses, evidence of special talent, and extracurricular activities record.

Procedure: Freshmen are admitted to all sessions. Entrance exams should be taken no later than December of the senior year. There is an early decision plan. Early decision applications should be filed by November 1; regular applications, by January 31 for fall entry and November 15 for spring entry, along with a $35 fee. Notification of early decision is sent December 15; regular decision, March 15. 548 early decision candidates were accepted for the 1999-2000 class. 4% of all applicants are on a waiting list.

Financial Aid: In 1999-2000, 92% of all freshmen and 61% of continuing students received some form of financial aid. 41% of freshmen and 40% of continuing students received need-based aid. The average freshman award was $5508. Of that total, scholarships or need-based grants averaged $2026 ($22,187 maximum); loans averaged $2655 ($23,140 maximum); work contracts averaged $199 ($1650 maximum); and external resources averaged $628 ($24,571 maximum). 30% of undergraduates work part time. Average annual earnings from campus work are $1084. The average financial indebtedness of the 1999 graduate was $16,710. Miami University is a member of CSS. The FAFSA is required. The fall application deadline is February 15.

Computers: The mainframes are an IBM ES/9121 Model 480, a DEC ALPHA 4710, an IBM 9672-R21, and a DEC ALPHA 2100 5/250. Computer facilities include statistical analysis, database programming, and E-mail via student computing facilities in academic departments, residence halls, or dial-up. More than 700 PCs and terminals are available. All students may access the system. There are no time limits. The fee is $90 per semester for full-time on campus and $15 per semester for part-time and off campus.

MICHIGAN STATE UNIVERSITY
East Lansing, MI 48824-1046

(517) 355-8332
Fax: (517) 353-1647

Full-time: 13,627 men, 15,823 women	**Faculty:** 2468; I, av$
Part-time: 2226 men, 2290 women	**Ph.D.s:** 95%
Graduate: 4116 men, 4956 women	**Student/Faculty:** 12 to 1
Year: semesters, summer session	**Tuition:** $5079 ($11,820)
Application Deadline: July 25	**Room & Board:** $4298
Freshman Class: 29,998 applied, 15,675 accepted, 6427 enrolled	
SAT I Verbal/Math: 550/560	**ACT:** 24 **VERY COMPETITIVE**

Michigan State University, a pioneer land-grant institution, was founded in 1855. Its 14 colleges and more than 100 departments offer undergraduate and graduate degrees in more than 200 fields of study. The university's Honors College offers students an alternative education program. There are 11 undergraduate and 13 graduate schools. In addition to regional accreditation, MSU has baccalaureate program accreditation with AACSB, ABET, ACEJMC, ADA, ASLA, CAHEA, CSWE, FIDER, NASM, NCATE, NLN, and SAF. The 16 libraries contain 4,206,032 volumes, 5,061,423 microform items, and 34,611 audiovisual forms/CDs, and subscribe to 28,007 periodicals. Computerized library services include the card catalog, interlibrary loans, and database searching. Special learning facilities include a learning resource center, art gallery, natural history museum, planetarium, radio station, and tv station. Other facilities include the Beal Botanical Garden, a superconducting cyclotron lab, the Center for Environmental Toxicology, the Pesticide Research Center, and the Case Center for Computer-Aided Engineering and Manufacturing. The 5239-acre campus is in a suburban area 80 miles west of Detroit. Including residence halls, there are 564 buildings.

Programs of Study: MSU confers B.A., B.S., B.F.A., B.Land.Arch., B.Mus., and B.S. in Nursing degrees. Master's and doctoral degrees are also awarded. Bachelor's degrees are awarded in AGRICULTURE (agriculture, animal science, forestry and related sciences, horticulture, and soil science), BIOLOGICAL SCIENCE (biochemistry, biology/biological science, botany, entomology, microbiology, nutrition, and zoology), BUSINESS (accounting, business administration and management, marketing management, marketing/retailing/merchandising, and personnel management), COMMUNICATIONS AND THE ARTS (advertising, applied music, art history and appreciation, communications, English, French, German, journalism, Latin, linguistics, music, music theory and composition, Russian, Spanish, studio art, and telecommunications), COMPUTER AND PHYSICAL SCIENCE (astrophysics, chemistry, computer science, earth science, geology, mathematics, physical sciences, physics, science, and statistics), EDUCATION (agricultural, art, early childhood, elementary, foreign languages, home economics, music, physical, science, secondary, and special), ENGINEERING AND ENVIRONMENTAL DESIGN (chemical engineering, city/community/regional planning, civil engineering, computer engineering, construction management, electrical/electronics engineering, engineering, interior design, landscape architecture/design, materials engineering, and mechanical engineering), HEALTH PROFESSIONS (clinical science, medical laboratory technology, music therapy, nursing, predentistry, premedicine, and speech pathology/audiology), SOCIAL SCIENCE (American studies, anthropology, classical/ancient civilization, criminal justice, dietetics, economics, family/consumer resource management, food production/management/services, food science, geography, history, humanities, international relations, philosophy, political science/government, prelaw, psychology, public administration, religion, social science, social work, and sociology). Teacher education, audiology and speech sciences are the strongest academically. Psychology, general business administration, and accounting are the largest.

Special: Special academic programs include an engineering co-op program with business and industry; internships in business, education, political science, agriculture, and communication arts; study abroad in more than 51 countries; on-campus work-study programs; and a sea semester. An accelerated degree program in all majors and student-designed majors are offered at the Honors College. Nondegree study, pass/fail options in some courses, and dual majors are possible. Educationally disadvantaged students may avail themselves of the College Achievement Admissions Program (CAAP). Cross-registration with the Committee on Institutional Cooperation schools is available. There are 48 national honor societies, including Phi Beta Kappa, and a freshman honors program.

Admissions: 52% of the 1999-2000 applicants were accepted. The SAT I scores for the 1999-2000 freshman class were: Verbal--29% below 500, 42% between 500 and 599, 24% between 600 and 700, and 6% above 700; Math--26% below 500, 37% between 500 and 599, 30% between 600 and 700, and 8% above 700. The ACT scores were 20% below 21, 28% between 21 and 23, 29% between 24 and 26, 12% between 27 and 28, and 11% above 28. 46% of the current freshmen were in the top fifth of their class; 81% were in the top two fifths.

Requirements: The SAT I or ACT is required. Applicants must be graduates of an accredited secondary school and have completed 4 years of English, 3 years each of math and social studies, including history, and 2 years of science. The GED is accepted. Music majors must audition. Applications are available on diskette for DOS, Macintosh, and Windows. AP and CLEP credits are accepted. Important factors in the admissions decision are recommendations by school officials, advanced placement or honor courses, and evidence of special talent.

Procedure: Freshmen are admitted to all sessions. Entrance exams should be taken during the junior year of high school. There is a deferred admissions plan. Applications should be filed by July 25 for fall entry, December 1 for spring entry, and April 15 for summer entry, along with a $30 fee. Notification is sent on a rolling basis. A waiting list is an active part of the admissions procedure.

Financial Aid: MSU is a member of CSS. The FAFSA is required.

Computers: The mainframes are an IBM 3090, a CONVEX 220, and a 96 Node GP1000. There are more than 5000 networked PCs from various vendors located in 25 public microlabs and numerous restricted micro-facilities. Seven residence halls have public labs with computers that are on the Internet. All residence halls have modem-compatible phone lines in the living quarters. All students may access the system 16 hours per day; 7 days per week. There are no time limits and no fees.

MICHIGAN TECHNOLOGICAL UNIVERSITY
Houghton, MI 49931-1295   (906) 487-2335; Fax: (906) 487-3343

Full-time: 3803 men, 1347 women	**Faculty:** 370; I, -$
Part-time: 340 men, 171 women	**Ph.D.s:** 93%
Graduate: 450 men, 210 women	**Student/Faculty:** 14 to 1
Year: quarters, summer session	**Tuition:** $4365 ($10,578)
Application Deadline: open	**Room & Board:** $4726
Freshman Class: 2689 applied, 2541 accepted, 1172 enrolled	
SAT I Verbal/Math: 581/620	**ACT:** 25 **VERY COMPETITIVE**

Michigan Technological University, founded in 1885, is a state-supported institution offering degrees in engineering, liberal arts, sciences, forestry, business, and

344

technology. There are 5 undergraduate schools and 1 graduate school. In addition to regional accreditation, Michigan Tech has baccalaureate program accreditation with ABET and SAF. The library contains 808,018 volumes, 508,303 microform items, and 3075 audiovisual forms/CDs, and subscribes to 2146 periodicals. Computerized library services include the card catalog, interlibrary loans, and database searching. Special learning facilities include a learning resource center, radio station, and mineral museum. The 240-acre campus is in a small town 380 miles northwest of Milwaukee, Wisconsin. Including residence halls, there are 42 buildings.

Programs of Study: Michigan Tech confers B.A. and B.S. degrees. Associate, master's, and doctoral degrees are also awarded. Bachelor's degrees are awarded in AGRICULTURE (forestry and related sciences), BIOLOGICAL SCIENCE (biology/biological science and ecology), BUSINESS (business administration and management and business economics), COMMUNICATIONS AND THE ARTS (communications and technical and business writing), COMPUTER AND PHYSICAL SCIENCE (chemistry, computer science, geology, geophysics and seismology, mathematics, and physics), ENGINEERING AND ENVIRONMENTAL DESIGN (chemical engineering, civil engineering, electrical/electronics engineering, engineering, environmental engineering, geological engineering, mechanical engineering, metallurgical engineering, mining and mineral engineering, and surveying engineering), HEALTH PROFESSIONS (medical laboratory technology), SOCIAL SCIENCE (liberal arts/general studies and social science). Engineering, forestry, and physical science are the strongest academically. Mechanical, electrical, and chemical engineering are the largest.

Special: Michigan Tech offers co-op programs in almost all majors, internships in medical technology and secondary teacher education, study abroad in 64 countries, dual majors, and a B.A.-B.S. degree in scientific and technical communication. There are interinstitutional programs with Central Michigan University, Northwestern Michigan College, Gogebic Community College, Oakland Community College, and Delta College. A 3-2 engineering degree is possible in conjunction with the University of Wisconsin/Superior, the College of St. Scholastica, and Adrian, Albion, Augsburg, Northland, and Mount Senario Colleges. There are 16 national honor societies.

Admissions: 94% of the 1999-2000 applicants were accepted. The ACT scores were 11% below 21, 20% between 21 and 23, 30% between 24 and 26, 18% between 27 and 28, and 21% above 28. 54% of the current freshmen were in the top fifth of their class; 82% were in the top two fifths. There were 7 National Merit finalists. 63 freshmen graduated first in their class.

Requirements: The SAT I or ACT is recommended. Scores are used for admission and placement. Admissions requirements include graduation from an accredited secondary school, with 15 academic credits. These must include 3 credits in English, 1 credit of chemistry or physics, and 3 credits in math for engineering and science curricula; credits in social studies and foreign language are recommended. The GED is accepted. Applications are accepted on computer disk and on-line at the school's web site. AP and CLEP credits are accepted. Important factors in the admissions decision are recommendations by school officials, advanced placement or honor courses, and personality/intangible qualities.

Procedure: Freshmen are admitted to all sessions. Entrance exams should be taken in the junior year. There is a deferred admissions plan. Application deadlines are open. The application fee is $30. Notification is sent on a rolling basis.

Financial Aid: In 1999-2000, 84% of all freshmen and 60% of continuing students received some form of financial aid. 50% of freshmen and 44% of continuing students received need-based aid. The average freshman award was $6560. Of that total, scholarships or need-based grants averaged $3814 ($16,030 maximum); loans averaged $4514 ($16,480 maximum); and work contracts averaged $1350 ($1545 maximum). 25% of undergraduates work part time. Average annual earnings from campus work are $4500. The average financial indebtedness of the 1999 graduate was $10,488. Michigan Tech is a member of CSS. The FAFSA is required. The fall application deadline is March 1.

Computers: Almost every department has 1 or more student computing labs. Equipment varies but includes PCs, Macs, Sun workstations, laser printers, electrostatic plotters, and scanners. Software includes general productivity packages, such as word processing and spreadsheets, and specialized applications, such as CAD/CAM, GIS, and publishing. All students may access the system 24 hours a day. There are no time limits. The fee varies with major.

MIDDLEBURY COLLEGE
Middlebury, VT 05753 (802) 443-3000; Fax: (802) 443-0258

Full-time: 1101 men, 1124 women	**Faculty:** 186; IIB, +$
Part-time: 10 men, 30 women	**Ph.D.s:** 97%
Graduate: 5 women	**Student/Faculty:** 11 to 1
Year: 4-1-4	**Tuition:** $31,790
Application Deadline: December 15	**Room & Board:** see profile
Freshman Class: 4869 applied, 1247 accepted, 527 enrolled	
SAT I Verbal/Math: 670/650	**ACT:** 28 **MOST COMPETITIVE**

Middlebury College, founded in 1800, is a small, independent liberal arts institution offering degree programs in languages, humanities, and social and natural sciences. Some of the information in this profile is approximate. The $31,790 comprehensive fee includes room and board. There are 2 graduate schools. The 3 libraries contain 775,000 volumes, 303,000 microform items, and 26,000 audiovisual forms/CDs, and subscribe to 2400 periodicals. Computerized library services include the card catalog, interlibrary loans, and database searching. Special learning facilities include a learning resource center, art gallery, and radio station. The 350-acre campus is in a small town 35 miles south of Burlington. Including residence halls, there are 61 buildings.

Programs of Study: Midd confers the A.B. degree. Master's and doctoral degrees are also awarded. Bachelor's degrees are awarded in BIOLOGICAL SCIENCE (biochemistry, biology/biological science, and molecular biology), BUSINESS (international economics), COMMUNICATIONS AND THE ARTS (American literature, art, Chinese, classics, dance, dramatic arts, English, film arts, French, German, Italian, Japanese, literature, music, Russian, Spanish, and studio art), COMPUTER AND PHYSICAL SCIENCE (chemistry, computer science, geology, mathematics, and physics), ENGINEERING AND ENVIRONMENTAL DESIGN (environmental science), SOCIAL SCIENCE (American studies, anthropology, classical/ancient civilization, East Asian studies, economics, geography, history, international relations, international studies, philosophy, political science/government, psychology, religion, Russian and Slavic studies, sociology, and women's studies). Foreign languages, international studies, and science are the strongest academically. English, political science, and history are the largest.

Special: Off-campus opportunities include an international major program at one of the Middlebury College schools abroad; exchange programs with Berea, St. Mary's, and Swarthmore; a junior year abroad; study through the American Collegiate Consortium for East-West Cultural and Academic Exchange; a 1-year program at Lincoln and Worcester Colleges, Oxford; a Washington, D.C., semester; and a maritime studies program with Williams College at Mystic Seaport. Middlebury also offers an independent scholar program, joint and double majors, various professional programs, dual degrees in business management, forestry/environmental studies, engineering, and nursing, and an early assurance premed program with Dartmouth, Rochester, Tufts, and the Medical College of Pennsylvania, which assures medical school acceptance by the end of the sophomore year. There is a chapter of Phi Beta Kappa, and 10 departmental honors programs.

Admissions: 26% of the 1999-2000 applicants were accepted. The ACT scores for the 1999-2000 freshman class were: 11% between 21 and 25, 56% between 26 and 30, and 33% above 31. 73% of the current freshmen were in the top tenth of their class; 92% were in the top quarter.

Requirements: The SAT I or ACT is required. Students should submit test scores as follows: the ACT or 3 SAT II: Subject tests, AP tests, or any combination thereof, including 1 English and 1 quantitative test. Secondary school preparation should include 4 years each of English, math and/or computer science, and 1 foreign language, 3 or more years of lab science and history and social science, and some study of music, art, and/or drama. Middlebury accepts applications on-line via ExPAN. AP credits are accepted. Important factors in the admissions decision are advanced placement or honor courses, recommendations by school officials, and evidence of special talent.

Procedure: Freshmen are admitted fall and spring. Entrance exams should be taken by December of the senior year. There are early decision and deferred admissions plans. Applications should be filed by December 15 for fall entry, along with a $55 fee. Notification of early decision is sent December 15; regular decision, by April 5.

Financial Aid: In 1999-2000, 42% of all freshmen and 36% of continuing students received some form of financial aid. 40% of freshmen and 34% of continuing students received need-based aid. The average freshman award was $23,354. The average financial indebtedness of the 1999 graduate was $18,731. The CSS/Profile, the college's own financial statement, and the federal tax form are required. The fall application deadline is January 15.

Computers: The mainframes are an IBM Model F70 AS/400 and 5 IBM RS/6000s. Individual student rooms are wired to the mainframe. More than half of the students have their own personal computers, and there are more than 150 public PCs easily available in 7 buildings on campus. There are connections to the Internet and to BITNET, and a variety of software is available. All students may access the system 24 hours a day. There are no time limits and no fees.

MILLIGAN COLLEGE
Milligan College, TN 37682

(423) 461-8730
(800) 262-8337; Fax: (423) 461-8982

Full-time: 316 men, 460 women	**Faculty:** 62; IIB, --$
Part-time: 9 men, 11 women	**Ph.D.s:** 64%
Graduate: 30 men, 88 women	**Student/Faculty:** 13 to 1
Year: semesters, summer session	**Tuition:** $11,480
Application Deadline: August 15	**Room & Board:** $4000
Freshman Class: 761 applied, 527 accepted, 213 enrolled	
SAT I Verbal/Math: 550/540	**ACT:** 24 **VERY COMPETITIVE**

Milligan College, founded in 1866, is a private institution affiliated with the Christian Churches and Churches of Christ. Its undergraduate and graduate programs stress the liberal arts and biblical studies. There are 2 graduate schools. In addition to regional accreditation, Milligan has baccalaureate program accreditation with NCATE. The library contains 153,571 volumes, 436,905 microform items, and 2782 audiovisual forms/CDs, and subscribes to 547 periodicals. Computerized library services include the card catalog, interlibrary loans, and database searching. Special learning facilities include a learning resource center, art gallery, radio station, radio and tv studios, editing rooms, and darkroom. The 145-acre campus is in a suburban area 4 miles south of Johnson City. Including residence halls, there are 23 buildings.

Programs of Study: Milligan confers B.A., B.S., and B.S.N. degrees. Master's degrees are also awarded. Bachelor's degrees are awarded in BIOLOGICAL SCIENCE (biology/biological science), BUSINESS (accounting and business administration and management), COMMUNICATIONS AND THE ARTS (communications, English, fine arts, and music), COMPUTER AND PHYSICAL SCIENCE (chemistry, computer science, and mathematics), EDUCATION (early childhood, elementary, and music), HEALTH PROFESSIONS (health care administration, nursing, and premedicine), SOCIAL SCIENCE (biblical studies, history, humanities, missions, paralegal studies, psychology, and sociology). Education, business, and communications are the largest.

Special: Milligan offers a Washington semester, study abroad in England, co-op programs and internships in several majors, dual degrees, cross-registration with East Tennessee State University, a 3-2 engineering degree with Tennessee Tech, work-study, nondegree study, and credit for life, military, or work experience. 6 credits are offered for students participating in the annual summer tour of Europe. There are 2 national honor societies.

Admissions: 69% of the 1999-2000 applicants were accepted. The SAT I scores for the 1999-2000 freshman class were: Verbal--25% below 500, 47% between 500 and 599, 26% between 600 and 700, and 2% above 700; Math--27% below 500, 44% between 500 and 599, 26% between 600 and 700, and 3% above 700. The ACT scores were 25% below 21, 22% between 21 and 23, 30% between 24 and 26, 13% between 27 and 28, and 10% above 28. 69% of the current freshmen were in the top fifth of their class; 98% were in the top two fifths.

Requirements: The SAT I or ACT is required. Milligan requires applicants to be in the upper 50% of their class. A GPA of 2.5 is required. Students must be graduates of an accredited secondary school, with 18 Carnegie units and 18 academic credits, including 4 years of English, 3 of math, 2 of science, and 1 each of history and social studies. An interview is advised, and music students must audition. The GED is accepted. Other factors in the admission decision include advanced placement or honor courses, character, recommendations by school officials, ability, preparation, and Christian commitment. AP and CLEP credits are accepted.

Procedure: Freshmen are admitted to all sessions. There are early admissions and deferred admissions plans. Applications should be filed by August 15 for fall entry, along with a $30 fee. Notification is sent on a rolling basis. 5% of all applicants are on a waiting list.

Financial Aid: In 1999-2000, 64% of all freshmen and 74% of continuing students received some form of financial aid. 61% of freshmen and 67% of continuing students received need-based aid. The average freshman award was $9499. Of that total, scholarships or need-based grants averaged $2500 ($6000 maximum); loans averaged $3000 ($4625 maximum); outside and athletic awards averaged $7134; and work contracts averaged $1082 ($1442 maximum). 47% of undergraduates work part time. Average annual earnings from campus work are $1185. The average financial indebtedness of the 1999 graduate was $13,621. Milligan is a member of CSS. The FAFSA and the college's own financial statement are required. The fall application deadline is March 1.

Computers: 78 PCs are available in 5 computer labs, the library, and specific departments. All have access to the Internet and the Web. Every dormitory room has a network connection available for each resident. All students may access the system. There are no time limits. The fee is $140 per semester. It is recommended that all students have Intel-based Pentium personal computers.

MILLS COLLEGE
Oakland, CA 94613

(510) 430-2135
(800) 87-MILLS; Fax: (510) 430-3314

Full-time: 688 women	**Faculty:** 81; IIA, ++$
Part-time: 43 women	**Ph.D.s:** 95%
Graduate: 80 men, 319 women	**Student/Faculty:** 8 to 1
Year: semesters	**Tuition:** $17,250
Application Deadline: February 15	**Room & Board:** $7296
Freshman Class: 461 applied, 360 accepted, 121 enrolled	
SAT I Verbal/Math: 600/550	**ACT:** 25 **VERY COMPETITIVE**

Mills College, founded in 1852, is a private women's college offering instruction in liberal and fine arts, sciences, and teacher preparation. Graduate programs are coeducational There is 1 graduate school. The library contains 206,555 volumes, 7657 microform items, and 5017 audiovisual forms/ CDs, and subscribes to 683 periodicals. Computerized library services include the card catalog, interlibrary loans, and database searching. Special learning facilities include an art gallery and a children's school, a small book press, an electronic/computer music studio, a botanical garden, and a computer learning studio. The 135-acre campus is in an urban area 12 miles east of San Francisco. Including residence halls, there are 84 buildings.

Programs of Study: Mills confers the B.A. degree. Master's degrees are also awarded. Bachelor's degrees are awarded in BIOLOGICAL SCIENCE (biochemistry and biology/biological science), BUSINESS (business economics), COMMUNICATIONS AND THE ARTS (art history and appreciation, communications, comparative literature, creative writing, dance, dramatic arts, English, French, German, music, and studio art), COMPUTER AND PHYSICAL SCIENCE (chemistry, computer science, and mathematics), EDUCATION (early childhood), SOCIAL SCIENCE (American studies, anthropology, child psychology/development, economics, ethnic studies, Hispanic American studies, history, international relations, philosophy, political science/government, prelaw, psychology, sociology, and women's studies). Art, biology, and computer science are the strongest academically. Communications, English, and psychology are the largest.

Special: There is cross-registration with the University of California/Berkeley and California State University, among others. Mills offers co-op programs, internships, study abroad, a Washington semester, work-study programs, dual, student-designed and interdisciplinary majors, including political, legal, and economic analysis, an accelerated degree program, a general studies degree, a 3-2 engineering program, a 5-year B.A./M.A. program in interdisciplinary computer science, credit by examination, and pass/fail options. There is 1 national honor society, Phi Beta Kappa.

Admissions: 78% of the 1999-2000 applicants were accepted. The SAT I scores for the 1999-2000 freshman class were: Verbal--15% below 500, 34% between 500 and 599, 41% between 600 and 700, and 10% above 700; Math--24% below 500, 51% between 500 and 599, 21% between 600 and 700, and 3% above 700. 57% of the current freshmen were in the top fifth of their class; 94% were in the top two fifths. 2 freshmen graduated first in their class.

Requirements: The SAT I or ACT is required. Mills requires applicants to be in the upper 50% of their class. A GPA of 3.0 is required. SAT II: Subject tests are recommended. Applicants should graduate from an accredited secondary school or have a GED. An essay is required; an interview, recommended. The common application is accepted on-line. AP credits are accepted. Important factors in the admissions decision are advanced placement or honor courses, personality/intangible qualities, and recommendations by school officials.

Procedure: Freshmen are admitted fall and spring. Entrance exams should be taken no later than 1 month prior to application. There are early admissions and deferred admissions plans. Early decision applications should be filed by November 15; regular applications by February 15 for fall entry and November 1 for spring entry, along with a $40 fee. Notification of early decision is sent December 20; regular decision, March 30.

Financial Aid: In 1999-2000, 86% of all students received some form of financial aid. Mills is a member of CSS. The FAFSA and the college's own financial statement are required. The fall application deadline is February 15.

Computers: The mainframe is a Sun SPARC 10. Students can access any one of 3 central systems servers from many locations on campus. The three systems provide E-mail services, file storage and sharing, and student financial and academic records. A mix of 132 Macs and PCs in residence halls, computing labs, academic departmental labs, the library, and student lounges give students access to the Internet and Web. All students may access the system 24 hours a day, year-round. There are no time limits. The fee is $100. It is recommended that students in computer science and book arts have personal computers. A Mac is recommended.

MILLSAPS COLLEGE
Jackson, MS 39210

(601) 974-1050
(800) 352-1050; Fax: (601) 974-1059

Full-time: 516 men, 601 women	**Faculty:** 89; IIB, av$
Part-time: 22 men, 52 women	**Ph.D.s:** 94%
Graduate: 78 men, 45 women	**Student/Faculty:** 13 to 1
Year: semesters, summer session	**Tuition:** $15,029
Application Deadline: February 1	**Room & Board:** $6106
Freshman Class: 912 applied, 792 accepted, 284 enrolled	
SAT I Verbal/Math: 600/580	**ACT:** 26 **VERY COMPETITIVE+**

Millsaps College, founded in 1890, is a private liberal arts institution affiliated with the United Methodist Church. In addition to regional accreditation, Millsaps has baccalaureate program accreditation with AACSB and NCATE. The library contains 200,302 volumes, 20,966 microform items, and 7531 audiovisual forms/CDs, and subscribes to 631 periodicals. Computerized library services include the card catalog, interlibrary loans, and database searching. Special learning facilities include an art gallery and an observatory. The 100-acre campus is in an urban area in the capital city of Jackson. Including residence halls, there are 36 buildings.

Programs of Study: Millsaps confers B.A., B.S., B.B.A., and B.L.S. degrees. Master's degrees are also awarded. Bachelor's degrees are awarded in BIOLOGICAL SCIENCE (biology/biological science), BUSINESS (accounting and business administration and management), COMMUNICATIONS AND THE ARTS (art, classics, dramatic arts, English, French, German, music, and Spanish), COMPUTER AND PHYSICAL SCIENCE (chemistry, computer science, geology, mathematics, and physics), EDUCATION (elementary), SOCIAL SCIENCE (economics, European studies, history, philosophy, political science/government, psychology, religion, and sociology). Business administration, biology, and chemistry are strongest academically and have the largest enrollments.

Special: Millsaps offers many opportunities for study abroad, a Washington semester, internships, dual majors, a B.A.-B.S. degree in most majors, 3-2 degree programs in engineering with Washington, Auburn, Vanderbilt, and Columbia universities, and a 3-2 degree in business administration. There are 23 national honor societies, including Phi Beta Kappa, and 23 departmental honors programs.

Admissions: 87% of the 1999-2000 applicants were accepted. The SAT I scores for the 1999-2000 freshman class were: Verbal--10% below 500, 35% between 500 and 599, 44% between 600 and 700, and 11% above 700; Math--15% below 500, 43% between 500 and 599, 35% between 600 and 700, and 7% above 700. The ACT scores were 7% below 21, 19% between 21 and 23, 26% between 24 and 26, 19% between 27 and 28, and 29% above 28. 63% of the current freshmen were in the top fifth of their class; 85% were in the top two fifths. 13 freshmen graduated first in their class.

Requirements: The SAT I or ACT is required. Millsaps requires applicants to be in the upper 50% of their class. A GPA of 2.5 is required. In addition, applicants should be graduates of an accredited secondary school or have a GED certificate and have completed at least 14 academic units of English, math, social studies, natural sciences, or foreign languages (4 units of English should be included). An essay is required. Applications are accepted on computer disk and on-line. AP and CLEP credits are accepted. Important factors in the admissions decision are advanced placement or honor courses, extracurricular activities record, and recommendations by school officials.

Procedure: Freshmen are admitted fall and spring. Entrance exams should be taken in the spring of the junior year or fall of the senior year. There are early admissions and deferred admissions plans. Early decision applications should be filed by December 1; regular applications, by February 1 for fall entry and December 1 for spring entry, along with a $25 fee. Notification is sent January 15.

Financial Aid: In 1999-2000, 98% of all freshmen and 67% of continuing students received some form of financial aid. 63% of freshmen and 58% of continuing students received need-based aid. The average freshman award was $13,561. Of that total, scholarships or need-based grants averaged $11,352 ($19,000 maximum); loans averaged $1433 ($6000 maximum); and work contracts averaged $484 ($2500 maximum). 90% of undergraduates work part time. Average annual earnings from campus work are $900. The average financial indebtedness of the 1999 graduate was $18,743. Millsaps is a member of CSS. The FAFSA and the college's own financial statement are required. The fall application deadline is March 1.

Computers: The mainframes are a VMS 2 VAX 4000-50 and 2 VAX 4000-500A, an ALPHA 4100 (Unix), an ALPHA 1000 (NT), plus additional area servers. There are also 55 PCs in 2 academic labs and 50 terminals in 6 student labs. All students may access the system at any time. There are no time limits and no fees. It is strongly recommended that students have personal computers. The Gateway or Pentium is recommended.

MILWAUKEE INSTITUTE OF ART AND DESIGN
Milwaukee, WI 53202-6003

(414) 291-8070
(888) 749-MIAD; Fax: (414) 291-8077

Full-time: 303 men, 246 women	**Faculty:** 26; III, av$
Part-time: 37 men, 39 women	**Ph.D.s:** 85%
Graduate: none	**Student/Faculty:** 21 to 1
Year: semesters, summer session	**Tuition:** $15,040
Application Deadline: April 1	**Room & Board:** $6458
Freshman Class: 290 applied, 244 accepted, 139 enrolled	
ACT: recommended	**SPECIAL**

Milwaukee Institute of Art and Design, founded in 1974, is a private, 4-year professional college of art and design. In addition to regional accreditation, MIAD has baccalaureate program accreditation with NASAD. The library contains 12, 831 volumes and 48,350 audiovisual forms/CDs, and subscribes to 361 periodicals. Computerized library services include the card catalog, interlibrary loans, and database searching. Special learning facilities include a learning resource center, art gallery, and museum. The campus is in an urban area in downtown Milwaukee. Including residence halls, there are 3 buildings.

Programs of Study: MIAD confers the B.F.A. degree. Bachelor's degrees are awarded in COMMUNICATIONS AND THE ARTS (drawing, fine arts, graphic design, illustration, industrial design, painting, photography, printmaking, and sculpture), ENGINEERING AND ENVIRONMENTAL DESIGN (interior design). Graphic design, illustration, and industrial design are the largest.

Special: Students may cross-register with Marquette University and 29 other nationally accredited art colleges. Study abroad in Japan, Germany, Poland, and France, a semester at New York Artists Studio, and internships in all design fields and photography are available. Nondegree study and credit for life, military, and work experience are possible.

Admissions: 84% of the 1999-2000 applicants were accepted.

Requirements: The ACT is recommended. A GPA of 2.0 is required. Applicants must be graduates of an accredited secondary school. 4 years of art are recommended. A portfolio review and an interview are required. AP and CLEP credits are accepted. Important factors in the admissions decision are evidence of special talent, advanced placement or honor courses, and personality/intangible qualities.

Procedure: Freshmen are admitted fall and spring. There is a deferred admissions plan. Early decision applications should be filed by December; regular applications, by April 1 for fall entry, along with a $25 fee. Notification is sent on a rolling basis beginning May 1.

Financial Aid: In 1999-2000, 74% of all freshmen and 87% of continuing students received some form of financial aid. 74% of freshmen and 93% of continuing students received need-based aid. The average freshman award was $13,425. Of that total, scholarships or need-based grants averaged $7161; and loans averaged $5200. The average financial indebtedness of the 1999 graduate was $21, 053. MIAD is a member of CSS. The FAFSA is required. The fall application deadline is March 1.

Computers: The main system is a Mac Power PC. There are 43 stations in the computer lab. All students may access the system more than 80 hours a week, for a suggested 1 hour at a time. There are no fees.

MILWAUKEE SCHOOL OF ENGINEERING

Milwaukee, WI 53202-3109
(414) 277-7481
(800) 332-6763; Fax: (414) 277-7475

Full-time: 1389 men, 305 women	**Faculty:** 110; IIB, +$
Part-time: 548 men, 101 women	**Ph.D.s:** 40%
Graduate: 296 men, 72 women	**Student/Faculty:** 15 to 1
Year: quarters, summer session	**Tuition:** $18,990
Application Deadline: open	**Room & Board:** $4440
Freshman Class: 1837 applied, 1312 accepted, 666 enrolled	
SAT I Verbal/Math: 590/620	**ACT:** 25 **VERY COMPETITIVE**

Milwaukee School of Engineering, established in 1903, is a private institution with programs in engineering, engineering technology, business, communication, and nursing. Some of the information in this profile is approximate. There is 1 graduate school. In addition to regional accreditation, MSOE has baccalaureate program accreditation with ABET. The library contains 60,000 volumes, 57,000 microform items, and 530 audiovisual forms/CDs, and subscribes to 675 periodicals. Computerized library services include the card catalog, interlibrary loans, and database searching. Special learning facilities include a learning resource center and radio station. The 12-acre campus is in an urban area in Milwaukee. Including residence halls, there are 10 buildings.

Programs of Study: MSOE confers B.A. and B.S. degrees. Associate and master's degrees are also awarded. Bachelor's degrees are awarded in BUSINESS (business administration and management), COMMUNICATIONS AND THE ARTS (technical and business writing), COMPUTER AND PHYSICAL SCIENCE (computer science), ENGINEERING AND ENVIRONMENTAL DESIGN (architectural engineering, biomedical engineering, computer engineering, electrical/electronics engineering, engineering technology, industrial engineering, and mechanical engineering). Architectural and mechanical engineering are the largest.

Special: MSOE offers summer internships in the student's discipline, on-campus work-study programs, and nondegree study. A 4-year engineering degree and a dual degree in engineering and business communication along with a 5-year dual degree with a bachelor's in engineering and a master's in environmental engineering are available. There are 2 national honor societies.

Admissions: 71% of the 1999-2000 applicants were accepted. The SAT I scores for the 1999-2000 freshman class were: Verbal--20% below 500, 53% between 500 and 599, 22% between 600 and 700, and 5% above 700; Math--11% below 500, 33% between 500 and 599, 38% between 600 and 700, and 18% above 700. The ACT scores were 1% below 21, 6% between 21 and 23, 20% between 24 and 26, 60% between 27 and 28, and 13% above 28. 14% of the current freshmen were in the top fifth of their class; 85% were in the top two fifths.

Requirements: The SAT I or ACT is recommended. A GPA of 2.5 is required. In addition, applicants must be graduates of an accredited secondary school, having completed 15 academic credits, including 4 units of English, 2 units each of science and mathematics, and 1 unit each of social studies and history. More units in mathematics, science, and English are strongly advised; 1 unit in computer science is helpful. The GED is accepted. An essay is required, and an interview is recommended. MSOE accepts applications on computer disk using CollegeView and ExPAN. AP and CLEP credits are accepted. Important factors in the admissions decision are advanced placement or honor courses, leadership record, and personality/intangible qualities.

Procedure: Freshmen are admitted to all sessions. Entrance exams should be taken in fall of the senior year. Application deadlines are open. There is a $25 fee. Notification is sent on a rolling basis.

Financial Aid: In 1999-2000, 88% of all freshmen and 67% of continuing students received some form of financial aid. 29% of freshmen and 49% of continuing students received need-based aid. The average freshman award was $16,203. The average financial indebtedness of the 1999 graduate was $11,477. The FAFSA is required. Check with the school for current deadlines.

Computers: The mainframes are 2 DEC VAXs. More than 150 PCs and terminals are located throughout the library, science building, and student center for student use. Students can also dial up the main computer center over the phone lines to access computer service. All students may access the system. There are no time limits and no fees.

MINNEAPOLIS COLLEGE OF ART AND DESIGN
Minneapolis, MN 55404 (612) 874-3762
(800) 874-6223; Fax: (612) 874-3701

Full-time: 300 men, 206 women	**Faculty:** 39; IIB, -$
Part-time: 34 men, 39 women	**Ph.D.s:** 67%
Graduate: 12 men, 13 women	**Student/Faculty:** 13 to 1
Year: semesters, summer session	**Tuition:** $18,190
Application Deadline: open	**Room & Board:** $4375
Freshman Class: 478 applied, 349 accepted, 158 enrolled	
SAT I Verbal/Math: 560/510	**ACT:** 22 SPECIAL

The Minneapolis College of Art and Design, founded in 1886, is a private college of art. There is 1 graduate school. In addition to regional accreditation, MCAD has baccalaureate program accreditation with NASAD. The library contains 59, 067 volumes, 9 microform items, and 2103 audiovisual forms/CDs, and subscribes to 192 periodicals. Computerized library services include interlibrary loans and database searching. Special learning facilities include a learning resource center and art gallery. The 7-acre campus is in an urban area 1 mile south of downtown Minneapolis. Including residence halls, there are 9 buildings.

Programs of Study: MCAD confers B.F.A. and B.S. degrees. Master's degrees are also awarded. Bachelor's degrees are awarded in COMMUNICATIONS AND THE ARTS (advertising, design, drawing, film arts, fine arts, graphic design, illustration, media arts, painting, photography, printmaking, sculpture, studio art, and video), ENGINEERING AND ENVIRONMENTAL DESIGN (furniture design). Design and illustration are the largest.

Special: MCAD offers cross-registration with Macalester College, internships, study abroad in Italy, Japan, Canada, Germany, France, England, Mexico, and Denmark, and work-study programs.

Admissions: 73% of the 1999-2000 applicants were accepted. The SAT I scores for the 1999-2000 freshman class were: Verbal--23% below 500, 46% between 500 and 599, and 31% between 600 and 700; Math--41% below 500, 36% between 500 and 599, and 23% between 600 and 700. The ACT scores were 35% below 21, 27% between 21 and 23, 22% between 24 and 26, 10% between 27 and 28, and 5% above 28. 21% of the current freshmen were in the top fifth of their class; 51% were in the top two fifths. One freshman graduated first in their class.

Requirements: The SAT I or ACT is required. Applicants must submit a personal statement of interest, an essay, a letter of recommendation, transcripts, and a portfolio (B.F.A.). An interview is strongly encouraged. The GED is accepted. AP credits are accepted. Important factors in the admissions decision are evidence of special talent, personality/intangible qualities, and recommendations by school officials.

Procedure: Freshmen are admitted fall and spring. Entrance exams should be taken spring of the junior year in high school. There is a deferred admissions plan. Application deadlines are open. The application fee is $35. Notification is sent within 2 weeks.

Financial Aid: In 1999-2000, 71% of all freshmen and 94% of continuing students received some form of financial aid. 62% of freshmen and 75% of continuing students received need-based aid. The average freshman award was $10,034. Of that total, scholarships or need-based grants averaged $4997 ($6500 maximum); loans averaged $2674 ($5000 maximum); and work contracts averaged $1825. 24% of undergraduates work part time. Average annual earnings from campus work are $1825. The average financial indebtedness of the 1999 graduate was $22,240. MCAD is a member of CSS. The FAFSA and parent and student federal income tax forms are required. The fall application deadline is April 1.

Computers: The Computer Center services more than 118 workstations in 7 locations. There is software for word processing, painting, drawing, 2- and 3-dimensional design, programming, electronic imaging (digitizing), scanning, image processing, page layout prepress color separation, 2- and 3-dimensional animation, and modeling on Mac IIcx, computers, a NeXT Dimension, NeXT stations, Apollo 3 AT&T Targa-based PCs, and Amigas. All students may access the system. There are no time limits. The fee is $60.

MISSISSIPPI STATE UNIVERSITY
Mississippi State, MS 39762

(601) 325-2224
Fax: (601) 325-7360

Full-time: 6199 men, 4985 women	**Faculty:** 346; I, --$
Part-time: 946 men, 749 women	**Ph.D.s:** 80%
Graduate: 1569 men, 1628 women	**Student/Faculty:** 32 to 1
Year: semesters, summer session	**Tuition:** $3017 ($6119)
Application Deadline: August 1	**Room & Board:** $3690
Freshman Class: 6046 applied, 4232 accepted, 1986 enrolled	
ACT: 23	**VERY COMPETITIVE**

Mississippi State University, founded in 1878 as a land-grant institution, offers degree programs in the arts and sciences, agriculture, business and industry, education, engineering, forest resources, architecture, accounting, and professional training in veterinary medicine. There are 7 undergraduate schools and 1 graduate school. In addition to regional accreditation, State has baccalaureate program accreditation with AACSB, ABET, ADA, AHEA, ASLA, CSWE, NAAB, NASAD, NASM, NCATE, and SAF. The 3 libraries contain 1,422,763 volumes, 440,000 microform items, and 11,915 audiovisual forms/CDs, and subscribe to 9952 periodicals. Computerized library services include the card catalog, interlibrary loans, and database searching. Special learning facilities include a learning resource center, art gallery, natural history museum, planetarium, radio station, TV station, music museum, archeology museum, and an entomology museum. The 4200-acre campus is in a small town 125 miles northeast of Jackson. Including residence halls, there are 325 buildings.

Programs of Study: State confers B.A., B.S., B.Arch., B.B.A., B.F.A., B.Land. Arch., B.Mus.Ed., B.P.A., and B.S.W. degrees. Master's and doctoral degrees are also awarded. Bachelor's degrees are awarded in AGRICULTURE (agricultural business management, agricultural economics, agriculture, agronomy, animal science, fishing and fisheries, forestry production and processing, horticulture, plant protection (pest management), poultry science, and wildlife management), BIOLOGICAL SCIENCE (biochemistry, biology/biological science, and microbiology), BUSINESS (accounting, banking and finance, business administration and management, insurance, marketing/retailing/merchandising, real estate, and trade and industrial supervision and management), COMMUNICATIONS AND THE ARTS (art, communications, English, and languages), COMPUTER AND PHYSICAL SCIENCE (chemistry, computer science, geoscience, information sciences and systems, mathematics, physics, and science), EDUCATION (agricultural, business, education, elementary, music, physical, secondary, special, and technical), ENGINEERING AND ENVIRONMENTAL DESIGN (aerospace studies, agricultural engineering technology, architecture, bioengineering, chemical engineering, civil engineering, computer engineering, electrical/electronics engineering, industrial engineering, industrial engineering technology, landscape architecture/design, and mechanical engineering), HEALTH PROFESSIONS (medical technology), SOCIAL SCIENCE (anthropology, economics, food science, history, interdisciplinary studies, liberal arts/general studies, philosophy, political science/government, psychology, social work, and sociology). Information technology, taxation and mathematical sciences are the strongest academically. General business administration, elementary education, and biology are the largest.

Special: Cooperative education, cross-registration with the Academic Common Market, internships, and study abroad in 15 countries are offered. Work-study programs, a Washington semester, a general studies degree, 3-2 engineering degrees, nondegree study, student-designed majors, B.A.-B.S. degrees, and pass/fail options for some courses are available. There are 43 national honor societies, a freshman honors program, and 27 departmental honors programs.

Admissions: 70% of the 1999-2000 applicants were accepted. The ACT scores for the 1999-2000 freshman class were: 33% below 21, 21% between 21 and 23, 19% between 24 and 26, 11% between 27 and 28, and 16% above 28. There were 40 National Merit finalists and 49 semifinalists. 62 freshmen graduated first in their class.

Requirements: The SAT I or ACT is required. Applicants should have completed 15 1/2 high school academic credits, including 4 in English, 3 each in math, science, and social science, 2 advanced electives (foreign language, world geography, 4th year lab-based science, or 4th year math), and 1/2 credit in the computer as a prodiuctivity tool (not keyboarding) Full admission is granted with all of the above and one of the following: minimum 3.2 GPA on required high school courses; 2.5 GPA on required high school classes or class standing in top 50% with ACT score of 16 or higher/SAT combined score of 750 or higher; 2.0 GPA on required high school classes with ACT score of 18 or higher/SAT combined 840 or higher; or satisfy National Collegiate Athletic Association standards for student-athletes who are full qualifiers under Division I guidelines. Students with a GED are accepted with the required ACT/SAT score. Applications may be sumbitted on-line at the school's web site. AP and CLEP credits are accepted.

Procedure: Freshmen are admitted to all sessions. There are early admissions and deferred admissions plans. Applications should be filed by August 1 for fall entry, December 15 for spring entry, and May 15 for summer entry, along with a $25 fee for out-of-state and international students only. Notification is sent on a rolling basis.

Financial Aid: In 1999-2000, 81% of all freshmen and 67% of continuing students received some form of financial aid. 36% of freshmen and 37% of continuing students received need-based aid. The average freshman award was $5507.

Of that total, scholarships or need-based grants averaged $2352 ($7500 maximum); loans averaged $4841 ($11,079 maximum); and work contracts averaged $2788 ($3160 maximum). 62% of undergraduates work part time. Average annual earnings from campus work are $2324. The average financial indebtedness of the 1999 graduate was $17,712. State is a member of CSS. The FAFSA is required. The fall application deadline is April 1.

Computers: The mainframes are a Sun E10000, a Sun Enterprise Server 6000, and a Sun Enterprise Server 2000. Mainframes, servers, and PCs are connected to a campus ATM/Ethernet network. 2 public labs and several departmental labs provide several hundred PC's for student use. All have access to the Internet. All students may access the system 24 hours a day. There are no time limits and no fees. It is recommended that students in preveterinary medicine, architecture, and engineering have personal computers.

MONMOUTH COLLEGE
Monmouth, IL 61462

(309) 457-2131
(800) 747-2687; Fax: (309) 457-2141

Full-time: 446 men, 595 women	**Faculty:** 65; IIB, av$
Part-time: 5 men, 11 women	**Ph.D.s:** 90%
Graduate: none	**Student/Faculty:** 16 to 1
Year: semesters	**Tuition:** $15,720
Application Deadline: May 1	**Room & Board:** $4410
Freshman Class: 1376 applied, 1062 accepted, 337 enrolled	
ACT: 22	**VERY COMPETITIVE**

Monmouth College, founded in 1853, is a private liberal arts institution affiliated with the Presbyterian Church (U.S.A.). The library contains 230,000 volumes, 75,000 microform items, and 700 audiovisual forms/CDs, and subscribes to 635 periodicals. Computerized library services include the card catalog, interlibrary loans, and database searching. Special learning facilities include a learning resource center, art gallery, radio station, TV station, biology field station on the Mississippi River, and prairie plot of native flora. The 50-acre campus is in a small town 45 miles south of Rock Island and Moline. Including residence halls, there are 26 buildings.

Programs of Study: MC confers the B.A. degree. Bachelor's degrees are awarded in BIOLOGICAL SCIENCE (biology/biological science), BUSINESS (accounting, business administration and management, and business economics), COMMUNICATIONS AND THE ARTS (art, classics, communications, dramatic arts, English, French, Greek, Latin, music, and Spanish), COMPUTER AND PHYSICAL SCIENCE (chemistry, computer programming, computer science, mathematics, and physics), EDUCATION (elementary, physical, secondary, and special), ENGINEERING AND ENVIRONMENTAL DESIGN (environmental science), SOCIAL SCIENCE (anthropology, history, philosophy, political science/government, psychology, religion, and sociology). Education, sciences, and business are the strongest academically. Business and education are the largest.

Special: Monmouth offers 3-2 nursing programs with Rush and Mennonite Hospitals, and a 3-2 engineering degree with Washington University, Case Western Reserve, and the University of Southern California. Students have the opportunity to study in more than 15 countries in Europe, Asia, and Africa. Internships, a Washington semester, and dual and student-designed synoptic majors are available. There are 12 national honor societies, a freshman honors program, and 8 departmental honors programs.

Admissions: 77% of the 1999-2000 applicants were accepted. The ACT scores for the 1999-2000 freshman class were: 24% below 21, 40% between 21 and 23,

20% between 24 and 26, 10% between 27 and 28, and 6% above 28. 10 freshmen graduated first in their class.

Requirements: Either the SAT I, with a recommended minimum composite score of 900, or the ACT, with a recommended minimum composite score of 19, is required. MC requires applicants to be in the upper 50% of their class. A GPA of 2.5 is required. Applicants must be graduates of accredited high schools and have completed 4 years of English, 3 each of math and social studies, 2 each of science, including 1 of lab, and a foreign language, and 1 of history. A GED is also accepted. The general college application is accepted on-line. AP credits are accepted. Important factors in the admissions decision are advanced placement or honor courses, evidence of special talent, and recommendations by school officials.

Procedure: Freshmen are admitted to all sessions. Entrance exams should be taken by the spring of the junior year. Applications should be filed by May 1 for fall entry and November 1 for spring entry. Notification is sent on a rolling basis.

Financial Aid: In 1999-2000, 98% of all students received need-based aid. The average freshman award was $14,900. Of that total, scholarships or need-based grants averaged $11,512 ($15,720 maximum); loans averaged $2795 ($3625 maximum); and work contracts averaged $593 ($1545 maximum). 36% of undergraduates work part time. Average annual earnings from campus work are $800. MC is a member of CSS. The FAFSA is required. The fall application deadline is May 1.

Computers: The mainframe is an HP 9000. There are also more than 150 PCs available, and individual rooms are wired for use. All students may access the system 24 hours a day. There are no time limits and no fees.

MORAVIAN COLLEGE
Bethlehem, PA 18018   (610) 861-1320; Fax: (610) 861-3956

Full-time: 563 men, 685 women	**Faculty:** 105; IIB, +$
Part-time: 15 men, 14 women	**Ph.D.s:** 93%
Graduate: 67 men, 32 women	**Student/Faculty:** 12 to 1
Year: semesters, summer session	**Tuition:** $18,605
Application Deadline: March 1	**Room & Board:** $5920
Freshman Class: 1356 applied, 995 accepted, 325 enrolled	
SAT I Verbal/Math: 563/569	**ACT:** 25 **VERY COMPETITIVE**

Moravian College, established in 1742, is a private, liberal arts institution affiliated with the Moravian Church. There are 2 graduate schools. In addition to regional accreditation, Moravian has baccalaureate program accreditation with CAHEA and NASM. The library contains 245,332 volumes, 9717 microform items, and 1230 audiovisual forms/CDs, and subscribes to 1298 periodicals. Computerized library services include the card catalog, interlibrary loans, and database searching. Special learning facilities include a learning resource center, art gallery, and radio station. The 80-acre campus is in a suburban area 60 miles north of Philadelphia, and 90 miles west of New York City. Including residence halls, there are 55 buildings.

Programs of Study: Moravian confers B.A., B.S., and B.Mus. degrees. Master's degrees are also awarded. Bachelor's degrees are awarded in BIOLOGICAL SCIENCE (biology/biological science), BUSINESS (accounting, business economics, international business management, and management science), COMMUNICATIONS AND THE ARTS (art history and appreciation, dramatic arts, English, French, German, graphic design, Greek, journalism, Latin, music, Spanish, and studio art), COMPUTER AND PHYSICAL SCIENCE (chemistry, computer science, information sciences and systems, mathematics, and physics), EDUCATION (art, elementary, music, and secondary), HEALTH PROFESSIONS (nursing), SOCIAL SCIENCE (counseling/psychology, criminal justice, developmental psychology, economics, experimental psychology, history, industrial and organizational psychology, philosophy, political science/government, prelaw, psychology, religion, social science, and sociology). Education, biology, and music are the strongest academically. Business, biology, and education are the largest.

Special: The college offers 3-2 engineering degrees in conjunction with Lafayette College, the University of Pennsylvania, and Washington University, and a 4-1 engineering program with the University of Pennsylvania. Moravian also offers cooperative programs in allied health, natural resource management, and geology with Lehigh, Duke, and Thomas Jefferson Universities. Cross-registration is available with Lehigh University and Lafayette, Muhlenberg, Cedar Crest, and Allentown Colleges. Internships, study abroad in 4 countries, a Washington semester, dual majors, and student-designed majors may be pursued. Students have a pass/fail grading option. They also may enroll in a core program composed of 7 courses that offer an integrated introduction to college study. There are 15 national honor societies and 17 departmental honors programs.

Admissions: 73% of the 1999-2000 applicants were accepted. The SAT I scores for the 1999-2000 freshman class were: Verbal--19% below 500, 54% between 500 and 599, 23% between 600 and 700, and 4% above 700; Math--16% below 500, 56% between 500 and 599, 24% between 600 and 700, and 4% above 700. The ACT scores were 8% below 21, 50% between 21 and 23, 17% between 24 and 26, and 25% between 27 and 28. 46% of the current freshmen were in the top fifth of their class; 79% were in the top two fifths. 5 freshmen graduated first in their class.

Requirements: The SAT I or ACT is required. Applicants must graduate from an accredited secondary school or have a GED. Moravian requires applicants to be in the upper 60% of their class. A minimum grade average of C+ is required. Moravian requires 16 Carnegie units, based on 4 years each of English and social science, 3 to 4 of math, and 2 each of lab science, foreign language, and electives. Essays are required and interviews are recommended. For music students, auditions are required; for art students, portfolios are recommended. Applications are accepted on computer disk via Apply, CollegeLink, and Common App. AP and CLEP credits are accepted. Important factors in the admissions decision are leadership record, recommendations by school officials, and advanced placement or honor courses.

Procedure: Freshmen are admitted fall and spring. Entrance exams should be taken prior to January of the senior year. There are early decision, early admissions, and deferred admissions plans. Early decision applications should be filed by January 15; regular applications, by March 1 for fall entry and December 1 for spring entry, along with a $30 fee. Notification of early decision is sent February 1; regular decision, March 15. 62 early decision candidates were accepted for the 1999-2000 class. 15% of all applicants are on a waiting list.

Financial Aid: In 1999-2000, 94% of all freshmen and 92% of continuing students received some form of financial aid. 81% of freshmen and 77% of continuing students received need-based aid. The average freshman award was $12,396. Of that total, scholarships or need-based grants averaged $9815 ($18,245 maximum); loans averaged $3179 ($5625 maximum); and work contracts averaged $1425 ($2000 maximum). 52% of undergraduates work part time. Average annual earnings from campus work are $712. The average financial indebtedness of the 1999 graduate was $12,505. Moravian is a member of CSS. The CSS/Profile and FAFSA are required. The fall application deadline is March 15.

Computers: A high-speed campus network accessible from dormitories includes public access labs, 32 PCs, and more than 15 Macs. The network provides students with shared applications, shared printing services, E-mail, and access to the Internet and the Web. All students may access the system 24 hours per day. There are no time limits and no fees.

MOUNT HOLYOKE COLLEGE
South Hadley, MA 01075 (413) 538-2023; Fax: (413) 538-2409

Full-time: 2 men, 1898 women	**Faculty:** 192; IIB, ++$
Part-time: 4 men, 71 women	**Ph.D.s:** 87%
Graduate: 1 men, 2 women	**Student/Faculty:** 10 to 1
Year: 4-1-4	**Tuition:** $23,349
Application Deadline: January 15	**Room & Board:** $7110
Freshman Class: 2435 applied, 1458 accepted, 563 enrolled	
SAT I Verbal/Math: 630/610	**ACT:** 27 **HIGHLY COMPETITIVE**

Mount Holyoke, founded in 1837, is one of the oldest institutions of higher learning for women in the United States. An independent liberal arts college, it affords students great freedom in selecting course studies. There is 1 graduate school. The library contains 649,000 volumes, 15,120 microform items, and 4411 audiovisual forms/CDs, and subscribes to 1636 periodicals. Computerized library services include the card catalog, interlibrary loans, and database searching. Special learning facilities include a learning resource center, art gallery, radio station, observatory, child study and language centers, and arboretum. The 800-acre campus is in a small town 90 miles west of Boston. Including residence halls, there are 40 buildings.

Programs of Study: Mount Holyoke confers the A.B. degree. Master's degrees are also awarded. Bachelor's degrees are awarded in BIOLOGICAL SCIENCE (biochemistry and biology/biological science), COMMUNICATIONS AND THE ARTS (art history and appreciation, classical languages, dance, dramatic arts, English, French, German, Greek, Italian, Latin, music, romance languages and literature, Russian, Spanish, and studio art), COMPUTER AND PHYSICAL SCIENCE (astronomy, chemistry, computer science, geology, mathematics, physics, and statistics), EDUCATION (bilingual/bicultural, early childhood, elementary, mathematics, science, and social science), SOCIAL SCIENCE (African American studies, American studies, anthropology, Asian/Oriental studies, economics, European studies, geography, history, international relations, Judaic studies, Latin American studies, medieval studies, philosophy, political science/government, psychobiology, psychology, religion, sociology, and women's studies). Sciences and mathematics are the strongest academically. English, politics, and biology are the largest.

Special: Mount Holyoke offers students cross-registration through a 12- and 5-college exchange plan. Internships, including those in science and international studies, study abroad worldwide, a Washington semester, work-study, student-designed majors, dual majors, a January program, A.B.-B.S. and accelerated degrees, nondegree study, and pass/fail options also are offered. The school, in addition, emphasizes humanities and math. There is a 3-2 engineering degree available with Dartmouth College. There are 2 national honor societies, including Phi Beta Kappa, a freshman honors program, and honors programs in nearly all majors.

Admissions: 60% of the 1999-2000 applicants were accepted. The SAT I scores for the 1999-2000 freshman class were: Verbal--1% below 500, 29% between 500 and 599, 50% between 600 and 700, and 21% above 700; Math--3% below 500, 38% between 500 and 599, 46% between 600 and 700, and 13% above 700.

The ACT scores were 3% between 21 and 23, 19% between 24 and 26, 47% between 27 and 28, and 31% above 28. There were 20 National Merit finalists. 21 freshmen graduated first in their class.

Requirements: The SAT I or ACT is required. The school recommends that applicants have 4 years each of English and foreign language, 3 each of math and science, and 2 of social studies. An essay is required and an interview is strongly recommended. AP credits are accepted. Important factors in the admissions decision are recommendations by school officials, leadership record, and advanced placement or honor courses.

Procedure: Freshmen are admitted in the fall. Entrance exams should be taken before the application deadline. There are early decision, early admissions, and deferred admissions plans. Early decision applications should be filed by December 1; regular applications, by January 15 for fall entry, along with a $55 fee. Notification of early decision is sent December 31; regular decision, April 1. 161 early decision candidates were accepted for the 1999-2000 class. 8% of all applicants are on a waiting list.

Financial Aid: In 1999-2000, 66% of all freshmen and 73% of continuing students received some form of financial aid, including need-based aid. The average freshman award was $21,398. Of that total, scholarships or need-based grants averaged $17,858 ($31,479 maximum); loans averaged $2755 ($4625 maximum); and work contracts averaged $1250 ($1500 maximum). 60% of undergraduates work part time. Average annual earnings from campus work are $950. The average financial indebtedness of the 1999 graduate was $15,000. Mount Holyoke is a member of CSS. The CSS/Profile or FAFSA and parent and student tax returns are required. The fall application deadline is January 15.

Computers: The mainframes are a DEC MicroVAX and a Sun system. A computer center houses several labs containing various PCs and workstations. There are 4 other labs distributed elsewhere. Computers are also available for use at the student center. Most residence halls contain word-processing facilities with 3 to 6 computers. The mainframes may be accessed via PCs connected to Ethernet or by modem. Network connections beyond the campus are through a DECnet to neighbor schools and through Bitnet and Internet to the world. All students may access the system. There are no time limits and no fees.

MOUNT SAINT MARY'S COLLEGE
Los Angeles, CA 90049

(310) 954-4250
(800) 999-9893; Fax: (310) 954-4259

Full-time: 17 men, 873 women	**Faculty:** 91
Part-time: 34 women	**Ph.D.s:** 43%
Graduate: 84 men, 229 women	**Student/Faculty:** 10 to 1
Year: semesters	**Tuition:** $17,328
Application Deadline: March 1	**Room & Board:** $6634
Freshman Class: 621 applied, 366 accepted, 136 enrolled	
SAT I Verbal/Math: 530/510	**VERY COMPETITIVE**

Mount Saint Mary's College, founded in 1925 and affiliated with the Catholic Church, is a private, primarily women's institution that offers programs in the liberal arts and sciences. There is 1 graduate school. In addition to regional accreditation, The Mount has baccalaureate program accreditation with NASM and NLN. The library contains 132,000 volumes, 318 microform items, and 2522 audiovisual forms/CDs, and subscribes to 690 periodicals. Computerized library services include the card catalog, interlibrary loans, and database searching. Special learning facilities include a learning resource center and art gallery. The 72-

acre campus is in an urban area 10 miles west of Los Angeles. Including residence halls, there are 26 buildings.

Programs of Study: The Mount confers B.A., B.S., and B.A.M. degrees. Associate and master's degrees are also awarded. Bachelor's degrees are awarded in BIOLOGICAL SCIENCE (biochemistry and biology/biological science), BUSINESS (business administration and management), COMMUNICATIONS AND THE ARTS (English, French, music, and Spanish), COMPUTER AND PHYSICAL SCIENCE (chemistry and mathematics), EDUCATION (art, elementary, and science), HEALTH PROFESSIONS (nursing), SOCIAL SCIENCE (American studies, gerontology, history, liberal arts/general studies, philosophy, political science/government, psychology, religion, and sociology). Nursing and biological science are the largest.

Special: The Mount offers cross-registration with UCLA, internships within the Business Department, study abroad in Spain, England, and France, a Washington semester through American University, the B.A.-B.S. degree in business, dual and student-designed majors, credit for prior experiences, and pass/fail options. There are 11 national honor societies, a freshman honors program, and 9 departmental honors programs.

Admissions: 59% of the 1999-2000 applicants were accepted. The SAT I scores for the 1999-2000 freshman class were: Verbal--36% below 500, 47% between 500 and 599, 16% between 600 and 700, and 2% above 700; Math--48% below 500, 38% between 500 and 599, 14% between 600 and 700, and 1% above 700. 43% of the current freshmen were in the top fifth of their class; 73% were in the top two fifths.

Requirements: The SAT I or ACT is required. A GPA of 3.25 is required. Applicants must be graduates of an accredited secondary school or have earned the GED, with 16 academic credits and 16 Carnegie units, including 4 years of English literature and composition, 2 or 3 years each of math, science, and social studies, and 1 or 2 years of history. An essay is required, and an interview is recommended. Applications are accepted on computer disk. AP and CLEP credits are accepted. Important factors in the admissions decision are recommendations by school officials, recommendations by alumni, and advanced placement or honor courses.

Procedure: Freshmen are admitted in the fall. Entrance exams should be taken at the end of the junior year or the beginning of the senior year. Applications should be filed by March 1 for fall entry, along with a $35 fee. Notification is sent on a rolling basis.

Financial Aid: In 1999-2000, 86% of all freshmen and 82% of continuing students received some form of financial aid. 66% of freshmen and 60% of continuing students received need-based aid. The average freshman award was $13,500. Of that total, scholarships or need-based grants averaged $8375 ($14,716 maximum); loans averaged $2625 ($6625 maximum); and work contracts averaged $2500 ($3000 maximum). 45% of undergraduates work part time. Average annual earnings from campus work are $1800. The average financial indebtedness of the 1999 graduate was $15,000. The Mount is a member of CSS. The FAFSA is required. The fall application deadline is March 2.

Computers: The mainframe is a Sequent S27. There are 40 PCs available in a lab for word processing, database use, computer programming, and Internet access. All students may access the system during regular working hours, 4 nights per week, and from 3 p.m. to 11 p.m. on Sunday. There are no time limits and no fees.

MUHLENBERG COLLEGE
Allentown, PA 18104   (484) 664-3200; Fax: (484) 664-3234

Full-time: 825 men, 1149 women	**Faculty:** 134; IIB, +$
Part-time: 64 men, 82 women	**Ph.D.s:** 93%
Graduate: none	**Student/Faculty:** 15 to 1
Year: semesters, summer session	**Tuition:** $20,085
Application Deadline: February 15	**Room & Board:** $5390
Freshman Class: 3274 applied, 1808 accepted, 551 enrolled	
SAT I Verbal/Math: 595/598	**HIGHLY COMPETITIVE**

Muhlenberg College, established in 1848, is a private liberal arts institution affiliated with the Lutheran Church. The library contains 199,220 volumes, 160,000 microform items, and 4400 audiovisual forms/CDs, and subscribes to 800 periodicals. Computerized library services include the card catalog, interlibrary loans, and database searching. Special learning facilities include a learning resource center, art gallery, natural history museum, radio station, TV station, and two 40-acre environmental field stations. The 75-acre campus is in a suburban area 50 miles north of Philadelphia and 90 miles west of New York City. Including residence halls, there are 32 buildings.

Programs of Study: Muhlenberg confers B.A. and B.S. degrees. Bachelor's degrees are awarded in BIOLOGICAL SCIENCE (biochemistry and biology/biological science), BUSINESS (accounting and business administration and management), COMMUNICATIONS AND THE ARTS (art, classics, communications, dramatic arts, English, fine arts, French, German, Greek, Latin, music, and Spanish), COMPUTER AND PHYSICAL SCIENCE (chemistry, computer science, mathematics, natural sciences, physical sciences, and physics), ENGINEERING AND ENVIRONMENTAL DESIGN (environmental science), SOCIAL SCIENCE (American studies, economics, German area studies, history, international studies, philosophy, political science/government, psychology, religion, Russian and Slavic studies, social science, social work, and sociology). Biology, drama, and English are the strongest academically. Biology, business administration, and psychology are the largest.

Special: Students may cross-register with Lehigh, Lafayette, Cedar Crest, Moravian and Allentown Colleges. Internships, work-study programs, study-abroad in Asia, Latin America, Russia, and Europe, and a Washington semester are available. Dual majors and student-designed majors may be pursued. A 3-2 engineering degree is available in cooperation with Columbia and Washington Universities, a 4-4 assured admission medical program is offered with MCP/Hahnemann University, a 3-4 dental program is offered with University of Pennsylvania and a 3-2 forestry degree is offered in cooperation with Duke University. Nondegree study and a pass/fail grading option are also offered. There are 12 national honor societies, including Phi Beta Kappa, a freshman honors program, and 9 departmental honors programs.

Admissions: 55% of the 1999-2000 applicants were accepted. The SAT I scores for the 1999-2000 freshman class were: Verbal--10% below 500, 46% between 500 and 599, 37% between 600 and 700, and 7% above 700; Math--9% below 500, 44% between 500 and 599, 39% between 600 and 700, and 8% above 700. 58% of the current freshmen were in the top fifth of their class; 88% were in the top two fifths. There was 1 National Merit finalist and 6 semifinalists. 7 freshmen graduated first in their class.

Requirements: Applicants must graduate from an accredited secondary school or have a GED. 16 Carnegie units are required, and students must complete 4 courses in English, 3 in math, and 2 each in history, science, and a foreign language. All students must submit essays. Interviews are recommended and are required for those who do not submit SAT I scores. AP and CLEP credits are accepted. Important factors in the admissions decision are advanced placement or honor courses, leadership record, and evidence of special talent.

Procedure: Freshmen are admitted fall and spring. Entrance exams should be taken during the spring of the junior year or the fall of the senior year. There are early decision, early admissions, and deferred admissions plans. Early decision applications should be filed by January 15; regular applications, by February 15 for fall entry, along with a $40 fee. Notification of early decision is sent February 1; regular decision, March 15. 201 early decision candidates were accepted for the 1999-2000 class. 10% of all applicants are on a waiting list.

Financial Aid: In 1999-2000, 68% of all freshmen and 67% of continuing students received some form of financial aid. 59% of freshmen and 58% of continuing students received need-based aid. The average freshman award was $14,495. Of that total, scholarships or need-based grants averaged $9452 ($20,000 maximum); loans averaged $2400 ($3625 maximum); work contracts averaged $1250, and state or federal aid averaged $1200-8320 maximum, 47% of undergraduates work part time. Average annual earnings from campus work are $1189. The average financial indebtedness of the 1999 graduate was $12,850. Muhlenberg is a member of CSS. The CSS/Profile, FAFSA, the college's own financial statement parent and student tax returns. and W-2 forms are required. The fall application deadline is February 15.

Computers: The mainframes are an HP 3000 Series 70 and 2 HP 9000s. Students may access the campus network and Internet from the computer labs. There are more than 150 PCs available to students in labs and computer lounges throughout the campus. Residence halls are wired to provide Internet and campus network access. All students may access the system 24 hours a day. There are no time limits and no fees. It is strongly recommended that all students have personal computers.

MURRAY STATE UNIVERSITY
Murray, KY 42071

(270) 762-3741
(800) 272-4678; Fax: (270) 762-3050

Full-time: 2806 men, 3511 women	**Faculty:** 371; IIA, -$
Part-time: 368 men, 612 women	**Ph.D.s:** 90%
Graduate: 509 men, 1108 women	**Student/Faculty:** 17 to 1
Year: semesters, summer session	**Tuition:** $2400 ($6440)
Application Deadline: August 1	**Room & Board:** $3700
Freshman Class: 2728 applied, 2115 accepted, 950 enrolled	
ACT: 24	**VERY COMPETITIVE**

Murray State University, founded in 1922, is a public institution offering degree programs in business and public affairs, education, fine arts and communication, humanistic studies, industry and technology, and science. There are 6 undergraduate and 6 graduate schools. In addition to regional accreditation, MSU has baccalaureate program accreditation with AACSB, ABET, ACEJMC, ADA, ASLA, CSWE, NASAD, NASM, NCATE, and NLN. The library contains 450,000 volumes, 185,000 microform items, and 9200 audiovisual forms CDs, and subscribes to 3000 periodicals. Computerized library services include the card catalog, interlibrary loans, and database searching. Special learning facilities include a learning resource center, art gallery, natural history museum, radio station, TV station, biological station, and interactive telecommunications network. The 236-acre campus is in a small town 130 miles northwest of Nashville. Including residence halls, there are 94 buildings.

Programs of Study: MSU confers B.A., B.S., B.F.A., B.I.S., B.M., B.M.E., B. S.A., B.S.B., B.S.N., B.S.V.T.E., and B.S.W. degrees. Associate and master's degrees are also awarded. Bachelor's degrees are awarded in AGRICULTURE (agricultural mechanics, agriculture, animal science, fishing and fisheries, and horticulture), BIOLOGICAL SCIENCE (biochemistry, biology/biological science, and wildlife biology), BUSINESS (accounting, banking and finance, business administration and management, business economics, marketing/retailing/merchandising, and personnel management), COMMUNICATIONS AND THE ARTS (advertising, broadcasting, communications, dramatic arts, English, fine arts, French, German, journalism, languages, music, Spanish, speech/debate/rhetoric, and telecommunications), COMPUTER AND PHYSICAL SCIENCE (chemistry, computer programming, computer science, earth science, geology, mathematics, and physics), EDUCATION (agricultural, art, business, early childhood, elementary, foreign languages, health, home economics, industrial arts, middle school, music, and secondary), ENGINEERING AND ENVIRONMENTAL DESIGN (civil engineering technology, computer technology, construction technology, electrical/electronics engineering technology, engineering technology, and occupational safety and health), HEALTH PROFESSIONS (nursing, predentistry, premedicine, speech pathology/audiology, and veterinary science), SOCIAL SCIENCE (criminal justice, crosscultural studies, dietetics, economics, geography, history, parks and recreation management, philosophy, political science/government, prelaw, psychology, social work, and sociology). Premedicine, engineering, and physics are the strongest academically. Business, nursing, and education are the largest.

Special: MSU offers cooperative programs in all majors, cross-registration through the National Student Exchange, internships, study abroad in 14 countries, dual majors, B.A.-B.S. degrees, and a 3-2 engineering degree with the universities of Louisville and Kentucky. Credit for life experience and a degree in independent studies are also offered. Nondegree study is possible. There are 12 national honor societies, including Phi Beta Kappa, and a freshman honors program. In addition, all departments have honors programs.

Admissions: 78% of the 1999-2000 applicants were accepted. The ACT scores for the 1999-2000 freshman class were: 20% below 21, 30% between 21 and 23, 30% between 24 and 26, 12% between 27 and 28, and 8% above 28. 60% of the current freshmen were in the top fifth of their class; 88% were in the top two fifths. There were 9 National Merit finalists and 11 semifinalists. 61 freshmen graduated first in their class.

Requirements: The ACT is required, with a minimum composite score of 18 instate. MSU requires applicants to be in the upper 50% of their class. In-state residents must rank in the top half of their class; out-of-state applicants must rank in the top half of their class and have a 22 on the ACT or be in the top third and have an 18 on the ACT. Applicants should have completed 22 high school academic credits, including 4 units in English, 3 in math, 2 each in science and social studies, and 9 in electives; in addition, MSU strongly recommends a fourth year of math, 2 of foreign language, and 1 of fine arts. A portfolio or audition is required for art and music majors. An interview is recommended. Applications are available on-line at the school's web site. AP and CLEP credits are accepted. Important factors in the admissions decision are advanced placement or honor courses and leadership record.

Procedure: Freshmen are admitted to all sessions. Entrance exams should be taken before January of the enrollment year. There is an early admissions plan. Applications should be filed by August 1 for fall entry, December 1 for spring entry, and May 1 for summer entry, along with a $20 fee. Notification is sent on a rolling basis.

Financial Aid: In 1999-2000, 70% of all students received some form of financial aid. 45% of all students received need-based aid. The average freshman award was $4487. Of that total, scholarships or need-based grants averaged $2300 ($6000 maximum); loans averaged $2500 ($2625 maximum); and work contracts averaged $1450 ($2500 maximum). 30% of undergraduates work part time. Average annual earnings from campus work are $1450. The average financial indebtedness of the 1999 graduate was $6863. MSU is a member of CSS. The FAFSA is required. The fall application deadline is April 1.

Computers: The mainframe is an IBM. Students may access the mainframe through computer labs in each of 6 colleges and the student center. PCs are available at these locations and throughout the campus, including the residential colleges. All students may access the system. There are no time limits and no fees. MSU strongly recommends that students have their own personal computers.

NAZARETH COLLEGE OF ROCHESTER
Rochester, NY 14618-3790
(716) 389-2860
(800) 462-3944; Fax: (716) 389-2826

Full-time: 412 men, 1131 women	**Faculty:** 122; IIA, av$
Part-time: 32 men, 218 women	**Ph.D.s:** 96%
Graduate: 202 men, 879 women	**Student/Faculty:** 13 to 1
Year: semesters, summer session	**Tuition:** $14,046
Application Deadline: March 1	**Room & Board:** $6376
Freshman Class: 1248 applied, 1007 accepted, 334 enrolled	
SAT I Verbal/Math: 564/559	**ACT:** 25 **VERY COMPETITIVE**

Nazareth College of Rochester, founded in 1924, is an independent institution offering programs in the liberal arts and sciences and preprofessional areas. There are 4 graduate schools. In addition to regional accreditation, Nazareth has baccalaureate program accreditation with CSWE, NASM, and NLN. The library contains 273,086 volumes, 357,343 microform items, and 17,886 audiovisual forms/CDs, and subscribes to 1646 periodicals. Computerized library services include the card catalog, interlibrary loans, and database searching. Special learning facilities include a learning resource center, art gallery, and radio station. The 75-acre campus is in a suburban area 7 miles east of Rochester. Including residence halls, there are 18 buildings.

Programs of Study: Nazareth confers B.A., B.S., and B.Mus. degrees. Master's degrees are also awarded. Bachelor's degrees are awarded in BIOLOGICAL SCIENCE (biochemistry and biology/biological science), BUSINESS (accounting and business administration and management), COMMUNICATIONS AND THE ARTS (art, art history and appreciation, dramatic arts, English, fine arts, French, German, Italian, music, music history and appreciation, music performance, and Spanish), COMPUTER AND PHYSICAL SCIENCE (chemistry and mathematics), EDUCATION (art, business, elementary, English, foreign languages, mathematics, middle school, music, science, social studies, and special), ENGINEERING AND ENVIRONMENTAL DESIGN (environmental science), HEALTH PROFESSIONS (music therapy, nursing, physical therapy, and speech pathology/audiology), SOCIAL SCIENCE (American studies, anthropology, economics, history, international studies, philosophy, political science/government, psychology, religion, social science, social work, and sociology). English, biology, and physical therapy are the strongest academically. Psychology, physical therapy, and education are the largest.

Special: There is cross-registration with members of the Rochester Area Colleges Consortium. Internships are available in political science, law, business, and all other majors. A Washington semester, college-sponsored study abroad in France, Italy, and Spain, and nondegree study are also available. There are 11 national honor societies and 10 departmental honors programs.

Admissions: 81% of the 1999-2000 applicants were accepted. The SAT I scores for the 1999-2000 freshman class were: Verbal--18% below 500, 50% between 500 and 599, 27% between 600 and 700, and 5% above 700; Math--19% below 500, 53% between 500 and 599, 26% between 600 and 700, and 3% above 700. The ACT scores were 20% below 21, 33% between 21 and 23, 27% between 24 and 26, 8% between 27 and 28, and 12% above 28. 52% of the current freshmen were in the top fifth of their class; 82% were in the top two fifths. 8 freshmen graduated first in their class in a recent year.

Requirements: The SAT I or ACT is required with minimum scores of 500 verbal and 500 math on the SAT I and 21 on the ACT. Nazareth requires applicants to be in the upper 50% of their class. A GPA of 2.8 is required. Applicants should graduate from an accredited secondary school or have a GED. A minimum of 16 academic credits is required, including 4 years of English, and 3 each of social studies, foreign language, math, and science. An essay is required, as are an audition for music students and a portfolio for art students. An interview is recommended. AP and CLEP credits are accepted. Important factors in the admissions decision are geographic diversity, advanced placement or honor courses, and evidence of special talent.

Procedure: Freshmen are admitted fall and spring. Entrance exams should be taken by December of the senior year. There are early decision, early admissions, and deferred admissions plans. Early decision applications should be filed by November 15; regular applications, by March 1 for fall entry and December 15 for spring entry, along with a $40 fee. Notification of early decision is sent December 15; regular decision, February 1. 56 early decision candidates were accepted for the 1999-2000 class. A waiting list is an active part of the admissions procedure.

Financial Aid: In 1999-2000, 97% of all freshmen and 92% of continuing students received some form of financial aid. 81% of freshmen and 80% of continuing students received need-based aid. The average freshman award was $12,186. Of that total, scholarships or need-based grants averaged $8525 ($13,060 maximum); loans averaged $2899 ($4325 maximum); and work contracts averaged $950 ($1500 maximum). 66% of undergraduates work part time. Average annual earnings from campus work are $1268. The average financial indebtedness of the 1999 graduate was $18,095. Nazareth is a member of CSS. The FAFSA and the college's own financial statement are required. The CSS/Profile is required only for early decision. The fall application deadline is February 15.

Computers: The mainframe is a DEC System 5260 ULTRIX. There are 150 PCs available for academic use in 6 labs. 2 labs are open 24 hours a day. All students may access the system. There are no time limits and no fees.

NEW COLLEGE OF THE UNIVERSITY OF SOUTH FLORIDA
Sarasota, FL 34243-2197   (941) 359-4269; Fax: (941) 359-4435

Full-time: 228 men, 389 women	**Faculty:** 55
Part-time: none	**Ph.D.s:** 98%
Graduate: none	**Student/Faculty:** 11 to 1
Year: 4-1-4	**Tuition:** $2492 ($10,878)
Application Deadline: May 1	**Room & Board:** $4663
Freshman Class: 298 applied, 223 accepted, 129 enrolled	
SAT I Verbal/Math: 680/630	**ACT:** 28 **MOST COMPETITIVE**

New College of the University of South Florida, established in 1960, is the honors college of the State University System of Florida. The library contains 254,889 volumes, 482,536 microform items, and 1168 audiovisual forms/CDs, and subscribes to 1592 periodicals. Computerized library services include the card catalog, interlibrary loans, and database searching. Special learning facilities include an art gallery, radio station, and media and technology center. The 144-acre campus is in a suburban area 50 miles south of Tampa. Including residence halls, there are 46 buildings.

Programs of Study: New College confers the B.A. degree. Bachelor's degrees are awarded in BIOLOGICAL SCIENCE (biology/biological science), COMMUNICATIONS AND THE ARTS (classics, fine arts, Germanic languages and literature, languages, literature, music, and Russian languages and literature), COMPUTER AND PHYSICAL SCIENCE (chemistry, mathematics, natural sciences, and physics), ENGINEERING AND ENVIRONMENTAL DESIGN (environmental science), SOCIAL SCIENCE (anthropology, economics, French studies, history, humanities, international studies, medieval studies, philosophy, political science/government, psychology, public administration, religion, social science, sociology, Spanish studies, urban studies, and women's studies). Biology, psychology, and literature are the largest.

Special: Cross-registration, domestic and international internships, study abroad in 11 countries at 24 universities, accelerated degree programs, student-designed and interdisciplinary majors, and independent study are available.

Admissions: 75% of the 1999-2000 applicants were accepted. The SAT I scores for the 1999-2000 freshman class were: Verbal--2% below 500, 7% between 500 and 599, 50% between 600 and 700, and 41% above 700; Math--5% below 500, 25% between 500 and 599, 55% between 600 and 700, and 16% above 700. The ACT scores were 7% between 21 and 23, 30% between 24 and 26, 30% between 27 and 28, and 33% above 28. 75% of the current freshmen were in the top fifth of their class; 93% were in the top two fifths. There were 11 National Merit finalists and 2 semifinalists. 5 freshmen graduated first in their class.

Requirements: The SAT I or ACT is required. A GPA of 3.0 is required. Graduation from an accredited secondary school (preferred) or the GED is required. High school students should pursue at least 5 academic courses each year, at the most rigorous level available, with a minimum distribution of 4 years of English, 3 years each of math, sciences, and social sciences, 2 consecutive years of the same foreign language, and 4 other academic courses. A writing sample must be submitted as well as application essays. A formal interview is recommended for all applicants. Applications may be accessed from the World Wide Web but must be submitted by mail. Important factors in the admissions decision are advanced placement or honor courses, evidence of special talent, and ability to finance college education.

Procedure: Freshmen are admitted in the fall. Entrance exams should be taken in time for the scores to be reported as part of the application. There are early admissions and deferred admissions plans. Applications should be filed by May 1 for fall entry and December 1 for spring entry, along with a $20 fee. Notification is sent on a rolling basis. 8% of all applicants are on a waiting list.

Financial Aid: In 1999-2000, 88% of all freshmen and 76% of continuing students received some form of financial aid. 43% of freshmen and 36% of continuing students received need-based aid. The average freshman award was $9945. Of that total, scholarships or non-need-based grants averaged $7107 ($14,440 maximum); loans averaged $1364 ($8800 maximum); work contracts averaged $2500 ($3500 maximum); and need-based grants averaged $2740 ($5200 maximum). The average financial indebtedness of the 1999 graduate was $15,800. New College is a member of CSS. The FAFSA is required. The fall application deadline is March 1.

Computers: 4 open-use computer labs exist on campus. All PCs are 486 or better, directly connected to the Internet, minimum 16MB RAM with Windows 95, some with multimedia capabilities. Each lab has a laser printer. 2 Mac open-use facilities are operated by the student government. All students have Internet accounts. All students may access the system 8 a.m. to 11 p.m. Monday through Thursday, and 8 a.m. to 9 p.m. Friday to Sunday. There are no time limits and no fees.

NEW ENGLAND CONSERVATORY OF MUSIC
Boston, MA 02115   (617) 585-1101; Fax: (617) 585-1115

Full-time: 730 men and women	**Faculty:** 54; IIA, --$
Part-time: 33 men and women	**Ph.D.s:** 22%
Graduate: 37 men and women	**Student/Faculty:** 14 to 1
Year: semesters	**Tuition:** $18,850
Application Deadline: December 1	**Room & Board:** $8600
Freshman Class: 696 applied, 350 accepted, 101 enrolled	
SAT I Verbal/Math: 575/600	**ACT:** 27 **SPECIAL**

The New England Conservatory of Music, founded in 1867, is the oldest private school of its kind in the United States. It combines classroom study of music with an emphasis on performance for talented young musicians. There is 1 graduate school. In addition to regional accreditation, NEC has baccalaureate program accreditation with NASM. The 3 libraries contain 70,000 volumes, 500 microform items, and 20,000 audiovisual forms/CDs, and subscribe to 250 periodicals. Computerized library services include interlibrary loans. Special learning facilities include an electronic music studio. The 8-acre campus is in an urban area 2 miles south of downtown Boston. Including residence halls, there are 4 buildings.

Programs of Study: NEC confers the B.Mus. degree. Master's and doctoral degrees are also awarded. Bachelor's degrees are awarded in COMMUNICATIONS AND THE ARTS (applied music, jazz, music, music history and appreciation, music performance, music theory and composition, and visual and performing arts), EDUCATION (music).

Special: NEC offers cross-registration with Northeastern, Simmons, and Tufts universities, as well as a 5 year double major degree program with Tufts University. There is a freshman honors program, and all departments have honors programs.

Admissions: 50% of the 1999-2000 applicants were accepted.

Requirements: The SAT I or ACT is required. A GPA of 2.8 is required. In addition, the applicant must be a graduate of an accredited secondary school or have a GED. An essay is required, as is an audition after submitting the formal application. In some cases, taped auditions are accepted; these must be submitted with the admissions application. Applicants are expected to have reached an advanced level of performance accomplishment. AP and CLEP credits are accepted. Important factors in the admissions decision are evidence of special talent, recommendations by school officials, and parents or siblings attending the school.

Procedure: Freshmen are admitted in the fall. Entrance exams should be taken by March 1. There is a deferred admissions plan. Applications should be filed by December 1 for fall entry, along with a $75 fee. Notification is sent by April 1. 5% of all applicants are on a waiting list.

Financial Aid: In 1999-2000, 90% of all freshmen and 90% of continuing students received some form of financial aid. 80% of freshmen and 85% of continuing students received need-based aid. The average freshman award was $17,500. Of that total, scholarships or need-based grants averaged $8700 ($19,650 maximum); loans averaged $7500 ($7500 maximum); and work contracts averaged $1500 ($2500 maximum). 80% of undergraduates work part time. Average annual earnings from campus work are $1500. The average financial indebtedness of the 1999 graduate was $15,000. NEC is a member of CSS. The FAFSA and the college's own financial statement are required. The fall application deadline is December 1.

Computers: Macs, a library of music software, and synthesizers are available in the computer studio. All students may access the system. There are no time limits and no fees.

NEW MEXICO INSTITUTE OF MINING AND TECHNOLOGY
Socorro, NM 87801

(505) 835-5424
(800) 428-TECH; Fax: (505) 835-5989

Full-time: 676 men, 315 women	**Faculty:** 92
Part-time: 97 men, 130 women	**Ph.D.s:** 98%
Graduate: 197 men, 98 women	**Student/Faculty:** 11 to 1
Year: semesters, summer session	**Tuition:** $2328 ($7328)
Application Deadline: August 1	**Room & Board:** $3584
Freshman Class: 829 applied, 563 accepted, 284 enrolled	
ACT: 26	**VERY COMPETITIVE+**

New Mexico Institute of Mining and Technology, founded in 1889 as the New Mexico School of Mines, is a science and engineering university. It has four research associated divisions: the New Mexico Bureau of Mines and Mineral Resources, the Energetic Materials Research and Testing Center, the Petroleum Recovery Research Center, and the Langmuir Laboratory for Atmospheric Research. In addition to regional accreditation, New Mexico Tech has baccalaureate program accreditation with ABET. The library contains 242,500 volumes, 180,000 microform items, and 1400 audiovisual forms/CDs, and subscribes to 900 periodicals. Computerized library services include the card catalog, interlibrary loans, and database searching. Special learning facilities include a radio station and mineral museum and seismic research mine. The 320-acre campus is in a small town 75 miles south of Albuquerque. Including residence halls, there are 27 buildings.

Programs of Study: New Mexico Tech confers B.S. and B.G.S. degrees. Associate, master's, and doctoral degrees are also awarded. Bachelor's degrees are awarded in BIOLOGICAL SCIENCE (biology/biological science), BUSINESS (business administration and management), COMMUNICATIONS AND THE

ARTS (technical and business writing), COMPUTER AND PHYSICAL SCIENCE (chemistry, computer science, geology, geophysics and seismology, mathematics, and physics), ENGINEERING AND ENVIRONMENTAL DESIGN (chemical engineering, electrical/electronics engineering, engineering, engineering mechanics, environmental engineering, environmental science, materials engineering, metallurgical engineering, mining and mineral engineering, and petroleum/natural gas engineering), SOCIAL SCIENCE (liberal arts/general studies and psychology). Computer science, physics, and electrical engineering are the strongest academically and have the largest enrollment.

Special: New Mexico Tech offers co-op programs in computer science and all engineering majors, internships in Technical Communications, and cross-registration with New Mexico State, University of New Mexico, and Los Alamos National Laboratories in the WERC consortium. Dual majors are offered in engineering, computer science, physics, and math, work programs, student-designed majors in environmental science, general studies, and basic science. Nondegree study and pass/fail options are also available. There are 3-2 accelerated degree programs in geology and in science or engineering and hydrology. There are 4 national honor societies, and 4 departmental honors programs.

Admissions: 68% of the 1999-2000 applicants were accepted. The ACT scores for the 1999-2000 freshman class were: 5% below 21, 25% between 21 and 23, 25% between 24 and 26, 19% between 27 and 28, and 26% above 28. 60% of the current freshmen were in the top fifth of their class; 87% were in the top two fifths.

Requirements: The ACT is required, with a minimum score of 21. A GPA of 2.0 is required. Applicants must be high school graduates or present a GED certificate. Students should have earned 15 academic credits, consisting of 4 units of English, 3 each of social science and math (2 beyond general math), and 2 of science (including 1 of lab science), and electives. On-line applications are available at http://www.nmt.edu/mainpage/uginfo/application.html, but the printout must be sent to the school. AP credits are accepted. Important factors in the admissions decision are advanced placement or honor courses, evidence of special talent, and extracurricular activities record.

Procedure: Freshmen are admitted to all sessions. Entrance exams should be taken by December of the senior year. There are early decision, early admissions, and deferred admissions plans. Applications should be filed by August 1 for fall entry and December 1 for spring entry, along with a $15 fee. Notification is sent on a rolling basis.

Financial Aid: In a recent year, 87% of all freshmen and 91% of continuing students received some form of financial aid. 40% of freshmen and 63% of continuing students received need-based aid. The average freshman award was $4337. Of that total, scholarships or need-based grants averaged $3768 ($13,225 maximum); loans averaged $1902 ($5228 maximum); and work contracts averaged $1200 ($3090 maximum). 47% of undergraduates work part time. Average annual earnings from campus work are $3500. The average financial indebtedness of the recent graduate was $14,000. New Mexico Tech is a member of CSS. The FAFSA is required. The fall application deadline is March 1.

Computers: The mainframes are a dual SPARC 20, DEC ALPHA 500 and DEC ALPHA 400. Students may access the mainframe from PCs located in the computer center and in most departments as well as from their rooms via Ethernet connection or modem. All students may access the system 16.5 hours a day on site; 24 hours a day via network. There are no time limits. The fee is $2 per semester. It is strongly recommended that all students have personal computers.

NEW YORK UNIVERSITY
New York, NY 10011   (212) 998-4500; Fax: (212) 995-4902

Full-time: 6587 men, 9396 women	**Faculty:** 1273; I, +$
Part-time: 873 men, 1348 women	**Ph.D.s:** 99%
Graduate: 8167 men, 10,761 women	**Student/Faculty:** 13 to 1
Year: semesters, summer session	**Tuition:** $23,456
Application Deadline: January 15	**Room & Board:** $8676
Freshman Class: 28,794 applied, 9140 accepted, 3492 enrolled	
SAT I Verbal/Math: 664/660 (mean)	**MOST COMPETITIVE**

New York University, founded in 1831, is a private research university offering undergraduate, graduate and professional degrees in arts and sciences, business, education, health professions, nursing, social work, and individualized study. NYU consists of 14 colleges and schools located in New York City. There are 7 undergraduate and 11 graduate schools. In addition to regional accreditation, NYU has baccalaureate program accreditation with AACSB, ACEJMC, ADA, APTA, CSWE, and NLN. The 9 libraries contain 4,282,065 volumes, 4,331,927 microform items, and 56,781 audiovisual forms/CDs, and subscribe to 31,492 periodicals. Computerized library services include the card catalog, interlibrary loans, and database searching. Special learning facilities include a learning resource center, art gallery, radio station, TV station, and a speech/language/ hearing clinic. The campus is in an urban area in New York City's Greenwich Village. Including residence halls, there are more than 150 buildings.

Programs of Study: NYU confers B.A., B.S., B.F.A., B.S./B.E., and Mus.B. degrees. Associate, master's, and doctoral degrees are also awarded. Bachelor's degrees are awarded in BIOLOGICAL SCIENCE (biochemistry, biology/biological science, neurosciences, and nutrition), BUSINESS (accounting, banking and finance, business administration and management, business economics, hotel/motel and restaurant management, international business management, marketing/ retailing/merchandising, operations research, and recreation and leisure services), COMMUNICATIONS AND THE ARTS (American literature, art history and appreciation, classics, communications, comparative literature, dance, dramatic arts, English, English literature, film arts, fine arts, French, German, Germanic languages and literature, Greek, Greek (classical), Hebrew, Italian, journalism, Latin, linguistics, music, music business management, music performance, music theory and composition, photography, Portuguese, radio/television technology, romance languages and literature, Russian, Spanish, speech/debate/rhetoric, studio art, theater design, and voice), COMPUTER AND PHYSICAL SCIENCE (actuarial science, chemistry, computer science, information sciences and systems, mathematics, physics, and statistics), EDUCATION (art, dance, early childhood, elementary, English, foreign languages, mathematics, music, science, secondary, social studies, and special), ENGINEERING AND ENVIRONMENTAL DESIGN (chemical engineering, civil engineering, computer engineering, electrical/electronics engineering, engineering physics, environmental engineering, environmental science, graphic arts technology, materials engineering, mechanical engineering, and urban design), HEALTH PROFESSIONS (nursing, predentistry, premedicine, preoptometry, prepodiatry, and speech pathology/audiology), SOCIAL SCIENCE (African studies, anthropology, Asian/American studies, classical/ancient civilization, East Asian studies, economics, European studies, history, Judaic studies, Latin American studies, Luso-Brazilian studies, medieval studies, Middle Eastern studies, peace studies, philosophy, political science/ government, prelaw, psychology, public administration, religion, social work, sociology, Western European studies, and women's studies). Finance, fine and performing arts, and film and television are the largest.

Special: A 3-2 engineering degree (B.S./B.E.) is available with the Stevens Institute of Technology in New Jersey. A vast array of internships is available, as well as study worldwide at 6 sites: Florence, Paris, Madrid, Prague, London and Buenos Aires. B.A.-B.S. degree options, accelerated degrees, dual and student-designed majors, credit by exam, and pass/fail options are also available. A Washington semester is available to political science majors. There are exchange programs with several historically black colleges. There is a chapter of Phi Beta Kappa and a freshman honors program.

Admissions: 32% of the 1999-2000 applicants were accepted. The SAT I scores for the 1999-2000 freshman class were: Verbal--1% below 500, 14% between 500 and 599, 53% between 600 and 700, and 33% above 700; Math--1% below 500, 16% between 500 and 599, 51% between 600 and 700, and 31% above 700. The ACT scores were 3% between 21 and 23, 7% between 24 and 26, 31% between 27 and 28, and 58% above 28. 86% of the current freshmen were in the top fifth of their class; 99% were in the top two fifths. There were 126 National Merit finalists.

Requirements: The SAT I or ACT is required. Applicants must graduate from an accredited secondary school. The GED is accepted. Students must present at least 16 Carnegie units, including 4 in English. All applicants must submit an essay and 2 letters of recommendation. Some majors require an audition or submission of a creative portfolio. Students may apply on computer disk via XAPplication or on-line at the school's web site. AP and CLEP credits are accepted. Important factors in the admissions decision are advanced placement or honor courses, leadership record, and evidence of special talent.

Procedure: Freshmen are admitted fall, spring, and summer. Entrance exams should be taken by November of the senior year. There are early decision, early admissions, and deferred admissions plans. Early decision applications should be filed by November 15; regular applications, by January 15 for fall entry, December 1 for spring entry, and May 1 for summer entry, along with a $50 fee. Notification of early decision is sent begining December 15; regular decision, April 1. 731 early decision candidates were accepted for the 1999-2000 class. A waiting list is an active part of the admissions procedure.

Financial Aid: In 1999-2000, 79% of all freshmen and 77% of continuing students received some form of financial aid. 58% of freshmen and 61% of continuing students received need-based aid. The average freshman award was $15,600. 25% of undergraduates work part time. Average annual earnings from campus work are $3000. NYU is a member of CSS. The FAFSA is required. The fall application deadline is February 15.

Computers: The mainframes are 1 Sun E 10000, 6 Sun E 3500s, 2 IBM Sp2s, an FBMES 9000 mainframe computer (9672-RB6) running both the UM/ESA and the OS/390 operating systems, an IBM RS/6000, SP2(9076-206) running the AIX operating system; and a number of Novell servers and AIX servers. Students in degree or diploma programs are eligible for an NYU Internet account. This account provides E-mail, a personal web page, software, and easy access to the World Wide Web, network news, and other Internet services. Computer facilities include Macs and PCs at Information Technology Services, 4 student computer labs, and more than 90 NYU Internet stations that allow walk-up access to E-mail and other Internet services. High-speed Ethernet connections are available from most residence halls; all residence halls support NYU-NET Dial Service to allow fast PPP phone and modem connections. All students may access the system 24 hours a day, 7 days a week in some cases. There are no time limits and no fees.

NORTH CAROLINA SCHOOL OF THE ARTS
Winston-Salem, NC 27127-2188

(336) 770-3290
Fax: (336) 770-3370

Full-time: 479 men, 317 women	**Faculty:** 24
Part-time: 20 men, 7 women	**Ph.D.s:** 16%
Graduate: 40 men, 26 women	**Student/Faculty:** 33 to 1
Year: trimesters	**Tuition:** $2427 ($11,055)
Application Deadline: March 1	**Room & Board:** $3970
Freshman Class: 998 applied, 386 accepted, 294 enrolled	
SAT I Verbal/Math: 586/551	**SPECIAL**

North Carolina School of the Arts, founded in 1963 and now part of the University of North Carolina system, is a public institution offering professional training in the performing arts. There are 5 undergraduate and 2 graduate schools. The library contains 102,000 volumes and 36,000 audiovisual forms/CDs, and subscribes to 450 periodicals. Computerized library services include the card catalog, interlibrary loans, and database searching. Special learning facilities include a learning resource center, art gallery, and numerous performance theaters, screening rooms, and CAD studios. The 45-acre campus is in an urban area 75 miles north of Charlotte. Including residence halls, there are 14 buildings.

Programs of Study: NCSA confers B.F.A. and B.M. degrees. Master's degrees are also awarded. Bachelor's degrees are awarded in COMMUNICATIONS AND THE ARTS (dance, dramatic arts, film arts, music, performing arts, and theater design).

Special: NCSA offers work-study programs, a general studies major, independent study, and design and production apprenticeships. An accelerated degree program is available to high school students in dance, drama, music, and visual arts.

Admissions: 39% of the 1999-2000 applicants were accepted.

Requirements: The SAT I or ACT is required. Applicants must be graduates of an accredited secondary school or have a GED certificate. They should have completed 4 units in English, 3 in math, 3 in science with 1 in a lab course, and 2 in social studies with 1 in U.S. history. Also recommended are 2 units in a foreign language and 1 unit each in foreign language and math in the senior year. An audition/interview demonstrating evidence of special talent is the primary admissions criterion. Applicants to the School of Design and Production must submit a portfolio. Filmmaking applicants must submit a creative writing sample. CLEP credit is accepted.

Procedure: Freshmen are admitted fall and winter. Applications should be filed by March 1 for fall entry, along with a $35 fee. Notification is sent on a rolling basis.

Financial Aid: In a recent year, 66% of all freshmen and 70% of continuing students received some form of financial aid. 51% of freshmen and 53% of continuing students received need-based aid. The average freshman award was $6893. Of that total, scholarships or need-based grants averaged $2263 ($1400 maximum); loans averaged $5139 ($1200 maximum); and work contracts averaged $447 ($984 maximum). 21% of undergraduates work part time. Average annual earnings from campus work are $412. The average financial indebtedness of the recent graduate was $15,930. NCSA is a member of CSS. The FAFSA is required. The fall application deadline is March 1.

NORTH CAROLINA STATE UNIVERSITY
Raleigh, NC 27695-7103   (919) 515-2434; Fax: (919) 515-5039

Full-time: 10,529 men, 7161 women	**Faculty:** 1489; I, av$
Part-time: 2275 men, 1719 women	**Ph.D.s:** 89%
Graduate: 3383 men, 2655 women	**Student/Faculty:** 12 to 1
Year: semesters, summer session	**Tuition:** $2414 ($11,580)
Application Deadline: February 1	**Room & Board:** $4560
Freshman Class: 12,227 applied, 7555 accepted, 3553 enrolled	
SAT I Verbal/Math: 570/600	**ACT:** 25 **HIGHLY COMPETITIVE**

North Carolina State University, founded in 1887, is a member of the University of North Carolina System. Its degree programs emphasize the arts and sciences, agriculture, business, education, engineering, and preprofessional training. There are 10 undergraduate and 10 graduate schools. In addition to regional accreditation, NC State has baccalaureate program accreditation with ABET, CSWE, NAAB, NCATE, NRPA, and SAF. The 5 libraries contain 2,820,312 volumes, 4,852,892 microform items, and 142,831 audiovisual forms/CDs, and subscribe to 22,001 periodicals. Computerized library services include the card catalog, interlibrary loans, and database searching. Special learning facilities include a learning resource center, art gallery, radio station, TV station, nuclear reactor, phytotron, electron microscope facilities, Materials Research Center, Integrated Manufacturing Systems Engineering Institute, Japan Center, and Precision Engineering Center. The 2110-acre campus is in an urban area in Raleigh. Including residence halls, there are 150 buildings.

Programs of Study: NC State confers B.A., B.S., B.Arch., B.E.D.A., B.L.A., and B.S.W. degrees. Associate, master's, and doctoral degrees are also awarded. Bachelor's degrees are awarded in AGRICULTURE (agricultural business management, agricultural economics, agriculture, agronomy, animal science, conservation and regulation, fishing and fisheries, forestry and related sciences, horticulture, natural resource management, poultry science, soil science, and wood science), BIOLOGICAL SCIENCE (biochemistry, biology/biological science, botany, microbiology, and zoology), BUSINESS (accounting, business administration and management, business economics, and recreation and leisure services), COMMUNICATIONS AND THE ARTS (communications, design, English, French, graphic design, industrial design, and Spanish), COMPUTER AND PHYSICAL SCIENCE (atmospheric sciences and meteorology, chemistry, computer science, earth science, geology, mathematics, physics, and statistics), EDUCATION (agricultural, education, foreign languages, industrial arts, marketing and distribution, mathematics, middle school, science, secondary, social studies, technical, and vocational), ENGINEERING AND ENVIRONMENTAL DESIGN (aeronautical engineering, agricultural engineering, architecture, chemical engineering, civil engineering, computer engineering, construction management, electrical/electronics engineering, engineering, environmental design, environmental engineering, environmental science, furniture design, industrial engineering, landscape architecture/design, materials science, mechanical engineering, nuclear engineering, paper and pulp science, and textile engineering), HEALTH PROFESSIONS (medical laboratory technology, predentistry, premedicine, preveterinary science, and speech pathology/audiology), SOCIAL SCIENCE (clothing and textiles management/production/services, criminal justice, economics, food science, history, interdisciplinary studies, parks and recreation management, philosophy, political science/government, prelaw, psychology, religion, social science, social work, sociology, and textiles and clothing). Electrical engineering, chemical engineering, and architecture are the strongest academically. Business management, mechanical engineering, and electrical engineering are the largest.

Special: NC State offers cross-registration within the Cooperating Raleigh Colleges network, study abroad in more than 90 countries, internships, work-study programs, an accelerated degree plan, dual majors within any program, a general studies degree in education, a 3-2 engineering degree with the University of North Carolina at Asheville, student-designed multidisciplinary studies majors, credit by examination, nondegree study, and pass/fail options. There are 15 national honor societies, including Phi Beta Kappa, a freshman honors program, and 44 departmental honors programs.

Admissions: 62% of the 1999-2000 applicants were accepted. The SAT I scores for the 1999-2000 freshman class were: Verbal--13% below 500, 50% between 500 and 599, 30% between 600 and 700, and 7% above 700; Math--8% below 500, 39% between 500 and 599, 41% between 600 and 700, and 12% above 700. The ACT scores were 13% below 21, 24% between 21 and 23, 32% between 24 and 26, 11% between 27 and 28, and 20% above 28. 67% of the current freshmen were in the top fifth of their class; 94% were in the top two fifths. There were 41 National Merit finalists.

Requirements: The SAT I or ACT is required. The SAT II: Math test is recommended. Applicants must be graduates of an accredited secondary school or have a GED certificate. They must have completed 20 academic credits, including 4 units of English, 3 each of science and math (4 of math is advised), 2 each of social studies and foreign language, and 1 of history. An essay is recommended for all applicants. A portfolio and interview are required for the School of Design. AP and CLEP credits are accepted. Important factors in the admissions decision are advanced placement or honor courses, leadership record, and evidence of special talent.

Procedure: Freshmen are admitted to all sessions. Entrance exams should be taken in the spring of the junior year and the fall of the senior year. There are early action and deferred admissions plans. Early action applications should be filed by November 15; regular applications, by February 1 for fall entry, November 1 for spring entry, and February 1 for summer entry, along with a $55 fee. Notification of early decision is sent December 15; regular decision, on a rolling basis. 3% of all applicants were on a waiting list in a recent year.

Financial Aid: NC State is a member of CSS. The FAFSA is required. The fall application deadline is March 1.

Computers: The mainframes are an IBM 3081, an IBM 4381/P12, and a DEC VAX 8700. There are also 2300 computer stations located campuswide. Several departments have additional stations available for their majors only. All students may access the system. Time limits vary by class. The fee is $100.

NORTH CENTRAL COLLEGE
Naperville, IL 60566
(630) 637-5800
(800) 411-1861; Fax: (630) 637-5121

Full-time: 736 men, 979 women	**Faculty:** 120; IIB, av$
Part-time: 182 men, 282 women	**Ph.D.s:** 86%
Graduate: 174 men, 192 women	**Student/Faculty:** 14 to 1
Year: trimesters, summer session	**Tuition:** $15,096
Application Deadline: open	**Room & Board:** $5400
Freshman Class: 1453 applied, 1111 accepted, 402 enrolled	
SAT I Verbal/Math: 570/565	**ACT:** 24 **VERY COMPETITIVE**

North Central College, founded in 1861, is a private liberal arts institution affiliated with the United Methodist Church. The library contains 129,336 volumes, 156,131 microform items, and 3393 audiovisual forms/CDs, and subscribes to 671 periodicals. Computerized library services include the card catalog, interlibrary loans, and database searching. Special learning facilities include a learning resource center, art gallery, radio station, advising center, foreign language lab, and writing center. The 54-acre campus is in a suburban area 30 miles west of Chicago. Including residence halls, there are 24 buildings.

Programs of Study: North Central confers B.A. and B.S. degrees. Master's degrees are also awarded. Bachelor's degrees are awarded in BIOLOGICAL SCIENCE (biochemistry, biology/biological science, and zoology), BUSINESS (accounting, banking and finance, business administration and management, international business management, and marketing/retailing/merchandising), COMMUNICATIONS AND THE ARTS (broadcasting, classics, communications, English, fine arts, French, German, Japanese, music, Spanish, and speech/debate/rhetoric), COMPUTER AND PHYSICAL SCIENCE (applied mathematics, chemistry, computer science, mathematics, and physics), EDUCATION (elementary and secondary), ENGINEERING AND ENVIRONMENTAL DESIGN (preengineering), HEALTH PROFESSIONS (nursing, predentistry, premedicine, and preveterinary science), SOCIAL SCIENCE (anthropology, economics, history, philosophy, political science/government, prelaw, psychology, religion, social science, and sociology). Business and education are the largest.

Special: North Central offers co-op programs in medical technology, nursing, and physical therapy, cross-registration with Benedictine University, Elmhurst College, and Aurora University, a Washington semester, and study abroad in more than 60 countries. Internships in all subject areas, work-study programs, a 3-2 engineering degree with Washington, Champaign-Urbana, and Marquette Universities and the Universities of Illinois and Minnesota, credit for life experience, and nondegree study are available. Students may pursue a B.A.-B.S. degree in all business areas and in psychology and physical science. Dual majors, a general studies degree, accelerated degree programs, and student-designed majors are also offered. There are 2 national honor societies, and a freshman honors program.

Admissions: 76% of the 1999-2000 applicants were accepted. The SAT I scores for the 1999-2000 freshman class were: Verbal--15% below 500, 53% between 500 and 599, 25% between 600 and 700, and 7% above 700; Math--23% below 500, 41% between 500 and 599, 30% between 600 and 700, and 5% above 700. The ACT scores were 14% below 21, 25% between 21 and 23, 34% between 24 and 26, 13% between 27 and 28, and 14% above 28. 50% of the current freshmen were in the top fifth of their class; 91% were in the top two fifths. There were 11 National Merit finalists. 10 freshmen graduated first in their class.

Requirements: The SAT I or ACT is required, a composite score of 20 on the ACT or a minimum score of 930 on the SAT I. North Central requires applicants to be in the upper 50% of their class. A GPA of 2.0 is required. Applicants must be graduates of an accredited secondary school. The GED is accepted. The recommended secondary school courses are 4 years of English, 3 each of math and science, and 2 each of a foreign language, history, and social studies. The school recommends an interview for all applicants. An essay is required. North Central accepts applications on computer disk and on-line. AP and CLEP credits are accepted. Important factors in the admissions decision are recommendations by school officials, leadership record, and evidence of special talent.

Procedure: Freshmen are admitted fall, winter, and spring. Entrance exams should be taken in the spring of the junior year or the fall of the senior year. There is a deferred admissions plan. Application deadlines are open. There is a $25 fee. Notification is sent on a rolling basis.

Financial Aid: In 1999-2000, 92% of all freshmen and 66% of continuing students received some form of financial aid. 64% of freshmen and 43% of continuing students received need-based aid. The average freshman award was $13,921. Of that total, scholarships or need-based grants averaged $10,679; loans averaged $2843; and work contracts averaged $399. 45% of undergraduates work part time. Average annual earnings from campus work are $936. The average financial indebtedness of the 1999 graduate was $14,061. North Central is a member of CSS. The FAFSA and the college's own financial statement are required. The fall application deadline is September 1.

Computers: The mainframes are a Compaq Proliant 1500 and an HP 9000 model K260. Students may use computers located in the on-campus center, computer labs, and the library. There are a total of 110 terminals and PCs available to students. All residence halls are connected to the campus network. All students may access the system 7 a.m. to midnight in the computer center or from a modem or residence hall room at any time. There are no time limits. The fee is $150 per year. It is strongly recommended that all students have personal computers.

NORTHEASTERN UNIVERSITY
Boston, MA 02115   (617) 373-2200; Fax: (617) 373-8780

Full-time: 6493 men, 6379 women	**Faculty:** 751; I, av$
Part-time: 3061 men, 3432 women	**Ph.D.s:** 80%
Graduate: 2176 men, 2152 women	**Student/Faculty:** 17 to 1
Year: quarters, summer session	**Tuition:** $18,867
Application Deadline: open	**Room & Board:** $9234
Freshman Class: 18,514 applied, 11,715 accepted, 2830 enrolled	
SAT I Verbal/Math: 560/570	**ACT:** 24 **VERY COMPETITIVE**

Northeastern University, founded in 1898, is a private, nonsectarian institution offering programs that include an experiential learning component and that integrate professional work experience with classroom study. The academic program usually requires 5 years to complete. There are 6 undergraduate and 9 graduate schools. In addition to regional accreditation, Northeastern has baccalaureate program accreditation with AACSB, ABET, ACPE, ADA, APTA, CAHEA, CSAB, and NLN. The 7 libraries contain 852,230 volumes, 2,015,238 microform items, and 18,941 audiovisual forms/CDs, and subscribe to 8285 periodicals. Computerized library services include the card catalog, interlibrary loans, and database searching. Special learning facilities include a learning resource center, art gallery, and radio station. The 60-acre campus is in an urban area in the heart of the Back Bay section of Boston. Including residence halls, there are 55 buildings.

Programs of Study: Northeastern confers B.A., B.S., and B.Ed. degrees. Associate, master's, and doctoral degrees are also awarded. Bachelor's degrees are awarded in BIOLOGICAL SCIENCE (biochemistry, biology/biological science, neurosciences, and toxicology), BUSINESS (accounting, business administration and management, human resources, insurance, international business management, management information systems, marketing/retailing/merchandising, small business management, and transportation management), COMMUNICATIONS AND THE ARTS (advertising, art, communications, dramatic arts, English, French, journalism, languages, linguistics, music, performing arts, public relations, Spanish, and speech/debate/rhetoric), COMPUTER AND PHYSICAL SCIENCE (applied physics, chemistry, computer programming, computer science, geology, information sciences and systems, mathematics, and physics), EDUCATION (athletic training, early childhood, and elementary), ENGINEERING AND ENVIRONMENTAL DESIGN (aerospace studies, chemical engineering, civil engineering, computer engineering, computer technology, electrical/electronics engineering, electrical/electronics engineering technology, engineering, engineering technology, industrial engineering, mechanical engineering, and mechanical engineering technology), HEALTH PROFESSIONS (dental hygiene, health science, medical laboratory science, nursing, pharmacy, physical therapy, rehabilitation therapy, respiratory therapy, and speech pathology/audiology), SOCIAL SCIENCE (African American studies, anthropology, criminal justice, economics, history, human services, interdisciplinary studies, international relations, interpreter for the deaf, philosophy, physical fitness/movement, political science/government, psychology, and sociology). Engineering, computer science, and business administration are the strongest academically. Arts and sciences and business administration are the largest.

Special: Northeastern offers many paid professional internships with area companies to integrate classroom instruction with professional experience. Cross-registration with the New England Conservatory of Music and Hebrew College, study abroad in numerous countries, a Washington semester, work-study through the university and public or private agencies, dual majors, and student-designed majors in arts and sciences are offered. Nondegree adult and continuing education and limited pass/fail options are possible. Also available are the School of General Studies and Ujima Scholars Program, an academic support program designed to assist minority students. The Women in Engineering Program Office maintains a database for academic support and networking. Accelerated degrees in engineering, nursing, and business are available. There are 26 national honor societies, a freshman honors program, and 10 departmental honors programs in all departments.

Admissions: 63% of the 1999-2000 applicants were accepted. The SAT I scores for the 1999-2000 freshman class were: Verbal--18% below 500, 52% between 500 and 599, 27% between 600 and 700, and 3% above 700; Math--14% below 500, 48% between 500 and 599, 32% between 600 and 700, and 6% above 700. The ACT scores were 15% below 21, 34% between 21 and 23, 29% between 24 and 26, 10% between 27 and 28, and 12% above 28. 40% of the current freshmen were in the top fifth of their class; 77% were in the top two fifths.

Requirements: The SAT I or ACT is required. Northeastern recommends that applicants have 17 academic units, including 4 in English, 3 each in math, science, and social studies, and 2 each in foreign language and history. An essay is required and an interview is recommended. Applications are accepted on-line at the school's web site. AP and CLEP credits are accepted. Important factors in the admissions decision are recommendations by school officials, advanced placement or honor courses, and leadership record.

Procedure: Freshmen are admitted fall and winter. Entrance exams should be taken sometime from October of the junior year through December of the senior year. There are early admissions and deferred admissions plans. Application deadlines are open. There is a $45 fee. Notification is sent on a rolling basis. A waiting list is an active part of the admissions procedure.

Financial Aid: In 1999-2000, 75% of all freshmen and 70% of continuing students received some form of financial aid, including need-based aid. The average freshman award was $13,024. Of that total, scholarships or need-based grants averaged $9991; loans averaged $2600; and work contracts averaged $1621. Average annual earnings from campus work are $1621. Northeastern is a member of CSS. The CSS/Profile or FAFSA ia required. Upperclassmen must submit the university's own financial statement. The fall application deadline is March 1.

Computers: The mainframe is a Super-miniVAX cluster consisting of 2 DEC VAX 6000-440 computers. Students may gain access to the mainframe systems from on-campus computer labs or off-campus dial-in modems. The computers accessed are utilized for various computer course work, E-mail, computer conferencing, and bulletin board purposes. All students may access the system 24 hours a day. There are no time limits and no fees.

NORTHWESTERN UNIVERSITY
Evanston, IL 60208
(847) 491-7271

Full-time: 3692 men, 4084 women	**Faculty:** I, ++$
Part-time: 36 men, 30 women	**Ph.D.s:** 100%
Graduate: 2560 men, 1933 women	**Student/Faculty:** n/av
Year: quarters, summer session	**Tuition:** $23,562
Application Deadline: January 1	**Room & Board:** $6847
Freshman Class: 15,460 applied, 4999 accepted, 1952 enrolled	
SAT I Verbal/Math: 680/700	**ACT:** 30 **MOST COMPETITIVE**

Northwestern University, founded in 1851, is an independent, nonprofit liberal arts institution offering undergraduate study in the arts and sciences, education and social policy, journalism, music, speech, and engineering and applied science. There are 6 undergraduate and 7 graduate schools. In addition to regional accreditation, Northwestern has baccalaureate program accreditation with AAC-SB, ABET, ACEJMC, ADA, APTA, ASLA, and NASM. The 3 libraries contain 4,800,000 volumes, 3,483,125 microform items, and 637,213 audiovisual forms/CDs, and subscribe to 40,008 periodicals. Computerized library services include the card catalog, interlibrary loans, and database searching. Special learning facilities include an art gallery, radio station, and TV station. The 231-acre campus is in a suburban area 12 miles north of Chicago on the shores of Lake Michigan. Including residence halls, there are 174 buildings.

Programs of Study: Northwestern confers B.A., B.A.M., B.M., B.M.E., B.S.E., B.S.Ed., B.S.J., and B.S.Sp. degrees. Master's and doctoral degrees are also awarded. Bachelor's degrees are awarded in BIOLOGICAL SCIENCE (biology/biological science, molecular biology, and neurosciences), COMMUNICATIONS AND THE ARTS (applied music, art, art history and appreciation, broadcasting, classics, communications, comparative literature, dance, dramatic arts, English, French, German, Italian, journalism, linguistics, music, percussion, performing arts, piano/organ, Portuguese, radio/television technology, Slavic languages, Spanish, voice, and winds), COMPUTER AND PHYSICAL SCIENCE (applied mathematics, astronomy, chemistry, computer science, geology, mathematics, physics, and statistics), EDUCATION (education, music, and secondary), ENGINEERING AND ENVIRONMENTAL DESIGN (biomedical engineering, chemical engineering, civil engineering, computer engineering, electrical/

electronics engineering, engineering, environmental engineering, industrial engineering, materials science, and mechanical engineering), HEALTH PROFESSIONS (speech pathology/audiology), SOCIAL SCIENCE (African American studies, American studies, anthropology, cognitive science, economics, Hispanic American studies, history, human development, international studies, philosophy, political science/government, psychology, religion, sociology, and urban studies). Journalism, speech, and physical and life sciences are the strongest academically. Economics, political science, and engineering are the largest.

Special: The university offers cooperative engineering programs throughout the country, internships in the arts, journalism, and teaching, study abroad at 11 universities around the world, a Washington semester, and numerous work-study programs both on and off campus. There is an accelerated degree program in medical education and B.A.-B.S. degrees in liberal arts and engineering, liberal arts and music, and music and engineering. An integrated science program, an interdisciplinary study in mathematical methods in social sciences, a variety of dual and student-designed majors, pass/fail options, and a teaching newspaper and television program are also available. There is a chapter of Phi Beta Kappa, a freshman honors program, and 28 departmental honors programs.

Admissions: 32% of the 1999-2000 applicants were accepted. The SAT I scores for the 1999-2000 freshman class were: Math--1% below 500, 8% between 500 and 599, 46% between 600 and 700, and 45% above 700. The ACT scores were 1% below 21, 3% between 21 and 23, 10% between 24 and 26, 14% between 27 and 28, and 72% above 28. 94% of the current freshmen were in the top fifth of their class; 99% were in the top two fifths.

Requirements: The SAT I or ACT is required. Applicants must be graduates of an accredited secondary school or have a GED certificate, and have completed a minimum of 16 units, including 4 units of English, 3 of math, 2 or 3 each of a foreign language and history, and 2 of laboratory sciences. SAT II: Subject tests are required for the accelerated honors program in medical education and the integrated science program. Auditions are required for applicants to the School of Music. Applications may be submitted on-line via Embark.com. AP credits are accepted. Important factors in the admissions decision are advanced placement or honor courses, recommendations by school officials, and extracurricular activities record.

Procedure: Freshmen are admitted to all sessions. Entrance exams should be taken by December of the senior year. There are early decision and deferred admissions plans. Early decision applications should be filed by November 1; regular applications, by January 1 for fall entry, November 1 for winter entry, February 1 for spring entry, and May 1 for summer entry, along with a $55 fee. Notification of early decision is sent December 15; regular decision, April 15. 388 early decision candidates were accepted for the 1999-2000 class. 2% of all applicants are on a waiting list.

Financial Aid: In 1999-2000, 57% of all freshmen and 60% of continuing students received some form of financial aid. 47% of freshmen and 54% of continuing students received need-based aid. The average freshman award was $20,000. Of that total, scholarships or need-based grants averaged $15,851 ($22,000 maximum); loans averaged $2735 ($5000 maximum); and work contracts averaged $1400 ($2200 maximum). 40% of undergraduates work part time. Average annual earnings from campus work are $1500. The average financial indebtedness of the 1999 graduate was $12,390. Northwestern is a member of CSS. The FAFSA and tax returns, under certain conditions, are required. The fall application deadline is February 15.

Computers: The mainframe is an IBM 3090/180J. All academic and administrative buildings, as well as student residences, are connected to the campus network, through which students have access to E-mail, the campus bulletin board and calendar, and the Internet, as well as the card catalog of the university library. All students may access the system 24 hours per day. There are no time limits and no fees. It is recommended that students in engineering have personal computers.

OBERLIN COLLEGE
Oberlin, OH 44074

(440) 775-8411
(800) 622-6243; Fax: (440) 775-6905

Full-time: 1187 men, 1715 women	**Faculty:** 242; IIB, ++$
Part-time: n/av	**Ph.D.s:** 94%
Graduate: 22 men and women	**Student/Faculty:** 12 to 1
Year: 4-1-4	**Tuition:** $24,264
Application Deadline: January 15	**Room & Board:** $6178
Freshman Class: 3819 applied, 2203 accepted, 634 enrolled	
SAT I Verbal/Math: 690/650	**ACT:** 29 **HIGHLY COMPETITIVE+**

Oberlin College, founded in 1833, is an independent institution offering degree programs in the liberal arts and sciences and music. There are 2 undergraduate schools. In addition to regional accreditation, Oberlin has baccalaureate program accreditation with NASAD and NASM. The 4 libraries contain 1,176,241 volumes, 364,506 microform items, and 61,303 audiovisual forms/CDs, and subscribe to 2685 periodicals. Computerized library services include the card catalog, interlibrary loans, and database searching. Special learning facilities include a learning resource center, art gallery, radio station, observatory, art museum, and art library. The 440-acre campus is in a small town 35 miles southwest of Cleveland. Including residence halls, there are 65 buildings.

Programs of Study: Oberlin confers B.A. and B.Mus. degrees. Master's degrees are also awarded. Bachelor's degrees are awarded in BIOLOGICAL SCIENCE (biochemistry, biology/biological science, and neurosciences), COMMUNICATIONS AND THE ARTS (art, classics, comparative literature, creative writing, dance, dramatic arts, English, fine arts, French, German, music, music history and appreciation, music performance, music theory and composition, romance languages and literature, Russian, and Spanish), COMPUTER AND PHYSICAL SCIENCE (astronomy, chemistry, computer science, geology, mathematics, and physics), EDUCATION (music), ENGINEERING AND ENVIRONMENTAL DESIGN (environmental science), SOCIAL SCIENCE (African American studies, anthropology, archeology, East Asian studies, economics, history, humanities, Judaic studies, Latin American studies, law, Near Eastern studies, philosophy, political science/government, psychology, religion, sociology, and women's studies). Sciences, art and humanities, and music are the strongest academically. English, government, and history are the largest.

Special: Internships are available through the Business Initiatives Program. Students may study abroad in more than 25 countries. The college offers independent and dual majors, 3-2 engineering programs with 3 other institutions, nondegree study for special and visiting students, and a 5-year B.A.-B.Mus. double degree. Pass/no credit options are available to all students. There are 4 national honor societies, including Phi Beta Kappa, and 25 departmental honors programs.

Admissions: 58% of the 1999-2000 applicants were accepted. The SAT I scores for the 1999-2000 freshman class were: Verbal--2% below 500, 10% between 500 and 599, 48% between 600 and 700, and 40% above 700; Math--2% below 500, 22% between 500 and 599, 55% between 600 and 700, and 21% above 700. The ACT scores were 2% below 21, 7% between 21 and 23, 14% between 24

and 26, 21% between 27 and 28, and 56% above 28. 81% of the current freshmen were in the top fifth of their class; 97% were in the top two fifths. There were 36 National Merit finalists. 33 freshmen graduated first in their class.

Requirements: The SAT I or ACT is required. Candidates for admission should have completed 4 years each of English and math and 3 each of science, social studies, and a foreign language. Oberlin accepts printouts from application services including Apply, CollegeLink, and Common App on disk. AP credits are accepted. Important factors in the admissions decision are advanced placement or honor courses, personality/intangible qualities, and leadership record.

Procedure: Freshmen are admitted fall and spring. Entrance exams should be taken in the junior year or early in the senior year. There are early decision, early admissions, and deferred admissions plans. Early decision applications should be filed by November 15; regular applications, by January 15 for fall entry and November 15 for spring entry, along with a $30 fee. Notification of early decision is sent December 15; regular decision, April 1. 106 early decision candidates were accepted for the 1999-2000 class. 11% of all applicants are on a waiting list.

Financial Aid: In 1999-2000, 59% of all students received some form of financial aid. 59% of freshmen and 59% of continuing students received need-based aid or some form of financial aid. The average freshman award was $20,545. Of that total, scholarships or need-based grants averaged $16,961 ($25,000 maximum); loans averaged $3766 ($4000 maximum); and work contracts averaged $1192 ($1550 maximum). 57% of undergraduates work part time. Average annual earnings from campus work are $1450. The average financial indebtedness of the 1999 graduate was $13,926. Oberlin is a member of CSS. The CSS/Profile or FAFSA and the college's own financial statement are required. The fall application deadline is February 15.

Computers: The mainframe is a DEC VAX 6410. There are 190 Mac, Zenith, and HP PCs and 47 terminals available for student use in the computing center, music conservatory, residence halls, and classrooms. All students may access the system. There are no time limits and no fees.

OCCIDENTAL COLLEGE
Los Angeles, CA 90041

(323) 259-2700
800-825-5262; Fax: (323) 259-2958

Full-time: 670 men, 875 women	**Faculty:** 138; IIB, ++$
Part-time: 16 men, 9 women	**Ph.D.s:** 93%
Graduate: 11 men, 22 women	**Student/Faculty:** 11 to 1
Year: semesters, summer session	**Tuition:** $24,030
Application Deadline: January 15	**Room & Board:** $6880
Freshman Class: 3002 applied, 1800 accepted, 422 enrolled	
SAT I Verbal/Math: 610/610	**HIGHLY COMPETITIVE**

Occidental College, founded in 1887, is a nonsectarian school of liberal arts and sciences. The library contains 500,000 volumes, 390,000 microform items, and 12,000 audiovisual forms/CDs, and subscribes to 1450 periodicals. Computerized library services include the card catalog, interlibrary loans, and database searching. Special learning facilities include a learning resource center, art gallery, radio station, ocean-going research vessel, and small nuclear reactor. The 120-acre campus is in an urban area in Los Angeles. Including residence halls, there are 44 buildings.

Programs of Study: Oxy confers the A.B. degree. Master's degrees are also awarded. Bachelor's degrees are awarded in BIOLOGICAL SCIENCE (biochemistry and biology/biological science), COMMUNICATIONS AND THE ARTS (art history and appreciation, comparative literature, dramatic arts, French, German, languages, music, and Spanish), COMPUTER AND PHYSICAL SCIENCE (chemistry, geochemistry, geology, geophysics and seismology, mathematics, and physics), ENGINEERING AND ENVIRONMENTAL DESIGN (electrical/electronics engineering, environmental science, and mechanical engineering), HEALTH PROFESSIONS (predentistry and premedicine), SOCIAL SCIENCE (American studies, anthropology, Asian/Oriental studies, cognitive science, economics, history, international relations, philosophy, physical fitness/movement, political science/government, psychobiology, psychology, public administration, religion, sociology, urban studies, and women's studies). Social sciences, biology, and chemistry are the strongest academically. Social sciences, biology, and diplomacy and world affairs are the largest.

Special: Cross-registration is permitted with the California Institute of Technology and the Art Center College of Design. Cooperative programs are available with Columbia University. Students may study abroad in 18 countries in Europe, Asia, and Latin America. Opportunities are provided for internships, a Washington semester, a U.N. semester in New York City, work-study programs, B.A.-B.S. degrees, dual and student-designed majors, a 3-2 engineering degree with the California Institute of Technology, credit by examination, nondegree study, and pass/fail options. There are 9 national honor societies, including Phi Beta Kappa.

Admissions: 60% of the 1999-2000 applicants were accepted. The SAT I scores for the 1999-2000 freshman class were: Verbal--11% below 500, 34% between 500 and 599, 44% between 600 and 700, and 13% above 700; Math--9% below 500, 36% between 500 and 599, 42% between 600 and 700, and 10% above 700. 75% of the current freshmen were in the top fifth of their class; 93% were in the top two fifths. 20 freshmen graduated first in their class.

Requirements: The SAT I or ACT is required. Applicants should be high school graduates of high academic standing with 4 years of English, 3 to 4 of math, 3 each of foreign language and social studies, and 1 each of biological and physical science. The GED is accepted. An essay is required and an interview is recommended. Applications are accepted on disk via the Common Application or online at the school's web site. AP credits are accepted. Important factors in the admissions decision are extracurricular activities record, advanced placement or honor courses, and recommendations by school officials.

Procedure: Freshmen are admitted in the fall. Entrance exams should be taken no later than January of the senior year. There are early decision and deferred admissions plans. Early decision applications should be filed by November 15; regular applications, by January 15 for fall entry, along with a $50 fee. Notification of early decision is sent December 15; regular decision, April 1. 29 early decision candidates were accepted for the 1999-2000 class. 14% of all applicants are on a waiting list.

Financial Aid: In 1999-2000, 54% of all freshmen and 60% of continuing students received some form of financial aid. 48% of freshmen and 50% of continuing students received need-based aid. The average freshman award was $23,507. Oxy is a member of CSS. The CSS/Profile or FAFSA and the SAAC for California residents are required. The fall application deadline is February 1.

Computers: The mainframe is a Sun SPARC Station 10 Model 512. Macs and PCs are available in the library's computer center. All students may access the system at any time. There are no time limits and no fees.

OHIO STATE UNIVERSITY
Columbus, OH 43210-1200   (614) 292-3980; Fax: (614) 292-4818

Full-time: 15,984 men, 14,974 women	**Faculty:** 2930; I, av$
Part-time: 2719 men, 2415 women	**Ph.D.s:** 99%
Graduate: 5701 men, 6210 women	**Student/Faculty:** 11 to 1
Year: quarters, summer session	**Tuition:** $4164 ($12,114)
Application Deadline: February 15	**Room & Board:** $5446
Freshman Class: 19,804 applied, 14,566 accepted, 6105 enrolled	
SAT I Verbal/Math: 560/580	**ACT:** 24 **VERY COMPETITIVE**

Ohio State University, founded in 1870, is a public land-grant institution offering programs in agriculture/natural resources, arts and sciences, business, education, architecture/engineering, nursing, pharmacy, social work, dental hygiene, and human ecology. There are 5 other campuses. There are 14 undergraduate schools and 1 graduate school. In addition to regional accreditation, Ohio State has baccalaureate program accreditation with AACSB, ABET, ACPE, ADA, APTA, ASLA, FIDER, NAAB, NASAD, NASM, NCATE, and NLN. The 18 libraries contain 5,178,171 volumes, 4,410,243 microform items, and 15,065 audiovisual forms/CDs, and subscribe to 36,020 periodicals. Computerized library services include the card catalog, interlibrary loans, and database searching. Special learning facilities include a learning resource center, art gallery, planetarium, radio station, TV station, Museum of Biological Diversity, The John Glenn Institute for Public Service and Public Policy, and the Cartoon Research Library. The 3390-acre campus is in an urban area 2 miles north of downtown Columbus. Including residence halls, there are 329 buildings.

Programs of Study: Ohio State confers B.A., B.S., B.F.A., B.Mus., and B.Mus. Ed. degrees. Master's and doctoral degrees are also awarded. Bachelor's degrees are awarded in AGRICULTURE (agricultural business management, agricultural economics, agricultural mechanics, agriculture, animal science, fishing and fisheries, forestry and related sciences, horticulture, natural resource management, plant protection (pest management), plant science, soil science, and wildlife management), BIOLOGICAL SCIENCE (biochemistry, biology/biological science, entomology, plant physiology, and zoology), BUSINESS (accounting, banking and finance, business economics, hospitality management services, human resources, insurance and risk management, international business management, management information systems, marketing and distribution, real estate, and transportation management), COMMUNICATIONS AND THE ARTS (Arabic, art, art history and appreciation, ceramic art and design, Chinese, classical languages, classics, communications, comparative literature, dance, dramatic arts, drawing, English, fine arts, folklore and mythology, French, German, glass, Greek (modern), Hebrew, industrial design, Italian, Japanese, jazz, journalism, linguistics, literature, music, music history and appreciation, music performance, music theory and composition, painting, photography, piano/organ, Portuguese, printmaking, Russian, sculpture, Spanish, and voice), COMPUTER AND PHYSICAL SCIENCE (actuarial science, astronomy, chemistry, computer science, geology, information sciences and systems, mathematics, optics, and physics), EDUCATION (agricultural, art, environmental, music, recreation, and technical), ENGINEERING AND ENVIRONMENTAL DESIGN (aeronautical engineering, agricultural engineering, airline piloting and navigation, architecture, ceramic engineering, chemical engineering, civil engineering, computer engineering, electrical/electronics engineering, engineering physics, environmental science, industrial engineering, landscape architecture/design, materials engineering, materials science, mechanical engineering, metallurgical engineering, systems engineering, and welding engineering), HEALTH PROFESSIONS (allied health, dental hygiene, medical records administration/services, medical technology, nursing, occupational therapy, physical therapy, radiograph medical technology, and respiratory therapy), SOCIAL SCIENCE (African American studies, anthropology, classical/ancient civilization, clothing and textiles management/production/services, criminal justice, criminology, economics, geography, history, human development, human ecology, humanities, industrial and organizational psychology, interdisciplinary studies, international studies, Islamic studies, Judaic studies, medieval studies, parks and recreation management, philosophy, political science/government, psychology, social work, sociology, theological studies, women's studies, and youth ministry). Engineering, business, and social and behavioral sciences are the largest.

Special: Students may cross-register with all central Ohio colleges. OSU offers internships, co-op programs, extensive study abroad, work-study programs, dual and student-designed majors, a general degree, a B.A.-B.S. degree, credit by examination, nondegree study, and pass/fail options. There are 22 national honor societies, including Phi Beta Kappa, a freshman honors program, and 18 colleges or schools honors programs.

Admissions: 74% of the 1999-2000 applicants were accepted. The SAT I scores for the 1999-2000 freshman class were: Verbal--22% below 500, 43% between 500 and 599, 29% between 600 and 700, and 6% above 700; Math--18% below 500, 38% between 500 and 599, 35% between 600 and 700, and 9% above 700. The ACT scores were 13% below 21, 28% between 21 and 23, 28% between 24 and 26, 14% between 27 and 28, and 17% above 28. 52% of the current freshmen were in the top fifth of their class; 83% were in the top two fifths. There were 104 National Merit finalists. 231 freshmen graduated first in their class.

Requirements: The SAT I or ACT is required. Applicants must complete high school with at least 18 academic credits, including 4 in English, 3 in math, 2 each in foreign language, science, and history/social studies, and 1 in art or music. The GED is accepted. Students may apply on-line at the school's web site. AP and CLEP credits are accepted. Important factors in the admissions decision are advanced placement or honor courses, evidence of special talent, and extracurricular activities record.

Procedure: Freshmen are admitted to all sessions. Entrance exams should be taken by October of the senior year. Applications should be filed by February 15 for fall entry, November 1 for winter entry, February 1 for spring entry, and February 15 for summer entry, along with a $30 fee. Notification is sent on a rolling basis. 3% of all applicants are on a waiting list.

Financial Aid: In 1999-2000, 91% of all freshmen and 79% of continuing students received some form of financial aid. 44% of freshmen and 47% of continuing students received need-based aid. The average freshman award was $5677. Of that total, scholarships or need-based grants averaged $3344 ($12,639 maximum); loans averaged $2113 ($5625 maximum); and work contracts averaged $220 ($2000 maximum). 40% of undergraduates work part time. Average annual earnings from campus work are $2500. The average financial indebtedness of the 1999 graduate was $5900. Ohio State is a member of CSS. The FAFSA is required. The fall application deadline is February 15.

Computers: The mainframes are an IBM 3081 and 4381, an HP 9000, HP3000, and a DEC VAX 20. More than 1000 PCs are available to students in the main computer center and in libraries, residence halls, labs, and student centers. Students may also connect through university-supplied software from their homes. All students may access the system 24 hours a day. There are no time limits. It is strongly recommended that all students have PCs.

OKLAHOMA BAPTIST UNIVERSITY

Shawnee, OK 74801

(405) 878-2030
(800) 654-3285; Fax: (405) 878-2046

Full-time: 674 men, 928 women	**Faculty:** 117; IIB, --$
Part-time: 320 men, 176 women	**Ph.D.s:** 77%
Graduate: 9 men, 16 women	**Student/Faculty:** 14 to 1
Year: 4-1-4, summer session	**Tuition:** $8946
Application Deadline: August 1	**Room & Board:** $3400
Freshman Class: 854 applied, 807 accepted, 418 enrolled	
SAT I Verbal/Math: 595/565	**ACT:** 25 **VERY COMPETITIVE**

Oklahoma Baptist University, founded in 1910, is a liberal arts institution affiliated with the Southern Baptist Convention. OBU offers degrees in Christian service, business, nursing, fine arts, telecommunications, teacher education, and the traditional liberal arts areas. There are 5 undergraduate schools and 1 graduate school. In addition to regional accreditation, OBU has baccalaureate program accreditation with ACBSP, NASM, NCATE, and NLN. The library contains 290,000 volumes, 230,000 microform items, and 1500 audiovisual forms/CDs, and subscribes to 600 periodicals. Computerized library services include the card catalog, interlibrary loans, and database searching. Special learning facilities include a learning resource center, planetarium, TV station, language lab, and Biblical research library. The 189-acre campus is in a small town 35 miles east of Oklahoma City and 90 miles southwest of Tulsa. Including residence halls, there are 25 buildings.

Programs of Study: OBU confers B.A., B.S., B.B.A., B.F.A., B.Hum., B.M., B.M.A., B.Mus.Ed., and B.S.E. degrees. Associate degrees are also awarded. Bachelor's degrees are awarded in BIOLOGICAL SCIENCE (biology/biological science), BUSINESS (accounting, banking and finance, business administration and management, and marketing/retailing/merchandising), COMMUNICATIONS AND THE ARTS (broadcasting, communications, dramatic arts, English, fine arts, French, German, journalism, music, Spanish, speech/debate/rhetoric, and telecommunications), COMPUTER AND PHYSICAL SCIENCE (chemistry, computer science, information sciences and systems, mathematics, and physics), EDUCATION (art, early childhood, elementary, foreign languages, music, physical, science, and secondary), HEALTH PROFESSIONS (nursing, physical therapy, predentistry, and premedicine), SOCIAL SCIENCE (history, political science/government, prelaw, psychology, religion, social science, social work, and sociology). Teacher education, biology, and religion are the strongest academically. Biology, elementary education, and nursing are the largest.

Special: OBU offers co-op programs in business, cross-registration with Saint Gregory's University, and a 3-2 engineering degree with Oklahoma State University. Students may study abroad in Europe, South America, Hungary, China, Japan, Spain, and Russia. Internships in several fields, student-designed majors, including an interdisciplinary program in humanities, and pass/fail options are available. There are 4 national honor societies, and a freshman honors program.

Admissions: 94% of the 1999-2000 applicants were accepted. The SAT I scores for the 1999-2000 freshman class were: Verbal--10% below 500, 46% between 500 and 599, 34% between 600 and 700, and 10% above 700; Math--20% below 500, 42% between 500 and 599, 35% between 600 and 700, and 3% above 700. The ACT scores were 11% below 21, 29% between 21 and 23, 24% between 24 and 26, 17% between 27 and 28, and 19% above 28. 60% of the current freshmen were in the top fifth of their class; 83% were in the top two fifths. There were

5 National Merit finalists and 5 semifinalists. 36 freshmen graduated first in their class.

Requirements: The SAT I or ACT is required. OBU requires applicants to be in the upper 50% of their class. A GPA of 2.5 is required. Admission is granted to students with composite scores of 950 on the SAT I or 20 on the ACT. Graduation from an accredited secondary school or satisfactory scores on the GED are required for admission. The recommended high school courses should include 4 units of English, 3 units of math, and 2 units each of social studies, lab science, and a foreign language. AP and CLEP credits are accepted. Important factors in the admissions decision are advanced placement or honor courses, recommendations by school officials, and leadership record.

Procedure: Freshmen are admitted to all sessions. Entrance exams should be taken during the spring of the junior year. There are early admissions and deferred admissions plans. Applications should be filed by August 1 for fall entry, December 15 for winter entry, January 15 for spring entry, and May 15 for summer entry, along with a $25 fee. Notification is sent on a rolling basis.

Financial Aid: In 1999-2000, 85% of all freshmen and 89% of continuing students received some form of financial aid. 69% of freshmen and 78% of continuing students received need-based aid. The average freshman award was $5750. Of that total, scholarships or need-based grants averaged $2580 ($10,000 maximum); loans averaged $2150 ($5500 maximum); and work contracts averaged $930 ($1800 maximum). 95% of undergraduates work part time. Average annual earnings from campus work are $958. The average financial indebtedness of the 1999 graduate was $13,000. The FAFSA is required. The fall application deadline is April 15.

Computers: The mainframe is an HP 3000/979. Students have access to about 175 networked Windows 95 and Mac PCs in residence halls, labs, and elsewhere on campus. All students have access to E-mail and the World Wide Web. All students may access the system 75 hours per week. There are no time limits. The fee is $20 per semester.

OKLAHOMA CITY UNIVERSITY
Oklahoma City, OK 73106-1493   (405) 521-5050
(800) 633-7242; Fax: (405) 521-5916

Full-time: 631 men, 866 women	**Faculty:** 138
Part-time: 262 men, 341 women	**Ph.D.s:** 79%
Graduate: 1235 men, 808 women	**Student/Faculty:** 11 to 1
Year: semesters, summer session	**Tuition:** $9496
Application Deadline: open	**Room & Board:** $4400
Freshman Class: 1033 applied, 639 accepted, 283 enrolled	
SAT I Verbal/Math: 540/520	**ACT:** 23 **VERY COMPETITIVE**

Oklahoma City University, founded in 1904, is a private, comprehensive university affiliated with the United Methodist Church, offering undergraduate and graduate programs in arts and sciences, business, music and performing arts, religion and church vocations, nursing, and law. There are 6 undergraduate and 5 graduate schools. In addition to regional accreditation, OCU has baccalaureate program accreditation with ACBSP, NASM, and NLN. The 2 libraries contain 269,035 volumes, 308,501 microform items, and 10,652 audiovisual forms/CDs, and subscribe to 1462 periodicals. Computerized library services include the card catalog, interlibrary loans, and database searching. Special learning facilities include a learning resource center, art gallery, and TV station. The 68-acre campus is in an urban area within Oklahoma City. Including residence halls, there are 28 buildings.

Programs of Study: OCU confers B.A., B.S., B.F.A., B.M., B.Perf.Arts, B.S.B., and B.S.N. degrees. Master's degrees are also awarded. Bachelor's degrees are awarded in BIOLOGICAL SCIENCE (biochemistry, biology/biological science, and biophysics), BUSINESS (accounting, banking and finance, and business administration and management), COMMUNICATIONS AND THE ARTS (advertising, art, broadcasting, communications, dance, dramatic arts, English, French, German, graphic design, journalism, music, piano/organ, Spanish, and speech/debate/rhetoric), COMPUTER AND PHYSICAL SCIENCE (chemistry, computer management, computer science, mathematics, physics, and science), EDUCATION (early childhood, elementary, foreign languages, music, physical, and science), HEALTH PROFESSIONS (nursing and premedicine), SOCIAL SCIENCE (Asian/Oriental studies, criminal justice, economics, history, humanities, philosophy, political science/government, prelaw, psychology, religion, and sociology). Business, performing arts, and dance are the strongest academically. Business, performing arts, and mass communications are the largest.

Special: OCU offers internships, a Washington semester, work-study programs, a general studies degree, dual and student-designed majors, credit for life experience, and study-abroad programs. There are 9 national honor societies, a freshman honors program, and 10 departmental honors programs.

Admissions: 62% of the 1999-2000 applicants were accepted. The SAT I scores for the 1999-2000 freshman class were: Verbal--29% below 500, 43% between 500 and 599, 20% between 600 and 700, and 8% above 700; Math--36% below 500, 40% between 500 and 599, and 24% between 600 and 700. The ACT scores were 27% below 21, 26% between 21 and 23, 26% between 24 and 26, 11% between 27 and 28, and 10% above 28. There was 1 National Merit finalist and 3 semifinalists. 5 freshmen graduated first in their class.

Requirements: OCU requires applicants to be in the upper 50% of their class. A GPA of 2.5 is required. The SAT I, with a minimum composite score of 930, or the ACT, with a minimum score of 20, is required. Graduation from an accredited secondary school or satisfactory scores on the GED are also required for admission. High school courses must include 4 units of English, 3 units each of science, social studies, and math, and 2 units of a foreign language. Music and dance students are required to audition. AP and CLEP credits are accepted. Important factors in the admissions decision are evidence of special talent, advanced placement or honor courses, and leadership record.

Procedure: Freshmen are admitted to all sessions. Entrance exams should be taken by February of the senior year. There are early admissions and deferred admissions plans. Application deadlines are open. The application fee is $20. Notification is sent on a rolling basis.

Financial Aid: In 1999-2000, 97% of all freshmen and 66% of continuing students received some form of financial aid. 58% of freshmen and 66% of continuing students received need-based aid. The average freshman award was $9818. Of that total, scholarships or need-based grants averaged $6121 ($10,540 maximum); loans averaged $5503 ($12,648 maximum); and work contracts averaged $2768 ($3296 maximum). 24% of undergraduates work part time. Average annual earnings from campus work are $2604. The average financial indebtedness of the 1999 graduate was $17,563. OCU is a member of CSS. The FAFSA and tax returns, if selected for verification are required. The fall application deadline is March 1.

Computers: The mainframes are an NCR 3455, NCR 3550, 2 DEC ALPHAs, a DEC 8250, and a VAX 4500. Students have access to academic computer systems from the labs, dorm rooms, and through a dial-up remote system. Students can access E-mail from any browser on and off campus. Home directories are only accessible on campus. Approximately 130 open access PCs are available to students in labs on campus. Internet access is available to students form all 8 computer labs and in the dorms. All students may access the system 24 hours a day. There are no time limits. The fee is $45 per semester.

OKLAHOMA STATE UNIVERSITY
Stillwater, OK 74078

(405) 744-6858
(800) 852-1255; Fax: (405) 744-5285

Full-time: 7710 men, 6930 women	**Faculty:** 681; I, -$
Part-time: 862 men, 701 women	**Ph.D.s:** 88%
Graduate: 2706 men, 2178 women	**Student/Faculty:** 22 to 1
Year: semesters, summer session	**Tuition:** $2412 ($6492)
Application Deadline: open	**Room & Board:** $4344
Freshman Class: 5717 applied, 5081 accepted, 2929 enrolled	
SAT I Verbal/Math: 550/570	**ACT:** 24 **VERY COMPETITIVE**

Oklahoma State University, founded in 1890, is a publicly funded land-grant institution, offering undergraduate programs in agricultural sciences and natural resources, arts and sciences, business, education, engineering, architecture, technology, and human environmental resources. There are 6 undergraduate schools and 1 graduate school. In addition to regional accreditation, OSU has baccalaureate program accreditation with AACSB, ABET, ACEJMC, ADA, AHEA, ASLA, FIDER, NAAB, NASM, NRPA, and SAF. The 5 libraries contain 2,025,168 volumes, 3,593,548 microform items, and 6041 audiovisual forms/CDs, and subscribe to 18,301 periodicals. Computerized library services include interlibrary loans and database searching. Special learning facilities include an art gallery, natural history museum, and radio station. The 415-acre campus is in a small town 65 miles north of Oklahoma City and 65 miles west of Tulsa. Including residence halls, there are 200 buildings.

Programs of Study: OSU confers B.A., B.S., B.Arch., B.Arch.Eng., B.F.A., B. Land.Arch., B.M., and B.U.S. degrees. Master's and doctoral degrees are also awarded. Bachelor's degrees are awarded in AGRICULTURE (agricultural business management, agricultural economics, agricultural mechanics, agriculture, animal science, conservation and regulation, forestry and related sciences, horticulture, plant science, and soil science), BIOLOGICAL SCIENCE (biochemistry, biology/biological science, botany, cell biology, entomology, microbiology, molecular biology, nutrition, physiology, and zoology), BUSINESS (accounting, banking and finance, business administration and management, business economics, hotel/motel and restaurant management, international business management, management information systems, management science, marketing/retailing/merchandising, personnel management, and recreation and leisure services), COMMUNICATIONS AND THE ARTS (art, broadcasting, communications, design, dramatic arts, English, French, German, journalism, music, Russian, Spanish, and speech/debate/rhetoric), COMPUTER AND PHYSICAL SCIENCE (chemistry, computer science, geology, mathematics, physics, and statistics), EDUCATION (agricultural, education administration, elementary, health, music, physical, secondary, speech correction, and technical), ENGINEERING AND ENVIRONMENTAL DESIGN (agricultural engineering, architectural engineering, architecture, aviation computer technology, chemical engineering, civil engineering, construction management, electrical/electronics engineering, electrical/electronics engineering technology, engineering, environmental science, industrial engineering, mechanical engineering, and mechanical engineering technology), HEALTH PROFESSIONS (medical technology, premedicine, and preveterinary science), SOCIAL SCIENCE (child care/child and family studies, child psychology/development, economics, fire control and safety technology, geography, history, philosophy, political science/government, prelaw, psychology, and sociology). Engineering and business are the strongest academically. Animal sciences is the largest.

Special: OSU offers internships in medical technology, engineering, home economics, and arts and sciences. A B.A.-B.S. degree, dual majors, an individualized university studies degree, a 3-2 engineering degree, an engineering co-op program, multidisciplinary majors in biosystems engineering and in cell and molecular biology, credit for life experience, nondegree study, and pass/fail options are available. Students may study abroad in several countries. The school also sponsors Semester at Sea, a 1-semester program of study on a ship traveling to ports throughout the world. There is a freshman honors program. All departments have honors programs.

Admissions: 89% of the 1999-2000 applicants were accepted. The SAT I scores for the 1999-2000 freshman class were: Verbal--25% below 500, 40% between 500 and 599, 27% between 600 and 700, and 9% above 700; Math--22% below 500, 38% between 500 and 599, 31% between 600 and 700, and 9% above 700. The ACT scores were 18% below 21, 28% between 21 and 23, 26% between 24 and 26, 14% between 27 and 28, and 14% above 28. 55% of the current freshmen were in the top fifth of their class; 83% were in the top two fifths. There were 22 National Merit finalists. 296 freshmen graduated first in their class.

Requirements: The SAT I or ACT is required. For admission in good standing, freshman applicants must have a cumulative high school GPA of 3.0 (4.0 scale) and rank in the upper third of their graduating class or achieve at least a 22 composite score on the ACT or 1010 on the SAT I. In addition, freshman applicants must have 15 specific curricular units from high school, including 4 years of English, 3 of math (algebra I and above), 2 each of history and lab science, 1 of citizenship skills, and 3 more from any of the above or computer science or foreign language. AP and CLEP credits are accepted. Important factors in the admissions decision are advanced placement or honor courses, evidence of special talent, and leadership record.

Procedure: Freshmen are admitted to all sessions. Application deadlines are open. There is a $25 fee. Notification is sent on a rolling basis.

Financial Aid: In 1999-2000, 74% of all freshmen and 70% of continuing students received some form of financial aid. 37% of freshmen and 41% of continuing students received need-based aid. The average freshman award was $6370. Of that total, scholarships or need-based grants averaged $3600; loans averaged $3157; and work contracts averaged $2037. 26% of undergraduates work part time. Average annual earnings from campus work are $1870. The average financial indebtedness of the 1999 graduate was $14,113. The FAFSA is required. The fall application deadline is March 1.

Computers: The mainframe is an IBM Model 9672 R25. There are some 2000 Mac and IBM PCs available throughout the campus with more than 15,000 active data ports. Access is also available in most residence halls. All students may access the system. There are no time limits. The fee is $5 per credit hour.

OLD DOMINION UNIVERSITY

Norfolk, VA 23529-0050

(757) 683-3637
(800) 348-7926; Fax: (757) 683-3255

Full-time: 3469 men, 4517 women	**Faculty:** 596; I, --$
Part-time: 2306 men, 2773 women	**Ph.D.s:** 87%
Graduate: 2488 men, 3318 women	**Student/Faculty:** 13 to 1
Year: semesters, summer session	**Tuition:** $3796 ($11,386)
Application Deadline: March 15	**Room & Board:** $5114
Freshman Class: 6393 applied, 4517 accepted, 1578 enrolled	
SAT I Verbal/Math: 510/510	**VERY COMPETITIVE**

Old Dominion University, founded in 1930, is a public institution with programs in arts and letters, business and public administration, engineering, education, sciences, and health sciences. Some of the information in this profile is approximate. There are 6 undergraduate and 6 graduate schools. In addition to regional accreditation, ODU has baccalaureate program accreditation with AACSB, ABET, ADA, APTA, ASLA, CAHEA, NASM, NCATE, NLN, and NRPA. The library contains 512,000 volumes, 11,200 microform items, and 19,300 audiovisual forms/CDs, and subscribes to 7000 periodicals. Computerized library services include the card catalog, interlibrary loans, and database searching. Special learning facilities include an art gallery, planetarium, radio station, and music library. The 187-acre campus is in an urban area in the Norfolk/Hampton Roads Metropolitan region. Including residence halls, there are 68 buildings.

Programs of Study: ODU confers B.A., B.S., B.F.A., B.M., B.S.B.A., B.S.C.E., B.S.C.P., B.S.C.S., B.S.D.H., B.S.E.E., B.S.E.H., B.S.E.T., B.S.Ev., B.S.H.S., B. S.M.E., B.S.M.T., and B.S.N. degrees. Master's and doctoral degrees are also awarded. Bachelor's degrees are awarded in BIOLOGICAL SCIENCE (biochemistry and biology/biological science), BUSINESS (accounting, banking and finance, business administration and management, international business management, management information systems, marketing/retailing/merchandising, recreational facilities management, and sports management), COMMUNICATIONS AND THE ARTS (art, art history and appreciation, communications, dance, design, dramatic arts, drawing, English, English literature, fine arts, French, German, graphic design, journalism, music, music history and appreciation, music performance, music theory and composition, painting, photography, printmaking, sculpture, Spanish, and speech/debate/rhetoric), COMPUTER AND PHYSICAL SCIENCE (chemistry, computer science, geology, information sciences and systems, mathematics, physics, and statistics), EDUCATION (art, athletic training, early childhood, elementary, English, foreign languages, mathematics, middle school, physical, science, secondary, social studies, and teaching English as a second/foreign language (TESOL/TEFOL)), ENGINEERING AND ENVIRONMENTAL DESIGN (aerospace studies, civil engineering, civil engineering technology, computer engineering, computer technology, electrical/electronics engineering, electrical/electronics engineering technology, engineering technology, environmental engineering, mechanical engineering, mechanical engineering technology, and nuclear engineering technology), HEALTH PROFESSIONS (dental hygiene, environmental health science, health science, medical laboratory technology, nuclear medical technology, nursing, premedicine, public health, recreation therapy, speech pathology/audiology, and sports medicine), SOCIAL SCIENCE (anthropology, criminal justice, economics, geography, history, human services, interdisciplinary studies, international relations, international studies, philosophy, political science/government, psychology, public administration, religion, social science, sociology, and women's studies). Engineering is the strongest academically. Education (teacher preparation), psychology, and nursing are the largest.

Special: Old Dominion offers cross-registration with schools in the Tidewater Consortium program. There are co-op programs, guaranteed internships, study abroad in 8 countries, and a work-study program. Students may take a B.A.-B.S. degree in engineering and liberal arts. An interdisciplinary program, dual majors, 3-2 engineering degrees in business and engineering, nondegree study, pass/fail options, and credit for military and life experience are available. There is 1 national honor society, Phi Beta Kappa, a freshman honors program, and 13 departmental honors programs.

Admissions: 71% of the 1999-2000 applicants were accepted. The SAT I scores for the 1999-2000 freshman class were: Verbal--75% between 500 and 599, 23% between 600 and 700, and 1% above 700; Math--74% between 500 and 599, 24% between 600 and 700, and 1% above 700. 40% of the current freshmen were in the top fifth of their class; 69% were in the top two fifths.

Requirements: A GPA of 2.5 is required. SAT I, with a minimum combined score of 850 (minimum 400 on each part), is required. The ACT is accepted. Applicants must be graduates of an accredited secondary school. The GED is accepted. Applicants should have completed 4 years of math, 3 years each of English, foreign languages, science, and social science. An essay and an interview are recommended. Applications are accepted on computer disk. AP and CLEP credits are accepted. Important factors in the admissions decision are advanced placement or honor courses, recommendations by school officials, and extracurricular activities record.

Procedure: Freshmen are admitted to all sessions. Entrance exams should be taken in May of the junior year or November/December of the senior year. There are early admissions and deferred admissions plans. Applications should be filed by March 15 for fall entry, November 1 for spring entry, and April 1 for summer entry, along with a $30 fee. Notification is sent on a rolling basis.

Financial Aid: In 1999-2000, 59% of all freshmen and 56% of continuing students received some form of financial aid. 44% of freshmen and 41% of continuing students received need-based aid. The average freshman award was $6685. ODU is a member of CSS. The FAFSA is required. The fall application deadline is May 2.

Computers: The mainframe is an IBM 3090. There are computer labs at various locations on campus. The system also may be accessed via modem from home or dormitory rooms. All students may access the system 24 hours a day. There are no time limits and no fees.

OREGON STATE UNIVERSITY
Corvallis, OR 97331-2106

(541) 737-4411
(800) 291-4192; Fax: (541) 737-2482

Full-time: 6444 men, 5386 women	**Faculty:** 1063; I, --$
Part-time: 500 men, 453 women	**Ph.D.s:** 85%
Graduate: 1624 men, 1684 women	**Student/Faculty:** 11 to 1
Year: quarters, summer session	**Tuition:** $3549 ($12,393)
Application Deadline: March 1	**Room & Board:** $5394
Freshman Class: 6493 applied, 3074 accepted, 2846 enrolled	
SAT I Verbal/Math: 530/550	**ACT:** 23 **VERY COMPETITIVE**

Oregon State University, founded in 1868, is the oldest institution in the Oregon state system, offering liberal arts and preprofessional programs. There are 10 undergraduate and 12 graduate schools. In addition to regional accreditation, OSU has baccalaureate program accreditation with AACSB, ABET, ACCE, ACEJMC, ACPE, AHEA, NASM, NCATE, and SAF. The 4 libraries contain 1.2 million volumes, 1,829,175 microform items, and 6225 audiovisual forms/CDs, and subscribe to 11,605 periodicals. Computerized library services include the card catalog and database searching. Special learning facilities include a learning resource center, art gallery, natural history museum, radio station, TV station, arboretum, wave research lab, research farm, research vessel, and the Linus Pauling Collection. The 400-acre campus is in a small town 80 miles south of Portland. Including residence halls, there are 201 buildings.

Programs of Study: OSU confers B.A., B.S., and B.F.A. degrees. Master's and doctoral degrees are also awarded. Bachelor's degrees are awarded in AGRICULTURE (agricultural business management, agricultural economics, agriculture, animal science, fishing and fisheries, forest engineering, forestry and related sciences, forestry production and processing, horticulture, poultry science, range/farm management, and soil science), BIOLOGICAL SCIENCE (biochemistry, biology/biological science, biophysics, botany, entomology, microbiology, plant pathology, wildlife biology, and zoology), BUSINESS (accounting, banking and finance, business administration and management, hotel/motel and restaurant management, international business management, management information systems, management science, marketing management, and marketing/retailing/merchandising), COMMUNICATIONS AND THE ARTS (communications, dramatic arts, English, French, German, journalism, music, Spanish, speech/debate/rhetoric, and visual and performing arts), COMPUTER AND PHYSICAL SCIENCE (atmospheric sciences and meteorology, chemistry, computer science, geology, mathematics, physics, and science), EDUCATION (health), ENGINEERING AND ENVIRONMENTAL DESIGN (chemical engineering, civil engineering, computer engineering, construction management, engineering physics, industrial engineering technology, landscape architecture/design, mechanical engineering, nuclear engineering, and urban design), HEALTH PROFESSIONS (health, health care administration, medical laboratory technology, nursing, occupational therapy, pharmacy, physical therapy, predentistry, and premedicine), SOCIAL SCIENCE (American studies, anthropology, consumer services, dietetics, economics, family/consumer studies, fashion design and technology, food science, geography, history, home economics, human development, liberal arts/general studies, philosophy, political science/government, psychology, religion, sociology, and textiles and clothing). Engineering, biochemistry, and forestry are the strongest academically. Business, liberal arts, and mechanical engineering are the largest.

Special: OSU offers cooperative veterinary medicine programs with Washington State University and the University of Idaho; geological, metallurgical, and mining engineering programs with the University of Idaho; and an education program with the University of Oregon. Students may cross-register at any college in the Oregon state system, at member colleges of the Western Interstate Commission, and with any member of the National Student Exchange. Study abroad is possible in any of 13 countries, including New Zealand and the former Soviet Union. There is a 5-year B.A.-B.S. program in civil engineering and forest engineering, and a 3-2 engineering program with the University of Oregon. Internships, a liberal studies degree, nondegree study, and pass/fail options are also available. There are 7 national honor societies, a freshman honors program, and 20 departmental honors programs.

Admissions: 47% of the 1999-2000 applicants were accepted. The SAT I scores for the 1999-2000 freshman class were: Verbal--34% below 500, 44% between 500 and 599, 20% between 600 and 700, and 2% above 700; Math--29% below 500, 41% between 500 and 599, 27% between 600 and 700, and 3% above 700.

The ACT scores were 28% below 21, 31% between 21 and 23, 20% between 24 and 26, 12% between 27 and 28, and 9% above 28.

Requirements: The SAT I or ACT is required. A GPA of 3.0 is required. Applicants should be high school graduates or hold the GED. Required high school preparation includes 4 years of English; 3 years of math, including algebra I; 2 years of natural science; and 1 year each of U.S history, world history, and social science. Among electives, government and foreign language are strongly recommended. Some subject requirements may be fulfilled by test scores. AP and CLEP credits are accepted. Advanced placement or honor courses is an important factor in the admission decision.

Procedure: Freshmen are admitted to all sessions. Entrance exams should be taken during the junior or senior year. There is an early admissions plan. Applications should be filed by March 1 for fall, spring, or summer entry, and December 1 for winter entry along with a $50 fee. Notification is sent on a rolling basis.

Financial Aid: OSU is a member of CSS. The FAFSA is required. The fall application deadline is February 1.

Computers: The mainframes are 2 Digital 7000/620 AXP open/VMS machines and 1 Digital 2100 AXP OSF/1. There are more than 2200 PC and Mac systems available to students in the computer lab, the library, and various academic buildings. All students may access the system at any time. There are no time limits and no fees.

OTIS COLLEGE OF ART AND DESIGN
Los Angeles, CA 90045

(310) 665-6820
(800) 527-6847; Fax: (310) 665-6821

Full-time: 360 men, 420 women	**Faculty:** 26
Part-time: 5 men, 5 women	**Ph.D.s:** 98%
Graduate: 10 men, 10 women	**Student/Faculty:** 30 to 1
Year: semesters, summer session	**Tuition:** $18,400
Application Deadline: August 15	**Room & Board:** n/app
Freshman Class: n/av	
SAT I or ACT: required	**SPECIAL**

Otis College of Art and Design, founded in 1918, is a private, not-for-profit college offering undergraduate programs in fine arts, ceramics, graphic design and illustration, environmental arts, fashion design, toy design, photography, and digital media design and graduate programs in fine arts and writing. As part of their instruction, students work directly with professional artists, designers, critics, and writers. The figures in the above capsule are approximate. There are 2 undergraduate and 1 graduate school. In addition to regional accreditation, Otis has baccalaureate program accreditation with NASAD. The library contains 27,000 volumes, and subscribes to 180 periodicals. Computerized library services include the card catalog, interlibrary loans, and database searching. Special learning facilities include a learning resource center, an art gallery, a photographic darkroom, printmaking studios, a fine books press room, a woodworking studio, a digital imaging room, a metalworking shop, and multiuse studios. The 5-acre campus is in an urban area on the west side of Los Angeles. There are 3 buildings.

Programs of Study: Otis confers the B.F.A. degree. Master's degrees are also awarded. Bachelor's degrees are awarded in COMMUNICATIONS AND THE ARTS (ceramic art and design, design, fine arts, graphic design, illustration, and photography), ENGINEERING AND ENVIRONMENTAL DESIGN (environmental design), SOCIAL SCIENCE (fashion design and technology). Graphic design and fine arts are the strongest academically. Fine arts, graphic design, and illustration are the largest.

Special: Study abroad is available in London, Paris, and Stockholm. There is a freshman honors program.

Requirements: The SAT I or ACT is required. applicants must be graduates of an accredited secondary school or have a GED certificate, and submit a portfolio. 75% of the admissions decision is based on the portfolio. Interviews are recommended for students living within 200 miles of campus; essays are required. AP credits are accepted. Important factors in the admissions decision are evidence of special talent, advanced placement or honor courses, and recommendations by school officials.

Procedure: Freshmen are admitted fall and spring. Entrance exams should be taken in the fall. There is a deferred admissions plan. Early decision applications should be filed by May 1; regular applications, by August 15 for fall entry, December 15 for spring entry, and August 15 for summer entry, along with a $50 fee. Notification is sent on a rolling basis.

Financial Aid: Otis is a member of CSS. The FAFSA, the college's own financial statement, and the SAAC for California residents are required.

Computers: The mainframe is an Apple 8150 server. There are 27 Power Mac 7100s and 15 Macs. There is also an Internet access station. All students may access the system. There are no time limits and no fees. It is strongly recommended that all students have personal computers.

OUACHITA BAPTIST UNIVERSITY
Arkadelphia, AR 71998-0001
(870) 245-5110
(800) 342-5628; Fax: (870) 245-5500

Full-time: 684 men, 854 women	**Faculty:** 103; IIB, -$
Part-time: 56 men, 44 women	**Ph.D.s:** 75%
Graduate: none	**Student/Faculty:** 15 to 1
Year: semesters, summer session	**Tuition:** $8930
Application Deadline: open	**Room & Board:** $3450
Freshman Class: 931 applied, 665 accepted, 485 enrolled	
SAT I Verbal/Math: 560/540	**ACT:** 24 **VERY COMPETITIVE**

Ouachita Baptist University, founded in 1886, is a private liberal arts institution affiliated with the Arkansas Baptist State Convention. There are 4 undergraduate schools. In addition to regional accreditation, Ouachita has baccalaureate program accreditation with NASM and NCATE. The 2 libraries contain 117,517 volumes, 205,614 microform items, and 3159 audiovisual forms/CDs, and subscribe to 1067 periodicals. Computerized library services include the card catalog, interlibrary loans, and database searching. Special learning facilities include a learning resource center, art gallery, and planetarium. The 60-acre campus is in a small town 65 miles southwest of Little Rock. Including residence halls, there are 33 buildings.

Programs of Study: Ouachita confers B.A., B.S., B.M., B.M.E., and B.S.E. degrees. Associate degrees are also awarded. Bachelor's degrees are awarded in BIOLOGICAL SCIENCE (biology/biological science), BUSINESS (accounting, business administration and management, and business economics), COMMUNICATIONS AND THE ARTS (communications, dramatic arts, English, French, music, musical theater, Russian languages and literature, Spanish, and speech/debate/rhetoric), COMPUTER AND PHYSICAL SCIENCE (chemistry, computer science, mathematics, and physics), EDUCATION (art, business, early childhood, elementary, foreign languages, health, home economics, middle school, music, science, and secondary), HEALTH PROFESSIONS (medical laboratory technology, predentistry, premedicine, and speech pathology/audiology), SO-

CIAL SCIENCE (biblical studies, dietetics, economics, history, ministries, philosophy, political science/government, prelaw, psychology, religion, sociology, and theological studies). Education, business, and religion are the largest.

Special: Ouachita offers cross-registration with Henderson State University, a Washington semester for political science majors, internships and co-op programs for business majors, B.A.-B.S. degrees, dual majors, pass/fail options, and nondegree study. Study-abroad opportunities are available in Germany, England, France, Italy, Russia, Japan, China, Hong Kong, Kazakhstan, Austria, Israel, Belize, and Morocco. There is a freshman honors program.

Admissions: 71% of the 1999-2000 applicants were accepted. The SAT I scores for the 1999-2000 freshman class were: Verbal--27% below 500, 43% between 500 and 599, 23% between 600 and 700, and 7% above 700; Math--31% below 500, 41% between 500 and 599, 21% between 600 and 700, and 7% above 700. The ACT scores were 21% below 21, 27% between 21 and 23, 27% between 24 and 26, 14% between 27 and 28, and 11% above 28. 59% of the current freshmen were in the top fifth of their class; 84% were in the top two fifths. There were 3 National Merit finalists. 15 freshmen graduated first in their class.

Requirements: The SAT I or ACT is required. Ouachita requires applicants to be in the upper 50% of their class. A GPA of 2.5 is required. Applicants should have completed 19 high school units, including 4 in English, 3 in social science, and 2 each in natural science and math; 2 in a foreign language and 1/2 in computer science are also recommended. AP and CLEP credits are accepted.

Procedure: Freshmen are admitted to all sessions. Entrance exams should be taken in the junior year. There are early decision, early admissions, and deferred admissions plans. Application deadlines are open. There is a $25 fee. Notification is sent on a rolling basis. 10 early decision candidates were accepted for a recent class.

Financial Aid: In 1999-2000, 95% of all freshmen and 90% of continuing students received some form of financial aid. 50% of freshmen and 48% of continuing students received need-based aid. The average freshman award was $10,152. Of that total, scholarships or need-based grants averaged $8636 ($12,960 maximum); loans averaged $2175 ($2625 maximum); and work contracts averaged $1450 ($1500 maximum). 50% of undergraduates work part time. Average annual earnings from campus work are $1500. The average financial indebtedness of the 1999 graduate was $13,865. Ouachita is a member of CSS. The FAFSA and the college's own financial statement are required. The fall application deadline is February 15.

Computers: The mainframe is an IBM AS/400. There are 5 computer labs available to students. All academic departments have PCs. All students may access the system. There are no time limits and no fees.

PACIFIC LUTHERAN UNIVERSITY
Tacoma, WA 98447

(253) 535-7151
(800) 274-6758; Fax: (253) 536-5136

Full-time: 1171 men, 1828 women	**Faculty:** 232; IIA, -$
Part-time: 143 men, 160 women	**Ph.D.s:** 83%
Graduate: 131 men, 169 women	**Student/Faculty:** 13 to 1
Year: 4-1-4, summer session	**Tuition:** $16,224
Application Deadline: open	**Room & Board:** $5038
Freshman Class: 1462 applied, 1413 accepted, 568 enrolled	
SAT I Verbal/Math: 556/549	**ACT:** 24 **VERY COMPETITIVE**

Pacific Lutheran University, founded in 1890, is an independent, nonprofit institution affiliated with the Evangelical Lutheran Church in America. PLU offers programs in arts and sciences, business, education, nursing, fine arts, and phys ed. There are 6 undergraduate schools and 1 graduate school. In addition to regional accreditation, PLU has baccalaureate program accreditation with AACSB, ABET, CSAB, CSWE, NASM, NCATE, and NLN. The library contains 582,707 volumes, 212,793 microform items, and 12,046 audiovisual forms/CDs, and subscribes to 1869 periodicals. Computerized library services include the card catalog, interlibrary loans, and database searching. Special learning facilities include a learning resource center, art gallery, radio station, TV station, herbarium, invertebrate and vertebrate museums, biology field station, Northwest history collections, Scandinavian history collection, and lanquage resource center. The 126-acre campus is in a suburban area 7 miles south of Tacoma. Including residence halls, there are 41 buildings.

Programs of Study: PLU confers B.A., B.S., B.A.E., B.A.P.E., B.A.Rec., B. B.A., B.F.A., B.M., B.M.A., B.M.Ed., B.S.N., and B.S.P.E. degrees. Master's degrees are also awarded. Bachelor's degrees are awarded in BIOLOGICAL SCIENCE (biology/biological science), BUSINESS (business administration and management), COMMUNICATIONS AND THE ARTS (art, classics, communications, English, fine arts, French, German, music, music performance, music theory and composition, piano/organ, Scandinavian languages, and Spanish), COMPUTER AND PHYSICAL SCIENCE (applied physics, chemistry, computer programming, computer science, geology, geoscience, mathematics, and physics), EDUCATION (education, music, and physical), ENGINEERING AND ENVIRONMENTAL DESIGN (computer engineering and engineering and applied science), HEALTH PROFESSIONS (nursing), SOCIAL SCIENCE (anthropology, Asian/Oriental studies, economics, history, international studies, philosophy, political science/government, psychology, religion, Scandinavian studies, social work, sociology, and women's studies). Business administration, education, and nursing are the largest.

Special: PLU offers 2 different bachelor's degrees simultaneously, 3-2 engineering degrees with Washington University in St. Louis and Columbia University, and accelerated degree programs in most majors. Dual majors and student-designed majors can be arranged. There are 55 study-abroad programs in 22 countries, extensive internships with local businesses and nonprofit organizations, and work-study programs. Credit is given by exam and through the AURA Program for adults age 30 or older. Nondegree study and pass/fail options are also available. There are 7 national honor societies, a freshman honors program, and 6 departmental honors programs.

Admissions: 97% of the 1999-2000 applicants were accepted. The SAT I scores for the 1999-2000 freshman class were: Verbal--26% below 500, 42% between 500 and 599, 27% between 600 and 700, and 5% above 700; Math--27% below

500, 45% between 500 and 599, 26% between 600 and 700, and 2% above 700. The ACT scores were 20% below 21, 24% between 21 and 23, 26% between 24 and 26, 15% between 27 and 28, and 15% above 28. 62% of the current freshmen were in the top fifth of their class; 89% were in the top two fifths. There were 5 National Merit finalists and 0 semifinalist. 32 freshmen graduated first in their class.

Requirements: The SAT I or ACT is required. PLU requires applicants to be in the upper 50% of their class. A GPA of 2.5 is required. Applicants should be graduates of accredited secondary schools, although GED certificates are accepted. PLU requires 2 years each of college preparatory math and a foreign language, and recommends 4 years of English, 2 each of social studies, and lab science, and 1 of fine or performing arts, and 3 of electives. An essay is required. Students may apply on-line vviaa PLU's Web site. AP and CLEP credits are accepted. Important factors in the admissions decision are advanced placement or honor courses, leadership record, and evidence of special talent.

Procedure: Freshmen are admitted fall and spring. Entrance exams should be taken by January of the senior year. There are early action, early admissions, and deferred admissions plans. Application for early action are due November 15, application deadlines are open. The fee is $35. Notification of early action is sent between October 1 and November 30; regular decision, on a rolling basis.

Financial Aid: In 1999-2000, 95% of all freshmen and 90% of continuing students received some form of financial aid. 74% of freshmen and 62% of continuing students received need-based aid. The average freshman award was $15,336. Of that total, scholarships or need-based grants averaged $7000 ($16,224 maximum); loans averaged $3500 ($8500 maximum); and work contracts averaged $1800 ($3000 maximum). 49% of undergraduates work part time. Average annual earnings from campus work are $2286. The average financial indebtedness of the 1999 graduate was $19,267. The FAFSA is required. The fall application deadline is January 31.

Computers: The mainframe is a DEC ALPHA 2100A clustered with a DEC VAX 4700A. There are 2 teaching labs and 2 open labs for student use. All students may access the system 18 hours per day, or 24 hours with a modem. There are no time limits and no fees.

PACIFIC UNION COLLEGE
Angwin, CA 94508

(707) 965-6336
(800) 862-7080; Fax: (707) 965-6432

Full-time: 678 men, 779 women	**Faculty:** 100; IIB, -$
Part-time: 47 men, 119 women	**Ph.D.s:** 56%
Graduate: 2 women	**Student/Faculty:** 15 to 1
Year: quarters, summer session	**Tuition:** $14,475
Application Deadline: open	**Room & Board:** $4425
Freshman Class: 859 applied, 459 accepted, 374 enrolled	
ACT: recommended	**VERY COMPETITIVE**

Pacific Union College, founded in 1888, is a private college affiliated with the Seventh-day Adventist Church and offering programs in liberal arts, religion, business, health science, and teacher preparation. In addition to regional accreditation, PUC has baccalaureate program accreditation with ADA, CSWE, NASM, and NLN. The library contains 130,252 volumes, 105,966 microform items, and 53,552 audiovisual forms/CDs, and subscribes to 925 periodicals. Computerized library services include the card catalog and interlibrary loans. Special learning facilities include a learning resource center, art gallery, natural history museum, and radio station. The 2000-acre campus is in a small town 70 miles north of San Francisco. Including residence halls, there are 60 buildings.

Programs of Study: PUC confers B.A., B.S., B.B.A., B.Mus., B.S.Med.Tech., and B.S.W. degrees. Associate and master's degrees are also awarded. Bachelor's degrees are awarded in BIOLOGICAL SCIENCE (biology/biological science and biophysics), BUSINESS (business administration and management, fashion merchandising, office supervision and management, and recreation and leisure services), COMMUNICATIONS AND THE ARTS (art history and appreciation, communications, design, English, fine arts, French, graphic design, journalism, music, public relations, Spanish, and studio art), COMPUTER AND PHYSICAL SCIENCE (applied mathematics, chemistry, computer science, mathematics, natural sciences, physical sciences, and physics), EDUCATION (business, early childhood, physical, and trade and industrial), ENGINEERING AND ENVIRONMENTAL DESIGN (engineering technology, graphic arts technology, industrial engineering technology, and interior design), HEALTH PROFESSIONS (medical laboratory technology and nursing), SOCIAL SCIENCE (behavioral science, family/consumer studies, food science, history, interdisciplinary studies, liberal arts/general studies, psychology, religion, social studies, social work, sociology, and theological studies). Business administration is the largest.

Special: Students may study abroad in Austria, Spain, and France, earn a B.A.-B.S. degree, take dual majors, earn a general studies degree in liberal studies, and pursue a student-designed major in interdisciplinary studies. The college offers nondegree study and credit for life, military, and work experience. There is a freshman honors program.

Admissions: 53% of the 1999-2000 applicants were accepted.

Requirements: The ACT is recommended. A GPA of 2.3 is required. Scores are used only for advising purposes. Candidates for admission should have completed 4 years of English, 2 of math, and 1 each of science and history. Applications are accepted on-line. AP and CLEP credits are accepted. Important factors in the admissions decision are recommendations by school officials, leadership record, and advanced placement or honor courses.

Procedure: Entrance exams should be taken in the junior or senior year. Application deadlines are open; the fee is $30. A waiting list is an active part of the admissions procedure.

Financial Aid: PUC is a member of CSS. The FAFSA and the college's own financial statement are required. The fall application deadline is March 2.

Computers: All students may access the system at any time. There are no time limits and no fees. The college strongly recommends that students have their own personal computers.

PACIFIC UNIVERSITY
Forest Grove, OR 97116

(503) 359-2218
(800) 677-6712; Fax: (503) 359-2975

Full-time: 381 men, 619 women	**Faculty:** 87; IIA, -$
Part-time: 33 men, 39 women	**Ph.D.s:** 78%
Graduate: 368 men, 624 women	**Student/Faculty:** 12 to 1
Year: 4-1-4, summer session	**Tuition:** $17,250
Application Deadline: February 15	**Room & Board:** $5294
Freshman Class: 989 applied, 853 accepted, 292 enrolled	
SAT I Verbal/Math: 550/570	**ACT:** 26 **VERY COMPETITIVE**

Pacific University, founded in 1849, is an independent institution affiliated with the Congregational Church (United Church of Christ), offering degree programs in liberal arts, science, business, education, and health professions. There are 6 graduate schools. In addition to regional accreditation, Pacific has baccalaureate program accreditation with NASM. The library contains 152,060 volumes, 76,609 microform items, and 3708 audiovisual forms/CDs, and subscribes to 945 periodicals. Computerized library services include the card catalog, interlibrary loans, and database searching. Special learning facilities include a learning resource center, art gallery, radio station, TV station, and museum of the history of the university. The 55-acre campus is in a small town 25 miles west of Portland. Including residence halls, there are 18 buildings.

Programs of Study: Pacific confers B.A., B.S., and B.M. degrees. Master's and doctoral degrees are also awarded. Bachelor's degrees are awarded in BIOLOGICAL SCIENCE (biology/biological science), BUSINESS (business administration and management), COMMUNICATIONS AND THE ARTS (creative writing, dramatic arts, Japanese, literature, music, and Spanish), COMPUTER AND PHYSICAL SCIENCE (chemistry, computer science, mathematics, and physics), SOCIAL SCIENCE (economics, history, humanities, philosophy, political science/government, psychology, social work, and sociology). Natural sciences, literature, and creative writing are the strongest academically. Business administration, English and psychology are the largest.

Special: Cross-registration is available with Oregon Independent Colleges and Oregon Graduate Institute of Science and Technology (OGIST). The university also offers cooperative programs with Washington University in St. Louis, OGIST, and Oregon School of Arts and Crafts, as well as study abroad in 13 countries. Full-time, semester-long internships, including one in Washington D.C., are possible. Dual majors, a general studies degree in humanities, nondegree study, 3-2 engineering programs with Washington University in St. Louis and OGIST, and an interdisciplinary program in peace and conflict studies are available. There are 2 national honor societies, a freshman honors program, and 1 departmental honors program.

Admissions: 86% of the 1999-2000 applicants were accepted. The SAT I scores for the 1999-2000 freshman class were: Verbal--21% below 500, 54% between 500 and 599, 20% between 600 and 700, and 5% above 700; Math--18% below 500, 45% between 500 and 599, 33% between 600 and 700, and 4% above 700. The ACT scores were 11% below 21, 10% between 21 and 23, 36% between 24 and 26, 17% between 27 and 28, and 26% above 28. 61% of the current freshmen were in the top fifth of their class; 88% were in the top two fifths. 18 freshmen graduated first in their class.

Requirements: The SAT I or ACT is required. A GPA of 3.0 is required. Applicants are expected to be high school graduates or to hold the GED. A personal essay is required, and an interview is recommended. Applications are accepted on-line at the school's web site or through Applied Technology (Princeton Review). AP and CLEP credits are accepted. Important factors in the admissions decision are advanced placement or honor courses, recommendations by school officials, and extracurricular activities record.

Procedure: Freshmen are admitted fall and spring. There is a deferred admissions plan. Applications should be filed by February 15 for fall entry, along with a $30 fee. Notification is sent on a rolling basis.

Financial Aid: In 1999-2000, 92% of all freshmen and 97% of continuing students received some form of financial aid. 82% of freshmen and 70% of continuing students received need-based aid. The average freshman award was $15,957. Of that total, scholarships or need-based grants averaged $10,225 ($18,683 maximum); and loans averaged $4674 ($17,789 maximum). 54% of undergraduates work part time. Average annual earnings from campus work are $823. The average financial indebtedness of the 1999 graduate was $18,500. Pacific is a member of CSS. The FAFSA is required. The fall application deadline is April 1.

Computers: There is a Mac-based LAN with 45 student terminals, plus 6 student-use PCs, 18 Macs in residence halls, a Sequent S-81, an Intel System 303 running UNIX System 5, and a Sun 3/80 workstation. All students may access the system. There are no time limits and no fees.

PARSONS SCHOOL OF DESIGN
New York, NY 10011
(212) 229-8910
(800) 252-0852; Fax: (212) 229-8975

Full-time: 501 men, 1325 women	**Faculty:** 33
Part-time: 34 men, 51 women	**Ph.D.s:** 6%
Graduate: 99 men, 220 women	**Student/Faculty:** 55 to 1
Year: semesters, summer session	**Tuition:** $20,640
Application Deadline: open	**Room & Board:** $8857
Freshman Class: 2030 applied, 866 accepted, 418 enrolled	
SAT I Verbal/Math: 530/530	**SPECIAL**

Parsons School of Design, founded in 1896, is a private professional art school and is part of the New School for Social Research. There is 1 graduate school. In addition to regional accreditation, Parsons has baccalaureate program accreditation with NASAD. The 2 libraries contain 177,000 volumes and 5000 audiovisual forms/CDs, and subscribe to 230 periodicals. Computerized library services include the card catalog and database searching. Special learning facilities include an art gallery. The 2-acre campus is in an urban area in Manhattan's Greenwich Village. Including residence halls, there are 8 buildings.

Programs of Study: Parsons confers B.A.-B.F.A., B.B.A., and B.F.A. degrees. Associate and master's degrees are also awarded. Bachelor's degrees are awarded in BUSINESS (marketing/retailing/merchandising), COMMUNICATIONS AND THE ARTS (advertising, design, fine arts, graphic design, illustration, photography, and studio art), ENGINEERING AND ENVIRONMENTAL DESIGN (architectural engineering and interior design), SOCIAL SCIENCE (fashion design and technology). Communication design, illustration, and fashion design are the largest.

Special: Students may cross-register at the New School for Social Research, Cooper Union, and Pratt Institute. Internships are required for some majors. Students may study abroad at the Parsons campus in Paris or in 4 other countries. The 5-year combined B.A.-B.F.A. degree requires 180 credits for graduation. A mobility semester or year at any AICAD school is available, and interdisciplinary majors, including architecture and environmental design and design marketing, are possible.

Admissions: 43% of the 1999-2000 applicants were accepted. The SAT I scores for the 1999-2000 freshman class were: Verbal--37% below 500, 36% between 500 and 599, 23% between 600 and 700, and 5% above 700; Math--36% below 500, 38% between 500 and 599, 22% between 600 and 700, and 5% above 700.

Requirements: The SAT I or ACT is required. A GPA of 2.0 is required. Applicants must be graduates of an accredited secondary school. The GED is accepted. Applicants should have completed 4 years each of art, English, history, and social studies. A portfolio and home examination are required, and an interview is recommended. AP credits are accepted. Important factors in the admissions decision are evidence of special talent, advanced placement or honor courses, and personality/intangible qualities.

Procedure: Freshmen are admitted fall and spring. Entrance exams should be taken by spring of the junior year. There is an early admissions plan. Application deadlines are open. There is a $40 fee. Notification is sent on a rolling basis. 15% of all applicants are on a waiting list.

Financial Aid: In a recent year, 70% of all freshmen and 80% of continuing students received some form of financial aid, including need-based aid. The average freshman award was $12,125. Of that total, scholarships or need-based grants averaged $7600 ($14,000 maximum); loans averaged $2625 ($4625 maximum); and work contracts averaged $2000 ($2500 maximum). 25% of undergraduates work part time. Average annual earnings from campus work are $1210. The average financial indebtedness of the 1999 graduate was $17,125. Parsons is a member of CSS. The FAFSA is required. International students must file an institutional application. The fall application deadline is April 1.

Computers: 800 Macs/PCs are available, as well as graphical software, E-mail and Internet access, and AutoCad and fashion-design labs. All students may access the system. There are no time limits and no fees. It is strongly recommended that all students have personal computers.

PENN STATE UNIVERSITY/UNIVERSITY PARK CAMPUS

University Park, PA 16802   (814) 863-0233; Fax: (814) 863-7590

Full-time: 17,330 men, 15,100 women	**Faculty:** 1721; I, -$
Part-time: 1236 men, 839 women	**Ph.D.s:** 88%
Graduate: 3410 men, 2743 women	**Student/Faculty:** 19 to 1
Year: semesters, summer session	**Tuition:** $6436 ($13,552)
Application Deadline: open	**Room & Board:** $4690
Freshman Class: 26,079 applied, 12,862 accepted, 5069 enrolled	
SAT I Verbal/Math: 589/614	**VERY COMPETITIVE**

Penn State University/University Park Campus, founded in 1855, is the oldest and largest of 24 campuses in the Penn State system, offering undergraduate and graduate degrees in agricultural science, arts and architecture, business administration, earth and mineral sciences, education, engineering, health and human development, liberal arts, science, and communications. Some of the information in this profile is approximate. There are 10 undergraduate and 1 graduate school. In addition to regional accreditation, Penn State has baccalaureate program accreditation with AACSB, ABET, ACEJMC, ADA, ASLA, CSWE, NAAB, NASAD, NASM, NCATE, NLN, NRPA, and SAF. The 10 libraries contain 2,452,370 volumes, 1,917,033 microform items, and 38,931 audiovisual forms/CDs, and subscribe to 26,157 periodicals. Computerized library services include the card catalog, interlibrary loans, and database searching. Special learning facilities include a learning resource center, an art gallery, a radio station, a TV station, museums of art, anthropology, and earth and mineral sciences, an observatory, and a nuclear reactor. The 5617-acre campus is in a suburban area 90 miles west of Harrisburg. Including residence halls, there are 403 buildings.

Programs of Study: Penn State confers B.A., B.S., B.Arch., B.Arch.Eng., B. F.A., B.M., B.Mus.Arts, and B.Ph. degrees. Associate, master's, and doctoral degrees are also awarded. Bachelor's degrees are awarded in AGRICULTURE (agricultural business management, agriculture, agronomy, animal science, dairy science, fishing and fisheries, forestry and related sciences, forestry production and processing, horticulture, natural resource management, plant science, poultry science, and soil science), BIOLOGICAL SCIENCE (biochemistry, biology/biological science, ecology, microbiology, molecular biology, nutrition, and wildlife biology), BUSINESS (accounting, banking and finance, business administration and management, hotel/motel and restaurant management, insurance, international business management, labor studies, management information systems, management science, marketing/retailing/merchandising, real estate, and transportation management), COMMUNICATIONS AND THE ARTS (advertising, art, art history and appreciation, broadcasting, classics, communications, comparative literature, dramatic arts, English, film arts, fine arts, French, German, Italian, journalism, music, Russian, Spanish, and speech/debate/rhetoric), COMPUTER AND PHYSICAL SCIENCE (actuarial science, astronomy, atmospheric sciences and meteorology, chemistry, computer science, earth science, geoscience, mathematics, physics, science, and statistics), EDUCATION (agricultural, art, elementary, health, industrial arts, music, secondary, and special), ENGINEERING AND ENVIRONMENTAL DESIGN (aeronautical engineering, agricultural engineering, architectural engineering, architecture, chemical engineering, civil engineering, computer engineering, electrical/electronics engineering, energy management technology, engineering, environmental engineering, industrial administration/management, industrial engineering, landscape architecture/design, materials science, mechanical engineering, mining and mineral engineering, nuclear engineering, and petroleum/natural gas engineering), HEALTH PROFESSIONS (health care administration, nursing, premedicine, public health, rehabilitation therapy, and speech pathology/audiology), SOCIAL SCIENCE (African American studies, American studies, anthropology, criminal justice, East Asian studies, economics, food science, geography, history, human development, international relations, Latin American studies, liberal arts/general studies, medieval studies, parks and recreation management, philosophy, physical fitness/movement, political science/government, prelaw, psychology, public administration, religion, sociology, and women's studies). Agriculture, architecture, and meteorology are the strongest academically. Electrical engineering, education, and accounting are the largest.

Special: Intercollegiate programs in marine sciences and military studies, as well as the B.Ph. program, are offered by faculty from several university colleges. There are internships available in many disciplines. Study abroad is possible through more than 70 programs in 30 countries. Dual and student-designed majors, a general studies degree in arts and sciences, and dual degrees in liberal arts and either earth/natural sciences or engineering are offered with 26 other institutions, as well as a 3-2 engineering program. Co-op programs are available in most engineering majors. There are limited pass/fail options, and nondegree study is possible. There are 45 national honor societies, including Phi Beta Kappa, and a freshman honors program.

Admissions: 49% of the 1999-2000 applicants were accepted. The SAT I scores for the 1999-2000 freshman class were: Verbal--11% below 500, 43% between 500 and 599, 36% between 600 and 700, and 10% above 700; Math--8% below 500, 30% between 500 and 599, 46% between 600 and 700, and 16% above 700. 74% of the current freshmen were in the top fifth of their class; 88% were in the top two fifths.

Requirements: The SAT I or ACT is required; the SAT I is preferred. A GPA of 2.0 is required. Applicants should be graduates of accredited high schools or have earned the GED. Required secondary preparation varies by the college or other academic unit applied to. Generally, all applicants should have 5 years in arts, humanities, and social studies, 4 of English, and 3 each of science and math. 2 years of the same foreign language are required for the College of Liberal Arts and School of Communications, and recommended for all other programs. AP and CLEP credits are accepted. Important factors in the admissions decision are advanced placement or honor courses and evidence of special talent.

Procedure: Freshmen are admitted to all sessions. Entrance exams should be taken in the junior year. Application deadlines are open. There is a $50 fee. Notification is sent on a rolling basis.

Financial Aid: The average financial indebtedness of the 1999 graduate was $17,125. The FAFSA, and for Pennsylvania residents, the PHEAA form are required. Check with the school for current application deadlines.

Computers: The mainframe is an IBM ES/3090-600s. The Center for Academic Computing is connected to a wide variety of academic facilities, the library, other Penn State campuses, the National Science Foundation network, Bitnet/CREN, and more than a thousand other organizations worldwide. PC classrooms and laboratories are available throughout the campus, and special facilities for graphics applications and desktop publishing are available. All students may access the system 24 hours a day, every day. There are no time limits and no fees.

PEPPERDINE UNIVERSITY
Malibu, CA 90263-4392   (310) 456-4392; Fax: (310) 456-4861

Full-time: 1049 men, 1612 women	**Faculty:** 167; IIA, ++$
Part-time: 53 men, 77 women	**Ph.D.s:** 100%
Graduate: 2269 men, 2386 women	**Student/Faculty:** 16 to 1
Year: semesters, summer session	**Tuition:** $23,070
Application Deadline: January 15	**Room & Board:** $7010
Freshman Class: 5219 applied, 1818 accepted, 612 enrolled	
SAT I Verbal/Math: 621/627	**ACT:** 27 **HIGHLY COMPETITIVE**

Pepperdine University, founded in 1937, is a private liberal arts university affiliated with the Church of Christ. There are 4 graduate schools. The library contains 470,236 volumes, 455,162 microform items, and 5817 audiovisual forms/CDs, and subscribes to 3134 periodicals. Computerized library services include the card catalog, interlibrary loans, and database searching. Special learning facilities include an art gallery, radio station, tv station, writing center, and Japanese tea ceremony room. The 830-acre campus is in a suburban area 35 miles northwest of Los Angeles, overlooking the Pacific Ocean. Including residence halls, there are 76 buildings.

Programs of Study: Pepperdine confers B.A., B.S., and B.S.M. degrees. Master's and doctoral degrees are also awarded. Bachelor's degrees are awarded in BIOLOGICAL SCIENCE (biology/biological science and nutrition), BUSINESS (accounting, business administration and management, and international business management), COMMUNICATIONS AND THE ARTS (advertising, art, communications, dramatic arts, English, French, German, journalism, music, public relations, Spanish, speech/debate/rhetoric, and telecommunications), COMPUTER AND PHYSICAL SCIENCE (chemistry, computer science, mathematics, and natural sciences), EDUCATION (elementary, physical, and secondary), ENGINEERING AND ENVIRONMENTAL DESIGN (engineering), HEALTH PROFESSIONS (sports medicine), SOCIAL SCIENCE (economics, history, humanities, international studies, liberal arts/general studies, philosophy, political science/government, psychology, religion, social science, and sociology). Natural sciences (premedical), sports medicine, and political science are the strongest academically. Communication and business are the largest.

Special: Students may earn 1 to 4 units for an internship, available in most majors, participate in a Washington or a Sacramento semester, and study abroad in 8 countries. The school offers a 3-2 engineering degree with Washington University in St. Louis the University of Southern California, and Boston University. There are dual majors in any discipline, student-designed contract majors, federal work-study programs, nondegree study, and pass/fail options. There are 12 national honor societies, a freshman honors program, and 3 departmental honors programs.

Admissions: 35% of the 1999-2000 applicants were accepted. The SAT I scores for the 1999-2000 freshman class were: Verbal--3% below 500, 33% between 500 and 599, 49% between 600 and 700, and 15% above 700; Math--4% below 500, 28% between 500 and 599, 50% between 600 and 700, and 18% above 700. The ACT scores were 3% below 21, 10% between 21 and 23, 27% between 24 and 26, 25% between 27 and 28, and 35% above 28.

Requirements: The SAT I or ACT is required. It is strongly recommended that candidates for admission present a college preparatory program that includes 4 years of English, 3 of math, 2 each of foreign language and science, and courses in speech communication, humanities, and social science. Applications are available on-line at www.wavelink.edu. AP and CLEP credits are accepted. Important factors in the admissions decision are advanced placement or honor courses, recommendations by school officials, and evidence of special talent.

Procedure: Freshmen are admitted fall and spring. Entrance exams should be taken in the fall. There are early decision and deferred admissions plans. Early decision applications should be filed by November 15; regular applications, by January 15 for fall entry and October 15 for spring entry, along with a $55 fee. Notification of early decision is sent December 15; regular decision, April 1. 319 early decision candidates were accepted for the 1999-2000 class. 7% of all applicants are on a waiting list.

Financial Aid: In 1999-2000, 79% of all freshmen and 70% of continuing students received some form of financial aid. 55% of all students received need-based aid. The average freshman need-based award was $23,364. Of that total, scholarships or need-based grants averaged $11,277; loans averaged $4744; and work contracts averaged $1914. 97% of undergraduates work part time. Average annual earnings from campus work are $1500. Pepperdine is a member of CSS. The FAFSA, the college's own financial statement, the federal income tax form, state scholarship/grant form (California residents), and W-2 wage statements are required. The fall application deadline is February 15.

Computers: The mainframe is an IBM ES/9000 Model 210. 292 PCs are available to students in residence halls, computer labs, electronic classrooms, the library, and the student center. Access to the minicomputer and mainframe, the library system, and the Internet is available. Students may access the system anytime, with permission from the faculty. Word-processing labs are open to all students. There are no time limits and no fees.

PITZER COLLEGE
Claremont, CA 91711-6101

(909) 621-8129
(800) PITZER-1; Fax: (909) 621-8770

Full-time: 321 men, 535 women	**Faculty:** 60; IIB, ++$
Part-time: 17 men, 57 women	**Ph.D.s:** 99%
Graduate: none	**Student/Faculty:** 13 to 1
Year: semesters	**Tuition:** $24,096
Application Deadline: February 1	**Room & Board:** $6240
Freshman Class: 1680 applied, 1234 accepted, 246 enrolled	
SAT I Verbal/Math: 590/580	**ACT:** 23 **VERY COMPETITIVE**

Pitzer College, founded in 1963, is a private liberal arts college emphasizing the social and behavioral sciences. Some of the information in this profile is approximate. It is one of the Claremont Colleges. There are 5 undergraduate schools and

1 graduate school. The library contains 2 million volumes and 1.3 million microform items, and subscribes to 6000 periodicals. Computerized library services include the card catalog, interlibrary loans, and database searching. Special learning facilities include an art gallery, radio station, TV station, a social science lab, and an arboretum. The 30-acre campus is in a suburban area 35 miles east of Los Angeles. Including residence halls, there are 13 buildings.

Programs of Study: Pitzer confers the B.A. degree. Bachelor's degrees are awarded in BIOLOGICAL SCIENCE (biology/biological science), BUSINESS (management engineering and organizational behavior), COMMUNICATIONS AND THE ARTS (classics, dramatic arts, English, film arts, fine arts, folklore and mythology, French, German, linguistics, and Spanish), COMPUTER AND PHYSICAL SCIENCE (chemistry, mathematics, physics, and science), ENGINEERING AND ENVIRONMENTAL DESIGN (environmental science), SOCIAL SCIENCE (anthropology, Asian/Oriental studies, economics, European studies, history, international relations, Latin American studies, Mexican-American/Chicano studies, philosophy, psychobiology, psychology, sociology, and women's studies). Social and behavioral sciences are the strongest academically and are the largest.

Special: Students may cross-register at any of the other Claremont Colleges, or study abroad in Africa, Asia, Europe, Latin America, North America, or Oceania. There is an extensive freshman seminar program, and interdisciplinary study is offered in areas such as science and technology, education, chemical dependency, and international or intercultural studies. Joint advanced degrees are offered in math, business administration, and public policy. Dual concentrations are possible in most areas. There are independent study and limited pass/fail options.

Admissions: 73% of the 1999-2000 applicants were accepted. The SAT I scores for the 1999-2000 freshman class were: Verbal--13% below 500, 37% between 500 and 599, 37% between 600 and 700, and 13% above 700; Math--16% below 500, 41% between 500 and 599, 36% between 600 and 700, and 6% above 700. The ACT scores were 23% below 21, 28% between 21 and 23, 22% between 24 and 26, 16% between 27 and 28, and 11% above 28. 55% of the current freshmen were in the top fifth of their class; 79% were in the top two fifths.

Requirements: The SAT I or ACT is required. Applicants must be graduates of an accredited secondary school or have earned the GED. Secondary school courses must include 4 years of English courses requiring extensive writing, and 3 years each of social and behavioral sciences including history, lab science, foreign language, and math. A personal essay is required, and a personal interview is recommended. AP credits are accepted. Important factors in the admissions decision are advanced placement or honor courses, geographic diversity, and recommendations by school officials.

Procedure: Freshmen are admitted fall and spring. There are early admissions and deferred admissions plans. Early decision applications should be filed by December 1; regular applications, by February 1 for fall entry and October 15 for spring entry, along with a $40 fee. Notification of early decision is sent December 31; regular decision, April 1.

Financial Aid: In 1999-2000, 50% of all freshmen and 55% of continuing students received some form of financial aid. 46% of freshmen and 53% of continuing students received need-based aid. The average freshman award was $21,942. The average financial indebtedness of the 1999 graduate was $20,080. Pitzer is a member of CSS. The CSS/Profile or FAFSA is required. The fall application deadline is February 1.

Computers: The mainframes are a VAX 4000/200, VAXstation 3100, and 16 NeXT workstations. Macintosh and IBM PCs are available in labs. All students may access the system. There are no time limits and no fees.

POLYTECHNIC UNIVERSITY/FARMINGDALE
Farmingdale, NY 11735

(516) 755-4200
(800) POLYTEC; Fax: (516) 755-4229

Full-time: 314 men, 46 women	**Faculty:** 154
Part-time: 14 men	**Ph.D.s:** 94%
Graduate: 169 men, 41 women	**Student/Faculty:** 2 to 1
Year: semesters, summer session	**Tuition:** $20,810
Application Deadline: open	**Room & Board:** $5470
Freshman Class: 306 applied, 225 accepted, 107 enrolled	
SAT I Verbal/Math: 570/650	**VERY COMPETITIVE+**

Polytechnic University, founded in 1854, is a private university offering undergraduate and graduate programs through the divisions of arts and sciences, engineering, and management. There are 3 graduate schools. In addition to regional accreditation, Polytechnic University/Farmingdale has baccalaureate program accreditation with ABET. The library contains 35,000 volumes and 100 audiovisual forms/CDs, and subscribes to 110 periodicals. Computerized library services include the card catalog, interlibrary loans, and database searching. Special learning facilities include a learning resource center. The 25-acre campus is in a suburban area in the center of Long Island. Including residence halls, there are 6 buildings.

Programs of Study: Polytechnic University/Farmingdale confers the B.S. degree. Master's and doctoral degrees are also awarded. Bachelor's degrees are awarded in COMPUTER AND PHYSICAL SCIENCE (computer science and information sciences and systems), ENGINEERING AND ENVIRONMENTAL DESIGN (civil engineering, computer engineering, electrical/electronics engineering, and mechanical engineering). Engineering, management, and arts and sciences are the strongest academically. Electrical, and computer engineering are the largest.

Special: Cross-registration is permitted through a consortium of Long Island colleges. Opportunities are provided for internships, work-study programs, study abroad, accelerated degree programs in computer science and computer or electrical engineering, dual majors, student-designed majors, and nondegree study. There are 5 national honor societies, a freshman honors program, and 3 departmental honors programs.

Admissions: 74% of the 1999-2000 applicants were accepted. The SAT I scores for the 1999-2000 freshman class were: Verbal--24% below 500, 45% between 500 and 599, 27% between 600 and 700, and 4% above 700; Math--1% below 500, 27% between 500 and 599, 56% between 600 and 700, and 16% above 700.

Requirements: The SAT I is required. A minimum ACT score of 24 may be substituted for the SAT I results. Graduation from an accredited secondary school is required; a GED will be accepted. Applicants must submit a minimum of 16 credit hours, including 4 each in English, math, and science, and 1 each in foreign language, art, music, and social studies. SAT II: English composition, math I or II, and chemistry or physics are recommended. An essay and an interview are also recommended. Applications are accepted on-line at the school's web site. AP credits are accepted. Important factors in the admissions decision are advanced placement or honor courses, evidence of special talent, and leadership record.

Procedure: Freshmen are admitted fall, spring, and summer. Entrance exams should be taken by November of the senior year. There is a deferred admissions plan. Application deadlines are open. There is a $40 fee. Notification is sent on a rolling basis.

Financial Aid: In 1999-2000, 97% of all freshmen and 88% of continuing students received some form of financial aid. 78% of all students received need-based aid. The average freshman award was $18,250. Of that total, scholarships or need-based grants averaged $9865 ($20,210 maximum); loans averaged $3522 ($4625 maximum); and work contracts averaged $1500 ($2000 maximum). 16% of undergraduates work part time. Average annual earnings from campus work are $1500. The average financial indebtedness of the 1999 graduate was $10,991. Polytechnic University/Farmingdale is a member of CSS. The CSS/Profile and the college's own financial statement are required. The fall application deadline is February 1.

Computers: 58 Win NT4 Pentiums II are located in 3 labs, and additional facilities are available as part of the Engineering 101 lab. All students may access the system 15 hours a day. There are no time limits and no fees.

POMONA COLLEGE
Claremont, CA 91711
(909) 621-8134; Fax: (909) 621-8952

Full-time: 814 men, 719 women	**Faculty:** 155; IIB, ++$
Part-time: 10 men, 6 women	**Ph.D.s:** 100%
Graduate: none	**Student/Faculty:** 10 to 1
Year: semesters	**Tuition:** $22,940
Application Deadline: January 1	**Room & Board:** $7750
Freshman Class: 3612 applied, 1147 accepted, 390 enrolled	
SAT I Verbal/Math: 720/710	**ACT:** 31 MOST COMPETITIVE

Pomona College, the oldest and largest of the Claremont Colleges (a consortium of colleges), is an independent, national liberal arts and sciences institution founded in 1887. There are 5 undergraduate and 2 graduate schools. The 3 libraries contain 2,022,481 volumes, 1,382,687 microform items, and 777 audiovisual forms/CDs, and subscribe to 6624 periodicals. Computerized library services include the card catalog, interlibrary loans, and database searching. Special learning facilities include an art gallery, radio station, observatory, and modern languages and international relations center. The 140-acre campus is in a suburban area 35 miles east of Los Angeles. Including residence halls, there are 47 buildings.

Programs of Study: Pomona confers the B.A. degree. Bachelor's degrees are awarded in BIOLOGICAL SCIENCE (biology/biological science, molecular biology, and neurosciences), COMMUNICATIONS AND THE ARTS (art history and appreciation, Chinese, classics, dramatic arts, English, fine arts, French, German, Japanese, languages, linguistics, literature, media arts, music, Russian, Spanish, and studio art), COMPUTER AND PHYSICAL SCIENCE (chemistry, computer science, geology, mathematics, physics, and science), ENGINEERING AND ENVIRONMENTAL DESIGN (technology and public affairs), SOCIAL SCIENCE (African American studies, American studies, anthropology, Asian/Oriental studies, economics, German area studies, history, international relations, Latin American studies, philosophy, political science/government, psychology, public affairs, religion, sociology, and women's studies). Social sciences and sciences are the largest.

Special: Pomona offers cross-registration with any of the Claremont Colleges, study abroad in 22 countries, a Washington semester, dual and student-designed majors, internships, independent study, and pass/fail options. A 3-2 engineering program is offered with California Institute of Technology or Washington University in St. Louis. Students may study for 1 semester at Colby, Smith, Spelman, or Swarthmore Colleges. There are 9 national honor societies, including Phi Beta Kappa.

Admissions: 32% of the 1999-2000 applicants were accepted. The SAT I scores for the 1999-2000 freshman class were: Verbal--6% between 500 and 599, 29%

between 600 and 700, and 65% above 700; Math--4% between 500 and 599, 37% between 600 and 700, and 59% above 700. The ACT scores were 1% below 21, 1% between 21 and 23, 2% between 24 and 26, 3% between 27 and 28, and 94% above 28. 95% of the current freshmen were in the top fifth of their class; All were in the top two fifths. There were 41 National Merit finalists. 32 freshmen graduated first in their class.

Requirements: The SAT I or ACT is required. Although applicants need not be graduates of accredited high schools (some may be admitted after the junior year), most are, or have earned the GED. Secondary preparation must include 4 years of English, 3 each of math and foreign languages, and 2 each of lab and social sciences. An essay is required and an interview is strongly recommended. Applications are accepted on-line at CollegeLink, Apply, Common Application, and the College Board's "Next Stop College". AP credits are accepted. Important factors in the admissions decision are recommendations by school officials, leadership record, and recommendations by alumni.

Procedure: Freshmen are admitted in the fall. Entrance exams should be taken before December of the senior year. There are early decision, early admissions, and deferred admissions plans. Early decision applications should be filed by November 15; regular applications, by January 1 for fall entry, along with a $55 fee. Notification of early decision is sent December 15; regular decision, April 10. 82 early decision candidates were accepted for the 1999-2000 class. A waiting list is an active part of the admissions procedure.

Financial Aid: In 1999-2000, 49% of all freshmen and 52% of continuing students received some form of financial aid, including need-based aid. The average freshman award was $21,310. Of that total, scholarships or need-based grants averaged $16,500; loans averaged $3500; and work contracts averaged $2110. 65% of undergraduates work part time. Average annual earnings from campus work are $2000. The average financial indebtedness of the 1999 graduate was $15,800. Pomona is a member of CSS. The CSS/Profile or FAFSA and tax returns are required. The fall application deadline is February 1.

Computers: The mainframe is a DEC ALPHA. Students may access the mainframe computer at several public facilities and from dormitory rooms. Macs and PCs are available in public work areas. All students may access the system. There are no time limits and no fees.

PRATT INSTITUTE
Brooklyn, NY 11205

(718) 636-3669
(800) 331-0834; Fax: (718) 636-3670

Full-time: 1233 men, 1213 women	**Faculty:** 67; IIA, --$
Part-time: 166 men, 160 women	**Ph.D.s:** 64%
Graduate: 497 men, 852 women	**Student/Faculty:** 37 to 1
Year: 4-1-4, summer session	**Tuition:** $19,162
Application Deadline: February 1	**Room & Board:** $7762
Freshman Class: 3342 applied, 1586 accepted, 622 enrolled	
SAT I Verbal/Math: 570/580	**SPECIAL**

Pratt Institute, founded in 1887, is a private institution offering undergraduate and graduate programs in architecture, art and design education, art history, industrial, interior and communication design, fine arts, design management, arts and cultural management, writing for publication, performance and media, and professional studies. There are 2 undergraduate and 3 graduate schools. In addition to regional accreditation, Pratt has baccalaureate program accreditation with FIDER, NAAB, and NASAD. The library contains 208,000 volumes, 50,000 microform items, and 3500 audiovisual forms/CDs, and subscribes to 500 periodicals. Computerized library services include the card catalog and database searching. Special learning facilities include a learning resource center, art gallery, radio station, bronze foundry, and metal forge. The 25-acre campus is in an urban area 25 miles east of downtown Manhattan. Including residence halls, there are 23 buildings.

Programs of Study: Pratt confers B.Arch., B.F.A., B.I.D., and B.P.S. degrees. Associate and master's degrees are also awarded. Bachelor's degrees are awarded in COMMUNICATIONS AND THE ARTS (art history and appreciation, communications, creative writing, film arts, fine arts, industrial design, and photography), EDUCATION (art), ENGINEERING AND ENVIRONMENTAL DESIGN (architecture, computer graphics, construction management, and interior design), SOCIAL SCIENCE (fashion design and technology). Fine arts, industrial design, and communications design are the strongest academically. Architecture and communications design are the largest.

Special: Pratt offers co-op programs with the East Coast Consortium (art and design schools) and cross-registration with St. John's College and Queens College. Internships, study abroad in 4 countries, accelerated degree programs, work-study programs, dual majors, credit for work experience, nondegree study, and pass/fail options are available. There are 4 national honor societies.

Admissions: 47% of the 1999-2000 applicants were accepted. The SAT I scores for the 1999-2000 freshman class were: Verbal--33% below 500, 36% between 500 and 599, 28% between 600 and 700, and 2% above 700; Math--27% below 500, 35% between 500 and 599, 36% between 600 and 700, and 2% above 700.

Requirements: The SAT I or ACT is required. A GPA of 3.0 is required. SAT II: Subject tests in writing and mathematics level I or II are recommended for architecture applicants. Applicants must be graduates of an accredited secondary school. The GED is accepted. Students should have completed 4 years of English, 3 of math, and 2 each of science, social studies, and history. A portfolio is required, as is an interview for all applicants who live within 100 miles of Pratt. Applications are accepted on-line at the school's web site, www.pratt.edu. AP and CLEP credits are accepted. Important factors in the admissions decision are evidence of special talent, advanced placement or honor courses, and recommendations by school officials.

Procedure: Freshmen are admitted fall and spring. Entrance exams should be taken by November of the senior year. There is an early decision plan. Early decision applications should be filed by November 15; regular applications, by February 1 for fall entry and November 1 for spring entry, along with a $40 fee. Notification of early decision is sent December 1; regular decision, March 1. 30 early decision candidates were accepted for the 1999-2000 class. 5% of all applicants are on a waiting list.

Financial Aid: In a recent year, 95% of all freshmen and 75% of continuing students received some form of financial aid. 93% of freshmen and 70% of continuing students received need-based aid. The average freshman award was $13,985. Of that total, scholarships or need-based grants averaged $8155; loans averaged $3330; and work contracts averaged $2500. 30% of undergraduates work part time. Average annual earnings from campus work are $1200. Pratt is a member of CSS. The CSS/Profile or FAFSA, the college's own financial statement, and the parents' and student's tax returns are required. The fall application deadline is February 1.

Computers: The mainframe is a DEC VAX 6210. The mainframe may be reached via 12 VT340 terminals in the engineering lab or by dial-up modem. All students may access the system 24-hour access 7 days a week. There are no time limits and no fees. The school strongly recommends that all students have PCs.

PRESBYTERIAN COLLEGE
Clinton, SC 29325
(864) 833-8230
(800) 476-7272; Fax: (864) 833-8481

Full-time: 513 men, 569 women	**Faculty:** 77; IIB, av$
Part-time: 26 men, 13 women	**Ph.D.s:** 90%
Graduate: none	**Student/Faculty:** 14 to 1
Year: semesters, summer session	**Tuition:** $16,524
Application Deadline: open	**Room & Board:** $4650
Freshman Class: 995 applied, 808 accepted, 339 enrolled	
SAT I Verbal/Math: 562/565	**ACT:** 24 **VERY COMPETITIVE**

Presbyterian College, founded in 1880, is a private liberal arts institution affiliated with the Presbyterian Church (U.S.A.). In addition to regional accreditation, PC has baccalaureate program accreditation with AACSB and NCATE. The library contains 168,992 volumes, 13,831 microform items, and 6702 audiovisual forms/CDs, and subscribes to 785 periodicals. Computerized library services include the card catalog, interlibrary loans, and database searching. Special learning facilities include a learning resource center, art gallery, and radio station. The 220-acre campus is in a small town 40 miles south of Greenville. Including residence halls, there are 39 buildings.

Programs of Study: PC confers B.A. and B.S degrees. Bachelor's degrees are awarded in BIOLOGICAL SCIENCE (biology/biological science), BUSINESS (accounting and business administration and management), COMMUNICATIONS AND THE ARTS (English, fine arts, French, German, music, Spanish, and visual and performing arts), COMPUTER AND PHYSICAL SCIENCE (chemistry, mathematics, and physics), EDUCATION (elementary, music, secondary, and special), SOCIAL SCIENCE (economics, history, political science/government, psychology, religion, and sociology). Business, biology, and English are the largest.

Special: Educational internships, study abroad in 40 countries, and a Washington semester are available. Dual majors, work-study programs, accelerated degree programs, B.A.-B.S. degrees, and a 3-2 engineering degree with Auburn, Clemson, Vanderbilt, and Mercer universities are offered. There is a forestry environmental studies program with Duke University and a Christian education program with Presbyterian School of Christian Education. Credit for life, military, or work experience, auditing courses, and pass/fail options are possible. There are 9 national honor societies, a freshman honors program, and 26 departmental honors programs.

Admissions: 81% of the 1999-2000 applicants were accepted. The SAT I scores for the 1999-2000 freshman class were: Verbal--19% below 500, 43% between 500 and 599, 32% between 600 and 700, and 6% above 700; Math--19% below 500, 46% between 500 and 599, 31% between 600 and 700, and 4% above 700. The ACT scores were 24% below 21, 20% between 21 and 23, 30% between 24 and 26, 18% between 27 and 28, and 8% above 28. 65% of the current freshmen were in the top fifth of their class; 90% were in the top two fifths. 4 freshmen graduated first in their class.

Requirements: The SAT I or ACT is required. A GPA of 2.3 is required. In addition, applicants must be graduates of an accredited secondary school with 18 academic credits, including 4 years of English, 3 years of math, and 2 or more years each of foreign language, history, science, and social studies. The GED is accepted. An essay is required. For music scholarships, an audition is necessary. Applications are accepted on-line via the college's Web page: http://www.presby.edu. AP and CLEP credits are accepted. Important factors in the admissions decision are advanced placement or honor courses, recommendations by school officials, and leadership record.

Procedure: Freshmen are admitted to all sessions. Entrance exams should be taken during the spring of the junior year. There are early decision, early admissions, and deferred admissions plans. Application deadlines are open; the fee is $30. Notification of early decision is sent December 5; regular decision, on a rolling basis. 110 early decision candidates were accepted for the 1999-2000 class.

Financial Aid: In 1999-2000, 90% of all freshmen and 89% of continuing students received some form of financial aid. 70% of freshmen and 69% of continuing students received need-based aid. The average freshman award was $13,662. Of that total, scholarships or need-based grants averaged $8776 (full); loans averaged $4886 (full); and work contracts averaged $800 ($1500 maximum). 30% of undergraduates work part time. Average annual earnings from campus work are $800. The average financial indebtedness of the 1999 graduate was $13,623. The FAFSA and the college's own financial statement are required. The fall application deadline is March 1.

Computers: The mainframes are a Prime 2755 and a Data General Avion. There are 120 PCs in 3 labs, including IBMs and Macs. Software and printers, including laser printers, are available. Computer assistance is provided during open hours. All academic buildings, residence halls, classrooms, labs, and faculty offices are networked through the Internet/Bitnet and other national and international networks. E-mail is available. All students may access the system any time. There are no time limits and no fees.

PRINCETON UNIVERSITY
Princeton, NJ 08544-0430 (609) 258-3060; Fax: (609) 258-6743

Full-time: 2460 men, 2140 women	**Faculty:** 704; I, ++$
Part-time: none	**Ph.D.s:** 83%
Graduate: 1100 men, 630 women	**Student/Faculty:** 7 to 1
Year: semesters	**Tuition:** $24,700
Application Deadline: see profile	**Room & Board:** $7000
Freshman Class: 14,875 applied, 1689 accepted, 1165 enrolled	
SAT I: required	**MOST COMPETITIVE**

Princeton University, established in 1746, is a private institution offering degrees in the liberal arts and sciences, engineering, applied science, architecture, public and international affairs, interdisciplinary and regional studies, and the creative arts. Figures given in the above capsule are approximate. There are 4 graduate schools. In addition to regional accreditation, Princeton has baccalaureate program accreditation with ABET and NAAB. The 20 libraries contain 5 million volumes, 3 million microform items, and 52,000 audiovisual forms/CDs, and subscribe to 30,000 periodicals. Computerized library services include the card catalog. Special learning facilities include an art gallery, a natural history museum, a radio station, a music center, a visual and performing arts center, several theaters, an observatory, a plasma physics lab, and a center for environmental and energy studies. The 600-acre campus is in a small town 50 miles south of New York City. Including residence halls, there are 140 buildings.

Programs of Study: Princeton confers A.B. and B.S.E. degrees. Master's and doctoral degrees are also awarded. Bachelor's degrees are awarded in BIOLOGICAL SCIENCE (biology/biological science), COMMUNICATIONS AND THE ARTS (classics, comparative literature, English, Germanic languages and literature, music, romance languages and literature, and Slavic languages), COMPUTER AND PHYSICAL SCIENCE (astrophysics, chemistry, computer science, geology, mathematics, and physics), ENGINEERING AND ENVIRONMENTAL DESIGN (aeronautical engineering, architectural engineering, architecture, chemical engineering, civil engineering, electrical/electronics engineering, and mechanical engineering), SOCIAL SCIENCE (anthropology, archeology, East Asian studies, economics, history, international relations, Near Eastern studies, philosophy, political science/government, psychology, religion, and sociology). History, political science, and English are the largest.

Special: Princeton offers independent study, preceptorials, accelerated degree programs, a program in teacher preparation, student-proposed courses and majors, field study, study abroad, seminars, and internships in public affairs. The university operates on an honor code whereby exams are not proctored by faculty members. There are 2 national honor societies, including Phi Beta Kappa.

Admissions: 11% of the 1999-2000 applicants were accepted. The SAT I scores for the 1999-2000 freshman class were: Verbal--25% below 680, 50% between 680 and 770, and 25% above 770; Math--25% below 690, 50% between 690 and 770, and 25% above 770. 97% of the current freshmen were in the top fifth of their class.

Requirements: The SAT I is required. The ACT is accepted. SAT II: Subject tests are also required. Applicants must be graduates of an accredited secondary school. Recommended college preparatory courses include 4 years each of English, math, and a foreign language; 2 years each of lab science and history; and some study of art, music, and, if possible, a second foreign language. An essay is required and an interview is recommended. Fine arts majors should submit an audition tape or portfolio. AP credits are accepted.

Procedure: Freshmen are admitted in the fall. Entrance exams should be taken by January of the senior year. There are early decision, early admissions, and deferred admissions plans. Check with the school for current application deadlines and fees. 3% of all applicants are on a waiting list.

Financial Aid: In 1999-2000, about 75% of all students received some form of financial aid., including 44% from the university adn 31% from outside sources. 67% of undergraduates work part time. Princeton is a member of CSS. The CSS/Profile and the university's own financial statement are required. Check with the school for current deadlines.

Computers: The mainframe is an IBM 9672-RC4 system. There are also 450 PCs, including Macs and IBMs, connected to a central TigerNet system. NeXT, Silicon Graphics, Bitnet, and the Internet are available through Sun workstations. All residence hall rooms are wired through Dormnet, and specialized clusters on campus provide access to very high bandwidth resources. All students may access the system. There are no fees. The university recommends that all students have PCs.

PROVIDENCE COLLEGE
Providence, RI 02918

(401) 865-2535
(800) 721-6444; Fax: (401) 865-2826

Full-time: 1601 men, 2211 women	**Faculty:** 241; IIA, ++$
Part-time: 252 men, 441 women	**Ph.D.s:** 84%
Graduate: 345 men, 592 women	**Student/Faculty:** 16 to 1
Year: semesters, summer session	**Tuition:** $17,945
Application Deadline: January 15	**Room & Board:** $7355
Freshman Class: 5328 applied, 3181 accepted, 983 enrolled	
SAT I Verbal/Math: 589/587	**ACT:** 26 **VERY COMPETITIVE**

Providence College, founded in 1917, is a liberal arts and sciences institution operated by the Dominican Order of the Catholic Church. There is 1 graduate school. In addition to regional accreditation, Providence has baccalaureate program accreditation with CSWE and NCATE. The library contains 347,968 volumes, 27,882 microform items, and 5364 audiovisual forms/CDs, and subscribes to 1610 periodicals. Computerized library services include interlibrary loans and database searching. Special learning facilities include a learning resource center, art gallery, radio station, and Blackfriars Theatre. The 105-acre campus is in a suburban area 50 miles south of Boston. Including residence halls, there are 40 buildings.

Programs of Study: Providence confers B.A. and B.S. degrees. Master's and doctoral degrees are also awarded. Bachelor's degrees are awarded in BIOLOGICAL SCIENCE (biology/biological science), BUSINESS (accounting, banking and finance, business administration and management, business economics, and marketing/retailing/merchandising), COMMUNICATIONS AND THE ARTS (art history and appreciation, dramatic arts, English, fine arts, French, Italian, music, and Spanish), COMPUTER AND PHYSICAL SCIENCE (applied mathematics, chemistry, computer science, and mathematics), EDUCATION (elementary, secondary, and special), ENGINEERING AND ENVIRONMENTAL DESIGN (preengineering), HEALTH PROFESSIONS (health care administration), SOCIAL SCIENCE (American studies, community services, economics, history, humanities, Latin American studies, philosophy, political science/government, psychology, social science, social work, sociology, systems science, and theological studies). Biology, chemistry, and business are the strongest academically. Education, business, political science, and English are the largest.

Special: Providence offers cross-registration with Rhode Island School of Design, internships in politics, broadcasting, journalism, and business, and study abroad in Europe and Japan and through the New England-Quebec Exchange Program. Also available are B.A.-B.S. degrees in science majors, dual and student-designed majors, a 3-2 engineering degree with Columbia University or Washington University in St. Louis, nondegree study, and pass/fail options. There are 14 national honor societies and a freshman honors program.

Admissions: 60% of the 1999-2000 applicants were accepted. The SAT I scores for the 1999-2000 freshman class were: Verbal--8% below 500, 47% between 500 and 599, 40% between 600 and 700, and 5% above 700; Math--8% below 500, 47% between 500 and 599, 41% between 600 and 700, and 4% above 700. The ACT scores were 16% below 21, 30% between 21 and 23, 34% between 24 and 26, 6% between 27 and 28, and 14% above 28. 65% of the current freshmen were in the top fifth of their class; 94% were in the top two fifths. There were 41 National Merit semifinalists. 16 freshmen graduated first in their class.

Requirements: The SAT I or ACT is required. SAT II: Subject tests in writing and 2 others of the applicant's choice are recommended. Applicants must be

415

graduates of an accredited secondary school or have a GED certificate. A GPA of 3.0 is recommended. High school preparation should include 4 years of English, 3 years each of foreign language and math, and 2 years each of history, science, and social studies. An essay is required. Students may file applications online via CollegeLink. AP and CLEP credits are accepted. Important factors in the admissions decision are advanced placement or honor courses, leadership record, and extracurricular activities record.

Procedure: Freshmen are admitted fall and spring. Entrance exams should be taken in the junior or senior year. There are early decision, early admissions, and deferred admissions plans. Early decision applications should be filed by November 15; regular applications, by January 15 for fall entry and November 1 for spring entry, along with a $40 fee. Notification of early decision is sent January 1; regular decision, April 1. 441 early decision candidates were accepted for the 1999-2000 class. 13% of all applicants are on a waiting list.

Financial Aid: In a recent year, 79% of all freshmen and 73% of continuing students received some form of financial aid. 64% of freshmen and 62% of continuing students received need-based aid. The average freshman award was $12,225. Of that total, scholarships or need-based grants averaged $7000 ($16,350 maximum); loans averaged $4000 ($4625 maximum); and work contracts averaged $1600 ($2000 maximum). 66% of undergraduates work part time. Average annual earnings from campus work were $1525. The average financial indebtedness of the recent graduate was $19,000. Providence is a member of CSS. The CSS/Profile or FAFSA is required. The fall application deadline is February 1.

Computers: The mainframe is a Wang VS 8000. There are 8 computer labs equipped with 130 PCs for student use. All students have access to the Internet. All students may access the system. There are no time limits.

PURDUE UNIVERSITY/WEST LAFAYETTE
West Lafayette, IN 47907   (765) 494-1776; Fax: (765) 494-0544

Full-time: 16,414 men, 12,354 women	**Faculty:** 2023; I, av$
Part-time: 1083 men, 984 women	**Ph.D.s:** 85%
Graduate: 4186 men, 2741 women	**Student/Faculty:** 14 to 1
Year: semesters, summer session	**Tuition:** $3724 ($12,348)
Application Deadline: open	**Room & Board:** $5500
Freshman Class: 19,625 applied, 16,499 accepted, 6964 enrolled	
SAT I Verbal/Math: 540/562	**ACT:** 24 **COMPETITIVE**

Purdue University, founded in 1869, is a publicly supported institution offering degree programs with an emphasis on engineering, business, communications, arts, and social sciences. There are 12 undergraduate schools and 1 graduate school. In addition to regional accreditation, Purdue has baccalaureate program accreditation with AACSB, ABET, ACCE, ACPE, ADA, ASLA, NCATE, NLN, and SAF. The 15 libraries contain 2,280,681 volumes, 2,280,092 microform items, and 10,066 audiovisual forms/CDs, and subscribe to 19,025 periodicals. Computerized library services include the card catalog, interlibrary loans, and database searching. Special learning facilities include a learning resource center, art gallery, and radio station. The 1579-acre campus is in a suburban area 65 miles northwest of Indianapolis. Including residence halls, there are 145 buildings.

Programs of Study: Purdue confers B.A., B.S., B.P.E, B.S.A.A.E., B.S.A.B.E., B.S.A.G.E., B.S.C.E., B.S.C.E.E., B.S.C.E.M., B.S.Ch., B.S.Ch.E., B.S.C.M. P.E., B.S.E., B.S.E.E., B.S.E.H., B.S.F., B.S.I.E., B.S.I.E.D., B.S.I.M., B.S.L.A., B.S.L.S., B.S.L.S.E., B.S.M.E., B.S.M.S.E., B.S.N.E., and B.S.Pharm. degrees.

Associate, master's, and doctoral degrees are also awarded. Bachelor's degrees are awarded in AGRICULTURE (agricultural business management, agricultural economics, agricultural mechanics, agriculture, agronomy, animal science, conservation and regulation, forestry and related sciences, horticulture, natural resource management, plant protection (pest management), and wildlife management), BIOLOGICAL SCIENCE (biochemistry, biology/biological science, entomology, and nutrition), BUSINESS (accounting, hotel/motel and restaurant management, management science, office supervision and management, recreation and leisure services, and retailing), COMMUNICATIONS AND THE ARTS (art history and appreciation, classics, communications, crafts, design, dramatic arts, English, film arts, fine arts, German, industrial design, journalism, languages, linguistics, media arts, photography, and Russian), COMPUTER AND PHYSICAL SCIENCE (actuarial science, atmospheric sciences and meteorology, chemistry, computer science, earth science, geology, information sciences and systems, mathematics, physics, science, and statistics), EDUCATION (agricultural, art, athletic training, educational media, elementary, English, foreign languages, health, industrial arts, mathematics, physical, science, secondary, social studies, and special), ENGINEERING AND ENVIRONMENTAL DESIGN (aeronautical engineering, aeronautical technology, agricultural engineering, biomedical engineering, chemical engineering, civil engineering, computer engineering, computer graphics, computer technology, construction engineering, construction technology, electrical/electronics engineering, electrical/electronics engineering technology, engineering, graphic arts technology, industrial administration/management, industrial engineering, industrial engineering technology, interior design, landscape architecture/design, materials engineering, mechanical engineering, mechanical engineering technology, nuclear engineering, preengineering, and surveying engineering), HEALTH PROFESSIONS (community health work, health science, medical technology, nursing, predentistry, premedicine, prepharmacy, and speech pathology/audiology), SOCIAL SCIENCE (African American studies, American studies, anthropology, child care/child and family studies, economics, food science, history, liberal arts/general studies, medieval studies, philosophy, political science/government, prelaw, psychology, religion, and sociology). Engineering, actuarial science, and industrial management are the strongest academically. Management, preengineering, and mechanical engineering are the largest.

Special: Cooperative programs are available in engineering, technology, agriculture, management, science, and consumer and family sciences. Cross-registration with Purdue's regional campuses, numerous internships, study abroad in 41 countries, dual majors, student-designed majors, nondegree study, and pass/fail options are also offered. There are 14 national honor societies, including Phi Beta Kappa, a freshman honors program, and 10 departmental honors programs.

Admissions: 84% of the 1999-2000 applicants were accepted. The SAT I scores for the 1999-2000 freshman class were: Verbal--30% below 500, 45% between 500 and 599, 21% between 600 and 700, and 4% above 700; Math--25% below 500, 39% between 500 and 599, 28% between 600 and 700, and 8% above 700. The ACT scores were 19% below 21, 25% between 21 and 23, 31% between 24 and 26, 13% between 27 and 28, and 12% above 28. 42% of the current freshmen were in the top fifth of their class; 71% were in the top two fifths. 185 freshmen graduated first in their class.

Requirements: The SAT I or ACT is required. Purdue recommends that most students have 15 semester credits, including 4 years of English, 3 to 4 of math, and 2 to 4 of lab science. The GED is accepted. Applications are accepted online. AP and CLEP credits are accepted. Important factors in the admissions decision are advanced placement or honor courses, recommendations by school officials, and parents or siblings attending the school.

Procedure: Freshmen are admitted to all sessions. Entrance exams should be taken at the end of the junior year. Application deadlines are open; the fee is $30. Notification is sent on a rolling basis.

Financial Aid: In a recent year, 58% of all freshmen and 50% of continuing students received some form of financial aid. 46% of freshmen and 40% of continuing students received need-based aid. The average freshman award was $9547. Of that total, scholarships or need-based grants averaged $2037 ($5700 maximum); loans averaged $7375; and work contracts averaged $136 ($1600 maximum). 34% of undergraduates work part time. Average annual earnings from campus work are $1259. The average financial indebtedness of the recent graduate was $13,783. Purdue is a member of CSS. The FAFSA is required. The fall application deadline is March 1.

Computers: Central computer services are provided on a variety of servers that include about 20 models of the IBM RS/6000 class, about 15 models of the Sun Enterprise 4000 family, an IBM SP2 machine, and an Intel Paragon. Students may access central computing facilities through approximately 80 lab locations containing about 2100 workstations (Windows, Mac, and Unix.) Direct network connections are also available in each residence hall room. Students are granted a career account that provides e-mail and Internet services during their entire time at Purdue. All students may access the system 24 hours daily. There are no time limits and no fees.

RAMAPO COLLEGE OF NEW JERSEY
Mahwah, NJ 07430

(201) 529-7600
(800) 9-RAMAPO; Fax: (201) 529-7603

Full-time: 1361 men, 1688 women	**Faculty:** 143; IIB, ++$
Part-time: 627 men, 979 women	**Ph.D.s:** n/av
Graduate: 69 men, 144 women	**Student/Faculty:** 21 to 1
Year: semesters, summer session	**Tuition:** $4980 ($7846)
Application Deadline: March 1	**Room & Board:** $6624
Freshman Class: 2705 applied, 1276 accepted, 536 enrolled	
SAT I Verbal/Math: 540/550	**VERY COMPETITIVE**

Ramapo College, founded in 1971, is a public institution offering undergraduate programs in the arts and sciences, American and international studies, business administration, and human services. Personal interaction is incorporated throughout the curriculum as is an international, multicultural component including telecommunications and computer technology. There are 5 undergraduate and 3 graduate schools. In addition to regional accreditation, Ramapo has baccalaureate program accreditation with NLN. The library contains 158,615 volumes, 975 microform items, and 19,057 audiovisual forms/CDs, and subscribes to 910 periodicals. Computerized library services include the card catalog, interlibrary loans, and database searching. Special learning facilities include an art gallery, radio station, and international telecommunications satellite center. The 314-acre campus is in a suburban area 25 miles northwest of New York City. Including residence halls, there are 46 buildings.

Programs of Study: Ramapo confers B.A., B.S., B.S.N., and B.S.W. degrees. Master's degrees are also awarded. Bachelor's degrees are awarded in BIOLOGICAL SCIENCE (biochemistry and biology/biological science), BUSINESS (accounting, business administration and management, and international business management), COMMUNICATIONS AND THE ARTS (communications, fine arts, and literature), COMPUTER AND PHYSICAL SCIENCE (chemistry, computer science, information sciences and systems, mathematics, and physics), ENGINEERING AND ENVIRONMENTAL DESIGN (environmental science), HEALTH PROFESSIONS (clinical science and nursing), SOCIAL SCIENCE (American studies, economics, history, human ecology, international studies, law, political science/government, psychology, social science, social work, and sociology). Accounting, nursing, and marketing are the strongest academically. Business administration, psychology, and communications are the largest.

Special: Ramapo's curriculum emphasizes the interdependence of global society and includes an international dimension in all academic programs. Students may study abroad in 6 countries. Cooperative programs are available with various corporations and in 12 foreign countries. Cross-registration is possible with local state colleges. Ramapo also offers a winter session, accelerated degree programs, dual, student-designed, and interdisciplinary majors (including law and society), credit for life experience, pass/fail options, and nondegree study. There are 6 national honor societies, a freshman honors program, and a centralized honor society.

Admissions: 47% of the 1999-2000 applicants were accepted. The SAT I scores for the 1999-2000 freshman class were: Verbal--27% below 500, 51% between 500 and 599, 20% between 600 and 700, and 2% above 700; Math--25% below 500, 53% between 500 and 599, 20% between 600 and 700, and 2% above 700. 36% of the current freshmen were in the top fifth of their class; 76% were in the top two fifths.

Requirements: The SAT I is required. A GPA of 3.0 is required. Applicants must be graduates of accredited secondary schools or have earned a GED. The college requires 16 academic credits, including 4 in English, 3 in math, 2 each in science and social studies, and the remaining 5 in academic electives. Students are encouraged to take 2 years of a foreign language. Students must also submit an essay. An interview is recommended. Applications are accepted on computer disk. AP and CLEP credits are accepted. Important factors in the admissions decision are advanced placement or honor courses, recommendations by school officials, and evidence of special talent.

Procedure: Freshmen are admitted fall and spring. There are early decision and deferred admissions plans. Applications should be filed by March 1 for fall entry and December 1 for spring entry, along with a $45 fee. Notification is sent on a rolling basis.

Financial Aid: In 1999-2000, 47% of all freshmen and 44% of continuing students received some form of financial aid. 40% of freshmen and 36% of continuing students received need-based aid. The average freshman award was $6703. Of that total, scholarships or need-based grants averaged $6295; loans averaged $2203; and work contracts averaged $1348. 93% of undergraduates work part time. Average annual earnings from campus work are $1800. The average financial indebtedness of the 1999 graduate was $11,498. The FAFSA is required. The fall application deadline is March 15.

Computers: The mainframe is a DEC 5500 running UNIX. In addition, 250 PCs are located in the residence halls, the computing lab, and the library. All students may access the system according to a posted schedule. There are no time limits and no fees.

RANDOLPH-MACON WOMAN'S COLLEGE
Lynchburg, VA 24503　　　　　　　　　　　　　　(804) 947-8100
(800) 745-7692; Fax: (804) 947-8996

Full-time: 669 women	**Faculty:** 73; IIB, av$
Part-time: 5 men, 36 women	**Ph.D.s:** 93%
Graduate: none	**Student/Faculty:** 9 to 1
Year: semesters	**Tuition:** $17,080
Application Deadline: February 15	**Room & Board:** $7010
Freshman Class: 719 applied, 604 accepted, 201 enrolled	
SAT I Verbal/Math: 600/560	**ACT:** 27　**VERY COMPETITIVE**

Randolph-Macon Woman's College, founded in 1891, is an independent, liberal arts institution affiliated with the United Methodist Church. In addition to regional accreditation, R-MWC has baccalaureate program accreditation with NASDT-EC. The library contains 167,900 volumes, 175,150 microform items, and 1400 audiovisual forms/CDs, and subscribes to 850 periodicals. Computerized library services include the card catalog, interlibrary loans, and database searching. Special learning facilities include a learning resource center, an art gallery, a radio station, an observatory, an art museum, 2 theaters, and 3 nature preserves. The 100-acre campus is in a suburban area in the foothills of the Blue Ridge Mountains, 1 hour south of Charlottesville. Including residence halls, there are 18 buildings.

Programs of Study: R-MWC confers B.A. and B.S. degrees. Bachelor's degrees are awarded in BIOLOGICAL SCIENCE (biology/biological science), COMMUNICATIONS AND THE ARTS (art, classics, communications, dance, dramatic arts, English, French, German, music, and Spanish), COMPUTER AND PHYSICAL SCIENCE (chemistry, mathematics, and physics), SOCIAL SCIENCE (economics, history, international relations, philosophy, political science/government, psychology, religion, Russian and Slavic studies, and sociology). Psychology, English, politics, sciences, and communications are the largest.

Special: R-MWC offers a junior year spring semester American Culture Program, as well as study abroad in 7 countries. A Washington semester at American University is available, as is cross-registration with Sweet Briar and Lynchburg colleges, and through the Tri-College Cnsortium and the Seven-College Exchange Program with Hampden-Sydney, Hollins, Mary Baldwin, Randolph-Macon, and Sweet Briar colleges, and Washington and Lee University. There are 3-2 nursing programs with Johns Hopkins and Vanderbilt universities and an accelerated program in public health with the University of Rochester School of Medicine and Dentistry. There are 5 national honor societies, including Phi Beta Kappa.

Admissions: 84% of the 1999-2000 applicants were accepted. The SAT I scores for the 1999-2000 freshman class were: Verbal--12% below 500, 35% between 500 and 599, 40% between 600 and 700, and 13% above 700; Math--23% below 500, 43% between 500 and 599, 31% between 600 and 700, and 3% above 700. The ACT scores were 3% below 21, 14% between 21 and 23, 29% between 24 and 26, 25% between 27 and 28, and 29% above 28. 62% of the current freshmen were in the top fifth of their class; 89% were in the top two fifths. 2 freshmen graduated first in their class.

Requirements: The SAT I or ACT is required. In addition, applicants must be graduates of an accredited secondary school with at least 16 academic credits, including 4 units in English, 3 to 4 in a foreign language, 3 in math, 2 in biology, chemistry, or physics with lab work, and 1 to 2 in electives from other academic study. An interview is strongly recommended. Applications are available on-line and are accepted on computer disk. AP and CLEP credits are accepted. Important factors in the admissions decision are advanced placement or honor courses, recommendations by school officials, and leadership record.

Procedure: Freshmen are admitted fall and spring. Entrance exams should be taken in the junior or senior year. There are early decision, early admissions, and deferred admissions plans. Early decision applications should be filed by November 15; regular applications, by February 15 for fall entry and December 1 for spring entry, along with a $25 fee. Notification of early decision is sent December 15; regular decision, on a rolling basis. 23 early decision candidates were accepted for the 1999-2000 class.

Financial Aid: In 1999-2000, all freshmen and 98% of continuing students received some form of financial aid. 62% of freshmen and 56% of continuing students received need-based aid. The average freshman award was $16,685. Of that total, scholarships or need-based grants averaged $11,370 ($17,875 maximum); loans averaged $3535 ($4625 maximum); and work contracts averaged $1780 ($1860 maximum). 61% of undergraduates work part time. Average annual earnings from campus work are $1090. The average financial indebtedness of the 1999 graduate was $13,171. R-MWC is a member of CSS. The FAFSA is required. The fall application deadline is March 1.

Computers: Students may access 90 PC and 20 Mac computers, all networked and software equipped, in several cluster locations on campus. All dorm rooms are also networked, and the campuswide information system provides access to global E-mail services and other information resources. Multimedia computers in the science building integrate and display digital video, audio, and text information on large display screens. Students have access to course schedules, grades, unofficial transcripts, financial aid, and billing information via the Web. All students may access the system. There are no time limits and no fees.

REED COLLEGE
Portland, OR 97202-8199

(503) 777-7511
(800) 547-4750; Fax: (503) 777-7553

Full-time: 598 men, 689 women	**Faculty:** 107; IIB, +$
Part-time: 28 men, 38 women	**Ph.D.s:** 85%
Graduate: 11 men, 9 women	**Student/Faculty:** 12 to 1
Year: semesters	**Tuition:** $24,050
Application Deadline: January 15	**Room & Board:** $6650
Freshman Class: 2018 applied, 1376 accepted, 337 enrolled	
SAT I Verbal/Math: 690/660	**ACT:** 29 **HIGHLY COMPETITIVE+**

Reed College, founded in 1908, is a private, nonsectarian institution offering programs in liberal arts and sciences and emphasizing instruction through small conference-style classes. There is 1 graduate school. The library contains 438,119 volumes, 229,485 microform items, and 14,543 audiovisual forms/CDs, and subscribes to 1621 periodicals. Computerized library services include the card catalog, interlibrary loans, and database searching. Special learning facilities include a learning resource center, art gallery, and radio station. The 100-acre campus is in an urban area in Portland. Including residence halls, there are 36 buildings.

Programs of Study: Reed confers the B.A. degree. Master's degrees are also awarded. Bachelor's degrees are awarded in BIOLOGICAL SCIENCE (biochemistry, biology/biological science, and molecular biology), COMMUNICATIONS AND THE ARTS (Chinese, classics, dance, dramatic arts, English, fine arts, French, German, linguistics, literature, music, Russian, and Spanish), COMPUTER AND PHYSICAL SCIENCE (chemistry, mathematics, and physics), SO-

CIAL SCIENCE (American studies, anthropology, economics, history, international studies, philosophy, political science/government, psychology, religion, and sociology). Biology is the largest.

Special: Cross-registration is available through the Oregon Independent Colleges organization. Also available are 3-2 engineering degrees with California Institute of Technology, Columbia University, and Rensselaer Polytechnic Institute, combined 3-2 programs in science, programs with the Pacific Northwest College of Art, and business programs with the university of Oregon. Study abroad in 6 countries, a domestic exchange program with Howard University in Washington, D.C., accelerated degree programs, dual majors, student-designed majors, numerous interdisciplinary majors, nondegree study, and pass/fail options are also offered. There is a chapter of Phi Beta Kappa.

Admissions: 68% of the 1999-2000 applicants were accepted. The SAT I scores for the 1999-2000 freshman class were: Verbal--1% below 500, 7% between 500 and 599, 43% between 600 and 700, and 49% above 700; Math--1% below 500, 19% between 500 and 599, 52% between 600 and 700, and 28% above 700. 72% of the current freshmen were in the top fifth of their class; 95% were in the top two fifths. There were 11 National Merit finalists. 19 freshmen graduated first in their class.

Requirements: The SAT I is required. The SAT II: Subject test in writing is recommended. Reed strongly recommends that applicants have 4 years of English, 3 each of math and science, and 2 each of foreign language, history, and social studies. An essay is required, and an interview is recommended. The GED is accepted. Applications are accepted on-line. AP credits are accepted. Important factors in the admissions decision are advanced placement or honor courses, personality/intangible qualities, and evidence of special talent.

Procedure: Freshmen are admitted fall; they are also admitted in the spring when space is available. There are early decision, early admissions, and deferred admissions plans. Early decision applications should be filed by November 15; regular applications, by January 15 for fall entry, along with a $40 fee. Notification of early decision is sent December 15; regular decision, April 1. 108 early decision candidates were accepted for the 1999-2000 class.

Financial Aid: In 1999-2000, 42% of all freshmen and 48% of continuing students received need-based aid or soe form of financial aid. The average freshman award was $18,282. Of that total, scholarships or need-based grants averaged $17,590 ($28,550 maximum); loans averaged $2500 (maximum); and work contracts averaged $600 ($1500 maximum). 56% of undergraduates work part time. Average annual earnings from campus work are $1640. The average financial indebtedness of the 1999 graduate was $14,010. Reed is a member of CSS. The CSS/Profile or FAFSA, the college's own financial statement, and parent and student federal tax forms are required. The fall application deadline is March 1.

Computers: The mainframes are DEC ALPHA servers with Sun and NT boxes. There are more than 800 Macs available. Various labs and workstations offer UNIX workstations and servers. The entire campus is networked with fiber-optic cable, and there is network access in each residence hall room. The library is also accessible on-line. All students may access the system 24 hours daily. There are no time limits and no fees.

REGIS UNIVERSITY
Denver, CO 80221-1099   **(303) 458-4900**
(800) 388-2366, ext. 4900; Fax: (303) 964-5534

Full-time: 466 men, 556 women	**Faculty:** 68
Part-time: none	**Ph.D.s:** 95%
Graduate: none	**Student/Faculty:** 15 to 1
Year: semesters, summer session	**Tuition:** $16,670
Application Deadline: open	**Room & Board:** $6700
Freshman Class: 1331 applied, 1121 accepted, 298 enrolled	
SAT I Verbal/Math: 564/562	**ACT:** 24 **VERY COMPETITIVE**

Regis University, founded in 1877, is a private, Roman Catholic liberal arts institution operated by the Jesuits. There are 3 undergraduate schools. In addition to regional accreditation, Regis has baccalaureate program accreditation with CAHEA, NCATE, and NLN. The library contains 420,799 volumes, 136,379 microform items, and 104,698 audiovisual forms/CDs, and subscribes to 3979 periodicals. Computerized library services include the card catalog, interlibrary loans, and database searching. Special learning facilities include a learning resource center and radio station. The 90-acre campus is in a suburban area in North Denver. Including residence halls, there are 12 buildings.

Programs of Study: Regis confers B.A., B.S., and B.S.N. degrees. Master's degrees are also awarded. Bachelor's degrees are awarded in BIOLOGICAL SCIENCE (biochemistry, biology/biological science, and neurosciences), BUSINESS (accounting, business administration and management, business economics, international business management, and marketing/retailing/merchandising), COMMUNICATIONS AND THE ARTS (communications, English, French, and Spanish), COMPUTER AND PHYSICAL SCIENCE (chemistry, computer science, and mathematics), ENGINEERING AND ENVIRONMENTAL DESIGN (engineering), HEALTH PROFESSIONS (medical records administration/services and nursing), SOCIAL SCIENCE (economics, history, philosophy, political science/government, prelaw, psychology, religion, and sociology). Business is the largest.

Special: Cross-registration is possible with Denver University and Metropolitan State. Internships, study abroad, and work-study programs with Regis are available. The college offers B.A.-B.S. degrees, dual majors, student-designed majors, a 3-2 engineering degree with Washington University, and pass/fail options. There is 1 national honor society and a freshman honors program.

Admissions: 84% of the 1999-2000 applicants were accepted. The SAT I scores for the 1999-2000 freshman class were: Verbal--17% below 500, 52% between 500 and 599, 24% between 600 and 700, and 7% above 700; Math--23% below 500, 46% between 500 and 599, 25% between 600 and 700, and 6% above 700. The ACT scores were 13% below 21, 33% between 21 and 23, 27% between 24 and 26, 13% between 27 and 28, and 14% above 28. 40% of the current freshmen were in the top fifth of their class; 63% were in the top two fifths. 8 freshmen graduated first in their class.

Requirements: The SAT I or ACT is required. A GPA of 2.2 is required. Applicants should be graduates of an accredited secondary school. The GED is accepted. Students should have completed 16 high school academic credits, including 4 years of English, 3 each of math, science, and history, 2 of a foreign language, and 1 to 2 of social studies. A recommendation from the high school counselor and an essay are required. An interview is recommended. Applications are accepted on-line or on computer disk. AP and CLEP credits are accepted. Important factors in the admissions decision are recommendations by school officials, leadership record, and extracurricular activities record.

Procedure: Freshmen are admitted fall and spring. Entrance exams should be taken in the fall. There is a deferred admissions plan. Application deadlines are open; the fee is $40. Notification is sent on a rolling basis. 3% of all applicants are on a waiting list.

Financial Aid: In a recent year, 72% of all students received some form of financial aid. 63% of freshmen and 65% of continuing students received need-based aid. 51% of undergraduates work part time. Average annual earnings from campus work are $1750. The average financial indebtedness of the 1999 graduate was $15,500. The FAFSA and the college's own financial statement are required. The fall application deadline is March 15.

Computers: The mainframe is a DEC VAX 11/785. The mainframe and PCs systems are available 24 hours a day in the computer labs. All students may access the system. There are no time limits and no fees. The school strongly recommends that all students have their own personal computers.

RENSSELAER POLYTECHNIC INSTITUTE
Troy, NY 12180-3590 (518) 276-6216
(800) 448-6562; Fax: (518) 276-4072

Full-time: 3696 men, 1154 women	**Faculty:** 357; I, ++$
Part-time: 12 men, 5 women	**Ph.D.s:** 99%
Graduate: 1303 men, 496 women	**Student/Faculty:** 14 to 1
Year: semesters, summer session	**Tuition:** $22,955
Application Deadline: January 1	**Room & Board:** $7380
Freshman Class: 5264 applied, 4126 accepted, 1323 enrolled	
SAT I Verbal/Math: 614/667	**ACT:** 27 **HIGHLY COMPETITIVE**

Rensselaer Polytechnic Institute, founded in 1824, is a private institution that emphasizes technology in its Schools of Engineering, Architecture, Management, Humanities, Social Sciences, and Science. There are 5 undergraduate and 5 graduate schools. In addition to regional accreditation, Rensselaer has baccalaureate program accreditation with AACSB, ABET, and NAAB. The 2 libraries contain 309,171 volumes, 615,477 microform items, and 4697 audiovisual forms/CDs, and subscribe to 3283 periodicals. Computerized library services include the card catalog, interlibrary loans, and database searching. Special learning facilities include a learning resource center, art gallery, radio station, and observatory. The 262-acre campus is in a suburban area 10 miles north of Albany. Including residence halls, there are 185 buildings.

Programs of Study: Rensselaer confers B.S. and B.Arch. degrees. Master's and doctoral degrees are also awarded. Bachelor's degrees are awarded in BIOLOGICAL SCIENCE (biochemistry, biology/biological science, and biophysics), BUSINESS (management information systems and management science), COMMUNICATIONS AND THE ARTS (communications and media arts), COMPUTER AND PHYSICAL SCIENCE (chemistry, computer science, geology, mathematics, physics, and science technology), ENGINEERING AND ENVIRONMENTAL DESIGN (aeronautical engineering, architecture, biomedical engineering, chemical engineering, civil engineering, computer engineering, construction engineering, electrical/electronics engineering, engineering, engineering physics, environmental engineering, industrial engineering, materials engineering, mechanical engineering, and nuclear engineering), HEALTH PROFESSIONS (predentistry and premedicine), SOCIAL SCIENCE (economics, interdisciplinary studies, philosophy, prelaw, and psychology). Mechanical engineering, electrical engineering, and computer and systems engineering are the strongest academically. General engineering, management, and computer science are the largest.

Special: Rensselaer offers an exchange program with Williams and Harvey Mudd Colleges and cross-registration with 15 regional colleges and universities. Co-op programs, internships, study abroad in several countries, and pass/fail options are available. Students may pursue dual and student-designed majors, a 3-2 engineering degree, and accelerated 4-year B.S.-M.S. degrees in engineering, computer science, geophysics, and math. Continuing education programs are broadcast via TV satellite to various industrial locations. There are 14 national honor societies and 3 departmental honors programs.

Admissions: 78% of the 1999-2000 applicants were accepted. The SAT I scores for the 1999-2000 freshman class were: Verbal--6% below 500, 34% between 500 and 599, 46% between 600 and 700, and 14% above 700; Math--15% between 500 and 599, 51% between 600 and 700, and 34% above 700. The ACT scores were 18% between 18 and 23, 68% between 24 and 29, and 14% above 30. 79% of the current freshmen were in the top fifth of their class; 96% were in the top two fifths. 101 freshmen graduated first in their class.

Requirements: The SAT I or ACT is required. In addition, SAT II: Subject tests in writing, math (level I, IC, II, or IIC), and chemistry or physics are recommended (required for accelerated-program applicants). Applicants must be graduates of an accredited secondary school and have completed 4 years each of English, math (through precalculus), and science (including chemistry and physics), and 3 years of social studies. An essay is required. Architecture applicants must submit a portfolio. Rensselaer offers its application for use on PC systems; an application can be accessed on-line from the school's web site. AP credits are accepted. Important factors in the admissions decision are advanced placement or honor courses, recommendations by school officials, and leadership record.

Procedure: Freshmen are admitted fall and spring. Entrance exams should be taken in the junior and/or senior year. There are early decision, early admissions, and deferred admissions plans. Early decision applications should be filed by November 15; regular applications, by January 1 for fall entry and November 1 for spring entry, along with a $50 fee. Notification of early decision is sent 3 weeks after the application is received; regular decision, March 15. 133 early decision candidates were accepted for the 1999-2000 class.

Financial Aid: In 1999-2000, 86% of all students received some form of financial aid. 60% of freshmen and 62% of continuing students received need-based aid. The average freshman award was $19,375. Of that total, scholarships or need-based grants averaged $14,961; loans averaged $3432; and work contracts averaged $981. 24% of undergraduates work part time. Average annual earnings from campus work are $740. The average financial indebtedness of the 1999 graduate was $22,300. Rensselaer is a member of CSS. The FAFSA is required. The fall application deadline is February 15.

Computers: The mainframe is an IBM ES/9000. There are several PC labs on campus as well as sites in the dormitories. Students use more than 720 networked workstations. All students may access the system. There are no time limits and no fees. The school requires all studetns to have an IBM ThinkPaqd 600E or equivalent.

RHODE ISLAND SCHOOL OF DESIGN
Providence, RI 02903

(401) 454-6300
(800) 364-7473; Fax: (401) 454-6309

Full-time: 840 men, 1000 women	**Faculty:** 143; IIB, ++$
Part-time: none	**Ph.D.s:** n/av
Graduate: 100 men, 130 women	**Student/Faculty:** 12 to 1
Year: 4-1-4	**Tuition:** $21,405
Application Deadline: December 15	**Room & Board:** $6490
Freshman Class: n/av	
SAT I: required	**SPECIAL**

Rhode Island School of Design, founded in 1877, is a private institution offering degree programs in fine arts, design, and architecture. Figures given in the above capsule are approximate. In addition to regional accreditation, RISD has baccalaureate program accreditation with ASLA, NAAB, and NASAD. The library contains 90,000 volumes and 780 audiovisual forms/CDs, and subscribes to 360 periodicals. Computerized library services include the card catalog, interlibrary loans, and database searching. Special learning facilities include an art gallery, art museum, and nature lab. The 13-acre campus is in an urban area 50 miles south of Boston, Massachusetts. Including residence halls, there are 41 buildings.

Programs of Study: RISD confers B.Arch., B.F.A., B.G.D., B.I.D., B.Int.Arch., and B.Land.Arch. degrees. Master's degrees are also awarded. Bachelor's degrees are awarded in COMMUNICATIONS AND THE ARTS (apparel design, ceramic art and design, design, film arts, glass, graphic design, illustration, industrial design, metal/jewelry, painting, photography, printmaking, and sculpture), EDUCATION (art), ENGINEERING AND ENVIRONMENTAL DESIGN (architecture, furniture design, interior design, and landscape architecture/design), SOCIAL SCIENCE (textiles and clothing). Illustration, graphic design, and architecture are the largest.

Special: RISD offers cross-registration with Brown University and through the AICAD mobility program, credit or noncredit summer programs, 6-week internships during the midyear winter session, and study abroad in 17 countries and through the senior-year European Honors Program in Rome.

Requirements: The SAT I is required; the ACT may be substituted. Applicants must be graduates of an accredited secondary school or have a GED. An essay, assigned drawings, and a portfolio (optional for architecture majors) are also required. AP credits are accepted. Important factors in the admissions decision are evidence of special talent, advanced placement or honor courses, and personality/intangible qualities.

Procedure: Freshmen are admitted fall and spring. Entrance exams should be taken at least 6 weeks before the application deadline. There are early admissions and deferred admissions plans. Applications should be filed by December 15 for fall entry and January 21 for spring entry, along with a $35 fee. 13% of all applicants are on a waiting list. Notification is sent by the last week of January for those who applied by December 15, or the first week of April, for those who filed in January.

Financial Aid: In a recent year, 56% of all freshmen and 61% of continuing students received some form of financial aid. 55% of freshmen and 60% of continuing students received need-based aid. The average freshman award was $12,453. Of that total, scholarships or need-based grants averaged $9129 ($20,500 maximum); loans averaged $2625 ($7375 maximum); and work contracts averaged $1100. 57% of undergraduates work part time. Average annual earnings from campus work are $1100. The average financial indebtedness of a recent graduate was $19,000. RISD is a member of CSS. The CSS/Profile, FAFSA, and parents' income tax returns are required. The fall application deadline is February 15.

Computers: There are more than 300 Macs, IBM, Silicon Graphic, and other workstations located in the computer center and various departments. All students have access to the Internet and Web. All students may access the system. There are no time limits and no fees.

RHODES COLLEGE
Memphis, TN 38112

(901) 843-3700
(800) 844-5969; Fax: (901) 843-3719

Full-time: 674 men, 811 women	**Faculty:** 121; IIB, ++$
Part-time: 8 men, 6 women	**Ph.D.s:** 99%
Graduate: 7 men, 4 women	**Student/Faculty:** 12 to 1
Year: semesters, summer session	**Tuition:** $18,719
Application Deadline: February 1	**Room & Board:** $5454
Freshman Class: 2247 applied, 1758 accepted, 448 enrolled	
SAT I Verbal/Math: 700/620	**ACT:** 28 **HIGHLY COMPETITIVE+**

Rhodes College, founded in 1848, is a nonprofit, private liberal arts institution affiliated with the Presbyterian Church (U.S.A.). There is 1 graduate school. The 6 libraries contain 250,000 volumes, 54,000 microform items, and 8400 audiovisual forms/CDs, and subscribe to 1200 periodicals. Computerized library services include the card catalog, interlibrary loans, and database searching. Special learning facilities include an art gallery, 2 electron microscopes, a 0.8-meter infrared optimized telescope, a cell culture lab, and the Human Relations Area Files, containing 2 million pages of human behavior resources materials on microfiche. The 100-acre campus is in a suburban area in Memphis. Including residence halls, there are 43 buildings.

Programs of Study: Rhodes confers B.A. and B.S. degrees. Master's degrees are also awarded. Bachelor's degrees are awarded in BIOLOGICAL SCIENCE (biology/biological science), BUSINESS (business administration and management), COMMUNICATIONS AND THE ARTS (art, dramatic arts, English, French, German, music, and Spanish), COMPUTER AND PHYSICAL SCIENCE (chemistry, mathematics, and physics), SOCIAL SCIENCE (anthropology, classical/ancient civilization, economics, history, international studies, Latin American studies, philosophy, political science/government, psychology, religion, Russian and Slavic studies, sociology, and urban studies). English, foreign languages, and business administration are the strongest academically. Biology, business administration, and English are the largest.

Special: More than half of Rhodes students have an internship experience, in which off-campus work and significant academic work are combined for credit. Study abroad in 7 countries, a Washington semester, cross-registration with Memphis College of Art, and a science semester at Oak Ridge National Laboratory are offered. A 3-2 engineering degree with Washington University is available. The B.A.-B.S. degree and dual majors, including anthropology/sociology, are offered in any combination, and student-designed majors can be arranged. Nondegree study and pass/fail options are possible. There are 11 national honor societies, including Phi Beta Kappa, and all departments offer honors programs.

Admissions: 78% of the 1999-2000 applicants were accepted. The SAT I scores for the 1999-2000 freshman class were: Verbal--2% below 500, 24% between 500 and 599, 45% between 600 and 700, and 29% above 700; Math--2% below 500, 20% between 500 and 599, 54% between 600 and 700, and 24% above 700. The ACT scores were 5% between 21 and 23, 28% between 24 and 26, 26% between 27 and 28, and 41% above 28. 75% of the current freshmen were in the top fifth of their class; 91% were in the top two fifths. There were 12 National Merit finalists and 29 semifinalists. 34 freshmen graduated first in their class.

Requirements: The SAT I or ACT is required. Graduation from an accredited secondary school is required, with 16 or more academic credits, including 4 years of English, 3 of math, and 2 each of a foreign language, science, and social studies/history. The GED is accepted. An essay is required; an interview is recommended. Applications may be submitted on-line through the Common Application. AP credits are accepted. Important factors in the admissions decision are advanced placement or honor courses, recommendations by school officials, and extracurricular activities record.

Procedure: Freshmen are admitted fall and spring. Entrance exams should be taken prior to December of the senior year. There are early decision, early admissions, and deferred admissions plans. Early decision applications should be filed by November 1 or January 1; regular applications, by February 1 for fall entry (or January 15 for competitive scholarship consideration) and December 1 for spring entry, along with a $40 fee. Notification of early decision is sent December 1 or February 1; regular decision, April 1. 36 early decision candidates were accepted for the 1999-2000 class. 12% of all applicants are on a waiting list; 2 were accepted in 1999.

Financial Aid: In 1999-2000, 77% of all freshmen and 75% of continuing students received some form of financial aid. 37% of freshmen and 42% of continuing students received need-based aid. The average freshman award was $11,402. Of that total, scholarships or need-based grants averaged $6462 ($34,000 maximum); loans averaged $3453 ($6625 maximum); and work contracts averaged $1487 ($1500 maximum). 30% of undergraduates work part time. Average annual earnings from campus work are $1019. The average financial indebtedness of the 1999 graduate was $15,598. Rhodes is a member of CSS. The CSS/Profile or FAFSA and the college's own financial statement are required. The fall application deadline is March 1.

Computers: The mainframe is a DEC ALPHA. PCs and Macs are available in 3 computer labs. The math department runs an additional lab of Sun and Digital servers and workstations. All residence hall rooms are networked to the campus-wide system and the Internet. All students may access the system 24 hours a day. There are no time limits and no fees. It is recommended that all students have personal computers that support a dual platform.

RICE UNIVERSITY
Houston, TX 77005

(713) 527-4036
(800) 527-OWLS; Fax: (713) 285-5952

Full-time: 1440 men, 1260 women	**Faculty:** 449; I, ++$
Part-time: 50 men, 30 women	**Ph.D.s:** 99%
Graduate: 885 men, 570 women	**Student/Faculty:** 6 to 1
Year: semesters, summer session	**Tuition:** $16,220
Application Deadline: see profile	**Room & Board:** $6300
Freshman Class: n/av	
SAT I or ACT: required	**MOST COMPETITIVE**

Rice University, founded in 1912, is a private institution offering undergraduate and graduate programs through the divisions of Engineering, Natural Sciences, Humanities, Social Sciences, Music, Architecture, and Administrative Sciences. Figures given in the above capsule are approximate. There are 6 undergraduate schools and 1 graduate school. In addition to regional accreditation, Rice has baccalaureate program accreditation with ABET and NAAB. The library contains 1.5 million volumes, 2.2 million microform items, and 3000 audiovisual forms/CDs, and subscribes to 14,000 periodicals. Computerized library services include the card catalog and database searching. Special learning facilities include an art gallery, radio station, and media center. The 300-acre campus is in a suburban area 3 miles southwest of downtown Houston. Including residence halls, there are 40 buildings.

Programs of Study: Rice confers B.A., B.S., B.Arch., B.F.A., and B.Mus. degrees. Master's and doctoral degrees are also awarded. Bachelor's degrees are awarded in BIOLOGICAL SCIENCE (biochemistry, biology/biological science, and ecology), BUSINESS (management science), COMMUNICATIONS AND THE ARTS (art, art history and appreciation, English, linguistics, music, and Spanish), COMPUTER AND PHYSICAL SCIENCE (applied mathematics, chemistry, computer science, geology, geophysics and seismology, mathematics, physics, and statistics), ENGINEERING AND ENVIRONMENTAL DESIGN (architecture, chemical engineering, civil engineering, computer engineering, electrical/electronics engineering, environmental science, and mechanical engineering), SOCIAL SCIENCE (anthropology, Asian/Oriental studies, classical/ancient civilization, cognitive science, economics, French studies, German area studies, Hispanic American studies, history, medieval studies, philosophy, physical fitness/movement, political science/government, psychology, public affairs, religion, Russian and Slavic studies, sociology, and women's studies). Engineering is the largest.

Special: Cross-registration at other colleges, internships, a semester studying deep-water oceanography in Massachusetts and the Caribbean, or maritime culture and commerce on a sailing vessel off the North American coastline, study abroad in a number of countries, dual and student-designed majors, nondegree study, and limited pass/fail options are offered. There are 10 national honor societies, including Phi Beta Kappa, and 9 departmental honors programs.

Requirements: The SAT I or ACT is required, along with 3 SAT II: Subject tests, including the writing test. Potential engineering and natural science majors should also take math I or II and either chemistry or physics. Applicants should be high school graduates or have earned the GED. Secondary preparation should include 4 years of English, 3 years each of math and academic electives, and 2 years each of a foreign language, science, and social studies. An interview is recommended and a personal essay is required; architecture majors should submit a portfolio, and music majors should audition. Candidates must submit evaluations from a counselor and a teacher. AP and CLEP credits are accepted. Important factors in the admissions decision are advanced placement or honor courses, extracurricular activities record, and personality/intangible qualities.

Procedure: Freshmen are admitted in the fall. Entrance exams should be taken between October and January of the senior year, depending on the decision plan. There is an early decision plan. 55 early decision candidates were accepted for a recent class. Check with the school for current application deadlines and fee. A waiting list is an active part of the admissions procedure.

Financial Aid: Rice is a member of CSS. The FAFSA, the college's own financial statement and the and the parents' and student's tax returns are required.

Computers: The mainframes are an NAS AS/9000 and an IBM 3081. There are also Mac and IBM PCs available in the computing center, the library, and academic labs. All students may access the system. There are no time limits and no fees. It is recommended that all students have personal computers.

RICHARD STOCKTON COLLEGE OF NEW JERSEY

Pomona, NJ 08240 **(609) 652-4261; Fax: (609) 748-5541**

Full-time: 2150 men, 2682 women	**Faculty:** 195; IIB, ++$
Part-time: 446 men, 697 women	**Ph.D.s:** 96%
Graduate: 114 men, 209 women	**Student/Faculty:** 25 to 1
Year: semesters, summer session	**Tuition:** $4400 ($6432)
Application Deadline: May 1	**Room & Board:** $5218
Freshman Class: 3138 applied, 1493 accepted, 733 enrolled	
SAT I Verbal/Math: 550/570	**VERY COMPETITIVE**

Richard Stockton College of New Jersey, founded in 1969, is a public liberal arts college with 27 undergraduate programs and 6 graduate specialty areas. There are 5 undergraduate and 3 graduate schools. In addition to regional accreditation, Stockton has baccalaureate program accreditation with APTA, CSWE, NASDT-EC, NCATE, and NLN. The library contains 248,150 volumes, 341,102 microform items, and 13,120 audiovisual forms/CDs, and subscribes to 1360 periodicals. Computerized library services include the card catalog, interlibrary loans, and database searching. Special learning facilities include a learning resource center, an art gallery, a radio station, a TV station, an astronomical observatory, a marine science field lab, a marina with a fleet of small boats, a holocaust resource center, and an educational technology training center. The 1600-acre campus is in a suburban area 12 miles northwest of Atlantic City. Including residence halls, there are 51 buildings.

Programs of Study: Stockton confers B.A., B.S., and B.S.N. degrees. Master's degrees are also awarded. Bachelor's degrees are awarded in BIOLOGICAL SCIENCE (biochemistry, biology/biological science, and marine science), BUSINESS (accounting, banking and finance, business administration and management, and management science), COMMUNICATIONS AND THE ARTS (dance, dramatic arts, fine arts, and music), COMPUTER AND PHYSICAL SCIENCE (chemistry, computer science, information sciences and systems, mathematics, and physics), ENGINEERING AND ENVIRONMENTAL DESIGN (environmental science and preengineering), HEALTH PROFESSIONS (nursing, physical therapy, public health, and speech pathology/audiology), SOCIAL SCIENCE (anthropology, criminal justice, economics, history, liberal arts/general studies, philosophy, political science/government, psychology, and social work). Sciences are the strongest academically. Business, psychology, and criminal justice are the largest.

Special: Stockton offers internships in all fields with a wide variety of companies, work-study with various government agencies and corporations, a Washington semester, independent study, and study abroad in 10 countries. Dual majors in all programs, student-designed majors, an accelerated degree in medicine, 3-2 engineering degrees with the New Jersey Institute of Technology and Rutgers University, and general studies degrees are also offered. Nondegree study, pass/fail options, and credit for life, military, and work experience are possible. There are 5 national honor societies and 1 departmental honors program.

Admissions: 48% of the 1999-2000 applicants were accepted. The SAT I scores for the 1999-2000 freshman class were: Verbal--23% below 500, 57% between 500 and 599, 18% between 600 and 700, and 2% above 700; Math--20% below 500, 59% between 500 and 599, 18% between 600 and 700, and 3% above 700. 50% of the current freshmen were in the top fifth of their class; 80% were in the top two fifths.

Requirements: The SAT I or ACT is required. Stockton requires applicants to be in the upper 50% of their class. A GPA of 2.5 is required. Applicants must be high school graduates; the GED is accepted. 16 academic credits are required, including 4 years in English, 3 each in math and social studies, 2 in science, and 4 additional years of any of the above or a foreign language, or both. An essay and an interview are recommended, and a portfolio or audition is necessary where appropriate. AP and CLEP credits are accepted. Important factors in the admissions decision are advanced placement or honor courses, leadership record, and evidence of special talent.

Procedure: Freshmen are admitted fall and spring. Entrance exams should be taken once in the junior year and again before January in the senior year. There is an early admissions plan. Early decision applications should be filed by January 15; regular applications, by May 1 for fall entry and December 1 for spring entry, along with a $35 fee. Notification is sent on a rolling basis. 15% of all applicants are on a waiting list.

Financial Aid: In 1999-2000, 91% of all freshmen and 84% of continuing students received some form of financial aid. 87% of freshmen and 46% of continuing students received need-based aid. The average freshman award was $8565. Of that total, scholarships or need-based grants averaged $4554 ($9129 maximum); loans averaged $5601 ($12,587 maximum); and work contracts averaged $1682 ($2800 maximum). 37% of undergraduates work part time. Average annual earnings from campus work are $1682. The average financial indebtedness of the 1999 graduate was $13,135. The FAFSA is required. The fall application deadline is March 1.

Computers: The mainframes are a DEC VAX 8600 and 6300 and an IBM 3090. There are also 2 Alpha 2104/275 servers, 1 Alpha 2000/233 server, and a DEC 5500 processor. Students may access the Caucus network for conferencing and linkage to the mainframe and the Internet. There are also more than 750 PCs dispersed in 20 computer labs, 34 electronic classrooms, the library, faculty offices, and academic support facilities. All students may access the system 24 hours a day. There are no time limits and no fees.

RINGLING SCHOOL OF ART AND DESIGN
Sarasota, FL 34234-5896 (941) 351-5100
(800) 255-7695; Fax: (941) 359-7517

Full-time: 497 men, 374 women	**Faculty:** 44
Part-time: 11 men, 10 women	**Ph.D.s:** 82%
Graduate: none	**Student/Faculty:** 20 to 1
Year: semesters	**Tuition:** $15,300
Application Deadline: open	**Room & Board:** $6800
Freshman Class: 751 applied, 416 accepted, 235 enrolled	
SAT I or ACT: recommended	**SPECIAL**

Ringling School of Art and Design, founded in 1931, is a private art college. In addition to regional accreditation, the college has baccalaureate program accreditation with FIDER and NASAD. The library contains 36,636 volumes and 2482 audiovisual forms/CDs, and subscribes to 325 periodicals. Computerized library services include the card catalog, interlibrary loans, and database searching. Special learning facilities include a learning resource center, art gallery, and a total of 85,000 slides. The 32-acre campus is in an urban area 50 miles south of Tampa. Including residence halls, there are 51 buildings.

Programs of Study: The college confers the B.F.A. degree. Bachelor's degrees are awarded in COMMUNICATIONS AND THE ARTS (fine arts, graphic design, illustration, and photography), ENGINEERING AND ENVIRONMENTAL DESIGN (computer graphics and interior design). Illustration is the largest.

Special: The college offers cross-registration with the Art College Exchange, internships with Walt Disney animation and Home Box Office, and study abroad in France. Also available are credit by portfolio, an accelerated degree program in interior design, and a nondegree, continuing education program.

Admissions: 55% of the 1999-2000 applicants were accepted.

Requirements: The SAT I or ACT is recommended. A GPA of 2.0 is required. Applicants must be graduates of an accredited secondary school or have a GED. Admission is based on the academic record and a portfolio. An essay is required, and an interview is recommended. AP and CLEP credits are accepted. Important factors in the admissions decision are evidence of special talent, advanced placement or honor courses, and recommendations by school officials.

Procedure: Freshmen are admitted in the fall. Application deadlines are open. There is a $30 fee. Notification is sent on a rolling basis. A waiting list is an active part of the admissions procedure.

Financial Aid: In 1999-2000, 68% of all freshmen and 76% of continuing students received some form of financial aid. 62% of freshmen and 66% of continuing students received need-based aid. The average freshman award was $11,512. Of that total, scholarships or need-based grants averaged $2978 ($5000 maximum); loans averaged $3429 ($7625 maximum); and noneed-based state tuition differential grants (F.R.A.G.) and state merit scholarships averaged $2400 ($4908 maximum). 35% of undergraduates work part time. Average annual earnings from campus work are $2500. The average financial indebtedness of the 1999 graduate was $16,500. The college is a member of CSS. The FAFSA and the college's own financial statement are required. The fall application deadline is March 1.

Computers: PCs are available in the computer center. All students may access the system. There are no time limits and no fees.

RIPON COLLEGE
Ripon, WI 54971

(920) 748-8185
(800) 94-RIPON; Fax: (920) 748-8335

Full-time: 349 men, 364 women	**Faculty:** 61; IIB, av$
Part-time: 9 men, 24 women	**Ph.D.s:** 95%
Graduate: none	**Student/Faculty:** 12 to 1
Year: semesters	**Tuition:** $18,240
Application Deadline: August 1	**Room & Board:** $4400
Freshman Class: 824 applied, 718 accepted, 283 enrolled	
SAT I Verbal/Math: 616/603	**ACT:** 25 **VERY COMPETITIVE**

Ripon College, established in 1851, is a private, residential, liberal arts institution. The library contains 164,378 volumes, 18,660 microform items, and 6000 audiovisual forms/CDs, and subscribes to 631 periodicals. Computerized library services include the card catalog, interlibrary loans, and database searching. Special learning facilities include a learning resource center, art gallery, radio station, music library, art slide library, and college archives. The 250-acre campus is in a small town 80 miles north of Milwaukee in the east-central part of the state. Including residence halls, there are 29 buildings.

Programs of Study: Ripon College confers the A.B. degree. Bachelor's degrees are awarded in BIOLOGICAL SCIENCE (biochemistry and biology/biological science), BUSINESS (business administration and management), COMMUNICATIONS AND THE ARTS (art history and appreciation, dramatic arts, English, French, German, music, Spanish, and speech/debate/rhetoric), COMPUTER AND PHYSICAL SCIENCE (chemistry, computer science, mathematics, and physics), EDUCATION (elementary, middle school, physical, and secondary), ENGINEERING AND ENVIRONMENTAL DESIGN (environmental science), SOCIAL SCIENCE (anthropology, economics, history, international studies, Latin American studies, philosophy, political science/government, psychobiology, psychology, religion, and sociology). Biology, chemistry, and physics are the strongest academically. Economics, history, and business management are the largest.

Special: Students may cross-register with the Associated Colleges of the Midwest. Internships, study abroad in 13 countries and study through 7 domestic programs, and a Washington semester are available. The college offers a 3-year degree in all areas, dual and student-designed majors, and pass/fail options. A 3-2 engineering degree is available with Rensselaer Polytechnic Institute, Washington University, and the University of Minnesota; other 3-2 programs are in environmental studies and in forestry with Duke University and in social welfare with the University of Chicago. A 2-2 nursing program is possible with Rush University. There are 11 national honor societies, including Phi Beta Kappa, and a freshman honors program.

Admissions: 87% of the 1999-2000 applicants were accepted. The SAT I scores for the 1999-2000 freshman class were: Verbal--9% below 500, 29% between 500 and 599, 46% between 600 and 700, and 16% above 700; Math--9% below 500, 33% between 500 and 599, 49% between 600 and 700, and 9% above 700. The ACT scores were 14% below 21, 26% between 21 and 23, 33% between 24 and 26, 12% between 27 and 28, and 15% above 28. 52% of the current freshmen were in the top fifth of their class; 77% were in the top two fifths. 15 freshmen graduated first in their class.

Requirements: The SAT I or ACT is required. Ripon College requires applicants to be in the upper 50% of their class. A GPA of 2.0 is required. In addition, applicants must be graduates of an accredited secondary school. The GED is accepted. Applicants should complete at least 17 Carnegie units including 4 of English, 2 to 4 each of math, social studies, and natural sciences, and up to 7 of other college-preparatory electives. An essay may be required, and an interview is recommended. Applications are accepted on-line via Common App, CollegeLink, and Ripon's web site. AP and CLEP credits are accepted. Important factors in the admissions decision are advanced placement or honor courses, recommendations by school officials, and extracurricular activities record.

Procedure: Freshmen are admitted fall and spring. Entrance exams should be taken in the junior year or fall of the senior year. There are early admissions and deferred admissions plans. Applications should be filed by August 1 for fall entry and December 15 for spring entry, along with a $25 fee. Notification is sent on a rolling basis.

Financial Aid: In 1999-2000, 99% of all freshmen and 93% of continuing students received some form of financial aid. 63% of freshmen and 67% of continuing students received need-based aid. The average freshman award was $18,103. Of that total, scholarships or need-based grants averaged $14,013 ($22,640 maximum); loans averaged $2625 ($40,000 maximum); and work contracts averaged $1300 ($1800 maximum). 68% of undergraduates work part time. Average annual earnings from campus work are $860. The average financial indebtedness of the 1999 graduate was $11,978. Ripon College is a member of CSS. The FAFSA is required. The fall application deadline is March 15.

Computers: The mainframes are 2 DEC VAX 11/750 models. The mainframes and Macs are in the computer center; the many terminals allow for easy access. A second computer resource center is on the second floor of Lane Library. VAX terminals are located in several buildings. Macs and PCs are supported through labs in the economics, math, computer science, and natural sciences departments. All students may access the system. There are no time limits and no fees.

ROCHESTER INSTITUTE OF TECHNOLOGY
Rochester, NY 14623   (716) 475-6631; Fax: (716) 475-7424

Full-time: 6108 men, 2972 women	**Faculty:** 670; IIA, ++$
Part-time: 1516 men, 869 women	**Ph.D.s:** 80%
Graduate: 1382 men, 855 women	**Student/Faculty:** 14 to 1
Year: quarters, summer session	**Tuition:** $17,637
Application Deadline: open	**Room & Board:** $6852
Freshman Class: 7497 applied, 5744 accepted, 2098 enrolled	
SAT I Verbal/Math: 590/610	**ACT:** 26 **VERY COMPETITIVE**

Rochester Institute of Technology, a private institution founded in 1829, offers programs in science, computer science, allied health, engineering, fine arts, business, hotel management, graphic arts, and photography, as well as liberal arts, and includes the National Technical Institute for the Deaf. Most programs include a cooperative education component, which provides full-time work experience to complement classroom studies. There are 12 undergraduate and 12 graduate schools. In addition to regional accreditation, RIT has baccalaureate program accreditation with AACSB, ABET, ADA, CAHEA, CSAB, CSWE, and NASAD. The library contains 350,000 volumes, 377,000 microform items, and 8200 audiovisual forms/CDs, and subscribes to 7300 periodicals. Computerized library services include the card catalog, interlibrary loans, and database searching. Special learning facilities include a learning resource center, art gallery, radio station, TV station, computer chip manufacturing facility, student-operated restaurant, electronic prepress lab, and imaging science facility. The 1300-acre campus is in a suburban area 5 miles south of Rochester. Including residence halls, there are 166 buildings.

Programs of Study: RIT confers B.S. and B.F.A. degrees. Associate, master's, and doctoral degrees are also awarded. Bachelor's degrees are awarded in BIOLOGICAL SCIENCE (biochemistry, biology/biological science, biotechnology, and nutrition), BUSINESS (accounting, banking and finance, business administration and management, business systems analysis, hotel/motel and restaurant management, international business management, management information systems, management science, marketing management, and tourism), COMMUNICATIONS AND THE ARTS (applied art, ceramic art and design, communications, crafts, design, film arts, fine arts, glass, graphic design, illustration, industrial design, metal/jewelry, painting, photography, publishing, sculpture, studio art, telecommunications, and video), COMPUTER AND PHYSICAL SCIENCE (applied mathematics, chemistry, computer mathematics, computer science, information sciences and systems, mathematics, physics, polymer science, statistics, and systems analysis), EDUCATION (education of the deaf and hearing impaired), ENGINEERING AND ENVIRONMENTAL DESIGN (aerospace studies, automotive technology, civil engineering technology, computer engineering, computer graphics, computer technology, electrical/electronics engineering, electrical/electronics engineering technology, engineering, engineering technology, environmental engineering technology, environmental science, furniture design, graphic and printing production, graphic arts technology, industrial engineering, interior design, manufacturing engineering, manufacturing technology, materials science, mechanical engineering, mechanical engineering technology, military science, printing technology, and woodworking), HEALTH PROFESSIONS (allied health, medical laboratory technology, medical technology, nuclear medical technology, physician's assistant, predentistry, premedicine, preveterinary science, and ultrasound technology), SOCIAL SCIENCE (criminal justice, dietetics, economics, experimental psychology, food production/management/services, interpreter for the deaf, prelaw, psychology, and social work). Engineering, computer science, and business are the strongest academically. Engineering, information technology, and photography are the largest.

Special: RIT offers internships in social science and allied health majors, and cooperative education programs with 1300 co-op employers. Cooperative education is required or recommended in most programs and provides full-time paid work experience. Cross-registration with Rochester area colleges is available. There are accelerated degree programs in science, engineering, math, computer science, and business. The school grants credit for military and work experience. Students may study abroad in 15 countries, and student-designed majors are permitted in applied arts and sciences. There are 6 national honor societies.

Admissions: 77% of the 1999-2000 applicants were accepted. The SAT I scores for the 1999-2000 freshman class were: Verbal--15% below 500, 44% between 500 and 599, 35% between 600 and 700, and 6% above 700; Math--8% below 500, 36% between 500 and 599, 46% between 600 and 700, and 10% above 700. The ACT scores were 10% below 21, 19% between 21 and 23, 29% between 24 and 26, 20% between 27 and 28, and 22% above 28. 51% of the current freshmen were in the top fifth of their class; 81% were in the top two fifths. There were 12 National Merit finalists and 4 semifinalists. 44 freshmen graduated first in their class.

Requirements: The SAT I or ACT is required. RIT requires applicants to be in the upper 50% of their class. Applicants must be high school graduates or have a GED certificate. Applicants are required to submit an essay, and an interview is recommended. The School of Art and the School of Design emphasize a required portfolio of artwork. Required high school math and science credits vary by program, with 3 years in each area generally acceptable. Applications are accepted on-line via RIT's web site and through ExPAN and the Common Application. AP and CLEP credits are accepted. Important factors in the admissions decision are advanced placement or honor courses, recommendations by school officials, and extracurricular activities record.

Procedure: Freshmen are admitted to all sessions. Entrance exams should be taken during the junior or senior year. There are early decision, early admissions, and deferred admissions plans. Early decision applications should be filed by December 15; regular applications, on a rolling basis, along with a $40 fee. Notification of early decision is sent January 15; regular decision, on a rolling basis. 714 early decision candidates were accepted for the 1999-2000 class. 1% of all applicants are on a waiting list.

Financial Aid: In 1999-2000, 70% of all students received some form of financial aid, including need-based aid. The average freshman award was $14,200. Of that total, scholarships or need-based grants averaged $7700 ($17,328 maximum); loans averaged $3700 ($6625 maximum); work contracts averaged $1600 ($2200 maximum); and federal and state grants averaged $2000 ($7600 maximum). 70% of undergraduates work part time. Average annual earnings from campus work are $1500. The FAFSA is required. The fall application deadline is March 15.

Computers: The mainframes are a VMS cluster of 5 DEC VAX Models 6000-620, 6000-430, and 6000-520, and 4 Dec VAXstation Models 4000-90. RIT has 17 computer centers and computer labs on campus for student use. There are more than 300 mainframe terminals available, as well as hundreds of PCs. Students may link their terminals or PCs to the mainframe system from individual dormitory rooms or from off-campus locations, and access to the Internet is available. All students may access the system 7 days per week, from 8 a.m. to 1 a.m. There are no time limits and no fees.

ROLLINS COLLEGE
Winter Park, FL 32789   (407) 646-2161; Fax: (407) 646-1502

Full-time: 608 men, 911 women	**Faculty:** 125; IIA, ++$
Part-time: none	**Ph.D.s:** 90%
Graduate: 341 men, 413 women	**Student/Faculty:** 12 to 1
Year: semesters	**Tuition:** $21,870
Application Deadline: February 15	**Room & Board:** $6700
Freshman Class: 1748 applied, 1275 accepted, 448 enrolled	
SAT I Verbal/Math: 585/585	**ACT:** 26 **VERY COMPETITIVE**

Rollins College, founded in 1885, is a private liberal arts institution. There are 5 graduate schools. In addition to regional accreditation, Rollins has baccalaureate program accreditation with NASM. The library contains 273,429 volumes, 32,635 microform items, and 3522 audiovisual forms/CDs, and subscribes to 1695 periodicals. Computerized library services include the card catalog, interlibrary loans, and database searching. Special learning facilities include a learning resource center, art gallery, radio station, TV station, art museum, theaters, writing center, and math lab. The 67-acre campus is in a suburban area 5 miles north of Orlando. Including residence halls, there are 54 buildings.

Programs of Study: Rollins confers the B.A. degree. Master's degrees are also awarded. Bachelor's degrees are awarded in BIOLOGICAL SCIENCE (biology/biological science), BUSINESS (international business management), COMMUNICATIONS AND THE ARTS (art history and appreciation, dramatic arts, English, French, German, music history and appreciation, music performance, Spanish, studio art, and voice), COMPUTER AND PHYSICAL SCIENCE (chemistry, computer science, mathematics, and physics), EDUCATION (elementary), ENGINEERING AND ENVIRONMENTAL DESIGN (environmental science), SOCIAL SCIENCE (anthropology, classical/ancient civilization, economics, history, international relations, Latin American studies, philosophy, political science/government, psychology, religion, and sociology). English, biology, and chemistry are the strongest academically. Psychology, economics, and English are the largest.

Special: Rollins offers cross-registration with the evening studies division, co-op programs with American University in Washington, D.C., and Paris and the Duke University School of Forestry and Environmental Studies, departmental and professional internships, study abroad in 2 countries, and a Washington semester. Also available are work-study programs, an accelerated degree program in management, a B.A.-B.S. degree in preengineering, dual majors in any combination, and student-designed majors in area studies. A 3-2 engineering degree with Washington University in St. Louis and Auburn, Case Western Reserve, Columbia, and Boston universities is offered. Nondegree study and pass/fail options are possible. There are 3 national honor societies and a freshman honors program.

Admissions: 73% of the 1999-2000 applicants were accepted. The SAT I scores for the 1999-2000 freshman class were: Verbal--15% below 500, 45% between 500 and 599, 35% between 600 and 700, and 5% above 700; Math--15% below 500, 45% between 500 and 599, 35% between 600 and 700, and 5% above 700. The ACT scores were 15% below 21, 25% between 21 and 23, 25% between 24 and 26, 20% between 27 and 28, and 15% above 28. 56% of the current freshmen were in the top fifth of their class; 81% were in the top two fifths. In a recent year, 18 freshmen graduated first in their class.

Requirements: The SAT I or ACT is required. Applicants must be graduates of an accredited secondary school or have a GED certificate and have completed 4 years of English, 3 years of math, and 2 years each of foreign language, science, and social studies. An essay is required. SAT II: Subject tests in writing, math, and foreign language and an interview are recommended. Applications are accepted on computer disk by contacting Admissions and specifying PC or Mac. AP credits are accepted. Important factors in the admissions decision are advanced placement or honor courses, evidence of special talent, and extracurricular activities record.

Procedure: Freshmen are admitted fall and spring. Entrance exams should be taken by the first semester of the senior year. There are early decision, early admissions, and deferred admissions plans. Early decision applications should be filed by January 15; regular applications, by February 15 for fall entry and December 1 for spring entry, along with a $40 fee. Notification of early decision is sent February 1; regular decision, April 1. 75 early decision candidates were accepted for the 1999-2000 class. 10% of all applicants are on a waiting list.

Financial Aid: In a recent year, 64% of all freshmen and 63% of continuing students received some form of financial aid. 30% of freshmen and 34% of continuing students received need-based aid. The average freshman award was $17,458. Of that total, scholarships or need-based grants averaged $13,726 ($22,007 maximum); loans averaged $2732 ($4625 maximum); and work contracts averaged $1000 ($1500 maximum). 15% of undergraduates work part time. Average annual earnings from campus work are $891. The average financial indebtedness of the 1999 graduate was $11,730. Rollins is a member of CSS. The CSS/Profile or FAFSA and the college's own financial statement are required. The fall application deadline is March 1.

Computers: The mainframe is a MicroVAX 3100. The student computing center is open 24 hours. More than 150 terminals and PCs for student use are located in the writing center, residence halls, the library, and departmental lounges. Students may bring their own PC and, with a modem, access the mainframe 24 hours per day. All students may access the system. There are no time limits and no fees.

ROSE-HULMAN INSTITUTE OF TECHNOLOGY
Terre Haute, IN 47803

(812) 877-1511
(800) 248-7448; Fax: (812) 877-8941

Full-time: 1249 men, 257 women	**Faculty:** 123; IIB, ++$
Part-time: 27 men, 6 women	**Ph.D.s:** 98%
Graduate: 114 men, 19 women	**Student/Faculty:** 12 to 1
Year: quarters, summer session	**Tuition:** $18,887
Application Deadline: March 1	**Room & Board:** $5475
Freshman Class: 3107 applied, 2029 accepted, 395 enrolled	
SAT I Verbal/Math: 650/700	**ACT:** 30 **HIGHLY COMPETITIVE+**

Rose-Hulman Institute of Technology, founded in 1874, is a private college emphasizing engineering, science, and math. There is 1 graduate school. In addition to regional accreditation, Rose-Hulman has baccalaureate program accreditation with ABET. The library contains 74,205 volumes, 532 microform items, and 305 audiovisual forms/CDs, and subscribes to 495 periodicals. Computerized library services include the card catalog, interlibrary loans, and database searching. Special learning facilities include a learning resource center, art gallery, and radio station. The 200-acre campus is in a suburban area on the east side of Terre Haute. Including residence halls, there are 35 buildings.

Programs of Study: Rose-Hulman confers the B.S. degree. Master's degrees are also awarded. Bachelor's degrees are awarded in COMPUTER AND PHYSICAL

SCIENCE (chemistry, computer science, mathematics, optics, and physics), ENGINEERING AND ENVIRONMENTAL DESIGN (chemical engineering, civil engineering, computer engineering, electrical/electronics engineering, and mechanical engineering), SOCIAL SCIENCE (economics). Engineering, science, and math are the strongest academically. Electrical and computer engineering, mechanical engineering, and chemical engineering are the largest.

Special: The institute offers co-op programs, independent study, cross-registration with Indiana State University, summer industrial internships, study abroad in 8 countries, dual majors, and pass/fail options. There are 10 national honor societies.

Admissions: 65% of the 1999-2000 applicants were accepted. The SAT I scores for the 1999-2000 freshman class were: Verbal--1% below 500, 29% between 500 and 599, 42% between 600 and 700, and 28% above 700; Math--5% between 500 and 599, 39% between 600 and 700, and 56% above 700. The ACT scores were 10% between 24 and 26, 50% between 27 and 28, and 40% above 28. 92% of the current freshmen were in the top fifth of their class; all were in the top two fifths. There were 19 National Merit finalists and 40 semifinalists. 42 freshmen graduated first in their class.

Requirements: The SAT I or ACT is required. Rose-Hulman requires applicants to be in the upper 25% of their class. A GPA of 3.5 is required. Candidates should have at least 16 units of credit, including 4 in English, 2 in social sciences, and 1 each in math, chemistry, physics, and electives. An essay and interview are recommended. Applications are accepted on-line off the Rose-Hulman web page. AP credits are accepted. Important factors in the admissions decision are advanced placement or honor courses, recommendations by school officials, and personality/intangible qualities.

Procedure: Freshmen are admitted in the fall. Entrance exams should be taken in the fall of the senior year or the spring of the junior year. Applications should be filed by March 1 for fall entry, along with a $40 fee. Notification is sent within 3 weeks of receipt of the completed application.

Financial Aid: In 1999-2000, 95% of all freshmen and 90% of continuing students received some form of financial aid. 63% of freshmen and 72% of continuing students received need-based aid. The average freshman award was $14,017. Of that total, scholarships or need-based grants averaged $4600 ($10,000 maximum); loans averaged $5500 ($6500 maximum); and work contracts averaged $1500 (maximum). 65% of undergraduates work part time. Average annual earnings from campus work are $1500. The average financial indebtedness of the 1999 graduate was $22,000. Rose-Hulman is a member of CSS. The FAFSA is required. The fall application deadline is March 1.

Computers: There are network connections in all residence hall rooms and most classrooms and labs. All students may access the system. There are no time limits and no fees.

ROWAN UNIVERSITY
Glassboro, NJ 08028

(856) 256-4200
(800) 447-1165; Fax: (856) 256-4430

Full-time: 2975 men, 3646 women	**Faculty:** 364
Part-time: 654 men, 1115 women	**Ph.D.s:** 80%
Graduate: 289 men, 956 women	**Student/Faculty:** 18 to 1
Year: semesters, summer session	**Tuition:** $4920 ($8670)
Application Deadline: March 15	**Room & Board:** $5820
Freshman Class: 5311 applied, 2851 accepted, 1129 enrolled	
SAT I Verbal/Math: 560/572	**VERY COMPETITIVE**

Rowan University was founded in 1923 as a public institution offering undergraduate programs in the arts and sciences, business administration, education, fine and performing arts, and engineering. There are 6 undergraduate schools and 1 graduate school. In addition to regional accreditation, Rowan has baccalaureate program accreditation with NASM and NCATE. The library contains 350,800 volumes, 77,000 microform items, and 43,500 audiovisual forms/CDs, and subscribes to 1725 periodicals. Computerized library services include database searching. Special learning facilities include an art gallery, planetarium, and radio station. The 200-acre campus is in a small town 20 miles southeast of Philadelphia. Including residence halls, there are 40 buildings.

Programs of Study: Rowan confers B.A., B.S., B.F.A., and B.M. degrees. Master's and doctoral degrees are also awarded. Bachelor's degrees are awarded in BIOLOGICAL SCIENCE (biology/biological science), BUSINESS (accounting, business administration and management, marketing/retailing/merchandising, personnel management, and small business management), COMMUNICATIONS AND THE ARTS (broadcasting, communications, dramatic arts, English, fine arts, journalism, music, Spanish, and speech/debate/rhetoric), COMPUTER AND PHYSICAL SCIENCE (chemistry and physics), EDUCATION (early childhood, elementary, foreign languages, music, and science), ENGINEERING AND ENVIRONMENTAL DESIGN (engineering), SOCIAL SCIENCE (criminal justice, economics, history, liberal arts/general studies, political science/government, psychology, and sociology). Communications, business administration, and elementary education are the strongest academically. and the largest.

Special: Students may study abroad in 8 countries. Internships are available both with and without pay. Rowan also offers accelerated degree programs and 3-2 degrees in optometry, podiatry, and pharmacy. There are dual majors, pass/fail options, and credit for military experience. There is a freshman honors program.

Admissions: 54% of the 1999-2000 applicants were accepted. The SAT I scores for the 1999-2000 freshman class were: Verbal--13% below 500, 59% between 500 and 599, 27% between 600 and 700, and 2% above 700; Math--10% below 500, 59% between 500 and 599, 28% between 600 and 700, and 4% above 700. 45% of the current freshmen were in the top fifth of their class; 86% were in the top two fifths.

Requirements: The SAT I is required. A GPA of 3.0 is required, with a recommended minimum composite score of 950, or no less than 450 on either part. Students submitting ACT scores should have a minimum composite score of 19. Applicants must be graduates of accredited secondary schools or have earned a GED. Rowan requires 16 academic credits or Carnegie units, including 4 in English, 3 each in math and college preparatory electives, and 2 each in foreign language, history, and a lab science. An essay is required of all students, and a portfolio or audition is required for specific majors. AP and CLEP credits are

439

accepted. Important factors in the admissions decision are advanced placement or honor courses, evidence of special talent, and leadership record.

Procedure: Freshmen are admitted fall and spring. Entrance exams should be taken in November or December of the senior year. There is a deferred admissions plan. Applications should be filed by March 15 for fall entry and November 15 for spring entry, along with a $50 fee. Notification is sent on a rolling basis. A waiting list is an active part of the admissions procedure.

Financial Aid: Scholarships or need-based grants averaged $3190 ($2000 maximum); loans averaged $2185 ($2500 maximum); and work contracts averaged $900 ($1500 maximum). 10% of undergraduates work part time. Average annual earnings from campus work are $1200. Rowan is a member of CSS. The CSS/Profile, the university's own financial statement, and financial aid transcripts are required. The fall application deadline is April 1.

Computers: The mainframes are 2 DEC VAX 8650, Series 6000-410. PCs are available in academic labs and student labs. All students may access the system from 7:30 a.m. to midnight. There are no time limits and no fees.

RUTGERS, THE STATE UNIVERSITY OF NEW JERSEY/CAMDEN COLLEGE OF ARTS AND SCIENCES

Camden, NJ 08102   (856) 225-6104; Fax: (856) 225-6498

Full-time: 797 men, 1246 women	**Faculty:** 223; IIA, ++$
Part-time: 179 men, 229 women	**Ph.D.s:** 98%
Graduate: none	**Student/Faculty:** 11 to 1
Year: semesters, summer session	**Tuition:** $6058 ($10,988)
Application Deadline: December 15	**Room & Board:** $5548
Freshman Class: 4332 applied, 2668 accepted, 379 enrolled	
SAT I Verbal/Math: 548/551	**VERY COMPETITIVE**

Rutgers University, The State University of New Jersey/Camden College of Arts and Sciences, established in 1927, is a liberal arts institution. In addition to regional accreditation, Camden College of Arts and Sciences has baccalaureate program accreditation with AACSB, CSWE, NASDTEC, and NLN. The 2 libraries contain 6,280,743 volumes, 5,285,009 microform items, and 116,306 audiovisual forms/CDs, and subscribe to 29,005 periodicals. Computerized library services include the card catalog, interlibrary loans, and database searching. Special learning facilities include a learning resource center, art gallery, and radio station. The 25-acre campus is in an urban area 1 mile from Philadelphia. Including residence halls, there are 28 buildings.

Programs of Study: Camden College of Arts and Sciences confers B.A. and B.S. degrees. Bachelor's degrees are awarded in BIOLOGICAL SCIENCE (biochemistry and biology/biological science), BUSINESS (accounting, banking and finance, management science, and marketing/retailing/merchandising), COMMUNICATIONS AND THE ARTS (art, art history and appreciation, dramatic arts, English, French, German, music, and Spanish), COMPUTER AND PHYSICAL SCIENCE (chemistry, computer science, mathematics, physics, and science), EDUCATION (elementary and secondary), ENGINEERING AND ENVIRONMENTAL DESIGN (ceramic engineering, chemical engineering, civil engineering, electrical/electronics engineering, engineering and applied science, environmental engineering, industrial engineering, and mechanical engineering), HEALTH PROFESSIONS (biomedical science, medical laboratory technology, nursing, predentistry, and premedicine), SOCIAL SCIENCE (African American studies, criminal justice, economics, history, philosophy, political science/

government, prelaw, psychology, social work, sociology, and urban studies). Psychology, accounting, and English are the largest.

Special: The college offers study abroad in numerous countries, some B.A.-B.S. degrees, and student-designed majors. Pass/fail options are available for 2 courses during matriculation. Students may take 2-2 and 2-3 (dual major) programs with the College of Engineering, a 1-3 program with Cook College (agriculture), and a 2-3 program with the College of Pharmacy. There are 11 national honor societies and a freshman honors program.

Admissions: 62% of the 1999-2000 applicants were accepted. The SAT I scores for the 1999-2000 freshman class were: Verbal--22% below 500, 54% between 500 and 599, 22% between 600 and 700, and 1% above 700; Math--26% below 500, 51% between 500 and 599, 19% between 600 and 700, and 3% above 700. 49% of the current freshmen were in the top fifth of their class; 88% were in the top two fifths. 3 freshmen graduated first in their class.

Requirements: The SAT I or ACT is required. The GED is accepted. Students must have completed 16 academic credits or Carnegie units, including 4 years of English, 3 years of math (algebra I and II and geometry), 2 years each of a foreign language and science, and 5 other approved academic subjects. Students may apply on-line by accessing the Rutgers web site. AP and CLEP credits are accepted. Important factors in the admissions decision are advanced placement or honor courses, evidence of special talent, and leadership record.

Procedure: Freshmen are admitted fall and spring. Entrance exams should be taken early in the senior year. There are early admissions and deferred admissions plans. Applications should be filed by December 15 for fall entry and November 15 for spring entry, along with a $50 fee. Notification is sent on a rolling basis. A waiting list is an active part of the admissions procedure.

Financial Aid: In 1999-2000, 88% of all freshmen and 70% of continuing students received some form of financial aid. 67% of freshmen and 57% of continuing students received need-based aid. The average freshman award was $7098. Of that total, scholarships or need-based grants averaged $5621 ($15,410 maximum); loans averaged $2962 ($14,375 maximum); work contracts averaged $1460 ($1500 maximum); and outside scholarships averaged $1370 ($7500 maximum). 10% of undergraduates work part time. Average annual earnings from campus work are $1483. The average financial indebtedness of the 1999 graduate was $15,446. The FAFSA is required. The fall application deadline is March 15.

Computers: The mainframes are a Sun Ultra SPARC Server, Sun 10/51 SPARC Server, and Sun Enterprise 3500. Workstations and networked Macs and PCs (a total of 187 systems) are located in public labs in 2 major academic buildings, the library, the Campus Center, and the dorms. All have access to the central systems, the Web, and the local Camden campus computers. On-campus computer network services include on-line admission, registration, transcripts, E-mail, library searches and catalog, and full access to the Internet. A complete intranet web service is available for all aspects of student services. All students may access the system either 24 hours a day by modem or whenever the buildings housing the public labs are open. The main lab is available Monday through Thursday, 8 a.m. to 11 p.m.; Friday and Saturday, 9 a.m. to 5 p.m.; and Sunday, 2 p.m. to 10 p.m. There are no time limits. The fee is $200 per year.

RUTGERS, THE STATE UNIVERSITY OF NEW JERSEY/COOK COLLEGE

New Brunswick, NJ 08903 (732) 932-INFO; Fax: (732) 445-0237

Full-time: 1477 men, 1490 women	**Faculty:** 256; I, ++$
Part-time: 146 men, 118 women	**Ph.Ds:** 98%
Graduate: none	**Student/Faculty:** 11 to 1
Year: semesters, summer session	**Tuition:** $6751 ($12,220)
Application Deadline: December 15	**Room & Board:** $6098
Freshman Class: 6673 applied, 4267 accepted, 630 enrolled	
SAT I Verbal/Math: 571/596	**HIGHLY COMPETITIVE**

Rutgers, The State University of New Jersey/Cook College, founded in 1864, is a residential college offering a program that emphasizes life, environmental, marine and coastal, and agricultural sciences. In addition to regional accreditation, Cook College has baccalaureate program accreditation with ASLA and NASDTEC. The 14 libraries contain 6,280,743 volumes, 5,285,009 microform items, and 116,306 audiovisual forms/CDs, and subscribe to 29,005 periodicals. Computerized library services include the card catalog, interlibrary loans, and database searching. Special learning facilities include a learning resource center, art gallery, radio station, TV station, geology museum, and various research centers and institutes. The 2695-acre campus is in a small town 33 miles south of New York City. Including residence halls, there are 176 buildings.

Programs of Study: Cook College confers B.A. and B.S. degrees. Bachelor's degrees are awarded in AGRICULTURE (agriculture, animal science, fishing and fisheries, horticulture, natural resource management, plant science, and wildlife management), BIOLOGICAL SCIENCE (biochemistry, biology/biological science, biotechnology, botany, cell biology, ecology, evolutionary biology, genetics, marine science, microbiology, molecular biology, nutrition, and physiology), BUSINESS (business economics), COMMUNICATIONS AND THE ARTS (communications and journalism), COMPUTER AND PHYSICAL SCIENCE (atmospheric sciences and meteorology, chemistry, computer science, earth science, and geology), EDUCATION (health and physical), ENGINEERING AND ENVIRONMENTAL DESIGN (bioengineering, environmental design, environmental science, and landscape architecture/design), HEALTH PROFESSIONS (biomedical science, predentistry, premedicine, preveterinary science, and public health), SOCIAL SCIENCE (food science, geography, human ecology, international studies, and physical fitness/movement). Environmental sciences, nutritional science, and animal science are the largest.

Special: Cook College offers an extensive cooperative education program, independent study programs, B.A.-B.S. degrees, a 2-3 engineering degree, a 5-year advanced degree in planning and public policy, and an 8-year medical degree with the University of Medicine and Dentistry of New Jersey. Seniors may elect to take 1 course each semester on a pass/fail basis. Study abroad is offered in numerous countries. A wide variety of professionally oriented majors in the life, environmental, marine, coastal, and agricultural sciences is offered. There are 9 national honor societies, a freshman honors program, and 5 departmental honors programs.

Admissions: 64% of the 1999-2000 applicants were accepted. The SAT I scores for the 1999-2000 freshman class were: Verbal--13% below 500, 52% between 500 and 599, 32% between 600 and 700, and 3% above 700; Math--8% below 500, 44% between 500 and 599, 43% between 600 and 700, and 5% above 700. 61% of the current freshmen were in the top fifth of their class; 97% were in the top two fifths. 6 freshmen graduated first in their class.

Requirements: The SAT I or ACT is required. Applicants must have completed 16 high school academic credits or Carnegie units, including 4 years of English, 3 years of math (algebra I and II and geometry), 2 years of science, and 7 other approved academic subjects. The GED is accepted. Students without a high school diploma, those from a nonaccredited high school, or those with academic unit entrance deficiencies must take the SAT II: Subject tests in writing, math, and 1 other subject. Students may apply on-line by accessing the Rutgers web site. AP and CLEP credits are accepted. Important factors in the admissions decision are advanced placement or honor courses, evidence of special talent, and leadership record.

Procedure: Freshmen are admitted in the fall. Entrance exams should be taken early in the senior year. There are early admissions and deferred admissions plans. Applications should be filed by December 15 for fall entry, along with a $50 fee. Notification is sent February 28. 1% of all applicants are on a waiting list; 75 were accepted in 1999.

Financial Aid: In 1999-2000, 74% of all freshmen and 66% of continuing students received some form of financial aid. 55% of freshmen and 47% of continuing students received need-based aid. The average freshman award was $7930. Of that total, scholarships or need-based grants averaged $6033 ($15,410 maximum); loans averaged $3921 ($15,000 maximum); work contracts averaged $1485 ($1500 maximum); and outside scholarships averaged $1670 ($6806 maximum). 12% of undergraduates work part time. Average annual earnings from campus work are $1485. The average financial indebtedness of the 1999 graduate was $16,078. The FAFSA is required. The fall application deadline is March 15.

Computers: Central systems include 11 Sun UNIX servers dedicated to student use. These systems may be accessed from Macs, Windows-based PCs, and X-terminals located in several large labs. Services include E-mail, newsgroups, software applications, a campuswide information system, and access to the Internet. All students may access the system 24 hours a day. There are no time limits. The fee is $200 a year.

RUTGERS, THE STATE UNIVERSITY OF NEW JERSEY/DOUGLASS COLLEGE

New Brunswick, NJ 08903   (732) 932-INFO; Fax: (732) 445-0237

Full-time: 2954 women	**Faculty:** 1410; I, ++$
Part-time: 145 women	**Ph.D.s:** 98%
Graduate: none	**Student/Faculty:** n/av
Year: semesters, summer session	**Tuition:** $6228 ($11,158)
Application Deadline: see profile	**Room & Board:** $6098
Freshman Class: 6453 applied, 4419 accepted, 651 enrolled	
SAT I Verbal/Math: 560/557	**VERY COMPETITIVE**

Rutgers, The State University of New Jersey/Douglass College, founded in 1918, is a women's liberal arts institution. In addition to regional accreditation, Douglass College has baccalaureate program accreditation with AACSB, NASDTEC, and NASM. The 14 libraries contain 6,280,743 volumes, 5,285,009 microform items, and 116,306 audiovisual forms/CDs, and subscribe to 29,005 periodicals. Computerized library services include the card catalog, interlibrary loans, and database searching. Special learning facilities include a learning resource center, art gallery, radio station, TV station, geology museum, and various research institutes and centers, including the Center for Women and Work, the Eagleton Institute of Politics, and the Institute for Research on Women. The 2695-acre campus is in a suburban area 33 miles south of New York City. Including residence halls, there are 112 buildings.

Programs of Study: Douglass College confers B.A. and B.S. degrees. Bachelor's degrees are awarded in BIOLOGICAL SCIENCE (biochemistry, biology/biological science, biometrics and biostatistics, biotechnology, cell biology, genetics, marine science, and nutrition), BUSINESS (accounting, banking and finance, business administration and management, labor studies, management information systems, and marketing/retailing/merchandising), COMMUNICATIONS AND THE ARTS (art history and appreciation, Chinese, classical languages, classics, communications, comparative literature, dance, dramatic arts, English, French, German, Greek (classical), Italian, journalism, Latin, linguistics, music, Portuguese, Russian, Spanish, and visual and performing arts), COMPUTER AND PHYSICAL SCIENCE (atmospheric sciences and meteorology, chemistry, computer science, geology, mathematics, physics, and statistics), HEALTH PROFESSIONS (medical laboratory technology, predentistry, premedicine, and public health), SOCIAL SCIENCE (African American studies, American studies, anthropology, Caribbean studies, East Asian studies, economics, food science, geography, history, human ecology, Judaic studies, Latin American studies, medieval studies, Middle Eastern studies, philosophy, physical fitness/movement, political science/government, prelaw, psychology, religion, Russian and Slavic studies, sociology, urban studies, and women's studies). Biological sciences, psychology, and English are the largest.

Special: Douglass offers an alumnae-sponsored externship program, a Washington semester, B.A.-B.S. degrees in liberal arts and engineering, dual majors, student-designed majors, an environmental policy major through Cook College, 2-3 degrees with the School of Engineering, and pass/fail options. Students may study abroad in numerous countries. There is a certificate program in international studies. There is 1 national honor society, Phi Beta Kappa, and a freshman honors program.

Admissions: 68% of the 1999-2000 applicants were accepted. The SAT I scores for the 1999-2000 freshman class were: Verbal--18% below 500, 56% between 500 and 599, 23% between 600 and 700, and 3% above 700; Math--20% below 500, 56% between 500 and 599, 22% between 600 and 700, and 2% above 700. 38% of the current freshmen were in the top fifth of their class; 93% were in the top two fifths. There were 3 National Merit finalists. 7 freshmen graduated first in their class.

Requirements: The SAT I or ACT is required. Applicants must have completed 16 high school academic credits or Carnegie units, including 4 years of English, 3 years of math (algebra I and II and geometry), 2 years each of science and foreign language, and 5 other academic subjects. Students without a high school diploma, those from a nonaccredited high school, or those with academic deficiencies must take the SAT II: Subject tests in writing, math, and 1 other subject. Applications are accepted on-line at the university's web site. AP credits are accepted. Important factors in the admissions decision are advanced placement or honor courses, evidence of special talent, and leadership record.

Procedure: Freshmen are admitted in the fall. Entrance exams should be taken early in the senior year. There are early admissions and deferred admissions plans. The priority deadline for applications is December 15. There is a $50 fee. Notification is sent February 28. 1% of all applicants are on a waiting list; 70 were accepted in 1999.

Financial Aid: In 1999-2000, 71% of all freshmen and 64% of continuing students received some form of financial aid. 53% of freshmen and 49% of continuing students received need-based aid. The average freshman award was $7792. Of that total, scholarships or need-based grants averaged $5674 ($15,410 maximum); loans averaged $3963 ($17,375 maximum); work contracts averaged $1479 ($1500 maximum); and outside scholarships averaged $1674 ($8000 maximum). 15% of undergraduates work part time. Average annual earnings from campus work are $1487. The average financial indebtedness of the 1999 graduate was $16,496. Douglass College is a member of CSS. The FAFSA is required. The fall application deadline is March 15.

Computers: Central systems include 11 Sun UNIX servers dedicated for student use. Individual departments have a variety of PCs. The central systems may be accessed from Macs, Windows-based PCs, and X-terminals located in several large public labs. Services available include E-mail, newsgroups, software applications, a campuswide information system, and access to the Internet. All students may access the system 24 hours a day. There are no time limits. The fee is $200 per year.

RUTGERS, THE STATE UNIVERSITY OF NEW JERSEY/LIVINGSTON COLLEGE
New Brunswick, NJ 08903   (732) 932-INFO; Fax: (732) 445-0237

Full-time: 2025 men, 1328 women	**Faculty:** 1410; I, ++$
Part-time: 117 men, 66 women	**Ph.D.s:** 98%
Graduate: none	**Student/Faculty:** n/av
Year: semesters, summer session	**Tuition:** $6250 ($11,180)
Application Deadline: open	**Room & Board:** $6098
Freshman Class: 14,995 applied, 8927 accepted, 814 enrolled	
SAT I Verbal/Math: 554/578	**VERY COMPETITIVE**

Rutgers, The State University of New Jersey/Livingston College, founded in 1969, is a residential liberal arts college. In addition to regional accreditation, Livingston College has baccalaureate program accreditation with AACSB, CSWE, NASDTEC, and NASM. The 14 libraries contain 6,280,743 volumes, 5,285,009 microform items, and 116,306 audiovisual forms CDs, and subscribe to 29,005 periodicals. Computerized library services include the card catalog, interlibrary loans, and database searching. Special learning facilities include a learning resource center, art gallery, radio station, TV station, geology museum, and various research institutes and centers. The 2695-acre campus is in a suburban area 33 miles south of New York City. Including residence halls, there are 78 buildings.

Programs of Study: Livingston College confers B.A. and B.S. degrees. Bachelor's degrees are awarded in BIOLOGICAL SCIENCE (biochemistry, biology/biological science, biometrics and biostatistics, cell biology, ecology, genetics, marine science, and physiology), BUSINESS (accounting, banking and finance, business administration and management, labor studies, management information systems, and marketing/retailing/merchandising), COMMUNICATIONS AND THE ARTS (art history and appreciation, Chinese, classical languages, classics, communications, comparative literature, dance, dramatic arts, English, French, German, Greek (classical), Italian, journalism, Latin, linguistics, music, Portuguese, Russian, Spanish, and visual and performing arts), COMPUTER AND PHYSICAL SCIENCE (chemistry, computer science, geology, mathematics, physics, and statistics), HEALTH PROFESSIONS (medical laboratory technology, predentistry, premedicine, and public health), SOCIAL SCIENCE (African American studies, American studies, anthropology, Caribbean studies, criminal justice, East Asian studies, Eastern European studies, economics, geography, history, Judaic studies, Latin American studies, medieval studies, Middle Eastern studies, philosophy, physical fitness/movement, political science/government, prelaw, psychology, religion, social work, sociology, urban studies, and women's studies). Biological sciences, psychology, and English are the largest.

Special: Internships, a Washington semester, and accelerated degree programs are offered, as well as B.A.-B.S. degrees in computer science and physics, dual majors in statistics/math and history/political science, student-designed majors, a 2-3 engineering degree, and nondegree study. Credit for life, military, and work experience (including summer work) is available. There are pass/fail options under certain circumstances. Students may study abroad in numerous countries. There is 1 national honor society, Phi Beta Kappa, and a freshman honors program.

Admissions: 60% of the 1999-2000 applicants were accepted. The SAT I scores for the 1999-2000 freshman class were: Verbal--17% below 500, 63% between 500 and 599, 18% between 600 and 700, and 1% above 700; Math--11% below 500, 52% between 500 and 599, 35% between 600 and 700, and 2% above 700. 26% of the current freshmen were in the top fifth of their class; 85% were in the top two fifths. 1 freshman graduated first in class.

Requirements: The SAT I or ACT is required. Students should have completed 16 high school academic credits or Carnegie units, including 4 years of English, 3 years of math (algebra I and II and geometry), 2 years each of 1 foreign language and science, and 5 other approved academic subjects. The GED is accepted. Students without a high school diploma, those from a nonaccredited high school, or those with academic unit deficiencies must take the SAT II: Subject tests in writing, math, and 1 other subject. Applications may be submitted on-line to the Rutgers University web site. AP and CLEP credits are accepted. Important factors in the admissions decision are advanced placement or honor courses, evidence of special talent, and leadership record.

Procedure: Freshmen are admitted in the fall. Entrance exams should be taken early in the senior year. There are early admissions and deferred admissions plans. Application deadlines are open; there is a $50 fee. Notification is sent February 28. 3% of all applicants are on a waiting list.

Financial Aid: In 1999-2000, 66% of all freshmen and 61% of continuing students received some form of financial aid. 51% of freshmen and 50% of continuing students received need-based aid. The average freshman award was $7883. Of that total, scholarships or need-based grants averaged $5907 ($15,410 maximum); loans averaged $4186 ($17,000 maximum); work contracts averaged $1486 ($2000 maximum), and outside scholarships averaged $1127 ($4762 maximum). 15% of undergraduates work part time. Average annual earnings from campus work are $1490. The average financial indebtedness of the 1999 graduate was $15,942. The FAFSA is required. The fall application deadline is March 15.

Computers: The mainframe includes 11 Sun UNIX servers dedicated to student use. Individual departments have a variety of PCs. The central systems may be accessed from Macs, Windows-based PCs, and X-terminals located in several large public labs. Services available include E-mail, newsgroups, software applications, a campuswide information system, and access to the Internet. All students may access the system 24 hours a day. There are no time limits. The fee is $200.

RUTGERS, THE STATE UNIVERSITY OF NEW JERSEY/RUTGERS COLLEGE

New Brunswick, NJ 08903   (732) 932-INFO; Fax: (732) 445-0237

Full-time: 5138 men, 5518 women	**Faculty:** 1410; I, ++$
Part-time: 203 men, 134 women	**Ph.D.s:** 98%
Graduate: none	**Student/Faculty:** n/av
Year: semesters, summer session	**Tuition:** $6250 ($11,180)
Application Deadline: open	**Room & Board:** $6098
Freshman Class: 20,441 applied, 9896 accepted, 2462 enrolled	
SAT I Verbal/Math: 607/630	**HIGHLY COMPETITIVE**

Rutgers, The State University of New Jersey/Rutgers College, founded in 1766, is a liberal arts institution and the largest residential college in the Rutgers system. In addition to regional accreditation, Rutgers College has baccalaureate program accreditation with AACSB, NASDTEC, and NASM. The 14 libraries contain 6,280,743 volumes, 5,285,009 microform items, and 116,306 audiovisual forms/CDs, and subscribe to 29,005 periodicals. Computerized library services include the card catalog, interlibrary loans, and database searching. Special learning facilities include a learning resource center, art gallery, radio station, TV station, geology museum, and various research institutes and centers. The 2695-acre campus is in a suburban area 33 miles south of New York City. Including residence halls, there are 109 buildings.

Programs of Study: Rutgers College confers B.A. and B.S. degrees. Bachelor's degrees are awarded in BIOLOGICAL SCIENCE (biochemistry, biology/biological science, biometrics and biostatistics, cell biology, genetics, marine science, and physiology), BUSINESS (accounting, banking and finance, business administration and management, labor studies, management information systems, and marketing/retailing/merchandising), COMMUNICATIONS AND THE ARTS (art history and appreciation, Chinese, classical languages, classics, communications, comparative literature, dance, dramatic arts, English, French, German, Greek (classical), Italian, journalism, Latin, linguistics, music, Portuguese, Russian, Spanish, and visual and performing arts), COMPUTER AND PHYSICAL SCIENCE (chemistry, computer science, geology, mathematics, physics, and statistics), HEALTH PROFESSIONS (predentistry, premedicine, and public health), SOCIAL SCIENCE (African American studies, American studies, anthropology, Caribbean studies, criminal justice, East Asian studies, economics, geography, history, Judaic studies, Latin American studies, medieval studies, Middle Eastern studies, philosophy, physical fitness/movement, political science/government, prelaw, psychology, religion, Russian and Slavic studies, sociology, urban studies, and women's studies). Biological sciences, psychology, and economics have the largest enrollments.

Special: Rutgers College offers internships, a Washington semester, study abroad in numerous countries, student-designed majors, accelerated degree programs in business and engineering, and dual majors in statistics/math and history/political science. A 2-3 degree with the College of Engineering is also offered. There is 1 national honor society, Phi Beta Kappa, and a freshman honors program.

Admissions: 48% of the 1999-2000 applicants were accepted. The SAT I scores for the 1999-2000 freshman class were: Verbal--6% below 500, 40% between 500 and 599, 44% between 600 and 700, and 10% above 700; Math--3% below 500, 31% between 500 and 599, 51% between 600 and 700, and 15% above 700. 76% of the current freshmen were in the top fifth of their class; 98% were in the top two fifths. There were 11 National Merit finalists. 31 freshmen graduated first in their class.

Requirements: The SAT I or ACT is required. Applicants must have completed 16 high school credits or Carnegie units, including 4 years of English, 3 years of math (algebra I and II, and plane geometry), 2 years each of a foreign language and science, and 5 other academic subjects. Students without a high school diploma, those from a nonaccredited high school, or those with academic unit deficiencies must take the SAT II: Subject tests in writing, math, and 1 other subject. Applications may be submitted on-line at the Rutgers web site. AP credits are accepted. Important factors in the admissions decision are advanced placement or honor courses, evidence of special talent, and leadership record.

Procedure: Freshmen are admitted in the fall. Entrance exams should be taken early in the senior year. There are early admissions and deferred admissions plans. Application deadlines are open. There is a $50 fee. Notification is sent February 28. A waiting list is an active part of the admissions procedure.

Financial Aid: In 1999-2000, 76% of all freshmen and 63% of continuing students received some form of financial aid. 49% of freshmen and 43% of continuing students received need-based aid. The average freshman award was $7712. Of that total, scholarships or need-based grants averaged $6065 ($15,410 maximum); loans averaged $3923 ($17,000 maximum); work contracts averaged $1477 ($1500 maximum) and outside scholarships averaged $1630 ($8348 maximum). 12% of undergraduates work part time. Average annual earnings from campus work are $1495. The average financial indebtedness of the 1999 graduate was $15,560. The FAFSA is required. The fall application deadline is March 15.

Computers: The mainframe includes 11 Sun UNIX servers dedicated for student use. Individual departments have a variety of PCs. The central systems may be accessed from Macs, Windows-based PCs, and X-terminals located in several large public labs. Services include E-mail, newsgroups, software applications, a campuswide information system, and access to the Internet. All students may access the system 24 hours a day. There are no time limits. The fee is $200.

RUTGERS, THE STATE UNIVERSITY OF NEW JERSEY/SCHOOL OF ENGINEERING
New Brunswick, NJ 08903   (732) 932-INFO; Fax: (732) 445-0237

Full-time: 1649 men, 463 women	**Faculty:** 141; I, ++$
Part-time: 58 men, 20 women	**Ph.D.s:** 98%
Graduate: none	**Student/Faculty:** 15 to 1
Year: semesters, summer session	**Tuition:** $6763 ($12,231)
Application Deadline: December 15	**Room & Board:** $6098
Freshman Class: 3806 applied, 2593 accepted, 567 enrolled	
SAT I Verbal/Math: 593/670	**HIGHLY COMPETITIVE**

Rutgers, The State University of New Jersey/School of Engineering (formerly College of Engineering), founded in 1864, offers bachelor of science programs in engineering. In addition to regional accreditation, the school of Engineering has baccalaureate program accreditation with ABET. The 14 libraries contain 6, 280,743 volumes, 5,285,009 microform items, and 116,306 audiovisual forms/ CDs, and subscribe to 29,005 periodicals. Computerized library services include the card catalog, interlibrary loans, and database searching. Special learning facilities include a learning resource center, art gallery, radio station, TV station, fiber-optics drawing towers, a center for ceramics research that has ongoing projects for the Space Shuttle, research labs for artificial intelligence and virtual reality, the Nabisco Center for Advanced Food Technology for chemical and mechanical engineering research, and automated manufacturing labs for robotics.

The 2694-acre campus is in a suburban area 33 miles south of New York City. Including residence halls, there are 158 buildings.

Programs of Study: The School of Engineering confers the B.S. degree. Bachelor's degrees are awarded in ENGINEERING AND ENVIRONMENTAL DESIGN (bioengineering, ceramic engineering, chemical engineering, civil engineering, computer engineering, electrical/electronics engineering, engineering and applied science, environmental engineering, industrial engineering, and mechanical engineering). Electrical, mechanical, and chemical engineering are the largest.

Special: The school offers study abroad in England, 2-3 dual degree programs in conjunction with other undergraduate colleges of Rutgers, and B.A.-B.S. degrees in all engineering majors and all B.A. majors offered on the New Brunswick campus. Pass/fail options are limited to 2 elective courses. Internships are offered through the engineering departments and Career Services. An extended business degree is offered with the Graduate School of Management, and an 8-year medical degree is available with the University of Medicine and Dentistry of New Jersey. There are 7 national honor societies, a freshman honors program, and 7 departmental honors programs.

Admissions: 68% of the 1999-2000 applicants were accepted. The SAT I scores for the 1999-2000 freshman class were: Verbal--10% below 500, 44% between 500 and 599, 40% between 600 and 700, and 6% above 700; Math--14% between 500 and 599, 59% between 600 and 700, and 28% above 700. 67% of the current freshmen were in the top fifth of their class; 93% were in the top two fifths. There was 1 National Merit finalist. 10 freshmen graduated first in their class.

Requirements: The SAT I or ACT is required. The GED is accepted. Students must have completed 16 academic credits or Carnegie units, including 4 years each of English and math (through precalculus), 1 year each of chemistry and physics, plus 6 other approved academic subjects. Computer programming is recommended. Students without a high school diploma, those from nonaccredited high schools, and those with academic unit entrance deficiencies must take SAT II: Subject tests in writing, math, and a science. Students may access the on-line application at the Rutgers web site. AP credits are accepted. Important factors in the admissions decision are advanced placement or honor courses, evidence of special talent, and leadership record.

Procedure: Freshmen are admitted in the fall. Entrance exams should be taken early in the senior year. There are early admissions and deferred admissions plans. Applications should be filed by December 15 for fall entry, along with a $50 fee. Notification is sent February 28. 1% of all applicants are on a waiting list.

Financial Aid: In 1999-2000, 74% of all freshmen and 64% of continuing students received some form of financial aid. 50% of freshmen and 44% of continuing students received need-based aid. The average freshman award was $7868. Of that total, scholarships or need-based grants averaged $6146 ($15,410 maximum); loans averaged $3549 ($15,375 maximum); work contracts averaged $1490 ($1500 maximum); and outside scholarships averaged $2094 ($18,553 maximum). 13% of undergraduates work part time. Average annual earnings from campus work are $1496. The average financial indebtedness of the 1999 graduate was $16,386. The FAFSA is required. The fall application deadline is March 15.

Computers: Central systems include 11 Sun UNIX servers dedicated to student use. Individual departments have a variety of PCs. The central systems may be accessed from Macs, Windows-based PCs, and X-terminals located in several large public labs. Services available include E-mail, newsgroups, software applications, a campuswide information system, and access to the Internet. All students may access the system 24 hours a day. There are no time limits. The fee is $200.

SAINT JOHN'S COLLEGE
Annapolis, MD 21404

(410) 626-2523
(800) 727-9238; Fax: (410) 269-7916

Full-time: 245 men, 206 women	**Faculty:** 68; IIB, +$
Part-time: 1 man	**Ph.D.s:** 71%
Graduate: 38 men, 26 women	**Student/Faculty:** 6 to 1
Year: semesters, summer session	**Tuition:** $23,490
Application Deadline: open	**Room & Board:** $6360

Freshman Class: 446 applied, 349 accepted, 133 enrolled
SAT I Verbal/Math: 700/630 **HIGHLY COMPETITIVE+**

St. John's College, founded as King William's School in 1696 and chartered as St. John's in 1784, is a private institution that offers a single all-required curriculum sometimes called the Great Books Program. Students and faculty work together in small discussion classes without lecture courses, written finals, or emphasis on grades. The program is a rigorous interdisciplinary curriculum based on the great works of literature, math, philosophy, theology, sciences, political theory, music, history, and economics. There is also a campus in Santa Fe, New Mexico. There is 1 graduate school. The 2 libraries contain 98,245 volumes, 961 microform items, and 10,526 audiovisual forms/CDs, and subscribe to 114 periodicals. Computerized library services include the card catalog, interlibrary loans, and database searching. Special learning facilities include an art gallery and planetarium. The 36-acre campus is in a small town 35 miles east of Washington, D.C., and 32 miles south of Baltimore. Including residence halls, there are 16 buildings.

Programs of Study: St. John's confers the B.A. degree. Master's degrees are also awarded. Bachelor's degrees are awarded in SOCIAL SCIENCE (liberal arts/general studies, Western civilization/culture, and Western European studies).

Admissions: 78% of the 1999-2000 applicants were accepted. The SAT I scores for the 1999-2000 freshman class were: Verbal--6% between 500 and 599, 39% between 600 and 700, and 54% above 700; Math--6% below 500, 27% between 500 and 599, 49% between 600 and 700, and 19% above 700. 63% of the current freshmen were in the top fifth of their class; 88% were in the top two fifths. There were 12 National Merit finalists and 7 semifinalists.

Requirements: Applicants need not be high school graduates; some students are admitted before they complete high school. Test scores may be submitted but are not required. Secondary preparation should include 4 years of English, 3 years of math, and 2 years each of foreign language, science, and history. Applicants must submit written essays, which are critical to the admissions decision, and are strongly urged to schedule an interview. Important factors in the admissions decision are recommendations by school officials, advanced placement or honor courses, and personality/intangible qualities.

Procedure: Freshmen are admitted fall and spring. There are early admissions and deferred admissions plans. Application deadlines are open. Notification is sent on a rolling basis.

Financial Aid: In 1999-2000, 65% of all freshmen and 58% of continuing students received some form of financial aid. 52% of freshmen and 55% of continuing students received need-based aid. The average freshman award was $19,826. Of that total, scholarships or need-based grants averaged $13,370 ($21,000 maximum); loans averaged $2625 ($5500 maximum); and work contracts averaged

$2200. 75% of undergraduates work part time. Average annual earnings from campus work are $2350. The average financial indebtedness of the 1999 graduate was $17,525. St. John's is a member of CSS. The CSS/Profile or FAFSA is required. The fall application deadline is February 15.

Computers: The mainframe is an IBM AS/400. There is a network of 8 Macs available for student use in a computer room, as well as 1 Mac and 10 PCs in the library. They are equipped with word-processing programs and a variety of other software. All student dormatories are connected to the network. All students may access the system 24 hours a day. There are no time limits and no fees.

SAINT JOHN'S COLLEGE
Santa Fe, NM 87501

(505) 984-6060
(800) 331-5232; Fax: (505) 984-6003

Full-time: 244 men, 191 women	**Faculty:** 54
Part-time: none	**Ph.D.s:** 76%
Graduate: 58 men, 53 women	**Student/Faculty:** 8 to 1
Year: semesters, summer session	**Tuition:** $22,200
Application Deadline: open	**Room & Board:** $6386
Freshman Class: 333 applied, 297 accepted, 125 enrolled	
SAT I Verbal/Math: 690/620	**ACT:** 29 **VERY COMPETITIVE+**

St. John's College, founded in 1696, offers a curriculum based on the Great Books Program, in which students and faculty work together in small discussion classes without lecture courses, written finals, or emphasis on grades. The program is a rigorous interdisciplinary curriculum based on great books -- literature, math, philosophy theology, sciences, political theory, music, history, economics -- from Homer to Freud, Euclid to Einstein. There is 1 graduate school. The library contains 50,000 volumes and 8205 audiovisual forms/CDs, and subscribes to 135 periodicals. Computerized library services include the card catalog, interlibrary loans, and database searching. Special learning facilities include an art gallery and a music library, a search and rescue headquarters, and music practice rooms. The 250-acre campus is in Santa Fe. Including residence halls, there are 31 buildings.

Programs of Study: St. John's confers the B.A. degree. Master's degrees are also awarded. Bachelor's degrees are awarded in SOCIAL SCIENCE (liberal arts/general studies).

Special: Internships with alumni in a wide range of fields are available and students may transfer between the Santa Fe and Annapolis campuses. Premedical studies at universities around the country and 4-1 teaching certification through the University of New Mexico are possible.

Admissions: 89% of the 1999-2000 applicants were accepted. The SAT I scores for the 1999-2000 freshman class were: Verbal--1% below 500, 9% between 500 and 599, 46% between 600 and 700, and 44% above 700; Math--7% below 500, 28% between 500 and 599, 48% between 600 and 700, and 17% above 700. 59% of the current freshmen were in the top fifth of their class; 85% were in the top two fifths. There were 8 National Merit finalists and 9 semifinalists. 4 freshmen graduated first in their class.

Requirements: Applicants must write 3 personel essays and submit 2 teacher references, a secondary school report including a reference from a school official, and transcript of all academic work in high school and college. A campus visit and interview are recommended. Three years of math and 2 years of foreign language are required; 4 years each of math, foreign language, English, and science are recommended. The GED is accepted for early admission candidates. The SAT

I or ACT is required of early admission candidates. Important factors in the admissions decision are advanced placement or honor courses, evidence of special talent, and recommendations by school officials.

Procedure: Freshmen are admitted fall and spring. There are early admissions and deferred admissions plans. Application deadlines are open. Notification is sent on a rolling basis.

Financial Aid: In 1999-2000, 82% of all freshmen and 75% of continuing students received some form of financial aid. 82% of freshmen and 69% of continuing students received need-based aid. The average freshman award was $18,272. Of that total, scholarships or need-based grants averaged $11,754 ($20,136 maximum); loans averaged $2625; and work contracts averaged $2015. 75% of undergraduates work part time. Average annual earnings from campus work are $2015. The average financial indebtedness of the 1999 graduate was $17,000. St. John's is a member of CSS. The CSS/Profile or FAFSA and the college's own financial statement are required. The fall application deadline is February 15.

Computers: A computer lab with both Mac and IBM PCs and printers is available to students. All students may access the system. There are no time limits. The fee is $20.

SAINT JOHN'S UNIVERSITY
Collegeville, MN 56321-7155　　　　　　　　(320) 363-2196
(800) 245-6467; Fax: (320) 363-3206

Full-time: 1753 men, 1 woman	**Faculty:** 121; IIB, av$
Part-time: 30 men, 19 women	**Ph.D.s:** 81%
Graduate: 65 men, 64 women	**Student/Faculty:** 14 to 1
Year: 4-1-4	**Tuition:** $16,441
Application Deadline: open	**Room & Board:** $4930
Freshman Class: 1159 applied, 950 accepted, 475 enrolled	
SAT I Verbal/Math: 580/590	**ACT:** 25　　**VERY COMPETITIVE**

St. John's University, founded in 1857 by Benedictine monks, is a private institution offering programs in the liberal arts. The university is a college for men but shares an academic calendar, academic curriculum, and most cocurricular programs with the College of St. Benedict, a college for women 4 miles away. There is 1 graduate school. In addition to regional accreditation, St. John's has baccalaureate program accreditation with ADA, CSWE, NASM, NCATE, and NLN. The 4 libraries contain 569,410 volumes, 114,851 microform items, and 19,589 audiovisual forms/CDs, and subscribe to 1717 periodicals. Computerized library services include the card catalog, interlibrary loans, and database searching. Special learning facilities include a learning resource center, art gallery, natural history museum, radio station, tv station, observatory, greenhouse, and arboretum. The 2400-acre campus is in a rural area 15 miles west of St. Cloud and 70 miles northwest of Minneapolis and St. Paul. Including residence halls, there are 35 buildings.

Programs of Study: St. John's confers the B.A. degree. Master's degrees are also awarded. Bachelor's degrees are awarded in AGRICULTURE (forestry and related sciences), BIOLOGICAL SCIENCE (biology/biological science and nutrition), BUSINESS (accounting and management science), COMMUNICATIONS AND THE ARTS (art, classics, communications, dramatic arts, English, fine arts, French, German, music, and Spanish), COMPUTER AND PHYSICAL SCIENCE (chemistry, computer science, mathematics, natural sciences, and physics), EDUCATION (elementary), ENGINEERING AND ENVIRONMENTAL DESIGN (preengineering), HEALTH PROFESSIONS (medical laboratory technology, nursing, occupational therapy, physical therapy, predentistry, premedicine, prepharmacy, and preveterinary science), SOCIAL SCIENCE (dietetics, economics, history, humanities, pastoral studies, peace studies, philosophy, political science/government, prelaw, psychology, social science, social work, sociology, and theological studies). Biology, chemistry, and economics are the strongest academically. Management, biology, and computer science are the largest.

Special: There is cross-registration with the College of St. Benedict. An extensive program of internships and fieldwork, including programs in Latin America, South America, and Scandinavia, is offered. Students may design their own majors and individual learning projects, and may study abroad in 12 countries. There is a 3-2 engineering program with several universities. Double majors, including math/computer science and preprofessional programs, nondegree study, and pass/fail options are available. There is 1 national honor society and a freshman honors program.

Admissions: 82% of the 1999-2000 applicants were accepted. The SAT I scores for the 1999-2000 freshman class were: Verbal--17% below 500, 44% between 500 and 599, 29% between 600 and 700, and 10% above 700; Math--11% below 500, 40% between 500 and 599, 38% between 600 and 700, and 11% above 700. The ACT scores were 8% below 21, 26% between 21 and 23, 33% between 24 and 26, 18% between 27 and 28, and 15% above 28. 47% of the current freshmen were in the top fifth of their class; 83% were in the top two fifths. There was 1 National Merit finalist. 17 freshmen graduated first in their class in a recent year.

Requirements: The SAT I or ACT is required. St. John's requires applicants to be in the upper 60% of their class. A GPA of 2.8 is required. Students should be graduates of an accredited secondary school. Academic preparation should include 17 units, including 4 of English, 3 of math, 2 each of science and social studies, and 6 electives; a foreign language is recommended. A GED equivalence is accepted. An essay is required and an interview is recommended. The university accepts electronic applications via CollegeLink and ExPAN. Details can be found at the on-line application site at http://www.csbsju.edu/admission/index.html. AP and CLEP credits are accepted. Important factors in the admissions decision are leadership record, advanced placement or honor courses, and evidence of special talent.

Procedure: Freshmen are admitted fall and winter. Entrance exams should be taken by the fall of the senior year. There is a deferred admissions plan. Application deadlines are open. There is a $25 fee. Notification is sent on a rolling basis. A waiting list is an active part of the admissions procedure.

Financial Aid: In 1999-2000, 88% of all freshmen and 86% of continuing students received some form of financial aid. 70% of freshmen and 69% of continuing students received need-based aid. The average freshman award was $13,719. Of that total, scholarships or need-based grants averaged $75,000 ($12,500 maximum); loans averaged $2750 ($4625 maximum); and work contracts averaged $2075 (maximum). 45% of undergraduates work part time. Average annual earnings from campus work are $2075. The average financial indebtedness of the 1999 graduate is $16,487. St. John's is a member of CSS. The FAFSA, the college's own financial statement, and federal tax returns and W-2s are required. The fall application deadline is March 1.

Computers: The mainframe is a Windows NT network. Networked PCs are available in the computer center, library, and academic buildings. Most student residences are connected to PC and Mac networks. All students may access the system 24 hours a day. There are no time limits and no fees.

SAINT JOSEPH'S UNIVERSITY

Philadelphia, PA 19131

(610) 660-1300
(888) BEAHAWK; Fax: (610) 660-1314

Full-time: 1540 men, 1858 women	**Faculty:** 208; IIA, ++$
Part-time: 425 men, 584 women	**Ph.D.s:** 91%
Graduate: 993 men, 1578 women	**Student/Faculty:** 16 to 1
Year: semesters, summer session	**Tuition:** $18,390
Application Deadline: open	**Room & Board:** $7514
Freshman Class: 5690 applied, 3450 accepted, 990 enrolled	
SAT I Verbal/Math: 575/631	**VERY COMPETITIVE**

Saint Joseph's University, founded in 1851, is a private Catholic affiliated with the Jesuit order. It offers undergraduate programs in arts and sciences and business administration. There are 3 undergraduate and 2 graduate schools. In addition to regional accreditation, Saint Joseph's has baccalaureate program accreditation with NCATE. The 2 libraries contain 335,000 volumes, 750,000 microform items, and 2000 audiovisual forms/CDs, and subscribe to 1800 periodicals. Computerized library services include the card catalog, interlibrary loans, and database searching. Special learning facilities include a learning resource center, art gallery, radio station, instructional media center, and foreign language labs. The 60-acre campus is in a suburban area on the western edge of Philadelphia. Including residence halls, there are 47 buildings.

Programs of Study: Saint Joseph's confers B.A. and B.S. degrees. Associate and master's degrees are also awarded. Bachelor's degrees are awarded in BIOLOGICAL SCIENCE (biology/biological science), BUSINESS (accounting, banking and finance, business administration and management, labor studies, management science, and marketing/retailing/merchandising), COMMUNICATIONS AND THE ARTS (English, fine arts, French, German, and Spanish), COMPUTER AND PHYSICAL SCIENCE (chemistry, computer science, information sciences and systems, mathematics, and physics), EDUCATION (elementary and secondary), ENGINEERING AND ENVIRONMENTAL DESIGN (environmental science), HEALTH PROFESSIONS (health care administration), SOCIAL SCIENCE (criminal justice, economics, food production/management/services, French studies, history, human services, humanities, industrial and organizational psychology, international relations, philosophy, political science/government, psychology, public administration, religion, social studies, and sociology). Social sciences, natural sciences, and English are the strongest academically. Biology, psychology, and food marketing are the largest.

Special: There is an exchange program with a Japanese university and study abroad in 8 countries. The college offers internships, a Washington semester, advanced 5-year degrees in international marketing and in psychology, dual majors, minor concentrations, and special programs in American, Latin American, European, Russian, gender, and medieval studies. There is a co-op program for food marketing majors and an interdisciplinary major in health services. There are 17 national honor societies and a freshman honors program.

Admissions: 61% of the 1999-2000 applicants were accepted. 15 freshmen graduated first in their class in a recent year.

Requirements: The SAT I or ACT is required. Saint Joseph's requires applicants to be in the upper 40% of their class. A GPA of 3.0 is required. The SAT II: Subject test in writing is also recommended. Applicants must graduate from an accredited secondary school and prepare with 4 years of English, 3 of math, 2 each of foreign language and science, and 1 each of history and social studies. Preference is given to students with 3 to 4 years of foreign language and natural science and 4 years of math. An interview is recommended. Applications are accepted on computer disk via CollegeLink and the Common Application. AP and CLEP credits are accepted. Important factors in the admissions decision are advanced placement or honor courses, extracurricular activities record, and parents or siblings attending the school.

Procedure: Freshmen are admitted fall and spring. Entrance exams should be taken in the spring of the junior year or the fall of the senior year. There are early admissions and deferred admissions plans. Application deadlines are open. There is a $40 fee. Notification is sent on a rolling basis. A waiting list is an active part of the admissions procedure.

Financial Aid: In 1999-2000, 87% of all freshmen and 81% of continuing students received some form of financial aid. 72% of freshmen and 75% of continuing students received need-based aid. The average freshman award was $10,625. Of that total, scholarships or need-based grants averaged $6170 ($16,130 maximum); loans averaged $3425 ($3625 maximum); and work contracts averaged $1200 ($2000 maximum). 50% of undergraduates work part time. Average annual earnings from campus work are $1100. The average financial indebtedness of a recent graduate was $13,379. Saint Joseph's is a member of CSS. The FAFSA and PHEAA are required. The fall application deadline is May 1.

Computers: There are minicomputers and servers. Campuswide access is provided by 6 computer labs and 3 PC classrooms (143 systems); in addition, residence facilities are networked for 150 students. Dial-up access is also available. All students may access the system whenever the labs are open (about 90 hours per week) or any time if students are connected in their dormitory rooms. There are no time limits and no fees.

SAINT LAWRENCE UNIVERSITY
Canton, NY 13617

(315) 229-5261
(800) 285-1856; Fax: (315) 229-5818

Full-time: 904 men, 957 women	**Faculty:** 150; IIB, +$
Part-time: 13 men, 21 women	**Ph.D.s:** 97%
Graduate: 38 men, 65 women	**Student/Faculty:** 13 to 1
Year: semesters, summer session	**Tuition:** $23,095
Application Deadline: February 15	**Room & Board:** $7205
Freshman Class: 2235 applied, 1647 accepted, 575 enrolled	
SAT I Verbal/Math: 560/560	**VERY COMPETITIVE**

Saint Lawrence University, established in 1856, is a private liberal arts institution. Some of the information in this profile is approximate. There is 1 graduate school. The 2 libraries contain 472,258 volumes and 519,078 microform items, and subscribe to 1948 periodicals. Computerized library services include the card catalog, interlibrary loans, and database searching. Special learning facilities include a learning resource center, art gallery, radio station, and TV station. The 1000-acre campus is in a rural area 80 miles south of Ottawa, Canada. Including residence halls, there are 30 buildings.

Programs of Study: St. Lawrence confers B.A. and B.S. degrees. Master's degrees are also awarded. Bachelor's degrees are awarded in BIOLOGICAL SCIENCE (biology/biological science), BUSINESS (recreation and leisure services), COMMUNICATIONS AND THE ARTS (dramatic arts, English, fine arts, French, German, music, and Spanish), COMPUTER AND PHYSICAL SCIENCE (chemistry, computer science, geology, mathematics, and physics), ENGINEERING AND ENVIRONMENTAL DESIGN (environmental science), SOCIAL SCIENCE (anthropology, Asian/Oriental studies, Canadian studies, economics, history, interdisciplinary studies, philosophy, political science/government, psychology, religion, and sociology). Physical sciences and modern languages are the strongest academically. Psychology, English, and economics are the largest.

Special: Students may cross-register with the Associated Colleges of the St. Lawrence Valley. Internships are available through the sociology, psychology, and English departments and through a service learning program. Study abroad in 12 countries, a Washington semester, and a semester at sea are offered. Dual majors and student-designed majors can be arranged. Students may earn 3-2 engineering degrees in conjunction with 7 engineering schools. A 3-2 nursing degree program is available with the University of Rochester. Nondegree study and pass/fail options are also available. There are 20 national honor societies, including Phi Beta Kappa, and 17 departmental honors programs. .

Admissions: 74% of the 1999-2000 applicants were accepted. The SAT I scores for the 1999-2000 freshman class were: Verbal--18% below 500, 51% between 500 and 599, 27% between 600 and 700, and 5% above 700; Math--18% below 500, 47% between 500 and 599, 31% between 600 and 700, and 4% above 700. 51% of the current freshmen were in the top fifth of their class; 79% were in the top two fifths. 15 freshmen graduated first in their class.

Requirements: The SAT I is required. The SAT II: Writing test is also required and 2 other subject tests are recommended. Applicants must be graduates of an accredited high school. 16 or more academic credits are required, including 4 years of English and 3 years each of foreign languages, math, science, and social studies. Essays are required and interviews are recommended for all applicants. Applications are accepted on-line. AP and CLEP credits are accepted. Important factors in the admissions decision are advanced placement or honor courses, extracurricular activities record, and recommendations by school officials.

Procedure: Freshmen are admitted fall, spring, and summer. Entrance exams should be taken during the spring of the junior year or the fall of the senior year. There are early decision and deferred admissions plans. Applications should be filed by February 15 for fall entry and December 1 for spring entry, along with a $50 fee. Notification is sent March 15. In a recent year, 106 early decision candidates were accepted. 3% of all applicants were on a waiting list.

Financial Aid: In 1999-2000, 86% of all freshmen and 81% of continuing students received some form of financial aid. 76% of freshmen and 71% of continuing students received need-based aid. The average freshman award was $16,599. Of that total, scholarships or need-based grants averaged $11,834 ($26,140 maximum); loans averaged $5545 ($5600 maximum); and work contracts averaged $1152 ($1700 maximum). 37% of undergraduates work part time. Average annual earnings from campus work are $1000. The average financial indebtedness of the 1999 graduate was $15,000. St. Lawrence is a member of CSS. The FAFSA is required. The fall application deadline is February 15.

Computers: The mainframe is an IBM 9121. 600 PCs are linked to the mainframe and card catalog. Word processing, spreadsheet, database, and course-specific software, E-mail, calendars, bulletin boards, and Internet and World Wide Web access are available. Computer labs are located in all residence halls and most academic buildings. All students may access the system 24 hours per day. There are no time limits. The fee is $275 for 4 years.

SAINT LOUIS UNIVERSITY

St. Louis, MO 63103-2097

(314) 977-2500
(800) SLUFORU; Fax: (314) 977-7136

Full-time: 2783 men, 3373 women	**Faculty:** 366; I, -$
Part-time: 331 men, 402 women	**Ph.D.s:** 95%
Graduate: 1803 men, 2377 women	**Student/Faculty:** 17 to 1
Year: semesters, summer session	**Tuition:** $17,268
Application Deadline: December 1	**Room & Board:** $5900
Freshman Class: 4990 applied, 3440 accepted, 1274 enrolled	
SAT I Verbal/Math: 580/585	**ACT:** 26 **VERY COMPETITIVE+**

Saint Louis University, founded in 1818, is a private institution affiliated with the Jesuit Order of the Roman Catholic Church. There are 9 undergraduate schools and 1 graduate school. In addition to regional accreditation, SLU has baccalaureate program accreditation with AACSB, ABET, AHEA, APTA, CSWE, NCATE, and NLN. The 3 libraries contain 1,728,587 volumes, 2,238,622 microform items, and 197,603 audiovisual forms/CDs, and subscribe to 14,389 periodicals. Computerized library services include the card catalog, interlibrary loans, and database searching. Special learning facilities include a learning resource center, art gallery, radio station, and TV station. The 254-acre campus is in an urban area in the Midtown Arts District of St. Louis. Including residence halls, there are 106 buildings.

Programs of Study: SLU confers B.A. and B.S. degrees. Associate, master's, and doctoral degrees are also awarded. Bachelor's degrees are awarded in BIOLOGICAL SCIENCE (biology/biological science and nutrition), BUSINESS (accounting, banking and finance, business administration and management, business economics, hospitality management services, human resources, international business management, marketing/retailing/merchandising, organizational behavior, personnel management, and tourism), COMMUNICATIONS AND THE ARTS (art history and appreciation, communications, dramatic arts, English, fine arts, French, German, Greek, Latin, music, Russian, Spanish, and studio art), COMPUTER AND PHYSICAL SCIENCE (applied mathematics, chemistry, computer science, earth science, geology, geophysics and seismology, information sciences and systems, mathematics, and physics), EDUCATION (early childhood, elementary, secondary, and special), ENGINEERING AND ENVIRONMENTAL DESIGN (aeronautical engineering, aircraft mechanics, airline piloting and navigation, aviation administration/management, biomedical engineering, computer technology, electrical/electronics engineering, electrical/electronics engineering technology, engineering management, environmental science, and mechanical engineering), HEALTH PROFESSIONS (clinical science, health care administration, nuclear medical technology, nursing, occupational therapy, physical therapy, physician's assistant, and speech pathology/audiology), SOCIAL SCIENCE (American studies, classical/ancient civilization, criminal justice, dietetics, economics, history, humanities, international studies, philosophy, political science/government, psychology, public administration, religion, social science, social work, sociology, theological studies, and urban studies). Physical therapy, aerospace engineering, and psychology are the strongest academically. Biology, psychology, and physical therapy are the largest.

Special: Students may study abroad in Spain, France, and Germany. SLU offers co-op programs through the School of Business, cross-registration with Washington University and the University of Missouri at St. Louis, internships with local financial institutions, work-study programs on campus, an accelerated degree program in nursing, a 3-2 engineering degree program with Washington Univer-

457

sity in St. Louis, dual majors, student-designed majors, and pass/fail options. There are 18 national honor societies, including Phi Beta Kappa, and a freshman honors program.

Admissions: 69% of the 1999-2000 applicants were accepted. The ACT scores for the 1999-2000 freshman class were: 8% below 21, 22% between 21 and 23, 28% between 24 and 26, 16% between 27 and 28, and 26% above 28. 56% of the current freshmen were in the top fifth of their class; 82% were in the top two fifths. There were 23 National Merit finalists. 45 freshmen graduated first in their class.

Requirements: The ACT is required. A GPA of 2.0 is required. Applicants must be graduates of accredited secondary schools or have earned a GED. Students are encouraged to take 4 or more academic courses each semester of high school including 4 years of English, 3 each of math, and academic electives, and 2 each of natural sciences, social sciences, and foreign language. Other requirements include courses in biology and chemistry for the School of Nursing and the School of Allied Health Professions; physics, an additional year of natural science, and 4 years of math for the physical therapy program; a third year of natural science (preferably physics) for admission to the occupational therapy and nutrition and dietetics programs; and a fourth year of math for the Parks College engineering or aviation programs. Applications are accepted on computer disk or on-line at http://www.slu.edu/admissions/. AP and CLEP credits are accepted. Important factors in the admissions decision are advanced placement or honor courses, extracurricular activities record, and leadership record.

Procedure: Freshmen are admitted to all sessions. Entrance exams should be taken in the fall of the senior year. There are early admissions and deferred admissions plans. Applications should be filed by December 1 for fall entry and January 1 for winter entry, along with a $25 fee. Notification is sent on a rolling basis.

Financial Aid: In 1999-2000, 96% of all freshmen and 82% of continuing students received some form of financial aid. 82% of freshmen and 75% of continuing students received need-based aid. The average freshman award was $18,067. Of that total, scholarships or need-based grants averaged $13,976 ($26,518 maximum); loans averaged $3791 ($5625 maximum); and work contracts averaged $2600 ($2603 maximum). 19% of undergraduates work part time. Average annual earnings from campus work are $1191. The average financial indebtedness of the 1999 graduate was $14,067. SLU is a member of CSS. The FAFSA is required. The fall application deadline is July 1.

Computers: The mainframe is a DEC ALPHA 2000 cluster. There are more than 600 PCs available for student use in various labs. All students may access the system. There are no time limits and no fees.

SAINT MARY'S COLLEGE
Notre Dame, IN 46556

(219) 284-4587
(800) 551-7621; Fax: (219) 284-4716

Full-time: 11 men, 1452 women	**Faculty:** 107; IIB, +$
Part-time: 46 women	**Ph.D.s:** 97%
Graduate: 2 men, 6 women	**Student/Faculty:** 14 to 1
Year: semesters	**Tuition:** $16,994
Application Deadline: March 1	**Room & Board:** $5962
Freshman Class: 1041 applied, 869 accepted, 424 enrolled	
SAT I Verbal/Math: 570/560	**ACT:** 25 **VERY COMPETITIVE**

Saint Mary's College, established in 1844, was founded and sponsored by the Congregation of the Sisters of the Holy Cross. It is a Catholic comprehensive college for women in the liberal arts tradition. In addition to regional accreditation, Saint Mary's College has baccalaureate program accreditation with CSWE, NASAD, NASM, NCATE, and NLN. The library contains 201,253 volumes, 13,515 microform items, and 3359 audiovisual forms/CDs, and subscribes to 758 periodicals. Computerized library services include the card catalog and database searching. Special learning facilities include an art gallery. The 275-acre campus is in a suburban area 90 miles east of Chicago. Including residence halls, there are 14 buildings.

Programs of Study: Saint Mary's College confers B.A., B.S., B.B.A., B.F.A., and B.Mus. degrees. Bachelor's degrees are awarded in BIOLOGICAL SCIENCE (biology/biological science), BUSINESS (business administration and management), COMMUNICATIONS AND THE ARTS (art, communications, dramatic arts, English, fine arts, French, music, and Spanish), COMPUTER AND PHYSICAL SCIENCE (chemistry and mathematics), EDUCATION (elementary), HEALTH PROFESSIONS (nursing), SOCIAL SCIENCE (economics, history, humanities, philosophy, political science/government, psychology, religion, social work, and sociology). Art, business, and English are the strongest academically. Letters and humanities, social sciences, and business are the largest.

Special: Cross-registration is permitted with the University of Notre Dame and a consortium of 6 northern Indiana colleges. Opportunities are provided for internships, a Washington semester, an accelerated degree program in nursing, dual and student-designed majors, a 3-2 engineering degree with the University of Notre Dame, nondegree study, pass/fail options, and study abroad in 18 countries. There are 9 national honor societies and 2 departmental honors programs.

Admissions: 83% of the 1999-2000 applicants were accepted. The SAT I scores for the 1999-2000 freshman class were: Verbal--13% below 500, 52% between 500 and 599, 31% between 600 and 700, and 4% above 700; Math--18% below 500, 49% between 500 and 599, 30% between 600 and 700, and 3% above 700. The ACT scores were 12% below 21, 20% between 21 and 23, 39% between 24 and 26, 15% between 27 and 28, and 14% above 28. 57% of the current freshmen were in the top fifth of their class; 89% were in the top two fifths. There were 2 National Merit finalists and 4 semifinalists. 18 freshmen graduated first in their class.

Requirements: The SAT I or ACT is required. SAT II: Subject tests are required in writing, math, and foreign languange. Graduation from an accredited secondary school is required; a GED will be accepted. Applicants must have completed 16 academic credits, including 4 in English, 3 in math, 2 in a foreign language, 2 in history or social studies, 1 in science, and the remainder from college-preparatory electives in the above areas. An essay is required. Students may access an on-line application at the college's web site. AP and CLEP credits are accepted. Important factors in the admissions decision are advanced placement or honor courses, evidence of special talent, and recommendations by school officials.

Procedure: Freshmen are admitted fall and spring. Entrance exams should be taken between March of the junior year and December of the senior year. There are early decision, early admissions, and deferred admissions plans. Early decision applications should be filed by November 15; regular applications, by March 1 for fall entry and November 15 for spring entry, along with a $30 fee. Notification of early decision is sent December 15; regular decision, on a rolling basis. 137 early decision candidates were accepted for the 1999-2000 class.

Financial Aid: In 1999-2000, 85% of all freshmen and 76% of continuing students received some form of financial aid. 66% of freshmen and 63% of continuing students received need-based aid. Scholarships or need-based grants averaged $8364 ($15,275 maximum); loans averaged $3556 ($5625 maximum); and work contracts averaged $1471 ($2300 maximum). 42% of undergraduates work part time. Average annual earnings from campus work are $1471. The average financial indebtedness of the 1999 graduate was $15,894. Saint Mary's College is a member of CSS. The CSS/Profile or FAFSA is required. The fall application deadline is March 1.

Computers: The mainframe is a Sun Ultra Enterprise 450. 162 PCs and Macs are available for student use in the computer labs and at various other locations around campus. All computers are networked and have Internet access. All students have direct access to the campus network from their dorm rooms. The Internet, on-line instructional materials, and the library catalog are available for college-related work. All students may access the system 24 hours a day. There are no time limits and no fees. It is recommended that all students have Mac (System 8.1 preferred) or Windows 95/98 personal computers with an appropriate Ethernet card. Dell or Gateway models are strongly recommended.

SAINT MARY'S COLLEGE OF MARYLAND
St. Mary's City, MD 20686-3001   (301) 862-0292
(800) 492-7181; Fax: (301) 862-0906

Full-time: 621 men, 798 women	**Faculty:** 116; IIB, ++$
Part-time: 57 men, 137 women	**Ph.D.s:** 94%
Graduate: none	**Student/Faculty:** 12 to 1
Year: semesters, summer session	**Tuition:** $7175 ($11,875)
Application Deadline: January 15	**Room & Board:** $5970
Freshman Class: 1285 applied, 837 accepted, 276 enrolled	
SAT I Verbal/Math: 640/610	**HIGHLY COMPETITIVE**

St. Mary's College of Maryland, founded in 1840, is a small public liberal arts college in the Maryland State College and University System. In addition to regional accreditation, St. Mary's has baccalaureate program accreditation with NASM. The library contains 173,288 volumes, 257 microform items, and 10,116 audiovisual forms/CDs, and subscribes to 1580 periodicals. Computerized library services include the card catalog, interlibrary loans, and database searching. Special learning facilities include a learning resource center, art gallery, radio station, TV station, historic archeological site, and estuarine research facilities. The 275-acre campus is in a rural area 70 miles south of Washington, D.C. Including residence halls, there are 34 buildings.

Programs of Study: St. Mary's confers the B.A. degree. Bachelor's degrees are awarded in BIOLOGICAL SCIENCE (biology/biological science), COMMUNICATIONS AND THE ARTS (dramatic arts, English, fine arts, languages, and music), COMPUTER AND PHYSICAL SCIENCE (chemistry, computer science, mathematics, natural sciences, and physics), SOCIAL SCIENCE (anthropology, economics, history, human development, philosophy, political science/government, psychology, public affairs, and religion). Biology is the strongest academically. Economics, psychology, and biology are the largest.

Special: St. Mary's offers exchange programs with Johns Hopkins University and the National Student Exchange, study abroad in 3 countries, dual and student-designed majors, and nondegree study. There are pass/fail options for some courses. Unpaid internships for credit, with placement worldwide, are also permitted. There are 5 national honor societies, including Phi Beta Kappa, a freshman honors program, and a collegewide honors program.

Admissions: 65% of the 1999-2000 applicants were accepted. The SAT I scores for the 1999-2000 freshman class were: Verbal--4% below 500, 23% between 500 and 599, 58% between 600 and 700, and 15% above 700; Math--6% below

500, 35% between 500 and 599, 52% between 600 and 700, and 7% above 700. 73% of the current freshmen were in the top fifth of their class; 92% were in the top two fifths. 13 freshmen graduated first in their class.

Requirements: The SAT I or ACT is required. A GPA of 2.0 is required. Applicants should have graduated from an accredited secondary school or earned the GED. Minimum high school preparation should include 4 units of English, 3 each of math, social studies, and science, and 7 electives. An essay and 3 letters of recommendation are required. AP and CLEP credits are accepted. Important factors in the admissions decision are advanced placement or honor courses, recommendations by school officials, and evidence of special talent.

Procedure: Freshmen are admitted fall and spring. Entrance exams should be taken in May of the junior year or November of the senior year. There are early decision and early admissions plans. Early decision applications should be filed by December 1; regular applications, by January 15 for fall entry and October 15 for spring entry, along with a $25 fee. Notification of early decision is sent January 1; regular decision, April 1. 108 early decision candidates were accepted for the 1999-2000 class. 9% of all applicants are on a waiting list.

Financial Aid: In a recent year, 66% of all freshmen and 68% of continuing students received some form of financial aid. 39% of freshmen and 47% of continuing students received need-based aid. The average freshman award was $5382. The average financial indebtedness of a recent graduate was $14,529. St. Mary's is a member of CSS. The FAFSA is required. The fall application deadline is March 1.

Computers: Students can use any of the 140 Pentium systems, 3 Mac workstations, or multimedia stand-alone workstations. Access to the Internet and E-mail is available. There are several computer labs on campus. All students may access the system during all lab hours. There are no time limits and no fees.

SAINT OLAF COLLEGE
Northfield, MN 55057-1098

(507) 646-3025
(800) 800-3025; Fax: (507) 646-3832

Full-time: 1248 men, 1679 women	**Faculty:** 256; IIB, +$
Part-time: 28 men, 43 women	**Ph.D.s:** 86%
Graduate: none	**Student/Faculty:** 11 to 1
Year: 4-1-4, summer session	**Tuition:** $18,250
Application Deadline: February 1	**Room & Board:** $4320
Freshman Class: 2359 applied, 1803 accepted, 754 enrolled	
SAT I Verbal/Math: 630/630	**ACT:** 27 **HIGHLY COMPETITIVE**

St. Olaf College, founded in 1874, is a private liberal arts institution affiliated with the Evangelical Lutheran Church in America. In addition to regional accreditation, St. Olaf has baccalaureate program accreditation with CSWE, NASAD, NASM, NCATE, and NLN. The 4 libraries contain 488,299 volumes, 58,066 microform items, and 15,313 audiovisual forms/CDs, and subscribe to 1703 periodicals. Computerized library services include the card catalog, interlibrary loans, and database searching. Special learning facilities include a learning resource center, art gallery, and radio station. The 350-acre campus is in a small town 40 miles south of Minneapolis. Including residence halls, there are 29 buildings.

Programs of Study: St. Olaf confers B.A., B.Mus., and B.S.N. degrees. Bachelor's degrees are awarded in BIOLOGICAL SCIENCE (biology/biological science), COMMUNICATIONS AND THE ARTS (art, art history and appreciation, communications, dance, dramatic arts, English, fine arts, French, German, Greek, Latin, music, performing arts, Russian, Scandinavian languages, Spanish, and speech/debate/rhetoric), COMPUTER AND PHYSICAL SCIENCE (chemistry, mathematics, and physics), EDUCATION (art, English, foreign languages, health, mathematics, science, secondary, and social studies), HEALTH PROFESSIONS (nursing), SOCIAL SCIENCE (American studies, Asian/Oriental studies, classical/ancient civilization, crosscultural studies, economics, family/consumer resource management, Hispanic American studies, history, medieval studies, philosophy, political science/government, psychology, religion, Russian and Slavic studies, social work, sociology, and women's studies). Math, English, and music are the strongest academically. Biology, English, and psychology are the largest.

Special: St. Olaf offers cross-registration with Carleton College, study abroad in more than 27 countries, a Washington semester, preprofessional programs, internships, an accelerated prelaw program with Columbia University, and a 3-2 B. A.-B.S.E. degree in engineering with Washington University in St. Louis. There are dual majors, nondegree study, and pass/fail options. The Center for Integrative studies allows students to design individual majors with an emphasis on tutorials and seminars. There are 14 national honor societies, including Phi Beta Kappa.

Admissions: 76% of the 1999-2000 applicants were accepted. The SAT I scores for the 1999-2000 freshman class were: Verbal--4% below 500, 30% between 500 and 599, 50% between 600 and 700, and 16% above 700; Math--3% below 500, 27% between 500 and 599, 54% between 600 and 700, and 16% above 700. The ACT scores were 1% below 21, 14% between 21 and 23, 31% between 24 and 26, 22% between 27 and 28, and 32% above 28. 73% of the current freshmen were in the top fifth of their class; 95% were in the top two fifths. There were 32 National Merit finalists. 61 freshmen graduated first in their class.

Requirements: The SAT I or ACT is required. Applicants should have completed 4 years of English, 3 to 4 each of math and social studies, and 2 to 3 each of science and a foreign language. Applications may be made on computer disk using Common App or CollegeLink. AP and CLEP credits are accepted. Important factors in the admissions decision are advanced placement or honor courses, leadership record, and personality/intangible qualities.

Procedure: Freshmen are admitted fall, winter, and spring. Entrance exams should be taken in the spring of the junior year or the fall of the senior year. There are early decision, early admissions, and deferred admissions plans. Early decision applications should be filed by November 15; regular applications, by February 1 for priority consideration for fall entry, along with a $35 fee. Notification of early decision is sent December 1; regular decision, on a rolling basis beginning February 15. 130 early decision candidates were accepted for the 1999-2000 class.

Financial Aid: In 1999-2000, 80% of all freshmen and 73% of continuing students received some form of financial aid. 60% of freshmen and 64% of continuing students received need-based aid. The average freshman award was $14,003. Of that total, scholarships or need-based grants averaged $8144 ($16,500 maximum); loans averaged $3559 ($5625 maximum); and work contracts averaged $1600 ($2100 maximum). 82% of undergraduates work part time. Average annual earnings from campus work are $1175. The average financial indebtedness of the 1999 graduate was $15,995. St. Olaf is a member of CSS. The FAFSA and the college's own financial statement are required. The fall application deadline is March 1.

Computers: The mainframes are 2 DEC VAX 11/780s. More than 180 public-area PCs and Macs are available. Many departments and all residence halls have computer rooms as well. All students may access the system. There are no time limits and no fees.

SALISBURY STATE UNIVERSITY

Salisbury, MD 21801   (410) 543-6161; Fax: (410) 546-6016

Full-time: 2027 men, 2681 women	**Faculty:** 261; IIA, -$
Part-time: 361 men, 467 women	**Ph.D.s:** 76%
Graduate: 153 men, 371 women	**Student/Faculty:** 18 to 1
Year: 4-1-4, summer session	**Tuition:** $4156 ($8550)
Application Deadline: January 15	**Room & Board:** $5590
Freshman Class: 4501 applied, 2572 accepted, 870 enrolled	
SAT I or ACT: required	**VERY COMPETITIVE**

Salisbury State University, founded in 1925, is a public institution within the University System of Maryland. SSU provides undergraduate programs in the liberal arts, sciences, preprofessional and professional programs, and select, mostly applied, graduate programs in business, education, nursing, psychology, English and history. There are 4 undergraduate schools and 6 graduate programs. In addition to regional accreditation, SSU has baccalaureate program accreditation with AACSB, CAHEA, CSWE, and NLN. The library contains 246,294 volumes, 686,751 microform items, and 10,638 audiovisual forms/CDs, and subscribes to 1662 periodicals. Computerized library services include the card catalog, interlibrary loans, and database searching. Special learning facilities include a learning resource center, art gallery, radio station, TV station, and Research Center for Delmarva History and Culture, Enterprise Development Group, Shorecan Small Business Resources Center, and Scarborough Leadership Center. The 140-acre campus is in a small town 110 miles southeast of Baltimore and 100 miles east of Washington, D.C. Including residence halls, there are 43 buildings.

Programs of Study: SSU confers B.A., B.S., B.A.S.W., and B.F.A. degrees. Master's degrees are also awarded. Bachelor's degrees are awarded in BIOLOGICAL SCIENCE (biology/biological science), BUSINESS (accounting and business administration and management), COMMUNICATIONS AND THE ARTS (art, communications, English, fine arts, French, music, and Spanish), COMPUTER AND PHYSICAL SCIENCE (chemistry, information sciences and systems, mathematics, and physics), EDUCATION (elementary and physical), HEALTH PROFESSIONS (environmental health science, medical laboratory technology, nursing, and respiratory therapy), SOCIAL SCIENCE (economics, geography, history, liberal arts/general studies, philosophy, political science/government, psychology, social work, and sociology). The sciences and business are the strongest academically. Business administration and elementary education are the largest.

Special: Cross-registration with schools in the University System of Maryland, and study abroad in numerous countries are offered. SSU also offers an Annapolis semester, a Washington semester, internships, work-study programs, accelerated degree programs, a general studies degree, dual, interdisciplinary, and student-designed majors including physics/microelectronics, a 3-2 engineering degree with the University of Maryland at College Park, Old Dominion University, and Widener University, and pass/fail options. There are 21 national honor societies, a freshman honors program, and 15 departmental honors programs.

Admissions: 57% of the 1999-2000 applicants were accepted. The SAT I scores for the 1999-2000 freshman class were: Verbal--16% below 500, 59% between 500 and 599, 22% between 600 and 700, and 3% above 700; Math--14% below 500, 58% between 500 and 599, 26% between 600 and 700, and 2% above 700. The ACT scores were 37% between 21 and 23, 42% between 24 and 26, 13% between 27 and 28, and 8% above 28. 46% of the current freshmen were in the top fifth of their class; 80% were in the top two fifths. 10 freshmen graduated first in their class.

Requirements: The SAT I or ACT is required. A GPA of 2.0 is required. Applicants must be graduates of accredited secondary schools or have earned a GED. The university requires 14 academic credits or 20 Carnegie units, including 4 in English, 3 each in math and social studies, 3 in science (2 with labs), and 2 in foreign language. A portfolio or audition is required for specific majors. A campus visit is recommended for all students. Applications are accepted on-line, at the school's web site. AP and CLEP credits are accepted. Important factors in the admissions decision are advanced placement or honor courses, leadership record, and extracurricular activities record.

Procedure: Freshmen are admitted fall and spring. Entrance exams should be taken by November of the senior year. There are early decision and early admissions plans. Early decision applications should be filed by December 15; regular applications, by January 15 for fall entry and January 1 for spring entry, along with a $30 fee. Notification of early decision is sent January 15; regular decision, March 15. 266 early decision candidates were accepted for the 1999-2000 class. 28% of all applicants are on a waiting list.

Financial Aid: In 1999-2000, 60% of all students received some form of financial aid. 45% of freshmen and 60% of continuing students received need-based aid. The average freshman award was $2900. Of that total, scholarships or need-based grants averaged $1550 ($9000 maximum); loans averaged $2500 ($4625 maximum); and work contracts averaged $1600 ($2000 maximum). 30% of undergraduates work part time. Average annual earnings from campus work are $1800. The average financial indebtedness of the 1999 graduate was $6000. SSU is a member of CSS. The FAFSA is required. The fall application deadline is March 1.

Computers: The mainframes are a DEC VAX 4000-705A, a DEC ALPHA 2100-4/275, a cluster DEC VAX 8350, and a DEC VAX 6310. There are 24 VAX graphics-capable terminals connected to the mainframe that are available for student use. The University Center has 30 PCs networked to a server. In addition, there are 6 computer labs, each containing approximately 30 PCs using the Novell network with a MicroVAX as a server; a 19-station, networked Mac lab; 1850 residence hall ports; and an academic help room. 9 out of 12 dorms have ResNet services, which allow 2 computers and the phone to be used at the same time. In the general academic lab, scanning and color printing are available to all students. All students may access the system 24 hours daily via modem or in residence halls. There are no time limits and no fees. Specialized equipment is necessary to have ResNet and is available for an additional cost. The college strongly recommends that all students have personal computers.

SAMFORD UNIVERSITY
Birmingham, AL 35229

(205) 726-2871
(800) 888-7218; Fax: (205) 726-2171

Full-time: 1028 men, 1622 women	**Faculty:** 162; IIA, +$
Part-time: 67 men, 138 women	**Ph.D.s:** 81%
Graduate: 788 men, 851 women	**Student/Faculty:** 16 to 1
Year: 4-1-4, summer session	**Tuition:** $10,300
Application Deadline: August 1	**Room & Board:** $4560
Freshman Class: 1974 applied, 1738 accepted, 668 enrolled	
SAT I Verbal/Math: 570/560	**ACT:** 25 **VERY COMPETITIVE**

Samford University, founded in 1841, is a private, liberal arts school and maintains a close relationship with the Alabama Baptist Convention. There are 5 undergraduate and 3 graduate schools. In addition to regional accreditation, Samford has baccalaureate program accreditation with AACSB, ACPE, ADA, AHEA, FIDER, NASAD, NASM, NCATE, and NLN. The 4 libraries contain 794,848 volumes, 839,963 microform items, and 12,676 audiovisual forms/CDs, and subscribe to 8906 periodicals. Computerized library services include the card catalog, interlibrary loans, and database searching. Special learning facilities include a learning resource center, art gallery, planetarium, radio station, TV station, and a Global Center. The 180-acre campus is in a suburban area 4 miles south of Birmingham. Including residence halls, there are 62 buildings.

Programs of Study: Samford confers B.A., B.S., B.B.A., B.Mus., B.S.B.A., B.S. Ed., and B.S.N. degrees. Associate, master's, and doctoral degrees are also awarded. Bachelor's degrees are awarded in AGRICULTURE (forestry and related sciences), BIOLOGICAL SCIENCE (biochemistry, biology/biological science, marine science, and nutrition), BUSINESS (accounting, fashion merchandising, international business management, and marketing/retailing/merchandising), COMMUNICATIONS AND THE ARTS (classics, communications, dramatic arts, English, fine arts, French, German, graphic design, Greek, journalism, Latin, music, piano/organ, Spanish, speech/debate/rhetoric, and voice), COMPUTER AND PHYSICAL SCIENCE (chemistry, computer science, mathematics, and physics), EDUCATION (art, athletic training, early childhood, elementary, foreign languages, health, home economics, library science, middle school, music, physical, science, and secondary), ENGINEERING AND ENVIRONMENTAL DESIGN (engineering physics, environmental science, and preengineering), HEALTH PROFESSIONS (medical laboratory technology, nursing, occupational therapy, pharmacy, premedicine, and sports medicine), SOCIAL SCIENCE (Asian/Oriental studies, community services, food science, geography, history, human development, international relations, Latin American studies, ministries, paralegal studies, philosophy, political science/government, prelaw, psychology, public administration, religion, religious music, sociology, and youth ministry). Premedicine, business, and education are the strongest academically. Business, pharmacy, and education are the largest.

Special: Co-op programs are offered in public administration, graphic design, business, computer science, art, and journalism. A 3-2 engineering degree is available with Auburn, Washington (St. Louis), and Mercer Universities. The School of Arts and Sciences offers an interdisciplinary core curriculum with team teaching. Cross-registration with Birmingham-Southern College, the University of Alabama at Birmingham, the University of Montevallo, and Miles College, study abroad in England and 5 other countries, additional major options, internships, work-study programs, credit for life experience, and pass/fail options are also offered. Accelerated degree programs and B.A.-B.S. degrees are possible in some majors. There are 11 national honor societies, a freshman honors program, and 1 departmental honors program.

Admissions: 88% of the 1999-2000 applicants were accepted. The SAT I scores for the 1999-2000 freshman class were: Verbal--17% below 500, 46% between 500 and 599, 32% between 600 and 700, and 5% above 700; Math--21% below 500, 48% between 500 and 599, 29% between 600 and 700, and 2% above 700. The ACT scores were 10% below 21, 31% between 21 and 23, 27% between 24 and 26, 18% between 27 and 28, and 14% above 28. 58% of the current freshmen were in the top fifth of their class; 84% were in the top two fifths. There were 5 National Merit finalists and 3 semifinalists. 35 freshmen graduated first in their class.

Requirements: The SAT I or ACT is required. Applicants need 18 academic credits and 16 Carnegie units, including 4 in English. The university also recommends that students have 3 units in math and science and 2 units each in foreign language and social studies. An essay is required and an interview suggested. The GED is accepted. AP and CLEP credits are accepted. Important factors in the admissions decision are advanced placement or honor courses, leadership record, and recommendations by school officials.

Procedure: Freshmen are admitted fall, spring, and summer. Entrance exams should be taken in the junior year. Applications should be filed by August 1 for fall entry, along with a $25 fee. Notification is sent on a rolling basis.

Financial Aid: In a recent year, 90% of all freshmen and 72% of continuing students received some form of financial aid. 43% of freshmen and 49% of continuing students received need-based aid. The average freshman award was $8728. Of that total, scholarships or need-based grants averaged $2299 ($15,485 maximum); loans averaged $3582 ($14,401 maximum); work contracts averaged $892 ($2318 maximum); and state grants averaged $847 ($850 maximum). 25% of undergraduates work part time. The FAFSA is required. The fall application deadline is March 1.

Computers: The server is an IBM RISC/6000 7026 H50. There are 17 computer labs available for academic and student use. During the last month in each term, one is available 24 hours a day. PCs include Dell and Power Mac. There is a voice/data connection for every resident student. All students may access the system. There are no time limits and no fees.

SAN DIEGO STATE UNIVERSITY
San Diego, CA 92182 (619) 594-7800; Fax: (619) 594-4902

Full-time: 8621 men, 11,116 women	**Faculty:** 886; IIA, ++$
Part-time: 2612 men, 3284 women	**Ph.D.s:** n/av
Graduate: 2243 men, 3541 women	**Student/Faculty:** 22 to 1
Year: semesters, summer session	**Tuition:** $1776 ($7380)
Application Deadline: November 1 to 30	**Room & Board:** $6838

Freshman Class: 21,857 applied, 11,651 accepted, 3836 enrolled
SAT I Verbal/Math: 510/520   **ACT:** 21   **COMPETITIVE**

San Diego State University, founded in 1897, is a public liberal arts university that is part of the California State University system. Some of the information in this profile is approximate. There are 8 undergraduate schools. In addition to regional accreditation, SDSU has baccalaureate program accreditation with ACEJMC, ADA, ASLA, CSWE, FIDER, NASAD, NASM, NCATE, NLN, and NRPA. The library contains 1,128,058 volumes, 3,674,545 microform items, and

8853 audiovisual forms/CDs, and subscribes to 3740 periodicals. Computerized library services include the card catalog, interlibrary loans, and database searching. Special learning facilities include a learning resource center, art gallery, planetarium, radio station, TV station, theater, and recital hall. The 282-acre campus is in an urban area 8 miles east of downtown San Diego. Including residence halls, there are 56 buildings.

Programs of Study: SDSU confers B.A. and B.S. degrees. Master's and doctoral degrees are also awarded. Bachelor's degrees are awarded in BIOLOGICAL SCIENCE (biology/biological science), BUSINESS (accounting and business administration and management), COMMUNICATIONS AND THE ARTS (broadcasting, dance, dramatic arts, English, fine arts, journalism, and music), COMPUTER AND PHYSICAL SCIENCE (chemistry, computer programming, computer science, geology, mathematics, and physics), EDUCATION (home economics), ENGINEERING AND ENVIRONMENTAL DESIGN (aeronautical engineering, civil engineering, electrical/electronics engineering, and mechanical engineering), HEALTH PROFESSIONS (nursing and speech pathology/audiology), SOCIAL SCIENCE (anthropology, criminal justice, economics, geography, history, philosophy, political science/government, psychology, public administration, religion, social science, social work, sociology, and urban studies). Business administration is the strongest academically and the largest.

Special: Students may study abroad in London and Paris and receive credit for life, military, and work experience. Cross-registration with the University of California, community colleges, and California State University, internships, dual majors, an interdisciplinary major, Washington aand Sacramento semesters, an off-campus public administration program, and a prelaw program in cooperation with California Western School of Law are avaialable. There are 30 national honor societies, including Phi Beta Kappa, a freshman honors program, and 24 departmental honors programs.

Admissions: 53% of the 1999-2000 applicants were accepted. The SAT I scores for the 1999-2000 freshman class were: Verbal--46% below 500, 42% between 500 and 599, and 12% between 600 and 700; Math--38% below 500, 45% between 500 and 599, and 16% between 600 and 700. The ACT scores were 41% below 21, 32% between 21 and 23, 20% between 24 and 26, 5% between 27 and 28, and 2% above 28.

Requirements: The SAT I or ACT is required. For California residents, a GPA of 2.0 is required; for nonresidents, 2.45. Candidates for admission should have completed 4 years of English, 3 of math, 2 of a foreign language, and 1 each of science with lab and visual and performing arts.

Procedure: Freshmen are admitted fall and spring. Entrance exams should be taken in high school. Applications should be filed between November 1 and November 30 for fall entry and between August 1 and Aaugust 30 for spring entry, along with a $55 fee. Notification is sent on a rolling basis.

Financial Aid: In 1999-2000, 60% of all students received some form of financial aid. 41% of freshmen and 46% of continuing students received need-based aid. The average freshman award was $4800. 20% of undergraduates work part time. The average financial indebtedness of the 1999 graduate was $13,600. The CSS/Profile or FFS and SAAC are required. The fall application deadline is March 2.

Computers: The mainframes are an IBM-390 MVS System, a VAX Sun SPARC-1000E, and a SPARC-20. Student accounts are available by application; there is both on-campus and off-campus access. Various labs on campus with approximately 2000 computers are available. All students may access the system. There are no time limits and no fees.

467

SAN FRANCISCO ART INSTITUTE
San Francisco, CA 94133

(415) 749-4500
(800) 345-SFAI; Fax: (415) 749-4592

Full-time: 225 men, 194 women	**Faculty:** 35
Part-time: 39 men, 42 women	**Ph.D.s:** 99%
Graduate: 46 men, 78 women	**Student/Faculty:** 12 to 1
Year: semesters, summer session	**Tuition:** $19,300
Application Deadline: September 1	**Room & Board:** n/app
Freshman Class: 193 applied, 133 accepted, 48 enrolled	
SAT I or ACT: required	**SPECIAL**

San Francisco Art Institute, founded in 1871, is a private, commuter college devoted solely to the fine arts. In addition to regional accreditation, SFAI has baccalaureate program accreditation with NASAD. The library contains 22,000 volumes and 1500 audiovisual forms/CDs, and subscribes to 210 periodicals. Special learning facilities include a learning resource center and art gallery. The 3-acre campus is in an urban area. There is 1 building.

Programs of Study: SFAI confers the B.F.A. degree. Master's degrees are also awarded. Bachelor's degrees are awarded in COMMUNICATIONS AND THE ARTS (film arts, fine arts, painting, photography, printmaking, sculpture, and video). Painting and photography are the largest.

Special: Students may participate in off-campus internships for credit. There are study-abroad opportunities in 9 countries. There is an interdisciplinary program in which studio curricula are chosen that support specific artistic direction. The institute offers dual majors in all subjects, nondegree study, work-study with SFAI, and pass/fail options in the senior year.

Admissions: 69% of the 1999-2000 applicants were accepted.

Requirements: The SAT I or ACT is required. A GPA of 2.5 is required, with a minimum required score of 20 on the ACT or 420 on the SAT I verbal. AP and CLEP credits are accepted. Important factors in the admissions decision are evidence of special talent, recommendations by school officials, and recommendations by alumni.

Procedure: Freshmen are admitted to all sessions. There is a deferred admissions plan. Applications should be filed by September 1 for fall entry, along with a $60 fee. Notification is sent on a rolling basis.

Financial Aid: In 1999-2000 77% of all freshmen and 69% of continuing students received some form of financial aid. 59% of freshmen and 64% of continuing students received need-based aid. The average freshman award was $18,578. Of that total, scholarships or need-based grants averaged $12,438; loans averaged $8375 ($10,500 maximum); and work contracts averaged $2601 ($3000) maximum. 32% of undergraduates work part time. Average annual earnings from campus work are $2500. Other grants, such as Pell and SEOG, average $1560 ($7000 maximum). The average financial indebtedness of the 1999 graduate was $12,000. The FAFSA is required. The fall application deadline is September 1.

Computers: The mainframe is an HP. Students have access to 3 computer labs. There are 6 Macs for students in the tutoring center, and 6 Amigas can be used for video processing. 24 Macs are available in the Center for Digital Media. All students may access the system. Students registered in CDM classes may access the system from 9 a.m. to 10 p.m. There are no time limits. The fee is $50.

SAN FRANCISCO STATE UNIVERSITY

San Francisco, CA 94132   (415) 338-2355; Fax: (415) 338-0903

Full-time: 14,640 men and women	**Faculty:** 977; IIA, ++$
Part-time: 6090 men and women	**Ph.D.s:** n/av
Graduate: 6260 men and women	**Student/Faculty:** 15 to 1
Year: semesters, summer session	**Tuition:** $1904 ($7804)
Application Deadline: see profile	**Room & Board:** $5313
Freshman Class: n/av	
SAT I or ACT: required	**LESS COMPETITIVE**

San Francisco State University, founded in 1899, is a public liberal arts institution offering graduate and undergraduate programs as part of the California State University system. Figures given in above capsule are approximate. There are 8 undergraduate and 8 graduate schools. In addition to regional accreditation, San Francisco State has baccalaureate program accreditation with AACSB, ACEJMC, ADA, AHEA, NASM, and NLN. The library contains 636,000 volumes and 970,000 microform items, and subscribes to 560,000 periodicals. Computerized library services include the card catalog. Special learning facilities include a learning resource center, art gallery, natural history museum, planetarium, radio station, TV station, a field campus, the Labor Archives and Research Center, a Media Access Center, and an anthropology museum. The 130-acre campus is in an urban area. Including residence halls, there are 23 buildings.

Programs of Study: San Francisco State confers B.A., B.S., B.M., and B.Voc. Ed. degrees. Associate, master's, and doctoral degrees are also awarded. Bachelor's degrees are awarded in BIOLOGICAL SCIENCE (biochemistry, biology/biological science, botany, cell biology, ecology, marine biology, microbiology, physiology, and zoology), BUSINESS (accounting, banking and finance, business administration and management, international business management, labor studies, management science, marketing/retailing/merchandising, personnel management, real estate, and transportation management), COMMUNICATIONS AND THE ARTS (broadcasting, Chinese, classics, comparative literature, dance, dramatic arts, English, film arts, fine arts, French, German, Italian, Japanese, journalism, music, Russian, and speech/debate/rhetoric), COMPUTER AND PHYSICAL SCIENCE (applied mathematics, chemistry, computer science, geology, information sciences and systems, mathematics, physics, science, and statistics), EDUCATION (early childhood, elementary, home economics, industrial arts, physical, recreation, secondary, special, and vocational), ENGINEERING AND ENVIRONMENTAL DESIGN (civil engineering, electrical/electronics engineering, engineering, industrial administration/management, interior design, and mechanical engineering), HEALTH PROFESSIONS (allied health, clinical science, health science, medical laboratory technology, nursing, physical therapy, public health, and speech pathology/audiology), SOCIAL SCIENCE (African American studies, American studies, anthropology, clothing and textiles management/production/services, dietetics, economics, geography, history, humanities, interdisciplinary studies, international relations, liberal arts/general studies, philosophy, political science/government, psychology, social work, sociology, urban studies, and women's studies).

Special: Students may cross-register with the California College of Podiatric Medicine, the City College of San Francisco, Cogswell College of Engineering, and several other area universities. Study abroad in numerous countries, a Washington semester, campus work-study, a general studies degree, dual and student-designed majors, credit for life experience, nondegree study, and pass/fail options are also offered. There is a chapter of Phi Beta Kappa, and 2 departmental honors programs.

Requirements: The SAT I or ACT is required. A GPA of 2.0 is required. Applicants should be graduates of an accredited secondary school with a minimum GPA of 2.0. The GED is accepted. High school courses should include 4 years of English, 3 of math, 2 of foreign language, and 1 each of U.S. history or government, lab science, and visual and performing arts. AP and CLEP credits are accepted.

Procedure: Freshmen are admitted fall and spring. Check with the school for current application deadlines and fees. Notification is sent on a rolling basis.

Financial Aid: In a recent year, 50% of all freshmen received some form of financial aid. San Francisco State is a member of CSS. The CSS/Profile or FFS is required.

Computers: The mainframes are a DEC VAX 6420 and an IBM 4381/R22. There are 46 dial-in modems, 50 CD-ROM and on-line databases, more than 100 networked terminals, and more than 1000 IBM, Mac, and other PCs available for student use. All students may access the system 24 hours daily. There are no time limits and no fees.

SAN JOSE STATE UNIVERSITY
San Jose, CA 95192   (408) 924-2000; Fax: (408) 924-2050

Full-time: 6974 men, 7614 women	**Faculty:** 868; IIA, +$
Part-time: 3434 men, 3395 women	**Ph.D.s:** 84%
Graduate: 1973 men, 3547 women	**Student/Faculty:** 17 to 1
Year: semesters, summer session	**Tuition:** $1939 ($7843)
Application Deadline: open	**Room & Board:** $6248
Freshman Class: 10,275 applied, 7434 accepted, 2406 enrolled	
SAT I Verbal/Math: 480/510	**ACT:** 20 **COMPETITIVE**

San Jose State University, founded in 1857 and part of the California State University system, is a public institution offering undergraduate and graduate programs in applied arts and science, social science, and social work to a primarily commuter student body. There are 8 undergraduate and 8 graduate schools. In addition to regional accreditation, SJSU has baccalaureate program accreditation with AACSB, ABET, ACEJMC, ADA, ASLA, NASAD, NASM, NCATE, and NLN. The 2 libraries contain 1,101,995 volumes, 1,621,426 microform items, and 37,146 audiovisual forms/CDs, and subscribe to 2504 periodicals. Computerized library services include the card catalog, interlibrary loans, and database searching. Special learning facilities include a learning resource center, art gallery, radio station, and TV station. The 104-acre campus is in an urban area in the center of San Jose. Including residence halls, there are 55 buildings.

Programs of Study: SJSU confers B.A., B.S., B.F.A., and B.Mus. degrees. Master's degrees are also awarded. Bachelor's degrees are awarded in BIOLOGICAL SCIENCE (biochemistry, biology/biological science, botany, microbiology, and zoology), BUSINESS (accounting, banking and finance, business administration and management, international business management, and marketing/retailing/merchandising), COMMUNICATIONS AND THE ARTS (advertising, broadcasting, dance, design, dramatic arts, English, film arts, fine arts, French, German, journalism, music, Spanish, and speech/debate/rhetoric), COMPUTER AND PHYSICAL SCIENCE (chemistry, computer science, geology, mathematics, physics, and statistics), EDUCATION (early childhood and teaching English as a second/foreign language (TESOL/TEFOL)), ENGINEERING AND ENVIRONMENTAL DESIGN (aeronautical engineering, chemical engineering, civil engineering, computer engineering, electrical/electronics engineering, engineering, industrial engineering, interior design, materials engineering, and mechanical engineering), HEALTH PROFESSIONS (nursing, occupational therapy, and speech pathology/audiology), SOCIAL SCIENCE (anthropology, criminal justice, economics, food science, geography, history, philosophy, political science/government, psychology, religion, social science, social work, and sociology). Accounting is the strongest academically. Accounting, electrical engineering, and management are the largest.

Special: SJSU has opportunities for cooperative programs in business, science, engineering, arts, and the humanities, work-study with many employers, internships (some required, some optional), study abroad in 16 countries, field experiences, and student teaching. An accelerated program is offered in nursing, and the B.A.-B.S. degree and dual majors are available in various areas of study. A general studies degree, student-designed majors, nondegree study, and credit/no-credit options are possible. There are 3 national honor societies, and 18 departmental honors programs.

Admissions: 72% of the 1999-2000 applicants were accepted. The SAT I scores for the 1999-2000 freshman class were: Verbal--59% below 500, 32% between 500 and 599, and 9% between 600 and 700; Math--45% below 500, 37% between 500 and 599, 17% between 600 and 700, and 1% above 700. The ACT scores were 57% below 21, 26% between 21 and 23, 10% between 24 and 26, 5% between 27 and 28, and 2% above 28.

Requirements: The SAT I or ACT is required. A GPA of 2.1 is required. Scores are used to calculate an eligibility index rating, which determines qualification for admission. Graduation from an accredited secondary school is required; the GED is accepted. Applicants must have completed 4 years of English, 3 each of math and electives, 2 of a foreign language, and 1 each of history, science, and art. Applications are accepted on-line. AP and CLEP credits are accepted. Important factors in the admissions decision are personality/intangible qualities, recommendations by alumni, and recommendations by school officials.

Procedure: Freshmen are admitted fall and spring. Entrance exams should be taken prior to the fall semester. There are early admissions and deferred admissions plans. Application deadlines are open, along with a $55 fee. Notification is sent on a rolling basis.

Financial Aid: SJSU is a member of CSS. The FAFSA is required. The fall application deadline is March 1.

Computers: The mainframe is an IBM 3090. About 50% of students use the 1597 PCs available, about 300 of which are networked. All students may access the system 9 a.m. to 8 p.m. Monday through Friday and 9 a.m. to 5 p.m. Saturday. There are no time limits and no fees.

SANTA CLARA UNIVERSITY
Santa Clara, CA 95053   (408) 554-4700; Fax: (408) 554-5255

Full-time: 1970 men, 2360 women	**Faculty:** 347; IIA, ++$
Part-time: 74 men, 73 women	**Ph.D.s:** 93%
Graduate: 1822 men, 1371 women	**Student/Faculty:** 12 to 1
Year: quarters, summer session	**Tuition:** $19,311
Application Deadline: January 15	**Room & Board:** $7644
Freshman Class: 5577 applied, 3878 accepted, 1103 enrolled	
SAT I Verbal/Math: 590/610	**ACT:** 25 **HIGHLY COMPETITIVE**

Santa Clara University, founded in 1851 by Jesuit priests, is a private institution offering degree programs in arts and sciences, engineering, and business. There are 3 undergraduate and 5 graduate schools. In addition to regional accreditation, SCU has baccalaureate program accreditation with AACSB, ABET, and NASM. The 2 libraries contain 472,352 volumes, 1,547,481 microform items, and 11,953 audiovisual forms/CDs, and subscribe to 8760 periodicals. Computerized library services include the card catalog, interlibrary loans, and database searching. Special learning facilities include a learning resource center, art gallery, planetarium, radio station, and TV station. The 104-acre campus is in a suburban area 46 miles south of San Francisco. Including residence halls, there are 51 buildings.

Programs of Study: SCU confers B.A., B.S., B.S.C., and B.S.Ch. degrees. Master's and doctoral degrees are also awarded. Bachelor's degrees are awarded in BIOLOGICAL SCIENCE (biology/biological science), BUSINESS (accounting, banking and finance, business economics, marketing/retailing/merchandising, and organizational behavior), COMMUNICATIONS AND THE ARTS (art, art history and appreciation, classics, communications, dramatic arts, English, French, German, Greek, Italian, Latin, music, Spanish, and studio art), COMPUTER AND PHYSICAL SCIENCE (chemistry, computer science, information sciences and systems, mathematics, physics, and science), ENGINEERING AND ENVIRONMENTAL DESIGN (civil engineering, computer engineering, electrical/electronics engineering, engineering, engineering physics, and mechanical engineering), SOCIAL SCIENCE (anthropology, economics, history, interdisciplinary studies, liberal arts/general studies, philosophy, political science/government, psychology, religion, and sociology). Psychology, biology, and communications are the largest.

Special: Study abroad through the Institute of European Studies and in conjunction with other universities is offered in such cities as Rome, Tokyo, Paris, Madrid, and Hong Kong. A co-op program in engineering, dual majors, internships, a general studies degree, student-designed majors, and pass/fail options also are available. SCU periodically establishes temporary institutes for the study of themes such as war and conscience, the family, poverty and conscience, and technology and society. The programs involve traditional-style classes as well as public lectures, dramatic productions, films, and social events. There are 13 national honor societies, including Phi Beta Kappa, and a freshman honors program.

Admissions: 70% of the 1999-2000 applicants were accepted. The SAT I scores for the 1999-2000 freshman class were: Verbal--9% below 500, 46% between 500 and 599, 40% between 600 and 700, and 5% above 700; Math--7% below 500, 36% between 500 and 599, 47% between 600 and 700, and 10% above 700. 61% of the current freshmen were in the top fifth of their class; 88% were in the top two fifths. There were 4 National Merit finalists and 7 semifinalists. 42 freshmen graduated first in their class.

Requirements: The SAT I is required. Applicants should have 16 academic units, including 4 years of English, 3 each in math and foreign language, 1 each in history and science, and 2 1/2 to 4 in electives. An essay is required. An audition is recommended for theater arts majors. The GED is not accepted. Free Mac and PC disks are available on request for application by computer. AP credits are accepted. Important factors in the admissions decision are advanced placement or honor courses, parents or siblings attending the school, and recommendations by school officials.

Procedure: Freshmen are admitted fall and spring. Entrance exams should be taken by February 1. Applications should be filed by January 15 for fall or spring entry, along with a $50 fee. Notification is sent on a rolling basis. 8% of all applicants are on a waiting list.

Financial Aid: In a recent year, 67% of all freshmen and 69% of continuing students received some form of financial aid. 74% of freshmen and 69% of continuing students received need-based aid. The average freshman award was $13,578.

Of that total, scholarships or need-based grants averaged $10,681 ($16,464 maximum); loans averaged $4148 ($5625 maximum); work contracts averaged $1738 ($2000 maximum); and athletic awards averaged $8109 ($24,291 maximum). 70% of undergraduates work part time. Average annual earnings from campus work are $1531. The average financial indebtedness of a recent graduate was $14,367. SCU is a member of CSS. The CSS/Profile or FAFSA is required. The fall application deadline is February 1.

Computers: The mainframes are an IBM 4381, a DEC VAX 8650, and a DEC VAX 750. There are also PCs available in computer labs. All students may access the system. There are no time limits and no fees.

SARAH LAWRENCE COLLEGE
Bronxville, NY 10708　　　　　　　　　　　　**(914) 395-2510**
　　　　　　　　　　　　(800) 888-2858; Fax: (914) 395-2515

Full-time: 305 men, 802 women	**Faculty:** 174; IIB, ++$
Part-time: 8 men, 63 women	**Ph.D.s:** 91%
Graduate: 48 men, 269 women	**Student/Faculty:** 6 to 1
Year: semesters	**Tuition:** $26,068
Application Deadline: February 1	**Room & Board:** $7991
Freshman Class: 2070 applied, 895 accepted, 278 enrolled	
SAT I Verbal/Math: 640/570	**ACT:** 25　**HIGHLY COMPETITIVE**

Sarah Lawrence College, established in 1926, is an independent institution conferring liberal arts degrees. The academic structure is based on the British don system. Students meet biweekly with professors in tutorials and are enrolled in small seminars. While there are no formal majors, students develop individual concentrations that are usually interdisciplinary. There are 8 graduate programs. The library contains 213,860 volumes, 4809 microform items, and 7100 audiovisual forms/CDs, and subscribes to 1042 periodicals. Computerized library services include the card catalog, interlibrary loans, and database searching. Special learning facilities include a radio station slide library with 75,000 slides of art and architecture, early childhood center, electronic music studio, music library, student-run theater, and student-run art gallery. The 40-acre campus is in a suburban area 15 miles north of Mid town Manhattan in New York City. Including residence halls, there are 50 buildings.

Programs of Study: Sarah Lawrence confers the B.A. degree. Master's degrees are also awarded. Bachelor's degrees are awarded in liberal arts students may concentrate in BIOLOGICAL SCIENCE (biology/biological science), COMMUNICATIONS AND THE ARTS (art history and appreciation, classics, creative writing, dance, dramatic arts, English, film arts, fine arts, French, German, Greek, Italian, Latin, literature, music, Russian, Spanish, and visual and performing arts), COMPUTER AND PHYSICAL SCIENCE (chemistry and mathematics), HEALTH PROFESSIONS (premedicine), SOCIAL SCIENCE (anthropology, Asian/Oriental studies, economics, history, philosophy, political science/government, psychology, religion, Russian and Slavic studies, sociology, and women's studies).

Special: Internships are available in a variety of fields, with the school offering proximity to New York City art galleries and agencies. Study abroad in many countries, work-study programs, the equivalent of dual majors, and a general degree may be pursued. All concentrations are self-designed and can be combined.

Admissions: 43% of the 1999-2000 applicants were accepted. The SAT I scores for the 1999-2000 freshman class were: Verbal--4% below 500, 26% between 500 and 599, 45% between 600 and 700, and 25% above 700; Math--16% below

500, 48% between 500 and 599, 34% between 600 and 700, and 2% above 700. The ACT scores were 8% below 21, 21% between 21 and 23, 38% between 24 and 26, 14% between 27 and 28, and 19% above 28. 63% of the current freshmen were in the top fifth of their class; 89% were in the top two fifths. There were 5 National Merit finalists. 4 freshmen graduated first in their class.

Requirements: The SAT I or ACT or 3 SAT II: Subject tests is required. The number of academic credits required depends on the high school attended. The college recommends completion of 4 years of English, 3 each of math, science, social studies, and a foreign language, 2 to 3 of history, and 1 each of art and music. 3 essays are required. An interview is recommended. Applications are accepted on-line via the Common Application web site. AP credits are accepted. Important factors in the admissions decision are advanced placement or honor courses and personality/intangible qualities.

Procedure: Freshmen are admitted fall and spring. There are early decision, early admissions, and deferred admissions plans. Early decision applications should be filed by November 15; regular applications, by February 1 for fall entry and December 1 for spring entry, along with a $50 fee. Notification of early decision is sent December 15; regular decision, April 1. 81 early decision candidates were accepted for the 1999-2000 class. 14% of all applicants are on a waiting list.

Financial Aid: In 1999-2000, 57% of all freshmen and 62% of continuing students received some form of financial aid. 45% of freshmen and 50% of continuing students received need-based aid. The average freshman award was $17,686. Of that total, scholarships or need-based grants averaged $17,152 ($33,800 maximum); loans averaged $2625 ($3500 maximum); and work contracts averaged $1800 maximum. 70% of undergraduates work part time. Average annual earnings from campus work are $1800. The average financial indebtedness of the 1999 graduate was $16,362. Sarah Lawrence is a member of CSS. The CSS/Profile or FAFSA and non custodial parent statement are required. The fall application deadline is February 1.

Computers: There are 40 PCs and Macs with laser printers located in the student computer center, 16 located in the library, and 26 divided between 2 computer classrooms. All PCs are networked with full access to the Internet. All students may access the system 24 hours a day. There are no time limits and no fees.

SAVANNAH COLLEGE OF ART AND DESIGN
Savannah, GA 31401-3146 (912) 525-5100
(800) 869-7223; Fax: (912) 525-5995

Full-time: 1935 men, 1436 women	**Faculty:** 199
Part-time: 226 men, 178 women	**Ph.D.s:** 88%
Graduate: 312 men, 344 women	**Student/Faculty:** 17 to 1
Year: quarters, summer session	**Tuition:** $15,350
Application Deadline: open	**Room & Board:** $6475
Freshman Class: 3244 applied, 2465 accepted, 881 enrolled	
SAT I Verbal/Math: 550/530	**ACT:** 23 SPECIAL

Savannah College of Art and Design, founded in 1978, is a private fine arts university emphasizing career preparation in the visual and performing arts, design, building arts, and the history of art and architecture. There are 4 undergraduate and 4 graduate schools. In addition to regional accreditation, SCAD has baccalaureate program accreditation with NAAB. The library contains 60,000 volumes, 2553 microform items, and 1849 audiovisual forms/CDs, and subscribes to 893 periodicals. Computerized library services include the card catalog, interlibrary loans, and database searching. Special learning facilities include a learning resource center, art gallery, TV station, international center, language lab, writing center, and Internet labs. The campus is in an urban area on the southeast coast of Georgia, midway between Charleston, South Carolina, and Jacksonville, Florida. Including residence halls, there are 41 buildings.

Programs of Study: SCAD confers B.Arch. and B.F.A. degrees. Master's degrees are also awarded. Bachelor's degrees are awarded in COMMUNICATIONS AND THE ARTS (art, art history and appreciation, fiber/textiles/weaving, graphic design, historic preservation, illustration, industrial design, media arts, metal/jewelry, painting, performing arts, photography, and video), ENGINEERING AND ENVIRONMENTAL DESIGN (architecture, computer graphics, furniture design, and interior design), SOCIAL SCIENCE (fashion design and technology). Computer art, graphic design, and photography are the largest.

Special: The college offers study abroad through various programs each summer, on-campus work-study programs, dual majors in all disciplines, sessions for credit in New York and other domestic locations, and internships with artists, designers, museums, agencies, and architectural firms in the United States and abroad. There are 2 national honor societies.

Admissions: 76% of the 1999-2000 applicants were accepted. The SAT I scores for the 1999-2000 freshman class were: Verbal--31% below 500, 44% between 500 and 599, 22% between 600 and 700, and 3% above 700; Math--36% below 500, 42% between 500 and 599, 20% between 600 and 700, and 2% above 700. The ACT scores were 31% below 21, 24% between 21 and 23, 26% between 24 and 26, 12% between 27 and 28, and 7% above 28. In a recent year, there were 4 National Merit semifinalists.

Requirements: The SAT I or ACT is required. SCAD requires applicants to be in the upper 50% of their class. A GPA of 2.0 is required. Students must submit a completed application and high school transcript indicating successful completion. Preference is given to students with a 3.0 GPA or above and to students whose SAT I or ACT scores are above the national average (B.Arch. candidates with math scores below 540 or 23, respectively, may be admitted on a conditional basis). 3 recommendations, an interview, and a portfolio are encouraged. Applications are accepted on-line. AP credits are accepted. Important factors in the admissions decision are evidence of special talent, recommendations by school officials, and leadership record.

Procedure: Freshmen are admitted to all sessions. Entrance exams should be taken by November of the senior year. There is an early admissions plan. Application deadlines are open; the fee is $50. Notification is sent on a rolling basis.

Financial Aid: In 1999-2000, 68% of all freshmen and 65% of continuing students received some form of financial aid. 37% of freshmen and 65% of continuing students received need-based aid. The average freshman award was $12,000. Of that total, scholarships or need-based grants averaged $1400 ($5000 maximum); loans averaged $9800 ($15,000 maximum); and work contracts averaged $800 ($1500 maximum). 74% of undergrads work part time. Average annual earnings from campus work are $800. The average financial indebtedness of the 1999 graduate was $17,000. The FAFSA is required. A customized packet of materials is sent to each applicant interested in financial aid.

Computers: There are approximately 29 computer labs located across the campus, including an Internet lab, a homework lab, a video lab, and 8 computer art labs. All students may access the system. Students may access the system at designated times. There are no fees.

SCHOOL OF THE ART INSTITUTE OF CHICAGO
Chicago, IL 60603

(312) 899-5219
(800) 232-7242; Fax: (312) 899-1840

Full-time: 599 men, 883 women	**Faculty:** 70; IIA, +$
Part-time: 51 men, 80 women	**Ph.D.s:** 88%
Graduate: 166 men, 383 women	**Student/Faculty:** 21 to 1
Year: semesters, summer session	**Tuition:** $19,140
Application Deadline: August 1	**Room & Board:** $5725
Freshman Class: 1069 applied, 839 accepted, 284 enrolled	
SAT I or ACT: required	**SPECIAL**

The School of the Art Institute of Chicago, founded in 1866, is a private institution that is affiliated with the museum of the Art Institute of Chicago. The school offers training in the fine arts and design. There is 1 graduate school. In addition to regional accreditation, SAIC has baccalaureate program accreditation with NASAD. The library contains 60,000 volumes, 155 microform items, and 2700 audiovisual forms/ CDs, and subscribes to 350 periodicals. Computerized library services include the card catalog, interlibrary loans, and database searching. Special learning facilities include a learning resource center, art gallery, TV station, film center, video data bank, fashion resource center, student galleries, and poetry center. The campus is in an urban area in downtown Chicago. Including residence halls, there are 5 buildings.

Programs of Study: SAIC confers B.F.A. and B.Int.Arch. degrees. Master's degrees are also awarded. Bachelor's degrees are awarded in COMMUNICATIONS AND THE ARTS (audio technology, ceramic art and design, design, fiber/textiles/weaving, film arts, painting, photography, printmaking, sculpture, video, and visual and performing arts), EDUCATION (art), ENGINEERING AND ENVIRONMENTAL DESIGN (drafting and design technology and interior design), SOCIAL SCIENCE (fashion design and technology).

Special: SAIC offers internships, student-designed majors, pass/fail options, visual arts co-op programs, cross-registration with Roosevelt University, and cooperative work-study with the Art Institute of Chicago, the John D. and Catherine T. MacArthur Foundation, *Chicago* magazine, and others. Dual and student-designed majors, a B.A.-B.S. degree, and study abroad in 20 countries with active exchange programs are possible.

Admissions: 78% of the 1999-2000 applicants were accepted.

Requirements: The SAT I or ACT is required, with a minimum score of 500 on the verbal section of the SAT I or an English score of 20 on the ACT. Applicants must be graduates of an accredited secondary school. The GED is accepted. All students must submit a portfolio and an essay. An interview is recommended. AP and CLEP credits are accepted.

Procedure: Freshmen are admitted fall and spring. There are early decision and is a deferred admissions plans. Early decision applications should be filed by March 1; regular applications, by August 1 for fall entry and January 15 for spring entry, along with a $45 fee. Notification of early decision and regular decision is sent on a rolling basis.

Financial Aid: In a recent year, 76% of all freshmen and 74% of continuing students received some form of financial aid. 74% of freshmen and 78% of continuing students received need-based aid. The average freshman award was $15,278. Of that total, scholarships or need-based grants averaged $7395 ($17,120 maximum); loans averaged $4223 ($6625 maximum); and work contracts averaged $1500 ($3000 maximum). 30% of undergraduates work part time. Average annual earnings from campus work are $1500. SAIC is a member of CSS. The FAF-SA and the college's own financial statement are required. The fall application deadline is April 1.

Computers: Students have access to 40 G3 Macs and 29 Power Macs in the computer lab. Additionally, there are 75 G3 Macs and 15 Power Macs in computer classrooms; 60 G3 Macs, 25 Power Macs, 2 IBM/NT workstations, and 15 SGI workstations in departmental labs; 6 IBM workstations in the library; and 8 Power Macs in the residence halls. With minor exceptions, all are connected to the Web via Ethernet. All students may access the system. There are no time limits and no fees.

SCHOOL OF VISUAL ARTS
New York, NY 10010-3994

(212) 592-2100
(800) 436-4204; Fax: (212) 592-2116

Full-time: 1500 men, 1200 women	**Faculty:** 94
Part-time: 1000 men, 1400 women	**Ph.D.s:** 36%
Graduate: 140 men, 170 women	**Student/Faculty:** 28 to 1
Year: semesters, summer session	**Tuition:** $15,320
Application Deadline: March 15	**Room & Board:** $6900
Freshman Class: 1650 applied, 1056 accepted, 491 enrolled	
SAT I Verbal/Math: 540/510	**ACT:** 21 **SPECIAL**

The School of Visual Arts, established in 1947, is a private institution conferring undergraduate and graduate degrees in fine arts. The figures in the above capsule are approximate. There are 8 undergraduate and 5 graduate schools. In addition to regional accreditation, SVA has baccalaureate program accreditation with NASAD. The library contains 68,800 volumes, 1025 microform items, and 1935 audiovisual forms/CDs, and subscribes to 296 periodicals. Computerized library services include the card catalog and database searching. Special learning facilities include a learning resource center, art gallery, radio station, 5 student galleries, 3 media arts workshops, 3 film and 2 video studios, numerous editing facilities, an animation studio with 3 pencil test facilities, a digital audio room, a tape transfer room, and a multimedia facility with digital printing and editing systems. The campus is in an urban area in the middle of Manhattan. Including residence halls, there are 8 buildings.

Programs of Study: SVA confers the B.F.A. degree. Master's degrees are also awarded. Bachelor's degrees are awarded in COMMUNICATIONS AND THE ARTS (advertising, film arts, fine arts, graphic design, illustration, photography, and video), EDUCATION (art), ENGINEERING AND ENVIRONMENTAL DESIGN (computer graphics and interior design). Graphic design and advertising, illustration and cartooning, and fine arts are the largest.

Special: SVA offers study abroad in 8 countries and for-credit internships with more than 200 media-related, design, and advertising firms including DC Comics, MTV, and Pentagram Design. A summer internship with Walt Disney Studios is possible for illustration/cartooning majors. A certificate in art education or art therapy is offered in combination with fine arts.

Admissions: 64% of the 1999-2000 applicants were accepted. The SAT I scores for the 1999-2000 freshman class were: Verbal--34% below 500, 42% between 500 and 599, 21% between 600 and 700, and 3% above 700; Math--45% below 500, 38% between 500 and 599, 14% between 600 and 700, and 3% above 700. The ACT scores were 43% below 21, 27% between 21 and 23, 16% between 24 and 26, 10% between 27 and 28, and 4% above 28.

Requirements: The SAT I or ACT is required. A GPA of 2.3 is required. applicants must graduate from an accredited secondary school or have a GED. A personal interview is required of all students living within a 250-mile radius of the school. An essay is required. A portfolio is also required, except for film applicants. AP and CLEP credits are accepted. Important factors in the admissions decision are evidence of special talent, personality/intangible qualities, and leadership record.

Procedure: Freshmen are admitted fall and spring. There are early decision and deferred admissions plans. Early decision applications should be filed by December 1; regular applications, by March 15 for fall entry and December 1 for spring entry, along with a $45 fee. Notification of early decision is sent January 16; regular decision, on a rolling basis. 48 early decision candidates were accepted for the 1999-2000 class.

Financial Aid: In 1999-2000, 75% of all freshmen and 81% of continuing students received some form of financial aid. 64% of freshmen and 71% of continuing students received need-based aid. The average freshman award was $9400. Of that total, scholarships or need-based grants averaged $4490 ($17,400 maximum); loans averaged $3600 ($8625 maximum); and work contracts averaged $4900 ($5000 maximum). 5% of undergraduates work part time. Average annual earnings from campus work are $5000. The average financial indebtedness of the 1999 graduate was $14,000. SVA is a member of CSS. The FAFSA is required. The fall application deadline is February 15.

Computers: The mainframe is a Sun Enterprise 3500. There are 555 PCs available in the computer art department, digital imaging center, writing resource center, and library. All students may access the system during normal operating hours of the library and the writing resource center; use in other buildings varies by major. There are no time limits and no fees. The school strongly recommends all students have PCs; the Power Mac is preferred.

SCRIPPS COLLEGE
Claremont, CA 91711-3948

(909) 621-8149
(800) 770-1333; Fax: (909) 607-7508

Full-time: 763 women	**Faculty:** 57; IIB, ++$
Part-time: 5 women	**Ph.D.s:** 97%
Graduate: none	**Student/Faculty:** 13 to 1
Year: semesters	**Tuition:** $21,130
Application Deadline: February 1	**Room & Board:** $7870
Freshman Class: 1063 applied, 749 accepted, 212 enrolled	
SAT I Verbal/Math: 640/610	**HIGHLY COMPETITIVE**

Scripps College, founded in 1926, is a private liberal arts institution for women. A member of The Claremont Colleges, Scripps emphasizes a challenging core curriculum based on interdisciplinary humanistic studies. The 4 libraries contain 1.9 million volumes, 1,367,536 microform items, and 606 audiovisual forms/CDs, and subscribe to 4321 periodicals. Computerized library services include the card catalog, interlibrary loans, and database searching. Special learning facilities include an art gallery, radio station, TV station, humanities museum, and biological field station. The 30-acre campus is in a suburban area 35 miles east of Los Angeles. Including residence halls, there are 20 buildings.

Programs of Study: Scripps confers the B.A. degree. Bachelor's degrees are awarded in BIOLOGICAL SCIENCE (biochemistry, biology/biological science, molecular biology, and neurosciences), BUSINESS (accounting and organizational behavior), COMMUNICATIONS AND THE ARTS (art history and appreciation, Chinese, classical languages, dance, dramatic arts, English, Germanic languages and literature, Italian, Japanese, languages, linguistics, media arts, music, Russian, and studio art), COMPUTER AND PHYSICAL SCIENCE (chemistry, computer science, geology, mathematics, physics, and science and management), ENGINEERING AND ENVIRONMENTAL DESIGN (engineering management, environmental science, preengineering, and technology and public affairs), SOCIAL SCIENCE (African American studies, American studies, anthropology, Asian/American studies, Asian/Oriental studies, classical/ancient civilization, economics, European studies, French studies, German area studies, Hispanic American studies, history, human ecology, humanities, international relations, international studies, Italian studies, Judaic studies, Latin American studies, Mexican-American/Chicano studies, philosophy, political science/government, prelaw, psychobiology, psychology, public affairs, religion, sociology, and women's studies). Premedicine, art, and English are the strongest academically. Social science is the largest.

Special: Students may cross-register with any of the other Claremont Colleges. Scripps also offers internships, work-study programs, study abroad in 34 countries, a Washington semester, and student-designed, dual, and interdisciplinary majors, including organizational studies and science, technology, and society. Many courses are offered as seminars. There are 3-2 accelerated degree programs in the arts and business administration. A 3-2 engineering program (B.A.-B.S.) is offered with Harvey Mudd College, Washington University in St. Louis, USC, UC Berkeley, and Columbia, Stanford, and Boston universities. There are 3 national honor societies, including Phi Beta Kappa.

Admissions: 70% of the 1999-2000 applicants were accepted. The SAT I scores for the 1999-2000 freshman class were: Verbal--2% below 500, 22% between 500 and 599, 58% between 600 and 700, and 18% above 700; Math--3% below 500, 37% between 500 and 599, 52% between 600 and 700, and 8% above 700. The ACT scores were 7% below 21, 7% between 21 and 23, 25% between 24 and 26, 27% between 27 and 28, and 34% above 28. 75% of the current freshmen were in the top fifth of their class; 95% were in the top two fifths. In a recent year, there was 1 National Merit finalist and 3 semifinalists. 6 freshmen graduated first in their class in a recent year.

Requirements: The SAT I or ACT is required. Scripps requires applicants to be in the upper 50% of their class. A GPA of 3.0 is required. applicants must have completed 4 units each of high school English and math, 3 each of lab science and social studies, and either 3 of a single foreign language or 2 each of 2 languages. SAT II: Subject tests and an interview are recommended. An essay and a graded writing assignment from the junior or senior year are required. Applications are accepted on computer disk, and on-line. AP and CLEP credits are accepted. Important factors in the admissions decision are advanced placement or honor courses, evidence of special talent, and leadership record.

Procedure: Freshmen are admitted fall and spring. Entrance exams should be taken by December of the senior year. There are early decisions, early admissions, and deferred admissions plans. Early decision applications should be filed by November 1; regular applications by February 1 for fall entry and November 15 for spring entry, along with a $50 fee. Notification of early decision is sent December 15; regular decision, April 1. 33 early decision candidates were accepted for the 1999-2000 class. 10% of all applicants are on a waiting list.

Financial Aid: In 1999-2000, 69% of all freshmen and 62% of continuing students received some form of financial aid. 51% of freshmen and 56% of continuing students received need-based aid. The average freshman award was $20,177. Of that total, scholarships or need-based grants averaged $16,033 ($29,510 maximum); loans averaged $3037 ($3625 maximum); and work contracts averaged $1416 ($1650 maximum). All of undergraduates work part time. Average annual earnings from campus work are $1650. The average financial indebtedness of the

1999 graduate was $18,278. Scripps is a member of CSS. The CSS/Profile or FAFSA is required. The fall application deadline is February 1.

Computers: The mainframe is a DEC VAX. Macs and PCs are available in computer labs and dormitories. Students are served by the Novell Network, with access to the Internet, including direct access from their rooms. All students may access the system. There are no time limits and no fees.

SEATTLE UNIVERSITY
Seattle, WA 98122

(206) 296-5800
(800) 426-7123; Fax: (206) 296-5656

Full-time: 1178 men, 1691 women	**Faculty:** IIA, +$
Part-time: 170 men, 206 women	**Ph.D.s:** 87%
Graduate: 1105 men, 1479 women	**Student/Faculty:** n/av
Year: quarters, summer session	**Tuition:** $16,110
Application Deadline: February 1	**Room & Board:** $5870
Freshman Class: 2596 applied, 2087 accepted, 579 enrolled	
SAT I Verbal/Math: 560/560	**ACT:** 25 **VERY COMPETITIVE**

Seattle University, founded in 1891, is a private, comprehensive institution affiliated with the Roman Catholic Church and operated by the Jesuit Fathers. The emphasis of the undergraduate and graduate programs is on the liberal arts and sciences, business, health science, teacher preparation, theological studies, and law. There are 5 undergraduate and 7 graduate schools. In addition to regional accreditation, Seattle U has baccalaureate program accreditation with AACSB, ABET, CAHEA, NCATE, and NLN. The 2 libraries contain 220,606 volumes, 490,171 microform items, and 2689 audiovisual forms/CDs, and subscribe to 2639 periodicals. Computerized library services include the card catalog, interlibrary loans, and database searching. Special learning facilities include a learning resource center, art gallery, planetarium, radio station, electron microscope, recording studio, and MRI. The 46-acre campus is in an urban area just east of downtown Seattle. Including residence halls, there are 27 buildings.

Programs of Study: Seattle U confers B.A., B.S., B.A.B.A., B.A.E., B.A.H., B.C.J., B.P.A., B.S.B., B.S.B.C., B.S.C., B.S.C.E., B.S.C.S., B.S.D.U., B.S.E.E., B.S.G.S., B.S.M., B.S.M.E., B.S.M.T., B.S.N., and B.S.P. degrees. Master's and doctoral degrees are also awarded. Bachelor's degrees are awarded in BIOLOGICAL SCIENCE (biochemistry, biology/biological science, and ecology), BUSINESS (accounting, banking and finance, business administration and management, business economics, international business management, marketing/retailing/merchandising, and operations research), COMMUNICATIONS AND THE ARTS (communications, creative writing, dramatic arts, English, fine arts, French, German, journalism, and Spanish), COMPUTER AND PHYSICAL SCIENCE (chemistry, computer science, mathematics, physics, and science), ENGINEERING AND ENVIRONMENTAL DESIGN (civil engineering, electrical/electronics engineering, environmental engineering, manufacturing engineering, and mechanical engineering), HEALTH PROFESSIONS (medical technology, nursing, and ultrasound technology), SOCIAL SCIENCE (criminal justice, economics, history, humanities, international studies, liberal arts/general studies, philosophy, political science/government, psychology, public administration, religion, social work, and sociology). Engineering, accounting, and nursing are the strongest academically and have the largest enrollments.

Special: Special academic programs include internships in numerous disciplines, study abroad in 5 countries, and both on- and off-campus work-study through the Washington State Work-Study Program. A liberal studies degree and an accelerated degree program in business are offered. Pass/fail options are possible. There is a freshman honors program, and 1 departmental honors program.

Admissions: 80% of the 1999-2000 applicants were accepted. The SAT I scores for the 1999-2000 freshman class were: Verbal--20% below 500, 47% between 500 and 599, 28% between 600 and 700, and 5% above 700; Math--20% below 500, 47% between 500 and 599, 29% between 600 and 700, and 3% above 700. 56% of the current freshmen were in the top quarter of their class; 86% were in the top half. 18 freshmen graduated first in their class.

Requirements: The SAT I or ACT is required. A GPA of 2.75 is required. Admissions requirements include graduation from an accredited secondary school with 16 academic credits, including 4 years of English, 3 each of math and social studies, 2 of foreign language, 2 of lab science, and 2 academic electives; 4 years of math and lab physics and chemistry are required of science and engineering students; lab biology and chemistry are needed by nursing students. The GED is also accepted. Applications are available on-line at the school's web site. AP and CLEP credits are accepted. Important factors in the admissions decision are advanced placement or honor courses, recommendations by school officials, and leadership record.

Procedure: Freshmen are admitted to all sessions. Entrance exams should be taken during the fall of the senior year. There are early admissions and deferred admissions plans. Applications should be filed by February 1 for fall entry, November 1 for winter entry, February 1 for spring entry, and May 1 for summer entry, along with a $50 fee. Notification is sent on a rolling basis. 7% of all applicants are on a waiting list.

Financial Aid: In 1999-2000, 65% of all freshmen and 64% of continuing students received some form of financial aid. 64% of freshmen and 56% of continuing students received need-based aid. The average freshman award was $15,860. Of that total, scholarships or need-based grants averaged $8532; loans averaged $6593; and work contracts averaged $3520. 46% of undergraduates work part time. Average annual earnings from campus work are $2100. The average financial indebtedness of the 1999 graduate was $20,580. Seattle U is a member of CSS. The FAFSA is required. The fall application deadline is February 1.

Computers: The mainframes are 4 IBM RISC systems with 5 UNIX-based Sun servers. There are 400 PCs in labs and 5 specialized LAN terminals. All students may access the system during posted hours or any time from networked residence hall rooms. There are no time limits and no fees.

SIMMONS COLLEGE
Boston, MA 02115

(617) 521-2051
(800) 345-8468; Fax: (617) 521-3190

Full-time: 1090 women	**Faculty:** 121; IIA, av$
Part-time: 145 women	**Ph.D.s:** 80%
Graduate: 271 men, 1789 women	**Student/Faculty:** 9 to 1
Year: semesters, summer session	**Tuition:** $19,520
Application Deadline: February 1	**Room & Board:** $8046
Freshman Class: 1184 applied, 849 accepted, 271 enrolled	
SAT I Verbal/Math: 546/531	**ACT:** 23 **VERY COMPETITIVE**

Simmons College, founded in 1899, is a private institution primarily for women that offers a comprehensive education combining the arts, sciences, and humanities with preprofessional training. There are 5 graduate schools. In addition to regional accreditation, Simmons has baccalaureate program accreditation with ADA, APTA, CSWE, and NLN. The 5 libraries contain 270,402 volumes, 11,242 microform items, and 2873 audiovisual forms/CDs, and subscribe to 1822 periodicals. Computerized library services include the card catalog, interlibrary loans, and database searching. Special learning facilities include an art gallery and TV studio, foreign language lab, physical therapy motion lab, nursing lab, and library science technology center. The 12-acre campus is in an urban area in Boston. Including residence halls, there are 26 buildings.

Programs of Study: Simmons confers B.A. and B.S. degrees. Master's and doctoral degrees are also awarded. Bachelor's degrees are awarded in BIOLOGICAL SCIENCE (biochemistry, biology/biological science, and nutrition), BUSINESS (accounting, banking and finance, management information systems, and marketing/retailing/merchandising), COMMUNICATIONS AND THE ARTS (advertising, art, arts administration/management, communications, English, French, graphic design, music, public relations, and Spanish), COMPUTER AND PHYSICAL SCIENCE (chemistry, computer science, and mathematics), EDUCATION (elementary, secondary, and special), ENGINEERING AND ENVIRONMENTAL DESIGN (environmental science), HEALTH PROFESSIONS (nursing, physical therapy, premedicine, and public health), SOCIAL SCIENCE (African American studies, dietetics, East Asian studies, economics, food science, history, human services, international relations, philosophy, political science/government, prelaw, psychobiology, psychology, public affairs, sociology, and women's studies). International relations and physical therapy are the strongest academically. Nursing, biology, and sociology are the largest.

Special: Cross-registration is available with the New England Conservatory of Music, and Hebrew, Emmanuel, Wheelock Colleges, Massachusetts College of Art, and Wentworth Institute of Technology. Simmons offers study abroad in Europe through the Institute of European studies and its own semester or year in Spain. A Washington semester at American University, internship programs, a B.A.-B.S. degree, dual majors, interdisciplinary majors, student-designed majors, work-study programs, and pass/fail options are also offered. There is a dual-degree program in chemistry and pharmacy with Massachusetts College of Pharmacy and Health Sciences. There is a freshman honors program, and 4 departmental honors programs.

Admissions: 72% of the 1999-2000 applicants were accepted. The SAT I scores for the 1999-2000 freshman class were: Verbal--22% below 500, 47% between 500 and 599, 26% between 600 and 700, and 5% above 700; Math--29% below 500, 53% between 500 and 599, 16% between 600 and 700, and 2% above 700. 44% of the current freshmen were in the top fifth of their class; 80% were in the top two fifths. 2 freshmen graduated first in their class.

Requirements: The SAT I or ACT is required. A GPA of 3.0 is required. Simmons recommends that applicants have 4 years of English, 3 each of math, science, and social studies, and 2 of foreign language. An essay is required, and an interview is strongly recommended. Applications are accepted on disk and online via CollegeLink and College Net. AP and CLEP credits are accepted. Important factors in the admissions decision are advanced placement or honor courses, recommendations by school officials, and extracurricular activities record.

Procedure: Freshmen are admitted fall and spring. Entrance exams should be taken by February 1 of the senior year. There are early action, early admissions, and deferred admissions plans. Early action applications should be filed by December 1; regular admissions, by February 1 for fall entry and December 1 for spring entry, along with a $35 fee. Notification of early action is sent January 20; regular decision, April 15. 32 early action candidates were accepted for the 1999-2000 class. 4% of all applicants are on a waiting list.

Financial Aid: In 1999-2000, 80% of all students received some form of financial aid. 74% of freshmen and 73% of continuing students received need-based aid. The average freshman award was $19,618. Of that total, scholarships or need-based grants averaged $12,441 ($23,135 maximum); loans averaged $3675 ($4125 maximum); and work contracts averaged $1900 ($2100 maximum). 75% of undergraduates work part time. Average annual earnings from campus work are $1500. The average financial indebtedness of the 1999 graduate was $21,125. Simmons is a member of CSS. The CSS/Profile or FAFSA, the college's own financial statement, and federal tax returns or W2 forms are required. The fall application deadline is February 1.

Computers: The mainframe is a DEC ALPHA server with an ATM network. There are 93 Macs and 91 PCs on the academic network, including public-access machines in the library and residence halls. These are available for course-related Web access, general Web access and E-mail, with Minitab and SAS statistics packages and personal productivity applications. All students may access the system. There are no time limits and no fees. The college strongly recommends that all students have PCs.

SIMON'S ROCK COLLEGE OF BARD
Great Barrington, MA 01230-9702 (413) 528-7313
(800) 235-7186; Fax: (413) 528-7334

Full-time: 158 men, 209 women	**Faculty:** 35; 3
Part-time: 14 men, 10 women	**Ph.D.s:** 94%
Graduate: none	**Student/Faculty:** 10 to 1
Year: semesters	**Tuition:** $23,300
Application Deadline: June 30	**Room & Board:** $6410
Freshman Class: 246 applied, 208 accepted, 142 enrolled	
SAT I Verbal/Math: 630/590	**ACT:** 27 **VERY COMPETITIVE+**

Simon's Rock College of Bard, founded in 1964, is a privated liberal arts school especially designed to permit students who have completed the 10th or 11th graades to enroll for collegiate studies in 8 interdisciplinary majors. The library contains 69,500 volumes, 9800 microform items, and 3500 audiovisual forms/CDs, and subscribes to 360 periodicals. Computerized library services include the card catalog, interlibrary loans, and database searching. Special learning facilities include a learning resource center, art gallery, radio station, and language lab. The 275-acre campus is in a small town 50 miles west of Springfield. Including residence halls, there are 38 buildings.

Programs of Study: Simon's Rock confers the B.A. degree. Associate degrees are also awarded. Bachelor's degrees are awarded in BIOLOGICAL SCIENCE (biology/biological science and ecology), COMMUNICATIONS AND THE ARTS (art, art history and appreciation, comparative literature, creative writing, dance, dramatic arts, drawing, English literature, fine arts, French, German, Germanic languages and literature, literature, modern language, music history and appreciation, music performance, music theory and composition, painting, performing arts, photography, printmaking, Spanish, studio art, and visual and performing arts), COMPUTER AND PHYSICAL SCIENCE (applied mathematics, chemistry, mathematics, natural sciences, physics, quantitative methods, and science), HEALTH PROFESSIONS (premedicine), SOCIAL SCIENCE (African American studies, American studies, anthropology, Asian/Oriental studies, community services, crosscultural studies, East Asian studies, Eastern European studies, ethics, politics, and social policy, European studies, French studies, German area studies, interdisciplinary studies, Latin American studies, philosophy, political science/government, psychology, religion, Russian and Slavic studies, and sociology).

Special: A major consists of selecting 2 concentrations from the 36 available; one concentration may be self-designed. Independent study internships in many fields, study abroad, a cooperative program with Bard College, and pass/fail options are also available.

Admissions: 85% of the 1999-2000 applicants were accepted. The SAT I scores for the 1999-2000 freshman class were: Verbal--8% below 500, 22% between 500 and 599, 42% between 600 and 700, and 28% above 700; Math--6% below 500, 41% between 500 and 599, 34% between 600 and 700, and 11% above 700. The ACT scores were 10% between 21 and 23, 22% between 24 and 26, 28% between 27 and 28, and 40% above 28.

Requirements: The SAT I is required and the ACT is recommended. The admissions committee looks more toward the required interview, essay, recommendations, and special talent. The school recommends that prospective students finish 2 years each of English, foreign languages, history, math, science, and social studies. Important factors in the admissions decision are advanced placement or honor courses, recommendations by school officials, and personality/intangible qualities.

Procedure: Freshmen are admitted fall and spring. Entrance exams should be taken prior to June 10. There are early admissions and deferred admissions plans. Applications should be filed by June 30 for fall entry and December 1 for spring entry, along with a $40 fee. Notification is sent on a rolling basis.

Financial Aid: In 1999-2000, 80% of all freshmen and 86% of continuing students received some form of financial aid. 63% of students received need-based aid. The average freshman award was $15,716. Of that total, scholarships or need-based grants averaged $7500 ($12,000 maximum); loans averaged $3000 ($5000 maximum); and work contracts averaged $1000 ($1500 maximum). 40 full merit scholarships are given each year through the Aceleration to Excellence Program. 50% of undergraduates work part time. Average annual earnings from campus work are $1000. The average financial indebtedness of the 1999 graduate was $10,000. Simon's Rock is a member of CSS. The CSS/Profile or FAFSA is required. The fall application deadline is June 15.

Computers: Students may access the central servers from PCs in their dorm rooms or from 2 computer labs. A network connection is available in each dorm room. All students may access the system. There are no time limits and no fees. It is recommended that all students have personal computers.

SIMPSON COLLEGE
Indianola, IA 50125

(515) 961-1624
(800) 362-2454; Fax: (515) 961-1870

Full-time: 606 men, 706 women	**Faculty:** 80
Part-time: 218 men, 367 women	**Ph.D.s:** 79%
Graduate: none	**Student/Faculty:** 16 to 1
Year: 4-4-1, summer session	**Tuition:** $14,430
Application Deadline: open	**Room & Board:** $4800
Freshman Class: 1164 applied, 973 accepted, 345 enrolled	
SAT I Verbal/Math: 600/590	**ACT:** 25 **VERY COMPETITIVE**

Simpson College, founded in 1860, is a private liberal arts institution affiliated with the United Methodist Church. In addition to regional accreditation, Simpson has baccalaureate program accreditation with NASM. The 2 libraries contain 142, 193 volumes, 17,435 microform items, and 3880 audiovisual forms/CDs, and subscribe to 575 periodicals. Computerized library services include the card catalog, interlibrary loans, and database searching. Special learning facilities include a learning resource center, art gallery, science reference library, and an extensive collection from the Antebellum era. The 63-acre campus is in a suburban area 12 miles south of Des Moines. Including residence halls, there are 34 buildings.

Programs of Study: Simpson confers B.A. and B.Mus. degrees. Bachelor's degrees are awarded in BIOLOGICAL SCIENCE (biochemistry and biology/ biological science), BUSINESS (accounting, international business management, and sports management), COMMUNICATIONS AND THE ARTS (art, communications, dramatic arts, English, French, German, music, music performance, and Spanish), COMPUTER AND PHYSICAL SCIENCE (chemistry, information sciences and systems, and mathematics), EDUCATION (art, business, drama, early childhood, elementary, foreign languages, health, middle school, music, physical, science, and secondary), ENGINEERING AND ENVIRONMENTAL DESIGN (environmental science and preengineering), HEALTH PROFESSIONS (predentistry, premedicine, and preveterinary science), SOCIAL SCIENCE (criminal justice, economics, history, international relations, philosophy, political science/government, prelaw, psychology, religion, and sociology). Natural sciences, management, and visual and performing arts are the strongest academically. Management, education, and biology are the largest.

Special: Simpson offers a 3-2 engineering degree with Washington University at St. Louis, cross-registration at American and Drew Universities, internships, a Washington semester, study abroad in 15 to 20 countries, and work-study programs. Also available are dual majors, student-designed majors, nondegree study, credit for life, military, and work experience, and a pass/fail option for 1 course per year. There are preprofessional programs in nursing, optometry, physical therapy, dentistry, medicine, pharmacy, and veterinary medicine. There are 13 national honor societies, a freshman honors program, and 8 departmental honors programs.

Admissions: 84% of the 1999-2000 applicants were accepted. The SAT I scores for the 1999-2000 freshman class were: Verbal--23% below 500, 45% between 500 and 599, 27% between 600 and 700, and 6% above 700; Math--30% below 500, 34% between 500 and 599, 31% between 600 and 700, and 6% above 700. The ACT scores were 8% below 21, 35% between 21 and 23, 30% between 24 and 26, 13% between 27 and 28, and 14% above 28. 50% of the current freshmen were in the top fifth of their class; 80% were in the top two fifths. There was 1 National Merit semifinalist in a recent year. 19 freshmen graduated first in their class.

Requirements: The SAT I or ACT is required. Applicants must be graduates of an accredited secondary school. The GED is accepted. Test scores, counselor recommendations, GPA, college prep course grades, and class rank are all considered in a selective admissions process. The college strongly recommends that applicants complete 4 years of English and 3 each of math, lab science, social science, and a foreign language. The college requires an audition for music and theater scholarships. A portfolio is required for art scholarships. AP and CLEP credits are accepted. Important factors in the admissions decision are advanced placement or honor courses, recommendations by school officials, and leadership record.

Procedure: Freshmen are admitted to all sessions. Entrance exams should be taken in the junior or senior year. There is a deferred admissions plan. Application deadlines are open. Notification is sent on a rolling basis.

Financial Aid: In 1999-2000, 99% of all freshmen and 98% of continuing students received some form of financial aid. 85% of freshmen and 86% of continuing students received need-based aid. The average freshman award was $15,436. Of that total, scholarships or need-based grants averaged $10,904 ($20,975 maximum); loans averaged $4315 ($20,625 maximum); and work contracts averaged

$741 ($1050 maximum). 50% of undergraduates work part time. Average annual earnings from campus work are $809. The average financial indebtedness of the 1999 graduate was $12,501. Simpson is a member of CSS. The FAFSA is required. The fall application deadline is April 20 for priority consideration.

Computers: The mainframe is a DEC ALPHA 2100. All campus-owned buildings are connected to the mainframe network and have Internet access. There are 218 PCs available for student use in the library, Carver Science Center, and McNeill Computer Lab, where computer consultants are available to assist students. PCs are also available in residence halls. All students may access the system 24 hours a day. There are no time limits and no fees.

SKIDMORE COLLEGE
Saratoga Springs, NY 12866-1632　　　　　　　　**(518) 580-5570**
(800) 867-6007; Fax: (518) 580-5584

Full-time: 935 men, 1329 women	**Faculty:** 185; IIB, +$
Part-time: 87 men, 189 women	**Ph.D.s:** 95%
Graduate: 20 men, 32 women	**Student/Faculty:** 12 to 1
Year: semesters, summer session	**Tuition:** $24,259
Application Deadline: January 15	**Room & Board:** $6950
Freshman Class: 5414 applied, 2647 accepted, 659 enrolled	
SAT I Verbal/Math: 610/610	**ACT:** 28　**HIGHLY COMPETITIVE**

Skidmore College, established in 1903, is an independent institution offering undergraduate programs in liberal arts and sciences, as well as business, social work, education, studio art, dance, and theater. Some of the information in this profile is approximate. There is 1 graduate school. In addition to regional accreditation, Skidmore has baccalaureate program accreditation with CSWE and NASAD. The library contains 400,000 volumes, 245,000 microform items, and 9800 audiovisual forms/CDs, and subscribes to 1700 periodicals. Computerized library services include the card catalog and database searching. Special learning facilities include a learning resource center, art gallery, radio station, TV station, electronic music studio, music and art studios, theater teaching facility, anthropology lab, and special biological habitats on campus. The 850-acre campus is in a small town 30 miles north of Albany. Including residence halls, there are 49 buildings.

Programs of Study: Skidmore confers B.A. and B.S. degrees. Master's degrees are also awarded. Bachelor's degrees are awarded in BIOLOGICAL SCIENCE (biochemistry and biology/biological science), BUSINESS (business administration and management and business economics), COMMUNICATIONS AND THE ARTS (art history and appreciation, classics, dance, dramatic arts, English, fine arts, French, German, music, and Spanish), COMPUTER AND PHYSICAL SCIENCE (chemistry, computer science, geology, mathematics, and physics), EDUCATION (art, elementary, and physical), SOCIAL SCIENCE (American studies, anthropology, economics, history, liberal arts/general studies, philosophy, political science/government, psychology, social work, and sociology). English, business, psychology, government, and art are the largest.

Special: Skidmore offers cross-registration with the Hudson-Mohawk Consortium, individually designed internships, various study-abroad programs, a Washington semester in conjunction with American University, dual and student-designed majors, credit for life and experience, and pass/fail options, as well as a nondegree study program for senior citizens. There are cooperative programs in engineering with Dartmouth College and Clarkson University, in business with Clarkson and Rensselaer Polytechnic Institute, in education with Union College, and in law with the Benjamin Cardozo Law School. There is a 6-week internship period available at the end of the spring term. There are 9 national honor societies, including Phi Beta Kappa.

Admissions: 49% of the 1999-2000 applicants were accepted. The SAT I scores for the 1999-2000 freshman class were: Verbal--5% below 500, 39% between 500 and 599, 48% between 600 and 700, and 8% above 700; Math--5% below 500, 40% between 500 and 599, 47% between 600 and 700, and 8% above 700. The ACT scores were 9% between 24 and 26, 69% between 27 and 28, and 23% above 28. 652% of the current freshmen were in the top fifth of their class; 83% were in the top two fifths.

Requirements: The SAT I or ACT is required. Skidmore recommends SAT II: Subject tests in writing, a foreign language, and 1 other subject. Applicants must be graduates of an accredited secondary school or have the GED. They must complete 16 academic units, including 4 years of English, 3 each of math, social science, and a foreign language, and 2 or more of lab science. An essay is required and interviews are recommended. Applicants to creative arts programs may want to submit representations of their work. AP and CLEP credits are accepted. Important factors in the admissions decision are advanced placement or honor courses, recommendations by school officials, and evidence of special talent.

Procedure: Freshmen are admitted fall and spring. Entrance exams should be taken by December of the senior year. There are early decision and deferred admissions plans. Applications should be filed by January 15 for fall entry and November 15 for spring entry, along with a $50 fee. Notification of early decision is sent January 1; regular decision, late Marc. 8% of all applicants are on a waiting list.

Financial Aid: In 1999-2000, 44% of all freshmen and 42% of continuing students received some form of financial aid. 40% of freshmen and 39% of continuing students received need-based aid. The average freshman award was $14,847. The average financial indebtedness of the 1999 graduate was $14,400. Skidmore is a member of CSS. The CSS/Profile or FAFSA is required. The fall application deadline is February 1.

Computers: The mainframe is a DEC VAX 11/780. There are 200 PCs available in 3 major computing clusters, with networking capabilities throughout campus and through the Internet and Bitnet. A computer graphics lab and teaching facility is available. A cluster of 9 Sun computers provides the backbone for time-shared computing, providing access to E-mail, electronic bulletin boards, and compilers. Statistical analysis software, free services, and technical support are provided. Students may connect to central computing facilities through PCs via modem capabilities in each dormitory room. All students may access the system 24 hours per day. There are no time limits and no fees.

SMITH COLLEGE
Northampton, MA 01063   (413) 585-2500; Fax: (413) 585-2527

Full-time: 2548 women	**Faculty:** 255; IIA, ++$
Part-time: 117 women	**Ph.D.s:** 97%
Graduate: 7 men, 84 women	**Student/Faculty:** 10 to 1
Year: semesters	**Tuition:** $22,622
Application Deadline: January 15	**Room & Board:** $7820
Freshman Class: 2998 applied, 1681 accepted, 667 enrolled	
SAT I Verbal/Math: 660/630	**ACT:** 28 **HIGHLY COMPETITIVE+**

Smith College, founded in 1871, is the largest independent women's college in the United States and offers a liberal arts education. There are 2 graduate schools.

The 4 libraries contain 1,246,821 volumes, 107,184 microform items, and 60,135 audiovisual forms/CDs, and subscribe to 2796 periodicals. Computerized library services include the card catalog, interlibrary loans, and database searching. Special learning facilities include a learning resource center, art gallery, radio station, TV studio, astronomy observatories, a center for foreign languages and culture, a digital design studio, plant and horticultural labs, art studios with casting, printmaking, and darkroom facilities, and specialized libraries for science, music, and art. The 125-acre campus is in a small town 90 miles west of Boston. Including residence halls, there are 105 buildings.

Programs of Study: Smith confers the A.B. degree. Master's and doctoral degrees are also awarded. Bachelor's degrees are awarded in BIOLOGICAL SCIENCE (biochemistry, biology/biological science, and neurosciences), COMMUNICATIONS AND THE ARTS (art history and appreciation, classics, comparative literature, dance, dramatic arts, East Asian languages and literature, English, French, Germanic languages and literature, Greek, Italian, Latin, music, Russian, Spanish, and studio art), COMPUTER AND PHYSICAL SCIENCE (astronomy, chemistry, computer science, geology, mathematics, and physics), EDUCATION (early childhood and elementary), SOCIAL SCIENCE (African American studies, American studies, anthropology, classical/ancient civilization, economics, French studies, history, Latin American studies, Luso-Brazilian studies, medieval studies, philosophy, political science/government, psychology, religion, Russian and Slavic studies, sociology, and women's studies). Biological sciences, English, and economics are the strongest academically. Government, psychology, and art are the largest.

Special: Smith offers a junior year exchange program called the Twelve College Exchange, and cross-registration with 5 area colleges and universities. Internships, including one at the Smithsonian Institution, study abroad in Rome, Geneva, Hamburg, and Paris, consortial programs in Spain, China, Russia, Italy, Japan, and South India, and a Washington semester are available as are accelerated degree programs, student-designed majors, dual majors, nondegree study, and satisfactory/unsatisfactory options. There are 3 national honor societies, including Phi Beta Kappa. Most departments have honors programs.

Admissions: 56% of the 1999-2000 applicants were accepted. The SAT I scores for the 1999-2000 freshman class were: Verbal--2% below 500, 17% between 500 and 599, 54% between 600 and 700, and 27% above 700; Math--4% below 500, 30% between 500 and 599, 53% between 600 and 700, and 13% above 700. The ACT scores were 3% below 21, 8% between 21 and 23, 22% between 24 and 26, 34% between 27 and 28, and 33% above 28. 82% of the current freshmen were in the top fifth of their class; 97% were in the top two fifths. 33 freshmen graduated first in their class.

Requirements: The SAT I or ACT is required. Smith highly recommends that applicants have 4 years of English, 3 years each of math, science, and a foreign language, and 2 years of history. SAT II: Subject tests, especially in writing, are strongly recommended, as are personal interviews. The GED is accepted. AP credits are accepted. Important factors in the admissions decision are advanced placement or honor courses, leadership record, and recommendations by school officials.

Procedure: Freshmen are admitted in the fall. Entrance exams should be taken before January of the senior year. There are early decision, early admissions, and deferred admissions plans. Early decision applications should be filed by November 15; regular applications, by January 15 for fall entry, along with a $50 fee. Notification of early decision is sent December 15; regular decision, early April. 131 early decision candidates were accepted for the 1999-2000 class. 16% of all applicants are on a waiting list.

Financial Aid: In 1999-2000, 68% of all freshmen and 65% of continuing students received some form of financial aid. 56% of all students received need-based aid. The average freshman award was $21,320. Of that total, scholarships or need-based grants averaged $17,384 ($28,810 maximum); loans averaged $2451 ($3625 maximum); and work contracts averaged $1471 ($1625 maximum). 51% of undergraduates work part time. Average annual earnings from campus work are $1143. The average financial indebtedness of the 1999 graduate was $15,142. Smith is a member of CSS. The CSS/Profile or FAFSA and the college's own financial statement are required. The fall application deadline is February 1.

Computers: The mainframes consists of 1 DEC VAX, 3 DEC ALPHAs, 4 Sun, 2 other UNIX systems, and 22 Novell servers. Computing facilities include more than 550 PCs and Mac computers in public labs, classrooms, the libraries, and the foreign language center. All dormitory rooms have high-speed Ethernet connections and offer unlimited Internet access at no cost. Computing resources are connected by a campuswide fiber-optic network. All students may access the system. There are no time limits and no fees.

SOUTHERN METHODIST UNIVERSITY
Dallas, TX 75275
(214) SMU-2058
(800) 323-0672; Fax: (214) 768-2507

Full-time: 2424 men, 2784 women	**Faculty:** 459; I, av$
Part-time: 150 men, 194 women	**Ph.D.s:** 88%
Graduate: 2716 men, 2093 women	**Student/Faculty:** 11 to 1
Year: semesters, summer session	**Tuition:** $18,510
Application Deadline: January 15	**Room & Board:** $6901
Freshman Class: 4280 applied, 3809 accepted, 1331 enrolled	
SAT I or ACT: recommended	**VERY COMPETITIVE**

Southern Methodist University, founded in 1911, is a private nonsectarian institution affiliated with the United Methodist Church. SMU offers undergraduate and graduate programs in humanities and sciences, business, arts, and engineering and applied sciences. There are 4 undergraduate and 6 graduate schools. In addition to regional accreditation, SMU has baccalaureate program accreditation with AACSB, ABET, NASAD, and NASM. The 8 libraries contain 1.5 million volumes, 791,908 microform items, and 39,305 audiovisual forms/CDs, and subscribe to 11,216 periodicals. Computerized library services include the card catalog, interlibrary loans, and database searching. Special learning facilities include a learning resource center, art gallery, natural history museum, radio station, art museum, research laboratories, TV studio, and several performing arts theaters, including Classical Thrust Stage. The 163-acre campus is in a suburban area 5 miles north of downtown Dallas. Including residence halls, there are 75 buildings.

Programs of Study: SMU confers B.A., B.S., B.B.A., B.F.A., B.Hum., B.M., B. S.Comp.Eng., B.S.E.E., B.S.Env.E., B.S.M.E., and B.Soc.Sci. degrees. Master's and doctoral degrees are also awarded. Bachelor's degrees are awarded in BIOLOGICAL SCIENCE (biochemistry and biology/biological science), BUSINESS (accounting, banking and finance, business administration and management, management information systems, management science, marketing/retailing/merchandising, organizational behavior, and real estate), COMMUNICATIONS AND THE ARTS (advertising, art history and appreciation, broadcasting, creative writing, dance, dramatic arts, English, film arts, French, German, journalism, languages, media arts, music performance, music theory and composition, piano/organ, public relations, Russian, Spanish, and studio art), COMPUTER

AND PHYSICAL SCIENCE (chemistry, computer science, geology, geophysics and seismology, mathematics, physics, and statistics), EDUCATION (music), ENGINEERING AND ENVIRONMENTAL DESIGN (computer engineering, electrical/electronics engineering, environmental engineering, and mechanical engineering), HEALTH PROFESSIONS (music therapy), SOCIAL SCIENCE (African American studies, anthropology, economics, German area studies, history, humanities, international studies, Italian studies, Latin American studies, liberal arts/general studies, medieval studies, Mexican-American/Chicano studies, philosophy, political science/government, psychology, public affairs, religion, Russian and Slavic studies, social science, sociology, and Southwest American studies). Performing arts, life sciences, history, and business are the strongest academically. Business, communications, and psychology are the largest.

Special: SMU offers a co-op program in engineering, work-study programs, B.A. -B.S. degrees, study abroad in 12 countries, dual majors in any combination, student-designed majors, numerous internships, and interdisciplinary majors, including economics with finance applications and economics with systems analysis. A 3-2 advanced degree in business is available, as are evening degree programs in humanities and social sciences, and teacher certification programs. There are 16 national honor societies, including Phi Beta Kappa, and a freshman honors program.

Admissions: 89% of the 1999-2000 applicants were accepted. The SAT I scores for the 1999-2000 freshman class were: Verbal--18% below 500, 46% between 500 and 599, 30% between 600 and 700, and 6% above 700; Math--16% below 500, 43% between 500 and 599, 34% between 600 and 700, and 7% above 700.

Requirements: The SAT I or ACT is recommended. In addition, applicants should graduate from an accredited high school with a minimum of 15 academic credits: 4 in English, 3 in higher math, including algebra I, II, and plane geometry, 3 each in natural science and social science, and 2 in a foreign language. Home School Certificate applicants may qualify with the SAT I or ACT and 3 SAT II: Subject tests, including writing and math. Performing arts majors must audition. AP and CLEP credits are accepted. Important factors in the admissions decision are advanced placement or honor courses, leadership record, and recommendations by school officials.

Procedure: Freshmen are admitted to all sessions. Entrance exams should be taken by December of the senior year. There are early decision and deferred admissions plans. Early decision applications should be filed by November 1; regular applications, by January 15 for fall entry and April 1 for spring entry, along with a $40 fee. Notification of early decision is sent December 30; regular decision, on a rolling basis. A waiting list is an active part of the admissions procedure.

Financial Aid: In 1999-2000, 83% of all freshmen and 73% of continuing students received some form of financial aid. 47% of students received need-based aid. The average freshman award was $15,642. SMU is a member of CSS. The FAFSA is required. The fall application deadline is February 1.

Computers: The mainframe is an IBM 3090. Access to campus administrative and academic computers systems is available from all campus offices and dormitory rooms. In addition, several hundred public workstations are available in campus libraries and computer labs. All students may access the system 24 hours a day. There are no time limits and no fees.

SOUTHERN OREGON UNIVERSITY

Ashland, OR 97520-5005

(541) 552-6411
(800) 482-7672; Fax: (541) 552-6614

Full-time: 1621 men, 2030 women	**Faculty:** 149; IIA, --$
Part-time: 548 men, 878 women	**Ph.D.s:** 95%
Graduate: 230 men, 435 women	**Student/Faculty:** 25 to 1
Year: quarters, summer session	**Tuition:** $3234 ($9897)
Application Deadline: open	**Room & Board:** $4658
Freshman Class: 1961 applied, 1251 accepted, 880 enrolled	
SAT I Verbal/Math: 524/509	**ACT:** 22 **VERY COMPETITIVE**

Southern Oregon University, founded in 1882, is a public comprehensive university providing undergraduate and graduate programs in humanities, science, business, fine and performing arts, social sciences, and teacher education. There are 4 undergraduate and 1 graduate school. In addition to regional accreditation, Southern has baccalaureate program accreditation with NASM and NLN. The library contains 290,000 volumes, 750,000 microform items, and 2500 audiovisual forms, CDs, and subscribes to 2125 periodicals. Computerized library services include interlibrary loans and database searching. Special learning facilities include a learning resource center, art gallery, radio station, TV station, and an art museum, 3 art galleries, wildlife forensics lab, music recital hall, 2 theaters, greenhouse, vertebrate natural history museum, and herbarium. The 175-acre campus is in a small town 10 miles southeast of Medford. Including residence halls, there are 36 buildings.

Programs of Study: Southern confers B.A., B.S., and B.F.A. degrees. Master's degrees are also awarded. Bachelor's degrees are awarded in BIOLOGICAL SCIENCE (biology/biological science), BUSINESS (accounting, business administration and management, and marketing/retailing/merchandising), COMMUNICATIONS AND THE ARTS (art, communications, dramatic arts, English, languages, music, music business management, Spanish, and visual and performing arts), COMPUTER AND PHYSICAL SCIENCE (chemistry, computer science, geology, mathematics, physics, and science), EDUCATION (physical), ENGINEERING AND ENVIRONMENTAL DESIGN (environmental science), HEALTH PROFESSIONS (health, nursing, and premedicine), SOCIAL SCIENCE (anthropology, criminology, economics, geography, history, international studies, liberal arts/general studies, political science/government, prelaw, psychology, social science, and sociology). Fine and performing arts, sciences, and social sciences are the strongest academically. Business and social sciences are the largest.

Special: Cross-registration through the National Student Exchange, study abroad in 16 countries, and work-study programs are available. Interdisciplinary degrees, student-designed majors, dual majors in business plus chemistry, math, or music, and pass/fail options up to 1 course per quarter also are offered. Internships, accelerated degree programs, and B.A.-B.S. degrees are possible. There are 13 national honor societies, and 3 departmental honors programs. .

Admissions: 64% of the 1999-2000 applicants were accepted. The SAT I scores for the 1999-2000 freshman class were: Verbal--40% below 500, 39% between 500 and 599, 18% between 600 and 700, and 3% above 700; Math--45% below 500, 39% between 500 and 599, 15% between 600 and 700, and 1% above 700. The ACT scores were 33% below 21, 33% between 21 and 23, 26% between 24 and 26, 5% between 27 and 28, and 3% above 28.

Requirements: The SAT I or ACT is required. A GPA of 2.8 is required. A minimum composite score of 1010 on the SAT I is needed if the high school GPA is less than 2.75. Applicants need 14 academic credits, including 4 years of English, 3 each of math and social studies, 2 of science, and 2 years of one foreign language. SAT II: Subject tests in English, math, and another area are needed if there is insufficient college-preparatory course work. GED is accepted. AP and CLEP credits are accepted.

Procedure: Freshmen are admitted to all sessions. Entrance exams should be taken in the senior year. There are early admissions and deferred admissions plans. Application deadlines are open. There is a $50 fee. Notification is sent on a rolling basis.

Financial Aid: In 1999-2000, 62% of all freshmen and 72% of continuing students received some form of financial aid. 52% of freshmen and 60% of continuing students received need-based aid. The average freshman award was $5609. Of that total, scholarships or need-based grants averaged $1852 ($5500 maximum); loans averaged $3266 ($12,825 maximum); and work contracts averaged $1113 ($1500 maximum). 46% of undergraduates work part time. Average annual earnings from campus work are $809. The average financial indebtedness of the 1999 graduate was $13,404. Southern is a member of CSS. The FAFSA is required. The fall application deadline is March 1.

Computers: The mainframe is a DEC VAX 4310. A $4.1 million computing services center for students houses 200 PCs. Smaller labs house an additional 200 computers for student use. All students may access the system 8 a.m. to 10 p.m. Monday through Thursday, 8 a.m. to 5 p.m. Friday, 1 to 5 p.m. Saturday, and 1 to 8 p.m. Sunday. There are no time limits and no fees.

SOUTHWEST TEXAS STATE UNIVERSITY
San Marcos, TX 78666-4616   (512) 245-2364
Fax: (512) 245-8044

Full-time: 6823 men, 8364 women	**Faculty:** 572; IIA, -$
Part-time: 1750 men, 1919 women	**Ph.D.s:** 75%
Graduate: 1118 men, 1795 women	**Student/Faculty:** 27 to 1
Year: semesters, summer session	**Tuition:** $3056 ($9536)
Application Deadline: July 1	**Room & Board:** $4349
Freshman Class: 7294 applied, 4747 accepted, 2514 enrolled	
SAT I Verbal/Math: 539/537	**ACT:** 22 **VERY COMPETITIVE**

Southwest Texas State University, founded in 1899, is part of the Texas State University System and offers programs in general studies, applied arts and technology, business, education, fine arts, health professions, liberal arts, and science. There are 8 undergraduate schools and 1 graduate school. In addition to regional accreditation, SWT has baccalaureate program accreditation with AACSB, ADA, AHEA, ASLA, CSAB, CSWE, FIDER, NASM, and NRPA. The library contains 3.1 million volumes, 1.7 million microform items, and 252,844 audiovisual forms/CDs, and subscribes to 5339 periodicals. Computerized library services include the card catalog, interlibrary loans, and database searching. Special learning facilities include a learning resource center, art gallery, radio station, TV station, and a recording studio. The 423-acre campus is in a small town 30 miles south of Austin. Including residence halls, there are 170 buildings.

Programs of Study: SWT confers B.A., B.S., B.A.A.S., B.A.I.S., B.B.A., B.E. S.S., B.F.A., B.H.A., B.H.W.P., B.M., B.S.A.G., B.S.A.S., B.S.C.D., B.S.C.J., B. S.C.L.S., B.S.F.C.S., B.S.H.I.M., B.S.H.P., B.S.R.A., B.S.R.T., B.S.R.C., B.S.T. C.H., and B.S.W. degrees. Master's and doctoral degrees are also awarded. Bachelor's degrees are awarded in AGRICULTURE (agricultural business management, agriculture, animal science, and horticulture), BIOLOGICAL SCIENCE (biology/biological science, botany, marine biology, microbiology, nutrition, physiology, wildlife biology, and zoology), BUSINESS (accounting, banking and finance, business administration and management, fashion merchandising, international business management, marketing/retailing/merchandising, recreational facilities management, and tourism), COMMUNICATIONS AND THE ARTS (advertising, applied art, art, audio technology, communications, dramatic arts, English, fine arts, French, German, graphic design, illustration, music, music performance, music theory and composition, public relations, Spanish, and studio art), COMPUTER AND PHYSICAL SCIENCE (chemistry, computer management, computer science, information sciences and systems, mathematics, and physics), EDUCATION (agricultural, art, athletic training, bilingual/bicultural, early childhood, elementary, foreign languages, health, home economics, music, physical, reading, science, secondary, and special), ENGINEERING AND ENVIRONMENTAL DESIGN (cartography, city/community/regional planning, engineering technology, environmental science, industrial engineering technology, interior design, and preengineering), HEALTH PROFESSIONS (clinical science, exercise science, health care administration, medical laboratory technology, predentistry, premedicine, prepharmacy, radiation therapy, respiratory therapy, and speech pathology/audiology), SOCIAL SCIENCE (African studies, American studies, anthropology, Asian/Oriental studies, child care/child and family studies, corrections, criminal justice, economics, European studies, family/consumer studies, food science, geography, history, interdisciplinary studies, international relations, international studies, law enforcement and corrections, Middle Eastern studies, philosophy, physical fitness/movement, political science/government, psychology, Russian and Slavic studies, social science, social work, and sociology). Geography, and education are the strongest academically. Education, management, and biology are the largest.

Special: Co-op programs in medicine, dentistry, engineering, architecture, law, pharmacy, nursing, occupational therapy, and veterinary medicine, internships in many departments, study abroad in 26 countries, and Washington semesters are available. Dual majors, credit for life experience, and nondegree study also are possible. A 3-2 engineering degree is possible with the University of Texas or Texas A&M or Texas Tech Universities. There are 34 national honor societies, a freshman honors program, and 1 departmental honors program.

Admissions: 65% of the 1999-2000 applicants were accepted. The SAT I scores for the 1999-2000 freshman class were: Verbal--25% below 500, 57% between 500 and 599, 17% between 600 and 700, and 1% above 700; Math--26% below 500, 54% between 500 and 599, 19% between 600 and 700, and 1% above 700. The ACT scores were 20% below 21, 45% between 21 and 23, 25% between 24 and 26, 8% between 27 and 28, and 2% above 28. 52% of the current freshmen were in the top fifth of their class; 78% were in the top two fifths. 20 freshmen graduated first in their class.

Requirements: The SAT I or ACT is required, with minimum scores determined by high school class rank. Applicants need 15 academic credits, including 4 units in English, 3 in math and social science, 3 in natural science, 2 in foreign language, and 1 in computer science. The GED is accepted; applicants with a GED are treated as though they were ranked in the 4th quarter. An electronic application can be accessed through the University's web site at http://www.applytexas.org/adappc/commonapp.html. AP and CLEP credits are accepted. Important factors in the admissions decision are advanced placement or honor courses, leadership record, and extracurricular activities record.

Procedure: Freshmen are admitted to all sessions. Entrance exams should be taken at the end of the junior year. There is an early admissions plan. Applications should be filed by July 1 for fall entry, December 1 for spring entry, and May 1 for summer entry, along with a $25 fee. Notification is sent on a rolling basis.

Financial Aid: In 1999-2000, 48% of all freshmen and 43% of continuing students received some form of financial aid. 33% of freshmen and 30% of continuing students received need-based aid. The average freshman award was $5640. Of that total, scholarships or need-based grants averaged $3673 ($5000 maximum); and loans averaged $2823 ($9000 maximum). 22% of undergraduates work part time. Average annual earnings from campus work are $1096. The average financial indebtedness of the 1999 graduate was $13,511. SWT is a member of CSS. The FAFSA is required. The fall application deadline is April 1.

Computers: The mainframes are a DEC VAX 7640, a DEC VAX 6620, a DEC ALPHA AXP 7640, and a DEC ALPHA AXP 4100. PCs and Macs are available for student use throughout the campus. All students may access the system 24 hours daily. There are no time limits. The fee is $6 per semester hour.

SOUTHWESTERN UNIVERSITY
Georgetown, TX 78626

(512) 863-1200
(800) 252-3166; Fax: (512) 863-9601

Full-time: 515 men, 716 women	**Faculty:** 100; IIB, ++
Part-time: 11 men, 14 women	**Ph.D.s:** 94%
Graduate: none	**Student/Faculty:** 12 to 1
Year: semesters, summer session	**Tuition:** $15,000
Application Deadline: February 15	**Room & Board:** $5342
Freshman Class: 1495 applied, 995 accepted, 354 enrolled	
SAT I Verbal/Math: 622/622	**ACT:** 27 **HIGHLY COMPETITIVE**

Southwestern University, founded in 1840, is a private liberal arts institution affiliated with the United Methodist Church. There are 2 undergraduate schools. In addition to regional accreditation, Southwestern has baccalaureate program accreditation with NASM. The library contains 295,432 volumes, 45,841 microform items, and 9122 audiovisual forms/CDs, and subscribes to 1433 periodicals. Computerized library services include the card catalog, interlibrary loans, and database searching. Special learning facilities include a learning resource center and art gallery. The 500-acre campus is in a suburban area 28 miles north of Austin. Including residence halls, there are 31 buildings.

Programs of Study: Southwestern confers B.A., B.S., B.F.A., and B.Mus. degrees. Bachelor's degrees are awarded in AGRICULTURE (animal science), BIOLOGICAL SCIENCE (biology/biological science), BUSINESS (accounting and business administration and management), COMMUNICATIONS AND THE ARTS (art, classics, communications, dramatic arts, English, French, German, Latin, music, and Spanish), COMPUTER AND PHYSICAL SCIENCE (chemistry, computer science, mathematics, and physics), ENGINEERING AND ENVIRONMENTAL DESIGN (environmental science), SOCIAL SCIENCE (American studies, early childhood studies, economics, history, international studies, philosophy, physical fitness/movement, political science/government, psychology, religion, sociology, and women's studies). Biology, sociology, and political science are the strongest academically. Psychology, biology, and business are the largest.

Special: Students may study abroad in England, France, Mexico, Korea, and other countries. The university offers a Washington semester, dual, student-designed, and independent majors, and internships in government, fine arts, psychology, science, and other fields. A 3-2 engineering program may be arranged with Washington, Texas A&M, and Arizona State Universities, and the University of Texas at Austin. Some pass/fail options are available. There are 7 national honor societies, including Phi Beta Kappa, and honors programs in most departments.

Admissions: 67% of the 1999-2000 applicants were accepted. The SAT I scores for the 1999-2000 freshman class were: Verbal--4% below 500, 35% between 500 and 599, 42% between 600 and 700, and 19% above 700; Math--3% below 500, 33% between 500 and 599, 48% between 600 and 700, and 16% above 700. The ACT scores were 3% below 21, 13% between 21 and 23, 31% between 24 and 26, 23% between 27 and 28, and 30% above 28. 81% of the current freshmen were in the top fifth of their class; 97% were in the top two fifths. There were 10 National Merit finalists and 12 semifinalists. 21 freshmen graduated first in their class.

Requirements: The SAT I or ACT is required. The applicant should be a graduate of an accredited high school or have the GED. Secondary preparation should include 4 years each of English and math, 3 each of science and social science or history, 2 of a foreign language, and 1 of an academic elective. An essay is required and an interview is recommmended. Applications are accepted via CollegeLink, Apply, and Common Application, and on-line via the school's web site. AP and CLEP credits are accepted. Important factors in the admissions decision are advanced placement or honor courses, recommendations by school officials, and leadership record.

Procedure: Freshmen are admitted fall and spring. Entrance exams should be taken in the fall of the senior year. There are early decision, early admissions, and deferred admissions plans. Early decision applications should be filed by November 1 (fall) or january 1 (spring); regular applications, by February 15 for fall entry and December 1 for spring entry, along with a $40 fee. Notification of early decision is sent December 1 (fall) or February 1 (spring); regular decision, March 31. 125 early decision candidates were accepted for the 1999-2000 class. 11% of all applicants are on a waiting list; 3 were accepted in 1999.

Financial Aid: In 1999-2000, 81% of all freshmen and 71% of continuing students received some form of financial aid. 51% of freshmen and 46% of continuing students received need-based aid. The average freshman award was $13,265. Of that total, scholarships or need-based grants averaged $10,087 ($21,420 maximum); loans averaged $1694 ($4500 maximum); and work contracts averaged $1483 ($2000 maximum). 64% of undergraduates work part time. Average annual earnings from campus work are $1744. The average financial indebtedness of the 1999 graduate was $16,251. Southwestern is a member of CSS. The FAFSA and the college's own financial statement are required. The fall application deadline is March 1.

Computers: The mainframes are an HP 855, an HP 9000/800K, an HP 9000/800D, and HP 9000/800 E-55 and E-35 models. There are approximately 150 PCs located throughout the campus for student use. Students may also use the facilities in 3 computer labs where there is access to the Internet (E-mail, World Wide Web, and Gopher), word processing, and instructional software. All students may access the system at any time. There are no time limits and no fees.

STANFORD UNIVERSITY
Stanford, CA 94305-2040   (650) 723-2091; Fax: (650) 723-6050

Full-time: 3356 men, 3238 women	**Faculty:** I, ++$
Part-time: none	**Ph.D.s:** 99%
Graduate: 5936 men, 3108 women	**Student/Faculty:** 7 to 1
Year: quarters, summer session	**Tuition:** $23,058
Application Deadline: December 15	**Room & Board:** $7881
Freshman Class: 17,919 applied, 2689 accepted, 1750 enrolled	
SAT I or ACT: required	**MOST COMPETITIVE**

Stanford University, founded in 1891, is a private coeducational research-intensive university offering a broad curriculum in undergraduate liberal arts, graduate education, and professional training. There are 3 undergraduate and 7 graduate schools. In addition to regional accreditation, Stanford has baccalaureate program accreditation with AACSB and ABET. The 18 libraries contain 7 million volumes, 1.5 million microform items, and 245,760 audiovisual forms/CDs. Computerized library services include the card catalog, interlibrary loans, and database searching. Special learning facilities include a learning resource center, art gallery, radio station, TV station, art museum, biological preserve, and linear accelerator. The 8180-acre campus is in a suburban area 30 miles south of San Francisco. Including residence halls, there are 678 buildings.

Programs of Study: Stanford confers A.B., B.S., and B.A.S. degrees. Master's and doctoral degrees are also awarded. Bachelor's degrees are awarded in BIOLOGICAL SCIENCE (biology/biological science and microbiology), COMMUNICATIONS AND THE ARTS (Chinese, classics, communications, comparative literature, dramatic arts, English, fine arts, French, Italian, Japanese, linguistics, music, and Spanish), COMPUTER AND PHYSICAL SCIENCE (chemistry, computer science, earth science, geology, geoscience, mathematics, and physics), ENGINEERING AND ENVIRONMENTAL DESIGN (chemical engineering, civil engineering, electrical/electronics engineering, engineering, industrial engineering, materials science, mechanical engineering, and petroleum/natural gas engineering), SOCIAL SCIENCE (African American studies, American studies, anthropology, crosscultural studies, East Asian studies, economics, history, humanities, international relations, Latin American studies, philosophy, political science/government, psychology, public affairs, religion, sociology, systems science, and urban studies). Biology, economics, and English are the largest.

Special: Internships, study abroad, a Washington semester, student-designed majors, dual majors, a B.A.-B.S. degree, a 3-2 engineering degree, pass/no credit options and numerous research opportunities are offered. There is a chapter of Phi Beta Kappa.

Admissions: 15% of the 1999-2000 applicants were accepted. The SAT I scores for the 1999-2000 freshman class were: Verbal--5% between 500 and 599, 27% between 600 and 700, and 67% above 700; Math--4% between 500 and 599, 25% between 600 and 700, and 71% above 700. The ACT scores were 11% between 21 and 25, 29% between 26 and 29, and 60% above 29. 97% of the current freshmen were in the top fifth of their class.

Requirements: The SAT I or ACT is required. The university recommends that applicants have strong preparation in high school English, math, a foreign language, science, and social studies. SAT II: Subject tests are strongly recommended. AP credits are accepted. Important factors in the admissions decision are advanced placement or honor courses, personality/intangible qualities, and recommendations by school officials.

Procedure: Freshmen are admitted in the fall. Entrance exams should be taken before December of the application year. There are early decision and deferred admissions plans. Early decision applications should be filed by November 1; regular applications, by December 15 for fall entry, along with a $60 fee. Notification of early decision is sent mid-December; regular decision, early April. 484 early decision candidates were accepted for the 1999-2000 class. A waiting list is an active part of the admissions procedure.

Financial Aid: In 1998-1999, 72% of all freshmen and 70% of continuing students received some form of financial aid. 39% of freshmen and 42% of continuing students received need-based aid. The average freshman award was $22,859. Of that total, scholarships or need-based grants averaged $18,372 ($34,642 maximum); loans averaged $3361 ($27,625 maximum); and work contracts averaged $1127 ($2700 maximum). The average financial indebtedness of the 1998 graduate was $15,892. Stanford is a member of CSS. The CSS/Profile or FAFSA is required. The fall application deadline is February 1.

Computers: PCs are available in residences, libraries, and other campus clusters. All students may access the system. There are no fees.

STATE UNIVERSITY OF NEW YORK AT ALBANY
Albany, NY 12222

(518) 442-5435
(800) 293-SUNY; Fax: (518) 442-5383

Full-time: 5441 men, 5144 women	**Faculty:** 531; I, av$
Part-time: 548 men, 604 women	**Ph.D.s:** 96%
Graduate: 1995 men, 3169 women	**Student/Faculty:** 20 to 1
Year: semesters, summer session	**Tuition:** $4338 ($9238)
Application Deadline: March 1	**Room & Board:** $5828
Freshman Class: 15,312 applied, 9414 accepted, 2294 enrolled	
SAT I or ACT: required	**VERY COMPETITIVE**

The State University of New York at Albany, established in 1844, is a public institution conferring undergraduate degrees in humanities and fine arts, science and math, social and behavioral sciences, business, public policy, education, and social welfare. There are 5 undergraduate and 8 graduate schools. In addition to regional accreditation, University at Albany has baccalaureate program accreditation with AACSB and CSWE. The 3 libraries contain 1,940,532 volumes, 2.7 million microform items, and 5662 audiovisual forms/CDs, and subscribe to 16,103 periodicals. Computerized library services include the card catalog, interlibrary loans, and database searching. Special learning facilities include a learning resource center, art gallery, radio station, linear accelerator, a sophisticated weather data system, a national lightning detection system, an interactive media center, extensive art studios, and a new state-of-the-art electronic library. The 560-acre campus is in a suburban area about 5 miles west of downtown Albany. Including residence halls, there are 90 buildings.

Programs of Study: University at Albany confers B.A. and B.S. degrees. Master's and doctoral degrees are also awarded. Bachelor's degrees are awarded in BIOLOGICAL SCIENCE (biochemistry, biology/biological science, and molecular biology), BUSINESS (accounting and business administration and management), COMMUNICATIONS AND THE ARTS (art history and appreciation, Chinese, communications, English, fine arts, French, Hebrew, Italian, Latin, linguistics, music, Portuguese, Russian, and Spanish), COMPUTER AND PHYSICAL SCIENCE (actuarial science, applied mathematics, chemistry, computer science, geology, information sciences and systems, mathematics, and physics),

EDUCATION (foreign languages, science, and secondary), HEALTH PROFESSIONS (medical laboratory technology, predentistry, and premedicine), SOCIAL SCIENCE (African American studies, anthropology, Asian/Oriental studies, Caribbean studies, classical/ancient civilization, criminal justice, Eastern European studies, economics, geography, Hispanic American studies, history, Latin American studies, medieval studies, philosophy, political science/government, prelaw, psychology, religion, Russian and Slavic studies, social work, sociology, and women's studies). Business and accounting, sociology, and criminal justice are the strongest academically. Psychology, English, and business are the largest.

Special: Cross-registration is available with Rensselaer Polytechnic Institute, Albany Law School, and Union, Siena, and Russell Sage Colleges. Internships may be arranged with state government agencies and private organizations. Study abroad in many countries, a Washington semester, work-study programs, B.A.-B.S. degrees in biology, math, and economics, and a 3-2 engineering degree with Rensselaer Polytechnic Institute and Clarkson University are offered. Dual and student-designed majors, nondegree study, and pass/fail grading options are available. There are 14 national honor societies, including Phi Beta Kappa, a freshman honors program, and 20 departmental honors programs.

Admissions: 61% of the 1999-2000 applicants were accepted. The SAT I scores for the 1999-2000 freshman class were: Verbal--13% below 500, 56% between 500 and 599, 26% between 600 and 700, and 4% above 700; Math--10% below 500, 53% between 500 and 599, 33% between 600 and 700, and 4% above 700. 36% of the current freshmen were in the top fifth of their class; 81% were in the top two fifths. There were 2 National Merit finalists and 8 semifinalists. 8 freshmen graduated first in their class.

Requirements: The SAT I or ACT is required. Applicants must be graduates of an accredited secondary school or have a GED. 18 academic credits are required, including 2 to 3 units of math and 2 units of lab sciences. Foreign language study is also recommended. Applications are accepted on-line at http://www.albany.edu/admissions/undergraduate/applying/application.htm . AP credits are accepted. Important factors in the admissions decision are advanced placement or honor courses, personality/intangible qualities, and leadership record.

Procedure: Freshmen are admitted fall, spring, and summer. Entrance exams should be taken by November of the senior year. There are early action and deferred admissions plans. Early action applications should be filed by December 1; regular applications, by March 1 for fall or summer entry, January 1 for spring entry, along with a $30 fee. Notification of early decision is sent January 1; regular decision, on a rolling basis from January to April. 700 early action candidates were accepted for the 1999-2000 class. A waiting list is an active part of the admissions procedure.

Financial Aid: In 1999-2000, 57% of all freshmen and 53% of continuing students received some form of financial aid. 47% of freshmen and 43% of continuing students received need-based aid. The average freshman award was $6750. Of that total, scholarships or need-based grants averaged $3904; and loans averaged $3102. 25% of undergraduates work part time. The average financial indebtedness of the 1999 graduate was $15,300. University at Albany is a member of CSS. The FAFSA is required. The fall application deadline is March 15.

Computers: The mainframes are an IBM 9672-R21 and VAX and UNIX clusters. The computing services center networks provide E-mail facilities and Internet access. Computer access rooms, terminals in residence halls, and phone hookups provide 24-hour access to mainframe computing facilities. All students may access the system. There are no time limits and no fees.

STATE UNIVERSITY OF NEW YORK AT BINGHAMTON
Binghamton, NY 13902-6000   (607) 777-2171
                                                        Fax: (607) 777-4445

Full-time: 4484 men, 5051 women	**Faculty:** 509; I, -$
Part-time: 137 men, 200 women	**Ph.Ds:** 95%
Graduate: 1351 men, 1341 women	**Student/Faculty:** 19 to 1
Year: semesters, summer session	**Tuition:** $4416 ($9316)
Application Deadline: February 15	**Room & Board:** $5516
Freshman Class: 16,386 applied, 6902 accepted, 2049 enrolled	
SAT I Verbal/Math: 590/620	**HIGHLY COMPETITIVE**

The State University of New York at Binghamton, founded in 1946, is part of the State University of New York System. The public institution offers programs through the Harpur College of Arts and Sciences and the Schools of Education and Human Development, Nursing, Management, and Engineering and Applied Science. There are 5 undergraduate schools and 1 graduate school. In addition to regional accreditation, Binghamton University has baccalaureate program accreditation with AACSB, ABET, CSAB, NASM, and NLN. The 2 libraries contain 1,632,194 volumes, 1,645,463 microform items, and 116,914 audiovisual forms/CDs, and subscribe to 7265 periodicals. Computerized library services include the card catalog, interlibrary loans, and database searching. Special learning facilities include a learning resource center, art gallery, radio station, TV station, nature preserve, and 4-climate greenhouse. The 828-acre campus is in a suburban area 1 mile west of Binghamton. Including residence halls, there are 74 buildings.

Programs of Study: Binghamton University confers B.A., B.S., B.F.A., and B. Mus. degrees. Master's and doctoral degrees are also awarded. Bachelor's degrees are awarded in BIOLOGICAL SCIENCE (biochemistry and biology/biological science), BUSINESS (accounting and business administration and management), COMMUNICATIONS AND THE ARTS (Arabic, art, art history and appreciation, classics, comparative literature, dramatic arts, English, film arts, fine arts, French, German, Hebrew, Italian, Latin, linguistics, music, music performance, Spanish, speech/debate/rhetoric, and studio art), COMPUTER AND PHYSICAL SCIENCE (chemistry, computer science, geology, mathematics, and physics), ENGINEERING AND ENVIRONMENTAL DESIGN (computer engineering, electrical/electronics engineering, environmental science, industrial engineering, and mechanical engineering), HEALTH PROFESSIONS (nursing), SOCIAL SCIENCE (African American studies, anthropology, Caribbean studies, classical/ancient civilization, economics, geography, history, human development, interdisciplinary studies, Judaic studies, Latin American studies, medieval studies, philosophy, political science/government, psychobiology, psychology, and sociology). Accounting and anthropology are the strongest academically. Psychology, English, management, and biology are the largest.

Special: The university offers innovative study through the Innovational Projects Board, internships, study abroad in more than 100 countries, a Washington semester through American University, on- and off-campus work-study programs, and B.A.-B.S. degrees in 28 departments in arts and sciences and in the professional schools. There are also dual and interdisciplinary majors such as philosophy, politics, and law, student-designed majors, pass/fail options, and independent study. The 3-2 engineering degree is possible with SUNY at Buffalo, SUNY at Stony Brook, Columbia University, Rochester Institute of Technology, University of Rochester, Clarkson University and Binghamton University. Binghampton is also a member of the National Student Exchange and International Student Exchange. There are 20 national honor societies, including Phi Beta Kappa, a freshman honors program, and 32 departmental honors programs.

Admissions: 42% of the 1999-2000 applicants were accepted. The SAT I scores for the 1999-2000 freshman class were: Verbal--12% below 500, 41% between 500 and 599, 40% between 600 and 700, and 7% above 700; Math--5% below 500, 33% between 500 and 599, 48% between 600 and 700, and 14% above 700. 91% of the current freshmen were in the top fifth of their class; 99% were in the top two fifths. 18 freshmen graduated first in their class.

Requirements: The SAT I or ACT is required. Applicants must be graduates of an accredited secondary school, or have a GED certificate, and complete 16 academic credits. These include 4 units of English, 2.5 of math, 2 each of science and social studies, and 3 units of 1 foreign language or 2 units each of 2 foreign languages. Students may submit slides of artwork, request an audition for music, prepare a videotape for dance or theater, or share athletic achievements. An essay is required. The SUNY application is available through the home page at www. binghamton.edu. Applications are also accepted on computer disk. AP and CLEP credits are accepted. Important factors in the admissions decision are advanced placement or honor courses, extracurricular activities record, and evidence of special talent.

Procedure: Freshmen are admitted fall, spring, and summer. Entrance exams should be taken in the spring of the junior year or the fall of the senior year. There are early admissions and deferred admissions plans. Early action applications should be filed by November 1; regular applications, by February 15 for fall entry and November 15 for spring entry, along with a $30 fee. Notification of early action is sent December 20; regular decision, on a rolling basis after January 15. 180 early decision candidates were accepted for the 1999-2000 class. 3% of all applicants are on a waiting list.

Financial Aid: In 1999-2000, 83% of all freshmen and 68% of continuing students received some form of financial aid. 82% of freshmen and 66% of continuing students received need-based aid. The average freshman award was $10,127. Of that total, scholarships or need-based grants averaged $4175 ($16,845 maximum); loans averaged $5882 ($16,845 maximum); and work contracts averaged $1460 ($1500 maximum). 10% of undergraduates work part time. Average annual earnings from campus work are $1000. The average financial indebtedness of the 1999 graduate was $11,856. Binghamton University is a member of CSS. The FAFSA is required. The fall application deadline is March 1.

Computers: The mainframes comprise 2 IBM 9000 series and a cluster of 5 Sun servers. Each student is given a computer account. Terminals and PCs are available in libraries, some academic areas, and some residence halls. All residence hall rooms have Ethernet and Internet connections. All students may access the system 24 hours per day. There are no time limits and no fees.

STATE UNIVERSITY OF NEW YORK AT BUFFALO

Buffalo, NY 14260   (716) 645-6900; Fax: (716) 645-6498

Full-time: 7617 men, 6513 women	**Faculty:** 1017; I, av$
Part-time: 1024 men, 1105 women	**Ph.D.s:** 98%
Graduate: 4066 men, 3932 women	**Student/Faculty:** 14 to 1
Year: semesters, summer session	**Tuition:** $4655 ($9555)
Application Deadline: see profile	**Room & Board:** $5903
Freshman Class: 14,835 applied, 11,031 accepted, 3265 enrolled	
SAT I Verbal/Math: 557/580	**ACT:** 24 **VERY COMPETITIVE**

The State University of New York at Buffalo, established in 1846, is a public institution offering undergraduate degrees in liberal arts and sciences, architecture and planning, engineering, health-related professions, medicine, and management. There are 9 undergraduate and 14 graduate schools. In addition to regional accreditation, UB has baccalaureate program accreditation with AACSB, ABET, ACPE, ADA, APTA, ASLA, CAHEA, CSWE, NAAB, NASAD, NASM, and NLN. The 7 libraries contain 3,162,696 volumes, 5,230,416 microform items, and 258,787 audiovisual forms/CDs, and subscribe to 21,188 periodicals. Computerized library services include the card catalog, interlibrary loans, and database searching. Special learning facilities include a learning resource center, art gallery, radio station, anthropology research museum, observatory, concert hall, theater, nature preserve, and nuclear reactor. The 1350-acre campus is in a suburban area 3 miles north of Buffalo. Including residence halls, there are 120 buildings.

Programs of Study: UB confers B.A., B.S., B.F.A., B.P.S., B.S.Pharm., and Mus.B. degrees. Master's and doctoral degrees are also awarded. Bachelor's degrees are awarded in BIOLOGICAL SCIENCE (biochemistry, biology/biological science, and biophysics), BUSINESS (accounting and business administration and management), COMMUNICATIONS AND THE ARTS (art history and appreciation, communications, dramatic arts, English, fine arts, French, German, Italian, linguistics, media arts, music, music performance, Spanish, and studio art), COMPUTER AND PHYSICAL SCIENCE (chemistry, computer science, geology, mathematics, physics, and statistics), ENGINEERING AND ENVIRONMENTAL DESIGN (aeronautical engineering, chemical engineering, civil engineering, electrical/electronics engineering, engineering physics, environmental design, industrial engineering, and mechanical engineering), HEALTH PROFESSIONS (medical laboratory technology, nuclear medical technology, nursing, occupational therapy, pharmacy, physical therapy, and speech pathology/audiology), SOCIAL SCIENCE (African American studies, anthropology, economics, geography, history, philosophy, political science/government, psychology, social science, sociology, and women's studies). Business administration, psychology, and interdisciplinary social science are the largest.

Special: Students may cross-register with the Western New York Consortium. Internships are available, and students may study abroad in 24 countries. UB offers a Washington semester; B.A.-B.S. degrees; dual, student-designed, and interdisciplinary majors, including biochemical pharmacology and medicinal chemistry; nondegree study; and credit for military experience. A 3-2 engineering degree can be pursued. Students may choose a successful/unsuccessful (S/U) grading option for selected courses. There is an early assurance of admission program to medical school for students who have completed 3 semesters with a GPA of 3.5. There are 20 national honor societies, including Phi Beta Kappa, and a freshman honors program.

Admissions: 74% of the 1999-2000 applicants were accepted. The SAT I scores for the 1999-2000 freshman class were: Verbal--20% below 500, 49% between 500 and 599, 26% between 600 and 700, and 5% above 700; Math--13% below 500, 46% between 500 and 599, 34% between 600 and 700, and 7% above 700. 42% of the current freshmen were in the top fifth of their class; 80% were in the top two fifths.

Requirements: The SAT I or ACT is required. Applicants must be graduates of an accredited secondary school or have a GED. Art applicants must submit a portfolio; music applicants must audition. For on-line applications, consult the SUNY web site at http://infostu.suny.edu. AP and CLEP credits are accepted. Important factors in the admissions decision are advanced placement or honor courses, recommendations by school officials, and evidence of special talent.

Procedure: Freshmen are admitted fall and spring. Entrance exams should be taken during the spring of the junior year or the fall of the senior year. There are early decision and early admissions plans. Early decision applications should be filed by November 1; regular application, on a rolling basis with early November recommended; there is a $30 fee. Notification of early decision is sent December 20; regular decision, on a rolling basis.

Financial Aid: In a recent year, 63% of all freshmen and 50% of continuing students received some form of financial aid. 60% of freshmen and 46% of continuing students received need-based aid. The average freshman award was $4508. Of that total, scholarships or need-based grants averaged $2414 ($5785 maximum) and loans averaged $2625. Average annual earnings from campus work are $1100. The average financial indebtedness of the 1999 graduate was $12,000. The FAFSA is required. The fall application deadline is March 1.

Computers: The mainframes are an IBM 3090/300J, a DEC 7100, and a DEC 6520. Students have access through 1190 public terminals, PCs, and workstations. Dial-up access is also available. Individual libraries offer numerous CD-ROMs and student access to the Web. All students may access the system any time. There are no time limits. The fee is $300.

STATE UNIVERSITY OF NEW YORK AT STONY BROOK

Stony Brook, NY 11794   (516) 632-6868; Fax: (516) 632-9027

Full-time: 5742 men, 5676 women	**Faculty:** I, av$
Part-time: 556 men, 717 women	**Ph.D.s:** 95%
Graduate: 2725 men, 3709 women	**Student/Faculty:** 11 to 1
Year: semesters, summer session	**Tuition:** $4141 ($9041)
Application Deadline: July 10	**Room & Board:** $6222
Freshman Class: 14,892 applied, 8649 accepted, 2248 enrolled	
SAT I Verbal/Math: 530/560	**VERY COMPETITIVE**

The State University of New York at Stony Brook, founded in 1957, is a public institution offering degree programs in arts and sciences, engineering and applied sciences, nursing, health technology and management, and social welfare. There are 5 undergraduate and 8 graduate schools. In addition to regional accreditation, Stony Brook has baccalaureate program accreditation with ABET, APTA, CAHEA, CSWE, and NLN. The 7 libraries contain 1,891,079 volumes, 3,296, 892 microform items, and 29,846 audiovisual forms CDs, and subscribe to 14, 024 periodicals. Computerized library services include the card catalog, interlibrary loans, and database searching. Special learning facilities include a learning resource center, art gallery, radio station, the Museum of Long Island Natural Sciences, and the Fine Arts Center, which includes a 1100-seat main theater, a

400-seat recital hall, and 3 experimental theaters. The 1100-acre campus is in a suburban area on Long Island, 60 miles from New York City. Including residence halls, there are 113 buildings.

Programs of Study: Stony Brook confers B.A., B.S., and B.E. degrees. Master's and doctoral degrees are also awarded. Bachelor's degrees are awarded in BIOLOGICAL SCIENCE (biochemistry and biology/biological science), BUSINESS (business administration and management), COMMUNICATIONS AND THE ARTS (art history and appreciation, comparative literature, dramatic arts, English, film arts, French, German, Germanic languages and literature, linguistics, music, Russian languages and literature, Spanish, and studio art), COMPUTER AND PHYSICAL SCIENCE (applied mathematics, astronomy, atmospheric sciences and meteorology, chemistry, computer science, earth science, geology, information sciences and systems, mathematics, oceanography, physics, and planetary and space science), ENGINEERING AND ENVIRONMENTAL DESIGN (chemical engineering, computer engineering, electrical/electronics engineering, engineering and applied science, and mechanical engineering), HEALTH PROFESSIONS (clinical science, cytotechnology, medical laboratory science, nursing, occupational therapy, pharmacy, physician's assistant, and respiratory therapy), SOCIAL SCIENCE (African studies, anthropology, economics, ethnic studies, history, humanities, interdisciplinary studies, Italian studies, philosophy, political science/government, psychology, religion, social science, social work, sociology, and women's studies). Applied mathematics and statistics, biochemistry, and biology are the strongest academically. Psychology, biology, and business are the largest.

Special: Cross-registration may be arranged through the Long Island Regional Advisory Council for Higher Education. The college offers a Washington semester and internships with a variety of government, legal, and social agencies, with hospitals and clinics, and in business and industry. The Federated Learning Communities enable students to concentrate on a major issue each year, and the URECA Program allows undergraduates to work with faculty on research and creative projects. An accelerated degree program in nursing, dual majors, student-designed majors, a national student exchange program, study abroad in 7 countries, pass/fail options, and B.A.-B.S. degrees in chemistry, earth and space science, and psychology are available. There are 4 national honor societies, including Phi Beta Kappa, a freshman honors program, and 22 departmental honors programs.

Admissions: 58% of the 1999-2000 applicants were accepted. The SAT I scores for the 1999-2000 freshman class were: Verbal--35% below 500, 45% between 500 and 599, 17% between 600 and 700, and 4% above 700; Math--20% below 500, 42% between 500 and 599, 29% between 600 and 700, and 9% above 700. 53% of the current freshmen were in the top fifth of their class; 92% were in the top two fifths.

Requirements: The SAT I is required. Applicants must be graduates of an accredited secondary school or have a GED certificate. 16 or 17 academic credits are required, including 4 years each of English and social studies, 3 or 4 of math, 3 of science (4 for engineering majors), and 2 or 3 of a foreign language. 3 SAT II: Subject tests, an essay, and an interview are recommended. Stony Brook participates in the SUNY system common application form, available on diskette and through ExPAN. Applications are accepted on-line at the school's Web site and via Apply. AP and CLEP credits are accepted. Important factors in the admissions decision are advanced placement or honor courses, extracurricular activities record, and evidence of special talent.

Procedure: Freshmen are admitted to all sessions. Entrance exams should be taken during the junior year or in the fall of the senior year. There are early decision, early admissions, and deferred admissions plans. Early decision applications should be filed by November 1; regular applications, by July 10 for fall entry and December 20 for spring entry, along with a $30 fee. Notification of early decision is sent December 15; regular decision, on a rolling basis.

Financial Aid: In aa recent year, 81% of all freshmen and 70% of continuing students received some form of financial aid. 64% of freshmen received need-based aid. The average freshman award was $7345. Of that total, scholarships or need-based grants averaged $2000 ($3000 maximum); loans averaged $3000 ($4000 maximum); and work contracts averaged $1466. 10% of undergraduates work part time. Average annual earnings from campus work are $1466. The average financial indebtedness of a recent graduate was $13,834. Stony Brook is a member of CSS. The FAFSA and state aid form are required. The fall application deadline is March 1.

Computers: The mainframes are an IBM 3090/180E and a DEC ALPHA 2100/200. There are IBM PCs and Macs throughout the campus. There are also large HP UNIX and SUNSPARC workstation networks for student use. All students may access the system 24 hours a day. There are no time limits and no fees.

STATE UNIVERSITY OF NEW YORK/COLLEGE AT FREDONIA

Fredonia, NY 14063   (716) 673-3251
(800) 252-1212; Fax: (716) 673-3249

Full-time: 1830 men, 2628 women	**Faculty:** 239; IIA, av$
Part-time: 93 men, 176 women	**Ph.D.s:** 95%
Graduate: 60 men, 233 women	**Student/Faculty:** 19 to 1
Year: semesters, summer session	**Tuition:** $4125 ($9025)
Application Deadline: open	**Room & Board:** $5190
Freshman Class: 5148 applied, 3213 accepted, 1071 enrolled	
SAT I Verbal/Math: 553/551	**ACT:** 24 **VERY COMPETITIVE**

The State University of New York at Fredonia, established in 1826, is a public institution offering undergraduate programs in the arts and sciences, business and professional curricula, teacher preparation, and the fine and performing arts. There is 1 graduate school. In addition to regional accreditation, Fredonia has baccalaureate program accreditation with NASAD and NASM. The library contains 402,298 volumes, 1,043,006 microform items, and 26,249 audiovisual forms CDs, and subscribes to 1983 periodicals. Computerized library services include the card catalog, interlibrary loans, and database searching. Special learning facilities include a learning resource center, art gallery, radio station, TV station, a greenhouse, a day-care center, a speech clinic, and an arts center. The 266-acre campus is in a small town 50 miles south of Buffalo and 45 miles north of Erie, Pennsylvania. Including residence halls, there are 25 buildings.

Programs of Study: Fredonia confers B.A., B.S., B.F.A., B.S.Ed., and Mus.B. degrees. Master's degrees are also awarded. Bachelor's degrees are awarded in BIOLOGICAL SCIENCE (biochemistry and biology/biological science), BUSINESS (accounting, business administration and management, and business economics), COMMUNICATIONS AND THE ARTS (audio technology, communications, dramatic arts, English, fine arts, French, graphic design, media arts, music, and Spanish), COMPUTER AND PHYSICAL SCIENCE (chemistry, computer science, earth science, geology, mathematics, and physics), EDUCATION (early childhood, elementary, foreign languages, middle school, music, science, and secondary), HEALTH PROFESSIONS (health care administration, medical laboratory technology, predentistry, premedicine, and speech pathology/

audiology), SOCIAL SCIENCE (history, interdisciplinary studies, philosophy, political science/government, psychology, social work, and sociology). Business, education, and music are the largest.

Special: Cooperative programs are available with many other institutions. Students may cross-register with colleges in the Western New York Consortium. Fredonia offers a variety of internships, study-abroad programs in more than 90 countries, and a Washington semester. Accelerated degrees, a general studies degree, dual and student-designed majors, a 3-2 engineering degree program, non-degree study, and pass/fail grading options are available. There are 19 national honor societies, a freshman honors program, and 19 departmental honors programs.

Admissions: 62% of the 1999-2000 applicants were accepted. The SAT I scores for the 1999-2000 freshman class were: Verbal--18% below 500, 58% between 500 and 599, 20% between 600 and 700, and 4% above 700; Math--18% below 500, 60% between 500 and 599, 20% between 600 and 700, and 2% above 700. The ACT scores were 16% below 21, 40% between 21 and 23, 28% between 24 and 26, 8% between 27 and 28, and 8% above 28. 31% of the current freshmen were in the top fifth of their class; 76% were in the top two fifths. 10 freshmen graduated first in their class.

Requirements: The SAT I or ACT is required with a minimum composite score of 950 on the SAT I or 198 on the ACT. Fredonia requires applicants to be in the upper 50% of their class. A GPA of 2.7 is required. Applicants must possess a high school diploma or have a GED. 16 academic credits are recommended, including 4 credits each in English and social studies and 3 each in math, science, and a foreign language. 4 years of math and science are encouraged. Essays and interviews are recommended, and, where applicable, an audition or portfolio is required. Applications are accepted on-line at http://www.fredonia.edu/admissions/applying.html. AP and CLEP credits are accepted. Important factors in the admissions decision are advanced placement or honor courses, evidence of special talent, and recommendations by school officials.

Procedure: Freshmen are admitted fall and spring. Entrance exams should be taken during the spring of the junior year or fall of the senior year. There are early decision, early admissions, and deferred admissions plans. Early decision applications should be filed by November 1; regular application deadlines are open for fall entry. There is a $30 fee. Notification of early decision is sent December 15; regular decision, January 2. 56 early decision candidates were accepted for the 1999-2000 class.

Financial Aid: In 1999-2000, 81% of all freshmen and 70% of continuing students received some form of financial aid. 60% of freshmen and 63% of continuing students received need-based aid. The average freshman award was $5299. Of that total, scholarships or need-based grants averaged $2559 ($10,000 maximum); loans averaged $4232 ($11,500 maximum); and work contracts averaged $1240. 20% of undergraduates work part time. Average annual earnings from campus work are $1100. The average financial indebtedness of the 1999 graduate was $12,691. Fredonia is a member of CSS. The FAFSA and TAP are required.

Computers: The mainframe is a Unisys A18 Enterprise Server. PCs for student use are located in the computer center, all academic buildings, and various residence halls. There is Ethernet access in all student residence hall rooms. All students may access the system. There are no time limits and no fees.

STATE UNIVERSITY OF NEW YORK/COLLEGE AT GENESEO

Geneseo, NY 14454 (716) 245-5571; Fax: (716) 245-5005

Full-time: 1768 men, 3445 women	**Faculty:** 249; IIA, -$
Part-time: 44 men, 65 women	**Ph.D.s:** 89%
Graduate: 44 men, 238 women	**Student/Faculty:** 21 to 1
Year: semesters, summer session	**Tuition:** $4221 ($9121)
Application Deadline: January 15	**Room & Board:** $4940
Freshman Class: 7974 applied, 4148 accepted, 1140 enrolled	
SAT I Verbal/Math: 597/602	**ACT:** 26 **HIGHLY COMPETITIVE**

The State University of New York/College at Geneseo, founded in 1871, is a public institution offering liberal arts, business, and accounting programs, teaching certification, and training in communicative disorders and sciences. There is 1 graduate school. In addition to regional accreditation, Geneseo has baccalaureate program accreditation with ASLA. The library contains 492,236 volumes, 809,888 microform items, and 4266 audiovisual forms CDs, and subscribes to 2618 periodicals. Computerized library services include the card catalog, interlibrary loans, and database searching. Special learning facilities include a learning resource center, art gallery, planetarium, radio station, TV station, and 3 theaters. The 220-acre campus is in a small town 30 miles south of Rochester. Including residence halls, there are 38 buildings.

Programs of Study: Geneseo confers B.A., B.S., and B.S.Ed. degrees. Master's degrees are also awarded. Bachelor's degrees are awarded in BIOLOGICAL SCIENCE (biochemistry, biology/biological science, and biophysics), BUSINESS (accounting, business administration and management, and management science), COMMUNICATIONS AND THE ARTS (art history and appreciation, communications, comparative literature, dramatic arts, English, French, music, Spanish, and studio art), COMPUTER AND PHYSICAL SCIENCE (applied physics, chemistry, computer science, geochemistry, geology, geophysics and seismology, mathematics, natural sciences, and physics), EDUCATION (elementary and special), HEALTH PROFESSIONS (speech pathology/audiology), SOCIAL SCIENCE (African American studies, American studies, anthropology, economics, geography, history, international relations, philosophy, political science/government, psychology, and sociology). Biology, special education, and psychology are the largest.

Special: The college offers a cooperative 3-2 engineering degree with Alfred, Case Western Reserve, Clarkson, Columbia, Penn State, and Syracuse Universities, SUNY at Binghamton and Buffalo, and the University of Rochester, as well as a 3-3 degree with Rochester Institute of Technology. Cross-registration is available with the Rochester Area Colleges Consortium. Geneseo offers internships in all majors, study abroad through more than 95 programs, a Washington semester, dual majors, including theater/English, credit for military experience, and pass/fail options. There are 14 national honor societies, a freshman honors program, and 5 departmental honors programs.

Admissions: 52% of the 1999-2000 applicants were accepted. The SAT I scores for the 1999-2000 freshman class were: Verbal--4% below 500, 45% between 500 and 599, 43% between 600 and 700, and 7% above 700; Math--3% below 500, 43% between 500 and 599, 49% between 600 and 700, and 5% above 700. The ACT scores were 2% below 21, 20% between 21 and 23, 31% between 24 and 26, 22% between 27 and 28, and 25% above 28. 85% of the current freshmen were in the top fifth of their class; all were in the top two fifths. 35 freshmen graduated first in their class.

Requirements: The SAT I or ACT is required. Geneseo requires applicants to be in the upper 50% of their class. A minimum B+ grade average is required. Applicants must be graduates of an accredited secondary school or have a GED certificate. The academic program must have included 4 years each of English, math, science, and social studies and 3 years of a foreign language. An essay is required. A portfolio or audition for certain programs and an interview are recommended. Applications are available on-line. AP and CLEP credits are accepted. Important factors in the admissions decision are advanced placement or honor courses, recommendations by school officials, and evidence of special talent.

Procedure: Freshmen are admitted fall and spring. Entrance exams should be taken during the spring of the junior year. There are early decision, early admissions, and deferred admissions plans. Early decision applications should be filed by November 15; regular applications, by January 15 for fall entry and September 15 for spring entry, along with a $30 fee. Notification of early decision is sent December 15; regular decision, on a rolling basis. 151 early decision candidates were accepted for the 1999-2000 class. 12% of all applicants are on a waiting list.

Financial Aid: In a recent year, 68% of all freshmen and 70% of continuing students received some form of financial aid. 65% of freshmen and 70% of continuing students received need-based aid. The average freshman award was $2830. Of that total, scholarships or need-based grants averaged $2000 ($6900 maximum); loans averaged $2135 ($4000 maximum); and work contracts averaged $1005 ($3500 maximum). 68% of undergraduates work part time. The average financial indebtedness of the 1999 graduate was $14,500. Geneseo is a member of CSS. The FAFSA is required. The fall application deadline is February 15.

Computers: The mainframe is a DEC ALPHA 2100. Mac, DOS/Windows, and Sun workstations are located in more than 30 computer labs, supported by fiber-optic network connectivity and full Internet access. All students may access the system 24 hours a day. There are no time limits. The fee is $100. It is strongly recommended that all students have personal computers.

STATE UNIVERSITY OF NEW YORK/COLLEGE AT NEW PALTZ
New Paltz, NY 12561-2443 (914) 257-3200
(800) (888) 639-7589; Fax: (914) 257-3209

Full-time: 1896 men, 3169 women	**Faculty:** 275; IIA, av$
Part-time: 329 men, 688 women	**Ph.D.s:** 82%
Graduate: 469 men, 1194 women	**Student/Faculty:** 18 to 1
Year: semesters, summer session	**Tuition:** $3915 ($8815)
Application Deadline: May 1	**Room & Board:** $5246
Freshman Class: 9116 applied, 4112 accepted, 984 enrolled	
SAT I Verbal/Math: 564/566	**VERY COMPETITIVE**

State University of New York at New Paltz, founded in 1828, is a public institution offering undergraduate and graduate programs in the liberal arts and sciences, business, education, engineering, fine and performing arts, and the health professions. There are 4 undergraduate schools and 1 graduate school. In addition to regional accreditation, SUNY New Paltz has baccalaureate program accreditation with ABET, ASLA, CSAB, NASAD, NASM, and NLN. The library contains 510,000 volumes, 1 million microform items, and 15,000 audiovisual forms/CDs, and subscribes to 1200 periodicals. Computerized library services include the card catalog, interlibrary loans, and database searching. Special learning facilities include a learning resource center, art gallery, planetarium, radio station, TV station, and greenhouse, robotics lab, electron microscope facility, speech and hearing clinic, music therapy training facility, observatory, Fournier transform mass spectrometer, honors center, and electronic media center. The 216-acre campus is in a small town 100 miles north of New York City and 65 miles south of Albany. Including residence halls, there are 55 buildings.

Programs of Study: SUNY New Paltz confers B.A., B.S., B.F.A., B.S.E.E., and B.S.N. degrees. Master's and doctoral degrees are also awarded. Bachelor's degrees are awarded in BIOLOGICAL SCIENCE (biology/biological science), BUSINESS (accounting, banking and finance, business administration and management, and marketing/retailing/merchandising), COMMUNICATIONS AND THE ARTS (art history and appreciation, broadcasting, communications, design, dramatic arts, English, fine arts, French, German, journalism, music, photography, Spanish, and speech/debate/rhetoric), COMPUTER AND PHYSICAL SCIENCE (chemistry, computer science, geology, mathematics, and physics), EDUCATION (art, early childhood, elementary, foreign languages, middle school, science, and secondary), ENGINEERING AND ENVIRONMENTAL DESIGN (computer engineering and electrical/electronics engineering), HEALTH PROFESSIONS (premedicine and speech pathology/audiology), SOCIAL SCIENCE (anthropology, economics, geography, history, international relations, Latin American studies, philosophy, political science/government, psychology, social science, and sociology). Math, geography, and business are the strongest academically. Business administration, communications, and education are the largest.

Special: There is cross-registration with the Mid-Hudson Consortium of Colleges. The university offers co-op programs and internships in most majors, work-study programs on campus and at the Children's Center of New Paltz, and opportunities for student-designed or dual majors. Students may study abroad in 18 countries. A 3-2 advanced degree in environmental biology is offered with SUNY Environmental Science and Forestry. There are 7-year medical and optometry accelerated degree programs. There are 4 national honor societies, a freshman honors program, and 6 departmental honors programs.

Admissions: 45% of the 1999-2000 applicants were accepted. The SAT I scores for the 1999-2000 freshman class were: Verbal--16% below 500, 57% between 500 and 599, 24% between 600 and 700, and 3% above 700; Math--18% below 500, 60% between 500 and 599, 21% between 600 and 700, and 2% above 700. 34% of the current freshmen were in the top fifth of their class; 76% were in the top two fifths. There were 5 National Merit semifinalists. 3 freshmen graduated first in their class.

Requirements: The SAT I is required and the ACT is recommended. SUNY New Paltz requires applicants to be in the upper 50% of their class. A GPA of 3.0 is required, with a recommended minimum composite score of 1000. Graduation from an accredited secondary school is required; a GED will be accepted. The applicant's academic record must include a college preparatory program of 4 years of English and 3 to 4 years each of social studies, a foreign language, math, and lab science. Where required, a portfolio and an audition are used for placement purposes only. AP and CLEP credits are accepted. Important factors in the admissions decision are advanced placement or honor courses, extracurricular activities record, and evidence of special talent.

Procedure: Freshmen are admitted fall and spring. Entrance exams should be taken on or before November 15. There are early decision, early admissions, and deferred admissions plans. Early decision applications should be filed by November 15; regular applications, by May 1 for fall entry and December 1 for spring entry, along with a $30 fee. Notification of early decision is sent December 15; regular decision, January 15. 16 early decision candidates were accepted for the 1999-2000 class. A waiting list is an active part of the admissions procedure.

Financial Aid: In a recent year, 70% of all freshmen and 75% of continuing students received some form of financial aid. 68% of freshmen and 75% of continuing students received need-based aid. The average freshman award was $5000. Of that total, scholarships or need-based grants averaged $1000 ($5900 maximum); loans averaged $2500 ($3300 maximum); and work contracts averaged $800 ($1200 maximum). 35% of undergraduates work part time. Average annual earnings from campus work are $800. The average financial indebtedness of the 1999 graduate was $10,000. The FAFSA is required. The fall application deadline is March 15.

Computers: The mainframe is an IBM ES/9000 9121-210. Computer facilities include 6 large public PC labs, PC classrooms, department-based PC labs and clusters, and PC labs in residence halls. Access is provided in all residence hall rooms to local UNIX and mainframe hosts as well as the Internet. All students may access the system during those hours that the buildings are open; residence hall terminals and personal PCs, 24 hours. There are no time limits and no fees. It is recommended that students have personal computers.

STATE UNIVERSITY OF NEW YORK/COLLEGE AT PURCHASE

Purchase, NY 10577-1400 (914) 251-6300; Fax: (914) 251-6314

Full-time: 1310 men, 1581 women	**Faculty:** 115; IIB, av$
Part-time: 374 men, 582 women	**Ph.D.s:** 100%
Graduate: 44 men, 73 women	**Student/Faculty:** 25 to 1
Year: semesters, summer session	**Tuition:** $3949 ($8849)
Application Deadline: August 15	**Room & Board:** $5842
Freshman Class: 4773 applied, 1892 accepted, 647 enrolled	
SAT I Verbal/Math: 510/515	**VERY COMPETITIVE**

State University of New York/College at Purchase, founded in 1967, is a public institution that offers programs in visual arts, music, acting, dance, film, theater/stage design technology, natural science, social science, and humanities. The library contains 261,598 volumes, 237,277 microform items, and 14,375 audiovisual forms/CDs, and subscribes to 1141 periodicals. Computerized library services include the card catalog and interlibrary loans. Special learning facilities include a learning resource center, art gallery, radio station, listening and viewing center, science and photography labs, music practice rooms and instruments, multitrack synthesizers, experimental stage, typesetting and computer graphics labs, a performing arts complex, an electron microscope, and the Children's Center at Purchase College. The 500-acre campus is in a suburban area 35 miles north of midtown Manhattan. Including residence halls, there are 40 buildings.

Programs of Study: Purchase College SUNY confers B.A., B.S., B.A.L.A., and B.F.A. degrees. Master's degrees are also awarded. Bachelor's degrees are awarded in BIOLOGICAL SCIENCE (biology/biological science), COMMUNICATIONS AND THE ARTS (art history and appreciation, creative writing, dance, dramatic arts, film arts, literature, music, theater design, and visual and performing arts), COMPUTER AND PHYSICAL SCIENCE (chemistry and mathematics), ENGINEERING AND ENVIRONMENTAL DESIGN (environmental science), SOCIAL SCIENCE (anthropology, economics, ethnic studies, history, liberal arts/general studies, philosophy, political science/government, psychology, sociology, and women's studies). Dance, drama, and film are the strongest academically. Visual arts, literature, and psychology are the largest.

Special: Purchase College offers cross-registration with Empire State colleges, internships with corporations, newspapers, and local agencies, and student-designed majors, dual majors, study abroad, work-study, nondegree study, and pass/fail options. There is also an arts conservatory program.

Admissions: 40% of the 1999-2000 applicants were accepted. The SAT I scores for the 1999-2000 freshman class were: Verbal--29% below 500, 43% between 500 and 599, 24% between 600 and 700, and 4% above 700; Math--43% below 500, 41% between 500 and 599, 14% between 600 and 700, and 2% above 700.

Requirements: The SAT I or ACT is required. Minimum composite scores are 1100 on the SAT I or 23 on the ACT. Applicants must be graduates of an accredited secondary school and have completed 16 academic credits and 16 Carnegie units. The GED is accepted. Visual arts students must submit an essay and portfolio and have an interview. Film students need an essay and an interview. Design technology students need a portfolio and an interview. Performing arts students must audition. Applications are accepted on-line at www.infostu.suny.edu/apply.html. AP and CLEP credits are accepted. Important factors in the admissions decision are evidence of special talent, recommendations by school officials, and personality/intangible qualities.

Procedure: Freshmen are admitted fall and spring. Entrance exams should be taken by the fall of the senior year. There is a deferred admissions plan. Applications should be filed by August 15 for fall entry and December 1 for spring entry, along with a $30 fee. Notification is sent on a rolling basis. 5% of all applicants are on a waiting list.

Financial Aid: In 1999-2000, 89% of all freshmen and 78% of continuing students received some form of financial aid. 72% of freshmen and 65% of continuing students received need-based aid. The average freshman award was $7244. Of that total, scholarships or need-based grants averaged $1500 ($8000 maximum); loans averaged $4504 ($7625 maximum); and work contracts averaged $1150 ($1400 maximum). 18% of undergraduates work part time. Average annual earnings from campus work are $1200. The average financial indebtedness of the 1999 graduate was $12,460. The FAFSA is required. The fall application deadline is February 15.

Computers: The mainframes are PCs and servers. PCs are available in the computer center in the social sciences building. The humanities building, music building, art and design building, art and design building, dance hall, natural sciences building, the library, and dormitories house PCs as well. There are approximately 350 PCs in total. All students may access the system when the computer center is open. There are no time limits. The fee is $85 per semester. It is recommended that all students have personal computers.

STATE UNIVERSITY OF NEW YORK/COLLEGE OF ENVIRONMENTAL SCIENCE AND FORESTRY

Syracuse, NY 13210-2779

(315) 470-6600
(800) 7777-ESF; Fax: (315) 470-6933

Full-time: 660 men, 400 women	**Faculty:** 120; IIA, +$
Part-time: 40 men, 40 women	**Ph.D.s:** 91%
Graduate: 340 men, 230 women	**Student/Faculty:** 9 to 1
Year: semesters	**Tuition:** $3800 ($8700)
Application Deadline: see profile	**Room & Board:** $6800
Freshman Class: n/av	
SAT I or ACT: required	**VERY COMPETITIVE**

The College of Environmental Science and Forestry, founded in 1911 and located adjacent to the campus of Syracuse University, is one of the colleges of the State

University of New York. The public institution specializes in undergraduate and graduate degrees in agricultural, biological, environmental, health, and physical sciences, landscape architecture, and engineering. Students have access to the academic, cultural, and social life at Syracuse University. Figures given in the above capsule are approximate. There is 1 graduate school. In addition to regional accreditation, ESF has baccalaureate program accreditation with ABET, ASLA, and SAF. The library contains 120,000 volumes, and subscribes to 950 periodicals. Computerized library services include the card catalog, interlibrary loans, and database searching. Special learning facilities include a learning resource center, art gallery, radio station, and TV station. The 12-acre campus is in an urban area in Syracuse. Including residence halls, there are 7 buildings.

Programs of Study: ESF confers B.S. and B.L.A. degrees. Associate, master's, and doctoral degrees are also awarded. Bachelor's degrees are awarded in AGRICULTURE (animal science, forest engineering, forestry and related sciences, natural resource management, plant science, and soil science), BIOLOGICAL SCIENCE (biology/biological science, botany, ecology, entomology, environmental biology, microbiology, molecular biology, plant genetics, and plant physiology), COMPUTER AND PHYSICAL SCIENCE (chemistry and polymer science), EDUCATION (environmental and science), ENGINEERING AND ENVIRONMENTAL DESIGN (chemical engineering, construction management, environmental design, environmental engineering, environmental science, landscape architecture/design, paper and pulp science, paper engineering, and survey and mapping technology), HEALTH PROFESSIONS (predentistry, premedicine, and prepharmacy), SOCIAL SCIENCE (prelaw). Engineering, chemistry, and biology are the strongest academically. Environmental and forest biology and environmental studies are the largest.

Special: Cross-registration is offered with Syracuse University. Co-op programs, accelerated degrees in biology and landscape architecture, and dual options in biology and forestry are available. There is 1 national honor society.

Admissions: In a recent year, there was 1 National Merit finalist and 3 semifinalists. 9 freshmen graduated first in their class.

Requirements: The SAT I or ACT is required. A high school average of 86. is required. Applicants are required to have a minimum of 4 years of math and science, including chemistry, in a college preparatory curriculum. An essay is required and an interview, letters of recommendation, and a personal portfolio or resume are recommended. Applications are accepted on-line via ESF's web site and on computer disk using Apply, CollegeNET, CollegeLink, CollegeView, and ExPAN. AP and CLEP credits are accepted. Important factors in the admissions decision are advanced placement or honor courses, leadership record, and extracurricular activities record.

Procedure: Freshmen are admitted fall and spring. Entrance exams should be taken by October of the senior year. There are early decision, early admissions, and deferred admissions plans. Check with the school for current applicaiton deadlines and fee. Notification is sent on a rolling basis. A waiting list is an active part of the admissions procedure.

Financial Aid: In a recent year, 80% of all students received some form of financial aid. 80% of freshmen and 80% of continuing students received need-based aid. The average freshman award was $6425. Of that total, scholarships or need-based grants averaged $600; loans averaged $2600 ($4625 maximum); and work contracts averaged $800 ($1200 maximum). 45% of undergraduates work part time. Average annual earnings from campus work are $1200. The average financial indebtedness of the recent graduate was $12,000. ESF is a member of CSS. The FAFSA and the college's own financial statement are required. Check with the school for current deadlines.

Computers: Macs and IBM PCs are available. There are several computer labs at ESF and Syracuse University. All students may access the system. There are no time limits and no fees.

STEPHENS COLLEGE
Columbia, MO 65215

(573) 876-7207
(800) 876-7207; Fax: (573) 876-7237

Full-time: 16 men, 439 women	**Faculty:** 52
Part-time: 35 men, 244 women	**Ph.D.s:** 85%
Graduate: 7 men, 47 women	**Student/Faculty:** 9 to 1
Year: semesters	**Tuition:** $15,160 ($15,160)
Application Deadline: open	**Room & Board:** $5790
Freshman Class: 2369 applied, 1415 accepted, 587 enrolled	
SAT I Verbal/Math: 500/570-520	**VERY COMPETITIVE**

Stephens College, founded in 1833, is a private college, primarily for women, offering undergraduate programs in the arts and sciences, business, education, and fine arts. Some of the information in this profile is approximate. The library contains 130,000 volumes, 10,938 microform items, and 5000 audiovisual forms/CDs, and subscribes to 375 periodicals. Computerized library services include interlibrary loans and database searching. Special learning facilities include a learning resource center, art gallery, radio station, and TV station. The 202-acre campus is in an urban area 126 miles west of St. Louis. Including residence halls, there are 50 buildings.

Programs of Study: Stephens confers B.A., B.S., and B.F.A. degrees. Associate and master's degrees are also awarded. Bachelor's degrees are awarded in AGRICULTURE (equine science), BIOLOGICAL SCIENCE (biology/biological science), BUSINESS (accounting, business administration and management, and fashion merchandising), COMMUNICATIONS AND THE ARTS (creative writing, dance, dramatic arts, English, and public relations), COMPUTER AND PHYSICAL SCIENCE (mathematics), EDUCATION (early childhood and elementary), ENGINEERING AND ENVIRONMENTAL DESIGN (environmental science), SOCIAL SCIENCE (fashion design and technology, international studies, liberal arts/general studies, philosophy, prelaw, and social science). Business, theater arts, communications, and fashion are the largest.

Special: Students may study abroad in England, Canada, Mexico, and Spain. Stephens also offers cross-registration with the Mid-Missouri Associated Colleges and Universities, a Washington semester, dual and student-designed majors, a 3-2 occupational therapy degree program, and pass/fail options for electives. There are 8 national honor societies, and a freshman honors program.

Admissions: 60% of the 1999-2000 applicants were accepted. The SAT I scores for the 1999-2000 freshman class were: Verbal--32% below 500, 47% between 500 and 599, 18% between 600 and 700, and 33% above 700; Math--6% below 500, 44% between 500 and 599, 41% between 600 and 700, and 9% above 700. 38% of the current freshmen were in the top fifth of their class; 75% were in the top two fifths.

Requirements: The SAT I is required. A GPA of 2.8 is required. Applicants must be graduates of accredited secondary schools or have earned a GED. An essay is also required, and an interview is recommended. Applications are accepted on computer disk and on-line. AP and CLEP credits are accepted. Important factors in the admissions decision are advanced placement or honor courses, leadership record, and recommendations by school officials.

Procedure: Freshmen are admitted fall and spring. There are early decision, early admissions, and deferred admissions plans. Application deadlines are open. There is a $35 fee. Notification of early decision is sent December 20; regular decision, on a rolling basis.

Financial Aid: In 1999-2000, 85% of all freshmen received some form of financial aid. The average freshman award was $8500. Of that total, scholarships or need-based grants averaged $8600 ($14,500 maximum); loans averaged $2015 ($4125 maximum); and work contracts averaged $1235 ($1500 maximum). 35% of undergraduates work part time. Average annual earnings from campus work are $1000. The average financial indebtedness of the 1999 graduate was $17,125. Stephens is a member of CSS. The FAFSA is required.

Computers: The mainframe is a DEC ALPHA 4100. There are also 36 PCs available for student use in the computer lab. All students may access the system. There are no time limits and no fees.

STERLING COLLEGE
Sterling, KS 67579

(316) 278-4275
(800) 346-1017; Fax: (316) 278-3690

Full-time: 185 men, 215 women	**Faculty:** 32; IIB, --$
Part-time: 11 men, 13 women	**Ph.D.s:** 44%
Graduate: none	**Student/Faculty:** 13 to 1
Year: 4-1-4	**Tuition:** $11,030
Application Deadline: open	**Room & Board:** $4586
Freshman Class: 434 applied, 315 accepted, 111 enrolled	
SAT I Verbal/Math: 560/530	**ACT:** 23 **VERY COMPETITIVE**

Sterling College, established in 1887, is a private liberal arts institution affiliated with the Presbyterian Church, U.S.A., offering undergraduate curricula in 17 majors plus teacher preparation. The library contains 80,000 volumes, 50 microform items, and 3631 audiovisual forms/ CDs, and subscribes to 371 periodicals. Computerized library services include the card catalog and database searching. Special learning facilities include a learning resource center, a museum, and a theater. The 43-acre campus is in a small town 70 miles northwest of Wichita. Including residence halls, there are 19 buildings.

Programs of Study: Sterling confers B.A. and B.S. degrees. Bachelor's degrees are awarded in BIOLOGICAL SCIENCE (biology/biological science), BUSINESS (accounting and business administration and management), COMMUNICATIONS AND THE ARTS (art, dramatic arts, English, fine arts, music, and speech/debate/rhetoric), COMPUTER AND PHYSICAL SCIENCE (computer science and mathematics), EDUCATION (elementary, music, and physical), SOCIAL SCIENCE (behavioral science, history, religious education, and theological studies).

Special: Sterling offers internships, co-op programs, and work-study programs. Students may study abroad, and may register for junior-year programs through other colleges. A Washington semester is also available. The college offers a B. A.-B.S. degree in conjunction with Kansas State University. Dual and student-designed majors may also be pursued. Nondegree study and a pass/fail grading option are available.

Admissions: 73% of the 1999-2000 applicants were accepted. The SAT I scores for the 1999-2000 freshman class were: Verbal--22% below 500, 44% between 500 and 599, and 33% between 600 and 700; Math--22% below 500, 44% between 500 and 599, and 33% between 600 and 700. The ACT scores were 33% below 21, 25% between 21 and 23, 18% between 24 and 26, 9% between 27 and 28, and 15% above 28. 9 freshmen graduated first in their class.

Requirements: The SAT I or ACT is required. A GPA of 2.2 is required. Applicants must graduate from an accredited secondary school or have a GED. An interview is recommended. An application is available at the college Web site. AP and CLEP credits are accepted.

Procedure: Entrance exams should be taken in the fall of senior year. There is an early admissions plan. Application deadlines are open. The application fee is $10. Notification is sent on a rolling basis.

Financial Aid: In 1999-2000, 98% of all freshmen and 90% of continuing students received some form of financial aid. 51% of freshmen and 47% of continuing students received need-based aid. The average freshman award was $9500. Of that total, scholarships or need-based grants averaged $3465 ($11,030 maximum); loans averaged $3500 ($7875 maximum); work contracts averaged $1100 ($1600 maximum); and other assistance, including scholarships, grants, loans, awards, and employment, averaged $950 ($7700 maximum). State, SEOG, and other college grants are available. 60% of undergraduates work part time. Average annual earnings from campus work are $756. The average financial indebtedness of the 1999 graduate was $17,500. The FAFSA is required. The fall application deadline is March 15.

Computers: The mainframe is a Novell Network. There are Internet-connected computer labs in the library, in an academic building, and in 2 of the 4 residence halls. All students may access the system 16 hours per day. There are no time limits and no fees.

STEVENS INSTITUTE OF TECHNOLOGY
Hoboken, NJ 07030

(201) 216-5194
(800) 458-5323; Fax: (201) 216-8348

Full-time: 1190 men, 351 women	**Faculty:** 110
Part-time: 19 men, 4 women	**Ph.D.s:** 84%
Graduate: 1553 men, 597 women	**Student/Faculty:** 14 to 1
Year: semesters, summer session	**Tuition:** $21,415
Application Deadline: February 15	**Room & Board:** $7264
Freshman Class: 2304 applied, 1354 accepted, 437 enrolled	
SAT I Verbal/Math: 620/680	**HIGHLY COMPETITIVE+**

Stevens Institute of Technology, founded in 1870, is a private institution offering programs of study in science, computer science, engineering, and humanities. There are 3 undergraduate schools and 1 graduate school. In addition to regional accreditation, Stevens has baccalaureate program accreditation with ABET, ACS, and CSAB. The library contains 110,575 volumes, 2141 microform items, and 1754 audiovisual forms/CDs, and subscribes to 137 periodicals. Computerized library services include the card catalog, interlibrary loans, and database searching. Special learning facilities include an art gallery, radio station, TV station, lab for ocean and coastal engineering, environmental lab, design and manufacturing institute, technology center, and telecommunications institute. The 55-acre campus is in an urban area 1 mile west of New York City. Including residence halls, there are 50 buildings.

Programs of Study: Stevens confers B.A., B.S., and B.E. degrees. Master's and doctoral degrees are also awarded. Bachelor's degrees are awarded in BIOLOGICAL SCIENCE (biochemistry), COMMUNICATIONS AND THE ARTS (literature), COMPUTER AND PHYSICAL SCIENCE (applied mathematics, applied physics, chemistry, computer science, mathematics, physics, and polymer science), ENGINEERING AND ENVIRONMENTAL DESIGN (chemical engineering, civil engineering, computer engineering, electrical/electronics engineering, engineering management, engineering physics, environmental engineering, materials engineering, and mechanical engineering), HEALTH PROFESSIONS (predentistry and premedicine), SOCIAL SCIENCE (history, philosophy, and prelaw). Engineering is the strongest academically and the largest.

Special: Stevens offers a 3-2 engineering degree with New York University, a work-study program within the school, co-op programs, corporate and research internships through the Undergraduate Projects in Technology and Medicine, study abroad in Scotland, Australia, and Lebanon, and pass/fail options for extra courses. Students may undertake dual majors as well as accelerated degree programs in medicine, dentistry, and law, and can receive a B.A.-B.E. degree or a B.A.-B.S. degree in all majors. Undergraduates may take graduate courses. There are 3 national honor societies and a freshman honors program.

Admissions: 59% of the 1999-2000 applicants were accepted. The SAT I scores for the 1999-2000 freshman class were: Verbal--12% below 500, 38% between 500 and 599, 38% between 600 and 700, and 11% above 700; Math--2% below 500, 16% between 500 and 599, 53% between 600 and 700, and 29% above 700. 84% of the current freshmen were in the top fifth of their class; 95% were in the top two fifths. 11 freshmen graduated first in their class.

Requirements: The SAT I or ACT is required; the SAT I is preferred. Stevens recommends a minimum of 2 SAT II: Subject tests, depending on the intended major. A GPA of 3.0 is required. In addition, applicants must provide official high school transcripts. Students should have taken 4 years of English, math, and science. An interview is required. Applications are accepted on computer disk and on-line via the school's web site. AP credits are accepted. Important factors in the admissions decision are advanced placement or honor courses and extra-curricular activities record.

Procedure: Freshmen are admitted in the fall. Entrance exams should be taken by February of the senior year. There are early decision, early admissions, and deferred admissions plans. Early decision applications should be filed by November 15; regular applications, by February 15 for fall entry and December 1 for spring entry, along with a $45 fee. The application fee is waaived for on-line submissions. Notification of early decision is sent December 15; regular decision, March 15. 36 early decision candidates were accepted for the 1999-2000 class. 3% of all applicants are on a waiting list.

Financial Aid: In 1999-2000, 91% of all freshmen and 85% of continuing students received some form of financial aid. 82% of freshmen and 81% of continuing students received need-based aid. The average freshman award was $17,010. Of that total, scholarships or need-based grants averaged $11,810 ($30,024 maximum); loans averaged $4000 ($8100 maximum); and work contracts averaged $1200 ($1400 maximum). 55% of undergraduates work part time. Average annual earnings from campus work are $1000. The average financial indebtedness of the 1999 graduate was $12,400. Stevens is a member of CSS. The FAFSA is required.

Computers: The mainframes include SGI Challenge and Challenge L servers, Sun SPARC servers, and Intel-based servers. All students may access campus servers, the Internet, the Web, and specialized facilities via the campuswide network that connects every academic, administrative, and residential building. Labs of systems and connections for notebooks are available throughout the campus, including all residence hall rooms, 1 per person. All students may access the system. There are no time limits and no fees. It is recommended that all students have Pentium III 500 Notebooks, 64 MB, 5 GB, with a 10/100 network card.

STONEHILL COLLEGE
Easton, MA 02357
(508) 565-1373; Fax: (508) 565-1545

Full-time: 887 men, 1180 women	**Faculty:** 123; IIB, +$
Part-time: 8 men, 9 women	**Ph.D.s:** 81%
Graduate: 7 men, 9 women	**Student/Faculty:** 17 to 1
Year: semesters, summer session	**Tuition:** $16,336
Application Deadline: February 1	**Room & Board:** $7852
Freshman Class: 4432 applied, 2366 accepted, 572 enrolled	
SAT I Verbal/Math: 570/570	**ACT:** 23 **VERY COMPETITIVE**

Stonehill College, founded in 1948 by the Holy Cross Fathers, is a private Roman Catholic college offering undergraduate degrees in business administration, liberal arts, and the sciences. The 2 libraries contain 185,000 volumes, 72,000 microform items, and 3461 audiovisual forms/CDs, and subscribe to 1029 periodicals. Computerized library services include the card catalog, interlibrary loans, and database searching. Special learning facilities include a learning resource center, a radio station, an observatory, and an institute for the study of law and society. The 375-acre campus is in a suburban area 20 miles south of Boston. Including residence halls, there are 26 buildings.

Programs of Study: Stonehill confers B.A., B.S., and B.S.B.A. degrees. A Master of Science in Accountancy (MSA) is also awarded. Bachelor's degrees are awarded in BIOLOGICAL SCIENCE (biology/biological science), BUSINESS (accounting, banking and finance, business economics, management science, and marketing/retailing/merchandising), COMMUNICATIONS AND THE ARTS (communications, English, fine arts, and languages), COMPUTER AND PHYSICAL SCIENCE (chemistry, computer mathematics, computer science, and mathematics), EDUCATION (education), ENGINEERING AND ENVIRONMENTAL DESIGN (computer engineering), HEALTH PROFESSIONS (health care administration and medical technology), SOCIAL SCIENCE (American studies, criminal justice, economics, history, interdisciplinary studies, international studies, philosophy, political science/government, psychology, public administration, religion, and sociology). Biology, chemistry, and accounting are the strongest academically. Education studies, psychology, and biology are the largest.

Special: On-campus work-study, international and domestic internships, and a Washington semester through the Washington Center are available. Cross-registration with 8 other Massachusetts schools in the SACHEM consortium is also available. A 3-2 computer engineering degree is offered with the University of Notre Dame. Opportunities for study abroad include an exchange program with Yaroslavl State University in the Russian Federation, the Stonehill Program in France, Stonehill-Quebec Exchange, a semester in Irish studies at University College Dublin, and a worldwide Foreign Studies Program. Nondegree, directed, and field study are available as well as a pass/fail option for upperclassmen. Programs in early childhood, elementary, and secondary education lead to the state's provisional teacher certification. Stonehill is also a member of the Massachusetts Bay Marine Studies Consortium. Preprofessional preparation is also available in medicine, dentistry, veterinary science, and law. There are 12 national honor societies, a freshman honors program, and 6 departmental honors programs.

Admissions: 53% of the 1999-2000 applicants were accepted. The SAT I scores for the 1999-2000 freshman class were: Verbal--11% below 500, 57% between 500 and 599, 30% between 600 and 700, and 2% above 700; Math--12% below 500, 50% between 500 and 599, 35% between 600 and 700, and 2% above 700. 67% of the current freshmen were in the top fifth of their class; 94% were in the top two fifths. 5 freshmen graduated first in their class.

Requirements: The SAT I or ACT is required. Applicants should be graduates of an accredited high school or have earned the GED. Secondary preparation should include 4 units of English, 3 units of the same foreign language, 3 units of science, 2 units of algebra, 1 unit of geometry, and 4 combined units of history, political science, and social sciences. To these units elective subjects are to be added. Additional units in math are generally suggested, and especially suggested for business and science majors. An essay and guidance counselor recommendation are also required. AP and CLEP credits are accepted. Important factors in the admissions decision are advanced placement or honor courses, evidence of special talent, and leadership record.

Procedure: Freshmen are admitted fall and spring. Entrance exams should be taken in October. There are early decision, early admissions, and deferred admissions plans. Early decision applications should be filed by November 1; regular applications, by February 1 for fall entry and November 1 for spring entry, along with a $50 fee. Notification of early decision is sent December 31; regular decision, by April 1. 35 early decision candidates were accepted for the 1999-2000 class. 10% of all applicants are on a waiting list.

Financial Aid: In 1999-2000, 89% of all freshmen and 86% of continuing students received some form of financial aid. 72% of freshmen and 65% of continuing students received need-based aid. The average freshman award was $10,300. Of that total, scholarships or need-based grants averaged $8839 ($24,188 maximum); loans averaged $3665 ($5625 maximum); and work contracts averaged $1350 ($1500 maximum). 33% of undergraduates work part time. Average annual earnings from campus work are $837. The average financial indebtedness of the 1999 graduate was $10,863. Stonehill is a member of CSS. The CSS/Profile or FAFSA is required. The fall application deadline is February 1.

Computers: The mainframe is a Windows NT server backbone with 13 members. 125 PCs are accessible to students. A variety of software, word processors, statistics, spreadsheets, and databases are available for student use. Students have individual network accounts, E-mail, and access to the college network from dormitories by direct Ethernet connection. All students may access the system 7 days a week, 24 hours a day. There are no time limits and no fees. It is strongly recommended that all students have personal computers.

SUSQUEHANNA UNIVERSITY
Selinsgrove, PA 17870-1001

(570) 372-4260
(800) 326-9672; Fax: (570) 372-2722

Full-time: 715 men, 955 women	**Faculty:** 108; IIB, +$
Part-time: 37 men, 65 women	**Ph.D.s:** 92%
Graduate: none	**Student/Faculty:** 15 to 1
Year: semesters, summer session	**Tuition:** $19,670
Application Deadline: March 1	**Room & Board:** $5550
Freshman Class: 2143 applied, 1603 accepted, 463 enrolled	

VERY COMPETITIVE

Susquehanna University, founded in 1858, is an independent, selective, residential institution affiliated with the Lutheran Church. It offers programs through schools of arts, humanities, and communications, natural and social sciences, and business. There are 3 undergraduate schools. In addition to regional accreditation, S.U. has baccalaureate program accreditation with AACSB and NASM. The library contains 260,000 volumes, 113,700 microform items, and 12,600 audiovisual forms/CDs, and subscribes to 2400 periodicals. Computerized library services include the card catalog, interlibrary loans, and database searching. Special learning facilities include a learning resource center, an art gallery, a radio station, multimedia classrooms, video studios, a campuswide telecommunications network, satellite dishes and distribution system for foreign-language broadcasts, a video conferencing facility, an ecological field station, an observatory, a child development center, and an electronic music lab. The 210-acre campus is in a small town 50 miles north of Harrisburg. Including residence halls, there are 52 buildings.

Programs of Study: S.U. confers B.A., B.S., and B.M. degrees. Associate degrees are also awarded. Bachelor's degrees are awarded in BIOLOGICAL SCIENCE (biochemistry and biology/biological science), BUSINESS (accounting and business administration and management), COMMUNICATIONS AND THE ARTS (art, art history and appreciation, communications, dramatic arts, English, French, German, music, music performance, and Spanish), COMPUTER AND PHYSICAL SCIENCE (chemistry, computer science, information sciences and systems, mathematics, and physics), EDUCATION (early childhood, education, elementary, and music), ENGINEERING AND ENVIRONMENTAL DESIGN (environmental science), SOCIAL SCIENCE (economics, history, international studies, philosophy, political science/government, psychology, religion, religious music, and sociology). Natural sciences, business administration, and psychology are the strongest academically. Business administration, communications and theater arts, and psychology are the largest.

Special: There is cross-registration with Bucknell University. Interships are offered in almost all majors and study abroad is available on 6 continents. The School of Business offers a fall semester in London for junior business majors. Two-week study seminars in Australia, Ecuador, Southern Africa, and the Caribbean are available, as are a Washington semester, a United Nations semester, a work and study semester through the Philadelphia Center, and an Appalachian semester in Kentucky. The university offers dual and student-design majors, work-study programs, credit by examination, nondegree study, and pass/fail options. The B.A.-B.S. degree is available in several majors and there is a 3-2 engineering program with Pennsylvania State University, a 3-2 program in forestry with Duke University, and a 2-2 program in allied health with Thomas Jefferson University. Highly motivated students have the option of earning their baccalaureate degree in 3 years. There are 20 national honor societies, a freshman honors program, and 15 departmental honors programs.

Admissions: 75% of the 1999-2000 applicants were accepted. The SAT I scores for the 1999-2000 freshman class were: Verbal--15% below 500, 50% between 500 and 599, 31% between 600 and 700, and 5% above 700; Math--18% below 500, 45% between 500 and 599, 31% between 600 and 700, and 6% above 700. 50% of the current freshmen were in the top fifth of their class; 83% were in the top two fifths. 4 freshmen graduated first in their class.

Requirements: The SAT I is required, except for students with a cumulative class rank in the top 20% in a strong college preparatory program. Such students have the option of submitting either the SAT I or 2 graded writing samples. Students should be graduates of an accredited high school. Preparation should include 4 years of English and math, 3 to 4 years of science, and 2 to 3 years each of social studies and foreign language. In addition, 1 unit of art or music is recommended. 3 SAT II: Subject tests are recommended, including writing and math. An essay is required, as are, for relevant fields, an art portfolio, music audition, or writing portfolio. An interview is strongly recommended. Applications are accepted online at www.susqu.edu/admissions, and on computer disk via Common Application. AP and CLEP credits are accepted. Important factors in the admissions decision are advanced placement or honor courses, evidence of special talent, and recommendations by school officials.

Procedure: Freshmen are admitted fall and spring. Entrance exams should be taken by January of the senior year. There are early decision, early admissions, and deferred admissions plans. Early decision applications should be filed by December 15; regular applications, by March 1 for fall entry and December 1 for spring entry, along with a $30 fee. Notification of early decision is sent January 15; regular decision, on a rolling basis. 70 early decision candidates were accepted for the 1999-2000 class. 5% of all applicants are on a waiting list.

Financial Aid: In 1999-2000, 94% of all students received some form of financial aid. 62% of freshmen and 74% of continuing students received need-based aid. The average freshman award was $13,060. Of that total, scholarships or need-based grants averaged $10,515 ($25,770 maximum); loans averaged $3300 ($4625 maximum); and work contracts averaged $1675 ($1800 maximum). 64% of undergraduates work part time. Average annual earnings from campus work are $835. The average financial indebtedness of the 1999 graduate was $12,515. S.U. is a member of CSS. The CSS/Profile or FAFSA and federal tax return are required. The fall application deadline is May 1.

Computers: The mainframe is an HP 3000 Series 947. All residence hall rooms are wired for computer access to the campus LAN and the Internet. 285 PCs are available for student use in various labs and in the library. A wide variety of software is available as well. Laptop dataports are available in the business and communications building. All students may access the system 24 hours a day. There are no time limits and no fees. S.U. strongly recommends that all students have Pentium PCs with a minimum 400 MHz, 64mb RAM, 6 gb hard drive, 56kb modem, and 10/100 Ethernet card.

SWARTHMORE COLLEGE
Swarthmore, PA 19081-1397

(610) 328-8300
(800) 667-3110; Fax: (610) 328-8580

Full-time: 694 men, 767 women	**Faculty:** 174; IIB, ++$
Part-time: 1 man, 5 women	**Ph.D.s:** 95%
Graduate: none	**Student/Faculty:** 8 to 1
Year: semesters	**Tuition:** $24,190
Application Deadline: January 1	**Room & Board:** $7500
Freshman Class: 4163 applied, 906 accepted, 368 enrolled	
SAT I Verbal/Math: 770/705	**MOST COMPETITIVE**

Swarthmore College, established in 1864, is a private, nonprofit institution offering undergraduate courses in engineering and liberal arts. In addition to regional accreditation, Swarthmore has baccalaureate program accreditation with ABET. The 5 libraries contain 701,134 volumes, 289,252 microform items, and 17,332 audiovisual forms/CDs, and subscribe to 2199 periodicals. Computerized library services include the card catalog, interlibrary loans, and database searching. Special learning facilities include an art gallery, a radio station, an observatory, a performing arts center, a solar energy lab, an arboretum, and a library of documents and memorabilia of the peace movement. The 357-acre campus is in a suburban area 10 miles southwest of Philadelphia. Including residence halls, there are 46 buildings.

Programs of Study: Swarthmore confers B.A. and B.S. degrees. Master's degrees are also awarded. Bachelor's degrees are awarded in BIOLOGICAL SCIENCE (biochemistry and biology/biological science), COMMUNICATIONS AND THE ARTS (art, art history and appreciation, classics, comparative literature, dance, dramatic arts, English literature, French, German, Greek, Latin, linguistics, literature, music, Russian, and Spanish), COMPUTER AND PHYSI-

CAL SCIENCE (astronomy, astrophysics, chemistry, computer science, mathematics, and physics), EDUCATION (education), ENGINEERING AND ENVIRONMENTAL DESIGN (engineering), SOCIAL SCIENCE (anthropology, Asian/Oriental studies, classical/ancient civilization, economics, German area studies, history, humanities, medieval studies, philosophy, political science/ government, psychobiology, psychology, religion, and sociology). Biology, economics, and political science are the largest.

Special: Students may cross-register with Haverford and Bryn Mawr Colleges and the University of Pennsylvania. They may study abroad in their country of choice. Dual majors in physics and astronomy and in sociology and anthropology, student-designed majors, and a 4-year program leading to a B.A.-B.S. degree in engineering and liberal arts are available. Swarthmore offers a unique honors program whose features are student independence and responsibility and collegial relationship with faculty; students are evaluated by external examiners. There are 2 national honor societies, including Phi Beta Kappa. All departments have honors programs.

Admissions: 22% of the 1999-2000 applicants were accepted. The SAT I scores for the 1999-2000 freshman class were: Verbal--1% below 500, 7% between 500 and 599, 32% between 600 and 700, and 60% above 700; Math--8% between 500 and 599, 35% between 600 and 700, and 56% above 700. 94% of the current freshmen were in the top fifth of their class; all were in the top two fifths. There were 32 National Merit finalists. 56 freshmen graduated first in their class.

Requirements: The SAT I is required. The ACT may be submitted in place of the SAT I. SAT II: Subject tests in writing and 2 other areas of choice are required; math level II is required for engineering majors. Swarthmore does not require a specific high school curriculum. It does, however, recommend the inclusion of English, math, 1 or 2 foreign languages, history and social studies, literature, art, music, and the sciences. Interviews are strongly recommended. An essay, 2 teacher recommendations, and a counselor recommendation are required. Apply and the Common Application are accessible through the college's web site, www.swarthmore.edu. Students may also apply through CollegeNet at www. collegenet.com. AP credits are accepted. Important factors in the admissions decision are advanced placement or honor courses, recommendations by school officials, and extracurricular activities record.

Procedure: Freshmen are admitted in the fall. Entrance exams should be taken in spring of the junior year or fall of the senior year. There are early decision and deferred admissions plans. Early decision applications should be filed by November 15 or January 1; regular applications, by January 1 for fall entry, along with a $60 fee. Notification of early decision is sent December 15 or February 1; regular decision, April 1. 139 early decision candidates were accepted for the 1999-2000 class. A waiting list is an active part of the admissions procedure.

Financial Aid: In 1999-2000, 60% of all students received some form of financial aid. 51% of freshmen and 48% of continuing students received need-based aid. The average freshman award was $22,843. Of that total, scholarships or need-based grants averaged $19,185 ($32,000 maximum); loans averaged $2298; and work contracts averaged $1360. 81% of undergraduates work part time. Average annual earnings from campus work are $1360. The average financial indebtedness of the 1999 graduate was $13,390. Swarthmore is a member of CSS. The CSS/Profile or FAFSA, the college's own financial statement, and tax returns, W-2 statements, and year-end paycheck stubs are required. The fall application deadline is February 15.

Computers: The mainframe consists of UNIX based servers. There are more than 125 networked Macs and PCs available throughout the campus in public areas for student use. Residence halls are fully hooked up to the network with a connection for each resident, giving students access to the Internet, the library database, E-mail, shared software, and many other resources. All students may access the system. There are no time limits and no fees.

SWEET BRIAR COLLEGE
Sweet Briar, VA 24595

(804) 381-6142
(800) 381-6142; Fax: (804) 381-6152

Full-time: 11 men, 653 women	**Faculty:** 69; IIB, ++$
Part-time: 11 men, 35 women	**Ph.D.s:** 85%
Graduate: none	**Student/Faculty:** 10 to 1
Year: semesters	**Tuition:** $16,585
Application Deadline: February 15	**Room & Board:** $6715
Freshman Class: 499 applied, 445 accepted, 188 enrolled	
SAT I Verbal/Math: 580/520	**ACT:** 24 **VERY COMPETITIVE**

Sweet Briar College, founded in 1901, is a private women's liberal arts institution. Men may be admitted as special students but may not receive a degree from Sweet Briar. The 4 libraries contain 247,385 volumes, 387,642 microform items, and 6650 audiovisual forms/CDs, and subscribe to 1650 periodicals. Computerized library services include the card catalog, interlibrary loans, and database searching. Special learning facilities include a learning resource center, art gallery, radio station, TV station, and and college museum. The 3300-acre campus is in a rural area 150 miles southwest of Washington, D.C., 100 miles west of Richmond, and 12 miles north of Lynchburg. Including residence halls, there are 38 buildings.

Programs of Study: Sweet Briar confers A.B. and B.S. degrees. Bachelor's degrees are awarded in BIOLOGICAL SCIENCE (biochemistry, biology/biological science, and molecular biology), COMMUNICATIONS AND THE ARTS (art history and appreciation, creative writing, dance, dramatic arts, English, languages, music, and studio art), COMPUTER AND PHYSICAL SCIENCE (chemistry, computer science, mathematics, and physics), ENGINEERING AND ENVIRONMENTAL DESIGN (preengineering), SOCIAL SCIENCE (anthropology, classical/ancient civilization, economics, history, international relations, philosophy, political science/government, psychology, religion, and sociology). International affairs, biology, and English are the strongest academically. Psychology, government, and English are the largest.

Special: The college offers a coordinate program in general business management and arts management, as well as internships to explore career opportunities and gain work experience. study abroad in 15 countries, and a Washington semester with American University. B.A.-B.S. degrees, student-designed and interdisciplinary majors, accelerated degree programs, and 3-2 engineering degrees with Columbia University, Washington University in St. Louis, Virginia Polytechnic Institute, and University of Virginia are available. Cross-registration with Lynchburg and Randolph-Macon Woman's colleges (the Tri-College Consortium) and the Seven College Exchange is also possible. There are 5 national honor societies, including Phi Beta Kappa, and a freshman honors program.

Admissions: 89% of the 1999-2000 applicants were accepted. The SAT I scores for the 1999-2000 freshman class were: Verbal--17% below 500, 43% between 500 and 599, 32% between 600 and 700, and 8% above 700; Math--36% below 500, 45% between 500 and 599, 16% between 600 and 700, and 3% above 700. The ACT scores were 18% below 21, 25% between 21 and 23, 28% between 24 and 26, 12% between 27 and 28, and 17% above 28. 50% of the current freshmen were in the top fifth of their class; 84% were in the top two fifths. There was 1 National Merit finalist. 5 freshmen graduated first in their class.

Requirements: The SAT I or ACT is required. If the SAT I is submitted, it is recommended that the applicant also take 3 SAT II: Subject tests, 1 in English and 2 in other areas. Applicants must be graduates of an accredited secondary school. Applicants must complete at least 16 high school academic credits (20 recommended), including 4 years of English and 3 each of math, social studies, science, history, and a foreign language. The college requires an essay and recommends an interview. AP credits are accepted. Important factors in the admissions decision are advanced placement or honor courses, evidence of special talent, and leadership record.

Procedure: Freshmen are admitted fall and spring. Entrance exams should be taken by January of the year of application; SAT II: Subject tests can be taken in the spring of the senior year. There are early decision, early admissions, and deferred admissions plans. Early decision applications should be filed by December 1; regular applications, by February 15 for fall entry and November 15 for spring entry, along with a $25 fee. Notification of early decision is sent December 15; regular decision, April 1. 43 early decision candidates were accepted for the 1999-2000 class.

Financial Aid: In 1999-2000, 99% of all freshmen and 93% of continuing students received some form of financial aid. 58% of freshmen and 52% of continuing students received need-based aid. The average freshman award was $15,576. Of that total, scholarships or need-based grants averaged $12,412 ($20,660 maximum); loans averaged $2525 ($6625 maximum); and work contracts averaged $639 ($1000 maximum). 61% of undergraduates work part time. Average annual earnings from campus work are $750. The average financial indebtedness of the 1999 graduate was $15,256. Sweet Briar is a member of CSS. The FAFSA and the college's own financial statement are required. The fall application deadline is March 1.

Computers: The mainframes are DEC ALPHA 2100, and an AXP2000. More than 95 Mac and Pentium computers for student use are located across campus in 24-hour multimedia labs, the libraries, study rooms, and academic buildings. The computer-student ratio is 1:6 and more than 600 fiber-optic connections to the campus network exist in academic buildings. Student residence hall rooms also have network connections. The college is connected to the Internet, including the World Wide Web. All students may access the system 24 hours a day. There are no time limits and no fees. It is recommended that all students have personal computers, and recommended Mac and Wintel configurations are available upon request.

SYRACUSE UNIVERSITY
Syracuse, NY 13244
(315) 443-3611

Full-time: 4828 men, 5654 women	**Faculty:** 778; I, -$
Part-time: 123 men, 80 women	**Ph.Ds:** 86%
Graduate: 1915 men, 2068 women	**Student/Faculty:** 13 to 1
Year: semesters, summer session	**Tuition:** $19,784
Application Deadline: January 15	**Room & Board:** $8400
Freshman Class: 12,663 applied, 7459 accepted, 2752 enrolled	
SAT I or ACT: required	**HIGHLY COMPETITIVE**

Syracuse University, founded in 1870, is a private institution offering undergraduate programs in liberal arts and sciences, architecture, public communications, education, management, human development, information studies, nursing, social work, visual and performing arts, engineering, and computer science. There are 11 undergraduate and 13 graduate schools. In addition to regional accreditation, Syracuse has baccalaureate program accreditation with AACSB, ABET, ACEJ-

MC, ADA, ASLA, CSWE, FIDER, NAAB, NASAD, NASM, NCATE, and NLN. The 6 libraries contain 3 million volumes, 3.7 million microform items, and 1.3 million audiovisual forms/CDs, and subscribe to 16,300 periodicals. Computerized library services include the card catalog, interlibrary loans, and database searching. Special learning facilities include a learning resource center, art gallery, radio station, TV station, Institute for Sensory Research, speech and hearing clinic, audio archives, Global Collaboratory multimedia classroom, a laser spectroscopy lab, and a Center for Science and Technology. The 200-acre campus is in an urban area 270 miles northwest of New York City. Including residence halls, there are 170 buildings.

Programs of Study: Syracuse confers A.B., B.S., B.Arch., B.F.A, B.I.D., and B. Mus. degrees. Master's and doctoral degrees are also awarded. Bachelor's degrees are awarded in BIOLOGICAL SCIENCE (biology/biological science, neurosciences, and nutrition), BUSINESS (accounting, banking and finance, business administration and management, entrepreneurial studies, management information systems, management science, marketing management, marketing/retailing/merchandising, and retailing), COMMUNICATIONS AND THE ARTS (advertising, art, art history and appreciation, broadcasting, ceramic art and design, classics, communications, comparative literature, design, dramatic arts, English, English literature, fiber/textiles/weaving, film arts, fine arts, French, Germanic languages and literature, graphic design, illustration, industrial design, journalism, languages, linguistics, media arts, metal/jewelry, modern language, music, music business management, music performance, music theory and composition, musical theater, painting, photography, printmaking, public relations, publishing, Russian, sculpture, Spanish, speech/debate/rhetoric, telecommunications, theater design, theater management, and video), COMPUTER AND PHYSICAL SCIENCE (chemistry, computer science, geology, information sciences and systems, mathematics, physics, and statistics), EDUCATION (art, athletic training, early childhood, elementary, English, mathematics, middle school, music, physical, science, secondary, social studies, and special), ENGINEERING AND ENVIRONMENTAL DESIGN (aerospace studies, architecture, bioengineering, chemical engineering, civil engineering, computer engineering, computer graphics, electrical/electronics engineering, engineering physics, environmental design, environmental engineering, environmental science, interior design, and mechanical engineering), HEALTH PROFESSIONS (exercise science, health science, nursing, predentistry, premedicine, preveterinary science, and speech pathology/audiology), SOCIAL SCIENCE (African American studies, American studies, anthropology, child care/child and family studies, classical/ancient civilization, consumer services, dietetics, economics, ethics, politics, and social policy, European studies, family/consumer studies, fashion design and technology, food production/management/services, geography, history, international relations, Italian studies, Latin American studies, medieval studies, peace studies, philosophy, political science/government, prelaw, psychology, public affairs, religion, Russian and Slavic studies, social science, social work, sociology, textiles and clothing, and women's studies). Information management and technology, philosophy, and geography are the strongest academically. Information management and technology, psychology, and broadcast journalism are the largest.

Special: The Syracuse University Internship Program (SUIP) places students in off-campus local or national field positions related to their major. Cooperative education programs are available in engineering, retailing, and information studies. Cross-registration is offered with SUNY College of Environmental Science and Forestry. Study abroad is available in 6 university-operated centers and through other special programs, and a Washington semester is offered through the International Relations Program. Syracuse also offers B.A.-B.S. degrees, dual and student-designed majors, accelerated degree programs, work-study programs, a general studies degree, pass/fail options, and nondegree study. There are 36 national honor societies, including Phi Beta Kappa, and a freshman honors program.

Admissions: 59% of the 1999-2000 applicants were accepted. The SAT I scores for the 1999-2000 freshman class were: Verbal--10% below 500, 42% between 500 and 599, 39% between 600 and 700, and 9% above 700; Math--6% below 500, 35% between 500 and 599, 47% between 600 and 700, and 12% above 700. 66% of the current freshmen were in the top fifth of their class; 92% were in the top two fifths. 39 freshmen graduated first in their class.

Requirements: The SAT I or ACT is required. Applicants should have a strong college preparatory record from an accredited secondary school or have a GED equivalent. An essay is required. A portfolio is required for art and architecture majors, and an audition is required for music and drama majors. A secondary school counselor evaluation, or 2 academic recommendations, and a high school transcript, are also required. AP and CLEP credits are accepted. Important factors in the admissions decision are advanced placement or honor courses, evidence of special talent, and recommendations by school officials.

Procedure: Freshmen are admitted fall and spring. Entrance exams should be taken before January of the senior year. There are early decision, early admissions, and deferred admissions plans. Early decision applications should be filed by November 15; regular applications, by January 15 for fall entry and November 15 for spring entry, along with a $40 fee. Notification of early decision is sent late December ; regular decision, early March. 437 early decision candidates were accepted for the 1999-2000 class.

Financial Aid: In 1999-2000, 78% of all freshmen and 80% of continuing students received some form of financial aid. 56% of freshmen and 55% of continuing students received need-based aid. The average freshman award was $15,100. Of that total, scholarships or need-based grants averaged $9700 ($19,360 maximum); loans averaged $3500 ($4625 maximum); and work contracts averaged $1900 ($2000 maximum). 45% of undergraduates work part time. Average annual earnings from campus work are $1500. The average financial indebtedness of the 1999 graduate was $18,600. The FAFSA is required. The fall application deadline is February 15.

Computers: Syracuse has a networked client/server computing environment that gives students access to almost 1000 Macs and UNIX workstations located throughout the campus. High-speed connections are available in many residence halls. All students may access the system 24 hours per day. There are no time limits and no fees. It is recommended that all students have personal computers.

TABOR COLLEGE
Hillsboro, KS 67063

(316) 947-3121
(800) TABOR-99; Fax: (316) 947-2607

Full-time: 209 men, 180 women	**Faculty:** 33; IIB, --$
Part-time: 64 men, 85 women	**Ph.D.s:** 67%
Graduate: none	**Student/Faculty:** 12 to 1
Year: 4-1-4	**Tuition:** $11,850
Application Deadline: August 1	**Room & Board:** $4000
Freshman Class: 302 applied, 197 accepted, 138 enrolled	
ACT: required	**VERY COMPETITIVE**

Tabor College, established in 1908, is a private liberal arts facility affiliated with the Mennonite Brethren Church. In addition to regional accreditation, Tabor has baccalaureate program accreditation with CSWE and NASM. The library contains 70,000 volumes and 2000 audiovisual forms/CDs, and subscribes to 450 periodicals. Computerized library services include the card catalog and database searching. Special learning facilities include a learning resource center and a writing center. The 26-acre campus is in a rural area 50 miles north of Wichita. Including residence halls, there are 28 buildings.

Programs of Study: Tabor confers B.A. and B.S. degrees. Associate degrees are also awarded. Bachelor's degrees are awarded in BIOLOGICAL SCIENCE (biology/biological science), BUSINESS (accounting, business administration and management, marketing/retailing/merchandising, and office supervision and management), COMMUNICATIONS AND THE ARTS (communications, English, and music), COMPUTER AND PHYSICAL SCIENCE (chemistry, computer programming, computer science, mathematics, and natural sciences), EDUCATION (athletic training, business, elementary, health, middle school, music, physical, science, secondary, and special), HEALTH PROFESSIONS (medical laboratory technology), SOCIAL SCIENCE (biblical studies, history, humanities, international studies, ministries, philosophy, psychology, religion, social science, and sociology). The sciences are the strongest academically. Business and education are the largest.

Special: Cross-registration is offered with the Association of Colleges of Central Kansas. Study abroad in 5 countries is possible. Dual majors, student-designed majors, a Washington semester for juniors or seniors, and pass/fail options are available, as is a 3-2 engineering degree with Wichita State University. An accelerated degree program in management organizational development and preprofessional curricula in allied health, law, and medicine are also offered. There is a freshman honors program and 1 departmental honors program.

Admissions: 65% of the 1999-2000 applicants were accepted. The ACT scores for the 1999-2000 freshman class were: 27% below 21, 32% between 21 and 23, 28% between 24 and 26, and 13% above 27. 57% of the current freshmen were in the top fifth of their class; 89% were in the top two fifths.

Requirements: The ACT is required. A GPA of 2.0 is required. An essay is required and an interview is recommended. Tabor is a part of the CollegeLink electronic application system. Applications are also accepted on-line via Tabor's web site: www.tabor.edu. AP and CLEP credits are accepted. Personality/intangible qualities is an important factor in the admission decision.

Procedure: Freshmen are admitted to all sessions. Entrance exams should be taken in October of the senior year. There is an early admissions plan. Early decision applications should be filed by February 1; regular applications, by August 1 for fall entry, along with a $10 fee. Notification is sent on a rolling basis.

Financial Aid: In a recent year, students received some form of financial aid. 74% of freshmen received need-based aid. The average freshman award was $5700. Of that total, scholarships or need-based grants averaged $3200 ($7850 maximum); loans averaged $2400; and work contracts averaged $1000 ($1500 maximum). 25% of undergraduates work part time. Average annual earnings from campus work are $1000. The average financial indebtedness of the 1999 graduate was $20,000. The FAFSA and a federal income tax form are required. The fall application deadline is March 1.

Computers: The mainframe is a Dual 83/80. There are also 60 PCs available in the administration building and labs. All students may access the system. There are no time limits and no fees.

TAYLOR UNIVERSITY
Upland, IN 46989-1001

(765) 998-5134
(800) 882-3456; Fax: (765) 998-4925

Full-time: 871 men, 973 women	**Faculty:** 113; IIB, -$
Part-time: 25 men, 28 women	**Ph.D.s:** 75%
Graduate: none	**Student/Faculty:** 16 to 1
Year: 4-1-4, summer session	**Tuition:** $15,118
Application Deadline: open	**Room & Board:** $4630
Freshman Class: 1624 applied, 1099 accepted, 474 enrolled	
SAT I Verbal/Math: 596/603	**ACT:** 26 **VERY COMPETITIVE**

Taylor University, founded in 1846, is a Christian interdenominational liberal arts institution. In addition to regional accreditation, Taylor has baccalaureate program accreditation with CSWE, NASM, and NCATE. The library contains 192,674 volumes, 10,735 microform items, and 6542 audiovisual forms/CDs, and subscribes to 660 periodicals. Computerized library services include the card catalog, interlibrary loans, and database searching. Special learning facilities include a learning resource center, art gallery, radio station, TV station, 65-acre arboretum, and C. S. Lewis Collection. The 250-acre campus is in a rural area 70 miles north of Indianapolis. Including residence halls, there are 26 buildings.

Programs of Study: Taylor confers B.A., B.S., and B.Mus. degrees. Associate degrees are also awarded. Bachelor's degrees are awarded in BIOLOGICAL SCIENCE (biology/biological science and environmental biology), BUSINESS (accounting, business administration and management, international business management, and recreation and leisure services), COMMUNICATIONS AND THE ARTS (art, communications, dramatic arts, English, French, music, and Spanish), COMPUTER AND PHYSICAL SCIENCE (chemistry, computer science, mathematics, natural sciences, and physics), EDUCATION (art, athletic training, Christian, elementary, and physical), ENGINEERING AND ENVIRONMENTAL DESIGN (computer graphics, engineering physics, and environmental science), SOCIAL SCIENCE (biblical studies, economics, history, international studies, philosophy, political science/government, psychology, social studies, social work, and sociology). Computer science and environmental science are the strongest academically. Business and education are the largest.

Special: Opportunities are provided for internships, cooperative programs, a Washington semester, study abroad in 11 countries, work-study programs, dual majors, student-designed majors, B.A.-B.S. degrees, and a 3-2 engineering degree with Washington University, St. Louis. There is cross-registration with the other members of the Coalition for Christian Colleges and Universities and the Christian College Consortium. There are 6 national honor societies and a freshman honors program.

Admissions: 68% of the 1999-2000 applicants were accepted. The SAT I scores for the 1999-2000 freshman class were: Verbal--15% below 500, 38% between 500 and 599, 32% between 600 and 700, and 15% above 700; Math--12% below 500, 42% between 500 and 599, 36% between 600 and 700, and 10% above 700. 64% of the current freshmen were in the top fifth of their class; 87% were in the top two fifths. In a recent year, there were 12 National Merit finalists. 37 freshmen graduated first in their class.

Requirements: The SAT I or ACT is required. Taylor requires applicants to be in the upper 40% of their class. A GPA of 2.8 is required, with composite scores of 1000 on the SAT I and 24 on the ACT recommended. Graduation from an accredited secondary school is required; a GED will be accepted. It is recommended that applicants complete 4 years of English, 3 to 4 each of math and lab science, 2 each of social studies and a foreign language, and course work in computing, typing/keyboarding, and the arts. An interview is recommended for all students, and an audition is required for music majors. AP and CLEP credits are accepted. Important factors in the admissions decision are personality/intangible qualities, evidence of special talent, and leadership record.

Procedure: Freshmen are admitted fall and spring. Entrance exams should be taken during the spring of the junior year or fall of the senior year. There are early admissions and deferred admissions plans. Application deadlines are open; there is a $20 application fee. Notification is sent on a rolling basis. A waiting list is an active part of the admissions procedure.

Financial Aid: In a recent year, 80% of all students received some form of financial aid. 55% of all students received need-based aid. The average freshman award was $11,600. Of that total, scholarships or need-based grants averaged $7200 ($17,894 maximum); loans averaged $3300 ($4125 maximum); and work contracts averaged $1100 ($1500 maximum). 78% of undergraduates work part time. Average annual earnings from campus work are $2300. The average financial indebtedness of the 1999 graduate was $14,200. Taylor is a member of CSS. The FAFSA and the college's own financial statement are required. The fall application deadline is March 1.

Computers: The mainframes are a DEC PDP 11/70 and MicroVAX 3600 models. There are PCs at sites throughout the campus in a ratio of 1 for each 13 students. All students may access the system. There are no time limits and no fees. It is strongly recommended that all students have IBM personal computers.

TEXAS A&M UNIVERSITY
College Station, TX 77843   (409) 845-3741; Fax: (409) 847-8737

Full-time: 17,391 men, 15,947 women	**Faculty:** 1294; I, -$
Part-time: 1492 men, 1252 women	**Ph.D.s:** 90%
Graduate: 4405 men, 2955 women	**Student/Faculty:** 26 to 1
Year: semesters, summer session	**Tuition:** $2639 ($7823)
Application Deadline: February 15	**Room & Board:** $4898
Freshman Class: 14,453 applied, 10,748 accepted, 6695 enrolled	
SAT I Verbal/Math: 570/600	**HIGHLY COMPETITIVE**

Texas A&M University, founded in 1876, is part of the Texas A&M University system. Undergraduate degrees are offered in agriculture and life sciences, architecture, business administration, education, engineering, geosciences, liberal arts, science, and biomedical science. There are 9 undergraduate and 10 graduate schools. In addition to regional accreditation, Texas A&M has baccalaureate program accreditation with AACSB, ABET, ACCE, ACEJMC, ADA, ASLA, CSAB, NAAB, NCATE, and SAF. The 3 libraries contain 2.5 million volumes,

4.7 million microform items, and 27,717 audiovisual forms/CDs, and subscribe to 29,671 periodicals. Computerized library services include the card catalog, interlibrary loans, and database searching. Special learning facilities include a learning resource center, art gallery, radio station, TV station, weather station, observatory, cyclotron, wind tunnel, visualization lab, nuclear reactor, ocean wave pool, and the Bush Museum and Library. The 5200-acre campus is in an urban area 90 miles northwest of Houston. Including residence halls, there are 751 buildings.

Programs of Study: Texas A&M confers B.A., B.S., B.B.A., B.Ed., and B.L.A. degrees. Master's and doctoral degrees are also awarded. Bachelor's degrees are awarded in AGRICULTURE (agricultural business management, agricultural economics, animal science, dairy science, fish and game management, fishing and fisheries, forestry and related sciences, horticulture, poultry science, and range/farm management), BIOLOGICAL SCIENCE (biochemistry, biology/biological science, botany, entomology, genetics, microbiology, and zoology), BUSINESS (accounting, banking and finance, business systems analysis, management science, marketing/retailing/merchandising, and personnel management), COMMUNICATIONS AND THE ARTS (English, French, German, journalism, Russian, Spanish, and speech/debate/rhetoric), COMPUTER AND PHYSICAL SCIENCE (atmospheric sciences and meteorology, chemistry, computer science, geology, geophysics and seismology, mathematics, and physics), EDUCATION (elementary, health, physical, and secondary), ENGINEERING AND ENVIRONMENTAL DESIGN (aeronautical engineering, agricultural engineering, bioengineering, chemical engineering, civil engineering, computer engineering, construction engineering, electrical/electronics engineering, engineering technology, environmental design, environmental science, industrial engineering technology, landscape architecture/design, mechanical engineering, nuclear engineering, and petroleum/natural gas engineering), HEALTH PROFESSIONS (biomedical science), SOCIAL SCIENCE (anthropology, economics, history, international studies, parks and recreation management, philosophy, political science/government, psychology, and sociology). Engineering, business administration, and life sciences are the strongest academically. Psychology, accounting, and biomedical science are the largest.

Special: The university offers extensive opportunities through the Career Center and Study Abroad Office. B.A.- B.S. degrees, credit for military experience, nondegree study, dual majors, and pass/fail options are available. A 5-year graduate business/liberal arts program is offered, as well as a 3-2 engineering degree with Sam Houston State University. There are 41 national honor societies, and a freshman honors program.

Admissions: 74% of the 1999-2000 applicants were accepted. The SAT I scores for the 1999-2000 freshman class were: Verbal--14% below 500, 48% between 500 and 599, 31% between 600 and 700, and 7% above 700; Math--8% below 500, 39% between 500 and 599, 40% between 600 and 700, and 13% above 700. 73% of the current freshmen were in the top fifth of their class; 94% were in the top two fifths. There were 149 National Merit finalists.

Requirements: The SAT I or ACT is required. Secondary school graduation is a condition of freshman admission. Required high school courses include 4 credits in English, 3 1/2 credits in math, 3 credits in science (2 from biology, chemistry, or physics), and 2 credits of the same foreign language. The state of Texas Common Application is accepted on-line via www.applytexas.org or through TAMU web site, www.tamu.edu/admissions. AP and CLEP credits are accepted. Important factors in the admissions decision are leadership record, evidence of special talent, and extracurricular activities record.

Procedure: Freshmen are admitted fall, spring, and summer. Entrance exams should be taken during the spring of the junior year or by December of the senior year. Applications should be filed by February 15 for fall entry, October 15 for spring entry, and February 15 for summer entry, along with a $50 fee. Notification is sent on a rolling basis. A waiting list is an active part of the admissions procedure.

Financial Aid: In 1999-2000, 65% of all freshmen and 68% of continuing students received some form of financial aid. 35% of freshmen and 40% of continuing students received need-based aid. The average freshman award was $4959. Of that total, scholarships or need-based grants averaged $3199 ($27,550 maximum); loans averaged $4650 ($16,172 maximum); and work contracts averaged $1282 ($8056 maximum). 26% of undergraduates work part time. Average annual earnings from campus work are $3628. The average financial indebtedness of the 1999 graduate was $12,401. Texas A&M is a member of CSS. The FAFSA is required. The fall application deadline is April 1.

Computers: The mainframes are an IBM 3090-600E, an Amdahl 5990, and DEC VAXs 880, 8650, and 9000-210V. About 2000 Macs and PCs are available throughout the campus. All students may access the system at any time. There are no time limits and no fees.

TEXAS CHRISTIAN UNIVERSITY
Fort Worth, TX 76129

(817) 257-7490
(800) TCU-FROG; Fax: (817) 257-7268

Full-time: 2413 men, 3474 women	**Faculty:** 357; I, -$
Part-time: 241 men, 328 women	**Ph.D.s:** 90%
Graduate: 535 men, 560 women	**Student/Faculty:** 17 to 1
Year: semesters, summer session	**Tuition:** $12,290
Application Deadline: February 15	**Room & Board:** $3970
Freshman Class: 5028 applied, 3769 accepted, 1426 enrolled	
SAT I or ACT: recommended	**VERY COMPETITIVE**

Texas Christian University, founded in 1873, is a private university affiliated with the Christian Church (Disciples of Christ). TCU is a teaching and research institution offering undergraduate programs in arts, sciences, business, education, fine arts, communications, nursing, and engineering. There are 5 undergraduate and 5 graduate schools. In addition to regional accreditation, TCU has baccalaureate program accreditation with AACSB, ACEJMC, ADA, ASLA, CSAB, CSWE, FIDER, and NASM. The library contains 1,885,702 volumes, 557,553 microform items, and 55,246 audiovisual forms/CDs, and subscribes to 4757 periodicals. Computerized library services include the card catalog, interlibrary loans, and database searching. Special learning facilities include a learning resource center, art gallery, radio station, TV station, an observatory, and a speech and hearing clinic. The more than 300-acre campus is in a suburban area 3 miles southwest of downtown Fort Worth. Including residence halls, there are 73 buildings.

Programs of Study: TCU confers B.A., B.S., B.B.A., B.F.A., B.G.S., B.Med., B.Mus., B.S.E., B.S.Ed., and B.S.N. degrees. Master's and doctoral degrees are also awarded. Bachelor's degrees are awarded in BIOLOGICAL SCIENCE (biology/biological science, neurosciences, and nutrition), BUSINESS (accounting, banking and finance, fashion merchandising, international business management, management science, and marketing/retailing/merchandising), COMMUNICATIONS AND THE ARTS (advertising, art history and appreciation, broadcasting, communications, dance, dramatic arts, English, film arts, French, graphic design, journalism, music, music history and appreciation, music performance, music theory and composition, Spanish, and studio art), COMPUTER AND PHYSICAL SCIENCE (astronomy, chemistry, computer science, geology, mathematics, and physics), EDUCATION (art, education of the deaf and hearing impaired, elementary, music, physical, and recreation), ENGINEERING AND ENVIRONMENTAL DESIGN (engineering, environmental science, and interior design), HEALTH PROFESSIONS (nursing and speech pathology/audiology), SOCIAL SCIENCE (criminal justice, economics, fashion design and technology, history, Latin American studies, liberal arts/general studies, philosophy, physical fitness/ movement, political science/government, psychology, religion, social work, and sociology). Psychology, biology, and nursing are the largest.

Special: A general studies degree and a combined B.A.-B.S. degree in numerous majors are offered. Student-designed majors, dual majors, nondegree study, and pass/no credit options are available. TCU also accepts credit by exam and credit for life, military, and work experience. 3-2 programs are available in business, education, and economics. Internships are available in almost all major areas. The university also offers a Washington semester, student exchange in Japan and Mexico, and study abroad in 28 countries. TCU also offers study at its London Center and through the American Airlines Leadership for the Americas program. There are 4 national honor societies, including Phi Beta Kappa, a freshman honors program, and 29 departmental honors programs.

Admissions: 75% of the 1999-2000 applicants were accepted. 56% of the current freshmen were in the top fifth of their class; 87% were in the top two fifths. 78 freshmen graduated first in their class.

Requirements: The SAT I or ACT is recommended. Candidates should be graduates of an accredited secondary school and have completed 2 years of academic electives and 15 Carnegie units, including 4 years of English, 3 years each of math, science, and social studies, and 2 of the same foreign language. TCU also recommends an interview and requires an essay and counselor's recommendation. Applications are accepted on computer disk and on-line. AP and CLEP credits are accepted. Important factors in the admissions decision are advanced placement or honor courses, leadership record, and evidence of special talent.

Procedure: Freshmen are admitted to all sessions. Entrance exams should be taken during or before the fall semester of the senior year. There are early admissions and deferred admissions plans. Applications should be filed by February 15 for fall entry and December 1 for spring entry, along with a $30 fee. Notification is sent April 1. A waiting list is an active part of the admissions procedure.

Financial Aid: In 1999-2000, 82% of all freshmen and 63% of continuing students received some form of financial aid. 39% of freshmen and 34% of continuing students received need-based aid. TCU is a member of CSS. The FAFSA is required. The fall application deadline is May 1.

Computers: The mainframes are a DEC ALPHA 2100 VMS, a DEC ALPHA 2000, a DEC ALPHA 1200 VMS, a Compaq Proliant 5000, and a Compaq Proliant 7000. There are 2,156 academic networks and 3,444 student network computer capabilities. There are 12 PC labs and 6 Mac labs; any PC equipped with a modem may also access the network. All residential facilities are hard wired to provide network connections to every student. All students may access the system any time. There are no time limits and no fees.

TEXAS TECH UNIVERSITY

Lubbock, TX 79409-5005 (806) 742-1482; Fax: (806) 742-0980

Full-time: 9663 men, 8372 women	**Faculty:** 905; I, --$
Part-time: 1183 men, 1009 women	**Ph.D.s:** 90%
Graduate: 2127 men, 1895 women	**Student/Faculty:** 20 to 1
Year: semesters, summer session	**Tuition:** $3107 ($9587)
Application Deadline: open	**Room & Board:** $4788
Freshman Class: 9000 applied, 6104 accepted, 3372 enrolled	
SAT I Verbal/Math: 600/615	**ACT:** 26 **VERY COMPETITIVE**

Texas Tech University, founded in 1923, is a large, comprehensive public university offering undergraduate and graduate programs in a variety of professional and vocational fields. There are 7 undergraduate and 2 graduate schools. In addition to regional accreditation, Texas Tech has baccalaureate program accreditation with AACSB, ABET, ACEJMC, ADA, APTA, ASLA, CSWE, FIDER, NAAB, NASAD, NASM, NCATE, and NLN. The 5 libraries contain 2,125,130 volumes, 1,981,391 microform items, and 79,471 audiovisual forms/CDs, and subscribe to 23,552 periodicals. Computerized library services include the card catalog, interlibrary loans, and database searching. Special learning facilities include a learning resource center, art gallery, natural history museum, planetarium, radio station, TV station, a ranching heritage center, an international cultural center, an international textile center, and a Southwest collection. The 1839-acre campus is in an urban area in Lubbock. Including residence halls, there are 172 buildings.

Programs of Study: Texas Tech confers B.A., B.S., B.Arch., B.B.A., B.F.A., B.G.S., B.I.D., B.Land.Arch., B.M., B.S.C.E., B.S.Ch.E., B.S.E.E., B.S.H.E., B.S.I.E., B.S. in E., B.S. in Eco., B.S. in Engineering Physics, B.S. in Environmental Engineering, B.S. in Family and Consumer Sciences, B.S. in Petroleum Engineering, B.S. in Restaurant, Hotel, and Institutional Management, B.S. in Textile Engineering, B.S.M.E., and B.S.Tech. degrees. Master's and doctoral degrees are also awarded. Bachelor's degrees are awarded in AGRICULTURE (agricultural business management, agricultural economics, agronomy, animal science, horticulture, plant protection (pest management), range/farm management, and wildlife management), BIOLOGICAL SCIENCE (biochemistry, biology/biological science, cell biology, microbiology, molecular biology, and zoology), BUSINESS (accounting, banking and finance, business administration and management, business economics, hotel/motel and restaurant management, international business management, international economics, management information systems, marketing/retailing/merchandising, and recreation and leisure services), COMMUNICATIONS AND THE ARTS (advertising, art history and appreciation, broadcasting, dance, design, dramatic arts, English, fine arts, French, German, journalism, Latin, music, music performance, music theory and composition, photography, public relations, Spanish, speech/debate/rhetoric, studio art, telecommunications, and visual and performing arts), COMPUTER AND PHYSICAL SCIENCE (chemistry, computer science, geology, geophysics and seismology, geoscience, mathematics, and physics), EDUCATION (agricultural, art, business, early childhood, education, elementary, and physical), ENGINEERING AND ENVIRONMENTAL DESIGN (architectural engineering, chemical engineering, civil engineering, construction technology, electrical/electronics engineering, electrical/electronics engineering technology, engineering, engineering physics, environmental engineering, industrial engineering technology, interior design, landscape architecture/design, mechanical engineering, mechanical engineering technology, petroleum/natural gas engineering, and textile engineering),

HEALTH PROFESSIONS (health), SOCIAL SCIENCE (anthropology, child care/child and family studies, clothing and textiles management/production/services, dietetics, economics, family/consumer resource management, fashion design and technology, food production/management/services, food science, geography, history, home economics, Latin American studies, liberal arts/general studies, parks and recreation management, philosophy, physical fitness/movement, political science/government, prelaw, psychology, Russian and Slavic studies, social work, and sociology). Business, human development and family studies, and educational curriculum and instruction are the largest.

Special: There are many work-study programs and internships, and students may study in 5 countries. Texas Tech also offers B.A.- B.S. degrees, an accelerated degree program, co-o programs, dual degrees, dual majors, cross-registration, a general studies degree, a 3-2 engineering program, student-designed majors, non-degree study, and pass/fail options. There are 7 national honor societies and a freshman honors program.

Admissions: 68% of the 1999-2000 applicants were accepted. The SAT I scores for the 1999-2000 freshman class were: Verbal--8% below 500, 41% between 500 and 599, 40% between 600 and 700, and 11% above 700; Math--7% below 500, 32% between 500 and 599, 49% between 600 and 700, and 13% above 700. The ACT scores were 7% below 21, 15% between 21 and 23, 33% between 24 and 26, 21% between 27 and 28, and 25% above 28. 43% of the current freshmen were in the top fifth of their class; 87% were in the top two fifths. There were 13 National Merit finalists. 79 freshmen graduated first in their class.

Requirements: The SAT I or ACT is required. A GPA of 2.0 is required. Applicants should be graduates of an accredited high school or have the GED. The university requires 17 credits of academic work in high school, including 4 credits in English, 3 credits in math, 2 1/2 in social studies, 2 credits in science, and 3 1/2 credits in academic electives. The university admits all students scoring 1200 (composite) on the SAT I or 29 on the ACT. Special circumstances may allow those not fulfilling the above requirements to be admitted. Applications for admissions are accepted on-line at the school's web site, http://www.srel.ttu.edu. AP and CLEP credits are accepted.

Procedure: Freshmen are admitted to all sessions. Entrance exams should be taken before July 1. There is an early admissions plan. Application deadlines are open. There is a $25 fee. Notification is sent on a rolling basis.

Financial Aid: In a recent year, 35% of all freshmen and 68% of continuing students received some form of financial aid. 27% of freshmen and 56% of continuing students received need-based aid. The average freshman award was $4097. Of that total, scholarships or need-based grants averaged $1998 ($12,787 maximum); loans averaged $3643 ($12,625 maximum); and work contracts averaged $1252 ($3309 maximum). 10% of undergraduates work part time. Average annual earnings from campus work are $3500. The FFS is required. The fall application deadline is April 15.

Computers: The mainframe is an IBM 9672-R34. There are also Macs and IBM, Zenith, Sun, and other PCs available in the Advanced Technology Learning Center and in academic departments. All students may access the system 24 hours per day. There are no time limits. The fee is $6 per semester hour. It is strongly recommended that all students have personal computers.

THOMAS AQUINAS COLLEGE

Santa Paula, CA 93060

(805) 525-4417
(800) 634-9797; Fax: (805) 525-0620

Full-time: 158 men, 109 women	**Faculty:** 24
Part-time: none	**Ph.D.s:** 79%
Graduate: none	**Student/Faculty:** 11 to 1
Year: semesters	**Tuition:** $14,900
Application Deadline: open	**Room & Board:** $4300
Freshman Class: 151 applied, 123 accepted, 86 enrolled	
SAT I Verbal/Math: 660/620	**ACT:** 27 **HIGHLY COMPETITIVE**

Thomas Aquinas College, founded in 1969 and affiliated with the Roman Catholic Church, is a small, private, liberal arts college offering an integrated studies curriculum based on the Great Books. All classes are conducted as conversations directed by teachers using the Socratic method. In addition to regional accreditation, TAC has baccalaureate program accreditation with AALE. The library contains 48,000 volumes and 7000 audiovisual forms/CDs, and subscribes to 48 periodicals. Computerized library services include the card catalog, interlibrary loans, and database searching. Special learning facilities include a learning resource center. The 170-acre campus is in a rural area 60 miles northwest of Los Angeles. Including residence halls, there are 22 buildings.

Programs of Study: TAC confers the B.A. degree. Bachelor's degrees are awarded in SOCIAL SCIENCE (liberal arts/general studies).

Special: There are no electives, majors, or minors. Students read original writings of Western civilization and discuss them in small seminar-style groups. Many examinations are oral.

Admissions: 81% of the 1999-2000 applicants were accepted. The SAT I scores for the 1999-2000 freshman class were: Verbal--11% between 500 and 599, 60% between 600 and 700, and 29% above 700; Math--3% below 500, 29% between 500 and 599, 57% between 600 and 700, and 11% above 700. The ACT scores were 15% between 21 and 23, 20% between 24 and 26, 30% between 27 and 28, and 35% above 28. There were 3 National Merit finalists and 1 semifinalist. 2 freshmen graduated first in their class.

Requirements: The SAT I or ACT is required. Candidates for admission should have completed 4 years of English, 3 years of math, and 2 years each of a foreign language, history, and science. Important factors in the admissions decision are personality/intangible qualities, advanced placement or honor courses, and recommendations by school officials.

Procedure: Freshmen are admitted in the fall. Entrance exams should be taken by March. There are early admissions and deferred admissions plans. Application deadlines are open. Notification is sent on a rolling basis.

Financial Aid: In 1999-2000, 78% of all freshmen and 85% of continuing students received some form of financial aid. 70% of freshmen and 82% of continuing students received need-based aid. The average freshman award was $13,691. Of that total, scholarships or need-based grants averaged $8076 ($12,064 maximum); loans averaged $2625 (maximum); and work contracts averaged $2990 (maximum). 71% of undergraduates work part time. Average annual earnings from campus work are $2990. The average financial indebtedness of the 1999 graduate was $13,250. TAC is a member of CSS. The FAFSA and the college's own financial statement are required. The fall application deadline is July 1.

Computers: 1 PC is available to students in each of the 7 dormitory buildings; there are 7 student computers in the library for E-mail, word processing, and limited access to the Web. All students may access the system whenever available, or during library hours. There are no time limits and no fees.

TOWSON UNIVERSITY
Towson, MD 21252-0001

(410) 830-2113
(800) (888) 4-TOWSON; Fax: (410) 830-3030

Full-time: 4627 men, 6909 women	**Faculty:** IIA, av$
Part-time: 1039 men, 1406 women	**Ph.D.s:** 79%
Graduate: 585 men, 2081 women	**Student/Faculty:** 16 to 1
Year: semesters, summer session	**Tuition:** $4710 ($11,140)
Application Deadline: May 1	**Room & Board:** $5800
Freshman Class: 7799 applied, 5390 accepted, 2108 enrolled	
SAT I Verbal/Math: 530/540	**ACT:** 20 **VERY COMPETITIVE**

Towson University, founded in 1866, is part of the University System of Maryland and offers undergraduate and graduate programs in liberal arts and sciences, allied health sciences, education, fine arts, communication, and business and economics. There are 6 undergraduate schools and 1 graduate school. In addition to regional accreditation, Towson has baccalaureate program accreditation with AACSB, CAHEA, NASDTEC, NASM, and NLN. The library contains 363,722 volumes, 792,810 microform items, and 17,178 audiovisual forms/CDs, and subscribes to 2302 periodicals. Computerized library services include the card catalog, interlibrary loans, and database searching. Special learning facilities include a learning resource center, art gallery, planetarium, radio station, TV station, curriculum center, herbarium, animal museum, observatory, and greenhouse. The 321-acre campus is in a suburban area 2 miles north of Baltimore. Including residence halls, there are 40 buildings.

Programs of Study: Towson confers B.A., B.S., B.F.A., and B.M. degrees. Master's degrees are also awarded. Bachelor's degrees are awarded in BIOLOGICAL SCIENCE (biology/biological science and molecular biology), BUSINESS (accounting, business administration and management, and sports management), COMMUNICATIONS AND THE ARTS (communications, dance, dramatic arts, English, fine arts, French, German, media arts, music, Spanish, speech/debate/rhetoric, and studio art), COMPUTER AND PHYSICAL SCIENCE (chemistry, computer science, geoscience, information sciences and systems, mathematics, and physics), EDUCATION (art, athletic training, early childhood, education, elementary, music, and physical), ENGINEERING AND ENVIRONMENTAL DESIGN (environmental science), HEALTH PROFESSIONS (exercise science, health, health care administration, medical laboratory technology, nursing, occupational therapy, speech pathology/audiology, and sports medicine), SOCIAL SCIENCE (economics, ethnic studies, family/consumer studies, geography, gerontology, history, interdisciplinary studies, international studies, law, philosophy, physical fitness/movement, political science/government, psychology, religion, social science, sociology, urban studies, and women's studies). Fine arts, business, and education are the strongest academically. Business disciplines, mass communications, and psychology are the largest.

Special: Towson University offers cooperative programs with other institutions in the University System of Maryland and at Loyola College, the College of Notre Dame, or Johns Hopkins University, cross-registration at more than 80 colleges through the National Student Exchange, and study abroad. Students may pursue a dual major in physics and engineering, an interdisciplinary studies degree, which allows them to design their own majors, a 3-2 engineering program with the University of Maryland at College Park, or nondegree study. There are pass/fail options, extensive evening offerings, and opportunities to earn credits between semesters. Internships are available in most majors and work-study programs are offered both on and off campus. There are 20 national honor societies, a freshman honors program, and 12 departmental honors programs.

Admissions: 69% of the 1999-2000 applicants were accepted. The SAT I scores for the 1999-2000 freshman class were: Verbal--28% below 500, 52% between 500 and 599, 18% between 600 and 700, and 2% above 700; Math--27% below 500, 52% between 500 and 599, 19% between 600 and 700, and 2% above 700.

Requirements: The SAT I is required, generally with a composite score of 1100. The ACT is recommended and will be acccepted in lieu of the SAT I. A GPA of 2.8 is required. Applicants should have graduated from an accredited secondary school or earned the GED. Secondary preparation should include 4 years of English, 3 each of math, lab science, and social studies, and 2 of foreign language. Prospective music and dance majors must audition. Applications are accepted via Towson's web site. AP and CLEP credits are accepted. Important factors in the admissions decision are advanced placement or honor courses, recommendations by school officials, and leadership record.

Procedure: Freshmen are admitted fall and spring. Entrance exams should be taken in the junior and senior year. There are early admissions and deferred admissions plans. Applications should be filed by May 1 for fall entry and December 1 for spring entry, along with a $35 fee. Notification is sent on a rolling basis beginning October 1.

Financial Aid: In 1999-2000, 66% of all freshmen and 60% of continuing students received some form of financial aid. 41% of freshmen and 39% of continuing students received need-based aid. The average freshman award was $7488. Of that total, scholarships or need-based grants averaged $3028 ($21,564 maximum); loans averaged $4434 ($19,984 maximum); and work contracts averaged $25 ($7048 maximum). 72% of undergraduates work part time. Average annual earnings from campus work are $1185. The average financial indebtedness of the 1999 graduate was $15,836. Towson is a member of CSS. The FAFSA is required. The fall application deadline is February 15.

Computers: The mainframes are 3 SGI Challenge/IRIX systems, 2 DEC VAX/VMS systems, and 2 DEC 5200/Ultrix systems. Each student receives a computer account that provides E-mail, personal web pages, and access to UNIX System software. There are 65 labs on campus with 1208 total workstations: 1009 PCs, 133 Macs, and 22 UNIX workstations. All students may access the system 24 hours daily except 5 p.m. to 9 p.m. Fridays. There are no time limits and no fees.

TRANSYLVANIA UNIVERSITY
Lexington, KY 40508-1797

(606) 233-8242
(800) 872-6798; Fax: (606) 233-8797

Full-time: 439 men, 624 women	**Faculty:** 70; IIB, ++$
Part-time: 5 men, 4 women	**Ph.D.s:** 96%
Graduate: none	**Student/Faculty:** 15 to 1
Year: 4-4-1, summer session	**Tuition:** $14,600
Application Deadline: March 1	**Room & Board:** $5350
Freshman Class: 1061 applied, 931 accepted, 308 enrolled	
SAT I Verbal/Math: 610/600	**ACT:** 26 **VERY COMPETITIVE+**

Transylvania University, founded in 1780, is an independent liberal arts institution affiliated with the Christian Church (Disciples of Christ). The library contains 118,000 volumes, 65 microform items, and 1768 audiovisual forms/CDs, and subscribes to 540 periodicals. Computerized library services include the card catalog, interlibrary loans, and database searching. Special learning facilities include a learning resource center, art gallery, natural history museum, and radio station. The 48-acre campus is in an urban area 80 miles east of Louisville and 80 miles south of Cincinnati, Ohio. Including residence halls, there are 23 buildings.

Programs of Study: Transylvania confers the B.A. degree. Bachelor's degrees are awarded in BIOLOGICAL SCIENCE (biology/biological science), BUSINESS (accounting and business administration and management), COMMUNICATIONS AND THE ARTS (dramatic arts, English, French, music, Spanish, and studio art), COMPUTER AND PHYSICAL SCIENCE (chemistry, computer science, mathematics, and physics), EDUCATION (elementary and middle school), HEALTH PROFESSIONS (exercise science), SOCIAL SCIENCE (economics, history, philosophy, political science/government, psychology, religion, and sociology). Business, biology, and psychology are the largest.

Special: 3-2 engineering degrees with the University of Kentucky, Vanderbilt University, and Washington University in St. Louis are offered. Cross-registration with May Term Consortium schools, internships, study abroad in many countries, work-study programs, a Washington semester, dual majors, and student-designed majors are available. There are 9 national honor societies.

Admissions: 88% of the 1999-2000 applicants were accepted. The SAT I scores for the 1999-2000 freshman class were: Verbal--15% below 500, 36% between 500 and 599, 34% between 600 and 700, and 15% above 700; Math--17% below 500, 32% between 500 and 599, 40% between 600 and 700, and 11% above 700. The ACT scores were 7% below 21, 14% between 21 and 23, 27% between 24 and 26, 23% between 27 and 28, and 29% above 28. 76% of the current freshmen were in the top fifth of their class; 94% were in the top two fifths. There were 16 National Merit finalists and 3 semifinalists. 31 freshmen graduated first in their class.

Requirements: The SAT I or ACT is required. Transylvania requires applicants to be in the upper 50% of their class. A GPA of 2.8 is required. In addition, 1 essay and 2 recommendations are required. An interview is strongly recommended. Applications are accepted via Transylvania's own on-line application. AP credits are accepted. Important factors in the admissions decision are advanced placement or honor courses, recommendations by school officials, and extracurricular activities record.

Procedure: Freshmen are admitted fall and winter. Entrance exams should be taken during the junior year, no later than December of the senior year for scholarship consideration or February for general admission. There are early admissions and deferred admissions plans. Applications should be filed by March 1 for fall entry and December 5 for winter entry, along with a $20 fee. Notification is sent on a rolling basis. 2% of all applicants are on a waiting list. Note: Applications should be filed by December 1 to be considered for Young and Pioneer scholarships and by February 1 for other merit-based scholarships.

Financial Aid: In 1999-2000, of all freshmen and 97% of continuing students received some form of financial aid. 63% of freshmen and 57% of continuing students received need-based aid. The average freshman award was $13,002. Of that total, scholarships or need-based grants averaged $8982 ($19,950 maximum); loans averaged $2499 ($4625 maximum); and work contracts averaged $1708 ($2000 maximum). 43% of undergraduates work part time. Average annual earnings from campus work are $1640. The average financial indebtedness of the 1999 graduate was $14,978. Transylvania is a member of CSS. The FAFSA is required. The fall application deadline is March 1.

Computers: The mainframe is an IBM 4381. There are about 60 terminals accessing the mainframe and 220 PCs in 8 computer labs available for student use. Word processing, programming languages, statistical software packages, E-mail, and the Internet are available. Computing facilities are available in all academic buildings and residence halls. Students can also access the campus network and the Internet from the dorm rooms. All students may access the system 24 hours a day. There are no time limits and no fees. The school strongly recommends that students have their own IBM personal computers.

TRINITY COLLEGE
Hartford, CT 06106
(860) 297-2180; Fax: (860) 297-2287

Full-time: 1032 men, 930 women	**Faculty:** 169; IIB, ++$
Part-time: 81 men, 126 women	**Ph.D.s:** 93%
Graduate: 110 men, 93 women	**Student/Faculty:** 12 to 1
Year: semesters	**Tuition:** $24,490
Application Deadline: January 15	**Room & Board:** $6890
Freshman Class: 4644 applied, 1855 accepted, 567 enrolled	
SAT I Verbal/Math: 630/640	**ACT:** 28 **HIGHLY COMPETITIVE**

Trinity College, founded in 1823, is an independent, nonsectarian liberal arts college offering a curriculum grounded in the traditional liberal arts with emphases on interdisciplinary studies, science, and engineering. There is 1 graduate school. In addition to regional accreditation, Trinity has baccalaureate program accreditation with ABET. The library contains 950,843 volumes, 383,737 microform items, and 20,309 audiovisual forms/CDs, and subscribes to 2405 periodicals. Computerized library services include the card catalog, interlibrary loans, and database searching. Special learning facilities include an art gallery, radio station, and TV station. Connecticut Public Television and Radio, located on campus, offers internships to Trinity students. The 100-acre campus is in an urban area southwest of downtown Hartford. Including residence halls, there are 76 buildings.

Programs of Study: Trinity confers B.A. and B.S. degrees. Master's degrees are also awarded. Bachelor's degrees are awarded in BIOLOGICAL SCIENCE (biochemistry, biology/biological science, and neurosciences), COMMUNICATIONS AND THE ARTS (art history and appreciation, classics, comparative literature, dance, dramatic arts, English, fine arts, French, German, Italian, modern language, music, Russian, Spanish, studio art, and theater management), COMPUTER AND PHYSICAL SCIENCE (chemistry, computer science, mathematics, and physics), EDUCATION (education), ENGINEERING AND ENVIRONMENTAL DESIGN (engineering), SOCIAL SCIENCE (American studies, anthropology, classical/ancient civilization, economics, history, interdisciplinary studies, international studies, Judaic studies, philosophy, political science/government, psychology, public affairs, religion, sociology, and women's studies). HISTORY, ENGLISH, and economics. are the largest.

Special: Trinity offers special programs for exceptional freshmen, including interdisciplinary studies in the sciences and the humanities. There is an intensive study program under which students can devote a semester to 1 subject. Cross-registration through the Hartford Consortium and the Twelve-College Exchange Program, hundreds of internships, a global study abroad program that includes Italy, South Africa, Trinidad, and Nepal, a Washington semester, dual majors in all disciplines, student-designed majors, nondegree study, and pass/fail options also are offered. A 5-year advanced degree in electrical or mechanical engineering with Rensselaer Polytechnic Institute is available. There are 4 national honor societies, including Phi Beta Kappa.

Admissions: 40% of the 1999-2000 applicants were accepted. The SAT I scores for the 1999-2000 freshman class were: Verbal--3% below 500, 27% between 500 and 599, 56% between 600 and 700, and 14% above 700; Math--6% below

500, 22% between 500 and 599, 58% between 600 and 700, and 14% above 700. The ACT scores were 5% below 21, 5% between 21 and 23, 20% between 24 and 26, 30% between 27 and 28, and 40% above 28. 77% of the current freshmen were in the top fifth of their class; 95% were in the top two fifths.

Requirements: The SAT I or ACT is required, along with the SAT II: Subject test in writing. Trinity strongly emphasizes individual character and personal qualities in admission. Consequently, an interview and essay are recommended. The college requires 4 years of English, 2 years each in foreign language and algebra, and 1 year each in geometry, history, and lab science. Applications are accepted on computer disk via ExPAN, CollegeLink, and Apply. AP credits are accepted. Important factors in the admissions decision are advanced placement or honor courses, extracurricular activities record, and evidence of special talent.

Procedure: Freshmen are admitted in the fall. Entrance exams should be taken in the fall of the senior year. There are early decision, early admissions, and deferred admissions plans. Early decision applications should be filed by November 15; regular applications, by January 15 for fall entry, along with a $50 fee. Notification of early decision is sent December 20; regular decision, April 2. 198 early decision candidates were accepted for the 1999-2000 class. 26% of all applicants are on a waiting list.

Financial Aid: In 1999-2000, 47% of all freshmen and 41% of continuing students received some form of financial aid, including need-based aid. The average freshman award was $20,014. Of that total, scholarships or need-based grants averaged $16,845 ($32,525 maximum); loans averaged $2048 ($5625 maximum); work contracts averaged $786 ($1500 maximum); and other unsubsidized loans averaged $10,460 ($31,250 maximum). 68% of undergraduates work part time. Average annual earnings from campus work are $1213. The average financial indebtedness of the 1999 graduate was $12,953. Trinity is a member of CSS. The CSS/Profile or FAFSA is required. The fall application deadline is February 1.

Computers: The mainframe is a Sun SPARC network. All dormitory rooms are equipped with Ethernet connections. In addition, more than 200 public workstations of various types are available for student use; all can access the Internet and campus-based network resources. The campus network supports UNIX, Windows 95, Windows NT, and Mac workstations. All students have E-mail accounts, and all are entitled to a personal home page on a campus server. All students may access the system 24 hours daily. There are no time limits and no fees. The college strongly recommends that all students have PCs. Either Windows 95 PCs or Macs are supported on the dormitory network.

TRINITY UNIVERSITY
San Antonio, TX 78212-7200

(210) 999-7207
(800) TRINITY; Fax: (210) 999-8164

Full-time: 1108 men, 1193 women	**Faculty:** 204; IIA, ++$
Part-time: 24 men, 20 women	**Ph.D.s:** 99%
Graduate: 84 men, 150 women	**Student/Faculty:** 11 to 1
Year: semesters, summer session	**Tuition:** $15,264
Application Deadline: February 1	**Room & Board:** $6180
Freshman Class: 2743 applied, 2076 accepted, 637 enrolled	
SAT I Verbal/Math: 630/640	**ACT:** 28 **HIGHLY COMPETITIVE**

Trinity University, founded in 1869, is a liberal arts and sciences institution affiliated with the Presbyterian Church (U.S.A.). There is 1 graduate school. In addition to regional accreditation, Trinity has baccalaureate program accreditation with AACSB, ABET, NASM, and NCATE. The library contains 854,825 volumes, 274,012 microform items, and 22,976 audiovisual forms/CDs, and subscribes to 2456 periodicals. Computerized library services include the card catalog, interlibrary loans, and database searching. Special learning facilities include a radio station and TV station. The 117-acre campus is in a suburban area 3 miles north of downtown San Antonio. Including residence halls, there are 45 buildings.

Programs of Study: Trinity confers B.A., B.S., and B.M. degrees. Master's degrees are also awarded. Bachelor's degrees are awarded in BIOLOGICAL SCIENCE (biochemistry and biology/biological science), BUSINESS (business administration and management), COMMUNICATIONS AND THE ARTS (communications, dramatic arts, English, French, German, music, Russian, Spanish, and speech/debate/rhetoric), COMPUTER AND PHYSICAL SCIENCE (chemistry, computer science, geoscience, mathematics, and physics), EDUCATION (art and foreign languages), ENGINEERING AND ENVIRONMENTAL DESIGN (engineering and applied science), SOCIAL SCIENCE (anthropology, economics, history, international relations, philosophy, political science/government, psychology, religion, sociology, and urban studies). Business, communication, and biology are the largest.

Special: The university offers study abroad in 35 countries. A Washington semester, dual majors, and pass/fail options are also available, as are teacher certification and a liberal arts/career combination. There are 5 national honor societies, including Phi Beta Kappa, and 14 departmental honors programs.

Admissions: 76% of the 1999-2000 applicants were accepted. The SAT I scores for the 1999-2000 freshman class were: Verbal--2% below 500, 29% between 500 and 599, 52% between 600 and 700, and 17% above 700; Math--1% below 500, 25% between 500 and 599, 61% between 600 and 700, and 13% above 700. The ACT scores were 1% below 21, 8% between 21 and 23, 28% between 24 and 26, 24% between 27 and 28, and 39% above 28. 72% of the current freshmen were in the top fifth of their class; 97% were in the top two fifths. There were 22 National Merit finalists. 26 freshmen graduated first in their class.

Requirements: The SAT I or ACT is required. At high school graduation, applicants should have completed 4 years of English, 3 1/2 of math, 3 each of lab science and social studies, and 2 of foreign language. A personal essay, an official high school transcript, a recommendation from a high school counselor, and a teacher's evaluation are also required. A campus visit and a visit with the university's counselor are also recommended. Applications are accepted on-line at the school's web site. AP credits are accepted.

Procedure: Freshmen are admitted fall, spring, and summer. Entrance exams should be taken late in the junior year or early in the senior year. There are early decision and deferred admissions plans. Early decision applications should be filed by November 15; regular applications, by February 1 for fall entry and November 15 for spring entry, along with a $30 fee. Notification of early decision is sent December 15; regular decision, April 1. 63 early decision candidates were accepted for the 1999-2000 class. 5% of all applicants are on a waiting list.

Financial Aid: In 1999-2000, 84% of all freshmen and 79% of continuing students received some form of financial aid. 45% of freshmen and 40% of continuing students received need-based aid. The average freshman award was $15,258. Of that total, scholarships or need-based grants averaged $10,508; loans averaged $2800; work contracts averaged $1218; and external awards averaged $7320. Average annual earnings from campus work are $1410. The average financial indebtedness of the 1999 graduate was $14,000. Trinity is a member of CSS. The CSS/Profile and FAFSA are required. The fall application deadline is February 1.

Computers: There are 3 general-use computing labs containing 60 Windows NT-based systems (with Pentium or Pentium II processors) and 15 Mac systems (with Power PC processors). All of these systems are connected to the campus network and have access to a suite of application software, including Microsoft Word, Excel, PowerPoint, Access, SPSS/PS, and utilities for Internet access. Laser printers are available in each lab. Access to the campus network and to the Internet is available in all residence halls for a small semester charge. All students may access the system 24 hours per day. There are no time limits. It is strongly recommended that all students have personal computers.

TRUMAN STATE UNIVERSITY
Kirksville, MO 63501

(660) 785-4114
(800) 892-7792; Fax: (660) 785-7456

Full-time: 2414 men, 3375 women	**Faculty:** 353; IIA, -$
Part-time: 82 men, 90 women	**Ph.D.s:** 82%
Graduate: 60 men, 167 women	**Student/Faculty:** 16 to 1
Year: semesters, summer session	**Tuition:** $3936 ($6462)
Application Deadline: March 1	**Room & Board:** $4400
Freshman Class: 5159 applied, 4166 accepted, 1472 enrolled	
ACT: 27	**VERY COMPETITIVE+**

Truman State University, founded in 1867, and formerly known as Northeast Missouri State University, is a public liberal arts institution offering undergraduate and graduate degree programs in business and accountancy, education, fine arts, human potential and performance, language and literature, mathematics and computer science, science, and social science. There are 7 undergraduate and 9 graduate schools. In addition to regional accreditation, Truman has baccalaureate program accreditation with AACSB, ASLA, NASM, NCATE, and NLN. The library contains 410,251 volumes, 1,477,304 microform items, and 17,878 audiovisual forms/CDs, and subscribes to 3427 periodicals. Computerized library services include the card catalog, interlibrary loans, and database searching. Special learning facilities include a learning resource center, art gallery, radio station, TV studio, a biofeedback lab, an independent learning center for nursing students, an observatory, and a greenhouse chamber. The 140-acre campus is in a small town 170 miles northeast of Kansas City and 200 miles north of St. Louis. Including residence halls, there are 39 buildings.

Programs of Study: Truman confers B.A., B.S., B.F.A., B.M., and B.S.N. degrees. Master's degrees are also awarded. Bachelor's degrees are awarded in AGRICULTURE (agricultural economics, agriculture, agronomy, animal science, and equine science), BIOLOGICAL SCIENCE (biology/biological science), BUSINESS (accounting and business administration and management), COMMUNICATIONS AND THE ARTS (art, art history and appreciation, classics, communications, dramatic arts, English, fine arts, French, German, journalism, music, music performance, Russian, Spanish, and speech/debate/rhetoric), COMPUTER AND PHYSICAL SCIENCE (chemistry, computer science, mathematics, and physics), EDUCATION (physical), ENGINEERING AND ENVIRONMENTAL DESIGN (preengineering), HEALTH PROFESSIONS (health science, medical technology, nursing, physical therapy, predentistry, premedicine, preoptometry, prepharmacy, preveterinary science, and speech pathology/audiology), SOCIAL SCIENCE (criminal justice, economics, history, philosophy, physical fitness/movement, political science/government, prelaw, psychology, religion, and sociology). Chemistry, physics, and mathematics are the strongest academically. Business administration, biology, and psychology are the largest.

Special: Study abroad in 49 countries is offered through Truman's own programs and those of the College Consortium for International Studies, the Council on International Educational Exchange, and the International Student Exchange Program. The university requires internships in education and agricultural science, but also offers voluntary legislative internships at the state capitol, and internships through the Wasington Center. There is a 2-2 engineering program with the University of Missouri's Rolla and Columbia campuses. Work-study programs, B.A.-B.S. degrees, dual majors, student-designed majors in health and exercise science, credit for military experience, pass/fail options for internships, and non-degree study are available. There are 13 national honor societies, a freshman honors program, and 11 departmental honors programs.

Admissions: 81% of the 1999-2000 applicants were accepted. The ACT scores for the 1999-2000 freshman class were: 1% below 21, 11% between 21 and 23, 34% between 24 and 26, 20% between 27 and 28, and 34% above 28. 74% of the current freshmen were in the top fifth of their class; 96% were in the top two fifths. There were 18 National Merit finalists. 137 freshmen graduated first in their class.

Requirements: The SAT I or ACT is required. Truman requires applicants to be in the upper 70% of their class. A GPA of 2.8 is required. The University prefers the ACT, with a recommended minimum score of 22. Recommended minimum composite score on the SAT I is 960, or 480 on each part. Applicants should have completed 4 units of English, 3 each of science and social studies, 2 of foreign language, and 1 of art or music, 4 units of math are strongly recommended. An essay is required and an interview or visit is recommended. Applications are accepted on-line via Apply, Next Stop College, CollegeLink, or the school's web site. AP and CLEP credits are accepted. Important factors in the admissions decision are leadership record, advanced placement or honor courses, and extracurricular activities record.

Procedure: Freshmen are admitted to all sessions. Entrance exams should be taken during the spring or summer following the junior year. There are early admissions and deferred admissions plans. Early decision applications should be filed by November 15; regular applications, by March 1 for fall entry. Notification of early decision is sent December 15; regular decision, on a rolling basis.

Financial Aid: In 1999-2000, 95% of all freshmen and 87% of continuing students received some form of financial aid. 31% of freshmen and 34% of continuing students received need-based aid. The average freshman award was $5342. Of that total, scholarships or need-based grants averaged $4004 ($10,744 maximum); loans averaged $3326 ($12,300 maximum); and work contracts averaged $860 ($3296 maximum). 67% of undergraduates work part time. Average annual earnings from campus work was $860. The average financial indebtedness of the 1999 graduate was $14,980. Truman is a member of CSS. The CSS/Profile, FAFSA, FFS, or SFS is required. The fall application deadline is April 1.

Computers: The mainframe is an IBM 4361. Students have access to both mainframe and PC-based networks. All students receive free computer accounts for E-mail, printing, and saving files. Approximately 230 workstations are available for student use; PCs are located in 8 residence halls and most academic buildings, and there are 2 large computer labs on campus. All residence hall rooms are wired for network connections. All students may access the system. Labs are open until midnight in the academic buildings, and 2 a.m. in the library. Residence hall labs have extended hours, and dial-ins with modems provide 24-hour access. An individual time limit of 30 minutes is imposed only when other students are waiting. There are no fees.

Full-time: 2333 men, 2598 women	**Faculty:** 371; I, av$
Part-time: 28 men, 18 women	**Ph.D.s:** 99%
Graduate: 1921 men, 2371 women	**Student/Faculty:** 13 to 1
Year: semesters, summer session	**Tuition:** $24,751
Application Deadline: January 1	**Room & Board:** $7375
Freshman Class: 13,471 applied, 4313 accepted, 1347 enrolled	

MOST COMPETITIVE

Tufts University, founded in 1852, is a private institution offering undergraduate programs in liberal arts and sciences and engineering. There are 2 undergraduate and 9 graduate schools. In addition to regional accreditation, Tufts has baccalaureate program accreditation with ABET, ADA, and CAHEA. The 2 libraries contain 965,000 volumes, 1,180,000 microform items, and 28,700 audiovisual forms/CDs, and subscribe to 5630 periodicals. Computerized library services include the card catalog, interlibrary loans, and database searching. Special learning facilities include a learning resource center, art gallery, radio station, TV station, and theater. The 140-acre campus is in a suburban area 5 miles northwest of Boston. Including residence halls, there are 167 buildings.

Programs of Study: Tufts confers B.A., B.S., B.S.C.E., B.S.Ch.E., B.S.Comp. Eng., B.S.E., B.S.E.E., B.S.E.S., B.S.Environmental Eng., and B.S.M.E. degrees. Master's and doctoral degrees are also awarded. Bachelor's degrees are awarded in BIOLOGICAL SCIENCE (biology/biological science), COMMUNICATIONS AND THE ARTS (art history and appreciation, classics, dramatic arts, English, French, German, Greek, Latin, music, Russian, and Spanish), COMPUTER AND PHYSICAL SCIENCE (chemistry, computer science, geology, mathematics, and physics), EDUCATION (early childhood), ENGINEERING AND ENVIRONMENTAL DESIGN (chemical engineering, civil engineering, computer engineering, electrical/electronics engineering, engineering, engineering and applied science, engineering physics, environmental science, and mechanical engineering), SOCIAL SCIENCE (American studies, anthropology, archeology, Asian/Oriental studies, clinical psychology, economics, experimental psychology, history, international relations, philosophy, political science/government, psychobiology, psychology, religion, Russian and Slavic studies, social psychology, and sociology). Biology, international relations, and English are the largest.

Special: The university offers cross-registration at Swarthmore College, Boston University, Boston College, and Brandeis University, a Washington semester, and study abroad in England, Spain, France, Moscow, Chile, Japan, Ghana, and Germany. Many internships are available. Double majors in the liberal arts are common; student-designed majors are possible. There is a 5-year B.A./M.A. or B.S./M.S. program in engineering or liberal arts, a B.A.-B.F.A. program with the Museum School of Fine Arts, and a B.A.-B.M. program with the New England Conservatory of Music. Pass/fail options are offered. There are 4 national honor societies, including Phi Beta Kappa.

Admissions: 32% of the 1999-2000 applicants were accepted. The SAT I scores for the 1999-2000 freshman class were: Verbal--1% below 500, 15% between 500 and 599, 56% between 600 and 700, and 29% above 700; Math--1% below 500, 10% between 500 and 599, 54% between 600 and 700, and 35% above 700. The ACT scores were 1% between 21 and 23, 19% between 24 and 26, 23% between 27 and 28, and 57% above 28. 90% of the current freshmen were in the top fifth of their class; 98% were in the top two fifths.

Requirements: The university accepts either the SAT I and the results of 3 SAT II: Subject tests, or the ACT. Liberal arts applicants should take the SAT II: Subject test in writing and 2 others; engineering applicants should take writing, math level I or II, and either physics or chemistry. In addition, all applicants should be high school graduates or hold the GED. Academic preparation is expected to include 4 years of English, 3 years each of humanities and a foreign language, 2 years each of social and natural sciences, and 1 year of history. A personal essay is required. Tufts provides an on-line Embark application via its web site, http://www.tufts.edu. AP credits are accepted. Important factors in the admissions decision are advanced placement or honor courses, recommendations by school officials, and extracurricular activities record.

Procedure: Freshmen are admitted in the fall. Entrance exams should be taken by January of the senior year. There are early decision, early admissions, and deferred admissions plans. Early decision applications should be filed by November 15 for round 1 and January 1 for round 2; regular applications, by January 1 for fall entry, along with a $55 fee. Notification of early decision is sent December 15 for round 1 and February 1 for round 2; regular decision, April 1. 450 early decision candidates were accepted for the 1999-2000 class. A waiting list is an active part of the admissions procedure.

Financial Aid: In a recent year, 40% of all freshmen and 42% of continuing students received some form of financial aid. 33% of freshmen and 38% of continuing students received need-based aid. The average freshman award was $18,048. Of that total, scholarships or need-based grants averaged $15,400 ($29,300 maximum); loans averaged $3525 ($4125 maximum); and work contracts averaged $1715 ($2000 maximum). 40% of undergraduates work part time. Average annual earnings from campus work are $1350. The average financial indebtedness of a recent year graduate was $14,564. Tufts is a member of CSS. The CSS/Profile or FAFSA is required. The fall application deadline is February 15.

Computers: The mainframes are a DEC ALPHA Server 8200 with 4 ALPHA processors and a DEC MicroVAX 3600 processor; the machines operate on VMS and UNIX. Mainframes and PC labs are networked on a universitywide computer network called Jumbonet. There are 254 terminals and PCs in 5 locations across campus, supported by 45 printers in various locations. A special computer-aided design (CAD) lab is available to undergraduates. All campus residence rooms are hard-wired for access to the university computer facilities and the Internet. All students may access the system 24 hours a day. There are no time limits and no fees.

TULANE UNIVERSITY
New Orleans, LA 70118

(504) 865-5731
(800) 873-9283; Fax: (504) 862-8715

Full-time: 2764 men, 2857 women	**Faculty:** 514; I, av$
Part-time: 635 men, 914 women	**Ph.D.s:** 91%
Graduate: 2484 men, 2291 women	**Student/Faculty:** 11 to 1
Year: semesters, summer session	**Tuition:** $24,214
Application Deadline: January 15	**Room & Board:** $6700
Freshman Class: 8189 applied, 6347 accepted, 1535 enrolled	
SAT I Verbal/Math: 641/655	**HIGHLY COMPETITIVE**

Tulane University, founded in 1834, is a private institution offering degree programs in liberal arts and sciences, business, architecture, and engineering. There are 6 undergraduate and 8 graduate schools. In addition to regional accreditation, Tulane has baccalaureate program accreditation with AACSB, ABET, CSAB,

CSWE, and NAAB. The 8 libraries contain 2,116,015 volumes, 1,253,648 micro-form items, and 83,774 audiovisual forms/CDs, and subscribe to 14,986 periodicals. Computerized library services include the card catalog, interlibrary loans, and database searching. Special learning facilities include a learning resource center, art gallery, planetarium, radio station, and TV station. The 110-acre campus is in an urban area in uptown New Orleans. Including residence halls, there are 70 buildings.

Programs of Study: Tulane confers B.A., B.S., B.Arch., B.F.A., B.G.S., B.S.E., and B.S.M. degrees. Associate, master's, and doctoral degrees are also awarded. Bachelor's degrees are awarded in BIOLOGICAL SCIENCE (biochemistry, cell biology, ecology, and evolutionary biology), BUSINESS (accounting, business administration and management, management science, marketing management, and sports management), COMMUNICATIONS AND THE ARTS (art history and appreciation, classics, communications, dramatic arts, English, French, German, Greek, Italian, Latin, linguistics, media arts, music, music history and appreciation, Portuguese, Russian, Spanish, and studio art), COMPUTER AND PHYSICAL SCIENCE (chemistry, computer science, earth science, geology, information sciences and systems, mathematics, and physics), EDUCATION (early childhood), ENGINEERING AND ENVIRONMENTAL DESIGN (architecture, biomedical engineering, chemical engineering, civil engineering, computer engineering, electrical/electronics engineering, engineering, environmental engineering, environmental science, and mechanical engineering), SOCIAL SCIENCE (American studies, anthropology, Asian/Oriental studies, cognitive science, economics, history, international relations, Judaic studies, Latin American studies, medieval studies, philosophy, political science/government, psychology, religion, Russian and Slavic studies, sociology, and women's studies). Environmental sciences, political economy, and preprofessional programs are the strongest academically. English, psychology, and biology are the largest.

Special: Cross-registration with Loyola and Xavier universities, numerous internships, study abroad in 15 countries, work-study programs, a Washington semester, and B.A.-B.S. degrees in liberal arts, engineering, and architecture are offered. Accelerated joint degrees with Tulane's schools of medicine, law, business and public health, student-designed, dual, and interdisciplinary majors, including art and biology, Greek and Latin, mathematical economics, political economy, and cognitive studies, and a 3-2 engineering degree with Loyola University in New Orleans are available. There are 32 national honor societies, including Phi Beta Kappa, and a freshman honors program.

Admissions: 78% of the 1999-2000 applicants were accepted. The SAT I scores for the 1999-2000 freshman class were: Verbal--1% below 500, 20% between 500 and 599, 49% between 600 and 700, and 31% above 700; Math--1% below 500, 25% between 500 and 599, 52% between 600 and 700, and 21% above 700. 78% of the current freshmen were in the top fifth of their class; 96% were in the top two fifths.

Requirements: The SAT I or ACT is required. Applicants must be graduates of an accredited secondary school or have a GED certificate. It is recommended that students have completed 4 years each of high school English and math and 3 each of foreign language, social studies, and the sciences. SAT II: Subject tests in writing, math, and foreign language are recommended for placement purposes and are required for home-schooled applicants. An essay is required. A portfolio is recommended for architecture applicants only. Applications printed from disks are accepted. The application form is available on-line via Embark.com, Apply, and Common Application. AP credits are accepted. Important factors in the admissions decision are advanced placement or honor courses, recommendations by school officials, and extracurricular activities record.

Procedure: Freshmen are admitted fall and spring. Entrance exams should be taken during the spring of the junior year or the fall of the senior year. There are early decision, early admissions, and deferred admissions plans. Early decision applications should be filed by November 1; regular applications, by January 15 for fall entry and November 1 for spring entry, along with a $45 fee. Notification of early decision is sent December 15; regular decision, by April 1. 1092 early action candidates were accepted for the 1999-2000 class.

Financial Aid: In 1999-2000, 74% of all freshmen and 66% of continuing students received some form of financial aid. 39% of freshmen and 46% of continuing students received need-based aid. The average freshman award was $19,634. Of that total, scholarships or need-based grants averaged $14,899 ($24,000 maximum); loans averaged $3534 ($5625 maximum); and work contracts averaged $1202 ($1700 maximum). 40% of undergraduates work part time. Average annual earnings from campus work are $960. The average financial indebtedness of the 1999 graduate was $19,781. Tulane is a member of CSS. The CSS/Profile or FAFSA is required. The fall application deadline is December 15.

Computers: The mainframe is a cluster of 8 IBM RS/6000s. There are 22 computer labs on campus housing more than 250 workstations, all of which are connected to the university network. Access to the mainframe is possible from any terminal, PC, or workstation and from residence hall rooms if students have their own PCs. The university network extends to all campus buildings. Each residence hall room has a data connection for each PC and a cable television connection. All students may access the system 24 hours a day. There are no time limits and no fees. It is strongly recommended that all students have personal computers.

UNION COLLEGE
Schenectady, NY 12308-2311　　　　　　　　**(518) 388-6112**
(800) (888) 843-6688; Fax: (518) 388-6986

Full-time: 1095 men, 1013 women	**Faculty:** 189; IIA, ++$
Part-time: 34 men, 8 women	**Ph.D.s:** 98%
Graduate: 170 men, 112 women	**Student/Faculty:** 11 to 1
Year: trimesters, summer session	**Tuition:** $24,099
Application Deadline: February 1	**Room & Board:** $6474
Freshman Class: 3761 applied, 1745 accepted, 535 enrolled	
SAT I Verbal/Math: 600/630	**ACT:** 26　**HIGHLY COMPETITIVE**

Union College, founded in 1795, is an independent liberal arts and engineering college. There is 1 graduate school. In addition to regional accreditation, Union has baccalaureate program accreditation with ABET. The library contains 281,165 volumes, 741,695 microform items, and 6799 audiovisual forms/CDs, and subscribes to 5289 periodicals. Computerized library services include the card catalog, interlibrary loans, and database searching. Special learning facilities include a radio station, theater, a high technology classroom, and lab center. The 100-acre campus is in an urban area 15 miles west of Albany. Including residence halls, there are 97 buildings.

Programs of Study: Union confers B.A., B.S., B.S.C.E., B.S.C.S.E., B.S.E.E., and B.S.M.E. degrees. Master's degrees are also awarded. Bachelor's degrees are awarded in BIOLOGICAL SCIENCE (biochemistry and biology/biological science), COMMUNICATIONS AND THE ARTS (classics, English, fine arts, modern language, and visual and performing arts), COMPUTER AND PHYSICAL SCIENCE (chemistry, computer science, geology, mathematics, physics, and science), ENGINEERING AND ENVIRONMENTAL DESIGN (civil engineering, electrical/electronics engineering, and mechanical engineering), SO-CIAL SCIENCE (American studies, anthropology, economics, history, humanities, liberal arts/general studies, philosophy, political science/government, psychology, social science, sociology, and women's studies). Math, chemistry, and classics are the strongest academically. Biology, political science, and psychology are the largest.

Special: Cross-registration is permitted with the Hudson Mohawk Consortium. Opportunities are provided for legislative internships in Albany and Washington, D.C. Union also offers pass/fail options, B.A.-B.S. degrees, dual and student-designed majors, a Washington semester, accelerated degree programs in law and medicine, and study abroad in 25 countries. There are 12 national honor societies, including Phi Beta Kappa, a freshman honors program, and 11 departmental honors programs.

Admissions: 46% of the 1999-2000 applicants were accepted. The SAT I scores for the 1999-2000 freshman class were: Verbal--4% below 500, 40% between 500 and 599, 48% between 600 and 700, and 7% above 700; Math--2% below 500, 30% between 500 and 599, 54% between 600 and 700, and 14% above 700. 77% of the current freshmen were in the top quarter of their class; 98% were in the top two half. There was 1 National Merit finalist.

Requirements: The SAT I or ACT is required. In place of these, 3 SAT II: Subject tests may be submitted, including 1 in writing. Graduation from an accredited secondary school is required. Applicants must submit a minimum of 16 full-year credits, distributed as follows: 4 years of English, 2 of a foreign language, 2 1/2 to 3 1/2 years of math, 2 years each of science and social studies, and the remainder in college-preparatory courses. Engineering and math majors are expected to have completed additional math and science courses beyond the minimum requirements. An essay is also required, and an interview is recommended. Applications prepared on the computer are accepted. AP credits are accepted. Important factors in the admissions decision are advanced placement or honor courses, recommendations by school officials, and extracurricular activities record.

Procedure: Freshmen are admitted in the fall. Entrance exams should be taken by January of the senior year. There are early decision, early admissions, and deferred admissions plans. Early decision applications should be filed by November 15; regular applications, by February 1 for fall entry, along with a $50 fee. Notification of early decision is sent December 15; regular decision, April 1. 165 early decision candidates were accepted for the 1999-2000 class. 27% of all applicants are on a waiting list.

Financial Aid: In 1999-2000, 58% of all students received some form of financial aid, including need-based aid. The average freshman award was $22,000. Of that total, scholarships or need-based grants averaged $17,900 ($30,440 maximum); loans averaged $2900 ($4625 maximum); and work contracts averaged $1200. 33% of undergraduates work part time. Average annual earnings from campus work are $900. The average financial indebtedness of the 1999 graduate was $16,700. Union is a member of CSS. The CSS/Profile or FAFSA is required. The fall application deadline is February 1.

Computers: The mainframes are 8 Compaq ALPHA servers and 6 Windows NT servers. There are more than 1,000 PCs and workstations on campus linking classrooms, labs, offices, and residence hall rooms. There are also 19 electronic classrooms. Departmental computer labs offer Windows and Mac-based systems. 3 computer labs are available 24 hours per day. Internet access is available through the colleg's membership in NYSERnet. Other on-line resources can be accessed from any point on the network. The college maintains a web page, at http://www.union.edu/. All students may access the system 24 hours per day, 7 days a week. There are no time limits and no fees.

UNITED STATES AIR FORCE ACADEMY

USAFA, CO 80840-5025

(719) 333-2520
(800) 443-9266; Fax: (719) 333-3012

Full-time: 3487 men, 674 women	**Faculty:** 577
Part-time: none	**Ph.D.s:** 50%
Graduate: none	**Student/Faculty:** 7 to 1
Year: semesters, summer session	**Tuition:** see profile
Application Deadline: January 31	**Room & Board:** n/app
Freshman Class: 8828 applied, 1762 accepted, 1335 enrolled	
SAT I Verbal/Math: 629/654	**ACT:** 28 **MOST COMPETITIVE**

The United States Air Force Academy, the newest of the United States service academies, was founded in 1954 and is a public institution. Graduates receive the B.S. degree and a second lieutenant's commission in the regular Air Force. All graduates are obligated to serve at least 5 years of active duty military service. Tuition, room, board, medical, and dental expenses are paid by the U.S. government. Each cadet receives a monthly salary from which to pay for uniforms, supplies, and personal expenses. Entering freshman are required to deposit $2,500 to defray the initial costs of uniforms and personal expenses incurred upon entry. Students who are unable to submit the full deposit will receive a reduced monthly cash allotment until prescribed levels are reached. In addition to regional accreditation, USAFA has baccalaureate program accreditation with ABET and CSAB. The 3 libraries contain 688,801 volumes, 621,792 microform items, and 4860 audiovisual forms/CDs, and subscribe to 2106 periodicals. Computerized library services include the card catalog, interlibrary loans, and database searching. Special learning facilities include a learning resource center, art gallery, planetarium, radio station, TV station, a field engineering and readiness lab, and an aeronautics lab/aeronautical research center. The 18,000-acre campus is in a suburban area 70 miles south of downtown Denver and 8 miles north of downtown Colorado Springs. Including residence halls, there are 12 buildings.

Programs of Study: USAFA confers the B.S. degree. Bachelor's degrees are awarded in BIOLOGICAL SCIENCE (biology/biological science), BUSINESS (management science and operations research), COMMUNICATIONS AND THE ARTS (English), COMPUTER AND PHYSICAL SCIENCE (atmospheric sciences and meteorology, chemistry, computer science, mathematics, physics, and science), ENGINEERING AND ENVIRONMENTAL DESIGN (aeronautical engineering, aerospace studies, civil engineering, computer engineering, electrical/electronics engineering, engineering, engineering and applied science, engineering mechanics, environmental engineering, mechanical engineering, and military science), SOCIAL SCIENCE (behavioral science, economics, geography, history, humanities, international studies, law, political science/government, psychology, and social science). Engineering and basic sciences are the strongest academically. Management, biology, and operations research are the largest.

Special: All cadets receive orientation flights in Air Force aircraft and take aviation science courses. A semester exchange program is available with the French Air Force Academy and U.S. Army, Naval, and Coast Guard academies. Freshman classes start in June, and basic cadet training must be completed before academics begin in August. Work-study programs are available, and dual majors are possible in all areas. There is an interdisciplinary space operations major. There are 2 national honor societies.

Admissions: 20% of the 1999-2000 applicants were accepted. The SAT I scores for the 1999-2000 freshman class were: Verbal--2% below 500, 28% between 500 and 599, 54% between 600 and 700, and 16% above 700; Math--13% between 500 and 599, 64% between 600 and 700, and 23% above 700. 80% of the current freshmen were in the top fifth of their class; 87% were in the top two fifths. There were 36 National Merit finalists and 35 semifinalists. 121 freshmen graduated first in their class.

Requirements: The SAT I or ACT is required. Candidates must be U.S. citizens between 17 and 22 years of age, unmarried and with no dependents, and nominated from a legal source. Students should have completed 4 years each of English, math, and lab sciences, and 2 years each of social sciences and foreign languages. A computer course is recommended. A personal interview is required, as is an essay and a drug and alcohol abuse certificate. AP credits are accepted. Important factors in the admissions decision are personality/intangible qualities, advanced placement or honor courses, and leadership record.

Procedure: Freshmen are admitted in the summer. Entrance exams should be taken in the spring of the junior year. Applications should be filed by January 31 for fall entry. Notification is sent April 1.

Computers: The mainframes are a Unisys and an HP. All cadets reimburse the academy for a PC upon entry. These PCs are all networked to a 10,000 drop fiberoptic LAN called USAFANET. Gateways to the Internet are provided as well, and cadets have limited access to the Unisys. All students may access the system 24 hours per day. There are no time limits and no fees. All students are required to have personal computers.

UNITED STATES COAST GUARD ACADEMY
New London, CT 06320-4195

(860) 444-8500
(800) 883-8724; Fax: (860) 701-6700

Full-time: 599 men, 231 women	**Faculty:** 112
Part-time: none	**Ph.D.s:** 30%
Graduate: none	**Student/Faculty:** 7 to 1
Year: semesters, summer session	**Tuition:** see profile
Application Deadline: December 15	**Room & Board:** n/app
Freshman Class: 2150 applied, 522 accepted, 321 enrolled	
SAT I Verbal/Math: 620/640	**ACT:** 26 **MOST COMPETITIVE**

The U.S. Coast Guard Academy, founded in 1876, is an Armed Forces Service Academy for men and women. Appointments are made solely on the basis of an annual nationwide competition. Except for an entrance fee of $3,000, the federal government covers all cadet expenses by providing a monthly allowance of $600 plus a daily food allowance. In addition to regional accreditation, the academy has baccalaureate program accreditation with ABET. The library contains 150,000 volumes, 60,000 microform items, and 1500 audiovisual forms/CDs, and subscribes to 850 periodicals. Computerized library services include the card catalog, interlibrary loans, and database searching. Special learning facilities include the Coast Guard Museum, a $5 million bridge simulator, and the Leadership Development Center for the Coast Guard. The 110-acre campus is in a suburban area 45 miles southeast of Hartford. Including residence halls, there are 25 buildings.

Programs of Study: The academy confers the B.S. degree. Bachelor's degrees are awarded in BIOLOGICAL SCIENCE (marine science), BUSINESS (management science and operations research), ENGINEERING AND ENVIRONMENTAL DESIGN (civil engineering, electrical/electronics engineering, mechanical engineering, and naval architecture and marine engineering), SOCIAL SCIENCE (political science/government). Political science/government is the largest.

Special: Cross-registration with Connecticut College, summer cruises to foreign ports, 6-week internships with various government agencies, and a 1-semester exchange program with the 3 other military academies are available. All graduates are commissioned in the U.S. Coast Guard. There are 2 national honor societies, a freshman honors program, and 3 departmental honors programs.

Admissions: 24% of the 1999-2000 applicants were accepted. The SAT I scores for the 1999-2000 freshman class were: Verbal--4% below 500, 31% between 500 and 599, 51% between 600 and 700, and 14% above 700; Math--1% below 500, 22% between 500 and 599, 61% between 600 and 700, and 16% above 700. 76% of the current freshmen were in the top fifth of their class; 92% were in the top two fifths. 9 freshmen graduated first in their class.

Requirements: The SAT I or ACT is required. Applicants must have reached the age of 17 but not the age of 22 by July 1 of the year of admission, be citizens of the United States, be single at the time of appointment and remain single while attending the academy. Required secondary school courses include 3 years each of English and math. Applications are accepted on-line. AP credits are accepted. Important factors in the admissions decision are leadership record, recommendations by school officials, and advanced placement or honor courses.

Procedure: Freshmen are admitted in the summer. Entrance exams should be taken by December 15. There is an early admissions plan. Applications should be filed by December 15 for fall entry. Notification is sent on a rolling basis. 5% of all applicants are on a waiting list.

Computers: Students may use computer rooms in the dormitories and academic building. Access to the Sun Model 10 main server is also available. All students receive a laptop computer upon entering the academy. All rooms are wired for Internet access. All students may access the system 24 hours a day. There are no time limits and no fees.

UNITED STATES MERCHANT MARINE ACADEMY
Kings Point, NY 11024-1699

(516) 773-5391
(800) 732-6267; Fax: (516) 773-5390

Full-time: 840 men, 100 women	**Faculty:** 74
Part-time: none	**Ph.D.s:** 85%
Graduate: none	**Student/Faculty:** 13 to 1
Year: semesters	**Tuition:** see profile
Application Deadline: March 1	**Room & Board:** n/app
Freshman Class: 910 applied, 430 accepted, 276 enrolled	
SAT I Verbal/Math: 608/610	**HIGHLY COMPETITIVE**

The United States Merchant Marine Academy, founded in 1943, is a publicly supported institution offering maritime, military, and engineering programs for the purpose of training officers for the U.S. merchant marine and the maritime industry. Students may have no conventional tuition and board payments. Required fees for freshmen are $4800; costs in subsequent years are less. In addition to regional accreditation, Kings Point has baccalaureate program accreditation with ABET. The library contains 225,000 volumes, 110,000 microform items, and 2000 audiovisual forms/CDs, and subscribes to 1000 periodicals. Computerized library services include database searching. Special learning facilities include a maritime museum. The 80-acre campus is in a suburban area 19 miles east of New York City. Including residence halls, there are 28 buildings.

Programs of Study: Kings Point confers the B.S. degree. Bachelor's degrees are awarded in BUSINESS (transportation management), ENGINEERING AND ENVIRONMENTAL DESIGN (engineering, marine engineering, and maritime science). Marine engineering systems is the strongest academically. Marine engineering is the largest.

Special: The college offers internships in the maritime industry and work-study programs with U.S. shipping companies.

Admissions: 47% of the 1999-2000 applicants were accepted. The SAT I scores for the 1999-2000 freshman class were: Verbal--5% below 500, 50% between 500 and 599, 35% between 600 and 700, and 10% above 700; Math--41% between 500 and 599, 50% between 600 and 700, and 9% above 700. 50% of the current freshmen were in the top fifth of their class; 99% were in the top two fifths.

Requirements: The SAT I or ACT is required. Kings Point requires applicants to be in the upper 40% of their class. SAT II: Subject tests are recommended. Candidates for admission to the academy must be nominated by a member of the U.S. Congress. They must be between the ages of 17 and 25, U.S. citizens (except by special arrangement), and in excellent physical condition. Applicants should be graduates of an accredited secondary school or have a GED equivalent. 16 academic credits are required, including 4 in English, 3 in math, 1 credit in physics or chemistry with a lab, and 8 in electives. An essay is required. Important factors in the admissions decision are advanced placement or honor courses, leadership record, and extracurricular activities record.

Procedure: Freshmen are admitted in the fall. Entrance exams should be taken by the first test date of the year of requested admission. Applications should be filed by March 1 for fall entry. Notification is sent around May 1. 50% of all applicants are on a waiting list.

Financial Aid: 1% of undergraduates work part time. Kings Point is a member of CSS. The FAFSA is required.

Computers: The mainframes are a DEC VAX 8600, an IBM 4381, and a Honeywell GPS. There are also 1200 PCs and Macs available in dorm and labs. Cadets are required to have their own personal notebook computers. All students may access the system 24 hours per day. There are no time limits and no fees.

UNITED STATES MILITARY ACADEMY
West Point, NY 10996-1797
(914) 938-4041
Fax: (914) 938-8121

Full-time: 3528 men, 637 women	**Faculty:** 577
Part-time: none	**Ph.D.s:** 39%
Graduate: none	**Student/Faculty:** 7 to 1
Year: semesters, summer session	**Tuition:** see profile
Application Deadline: March 20	**Room & Board:** see profile
Freshman Class: 11,490 applied, 1483 accepted, 1134 enrolled	
SAT I Verbal/Math: 627/641	**ACT:** 28 **MOST COMPETITIVE**

The United States Military Academy, founded in 1802, offers military, engineering, and comprehensive arts and sciences programs leading to a bachelor's degree and a commission as a second lieutenant in the U.S. Army, with a 5-year active duty service obligation. All students receive free tuition and room and board as well as an annual salary of more than $6700. An initial deposit of $2400 is required. In addition to regional accreditation, West Point has baccalaureate program accreditation with ABET. The library contains 442,169 volumes, 748,443 microform items, and 12,378 audiovisual forms/CDs, and subscribes to 1963 periodicals. Computerized library services include the card catalog, interlibrary loans, and database searching. Special learning facilities include a learning resource center, art gallery, radio station, TV station, and military museum. Cadets may conduct research in conjunction with the academic departments through the Operations Research Center, the Photonics Research Center, the Mechanical Engineering Research Center, and the Office of Artificial Intelligence, Analysis, and Evaluation. There is also a visiting artist program featuring painting, sculpture, and photography. The 16,080-acre campus is in a small town 56 miles north of New York City. Including residence halls, there are 902 buildings.

Programs of Study: West Point confers the B.S. degree. Bachelor's degrees are awarded in BIOLOGICAL SCIENCE (life science), BUSINESS (management science and operations research), COMMUNICATIONS AND THE ARTS (languages and literature), COMPUTER AND PHYSICAL SCIENCE (chemistry, computer science, mathematics, and physics), ENGINEERING AND ENVIRONMENTAL DESIGN (civil engineering, electrical/electronics engineering, engineering management, engineering physics, environmental engineering, mechanical engineering, military science, nuclear engineering, and systems engineering), SOCIAL SCIENCE (behavioral science, economics, geography, history, international studies, law, philosophy, and political science/government). Engineering, behavioral sciences, and history are the largest.

Special: Junior and senior cadets may participate in 3-week summer educational experiences, including Operations Crossroads Africa, research work in technical areas throughout the country, medical internships at Walter Reed Medical Center, workfellow positions with federal and Department of Defense agencies, language training in foreign countries, and study at other military and civilian institutions. There are 7 national honor societies, including Phi Beta Kappa, a freshman honors program, and 5 departmental honors programs.

Admissions: 13% of the 1999-2000 applicants were accepted. The SAT I scores for the 1999-2000 freshman class were: Verbal--5% below 500, 28% between 500 and 599, 49% between 600 and 700, and 18% above 700; Math--1% below 500, 24% between 500 and 599, 53% between 600 and 700, and 22% above 700. 73% of the current freshmen were in the top fifth of their class; 93% were in the top two fifths. In a recent year, there were 28 National Merit finalists and 17 semifinalists, and 81 freshmen graduated first in their class.

Requirements: The SAT I or ACT is required. Applicants must be qualified academically, physically, and medically. Candidates must be nominated for admission by members of the U.S. Congress or executive sources. West Point recommends that applicants have 4 years each of English and math, 2 years each of foreign language and lab science, such as chemistry and physics, and 1 year of U.S. history. Courses in geography, government, and economics are also suggested. An essay is required, and an interview is recommended. The GED is accepted. Applicants must be 17 to 22 years old, a U.S. citizen at the time of enrollment (except by agreement with another country), unmarried, and not pregnant or legally obligated to support children. AP credits are accepted. Important factors in the admissions decision are leadership record, extracurricular activities record, and recommendations by school officials.

Procedure: Freshmen are admitted in the summer. Entrance exams should be taken in the spring of the junior year and not later than the fall of the senior year. There are early decision and early admissions plans. Applications should be filed by March 20. Notification of early decision is sent January 15; regular decision, on a rolling basis. 493 early decision candidates were accepted for a recent class. 5% of all applicants are on a waiting list.

Computers: The mainframe is a Unisys 2200/425. Virtually every course requires a computer. There is a PC at each desk connected to academic computing services, word processing, worldwide E-mail, spreadsheets, and database access. All students may access the system 24 hours daily. There are no time limits and no fees.

UNITED STATES NAVAL ACADEMY

Annapolis, MD 21402-5018

(410) 293-4361
(800) 638-9156; Fax: (410) 293-4348

Full-time: 3500 men, 600 women	**Faculty:** 600; IIB, +$
Part-time: none	**Ph.D.s:** 90%
Graduate: none	**Student/Faculty:** 7 to 1
Year: semesters, summer session	**Tuition:** see profile
Application Deadline: see profile	**Room & Board:** n/app
Freshman Class: n/av	
SAT I or ACT: required	**MOST COMPETITIVE**

The United States Naval Academy, founded in 1845, is a national military service college offering undergraduate degree programs and professional training in aviation, surface ships, submarines, and various military, maritime, and technical fields. The U.S. Navy pays tuition, room and board, medical and dental care, and a monthly stipend to all Naval Academy students. Figures given in the above capsule are approximate. In addition to regional accreditation, Annapolis has baccalaureate program accreditation with ABET and CSAB. The library contains 530,000 volumes and subscribes to 2000 periodicals. Computerized library services include the card catalog, interlibrary loans, and database searching. Special learning facilities include a learning resource center, art gallery, planetarium, radio station, TV station, propulsion lab, nuclear reactor, oceanographic research vessel, towing tanks, flight simulator, and naval history museum. The 329-acre campus is in a small town 30 miles southeast of Baltimore. Including the residence hall, there are 25 buildings.

Programs of Study: Annapolis confers the B.S. degree. Bachelor's degrees are awarded in COMMUNICATIONS AND THE ARTS (English), COMPUTER AND PHYSICAL SCIENCE (chemistry, computer science, mathematics, oceanography, physics, and science), ENGINEERING AND ENVIRONMENTAL DESIGN (aeronautical engineering, electrical/electronics engineering, engineering, marine engineering, mechanical engineering, naval architecture and marine engineering, ocean engineering, and systems engineering), SOCIAL SCIENCE (economics, history, and political science/government). Chemistry, aeronautical engineering, and systems engineering are the strongest academically. Mechanical engineering, math, and oceanography are the largest.

Special: Study in Washington, D.C., is available during 1 semester of the senior year. A voluntary graduate program is available for those who complete requirements early and wish to begin master's work at nearby institutions, such as Georgetown or Johns Hopkins Universities. Trident Scholars may spend their senior year in independent research. There are 10 national honor societies and 5 departmental honors programs.

Requirements: The SAT I or ACT is required. Candidates must be unmarried with no dependents, U.S. citizens of good moral character, and between 17 and 23 years of age. Candidates should have a sound secondary school background, including 4 years each of English and math, 2 years of a foreign language, and 1 year each of U.S. history, world or European history, chemistry, physics, and computer literacy. Candidates must obtain an official nomination from congressional or military sources. An interview is conducted, and medical and physical examinations must be passed in order to qualify for admission. AP credits are accepted. Important factors in the admissions decision are advanced placement or honor courses, recommendations by school officials, and leadership record.

Procedure: Freshmen are admitted in the summer. Entrance exams should be taken after December of the junior year. Check with the school for current application deadlines. Notification is sent on a rolling basis.

Computers: The mainframe is a Honeywell DPS8. There are also 1500 PCs available in the dormitory, library, computer center, and computer lab. All students may access the system. There are no time limits and no fees. Each student is issued a personal computer.

UNIVERSITY OF ALABAMA AT HUNTSVILLE

Huntsville, AL 35899 (256) 890-6070
(800) UAH-CALL; Fax: (256) 890-6073

Full-time: 1474 men, 1614 women	**Faculty:** 281
Part-time: 1258 men, 1167 women	**Ph.D.s:** 92%
Graduate: 792 men, 569 women	**Student/Faculty:** 11 to 1
Year: semesters, summer session	**Tuition:** $3112 ($6516)
Application Deadline: August 15	**Room & Board:** $3780
Freshman Class: 1100 applied, 1013 accepted, 538 enrolled	
SAT I Verbal/Math: 580/580	**ACT:** 25 **VERY COMPETITIVE**

The University of Alabama in Huntsville, founded in 1950 and part of the University of Alabama system, is a public institution offering programs in liberal arts and sciences, business, nursing, and engineering. There are 5 undergraduate schools and 1 graduate school. In addition to regional accreditation, UAH has baccalaureate program accreditation with AACSB, ABET, CSAB, NASM, and NLN. The library contains 331,353 volumes, 288,536 microform items, and 9563 audiovisual forms/CDs, and subscribes to 2766 periodicals. Computerized library services include the card catalog, interlibrary loans, and database searching. Special learning facilities include an art gallery and radio station. The 376-acre campus is in a suburban area 100 miles north of Birmingham and south of Nashville. Including residence halls, there are 31 buildings.

Programs of Study: UAH confers B.A., B.S., B.S.B.A., B.S.E., and B.S.N. degrees. Master's and doctoral degrees are also awarded. Bachelor's degrees are awarded in BIOLOGICAL SCIENCE (biology/biological science), BUSINESS (accounting, banking and finance, business administration and management, management information systems, marketing/retailing/merchandising, and purchasing/inventory management), COMMUNICATIONS AND THE ARTS (communications, English, fine arts, French, German, languages, music, and Spanish), COMPUTER AND PHYSICAL SCIENCE (chemistry, computer science, mathematics, optics, and physics), EDUCATION (education), ENGINEERING AND ENVIRONMENTAL DESIGN (chemical engineering, civil engineering, computer engineering, electrical/electronics engineering, industrial engineering, mechanical engineering, and optical engineering), HEALTH PROFESSIONS (nursing), SOCIAL SCIENCE (history, philosophy, political science/government, psychology, Russian and Slavic studies, and sociology). Engineering and nursing are the strongest academically. Computer science, nursing, and biological sciences are the largest.

Special: UAH offers co-op programs in all majors, cross-registration with Alabama Agricultural and Mechanical University and Athens State and Calhoun Community Colleges, and internships in administrative science, communications, education, and political science. A 3-2 engineering degree is available with Oakwood College, Fisk University, Atlanta University Center, and the American University of Paris. Dual majors, B.A.-B.S. degrees in math and biology, nondegree study, and a pass/fail option are also offered. There are 22 national honor societies and a freshman honors program.

Admissions: 92% of the 1999-2000 applicants were accepted. The SAT I scores for the 1999-2000 freshman class were: Verbal--15% below 500, 41% between 500 and 599, 37% between 600 and 700, and 8% above 700; Math--21% below 500, 36% between 500 and 599, 35% between 600 and 700, and 8% above 700. The ACT scores were 14% below 21, 22% between 21 and 23, 31% between 24 and 26, 17% between 27 and 28, and 16% above 28. 52% of the current freshmen were in the top fifth of their class; 79% were in the top two fifths. There were 2 National Merit finalists. 1 freshman graduated first in the class.

Requirements: The SAT I or ACT is required. A sliding scale with the GPA determines the minimum test score needed. The GED is accepted. Students should present a minimum of 20 Carnegie units, including 4 years of English, 3 each of math and social studies, and 2 of science. AP and CLEP credits are accepted.

Procedure: Freshmen are admitted to all sessions. Entrance exams should be taken during the junior year. There are early admissions and deferred admissions plans. Applications should be filed by August 15 for fall entry, January 15 for spring entry, and May 15 for summer entry, along with a $20 fee. Notification is sent on a rolling basis.

Financial Aid: In 1999-2000, 90% of all freshmen and 49% of continuing students received some form of financial aid. 49% of freshmen and 38% of continuing students received need-based aid. The average freshman award was $3542. Of that total, scholarships or need-based grants averaged $2468 ($13,693 maximum); loans averaged $3714 ($11,304 maximum); and work contracts averaged $3155. 10% of undergraduates work part time. Average annual earnings from campus work are $2100. The average financial indebtedness of the 1999 graduate was $15,235. UAH is a member of CSS. The FAFSA is required. The fall application deadline is July 1 (February 1 for institutional scholarships).

Computers: The mainframe is a DEC 7000/610. Terminals are located in 8 buildings across campus. The campus is served by Ethernet and provides access to the Alabama Supercomputer Cray X-MP24. All students may access the system 24 hours a day. There are no time limits and no fees.

UNIVERSITY OF ARIZONA
Tucson, AZ 85721   (520) 621-3237; Fax: (520) 621-9799

Full-time: 10,229 men, 11,375 women	**Faculty:** 1495; I, av$
Part-time: 2154 men, 2500 women	**Ph.Ds:** 94%
Graduate: 3952 men, 4116 women	**Student/Faculty:** 14 to 1
Year: semesters, summer session	**Tuition:** $2158 ($9110)
Application Deadline: April 1	**Room & Board:** $5038
Freshman Class: 17,700 applied, 14,868 accepted, 5369 enrolled	
SAT I Verbal/Math: 540/550	**ACT:** 23 **VERY COMPETITIVE**

The University of Arizona, founded in 1885, is a public land-grant institution controlled by the state of Arizona. Undergraduate programs are offered in agriculture, architecture, arts and sciences, business and public administration, education, engineering and mines, and nursing, pharmacy, and other health-related professions. There are 13 undergraduate and 5 graduate schools. In addition to regional accreditation, UA has baccalaureate program accreditation with AACSB, ABET, ACPE, ADA, ASLA, NAAB, NASAD, NASM, NCATE, and NLN. The 7 libraries contain 4,620,234 volumes, 5,636,841 microform items, and 47,012 audiovisual forms/CDs, and subscribe to 30,000 periodicals. Computerized library services include the card catalog, interlibrary loans, and database searching. Special learning facilities include a learning resource center, art gallery, natural history museum, planetarium, radio station, TV station, and the Ansel Adams Center for creative photography. The 353-acre campus is in an urban area in Tucson. Including residence halls, there are 172 buildings.

Programs of Study: UA confers B.A., B.S., B.Arch., B.F.A., B.L.A., B.M., B.S. B.A., B.S.H.S., B.S.N., and B.S.P.A. degrees. Master's and doctoral degrees are also awarded. Bachelor's degrees are awarded in AGRICULTURE (agricultural economics, animal science, natural resource management, plant science, range/farm management, and soil science), BIOLOGICAL SCIENCE (biochemistry, biology/biological science, ecology, evolutionary biology, microbiology, molecular biology, nutrition, physiology, and wildlife biology), BUSINESS (accounting, banking and finance, business administration and management, business economics, entrepreneurial studies, human resources, management information systems, management science, marketing/retailing/merchandising, and retailing), COMMUNICATIONS AND THE ARTS (art history and appreciation, classics, communications, creative writing, dance, dramatic arts, English, fine arts, French, German, Italian, journalism, language arts, Latin, linguistics, media arts, music, music performance, music theory and composition, musical theater, Portuguese, Russian, Spanish, studio art, and theater design), COMPUTER AND PHYSICAL SCIENCE (astronomy, atmospheric sciences and meteorology, chemistry, computer science, earth science, geology, geoscience, hydrology, mathematics, natural sciences, and physics), EDUCATION (agricultural, art, drama, early childhood, elementary, health, home economics, music, physical, secondary, and special), ENGINEERING AND ENVIRONMENTAL DESIGN (aeronautical engineering, agricultural engineering, agricultural engineering technology, architecture, chemical engineering, city/community/regional planning, civil engineering, computer engineering, electrical/electronics engineering, engineering, engineering physics, environmental science, geological engineering, industrial engineering, landscape architecture/design, materials engineering, mechanical engineering, mining and mineral engineering, nuclear engineering, optical engineering, and systems engineering), HEALTH PROFESSIONS (health care administration, medical laboratory technology, nursing, pharmacy, speech pathology/audiology, and veterinary science), SOCIAL SCIENCE (anthropology, child care/child and family studies, criminal justice, East Asian studies, economics, ethnic studies, family/consumer resource management, family/consumer studies, geography, German area studies, history, humanities, interdisciplinary studies, Judaic studies, Latin American studies, liberal arts/general studies, Mexican-American/Chicano studies, Near Eastern studies, philosophy, political science/government, psychology, public administration, religion, social science, social studies, sociology, theological studies, water resources, and women's studies). Sciences, social sciences, and management information systems are the strongest academically. Social sciences and business are the largest.

Special: Co-op programs are available in almost all majors. B.A.-B.S. degrees, dual majors, interdisciplinary degrees such as engineering-math and theater arts-education, a 3-2 arts and sciences-business degree, and student-designed majors are offered. Internships in almost all disciplines, Washington semester, study abroad in numerous countries, work-study programs on campus, a general studies degree, and pass/fail options are offered. Nondegree study is possible. There are 19 national honor societies, including Phi Beta Kappa, and a freshman honors program.

Admissions: 84% of the 1999-2000 applicants were accepted. The SAT I scores for the 1999-2000 freshman class were: Verbal--29% below 500, 42% between 500 and 599, 23% between 600 and 700, and 5% above 700; Math--27% below 500, 41% between 500 and 599, 26% between 600 and 700, and 6% above 700. The ACT scores were 25% below 21, 27% between 21 and 23, 24% between 24 and 26, 13% between 27 and 28, and 11% above 28. 51% of the current freshmen

were in the top fifth of their class; 78% were in the top two fifths. There were 54 National Merit finalists. 105 freshmen graduated first in their class.

Requirements: The SAT I or ACT is required. UA requires applicants to be in the upper 25% of their class. A GPA of 3.0 is required. Applicants should have completed 4 years each in high school English and math, 3 in science, 2 in a foreign language, and 1 each in history, fine arts, and social studies. A GED may be considered in place of a high school diploma. Some fine arts programs require auditions prior to admission. Applications are accepted on-line at the UA web site. AP and CLEP credits are accepted. Important factors in the admissions decision are advanced placement or honor courses, leadership record, and extracurricular activities record.

Procedure: Freshmen are admitted to all sessions. Entrance exams should be taken from june of the junior year through February of the senior year. There is a deferred admissions plan. Applications should be filed by April 1 for fall entry, October 1 for spring entry, and May 1 for summer entry, along with a $40 fee (out-of-state only). Notification is sent on a rolling basis.

Financial Aid: In 1999-2000, 85% of all students received some form of financial aid. 52% of students received need-based aid. The average freshman award was $5635. Of that total, scholarships or need-based grants averaged $2426 ($4710 maximum); loans averaged $5499 ($10,500 maximum); and work contracts averaged $1292 ($3500 maximum). 31% of undergraduates work part time on campus. Average annual earnings from campus work are $2200. The average financial indebtedness of the 1999 graduate was $16,882. UA is a member of CSS. The FAFSA is required. The fall application deadline is March 1.

Computers: The mainframes are IBM 9672 and HP UNIX systems. There are 1913 terminals, all with Internet web access. All students may access the system 18 hours a day. There are no fees. Students in architecture must provide their own PCs.

UNIVERSITY OF CALIFORNIA AT BERKELEY
Berkeley, CA 94720-5800   (510) 642-3175; Fax: (510) 642-7333

Full-time: 11,109 men, 11,596 women	**Faculty:** 1604; I, ++$
Part-time: none	**Ph.Ds:** 95%
Graduate: 4763 men, 3879 women	**Student/Faculty:** 14 to 1
Year: semesters, summer session	**Tuition:** $3628 ($13,802)
Application Deadline: November 30	**Room & Board:** $8266
Freshman Class: 30,042 applied, 8443 accepted, 3735 enrolled	
SAT I or ACT: required	**MOST COMPETITIVE**

The University of California at Berkeley, founded in 1868, is a public institution offering a wide variety of programs in the social and physical sciences, liberal arts, and professional fields. It is the oldest campus of the University of California system. There are 7 undergraduate schools. In addition to regional accreditation, Cal has baccalaureate program accreditation with AACSB, ABET, ADA, ASLA, CSWE, NAAB, and SAF. The 30 libraries contain 8,450,000 volumes, 5,675,000 microform items, and 60,000 audiovisual forms/CDs, and subscribe to 83,000 periodicals. Computerized library services include the card catalog, interlibrary loans, and database searching. Special learning facilities include a learning resource center, art gallery, natural history museum, radio station, TV station, botanical garden, anthropology museum, hall of science, the University Art Museum and Pacific Film Archive, seismographic station, herberia, the Hall for the Performing Arts, observatory, and many off-campus facilities. The 1232-acre campus is in an urban area 10 miles east of San Francisco. Including residence halls, there are 100 buildings.

Programs of Study: Cal confers A.B. and B.S. degrees. Master's and doctoral degrees are also awarded. Bachelor's degrees are awarded in BIOLOGICAL SCIENCE (biology/biological science, cell biology, entomology, genetics, molecular biology, neurosciences, nutrition, and plant genetics), BUSINESS (business administration and management and operations research), COMMUNICATIONS AND THE ARTS (art history and appreciation, Chinese, classical languages, communications, comparative literature, dramatic arts, Dutch, English, film arts, French, German, Greek, Italian, Japanese, Latin, linguistics, music, Scandinavian languages, Slavic languages, Spanish, and speech/debate/rhetoric), COMPUTER AND PHYSICAL SCIENCE (applied mathematics, astrophysics, chemistry, computer science, earth science, geology, geophysics and seismology, mathematics, paleontology, physical sciences, physics, and statistics), ENGINEERING AND ENVIRONMENTAL DESIGN (architecture, bioengineering, chemical engineering, civil engineering, electrical/electronics engineering, engineering and applied science, engineering physics, environmental engineering, environmental science, industrial engineering, landscape architecture/design, manufacturing engineering, materials engineering, materials science, mechanical engineering, mining and mineral engineering, nuclear engineering, and petroleum/natural gas engineering), HEALTH PROFESSIONS (health science and optometry), SOCIAL SCIENCE (African American studies, American studies, anthropology, archeology, Asian/American studies, Asian/Oriental studies, Celtic studies, classical/ancient civilization, cognitive science, economics, ethnic studies, geography, history, humanities, Latin American studies, Mexican-American/Chicano studies, Middle Eastern studies, Native American studies, Near Eastern studies, peace studies, philosophy, political science/government, psychology, religion, social science, social work, sociology, South Asian studies, and women's studies). Molecular and cell biology, English, and psychology are the largest.

Special: Co-op programs, cross-registration with many area schools, internships, work-study programs, and study abroad in 33 countries are available. Interdisciplinary majors are also available. Students may double-major, earn dual degrees, design their own majors, study independently, and choose pass/fail options. Students have opportunities for independent or team research. There is a 3-2 engineering degree program with the University of California at Santa Cruz. There are 6 national honor societies, including Phi Beta Kappa.

Admissions: 28% of the 1999-2000 applicants were accepted. The SAT I scores for the 1999-2000 freshman class were: Verbal--6% below 500, 18% between 500 and 599, 44% between 600 and 700, and 32% above 700; Math--3% below 500, 11% between 500 and 599, 37% between 600 and 700, and 50% above 700. 95% of the current freshmen were in the top fifth of their class.

Requirements: The SAT I or ACT is required, along with 3 SAT II: Subject tests. A GPA of 3.3 is required. Also required are 4 years of English, 3 of math (4 recommended), and 2 each of history/social sciences, lab science (3 recommended), foreign language (3 recommended), and college-preparatory electives. Applications are accepted on-line at http://www.ucop.edu/pathways. AP credits are accepted. Important factors in the admissions decision are advanced placement or honor courses, evidence of special talent, and leadership record.

Procedure: Freshmen are admitted in the fall. Entrance exams should be taken no later than December of the senior year. There is a deferred admissions plan. Applications should be filed by November 30 for fall entry, along with a $40 fee. Notification is sent March 30.

Financial Aid: In a recent year, 73% of all freshmen and 64% of continuing students received some form of financial aid. 49% of freshmen and 54% of continuing students received need-based aid. The average freshman award was $12,050. 26% of undergraduates work part time. Average annual earnings from campus work are $2711. Cal is a member of CSS. The FAFSA is required. The fall application deadline is March 2.

Computers: The mainframes are an IBM 3090 and a DEC UNIX. There are 12 general-access computer facilities on campus, with about 600 computers, including Macs, PCs, and UNIX workstations. Additional computer labs are located in residence halls, libraries, and academic departments. Internet access and E-mail accounts are available. Home computers can be linked to the campus data network. All students may access the system. There are no fees.

UNIVERSITY OF CALIFORNIA AT DAVIS
Davis, CA 95616-8507   (530) 752-2971; Fax: (530) 752-1280

Full-time: 7710 men, 9220 women	**Faculty:** 1331; I, ++$
Part-time: 1100 men, 1160 women	**Ph.D.s:** 98%
Graduate: 2300 men, 1800 women	**Student/Faculty:** 13 to 1
Year: quarters, summer session	**Tuition:** $4330 ($13,320)
Application Deadline: see profile	**Room & Board:** $6830
Freshman Class: n/av	
SAT I or ACT: required	**COMPETITIVE**

University of California at Davis, founded in 1905, is a public, comprehensive institution offering programs in arts and science, agricultural and environmental sciences, and engineering. Figures given in the above capsule are approximate. There are 3 undergraduate and 5 graduate schools. In addition to regional accreditation, UCD has baccalaureate program accreditation with ABET, ADA, and ASLA. The 5 libraries contain 2,807,863 volumes, 3,464,667 microform items, and 13,937 audiovisual forms/CDs, and subscribe to 47,133 periodicals. Computerized library services include the card catalog and database searching. Special learning facilities include a learning resource center, art gallery, radio station, experimental farms, a 150-acre arboretum, a raptor center, an equestrian center, a primate research center, and the Crocker Nuclear Laboratory. The 5980-acre campus is in a suburban area 15 miles west of Sacramento and 72 miles northeast of San Francisco. Including residence halls, there are 1083 buildings.

Programs of Study: UCD confers A.B., B.S., and B.A.S. degrees. Master's and doctoral degrees are also awarded. Bachelor's degrees are awarded in AGRICULTURE (agricultural business management, agricultural economics, animal science, international agriculture, plant science, range/farm management, and soil science), BIOLOGICAL SCIENCE (avian sciences, bacteriology, biochemistry, biology/biological science, botany, ecology, entomology, environmental biology, genetics, microbiology, nutrition, physiology, toxicology, wildlife biology, and zoology), BUSINESS (organizational behavior), COMMUNICATIONS AND THE ARTS (art history and appreciation, Chinese, communications, comparative literature, design, dramatic arts, English, fine arts, French, German, Greek, Italian, Japanese, Latin, linguistics, music, Russian, Spanish, speech/debate/rhetoric, and studio art), COMPUTER AND PHYSICAL SCIENCE (atmospheric sciences and meteorology, chemistry, computer science, geology, hydrology, mathematics, physics, polymer science, and statistics), EDUCATION (physical), ENGINEERING AND ENVIRONMENTAL DESIGN (aeronautical engineering, agricultural engineering, bioengineering, chemical engineering, civil engineering, computer engineering, electrical/electronics engineering, environmental design, environmental science, landscape architecture/design, materials engineering, and mechanical engineering), HEALTH PROFESSIONS (community health work and environmental health science), SOCIAL SCIENCE (African studies, American studies, anthropology, behavioral science, classical/ancient civilization, dietetics, East Asian studies, economics, food science, geography, history, human development, human ecology, international relations, medieval studies, Mexican-American/Chicano studies, Native American studies, philosophy, political science/government, psychology, religion, social science, sociology, textiles and clothing, and women's studies). Agricultural, biological, and biotechnical sciences are the strongest academically. Biological science, biochemistry, and psychology are the largest.

Special: There are credit and noncredit internship programs. Study abroad in more than 32 countries and a Washington semester are offered. Students may participate in college work-study, federal work-study, and California work-study programs. Several A.B.-B.S. degrees are offered. Students may design their own majors, take dual majors, and elect pass/fail options. Interdisciplinary majors are offered in African American and African studies, American Studies, Chicana/Chicano (Mexican-American) studies, comparative literature, East Asian studies, exercise science, international relations, linguistics, medieval studies, Native American studies, religious studies, and women's studies. There are 24 national honor societies, including Phi Beta Kappa, a freshman honors program, and 3 departmental honors programs.

Requirements: The SAT I or ACT is required. A GPA of 3.3 is required. Candidates for admission should have completed 4 units of English, 3 of math, and 2 each of foreign language, history/social science, lab science, and college preparatory electives, for a total of 15 units. SAT II: Subject tests are required in writing, math, and 1 other subject chosen from English literature, foreign language, science, or social studies. AP credits are accepted. Important factors in the admissions decision are advanced placement or honor courses, evidence of special talent, and leadership record.

Procedure: Freshmen are admitted fall, winter, and spring. Entrance exams should be taken no later than December of the senior year. There is a deferred admissions plan. Check with the school for current application deadlines and fee.

Financial Aid: 44% of undergraduates work part time. The average financial indebtedness of the 1999 graduate was $8300. UCD is a member of CSS. The CSS/Profile or FFS is required.

Computers: There are hundreds of PCs and terminals located in numerous computer labs and classrooms throughout the campus. In addition, many PCs are provided for student use in the residence halls. All students may access the system. There are no time limits and no fees.

UNIVERSITY OF CALIFORNIA AT IRVINE
Irvine, CA 92697-1075
(949) 824-6701; Fax: (949) 824-2711

Full-time: 7264 men, 8132 women	**Faculty:** 1207; I, ++$
Part-time: none	**Ph.D.s:** 99%
Graduate: 1696 men, 981 women	**Student/Faculty:** 13 to 1
Year: quarters, summer session	**Tuition:** $3870 ($13674)
Application Deadline: November 30	**Room & Board:** $6407
Freshman Class: 22,157 applied, 13,311 accepted, 3706 enrolled	
SAT I Verbal/Math: 560/610	**HIGHLY COMPETITIVE**

The University of California, Irvine, founded in 1965, is a public research university and part of the University of California System. There are 8 undergraduate and 3 graduate schools. In addition to regional accreditation, UCI has baccalaureate program accreditation with AACSB and ABET. The 3 libraries contain 2.3 million volumes, 2,284,641 microform items, and 87,375 audiovisual forms/CDs, and subscribe to 18,187 periodicals. Computerized library services include the card catalog, interlibrary loans, and database searching. Special learning facilities include a learning resource center, art gallery, planetarium, radio station, freshwater marsh reserve, arboretum, laser institute, and numerous research centers. The 1489-acre campus is in a suburban area 40 miles south of Los Angeles. Including residence halls, there are 418 buildings.

Programs of Study: UCI confers B.A., B.S., B.F.A., and B.Mus. degrees. Master's and doctoral degrees are also awarded. Bachelor's degrees are awarded in BIOLOGICAL SCIENCE (biology/biological science and ecology), COMMUNICATIONS AND THE ARTS (art history and appreciation, Chinese, classics, comparative literature, dance, dramatic arts, English, film arts, fine arts, French, German, Japanese, linguistics, music, Russian, Spanish, and studio art), COMPUTER AND PHYSICAL SCIENCE (chemistry, information sciences and systems, mathematics, and physics), ENGINEERING AND ENVIRONMENTAL DESIGN (aeronautical engineering, chemical engineering, civil engineering, computer engineering, electrical/electronics engineering, engineering, environmental design, environmental engineering, and mechanical engineering), SOCIAL SCIENCE (anthropology, classical/ancient civilization, criminology, crosscultural studies, East Asian studies, economics, geography, history, human ecology, humanities, international studies, philosophy, political science/government, psychology, social science, sociology, and women's studies). Biological sciences, political science, and economics are the strongest academically. Biological sciences, social ecology, and economics are the largest.

Special: Students may study abroad in Spain, England, India, Kenya, Sweden, and Egypt. UCI also offers internships, a Washington semester, work-study programs with the university, B.A.-B.S. degrees, dual majors, and pass/fail options. There are 3 national honor societies, including Phi Beta Kappa, a freshman honors program, and 14 departmental honors programs.

Admissions: 60% of the 1999-2000 applicants were accepted. The SAT I scores for the 1999-2000 freshman class were: Verbal--22% below 500, 48% between 500 and 599, 25% between 600 and 700, and 5% above 700; Math--9% below 500, 36% between 500 and 599, 40% between 600 and 700, and 15% above 700. All of the current freshmen were in the top fifth of their class. There were 9 National Merit finalists.

Requirements: The SAT I or ACT is required as is a GPA of 2.8. Required minimum scores are determined by an eligibility index. In addition, SAT II: Subject tests in writing, math, and a third chosen from science, social science, foreign language, or English literature are required. Applicants need 15 academic credits, including 4 years of English, 3 in math, and 2 each in foreign language, history/social science, lab science, and electives. An additional year each in foreign language, math, and science is recommended. An essay also is needed. The GED is accepted. Applications are accepted on-line at www.ucop.edu/pathways/. AP credits are accepted.

Procedure: Freshmen are admitted in the fall. Entrance exams should be taken no later than December of the senior year. Applications should be filed by November 30 for fall entry, July 31 for winter entry, and October 31 for spring entry, along with a $40 fee. Notification is sent March 1.

Financial Aid: In 1999-2000, 75% of all freshmen and 62% of continuing students received some form of financial aid. 50% of freshmen and 52% of continuing students received need-based aid. The average freshman award was $11,254. Of that total, scholarships or need-based grants averaged $5820; loans averaged $6450; and work contracts averaged $1640. Average annual earnings from campus work are $1640. The average financial indebtedness of the 1999 graduate was $9680. UCI is a member of CSS. The FAFSA is required.

Computers: There are approximately 500 computer terminals/PCs located in the computer center, the student center, the library, and departmental computer labs.

All students may access the system 24 hours a day, for 2-hour sessions. There are no fees.

UNIVERSITY OF CALIFORNIA AT LOS ANGELES
Los Angeles, CA 90095   (213) 825-3101; Fax: (310) 206-1206

Full-time: 11,129 men, 13,539 women	**Faculty:** 1528; I, ++$
Part-time: none	**Ph.D.s:** 100%
Graduate: 5911 men, 5772 women	**Student/Faculty:** 16 to 1
Year: quarters, summer session	**Tuition:** $3683 ($13,487)
Application Deadline: November 30	**Room & Board:** $7692
Freshman Class: 35,681 applied, 10,296 accepted, 4131 enrolled	
SAT I Verbal/Math: 620/655	**ACT:** 26 **MOST COMPETITIVE**

University of California at Los Angeles (UCLA), founded in 1919, is a public institution offering undergraduate and graduate degrees in arts and sciences, engineering, applied science, nursing, and theater, film, and television. There are 5 undergraduate and 12 graduate schools. In addition to regional accreditation, UCLA has baccalaureate program accreditation with AACSB, ABET, ADA, CSWE, NAAB, and NLN. The 13 libraries contain 7,401,780 volumes, 6,001,443 microform items, and 237,661 audiovisual forms/CDs, and subscribe to 96,021 periodicals. Computerized library services include the card catalog and database searching. Special learning facilities include a learning resource center, art gallery, natural history museum, and radio station. The 419-acre campus is in an urban area. Including residence halls, there are 272 buildings.

Programs of Study: UCLA confers B.A. and B.S. degrees. Master's and doctoral degrees are also awarded. Bachelor's degrees are awarded in BIOLOGICAL SCIENCE (biochemistry, biology/biological science, microbiology, molecular biology, neurosciences, and physiology), BUSINESS (business economics and international economics), COMMUNICATIONS AND THE ARTS (African languages, Arabic, art, art history and appreciation, Chinese, communications, comparative literature, design, dramatic arts, English, film arts, French, German, Greek, Hebrew, Italian, Japanese, Korean, Latin, linguistics, music, music history and appreciation, Portuguese, Scandinavian languages, Slavic languages, and Spanish), COMPUTER AND PHYSICAL SCIENCE (applied mathematics, astrophysics, atmospheric sciences and meteorology, chemistry, computer mathematics, computer science, cybernetics, earth science, geology, geophysics and seismology, mathematics, paleontology, and physics), ENGINEERING AND ENVIRONMENTAL DESIGN (aeronautical engineering, chemical engineering, civil engineering, computer engineering, electrical/electronics engineering, geological engineering, geophysical engineering, materials engineering, materials science, and mechanical engineering), HEALTH PROFESSIONS (nursing), SOCIAL SCIENCE (African American studies, American studies, anthropology, Asian/American studies, classical/ancient civilization, cognitive science, East Asian studies, economics, European studies, geography, Hispanic American studies, history, human ecology, interdisciplinary studies, international studies, Italian studies, Judaic studies, Latin American studies, Near Eastern studies, philosophy, political science/government, psychobiology, psychology, religion, Russian and Slavic studies, sociology, and women's studies). Biology, psychology, and economics are the largest.

Special: Opportunities are provided for internships, work-study programs, study abroad in 33 countries, B.A.-B.S. degrees, student-designed majors, dual majors, and interdisciplinary majors, including chemistry/materials science, Chicana and

Chicano studies, engineering geology, economics/systems science, ethnomusicology, and computer science and engineering. There is a Washington, D.C. program for 20 to 30 students selected each fall and spring. There are 4 national honor societies, including Phi Beta Kappa, a freshman honors program, and 7 departmental honors programs.

Admissions: 29% of the 1999-2000 applicants were accepted. The SAT I scores for the 1999-2000 freshman class were: Verbal--8% below 500, 28% between 500 and 599, 47% between 600 and 700, and 18% above 700; Math--5% below 500, 18% between 500 and 599, 42% between 600 and 700, and 35% above 700.

Requirements: The SAT I or ACT is required. UCLA requires applicants to be in the upper 13% of their class. A GPA of 3.3 is required. Graduation from an accredited secondary school is required. Applicants must submit a challenging academic program, including honors and AP-level courses in English, math, a language other than English, science, and history and social science; most students complete at least 42 semester courses in these areas. SAT II: Subject tests in writing, math, and 1 subject of the student's choice are required. An essay is required, and a portfolio and audition are required for all art and theater, film and television majors. Applications may be submitted on-line at www.ucop.edu/pathways or via UC Application. AP credits are accepted. Important factors in the admissions decision are advanced placement or honor courses, evidence of special talent, and leadership record.

Procedure: Freshmen are admitted in the fall. Entrance exams should be taken preferably in the junior year, but no later than December of the senior year. Applications should be filed by November 30 for fall entry, along with a $40 fee. Notification is sent March 31.

Financial Aid: In 1998-99, 60% of all freshmen and 58% of continuing students received some form of financial aid. 52% of freshmen and 59% of continuing students received need-based aid. The average freshman award was $8461. Of that total, scholarships or need-based grants averaged $6723 ($6900 maximum); loans averaged $4531 ($5500 maximum); and work contracts averaged $1400 ($5000 maximum). 37% of undergraduates work part time. Average annual earnings from campus work are $3424. The average financial indebtedness of the 1998 graduate was $15,393. UCLA is a member of CSS. The FAFSA and the university's own financial statement are required. The fall application deadline is March 2.

Computers: The mainframe is an IBM 3090 Model 600S. There are also IBM, HP, Zenith, and DEC VAX PCs available throughout the campus. All students may access the system 24 hours a day, 7 days a week. Time limits vary by individual department. There are no fees.

UNIVERSITY OF CALIFORNIA AT SAN DIEGO
La Jolla, CA 92093 (858) 534-4480

Full-time and Part-Time: 16,230 men and women	Faculty: I, ++$
	Ph.D.s: 95%
Part-time: none	Student/Faculty: 19 to 1
Graduate: 2648 men and women	Tuition: $3848 ($13,652)
Year: quarters, summer session	Room & Board: $7134
Application Deadline: November 30	

Freshman Class: 32,539 applied, 13,249 accepted, 3286 enrolled
SAT I Verbal/Math: 609/647   ACT: 25   **HIGHLY COMPETITIVE**

University of California at San Diego, founded in 1959, is a public liberal arts institution. There are 5 undergraduate and 5 graduate schools. In addition to regional accreditation, UCSD has baccalaureate program accreditation with ABET. The 7 libraries contain 2,616,776 volumes, 2,880,645 microform items, and 87,625 audiovisual forms/CD, and subscribe to 24,986 periodicals. Computerized library services include the card catalog, interlibrary loans, and database searching. Special learning facilities include an art gallery, radio station, TV station, and aquarium-museum. The 1976-acre campus is in a suburban area 12 miles north of downtown San Diego. Including residence halls, there are 501 buildings.

Programs of Study: UCSD confers B.A. and B.S. degrees. Master's and doctoral degrees are also awarded. Bachelor's degrees are awarded in AGRICULTURE (animal science), BIOLOGICAL SCIENCE (biochemistry, biology/biological science, biophysics, ecology, microbiology, molecular biology, and physiology), BUSINESS (management science), COMMUNICATIONS AND THE ARTS (art history and appreciation, Chinese, classics, communications, dance, dramatic arts, English literature, Germanic languages and literature, linguistics, literature, music, music history and appreciation, music technology, studio art, and visual and performing arts), COMPUTER AND PHYSICAL SCIENCE (applied mathematics, applied physics, chemistry, computer science, earth science, information sciences and systems, mathematics, physical chemistry, and physics), EDUCATION (mathematics and science), ENGINEERING AND ENVIRONMENTAL DESIGN (aerospace studies, bioengineering, chemical engineering, computer engineering, construction engineering, electrical/electronics engineering, engineering, engineering physics, environmental science, and mechanical engineering), SOCIAL SCIENCE (anthropology, cognitive science, economics, ethnic studies, French studies, gender studies, history, human development, Italian studies, Japanese studies, Judaic studies, Latin American studies, philosophy, political science/government, psychology, religion, Russian and Slavic studies, sociology, Spanish studies, Third World studies, and urban studies). Sciences, the arts, and social sciences are the strongest academically. Biology, psychology, and applied mechanics and engineering are the largest.

Special: Internships, work-study, study abroad in more than 30 countries, and a Washington semester are offered. B.A.-B.S. degrees, an accelerated degree, dual majors, student-designed majors, and exchange programs with Dartmouth College, Spelman College, and Morehouse College are available. Nondegree study, credit for military experience, and pass/fail options are possible. There are 2 national honor societies, including Phi Beta Kappa, a freshman honors program, and 14 departmental honors programs.

Admissions: 41% of the 1999-2000 applicants were accepted.

Requirements: The SAT I or ACT is required. A GPA of 3.3 is required. The SAT I or ACT and 3 SAT II: Subject tests, including writing, math I or II, and a choice of English literature, foreign language, science, or social studies, are required. Candidates for admission should have completed 4 years of English, 3 of math, and 2 each of a foreign language, lab science, history, and college preparatory electives. AP credits are accepted. Important factors in the admissions decision are advanced placement or honor courses, evidence of special talent, and leadership record.

Procedure: Freshmen are admitted in the fall. Entrance exams should be taken by December of the senior year. There is an early admissions plan. Applications should be filed by November 30 for fall entry, along with a $40 fee. Notification is sent March 1 to March 15.

Financial Aid: In 1999-2000, 51% of all students received some form of financial aid. Need-based aid averaged $5504; and non-need-based-aid averaged $3733. 75% of undergraduates work part time. Average annual earnings from campus work are $1325. UCSD is a member of CSS. The FAFSA is required. The fall application deadline is May 1.

Computers: There are 1020 computer terminals available for student use in computer labs, libraries, the student center, and each undergraduate college. Students have access to E-mail, the Internet, and the World Wide Web. There is a campus-wide network. All students may access the system 24 hours every day. There are no fees. The school strongly recommends that students have their own personal computers.

UNIVERSITY OF CALIFORNIA AT SANTA BARBARA

Santa Barbara, CA 93106   (805) 893-2881; Fax: (805) 893-2676

Full-time: 7749 men, 9337 women	**Faculty:** I, ++$
Part-time: 318 men, 295 women	**Ph.D.s:** 100%
Graduate: 1347 men, 1010 women	**Student/Faculty:** n/av
Year: quarters, summer session	**Tuition:** $3844 ($14,018)
Application Deadline: November 30	**Room & Board:** $7156
Freshman Class: 26,964 applied, 14,384 accepted, 3781 enrolled	
SAT I Verbal/Math: 580/610	**ACT:** 24 **VERY COMPETITIVE**

The University of California at Santa Barbara, founded in 1909, is a public liberal arts institution offering programs in creative studies, engineering, and letters and science. Some of the information in this profile is approximate. There are 3 undergraduate and 1 graduate school. In addition to regional accreditation, UCSB has baccalaureate program accreditation with ABET and CSAB. The library contains 2,200,000 volumes, 3,757,000 microform items, and 93,000 audiovisual forms/CDs, and subscribes to 24,325 periodicals. Computerized library services include the card catalog, interlibrary loans, and database searching. Special learning facilities include a learning resource center, art gallery, radio station, language and learning lab, and numerous national and multicampus research institutes. The 813-acre campus is in a suburban area 10 miles west of Santa Barbara. Including residence halls, there are 300 buildings.

Programs of Study: UCSB confers B.A., B.S., B.F.A., and B.M. degrees. Master's and doctoral degrees are also awarded. Bachelor's degrees are awarded in BIOLOGICAL SCIENCE (biochemistry, biology/biological science, cell biology, evolutionary biology, marine biology, microbiology, physiology, and zoology), BUSINESS (business economics), COMMUNICATIONS AND THE ARTS (art, art history and appreciation, Chinese, classics, communications, comparative literature, dance, dramatic arts, English, film arts, French, German, Germanic languages and literature, Japanese, linguistics, literature, music, music performance, music theory and composition, Portuguese, Slavic languages, and Spanish), COMPUTER AND PHYSICAL SCIENCE (chemistry, computer science, geology, geophysics and seismology, hydrology, mathematics, physics, and statistics), ENGINEERING AND ENVIRONMENTAL DESIGN (chemical engineering, electrical/electronics engineering, environmental science, and mechanical engineering), HEALTH PROFESSIONS (pharmacy), SOCIAL SCIENCE (African American studies, anthropology, Asian/American studies, Asian/Oriental studies, biopsychology, economics, geography, history, interdisciplinary studies, Islamic studies, Italian studies, Latin American studies, law, medieval studies, Mexican-American/Chicano studies, philosophy, political science/government, psychology, public affairs, religion, sociology, and women's studies). Business economics, political science, and biological science are the largest.

Special: A Washington semester, internships, study abroad in 32 countries, work-study programs, student-designed majors, the B.A.-B.S. degree, and an accelerated degree program in electrical engineering are offered. There are 6 national honor societies, including Phi Beta Kappa, and a freshman honors program.

Admissions: 53% of the 1999-2000 applicants were accepted. The SAT I scores for the 1999-2000 freshman class were: Verbal--16% below 500, 40% between 500 and 599, 37% between 600 and 700, and 7% above 700; Math--11% below 500, 34% between 500 and 599, 43% between 600 and 700, and 12% above 700. The ACT scores were 16% below 21, 22% between 21 and 23, 33% between 24 and 26, 16% between 27 and 28, and 13% above 28.

Requirements: The SAT I, or ACT is required. The minimum GPA depends on standardized test scores: 2.8 is required with a combined SAT I score of 1600. SAT II: Subject tests in writing, math, and 1 other choice are also required. Candidates for admission must have completed 4 years of English, 3 of math, and 2 each of foreign language, lab science, history/social science, and college-preparatory electives. An additional year each in foreign language, math, and science is recommended. AP and CLEP credits are accepted.

Procedure: Freshmen are admitted in the fall. Entrance exams should be taken by November of the senior year. Applications should be filed by November 30 for fall entry, along with a $40 fee.

Financial Aid: UCSB is a member of CSS. The FAFSA is required.

Computers: They are accessed via numerous systems and networks on campus. There are more than 1800 terminals available in PC and departmental labs. All students may access the system at any time, if students have their own computer and modem.

UNIVERSITY OF CALIFORNIA AT SANTA CRUZ

Santa Cruz, CA 95064   (831) 459-4008; Fax: (831) 459-4452

Full-time: 10,242 men and women	**Faculty:** 420; I, +$
Part-time: n/av	**Ph.D.s:** 100%
Graduate: 1060 men and women	**Student/Faculty:** 24 to 1
Year: quarters, summer session	**Tuition:** $4255 ($14,409)
Application Deadline: November 30	**Room & Board:** $7337
Freshman Class: 14,485 applied, 11,098 accepted, 2410 enrolled	
SAT I Verbal/Math: 580/580	**ACT:** 24 **HIGHLY COMPETITIVE**

University of California, at Santa Cruz, opened in 1965, is a public institution in a small-college setting with the academic resources of a major university, offering programs in the arts, engineering, humanities, natural sciences, and social sciences. There are 9 undergraduate and 24 graduate schools. In addition to regional accreditation, UCSC has baccalaureate program accreditation with ABET. The 10 libraries contain 1,367,955 volumes, 780,387 microform items, and 26,833 audiovisual forms/CDs, and subscribe to 26,599 periodicals. Computerized library services include the card catalog, interlibrary loans, and database searching. Special learning facilities include a learning resource center, art gallery, radio station, agroecology program farm, arboretum, Long Marine Lab, and Lick Observatory on Mt. Hamilton. The 2000-acre campus is in a small town 40 miles north of Monterey and 75 miles south of San Francisco. Including residence halls, there are 467 buildings.

Programs of Study: UCSC confers B.A. B.S., and B.M. degrees. Master's and doctoral degrees are also awarded. Bachelor's degrees are awarded in BIOLOGICAL SCIENCE (biochemistry, biology/biological science, and marine biology), BUSINESS (business economics), COMMUNICATIONS AND THE ARTS (art, dramatic arts, film arts, French, Italian, Japanese, linguistics, literature, music, photography, Russian, and Spanish), COMPUTER AND PHYSICAL SCIENCE (chemistry, earth science, geology, information sciences and systems, mathematics, and physics), ENGINEERING AND ENVIRONMENTAL DESIGN (computer engineering), SOCIAL SCIENCE (American studies, anthropology, economics, German area studies, history, Latin American studies, philosophy, political science/government, psychobiology, psychology, religion, sociology, and Western civilization/culture). Psychology, biology, and literature are the largest.

Special: Cross-registration is possible with other University of California campuses, Hampshire College, the University of New Hampshire, and the University of New Mexico. UCSC also offers work-study, internships in many arenas, study abroad in 36 countries, a Washington quarter, student-designed majors, dual majors, a 3-2 engineering degree with the University of California at Berkeley, and a B.A.-B.S. degree in earth sciences, chemistry and biochemistry, and computer science. Students receive a written narrative evaluation of their academic performance. Grades are optional. There is a chapter of Phi Beta Kappa, a freshman honors program through Merrill College and 1 College honors program.

Admissions: 77% of the 1999-2000 applicants were accepted. The SAT I scores for the 1999-2000 freshman class were: Verbal--19% below 500, 39% between 500 and 599, 32% between 600 and 700, and 10% above 700; Math--17% below 500, 42% between 500 and 599, 34% between 600 and 700, and 7% above 700. The ACT scores were 9% between 12 and 17, 39% between 18 and 23, 43% between 24 and 29, and 8% between 30 and 36. 96% of the current freshmen were in the top fifth of their class; All were in the top two fifths.

Requirements: The SAT I or ACT is required, as are SAT II: Subject tests in writing, math, and a choice of English literature, social science, foreign language, or science. Applicants must be graduates of an accredited secondary school or have a GED certificate. They should have completed 15 academic credits, including 4 years of English, 3 of math, and 2 each of foreign language, history, lab science, and college preparatory electives. Auditions are required for music majors, and portfolios are recommended for art majors. All students must submit a personal statement. Nonresidents must meet additional requirements. Applications are accepted on-line at http://www.ucop.edu/pathways. AP credits are accepted. Important factors in the admissions decision are advanced placement or honor courses, evidence of special talent, and extracurricular activities record.

Procedure: Freshmen are admitted in the fall. Entrance exams should be taken by December of the senior year. Applications should be filed by November 30 for fall entry, July 31 for winter entry, and October 31 for spring entry, along with a $40 fee. Notification is sent March 1.

Financial Aid: UCSC is a member of CSS. The FAFSA is required. The fall application deadline is March 2.

Computers: The mainframe is a Sun SPARC Station 10. There are Mac and IBM PCs available in 13 open-access computer labs and in classrooms throughout the campus, providing e-mail and Internet access. ResNet provides Internet access to all students in University-sponsored housing. All students may sign up for e-mail addresses. All students may access the system. There are no time limits and no fees. The school strongly recommends that students have their own personal computers.

UNIVERSITY OF CENTRAL ARKANSAS

Conway, AR 72035-0001   **(501) 450-3128; (800) 243-8245**

Full-time: 2668 men, 4189 women	**Faculty:** IIA, --$
Part-time: 344 men, 452 women	**Ph.D.s:** 68%
Graduate: 270 men, 772 women	**Student/Faculty:** n/av
Year: semesters, summer session	**Tuition:** $3238 ($5902)
Application Deadline: open	**Room & Board:** $3150

Freshman Class: 3373 applied, 2736 accepted, 1762 enrolled
ACT: 23   **VERY COMPETITIVE**

The University of Central Arkansas, established in 1907, is a comprehensive public institution offering undergraduate and graduate degrees in liberal arts, business, health-related sciences, and education. There are 7 undergraduate and 1 graduate school. In addition to regional accreditation, UCA has baccalaureate program accreditation with AACSB, ADA, APTA, CAHEA, NASAD, NASM, NCATE, and NLN. The library contains 405,245 volumes, 866,559 microform items, and 6200 audiovisual forms/CDs, and subscribes to 2000 periodicals. Computerized library services include the card catalog, interlibrary loans, and database searching. Special learning facilities include a learning resource center, art gallery, planetarium, radio station, and TV station. The 262-acre campus is in a small town 29 miles north of Little Rock. Including residence halls, there are 52 buildings.

Programs of Study: UCA confers B.A., B.S., B.B.A., B.M., B.M.E., and B.S.E. degrees. Associate, master's, and doctoral degrees are also awarded. Bachelor's degrees are awarded in BIOLOGICAL SCIENCE (biology/biological science), BUSINESS (accounting, business administration and management, business economics, and marketing/retailing/merchandising), COMMUNICATIONS AND THE ARTS (communications, English, French, journalism, music, Spanish, and speech/debate/rhetoric), COMPUTER AND PHYSICAL SCIENCE (chemistry, computer science, information sciences and systems, mathematics, physics, and quantitative methods), EDUCATION (art, early childhood, education of the exceptional child, elementary, foreign languages, guidance, health, home economics, industrial arts, library science, middle school, music, physical, science, secondary, and special), HEALTH PROFESSIONS (medical laboratory technology, nursing, occupational therapy, physical therapy, radiological science, respiratory therapy, and speech pathology/audiology), SOCIAL SCIENCE (economics, geography, history, philosophy, political science/government, psychology, public administration, and sociology). Business, health-related sciences, and education are the strongest academically. Business and health-related sciences are the largest.

Special: Study abroad, work-study programs, a B.S.-B.A. degree, a 3-2 engineering degree with Arkansas State University, dual majors, nondegree study, and pass/fail options are available. Co-op programs in business, computer science, and health sciences and internships in education are also possible. There are 18 national honor societies, a freshman honors program, and 25 departmental honors programs.

Admissions: 81% of the 1999-2000 applicants were accepted. The ACT scores for the 1999-2000 freshman class were: 32% below 21, 22% between 21 and 23, 22% between 24 and 26, 14% between 27 and 28, and 10% above 28. 48% of the current freshmen were in the top fifth of their class; 74% were in the top two fifths.

Requirements: The SAT I or ACT is required, with a minimum ACT score of 19. UCA requires applicants to be in the upper 33% of their class. A GPA of 3.0

is required. The GED is accepted. AP and CLEP credits are accepted. Important factors in the admissions decision are advanced placement or honor courses, evidence of special talent, and recommendations by school officials.

Procedure: Freshmen are admitted to all sessions. Application deadlines are open. Notification is sent on a rolling basis.

Financial Aid: In a recent year, 79% of all freshmen received some form of financial aid. 31% of freshmen received need-based aid. The average freshman award was $2519. Of that total, loans averaged $1365; and work contracts averaged $465. 10% of undergraduates work part time. Average annual earnings from campus work are $601. The FAFSA or FFS is required.

Computers: The mainframe is an IBM 5390 Multipurpose 2000. There are also 110 PCs and Macs available in academic buildings, the library, and dormitories. All students may access the system. There are no time limits and no fees. It is strongly recommended that all students have personal computers.

UNIVERSITY OF CENTRAL FLORIDA
Orlando, FL 32816-0111   (407) 823-3000; Fax: (407) 823-3419

Full-time: 8258 men, 10,282 women	**Faculty:** 877; I, --$
Part-time: 3617 men, 4328 women	**Ph.D.s:** 80%
Graduate: 2220 men, 2968 women	**Student/Faculty:** 21 to 1
Year: semesters, summer session	**Tuition:** $2297 ($9285)
Application Deadline: May 15	**Room & Board:** $5429
Freshman Class: 13,703 applied, 8541 accepted, 3470 enrolled	
SAT I Verbal/Math: 568/580	**ACT:** 25 **VERY COMPETITIVE**

University of Central Florida, founded in 1963 and part of the State University System of Florida, offers programs in liberal and fine arts, business, engineering, health science, professional training, and teacher preparation. There are 6 undergraduate and 5 graduate schools. In addition to regional accreditation, UCF has baccalaureate program accreditation with AACSB, ABET, CSAB, CSWE, NASM, NCATE, and NLN. The library contains 1,256,294 volumes, 2,118,032 microform items, and 30,889 audiovisual forms/CDs, and subscribes to 8092 periodicals. Computerized library services include the card catalog, interlibrary loans, and database searching. Special learning facilities include a learning resource center, art gallery, FM and AM radio stations, an observatory, a center for research and education in optics and lasers, an institute for simulation and training, and the Florida Solar Energy Center. The 1445-acre campus is in an urban area 13 miles northeast of downtown Orlando. Including residence halls, there are 79 buildings.

Programs of Study: UCF confers B.A., B.S., B.F.A., B.M., B.M.E., B.S.B.A., B.S.A.E., B.S.C.E., B.S.Cp.E., B.S.E.E., B.S.E.E.T., B.S.Env.E., B.S.E.T., B.S. I.E., B.S.M.E., B.S.N., and B.S.W. degrees. Associate, master's, and doctoral degrees are also awarded. Bachelor's degrees are awarded in BIOLOGICAL SCIENCE (biology/biological science and microbiology), BUSINESS (accounting, banking and finance, business administration and management, hospitality management services, management information systems, management science, and marketing/retailing/merchandising), COMMUNICATIONS AND THE ARTS (advertising, art, broadcasting, communications, dramatic arts, English, film arts, fine arts, French, journalism, languages, music, public relations, and Spanish), COMPUTER AND PHYSICAL SCIENCE (chemistry, computer science, mathematics, physics, and statistics), EDUCATION (art, business, early childhood, education of the exceptional child, elementary, English, foreign languages, mathematics, music, physical, science, social science, special, and vocational),

ENGINEERING AND ENVIRONMENTAL DESIGN (aeronautical engineering, aerospace studies, civil engineering, computer engineering, electrical/electronics engineering, electrical/electronics engineering technology, engineering technology, environmental engineering, industrial engineering technology, and mechanical engineering), HEALTH PROFESSIONS (health care administration, health science, medical laboratory technology, nursing, radiological science, respiratory therapy, and speech pathology/audiology), SOCIAL SCIENCE (anthropology, criminal justice, economics, forensic studies, history, humanities, law, liberal arts/general studies, philosophy, political science/government, psychology, public administration, social science, social work, and sociology). Engineering, business administration, and computer science are the strongest academically. Psychology, elementary education, and liberal studies are the largest.

Special: Internships are available in most majors through UCF's extensive partnerships with area businesses and industries such as NASA, Disney, Universal Studios, and AT&T. Students may participate in study abroad and co-op and work-study programs, earn B.A.-B.S. degrees or a liberal studies degree, or pursue dual majors. Nondegree study and pass/fail options are available. There are 2 national honor societies, including Phi Beta Kappa, and a freshman honors program. All departments have honors programs.

Admissions: 62% of the 1999-2000 applicants were accepted. The SAT I scores for the 1999-2000 freshman class were: Verbal--13% below 500, 56% between 500 and 599, 28% between 600 and 700, and 4% above 700; Math--12% below 500, 50% between 500 and 599, 34% between 600 and 700, and 4% above 700. The ACT scores were 7% below 21, 31% between 21 and 23, 38% between 24 and 26, 14% between 27 and 28, and 11% above 28. There were 19 National Merit finalists and 3 semifinalists.

Requirements: The SAT I or ACT is required. A GPA of 2.0 is required. GPA and standardized test scores are rated on a sliding scale. A high school diploma or GED is required. Applicants should have completed 4 units of English, 3 each of math, science (2 with labs), and social studies, and 2 of a foreign language, plus 4 of academic electives. Applications are accepted on-line at the UCF web site. AP and CLEP credits are accepted. Important factors in the admissions decision are advanced placement or honor courses, evidence of special talent, and leadership record.

Procedure: Freshmen are admitted to all sessions. Entrance exams should be taken during the junior year or the first semester of the senior year. There is an early admissions plan. Applications should be filed by May 15 for fall entry, November 15 for spring entry, and April 15 for summer entry, along with a $20 fee. Notification is sent on a rolling basis. 2% of all applicants are on a waiting list.

Financial Aid: In 1999-2000, 49% of all freshmen and 52% of continuing students received some form of financial aid. 36% of freshmen and 47% of continuing students received need-based aid. The average freshman award was $4315. Of that total, scholarships or need-based grants averaged $969 ($9000 maximum); loans averaged $2754 ($17,146 maximum); and work contracts averaged $2881 ($4000 maximum). 50% of undergraduates work part time. Average annual earnings from campus work are $2500. UCF is a member of CSS. The FAFSA is required. The fall application deadline is March 1.

Computers: The mainframes are a Sun Enterprise 450, an IBM ES/9000 Model 170, and several Novell LAN file servers. 5 public-access computer labs with 500 terminals are available. Students use E-mail to communicate with faculty and classmates, and have free Internet access. All students may access the system at all times. There are no time limits and no fees.

UNIVERSITY OF CHICAGO

Chicago, IL 60637   (773) 702-8650; Fax: (773) 702-4199

Full-time: 1941 men, 1846 women	**Faculty:** 878; I, ++$
Part-time: 28 men, 21 women	**Ph.D.s:** 99%
Graduate: 4265 men, 2542 women	**Student/Faculty:** 4 to 1
Year: quarters, summer session	**Tuition:** $24,484
Application Deadline: January 1	**Room & Board:** $7835
Freshman Class: 6844 applied, 3252 accepted, 1011 enrolled	
SAT I Verbal/Math: 680/680	**ACT:** 29 **MOST COMPETITIVE**

The University of Chicago, founded in 1891, is a private liberal arts institution offering undergraduate and graduate programs with emphases on the biological and physical sciences, the humanities, and the social sciences. There are 10 graduate schools. In addition to regional accreditation, Chicago has baccalaureate program accreditation with NCATE. The 8 libraries contain 5.7 million volumes, 2 million microform items, and 15,000 audiovisual forms/CDs, and subscribe to 47,000 periodicals. Computerized library services include the card catalog, interlibrary loans, and database searching. Special learning facilities include a learning resource center, art gallery, radio station, film studies center, language labs, museum of Near Eastern antiquities, and Renaissance Society (contemporary art). The 190-acre campus is in an urban area in Chicago. Including residence halls, there are 200 buildings.

Programs of Study: Chicago confers B.A. and B.S. degrees. Master's and doctoral degrees are also awarded. Bachelor's degrees are awarded in BIOLOGICAL SCIENCE (biochemistry and biology/biological science), COMMUNICATIONS AND THE ARTS (art, art history and appreciation, Chinese, classics, English, fine arts, German, Japanese, Korean, linguistics, music, romance languages and literature, and Russian), COMPUTER AND PHYSICAL SCIENCE (chemistry, computer science, mathematics, physics, and statistics), ENGINEERING AND ENVIRONMENTAL DESIGN (environmental science), SOCIAL SCIENCE (African American studies, anthropology, Asian/Oriental studies, economics, geography, history, humanities, Judaic studies, Latin American studies, medieval studies, Near Eastern studies, philosophy, political science/government, psychology, religion, and sociology). Biology, philosophy, and chemistry are the strongest academically. Biology, economics, and English are the largest.

Special: Special academic programs include international, national, and local internships in most disciplines as well as a summer internship in Washington, study abroad in 12 countries, and work-study in most departments. There are 3-2 programs available through the schools of law, business, social service administration, and public policy. B.A.-B.S. and general studies degrees are offered, as are student designed majors. Nondegree study and pass/fail options are possible. There are 2 national honor societies, including Phi Beta Kappa.

Admissions: 48% of the 1999-2000 applicants were accepted. The SAT I scores for the 1999-2000 freshman class were: Verbal--1% below 500, 13% between 500 and 599, 44% between 600 and 700, and 42% above 700; Math--1% below 500, 11% between 500 and 599, 45% between 600 and 700, and 43% above 700. The ACT scores were 1% below 21, 3% between 21 and 23, 14% between 24 and 26, 22% between 27 and 28, and 60% above 28. 97% of the current freshmen were in the top quarter of their class; All were in the top half. In a recent year, there were 102 National Merit finalists. 66 freshmen graduated first in their class.

Requirements: The SAT I or ACT is required. Other admissions criteria include a recommended secondary school curriculum of 4 years of English, 3 to 4 years each of history, social studies, math, and science, and 2 to 3 years of a foreign language. The GED is accepted. An essay must be submitted and an interview is recommended. Applications may be submitted on disk using Apply. AP credits are accepted. Important factors in the admissions decision are advanced placement or honor courses, personality/intangible qualities, and evidence of special talent.

Procedure: Freshmen are admitted in the fall. Entrance exams should be taken during the senior year. There are early action, early admissions, and deferred admissions plans. Early action applications should be filed by November 15; regular applications, by January 1 for fall entry, along with a $60 fee. Notification of early action is sent December 15; regular decision, April 1. 11% of all applicants are on a waiting list.

Financial Aid: In a recent year, 76% of all freshmen and 68% of continuing students received some form of financial aid. 62% of freshmen and 56% of continuing students received need-based aid. The average freshman award was $20,522. Of that total, scholarships or need-based grants averaged $13,920 ($22,086 maximum); loans averaged $3460 ($3625 maximum); work contracts averaged $1422 ($1700 maximum) and Pell, FSEOG, and state and other noninstitutional grants averaged $5172 ($9800 maximum). 60% of undergraduates work part time. Average annual earnings from campus work are $1868. The average financial indebtedness of the 1999 graduate was $12,560. Chicago is a member of CSS. The CSS/Profile or FAFSA and the college's own financial statement are required. The fall application deadline is January 15.

Computers: The mainframes include an Amdahl 5880, 2 Sun minicomputers, and a Silicon Graphics 4D/240 minicomputer. Students are able to access the Amdahl or the Suns through personal user accounts. In addition, there are 7 public computer clusters with PCs and Macs as well as computer clusters in many of the residence halls. All residence hall rooms are linked to the campus computer network. All students may access the system any time. There are no time limits and no fees.

UNIVERSITY OF CINCINNATI
Cincinnati, OH 45221-0063   (513) 556-1100; Fax: (513) 556-1105

Full-time: 8215 men, 7365 women	**Faculty:** 1229; I, -$
Part-time: 2830 men, 2580 women	**Ph.D.s:** 82%
Graduate: 2880 men, 3335 women	**Student/Faculty:** 13 to 1
Year: quarters, summer session	**Tuition:** $4998 ($11,000)
Application Deadline: open	**Room & Board:** $5650
Freshman Class: 10,704 applied, 9169 accepted, 3943 enrolled	
SAT I Verbal/Math: 518/533	**ACT:** 22 **COMPETITIVE**

The University of Cincinnati, founded in 1819, is a state-supported institution offering undergraduate programs in art and architecture, business, engineering, health science, liberal arts and sciences, music, and technical training. Some of the information in this profile is approximate. There are 17 undergraduate and 10 graduate schools. In addition to regional accreditation, UC has baccalaureate program accreditation with AACSB and NCATE. The 18 libraries contain 1,948,000 volumes, 2,691,000 microform items, and 21,000 audiovisual forms/CDs, and subscribe to 19,600 periodicals. Computerized library services include the card catalog. Special learning facilities include a learning resource center, art gallery, and radio station. The 270-acre campus is in an urban area downtown Cincinnati. Including residence halls, there are 90 buildings.

Programs of Study: UC confers B.A., B.S., B.Arch., B.B.A., B.F.A., B.G.S., B.M., B.S.Des., B.S.E., B.S.N., B.S.Pharm., B.S.W, B.S.I.M, and B.U.P. degrees.

Associate, master's, and doctoral degrees are also awarded. Bachelor's degrees are awarded in BIOLOGICAL SCIENCE (biochemistry and biology/biological science), BUSINESS (accounting, banking and finance, business administration and management, management science, marketing/retailing/merchandising, and real estate), COMMUNICATIONS AND THE ARTS (broadcasting, communications, comparative literature, dance, design, dramatic arts, English, fine arts, French, German, jazz, linguistics, music, music history and appreciation, music theory and composition, piano/organ, Spanish, theater design, and voice), COMPUTER AND PHYSICAL SCIENCE (chemical technology, chemistry, computer science, geology, information sciences and systems, mathematics, physics, and quantitative methods), EDUCATION (art, business, early childhood, elementary, foreign languages, guidance, health, industrial arts, middle school, music, nutrition, science, secondary, and special), ENGINEERING AND ENVIRONMENTAL DESIGN (aeronautical engineering, architectural engineering, architectural technology, chemical engineering, city/community/regional planning, civil engineering, computer engineering, construction management, electrical/electronics engineering, electrical/electronics engineering technology, engineering, engineering mechanics, engineering technology, industrial administration/management, industrial engineering technology, materials engineering, mechanical engineering, mechanical engineering technology, metallurgical engineering, and nuclear engineering), HEALTH PROFESSIONS (medical laboratory technology, nuclear medical technology, nursing, pharmacy, predentistry, premedicine, and speech pathology/audiology), SOCIAL SCIENCE (African American studies, anthropology, Asian/Oriental studies, classical/ancient civilization, criminal justice, economics, geography, history, international studies, Judaic studies, Latin American studies, philosophy, political science/government, prelaw, psychology, social science, social work, sociology, and urban studies). Engineering is the strongest academically. Arts and sciences are the largest.

Special: The Professional Practice Program, a 5-year cooperative plan offering alternate work in academic subjects and industry, is available for students in engineering, business, arts and sciences, and design, architecture, and art. Study abroad opportunities include a winter quarter in Spain, an academic program in Paris, and a language/area studies work program in Germany. A general studies degree and nondegree study are available. There is a chapter of Phi Beta Kappa, and a freshman honors program.

Admissions: 86% of the 1999-2000 applicants were accepted. The SAT I scores for the 1999-2000 freshman class were: Verbal--41% below 500, 37% between 500 and 599, 19% between 600 and 700, and 3% above 700; Math--37% below 500, 35% between 500 and 599, 22% between 600 and 700, and 6% above 700. The ACT scores were 37% below 21, 23% between 21 and 23, 19% between 24 and 26, 10% between 27 and 28, and 9% above 28. 29% of the current freshmen were in the top fifth of their class; 54% were in the top two fifths.

Requirements: The SAT I or ACT is required. A GPA of 2.0 is required. Applicants should be graduates of an accredited secondary school with 4 units of high school English, 3 of math, 2 each of science, social science, foreign language, and electives, and 1 of fine arts.

Procedure: Freshmen are admitted to all sessions. Entrance exams should be taken In May of the junior year or January or March of the senior year. Application deadlines are open. There is a $30 fee. Notification is sent on a rolling basis.

Financial Aid: The CSS/Profile or FAFSA is required. The fall application deadline is March 1.

Computers: The mainframes are an Amdahl 5880 and 470, and a DEC VAX. There are also 350 Mac, IBM, and Zenith PCs available in all colleges and in the library. All students may access the system. There are no time limits and no fees.

UNIVERSITY OF COLORADO AT BOULDER

Boulder, CO 80309-0030 (303) 492-6301; Fax: (303) 492-7115

Full-time: 10,452 men, 9772 women
Part-time: 1287 men, 1149 women
Graduate: 3141 men, 2572 women
Year: semesters, summer session
Application Deadline: February 15
Freshman Class: 14,647 applied, 12,386 accepted, 4595 enrolled
SAT I Verbal/Math: 570/590

Faculty: 1104; I, av$
Ph.D.s: 86%
Student/Faculty: 18 to 1
Tuition: $3118 ($15,898)
Room & Board: $5200

ACT: 25   **COMPETITIVE+**

The University of Colorado at Boulder, established in 1876, is a public institution offering undergraduate and graduate programs in arts and sciences, business, engineering, architecture and planning, music, education, and journalism. There are 7 undergraduate and 3 graduate schools. In addition to regional accreditation, CU-Boulder has baccalaureate program accreditation with AACSB, ABET, ACEJMC, NASM, and NCATE. The 7 libraries contain 2,789,579 volumes, 5,902, 528 microform items, and 57,656 audiovisual forms/CDs, and subscribe to 25, 712 periodicals. Computerized library services include the card catalog, interlibrary loans, and database searching. Special learning facilities include a learning resource center, art gallery, natural history museum, planetarium, radio station, TV station, interactive foreign language video center, mountain research station, and integrated teaching and learning lab in engineering. The 600-acre campus is in a suburban area 30 miles northwest of Denver. Including residence halls, there are 155 buildings.

Programs of Study: CU-Boulder confers B.A., B.S., B.Env.D., B.F.A., B.Mus., and B.Mus.Ed. degrees. Master's and doctoral degrees are also awarded. Bachelor's degrees are awarded in BIOLOGICAL SCIENCE (biochemistry, cell biology, environmental biology, and molecular biology), BUSINESS (business administration and management), COMMUNICATIONS AND THE ARTS (art history and appreciation, Chinese, classics, communications, dance, dramatic arts, English, film arts, fine arts, French, Germanic languages and literature, Italian, Japanese, journalism, linguistics, music, Spanish, and studio art), COMPUTER AND PHYSICAL SCIENCE (applied mathematics, chemistry, computer science, geology, mathematics, and physics), EDUCATION (music), ENGINEERING AND ENVIRONMENTAL DESIGN (aeronautical engineering, architectural engineering, chemical engineering, civil engineering, computer engineering, electrical/electronics engineering, engineering, engineering physics, environmental design, environmental engineering, environmental science, and mechanical engineering), HEALTH PROFESSIONS (speech pathology/audiology), SOCIAL SCIENCE (American studies, anthropology, Asian/Oriental studies, Eastern European studies, economics, ethnic studies, geography, German area studies, history, humanities, interdisciplinary studies, international relations, Latin American studies, philosophy, physical fitness/movement, political science/government, psychology, religion, Russian and Slavic studies, sociology, and women's studies). Engineering, biological sciences, and chemistry are the strongest academically. Psychology, environmental studies, and biology. are the largest.

Special: Sewall, Farrand, and other residential programs for freshmen and sophomores offer a small liberal arts college atmosphere while taking advantage of the resources of a major university. A residential program in Baker Hall Village offers courses in the environmental sciences. Student-designed and dual majors, internships, 5-year B.A.-B.S. degrees, 5-year B.A.- M.A. degrees, and cooperative programs in business and engineering are available. Study abroad in 45 countries, work-study programs in federal labs, internships, a 3-2 engineering degree, and cross registration with other University of Colorado campuses are offered. There are 19 national honor societies, including Phi Beta Kappa, a freshman honors program, and 47 departmental honors programs.

Admissions: 85% of the 1999-2000 applicants were accepted. The SAT I scores for the 1999-2000 freshman class were: Verbal--15% below 500, 47% between 500 and 599, 32% between 600 and 700, and 6% above 700; Math--12% below 500, 42% between 500 and 599, 38% between 600 and 700, and 8% above 700. The ACT scores were 11% below 21, 25% between 21 and 23, 33% between 24 and 26, 16% between 27 and 28, and 16% above 28. 44% of the current freshmen were in the top fifth of their class; 79% were in the top two fifths. 135 freshmen graduated first in their class.

Requirements: The SAT I or ACT is required. A GPA of 2.0 is required. Applicants must have completed 16 credits of high school work as identified by the University of Colorado minimum Academic Preparation Standards. Students are asked to write a personal statement. Interviews are not used in the decision-making process. Auditions are required for consideration to the College of Music. Portfolios are discouraged. Students with a GED are considered on an individual basis. Applications are accepted on-line at http://www.colorado.edu/admissions/app/appintro.html. AP and CLEP credits are accepted. Important factors in the admissions decision are advanced placement or honor courses, geographic diversity, and leadership record.

Procedure: Freshmen are admitted to all sessions. Entrance exams should be taken no later than December of the senior year. There is a deferred admissions plan. Applications should be filed by February 15 for fall entry, October 1 for spring entry, and February 15 for summer entry, along with a $40 fee. Notification is sent on a rolling basis.

Financial Aid: In 1999-2000, 54% of all freshmen and 50% of continuing students received some form of financial aid. 31% of freshmen and 36% of continuing students received need-based aid. The average freshman award was $5515. Of that total, scholarships or need-based grants averaged $2693 ($25,400 maximum); loans averaged $2613 ($26,342 maximum); and work contracts averaged $209 ($4694 maximum). 61% of undergraduates work part time. The average financial indebtedness of the 1999 graduate was $16,422. CU-Boulder is a member of CSS. The FAFSA and tax returns are required. The fall application deadline is March 1.

Computers: The mainframe is an Hitachi Data Systems 3090 done. More than 1200 public access PCs are available in the computer labs, classroom buildings, dormitories, and libraries. All have Internet, Web,and Personal Lookup access. All students have e-mail and Internet accounts on the academic mainframe. All students may access the system 24 hours per day. There are no time limits and no fees. CU Boulder strongly recommends that all students have PCs.

UNIVERSITY OF COLORADO AT DENVER
Denver, CO 80217-3364   (303) 556-3287; Fax: (303) 556-4838

Full-time: 1947 men, 2523 women	**Faculty:** 479; IIA, +$
Part-time: 1693 men, 2191 women	**Ph.Ds:** n/av
Graduate: 2567 men, 3154 women	**Student/Faculty:** 9 to 1
Year: semesters, summer session	**Tuition:** $2443 ($11,569)
Application Deadline: July 22	**Room & Board:** n/app
Freshman Class: 1122 applied, 855 accepted, 385 enrolled	
SAT I or ACT: required	**VERY COMPETITIVE**

The University of Colorado at Denver, established in 1912, is a public, commuter institution with programs in the liberal arts and sciences, business, engineering and applied sciences, music, architecture and planning, and education. There are 3 undergraduate and 6 graduate schools. In addition to regional accreditation, CU-Denver has baccalaureate program accreditation with AACSB, ABET, NAAB, NASM, and NCATE. The library contains 533,821 volumes, 911,831 microform items, and 18,718 audiovisual forms/CDs, and subscribes to 4719 periodicals. Computerized library services include the card catalog, interlibrary loans, and database searching. Special learning facilities include a learning resource center, art gallery, TV station, and writing center. The 127-acre campus is in an urban area in downtown Denver. There are 30 buildings.

Programs of Study: CU-Denver confers B.A., B.S., and B.F.A degrees. Master's and doctoral degrees are also awarded. Bachelor's degrees are awarded in BIOLOGICAL SCIENCE (biology/biological science), BUSINESS (business administration and management), COMMUNICATIONS AND THE ARTS (communications, creative writing, dramatic arts, English, fine arts, French, music, and Spanish), COMPUTER AND PHYSICAL SCIENCE (applied mathematics, chemistry, computer science, geology, mathematics, and physics), ENGINEERING AND ENVIRONMENTAL DESIGN (civil engineering, electrical/electronics engineering, and mechanical engineering), SOCIAL SCIENCE (anthropology, economics, geography, history, interdisciplinary studies, philosophy, political science/government, psychology, and sociology). Business, engineering, and psychology are the strongest academically. Business administration, biology, and psychology are the largest.

Special: Cross-registration is possible with Metropolitan State College and Community College of Denver. Concurrent enrollment with any University of Colorado campus is possible. Cooperative programs, 1-semester internships, study abroad in 12 countries, work-study programs, an accelerated degree program in business, and B.A.-B.S. degrees are available. The university offers dual majors, a general studies degree, nondegree study, and pass/fail options. Student-designed majors and a 3-2 engineering degree are available. There are small, individualized classes, peer advocates, and workshops. There are 8 national honor societies.

Admissions: 76% of the 1999-2000 applicants were accepted. The SAT I scores for the 1999-2000 freshman class were: Verbal--38% below 500, 41% between 500 and 599, 19% between 600 and 700, and 3% above 700; Math--33% below 500, 42% between 500 and 599, 22% between 600 and 700, and 3% above 700. The ACT scores were 17% below 19, 62% between 19 and 24, 20% between 25 and 30, and 1% between 31 and 36. 57% of the current freshmen were in the top quarter of their class; 84% were in the top half.

Requirements: The SAT I or ACT is required. A GPA of 2.5 is required. Preference for admission is given to applicants who rank in the top 30% of their high school graduating class and present a composite score of 21 or higher on the ACT or a combined score of 950 or higher on the SAT I. Applications are accepted on-line via Entrata. AP and CLEP credits are accepted. Important factors in the admissions decision are advanced placement or honor courses, evidence of special talent, and extracurricular activities record.

Procedure: Freshmen are admitted to all sessions. Entrance exams should be taken in the junior or senior year of high school. There is a deferred admissions plan. Applications should be filed by July 22 for fall entry, December 1 for spring entry, and May 3 for summer entry, along with a $40 fee. Notification is sent on a rolling basis.

Financial Aid: In 1999-2000, 36% of all freshmen and 44% of continuing students received some form of financial aid. 23% of freshmen and 26% of continuing students received need-based aid. The average freshman award was $3514. 80% of undergraduates work part time. Average annual earnings from campus work are $2000. The average financial indebtedness of the 1999 graduate was $15,275. CU-Denver is a member of CSS. The FAFSA, the university's own financial statement, and tax returns are required. The priority date for fall application is March 1.

Computers: The mainframe is a Hitachi Model EX-90. There are computer labs with more than 100 PCs and Macs available. Internet access and word processing, spreadsheet, and graphics applications are provided. Remote access is available, as is a fullystaffed help center. All students may access the system any time. There are no time limits.

UNIVERSITY OF DALLAS
Irving, TX 75062-4799

(972) 721-5266
(800) 628-6999; Fax: (972) 721-5017

Full-time: 451 men, 668 women	**Faculty:** 98; IIA, -$
Part-time: 38 men, 32 women	**Ph.D.s:** 92%
Graduate: 1129 men, 898 women	**Student/Faculty:** 11 to 1
Year: semesters, summer session	**Tuition:** $14,420
Application Deadline: February 15	**Room & Board:** $5416
Freshman Class: 1213 applied, 927 accepted, 310 enrolled	
SAT I Verbal/Math: 630/600	**ACT:** 26 **VERY COMPETITIVE+**

The University of Dallas, founded in 1955, is a private liberal arts institution affiliated with the Roman Catholic Church. Undergraduate programs are offered through the Constantin College of Liberal Arts and the Braniff Graduate School, which has liberal arts and management divisions. A second campus is located in Rome, Italy. There are 2 graduate schools. In addition to regional accreditation, UD has baccalaureate program accreditation with AALE. The library contains 295,018 volumes, 75,565 microform items, and 946 audiovisual forms/CDs, and subscribes to 1074 periodicals. Computerized library services include the card catalog, interlibrary loans, and database searching. Special learning facilities include a learning resource center and 80-seat theater, observatory, and several art galleries. The 750-acre campus is in a suburban area 12 miles west of Dallas. Including residence halls, there are 28 buildings.

Programs of Study: UD confers B.A. and B.S. degrees. Master's and doctoral degrees are also awarded. Bachelor's degrees are awarded in BIOLOGICAL SCIENCE (biochemistry and biology/biological science), COMMUNICATIONS AND THE ARTS (art history and appreciation, ceramic art and design, classics, dramatic arts, English, French, German, painting, printmaking, and Spanish), COMPUTER AND PHYSICAL SCIENCE (chemistry, computer science, mathematics, and physics), EDUCATION (art and elementary), SOCIAL SCIENCE (economics, history, philosophy, political science/government, psychology, and theological studies). Classics, English, and politics are the strongest academically. Biology, English, and politics are the largest.

Special: UD offers Air Force and Army ROTC cross-registration with the University of North Texas, internships in field experience or off-campus research semester, and summer study abroad, a Washington semester, on-campus work-study programs, an accelerated 5-year business degree program, B.A.-B.S. degrees, dual and student-designed majors, and pass/fail options. A 3-2 engineering degree or 3-2 architecture degree may be arranged with Washington University in St. Louis and the University of Texas. There are 4 national honor societies, including Phi Beta Kappa.

Admissions: 76% of the 1999-2000 applicants were accepted. The SAT I scores for the 1999-2000 freshman class were: Verbal--5% below 500, 29% between 500 and 599, 47% between 600 and 700, and 19% above 700; Math--11% below 500, 37% between 500 and 599, 42% between 600 and 700, and 10% above 700. The ACT scores were 4% below 21, 17% between 21 and 23, 32% between 24 and 26, 22% between 27 and 28, and 25% above 28. 71% of the current freshmen were in the top fifth of their class; 96% were in the top two fifths. There were 16 National Merit finalists. 18 freshmen graduated first in their class.

Requirements: The SAT I or ACT is required. UD requires applicants to be in the upper 50% of their class. A GPA of 2.4 is required. Applicants must be graduates of an accredited secondary school or have a GED certificate. 16 academic or Carnegie credits are required, including courses in English, social studies, math, science, and a foreign language. An interview is recommended, and an essay is required. Applications are accepted on disk and on-line. AP credits are accepted. Important factors in the admissions decision are advanced placement or honor courses, leadership record, and extracurricular activities record.

Procedure: Freshmen are admitted fall and spring. Entrance exams should be taken during the junior year or by the fall of the senior year. There are early decision and deferred admissions plans. Early decision applications should be filed by December 1; regular applications, by February 15 for fall entry and December 15 for spring entry, along with a $40 fee. Notification is sent on a rolling basis. 102 early decision candidates were accepted for the 1999-2000 class.

Financial Aid: In 1999-2000, 96% of all freshmen and 91% of continuing students received some form of financial aid. 71% of freshmen and 70% of continuing students received need-based aid. The average freshman award was $14,917. Of that total, scholarships or need-based grants averaged $9157 ($14,354 maximum); loans averaged $4477 ($17,500 maximum); and work contracts averaged $1049 ($2318 maximum). 47% of undergraduates work part time. Average annual earnings from campus work are $1224. The average financial indebtedness of the 1999 graduate was $15,300. The FAFSA and the college's own financial statement are required. The fall application deadline is February 15.

Computers: The mainframe is an IBM RISC 6000. A network of IBM RISC 6000s and other servers supports all university students. 4 computer labs are available for student use, as well as individual workstations in the library, in the foreign language and math departments, and at various other sites across campus. All students are given Internet access. All students may access the system. There are no time limits and no fees. It is recommedned that all students have personal computers.

UNIVERSITY OF DAYTON
Dayton, OH 45469

(937) 229-4411
(800) 837-7433; Fax: (937) 229-4729

Full-time: 3075 men, 3383 women	**Faculty:** 340; IIA, +$
Part-time: 330 men, 230 women	**Ph.D.s:** 93%
Graduate: 1422 men, 1783 women	**Student/Faculty:** 19 to 1
Year: semesters, summer session	**Tuition:** $15,530
Application Deadline: open	**Room & Board:** $4870
Freshman Class: 7182 applied, 5773 accepted, 1766 enrolled	
SAT I Verbal/Math: 560/580	**ACT:** 24 **VERY COMPETITIVE**

The University of Dayton, founded in 1850, is a nonprofit, private, comprehensive institution affiliated with the Roman Catholic Church. Part of the Southwestern Ohio Council for Higher Education, it has undergraduate and graduate programs emphasizing the arts and sciences, business administration, engineering, education, and allied professions and law. There are 4 undergraduate schools and 1 graduate school. In addition to regional accreditation, UD has baccalaureate program accreditation with AACSB, ABET, ADA, NASM, and NCATE. The 2 libraries contain 991,020 volumes, 800,531 microform items, and 1858 audiovisual forms/CDs, and subscribe to 5153 periodicals. Computerized library services include the card catalog, interlibrary loans, and database searching. Special learning facilities include a learning resource center, art gallery, radio station, TV station, engineering and science research institute, information sciences center, and day-care facility that provides a learning environment for education majors. The 110-acre campus is in a suburban area 2 miles south of downtown Dayton. Including residence halls, there are 44 buildings.

Programs of Study: UD confers B.A., B.S., B.C.E., B.Ch.E., B.E.E., B.F.A., B. G.S., B.M., and B.M.E. degrees. Master's and doctoral degrees are also awarded. Bachelor's degrees are awarded in BIOLOGICAL SCIENCE (biochemistry, biology/biological science, environmental biology, and nutrition), BUSINESS (accounting, banking and finance, business economics, management information systems, management science, marketing/retailing/merchandising, and sports management), COMMUNICATIONS AND THE ARTS (broadcasting, communications, design, dramatic arts, English, fine arts, French, German, journalism, music, photography, public relations, and Spanish), COMPUTER AND PHYSICAL SCIENCE (chemistry, computer science, geology, information sciences and systems, mathematics, physical sciences, and physics), EDUCATION (art, business, early childhood, elementary, health, music, secondary, and special), ENGINEERING AND ENVIRONMENTAL DESIGN (chemical engineering, civil engineering, computer engineering, electrical/electronics engineering, electrical/electronics engineering technology, engineering, engineering technology, industrial engineering technology, manufacturing technology, mechanical engineering, and mechanical engineering technology), HEALTH PROFESSIONS (music therapy, predentistry, and premedicine), SOCIAL SCIENCE (American studies, criminal justice, dietetics, economics, history, international studies, philosophy, physical fitness/movement, political science/government, psychology, religion, and sociology). Engineering, business, and exercise science are the strongest academically. Communication and psychology are the largest.

Special: Special academic programs include co-op and work-study programs, internships, summer study abroad at 5 European sites chosen each year, a summer program in Germany or semester exchange in France for business students, a Washington semester, one-month immersion language programs, and cross-registration with the Southwestern Ohio Council for Higher Education (SOCHE) consortium. Dual major programs are available, as is a B.A.-B.S. degree in economics, chemistry, math, and psychology. A 3-2 engineering degree is offered with Wilberforce University and Thomas More College. A general studies degree, credit for life, military, or work experience, and pass/fail options are also available. There are 23 national honor societies and a freshman honors program.

Admissions: 80% of the 1999-2000 applicants were accepted. The SAT I scores for the 1999-2000 freshman class were: Verbal--17% below 500, 47% between 500 and 599, 30% between 600 and 700, and 6% above 700; Math--17% below 500, 37% between 500 and 599, 35% between 600 and 700, and 11% above 700. The ACT scores were 11% below 21, 28% between 21 and 23, 30% between 24 and 26, 14% between 27 and 28, and 17% above 28. 42% of the current freshmen were in the top fifth of their class; 70% were in the top two fifths. There were 13 National Merit finalists. 39 freshmen graduated first in their class.

Requirements: The SAT I or ACT is required. In addition, applicants should be graduates of an accredited secondary school with 15 to 18 units in English, social sciences, math, foreign language, and lab science. Additional math and science courses may be neessary for certain programs. The GED is accepted. High school transcripts and official scores from the ACT or SAT I must be submitted. An essay or personal statement, recommendation from the high school guidance counselor, and an interview are recommended. Music students must audition. Applications are accepted on-line at admission.udayton.edu/application.asp. AP and CLEP credits are accepted. Important factors in the admissions decision are advanced placement or honor courses, leadership record, and extracurricular activities record.

Procedure: Freshmen are admitted fall, winter, and summer. Entrance exams should be taken by December of the senior year. There is a deferred admissions plan. The priority admission application date is January 1, but open; the fee is $30. Notification is sent on a rolling basis. 10% of all applicants are on a waiting list.

Financial Aid: In 1999-2000, 93% of all freshmen and 96% of continuing students received some form of financial aid. 52% of freshmen and 50% of continuing students received need-based aid. The average freshman award was $12,847. Of that total, scholarships or need-based grants averaged $7219 ($15,020 maximum); loans averaged $4851 ($5625 maximum); and work contracts averaged $1790 ($2100 maximum). 77% of undergraduates work part time. Average annual earnings from campus work are $1460. The average financial indebtedness of the 1999 graduate was $16,252. UD is a member of CSS. The FAFSA is required. The fall application deadline is March 31.

Computers: The mainframe is an NCR 3600. All student housing is connected to the campus voice, video, and data networks. In addition, more than 550 PC, Mac, and Sun computers are available in more than 21 labs around the campus. The university also operates a computer store. All students may access the network system 24 hours a day, 7 day a week. There are no time limits and no fees. All entering first-year students are required to purchase one of three preconfigured computer systems through the university: the Tangent Medallion 600, Tangent Medallion 667, or Tangent Shuttle XI 400.

UNIVERSITY OF DELAWARE
Newark, DE 19716   (302) 831-8123; Fax: (302) 831-6905

Full-time: 5960 men, 8476 women	**Faculty:** 998; I, +$
Part-time: 1309 men, 1754 women	**Ph.D.s:** 87%
Graduate: 1579 men, 1529 women	**Student/Faculty:** 14 to 1
Year: 4-1-4, summer session	**Tuition:** $4858 ($13,228)
Application Deadline: February 15	**Room & Board:** $5132
Freshman Class: 14,107 applied, 8891 accepted, 3534 enrolled	
SAT I Verbal/Math: 560/570	**VERY COMPETITIVE**

The University of Delaware, founded in 1743 and chartered in 1833, is an independently chartered institution with state assistance. It offers programs in agricultural and natural resources, liberal arts and sciences, business, education, human resources, health and nursing sciences, and engineering. There are 6 undergraduate and 2 graduate schools. In addition to regional accreditation, Delaware has baccalaureate program accreditation with AACSB, ABET, ADA, APTA, CAHEA, NASDTEC, NASM, NCATE, and NLN. The 5 libraries contain 2,358,006 volumes, 2,993,864 microform items, and 134,716 audiovisual forms/CDs, and subscribe to 12,220 periodicals. Computerized library services include the card catalog, interlibrary loans, and database searching. Special learning facilities include a learning resource center, art gallery, radio station, TV station, preschool lab, development ice skating science center, computer-controlled greenhouse, nursing practice labs, physical therapy clinic, 400-acre agricultural research complex, exercise physiology biomechanics labs, foreign language media center, and composite materials center. The 1000-acre campus is in a small town 12 miles southwest of Wilmington; centered on the east coast between New York City and Washington D.C., and Philadeplphia and Baltimore. Including residence halls, there are 400 buildings.

Programs of Study: Delaware confers B.A., B.S., B.A. Liberal Studies, B.A.S., B.C.E., B.Ch.E., B.C.P.E., B.E.E., B.E.N.E., B.F.A., B.M.E., B.Mus., B.S.Acc., B.S.Ag., B.S.A.T., B.S.B.A., B.S.Ed., B.S.N., and B.S.P.E. degrees. Associate, master's, and doctoral degrees are also awarded. Bachelor's degrees are awarded in AGRICULTURE (agricultural business management, agricultural economics, agriculture, animal science, natural resource management, plant science, and soil science), BIOLOGICAL SCIENCE (biochemistry, biology/biological science, biotechnology, entomology, nutrition, and plant pathology), BUSINESS (accounting, banking and finance, business administration and management, hotel/motel and restaurant management, management science, marketing/retailing/merchandising, and recreation and leisure services), COMMUNICATIONS AND THE ARTS (art, art history and appreciation, communications, comparative literature, English, fine arts, historic preservation, Italian, journalism, languages, music, music theory and composition, and theater management), COMPUTER AND PHYSICAL SCIENCE (astronomy, chemistry, computer science, geology, geophysics and seismology, information sciences and systems, mathematics, and physics), EDUCATION (agricultural, athletic training, early childhood, education, elementary, English, foreign languages, mathematics, music, physical, psychology, science, secondary, and special), ENGINEERING AND ENVIRONMENTAL DESIGN (bioengineering, chemical engineering, civil engineering, computer engineering, electrical/electronics engineering, engineering technology, environmental engineering, environmental science, landscape architecture/design, and mechanical engineering), HEALTH PROFESSIONS (medical laboratory technology and nursing), SOCIAL SCIENCE (anthropology, community services, consumer services, criminal justice, dietetics, economics, family and community services, fashion design and technology, food science, geography, history, human development, interdisciplinary studies, international relations, Latin American studies, parks and recreation management, philosophy, physical fitness/movement, political science/government, psychology, sociology, textiles and clothing, and women's studies). Engineering, all sciences, and business are the strongest academically. Biological sciences, elementary teacher education, and engineering are the largest.

Special: Students may participate in cooperative programs, internships, study abroad in 19 countries, a Washington semester, and work-study programs. The university offers accelerated degree programs, B.A.-B.S. degrees, dual majors, 68 minors, student-designed majors (Bachelor of Arts in Liberal Studies), and pass/fail options. There are 4-1 degree programs in business, engineering, and hotel and restaurant management. Nondegree study is available through the Division of Continuing Education. There is an extensive undergraduate research program. Students may earn an enriched degree through the University Honors Program. There are 37 national honor societies, including Phi Beta Kappa, and a freshman honors program.

Admissions: 63% of the 1999-2000 applicants were accepted. The SAT I scores for the 1999-2000 freshman class were: Verbal--16% below 500, 52% between 500 and 599, 27% between 600 and 700, and 5% above 700; Math--14% below 500, 46% between 500 and 599, 33% between 600 and 700, and 7% above 700. The ACT scores were 11% below 21, 31% between 21 and 23, 31% between 24 and 26, 17% between 27 and 28, and 9% above 28. 50% of the current freshmen were in the top fifth of their class; 86% were in the top two fifths. There were 17 National Merit finalists. 40 freshmen graduated first in their class.

Requirements: The SAT I or ACT is required. Applicants should be graduates of an accredited secondary school. The GED is accepted. Students should have completed a minimum of 16 high school academic credits, including 4 years of English, 2 years each of math, science, foreign language, and history, 1 year of social studies, and 3 years of academic course electives. SAT II: Subject tests are recommended, especially for honors program applicants. A writing sample and at least 1 letter of recommendation are required for all applicants. Applicants may apply on-line at the school's web site or through Apply. AP credits are accepted. Important factors in the admissions decision are advanced placement or honor courses, recommendations by school officials, and personality/intangible qualities.

Procedure: Freshmen are admitted fall and spring. Entrance exams should be taken at the end of the junior year or the beginning of the senior year. There are early decision, early admissions, and deferred admissions plans. Early decision applications should be filed by November 15; regular applications, by February 15 for fall entry and November 15 for spring entry, along with a $45 fee. Notification of early decision is sent December 15; regular decision, mid-March. 470 early decision candidates were accepted for the 1999-2000 class. 5% of all applicants are on a waiting list.

Financial Aid: In 1999-2000, 72% of all freshmen and 60% of continuing students received some form of financial aid. 48% of freshmen and 41% of continuing students received need-based aid. The average freshman award was $5500. Of that total, scholarships or need-based grants averaged $4500 ($19,500 maximum); loans averaged $2625 ($4000 maximum); and work contracts averaged $1400 ($2500 maximum). 50% of undergraduates work part time. Average annual earnings from campus work are $1000. The average financial indebtedness of the 1999 graduate was $14,000. Delaware is a member of CSS. The FAFSA is required. The fall application deadline is March 15.

Computers: Mainframes consist of 2 IBM RS/6000-990, 1 Silicon Graphics Power Challenge, 1 Cray Research J916/8-1024, 2 Sun Microsystems Ultra Enterprise 4000, and 1 Sun Microsystems Ultra Enterprise 5000. 35 computing sites are available to students, offering more than 900 terminals, PCs, and Macs. All residence hall rooms and many classrooms are equipped with data outlets for network connection. Those registered in computer courses or doing research that requires it may access the system 24 hours a day. There are no time limits and no fees.

UNIVERSITY OF DENVER
Denver, CO 80208

(303) 871-2036
(800) 525-9495; Fax: (303) 871-3301

Full-time: 1458 men, 1607 women	**Faculty:** 402; I, -$
Part-time: 92 men, 491 women	**Ph.D.s:** 91%
Graduate: 1836 men, 2344 women	**Student/Faculty:** 8 to 1
Year: quarters, summer session	**Tuition:** $19,440
Application Deadline: February 1	**Room & Board:** $6165
Freshman Class: 3469 applied, 2773 accepted, 816 enrolled	
SAT I Verbal/Math: 568/573	**ACT:** 25 **VERY COMPETITIVE**

The University of Denver, established in 1864 and affiliated with the Methodist Church, is a private institution offering degrees in arts and sciences, fine arts, music, business, engineering, and education. There are 7 undergraduate and 6 graduate schools. In addition to regional accreditation, DU has baccalaureate program accreditation with AACSB, ABET, CSWE, NASAD, and NASM. The 2 libraries contain 1,896,796 volumes, 931,335 microform items, and 2725 audiovisual forms/CDs, and subscribe to 5540 periodicals. Computerized library services include the card catalog, interlibrary loans, and database searching. Special learning facilities include a learning resource center, art gallery, a high-altitude research field station, an observatory, and elementary, middle, and high schools. The 123-acre campus is in a suburban area 8 miles southeast of the Denver business district. Including residence halls, there are 90 buildings.

Programs of Study: DU confers B.A., B.S., B.F.A., B.M., B.S.Acc., B.S.A.T., B.S.B.A., B.S.Ch., B.S.Comp.E., B.S.E.E., and B.S.M.E. degrees. Master's and doctoral degrees are also awarded. Bachelor's degrees are awarded in AGRICULTURE (animal science), BIOLOGICAL SCIENCE (biochemistry and biology/biological science), BUSINESS (accounting, banking and finance, business administration and management, business economics, hospitality management services, international business management, marketing/retailing/merchandising, and real estate), COMMUNICATIONS AND THE ARTS (applied art, art, art history and appreciation, classics, communications, comparative literature, dramatic arts, English, French, German, graphic design, Italian, Japanese, jazz, journalism, languages, music, music history and appreciation, music performance, music theory and composition, Spanish, and telecommunications), COMPUTER AND PHYSICAL SCIENCE (astronomy, chemistry, computer science, geology, mathematics, physics, science, and statistics), EDUCATION (music), ENGINEERING AND ENVIRONMENTAL DESIGN (computer engineering, construction management, electrical/electronics engineering, environmental science, materials science, and mechanical engineering), HEALTH PROFESSIONS (physical therapy), SOCIAL SCIENCE (anthropology, Asian/Oriental studies, cognitive science, economics, geography, history, international studies, Latin American studies, philosophy, political science/government, psychology, public affairs, religion, Russian and Slavic studies, social science, sociology, and women's studies). Communications, psychology, and business are the strongest academically. Communications, accounting, and political science are the largest.

Special: DU offers co-op programs, study abroad, internships, a Washington quarter, work-study programs, dual majors, a 3-2 engineering program, and B.A.-B.S. programs in psychology, environmental science, and math. Nondegree study and pass/fail options are also available. There are 13 national honor societies, including Phi Beta Kappa, a freshman honors program, and 13 departmental honors programs.

Admissions: 80% of the 1999-2000 applicants were accepted. The SAT I scores for the 1999-2000 freshman class were: Verbal--15% below 500, 50% between 500 and 599, 29% between 600 and 700, and 6% above 700; Math--16% below 500, 46% between 500 and 599, 32% between 600 and 700, and 6% above 700. The ACT scores were 15% below 21, 24% between 21 and 23, 31% between 24 and 26, 15% between 27 and 28, and 15% above 28. 52% of the current freshmen were in the top fifth of their class; 78% were in the top two fifths.

Requirements: The SAT I or ACT is required. A GPA of 2.0 is required. In addition, applicants must be graduates of an accredited secondary school. The GED is accepted. The university recommends that applicants have 15 to 20 high school academic credits, including 4 in English, 3 to 4 each in math, and 2 to 4 each in foreign language, social science, and natural sciences (2 with lab). Course work in the arts is encouraged. An essay is required of all students, and an interview is recommended. An audition is required for music applicants, and a portfolio is recommended for art students. Students may apply on-line using Common App, CollegeLink, or CollegeView. AP and CLEP credits are accepted. Important factors in the admissions decision are advanced placement or honor courses, recommendations by school officials, and evidence of special talent.

Procedure: Freshmen are admitted to all sessions. Entrance exams should be taken by February of the senior year. There is a deferred admissions plan. Applications should be filed by February 1 for fall entry, December 1 for winter entry, February 15 for spring entry, and May 15 for summer entry, along with a $45 fee. Notification is sent on a rolling basis beginning December 1.

Financial Aid: In a recent year, 74% of all freshmen and 60% of continuing students received some form of financial aid. 44% of freshmen and 34% of continuing students received need-based aid. The average freshman award was $16,314. Of that total, scholarships or need-based grants averaged $8425 ($15,948 maximum); loans averaged $3295 ($4125 maximum); and work contracts averaged $1500 ($1800 maximum). 26% of undergraduates work part time. Average annual earnings from campus work are $1400. The average financial indebtedness of a recent graduate was $9700. DU is a member of CSS. The FAFSA is required. The fall application deadline is February 15.

Computers: The mainframes are DEC ALPHA 4000 and 4100 servers running both VMS and Digitial UNIX. There are more than 500 PCs available in dormitories, computer labs, the library, and most classrooms, Internet access in all residence rooms, and a laptop computing program for undergraduates. Access to the Internet and the Web is available on and off campus. All students may access the system 24 hours a day. There are no time limits and no fees. Incoming freshmen are required to have laptop computers.

UNIVERSITY OF EVANSVILLE

Evansville, IN 47722-0329

(812) 479-2468
(800) 423-8633; Fax: (812) 474-4076

Full-time: 979 men, 1595 women	**Faculty:** 179; IIA, -$
Part-time: 131 men, 274 women	**Ph.D.s:** 83%
Graduate: 3 men, 22 women	**Student/Faculty:** 14 to 1
Year: semesters, summer session	**Tuition:** $15,504
Application Deadline: see profile	**Room & Board:** $5100
Freshman Class: n/av	
SAT I Verbal/Math: 570/573	**ACT:** 25 **VERY COMPETITIVE**

The University of Evansville, founded in 1854, is a private institution affiliated with the United Methodist Church. The university offers undergraduate degree programs in arts and sciences, business administration, education, engineering and computing sciences, fine arts, and nursing and health sciences. There are 4 undergraduate schools and 1 graduate school. In addition to regional accreditation, UE has baccalaureate program accreditation with ABET, APTA, NASM, NCATE, and NLN. The library contains 263,627 volumes, 419,776 microform items, and 7874 audiovisual forms/CDs, and subscribes to 1380 periodicals. Computerized library services include interlibrary loans and database searching. Special learning facilities include a learning resource center and radio station. The 75-acre campus is in an urban area 120 miles west of Louisville. Including residence halls, there are 39 buildings.

Programs of Study: UE confers B.A., B.S., B.F.A., B.L.S., B.M., B.M.M.E., and B.M.M.T. degrees. Associate and master's degrees are also awarded. Bachelor's degrees are awarded in BIOLOGICAL SCIENCE (biology/biological science), BUSINESS (accounting, banking and finance, business administration and management, international business management, and marketing/retailing/merchandising), COMMUNICATIONS AND THE ARTS (art, art history and appreciation, communications, creative writing, dramatic arts, English, French, German, graphic design, literature, music, music business management, music performance, Spanish, studio art, theater design, and theater management), COMPUTER AND PHYSICAL SCIENCE (chemistry, computer programming, computer science, mathematics, and physics), EDUCATION (art, athletic training, elementary, English, mathematics, middle school, music, physical, science, secondary, social studies, and special), ENGINEERING AND ENVIRONMENTAL DESIGN (civil engineering, computer engineering, electrical/electronics engineering, engineering management, environmental science, and mechanical engineering), HEALTH PROFESSIONS (music therapy, nursing, physical therapy, premedicine, and sports medicine), SOCIAL SCIENCE (anthropology, archeology, behavioral science, biblical studies, classical/ancient civilization, criminal justice, economics, gerontology, history, international studies, liberal arts/general studies, paralegal studies, philosophy, physical fitness/movement, political science/government, prelaw, psychobiology, psychology, religion, sociology, and theological studies). Business, engineering, and education are the largest.

Special: Students may study abroad in the United Kingdom and Germany. UE also offers cooperative programs in engineering and business with various industries, internships in such fields as communications and business, credit for life experience through the Center for Continuing Education, student-designed majors, and pass/fail options in elective courses. There are 18 national honor societies, a freshman honors program, and 20 departmental honors programs.

Admissions: The SAT I scores for the 1999-2000 freshman class were: Verbal-- 16% below 500, 46% between 500 and 599, 32% between 600 and 700, and 6%

above 700; Math--14% below 500, 47% between 500 and 599, 34% between 600 and 700, and 5% above 700. The ACT scores were 29% between 21 and 23, 34% between 24 and 26, 20% between 27 and 28, and 17% above 28. 54% of the current freshmen were in the top fifth of their class; 89% were in the top two fifths. In a recent year, there were 13 National Merit finalists. 39 freshmen graduated first in their class.

Requirements: The SAT I or ACT is required. To be competitive for admission, students should submit a minimum SAT I composite score of 1100 or ACT composite of 24. UE requires applicants to be in the upper 50% of their class. A GPA of 2.0 is required. Applicants must be graduates of accredited secondary schools; applicants who have been home-schooled are also considered. The university recommends completion of 4 years of college-preparatory English, 3 each of math (algebra I and II, geometry) and social science, and 2 of a foreign language. An interview is recommended, but not required. Applications are accepted on-line via ExPAN and UE's own on-line application. AP and CLEP credits are accepted. Important factors in the admissions decision are advanced placement or honor courses, leadership record, and recommendations by school officials.

Procedure: Freshmen are admitted fall and spring. Entrance exams should be taken by December of the senior year. There are early action, early admissions, and deferred admissions plans. Early action applications should be filed by December 1; thereafter applications are accepted as space permits. The application fee is $30. Notification of early action is sent December 15; regular decision, on a rolling basis.

Financial Aid: In 1999-2000, 97% of all freshmen and 91% of continuing students received some form of financial aid. 68% of freshmen and 70% of continuing students received need-based aid. The average freshman award was $11,491. Of that total, scholarships or need-based grants averaged $9788 ($17,704 maximum); loans averaged $3459 ($9625 maximum); work contracts averaged $1300 ($1650 maximum); and non-need-based scholarships averaged $5203 ($21,004 maximum). 20% of undergraduates work part time. Average annual earnings from campus work are $1256. The average financial indebtedness of the 1999 graduate was $15,688. UE is a member of CSS. The FAFSA and the college's own financial statement are required. The fall application deadline is March 1.

Computers: The mainframe is an IBM Multiprise 2003-206. There are 7 public computer labs and several departmental computer clusters connected to a LAN using UNIX, Novell, Windows NT, and Mac servers. Almost every computer on campus has access to the network, including student-owned computers in the residence halls. All students may access the system at any time. There are no time limits and no fees. It is recommended that students in some courses have personal computers.

UNIVERSITY OF FLORIDA
Gainesville, FL 32611-4000 (352) 392-1365

Full-time: 13,527 men, 15,115 women	**Faculty:** 1600; I, av$
Part-time: 1624 men, 1367 women	**Ph.D.s:** 97%
Graduate: 6160 men, 5589 women	**Student/Faculty:** 18 to 1
Year: semesters, summer session	**Tuition:** $2141 ($9130)
Application Deadline: January 29	**Room & Board:** $5040
Freshman Class: 13,967 applied, 8397 accepted, 3705 enrolled	
SAT I Verbal/Math: 625/642	**ACT:** 27 **HIGHLY COMPETITIVE**

The University of Florida, founded in 1853, is a public, liberal arts institution that is part of the state university system of Florida. There are 14 undergraduate and

17 graduate schools. In addition to regional accreditation, UF has baccalaureate program accreditation with AACSB, ABET, ACCE, ACEJMC, ACPE, ADA, AHEA, APTA, ASLA, FIDER, NAAB, NASAD, NASM, NCATE, NLN, and SAF. The 15 libraries contain 3,401,279 volumes, 6,340,498 microform items, and 30,864 audiovisual forms/CDs, and subscribe to 25,213 periodicals. Computerized library services include the card catalog, interlibrary loans, and database searching. Special learning facilities include a learning resource center, art gallery, natural history museum, radio station, TV station, a performing arts center, and a teaching hospital. The 2000-acre campus is in a suburban area 75 miles from Jacksonville. Including residence halls, there are 850 buildings.

Programs of Study: UF confers B.A., B.S., B.A.E., B.F.A., B.H.S., B.M.E., B. Mus., B.S.A., B.S.B.A., B.S.F., B.S.N., and B.S.P. degrees. Master's and doctoral degrees are also awarded. Bachelor's degrees are awarded in AGRICULTURE (agricultural business management, agronomy, animal science, dairy science, forestry and related sciences, horticulture, natural resource management, plant science, poultry science, and soil science), BIOLOGICAL SCIENCE (botany, entomology, microbiology, plant pathology, wildlife biology, and zoology), BUSINESS (accounting, banking and finance, insurance, management science, marketing/retailing/merchandising, real estate, and recreation and leisure services), COMMUNICATIONS AND THE ARTS (advertising, art, art history and appreciation, English, French, German, graphic design, journalism, linguistics, music, music history and appreciation, performing arts, photography, Portuguese, public relations, Russian, Spanish, speech/debate/rhetoric, telecommunications, and theater design), COMPUTER AND PHYSICAL SCIENCE (astronomy, chemistry, computer science, geology, mathematics, physics, and statistics), EDUCATION (agricultural, art, elementary, health, music, and special), ENGINEERING AND ENVIRONMENTAL DESIGN (aeronautical engineering, agricultural engineering, architecture, chemical engineering, civil engineering, computer engineering, construction engineering, electrical/electronics engineering, engineering and applied science, environmental engineering, industrial engineering technology, interior design, landscape architecture/design, materials engineering, mechanical engineering, nuclear engineering, nuclear engineering technology, and surveying engineering), HEALTH PROFESSIONS (allied health, nursing, occupational therapy, pharmacy, physical therapy, physician's assistant, and speech pathology/audiology), SOCIAL SCIENCE (American studies, anthropology, Asian/Oriental studies, classical/ancient civilization, criminal justice, East Asian studies, economics, food science, geography, history, home economics, interdisciplinary studies, Judaic studies, philosophy, physical fitness/movement, political science/government, psychology, religion, and sociology). Engineering, pharmacy, and tax law are the strongest academically. Business, engineering, and liberal arts are the largest.

Special: UF offers many internships, dual and student-designed majors, and study abroad in 32 countries. Cross-registration is possible through the Undergraduate Inter-institutional Registration program. Work-study programs, accelerated degree programs, co-op programs, and B.A.-B.S. degrees are available. There are 53 national honor societies, including Phi Beta Kappa, and a freshman honors program.

Admissions: 60% of the 1999-2000 applicants were accepted. The SAT I scores for the 1999-2000 freshman class were: Verbal--3% below 500, 31% between 500 and 599, 51% between 600 and 700, and 15% above 700; Math--2% below 500, 20% between 500 and 599, 60% between 600 and 700, and 18% above 700. The ACT scores were 1% below 21, 6% between 21 and 23, 25% between 24 and 26, 30% between 27 and 28, and 38% above 28. 88% of the current freshmen were in the top fifth of their class; 97% were in the top two fifths.

Requirements: The SAT I or ACT is required. The SAT I is preferred. Minimum composite scores are 950 on the SAT I and 19 on the ACT. Candidates should have graduated from an accredited secondary school or have a GED and have completed 4 years of English, 3 years each of math, science, and social studies, 2 years of a foreign language, and 4 units of academic electives. Applications are accepted on-line at http://www.reg.ufl.edu. AP and CLEP credits are accepted. Important factors in the admissions decision are advanced placement or honor courses, parents or siblings attending the school, and recommendations by school officials.

Procedure: Freshmen are admitted to all sessions. Entrance exams should be taken in the junior year. There are early decision and early admissions plans. Early decision applications should be filed by September 26; regular applications, by January 29 for fall entry, October 1 for spring entry, and January 29 for summer entry, along with a $20 fee. Notification of early decision is sent October 31; regular decision, March 20.

Financial Aid: The average freshman award was $6376. Of that total, scholarships or need-based rewards averaged $3082 (maximum); need based loans averaged $2222 (maximum); and need-based self-help averaged $2087 (maximum). 17% of undergraduates work part time. Average annual earnings from campus work are $1800. The average financial indebtedness of the 1999 graduate was $13,968. UF is a member of CSS. The FAFSA and the college's own financial statement are required. The fall application deadline is April 15.

Computers: The mainframes are an IBM ES9000-831/3VF, an IBM RS6000/SP(9 nodes), and a DEC ALPHA cluster. There are also 353 PCs and 100 Macs available for general student use. Upper-division teaching labs restricted to department majors add several hundred more. All students may access the system via 151 terminals for general student use. There is a limit on the IBM systems but no limit on the DEC cluster. There are no fees. The college requires all students to have personal computers.

UNIVERSITY OF GEORGIA
Athens, GA 30602   (706) 542-2112; Fax: (706) 542-1466

Full-time: 9677 men, 11,858 women	**Faculty:** 1809; I, av$
Part-time: 1272 men, 1233 women	**Ph.D.s:** 95%
Graduate: 2819 men, 4053 women	**Student/Faculty:** 12 to 1
Year: semesters, summer session	**Tuition:** $3034 ($10,276)
Application Deadline: February 1	**Room & Board:** $4902
Freshman Class: 13,402 applied, 8466 accepted, 4285 enrolled	
SAT I Verbal/Math: 598/597	**HIGHLY COMPETITIVE**

The University of Georgia, chartered in 1785 and part of the University System of Georgia, offers degree programs in the arts and sciences, marine studies, music, business, agricultural and environmental sciences, education, family and consumer sciences, forest resources, journalism, social work, pharmacy, law, veterinary medicine, and preprofessional studies. There are 12 undergraduate schools and 1 graduate school. In addition to regional accreditation, UGA has baccalaureate program accreditation with AACSB, ABET, ACEJMC, ACPE, ADA, ASLA, CSWE, FIDER, NASAD, NASM, NCATE, NRPA, and SAF. The 3 libraries contain 3,622,094 volumes, 6,001,206 microform items, and 174,967 audiovisual forms/CDs, and subscribe to 39,784 periodicals. Computerized library services include the card catalog, interlibrary loans, and database searching. Special learning facilities include a learning resource center, art gallery, natural history museum, radio station, bioscience learning center, rare book and manuscript library, performing arts center, State Botanical Garden of Georgia, Peabody Awards Archives, and Institute for Newspaper Management Studies. The 605-acre campus is in a small town 80 miles east of Atlanta. Including residence halls, there are 335 buildings.

Programs of Study: UGA confers B.A., B.S., A.B.J., B.B.A., B.F.A., B.L.A., B.Mus., B.S.A., B.S.A.E., B.S.BioEng., B.S.Chem., B.S.Ed., B.S.E.H., B.S.F.R., B.S.Family and Consumer Services, B.S.H.E., B.S.P.A., B.S.Pcs., B.S.Phr., and B.S.W., degrees. Associate, master's, and doctoral degrees are also awarded. Bachelor's degrees are awarded in AGRICULTURE (agricultural economics, agriculture, dairy science, fishing and fisheries, forestry and related sciences, horticulture, plant protection (pest management), poultry science, and wildlife management), BIOLOGICAL SCIENCE (biochemistry, biology/biological science, botany, ecology, entomology, genetics, microbiology, nutrition, and zoology), BUSINESS (accounting, business administration and management, fashion merchandising, international business management, management information systems, management science, marketing/retailing/merchandising, real estate, and recreation and leisure services), COMMUNICATIONS AND THE ARTS (advertising, art, broadcasting, communications, comparative literature, design, dramatic arts, English, French, German, Germanic languages and literature, Greek, Italian, journalism, Latin, linguistics, music, music performance, music theory and composition, public relations, romance languages and literature, Spanish, speech/ debate/rhetoric, studio art, and telecommunications), COMPUTER AND PHYSICAL SCIENCE (astronomy, chemistry, computer science, geology, mathematics, physics, and statistics), EDUCATION (agricultural, art, business, early childhood, elementary, English, foreign languages, health, marketing and distribution, mathematics, middle school, music, science, social science, special, and trade and industrial), ENGINEERING AND ENVIRONMENTAL DESIGN (agricultural engineering, bioengineering, environmental science, interior design, landscape architecture/design, preengineering, and technology and public affairs), HEALTH PROFESSIONS (environmental health science, music therapy, pharmacy, predentistry, premedicine, preveterinary science, and speech pathology/audiology), SOCIAL SCIENCE (anthropology, child care/child and family studies, classical/ ancient civilization, clothing and textiles management/production/services, cognitive science, criminal justice, dietetics, economics, family/consumer studies, food science, geography, history, home furnishings and equipment management/ production/services, interdisciplinary studies, Japanese studies, philosophy, political science/government, psychology, religion, social science, social work, and sociology). Business, journalism, and genetics are the strongest academically. Finance, marketing, and psychology are the largest.

Special: UGA offers co-op programs with the Medical College of Georgia and the Georgia Institute of Technology, as well as cross-registration with University Center institutions in urban Atlanta. With the Governor's Intern Program, students may serve a full-time 10-week internship in a state government agency; many other internships are available within departments, as well as work-study programs within the university and with many area businesses. Students may study abroad in 26 countries. A Washington semester, an accelerated degree program in business, general studies and 3-2 engineering degrees, student-designed majors, dual degrees and double majors, and nondegree study are also available. There are 48 national honor societies, including Phi Beta Kappa, a freshman honors program, and 51 departmental honors programs.

Admissions: 63% of the 1999-2000 applicants were accepted. The SAT I scores for the 1999-2000 freshman class were: Verbal--6% below 500, 44% between 500 and 599, 40% between 600 and 700, and 10% above 700; Math--6% below 500, 44% between 500 and 599, 42% between 600 and 700, and 8% above 700. There were 65 National Merit finalists.

Requirements: The SAT I or ACT is required. UGA admits freshmen primarily on the basis of high school curriculum, grades earned, and college admissions test scores. The University may consider qualitative information to determine a student's potential for success. Applicants should be high school graduates or present a GED certificate. Students should have taken 4 years of English, 3 each of math, science, and social studies, and 2 of a foreign language. An audition is required for music majors. Applications may be submitted on-line at the UGA web site. AP and CLEP credits are accepted.

Procedure: Freshmen are admitted to all sessions. Entrance exams should be taken in January of the senior year. Applications should be filed by February 1 for fall entry, along with a $25 fee. Notification is sent on a rolling basis.

Financial Aid: In 1999-2000, 97% of all freshmen and 59% of continuing students received some form of financial aid. 33% of all students received need-based aid. The average freshman award was $4000. Of that total, scholarships or need-based grants averaged $3000; loans averaged $1000 ($2625 maximum); and work contracts averaged $1500 ($3000 maximum). 60% of undergraduates work part time. The average financial indebtedness of the 1999 graduate was $13,600. UGA is a member of CSS. The FAFSA is required. The fall application deadline is August 1.

Computers: The mainframes comprise an IBM 3090 model 400; CDC CYBERs 180/850, 180/845, and 205; and a DEC VAX 11/780. Computers for student use are located at various points across campus, including the library, residence halls, the computer center, academic departments, and computer labs. All students may access the system at designated times for the various locations. There are no time limits and no fees.

UNIVERSITY OF HAWAII AT MANOA
Honolulu, HI 96822

(808) 956-8975
(800) 823-9771; Fax: (808) 956-4148

Full-time: 4369 men, 5462 women	**Faculty:** I, av$
Part-time: 1008 men, 1096 women	**Ph.D.s:** 86%
Graduate: 2405 men, 3272 women	**Student/Faculty:** n/av
Year: semesters, summer session	**Tuition:** $3142 ($9622)
Application Deadline: June 1	**Room & Board:** $3970
Freshman Class: 4715 applied, 3353 accepted, 1735 enrolled	
SAT I Verbal/Math: 523/566	**VERY COMPETITIVE**

The University of Hawaii at Manoa, founded in 1907, is the major research institution in the University of Hawaii system. The undergraduate programs offered include liberal arts and sciences, business, education, engineering, nursing, tropical agriculture, architecture, travel industry management, physical science, technology, Hawaiian, Asian-Pacific Studies, social work, and medicine. There are 13 undergraduate and 6 graduate schools. In addition to regional accreditation, UHM has baccalaureate program accreditation with AACSB, ABET, ACEJMC, ADA, CSWE, NAAB, NASM, and NLN. The 2 libraries contain 2,925,821 volumes, 5,729,691 microform items, and 35,315 audiovisual forms/CDs, and subscribe to 27,316 periodicals. Computerized library services include the card catalog, interlibrary loans, and database searching. Special learning facilities include a learning resource center, art gallery, radio station, and TV station. The 300-acre campus is in an urban area in Honolulu. Including residence halls, there are 247 buildings.

Programs of Study: UHM confers B.A., B.S., B.Arch., B.B.A., B.Ed., B.F.A., B.Mus., and B.S.W. degrees. Master's and doctoral degrees are also awarded.

Bachelor's degrees are awarded in AGRICULTURE (agricultural economics, agriculture, agronomy, animal science, and horticulture), BIOLOGICAL SCIENCE (biology/biological science, botany, entomology, microbiology, and zoology), BUSINESS (accounting, banking and finance, business administration and management, business economics, fashion merchandising, human resources, international business management, management information systems, management science, marketing/retailing/merchandising, real estate, recreation and leisure services, and tourism), COMMUNICATIONS AND THE ARTS (art, Chinese, classics, communications, dance, dramatic arts, English, fine arts, French, German, Hawaiian, Japanese, journalism, Korean, music, Russian, Spanish, and speech/debate/rhetoric), COMPUTER AND PHYSICAL SCIENCE (atmospheric sciences and meteorology, chemistry, computer science, geology, geophysics and seismology, information sciences and systems, mathematics, and physics), EDUCATION (athletic training, elementary, physical, recreation, secondary, and special), ENGINEERING AND ENVIRONMENTAL DESIGN (architecture, civil engineering, electrical/electronics engineering, environmental science, and mechanical engineering), HEALTH PROFESSIONS (dental hygiene, health science, medical laboratory technology, nursing, and speech pathology/audiology), SOCIAL SCIENCE (American studies, anthropology, Asian/Oriental studies, economics, ethnic studies, family/consumer resource management, food science, geography, Hawaiian studies, history, liberal arts/general studies, philosophy, political science/government, psychology, religion, social work, sociology, and women's studies). Education, nursing, and social work are the strongest academically. Psychology, biology, and art are the largest.

Special: Internships are available with the state legislature and through 55 different offices, as well as academic departments via career services. Co-op, work-study programs, and internships are also offered. Dual majors, nondegree study, and pass/fail options are available. The liberal studies program offers student-designed majors. Students may study abroad in any one of 20 countries for a summer, a semester, or a year. There are 13 national honor societies, including Phi Beta Kappa, a freshman honors program. All departments have honors programs.

Admissions: 71% of the 1999-2000 applicants were accepted. The SAT I scores for the 1999-2000 freshman class were: Verbal--35% below 500, 48% between 500 and 599, 15% between 600 and 700, and 2% above 700; Math--17% below 500, 46% between 500 and 599, 31% between 600 and 700, and 6% above 700.

Requirements: The SAT I or ACT is required. UHM requires applicants to be in the upper 40% of their class. A GPA of 3.2 is required. The minimum required score on the SAT I is 550 for each section or on the ACT, 22 composite. Applicants must be graduates of an accredited secondary school. The GED is accepted. UHM requires 22 Carnegie units or 17 academic credits, including 4 units of English and 3 units each of math, science, and social studies, as well as 4 additional units of college preparatory courses and 5 electives. AP and CLEP credits are accepted. Important factors in the admissions decision are advanced placement or honor courses, personality/intangible qualities, and leadership record.

Procedure: Freshmen are admitted to all sessions. Entrance exams should be taken by December of the senior year for fall admission. There is an early admissions plan. Applications should be filed by June 1 for fall entry and November 1 for spring entry, along with a $25 fee. Notification is sent on a rolling basis.

Financial Aid: In 1999-2000, 43% of all freshmen and 32% of continuing students received some form of financial aid. 35% of freshmen and 28% of continuing students received need-based aid. The average freshman award was $5010. Of that total, scholarships or need-based grants averaged $2943 ($7199 maximum); loans averaged $4458 ($17,515 maximum); work contracts averaged

$1557 ($2400 maximum), and external scholarships and academic waivers averaged $887 ($3213 maximum). Average annual earnings from campus work are $2017. The average financial indebtedness of the 1999 graduate was $7086. UHM is a member of CSS. The FAFSA and the college's own financial statement are required. The fall application deadline is March 1.

Computers: The mainframes are an IBM 9672 -RA5 and numerous Sun servers (various models). There are networked Macs and PCs available in labs, academic departments, and offices. Access is also available via modem dial-up or cable modem from home. All students may access the system. There are no time limits and no fees. It is recommended that students in architecture have personal computers.

UNIVERSITY OF HOUSTON
Houston, TX 77004

(713) 743-1010
(800) 741-4449; Fax: (713) 743-9633

Full-time: 7563 men, 9030 women	**Faculty:** 653; I, av$
Part-time: 3915 men, 4164 women	**Ph.D.s:** 86%
Graduate: 3640 men, 4339 women	**Student/Faculty:** 25 to 1
Year: semesters, summer session	**Tuition:** $2830 ($9310)
Application Deadline: July 1	**Room & Board:** $4513
Freshman Class: 6863 applied, 5666 accepted, 3261 enrolled	
SAT I Verbal/Math: 500/525	**ACT:** 20 **COMPETITIVE**

The University of Houston, established in 1927, is a public institution with programs in arts and sciences, business, education, engineering, and health professions. There are 13 undergraduate schools and 1 graduate school. In addition to regional accreditation, UH has baccalaureate program accreditation with AACSB, ABET, ACPE, ADA, CSWE, NAAB, NASM, and NCATE. The 5 libraries contain 2,035,040 volumes, 3,878,346 microform items, and 6343 audiovisual forms/CDs, and subscribe to 27,109 periodicals. Computerized library services include the card catalog, interlibrary loans, and database searching. Special learning facilities include a learning resource center, art gallery, radio station, tv station, and observatory. The 550-acre campus is in an urban area 3 miles from the Houston business district. Including residence halls, there are 98 buildings.

Programs of Study: UH confers B.A., B.S., B.Acc., B.Arch., B.B.A., B.F.A., B.M., B.S.C.E., B.S.Ch.E., B.S.E.E., B.S.I.E., B.S.M.E., B.S.Pharm., and B.S. Tech degrees. Master's and doctoral degrees are also awarded. Bachelor's degrees are awarded in BIOLOGICAL SCIENCE (biochemistry, biology/biological science, biophysics, and nutrition), BUSINESS (accounting, banking and finance, business administration and management, hotel/motel and restaurant management, management information systems, marketing and distribution, marketing/retailing/merchandising, operations research, personnel management, and sports management), COMMUNICATIONS AND THE ARTS (applied music, art, art history and appreciation, classical languages, classics, communications, creative writing, dramatic arts, English, fine arts, French, German, journalism, music, music theory and composition, painting, photography, printmaking, radio/television technology, sculpture, Spanish, speech/debate/rhetoric, and studio art), COMPUTER AND PHYSICAL SCIENCE (chemistry, computer science, earth science, geology, geophysics and seismology, information sciences and systems, mathematics, physics, quantitative methods, and statistics), EDUCATION (trade and industrial), ENGINEERING AND ENVIRONMENTAL DESIGN (architectural engineering, architecture, biomedical equipment technology, chemical engineering, civil engineering, civil engineering technology, computer engineering, computer technology, construction management, construction technology, drafting and design technology, electrical/electronics engineering, electrical/electronics engineering technology, electromechanical technology, environmental design, graphic arts technology, industrial administration/management, industrial engineering, industrial engineering technology, interior design, manufacturing technology, mechanical engineering, and mechanical engineering technology), HEALTH PROFESSIONS (health, optometry, pharmacy, predentistry, premedicine, prepharmacy, and preveterinary science), SOCIAL SCIENCE (anthropology, economics, family/consumer studies, history, human development, interdisciplinary studies, Italian studies, philosophy, physical fitness/movement, political science/government, prelaw, psychology, Russian and Slavic studies, social science, and sociology). Chemical engineering is the strongest academically. Business, engineering, and biological sciences are the largest.

Special: There is cross-registration with the University of Texas and Rice and Texas Wesleyan Universities. UH also offers internships and co-op programs in many majors, study abroad in 12 countries, work-study programs, and programs in Mexican American studies, Asian American studies, and inter-university African studies, as well as the Mickey Leland Internship in Washington, D.C. Also available are B.A.-B.S. degrees and dual majors in all areas of study, nondegree study, and pass/fail options. There are 10 national honor societies, a freshman honors program, and 13 departmental honors programs.

Admissions: 83% of the 1999-2000 applicants were accepted. The SAT I scores for the 1999-2000 freshman class were: Verbal--47% below 500, 37% between 500 and 599, 14% between 600 and 700, and 2% above 700; Math--40% below 500, 39% between 500 and 599, 18% between 600 and 700, and 3% above 700. The ACT scores were 50% below 21, 26% between 21 and 23, 14% between 24 and 26, 4% between 27 and 28, and 6% above 28. 48% of the current freshmen were in the top fifth of their class; 69% were in the top two fifths. There were 44 National Merit finalists. 17 freshmen graduated first in their class.

Requirements: The SAT I or ACT is required. A minimum composite score of 800 (400 verbal and 400 math) on the SAT I or 19 on the ACT is required if the student is in the top 10% of the high school class. Lower ranks require higher scores. A GPA of 2.0 is required. Applicants must be graduates of an accredited secondary school or have the GED. Students should complete 4 credits of English, 3 of math and social sciences, and 2 of lab science, with 2 of foreign language strongly recommended. There are special requirements for the College of Engineering and the School of Music, including an audition for music candidates. AP and CLEP credits are accepted. Important factors in the admissions decision are evidence of special talent, advanced placement or honor courses, and recommendations by school officials.

Procedure: Freshmen are admitted to all sessions. Entrance exams should be taken no later than February of the senior year. Applications should be filed by July 1 for fall entry, December 15 for spring entry, and May 1 for summer entry, along with a $30 fee. Notification is sent on a rolling basis.

Financial Aid: In 1999-2000, 50% of all freshmen received some form of financial aid. UH is a member of CSS. The FAFSA is required. The fall application deadline is April 1.

Computers: The mainframe is a DEC VAX 7000. Registered students have access to computer facilities that are located throughout the campus, including at the library and at a 24-hour site. In addition, individual departments, the Honors College, and the residence halls have their own computer facilities. All students may access the system. There are no time limits. The fee is $5 per credit hour.

UNIVERSITY OF ILLINOIS AT CHICAGO
Chicago, IL 60680 (312) 996-4350; Fax: (312) 413-7628

Full-time: 6288 men, 7741 women	**Faculty:** 988; I, av$
Part-time: 1076 men, 1055 women	**Ph.D.s:** 90%
Graduate: 3689 men, 4580 women	**Student/Faculty:** 14 to 1
Year: semesters, summer session	**Tuition:** $4644 ($10,920)
Application Deadline: February 1	**Room & Board:** $5856
Freshman Class: 10,757 applied, 6250 accepted, 2616 enrolled	
ACT: 23	**VERY COMPETITIVE**

The University of Illinois at Chicago, founded in 1946, is a public institution with undergraduate and graduate programs in the liberal arts, art and fine arts, business, engineering, architecture, health sciences, music, teacher preparation, social work, and professional training in dentistry, medicine, and pharmacy. There are 9 undergraduate and 1 graduate school. In addition to regional accreditation, UIC has baccalaureate program accreditation with AACSB, ABET, ACPE, ADA, APTA, CSAB, CSWE, NAAB, NASAD, and NLN. The 5 libraries contain 1, 989,739 volumes, 2,662,159 microform items, and 25,755 audiovisual forms/CDs, and subscribe to 15,538 periodicals. Computerized library services include the card catalog, interlibrary loans, and database searching. Special learning facilities include a learning resource center, art gallery, radio station, Jane Addams Hull House, which is a restored settlement house, and James Woodworth Prairie Reserve. The 216-acre campus is in an urban area just west of downtown Chicago. Including residence halls, there are 105 buildings.

Programs of Study: UIC confers B.A., B.S., B.Arch., B.F.A., B.S.C. and E., B. S.C.E., B.S.Ch.E., B.S.E.E., B.S.E.M., B.S.E.M.A.N., B.S.M.E., B.S.N., and B. S.W. degrees. Master's and doctoral degrees are also awarded. Bachelor's degrees are awarded in BIOLOGICAL SCIENCE (biochemistry, biology/biological science, and nutrition), BUSINESS (accounting, banking and finance, business administration and management, business statistics, management science, and marketing/retailing/merchandising), COMMUNICATIONS AND THE ARTS (art history and appreciation, classics, design, dramatic arts, French, German, graphic design, industrial design, Italian, literature, music, photography, Polish, Russian, Spanish, speech/debate/rhetoric, and studio art), COMPUTER AND PHYSICAL SCIENCE (chemistry, computer science, geology, information sciences and systems, mathematics, physics, and statistics), EDUCATION (art, education, elementary, English, foreign languages, mathematics, physical, science, and secondary), ENGINEERING AND ENVIRONMENTAL DESIGN (architecture, bioengineering, chemical engineering, civil engineering, computer engineering, electrical/electronics engineering, engineering, engineering management, engineering physics, industrial engineering technology, and mechanical engineering), HEALTH PROFESSIONS (medical laboratory science, nursing, occupational therapy, and pharmacy), SOCIAL SCIENCE (African American studies, anthropology, classical/ancient civilization, criminal justice, economics, geography, history, Latin American studies, philosophy, political science/government, psychology, social work, and sociology). Math, nursing, and philosophy are the strongest academically. Accounting, engineering, and psychology are the largest.

Special: Special academic programs include a wide variety of co-op and program internships, work-study with some 70 on- and off-campus employers, and study-abroad opportunities at accredited foreign universities, as well as special programs in France, Italy, Canada, Austria, Spain, and Mexico. There is cross-registration with the City Colleges of Chicago. Interdisciplinary majors are offered in architectural studies, communications and theater, French business studies, math and computer science, thermomechanics and energy information and bioengineering, and information and decision sciences. Students may pursue a 3-2 engineering degree with Chicago State, Eastern Illinois, Illinois State, Northeastern Illinois, and Western Illinois Universities. Up to 4 semester hours of credit may be granted for military experience. Dual and student-designed majors, nondegree study, and pass/fail options are available. There are 10 national honor societies, including Phi Beta Kappa, and a freshman honors program.

Admissions: 58% of the 1999-2000 applicants were accepted. The ACT scores for the 1999-2000 freshman class were: 27% below 21, 31% between 21 and 23, 23% between 24 and 26, 10% between 27 and 28, and 9% above 28. 48% of the current freshmen were in the top fifth of their class; 84% were in the top two fifths.

Requirements: The SAT I or ACT is required. UIC requires applicants to be in the upper 30% of their class. Applicants should be graduates of an accredited secondary school; the GED is accepted. The recommended secondary school curriculum varies according to the college program chosen, but 16 high school credits are required. AP and CLEP credits are accepted. Important factors in the admissions decision are recommendations by school officials, evidence of special talent, and advanced placement or honor courses.

Procedure: Freshmen are admitted to all sessions. Entrance exams should be taken in the spring of the junior year or the fall of the senior year. There are early admissions and deferred admissions plans. Applications should be filed by February 1 for fall entry, October 1 for spring entry, and April 1 for summer entry, along with a $40 fee. Notification is sent on a rolling basis.

Financial Aid: The FAFSA is required. The fall application priority deadline is March 1.

Computers: The mainframe is an IBM 3090/300J. Numerous terminals and PCs are located in labs, classrooms, libraries, and residence halls throughout the campus. All students may access the system 24 hours a day. There are no time limits and no fees.

UNIVERSITY OF ILLINOIS AT URBANA-CHAMPAIGN
Urbana, IL 61801   (217) 333-0302

Full-time: 14,739 men, 12,863 women	Faculty: 1684; I, +$
Part-time: 296 men, 194 women	Ph.D.s: 96%
Graduate: 5080 men, 4112 women	Student/Faculty: 16 to 1
Year: semesters, summer session	Tuition: $4770 ($11,862)
Application Deadline: January 6	Room & Board: $5560
Freshman Class: 17,867 applied, 12,636 accepted, 6479 enrolled	
SAT I Verbal/Math: 610/640	ACT: 27 HIGHLY COMPETITIVE

The University of Illinois at Urbana-Champaign, founded in 1867, is the oldest and largest campus in the University of Illinois system, offering some 150 undergraduate and more than 100 graduate degree programs. There are 9 undergraduate schools and 1 graduate school. In addition to regional accreditation, Illinois has baccalaureate program accreditation with AACSB, ABET, ACEJMC, ADA, AHEA, ASLA, CSWE, NAAB, NASAD, NASM, NCATE, NRPA, and SAF. The 39 libraries contain 9,171,693 volumes, 8,742,985 microform items, and 868,358 audiovisual forms/CDs, and subscribe to 90,954 periodicals. Computerized library services include the card catalog, interlibrary loans, and database searching. Special learning facilities include a learning resource center, art gallery, natural history museum, radio station, tv station, language learning lab, performing arts center, and graphic technologies lab. The 1470-acre campus is in a small town 130 miles south of Chicago. Including residence halls, there are 200 major buildings.

Programs of Study: Illinois confers A.B., B.S., B.A.U.P., B.F.A., B.Land.Arch., B.Mus., B.S.Ed., B.S.J., B.S.W., and B.V.M. degrees. Master's and doctoral degrees are also awarded. Bachelor's degrees are awarded in AGRICULTURE (agriculture, animal science, forestry and related sciences, horticulture, and soil science), BIOLOGICAL SCIENCE (biochemistry, biology/biological science, biophysics, cell biology, ecology, entomology, microbiology, and molecular biology), BUSINESS (accounting, banking and finance, business administration and management, hotel/motel and restaurant management, marketing/retailing/merchandising, and recreation and leisure services), COMMUNICATIONS AND THE ARTS (advertising, art history and appreciation, broadcasting, classics, communications, comparative literature, crafts, dance, dramatic arts, English, French, Germanic languages and literature, graphic design, industrial design, Italian, journalism, linguistics, media arts, music, music history and appreciation, music theory and composition, painting, photography, Portuguese, Russian, sculpture, Spanish, speech/debate/rhetoric, and voice), COMPUTER AND PHYSICAL SCIENCE (actuarial science, astronomy, chemistry, computer science, geology, mathematics, physics, and statistics), EDUCATION (agricultural, art, business, early childhood, education of the mentally handicapped, elementary, English, foreign languages, health, mathematics, music, physical, science, secondary, social studies, special, and speech correction), ENGINEERING AND ENVIRONMENTAL DESIGN (aeronautical engineering, agricultural engineering, architecture, bioengineering, ceramic engineering, chemical engineering, city/community/regional planning, civil engineering, computer engineering, electrical/electronics engineering, engineering, engineering mechanics, engineering physics, environmental science, industrial engineering, landscape architecture/design, materials science, mechanical engineering, metallurgical engineering, nuclear engineering, technological management, and urban design), HEALTH PROFESSIONS (community health work, speech pathology/audiology, and veterinary science), SOCIAL SCIENCE (anthropology, East Asian studies, Eastern European studies, economics, family/consumer studies, food production/management/services, food science, geography, history, home economics, human development, humanities, Latin American studies, liberal arts/general studies, philosophy, political science/government, psychology, Russian and Slavic studies, social work, sociology, and theological studies). Advertising, engineering and music are the strongest academically. Psychology, accountancy, and electrical and computer engineering are the largest.

Special: Illinois offers cooperative engineering programs with 30 midwestern liberal arts colleges; 16 summer, semester, and full-year programs abroad and numerous exchange opportunities; and cross-registration with Parkland Community College. Unusual opportunities include a leisure studies semester in Scotland and a summer parliamentary internship in London. A dual degree in liberal arts and engineering is offered, as well as student-designed majors and a 3-2 engineering program with numerous universities. On-campus work-study and pass/fail options are possible. There are more than 50 national honor societies, including Phi Beta Kappa, and a freshman honors program.

Admissions: 71% of the 1999-2000 applicants were accepted. The SAT I scores for the 1999-2000 freshman class were: Verbal--9% below 500, 35% between 500 and 599, 45% between 600 and 700, and 11% above 700; Math--5% below 500, 21% between 500 and 599, 48% between 600 and 700, and 26% above 700. The ACT scores were 6% below 21, 11% between 21 and 23, 27% between 24

and 26, 24% between 27 and 28, and 33% above 28. 76% of the current freshmen were in the top fifth of their class; 95% were in the top two fifths. There were 53 National Merit finalists. 583 freshmen graduated first in their class.

Requirements: Applicants should be graduates of accredited secondary schools or have the GED. High school preparation must include 4 years of English, 3 or more of math, 2 each of lab science and social studies, and, for most programs, 2 of foreign languages. A personal essay is optional. Visual arts applicants must submit a portfolio; performing arts applicants are required to audition. AP and CLEP credits are accepted. Important factors in the admissions decision are evidence of special talent, advanced placement or honor courses, and geographic diversity.

Procedure: Freshmen are admitted fall and spring. Entrance exams should be taken by the spring of the junior year and no later than October of the senior year. There are early admissions and deferred admissions plans. Applications should be filed by January 6 for fall entry and November 1 for spring entry, along with a $40 fee. Notification is sent February 20.

Financial Aid: In 1999-2000, 83% of all freshmen and 80% of continuing students received some form of financial aid. 46% of freshmen and 49% of continuing students received need-based aid. The average freshman award was $7500. Of that total, scholarships or need-based grants averaged $4719 ($6900 maximum); loans averaged $2794 ($4125 maximum); and work contracts averaged $1500 ($2000 maximum). 53% of undergraduates work part time. Average annual earnings from campus work are $1300. The average financial indebtedness of the 1999 graduate was $10,394. Illinois is a member of CSS. The FAFSA and the college's own financial statement are required. The fall application deadline is March 15.

Computers: The mainframes are an IBM RS/6000/540, an IBM 380, a Sequent Symmetry S81, a Convex C240, and an IBM 3801/KX6. About 3000 computer workstations are located in classrooms, labs, and residence halls across campus. All students may access the system 24 hours a day. Students may access the system 20 hours per week on dial-in access only; there is no limit from networked PCs. There are no fees. It is recommended that students in law school have personal computers, preferably a Pentium 120.

UNIVERSITY OF IOWA
Iowa City, IA 52242-1396

(319) 335-3847
(800) 553-IOWA; Fax: (319) 335-1535

Full-time: 7692 men, 9192 women	**Faculty:** 1620; I, +$
Part-time: 1208 men, 1445 women	**Ph.D.s:** 99%
Graduate: 4744 men, 4565 women	**Student/Faculty:** 10 to 1
Year: semesters, summer session	**Tuition:** $2786 ($10,228)
Application Deadline: May 15	**Room & Board:** $4370
Freshman Class: 11,358 applied, 9437 accepted, 3859 enrolled	
SAT I Verbal/Math: 590/600	**ACT:** 25 **VERY COMPETITIVE**

The University of Iowa, founded in 1847, is a comprehensive, public institution. Its undergraduate and graduate programs emphasize the liberal and fine arts, business, engineering, health science, and the professions. There are 6 undergraduate and 5 graduate schools. In addition to regional accreditation, Iowa has baccalaureate program accreditation with AACSB, ABET, ACEJMC, ACPE, ADA, AHEA, APTA, CAHEA, CSWE, NASM, NCATE, and NLN. The 13 libraries contain 3.75 million volumes, 5.8 million microform items, and 33,200 audiovisual forms/CDs, and subscribe to 38,400 periodicals. Computerized library services include the card catalog, interlibrary loans, and database searching. Special learning facilities include an art gallery, natural history museum, radio station, UI hospitals and clinics, the Iowa Center for the Arts, and a driving simulator. The 1900-acre campus is in a small town 110 miles east of Des Moines and 220 miles west of Chicago. Including residence halls, there are 115 buildings.

Programs of Study: Iowa confers B.A., B.S., B.B.A., B.F.A., B.L.S., B.M., B.S.E., B.S.M., B.S.N., and B.S.Ph. degrees. Master's and doctoral degrees are also awarded. Bachelor's degrees are awarded in BIOLOGICAL SCIENCE (biochemistry, biology/biological science, and microbiology), BUSINESS (accounting, banking and finance, business administration and management, business economics, management science, marketing/retailing/merchandising, and recreation and leisure services), COMMUNICATIONS AND THE ARTS (art, art history and appreciation, broadcasting, classics, communications, comparative literature, dance, dramatic arts, English, film arts, fine arts, French, German, Greek, Italian, journalism, Latin, linguistics, music, Portuguese, Russian, Spanish, and speech/debate/rhetoric), COMPUTER AND PHYSICAL SCIENCE (actuarial science, astronomy, chemistry, computer science, geology, information sciences and systems, mathematics, physics, and statistics), EDUCATION (art, elementary, foreign languages, health, middle school, music, science, and secondary), ENGINEERING AND ENVIRONMENTAL DESIGN (biomedical engineering, chemical engineering, civil engineering, computer engineering, electrical/electronics engineering, engineering, environmental science, industrial administration/management, industrial engineering, and mechanical engineering), HEALTH PROFESSIONS (medical laboratory technology, nuclear medical technology, nursing, pharmacy, predentistry, premedicine, and speech pathology/audiology), SOCIAL SCIENCE (African American studies, American studies, anthropology, Asian/Oriental studies, classical/ancient civilization, economics, geography, history, liberal arts/general studies, parks and recreation management, philosophy, political science/government, prelaw, psychology, religion, Russian and Slavic studies, social science, social work, and sociology). Business, engineering, and psychology are the largest.

Special: The University of Iowa offers cooperative education programs and internships in more than 70 academic departments; combined degree programs in liberal arts and engineering, liberal arts and business, liberal arts and nursing, and liberal arts and medicine; and study abroad in more than 45 countries. Dual and student-designed majors, B.A. and B.S. degrees, certificate programs including Native American studies, global studies, international business, and women's studies, credit for military experience, and pass/nonpass options are also available. There are 21 national honor societies, including Phi Beta Kappa, a freshman honors program, and 52 departmental honors programs.

Admissions: 83% of the 1999-2000 applicants were accepted. The SAT I scores for the 1999-2000 freshman class were: Verbal--20% below 500, 35% between 500 and 599, 31% between 600 and 700, and 14% above 700; Math--14% below 500, 36% between 500 and 599, 35% between 600 and 700, and 15% above 700. 40% of the current freshmen were in the top fifth of their class; 76% were in the top two fifths. There were 30 National Merit finalists. 146 freshmen graduated first in their class.

Requirements: The SAT I or ACT is required. Iowa residents must rank in the upper 50% of their high school class (nonresidents in the upper 30%) or must meet an acceptable combination of class rank and test scores. All applicants must have completed 4 years of high school English, 3 years each of social studies and science, 3 years of math (including 2 years of algebra and 1 of geometry), and 2 years of a single foreign language. Music students must audition. Applications are accepted on-line at the university's web site. AP and CLEP credits are accepted.

Procedure: Freshmen are admitted to all sessions. Entrance exams should be taken in the junior year. There is a deferred admissions plan. Applications should be filed by May 15 for fall entry, November 15 for spring entry, and May 15 for summer entry, along with a $30 fee. Notification is sent on a rolling basis.

Financial Aid: In 1999-2000, 63% of all freshmen and 59% of continuing students received some form of financial aid. 41% of all students received need-based aid. The average freshman award was $5300. Of that total, scholarships or need-based grants averaged $1600 ($11,600 maximum); loans averaged $2300 ($8000 maximum); and work contracts averaged $3000 (maximum). Average annual earnings from campus work are $1900. The average financial indebtedness of the 1999 graduate was $11,000. Iowa is a member of CSS. The CSS/Profile, FAFSA, FFS, or SFS and the college's own financial statement are required.

Computers: The mainframes are an IBM 9672, an IBM RS6000-SP2, and an SG1 Power Challenge XL-16. There are 1100 networked PCs at 26 public computer centers on campus. There are an additional 500 PCs in 33 departmental instructional labs on campus. All students may access the system 24 hours a day, 7 days a week. There are no time limits. The fee varies by college.

UNIVERSITY OF KENTUCKY
Lexington, KY 40506-0032   (606) 257-2000; Fax: (606) 257-3823

Full-time: 7139 men, 7713 women	**Faculty:** 1239; I, -$
Part-time: 969 men, 1020 women	**Ph.D.s:** 98%
Graduate: 2868 men, 3351 women	**Student/Faculty:** 12 to 1
Year: semesters, summer session	**Tuition:** $3296 ($9216)
Application Deadline: August 1	**Room & Board:** $3722
Freshman Class: 8320 applied, 6096 accepted, 2681 enrolled	
ACT: 24.5	**VERY COMPETITIVE**

The University of Kentucky, founded in 1865, is a public land-grant institution offering undergraduate and graduate programs in a variety of areas. There are 13 undergraduate schools and 1 graduate school. In addition to regional accreditation, UK has baccalaureate program accreditation with AACSB, ABET, ACEJ-MC, ACPE, ADA, AHEA, APTA, ASLA, CAHEA, CSWE, FIDER, NAAB, NASAD, NASM, NCATE, NLN, NRPA, and SAF. The 13 libraries contain 2, 792,293 volumes, 5,872,795 microform items, and 73,600 audiovisual forms/CDs, and subscribe to 26,539 periodicals. Computerized library services include the card catalog and database searching. Special learning facilities include a learning resource center, art gallery, natural history museum, radio station, and TV station. The 764-acre campus is in a suburban area 75 miles south of Cincinnati. Including residence halls, there are 335 buildings.

Programs of Study: UK confers B.A., B.S., B.Arch., B.B.A., B.F.A., B.H.S., and B.M. degrees. Master's and doctoral degrees are also awarded. Bachelor's degrees are awarded in AGRICULTURE (agricultural economics, agriculture, animal science, and forestry and related sciences), BIOLOGICAL SCIENCE (biology/biological science, botany, and zoology), BUSINESS (accounting, banking and finance, business economics, hotel/motel and restaurant management, and marketing/retailing/merchandising), COMMUNICATIONS AND THE ARTS (advertising, art history and appreciation, arts administration/management, communications, dramatic arts, English, French, German, Italian, journalism, linguistics, music, music performance, Russian, Spanish, and telecommunications), COMPUTER AND PHYSICAL SCIENCE (chemistry, computer science, geology, mathematics, and physics), EDUCATION (agricultural, art, business, early childhood, elementary, foreign languages, health, mathematics, middle school, music, physical, science, secondary, social studies, and special), ENGINEERING AND ENVIRONMENTAL DESIGN (chemical engineering, civil engineering, electrical/electronics engineering, landscape architecture/design, materials engineering, mechanical engineering, and mining and mineral engineering), HEALTH PROFESSIONS (nursing, physical therapy, and physician's assistant), SOCIAL SCIENCE (anthropology, economics, food science, geography, history, Latin American studies, philosophy, political science/government, psychology, social work, sociology, and textiles and clothing). Pharmacy, architecture, and allied health are the strongest academically. Finance, accounting, and marketing are the largest.

Special: Co-op programs are offered in engineering, business, computer science, math, and agriculture. The Academic Common Market allows students in 14 southern states to study outside the university. Internships in a variety of fields, study abroad in 36 countries, work-study programs with the university and local businesses, and credit for life experience are also available. An accelerated degree program, B.A.-B.S. degrees, dual and double majors, a general studies degree, student-designed majors, a 3-2 engineering degree with several smaller schools in Kentucky, nondegree study, and pass/fail options are also offered. There are 12 national honor societies, including Phi Beta Kappa, and a freshman honors program.

Admissions: 73% of the 1999-2000 applicants were accepted. There were 65 National Merit finalists. 106 freshmen graduated first in their class.

Requirements: The SAT I or ACT is required. A GPA of 2.0 is required. Minimum scores vary with the GPA. Applicants must complete 20 Carnegie units, including 4 years of English, 3 of math, and 2 each of science and social studies. A fourth year of math, 2 years of foreign language, and 1 year of fine arts also are recommended. A portfolio is required for art studio courses, and an audition is required for music performance. AP and CLEP credits are accepted.

Procedure: Freshmen are admitted to all sessions. Entrance exams should be taken before Christmas of the senior year. Applications should be filed by August 1 for fall entry and February 15 for summer entry, along with a $20 fee. Notification is sent on a rolling basis.

Financial Aid: 32% of freshmen and 34% of continuing students received need-based aid. The average freshman award was $6007. Of that total, need-based gifts averaged $2967; need-based loans averaged $2765; and need-based self-help averaged $2893. UK is a member of CSS. The FAFSA is required. The fall application deadline is February 15.

Computers: The mainframes are an IBM 3090/6055 and a Convex/HP Meta Series System. 21 terminals access the mainframe in the UK computing center. There are 831 PCs in 13 public computer labs, and students may access the university system via phone modem. Several colleges also operate computer labs and classrooms for their students. All students may access the system 24 hours daily in the computing center and at various hours in labs. There are no time limits and no fees.

UNIVERSITY OF MARYLAND/BALTIMORE COUNTY

Baltimore, MD 21250

(410) 455-2291
(800) UMBC-4U2; Fax: (410) 455-1094

Full-time: 3470 men, 3513 women	**Faculty:** 483; I, --$
Part-time: 927 men, 944 women	**Ph.D.s:** 87%
Graduate: 620 men, 791 women	**Student/Faculty:** 14 to 1
Year: 4-1-4, summer session	**Tuition:** $5148 ($9620)
Application Deadline: March 15	**Room & Board:** $5694
	(Maximum)

Freshman Class: 5128 applied, 3542 accepted, 1423 enrolled
SAT I Verbal/Math: 570/590   **ACT:** 24   **VERY COMPETITIVE**

University of Maryland/Baltimore County, founded in 1966, is a public research university offering programs in liberal arts and sciences and engineering. There are 3 undergraduate schools and 1 graduate school. In addition to regional accreditation, UMBC has baccalaureate program accreditation with ABET, CSWE, and NCATE. The library contains 690,000 volumes, 1,005,000 microform items, and 38,000 audiovisual forms/CDs, and subscribes to 4200 periodicals. Computerized library services include the card catalog, interlibrary loans, and database searching. Special learning facilities include a learning resource center, art gallery, radio station, centers for imaging research, earth systems technology, and telecommunications research, and institutes for medicine and policy analysis and research. The 530-acre campus is in a suburban area 5 miles southwest of Baltimore. Including residence halls, there are 50 buildings.

Programs of Study: UMBC confers B.A., B.S., and B.S.E. degrees. Master's and doctoral degrees are also awarded. Bachelor's degrees are awarded in BIOLOGICAL SCIENCE (biochemistry and biology/biological science), COMMUNICATIONS AND THE ARTS (dance, dramatic arts, English, fine arts, French, German, linguistics, modern language, music, Russian, Spanish, and visual and performing arts), COMPUTER AND PHYSICAL SCIENCE (chemistry, computer science, information sciences and systems, mathematics, and physics), ENGINEERING AND ENVIRONMENTAL DESIGN (chemical engineering, computer engineering, and mechanical engineering), HEALTH PROFESSIONS (emergency medical technologies and health science), SOCIAL SCIENCE (African American studies, American studies, classical/ancient civilization, crosscultural studies, economics, geography, history, interdisciplinary studies, philosophy, political science/government, psychology, social work, and sociology). Chemistry, biology, and engineering are the strongest academically. Information systems, computer science, and biological sciences are the largest.

Special: Dual and student-designed majors, cooperative education programs in all majors, cross-registration with University of Maryland schools and Johns Hopkins University, internships, study abroad, work-study programs, B.A.-B.S. degrees, pass/fail options, and nondegree study are available. UMBC also offers various opportunities in interdisciplinary studies and in such fields as artificial intelligence and optical communications. There are 15 national honor societies, including Phi Beta Kappa, a freshman honors program, and 14 departmental honors programs.

Admissions: 69% of the 1999-2000 applicants were accepted. The SAT I scores for the 1999-2000 freshman class were: Verbal--15% below 500, 46% between 500 and 599, 30% between 600 and 700, and 8% above 700; Math--9% below 500, 41% between 500 and 599, 40% between 600 and 700, and 10% above 700. The ACT scores were 16% below 21, 28% between 21 and 23, 27% between 24

and 26, 12% between 27 and 28, and 17% above 28. 52% of the current freshmen were in the top fifth of their class; 76% were in the top two fifths. There were 4 National Merit finalists.

Requirements: The SAT I or ACT is required. UMBC requires applicants to be in the upper 30% of their class. A GPA of 2.5 is required; 3.0 is recommended. Minimum high school preparation should include 4 years of English, 3 years each of social science/history and math, including algebra I and II and geometry, and 3 years of lab sciences and a 2 of a foreign language. An essay is required of all freshman applicants. Applications are accepted on-line at the school's web site at http://www.umbc.edu through College Net. AP and CLEP credits are accepted. Important factors in the admissions decision are advanced placement or honor courses, parents or siblings attending the school, and recommendations by school officials.

Procedure: Freshmen are admitted to all sessions. Entrance exams should be taken by fall of the senior year. There is an early admissions plan. Applications should be filed by March 15 for fall entry, December 1 for winter entry, December 15 for spring entry, and May 15 for summer entry, along with a $45 fee. 8% of all applicants are on a waiting list.

Financial Aid: In 1999-2000, 68% of all freshmen and 64% of continuing students received some form of financial aid. 49% of freshmen and 42% of continuing students received need-based aid. The average freshman award was $6000. Of that total, scholarships or need-based grants averaged $3000 ($16,000 maximum); loans averaged $2500 ($10,500 maximum); and work contracts averaged $500 ($1600 maximum). 7% of undergraduates work part time. Average annual earnings from campus work are $820. The average financial indebtedness of the 1999 graduate was $12,000. UMBC is a member of CSS. The FAFSA is required. The fall application deadline is March 1.

Computers: UMBC's network consists of 10 Sun and SGI Unix servers. Many of UMBC's research projects rely on high-end computers such as the Silicon Graphics, Inc., Challenge XL 20-processor supercomputer. UMBC has approximately 3,000 computers on campus, all of which have access to the Internet and the Web. Roughly 700 of these are available to students. These include more than 140 Silicon Graphics machines, 220 Macs, 20 Sun Workstations, and 300 PCs. The campus also has 120 modems for resident students and 300 modems for off-campus access. More than 75% of all residential spaces are networked. All students may access the system. There are no time limits and no fees.

UNIVERSITY OF MARYLAND/COLLEGE PARK
College Park, MD 20742

(301) 314-8385
(800) 422-5867; Fax: (301) 314-9693

Full-time: 11,083 men, 10,624 women	**Faculty:** 1389; I, av$
Part-time: 1269 men, 1052 women	**Ph.D.s:** 91%
Graduate: 3944 men, 3479 women	**Student/Faculty:** 16 to 1
Year: 4-1-4, summer session	**Tuition:** $4939 ($11,827)
Application Deadline: February 15	**Room & Board:** $6076
Freshman Class: 18,810 applied, 10,243 accepted, 3937 enrolled	
SAT I or ACT: required	**VERY COMPETITIVE**

University of Maryland/College Park, founded in 1856, is a land-grant institution, the flagship campus of the state's university system, offering undergraduate and graduate degrees. There are 11 undergraduate and 13 graduate schools. In addition to regional accreditation, Maryland has baccalaureate program accreditation with AACSB, ABET, ACEJMC, ACPE, ADA, ASLA, CSWE, NAAB, NASM,

NCATE, and NLN. The 7 libraries contain 2,772,663 volumes, 5,354,085 microform items, and 166,244 audiovisual forms/CDs, and subscribe to 30,030 periodicals. Computerized library services include the card catalog, interlibrary loans, and database searching. Special learning facilities include a learning resource center, art gallery, radio station, TV station, and observatory. The 1203-acre campus is in a suburban area 3 miles northeast of Washington, D.C., and 35 miles south of Baltimore. Including residence halls, there are 340 buildings.

Programs of Study: Maryland confers B.A., B.S., B.L.A., and B.M. degrees. Master's and doctoral degrees are also awarded. Bachelor's degrees are awarded in AGRICULTURE (agricultural business management, agricultural economics, agriculture, agronomy, animal science, conservation and regulation, horticulture, natural resource management, and plant science), BIOLOGICAL SCIENCE (biochemistry, biology/biological science, cell biology, genetics, marine biology, microbiology, molecular biology, nutrition, physiology, and zoology), BUSINESS (accounting, banking and finance, business administration and management, human resources, international business management, international economics, management information systems, marketing management, operations research, and personnel management), COMMUNICATIONS AND THE ARTS (art history and appreciation, Chinese, classics, communications, dance, dramatic arts, English, French, Germanic languages and literature, Japanese, journalism, linguistics, music, music performance, romance languages and literature, Russian, Spanish, and studio art), COMPUTER AND PHYSICAL SCIENCE (astronomy, chemistry, computer science, geology, information sciences and systems, mathematics, physical sciences, and physics), EDUCATION (art, drama, early childhood, elementary, English, foreign languages, health, mathematics, music, physical, science, secondary, social science, special, and speech correction), ENGINEERING AND ENVIRONMENTAL DESIGN (aeronautical engineering, agricultural engineering, architecture, bioengineering, chemical engineering, civil engineering, computer engineering, electrical/electronics engineering, engineering, environmental science, fire protection engineering, landscape architecture/design, materials engineering, materials science, mechanical engineering, nuclear engineering, and transportation engineering), HEALTH PROFESSIONS (preveterinary science and speech pathology/audiology), SOCIAL SCIENCE (African American studies, American studies, anthropology, criminal justice, criminology, dietetics, economics, family/consumer studies, food science, geography, history, Italian studies, Judaic studies, philosophy, physical fitness/movement, political science/government, psychology, Russian and Slavic studies, sociology, and women's studies). Engineering, computer science, and business are the strongest academically. Computer science, criminology and criminal justice, and psychology are the largest.

Special: Each of the 11 undergraduate schools offers special programs, and there is a campuswide cooperative education program. In addition, the university offers cross-registration with other colleges in the Consortium of Universities of the Washington Metropolitan Area, the B.A.-B.S. degree in most majors, dual and student-designed majors, nondegree study, an accelerated veterinary medicine program, study abroad, work-study programs with government and nonprofit organizations, and internship opportunities with members of Congress and the Maryland State House, the local media, and various federal agencies. There are 48 national honor societies, including Phi Beta Kappa, a freshman honors program, and 39 departmental honors programs.

Admissions: 54% of the 1999-2000 applicants were accepted. The SAT I scores for the 1999-2000 freshman class were: Verbal--8% below 500, 36% between 500 and 599, 43% between 600 and 700, and 13% above 700; Math--7% below 500, 26% between 500 and 599, 46% between 600 and 700, and 21% above 700.

38% of the current freshmen were in the top fifth of their class. There were 52 National Merit finalists and 5 semifinalists. 92 freshmen graduated first in their class.

Requirements: The SAT I or ACT is required. The university evaluates exam scores along with GPA, curriculum, and other criteria. Applicants should be graduates of accredited secondary schools or have the GED. Secondary preparation should include 4 years of English, 3 of history or soical sciences, 2 each of lab sciences and algebra, and 1 of plane geometry. An essay and counselor recommendation are required. Music majors must also audition. Applications may be submitted on-line. AP and CLEP credits are accepted. Important factors in the admissions decision are advanced placement or honor courses, recommendations by school officials, and evidence of special talent.

Procedure: Freshmen are admitted fall, spring, and summer. Entrance exams should be taken at the end of the junior year or the beginning of the senior year. There are early action and early admissions plans. Early action applications should be filed by December 1; regular applications, by February 15 for fall entry and December 15 for spring entry, along with a $45 fee ($65 for nonresidents). Notification of early decision is sent February 1; regular decision, on a rolling basis. 16% of all applicants are on a waiting list; none were accepted in 1999.

Financial Aid: In 1999-2000, 71% of all freshmen and 64% of continuing students received some form of financial aid. 42% of freshmen and 44% of continuing students received need-based aid. The average freshman award was $7016. Of that total, scholarships or need-based grants averaged $4858 ($17,162 maximum); loans averaged $3301 ($12,243 maximum); and work contracts averaged $1012 ($1341 maximum). 3% of undergraduates work part time. Average annual earnings from campus work are $1348. The average financial indebtedness of the 1999 graduate was $14,076. Maryland is a member of CSS. The FAFSA is required. The fall application deadline is February 15.

Computers: The mainframe is an IBM 9672/RC4. There are 1600 PCs available for student use in academic buildings, computer centers and libraries, and residence halls are wired for PCs. IBM and Mac word-processing programs are available to all registered students. The Computer Science Center supports advanced workstation and PC labs across campus for day and evening self-study and class projects. 9 labs house Dell Pentium and IBM PS Valuepoint 433 DX/S PCs with 334 connected workstations by Novell Network, and there are 37 other open work labs in various colleges and campus buildings. Software includes WordPerfect, all Microsoft products, Paradox, Systat, SPSS/PC, Maple and Math, Borland C++, Netscape, and various desktop publishing programs. All students may access the system 24 hours a day, 7 days a week. There are no time limits and no fees.

Full-time: 8810 men, 8933 women	**Faculty:** 1161; I, av$
Part-time: 763 men, 866 women	**Ph.D.s:** 94%
Graduate: 2758 men, 2901 women	**Student/Faculty:** 15 to 1
Year: semesters, summer session	**Tuition:** $5212 ($13,365)
Application Deadline: February 1	**Room & Board:** $4790
Freshman Class: 19,914 applied, 13,727 accepted, 4060 enrolled	
SAT I Verbal/Math: 570/570	**VERY COMPETITIVE**

Established in 1863, University of Massachusetts Amherst is a major public, research, land-grant institution offering nearly 100 academic majors in 9 schools and colleges. There are 9 undergraduate and 9 graduate schools. In addition to regional accreditation, UMass has baccalaureate program accreditation with AACSB, ABET, ASLA, FIDER, NASM, NCATE, NLN, and SAF. The 4 libraries contain 2,935,739 volumes, 2,373,469 microform items, and 14,622 audiovisual forms/CDs, and subscribe to 15,510 periodicals. Computerized library services include the card catalog, interlibrary loans, and database searching. Special learning facilities include a learning resource center, art gallery, radio station, and TV station. The 1463-acre campus is in a small town 90 miles west of Boston and 60 miles north of Hartford, Connecticut. Including residence halls, there are more than 200 major buildings.

Programs of Study: UMass confers B.A., B.S., B.B.A., B.F.A., B.G.S., and B. Mus. degrees. Associate, master's, and doctoral degrees are also awarded. Bachelor's degrees are awarded in AGRICULTURE (animal science, conservation and regulation, forestry and related sciences, natural resource management, plant science, soil science, wildlife management, and wood science), BIOLOGICAL SCIENCE (biochemistry, biology/biological science, microbiology, and nutrition), BUSINESS (accounting, apparel and accessories marketing, banking and finance, business administration and management, hotel/motel and restaurant management, marketing management, and sports management), COMMUNICATIONS AND THE ARTS (art history and appreciation, Chinese, classics, communications, comparative literature, dance, design, dramatic arts, English, French, German, Japanese, journalism, linguistics, music, music performance, Portuguese, Spanish, and studio art), COMPUTER AND PHYSICAL SCIENCE (astronomy, chemistry, computer science, earth science, geology, mathematics, physics, and science), EDUCATION (early childhood, elementary, middle school, and secondary), ENGINEERING AND ENVIRONMENTAL DESIGN (chemical engineering, civil engineering, computer engineering, electrical/electronics engineering, environmental design, environmental science, industrial engineering, landscape architecture/design, and mechanical engineering), HEALTH PROFESSIONS (medical laboratory technology, nursing, predentistry, premedicine, preveterinary science, and speech pathology/audiology), SOCIAL SCIENCE (African American studies, anthropology, economics, ethics, politics, and social policy, family/consumer studies, food science, geography, history, interdisciplinary studies, Italian studies, Judaic studies, liberal arts/general studies, Middle Eastern studies, philosophy, physical fitness/movement, political science/government, prelaw, psychology, Russian and Slavic studies, sociology, and women's studies). Chemical engineering, computer science, and electrical engineering are the strongest academically. Psychology, communication, and English are the largest.

Special: Cross-registration is possible with the Five-College Consortium (Smith, Mt. Holyoke, Hampshire, and Amherst) and other University of Massachusetts campuses. Students may participate in co-op programs, internships in every major, study abroad in more than 30 countries, a Washington semester, work-study programs in various university departments, dual majors in most subjects, and student-designed majors. The University Without Walls program gives credit for life, military, and work experience. Other special academic features include the Commonwealth Honors College, the National and International Exchange Programs, Learning Support Services, the Native American Student Support Services Program, the Minority and Women Engineering Programs, the Bilingual Collegiate Program, the Committee for the College Education of Black and Other Minority Students, the United Asian Learning Resource Center, and the Residential Academic Programs. There are 10 national honor societies, including Phi Beta Kappa, a freshman honors program, and 70 departmental honors programs.

Admissions: 69% of the 1999-2000 applicants were accepted. The SAT I scores for the 1999-2000 freshman class were: Verbal--16% below 500, 49% between 500 and 599, 29% between 600 and 700, and 6% above 700; Math--17% below 500, 46% between 500 and 599, 30% between 600 and 700, and 7% above 700. 39% of the current freshmen were in the top fifth of their class; 80% were in the top two fifths. 40 freshmen graduated first in their class.

Requirements: The SAT I or ACT is required. A GPA of 2.0 is required. In addition, applicants must be graduates of an accredited secondary school, or have the GED. The university recommends that students complete 16 Carnegie units, including 4 years of English, 3 years of math, 3 years of natural sciences (including 2 years lab), 2 years of electives, 2 years of foreign language, and 2 years of social sciences. 4 years of math are required for business, computer science, and engineering majors. Students must present a portfolio for admission to the art program and must audition for admission to music and dance. Applications are accepted on-line at the school's web site. AP and CLEP credits are accepted. Important factors in the admissions decision are geographic diversity, advanced placement or honor courses, and leadership record.

Procedure: Freshmen are admitted fall and spring. Entrance exams should be taken before February 1. There are early admissions and deferred admissions plans. Applications should be filed by February 1 for fall entry and October 15 for spring entry, along with a $25 fee in state, $40 out of state. Notification is sent on a rolling basis beginning December 15.

Financial Aid: In 1999-2000, 42% of all freshmen and 56% of continuing students received some form of financial aid. 48% of freshmen and 39% of continuing students received need-based aid. The average freshman award was $5588. 90% of undergraduates work part time. Average annual earnings from campus work are $1600. The average financial indebtedness of the 1999 graduate was $16,255. UMass is a member of CSS. The FAFSA is required. The fall application deadline is March 1.

Computers: Students have access to general computing and networking services. PC labs and classrooms (in both Mac and Windows NT environments), and central host computers running the UNIX operating system, support a wide range of applications, including E-mail, web browsing, and worldwide discussion groups through USENET. Most administrative and academic buildings, and some residence halls, have direct high-speed Ethernet connections that allow for access to the Internet and World Wide Web. Other campus locations can access the Internet and Web through the campus telephone system by use of a "terminal adapter unit" or TAU (available at no charge to students living in on-campus housing). All students may access the system. There are no time limits. The fee is $20 per semester.

UNIVERSITY OF MASSACHUSETTS BOSTON
Boston, MA 02125-3393   (617) 287-6000; Fax: (617) 287-6242

Full-time: 2566 men, 3413 women	**Faculty:** 456; IIA, ++$
Part-time: 1724 men, 2108 women	**Ph.D.s:** 91%
Graduate: 1021 men, 2091 women	**Student/Faculty:** 13 to 1
Year: semesters, summer session	**Tuition:** $4227 ($12,357)
Application Deadline: March 1	**Room & Board:** n/app
Freshman Class: 3461 applied, 1694 accepted, 789 enrolled	
SAT I Verbal/Math: 518/515	**VERY COMPETITIVE**

The University of Massachusetts Boston, established in 1964, is a public commuter institution offering undergraduate studies in arts and sciences and in preprofessional training. There are 4 undergraduate and 5 graduate schools. In addition to regional accreditation, UMass Boston has baccalaureate program accreditation with NLN. The library contains 575,438 volumes, 759,550 microform items, and 1939 audiovisual forms/CDs, and subscribes to 2691 periodicals. Computerized library services include the card catalog, interlibrary loans, and database searching. Special learning facilities include a learning resource center, art gallery, radio station, tropical greenhouse, observatory, adaptive computer lab, languages lab, and applied language and math center. The 177-acre campus is in an urban area 5 miles south of downtown Boston. There are 10 buildings.

Programs of Study: UMass Boston confers B.A. and B.S. degrees. Master's and doctoral degrees are also awarded. Bachelor's degrees are awarded in BIOLOGICAL SCIENCE (biochemistry and biology/biological science), BUSINESS (management science), COMMUNICATIONS AND THE ARTS (classics, dramatic arts, English, French, German, Greek (classical), Italian, Latin, music, Russian, and Spanish), COMPUTER AND PHYSICAL SCIENCE (applied mathematics, chemistry, computer science, mathematics, and physics), EDUCATION (physical), ENGINEERING AND ENVIRONMENTAL DESIGN (engineering physics), HEALTH PROFESSIONS (medical laboratory technology and nursing), SOCIAL SCIENCE (African American studies, anthropology, community services, criminal justice, economics, geography, gerontology, history, human services, philosophy, political science/government, psychology, sociology, and women's studies). Management, nursing, and psychology are the largest.

Special: Students may cross-register with Massachusetts College of Art, Bunker Hill Community College, Roxbury Community College, and Hebrew College. UMass Boston also offers cooperative programs, internships, study abroad, work-study programs, student-designed majors, B.A.-B.S. degrees, nondegree study, pass/fail options, and dual and interdisciplinary majors, including anthropology/history, biology/medical technology, philosophy/public policy, and psychology/sociology. A 2-2 engineering program is possible with various area institutions, and the College of Public and Community Service provides social-oriented education, generally to older students. There are 3 national honor societies and a freshman honors program.

Admissions: 49% of the 1999-2000 applicants were accepted.

Requirements: The SAT I or ACT is required, with a minimum composite score of 890 on the SAT I; test scores are not required of students who have been out of high school for 3 or more years. A GED of 3.0 is required. Applicants should be graduates of an accredited secondary school. The GED is accepted. The university requires the completion of 16 Carnegie units, including 4 years of English, 3 of college-preparatory math and science, 2 each of a foreign language and social studies, and 2 electives in the above academic areas or in humanities, arts, or computer science. An essay is recommended. Applications are accepted on-line via ExPAN and the school's web site. AP and CLEP credits are accepted. Important factors in the admissions decision are advanced placement or honor courses, recommendations by school officials, and personality/intangible qualities.

Procedure: Freshmen are admitted fall and spring. Entrance exams should be taken by the fall of the senior year. There is a deferred admissions plan. Applications should be filed by March 1 for fall entry and November 1 for spring entry, along with a $25 fee. Notification is sent on a rolling basis.

Financial Aid: In a recent year, 85% of all freshmen and 71% of continuing students received some form of financial aid. 78% of freshmen and 66% of continuing students received need-based aid. The average freshman award was $7441. Of that total, scholarships or need-based grants averaged $2981 ($4297 maximum); loans averaged $3660 ($5500 maximum); and work contracts averaged $1507 ($3500 maximum). 16% of undergraduates work part time. Average annual earnings from campus work are $2477. The average financial indebtedness of a recent graduate was $16,353. The FAFSA, the college's own financial statement, and the SAFA are required. The fall application deadline is March 1.

Computers: The mainframes are DEC VAX models 8800, 6000-410, and 6000-510. Students may access the mainframe through terminals located in the terminal room. There are also a number of PC labs containing Macs, IBMs, and other PCs. Most of the 390 terminals and PCs are located in the library, with the remainder in classroom buildings. All students may access the system 24 hours a day. There are no time limits and no fees.

UNIVERSITY OF MIAMI
Coral Gables, FL 33124   (305) 284-4323; Fax: (305) 284-2507

Full-time: 3625 men, 4201 women	**Faculty:** 578; I, av$
Part-time: 277 men, 525 women	**Ph.D.s:** 96%
Graduate: 2603 men, 2484 women	**Student/Faculty:** 14 to 1
Year: semesters, summer session	**Tuition:** $21,354
Application Deadline: March 1	**Room & Board:** $7782
Freshman Class: 12,264 applied, 6756 accepted, 1859 enrolled	
SAT I or ACT: required	**HIGHLY COMPETITIVE**

The University of Miami, founded in 1925, is a private university that offers degrees in more than 125 majors and areas of study. There are 9 undergraduate and 14 graduate schools. In addition to regional accreditation, UM has baccalaureate program accreditation with AACSB, ABET, ACEJMC, APTA, NAAB, NASM, NCATE, and NLN. The 3 libraries contain 2 million volumes and 3 million microform items, and subscribe to 19,551 periodicals. Computerized library services include the card catalog, interlibrary loans, and database searching. Special learning facilities include a learning resource center, art gallery, radio station, TV station, and a 600-seat acoustically perfect concert hall. The 260-acre campus is in a suburban area 6 miles south of Miami. Including residence halls, there are 101 buildings.

Programs of Study: UM confers B.A., B.S., B.Arch., B.B.A., B.C.S., B.F.A., B.G.S., B.H.S., B. M., B.S.A.E., B.S.B.E., B.S.C., B.S.C.E., B.S.Cp.E., B.S.E.E., B.S.E.S., B.S.I.E., B.S.M.E., and B.S.N. degrees. Master's and doctoral degrees are also awarded. Bachelor's degrees are awarded in AGRICULTURE (wildlife management), BIOLOGICAL SCIENCE (biochemistry, biology/biological science, ecology, marine science, microbiology, and toxicology), BUSINESS (accounting, banking and finance, business administration and management, business economics, business law, entrepreneurial studies, human resources, international business management, marketing/retailing/merchandising, real estate, and sports management), COMMUNICATIONS AND THE ARTS (advertising, art, art history and appreciation, audio technology, broadcasting, ceramic art and design, communications, dramatic arts, English, fiber/textiles/weaving, film arts, fine arts, French, German, graphic design, jazz, journalism, music, music business management, music history and appreciation, music performance, music theory and composition, musical theater, painting, photography, printmaking, public relations, sculpture, Spanish, speech/debate/rhetoric, technical and business writing, telecommunications, and video), COMPUTER AND PHYSICAL SCIENCE (applied mathematics, chemistry, computer science, geology, information sciences and systems, mathematics, physics, and systems analysis), EDUCATION (elementary, music, secondary, and special), ENGINEERING AND ENVIRONMENTAL DESIGN (aeronautical engineering, architectural engineering, architecture, biomedical engineering, civil engineering, computer engineering, electrical/electronics engineering, engineering, engineering technology, environmental engineering technology, environmental science, industrial engineering, manufacturing engineering, mechanical engineering, and ocean engineering), HEALTH PROFESSIONS (cytotechnology, environmental health science, health science, medical laboratory technology, music therapy, nuclear medical technology, nursing, and ultrasound technology), SOCIAL SCIENCE (American studies, anthropology, Caribbean studies, criminology, economics, geography, history, human ecology, international relations, international studies, Judaic studies, Latin American studies, law, philosophy, political science/government, psychobiology, psychology, religion, and sociology). Marine science, international finance and marketing, and music are the strongest academically. Biology, psychology, and business management are the largest.

Special: UM offers many opportunities for internships in communications, business, engineering, architecture, and science, work-study programs with local employers, and study abroad in 22 countries. There are special honors programs offered in medicine, law, biomedical engineering, physical therapy, and business. There are 42 national honor societies, including Phi Beta Kappa, a freshman honors program, and 20 departmental honors programs.

Admissions: 55% of the 1999-2000 applicants were accepted. The SAT I scores for the 1999-2000 freshman class were: Verbal--15% below 500, 44% between 500 and 599, 32% between 600 and 700, and 8% above 700; Math--14% below 500, 42% between 500 and 599, 33% between 600 and 700, and 11% above 700. The ACT scores were 14% below 21, 25% between 21 and 23, 27% between 24 and 26, 17% between 27 and 28, and 18% above 28. 68% of the current freshmen were in the top fifth of their class; 91% were in the top two fifths. There were 24 National Merit finalists.

Requirements: The SAT I or ACT is required. In addition, it is recommended that applicants have completed 4 years of English, 3 each of math, science, and social sciences, and 2 of foreign language. Also considered in the admissions decision are a recommendation from a high school counselor and an essay. The GED is accepted. Students may use the Common Application or the university's application forms available on paper and on the Web site via E-mail at www. miami.edu to apply for admission. Applications are also accepted on computer disk. AP and CLEP credits are accepted. Important factors in the admissions decision are advanced placement or honor courses, recommendations by school officials, and evidence of special talent.

Procedure: Freshmen are admitted to all sessions. Entrance exams should be taken in the fall of the senior year or earlier. There are early decision, early admissions, and deferred admissions plans. Early decision applications should be filed by November 15; regular applications, by March 1 for fall entry, November 15 for spring entry, and March 1 for summer entry, along with a $50 fee. Notification of early decision is sent December 15; regular decision, April 1. 320 early decision candidates were accepted for the 1999-2000 class. 5% of all applicants are on a waiting list.

Financial Aid: In 1999-2000, 87% of all freshmen and 82% of continuing students received some form of financial aid. 49% of freshmen and 48% of continuing students received need-based aid. The average freshman award was $15,303. Of that total, scholarships or need-based grants averaged $14,265 ($34,217 maximum); loans averaged $7565 ($33,983 maximum); and work contracts averaged $1954 ($2500 maximum). 26% of undergraduates work part time. Average annual earnings from campus work are $1600. The average financial indebtedness of the 1999 graduate was $19,101. UM is a member of CSS. The FAFSA and state aid form are required. The fall application deadline is February 15.

Computers: The mainframes are an IBM ES/9021 model 580, a DEC VAX cluster, with 2 VAX 4000-600 systems, and 2 VAX 3000 systems. Numerous DEC workstations and more than 40 computer labs are located in residential colleges, libraries, and schools across campus. More than 1000 PCs, workstations, and terminals are available to students. Each residential college has a computer lab with IBM PS/2 and Mac systems, laser printers, and connections to the campuswide network. E-mail access is available. All students may access the system 24 hours a day. There are no time limits and no fees.

UNIVERSITY OF MICHIGAN/ANN ARBOR
Ann Arbor, MI 48109　　　　(734) 764-7433; Fax: (734) 936-0740

Full-time: 11,580 men, 11,483 women	**Faculty:** 2993; I, ++$
Part-time: 648 men, 782 women	**Ph.D.s:** 95%
Graduate: 7732 men, 5621 women	**Student/Faculty:** 8 to 1
Year: trimesters, summer session	**Tuition:** $6148 ($19,576)
Application Deadline: February 1	**Room & Board:** $5614
Freshman Class: 21,328 applied, 12,592 accepted, 5253 enrolled	
SAT I or ACT: required	**HIGHLY COMPETITIVE+**

The University of Michigan/Ann Arbor, founded in 1817, is the main campus of the University of Michigan. The public institution offers undergraduate programs in the arts and sciences, architecture, business administration, education, engineering, fine arts, kinesiology, natural resources, nursing, and preprofessional studies, as well as a wide range of graduate and professional programs. There are 12 undergraduate and 19 graduate schools. In addition to regional accreditation, UM has baccalaureate program accreditation with AACSB, ABET, ACEJMC, ACPE, ADA, ASLA, CSWE, NAAB, NASAD, NASM, NCATE, NLN, and SAF. The 24 libraries contain 7,071,842 volumes, 5,879,325 microform items, and 54,279 audiovisual forms/CDs, and subscribe to 69,170 periodicals. Computerized library services include the card catalog, interlibrary loans, and database searching. Special learning facilities include a learning resource center, art gallery, natural history museum, planetarium, radio station, TV station, archeology museum, botanical gardens, and 2 historical museums. The 3114-acre campus is in a suburban area 38 miles west of Detroit. Including residence halls, there are 210 buildings.

Programs of Study: UM confers A.B., B.S., A.B.E.D., B.B.A., B.D.A., B.F.A., B.F.A.D., B.F.A.M.T., B.F.A.(T), B.G.S., B.Mus., B.Mus.A., B.S.A.O.S., B.S. Chem., B.S.D.Hyg., B.S.E.Aet., B.S.E.C.E., B.S.E.Ch., B.S.E.Civ., B.S.E.Comp., B.S.Ed., B.S.E.E.E., B.S.E.E.P., B.S.E.E.S., B.S.E.I.O., B.S.E.I.S., B.S.E.M.A., B.S.E.M.E., B.S.E.Met., B.S.E.M.S., B.S.E.Nav., B.S.Eng., B.S.M.C., B.S.Met., B.S.N., B.S.(NRE), B.S.P.O., and B.S.P.S. degrees. Master's and doctoral degrees are also awarded. Bachelor's degrees are awarded in AGRICULTURE (natural resource management), BIOLOGICAL SCIENCE (biochemistry, biology/biological science, biophysics, botany, cell biology, ecology, microbiology, nutrition, wildlife biology, and zoology), BUSINESS (business administration and management, recreation and leisure services, and sports management), COMMUNICATIONS AND THE ARTS (applied music, Arabic, art history and appreciation, ceramic art and design, Chinese, classical languages, communications, comparative literature, creative writing, dance, design, dramatic arts, English, fiber/textiles/weaving, film arts, French, German, graphic design, Greek, Hebrew, industrial design, Italian, Japanese, jazz, journalism, Latin, linguistics, literature, media arts, metal/jewelry, music, music history and appreciation, music performance, music theory and composition, musical theater, painting, percussion, performing arts, photography, piano/organ, printmaking, romance languages and literature, Russian, sculpture, Spanish, speech/debate/rhetoric, strings, voice, and winds), COMPUTER AND PHYSICAL SCIENCE (applied mathematics, astronomy, astrophysics, atmospheric sciences and meteorology, chemistry, computer science, geoscience, mathematics, oceanography, physics, and statistics), EDUCATION (art, elementary, music, physical, and secondary), ENGINEERING AND ENVIRONMENTAL DESIGN (aeronautical engineering, architecture, chemical engineering, civil engineering, computer engineering, electrical/electronics engineering, engineering, engineering and applied science, engineering physics, environmental engineering, environmental science, industrial engineering, interior design, landscape architecture/design, materials engineering, materials science, mechanical engineering, naval architecture and marine engineering, and nuclear engineering), HEALTH PROFESSIONS (biomedical science, dental hygiene, medical technology, nursing, and pharmacy), SOCIAL SCIENCE (African American studies, African studies, American studies, anthropology, archeology, Asian/Oriental studies, biblical languages, biblical studies, biopsychology, classical/ancient civilization, economics, geography, Hispanic American studies, history, humanities, Islamic studies, Judaic studies, Latin American studies, liberal arts/general studies, medieval studies, Middle Eastern studies, Near Eastern studies, philosophy, physical fitness/movement, political science/government, psychology, religion, Russian and Slavic studies, Scandinavian studies, social science, sociology, Western European studies, and women's studies). Classics, English, and political science are the strongest academically. Psychology, engineering, and business administration are the largest.

Special: A co-op program in engineering and cross-registration with Big Ten institutions and the University of Chicago are available, as are internships, study abroad in more than 28 countries, and a Washington semester. B.A.-B.S. degrees, dual and student-designed majors, and a 3-2 engineering degree with several colleges and universities are possible. Interdisciplinary majors are offered in anthropology and zoology, music and technology, natural resources and biometry, materials and metallurgical engineering, materials science and engineering, biopsychology and cognitive science, and social anthropology. Interdisciplinary liberal arts programs offering small group living/learning environments are available in the Residential College and the Lloyd Scholars Program. Also available are Honors College preferred admission to professional programs and a Women in Science Program. There are 21 national honor societies, including Phi Beta Kappa, and a freshman honors program.

Admissions: 59% of the 1999-2000 applicants were accepted. The SAT I scores for the 1999-2000 freshman class were: Verbal--7% below 500, 33% between 500 and 599, 45% between 600 and 700, and 15% above 700; Math--4% below 500, 19% between 500 and 599, 47% between 600 and 700, and 30% above 700. The ACT scores were 3% below 21, 9% between 21 and 23, 25% between 24

and 26, 22% between 27 and 28, and 41% above 28. 85% of the current freshmen were in the top fifth of their class; 98% were in the top two fifths. There were 38 National Merit finalists.

Requirements: The SAT I or ACT is required. Applicants must be graduates of accredited secondary schools or have earned a GED. The university requires 15 academic credits or 20 Carnegie units, including 4 in English, 3 in math (4 for engineering majors), 3 in history and social studies, 2 in foreign language, and 2 in science, with 1 each in hands-on computer study and fine or performing arts recommended as electives. An essay is required for all applicants. Students applying to the School of Art must submit a portfolio; those applying to the School of Music must present an audition. Applications are available on CD-ROM at www.weapply.com, or a PDF application can be downloaded from the school's web site. AP and CLEP credits are accepted.

Procedure: Freshmen are admitted to all sessions. Entrance exams should be taken at the end of the junior year or the beginning of the senior year. There is a deferred admissions plan. Applications should be filed by February 1 for fall entry, spring, or summer and November 1 for winter entry, along with a $40 fee. Notification is sent on a rolling basis. A waiting list is an active part of the admissions procedure.

Financial Aid: In 1999-2000, 40% of all freshmen and 53% of continuing students received some form of financial aid. 35% of freshmen and 45% of continuing students received need-based aid. The average freshman award was $14,026. Of that total, scholarships or need-based grants averaged $3399 ($8541 nonresident; $20,000 maximum); loans averaged $3828 ($7567 nonresident; $10,500 maximum); and work contracts averaged $1153 ($1144 nonresident; $2400 maximum). 42% of undergraduates work part time. Average annual earnings from campus work are $1148. The average financial indebtedness of the 1999 graduate was $14,501. UM is a member of CSS. The FAFSA and tax returns are required. The fall application deadline is September 30.

Computers: The mainframe is comprised of an IBM system 390 Multiprise 2000 Series Processor, CMOS, Model 2003-135. 1,400 PCs are available to members of the university community. The 15 campus computing sites provide networked computers, laser printers, and hundreds of software programs. There are also 15 residence hall sites, 10 computer-equipped classrooms, special multimedia labs, and an adaptive technology computing site for users with disabilities. All resident hall rooms are wired with Ethernet for Internet connectivity. Business administration provides an additional 155 workstations for its students' use only. Engineering provides an additional 440 workstations for it students' use only. Students also have access to 550 workstations in the Media Union. All students may access the system at any time. There are no time limits and no fees.

UNIVERSITY OF MICHIGAN/DEARBORN

Dearborn, MI 48128   (313) 593-5658/ (313) 593-5550
Fax: (313) 436-9167

Full-time: 392 men, 350 women	**Faculty:** 219; IIA, av$
Part-time: none	**Ph.Ds:** 85%
Graduate: none	**Student/Faculty:** 16 to 1
Year: semesters, summer session	**Tuition:** $4024 ($11,212)
Application Deadline: open	**Room & Board:** n/app
Freshman Class: 2187 applied, 1577 accepted, 742 enrolled	
ACT: 23	**VERY COMPETITIVE**

The University of Michigan/Dearborn, founded in 1959, is a public, comprehensive commuter institution that is part of the University of Michigan System. Some information in this profile is approximate. The emphasis of its degree programs is on the liberal arts, management, engineering, and education. There are 4 undergraduate and 4 graduate schools. In addition to regional accreditation, UM-Dearborn has baccalaureate program accreditation with ABET and NCATE. The library contains 300,000 volumes, 385,000 microform items, and 2000 audiovisual forms/CDs, and subscribes to 1600 periodicals. Computerized library services include the card catalog, interlibrary loans, and database searching. Special learning facilities include a learning resource center, art gallery, natural history museum, radio station, tv station, nature preserve, Armenian research center, child development center, engineering education and practice center, and the Henry Ford Estate, a National Historic Landmark. The 196-acre campus is in a suburban area 10 miles from Detroit. There are 20 buildings.

Programs of Study: University of Michigan/Dearborn confers B.A., B.S., B.B.A., B.G.S., B.S.A., and B.S.E. degrees. Master's degrees are also awarded. Bachelor's degrees are awarded in BIOLOGICAL SCIENCE (biochemistry, biology/biological science, and microbiology), BUSINESS (business administration and management), COMMUNICATIONS AND THE ARTS (art history and appreciation, arts administration/management, English, fine arts, languages, music, and music history and appreciation), COMPUTER AND PHYSICAL SCIENCE (chemistry, computer science, mathematics, physics, and science), EDUCATION (business, early childhood, elementary, science, secondary, and social studies), ENGINEERING AND ENVIRONMENTAL DESIGN (computer engineering, electrical/electronics engineering, environmental science, industrial engineering, manufacturing engineering, and mechanical engineering), SOCIAL SCIENCE (American studies, anthropology, behavioral science, economics, history, humanities, international studies, liberal arts/general studies, philosophy, political science/government, psychology, public administration, social science, and sociology). Electrical engineering and business administration are the strongest academically. Mechanical engineering, prebusiness, and business administration are the largest.

Special: UMD offers internships, study abroad, work-study and accelerated degree programs, a general studies degree, dual and student-designed majors, and co-op programs in engineering, business administration, and arts and sciences. Nondegree study and pass/fail options are possible. There is a freshman honors program.

Admissions: 72% of the 1999-2000 applicants were accepted. The ACT scores for the 1999-2000 freshman class were: 17% below 21, 37% between 21 and 23, 30% between 24 and 26, 10% between 27 and 28, and 7% above 28. 12 freshmen graduated first in their class.

Requirements: The SAT I or ACT is required. A GPA of 3.0 is required. The ACT, with a minimum composite score of 22, or the SAT I is required. Other admissions requirements normally include graduation from an accredited secondary school, with 4 years each in math and English, 3 in science, and 2 each in art, foreign language, and history. The GED is accepted with a minimum score of 55. An essay and interview are recommended. AP credits are accepted. Important factors in the admissions decision are advanced placement or honor courses, recommendations by school officials, and leadership record.

Procedure: Freshmen are admitted to all sessions. Entrance exams should be taken in the spring of the junior year or the fall of the senior year. There is an early admissions plan. Applications should be filed before the first day of the entering semester for fall entry, along with a $30 fee. Notification is sent on a rolling basis.

Financial Aid: 2% of undergraduates work part time. Average annual earnings from campus work are $700. University of Michigan/Dearborn is a member of CSS. The FAFSA is required. The fall application deadline is March 1.

Computers: There is a minicomputer with 400 networked PCs for students, including IBM PCs, Macs, and Sun models. All students may access the system. There are no time limits and no fees.

UNIVERSITY OF MINNESOTA/MORRIS
Morris, MN 56267-2199
(320) 589-6035
(800) 992-8863; Fax: (320) 589-1673

Full-time: 730 men, 1035 women	**Faculty:** 122; IIB, av$
Part-time: 39 men, 63 women	**Ph.D.s:** 87%
Graduate: none	**Student/Faculty:** 14 to 1
Year: Semesters, May intersession, summer	**Tuition:** $5312 ($10,014)
	Room & Board: $3910
Application Deadline: March 15	
Freshman Class: 1002 applied, 888 accepted, 462 enrolled	
SAT I Verbal/Math: 580/600	**ACT:** 24 **VERY COMPETITIVE**

The University of Minnesota/Morris, founded in 1959, is a public liberal arts institution within the University of Minnesota system. In addition to regional accreditation, UMM has baccalaureate program accreditation with NCATE. The library contains 180,000 volumes, 212,932 microform items, and 1900 audiovisual forms/CDs, and subscribes to 991 periodicals. Computerized library services include the card catalog, interlibrary loans, and database searching. Special learning facilities include a learning resource center, art gallery, radio station, TV studios, language lab, observatory, and agricultural experiment station. The 130-acre campus is in a small town 150 miles northwest of Minneapolis. Including residence halls, there are 36 buildings.

Programs of Study: UMM confers the B.A. degree. Bachelor's degrees are awarded in BIOLOGICAL SCIENCE (biology/biological science), BUSINESS (management science), COMMUNICATIONS AND THE ARTS (art history and appreciation, dramatic arts, English, French, German, music, Spanish, speech/debate/rhetoric, and studio art), COMPUTER AND PHYSICAL SCIENCE (chemistry, computer science, geology, mathematics, and physics), EDUCATION (elementary and secondary), HEALTH PROFESSIONS (premedicine), SOCIAL SCIENCE (economics, European studies, history, Latin American studies, liberal arts/general studies, philosophy, political science/government, prelaw, psychology, social science, and sociology). Psychology and sciences are the strongest academically. Economics, education, and English are the largest.

Special: UMM offers work-study programs, internships, study abroad, dual majors, student-designed majors, nondegree study, pass/fail options, and credit for life, military, and work experience. There is a 2-3 engineering degree with the University of Minnesota at Twin Cities. A competitive, merit-based program that pairs students and professors in order to undertake creative projects is available. There is a freshman honors program.

Admissions: 89% of the 1999-2000 applicants were accepted. The SAT I scores for the 1999-2000 freshman class were: Verbal--17% below 500, 42% between 500 and 599, 31% between 600 and 700, and 10% above 700; Math--12% below 500, 30% between 500 and 599, 45% between 600 and 700, and 13% above 700. The ACT scores were 20% below 21, 26% between 21 and 23, 27% between 24 and 26, 14% between 27 and 28, and 16% above 28. 74% of the current freshmen were in the top fifth of their class; 92% were in the top two fifths. There were 5 National Merit finalists. 42 freshmen graduated first in their class.

Requirements: The SAT I or ACT is required. A GPA of 3.0 is required. Applicants should be graduates of an accredited secondary school or have a GED certificate. They must have completed 4 years of English, 3 each of math and science, 2 of a single foreign language, and 1 each of social studies and American history. Applications are accepted on-line at http://www.mrs.umn.edu/admissions. AP and CLEP credits are accepted. Important factors in the admissions decision are leadership record, extracurricular activities record, and advanced placement or honor courses.

Procedure: Freshmen are admitted fall and spring. Entrance exams should be taken before December 1 of the senior year. There are early admissions and deferred admissions plans. Early decision applications should be filed by December 1; regular applications, by March 15 for fall entry and November 1 for winter entry, along with a $25 fee. The on-line application fee is $5. Notification of early decision is sent December 15; regular decision, April 1.

Financial Aid: In a recent year, 78% of all freshmen and 91% of continuing students received some form of financial aid. 76% of freshmen and 80% of continuing students received need-based aid. The average freshman award was $5000. Of that total, scholarships or need-based grants averaged $2500; loans averaged $2000; and work contracts averaged $500. 89% of undergraduates work part time. Average annual earnings from campus work are $690. The average financial indebtedness of the recent graduate was $10,300. UMM is a member of CSS. The FAFSA is required. The fall application deadline is April 1.

Computers: The mainframes are a cluster of VAX and UNIX computers and shared mainframe resources with U of M/Twin Cities. There are 7 PC and Mac computer labs on campus, with a student-to-computer ratio of about 13 to 1. All dorm rooms have access to the system. All students may access the system 24 hours per day. There are no time limits and no fees.

UNIVERSITY OF MINNESOTA/TWIN CITIES

Minneapolis, MN 55455
(612) 625-2008
(800) 752-1000; Fax: (612) 625-1693

Full-time: 9922 men, 10,835 women	**Faculty:** 2463; I, +$
Part-time: 2937 men, 3274 women	**Ph.D.s:** 91%
Graduate: 6032 men, 6186 women	**Student/Faculty:** 8 to 1
Year: semesters, summer session	**Tuition:** $4649 ($12,789)
Application Deadline: December 15	**Room & Board:** $4670
Freshman Class: 15,319 applied, 11,216 accepted, 5195 enrolled	
SAT I Verbal/Math: 600/620	**ACT:** 25 **VERY COMPETITIVE**

University of Minnesota/Twin Cities, founded in 1851, is a land-grant institution offering programs in liberal and fine arts, physical and biological sciences, health sciences, education, natural resources, human ecology, business, agriculture, engineering, and professional training in law, medicine, dentistry, pharmacy, and veterinary medicine. There are 18 undergraduate and 1 graduate school. In addition to regional accreditation, the university has baccalaureate program accreditation with AACSB, ABET, ABFSE, ACEJMC, ADA, APTA, ASLA, CSWE, FIDER, NAAB, NASM, NCATE, NLN, and SAF. The 17 libraries contain 565 million volumes, 5.4 million microform items, 500,000 audiovisual forms, CDs, and subscribe to 48,105 periodicals. Computerized library services include the card catalog, interlibrary loans, and database searching. Special learning facilities include a learning resource center, art gallery, natural history museum, planetarium, radio station, and TV station. The 2000-acre campus is in an urban area within both Minneapolis and St. Paul. Including residence halls, there are 205 buildings.

Programs of Study: The university confers B.A., B.S., B.Aerospace Eng., B. Agr.Eng., B.C.E., B.Ch., B.Ch.E., B.Comp.Sci., B.E.E., B.F.A., B.G.E., B.I.S., B.M., B.Materials Sci., B.Mathematics, B.M.E., B.Pcs., B.S.Bus., B.S.G., B.S. in Astrophysics, B.S. in Geophysics, B.S.N., and B.Statistics. degrees. Master's and doctoral degrees are also awarded. Bachelor's degrees are awarded in AGRICULTURE (agricultural business management, agricultural economics, fishing and fisheries, forestry and related sciences, forestry production and processing, and natural resource management), BIOLOGICAL SCIENCE (biochemistry, biology/biological science, botany, cell biology, ecology, evolutionary biology, genetics, microbiology, nutrition, physiology, and wildlife biology), BUSINESS (accounting, business administration and management, management science, marketing/retailing/merchandising, recreation and leisure services, recreational facilities management, and retailing), COMMUNICATIONS AND THE ARTS (art history and appreciation, Chinese, classical languages, dance, English, film arts, French, German, Greek, Hebrew, Italian, Japanese, languages, Latin, linguistics, music, Russian, Scandinavian languages, Spanish, speech/debate/rhetoric, and studio art), COMPUTER AND PHYSICAL SCIENCE (actuarial science, astronomy, astrophysics, chemistry, computer science, geology, geophysics and seismology, mathematics, physics, and statistics), EDUCATION (agricultural, art, bilingual/bicultural, business, early childhood, elementary, English, home economics, industrial arts, mathematics, music, physical, science, social studies, and teaching English as a second/foreign language (TESOL/TEFOL)), ENGINEERING AND ENVIRONMENTAL DESIGN (aeronautical engineering, agricultural engineering, architecture, chemical engineering, civil engineering, electrical/electronics engineering, environmental design, geological engineering, industrial engineering, interior design, landscape architecture/design, materials engineering, materials science, mechanical engineering, and metallurgical engineering), HEALTH PROFESSIONS (dental hygiene, medical laboratory technology, music therapy, nursing, occupational therapy, pharmacy, physical therapy, predentistry, premedicine, prepharmacy, preveterinary science, and speech pathology/audiology), SOCIAL SCIENCE (African American studies, African studies, American Indian studies, American studies, anthropology, child psychology/development, East Asian studies, economics, food science, geography, history, humanities, international relations, Mexican-American/Chicano studies, Middle Eastern studies, philosophy, political science/government, prelaw, psychology, Russian and Slavic studies, sociology, South Asian studies, textiles and clothing, urban studies, and women's studies). Chemical engineering, psychology, and economics are the strongest academically. Mechanical engineering, psychology, and electrical engineering are the largest.

Special: The university offers cooperative programs, cross-registration with the Minnesota Community College system, internships, study abroad in 65 countries, work-study programs both on and off campus, a B.A.-B.S. degree in all majors, a general studies degree, and dual and student-designed majors. Pass/fail options and credit for life, military, or work experience are available. There are 21 national honor societies, including Phi Beta Kappa, a freshman honors program, and 8 departmental honors programs.

Admissions: 73% of the 1999-2000 applicants were accepted. The SAT I scores for the 1999-2000 freshman class were: Verbal--14% below 500, 33% between 500 and 599, 39% between 600 and 700, and 13% above 700; Math--11% below 500, 29% between 500 and 599, 42% between 600 and 700, and 19% above 700. The ACT scores were 17% below 21, 22% between 21 and 23, 28% between 24 and 26, 16% between 27 and 28, and 17% above 28. 50% of the current freshmen were in the top fifth of their class; 83% were in the top two fifths. 266 freshmen graduated first in their class.

Requirements: The SAT I or ACT is required. The university uses a formula index in evaluating high school rank and ACT test scores. A portfolio is required for studio arts and architecture, an audition for music, and an interview for architecture and education. Applications are accepted on-line through the university's web site, http://admissions.tc.umn.edu. AP and CLEP credits are accepted. Important factors in the admissions decision are advanced placement or honor courses, evidence of special talent, and leadership record.

Procedure: Freshmen are admitted to all sessions. Entrance exams should be taken by the end of the junior year or October to December of the senior year. There is an early admissions plan. Applications should be filed by December 15 for fall entry and October 15 for spring entry, along with a $25 fee. Notification is sent on a rolling basis.

Financial Aid: In a recent year, 70% of all freshmen and 61% of continuing students received some form of financial aid. 52% of freshmen and 50% of continuing students received need-based aid. The average freshman award was $10,359. Of that total, scholarships or need-based grants averaged $2556; loans averaged $3589; and work contracts averaged $2160. The FAFSA is required. The fall application deadline is open.

Computers: The mainframes are an IBM/CMS, CDC CYBER NOSNE, NOS, EP/IX, and DEC VMS. There are about 250 terminals and 1000 PCs for public use. All the PCs are networked. All students may access the system 24 hours a day, 7 days a week. Students may access the system 2 hours per session if there are others waiting or signed on. The fee is $45 per semester. It is strongly recommended that all students have personal computers.

UNIVERSITY OF MISSISSIPPI

University, MS 38677

(662) 915-7226
(800) OLE-MISS; Fax: (662) 915-5869

Full-time: 4074 men, 4336 women	**Faculty:** 495; I, --$
Part-time: 249 men, 335 women	**Ph.D.s:** 83%
Graduate: 973 men, 949 women	**Student/Faculty:** 17 to 1
Year: semesters, summer session	**Tuition:** $3054 ($6156)
Application Deadline: August 1	**Room & Board:** $3580
Freshman Class: 6138 applied, 4264 accepted, 2305 enrolled	
SAT I or ACT: required	**VERY COMPETITIVE**

The University of Mississippi, founded in 1844, is a public institution offering undergraduate and graduate programs in the liberal arts, business, pharmacy, engineering, accountancy, and education. There are 6 undergraduate and 2 graduate schools. In addition to regional accreditation, Ole Miss has baccalaureate program accreditation with AACSB, ABET, ACEJMC, CSAB, CSWE, NASAD, NASM, and NCATE. The 3 libraries contain 1 million volumes and 42,056 audiovisual forms/CDs, and subscribe to 6427 periodicals. Computerized library services include the card catalog, interlibrary loans, and database searching. Special learning facilities include a learning resource center, art gallery, radio station, TV station, and a museum, the Center for the Study of Southern Culture, the National Center for Physical Acoustics, Rowan Oak, the home of William Faulkner, the National Center for Development of Natural Products, National Food Service Management Institute, and the Croft Institute for International Studies. The 2000-acre campus is in a small town 70 miles southeast of Memphis, Tennessee. Including residence halls, there are 193 buildings.

Programs of Study: Ole Miss confers B.A., B.S., B.Ac., B.A.E., B.A.Ed., B.A.L.M., B.B.A, B.C.R., B.E., B.F.A., B.Mus., B.P.A., B.S.C.E., B.S.Ch.E., B.S.C.S., B.S.E.E., B.S.E.S., B.S.F.C.S., B.S.G.E., B.S.J., B.S.M.E., B.S.Pharm., and B.S.W. degrees. Master's and doctoral degrees are also awarded. Bachelor's degrees are awarded in BIOLOGICAL SCIENCE (biology/biological science), BUSINESS (accounting, banking and finance, business administration and management, business economics, court reporting, insurance, international business management, investments and securities, management information systems, management science, marketing/retailing/merchandising, real estate, recreation and leisure services, and recreational facilities management), COMMUNICATIONS AND THE ARTS (advertising, art, art history and appreciation, broadcasting, design, dramatic arts, English, French, German, journalism, linguistics, music, radio/television technology, and Spanish), COMPUTER AND PHYSICAL SCIENCE (chemistry, computer science, geology, and physics), EDUCATION (elementary, English, foreign languages, home economics, mathematics, science, social science, and special), ENGINEERING AND ENVIRONMENTAL DESIGN (chemical engineering, civil engineering, electrical/electronics engineering, engineering, geological engineering, and mechanical engineering), HEALTH PROFESSIONS (biomedical science, exercise science, medical laboratory technology, medical technology, pharmacy, speech pathology/audiology, and speech therapy), SOCIAL SCIENCE (anthropology, area studies, classical/ancient civilization, economics, family/consumer studies, forensic studies, history, international studies, liberal arts/general studies, philosophy, political science/government, psychology, public administration, social work, and sociology). General business, accountancy, and biological sciences are the largest.

Special: Internships in journalism, accounting, and engineering, study abroad in numerous countries, and work-study programs within the college are offered.

Dual majors, a general studies degree, credit by exam, special testing in music and languages, credit for military experience, and limited pass/fail options also are available. There are 24 national honor societies, and a freshman honors program.

Admissions: 69% of the 1999-2000 applicants were accepted. The ACT scores for the 1999-2000 freshman class were: 27% below 21, 25% between 21 and 23, 22% between 24 and 26, 11% between 27 and 28, and 15% above 28. There were 27 National Merit finalists and 10 semifinalists.

Requirements: The SAT I or ACT is required. A GPA of 2.0 is required. with a minimum composite score of 840 on the SAT I or 18 on the ACT. Applicants need 15 academic credits, including 4 units in English, 3 each in math, science lab courses, and social studies, 2 in foreign language or world geography, and 1/2 in computer applications. A portfolio for art majors and an audition for theater and music majors are required. The GED is not accepted. Applications are accepted on-line. AP and CLEP credits are accepted.

Procedure: Freshmen are admitted to all sessions. There are early admissions and deferred admissions plans. Applications should be filed by August 1 for fall entry, December 1 for spring entry, and May 1 for summer entry, along with a $25 fee for out-of-state applicants. Notification is sent on a rolling basis.

Financial Aid: In 1999-2000, 74% of all freshmen and 73% of continuing students received some form of financial aid. 28% of freshmen and 32% of continuing students received need-based aid. The average freshman award was $5351. Of that total, scholarships or need-based grants averaged $3136 ($16,510 maximum); loans averaged $2043 ($12,000 maximum); and work contracts averaged $172 ($2400 maximum). The average financial indebtedness of the 1999 graduate was $11,658. Ole Miss is a member of CSS. The FAFSA is required. The fall application deadline is March 15.

Computers: The mainframes are an IBM ES 9000, an SGI Challenge L, an SGI Power Challenge L, a CRAY Y-MP83, and a CRAY J916. The computer center runs a 120-unit general-access lab housing Novell networked PCs with mainframe connection via the campus fiber optic network. Various academic departments operate their own PC labs, some of which are networked and connected to the campus backbone fiber. All students may access the system 24 hours daily. There are no time limits and no fees. It is recommended that all students have personal computers. Pharmacy students are required to have personal computers.

UNIVERSITY OF MISSOURI/COLUMBIA
Columbia, MO 65211

(573) 882-7786
(800) 225-6075; Fax: (573) 882-7887

Full-time: 7816 men, 8752 women	**Faculty:** 1669; I, -$
Part-time: 636 men, 607 women	**Ph.D.s:** 87%
Graduate: 2506 men, 2613 women	**Student/Faculty:** 10 to 1
Year: semesters, summer session	**Tuition:** $5285 ($11,027)
Application Deadline: May 1	**Room & Board:** $4635
Freshman Class: 9091 applied, 8143 accepted, 3932 enrolled	
ACT: 26	**VERY COMPETITIVE+**

The University of Missouri/Columbia, established in 1839, offers a comprehensive array of undergraduate and graduate programs as well as professional training in law, medicine, and veterinary medicine. There are 10 undergraduate and 17 graduate schools. In addition to regional accreditation, MU has baccalaureate program accreditation with AACSB, ABET, ACEJMC, ADA, APTA, CAHEA, CSWE, FIDER, NASAD, NASM, NRPA, and SAF. The 8 libraries contain 2.85

million volumes, and 6.46 million microform items, and subscribe to 23,522 periodicals. Computerized library services include the card catalog, interlibrary loans, and database searching. Special learning facilities include a learning resource center, art gallery, natural history museum, radio station, TV station, astronomy observatory, freedom of information center, herbarium, and anthropology, fishery, and wildlife collections. The 1377-acre campus is in a small town 120 miles west of St. Louis and 120 miles east of Kansas City. Including residence halls, there are 375 buildings.

Programs of Study: MU confers A.B., B.S., B.E.S., B.F.A., B.G.S., B.H.S., B.J., B.M., B.S.Acc., B.S.B.A., B.S.B.E., B.S.ChE., B.S.CiE., B.S.C.E., B.S.E.E., B.S. Ed., B.S.F., B.S.F.W., B.S.H.E.S., B.S.I.E., B.S.M.E., B.S.N., and B.S.W. degrees. Master's and doctoral degrees are also awarded. Bachelor's degrees are awarded in AGRICULTURE (agricultural economics, agriculture, animal science, and soil science), BIOLOGICAL SCIENCE (biochemistry and biology/biological science), BUSINESS (accounting, banking and finance, business administration and management, business economics, hotel/motel and restaurant management, marketing/retailing/merchandising, real estate, and tourism), COMMUNICATIONS AND THE ARTS (advertising, art history and appreciation, broadcasting, classics, communications, design, dramatic arts, English, French, German, journalism, music, Russian, and Spanish), COMPUTER AND PHYSICAL SCIENCE (atmospheric sciences and meteorology, chemistry, computer science, geology, mathematics, physics, and statistics), EDUCATION (art, early childhood, education, elementary, middle school, music, and secondary), ENGINEERING AND ENVIRONMENTAL DESIGN (chemical engineering, civil engineering, computer engineering, electrical/electronics engineering, industrial engineering, and mechanical engineering), HEALTH PROFESSIONS (nursing, occupational therapy, physical therapy, radiological science, and respiratory therapy), SOCIAL SCIENCE (anthropology, archeology, dietetics, economics, food science, geography, history, international studies, parks and recreation management, philosophy, political science/government, psychology, religion, social science, social work, and sociology). Biological sciences, business administration, and psychology are the strongest academically. Business and public administration, journalism, and engineering are the largest.

Special: Available academic programs include co-op programs and cross-registration with other schools, internships, study abroad, a Washington semester, and work-study programs. Special degrees or studies include an accelerated degree, dual majors, a general studies degree, and student-designed majors. Nondegree study and pass/fail options are available. For highly motivated students there is an honors college and the possibility of early admission to the schools of law and medicine. The university also has an easy-access program for nondegree-seeking community residents. There are 31 national honor societies, including Phi Beta Kappa, and a freshman honors program.

Admissions: 90% of the 1999-2000 applicants were accepted. The ACT scores for the 1999-2000 freshman class were: 7% below 21, 24% between 21 and 23, 30% between 24 and 26, 17% between 27 and 28, and 22% above 28. 53% of the current freshmen were in the top fifth of their class; 82% were in the top two fifths. There were 33 National Merit finalists. 133 freshmen graduated first in their class.

Requirements: The ACT is required. Students may gain probationary admission with sufficient GED scores. The usual requirements are completion of 17 Carnegie units, including 4 each in English and math, 3 each in social studies and science, 2 in a foreign language, and 1 in fine arts. Admission is determined by these units and a combination of class rank and ACT score. AP and CLEP credits are accepted. Important factors in the admissions decision are ability to finance

619

college education, advanced placement or honor courses, and evidence of special talent.

Procedure: Freshmen are admitted to all sessions. Entrance exams should be taken late in the junior year or in the senior year. Applications should be filed by May 1 for fall entry, along with a $25 fee. Notification is sent on a rolling basis.

Financial Aid: In a recent year, 81% of all freshmen and 71% of continuing students received some form of financial aid. 57% of freshmen and 41% of continuing students received need-based aid. The average freshman award was $6218. The average financial indebtedness at a recent graduate was $23214. MU is a member of CSS. The FAFSA is required. The fall application deadline is March 1.

Computers: The mainframe is an IBM 9672-R25. There are 15 general access computing sites with more than 850 workstations equipped with Macs, IBM's, and Silicon Graphics, and laser printers for output from the mainframe or PCs. 29 sites house 200 IBM and Mac workstations for students in residence halls. E-mail accounts for students are automatically generated with enrollment. 9 of 19 residence halls are wired for in-room Ethernet access to MU's high speed data backbone. All students may access the system 24 hours daily by modem; lab hours vary, but they are open 7 days a week and 2 are 24-hour facilities. There are no time limits. The fee is $8.30 per credit hour.

UNIVERSITY OF MISSOURI/KANSAS CITY
Kansas City, MO 64110　　　　(816) 235-1111; Fax: (816) 235-5544

Full-time: 1610 men, 2289 women	**Faculty:** 592; I, -$
Part-time: 1228 men, 1663 women	**Ph.D.s:** 84%
Graduate: 2002 men, 2726 women	**Student/Faculty:** 7 to 1
Year: semesters, summer session	**Tuition:** $4421 ($12,501)
Application Deadline: open	**Room & Board:** $4587
Freshman Class: 2592 applied, 1771 accepted, 714 enrolled	
ACT: 25	**VERY COMPETITIVE**

The University of Missouri/Kansas City, which opened in 1933, is a public institution offering undergraduate and graduate programs in the arts and sciences, engineering, business, education, health fields, preprofessional, and professional studies. It offers most of the degree programs in the evening to a primarily commuter student body. There are 9 undergraduate and 13 graduate schools. In addition to regional accreditation, UMKC has baccalaureate program accreditation with AACSB, ABET, ACPE, ADA, NASM, NCATE, and NLN. The 4 libraries contain 1,634,154 volumes, 19,373,323 microform items, and 387,982 audiovisual forms/CDs, and subscribe to 6848 periodicals. Computerized library services include the card catalog, interlibrary loans, and database searching. Special learning facilities include a learning resource center, art gallery, planetarium, and radio station. The 262-acre campus is in an urban area in Kansas City. Including residence halls, there are 42 buildings.

Programs of Study: UMKC confers B.A., B.S., B.B.A., B.F.A., B.I.T., B.L.A., B.M., B.M.E., B.S.C.I.E., B.S.D.H., B.S.E.E., B.S.M.E., and B.S.N. degrees. Master's and doctoral degrees are also awarded. Bachelor's degrees are awarded in BIOLOGICAL SCIENCE (biology/biological science), BUSINESS (accounting and business administration and management), COMMUNICATIONS AND THE ARTS (art, art history and appreciation, communications, dance, dramatic arts, English, fine arts, French, German, music, music performance, music theory and composition, performing arts, Spanish, speech/debate/rhetoric, and studio art), COMPUTER AND PHYSICAL SCIENCE (chemistry, computer science, earth science, geology, information sciences and systems, mathematics, and physics), EDUCATION (elementary, health, music, physical, and secondary), ENGINEERING AND ENVIRONMENTAL DESIGN (civil engineering, electrical/electronics engineering, environmental science, and mechanical engineering), HEALTH PROFESSIONS (dental hygiene, medical technology, music therapy, and nursing), SOCIAL SCIENCE (American studies, criminal justice, economics, geography, history, Judaic studies, liberal arts/general studies, philosophy, political science/government, psychology, sociology, and urban studies). Health sciences and performing arts are the strongest academically. Liberal arts is the largest.

Special: Special academic programs include co-op programs and internships in several majors, study abroad in 8 countries, an accelerated degree program, and numerous work-study opportunities in the Kansas City area. Special degrees include a B.A.-B.S. degree in the computer science program and a liberal arts degree offered by the adult program. The pass/fail option is available in some courses. Freshmen may enter 6-year medical and dental programs. There are 4 national honor societies, a freshman honors program, and 1 departmental honors program.

Admissions: 68% of the 1999-2000 applicants were accepted. The ACT scores for the 1999-2000 freshman class were: 15% below 21, 24% between 21 and 23, 28% between 24 and 26, 16% between 27 and 28, and 17% above 28. 54% of the current freshmen were in the top fifth of their class; 80% were in the top two fifths. 38 freshmen graduated first in their class.

Requirements: The ACT is required. A GPA of 2.0 is required. A combination of the student's test score and class rank determines admissibility; if the rank is 47 or below, the ACT score must be 24 or higher. Graduation from an accredited secondary school is a requirement for admission; the GED is also accepted. Required high school subjects include 4 units of English, 3 each of math and social studies, 2 of science, 1 of arts, and 3 more units selected from the above subjects or from a foreign language. A portfolio is required for art majors, an audition for music majors, and an interview for only those students applying for the pharmacy degree or the 6-year medical and dental programs. AP and CLEP credits are accepted.

Procedure: Freshmen are admitted to all sessions. Entrance exams should be taken by March of the senior year. Application deadlines are open. There is a $25 fee. Notification is sent on a rolling basis.

Financial Aid: In 1999-2000, 71% of all freshmen and 58% of continuing students received some form of financial aid. 40% of freshmen and 41% of continuing students received need-based aid. The average freshman award was $8374. Of that total, scholarships or need-based grants averaged $2227 ($19,704 maximum); loans averaged $2305 ($4000 maximum); work contracts averaged $3096 ($5000 maximum); and VA benefits averaged $4713 ($8648 maximum). 10% of undergraduates work part time. Average annual earnings from campus work are $3096. The FAFSA is required. The fall application deadline is March 1.

Computers: The mainframe is a 5 Compaq ALPHA 2100 minicomputers. There are more than 300 PCs available at various student computer labs and 322 high-speed modem ports for remote access. All students may access the system 24 hours, 7 days a week. Students may access the system dial-up limit of 15 hours; no limit for lab use. The fee is $30 per credit hour.

UNIVERSITY OF MISSOURI/ROLLA
Rolla, MO 65409-0910

(573) 341-4164
(800) 522-0938; Fax: (573) 341-4082

Full-time: 2646 men, 772 women	**Faculty:** 320; I, +$
Part-time: 332 men, 132 women	**Ph.Ds:** 90%
Graduate: 673 men, 160 women	**Student/Faculty:** 11 to 1
Year: semesters, summer session	**Tuition:** $4665 ($12,579)
Application Deadline: July 1	**Room & Board:** $4557
Freshman Class: 1699 applied, 1508 accepted, 697 enrolled	
SAT I Verbal/Math: 612/646	**ACT:** 28 **VERY COMPETITIVE+**

The University of Missouri/Rolla, founded in 1870, is part of the University of Missouri system. A public institution, it offers comprehensive undergraduate and graduate programs and confers degrees in arts and sciences, engineering, and mining and metallurgy. There are 3 undergraduate and 3 graduate schools. In addition to regional accreditation, UMR has baccalaureate program accreditation with ABET and CSAB. The library contains 372,804 volumes, 566,064 microform items, and 3993 audiovisual forms/CDs, and subscribes to 1501 periodicals. Computerized library services include the card catalog, interlibrary loans, and database searching. Special learning facilities include a learning resource center and working mine, nuclear reactor, and observatory. The 284-acre campus is in a small town 90 miles southwest of St. Louis. Including residence halls, there are 71 buildings.

Programs of Study: UMR confers B.A. and B.S. degrees. Master's and doctoral degrees are also awarded. Bachelor's degrees are awarded in BIOLOGICAL SCIENCE (life science), BUSINESS (management information systems), COMMUNICATIONS AND THE ARTS (English), COMPUTER AND PHYSICAL SCIENCE (applied mathematics, chemistry, computer science, geology, and physics), ENGINEERING AND ENVIRONMENTAL DESIGN (aeronautical engineering, ceramic engineering, chemical engineering, civil engineering, computer engineering, electrical/electronics engineering, engineering management, geological engineering, mechanical engineering, metallurgical engineering, mining and mineral engineering, nuclear engineering, and petroleum/natural gas engineering), SOCIAL SCIENCE (economics, history, philosophy, and psychology). Engineering is the strongest academically and the largest.

Special: UMR offers internships in business and government, co-op programs in which students work and attend school on alternating schedules, and study abroad in 8 countries. Accelerated degrees in science and engineering, dual majors, B.A.-B.S. degrees, a 3-2 engineering degree, a 5 year masters program, credit for life/military/work experience, and pass/fail options in certain courses are also available. There are 23 national honor societies, a freshman honors program. All 5 department's have honors programs.

Admissions: 89% of the 1999-2000 applicants were accepted. The SAT I scores for the 1999-2000 freshman class were: Verbal--8% below 500, 34% between 500 and 599, 47% between 600 and 700, and 11% above 700; Math--1% below 500, 24% between 500 and 599, 52% between 600 and 700, and 23% above 700. The ACT scores were 2% below 21, 13% between 21 and 23, 21% between 24 and 26, 18% between 27 and 28, and 46% above 28. 71% of the current freshmen were in the top fifth of their class; 90% were in the top two fifths. There were 20 National Merit finalists. 59 freshmen graduated first in their class.

Requirements: The SAT I or ACT is required. The sum of the high school student's class rank percentile and aptitude exam percentile must be 140 or higher. Candidates must be graduates of an accredited secondary school or have the

GED. The applicant must have completed 16 academic credit units, including 4 each in English and math, 3 each in science and social studies, and 2 in a foreign language. Applications are accepted on-line at http://www.umr.edu/enrol. AP and CLEP credits are accepted. Important factors in the admissions decision are leadership record, advanced placement or honor courses, and evidence of special talent.

Procedure: Freshmen are admitted to all sessions. Entrance exams should be taken late in the junior year or early in the senior year. Applications should be filed by July 1 for fall entry, December 1 for spring entry, and May 1 for summer entry, along with a $25 fee. Notification is sent on a rolling basis.

Financial Aid: In 1999-2000, 92% of all freshmen and 84% of continuing students received some form of financial aid. 68% of freshmen and 56% of continuing students received need-based aid. The average freshman award was $8500. Of that total, scholarships or need-based grants averaged $6350 ($18,600 maximum); loans averaged $3200 ($18,600 maximum); and work contracts averaged $1180 (maximum). 32% of undergraduates work part time. Average annual earnings from campus work are $1000. The average financial indebtedness of the 1999 graduate was $15,000. UMR is a member of CSS. The FAFSA is required. The fall application deadline is February 1 (November 1 priority).

Computers: The mainframes are a UNIX and Novell Servers. All students have free access to campus servers and to 700 networked PCs and Macs at 40 locations. Also available are 100 UNIX workstations (HP, HP/Apollo, and Sun). A complete array of software is provided on all platforms, and 24-hour service is offered. All students may access the system. There are no time limits and no fees.

UNIVERSITY OF NORTH CAROLINA AT ASHEVILLE
Asheville, NC 28804-8510

(828) 251-6481
(800) 531-9842; Fax: (828) 251-6482

Full-time: 994 men, 1371 women	**Faculty:** 156; IIB, +$
Part-time: 311 men, 446 women	**Ph.D.s:** 86%
Graduate: 19 men, 20 women	**Student/Faculty:** 15 to 1
Year: semesters, summer session	**Tuition:** $1960 ($8580)
Application Deadline: April 1	**Room & Board:** $4179
Freshman Class: 1866 applied, 1137 accepted, 460 enrolled	
SAT I Verbal/Math: 580/560	**ACT:** 23 **VERY COMPETITIVE**

The University of North Carolina at Asheville, founded in 1927, is a publicly assisted liberal arts institution in the University of North Carolina system. There is 1 graduate school. In addition to regional accreditation, UNC Asheville has baccalaureate program accreditation with NCATE. The library contains 245,429 volumes, 769,154 microform items, and 8292 audiovisual forms/CDs, and subscribes to 2240 periodicals. Computerized library services include the card catalog, interlibrary loans, and database searching. Special learning facilities include a learning resource center, an art gallery, the Environmental Quality Institute, aa distance learning facility, a center for creative retirement, an undergraduate research center, botanical gardens, and a music recording center. The 265-acre campus is in a suburban area 130 miles west of Charlotte. Including residence halls, there are 28 buildings.

Programs of Study: UNC Asheville confers B.A., B.S., and B.F.A. degrees. Master's degrees are also awarded. Bachelor's degrees are awarded in BIOLOGICAL SCIENCE (biology/biological science), BUSINESS (accounting and business administration and management), COMMUNICATIONS AND THE ARTS (art, classics, communications, dramatic arts, English, fine arts, French, German, multimedia, music, music technology, and Spanish), COMPUTER AND PHYSICAL SCIENCE (atmospheric sciences and meteorology, chemistry, computer science, mathematics, and physics), ENGINEERING AND ENVIRONMENTAL DESIGN (environmental science and industrial administration/management), SOCIAL SCIENCE (economics, history, philosophy, political science/government, psychology, and sociology). Management, psychology, and environmental science are the largest.

Special: Students may participate in cooperative programs in nursing, forestry, and textile chemistry. UNC Asheville participates in a consortium with Warren Wilson and Mars Hill Colleges, and there is cross-registration with a number of North Carolina universities and colleges. Study-abroad programs are available in more than 7 countries. The school offers internships, dual majors, student-designed interdisciplinary majors, a 2-2 engineering degree with North Carolina State University, and a Washington semester. Nondegree study is available. There are 12 national honor societies, a freshman honors program, and 10 departmental honors programs.

Admissions: 61% of the 1999-2000 applicants were accepted. The SAT I scores for the 1999-2000 freshman class were: Verbal--14% below 500, 45% between 500 and 599, 35% between 600 and 700, and 6% above 700; Math--17% below 500, 46% between 500 and 599, 35% between 600 and 700, and 3% above 700. The ACT scores were 19% below 21, 33% between 21 and 23, 28% between 24 and 26, 14% between 27 and 28, and 6% above 28. 51% of the current freshmen were in the top fifth of their class; 90% were in the top two fifths. 2 freshmen graduated first in their class.

Requirements: The SAT I or ACT is required. UNC Asheville requires applicants to be in the upper 50% of their class with a GPA of 2.0. In addition, graduation from an accredited secondary school or the GED is required. UNCA requires a minimum of 16 high school academic units, including 4 credits of English, 3 each of math (algebra I, geometry, algebra II) and science (biology, physical science, and a lab course), and 2 each of a foreign language and social studies/history. Applicants are evaluated primarily on their academic achievement record, extracurricular activities that support academic achievement, and SAT I or ACT scores. Applications are accepted on-line at the school's web site or at embark.com. AP and CLEP credits are accepted. Other important factors in the admissions decision are advanced placement or honor courses, leadership record, and evidence of special talent.

Procedure: Freshmen are admitted to all sessions. Entrance exams should be taken at the end of the junior year or the beginning of the senior year. There are early decision, early admissions, and deferred admissions plans. Early decision applications should be filed by October 15; regular applications, by April 1 for fall entry and December 1 for spring entry, along with a $45 fee. Notification of early decision and regular decision is sent monthly.

Financial Aid: In 1998-99, 67% of all freshmen and 52% of continuing students received some form of financial aid. 41% of freshmen and 38% of continuing students received need-based aid. The average freshman award was $4613. Of that total, scholarships or need-based grants averaged $1761 ($7267 maximum); loans averaged $3609 ($16,133 maximum); work contracts averaged $1079 ($1800 maximum); and non-need-based grants from outside agencies averaged $2938 ($12,914 maximum). 23% of undergraduates work part time. Average annual earnings from campus work are $1064. The average financial indebtedness of the 1998 graduate was $13,118. UNC Asheville is a member of CSS. The FAFSA is required. The fall application deadline is March 1.

Computers: The mainframes are a Compaq VAX 4000, a Compaq Alpha server 2100, and a Compaq Alpha server 4100. Students can access the central computing resources and the Internet from one of more than 250 PCs and Macs in campus labs, department labs, residence hall labs, and the library. Additionally, all dorms have a network port for every resident with a PC. The 9 general purpose computer labs offer a vaariety of personal productivity software, Internet browsers, and course-specific software and are available 7 days a week. There are 12 modems available for access to campus E-mail and text-based Internet services. All students may access the system 24 hours per day. There are no time limits and no fees.

UNIVERSITY OF NORTH CAROLINA AT CHAPEL HILL
Chapel Hill, NC 27599-2200

(919) 966-3623
Fax: (919) 962-3045

Full-time: 5714 men, 8878 women	**Faculty:** 2328; I, +$
Part-time: 365 men, 477 women	**Ph.D.s:** 94%
Graduate: 3945 men, 5274 women	**Student/Faculty:** 6 to 1
Year: semesters, summer session	**Tuition:** $2364 ($11,530)
Application Deadline: January 15	**Room & Board:** $5280
Freshman Class: 16,813 applied, 6178 accepted, 3405 enrolled	
SAT I Verbal/Math: 620/630	**HIGHLY COMPETITIVE**

The University of North Carolina at Chapel Hill, chartered in 1789 and the nation's first public university, offers academic programs leading to 95 bachelor's, 169 master's, and 109 doctoral degrees, as well as professional degrees. Some of the information in this profile is a approximate. There are 9 undergraduate and 12 graduate schools. The 15 libraries contain 4,263,684 volumes, 3,897,013 microform items, and 662,203 audiovisual forms/CDs, and subscribe to 39,044 periodicals. Computerized library services include the card catalog, interlibrary loans, and database searching. Special learning facilities include an art gallery, planetarium, radio station, TV station, and botanical garden. The 720-acre campus is in a suburban area 25 miles west of Raleigh.

Programs of Study: UNC-Chapel Hill confers B.A., B.S., B.A.Ed., B.F.A., B.M., B.Med., B.S.B.A., B.S.N., and B.S.S.T. degrees. Master's and doctoral degrees are also awarded. Bachelor's degrees are awarded in BIOLOGICAL SCIENCE (biology/biological science and zoology), BUSINESS (business administration and management and recreation and leisure services), COMMUNICATIONS AND THE ARTS (art history and appreciation, classical languages, classics, comparative literature, dramatic arts, English, French, German, Greek, Italian, journalism, Latin, linguistics, music, Portuguese, Russian, Slavic languages, Spanish, speech/debate/rhetoric, and studio art), COMPUTER AND PHYSICAL SCIENCE (astronomy, chemistry, geology, mathematics, physics, and statistics), EDUCATION (art, early childhood, education, elementary, foreign languages, middle school, music, physical, science, and secondary), ENGINEERING AND ENVIRONMENTAL DESIGN (industrial administration/management), HEALTH PROFESSIONS (dental hygiene, medical laboratory technology, nursing, pharmacy, public health, and radiological science), SOCIAL SCIENCE (African American studies, African studies, American studies, anthropology, East Asian studies, economics, geography, history, international studies, Latin American studies, liberal arts/general studies, peace studies, philosophy, political science/government, psychology, public affairs, religion, Russian and

Slavic studies, sociology, and women's studies). Sociology is the strongest academically. Biology, psychology, and English are the largest.

Special: Students may participate in joint programs with Duke University and North Carolina State University. Internships, study abroad, work-study programs, B.A.-B.S. degrees, and student-designed majors are available. The university offers a 2-2 engineering operations program with North Carolina State University. There are pass/fail options and nondegree study. There are 2 national honor societies, including Phi Beta Kappa, and a freshman honors program.

Admissions: 37% of the 1999-2000 applicants were accepted. The SAT I scores for the 1999-2000 freshman class were: Verbal--7% below 500, 33% between 500 and 599, 45% between 600 and 700, and 16% above 700; Math--6% below 500, 30% between 500 and 599, 47% between 600 and 700, and 17% above 700. 88% of the current freshmen were in the top fifth of their class; 97% were in the top two fifths.

Requirements: The SAT I or ACT is required. A GPA of 2.0 is required. In addition, applicants must be graduates of an accredited secondary school. They should complete 16 high school academic credits, including 4 in English, 3 each in math (2 in algebra and 1 in geometry) and science (including at least 1 physical science and 1 lab course), and 2 each in a single foreign language, history, and social studies. A portfolio and an audition are recommended for art and music majors. AP and CLEP credits are accepted. Important factors in the admissions decision are advanced placement or honor courses, leadership record, and recommendations by school officials.

Procedure: Freshmen are admitted in the fall. Entrance exams should be taken in the junior and senior years. There is an early admissions plan. Early decision applications should be filed by October 15; regular applications, by January 15 for fall entry, along with a $55 fee. Notification is sent on a rolling basis. 5% of all applicants are on a waiting list.

Financial Aid: In 1999-2000, 58% of all freshmen and 51% of continuing students received some form of financial aid. 30% of freshmen and 29% of continuing students received need-based aid. The average freshman award was $6114. The average financial indebtedness of the 1999 graduate was $12,800. UNC-Chapel Hill is a member of CSS. The CSS/Profile or FAFSA is required. The fall application deadline is March 1.

Computers: The mainframes are a CONVEX supercomputer and a variety of UNIX workstations. More than 300 microcomputers are available for student use throughout the campus. Accounts are available for E-mail and instructional computing. All students may access the system for E-mail; others for course work or independent research may access the system 24 hours a day. There are no time limits and no fees.

UNIVERSITY OF NORTH FLORIDA
Jacksonville, FL 32224   (904) 620-2624; Fax: (904) 620-2414

Full-time: 2545 men, 3678 women	**Faculty:** 363; IIA, -$
Part-time: 1785 men, 2420 women	**Ph.D.s:** 88%
Graduate: 576 men, 1188 women	**Student/Faculty:** 17 to 1
Year: semesters, summer session	**Tuition:** $2275 ($9264)
Application Deadline: July 23	**Room & Board:** $5100
Freshman Class: 4581 applied, 3066 accepted, 1286 enrolled	
SAT I Verbal/Math: 560/570	**ACT:** 22 **VERY COMPETITIVE**

The University of North Florida, founded in 1965, is a public university that is part of the state university system. There are 5 undergraduate and 5 graduate schools. In addition to regional accreditation, UNF has baccalaureate program accreditation with AACSB, ABET, NASM, NCATE, and NLN. The library contains 704,799 volumes, 1,272,603 microform items, and 60,776 audiovisual forms/CDs, and subscribes to 3000 periodicals. Computerized library services include the card catalog, interlibrary loans, and database searching. Special learning facilities include a learning resource center, art gallery, radio station, theater, auditorium, and nature preserve. The 1300-acre campus is in an urban area 12 miles southeast of downtown Jacksonville. Including residence halls, there are 44 buildings.

Programs of Study: UNF confers B.A., B.S., B.A.E., B.B.A., B.F.A., B.M., B.S. E.E., B.S.H., and B.S.N. degrees. Associate, master's, and doctoral degrees are also awarded. Bachelor's degrees are awarded in BIOLOGICAL SCIENCE (biology/biological science), BUSINESS (accounting, banking and finance, business administration and management, business economics, marketing/retailing/merchandising, and transportation management), COMMUNICATIONS AND THE ARTS (art, art history and appreciation, communications, English, fine arts, jazz, music, and Spanish), COMPUTER AND PHYSICAL SCIENCE (chemistry, computer science, information sciences and systems, mathematics, and statistics), EDUCATION (art, early childhood, elementary, mathematics, music, physical, science, secondary, social science, and special), ENGINEERING AND ENVIRONMENTAL DESIGN (construction technology and electrical/electronics engineering), HEALTH PROFESSIONS (health science and nursing), SOCIAL SCIENCE (criminal justice, economics, history, philosophy, political science/government, prelaw, psychology, and sociology). Special education, elementary education, and nursing are the strongest academically. Business, health science, and computer science are the largest.

Special: There are cooperative programs for preprofessional majors with the University of Florida, internships in most majors, and work-study programs with several Jacksonville businesses. Study abroad, a Washington semester, dual majors, and student-designed majors also are available. Credit is given for military experience. There are 2 national honor societies, a freshman honors program, and 8 departmental honors programs.

Admissions: 67% of the 1999-2000 applicants were accepted. The SAT I scores for the 1999-2000 freshman class were: Verbal--18% below 500, 49% between 500 and 599, 30% between 600 and 700, and 3% above 700; Math--18% below 500, 53% between 500 and 599, 27% between 600 and 700, and 2% above 700. The ACT scores were 30% below 21, 45% between 21 and 23, 19% between 24 and 26, 5% between 27 and 28, and 1% above 28. There were 4 National Merit finalists and 5 semifinalists. 8 freshmen graduated first in their class.

Requirements: The SAT I or ACT is required, with minimum acceptable composite scores of 970 on the SAT I and 20 on the ACT. A GPA of 2.5 is required. In addition, applicants must be graduates of an accredited secondary school or have a GED. A total of 15 academic credits plus 4 additional academic electives or 19 Carnegie units is required. Secondary school course work must include 4 years of English, 3 each of math, science, and social studies, and 2 of foreign language. AP and CLEP credits are accepted. Important factors in the admissions decision are advanced placement or honor courses, recommendations by school officials, and evidence of special talent.

Procedure: Freshmen are admitted to all sessions. Entrance exams should be taken during the spring of the junior year or the fall of the senior year. There are early admissions and deferred admissions plans. Applications should be filed by July 23 for fall entry, November 19 for spring entry, and April 1 for summer entry, along with a $20 fee. Notification is sent on a rolling basis.

Financial Aid: In 1999-2000, 77% of all freshmen and 54% of continuing students received some form of financial aid. 26% of freshmen and 33% of continuing students received need-based aid. The average freshman award was $1837. Of that total, scholarships or need-based grants averaged $1358 ($8000 maximum); loans averaged $2871 ($14,631 maximum); and work contracts averaged $3165 ($4000 maximum). 6% of undergraduates work part time. Average annual earnings from campus work are $4964. The average financial indebtedness of the 1999 graduate was $11,141. UNF is a member of CSS. The FAFSA is required. The fall application deadline is April 1.

Computers: The mainframes are 3 UNIX DEC ALPHA 2100s. The UNIX systems, as well as Internet access and E-mail, are accessible via dial-up and network connections in labs and residence halls. There are approximately 600 Pentium-level PCs in general-purpose and distributed labs with application software, including statistics and graphics packages. The general-purpose labs are open 8 a.m. to 1 a.m. Monday to Thursday, 8 a.m. to 9 p.m. Friday, 9 a.m. to 8 p.m. Saturday, and 12 p.m. to 12 a.m. Sunday. The UNIX systems are available 24 hours a day. There are no time limits and no fees. It is recommended that students in building construction management have personal computers. A Pentium 200, notebook, 128 MB RAM, 6 GB hard drive is recommended.

UNIVERSITY OF NORTH TEXAS
Denton, TX 76203

(940) 565-2681
(800) UNT-8211; Fax: (940) 565-2408

Full-time: 7136 men, 8527 women	**Faculty:** 769; I, --$
Part-time: 2354 men, 2435 women	**Ph.D.s:** 86%
Graduate: 2506 men, 3543 women	**Student/Faculty:** 20 to 1
Year: semesters, summer session	**Tuition:** $2852 ($9332)
Application Deadline: June 15	**Room & Board:** $4096
Freshman Class: 7189 applied, 5350 accepted, 3037 enrolled	
SAT I Verbal/Math: 530/530	**ACT:** 21 **COMPETITIVE**

The University of North Texas, founded in 1890, is a public institution offering programs through its colleges of arts and sciences, education, business administration, community services, library and information sciences, music, and merchandising and hospitality management. There are 8 undergraduate schools and 1 graduate school. In addition to regional accreditation, UNT has baccalaureate program accreditation with AACSB, ACEJMC, CSAB, CSWE, FIDER, NASM, and NRPA. The 4 libraries contain 1,905,113 volumes, 3,064,606 microform items, and 73,367 audiovisual forms/CDs, and subscribe to 9606 periodicals. Computerized library services include the card catalog, interlibrary loans, and database searching. Special learning facilities include a learning resource center, art gallery, radio station, observatory, and tv and film production unit. The 500-acre campus is in an urban area 35 miles north of Dallas/Fort Worth. Including residence halls, there are 138 buildings.

Programs of Study: UNT confers B.A., B.S., B.A.A.S., B.B.A., B.F.A., B.M., B.S.B.C., B.S.Bio., B.S.Chem., B.S.Eco., B.S.E.T., B.S.Math., B.S.M.T., B.S. Phy., and B.S.W. degrees. Master's and doctoral degrees are also awarded. Bachelor's degrees are awarded in BIOLOGICAL SCIENCE (biochemistry and biology/biological science), BUSINESS (accounting, banking and finance, business administration and management, business economics, entrepreneurial studies, hotel/motel and restaurant management, human resources, insurance, management information systems, management science, marketing/retailing/merchandising, operations research, organizational behavior, personnel management, real estate, recreation and leisure services, and small business management), COMMUNI-

CATIONS AND THE ARTS (applied art, art, art history and appreciation, ceramic art and design, communications, dance, dramatic arts, drawing, English, fiber/textiles/weaving, film arts, French, German, jazz, journalism, metal/jewelry, music, music history and appreciation, music performance, music theory and composition, painting, photography, printmaking, radio/television technology, sculpture, Spanish, and visual and performing arts), COMPUTER AND PHYSICAL SCIENCE (chemistry, computer science, information sciences and systems, mathematics, and physics), EDUCATION (business, early childhood, elementary, health, physical, reading, and vocational), ENGINEERING AND ENVIRONMENTAL DESIGN (commercial art, emergency/disaster science, engineering technology, industrial administration/management, and interior design), HEALTH PROFESSIONS (cytotechnology, medical laboratory technology, rehabilitation therapy, and speech pathology/audiology), SOCIAL SCIENCE (anthropology, child psychology/development, clothing and textiles management/production/services, counseling/psychology, criminal justice, economics, fashion design and technology, geography, history, home furnishings and equipment management/production/services, interdisciplinary studies, liberal arts/general studies, philosophy, physical fitness/movement, political science/government, psychology, social science, social work, and sociology). Accounting, jazz studies, and city management are the strongest academically. Biology, psychology, and interdisciplinary studies (teacher education department) are the largest.

Special: UNT offers co-op programs in 34 majors, internships, and work-study programs with the university. Students may study abroad in the United Kingdom, France, Japan, Germany, Mexico, and Australia. An accelerated degree program in math and science allows Texas high school students to obtain 2 years of college credit during their last 2 years in high school. Dual degrees, a general studies degree, and pass/fail options are also offered. There are 3 national honor societies, a freshman honors program, and 1 departmental honors program.

Admissions: 74% of the 1999-2000 applicants were accepted. The SAT I scores for the 1999-2000 freshman class were: Verbal--34% below 500, 43% between 500 and 599, 20% between 600 and 700, and 3% above 700; Math--36% below 500, 39% between 500 and 599, 21% between 600 and 700, and 4% above 700. The ACT scores were 38% below 21, 30% between 21 and 23, 21% between 24 and 26, 7% between 27 and 28, and 4% above 28. 40% of the current freshmen were in the top fifth of their class; 71% were in the top two fifths.

Requirements: The SAT I or ACT is required. Applicants must be graduates of an accredited high school and submit a high school transcript. The required minimum score for entrance exams is determined by high school class rank. AP and CLEP credits are accepted. Important factors in the admissions decision are recommendations by school officials, advanced placement or honor courses, and evidence of special talent.

Procedure: Freshmen are admitted to all sessions. Entrance exams should be taken at least 2 months before admissions deadlines. There are early admissions and deferred admissions plans. Applications should be filed by June 15 for fall entry, December 1 for spring entry, and May 15 for summer entry, along with a $25 fee. Notification is sent on a rolling basis.

Financial Aid: In 1999-2000, 49% of all freshmen received some form of financial aid. 39% of freshmen received need-based aid. The average freshman award was $3800. 80% of undergraduates work part time. Average annual earnings from campus work are $2400. The average financial indebtedness of the 1999 graduate was $12,000. The FAFSA is required. The fall application deadline is June 1.

Computers: The mainframes are an HDS-80-83, a Solbourne SE/904, an NBIV16S, an NAS8000, and an IBM 43004. More than 5000 PCs are available on campus. All students may access the system. Students may access the system 1 hour if labs are busy. The fee is $3.25 per semester hour.

UNIVERSITY OF NOTRE DAME
Notre Dame, IN 46556
(219) 631-7505

Full-time: 4347 men, 3636 women	**Faculty:** I, ++$
Part-time: 25 men, 6 women	**Ph.D.s:** n/av
Graduate: 1641 men, 999 women	**Student/Faculty:** 13 to 1
Year: semesters, summer session	**Tuition:** $22,187
Application Deadline: January 7	**Room & Board:** $5750
Freshman Class: 10,010 applied, 3500 accepted, 1971 enrolled	
SAT I Verbal/Math: 680/670	**ACT:** 31 **MOST COMPETITIVE**

The University of Notre Dame, founded in 1842, is a private institution affiliated with the Roman Catholic Church and offering degree programs in architecture, arts and letters, business administration, engineering, and science. There are 5 undergraduate and 6 graduate schools. In addition to regional accreditation, Notre Dame has baccalaureate program accreditation with AACSB, ABET, NAAB, and NASM. The 9 libraries contain 2,704,394 volumes, 3,272,037 microform items, and 18,765 audiovisual forms/CDs, and subscribe to 24,334 periodicals. Computerized library services include the card catalog, interlibrary loans, and database searching. Special learning facilities include a learning resource center, art gallery, radio station, tv station, and art museum. The 1250-acre campus is in a suburban area 90 miles east of Chicago. Including residence halls, there are 156 buildings.

Programs of Study: Notre Dame confers B.A., B.S., B.Arch., B.B.A., and B.F.A. degrees. Master's and doctoral degrees are also awarded. Bachelor's degrees are awarded in BIOLOGICAL SCIENCE (biochemistry and biology/biological science), BUSINESS (accounting, banking and finance, business economics, management information systems, management science, and marketing/retailing/merchandising), COMMUNICATIONS AND THE ARTS (art history and appreciation, communications, English, French, German, graphic design, Greek, Italian, Japanese, Latin, music, Russian, Spanish, and studio art), COMPUTER AND PHYSICAL SCIENCE (applied physics, chemistry, computer science, geoscience, mathematics, and physics), EDUCATION (science), ENGINEERING AND ENVIRONMENTAL DESIGN (aeronautical engineering, architecture, chemical engineering, civil engineering, computer engineering, electrical/electronics engineering, environmental engineering, environmental science, geological engineering, and mechanical engineering), HEALTH PROFESSIONS (predentistry and premedicine), SOCIAL SCIENCE (American studies, anthropology, classical/ancient civilization, economics, history, international studies, liberal arts/general studies, medieval studies, philosophy, political science/government, psychology, sociology, and theological studies). Engineering, theology, and business are the strongest academically. Accounting, government, and English are the largest.

Special: Cross-registration is offered with Saint Mary's College. Study abroad is possible in France, Austria, Australia, Chile, Mexico, Japan, Spain, Ireland, Italy, Egypt, Israel, and England. A 5-year arts and letters/engineering B.A.-B.S. degree is offered. There is a program of liberal studies, centered on the discussion of great books. Internships, an accelerated degree program, a Washington semester, dual majors, 3-2 engineering degrees, and pass/fail options are available. There are 15 national honor societies, including Phi Beta Kappa, and 2 departmental honors programs.

Admissions: 35% of the 1999-2000 applicants were accepted. The SAT I scores for the 1999-2000 freshman class were: Verbal--2% below 500, 15% between

500 and 599, 51% between 600 and 700, and 32% above 700; Math--1% below 500, 10% between 500 and 599, 46% between 600 and 700, and 42% above 700. The ACT scores were 1% below 21, 4% between 21 and 23, 6% between 24 and 26, 11% between 27 and 28, and 78% above 28. 94% of the current freshmen were in the top fifth of their class; 99% were in the top two fifths. 298 freshmen graduated first in their class.

Requirements: The SAT I or ACT is required. Applicants should be graduates of an accredited secondary school with 16 Carnegie credits completed, including 4 years of English, 3 of math, and 2 each of science, foreign language, and history. The SAT II: Subject test in a foreign language is recommended. An essay is required. An audition or a portfolio is recommended for some majors. Students can apply on-line through the university's Web site or through ExPAN and CollegeView. AP credits are accepted.

Procedure: Freshmen are admitted in the fall. Entrance exams should be taken by the fall of the senior year. There are early action and deferred admissions plans. Early action applications should be filed by November 1; regular applications, by January 7 for fall entry, along with a $40 fee. Notification of early action is sent December 15; regular decision, April 2. 6% of all applicants are on a waiting list.

Financial Aid: In 1999-2000, 77% of all freshmen and 71% of continuing students received some form of financial aid. 48% of freshmen and 46% of continuing students received need-based aid. The average freshman award was $13,950. Of that total, scholarships or need-based grants averaged $15,525 ($30,100 maximum); loans averaged $3755 ($5625 maximum); and work contracts averaged $1800 ($2100 maximum). 52% of undergraduates work part time. Average annual earnings from campus work are $1300. The average financial indebtedness of the 1999 graduate was $18,150. Notre Dame is a member of CSS. The CSS/Profile or FAFSA and federal income tax return are required. The fall application deadline is February 15.

Computers: The mainframes are an HP 3000 and two ORIGEN 2000s. There are 880 PCs, Macs, and UNIX computers in open clusters that students can use to complete their course work and access the Internet. All students may access the system 24 hours a day. There are no time limits and no fees. It is recommended that all students have personal computers.

UNIVERSITY OF OKLAHOMA
Norman, OK 73019

(405) 325-2251
(800) 234-6868; Fax: (405) 325-7124

Full-time: 7655 men, 7103 women	**Faculty:** 880; I, --$
Part-time: 1341 men, 1165 women	**Ph.D.s:** 88%
Graduate: 2177 men, 1898 women	**Student/Faculty:** 17 to 1
Year: semesters, summer session	**Tuition:** $1890 ($6225)
Application Deadline: July 15	**Room & Board:** $4384
Freshman Class: 5933 applied, 5687 accepted, 3298 enrolled	
ACT: 25	**VERY COMPETITIVE**

The University of Oklahoma, founded in 1890, is a comprehensive research university offering 160 areas for undergraduate study. There are 9 undergraduate and 9 graduate schools. In addition to regional accreditation, OU has baccalaureate program accreditation with AACSB, ABET, ACCE, ACEJMC, ADA, APTA, CSWE, FIDER, NAAB, NASM, and NCATE. The 8 libraries contain 4,107,132 volumes, 3,820,663 microform items, and 560,826 audiovisual forms/CDs, and subscribe to 16,989 periodicals. Computerized library services include the card catalog, interlibrary loans, and database searching. Special learning facilities include an art gallery, natural history museum, radio station, TV station, and an observatory. The 3136-acre campus is in a suburban area 18 miles south of Oklahoma City. Including residence halls, there are 231 buildings.

Programs of Study: OU confers B.A., B.S., B.Acct., B.B.A. B.F.A., B.L.S., B. Music, B.Mus.Educ., and B.S.Ed. degrees. Master's and doctoral degrees are also awarded. Bachelor's degrees are awarded in BIOLOGICAL SCIENCE (botany, microbiology, and zoology), BUSINESS (accounting, banking and finance, business administration and management, business economics, international business management, management information systems, marketing/retailing/merchandising, and real estate), COMMUNICATIONS AND THE ARTS (advertising, art, art history and appreciation, broadcasting, classics, communications, dance, dramatic arts, English, film arts, fine arts, French, German, journalism, languages, linguistics, music, photography, public relations, Russian, Spanish, and video), COMPUTER AND PHYSICAL SCIENCE (astronomy, astrophysics, atmospheric sciences and meteorology, chemistry, computer science, geology, geophysics and seismology, geoscience, mathematics, and physics), EDUCATION (early childhood, elementary, foreign languages, mathematics, music, science, social studies, and special), ENGINEERING AND ENVIRONMENTAL DESIGN (aeronautical engineering, architecture, aviation administration/management, chemical engineering, civil engineering, computer engineering, electrical/electronics engineering, engineering, engineering physics, environmental design, environmental engineering, environmental science, geological engineering, industrial engineering, interior design, land use management and reclamation, mechanical engineering, and petroleum/natural gas engineering), HEALTH PROFESSIONS (health science and medical laboratory technology), SOCIAL SCIENCE (African American studies, anthropology, area studies, Asian/Oriental studies, economics, geography, history, international studies, liberal arts/general studies, Native American studies, philosophy, political science/government, psychology, public affairs, religion, social work, sociology, and women's studies). Chemistry and biochemistry, history of science, and petroleum engineering are the strongest academically. Accounting, psychology, and management information systems are the largest.

Special: Co-op programs are available in engineering and business. A variety of voluntary and required internships are available in more than 50 fields of study. OU offers study abroad in 46 countries, work-study programs, a Washington semester, a general studies degree, dual and student-designed majors, nondegree study, pass/fail options, and credit for life experience. B.A.-B.S. degrees are offered in many subjects. The interdisciplinary major in letters combines the classics, history, philosophy, and languages. A professional studies major is offered through the continuing education program. There are 37 national honor societies, including Phi Beta Kappa, a freshman honors program, and a universitywide honors program.

Admissions: 96% of the 1999-2000 applicants were accepted. 52% of the current freshmen were in the top fifth of their class; 82% were in the top two fifths. There were 134 National Merit finalists.

Requirements: The SAT I or ACT is required. OU requires applicants to be in the upper 30% of their class. A GPA of 3.0 is required. Performance requirements can be met with a high school GPA of 3.0 and a class ranking in the upper 30% or a minimum composite score of 1090 on the SAT I or 24 on the ACT. Graduation from an accredited secondary school or a satisfactory score on the GED is required. Students must have a total of 15 curricular units, including 4 years of English, 3 of math, and 2 each of history and science, history, citizenship, computer science, or foreign language. Alternative admission opportunities include summer provisional admission, adult admission, and an alternative admission program. Applications are available on-line at http://www.ou.edu/admrec/admappl.htm. AP and CLEP credits are accepted. Recommendations by school officials is an important factor in the admission decision.

Procedure: Freshmen are admitted to all sessions. Entrance exams should be taken during the junior year or first part of the senior year. Applications should be filed by July 15 for fall entry, December 1 for spring entry, and May 1 for summer entry, along with a $25 fee. Notification is sent on a rolling basis.

Financial Aid: In 1999-2000, 62% of all freshmen and 71% of continuing students received some form of financial aid. 39% of freshmen and 51% of continuing students received need-based aid. The average freshman award was $5747. Of that total, scholarships or need-based grants averaged $3176 ($10,000 maximum); loans averaged $3296 ($7000 maximum); and work contracts averaged $1496 ($3200 maximum). 69% of undergraduates work part time. Average annual earnings from campus work are $3717. The average financial indebtedness of the 1999 graduate was $19,821. OU is a member of CSS. The FAFSA is required. The recommended fall application deadline is June 1.

Computers: The mainframes are an IBM 9672-R22, VAX 6520, and several networked SUN systems. Students may access several hundred computers distributed throughout the campus with a wide range of software, including word processing, presentation graphics, and Internet access. An extensive modem pool provides off-campus access to OU resources. All students may access the system 24 hours per day. There are no time limits. The fee is $5.00/credit hour. It is recommended that students in engineering programs have personal computers. A special OU student PC package is recommended.

UNIVERSITY OF PENNSYLVANIA
Philadelphia, PA 19104   (215) 898-7507

Full-time: 4765 men, 4558 women	**Faculty:** 2722; I, ++$
Part-time: 282 men, 222 women	**Ph.D.s:** 99%
Graduate: 5065 men, 4920 women	**Student/Faculty:** 3 to 1
Year: semesters, summer session	**Tuition:** $24,230
Application Deadline: January 1	**Room & Board:** $7362
Freshman Class: 17,666 applied, 4668 accepted, 2507 enrolled	
SAT I Verbal/Math: 680/710	**ACT:** 30 **MOST COMPETITIVE**

University of Pennsylvania, founded in 1740, is a private institution offering undergraduate and graduate degrees in arts and sciences, business, engineering and applied science, and nursing. There are 4 undergraduate and 12 graduate schools. In addition to regional accreditation, Penn has baccalaureate program accreditation with AACSB, ABET, NAAB, NCATE, and NLN. The 16 libraries contain 4,546,667 volumes, 3,155,776 microform items, and 48,794 audiovisual forms/CDs, and subscribe to 33,816 periodicals. Computerized library services include the card catalog, interlibrary loans, and database searching. Special learning facilities include a learning resource center, an art gallery, a natural history museum, a planetarium, a radio station, a TV station, an arboretum, an animal research center, a primate research center, a language lab, a center for performing arts, an institute for contemporary art, a wind tunnel, and an electron microscope. The 260-acre campus is in an urban area in Philadelphia. Including residence halls, there are 122 buildings.

Programs of Study: Penn confers B.A., B.S., B.Applied Sc., B.S. in Econ., B.S.E., and B.S.N. degrees. Associate, master's, and doctoral degrees are also awarded. Bachelor's degrees are awarded in BIOLOGICAL SCIENCE (biochemistry, biology/biological science, biophysics, and physiology), BUSINESS (accounting, banking and finance, business administration and management, business data processing, entrepreneurial studies, human resources, insurance and risk management, management information systems, management science, marketing/retailing/merchandising, purchasing/inventory management, and real estate), COMMUNICATIONS AND THE ARTS (art, art history and appreciation, classics, communications, comparative literature, dramatic arts, English literature, folklore and mythology, French, German, Italian, linguistics, music, romance languages and literature, Russian, and Spanish), COMPUTER AND PHYSICAL SCIENCE (actuarial science, astrophysics, chemistry, geology, mathematics, physics, and statistics), EDUCATION (education and elementary), ENGINEERING AND ENVIRONMENTAL DESIGN (bioengineering, chemical engineering, civil engineering, computer engineering, electrical/electronics engineering, environmental design, environmental science, materials engineering, mechanical engineering, and systems engineering), HEALTH PROFESSIONS (health care administration, hospital administration, and nursing), SOCIAL SCIENCE (African American studies, African studies, American studies, anthropology, East Asian studies, economics, history, history of science, humanities, international relations, Judaic studies, Latin American studies, law, liberal arts/general studies, Middle Eastern studies, philosophy, political science/government, psychology, public affairs, religion, social science, sociology, South Asian studies, urban studies, and women's studies).

Special: Cross-registration is permitted with Haverford, Swarthmore, and Bryn Mawr Colleges. Opportunities are provided for internships, a Washington semester, accelerated degree programs, preprofessional programs, B.A.-B.S. degrees, dual and student-designed majors, a 3-2 engineering degree, credit by examination, nondegree study, limited pass/fail options, and study abroad in 14 countries. Through the "one university" concept, students in 1 undergraduate school may study in any of the other 3. There are 10 national honor societies, including Phi Beta Kappa, a freshman honors program, and 27 departmental honors programs.

Admissions: 26% of the 1999-2000 applicants were accepted. The SAT I scores for the 1999-2000 freshman class were: Verbal--10% between 500 and 599, 46% between 600 and 700, and 43% above 700; Math--4% between 500 and 599, 34% between 600 and 700, and 61% above 700. 98% of the current freshmen were in the top fifth of their class; all were in the top two fifths. 235 freshmen graduated first in their class.

Requirements: The SAT I or ACT is required. Graduation from an accredited secondary school is not required. Recommended preparation includes 4 years of high school English, 3 or 4 each of a foreign language and math, and 3 each of history and science. An essay is required. A portfolio and an audition are recommended for prospective art and music majors, respectively. AP credits are accepted. Important factors in the admissions decision are advanced placement or honor courses, leadership record, and recommendations by school officials.

Procedure: Freshmen are admitted in the fall. Entrance exams should be taken by January of the senior year. There are early decision, early admissions, and deferred admissions plans. Early decision applications should be filed by November 1; regular applications, by January 1 for fall entry, along with a $55 fee. Notification of early decision is sent December 15; regular decision, April 1. 1007 early decision candidates were accepted for the 1999-2000 class. 5% of all applicants are on a waiting list.

Financial Aid: In a recent year, 44% of all freshmen and 45% of continuing students received some form of financial aid. 45% of all students received need-based aid. The average freshman award was $20,285. Of that total, scholarships or need-based grants averaged $14,317 ($28,650 maximum); loans averaged

$4199 ($12,125 maximum); and work contracts averaged $1769 ($2175 maximum). 47% of undergraduates work part time. Average annual earnings from campus work are $1360. The average financial indebtedness of the recent graduate was $19,149. Penn is a member of CSS. The CSS/Profile and the university's own financial statement are required. The fall application deadline is February 15.

Computers: The mainframe is an IBM 3090. Students may use the 550 networked PCs to access information sources, including the on-line library catalog, a campuswide information system (Penn Info), and worldwide resources via the Internet. All students may access the system. There are no time limits and no fees. It is recommended that students in engineering and business have personal computers.

UNIVERSITY OF PITTSBURGH AT PITTSBURGH
Pittsburgh, PA 15260　　　　　(412) 624-PITT; Fax: (412) 648-8815

Full-time: 7009 men, 7591 women	**Faculty:** 2892; I, av$
Part-time: 1115 men, 1453 women	**Ph.D.s:** 87%
Graduate: 4218 men, 4776 women	**Student/Faculty:** 5 to 1
Year: semesters, summer session	**Tuition:** $6698 ($14,014)
Application Deadline: open	**Room & Board:** $5766
Freshman Class: 12,863 applied, 7705 accepted, 2781 enrolled	
SAT I Verbal/Math: 581/584　　**ACT:** 25	**VERY COMPETITIVE**

The University of Pittsburgh, founded in 1787, is a state-related, public research university with programs in arts and sciences, education, engineering, law, social work, business, health science, information sciences, and public and international affairs. There are 10 undergraduate and 14 graduate schools. In addition to regional accreditation, Pitt has baccalaureate program accreditation with AACSB, ABET, ACPE, ADA, CSWE, and NLN. The 26 libraries contain 3,634,488 volumes and 3,955,811 microform items, and subscribe to 21,787 periodicals. Computerized library services include the card catalog, interlibrary loans, and database searching. Special learning facilities include a learning resource center, art gallery, radio station, international classrooms located in the 42-story Cathedral of Learning, observatory, and music hall. The 132-acre campus is in an urban area 3 miles east of downtown Pittsburgh. Including residence halls, there are 90 buildings.

Programs of Study: Pitt confers B.A., B.S., B.A.S.W., B.Phil., B.S.E., B.S.N., and B.S.B.A. degrees. Master's and doctoral degrees are also awarded. Bachelor's degrees are awarded in BIOLOGICAL SCIENCE (biology/biological science, ecology, evolutionary biology, microbiology, molecular biology, neurosciences, and nutrition), BUSINESS (accounting, banking and finance, business administration and management, management science, and marketing/retailing/merchandising), COMMUNICATIONS AND THE ARTS (Chinese, classics, communications, creative writing, dramatic arts, English literature, film arts, fine arts, French, German, Italian, Japanese, linguistics, music, Polish, Russian, Spanish, speech/debate/rhetoric, and studio art), COMPUTER AND PHYSICAL SCIENCE (astronomy, chemistry, computer science, geology, information sciences and systems, mathematics, natural sciences, physics, and statistics), ENGINEERING AND ENVIRONMENTAL DESIGN (bioengineering, chemical engineering, civil engineering, computer engineering, electrical/electronics engineering, engineering physics, environmental science, industrial engineering, materials engineering, materials science, mechanical engineering, and metallurgical engineering), HEALTH PROFESSIONS (emergency medical technologies, exercise science, medical laboratory technology, medical records administration/services, nursing, and occupational therapy), SOCIAL SCIENCE (African American studies, anthropology, child psychology/development, economics, history, humanities, law, law enforcement and corrections, liberal arts/general studies, paralegal studies, philosophy, physical fitness/movement, political science/government, psychology, public administration, religion, social science, social work, sociology, and urban studies). Philosophy, history and philosophy of science, and chemistry are the strongest academically. Engineering, psychology, and communications are the largest.

Special: Students may cross-register with 10 neighboring colleges and universities. Internships, study abroad, a semester at sea, a Washington semester, work-study programs, a dual major in business and any other subject in arts and sciences, and student-designed majors are available. There are freshman seminars and a 5-year joint degree in arts and sciences/engineering. There are 27 national honor societies, including Phi Beta Kappa, and a freshman honors program.

Admissions: 60% of the 1999-2000 applicants were accepted. The SAT I scores for the 1999-2000 freshman class were: Verbal--11% below 500, 50% between 500 and 599, 33% between 600 and 700, and 6% above 700; Math--11% below 500, 46% between 500 and 599, 37% between 600 and 700, and 6% above 700. The ACT scores were 8% below 21, 23% between 21 and 23, 29% between 24 and 26, 19% between 27 and 28, and 21% above 28. 55% of the current freshmen were in the top fifth of their class; 88% were in the top two fifths. There were 10 National Merit finalists. 60 freshmen graduated first in their class.

Requirements: The SAT I or ACT is required. Applicants for admission to the College of Arts and Sciences must be graduates of an accredited secondary school. Students must have 15 high school academic credits, including 4 units of English, 3 each of math and lab science, and 1 of social studies, plus 4 units in academic electives. Pitt recommends that the student have 3 or more years of a single foreign language. An essay is recommended if the student is seeking scholarship consideration, and music students must audition. Requirements for other colleges or schools may vary. Applications are accepted on disk and on-line at the Pitt web site. AP and CLEP credits are accepted. Important factors in the admissions decision are advanced placement or honor courses, evidence of special talent, and extracurricular activities record.

Procedure: Freshmen are admitted to all sessions. Entrance exams should be taken preferably by January for September admission. There is a deferred admissions plan. Application deadlines are open; there is a $35 fee. Notification is sent on a rolling basis.

Financial Aid: In 1999-2000, 65% of all freshmen and 60% of continuing students received some form of financial aid. The average freshman award was $7922. Of that total, scholarships or need-based grants averaged $4006; and loans and work contracts combined averaged $3916. 40% of undergraduates work part time. Average annual earnings from campus work are $1800. The average financial indebtedness of the 1999 graduate was $16,000. Pitt is a member of CSS. The FAFSA and the university's own financial statement are required. The fall application deadline is January 15.

Computers: 6 public computing labs, with more than 700 PCs and workstations, provide access to a variety of software, printers, and graphic plotters. All students may access the system, with a 4-hour limit on remote access. There are no fees.

UNIVERSITY OF PORTLAND
Portland, OR 97203

(503) 943-7147
(800) (888) 627-5601; Fax: (503) 943-7315

Full-time: 990 men, 1292 women	**Faculty:** 161; IIA, av$
Part-time: 57 men, 53 women	**Ph.D.s:** 93%
Graduate: 157 men, 298 women	**Student/Faculty:** 14 to 1
Year: semesters, summer session	**Tuition:** $17,299
Application Deadline: February 1	**Room & Board:** $5190
Freshman Class: 1813 applied, 1616 accepted, 626 enrolled	
SAT I Verbal/Math: 571/570	**VERY COMPETITIVE**

The University of Portland, founded in 1901, is an independent institution affiliated with the Roman Catholic Church and offering degree programs in the arts and sciences, business administration, education, engineering, and nursing. There are 5 undergraduate schools and 1 graduate school. In addition to regional accreditation, UP has baccalaureate program accreditation with AACSB, ABET, NASM, and NLN. The library contains 380,000 volumes, 524,861 microform items, and 7827 audiovisual forms/CDs, and subscribes to 1446 periodicals. Computerized library services include interlibrary loans and database searching. Special learning facilities include a learning resource center, art gallery, radio station, and observatory. The 125-acre campus is in a suburban area 4 miles north of downtown Portland. Including residence halls, there are 30 buildings.

Programs of Study: UP confers B.A., B.S., B.A.Ed., B.B.A., B.M.Ed., B.S.C.E., B.S.E.E., B.S.E.M., B.S.E.S., B.S.M.E., B.S.N., and B.S.S.E. degrees. Master's degrees are also awarded. Bachelor's degrees are awarded in BIOLOGICAL SCIENCE (biology/biological science), BUSINESS (accounting, banking and finance, international business management, and marketing/retailing/merchandising), COMMUNICATIONS AND THE ARTS (communications, dramatic arts, English, journalism, music, Spanish, and theater management), COMPUTER AND PHYSICAL SCIENCE (chemistry, computer science, mathematics, and physics), EDUCATION (elementary, music, and secondary), ENGINEERING AND ENVIRONMENTAL DESIGN (civil engineering, electrical/electronics engineering, engineering, engineering management, environmental science, and mechanical engineering), HEALTH PROFESSIONS (nursing), SOCIAL SCIENCE (criminal justice, history, interdisciplinary studies, philosophy, political science/government, psychology, social work, sociology, and theological studies). Engineering, business, and nursing are the strongest academically. Business administration, education, and nursing are the largest.

Special: UP offers internships through individual departments, cross-registration with members of the Oregon Independent College Association, dual and interdisciplinary majors, including engineering chemistry and organizational communications, work-study programs, and pass/fail options. Study abroad may be arranged in Japan, Mexico, and several European countries. There are 9 national honor societies, and a freshman honors program.

Admissions: 89% of the 1999-2000 applicants were accepted. The SAT I scores for the 1999-2000 freshman class were: Verbal--16% below 500, 49% between 500 and 599, 29% between 600 and 700, and 6% above 700; Math--17% below 500, 43% between 500 and 599, 36% between 600 and 700, and 4% above 700.

Requirements: The SAT I or ACT is required. A GPA of 2.8 is required, with a minimum score of 450 on each section of the SAT I or a composite of 19 on the ACT. Graduation from an accredited secondary school or satisfactory scores on the GED are required. The high school curriculum should include courses in English composition, math, social studies, science, and a foreign language. 2 essays are required, as is a letter of recommendation from the high school counselor or principal. Electronic application is available on disk through the Admissions Office or on-line via Common App or other services. AP and CLEP credits are accepted. Important factors in the admissions decision are advanced placement or honor courses, recommendations by school officials, and leadership record.

Procedure: Freshmen are admitted to all sessions. Entrance exams should be taken preferably before February 1 but no later than June 1 of the senior year. There are early decision and deferred admissions plans. Early decision applications should be filed by November 16; regular applications, by February 1 for fall entry, along with a $40 fee. Notification of early decision is sent December 15; regular decision, on a rolling basis. 34 early decision candidates were accepted for the 1999-2000 class.

Financial Aid: In 1999-2000, 89% of all freshmen and 84% of continuing students received some form of financial aid. 56% of all students received need-based aid. The average freshman award was $15,143. 41% of undergraduates work part time. Average annual earnings from campus work are $1807. The average financial indebtedness of the 1999 graduate was $19,319. UP is a member of CSS. The FAFSA and the college's own financial statement are required. The fall application deadline is March 1.

Computers: The mainframe is a Sun UNIX. All students may utilize more than 240 PCs for various projects, with additional terminals designated specifically for computer-intensive majors such as computer science, engineering, and education. Students have access to the Internet and to E-mail. All students may access the system. There are no time limits and no fees.

UNIVERSITY OF PUGET SOUND
Tacoma, WA 98416

(253) 879-3211
(800) 396-7191; Fax: (253) 879-3993

Full-time: 1036 men, 1561 women	**Faculty:** 206; IIB, +$
Part-time: 22 men, 68 women	**Ph.D.s:** 84%
Graduate: 71 men, 207 women	**Student/Faculty:** 13 to 1
Year: semesters, summer session	**Tuition:** $20,605
Application Deadline: February 1	**Room & Board:** $5270
Freshman Class: 4138 applied, 3069 accepted, 684 enrolled	
SAT I Verbal/Math: 620/620	**ACT:** 27 **HIGHLY COMPETITIVE**

The University of Puget Sound, founded in 1888, is an independent, residential, undergraduate liberal arts and sciences college with selected graduate programs building effectively on a liberal arts foundation. There are 2 graduate schools. In addition to regional accreditation, Puget Sound has baccalaureate program accreditation with NASM. The library contains 507,725 volumes, 593,092 microform items, and 15,450 audiovisual forms/CDs, and subscribes to 3600 periodicals. Computerized library services include the card catalog, interlibrary loans, and database searching. Special learning facilities include a learning resource center, art gallery, natural history museum, radio station, student science labs, observatory, computer labs, seminar rooms, media center, language houses, theater workshops, newspaper, center for writing and learning, and bibliographic instrumentation room. The 97-acre campus is in a suburban area 35 miles south of Seattle, 1 mile from Commencement Bay on Puget Sound. Including residence halls, there are 40 buildings.

Programs of Study: Puget Sound confers B.A., B.S., and B.M. degrees. Master's degrees are also awarded. Bachelor's degrees are awarded in BIOLOGICAL SCIENCE (biology/biological science), BUSINESS (business administration and management and international economics), COMMUNICATIONS AND THE ARTS (communications, dramatic arts, English, fine arts, French, German, music, music performance, and Spanish), COMPUTER AND PHYSICAL SCIENCE (chemistry, computer science, geology, mathematics, natural sciences, and physics), EDUCATION (music), HEALTH PROFESSIONS (occupational therapy), SOCIAL SCIENCE (Asian/Oriental studies, economics, history, philosophy, physical fitness/movement, political science/government, psychology, public administration, religion, and sociology). Chemistry, history, and music are the strongest academically. Business, English, and biology are the largest.

Special: Special academic programs include on- and off-campus work-study, paid and unpaid internships in the community in conjunction with an internship seminar, and study abroad in more than 40 countries. There are 3-2 engineering degrees with Washington University at St. Louis, Columbia, Boston, and Duke universities, and the University of Southern California. Dual majors in foreign language/international affairs, music/business, and computer science/business, as well as pass/fail options, are possible. 2 special features of the curriculum are the intensive 4-year study of the classics of Western civilization and the Business Leadership Program, combining traditional business and liberal arts study. A required science in context program integrates the sciences and humanities. There are 12 national honor societies, including Phi Beta Kappa, a freshman honors program, and 19 departmental honors programs.

Admissions: 74% of the 1999-2000 applicants were accepted. The SAT I scores for the 1999-2000 freshman class were: Verbal--3% below 500, 34% between 500 and 599, 50% between 600 and 700, and 13% above 700; Math--4% below 500, 33% between 500 and 599, 51% between 600 and 700, and 12% above 700. The ACT scores were 4% below 21, 13% between 21 and 23, 29% between 24 and 26, 21% between 27 and 28, and 33% above 28. 69% of the current freshmen were in the top fifth of their class; 92% were in the top two fifths. There were 28 National Merit finalists. 50 freshmen graduated first in their class.

Requirements: The SAT I or ACT is required. The SAT I is preferred. Other admission requirements include graduation from an accredited secondary school, with a recommended 4 years of English, 3 to 4 of math and natural/physical lab science, 3 of social studies/history, 2 to 3 of foreign language, and 1 of fine/visual/performing arts. Also required are letters of personal recommendation from a teacher and counselor; 2 are preferred. An essay must be submitted, and an interview is recommended. It is recommended that art students present a portfolio and that music students audition. The GED is also accepted. The Common Application is accepted on-line through ExPAN. CollegeView and CollegeLink disk/forms are also accepted. AP credits are accepted. Important factors in the admissions decision are advanced placement or honor courses, evidence of special talent, and extracurricular activities record.

Procedure: Freshmen are admitted to all sessions. Entrance exams should be taken during the fall of the senior year. There are early decision, early admissions, and deferred admissions plans. Early Decision I applications should be filed by November 15; Early Decision II by December 15; and regular applications, by February 1 for fall entry and November 1 for spring entry, along with a $40 fee. Notification of Early Decision I is sent December 15; Early Decision II, January 15; and regular decision by April. 114 early decision candidates were accepted for the 1999-2000 class. 8% of all applicants are on a waiting list.

Financial Aid: In 1999-2000, 84% of all freshmen and 87% of continuing students received some form of financial aid. 65% of all students received need-based aid. The average freshman award was $15,950. Of that total, scholarships or need-based grants averaged $8375 ($15,950 maximum); loans averaged $5130 ($5800 maximum); and work contracts averaged $2000 ($2300 maximum). 70%

of undergraduates work part time. Average annual earnings from campus work are $1900. The average financial indebtedness of the 1999 graduate was $20,259. Puget Sound is a member of CSS. The FAFSA is required. The CSS/Profile is also required of early decision candidates. The fall application deadline is February 1.

Computers: The mainframe is a DEC VAX 4000 series. The mainframe can be reached through the campus network. There are 2 large Mac and 3 IBM labs (open 24 hours), satellite labs in departments, and a network of Compaq workstations. All lab systems and workstations have full access to the Internet and Web. All students may access the system. There are no time limits and no fees. The university strongly recommends that students have their own personal computer.

UNIVERSITY OF REDLANDS
Redlands, CA 92373-0999

(909) 335-4074
(800) 455-5064; Fax: (909) 335-4089

Full-time: 730 men, 917 women	**Faculty:** 108; IIA, +$
Part-time: 9 men, 11 women	**Ph.D.s:** 91%
Graduate: 13 men, 56 women	**Student/Faculty:** 15 to 1
Year: 4-1-4	**Tuition:** $19,811
Application Deadline: February 1	**Room & Board:** $7368
Freshman Class: 1975 applied, 1581 accepted, 474 enrolled	
SAT I Verbal/Math: 550/550	**ACT:** 24 **VERY COMPETITIVE**

University of Redlands, founded in 1907, is an independent institution that offers programs in liberal and fine arts, business, and teacher preparation. There are 2 undergraduate and 4 graduate schools. The library contains 264,385 volumes, 281,894 microform items, and 7297 audiovisual forms/CDs, and subscribes to 1835 periodicals. Computerized library services include the card catalog, interlibrary loans, and database searching. Special learning facilities include an art gallery, radio station, language lab, computer center, and geographic information systems lab. The 130-acre campus is in a small town 60 miles east of Los Angeles. Including residence halls, there are 40 buildings.

Programs of Study: Redlands confers B.A., B.S., and B.Mus. degrees. Master's degrees are also awarded. Bachelor's degrees are awarded in BIOLOGICAL SCIENCE (biochemistry, biology/biological science, and molecular biology), BUSINESS (accounting and business administration and management), COMMUNICATIONS AND THE ARTS (art, English, French, German, music, and Spanish), COMPUTER AND PHYSICAL SCIENCE (chemistry, computer science, mathematics, and physics), ENGINEERING AND ENVIRONMENTAL DESIGN (environmental science), SOCIAL SCIENCE (anthropology, Asian/Oriental studies, economics, history, international relations, liberal arts/general studies, philosophy, political science/government, psychology, religion, and sociology). Liberal arts is the strongest academically. Business is the largest.

Special: Cross-registration with sister colleges, various internships, and study abroad in 50 countries are offered. A Washington semester, a Sacramento progtram, various work-study programs, B.A.-B.S. degrees, a liberal studies degree, dual majors, and accelerated degree programs are available. Students may pursue nondegree study, take advantage of pass/fail options, and receive credit for life or work experience. At the Johnston Center for Integrative studies, students design their own majors and courses of study. There are 6 national honor societies, including Phi Beta Kappa, and a freshman honors program.

Admissions: 80% of the 1999-2000 applicants were accepted. The SAT I scores for the 1999-2000 freshman class were: Verbal--24% below 500, 48% between

500 and 599, 22% between 600 and 700, and 6% above 700; Math--21% below 500, 49% between 500 and 599, 28% between 600 and 700, and 2% above 700. The ACT scores were 19% below 21, 29% between 21 and 23, 31% between 24 and 26, 17% between 27 and 28, and 4% above 28. There were 5 National Merit finalists.

Requirements: The SAT I or ACT is required. A GPA of 2.9 is required. Redlands recommends that applicants have completed a minimum of 16 units in solid academic areas. The student should have completed at least 4 years of high school English, 2 to 3 years each of math, lab sciences, and social science, and 2 years of a foreign language. Applications are available and can be completed at the school's web site. AP credits are accepted. Important factors in the admissions decision are advanced placement or honor courses, extracurricular activities record, and leadership record.

Procedure: Freshmen are admitted to all sessions. Entrance exams should be taken prior to application. There is a deferred admissions plan. Early decision applications should be filed by December 15; regular applications, by February 1 for fall entry and January 1 for spring entry, along with a $40 fee. Notification is sent on a rolling basis.

Financial Aid: In 1999-2000, 89% of all freshmen and 87% of continuing students received some form of financial aid, including need-based aid. The average freshman award was $17,146. Of that total, scholarships or need-based grants averaged $9749 ($19,490 maximum); loans averaged $3816 ($5625 maximum); work contracts averaged $1699 ($1950 maximum); other sources averaged $7690 ($20625 maximum). 54% of undergraduates work part time. Redlands is a member of CSS. The FAFSA, the college's own financial statement, and the GPA verification Form for California residents are required.

Computers: The academic computing center provides 150 networked Mac and Windows computers connecting to Mac, NT, and UNIX servers and the Internet. These include specialized graphics/desktop publishing and geographic information systems (GIS) labs as well as general-purpose teaching and drop-in labs. All students may access the system. There are no time limits. The fee is $300.

UNIVERSITY OF RICHMOND
University of Richmond, VA 23173 (804) 289-8640
(800) 700-1662; Fax: (804) 287-6003

Full-time: 1509 men, 1525 women	**Faculty:** 253; IIA, ++$
Part-time: 15 men, 9 women	**Ph.D.s:** 95%
Graduate: 403 men, 345 women	**Student/Faculty:** 12 to 1
Year: semesters, summer session	**Tuition:** $19,610
Application Deadline: January 15	**Room & Board:** $4150
Freshman Class: 6234 applied, 2787 accepted, 886 enrolled	
SAT I or ACT: required	**HIGHLY COMPETITIVE+**

The University of Richmond, founded in 1830, is a private independent institution offering programs in arts and sciences, business, and leadership studies. There are 4 undergraduate and 3 graduate schools. In addition to regional accreditation, UR has baccalaureate program accreditation with AACSB and NASM. The 4 libraries contain 704,490 volumes, 362,996 microform items, and 26,624 audiovisual forms/CDs, and subscribe to 3556 periodicals. Computerized library services include the card catalog, interlibrary loans, and database searching. Special learning facilities include a learning resource center, art gallery, radio station, TV station, and the Lora Robins Gallery of Design from Nature. The 350-acre campus is in a suburban area 6 miles west of Richmond. Including residence halls, there are 50 buildings.

Programs of Study: UR confers B.A., B.S., B.M., and B.S.B.A. degrees. Associate and master's degrees are also awarded. Bachelor's degrees are awarded in BIOLOGICAL SCIENCE (biology/biological science), BUSINESS (accounting, banking and finance, business administration and management, business economics, and marketing/retailing/merchandising), COMMUNICATIONS AND THE ARTS (art history and appreciation, dramatic arts, English, French, German, Greek, journalism, Latin, music, Russian, Spanish, speech/debate/rhetoric, and studio art), COMPUTER AND PHYSICAL SCIENCE (chemistry, computer science, mathematics, and physics), EDUCATION (art, early childhood, middle school, physical, science, and secondary), SOCIAL SCIENCE (American studies, classical/ancient civilization, criminal justice, economics, history, interdisciplinary studies, international relations, philosophy, political science/government, psychology, religion, sociology, urban studies, and women's studies). Business, biology, and political science are the largest.

Special: Internships in nearly every major, study abroad in 18 countries, and a Washington semester with American University are available. The university offers work-study programs, accelerated degree programs, B.A.-B.S. degrees, dual majors, student-designed majors, and a general studies degree through the School of Continuing Studies. The interdisciplinary leadership studies major includes a minor in arts and sciences or business. There is a marine biology study option with the Marine Sciences Laboratory at Duke University. There are 32 national honor societies, including Phi Beta Kappa, and 7 departmental honors programs.

Admissions: 45% of the 1999-2000 applicants were accepted. The SAT I scores for the 1999-2000 freshman class were: Verbal--1% below 500, 22% between 500 and 599, 59% between 600 and 700, and 18% above 700; Math--1% below 500, 15% between 500 and 599, 62% between 600 and 700, and 22% above 700. The ACT scores were 1% below 21, 6% between 21 and 23, 14% between 24 and 26, 38% between 27 and 28, and 42% above 28. 78% of the current freshmen were in the top fifth of their class; 98% were in the top two fifths. There were 19 National Merit finalists and 23 semifinalists. 36 freshmen graduated first in their class.

Requirements: The SAT I or ACT is required. In addition, SAT II: Subject tests are required in writing and math I or II if the student is taking the SAT I. Applicants must be graduates of an accredited secondary school. The GED is accepted. Applicants must complete 16 high school academic credits, including 4 years of English, 3 of math, and at least 2 each of history, foreign language, and lab science. An essay, a counselor recommendation, and auditions for music scholarships are required. Common Application is accepted on computer disk. AP and CLEP credits are accepted. Important factors in the admissions decision are advanced placement or honor courses, leadership record, and evidence of special talent.

Procedure: Freshmen are admitted in the fall. Entrance exams should be taken by January 1 of the senior year. There are early decision and deferred admissions plans. Early decision applications should be filed by November 15; regular applications, by January 15 for fall entry, along with a $40 fee. Notification of early decision is sent December 15; regular decision, April 1. 208 early decision candidates were accepted for the 1999-2000 class. 9% of all applicants are on a waiting list.

Financial Aid: In 1999-2000, 61% of all freshmen and 63% of continuing students received some form of financial aid. 31% of freshmen and 30% of continuing students received need-based aid. The average freshman award was $14,660. Of that total, scholarships or need-based grants averaged $10,407 ($23,480 maximum); loans averaged $5480 ($23,480 maximum); and work contracts averaged $1000 ($1500 maximum). 25% of undergraduates work part time. Average annual earnings from campus work are $800. The average financial indebtedness of the 1999 graduate was $14,300. The FAFSA and the college's own financial statement are required. The fall application deadline is February 25.

Computers: The mainframes are DEC VAX 11/750 and 11/785 models. All students have access to labs housing Mac, NeXT, IBM, UNIX, Sun, MS-DOS, Pentium, and DEC VAX equipment. Bitnet, Internet, LEXIS, and WESTLAW networks are also available. All students may access the system. There are no time limits and no fees.

UNIVERSITY OF ROCHESTER
Rochester, NY 14627-0251

(716) 275-3221
(888) 822-2256; Fax: (716) 461-4595

Full-time: 2265 men, 2046 women	**Faculty:** 433; 1, ++$
Part-time: 82 men, 135 women	**Ph.D.s:** 98%
Graduate: 1834 men, 1334 women	**Student/Faculty:** 10 to 1
Year: semesters, summer session	**Tuition:** $22,864
Application Deadline: January 15	**Room & Board:** $7512
Freshman Class: 7217 applied, 5714 accepted, 1087 enrolled	
SAT I or ACT: required	**HIGHLY COMPETITIVE**

The University of Rochester, founded in 1850, is a private institution offering programs in the arts and sciences, engineering and applied science, nursing, medicine and dentistry, business administration, music, and education. There are 4 undergraduate and 7 graduate schools. In addition to regional accreditation, UR has baccalaureate program accreditation with AACSB, ABET, ACPE, NASM, and NLN. The 7 libraries contain 2,922,335 volumes, 4,102,438 microform items, and 69,259 audiovisual forms/CDs, and subscribe to 9829 periodicals. Computerized library services include the card catalog, interlibrary loans, and database searching. Special learning facilities include a learning resource center, art gallery, radio station, labs for nuclear structure research and laser energetics, a center for visual science, the Strong Memorial Hospital, an art center, an observatory, an institute of optics, a center for electronic imaging systems, and the National Science Foundation Center for Photoinduced Charge Transfer. The 600-acre campus is in a suburban area 2 miles south of downtown Rochester. Including residence halls, there are 143 buildings.

Programs of Study: UR confers B.A., B.S., and B.M. degrees. Master's and doctoral degrees are also awarded. Bachelor's degrees are awarded in BIOLOGICAL SCIENCE (biochemistry, biology/biological science, cell biology, ecology, genetics, microbiology, and neurosciences), COMMUNICATIONS AND THE ARTS (art history and appreciation, classics, comparative literature, English, film arts, fine arts, French, German, Japanese, linguistics, music, Russian, Spanish, and studio art), COMPUTER AND PHYSICAL SCIENCE (applied mathematics, chemistry, computer science, geology, mathematics, optics, physics, and statistics), ENGINEERING AND ENVIRONMENTAL DESIGN (biomedical engineering, chemical engineering, electrical/electronics engineering, engineering and applied science, geological engineering, and mechanical engineering), HEALTH PROFESSIONS (nursing and public health), SOCIAL SCIENCE (anthropology, cognitive science, economics, history, interpreter for the deaf, philosophy, political science/government, psychology, religion, and women's studies). Psychology, biology, and political science are the largest.

Special: Cross-registration is offered with other Rochester area colleges. Internships, a Washington semester, B.A.-B.S. degrees, dual and student-designed majors, nondegree study, and pass/fail options are available. Study abroad is possible in 46 university-sponsored programs including: Australia, China, Japan, Egypt, Israel, and the former Soviet Union, and in several European countries. Other options include a fifth year of courses tuition-free, courses designed to teach first-year students how to learn and how to make learning a lifetime habit, a management studies certificate, and music lessons for credit at the Eastman School of Music. Qualified freshmen may obtain early assurance of admission to the university's medical school through the Rochester Early Medical Scholars program. Internships are available in the United States and abroad. There are 5 national honor societies, including Phi Beta Kappa, and 13 departmental honors programs.

Admissions: 79% of the 1999-2000 applicants were accepted. The SAT I scores for the 1999-2000 freshman class were: Verbal--3% below 500, 20% between 500 and 599, 50% between 600 and 700, and 27% above 700; Math--2% below 500, 11% between 500 and 599, 52% between 600 and 700, and 35% above 700. The ACT scores were 1% below 21, 5% between 21 and 23, 22% between 24 and 26, 25% between 27 and 28, and 47% above 28. 82% of the current freshmen were in the top fifth of their class; 97% were in the top two fifths. There were 25 National Merit finalists. 53 freshmen graduated first in their class.

Requirements: The SAT I or ACT is required. SAT II: Subject tests are recommended. Applicants should be graduates of an accredited secondary school or have a GED equivalent. An audition is required for music majors. The school accepts the institutional application through Embark linked to the UR admissions home page. AP credits are accepted. Important factors in the admissions decision are advanced placement or honor courses, recommendations by school officials, and leadership record.

Procedure: Freshmen are admitted fall and spring. Entrance exams should be taken by December of the senior year. There are early decision, early admissions, and deferred admissions plans. Early decision applications should be filed by November 15; regular applications, by January 15 for fall entry and November 15 for spring entry, along with a $50 fee. Notification of early decision is sent December 15; regular decision, April 1. 83 early decision candidates were accepted for the 1999-2000 class. 3% of all applicants are on a waiting list.

Financial Aid: In 1999-2000, 90% of all students received some form of financial aid. 65% of all students received need-based aid. The average freshman award was $18,400. Of that total, scholarships or need-based grants averaged $12,000 ($22,300 maximum); loans averaged $4400 ($4875 maximum); and work contracts averaged $2000 ($2250 maximum). 50% of undergraduates work part time. Average annual earnings from campus work are $1100. The average financial indebtedness of the 1999 graduate was $18,700. UR is a member of CSS. The CSS/Profile or FFS and the college's own financial statement are required. The fall application deadline is January 31.

Computers: The mainframes are an IBM 4381, DEC VAX systems, SUN systems, and a Solbourne computer. Students have access to hundreds of PCs, workstations, printers, and terminals in the libraries, classrooms, labs, and resource centers on campus. All residence hall rooms have lines accessing the mainframe computers and the Internet. All students may access the system 24 hours daily. There are no time limits and no fees.

UNIVERSITY OF SAINT THOMAS
St. Paul, MN 55105

(651) 962-6150
(800) 328-6819; Fax: (651) 962-6160

Full-time: 2127 men, 2499 women	**Faculty:** 256; IIA, av$
Part-time: 335 men, 438 women	**Ph.D.s:** 83%
Graduate: 2715 men, 2815 women	**Student/Faculty:** 18 to 1
Year: 4-1-4, summer session	**Tuition:** $16,353
Application Deadline: open	**Room & Board:** $5180
Freshman Class: 2853 applied, 2437 accepted, 1046 enrolled	
SAT I Verbal/Math: 560/580	**ACT:** 24 **VERY COMPETITIVE**

The University of Saint Thomas, founded in 1885, is a private liberal arts institution affiliated with the Roman Catholic Church. There are 2 undergraduate and 7 graduate schools. In addition to regional accreditation, Saint Thomas has baccalaureate program accreditation with CSWE, NASM, and NCATE. The 3 libraries contain 465,998 volumes, 589,362 microform items, and 3300 audiovisual forms/CDs, and subscribe to 2575 periodicals. Computerized library services include the card catalog, interlibrary loans, and database searching. Special learning facilities include a learning resource center and TV station. The 78-acre campus is in an urban area 5 miles west of St. Paul and 5 miles east of Minneapolis. Including residence halls, there are 74 buildings.

Programs of Study: Saint Thomas confers B.A., B.S. and B.S.M.E. degrees. Master's and doctoral degrees are also awarded. Bachelor's degrees are awarded in BIOLOGICAL SCIENCE (biology/biological science and neurosciences), BUSINESS (accounting, banking and finance, business administration and management, entrepreneurial studies, international business management, marketing management, personnel management, and real estate), COMMUNICATIONS AND THE ARTS (art history and appreciation, classical languages, communications, dramatic arts, English, French, German, journalism, Latin, literature, music, music business management, Russian, and Spanish), COMPUTER AND PHYSICAL SCIENCE (actuarial science, chemistry, computer science, geology, mathematics, and physics), EDUCATION (elementary, health, music, physical, science, and secondary), ENGINEERING AND ENVIRONMENTAL DESIGN (environmental science, manufacturing engineering, and mechanical engineering), HEALTH PROFESSIONS (community health work), SOCIAL SCIENCE (Christian studies, classical/ancient civilization, criminal justice, East Asian studies, economics, geography, history, international studies, peace studies, philosophy, political science/government, psychology, Russian and Slavic studies, social science, social studies, social work, sociology, theological studies, and women's studies). Business is the largest.

Special: Students may cross-register with Augsburg and Macalester Colleges, the College of Saint Catherine, and Hamline University. Study abroad is available in more than 10 countries, and there are several work-study programs. There are formal 3-2 engineering degree arrangements with Washington and Notre Dame Universities and the University of Minnesota, and 3-2 engineering degrees can also be arranged with many other accredited engineering programs. Nondegree study and pass/fail options also are available. There are 11 national honor societies and a freshman honors program.

Admissions: 85% of the 1999-2000 applicants were accepted. The SAT I scores for the 1999-2000 freshman class were: Verbal--14% below 500, 49% between 500 and 599, 32% between 600 and 700, and 5% above 700; Math--13% below 500, 43% between 500 and 599, 36% between 600 and 700, and 8% above 700. The ACT scores were 11% below 21, 29% between 21 and 23, 28% between 24

and 26, 17% between 27 and 28, and 15% above 28. 53% of the current freshmen were in the top fifth of their class; 82% were in the top two fifths. There were 2 National Merit finalists. 19 freshmen graduated first in their class.

Requirements: The SAT I or ACT is required, with a minimum composite score of 970 or 20 respectively. Saint Thomas requires applicants to be in the upper 60% of their class. In addition, Saint Thomas recommends 4 units each of English and math (with 3 units of math required), 3 of foreign language, and 2 each of science and history or social sciences. An essay is required. The GED is accepted. Applications are accepted on computer disk and on-line through the Admissions Office at the school's web site. AP and CLEP credits are accepted. Important factors in the admissions decision are recommendations by school officials, geographic diversity, and parents or siblings attending the school.

Procedure: Freshmen are admitted fall and spring. Entrance exams should be taken by the fall of the senior year. There is a deferred admissions plan. Application deadlines are open. There is a $30 fee. Notification is sent on a rolling basis.

Financial Aid: In 1999-2000, 86% of all freshmen and 81% of continuing students received some form of financial aid. 51% of all students received need-based aid. The average freshman award was $11,794. Of that total, scholarships or need-based grants averaged $6906 ($24,439 maximum); loans averaged $3249 ($20,600 maximum); and work contracts averaged $1639 ($4600 maximum). 47% of undergraduates work part time. Average annual earnings from campus work are $2225. The average financial indebtedness of the 1999 graduate was $16,321. The FAFSA is required. The fall application deadline is April 1.

Computers: The mainframes are a VMS cluster, comprised of a Compaq F.S. (Enterprise Server) 40 and a AXP4100. Connection to the network is via fastnet, with full access from all residence hall rooms. Students are given access to the internet via our network, a personal E-mail account, personal webpage space, and NT storage space. All computers in all labs have Internet access. There are 7 public labs, 7 residence hall labs, and 58 discipline specific labs with a total of 570 PCs and 275 Macs. All students may access the system any time. There are no time limits and no fees.

UNIVERSITY OF SAINT THOMAS
Houston, TX 77006-4696

(713) 525-3500
(800) 856-8565; Fax: (713) 525-3558

Full-time: 436 men, 789 women	**Faculty:** 102
Part-time: 153 men, 288 women	**Ph.D.s:** 87%
Graduate: 729 men, 546 women	**Student/Faculty:** 12 to 1
Year: semesters, summer session	**Tuition:** $11,812
Application Deadline: open	**Room & Board:** $5326
Freshman Class: 547 applied, 445 accepted, 216 enrolled	
SAT I Verbal/Math: 570/570	**ACT:** 24 **VERY COMPETITIVE**

The University of St. Thomas is a private institution committed to the liberal arts and to the religious, ethical, and intellectual tradition of Catholic higher education. There is an optional winter break term. The room and board fee includes 15 meals. There are 3 undergraduate and 9 graduate schools. In addition to regional accreditation, UST has baccalaureate program accreditation with ACBSP. The 2 libraries contain 190,321 volumes, 494,604 microform items, and 808 audiovisual forms/CDs, and subscribe to 2800 periodicals. Computerized library services include the card catalog, interlibrary loans, and database searching. Special learning facilities include a learning resource center and art gallery. The 21-acre campus is in an urban area in downtown Houston. Including residence halls, there are 49 buildings.

Programs of Study: UST confers B.A., B.B.A., B.S., and B.Th. degrees. Master's and doctoral degrees are also awarded. Bachelor's degrees are awarded in BIOLOGICAL SCIENCE (biology/biological science), BUSINESS (accounting, banking and finance, business administration and management, management information systems, and marketing/retailing/merchandising), COMMUNICATIONS AND THE ARTS (communications, dramatic arts, English, fine arts, French, music, and Spanish), COMPUTER AND PHYSICAL SCIENCE (chemistry and mathematics), EDUCATION (elementary, music, and secondary), ENGINEERING AND ENVIRONMENTAL DESIGN (environmental science), SOCIAL SCIENCE (economics, history, international studies, liberal arts/general studies, pastoral studies, philosophy, political science/government, psychology, and theological studies). Business administration, education, and international studies are the largest.

Special: UST offers cooperative programs with other universities in math, 3-2 engineering, and business administration; cross-registration with Houston, Notre Dame, Texas A&M, and Texas Southern Universities, internships, and study abroad in more than 19 countries. General studies, accelerated, and B.A.-B.S. degrees are available. Nondegree study, dual majors, and a NASA Cooperative Program are available. There are 20 national honor societies, and a freshman honors program.

Admissions: 81% of the 1999-2000 applicants were accepted. The SAT I scores for the 1999-2000 freshman class were: Verbal--16% below 500, 47% between 500 and 599, 30% between 600 and 700, and 7% above 700; Math--23% below 500, 41% between 500 and 599, 28% between 600 and 700, and 7% above 700. 63% of the current freshmen were in the top fifth of their class; 84% were in the top two fifths.

Requirements: The SAT I or ACT is required. UST requires applicants to be in the upper 50% of their class. A GPA of 2.0 is required. A minimum composite score equal to or above the national average on SAT I or on the ACT is required. Applicants must be graduates of an accredited secondary school and have 16 academic credits, 4 years of English, 3 years of math, 2 years each of foreign language, science, and social studies, and 1 year of history, or have a GED certificate. Applications are accepted on-line. AP and CLEP credits are accepted.

Procedure: Freshmen are admitted to all sessions. Entrance exams should be taken as early as possible. There is a deferred admissions plan. Application deadlines are open, and there is a $35 application fee. Notification is sent on a rolling basis.

Financial Aid: In 1999-2000, 80% of all freshmen and 48% of continuing students received some form of financial aid. 50% of freshmen and 57% of continuing students received need-based aid. The average freshman award was $10,808. Of that total, scholarships or need-based grants averaged $3730 ($13,260 maximum); loans averaged $3558 ($12,748 maximum); and work contracts averaged $1875 ($2000 maximum). The average financial indebtedness of the 1999 graduate was $10,000. UST is a member of CSS. The FAFSA, the college's own financial statement, and income tax forms are required. The fall application deadline is March 1.

Computers: The mainframe is a Sun workstation 4N. There are more than 450 PCs located in the dormitory and throughout the campus. The mainframe and networks can be accessed via TCP/IP or dial-up for E-mail and other services. All students may access the system 9 a.m. to 10 p.m., 7 days a week; dial-up, 24 hours a day. There are no time limits and no fees.

UNIVERSITY OF SAN DIEGO
San Diego, CA 92110

(619) 260-4506
(800) 248-4873; Fax: (619) 260-6836

Full-time: 1822 men, 2428 women	**Faculty:** 288; I, av\$
Part-time: 80 men, 109 women	**Ph.D.s:** 98%
Graduate: 1099 men, 1215 women	**Student/Faculty:** 15 to 1
Year: 4-1-4, summer session	**Tuition:** $17,885
Application Deadline: January 5	**Room & Board:** $7620
Freshman Class: 6291 applied, 3286 accepted, 991 enrolled	
SAT I Verbal/Math: 570/580	**ACT:** 26 **HIGHLY COMPETITIVE**

The University of San Diego, founded in 1949, is an independent, Catholic liberal arts university. There are 4 undergraduate and 5 graduate schools. In addition to regional accreditation, USD has baccalaureate program accreditation with AACSB, ABET, and NLN. The 2 libraries contain 475,000 volumes and 130,000 microform items, and subscribe to 2000 periodicals. Computerized library services include the card catalog, interlibrary loans, and database searching. Special learning facilities include a learning resource center, art gallery, media center, and child development center. The 180-acre campus is in an urban area 10 miles north of downtown San Diego. Including residence halls, there are 24 buildings.

Programs of Study: USD confers B.A., B.A./B.S., B.Acc., B.B.A., and B.S.N. degrees. Master's and doctoral degrees are also awarded. Bachelor's degrees are awarded in BIOLOGICAL SCIENCE (biology/biological science and marine science), BUSINESS (accounting, business administration and management, and business economics), COMMUNICATIONS AND THE ARTS (communications, English, fine arts, French, music, and Spanish), COMPUTER AND PHYSICAL SCIENCE (chemistry, computer science, mathematics, oceanography, and physics), EDUCATION (elementary and secondary), ENGINEERING AND ENVIRONMENTAL DESIGN (electrical/electronics engineering and industrial engineering), HEALTH PROFESSIONS (nursing), SOCIAL SCIENCE (anthropology, economics, history, humanities, international relations, liberal arts/general studies, philosophy, political science/government, psychology, religion, sociology, and urban studies). Business administration is the largest.

Special: A co-op program and a B.A.-B.S. degree are offered in electrical engineering. Internships in all disciplines, study abroad in 7 countries, work-study programs on campus, dual majors in marine science and ocean studies, nondegree study through the lawyer assistance program, and pass/fail options are available. There are 15 national honor societies and a freshman honors program.

Admissions: 52% of the 1999-2000 applicants were accepted. The SAT I scores for the 1999-2000 freshman class were: Verbal--11% below 500, 55% between 500 and 599, 30% between 600 and 700, and 4% above 700; Math--10% below 500, 45% between 500 and 599, 42% between 600 and 700, and 3% above 700. The ACT scores were 18% between 21 and 23, 30% between 24 and 26, 22% between 27 and 28, and 30% above 28. 85% of the current freshmen were in the top fifth of their class; 98% were in the top two fifths. 53 freshmen graduated first in their class.

Requirements: The SAT I is required, with a recommended score of 500 verbal and 500 math. In addition, the university recommends that applicants have 4 units each in high school English and math, 3 or 4 in foreign language, 2 or 3 in science, and 2 each in history and social studies. An essay also is necessary. The GED is accepted. Applications are accepted on-line via CollegeView, College Net, Apply, and XAPlication. AP and CLEP credits are accepted. Important factors in the admissions decision are advanced placement or honor courses, extracurricular activities record, and recommendations by school officials.

Procedure: Freshmen are admitted fall, spring, and summer. Entrance exams should be taken before December 30. There is an early admissions plan. Applications should be filed by January 5 for fall entry and November 1 for spring entry, along with a $45 fee. Notification is sent April 15. 5% of all applicants are on a waiting list.

Financial Aid: In 1999-2000, 69% of all freshmen and 61% of continuing students received some form of financial aid. 49% of freshmen and 45% of continuing students received need-based aid. The average freshman award was $13,445. Of that total, scholarships or need-based grants averaged $9748; loans averaged $4600; work contracts averaged $2250; and athletic awards averaged $9237. 21% of undergraduates work part time. Average annual earnings from campus work are $18,000. The average financial indebtedness of the 1999 graduate was $22,000. The FAFSA and the university's own financial statement are required. The fall application deadline is February 20.

Computers: The mainframes are a DEC VAX 6300 and 6330. There are 300 Apple II, IBM, and Rainbow PCs located in buildings across campus. All students may access the system. There are no time limits and no fees.

UNIVERSITY OF SAN FRANCISCO
San Francisco, CA 94117-1080
(415) 422-6563
(800) CALLUSF; Fax: (415) 422-2217

Full-time: 1539 men, 2580 women	**Faculty:** 250
Part-time: 115 men, 157 women	**Ph.D.s:** 91%
Graduate: 1198 men, 1794 women	**Student/Faculty:** 16 to 1
Year: 4-1-4, summer session	**Tuition:** $17,910
Application Deadline: February 15	**Room & Board:** $7838
Freshman Class: 3505 applied, 2805 accepted, 765 enrolled	
SAT I Verbal/Math: 550/550	**ACT:** 23 **VERY COMPETITIVE**

The University of San Francisco, founded in 1855, is a private Roman Catholic institution run by the Jesuit Fathers and offering degree programs in the arts and sciences, business, education, nursing, and law. There are 4 undergraduate and 6 graduate schools. In addition to regional accreditation, USF has baccalaureate program accreditation with AACSB, CSAB, and NLN. The 2 libraries contain 831,905 volumes, 833,179 microform items, and 5420 audiovisual forms/CDs, and subscribe to 3000 periodicals. Computerized library services include the card catalog, interlibrary loans, and database searching. Special learning facilities include a learning resource center, radio station, rare book room, the Institute for Chinese-Western Cultural History, and the Center for Pacific Rim Studies. The 55-acre campus is in an urban area in the heart of the city. Including residence halls, there are 17 buildings.

Programs of Study: USF confers B.A., B.S., B.Arch., B.F.A., B.P.A., B.S.B.A., and B.S.N. degrees. Master's and doctoral degrees are also awarded. Bachelor's degrees are awarded in BIOLOGICAL SCIENCE (biology/biological science), BUSINESS (accounting, banking and finance, business administration and management, hospitality management services, international business management, management information systems, marketing/retailing/merchandising, and organizational behavior), COMMUNICATIONS AND THE ARTS (communications, drawing, English, French, graphic design, illustration, industrial design, media arts, painting, performing arts, and Spanish), COMPUTER AND PHYSICAL SCIENCE (chemistry, computer science, information sciences and systems, mathematics, and physics), EDUCATION (athletic training, elementary, middle school, and secondary), ENGINEERING AND ENVIRONMENTAL DESIGN (architecture and environmental science), HEALTH PROFESSIONS (exercise science and nursing), SOCIAL SCIENCE (economics, fashion design and technology, history, law enforcement and corrections, philosophy, political science/government, psychology, public administration, religion, sociology, and theological studies). Sciences and business are the strongest academically. Communications, nursing, and psychology are the largest.

Special: USF offers co-op programs with the California College of Arts and Crafts, cross-registration with the San Francisco Consortium, internships with local businesses, and social services, and research opportunities. Study abroad in Europe and Japan, work-study programs both on and off campus, a B.A.-B.S. degree in exercise and sports medicine, dual majors in liberal arts and education, 3-2 engineering degrees with the University of Southern California, student-designed majors, nondegree study, and limited pass/fail options are also available. The College of Professional Studies is a degree completion program for working adults. There are 3 national honor societies, a freshman honors program, and 1 departmental honors program.

Admissions: 80% of the 1999-2000 applicants were accepted. The SAT I scores for the 1999-2000 freshman class were: Verbal--23% below 500, 45% between 500 and 599, 27% between 600 and 700, and 5% above 700; Math--24% below 500, 46% between 500 and 599, 27% between 600 and 700, and 3% above 700. The ACT scores were 19% below 21, 36% between 21 and 23, 24% between 24 and 26, 12% between 27 and 28, and 9% above 28. 49% of the current freshmen were in the top fifth of their class; 80% were in the top two fifths. 5 freshmen graduated first in their class.

Requirements: The SAT I or ACT is required. A GPA of 2.8 is required. In addition, applicants are required to have 20 academic units, based on 6 years of academic electives, 4 of English, 3 each of math and social studies, and 2 each of foreign language and lab science. An essay is required. The GED is accepted. Upon request, the Office of Admissions will send for completion a prepared IBM or Mac disk to those students who wish to apply by computer. AP and CLEP credits are accepted. Important factors in the admissions decision are advanced placement or honor courses, recommendations by school officials, and leadership record.

Procedure: Freshmen are admitted fall and spring. Entrance exams should be taken during the first half of the senior year. There are early admissions and deferred admissions plans. Early decision applications should be filed by December 1; regular applications, by February 15 for fall entry and December 15 for spring entry, along with a $45 fee. Notification is sent on a rolling basis.

Financial Aid: In 1999-2000, 59% of all freshmen and 65% of continuing students received some form of financial aid. 64% of freshmen and 44% of continuing students received need-based aid. The average freshman award was $16,715. Of that total, scholarships or need-based grants averaged $10,198 ($25,444 maximum); loans averaged $2940 ($12,425 maximum); and work contracts averaged $1974 ($2000 maximum). 16% of undergraduates work part time. Average annual earnings from campus work are $1500. The average financial indebtedness of the 1999 graduate was $22,238. USF is a member of CSS. The FAFSA and the university's own financial statement are required. The fall application deadline is February 15.

Computers: The mainframe is a DEC ALPHA/VMS administrative computer. There are 250 PCs available in 10 locations and operating on a LAN system. Each residence room is linked to the network, allowing E-mail and other applications. All students may access the system. There are no time limits and no fees.

UNIVERSITY OF SOUTH CAROLINA AT COLUMBIA

Columbia, SC 29208

(803) 777-7700
(800) 868-5872; Fax: (803) 777-0101

Full-time: 5734 men, 6942 women	**Faculty:** 761; I, -$
Part-time: 1253 men, 1622 women	**Ph.D.s:** 84%
Graduate: 3290 men, 4589 women	**Student/Faculty:** 17 to 1
Year: semesters, summer session	**Tuition:** $3740 ($9814)
Application Deadline: see profile	**Room & Board:** $4167
Freshman Class: 10,162 applied, 6844 accepted, 2668 enrolled	
SAT I Verbal/Math: 540/550	**ACT:** 23 **VERY COMPETITIVE**

The University of South Carolina at Columbia, founded in 1801, is a publicly assisted institution serving the entire state of South Carolina. In addition to the main campus at Columbia, there are 2 senior campuses at Aiken and Spartanburg and 5 regional campuses. There are 16 undergraduate and 18 graduate schools. In addition to regional accreditation, Carolina has baccalaureate program accreditation with AACSB, ABET, ACEJMC, ACPE, CSAB, NASM, NCATE, and NLN. The 7 libraries contain 3,143,505 volumes, 4,789,734 microform items, and 42,866 audiovisual forms/CDs, and subscribe to 18,976 periodicals. Computerized library services include the card catalog, interlibrary loans, and database searching. Special learning facilities include a learning resource center, art gallery, natural history museum, planetarium, and radio station. The 250-acre campus is in an urban area in the downtown area of Columbia. Including residence halls, there are 171 buildings.

Programs of Study: Carolina confers B.A., B.S., B.A.I.S., B.A.J., B.A.P.E./B.S. P.E., B.A.R.S.C., B.F.A., B.M., B.M.A., B.S.B.A., B.S.Chem., B.S.C.S., B.S.E., B.S.I.S., B.S.Med.Tech., and B.S.N. degrees. Associate, master's, and doctoral degrees are also awarded. Bachelor's degrees are awarded in BIOLOGICAL SCIENCE (biology/biological science and marine science), BUSINESS (accounting, banking and finance, business administration and management, business economics, hotel/motel and restaurant management, insurance, management science, marketing/retailing/merchandising, office supervision and management, real estate, retailing, and sports management), COMMUNICATIONS AND THE ARTS (advertising, art history and appreciation, broadcasting, classics, communications, dramatic arts, English, fine arts, French, German, Greek, Italian, journalism, Latin, media arts, music, music performance, public relations, Spanish, speech/debate/rhetoric, and studio art), COMPUTER AND PHYSICAL SCIENCE (chemistry, computer science, geology, geophysics and seismology, mathematics, physics, and statistics), EDUCATION (art, early childhood, elementary, music, physical, and secondary), ENGINEERING AND ENVIRONMENTAL DESIGN (chemical engineering, civil engineering, computer engineering, electrical/electronics engineering, and mechanical engineering), HEALTH PROFESSIONS (exercise science, medical laboratory technology, and nursing), SOCIAL SCIENCE (African American studies, anthropology, criminal justice, economics, European studies, geography, history, interdisciplinary studies, international relations, Latin American studies, philosophy, political science/government, psychology, religion, sociology, and women's studies). Biology, experimental psychology, and engineering are the largest.

Special: USC transmits live interactive televised instruction to more than 20 locations in the state. Cross-registration is offered with the National Technological University in Engineering and through the National Student Exchange. Internships in many fields, study abroad in many countries through the Byrnes International Center, co-op programs, and work-study programs are available. Double majors through the colleges of humanities and social sciences and science and math, student-designed majors, an interdisciplinary studies degree, and a 3-2 engineering degree with the College of Charleston are offered. Credit for military experience, nondegree study, and pass/fail options also are possible. There are 32 national honor societies, including Phi Beta Kappa, and a freshman honors program.

Admissions: 67% of the 1999-2000 applicants were accepted. The SAT I scores for the 1999-2000 freshman class were: Verbal--33% below 500, 42% between 500 and 599, 20% between 600 and 700, and 5% above 700; Math--28% below 500, 41% between 500 and 599, 26% between 600 and 700, and 5% above 700. The ACT scores were 26% below 21, 26% between 21 and 23, 22% between 24 and 26, 12% between 27 and 28, and 14% above 28. 56% of the current freshmen were in the top fifth of their class; 86% were in the top two fifths. There were 38 National Merit finalists. 82 freshmen graduated first in their class.

Requirements: The SAT I or ACT is required. Applicants must have 16 academic credits, including 4 in English, 3 each in math and social studies (1 of which must be U.S. history), 2 each in foreign language and lab science, 1 academic elective, and 1 phys ed or ROTC. The GED is accepted. Applications are accepted on-line at the school's web site, http://web.csd.sc.edu/app/ugrad-cola/. AP and CLEP credits are accepted. Important factors in the admissions decision are advanced placement or honor courses, evidence of special talent, and recommendations by school officials.

Procedure: Freshmen are admitted to all sessions. Entrance exams should be taken during spring of the junior year and fall of the senior year, if necessary. Application deadlines are noon of the last work-day prior to the start of classes. There is a $35 fee. Notification is sent on a rolling basis.

Financial Aid: In 1998-99, 60% of all freshmen and 65% of continuing students received some form of financial aid. 45% of freshmen and 50% of continuing students received need-based aid. The average freshman award was $2750. Of that total, scholarships or need-based grants averaged $900 ($2000 maximum); loans averaged $1750 ($2625 maximum); and work contracts averaged $2000 ($2550 maximum). 12% of undergraduates work part time. Average annual earnings from campus work are $3316. The average financial indebtedness of the 1998 graduate was $16,200. Carolina is a member of CSS. The FAFSA is required. The fall application deadline is April 15.

Computers: The mainframe is an IBM 9672-R53. Students may use the system to check on grades, make fee payments, search the Internet, visit web sites, and access the library, lists, and E-mail. All students may access the system. There are no time limits and no fees. It is recommended that all students have personal computers.

UNIVERSITY OF SOUTH FLORIDA
Tampa, FL 33620   (813) 974-3350; Fax: (813) 974-9689

Full-time: 6843 men, 9445 women	**Faculty:** 1492; I, --$
Part-time: 5069 men, 7559 women	**Ph.D.s:** 93%
Graduate: 2510 men, 3692 women	**Student/Faculty:** 11 to 1
Year: semesters, summer session	**Tuition:** $2256 ($9245)
Application Deadline: May 1	**Room & Board:** $4606
Freshman Class: 10,005 applied, 7267 accepted, 3287 enrolled	
SAT I Verbal/Math: 530/540	**ACT:** 22 **VERY COMPETITIVE**

The University of South Florida, founded in 1956, is a comprehensive public institution, part of the state university system of Florida, offering programs in liberal and fine arts, business, engineering, health science, and education. USF also maintains campuses at Lakeland, Sarasota, and St. Petersburg. There are 6 undergraduate and 9 graduate schools. In addition to regional accreditation, USF has baccalaureate program accreditation with AACSB, ABET, ACEJMC, ASLA, CSAB, CSWE, NAAB, NASAD, NASM, NCATE, and NLN. The 5 libraries contain 2.3 million volumes, 3.8 million microform items, and 148,986 audiovisual forms/CDs, and subscribe to 10,155 periodicals. Computerized library services include the card catalog, interlibrary loans, and database searching. Special learning facilities include a learning resource center, art gallery, radio station, TV station, mock broadcasting studio, anthropology museum, and botanical gardens. The 1913-acre campus is in an urban area 10 miles northeast of downtown Tampa. Including residence halls, there are 382 buildings.

Programs of Study: USF confers B.A., B.S., B.F.A., B.I.S., B.M., and B.S.W. degrees, and several engineering degrees. Associate, master's, and doctoral degrees are also awarded. Bachelor's degrees are awarded in BIOLOGICAL SCIENCE (biology/biological science and microbiology), BUSINESS (accounting, banking and finance, business administration and management, business economics, management information systems, management science, and marketing/retailing/merchandising), COMMUNICATIONS AND THE ARTS (art, classics, communications, dance, dramatic arts, English literature, French, German, Italian, languages, music, Russian, Spanish, and speech/debate/rhetoric), COMPUTER AND PHYSICAL SCIENCE (chemistry, geology, mathematics, physical sciences, and physics), EDUCATION (art, business, education, education of the emotionally handicapped, education of the mentally handicapped, elementary, English, foreign languages, mathematics, music, physical, science, social studies, special, specific learning disabilities, and vocational), ENGINEERING AND ENVIRONMENTAL DESIGN (chemical engineering, civil engineering, computer engineering, electrical/electronics engineering, engineering, environmental science, industrial engineering, and mechanical engineering), HEALTH PROFESSIONS (medical technology and nursing), SOCIAL SCIENCE (African American studies, American studies, anthropology, criminology, economics, geography, gerontology, history, humanities, international relations, liberal arts/general studies, philosophy, political science/government, psychology, religion, social science, social work, sociology, and women's studies). Education, fine arts, and sciences are the strongest academically. Business and education are the largest.

Special: USF offers co-op programs in business and engineering, study abroad, work-study programs, accelerated degree programs in public health and medicine, internships, a Washington semester, dual and student-designed majors, a liberal arts degree, nondegree study, and pass/fail options for some courses.

There are 21 national honor societies, a freshman honors program, and 18 departmental honors programs.

Admissions: 73% of the 1999-2000 applicants were accepted. The SAT I scores for the 1999-2000 freshman class were: Verbal--31% below 500, 45% between 500 and 599, 20% between 600 and 700, and 4% above 700; Math--29% below 500, 47% between 500 and 599, 21% between 600 and 700, and 3% above 700. The ACT scores were 9% below 21, 58% between 21 and 23, 33% between 24 and 26, and 3% between 27 and 28. 52% of the current freshmen were in the top fifth of their class; 85% were in the top two fifths. There were 65 National Merit finalists.

Requirements: The SAT I or ACT is required. A GPA of 2.0 is required. Candidates for admission should have completed 4 units each of English and academic electives, 3 each of math, science, and social studies, and 2 of a foreign language. The GED is accepted. Applicants who do not meet minimum requirements but have important attributes, special talents, or unique circumstances are considered for admission by an academic faculty committee. Applications are accepted online. AP and CLEP credits are accepted. Important factors in the admissions decision are advanced placement or honor courses, evidence of special talent, and recommendations by school officials.

Procedure: Freshmen are admitted to all sessions. Entrance exams should be taken at the end of the junior year or the beginning of the senior year. There is an early admissions plan. Applications should be filed by May 1 for fall entry, October 25 for spring entry, and March 1 for summer entry, along with a $20 fee. Notification is sent on a rolling basis.

Financial Aid: 23% of undergraduates work part time. Average annual earnings from campus work are $2015. USF is a member of CSS. The FAFSA is required. The fall application deadline is March 1.

Computers: The mainframe is an IBM 9672-R32 Enterpriser server MVS OS/ 390. Student computer labs exist throughout campus. All students may access the system. There are no time limits and no fees.

UNIVERSITY OF TENNESSEE AT KNOXVILLE
Knoxville, TN 37996-0230 (423) 974-2184
(800) 221-VOLS; Fax: (423) 974-6341

Full-time: 8885 men, 9106 women	**Faculty:** 1253
Part-time: 1027 men, 1241 women	**Ph.D.s:** 86%
Graduate: 2581 men, 3141 women	**Student/Faculty:** 14 to 1
Year: semesters, summer session	**Tuition:** $3104 ($9172)
Application Deadline: February 1	**Room & Board:** $4430
Freshman Class: 10,634 applied, 7148 accepted, 4155 enrolled	
SAT I Verbal/Math: 552/551	**ACT:** 24 **COMPETITIVE+**

The University of Tennessee, Knoxville, founded in 1794 and the original campus of the state university system, is now a large public institution offering more than 300 graduate and undergraduate programs. There are 11 undergraduate and 14 graduate schools. In addition to regional accreditation, UT Knoxville has baccalaureate program accreditation with AACSB, ABET, ACEJMC, ADA, AHEA, ASLA, CSWE, FIDER, NAAB, NASAD, NASM, NCATE, NLN, NRPA, and SAF. The 4 libraries contain 2,492,953 volumes, 3,502,541 microform items, and 173,506 audiovisual forms/CDs, and subscribe to 16,656 periodicals. Computerized library services include the card catalog, interlibrary loans, and database searching. Special learning facilities include a learning resource center, art gallery, natural history museum, radio station, and a science and engineering research facility. The 533-acre campus is in an urban area adjacent to downtown Knoxville. Including residence halls, there are 220 buildings.

Programs of Study: UT Knoxville confers B.A., B.S., B.Arch., B.F.A., B.M., and specialized B.S. degrees in 25 fields, including business administration, nursing, and social work. Master's and doctoral degrees are also awarded. Bachelor's degrees are awarded in AGRICULTURE (agricultural economics, agriculture, animal science, fishing and fisheries, forestry and related sciences, plant science, and soil science), BIOLOGICAL SCIENCE (biochemistry, biology/biological science, botany, microbiology, and nutrition), BUSINESS (accounting, banking and finance, business administration and management, business economics, hotel/motel and restaurant management, management science, marketing/retailing/merchandising, retailing, sports management, tourism, and transportation management), COMMUNICATIONS AND THE ARTS (advertising, art history and appreciation, broadcasting, classics, comparative literature, dramatic arts, English, film arts, fine arts, French, German, graphic design, Italian, journalism, languages, linguistics, music, Russian, Spanish, speech/debate/rhetoric, and studio art), COMPUTER AND PHYSICAL SCIENCE (chemistry, computer science, geology, mathematics, physics, and statistics), EDUCATION (agricultural, art, elementary, health, marketing and distribution, music, physical, recreation, and special), ENGINEERING AND ENVIRONMENTAL DESIGN (aerospace studies, agricultural engineering, architecture, chemical engineering, civil engineering, electrical/electronics engineering, engineering, engineering and applied science, engineering physics, environmental science, food services technology, industrial engineering, interior design, landscape architecture/design, materials engineering, materials science, mechanical engineering, and nuclear engineering), HEALTH PROFESSIONS (community health work, health science, nursing, predentistry, premedicine, preveterinary science, and speech pathology/audiology), SOCIAL SCIENCE (African American studies, anthropology, Asian/Oriental studies, child care/child and family studies, classical/ancient civilization, economics, food science, geography, history, human services, Latin American studies, medieval studies, philosophy, political science/government, psychology, public administration, religion, Russian and Slavic studies, social work, sociology, textiles and clothing, urban studies, and women's studies). Engineering, physical sciences, and English are the strongest academically. Business administration is the largest.

Special: Cooperative programs are offered in engineering, communications, liberal arts, and business. Cross-registration is possible through the Academic Common Market, a southern 14-state consortium, in any of 11 programs. Internships are available in social work, education, and architecture, and there are a number of work-study programs. Study abroad in more than 25 countries is possible. Dual and student-designed majors, accelerated study, nondegree study, and pass/fail options are offered. There are 51 national honor societies, including Phi Beta Kappa, a freshman honors program, and 13 departmental honors programs.

Admissions: 67% of the 1999-2000 applicants were accepted. The SAT I scores for the 1999-2000 freshman class were: Verbal--24% below 500, 48% between 500 and 599, 22% between 600 and 700, and 6% above 700; Math--26% below 500, 44% between 500 and 599, 24% between 600 and 700, and 6% above 700. The ACT scores were 23% below 21, 29% between 21 and 23, 26% between 24 and 26, 10% between 27 and 28, and 12% above 28. 43% of the current freshmen were in the top fifth of their class; 73% were in the top two fifths. There were 44 National Merit finalists.

Requirements: The SAT I or ACT is required. A GPA of 2.0 is required. The ACT is preferred. Applicants should be high school graduates or have the GED. Required secondary school courses include 4 credits in English, 3 in math, 2 each in science and a single foreign language, 1 each in history and world history or world geography, and 1 unit of visual/performing arts. AP and CLEP credits are accepted. Important factors in the admissions decision are advanced placement or honor courses, leadership record, and parents or siblings attending the school.

Procedure: Freshmen are admitted to all sessions. Entrance exams should be taken in spring of the junior year or fall of the senior year. There are early admissions and deferred admissions plans. Applications should be filed by February 1 for fall entry, November 1 for spring entry, and April 1 for summer entry, along with a $25 fee. Notification is sent on a rolling basis.

Financial Aid: In 1999-2000, 76% of all freshmen and 60% of continuing students received some form of financial aid. 68% of freshmen and 60% of continuing students received need-based aid. The average freshman award was $5548. Of that total, scholarships or need-based grants averaged $4379 ($7500 maximum); and loans averaged $2502 ($2625 maximum). The average financial indebtedness of the 1999 graduate was $19,624. UT Knoxville is a member of CSS. The CSS/Profile or FFS and Academic College Scholarship Application are required. The fall application deadline is April 1.

Computers: The mainframe is an IBM 9672-R42. There are also Macs, PCs, and Sun workstations available throughout the campus. Students can access the library mainframe from apartment or dormitory rooms via modem. All students may access the system. There are no time limits and no fees.

UNIVERSITY OF TEXAS AT AUSTIN
Austin, TX 78712
(512) 475-7440; Fax: (512) 475-7475

Full-time: 15,922 men, 16,614 women	**Faculty:** 2313; I, av$
Part-time: 2511 men, 2112 women	**Ph.D.s:** 90%
Graduate: 6245 men, 5605 women	**Student/Faculty:** 14 to 1
Year: semesters, summer session	**Tuition:** $3128 ($9608)
Application Deadline: February 1	**Room & Board:** $4854
Freshman Class: 18,930 applied, 11,948 accepted, 7040 enrolled	
SAT I Verbal/Math: 590/610	**ACT:** 25 **HIGHLY COMPETITIVE**

University of Texas at Austin, founded in 1883, is a major research institution within the University of Texas System and provides a broad range of degree programs. There are 11 undergraduate and 14 graduate schools. In addition to regional accreditation, UT has baccalaureate program accreditation with AACSB, ABET, ACEJMC, ACPE, ADA, CSWE, FIDER, NAAB, NASM, and NCATE. The 17 libraries contain 7,783,847 volumes, 5,624,783 microform items, and 124,399 audiovisual forms/CDs, and subscribe to 52,536 periodicals. Computerized library services include the card catalog, interlibrary loans, and database searching. Special learning facilities include a learning resource center, art gallery, natural history museum, radio station, TV station, observatory, marine science institute, fusion reactor, and the Lyndon Baines Johnson Library and Museum. The 350-acre campus is in an urban area near downtown Austin, just off the interstate. Including residence halls, there are 115 buildings.

Programs of Study: UT confers B.A., B.S., B.Arch., B.B.A., B.F.A., B.M., B.J., and B.S.W. degrees, among more than 50 specific degrees. Master's and doctoral degrees are also awarded. Bachelor's degrees are awarded in BIOLOGICAL SCIENCE (biochemistry, biology/biological science, botany, microbiology, molecular biology, nutrition, and zoology), BUSINESS (accounting, business administration and management, management information systems, and marketing/retailing/merchandising), COMMUNICATIONS AND THE ARTS (advertising, applied music, Arabic, art history and appreciation, classics, dance, design, dramatic arts, English, film arts, French, German, Greek, Hebrew, Italian, journalism, Latin, linguistics, music, music theory and composition, Portuguese, public relations, Russian, Scandinavian languages, Slavic languages, Spanish, speech/debate/rhetoric, studio art, and visual and performing arts), COMPUTER AND PHYSICAL SCIENCE (astronomy, chemistry, computer science, geology, geophysics and seismology, mathematics, and physics), ENGINEERING AND ENVIRONMENTAL DESIGN (aerospace studies, architectural engineering, architecture, chemical engineering, civil engineering, electrical/electronics engineering, environmental science, geophysical engineering, interior design, mechanical engineering, and petroleum/natural gas engineering), HEALTH PROFESSIONS (medical technology, nursing, pharmacy, and speech pathology/audiology), SOCIAL SCIENCE (American studies, anthropology, archeology, Asian/Oriental studies, child care/child and family studies, community services, dietetics, Eastern European studies, economics, ethnic studies, geography, history, home economics, humanities, Islamic studies, Latin American studies, liberal arts/general studies, Middle Eastern studies, philosophy, physical fitness/movement, political science/government, psychology, Russian and Slavic studies, social work, sociology, and textiles and clothing). Liberal arts, business administration, and natural sciences are the largest.

Special: Cooperative programs are available in all engineering courses, microbiology, chemistry, computer science, geology, and actuarial studies. Cross-registration is provided in pharmacy with the University of Texas at San Antonio. Internships, study abroad, B.A.-B.S. degrees in sciences and math, dual majors in architecture, student-designed majors for humanities students, and pass/fail options are offered. There are 45 national honor societies, including Phi Beta Kappa, a freshman honors program, and 52 departmental honors programs.

Admissions: 63% of the 1999-2000 applicants were accepted. The SAT I scores for the 1999-2000 freshman class were: Verbal--12% below 500, 40% between 500 and 599, 39% between 600 and 700, and 9% above 700; Math--9% below 500, 32% between 500 and 599, 45% between 600 and 700, and 14% above 700. The ACT scores were 11% below 21, 22% between 21 and 23, 32% between 24 and 26, 17% between 27 and 28, and 19% above 28. 73% of the current freshmen were in the top fifth of their class; 93% were in the top two fifths. There were 238 National Merit finalists. 174 freshmen graduated first in their class.

Requirements: The SAT I or ACT is required. All students graduating in the top 10% of their class from an accredited Texas high school are eligible for admission. Applicants not meeting that requirement are reviewed based on SAT I or ACT scores, class rank, writing samples, and related factors; consideration may be given to socioeconomic and geographic information. In addition, applicants need 15 1/2 academic credits, including 4 in English, 3 each in math and social studies, 2 each in science and foreign language, and 1 1/2 in electives. An audition is required for applied music majors. The GED is accepted, with supportive information. Home-schooled students are required to submit the results of either the SAT II: Subject tests or AP exams in English, math, and a third subject of the student's choosing. UT accepts applications on-line via ExPAN. AP and CLEP credits are accepted. Important factors in the admissions decision are leadership record, extracurricular activities record, and evidence of special talent.

Procedure: Freshmen are admitted to all sessions. Entrance exams should be taken in the junior year or early in the senior year. There is a deferred admissions plan. Applications should be filed by February 1 for fall entry, October 1 for spring entry, and February 1 for summer entry, along with a $50 fee. Notification is sent on a rolling basis.

Financial Aid: In 1999-2000, 50% of all freshmen and 61% of continuing students received some form of financial aid. 40% of freshmen and 43% of continu-

ing students received need-based aid. The average freshman award was $7260. Of that total, scholarships or need-based grants averaged $4440; loans averaged $2950; and work contracts averaged $3450. 20% of undergraduates work part time. Average annual earnings from campus work are $2200. The average financial indebtedness of the 1999 graduate was $17,000. UT is a member of CSS. The FAFSA is required. The fall application deadline is April 1.

Computers: A UNIX Timesharing Services (UTS) system provides general access interactive UNIX timesharing. The UTS cluster consists of 2 DEC Alpha servers running Digital UNIX. Students have access to the mainframe computers through classes that require computer use, or through individually funded computer user numbers. A 200-seat student facility includes Mac and DOS-compatible PCs. Workstations are located in public facilities for hands-on access and are also available through remote log-in. Some 57 campus buildings and thousands of computers and PCs are on the campuswide network. All student dormitory rooms are wired for access to the Internet. All students may access the system 24 hours a day. There are no time limits. The fee is $6 per semester credit hour.

UNIVERSITY OF TEXAS AT DALLAS
Richardson, TX 75083-0688

(972) 883-2342
(800) 889-2443; Fax: (972) 883-6803

Full-time: 1530 men, 1475 women	**Faculty:** 293; I, +$
Part-time: 1110 men, 1170 women	**Ph.D.s:** 97%
Graduate: 2235 men, 1835 women	**Student/Faculty:** 10 to 1
Year: semesters, summer session	**Tuition:** $2420 ($7560)
Application Deadline: see profile	**Room & Board:** n/app
Freshman Class: n/av	
SAT I or ACT: required	**VERY COMPETITIVE**

The University of Texas at Dallas, founded in 1969 as part of the University of Texas system, offers undergraduate and graduate programs in the liberal arts and sciences, business, engineering, computer science, cognitive science, and neuroscience. Figures given in the above capsule are approximate. There are 8 undergraduate and 8 graduate schools. In addition to regional accreditation, UTD has baccalaureate program accreditation with ABET. The library contains 632,690 volumes, 1,709,618 microform items, and 3500 audiovisual forms/CDs, and subscribes to 3811 periodicals. Computerized library services include the card catalog, interlibrary loans, and database searching. Special learning facilities include a learning resource center, art gallery, and the Callier Center for Communications Disorders. The 455-acre campus is in a suburban area 18 miles north of downtown Dallas. There are 41 buildings.

Programs of Study: UTD confers B.A., B.S., and B.S.E.E. degrees. Master's and doctoral degrees are also awarded. Bachelor's degrees are awarded in BIOLOGICAL SCIENCE (biology/biological science and neurosciences), BUSINESS (accounting and business administration and management), COMMUNICATIONS AND THE ARTS (literature and telecommunications), COMPUTER AND PHYSICAL SCIENCE (applied mathematics, chemistry, computer science, geoscience, mathematics, physics, and statistics), ENGINEERING AND ENVIRONMENTAL DESIGN (electrical/electronics engineering), HEALTH PROFESSIONS (speech pathology/audiology), SOCIAL SCIENCE (American studies, cognitive science, economics, history, interdisciplinary studies, political science/government, psychology, public administration, and sociology). Electrical engineering, biology, and neuroscience are the strongest academically. Business administration, computer science, and electrical engineering are the largest.

Special: Cross-registration is available with other University of Texas campuses. Accelerated degree programs and B.A.-B.S. degrees are offered in several majors, as is a 3-2 engineering degree with Austin College, Texas Women's University, or Abilene Christian University. Co-op programs, internships, study abroad, and work-study programs, as well as dual and student-designed majors, are possible. There are 3 national honor societies, a freshman honors program, and 1 departmental honors program.

Admissions: In a recent year, there were 25 National Merit finalists and 2 semifinalists. 11 freshmen graduated first in their class.

Requirements: The SAT I or ACT is required. UTD requires applicants to be in the upper 25% of their class. Applicants should be graduates of an accredited secondary school. Applications are accepted on-line at the school's web site. AP and CLEP credits are accepted.

Procedure: Freshmen are admitted to all sessions. Entrance exams should be taken at the end of the junior year or beginning of the senior year. There are early decision, early admissions, and deferred admissions plans. Check with the school for c'urrent application deadlines and fee. Notification is sent on a rolling basis.

Financial Aid: In a recent year, 26% of all freshmen and 25% of continuing students received some form of financial aid. 20% of freshmen and 23% of continuing students received need-based aid. The average freshman award was $2392. Of that total, scholarships or need-based grants averaged $550 ($2700 maximum); loans averaged $1285 ($2500 maximum); and work contracts averaged $1200 ($3800 maximum). 67% of undergraduates work part time. Average annual earnings from campus work are $2018. The average financial indebtedness of the 1999 graduate was $12,000. UTD is a member of CSS. The CSS/Profile or FAFSA and the university's own financial statement are required. Check with the school for cu;rrent deadlines.

Computers: The mainframes are a Sun E6000, Sun SPARC Station 10, and Sun SPARC 1. Student facilities include more than 260 Pentium PCs, 57 Macs, 23 UCDX terminals, and 20 Wyse terminals, plus microlabs. Individual schools provide additional SPARC stations with terminals. All students have E-mail, Internet, and Web access. All students may access the system 8 a.m. to midnight in most labs, 24 hours in specific labs, and 24 hours a day from remote locations via modem. There are no time limits. The fee is $6 per credit hour.

UNIVERSITY OF THE ARTS
Philadelphia, PA 19102

(215) 717-6030
(800) 616-2787; Fax: (215) 717-6045

Full-time: 833 men, 921 women	**Faculty:** 93; IIB, av$
Part-time: 24 men, 28 women	**Ph.D.s:** 58%
Graduate: 45 men, 87 women	**Student/Faculty:** 19 to 1
Year: semesters, summer session	**Tuition:** $16,800
Application Deadline: open	**Room & Board:** $4500
Freshman Class: 1634 applied, 891 accepted, 439 enrolled	
SAT I Verbal/Math: 520/480	**SPECIAL**

University of the Arts, founded in 1870, is a private, nonprofit institution offering education and professional training in visual, media, and performing arts, with an emphasis on the humanities and interdisciplinary exploration. There are 3 undergraduate and 2 graduate schools. In addition to regional accreditation, UArts has baccalaureate program accreditation with NASAD and NASM. The 3 libraries contain 189,658 volumes, 461 microform items, and 14,838 audiovisual forms/CDs, and subscribe to 501 periodicals. Computerized library services include the card catalog, interlibrary loans, and database searching. Special learning facilities include an art gallery, several theaters, and music, animation, and recording studios. The 18-acre campus is in an urban area in Philadelphia. Including residence halls, there are 8 buildings.

Programs of Study: UArts confers B.S., B.F.A., and B.M. degrees. Associate and master's degrees are also awarded. Bachelor's degrees are awarded in COMMUNICATIONS AND THE ARTS (ceramic art and design, communications, dance, dramatic arts, fiber/textiles/weaving, film arts, graphic design, illustration, industrial design, jazz, media arts, metal/jewelry, multimedia, music performance, music theory and composition, musical theater, painting, performing arts, photography, printmaking, radio/television technology, and sculpture), EDUCATION (dance), ENGINEERING AND ENVIRONMENTAL DESIGN (computer graphics). Dance, graphic design, and illustration are the largest.

Special: UArts offers cross-registration with the 10-member Consortium East Coast Art Schools as well as with the Pennsylvania Academy of Fine Arts and Philadelphia College of Textiles and Sciences. Internships may be arranged, and there are extensive summer programs and opportunities to study abroad.

Admissions: 55% of the 1999-2000 applicants were accepted. The SAT I scores for the 1999-2000 freshman class were: Verbal--37% below 500, 43% between 500 and 599, 19% between 600 and 700, and 1% above 700; Math--57% below 500, 31% between 500 and 599, 11% between 600 and 700, and 1% above 700. 7% of the current freshmen were in the upper 10% of their class; 31% were in the upper quarter; 68% were in the upper half.

Requirements: The SAT I or ACT is required. A GPA of 2.0 is required. Students must have graduated from an accredited secondary school or hold a GED certificate. A minimum of 16 academic credits consisting of 4 each in English and math and 2 each in music or art and history, is recommended. An essay and either a portfolio or an audition are required of all applicants. An interview is recommended. Applications are accepted on computer disk via CollegeLink. AP and CLEP credits are accepted. Important factors in the admissions decision are evidence of special talent, advanced placement or honor courses, and personality/intangible qualities.

Procedure: Freshmen are admitted fall and spring. Entrance exams should be taken late in the junior year or early in the senior year. There are early admissions and deferred admissions plans. Application deadlines are open. There is a $40 fee. Notification is sent on a rolling basis.

Financial Aid: In 1999-2000, 66% of all freshmen and 85% of continuing students received some form of financial aid, including need-based aid. The average freshman award was $11,628. Of that total, scholarships or need-based grants averaged $6500 ($10,000 maximum); loans averaged $2425 ($3625 maximum); work contracts averaged $1300 ($1500 maximum); and Presidential Merit Scholarships averaged $5000 ($7000 maximum). 30% of undergraduates work part time. Average annual earnings from campus work are $1500. The average financial indebtedness of the 1999 graduate was $17,000. UArts is a member of CSS. The FAFSA is required. The fall application deadline is February 15.

Computers: All 18 computer labs and 8 student lounges are networked with Internet and web access. Additional access is available in the university library. There are time limits at some stations, which vary from 30 minutes to 2 hours. Most labs do not have time limits. There are no fees. It is strongly recommended that all students have personal computers.

Full-time: 1201 men, 1651 women	**Faculty:** 327; IIA, ++$
Part-time: 47 men, 45 women	**Ph.D.s:** 86%
Graduate: 225 men, 361 women	**Student/Faculty:** 9 to 1
Year: semesters, summer session	**Tuition:** $19,935
Application Deadline: February 15	**Room & Board:** $6192
Freshman Class: 2831 applied, 2312 accepted, 745 enrolled	
SAT I Verbal/Math: 540/560	**ACT:** 23 **VERY COMPETITIVE**

The University of the Pacific, founded in 1851, is an independent institution. It offers undergraduate and graduate programs in arts and sciences and in the professions. There are 8 undergraduate schools and 1 graduate school. In addition to regional accreditation, Pacific has baccalaureate program accreditation with AACSB, ABET, ACPE, NASAD, NASM, and NCATE. The 2 libraries contain 400,000 volumes, 555,000 microform items, and 18,600 audiovisual forms/CDs, and subscribe to 2700 periodicals. Computerized library services include the card catalog, interlibrary loans, and database searching. Special learning facilities include a learning resource center, art gallery, and radio station. The 175-acre campus is in a suburban area 80 miles east of San Francisco and 40 miles south of Sacramento. Including residence halls, there are 98 buildings.

Programs of Study: Pacific confers B.A., B.S., B.F.A., B.M., and B.S. in Eng. degrees. Master's and doctoral degrees are also awarded. Bachelor's degrees are awarded in BIOLOGICAL SCIENCE (biochemistry, biology/biological science, and life science), BUSINESS (business administration and management, international business management, and sports management), COMMUNICATIONS AND THE ARTS (art, art history and appreciation, arts administration/management, classics, communications, dramatic arts, English, French, German, graphic design, Japanese, music, music business management, music performance, Spanish, and studio art), COMPUTER AND PHYSICAL SCIENCE (chemistry, computer science, geology, geophysics and seismology, information sciences and systems, mathematics, physical sciences, and physics), EDUCATION (art, elementary, foreign languages, middle school, music, physical, recreation, science, secondary, special, and teaching English as a second/foreign language (TESOL/TEFOL)), ENGINEERING AND ENVIRONMENTAL DESIGN (civil engineering, computer engineering, electrical/electronics engineering, engineering management, engineering physics, environmental science, and mechanical engineering), HEALTH PROFESSIONS (music therapy, predentistry, speech pathology/audiology, and sports medicine), SOCIAL SCIENCE (African American studies, crosscultural studies, economics, German area studies, history, international relations, international studies, Japanese studies, philosophy, political science/government, prelaw, psychology, religion, social science, sociology, and urban studies). Natural sciences and the professions are the strongest academically. Arts/sciences, pharmacy, and business are the largest.

Special: The engineering school requires and guarantees a co-op program for specialized training in the field. Internships for credit/pay in all majors, more than 230 study-abroad programs in more than 70 countries, a Washington semester, and more than 20 work-study programs also are available. An accelerated degree in dentistry, law, education, business, or pharmacy, student-designed majors, dual majors in most disciplines, and pass/fail options are possible. There are 13 national honor societies and a freshman honors program.

Admissions: 82% of the 1999-2000 applicants were accepted. The SAT I scores for the 1999-2000 freshman class were: Verbal--31% below 500, 43% between 500 and 599, 23% between 600 and 700, and 3% above 700; Math--22% below 500, 42% between 500 and 599, 30% between 600 and 700, and 5% above 700. The ACT scores were 26% below 21, 28% between 21 and 23, 24% between 24 and 26, 13% between 27 and 28, and 9% above 28. 61% of the current freshmen were in the top fifth of their class; 84% were in the top two fifths.

Requirements: The SAT I or ACT is required. A GPA of 2.5 is required. Applicants must have 16 academic credits, including a recommended 4 years of high school English, 3 of math, 2 of the same foreign language, 2 of lab science, 1 of U.S history or government, and 4 additional academic courses. An essay is required; an interview is recommended. An audition is necessary for music students. The GED is accepted. Applications are accepted on computer disk and online via XAPplication and the school's web site. AP and CLEP credits are accepted.

Procedure: Freshmen are admitted fall and spring. Entrance exams should be taken in the spring of the junior year or fall of the senior year. There are early action and deferred admissions plans. Early action applications should be filed by December 15; regular applications, by February 15 for fall entry and December 15 for spring entry, along with a $50 fee. Notification of early action is sent in January; regular decision, on a rolling basis.

Financial Aid: In 1999-2000, 78% of all freshmen and 80% of continuing students received some form of financial aid. 71% of freshmen and 73% of continuing students received need-based aid. 36% of undergraduates work part time. Average annual earnings from campus work are $1300. Pacific is a member of CSS. The FAFSA is required. The fall application deadline is February 15.

Computers: The mainframe is a SUN Enterprise 450. 185 PCs, primarily IBMs and Macs, are available for student use in residence halls and computer labs. All students may access the system any time. There are no time limits and no fees. It is recommended that students in pharmacy have PCs.

UNIVERSITY OF THE SCIENCES IN PHILADELPHIA
Philadelphia, PA 19104-4495   **(215) 596-8810**
                                        (800) (888) 996-8747; Fax: (215) 596-8821

Full-time: 701 men, 1305 women	**Faculty:** 127; IIA, av$
Part-time: 37 men, 62 women	**Ph.D.s:** 70%
Graduate: 40 men, 80 women	**Student/Faculty:** 16 to 1
Year: semesters, summer session	**Tuition:** $14,684
Application Deadline: open	**Room & Board:** $6902
Freshman Class: 1205 applied, 931 accepted, 323 enrolled	
SAT I Verbal/Math: 540/570	**ACT:** 24 **VERY COMPETITIVE**

University of the Sciences in Philadelphia, founded in 1821, is a private institution offering degree programs in the health sciences, pharmaceutical sciences, and arts and sciences. There are 4 undergraduate and 1 graduate school. In addition to regional accreditation, USP has baccalaureate program accreditation with ACPE and APTA. The library contains 73,571 volumes, 420 microform items, and 150 audiovisual forms, CDs, and subscribes to 809 periodicals. Computerized library services include the card catalog, interlibrary loans, and database searching. Special learning facilities include a learning resource center and and a pharmaceutical history museum. The 30-acre campus is in an urban area in the

University City section of Philadelphia. Including residence halls, there are 16 buildings.

Programs of Study: USP confers B.S. and B.S.Ed. degrees. Master's and doctoral degrees are also awarded. Bachelor's degrees are awarded in BIOLOGICAL SCIENCE (biochemistry, biology/biological science, microbiology, and toxicology), BUSINESS (marketing management), COMMUNICATIONS AND THE ARTS (technical and business writing), COMPUTER AND PHYSICAL SCIENCE (chemistry), ENGINEERING AND ENVIRONMENTAL DESIGN (environmental science), HEALTH PROFESSIONS (medical laboratory technology, medical technology, occupational therapy, pharmacy, physical therapy, physician's assistant, and premedicine), SOCIAL SCIENCE (psychology). Pharmacy and physical therapy are the strongest academically. Pharmacy, physical therapy, and biology are the largest.

Special: USP offers 5-year integrated professional program in occupational therapy, physical therapy, and physician's assistant. Internships are required in all health science disciplines. A one-year open major program is offered, as is a program of curriculum and advisement to prepare students to enter medical school. Students may elect a minor in communications, economics, psychology, sociology, math, physics, or computer science. There are 4 national honor societies.

Admissions: 77% of the 1999-2000 applicants were accepted. The SAT I scores for the 1999-2000 freshman class were: Verbal--22% below 500, 59% between 500 and 599, 17% between 600 and 700, and 2% above 700; Math--15% below 500, 51% between 500 and 599, 32% between 600 and 700, and 2% above 700.

Requirements: The SAT I is required. USP requires applicants to be in the upper 50% of their class. A GPA of 3.0 is required. Applicants must be high school graduates or hold the GED. Minimum academic requirements include 4 credits in English, 1 credit each in American history and social science, and 4 credits in academic electives. Math requirements include 2 years of algebra and 1 year of plane geometry; the college strongly recommends an additional year of higher-level math, such as precalculus or calculus. 3 science credits are required; strongly recommended are 1 credit each in biology, chemistry, and physics. All applicants must submit a personal 300-to 400- word essay. Applicants to the 5-year physical therapy and physician assistant programs must present evidence of at least 20 hours of volunteer experience in a clinical setting. Applications are accepted on-line via Apply Tech or CollegeLink. Applications can be downloaded from the USP web site. AP and CLEP credits are accepted. Important factors in the admissions decision are advanced placement or honor courses, personality/intangible qualities, and geographic diversity.

Procedure: Freshmen are admitted in the fall. Entrance exams should be taken at the end of the junior year and the fall of the senior year. There is a deferred admissions plan. Application deadlines are open; there is a $45 application fee. Notification is sent on a rolling basis. 10% of all applicants are on a waiting list.

Financial Aid: In 1999-2000, 94% of all freshmen and 74% of continuing students received some form of financial aid. 76% of freshmen and 61% of continuing students received need-based aid. The average freshman award was $8577. Of that total, scholarships or need-based grants averaged $5500 ($16,180 maximum); loans averaged $3850 ($10,500 maximum); work contracts averaged $800. (maximum), and other funds averaged $1320 ($10,000 maximum). All of undergraduates work part time. Average annual earnings from campus work are $640. The average financial indebtedness of the 1999 graduate was $34,000. The FAFSA and parent and student federal tax returns are required. The fall application deadline is March 15.

Computers: There are more than 35 PCs available in several computer centers. All students may access the system. There are no time limits and no fees.

UNIVERSITY OF TULSA
Tulsa, OK 74104-3189

(918) 631-2307
(800) 331-3050; Fax: (918) 631-5003

Full-time: 1260 men, 1396 women	**Faculty:** 274
Part-time: 138 men, 130 women	**Ph.D.s:** 96%
Graduate: 680 men, 588 women	**Student/Faculty:** 10 to 1
Year: semesters, summer session	**Tuition:** $13,480
Application Deadline: open	**Room & Board:** $4660
Freshman Class: 2037 applied, 1623 accepted, 615 enrolled	
SAT I Verbal/Math: 620/620	**ACT:** 26 **VERY COMPETITIVE+**

The University of Tulsa, founded in 1894, is a private, comprehensive institution offering more than 70 major areas of study through its programs in liberal arts and sciences, engineering and natural sciences, and business administration. There are 3 undergraduate and 2 graduate schools. In addition to regional accreditation, TU has baccalaureate program accreditation with AACSB, ABET, CSAB, NASM, NCATE, and NLN. The 2 libraries contain 959,685 volumes, 2,930,495 microform items, and 13,025 audiovisual forms/CDs, and subscribe to 7239 periodicals. Computerized library services include the card catalog, interlibrary loans, and database searching. Special learning facilities include an art gallery, radio station, and TV station. The 200-acre campus is in an urban area in the city of Tulsa. Including residence halls, there are 35 buildings.

Programs of Study: TU confers B.A., B.S., B.F.A., B.Mus., B.Mus.Ed., B.S. B.A., B.S.C.E., B.S.E.E., B.S.M.E., and B.S.N. degrees. Master's and doctoral degrees are also awarded. Bachelor's degrees are awarded in BIOLOGICAL SCIENCE (biology/biological science), BUSINESS (accounting, banking and finance, international business management, management information systems, management science, marketing/retailing/merchandising, and sports management), COMMUNICATIONS AND THE ARTS (art, communications, design, English, French, German, music, musical theater, and Spanish), COMPUTER AND PHYSICAL SCIENCE (chemistry, computer programming, computer science, geology, geoscience, information sciences and systems, mathematics, and physics), EDUCATION (athletic training, education of the deaf and hearing impaired, elementary, and music), ENGINEERING AND ENVIRONMENTAL DESIGN (chemical engineering, electrical/electronics engineering, engineering physics, environmental science, mechanical engineering, and petroleum/natural gas engineering), HEALTH PROFESSIONS (nursing, premedicine, and speech pathology/audiology), SOCIAL SCIENCE (anthropology, economics, history, international studies, philosophy, political science/government, prelaw, psychology, and sociology). Petroleum engineering, psychology, and English are the strongest academically. Biological science, accounting, and psychology are the largest.

Special: Internships are available in the Tulsa area during the school year and in cities throughout the United States during the summer. Students may participate in more than 40 study-abroad programs, most of them arranged through the Institute of European Studies. TU offers a Washington semester, B.A.-B.S. degrees, cross-registration with the 3 undergraduate schools, dual and student-designed majors, nondegree study, work-study programs, and pass/fail options. There are 35 national honor societies, including Phi Beta Kappa, and a freshman honors program. All departments have honors programs.

Admissions: 80% of the 1999-2000 applicants were accepted. The SAT I scores for the 1999-2000 freshman class were: Verbal--9% below 500, 35% between 500 and 599, 37% between 600 and 700, and 19% above 700; Math--13% below

500, 30% between 500 and 599, 39% between 600 and 700, and 18% above 700. The ACT scores were 9% below 21, 22% between 21 and 23, 29% between 24 and 26, 16% between 27 and 28, and 24% above 28. 69% of the current freshmen were in the top fifth of their class; 88% were in the top two fifths. There were 21 National Merit finalists. 140 freshmen graduated first in their class.

Requirements: The SAT I or ACT is required. TU requires applicants to be in the upper 33% of their class. A GPA of 3.0 is required. Graduation from an accredited secondary school or satisfactory scores on the GED are also required for admission. The school recommends a minimum of 15 academic credits, including 4 years of English, 3 to 4 years each of math, science, and social studies (including history), and 2 years of a single foreign language. An essay and an interview are highly recommended. An audition or a portfolio is required for students applying for music, theater, or art scholarships. The university accepts applications on computer disk through CollegeLink as well as on-line.

Procedure: Freshmen are admitted fall, spring, and summer. Entrance exams should be taken during spring of the junior year or fall of the senior year. There is a deferred admissions plan. Application deadlines are open. There is a $25 fee. Notification is sent on a rolling basis.

Financial Aid: In 1999-2000, 88% of all freshmen and 71% of continuing students received some form of financial aid. 54% of freshmen and 45% of continuing students received need-based aid. The average freshman award was $12,250. Of that total, scholarships or need-based grants averaged $4000 ($17,880 maximum); loans averaged $2400 ($6625 maximum); and work contracts averaged $1850 ($2300 maximum). 16% of undergraduates work part time. Average annual earnings from campus work are $1200. The average financial indebtedness of the 1999 graduate was $21,376. TU is a member of CSS. The FAFSA and the college's own financial statement are required. The fall application deadline is April 1.

Computers: The mainframe is a DEC VAX 6630. There are more than 500 PCs and Macs available throughout the campus. Connections are available in university housing, as are E-mail and Internet access. All students may access the system 24 hours per day. There are no time limits and no fees.

UNIVERSITY OF UTAH
Salt Lake City, UT 84112
(801) 581-7281; (800) 444-8638

Full-time: 7091 men, 5844 women	**Faculty:** 1456; I, -$
Part-time: 5262 men, 3759 women	**Ph.D.s:** 97%
Graduate: 2774 men, 2258 women	**Student/Faculty:** 9 to 1
Year: quarters, summer session	**Tuition:** $2351 ($7118)
Application Deadline: July 1	**Room & Board:** $4680
Freshman Class: 5540 applied, 5225 accepted, 2424 enrolled	
SAT I Verbal/Math: 550/490	**ACT:** 23 **COMPETITIVE**

University of Utah, founded in 1850, is a part of the Utah System of Higher Education. The university offers undergraduate degrees through the colleges of architecture, business, education, engineering, fine arts, health, humanities, nursing, medicine, mines and earth sciences, pharmacy, science, and social and behavioral science. There are 13 undergraduate and 15 graduate schools. In addition to regional accreditation, the university has baccalaureate program accreditation with AACSB, ABET, ACPE, ADA, APTA, ASLA, CSWE, NAAB, NASM, NCATE, NLN, and NRPA. The 3 libraries contain 3,497,121 volumes, 3,344,499 microform items, and 47,418 audiovisual forms/CDs, and subscribe to 21,807 periodicals. Computerized library services include the card catalog, interlibrary loans, and database searching. Special learning facilities include a learning resource center, art gallery, natural history museum, radio station, TV station, and an arboretum. The 1535-acre campus is in an urban area in Salt Lake City. Including residence halls, there are 303 buildings.

Programs of Study: The university confers B.A., B.S., B.F.A., and B.U.S. degrees. Master's and doctoral degrees are also awarded. Bachelor's degrees are awarded in BIOLOGICAL SCIENCE (biology/biological science), BUSINESS (accounting, banking and finance, management science, marketing/retailing/merchandising, and recreation and leisure services), COMMUNICATIONS AND THE ARTS (art history and appreciation, Chinese, classics, communications, dance, dramatic arts, English, film arts, French, German, Japanese, linguistics, music, performing arts, Russian, Spanish, and speech/debate/rhetoric), COMPUTER AND PHYSICAL SCIENCE (atmospheric sciences and meteorology, chemistry, computer science, geology, geophysics and seismology, mathematics, and physics), EDUCATION (art, athletic training, early childhood, elementary, health, home economics, and special), ENGINEERING AND ENVIRONMENTAL DESIGN (architecture, bioengineering, chemical engineering, civil engineering, computer engineering, electrical/electronics engineering, environmental engineering, geological engineering, materials engineering, mechanical engineering, metallurgical engineering, mining and mineral engineering, and urban planning technology), HEALTH PROFESSIONS (medical laboratory science, nursing, pharmacy, physical therapy, and speech pathology/audiology), SOCIAL SCIENCE (anthropology, Asian/Oriental studies, behavioral science, child care/child and family studies, economics, family/consumer studies, geography, history, Middle Eastern studies, philosophy, political science/government, psychology, social science, sociology, and women's studies). Social and behavioral sciences are the largest.

Special: The university offers numerous opportunities for cooperative programs, cross-registration through the Western Interstate Commission for Higher Education (WICHE), study abroad, internships, work-study and accelerated degree programs, and B.A.-B.S. degrees. Also available are the general studies degree, a Washington semester, student-designed and dual majors, credit for telecourses and military experience, nondegree study, and pass/fail options. There are 32 national honor societies, including Phi Beta Kappa, a freshman honors program, and 1 departmental honors program.

Admissions: 94% of the 1999-2000 applicants were accepted. The SAT I scores for the 1999-2000 freshman class were: Verbal--40% below 500, 40% between 500 and 599, and 20% between 600 and 700; Math--60% below 500, 20% between 500 and 599, and 20% between 600 and 700. The ACT scores were 30% below 21, 29% between 21 and 23, 24% between 24 and 26, 11% between 27 and 28, and 6% above 28. There were 35 National Merit finalists and 152 semifinalists.

Requirements: The SAT I or ACT is required. The ACT, with a minimum composite score of 20, is preferred. The SAT I, with a minimum composite score of 880, is accepted. A GPA of 2.0 is required. In addition, applicants must be graduates of an accredited secondary school or have the GED. 15 academic credits are required, including 4 years each of English and electives, 2 years each of foreign language, math, and science/lab, and 1 year of U.S. history. AP and CLEP credits are accepted.

Procedure: Freshmen are admitted to all sessions. Entrance exams should be taken in the junior year of high school. There are early admissions and deferred admissions plans. Applications should be filed by July 1 for fall entry, November 15 for winter entry, February 15 for spring entry, and May 15 for summer entry, along with a $30 fee. Notification is sent 2 to 3 weeks aftrr the application is received. A waiting list is an active part of the admissions procedure.

Financial Aid: In a recent year, 91% of freshmen and 82% of continuing students received need-based aid. The average freshman award was $3146. Of that total, scholarships or need-based grants averaged $1378 ($6000 maximum); loans averaged $3146 ($5000 maximum); and work contracts averaged $1500 ($4000 maximum). 13% of undergraduates work part time. Average annual earnings from campus work are $1500. The average financial indebtedness of a recent year's graduate was $13,000. The university is a member of CSS. The FAFSA is required. The fall application deadline is February 15.

Computers: The mainframe is an IBM 3090. There are 900 PCs for student use located in the library, engineering, business, student housing, student union, and math buildings. Other facilities include an IBM 9090 Model 600-S supercomputer, 25 mainframes, 75 minicomputers, and 125 workstation computers. All students may access the system 24 hours per day. There are no time limits and no fees.

UNIVERSITY OF VIRGINIA
Charlottesville, VA 22906   (804) 982-3200; Fax: (804) 924-3587

Full-time: 5847 men, 6793 women	**Faculty:** 923; I, ++$
Part-time: 371 men, 559 women	**Ph.D.s:** 93%
Graduate: 3662 men, 5201 women	**Student/Faculty:** 14 to 1
Year: semesters, summer session	**Tuition:** $4130 ($16,603)
Application Deadline: January 2	**Room & Board:** $4589
Freshman Class: 16,461 applied, 5588 accepted, 2924 enrolled	
SAT I Verbal/Math: 650/660	**ACT:** 29 **MOST COMPETITIVE**

The University of Virginia, founded in 1819, is a public institution with undergraduate programs in architecture, arts and sciences, commerce, education, engineering and applied science, and nursing. There are 6 undergraduate and 8 graduate schools. In addition to regional accreditation, UVA has baccalaureate program accreditation with AACSB, ABET, ASLA, NAAB, NASM, NCATE, and NLN. The 15 libraries contain 4,588,606 volumes, 5,161,698 microform items, and 72,854 audiovisual forms/CDs, and subscribe to 49,800 periodicals. Computerized library services include the card catalog, interlibrary loans, and database searching. Special learning facilities include a learning resource center, art gallery, radio station, TV station, and art museum. The 1138-acre campus is in a suburban area 70 miles northwest of Richmond. Including residence halls, there are 436 buildings.

Programs of Study: UVA confers B.A., B.S., B.A.R.H., B.C.P., B.I.S., B.S.C., B.S.Ed., and B.S.N. degrees. Master's and doctoral degrees are also awarded. Bachelor's degrees are awarded in BIOLOGICAL SCIENCE (biology/biological science), BUSINESS (business economics), COMMUNICATIONS AND THE ARTS (art, classics, comparative literature, dramatic arts, English, French, German, Italian, music, Slavic languages, and Spanish), COMPUTER AND PHYSICAL SCIENCE (applied mathematics, astronomy, chemistry, computer science, mathematics, and physics), EDUCATION (health and physical), ENGINEERING AND ENVIRONMENTAL DESIGN (aerospace studies, architecture, chemical engineering, city/community/regional planning, civil engineering, electrical/electronics engineering, engineering and applied science, environmental science, mechanical engineering, and systems engineering), HEALTH PROFESSIONS (nursing and speech pathology/audiology), SOCIAL SCIENCE (African American studies, anthropology, area studies, economics, history, interdisciplinary studies, international relations, philosophy, political science/government, psychology, religion, and sociology). English, history, biology, and commerce are the strongest academically. Commerce, English, and psychology are the largest.

Special: The college offers internships, study abroad in 8 countries, accelerated degree programs, B.A.-B.S. degrees in chemistry and physics, co-op programs in both aerospace and mechanical engineering, and nondegree study. Dual majors in most arts and sciences programs, student-designed majors, an interdisciplinary major and Echols Scholars program, and pass/fail options are available. There are 24 national honor societies, including Phi Beta Kappa, a freshman honors program, and 30 departmental honors programs.

Admissions: 34% of the 1999-2000 applicants were accepted. The SAT I scores for the 1999-2000 freshman class were: Verbal--4% below 500, 20% between 500 and 599, 46% between 600 and 700, and 30% above 700; Math--2% below 500, 16% between 500 and 599, 48% between 600 and 700, and 34% above 700. 95% of the current freshmen were in the top fifth of their class; 98% were in the top two fifths. 211 freshmen graduated first in their class.

Requirements: The SAT I or ACT is required. In addition, SAT II: Subject tests in writing, math I, IC, or IIC, and a choice of foreign language, history, or science are required. With few exceptions, candidates graduate from accredited secondary schools. While the GED is accepted, it is rare for candidates for first-year admission who have this credential to be competitive in the admissions process. Applicants should complete 16 high school academic courses, including 4 courses of English, 4 courses of math, beginning with algebra I, 2 courses of physics, biology, or chemistry (3 if applying to engineering), 2 years of foreign language, and 1 course of social studies. An essay is also required. Applications may be obtained via the World Wide Web. Applications are accepted at the school's web site. AP credits are accepted. Important factors in the admissions decision are evidence of special talent, advanced placement or honor courses, and grades earned.

Procedure: Freshmen are admitted in the fall. Entrance exams should be taken by December of the senior year. There are early decision and deferred admissions plans. Early decision applications should be filed by November 1; regular applications, by January 2 for fall entry, along with a $60 fee. Notification of early decision is sent December 1; regular decision, April 1. 799 early decision candidates were accepted for the 1999-2000 class. 17% of all applicants are on a waiting list.

Financial Aid: In 1999-2000, 49% of all freshmen and 41% of continuing students received some form of financial aid. 22% of freshmen and 24% of continuing students received need-based aid. The average freshman award was $7206. Of that total, scholarships or need-based grants averaged $4400 ($24,550 maximum); loans averaged $2705 ($25,620 maximum); and work contracts averaged $101 ($1440 maximum). 25% of undergraduates work part time. Average annual earnings from campus work are $1200. The average financial indebtedness of the 1999 graduate was $13,913. The FAFSA and the college's own financial statement are required. The fall application deadline is March 1.

Computers: The mainframes include UNIX-based IBM RS/600s and Suns, which are accessible anywhere on campus and in residence hall rooms and via remote dial-up. Access to the Internet is possible from more than 30 university-operated public computing facilities with more than 900 PCs or workstations. All students may access the system 24 hours a day, 7 days a week. There are no time limits and no fees. It is recommended that all students have personal computers.

UNIVERSITY OF WASHINGTON
Seattle, WA 98195

(206) 543-9686

Full-time: 10,380 men, 11,254 women	**Faculty:** 3048; I, -$
Part-time: 1877 men, 2087 women	**Ph.D.s:** 99%
Graduate: 4986 men, 4935 women	**Student/Faculty:** 7 to 1
Year: quarters, summer session	**Tuition:** $3638 ($12,029)
Application Deadline: January 31	**Room & Board:** $4905
Freshman Class: 12,785 applied, 9817 accepted, 4515 enrolled	
SAT I Verbal/Math: 569/590 (mean)	**ACT:** 25 (mean)

VERY COMPETITIVE

The University of Washington, founded in 1861, is a state-controlled institution offering a broad range of degree programs. There are 17 undergraduate schools and 1 graduate school. In addition to regional accreditation, UW has baccalaureate program accreditation with AACSB, ABET, NCATE, and NLN. The 19 libraries contain 5,601,263 volumes, 6,432,950 microform items, and 56,295 audiovisual forms/CDs. Computerized library services include the card catalog, interlibrary loans, and database searching. Special learning facilities include a learning resource center, art gallery, natural history museum, planetarium, radio station, state museum, full teaching hospital, marine science lab, 200-acre arboretum, and field research forest. The 703-acre campus is in an urban area 5 miles from downtown Seattle. Including residence halls, there are 213 buildings.

Programs of Study: UW confers B.A., B.S., B.A.B.A., B.C.H.S., B.L.Arch., B. Mus., B.S.A.& A., B.S.B.C., B.S.Cer.E., B.S.Comp.E., B.S.F., B.S.Fish., B.S. I.E., B.S.M.E., B.S.Med.Tech., B.S.Met.E., and B.S.Nur. degrees. Master's and doctoral degrees are also awarded. Bachelor's degrees are awarded in AGRICULTURE (fishing and fisheries, forest engineering, forestry production and processing, and wood science), BIOLOGICAL SCIENCE (biochemistry, biology/biological science, botany, microbiology, neurosciences, and zoology), BUSINESS (accounting, banking and finance, business administration and management, business economics, international business management, marketing/retailing/merchandising, and personnel management), COMMUNICATIONS AND THE ARTS (art history and appreciation, classics, communications, comparative literature, dance, dramatic arts, English, fiber/textiles/weaving, French, Germanic languages and literature, graphic design, Italian, Japanese, jazz, metal/jewelry, music history and appreciation, music performance, painting, photography, printmaking, Scandinavian languages, sculpture, Slavic languages, Spanish, speech/debate/rhetoric, studio art, and technical and business writing), COMPUTER AND PHYSICAL SCIENCE (astronomy, atmospheric sciences and meteorology, computer science, geology, information sciences and systems, mathematics, oceanography, physics, quantitative methods, and statistics), EDUCATION (music), ENGINEERING AND ENVIRONMENTAL DESIGN (aeronautical engineering, ceramic engineering, chemical engineering, civil engineering, computer engineering, construction engineering, electrical/electronics engineering, engineering, landscape architecture/design, materials science, ocean engineering, and paper and pulp science), HEALTH PROFESSIONS (dental hygiene, environmental health science, health care administration, medical laboratory technology, nursing, and speech pathology/audiology), SOCIAL SCIENCE (African American studies, anthropology, Asian/American studies, Asian/Oriental studies, Canadian studies, economics, ethnic studies, food science, geography, history, international relations, Judaic studies, liberal arts/general studies, Near Eastern studies, peace studies, philosophy, political science/government, psychology, religion, Russian and Slavic studies, social work, sociology, South

Asian studies, and women's studies). Biological and life sciences, computer science and engineering, and physics are the strongest academically. Business, political science, and art are the largest.

Special: A wide variety of internships, including those for minority students in engineering, concurrent dual majors, study abroad in 21 countries, a Washington semester, a general studies degree, and co-op programs are available. Work-study programs, credit/no credit options, student-designed majors, accelerated degree programs, nondegree study, and a 5-year B.A.-B.S. degree also are offered. There are 20 national honor societies, including Phi Beta Kappa, a freshman honors program, and 36 departmental honors programs.

Admissions: 77% of the 1999-2000 applicants were accepted. The SAT I scores for the 1999-2000 freshman class were: Verbal--22% below 500, 43% between 500 and 599, 28% between 600 and 700, and 7% above 700; Math--15% below 500, 40% between 500 and 599, 35% between 600 and 700, and 10% above 700. The ACT scores were 16% below 21, 24% between 21 and 23, 28% between 24 and 26, 15% between 27 and 28, and 17% above 28. 72% of the current freshmen were in the top fifth of their class; 96% were in the top two fifths.

Requirements: The SAT I or ACT is required. A GPA of 2.0 is required. Applicants must have completed 15 academic units, including 4 years of English, 3 each of math and social sciences, 2 each of foreign language and science, and 1/2 year each in fine/visual performing arts and electives. Admission is based on an indexing system. Applications are accepted on computer disk via CollegeLink or ExPAN. AP credits are accepted. Important factors in the admissions decision are advanced placement or honor courses and evidence of special talent.

Procedure: Freshmen are admitted to all sessions. Entrance exams should be taken by December of the senior year. There is an early admissions plan. Applications should be filed by January 31 for fall entry, September 15 for winter entry, December 15 for spring entry, and January 31 for summer entry, along with a $35 fee. Notification is sent March 15.

Financial Aid: UW is a member of CSS. The CSS/Profile is required. The fall application deadline is February 28.

Computers: The mainframes are an IBM 3090, several DEC VAX systems, and a Sequent. There are several public labs containing 10,000 Macs, IBM, Sun, DEC, and NeXT PCs and terminals. Dial-up is also used because most students live off campus. All students may access the system 24 hours daily. There are no time limits and no fees.

UNIVERSITY OF WISCONSIN/EAU CLAIRE
Eau Claire, WI 54701   (715) 836-5415; Fax: (715) 836-2409

Full-time: 3620 men, 5440 women	**Faculty:** 415; IIA, av$
Part-time: 359 men, 500 women	**Ph.D.s:** 88%
Graduate: 130 men, 346 women	**Student/Faculty:** 15 to 1
Year: semesters, summer session	**Tuition:** $3210 ($10,074)
Application Deadline: open	**Room & Board:** $3301
Freshman Class: 5690 applied, 4195 accepted, 2016 enrolled	
SAT I Verbal/Math: 540/550	**ACT:** 23 **VERY COMPETITIVE**

The University of Wisconsin/Eau Claire, founded in 1916, is a public institution offering programs in the liberal arts and sciences, business, teacher education, nursing, music, and the fine arts. There are 6 undergraduate schools. In addition to regional accreditation, UW/Eau Claire has baccalaureate program accreditation with AACSB, ACEJMC, CSWE, NASM, and NLN. The library contains 540,294 volumes, 1,238,402 microform items, and 61,809 audiovisual forms/CDs, and subscribes to 1543 periodicals. Computerized library services include the card catalog, interlibrary loans, and database searching. Special learning facilities include a learning resource center, art gallery, planetarium, radio station, TV station, geographic research center, bird museum, and observatory. The 333-acre campus is in an urban area 95 miles east of Minneapolis, Minnesota. Including residence halls, there are 26 buildings.

Programs of Study: UW/Eau Claire confers B.A., B.S., B.B.A., B.F.A., B.M., B.M.E., B.M.T.H., B.S.E.Ph., B.S.H.C.A., B.S.M.T., B.S.N., and B.S.W. degrees. Associate and master's degrees are also awarded. Bachelor's degrees are awarded in BIOLOGICAL SCIENCE (biochemistry and biology/biological science), BUSINESS (accounting, banking and finance, business administration and management, business economics, and marketing/retailing/merchandising), COMMUNICATIONS AND THE ARTS (advertising, art, broadcasting, communications, dramatic arts, English, fine arts, French, German, journalism, music, photography, and Spanish), COMPUTER AND PHYSICAL SCIENCE (chemistry, computer programming, computer science, geology, information sciences and systems, mathematics, physical sciences, physics, and statistics), EDUCATION (art, business, elementary, foreign languages, music, physical, science, secondary, and special), HEALTH PROFESSIONS (health care administration, music therapy, nursing, public health, and speech pathology/audiology), SOCIAL SCIENCE (American Indian studies, criminal justice, economics, geography, history, Latin American studies, philosophy, political science/government, psychology, religion, social science, social work, and sociology). Elementary education, nursing, and biology are the largest.

Special: Numerous internships, work-study programs, and study abroad in 13 countries are offered. Dual majors and interdisciplinary majors are possible. Credit by examination, nondegree study, and pass/fail options are offered. There are 27 national honor societies, a freshman honors program, and 11 departmental honors programs.

Admissions: 74% of the 1999-2000 applicants were accepted. The SAT I scores for the 1999-2000 freshman class were: Verbal--20% below 500, 53% between 500 and 599, 25% between 600 and 700, and 2% above 700; Math--15% below 500, 50% between 500 and 599, 28% between 600 and 700, and 7% above 700. The ACT scores were 14% below 21, 39% between 21 and 23, 28% between 24 and 26, 12% between 27 and 28, and 7% above 28. 43% of the current freshmen were in the top fifth of their class; 84% were in the top two fifths. There were 4 National Merit finalists. 52 freshmen graduated first in their class.

Requirements: The SAT I or ACT is recommended. UW/Eau Claire requires applicants to be in the upper 50% of their class. Applicants should graduate from an accredited secondary school or present its equivalent, with 17 academic credits, including 4 in English, 3 each in social studies, college preparatory math, and science, and 2 years of a single foreign language. Students must graduate in the upper 50% of their class or present a minimum composite score of 1100 on the SAT I or 22 on the ACT. Probationary admission is sometimes offered for the spring semester. Music majors or minors must audition. Students may apply online at the school's web site. AP and CLEP credits are accepted. Important factors in the admissions decision are advanced placement or honor courses, recommendations by school officials, and leadership record.

Procedure: Freshmen are admitted to all sessions. Entrance exams should be taken by December of the senior year. There is an early admissions plan. Application deadlines are open; the fee is $35. Notification is sent on a rolling basis. 14% of all applicants are on a waiting list.

Financial Aid: In 1999-2000, 61% of all freshmen and 59% of continuing students received some form of financial aid. 44% of all students received need-based aid. The average freshman award was $5085. Of that total, scholarships or need-based grants averaged $2809 ($9270 maximum); loans averaged $2912 ($14,058 maximum); and work contracts averaged $2029 ($4275 maximum). 97% of undergraduates work part time. Average annual earnings from campus work are $1076. The average financial indebtedness of the 1999 graduate was $13,252. The FAFSA is required. The fall application deadline is April 15.

Computers: The mainframe is a Unisys NX5602-22. Students may use computer facilities for classroom assignments, research, network access to other resources, and mail. Terminals and PCs are located across campus. There are 17 supported labs plus labs in housing and the library. Dial-in access is offered. All students may access the system 24 hours a day, 7 days per week. There are no time limits and no fees.

UNIVERSITY OF WISCONSIN/LA CROSSE
La Crosse, WI 54601
(608) 785-8067; Fax: (608) 785-8940

Full-time: 3337 men, 4625 women	**Faculty:** 350; IIA, av$
Part-time: 353 men, 335 women	**Ph.D.s:** 84%
Graduate: 251 men, 408 women	**Student/Faculty:** 23 to 1
Year: semesters, summer session	**Tuition:** $3239 ($8890)
Application Deadline: open	**Room & Board:** $3300
Freshman Class: 5007 applied, 3503 accepted, 1639 enrolled	
ACT: 24	**VERY COMPETITIVE**

The University of Wisconsin/La Crosse, founded in 1909, is a public institution offering undergraduate and graduate studies in arts and sciences, health and human services, business administration, education, phys ed and recreation, professional development, and educational administration. There are 6 undergraduate schools and 1 graduate school. In addition to regional accreditation, UW-L has baccalaureate program accreditation with AACSB, APTA, NASM, and NCATE. The library contains 862,831 volumes, 1,073,625 microform items, and 1358 audiovisual forms/CDs, and subscribes to 3974 periodicals. Computerized library services include the card catalog, interlibrary loans, and database searching. Special learning facilities include a learning resource center, art gallery, planetarium, radio station, TV station, and the River Studies Center. The 119-acre campus is in a small town 140 miles west of Madison and 150 miles southeast of Minneapolis/St. Paul. Including residence halls, there are 31 buildings.

Programs of Study: UW-L confers B.A. and B.S. degrees. Associate and master's degrees are also awarded. Bachelor's degrees are awarded in BIOLOGICAL SCIENCE (biology/biological science and microbiology), BUSINESS (accounting, banking and finance, business administration and management, international business management, and marketing/retailing/merchandising), COMMUNICATIONS AND THE ARTS (art, communications, dramatic arts, English, fine arts, French, music, Spanish, and speech/debate/rhetoric), COMPUTER AND PHYSICAL SCIENCE (chemistry, computer science, information sciences and systems, mathematics, and physics), EDUCATION (elementary, health, physical, secondary, and social studies), HEALTH PROFESSIONS (medical laboratory technology, nuclear medical technology, occupational therapy, physician's assistant, radiation therapy, and recreation therapy), SOCIAL SCIENCE (archeology, economics, geography, German area studies, history, parks and recreation management, philosophy, political science/government, psychology, public administration, social work, and sociology). Microbiology, nuclear medicine technology, and physics are the strongest academically. Business administration, elementary education, and biology are the largest.

Special: Cooperative programs and cross-registration are available with Viterbo College. There are study-abroad programs in 8 countries and an international student exchange program. UW-L also offers a 3-2 engineering degree with the University of Wisconsin/Madison, the University of Wisconsin/Milwaukee, and the University of Minnesota, work-study programs, internships, nondegree study, credit by exam, and pass/fail options. There are 10 national honor societies, a freshman honors program, and 11 departmental honors programs.

Admissions: 70% of the 1999-2000 applicants were accepted. The ACT scores for the 1999-2000 freshman class were: 9% below 21, 39% between 21 and 23, 34% between 24 and 26, 12% between 27 and 28, and 6% above 28. 50% of the current freshmen were in the top fifth of their class; 91% were in the top two fifths. 29 freshmen graduated first in their class.

Requirements: The ACT is required. UW-L requires applicants to be in the upper 40% of their class. A GPA of 3.2 is required. Candidates must be graduates of an accredited secondary school or hold a GED certificate. They must have completed 17 academic credits, including 4 courses in English, 3 each in social studies and science, 2 in algebra and 1 in geometry, and 3 other academic courses. Students completing rigorous courses, including in the senior year, will be stronger candidates for admission. Students must rank in the top 35% of their high school graduating class and score at least 22 on the ACT, or rank in the top 40% and score 23 on the ACT. Applications are accepted on-line. AP and CLEP credits are accepted. Important factors in the admissions decision are advanced placement or honor courses, leadership record, and recommendations by school officials.

Procedure: Freshmen are admitted to all sessions. Entrance exams should be taken at the end of the junior year or at the beginning of the senior year. Application deadlines are open; there is a $35 fee. Notification is sent on a rolling basis. 10% of all applicants are on a waiting list.

Financial Aid: In 1999-2000, 53% of all freshmen and 58% of continuing students received some form of financial aid. 46% of freshmen and 52% of continuing students received need-based aid. The average freshman award was $3830. Of that total, scholarships or need-based grants averaged $860 ($4100 maximum); loans averaged $2110 ($2625 maximum); and work contracts averaged $980 ($1400 maximum). 79% of undergraduates work part time. Average annual earnings from campus work are $980. The average financial indebtedness of the 1999 graduate was $12,800. The FAFSA, the university's own financial statement, and tax returns are required. The fall application deadline is March 15.

Computers: The mainframe is a Unisys 4600. There are 500 PCs, primarily Dell, Compaq, NEXT, and Mac, available in open labs and residence halls. All students have access to E-mail and the Internet. All students may access the system 24 hours a day. There are no time limits and no fees.

UNIVERSITY OF WISCONSIN/MADISON
Madison, WI 53706   (608) 262-3961

Full-time: 11,859 men, 13,178 women	**Faculty:** 2301; I, +$
Part-time: 276 men, 293 women	**Ph.D.s:** 97%
Graduate: 11,000 men and women	**Student/Faculty:** 11 to 1
Year: semesters, summer session	**Tuition:** $4056 ($12,806)
Application Deadline: February 1	**Room & Board:** $4206
Freshman Class: 17,625 applied, 12,008 accepted, 5625 enrolled	
SAT I Verbal/Math: 620/640	**ACT:** 27 **HIGHLY COMPETITIVE**

The University of Wisconsin/Madison, founded in 1849, is a public, land-grant institution offering undergraduate and graduate study in almost every major field. Some of the information in this profile is approximate. There are 9 undergraduate and 4 graduate schools. In addition to regional accreditation, Wisconsin has baccalaureate program accreditation with AACSB, ABET, ACEJMC, AHEA, ASLA, CSWE, NASAD, NASM, NCATE, and NLN. The 40 libraries contain 5, 800,000 volumes and 1,300,000 microform items, and subscribe to 55,000 periodicals. Computerized library services include the card catalog and database searching. Special learning facilities include a learning resource center, art gallery, natural history museum, planetarium, radio station, TV station, and arboretum, several wildlife areas, 40,000 acres of agricultural research and teaching areas, and 2 limnology research and teaching facilities. The 1000-acre campus is in an urban area 75 miles west of Milwaukee and 150 miles north of Chicago. Including residence halls, there are 192 buildings.

Programs of Study: Wisconsin confers B.A., B.S., B.Art Ed., B.B.A., B.F.A., B.M., B.S.Ch., B.S.E., and B.S.P. degrees. Master's and doctoral degrees are also awarded. Bachelor's degrees are awarded in AGRICULTURE (agricultural business management, agricultural economics, agricultural mechanics, animal science, conservation and regulation, dairy science, forestry and related sciences, horticulture, poultry science, and soil science), BIOLOGICAL SCIENCE (bacteriology, biochemistry, botany, entomology, genetics, microbiology, molecular biology, nutrition, plant pathology, toxicology, wildlife biology, and zoology), BUSINESS (accounting, banking and finance, business administration and management, insurance and risk management, marketing/retailing/merchandising, real estate, recreation and leisure services, and retailing), COMMUNICATIONS AND THE ARTS (African languages, art history and appreciation, Chinese, classics, communications, comparative literature, dramatic arts, English, French, German, Greek, Hebrew, Italian, Japanese, journalism, Latin, linguistics, music, Polish, Portuguese, Russian, and Spanish), COMPUTER AND PHYSICAL SCIENCE (actuarial science, applied mathematics, astronomy, atmospheric sciences and meteorology, chemistry, computer science, geology, information sciences and systems, mathematics, physics, quantitative methods, and statistics), EDUCATION (agricultural, art, elementary, physical, and secondary), ENGINEERING AND ENVIRONMENTAL DESIGN (agricultural engineering, biomedical engineering, cartography, chemical engineering, civil engineering, electrical/electronics engineering, engineering mechanics, engineering physics, geological engineering, industrial engineering, interior design, landscape architecture/design, materials science, mechanical engineering, metallurgical engineering, nuclear engineering, and textile technology), HEALTH PROFESSIONS (medical laboratory technology, medical science, nursing, occupational therapy, pharmacy, physician's assistant, and speech pathology/audiology), SOCIAL SCIENCE (African American studies, anthropology, Asian/Oriental studies, behavioral science, child care/child and family studies, consumer services, dietetics, economics, family/consumer studies, food science, geography, history, history of science, humanities, international relations, Judaic studies, Latin American studies, philosophy, political science/government, psychology, rural sociology, Scandinavian studies, social work, sociology, South Asian studies, textiles and clothing, and women's studies). Political science, psychology, and English are the largest.

Special: Co-op programs in engineering and internships in political science in Washington, D.C., and the state capital are possible. Study abroad is offered in more than 40 countries in Europe, Asia, and South America. Work-study programs, accelerated degrees, credit by examination, and pass/fail options are available. Students in the College of Letters and Science may select dual or self-designed majors, or an integrated liberal studies program. There are 24 national honor societies, including Phi Beta Kappa, and a freshman honors program.

Admissions: 68% of the 1999-2000 applicants were accepted. The SAT I scores for the 1999-2000 freshman class were: Verbal--6% below 500, 31% between 500 and 599, 45% between 600 and 700, and 17% above 700; Math--6% below 500, 22% between 500 and 599, 52% between 600 and 700, and 19% above 700. The ACT scores were 2% below 21, 17% between 21 and 23, 10% between 24 and 26, 36% between 27 and 28, and 35% above 28. 81% of the current freshmen were in the top fifth of their class; 99% were in the top two fifths.

Requirements: The ACT is required for in-state students, and either the ACT or the SAT I for out-of-state students. Candidates should be graduates of an accredited secondary school or hold a GED certificate. They must have completed the following academic credits: 4 in English, 3 each in math, history, science, and social studies, 2 in a foreign language, and college-preparatory electives. Grades, rank in class, and scores, as well as rigor of senior class course selection, are considered. The school accepts applications on its own PC and Mac disks, on other vendor disks, and via CollegeLink. AP and CLEP credits are accepted. Important factors in the admissions decision are advanced placement or honor courses and evidence of special talent.

Procedure: Freshmen are admitted to all sessions. Entrance exams should be taken in the junior year. There are early admissions and deferred admissions plans. Applications should be filed by February 1 for fall entry, November 15 for spring entry, and February 1 for summer entry, along with a $35 fee. Notification is sent on a rolling basis.

Financial Aid: In 1999-2000, 60% of all freshmen and 65% of continuing students received some form of financial aid. 55% of freshmen and 62% of continuing students received need-based aid. Wisconsin is a member of CSS. The FAFSA, the college's own financial statement, and a federal income tax return are required. Check with the school for current application deadlines.

Computers: There are 2800 IBM PS/2 and Mac PCs available in 15 open labs and dormitories. There are data ports in all dormitory rooms. All students have E-mail. All students may access the system. There are no time limits and no fees.

UNIVERSITY OF WISCONSIN/STEVENS POINT

Stevens Point, WI 54481-3897

(715) 346-2441
Fax: (715) 346-2558

Full-time: 3338 men, 4223 women	**Faculty:** 365; IIA, av$
Part-time: 327 men, 512 women	**Ph.D.s:** 83%
Graduate: 138 men, 430 women	**Student/Faculty:** 21 to 1
Year: semester, Winterim, summer session	**Tuition:** $3140 ($10,004)
	Room & Board: $3524

Application Deadline: open
Freshman Class: 3918 applied, 2345 accepted, 1515 enrolled
ACT: required

VERY COMPETITIVE

The University of Wisconsin/Stevens Point, founded in 1894, offers undergraduate programs in natural resources, education, business, arts and sciences, and professional studies. There are 4 undergraduate schools and 1 graduate school. In addition to regional accreditation, UW/Stevens Point has baccalaureate program accreditation with ADA, ASLA, FIDER, NASAD, NASM, and SAF. The library contains 370,000 volumes, 845,000 microform items, and 12,000 audiovisual forms/CDs, and subscribes to 1800 periodicals. Computerized library services include the card catalog, interlibrary loans, and database searching. Special learning facilities include a learning resource center, art gallery, natural history museum, planetarium, radio station, observatory, map center, 200-acre nature preserve, groundwater center, and wellness institute. The 335-acre campus is in a small town 110 miles north of Madison. Including residence halls, there are 35 buildings.

Programs of Study: UW/Stevens Point confers B.A., B.S., B.F.A, and B.M. degrees. Associate and master's degrees are also awarded. Bachelor's degrees are awarded in AGRICULTURE (forestry and related sciences, natural resource management, and soil science), BIOLOGICAL SCIENCE (biology/biological science and wildlife biology), BUSINESS (accounting, business administration and management, and management science), COMMUNICATIONS AND THE ARTS (arts administration/management, communications, dance, dramatic arts, English, fine arts, French, German, music, and Spanish), COMPUTER AND PHYSICAL SCIENCE (chemistry, mathematics, natural sciences, and physics), EDUCATION (athletic training, early childhood, education of the exceptional child, elementary, health, home economics, music, and physical), ENGINEERING AND ENVIRONMENTAL DESIGN (interior design and paper and pulp science), HEALTH PROFESSIONS (medical technology, nursing, and speech pathology/audiology), SOCIAL SCIENCE (dietetics, economics, geography, history, international studies, liberal arts/general studies, philosophy, physical fitness/movement, political science/government, psychology, public administration, social science, sociology, and water resources). Business administration, elementary education, and communication are the largest.

Special: A co-op program in nursing is offered with UW/Eau Claire and St. Joseph's Hospital. Internships, study abroad in 7 countries, work-study programs, dual and student-designed majors, independent study, and pass/fail options are also available. Credit is given for military, life, and work experience. There are 9 national honor societies.

Admissions: 60% of the 1999-2000 applicants were accepted. The ACT scores for the 1999-2000 freshman class were: 26% below 21, 34% between 21 and 23, 26% between 24 and 26, 9% between 27 and 28, and 5% above 28. 36% of the current freshmen were in the top fifth of their class; 81% were in the top two fifths. 40 freshmen graduated first in their class.

Requirements: The ACT is required, with a composite score of 21 or above. UW/Stevens Point requires applicants to be in the upper 60% of their class. A GPA of 3.0 is required. The GED is accepted. Required academic preparation includes 4 units of English, 3 of social studies, and 2 each of math and lab science, along with 5 electives. 2 units of foreign language are recommended. An interview is suggested. Applications are accepted on-line at http://apply.wisconsin.edu. AP and CLEP credits are accepted.

Procedure: Freshmen are admitted fall and spring. Entrance exams should be taken by February of the senior year. Application deadlines are open; the fee is $35. Notification is sent on a rolling basis.

Financial Aid: 45% of freshmen and 48% of all students received need-based aid. The average freshman award was $4200. Of that total, need-based aid averaged $2607; loans averaged $2586; and need-based self-help aid averaged $3055. 30% of undergraduates work part time. The average financial indebtedness of the 1999 graduate was $12,921. The FAFSA is required. The fall application deadline is June 15.

Computers: There are more than 500 networked PCs on campus. The Internet and World Wide Web are fully accessible. Networked computers with a wide variety of software packages are available in residence halls. All students may access the system. There are no time limits and no fees.

URSINUS COLLEGE
Collegeville, PA 19426   (610) 409-3200; Fax: (610) 489-0627

Full-time: 586 men, 690 women	**Faculty:** 100; IIB, ++$
Part-time: 2 men, 12 women	**Ph.D.s:** 92%
Graduate: none	**Student/Faculty:** 12 to 1
Year: semesters	**Tuition:** $20,230
Application Deadline: February 15	**Room & Board:** $5970
Freshman Class: 1491 applied, 1158 accepted, 337 enrolled	
SAT I Verbal/Math: 575/589	**VERY COMPETITIVE**

Ursinus College, founded in 1869, is a private residential college offering programs in the liberal arts. The library contains 200,000 volumes, 155,000 microform items, and 17,500 audiovisual forms/CDs, and subscribes to 900 periodicals. Computerized library services include the card catalog, interlibrary loans, and database searching. Special learning facilities include an art gallery, radio station, and TV station. The 160-acre campus is in a suburban area 24 miles west of Philadelphia. Including residence halls, there are 50 buildings.

Programs of Study: Ursinus confers B.A. and B.S. degrees. Bachelor's degrees are awarded in BIOLOGICAL SCIENCE (biochemistry and biology/biological science), BUSINESS (accounting, business administration and management, and business economics), COMMUNICATIONS AND THE ARTS (communications, English, French, German, music, and Spanish), COMPUTER AND PHYSICAL SCIENCE (chemistry, computer science, mathematics, and physics), EDUCATION (secondary), ENGINEERING AND ENVIRONMENTAL DESIGN (environmental science), HEALTH PROFESSIONS (premedicine), SOCIAL SCIENCE (anthropology, East Asian studies, economics, history, international relations, political science/government, prelaw, psychology, religion, and sociology). Biology, English, and politics are the strongest academically. Economics, business administration, and biology are the largest.

Special: The college offers study abroad, student-designed majors, internships, a Washington semester, a Harrisburg and Philadelphia semester, dual majors, and a 3-2 engineering degree with the University of Pennsylvania and the University of Southern California. There are 14 national honor societies, including Phi Beta Kappa, and 14 departmental honors programs.

Admissions: 78% of the 1999-2000 applicants were accepted. The SAT I scores for the 1999-2000 freshman class were: Verbal--15% below 500, 46% between 500 and 599, 33% between 600 and 700, and 6% above 700; Math--10% below 500, 41% between 500 and 599, 43% between 600 and 700, and 6% above 700. 63% of the current freshmen were in the top fifth of their class; 90% were in the top two fifths. There were 7 National Merit finalists in a recent year. 4 freshmen graduated first in their class.

Requirements: The SAT I or ACT is required. SAT II: Subject tests are recommended. A GED is accepted. Applicants should prepare with 16 academic credits, including 4 years of English, 3 of math, 2 of foreign language, and 1 each of science and social studies. An interview is recommended. Applications are accepted on computer disk and on-line via Common App and ExPAN. AP and CLEP credits are accepted. Important factors in the admissions decision are advanced placement or honor courses, recommendations by school officials, and leadership record.

Procedure: Freshmen are admitted fall and spring. Entrance exams should be taken in the junior or senior year. There are early decision, early admissions, and deferred admissions plans. Early decision applications should be filed by January 15; regular applications, by February 15 for fall entry and December 1 for spring entry, along with a $30 fee. Notification of early decision is sent January 15; regular decision, April 1. 51 early decision candidates were accepted for the 1999-2000 class. 5% of all applicants are on a waiting list.

Financial Aid: In 1999-2000, 90% of all freshmen and 74% of continuing students received some form of financial aid. 80% of freshmen and 70% of continuing students received need-based aid. Scholarships or need-based grants averaged $12,915 ($19,950 maximum); loans averaged $2562 ($4125 maximum); and work contracts averaged $739 ($1500 maximum). 50% of undergraduates work part time. Average annual earnings from campus work are $1000. The average financial indebtedness of the 1999 graduate was $16,000. Ursinus is a member of CSS. The CSS/Profile and FAFSA are required. The fall application deadline is February 15.

Computers: The mainframe is a DEC VAX. 200 IBM PCs and 100 Macs are available for student use; all are linked to the VAX. All entering students receive a laptop computer. All students may access the system during library hours, a total of 102 hours per week. There are no time limits and no fees.

VALPARAISO UNIVERSITY
Valparaiso, IN 46383

(219) 464-5011
(800) (888) GO-VALPO; Fax: (219) 464-6898

Full-time: 1311 men, 1441 women	**Faculty:** 206; IIA, av$
Part-time: 83 men, 151 women	**Ph.D.s:** 90%
Graduate: 271 men, 393 women	**Student/Faculty:** 13 to 1
Year: semesters, 2 summer sessions	**Tuition:** $16,806
Application Deadline: open	**Room & Board:** $4360
Freshman Class: 3301 applied, 2536 accepted, 780 enrolled	
SAT I Verbal/Math: 592/601	**ACT:** 26 **VERY COMPETITIVE**

Valparaiso University, founded in 1859, is an independent institution affiliated with the Lutheran Church. The university offers degree programs in arts and sciences, business administration, engineering, and nursing. There are 5 undergraduate and 2 graduate schools. In addition to regional accreditation, Valpo has baccalaureate program accreditation with AACSB, ABET, CSWE, NASM, NCATE, and NLN. The 2 libraries contain 673,853 volumes, 1,717,954 microform items, and 10,863 audiovisual forms/CDs, and subscribe to 5406 periodicals. Computerized library services include the card catalog, interlibrary loans, and database searching. Special learning facilities include a learning resource center, art gallery, planetarium, radio station, TV station, and observatory, weather station, center for visual and performing arts, and nuclear physics lab. The 310-acre campus is in a small town 45 miles southeast of Chicago. Including residence halls, there are 53 buildings.

Programs of Study: Valpo confers B.A., B.S., B.Mus., B.Mus.Ed., B.S.Acc., B.S.Bus.Adm., B.S.C.E., B.S.Comp.Eng., B.S.Ed., B.S.E.E., B.S.F.A., B.S.M.E., B.S.N., B.S.P.E., and B.S.W. degrees. Associate, master's, and doctoral degrees are also awarded. Bachelor's degrees are awarded in BIOLOGICAL SCIENCE (biology/biological science), BUSINESS (accounting, banking and finance, business administration and management, international business management, international economics, marketing/retailing/merchandising, personnel management, and sports management), COMMUNICATIONS AND THE ARTS (art, broadcasting, classics, communications, dramatic arts, English, fine arts, French, German, Greek, journalism, Latin, music, photography, and Spanish), COMPUTER AND PHYSICAL SCIENCE (atmospheric sciences and meteorology, chemistry, computer science, geology, mathematics, and physics), EDUCATION (athletic training, elementary, foreign languages, middle school, music, physical, science, and secondary), ENGINEERING AND ENVIRONMENTAL DESIGN (civil engineering, electrical/electronics engineering, engineering, environmental science, and mechanical engineering), HEALTH PROFESSIONS (nursing, predentistry, and premedicine), SOCIAL SCIENCE (American studies, Asian/Oriental studies, criminology, economics, European studies, geography, history, international public service, Japanese studies, philosophy, political science/government, prelaw, psychology, religion, social work, sociology, and theological studies). Biology, engineering, and English are the strongest academically. Education, communications, and engineering are the largest.

Special: There is cross-registration with Indiana University Northwest. Valparaiso maintains cooperative programs in most majors, including one in urban studies with the Association of Midwest Colleges, as well as a United Nations semester with Drew University and a Washington semester with American University. Students may study abroad in England, Germany, Mexico, France, Greece, Namibia, Japan, and China. Internships, the B.A.-B.S. degree, work-study programs, dual majors, student-designed majors, an accelerated degree program in numerous majors, pass/fail options, and nondegree study are also available. Other special academic features include Christ College, which is an autonomous honors college. There are 6 national honor societies, a freshman honors program, and 25 departmental honors programs. All arts and sciences and engineering departments have an honors program.

Admissions: 77% of the 1999-2000 applicants were accepted. The SAT I scores for the 1999-2000 freshman class were: Verbal--13% below 500, 41% between 500 and 599, 35% between 600 and 700, and 11% above 700; Math--11% below 500, 35% between 500 and 599, 41% between 600 and 700, and 13% above 700. The ACT scores were 4% below 21, 17% between 21 and 23, 30% between 24 and 26, 21% between 27 and 28, and 28% above 28. 69% of the current freshmen were in the top fifth of their class; 91% were in the top two fifths. There were 22 National Merit finalists; 43 freshmen graduated first in their class.

Requirements: The SAT I or ACT is required. Applicants must be graduates of accredited secondary schools or have earned a GED. Valpo requires completion of 4 years of English, 3 to 4 of math, 3 of social science, 2 to 3 of a foreign language, and 2 of lab science. An essay and an interview are recommended for all applicants, and an audition is required for music majors. Students can apply online via the school's web site. AP and CLEP credits are accepted. Important factors in the admissions decision are advanced placement or honor courses, extracurricular activities record, and evidence of special talent.

Procedure: Freshmen are admitted to all sessions. Entrance exams should be taken prior to the senior year. There are early admissions and deferred admissions plans. Application deadlines are open; there is a $30 application fee. Notification is sent on a rolling basis.

Financial Aid: In 1999-2000, 78% of all freshmen and 72% of continuing students received some form of financial aid. 62% of freshmen and 65% of continuing students received need-based aid. The average freshman award was $15,189. Of that total, scholarships or need-based grants averaged $9730 ($16,280 maximum); loans averaged $3643 (maximum); and work contracts averaged $1500 (maximum). 50% of undergraduates work part time. Average annual earnings from campus work are $950. The average financial indebtedness of the 1999 graduate was $17,435. The FAFSA is required. The fall application deadline is March 1.

Computers: The mainframe is a DEC VAX 4000 Model 500A. Services available to students include academic applications, the library bibliographic system and periodic indexes, the Internet and World Wide Web, and E-mail. There are 561 student computers, primarily Pentiums, Power Macs, and 486s, located throughout the campus. UNIX workstations are available in some departments. All residence halls have 24-hour computer clusters. Remote access to university resources includes a high-speed modem pool with PPP capability. All students may access the system 7 days a week. There are no time limits and no fees. It is recommended that students in engineering have personal computers. A PC with Pentium is recommended.

VANDERBILT UNIVERSITY
Nashville, TN 37203-1700
(615) 322-2561
(800) 288-0432; Fax: (615) 343-7765

Full-time: 2706 men, 3016 women	**Faculty:** 643; I, ++$
Part-time: 26 men, 32 women	**Ph.Ds:** 96%
Graduate: 2156 men, 2086 women	**Student/Faculty:** 9 to 1
Year: semesters, summer session	**Tuition:** $23,598
Application Deadline: January 7	**Room & Board:** $8032
Freshman Class: 8494 applied, 5216 accepted, 1633 enrolled	
ACT: 27-30 (mean)	**HIGHLY COMPETITIVE**

Vanderbilt University, founded in 1873, is a private university offering programs in liberal and fine arts, business, engineering, health science, military science, religion, law, music, and teacher preparation. There are 4 undergraduate and 6 graduate schools. In addition to regional accreditation, Vanderbilt has baccalaureate program accreditation with AACSB, ABET, CAHEA, and NCATE. The 9 libraries contain 2,442,711 volumes, 2,719,759 microform items, and 27,989 audiovisual forms/CDs, and subscribe to 19,768 periodicals. Computerized library services include the card catalog, interlibrary loans, and database searching. Special learning facilities include a learning resource center, art gallery, radio station, tv station, 2 observatories, and a tv news archive. The 330-acre campus is in an urban area less than a mile and a half from downtown Nashville. Including residence halls, there are 207 buildings.

Programs of Study: Vanderbilt confers B.A., B.S., B.Eng., and B.M. degrees. Master's and doctoral degrees are also awarded. Bachelor's degrees are awarded in BIOLOGICAL SCIENCE (biology/biological science and molecular biology), COMMUNICATIONS AND THE ARTS (classical languages, classics, communications, English, fine arts, French, German, music history and appreciation, music performance, music theory and composition, Russian, Spanish, and theater design), COMPUTER AND PHYSICAL SCIENCE (chemistry, geology, mathematics, and physics), EDUCATION (early childhood, education, elementary, secondary, and special), ENGINEERING AND ENVIRONMENTAL DESIGN (bioengineering, chemical engineering, civil engineering, computer engineering, electrical/electronics engineering, engineering and applied science, and mechanical engineering), SOCIAL SCIENCE (African American studies, American studies, anthropology, child psychology/development, cognitive science, East Asian studies, economics, European studies, history, human development, interdisciplinary studies, Latin American studies, philosophy, political science/government, psychology, public affairs, religion, sociology, and urban studies). Social science, engineering, and education are the largest.

Special: Vanderbilt offers cross-registration with Fisk and Howard Universities and Meharry Medical College, study abroad in 15 countries, a Washington semester, a work-study program, B.A.-B.S. degrees, dual and student-designed majors, nondegree study, and pass/fail options. Internships, required for human development majors, are available in human service agencies, city and state government, and businesses. A 3-2 engineering degree is offered with Fisk University. The school belongs to NASA's Tennessee Space Grant Consortium, the Intercollegiate Center for Classical Studies in Rome, the Tennessee Transportation Technology Coalition (research, development, and evaluation of transportation-related initiatives), and the Southeastern Consortium of University Transportation Centers. There are 19 national honor societies, including Phi Beta Kappa, a freshman honors program, and 21 departmental honors programs.

Admissions: 61% of the 1999-2000 applicants were accepted. The SAT I scores for the 1999-2000 freshman class were: Verbal--2% below 500, 23% between 500 and 599, 58% between 600 and 700, and 17% above 700; Math--1% below 500, 15% between 500 and 599, 59% between 600 and 700, and 25% above 700. The ACT scores were 1% below 21, 4% between 21 and 23, 19% between 24 and 26, 28% between 27 and 28, and 48% above 28. 88% of the current freshmen were in the top fifth of their class; 98% were in the top two fifths. There were 103 National Merit finalists. 124 freshmen graduated first in their class.

Requirements: The SAT I or ACT is required. SAT II: Subject tests are recommended in math level I, II, or IIc, writing, and foreign language. Admission requirements vary by school. Candidates should be graduates of an accredited secondary school with a minimum of 15 academic credits. Most programs require 4 years of English, 3 of math, and 2 of a foreign language and recommend 2 of history and 1 of social studies. An essay is required. An audition is required for Blair School of Music. Applications are accepted on computer disk provided a printout is included. Students may apply on-line at www.vanderbilt.edu/admissions/apply.html. AP credits are accepted.

Procedure: Freshmen are admitted in the fall. Entrance exams should be taken in the spring of the junior year or the fall of the senior year. There are early decision, early admissions, and deferred admissions plans. Early decision applications should be filed by November 1 or January 7; regular applications, by January 7 for fall entry, along with a $50 fee. Notification of early decision is sent December 15 or February 15; regular decision, April 1. 369 early decision candidates were accepted for the 1999-2000 class. 16% of all applicants are on a waiting list.

Financial Aid: In 1999-2000, 59% of all freshmen and 53% of continuing students received some form of financial aid. 42% of freshmen and 36% of continuing students received need-based aid. The average freshman award was $22,748. Of that total, scholarships or need-based grants averaged $16,801 ($32,030 maximum); loans averaged $5103 ($7625 maximum); and work contracts averaged $1752 ($1800 maximum). 24% of undergraduates work part time. Average annual earnings from campus work are $3700. The average financial indebtedness of the 1999 graduate was $19,900. Vanderbilt is a member of CSS. The CSS/Profile or FAFSA and tax return information are required. The fall application deadline is February 1.

Computers: The mainframe is a DEC ALPHA server 2100A Model 4/275. About 400 PCs and terminals are located in public and departmental labs. Most have Ethernet connections to the campus backbone, which is part of the Internet. All campus residences have Ethernet connections, and students who live off campus can access the network via modem. All students may access the system any time. There are no time limits and no fees.

VASSAR COLLEGE
Poughkeepsie, NY 12604

(914) 437-7300
(800) 827-7270; Fax: (914) 437-7063

Full-time: 892 men, 1384 women	**Faculty:** 247; IIB, +$
Part-time: 19 men, 27 women	**Ph.D.s:** 99%
Graduate: none	**Student/Faculty:** 9 to 1
Year: semesters	**Tuition:** $24,030
Application Deadline: January 1	**Room & Board:** $6770
Freshman Class: 4777 applied, 2039 accepted, 640 enrolled	
SAT I Verbal/Math: 677/654	**MOST COMPETITIVE**

Vassar College, founded in 1861, is a private, independent college of the liberal arts and sciences. The 2 libraries contain 788,857 volumes and 458,072 microform items, and subscribe to 4300 periodicals. Computerized library services include the card catalog, interlibrary loans, and database searching. Special learning facilities include a learning resource center, art gallery, radio station, studio art building, geological museum, observatory, 3 theaters, concert hall, environmental field station, intercultural center, and research-oriented lab facilities for natural sciences. The 1000-acre campus is in a suburban area 75 miles north of New York City. Including residence halls, there are 100 buildings.

Programs of Study: Vassar confers the A.B. degree. Master's degrees are also awarded. Bachelor's degrees are awarded in BIOLOGICAL SCIENCE (biochemistry and biology/biological science), COMMUNICATIONS AND THE ARTS (art, dramatic arts, English, film arts, fine arts, languages, and music), COMPUTER AND PHYSICAL SCIENCE (astronomy, chemistry, computer science, geology, mathematics, and physics), EDUCATION (foreign languages), ENGINEERING AND ENVIRONMENTAL DESIGN (technology and public affairs), HEALTH PROFESSIONS (premedicine), SOCIAL SCIENCE (African studies, American studies, anthropology, Asian/Oriental studies, biopsychology, British studies, cognitive science, economics, geography, history, international studies, Latin American studies, medieval studies, philosophy, political science/government, prelaw, psychology, religion, social studies, sociology, Spanish studies, urban studies, and women's studies). English, psychology, and political science are the largest.

Special: The school offers fieldwork in social agencies and schools, a Washington semester, dual majors, independent majors, a 4-year advanced degree program in chemistry, cross-registration with the 12 College Consortium, and nonrecorded grade options. Study-abroad programs may be arranged in 7 countries. A 3-2 engineering degree with Dartmouth College is offered. There is a chapter of Phi Beta Kappa.

Admissions: 43% of the 1999-2000 applicants were accepted. The SAT I scores for the 1999-2000 freshman class were: Verbal--1% below 500, 10% between 500 and 599, 48% between 600 and 700, and 41% above 700; Math--1% below 500, 16% between 500 and 599, 58% between 600 and 700, and 25% above 700. 86% of the current freshmen were in the top fifth of their class; 98% were in the top two fifths. There were 45 National Merit finalists and 47 semifinalists. 28 freshmen graduated first in their class.

Requirements: The SAT I and 3 SAT II: Subject tests, preferably 1 in writing, or the ACT, is required. In addition, graduation from an accredited secondary school or satisfactory scores on the GED are required for admission. The high school program should typically include 4 years of English, 3 or more years of a foreign language, 3 or 4 years of social studies, 3 or 4 years of math, and 2 or 3 years of science. An essay and a writing sample are required. AP credits are accepted. Important factors in the admissions decision are advanced placement or honor courses, recommendations by school officials, and leadership record.

Procedure: Freshmen are admitted in the fall. Entrance exams should be taken as early as possible, but no later than December of the senior year. There are early decision and deferred admissions plans. Early decision applications should be filed by November 15 for Roundd I, and January 1 for Round II; regular applications, by January 1 for fall entry, along with a $60 fee. Notification of early decision is sent December 15; regular decision, April 1. 165 early decision candidates were accepted for the 1999-2000 class. 10% of all applicants are on a waiting list.

Financial Aid: In 1999-2000, 62% of all freshmen and 61% of continuing students received some form of financial aid. 53% of freshmen and 55% of continuing students received need-based aid. The average freshman award was $19,662. Of that total, scholarships or need-based grants averaged $16,313 ($29,970 maximum); loans averaged $2157 ($4125 maximum); and work contracts averaged $1194 ($1300 maximum). 60% of undergraduates work part time. Average annual earnings from campus work are $1040. The average financial indebtedness of the 1999 graduate was $15,507. Vassar is a member of CSS. The CSS/Profile or FAFSA and the college's own financial statement are required. The fall application deadline is January 10.

Computers: The mainframes are a DEC VAX 6200, an 11/780, an 11/750, and a MicroVAX II. There are also 350 Mac and IBM PCs available throughout the campus. All students may access the system 24 hours per day. There are no time limits and no fees.

VILLANOVA UNIVERSITY
Villanova, PA 19085-1672

(610) 519-4000
(800) 338-7927; Fax: (610) 519-6450

Full-time: 3162 men, 3212 women	**Faculty:** 499; IIA, ++$
Part-time: 422 men, 337 women	**Ph.D.s:** 90%
Graduate: 1112 men, 985 women	**Student/Faculty:** 13 to 1
Year: semesters, summer session	**Tuition:** $20,855
Application Deadline: January 15	**Room & Board:** $8000
Freshman Class: 9826 applied, 5580 accepted, 1676 enrolled	
SAT I Verbal/Math: 550/570	**HIGHLY COMPETITIVE**

Villanova University, founded in 1842 and affiliated with the Catholic Church, offers undergraduate programs in liberal arts and sciences, commerce and finance, engineering, and nursing. There are 4 undergraduate and 5 graduate schools. In addition to regional accreditation, Villanova has baccalaureate program accreditation with AACSB, ABET, and NLN. The 2 libraries contain 888,000 volumes, 1,789,816 microform items, and 7600 audiovisual forms/CDs, and subscribe to 5500 periodicals. Computerized library services include the card catalog, interlibrary loans, and database searching. Special learning facilities include an art gallery, planetarium, radio station, TV station, and 2 observatories. The 254-acre campus is in a suburban area 12 miles west of Philadelphia. Including residence halls, there are 60 buildings.

Programs of Study: Villanova confers B.A., B.S., B.E., and B.S.N. degrees. Associate, master's, and doctoral degrees are also awarded. Bachelor's degrees are awarded in BIOLOGICAL SCIENCE (biology/biological science), BUSINESS (accounting, banking and finance, business administration and management, business economics, management information systems, and marketing/retailing/merchandising), COMMUNICATIONS AND THE ARTS (art history and appreciation, classics, communications, English, French, German, and Spanish), COMPUTER AND PHYSICAL SCIENCE (astronomy, astrophysics, chemistry, computer science, information sciences and systems, mathematics, physics, and science), EDUCATION (elementary and secondary), ENGINEERING AND ENVIRONMENTAL DESIGN (chemical engineering, civil engineering, computer engineering, electrical/electronics engineering, and mechanical engineering), HEALTH PROFESSIONS (nursing), SOCIAL SCIENCE (economics, geography, history, human services, liberal arts/general studies, philosophy, political science/government, psychology, religion, sociology, and theological studies). Sciences, business, and liberal arts are the strongest academically. Liberal arts, and commerce and finance are the largest.

Special: Cross-registration is possible with Rosemont College. Internships are available for each college in the Philadelphia area as well as in New York City and Washington. Students may study abroad in the British Isles, the Pacific Rim, East Africa, the former Soviet Union, and the Caribbean. Villanova offers a Washington semester, an accelerated degree program in biology for allied health programs, dual majors, a general studies degree, and credit by exam. There are 31 national honor societies, including Phi Beta Kappa, and a freshman honors program.

Admissions: 57% of the 1999-2000 applicants were accepted. The SAT I scores for the 1999-2000 freshman class were: Verbal--7% below 500, 43% between 500 and 599, 42% between 600 and 700, and 7% above 700; Math--7% below 500, 31% between 500 and 599, 49% between 600 and 700, and 13% above 700. 65% of the current freshmen were in the top fifth of their class; 92% were in the

top two fifths. There were 5 National Merit finalists. 27 freshmen graduated first in their class.

Requirements: The SAT I or ACT is required. Applicants must be graduates of an accredited secondary school and should have completed 16 academic units. The specific courses required vary according to college. A GED is accepted. An essay is required. Students may apply on-line at www.admission.villanova.edu. AP and CLEP credits are accepted. Important factors in the admissions decision are advanced placement or honor courses, leadership record, and extracurricular activities record.

Procedure: Freshmen are admitted in the fall. Entrance exams should be taken by December of the senior year. There are early admissions and deferred admissions plans. Early action applications should be filed by November 15; regular applications, by January 7 for fall entry, along with a $50 fee. Notification of early action is sent January 15; regular decision, April 1. 28% of all applicants are on a waiting list.

Financial Aid: In 1999-2000, 71% of all freshmen and 61% of continuing students received some form of financial aid. 52% of freshmen and 48% of continuing students received need-based aid. The average freshman award was $15,907. Of that total, scholarships or need-based grants averaged $11,230 ($28,732 maximum); loans averaged $6960 ($30,625 maximum); and work contracts averaged $1717 ($4000 maximum). 20% of undergraduates work part time. Average annual earnings from campus work are $963. The average financial indebtedness of the 1999 graduate was $16,652. Villanova is a member of CSS. The FAFSA, the college's own financial statement and the parent and student federal income tax return and W2s are required. The fall application deadline is February 15.

Computers: The mainframe consists of Sun 4500 Enterprise servers. Students in the College of Commerce and Finance are provided with laptop computers. There are 3 main PC labs as well as various other labs for specific majors. All students have access to the network and E-mail, on and off campus, and all residence hall rooms have network and web connections. All students may access the system. There are no time limits and no fees.

VIRGINIA MILITARY INSTITUTE
Lexington, VA 24450

(540) 464-7211
(800) 767-4207; Fax: (540) 464-7746

Full-time: 1268 men, 67 women	**Faculty:** 100; IIB, ++$
Part-time: none	**Ph.D.s:** 93%
Graduate: none	**Student/Faculty:** 13 to 1
Year: semesters, summer session	**Tuition:** $5014 ($15,454)
Application Deadline: April 1	**Room & Board:** $4376
Freshman Class: 1162 applied, 848 accepted, 429 enrolled	
SAT I Verbal/Math: 561/564	**ACT:** 23　　**VERY COMPETITIVE**

Virginia Military Institute, established in 1839, is the nation's first state-supported military college. It offers academic programs in engineering, sciences, and liberal arts. All students are members of the Corps of Cadets, live in barracks, eat together in the mess hall, wear uniforms, and adhere to the Honor System. In addition to regional accreditation, VMI has baccalaureate program accreditation with ABET. The 2 libraries contain 239,318 volumes, 17,619 microform items, and 4540 audiovisual forms/CDs, and subscribe to 803 periodicals. Computerized library services include the card catalog, interlibrary loans, and database searching. Special learning facilities include a learning resource center, an observatory, and a research library. The 134-acre campus is in a small town 50 miles north of Roanoke. Including residence halls, there are 68 buildings.

Programs of Study: VMI confers B.A. and B.S. degrees. Bachelor's degrees are awarded in BIOLOGICAL SCIENCE (biology/biological science), BUSINESS (business economics), COMMUNICATIONS AND THE ARTS (English), COMPUTER AND PHYSICAL SCIENCE (chemistry, computer science, mathematics, and physics), ENGINEERING AND ENVIRONMENTAL DESIGN (civil engineering, electrical/electronics engineering, and mechanical engineering), SOCIAL SCIENCE (history, international studies, and psychology). Engineering (civil, electrical, and mechanical) and sciences are the strongest academically. History, business/economics, and civil and mechanical engineering are the largest.

Special: Study abroad in 14 countries and work-study programs are available, as are for-credit internships in English and international studies and summer internships in foreign countries. VMI offers dual majors in any combination and B.A.-B.S. degrees in liberal arts, physical sciences, and engineering. Minors are offered in each field of study. There are 11 national honor societies, a freshman honors program, and 3 departmental honors programs.

Admissions: 73% of the 1999-2000 applicants were accepted. The SAT I scores for the 1999-2000 freshman class were: Verbal--18% below 500, 50% between 500 and 599, 30% between 600 and 700, and 3% above 700; Math--15% below 500, 54% between 500 and 599, 29% between 600 and 700, and 2% above 700. The ACT scores were 26% below 21, 26% between 21 and 23, 25% between 24 and 26, 13% between 27 and 28, and 10% above 28. 41% of the current freshmen were in the top quarter of their class; 82% were in the top half. 3 freshmen graduated first in their class.

Requirements: The SAT I or ACT is required. In addition, applicants must be graduates of an accredited secondary school. Applicants should complete 19 to 20 high school academic units, including 4 years of English and math, 3 of science, history, and foreign language, and 2 of social studies. An essay is encouraged and an interview is recommended. Applications are accepted on computer disk. AP credits are accepted. Important factors in the admissions decision are advanced placement or honor courses, extracurricular activities record, and leadership record.

Procedure: Freshmen are admitted in the fall. Entrance exams should be taken during the second semester of the junior year. There is an early decision plan. Early decision applications should be filed by November 15; regular applications, by April 1 for fall entry, along with a $25 fee. Notification of early decision is sent December 15; regular decision, on a rolling basis. 8% of all applicants are on a waiting list.

Financial Aid: In 1999-2000, 59% of all freshmen and 81% of continuing students received some form of financial aid. 37% of freshmen and 34% of continuing students received need-based aid. The average freshman award was $11,613. Of that total, scholarships or need-based grants averaged $6950 ($15,000 maximum); and loans averaged $4326 ($5625 maximum). 9% of undergraduates work part time; freshmen are not permitted to work. Average annual earnings from campus work are $800. The average financial indebtedness of the 1999 graduate was $13,000. VMI is a member of CSS. The FAFSA and the college's own financial statement are required. The fall application deadline is April 1.

Computers: The mainframe is a DEC ALPHA server 4100. There are 200 networked PCs available to cadets with access to the local area network and the Internet. All student rooms are wired for Internet access. All students may access the system. There are no time limits and no fees. It is recommended that all students have either a desktop PC or a laptop (IBM Thinkpad or Toshiba laptop).

VIRGINIA POLYTECHNIC INSTITUTE AND STATE UNIVERSITY

Blacksburg, VA 24061 (540) 231-6267; Fax: (540) 231-3242

Full-time: 12,636 men, 8633 women	**Faculty:** 925; I, -$
Part-time: 341 men, 200 women	**Ph.D.s:** 82%
Graduate: 2257 men, 1361 women	**Student/Faculty:** 23 to 1
Year: semesters, summer session	**Tuition:** $3620 ($11,844)
Application Deadline: February 1	**Room & Board:** $3780
Freshman Class: 16,500 applied, 11,616 accepted, 4659 enrolled	
SAT I Verbal/Math: 572/592	**VERY COMPETITIVE**

Virginia Polytechnic Institute and State University, founded in 1872, is a public land-grant institution. It offers a cadet program within the larger, nonmilitary student body. There are 7 undergraduate and 2 graduate schools. In addition to regional accreditation, Virginia Tech has baccalaureate program accreditation with AACSB, ABET, ACCE, ADA, AHEA, ASLA, FIDER, and SAF. The 4 libraries contain 2 million volumes, 6 million microform items, and 17,510 audiovisual forms/CDs, and subscribe to 18,737 periodicals. Computerized library services include the card catalog, interlibrary loans, and database searching. Special learning facilities include a learning resource center, art gallery, natural history museum, radio station, TV station, airport, wind tunnels, agricultural stations, radio/visual observatories, satellite up-link station, math emporium, CAVE (cave automatic virtual environment), and multimedia, digital musi, writing, and CAD/CAM labs. The 2600-acre campus is in a rural area 40 miles southwest of Roanoke. Including residence halls, there are 110 buildings.

Programs of Study: Virginia Tech confers B.A., B.S., B.Arch., B.F.A., B.Land. Arch., B.S.Bus., B.S.E., and B.S.Ed. degrees. Associate, master's, and doctoral degrees are also awarded. Bachelor's degrees are awarded in AGRICULTURE (agricultural economics, animal science, dairy science, forestry and related sciences, horticulture, poultry science, and soil science), BIOLOGICAL SCIENCE (biochemistry and biology/biological science), BUSINESS (accounting, banking and finance, business economics, hotel/motel and restaurant management, management science, and marketing/retailing/merchandising), COMMUNICATIONS AND THE ARTS (communications, dramatic arts, English, French, German, music, and Spanish), COMPUTER AND PHYSICAL SCIENCE (chemistry, computer science, geology, mathematics, physics, and statistics), EDUCATION (agricultural, business, early childhood, health, home economics, marketing and distribution, physical, technical, and vocational), ENGINEERING AND ENVIRONMENTAL DESIGN (agricultural engineering, architecture, chemical engineering, civil engineering, computer engineering, construction engineering, construction management, electrical/electronics engineering, environmental science, interior design, landscape architecture/design, materials engineering, mechanical engineering, mining and mineral engineering, and ocean engineering), SOCIAL SCIENCE (child care/child and family studies, economics, food science, geography, history, international studies, liberal arts/general studies, philosophy, political science/government, psychology, public administration, sociology, textiles and clothing, and urban studies). Engineering, architecture, and business are the strongest academically. Engineering, computer science, and biology are the largest.

Special: Students may cross-register with Miami University in Ohio, Oxford Polytechnic Institute, California Polytechnic Institute, and Florida A&M. Study abroad in 36 countries, a Washington semester, and a wide range of work-study programs are available, including co-ops in 48 majors. There are honors options for most majors, B.A.-B.S. degrees, dual and student-designed majors, credit for independent study or research, nondegree study, and pass/fail options. The Corps of Cadets, a militarily structured organization, is open to men and women. Undergraduate advising programs are available to students wishing to prepare for professional school in law, dentistry, medicine, pharmacy, physical therapy, or veterinary medicine. There are 13 national honor societies, including Phi Beta Kappa, and a freshman honors program.

Admissions: 70% of the 1999-2000 applicants were accepted. The SAT I scores for the 1999-2000 freshman class were: Verbal--14% below 500, 48% between 500 and 599, 31% between 600 and 700, and 7% above 700; Math--10% below 500, 40% between 500 and 599, 39% between 600 and 700, and 11% above 700. 63% of the current freshmen were in the top fifth of their class; 98% were in the top two fifths. There were 36 National Merit finalists. 77 freshmen graduated first in their class.

Requirements: The SAT I or ACT is required. A GPA of 2.0 is required. Students must also take SAT II: Subject tests in writing and history. Applicants must be graduates of an accredited secondary school, or the GED is accepted. Applicants should complete 18 high school academic credits, including 4 years of English, 3 of math, including algebra II and geometry, 2 of lab science, to be chosen from biology, chemistry, or physics, and 1 each of history and social studies. An additional 3 years from college preparatory courses and 4 from any credit course offerings are required. A portfolio and an audition are required for art and music students. Applications are accepted on-line via CollegeNET. AP and CLEP credits are accepted. Important factors in the admissions decision are advanced placement or honor courses, evidence of special talent, and recommendations by school officials.

Procedure: Freshmen are admitted to all sessions. Entrance exams should be taken by January 1 of the senior year. There are early decision, early admissions, and deferred admissions plans. Early decision applications should be filed by November 1; regular applications, by February 1 for fall entry, October 1 for spring entry, and April 22 for summer entry, along with a $25 fee. Notification of early decision is sent December 15; regular decision, on or before April 15. A waiting list is an active part of the admissions procedure.

Financial Aid: In 1999-2000, 65% of all freshmen and 63% of continuing students received some form of financial aid. 60% of freshmen and 63% of continuing students received need-based aid. The average freshman award was $6993. Of that total, scholarships or need-based grants averaged $3816 ($24,062 maximum); loans averaged $6728 ($18,500 maximum); and work contracts averaged $799 ($3500 maximum). 23% of undergraduates work part time. Average annual earnings from campus work are $1500. The average financial indebtedness of the 1999 graduate was $12,053. Virginia Tech is a member of CSS. The FAFSA is required. The fall application deadline is March 1.

Computers: Undergraduates receive guidance on using PCs and the Internet from their professors. They may access the Internet or use PCs in any one of many computer labs on campus, or from their dormitory rooms. Dormitory rooms are wired for data, voice, and video transmission. All students may access the system any time. There are no time limits and no fees. It is recommended that students in all programs have personal computers; specs will vary by major.

WABASH COLLEGE

Crawfordsville, IN 47933-0352

(765) 361-6253
(800) 345-5385; Fax: (765) 361-6437

Full-time: 853 men	**Faculty:** 81; IIB, +$
Part-time: 8 men	**Ph.D.s:** 97%
Graduate: none	**Student/Faculty:** 11 to 1
Year: semesters	**Tuition:** $17,275
Application Deadline: March 1	**Room & Board:** $5435
Freshman Class: 894 applied, 669 accepted, 292 enrolled	
SAT I Verbal/Math: 576/598	**ACT:** 25 **VERY COMPETITIVE**

Wabash College, founded in 1832, is a private liberal arts men's college with a strong emphasis on preprofessional programs. The library contains 253,024 volumes, 9460 microform items, and 8756 audiovisual forms CDs, and subscribes to 1072 periodicals. Computerized library services include the card catalog, interlibrary loans, and database searching. Special learning facilities include a learning resource center, art gallery, radio station, the Ramsay Archival Center, a quantitive skills center, and a writing center. The 55-acre campus is in a small town 45 miles northwest of Indianapolis. Including residence halls, there are 33 buildings.

Programs of Study: Wabash confers the A.B. degree. Bachelor's degrees are awarded in BIOLOGICAL SCIENCE (biology/biological science), COMMUNICATIONS AND THE ARTS (classics, dramatic arts, English, fine arts, French, German, Greek, Latin, music, Spanish, and speech/debate/rhetoric), COMPUTER AND PHYSICAL SCIENCE (chemistry, mathematics, and physics), SOCIAL SCIENCE (economics, history, philosophy, political science/government, psychology, and religion). Premedical and prelaw are the strongest academically. Biology, history, and psychology are the largest.

Special: Wabash offers internships with off-campus organizations, study abroad in unlimited countries, a Washington semester with American University, dual majors, and both a 3-2 engineering program and a 3-3 law program with Columbia University and Washington University in St. Louis. A Ninth Semester Teacher Education Program (tuition-free) is also available. There are 9 national honor societies, including Phi Beta Kappa.

Admissions: 75% of the 1999-2000 applicants were accepted. The SAT I scores for the 1999-2000 freshman class were: Verbal--19% below 500, 41% between 500 and 599, 33% between 600 and 700, and 7% above 700; Math--13% below 500, 36% between 500 and 599, 38% between 600 and 700, and 13% above 700. The ACT scores were 12% below 21, 25% between 21 and 23, 24% between 24 and 26, 19% between 27 and 28, and 20% above 28. 55% of the current freshmen were in the top fifth of their class; 85% were in the top two fifths. There were 4 National Merit finalists. 12 freshmen graduated first in their class.

Requirements: The SAT I or ACT is required. Wabash recommends applicants have 4 high school courses in English, 3 to 4 in math, and 2 each in foreign language, lab science, and social studies. An essay is required and an interview is recommended. Students can apply on-line via CollegeLink, ExPAN, Common App, or the school's web site. AP and CLEP credits are accepted. Important factors in the admissions decision are advanced placement or honor courses, leadership record, and extracurricular activities record.

Procedure: Freshmen are admitted fall and spring. Entrance exams should be taken by the spring of the junior year or fall of the senior year. There are early decision, early admissions, and deferred admissions plans. Early decision applications should be filed by November 1; regular applications, by March 1 for fall entry and December 1 for spring entry, along with a $30 fee. Notification of early decision is sent December 15; regular decision, on December 15, February 15, and March 15. 18 early decision candidates were accepted for the 1999-2000 class.

Financial Aid: In 1999-2000, 98% of all freshmen and 95% of continuing students received some form of financial aid. 77% of freshmen and 67% of continuing students received need-based aid. The average freshman award was $16,075. Of that total, scholarships or need-based grants averaged $13,208 ($24,310 maximum); loans averaged $3775 ($7625 maximum); and work contracts averaged $978 ($1750 maximum). 67% of undergraduates work part time. Average annual earnings from campus work are $886. The average financial indebtedness of the 1999 graduate was $9393. Wabash is a member of CSS. The CSS/Profile or FAFSA and federal tax form with W-2 statements are required. The fall application deadline is March 1.

Computers: The mainframe is a DEC ALPHA 2100 server. Every student has an account on a Novell server, with a network connection in his living unit. There are more than 100 Macs and PCs in 6 public classrooms. All students may access the system 24 hours per day or at designated times for specific computers. There are no time limits and no fees.

WAGNER COLLEGE
Staten Island, NY 10301

(718) 390-3411
(800) 221-1010; Fax: (718) 390-3105

Full-time: 626 men, 913 women	**Faculty:** 83; IIB, -$
Part-time: 23 men, 54 women	**Ph.D.s:** 85%
Graduate: 120 men, 264 women	**Student/Faculty:** 17 to 1
Year: semesters, summer session	**Tuition:** $18,000
Application Deadline: February 15	**Room & Board:** $6500
Freshman Class: 2156 applied, 1518 accepted, 478 enrolled	
SAT I Verbal/Math: 542/565	**ACT:** 25 **VERY COMPETITIVE**

Wagner College, founded in 1883, is a private liberal arts institution. Some of the information in this profile is approximate. There is 1 graduate school. In addition to regional accreditation, Wagner has baccalaureate program accreditation with NLN. The library contains 300,000 volumes and 225,000 microform items, and subscribes to 1000 periodicals. Computerized library services include interlibrary loans and database searching. Special learning facilities include an art gallery and planetarium. The 105-acre campus is in a suburban area 10 miles from Manhattan. Including residence halls, there are 18 buildings.

Programs of Study: Wagner confers B.A. and B.S. degrees. Master's degrees are also awarded. Bachelor's degrees are awarded in BIOLOGICAL SCIENCE (biology/biological science and microbiology), BUSINESS (accounting and business administration and management), COMMUNICATIONS AND THE ARTS (arts administration/management, dramatic arts, English, fine arts, and music), COMPUTER AND PHYSICAL SCIENCE (chemistry, computer science, mathematics, and physics), EDUCATION (elementary, middle school, and secondary), HEALTH PROFESSIONS (medical laboratory technology, nursing, and physician's assistant), SOCIAL SCIENCE (anthropology, gerontology, history, political science/government, psychology, public administration, social work, and sociology). Natural sciences is the strongest academically. Business is the largest.

Special: Internships are required for business and English majors and are recommended for all majors. Students may earn B.A.-B.S. degrees in math, physics, and psychology. Student-designed and dual majors, credit for life experience, a

Washington semester, nondegree study, and pass/fail options are available. Study abroad in 14 countries is possible. There are 9 national honor societies, and a freshman honors program.

Admissions: 70% of the 1999-2000 applicants were accepted. The SAT I scores for the 1999-2000 freshman class were: Verbal--22% below 500, 53% between 500 and 599, 22% between 600 and 700, and 2% above 700; Math--20% below 500, 55% between 500 and 599, 22% between 600 and 700, and 3% above 700. The ACT scores were 8% below 21, 24% between 21 and 23, 51% between 24 and 26, 10% between 27 and 28, and 7% above 28. 31% of the current freshmen were in the top fifth of their class; 69% were in the top two fifths.

Requirements: The SAT I or ACT is required. For SAT I, the recommended minimum scores are 510 verbal and 500 math. A composite score of 21 is recommended on the ACT. A GPA of 2.5 is required. Graduation from an accredited secondary school is required, with 18 academic credits or Carnegie units, including 4 years of English, 3 years each of history and math, 2 years each of foreign language, science, and social studies, and 1 year each of art and music. An essay is required, and an interview is recommended. Auditions are required for music and theater applicants. Applications are accepted on computer disk. AP and CLEP credits are accepted. Important factors in the admissions decision are advanced placement or honor courses, recommendations by school officials, and extracurricular activities record.

Procedure: Freshmen are admitted fall and spring. Entrance exams should be taken by December of the senior year. There are early decision, early admissions, and deferred admissions plans. Early decision applications should be filed by December 1; regular applications, by February 15 for fall entry and December 1 for spring entry, along with a $45 fee. Notification of early decision is sent January 1; regular decision, March 1.

Financial Aid: In 1999-2000, 78% of all freshmen and 80% of continuing students received some form of financial aid. The average freshman award was $6200. eraged $3200 ($5000 maximum); and work contracts averaged $1000 ($1200 maximum). 25% of undergraduates work part time. Average annual earnings from campus work are $800. Wagner is a member of CSS. The FAFSA and the college's own financial statement are required. The fall application deadline is April 1.

Computers: The mainframe is a DEC VAX. 75 IBM PCs in the computer center are connected to the mainframe. An additional 52 IBM PCs are available for student use. Printers include 4 HP LaserJet, 2 Epson LQ dot-matrix, and 1 HP PaintJet. All students may access the system Monday through Thursday, 9 a.m. to 10 p.m.; Friday, 9 a.m. to 6 p.m.; and Saturday and Sunday, 11 a.m. to 5 p.m. There are no time limits and no fees.

WAKE FOREST UNIVERSITY
Winston-Salem, NC 27109-7305   (336) 758-5201

Full-time: 1847 men, 1970 women	**Faculty:** 347; IIA, ++$
Part-time: 20 men, 13 women	**Ph.D.s:** 90%
Graduate: 1194 men, 970 women	**Student/Faculty:** 11 to 1
Year: semesters, summer session	**Tuition:** $21,420
Application Deadline: January 15	**Room & Board:** $5900
Freshman Class: 4982 applied, 2465 accepted, 979 enrolled	
SAT I: required	**MOST COMPETITIVE**

Wake Forest University, established in 1834, is a private institution offering undergraduate programs in the liberal arts and sciences, education, and preprofessional fields. There are 2 undergraduate and 5 graduate schools. In addition to regional accreditation, Wake Forest has baccalaureate program accreditation with AACSB. The 3 libraries contain 1.61 million volumes, 1,696,208 microform items, and 13,230 audiovisual forms/CDs, and subscribe to 17,842 periodicals. Computerized library services include the card catalog, interlibrary loans, and database searching. Special learning facilities include a learning resource center, art gallery, radio station, TV station, fine arts center, anthropology museum, and laser research facility. The 340-acre campus is in a suburban area 4 miles northwest of Winston-Salem. Including residence halls, there are 41 buildings.

Programs of Study: Wake Forest confers B.A. and B.S. degrees. Master's and doctoral degrees are also awarded. Bachelor's degrees are awarded in BIOLOGICAL SCIENCE (biology/biological science), BUSINESS (accounting and business administration and management), COMMUNICATIONS AND THE ARTS (art, communications, dramatic arts, English, French, German, music, and Spanish), COMPUTER AND PHYSICAL SCIENCE (chemistry, computer science, mathematics, and physics), EDUCATION (education), SOCIAL SCIENCE (anthropology, economics, history, philosophy, political science/government, psychology, religion, and sociology). Business, biology, and psychology are the largest.

Special: The school offers cooperative programs in forestry with Duke University. Cross-registration with Salem College is available. The school sponsors study-abroad programs in more than 10 countries. A Washington semester, internships, work-study programs, dual majors, a 3-2 engineering degree with North Carolina State University, a B.A.-B.S. degree in chemistry/physics, and pass/fail options are available. Accelerated degree programs may be arranged in dentistry and medical technology. Interdisciplinary honors courses and the Open Curriculum program are available for selected students. Wake Forest owns residences in London, Venice, and Vienna where students and professors may attend semester-long courses in a variety of disciplines. There are 11 national honor societies, including Phi Beta Kappa, a freshman honors program, and 21 departmental honors programs.

Admissions: 49% of the 1999-2000 applicants were accepted. The SAT I scores for the 1999-2000 freshman class were: Verbal--3% below 500, 17% between 500 and 599, 59% between 600 and 700, and 20% above 700; Math--3% below 500, 15% between 500 and 599, 57% between 600 and 700, and 26% above 700. 87% of the current freshmen were in the top fifth of their class; 98% were in the top two fifths. 70 freshmen graduated first in their class.

Requirements: The SAT I is required. 3 SAT II: Subject tests, including writing and mathematics, are recommended. Graduation from an accredited secondary school or the GED is required. The school requires 16 academic credits, including 4 credits of English, 2 each of a foreign language, history, and social studies, 3 of math, and 1 of science. 1 credit each of art and music is recommended. All students must submit an essay. Applications can be downloaded and are accepted at the university's web site. AP and CLEP credits are accepted. Important factors in the admissions decision are recommendations by school officials, leadership record, and advanced placement or honor courses.

Procedure: Freshmen are admitted fall and spring. Entrance exams should be taken during the junior year, and at least 1 SAT I should be taken during the senior year. There are early decision and early admissions plans. Early decision applications should be filed by November 15; regular applications, by January 15 for fall entry and November 1 for spring entry, along with a $40 fee. Notification of early decision is sent December 15; regular decision, April 1. 298 early decision candidates were accepted for the 1999-2000 class. A waiting list is an active part of the admissions procedure.

Financial Aid: In a recent year, 67% of all freshmen and 64% of continuing students received some form of financial aid. 32% of freshmen and 30% of continuing students received need-based aid. The average freshman award was $12,965. Of that total, scholarships or need-based grants averaged $9853 ($26,950 maximum); loans averaged $6237 ($26,950 maximum); and work contracts averaged $1993 ($2000 maximum). 25% of undergraduates work part time. Average annual earnings from campus work are $2000. The average financial indebtedness of a recent graduate was $14,800. Wake Forest is a member of CSS. The CSS/Profile or FAFSA and the college's own financial statement are required. The fall application deadline is March 1.

Computers: The mainframes are an IBM SP2 and an HP 3000. Each incoming student receives an IBM ThinkPad laptop computer with mainframe capability. Internet access is available directly from each residence hall room, faculty office, classroom, and the campus library. The Class of 2000 and all subsequent classes receive color inkjet printers. Students choosing not to use the inkjet printer have access to networked laser printers in each residence hall. All students may access the system 24 hours per day. There are no time limits and no fees.

WARREN WILSON COLLEGE
Asheville, NC 28815-9000

(828) 298-3325
(800) 934-3536; Fax: (828) 298-1440

Full-time: 294 men, 452 women	**Faculty:** 57; IIB, --$
Part-time: 5 men, 12 women	**Ph.D.s:** 81%
Graduate: 12 men, 56 women	**Student/Faculty:** 13 to 1
Year: semesters	**Tuition:** $13,600
Application Deadline: March 15	**Room & Board:** $4444
Freshman Class: 619 applied, 513 accepted, 195 enrolled	
SAT I Verbal/Math: 598/550	**ACT:** 24 **VERY COMPETITIVE**

Warren Wilson College, founded in 1894, is a liberal arts institution affiliated with the Presbyterian Church (U.S.A.). All students work 15 hours per week in jobs related to the operation and maintenance of the college. In exchange, tuition and room and board is reduced by $2472. In addition to regional accreditation, Warren Wilson College has baccalaureate program accreditation with CSWE and NCATE. The library contains 95,000 volumes, 25,000 microform items, and 5500 audiovisual forms/CDs. Students have access to more than 4000 periodicals and 2000 abstracts.Computerized library services include the card catalog, interlibrary loans, and database searching. Special learning facilities include a learning resource center, art gallery, and radio station. The 1100-acre campus is in a small town 10 miles east of Asheville. Including residence halls, there are 25 buildings.

Programs of Study: Warren Wilson College confers B.A. and B.S. degrees. Master's degrees are also awarded. Bachelor's degrees are awarded in BIOLOGICAL SCIENCE (biology/biological science), BUSINESS (business economics), COMMUNICATIONS AND THE ARTS (art and English), COMPUTER AND PHYSICAL SCIENCE (chemistry and mathematics), EDUCATION (elementary, middle school, and recreation), ENGINEERING AND ENVIRONMENTAL DESIGN (environmental science), SOCIAL SCIENCE (behavioral science, history, humanities, psychology, and social work). Biology is the strongest academically. Environmental studies, biology, and English are the largest.

Special: Cross registration is offered with Mars Hill College and the University of North Carolina at Asheville. Internships related to the major may be arranged. Study-abroad programs in South America, Europe, Japan, and India are available. The college offers an accelerated degree program in education, student-designed majors, nondegree study, and pass/fail options. There are dual majors in history/political science and English/theater arts. Cooperative programs are available in engineering with Washington University in St. Louis. On campus work-study is required. 3 departments have honors programs.

Admissions: 83% of the 1999-2000 applicants were accepted. The SAT I scores for the 1999-2000 freshman class were: Verbal--11% below 500, 41% between 500 and 599, 37% between 600 and 700, and 10% above 700; Math--11% below 500, 41% between 500 and 599, 37% between 600 and 700, and 10% above 700. The ACT scores were 11% below 21, 27% between 21 and 23, 38% between 24 and 26, 13% between 27 and 28, and 12% above 28. 40% of the current freshmen were in the top fifth of their class; 82% were in the top half. There were 3 National Merit finalists and 6 semifinalists. 2 freshmen graduated first in their class.

Requirements: The SAT I or ACT is required, with a score of 500 on each section of the SAT I or a composite score of 21 on the ACT. Warren Wilson College requires applicants to be in the upper 50% of their class. A GPA of 2.5 is required. Graduation from an accredited secondary school or the GED is required. Applicants should have a total of 12 academic credits. An essay and an interview are recommended. Applications are accepted on computer disk through CollegeLink. AP credits are accepted. Important factors in the admissions decision are advanced placement or honor courses, evidence of special talent, and recommendations by school officials.

Procedure: Freshmen are admitted fall and winter. Entrance exams should be taken by January 20 of the senior year. There are early decision, early admissions, and deferred admissions plans. Early decision applications should be filed by November 15; regular applications, by March 15 for fall entry and November 1 for winter entry. Notification of early decision is sent December 1; regular decision, April 1. 48 early decision candidates were accepted for the 1999-2000 class. 10% of all applicants are on a waiting list.

Financial Aid: All students work to offset tuition costs. In addition, in 1999-2000, 87% of all freshmen and 70% of continuing students received some form of financial aid. 70% of freshmen and 66% of continuing students received need-based aid. The average freshman award was $9835, excluding work program awards. Of that total, scholarships or need-based grants averaged $4738; loans averaged $2625; and work contracts averaged $2422. 88% of undergraduates work part time. Average annual earnings from campus work are $2472. The average financial indebtedness of the 1999 graduate was $14,942. The FAFSA and the college's own financial statement are required. The fall application deadline is April 1.

Computers: The mainframe is a McDonnel-Douglas Spirit 6000. PCs and Macs are available for student use in academic buildings and the library. All students may access the system. There are no time limits and no fees. It is recommended that all students have personal computers.

WARTBURG COLLEGE
Waverly, IA 50677-0903

(319) 352-8264
(800) 772-2085; Fax: (319) 352-8579

Full-time: 628 men, 850 women	**Faculty:** 94; IIB, av$
Part-time: 39 men, 29 women	**Ph.D.s:** 79%
Graduate: none	**Student/Faculty:** 16 to 1
Year: 4-4-1, summer session	**Tuition:** $14,955
Application Deadline: August 1	**Room & Board:** $4250
Freshman Class: 1385 applied, 1201 accepted, 411 enrolled	
SAT I Verbal/Math: 569/577	**ACT:** 24 **VERY COMPETITIVE**

Wartburg College, established in 1852, is a private institution affiliated with the Evangelical Lutheran Church in America. In addition to regional accreditation, Wartburg has baccalaureate program accreditation with CSWE, NASM, and NCATE. The library contains 133,910 volumes, 7153 microform items, and 2294 audiovisual forms/CDs, and subscribes to 732 periodicals. Computerized library services include the card catalog, interlibrary loans, and database searching. Special learning facilities include a learning resource center, art gallery, natural history museum, planetarium, radio station, tv station, state-of-the-art learning library, a business center, classroom technology center, fine arts center, journalism lab, symbolic computation lab, music computer lab, 6 acres of native grasses and prairie plants, and more than 100 acres of native timber used for field trips and research. The 118-acre campus is in a small town 15 miles north of Waterloo/Cedar Falls. Including residence halls, there are 34 buildings.

Programs of Study: Wartburg confers B.A., B.A.A., B.A.S., B.M., and B.M.E. degrees. Bachelor's degrees are awarded in BIOLOGICAL SCIENCE (biochemistry and biology/biological science), BUSINESS (accounting, banking and finance, business administration and management, international business management, marketing/retailing/merchandising, and recreation and leisure services), COMMUNICATIONS AND THE ARTS (art, broadcasting, communications, creative writing, English, French, German, graphic design, journalism, music, public relations, and Spanish), COMPUTER AND PHYSICAL SCIENCE (chemistry, computer programming, computer science, mathematics, and physics), EDUCATION (art, elementary, foreign languages, mathematics, music, physical, science, secondary, and social studies), HEALTH PROFESSIONS (medical laboratory technology, music therapy, and occupational therapy), SOCIAL SCIENCE (economics, history, international relations, law enforcement and corrections, philosophy, physical fitness/movement, political science/government, psychology, religion, religious music, social work, and sociology). Math, biology, and chemistry are the strongest academically. Biology, education, and business are the largest.

Special: Special academic programs at Wartburg include those in leadership education and global and multicultural studies. Internships are available in all majors and there are internship programs in Denver, Washington, D.C., and abroad. Study abroad in 15 countries, on-campus work-study, many B.A.-B.S. degrees, dual majors in any combination, and individualized majors are possible. A 3-2 engineering degree is offered with Iowa State University, the universities of Iowa and Illinois, and Washington University in St. Louis. Other 3-2 degrees are possible in medical technology and occupational therapy. A deferred admit program with the University of Iowa College of Dentistry is offered as is an array of experiential learning opportunities. There are 8 national honor societies.

Admissions: 87% of the 1999-2000 applicants were accepted. The SAT I scores for the 1999-2000 freshman class were: Verbal--23% below 500, 36% between

500 and 599, 33% between 600 and 700, and 8% above 700; Math--20% below 500, 36% between 500 and 599, 36% between 600 and 700, and 8% above 700. The ACT scores were 20% below 21, 22% between 21 and 23, 28% between 24 and 26, 15% between 27 and 28, and 15% above 28. 53% of the current freshmen were in the top fifth of their class; 79% were in the top two fifths. There were 4 National Merit finalists. 45 freshmen graduated first in their class.

Requirements: The SAT I or ACT is required. Wartburg requires applicants to be in the upper 50% of their class. A GPA of 2.2 is required. Candidates for admission must be graduates of an accredited secondary school, having completed 4 years of English, 3 years each of math, science, and social studies, 2 years of foreign language, and 1 year of introduction to computers. AP and CLEP credits are accepted. Important factors in the admissions decision are advanced placement or honor courses, recommendations by school officials, and leadership record.

Procedure: Freshmen are admitted fall and winter. Entrance exams should be taken before the senior year. There is an early admissions plan. Early decision applications should be filed by December 1; regular applications, by August 1 for fall entry and December 30 for winter entry, along with a $20 fee. Notification of early decision; and regular decision is sent on a rolling basis. 1% of all applicants are on a waiting list.

Financial Aid: In 1999-2000, 97% of all students received some form of financial aid. 67% of freshmen and 61% of continuing students received need-based aid. The average freshman award was $14,136. Of that total, scholarships or need-based grants averaged $9305; loans averaged $4010; and work contracts averaged $821 ($1500 maximum). 60% of undergraduates work part time. Average annual earnings from campus work are $1441. The average financial indebtedness of the 1999 graduate was $14,826. Wartburg is a member of CSS. The FAFSA is required. The fall application deadline is March 1.

Computers: The mainframes are a DEC VAX 4000-300, DEC ALPHA 2000, DEC VAX Station 3100, DEC VAX 3300 l, and two ALPHA 1000A. All students may use the mainframe system, Internet, and World Wide Web. Students are assigned a password and a user ID. More than 200 Macs and PCs are also available. All students may access the system. There are no time limits. The fee is $75.

WASHINGTON AND JEFFERSON COLLEGE
Washington, PA 15301
(724) 223-6025
(800) (888) 926-3529; Fax: (724) 223-6534

Full-time: 581 men, 554 women	**Faculty:** 88; IIB, +$
Part-time: 34 men, 48 women	**Ph.D.s:** 89%
Graduate: none	**Student/Faculty:** 13 to 1
Year: 4-1-4, summer session	**Tuition:** $19,000
Application Deadline: March 1	**Room & Board:** $4750
Freshman Class: 1262 applied, 1008 accepted, 327 enrolled	
SAT I Verbal/Math: 540/550	**ACT:** 23 **VERY COMPETITIVE**

Washington & Jefferson College, founded in 1781, is a private institution offering instruction in liberal arts. The library contains 195,525 volumes, 14,397 microform items, and 7495 audiovisual forms/CDs, and subscribes to 536 periodicals. Computerized library services include the card catalog, interlibrary loans, and database searching. Special learning facilities include a learning resource center, art gallery, radio station, and a biological field station. The 40-acre campus is in a small town 25 miles south of Pittsburgh. Including residence halls, there are 36 buildings.

Programs of Study: Washington & Jefferson confers the B.A. degree. Bachelor's degrees are awarded in BIOLOGICAL SCIENCE (biology/biological science), BUSINESS (accounting and business administration and management), COMMUNICATIONS AND THE ARTS (English, French, German, and Spanish), COMPUTER AND PHYSICAL SCIENCE (chemistry, computer science, mathematics, and physics), EDUCATION (art and foreign languages), SOCIAL SCIENCE (economics, history, philosophy, political science/government, psychology, and sociology). Business, English, and psychology are the largest.

Special: The college offers study abroad in England, Russsia, and Colombia, as well as other countries, internships in all majors, a Washington semester with American University, dual and student-designed majors, credit by exam, and pass/fail options. There is a 3-2 engineering program with Case Western Reserve University in Cleveland and Washington University in St. Louis. The college offers special human resources management and entrepreneurial studies programs. There is also a 3-4 podiatry program with the Pennsylvania and Ohio Colleges of Podiatry and a 3-4 optometry program with Pennsylvania College of Optometry. There is a 3-3 program with Duquesue University School of Law. There are 11 national honor societies, including Phi Beta Kappa, and 12 departmental honors programs.

Admissions: 80% of the 1999-2000 applicants were accepted. The SAT I scores for the 1999-2000 freshman class were: Verbal--25% below 500, 48% between 500 and 599, 25% between 600 and 700, and 2% above 700; Math--23% below 500, 51% between 500 and 599, 22% between 600 and 700, and 4% above 700. The ACT scores were 21% below 21, 30% between 21 and 23, 29% between 24 and 26, 14% between 27 and 28, and 6% above 28. 55% of the current freshmen were in the top fifth of their class; 82% were in the top two fifths. 17 freshmen graduated first in their class.

Requirements: The SAT I or ACT is required. Washington & Jefferson requires applicants to be in the upper 40% of their class. the SAT II: Subject tests in writing and 2 other subjects are required if submitting the SAT I. A GED is accepted. Applicants must complete 15 academic credits or Carnegie units, including 3 credits of English and math, 2 of foreign language, and 1 of science. An essay and interview are recommended. Applications are accepted on-line via the school's web site, CollegeView, CollegeLink, ExPAN and others. AP and CLEP credits are accepted. Important factors in the admissions decision are advanced placement or honor courses, recommendations by school officials, and personality/intangible qualities.

Procedure: Freshmen are admitted to all sessions. Entrance exams should be taken in the junior or senior year. There are early decision, early admissions, and deferred admissions plans. Early decision applications should be filed by November 1; regular applications, by March 1 for fall entry, January 1 for winter entry, February 1 for spring entry, and June 1 for summer entry, along with a $25 fee. Notification of early decision is sent November 15; regular decision, February 1. 15 early decision candidates were accepted for the 1999-2000 class.

Financial Aid: In 1999-2000, 80% of all freshmen and 75% of continuing students received some form of financial aid. 75% of all students received need-based aid. The average freshman award was $12,966. Of that total, scholarships or need-based grants averaged $9396 (maximum); loans averaged $2625 ($4125 maximum); and work contracts averaged $1200 (maximum). 15% of undergraduates work part time. Average annual earnings from campus work are $1200. The average financial indebtedness of the 1999 graduate was $13,900. Washington & Jefferson is a member of CSS. The FAFSA is required. The fall application deadline is March 15.

Computers: The mainframe is a Digital Vax 4000-500. 400 terminals, PCs, and Macs are located in the computer center and classrooms. Each dorm room has 2 free Internet connections. All students may access the system as needed. There are no time limits and no fees.

WASHINGTON AND LEE UNIVERSITY
Lexington, VA 24450   (540) 463-8710; Fax: (540) 463-8062

Full-time: 968 men, 758 women	**Faculty:** 155; IIB, ++$
Part-time: 3 women	**Ph.D.s:** 95%
Graduate: 215 men, 153 women	**Student/Faculty:** 11 to 1
Year: 4-4-2	**Tuition:** $17,105
Application Deadline: January 15	**Room & Board:** $5547
Freshman Class: 3082 applied, 1101 accepted, 467 enrolled	
SAT I or ACT: required	**MOST COMPETITIVE**

Washington and Lee University, established in 1749, is a private institution offering undergraduate liberal arts degrees. There are 2 undergraduate schools and 1 graduate school. In addition to regional accreditation, Washington and Lee has baccalaureate program accreditation with AACSB and ACEJMC. The 2 libraries contain 503,931 volumes, 124,056 microform items, and 7571 audiovisual forms/CDs, and subscribe to 1816 periodicals. Computerized library services include the card catalog, interlibrary loans, and database searching. Special learning facilities include an art gallery, radio station, tv station, and performing arts center. The 305-acre campus is in a small town 50 miles northeast of Roanoke. Including residence halls, there are 66 buildings.

Programs of Study: Washington and Lee confers B.A. and B.S. degrees. Doctoral degrees are also awarded. Bachelor's degrees are awarded in AGRICULTURE (forestry and related sciences), BIOLOGICAL SCIENCE (biology/biological science and neurosciences), BUSINESS (accounting and business administration and management), COMMUNICATIONS AND THE ARTS (art history and appreciation, classics, dramatic arts, English, French, German, Germanic languages and literature, journalism, music, romance languages and literature, Spanish, and studio art), COMPUTER AND PHYSICAL SCIENCE (chemistry, computer science, geology, mathematics, natural sciences, and physics), ENGINEERING AND ENVIRONMENTAL DESIGN (chemical engineering, engineering physics, and environmental science), SOCIAL SCIENCE (archeology, cognitive science, East Asian studies, economics, history, interdisciplinary studies, medieval studies, philosophy, political science/government, psychology, religion, Russian and Slavic studies, and sociology). The preprofessional commerce program, journalism, and mass media, and history are the strongest academically and the largest.

Special: There is cross-registration with area colleges, including VMI, and various internships, including commerce, government, and journalism, are available. Study-abroad programs are offered in several countries. There is a 3-3 law program, a 3-2 engineering degree with Rensselaer Polytechnic Institute and Washington and Columbia Universities, and a 3-2 program in forestry or environmental management with Duke University. Washington and Lee also offers interdisciplinary majors, including chemistry-engineering and natural science and math, and student-designed majors. There are 9 national honor societies, including Phi Beta Kappa, and a freshman honors program.

Admissions: 36% of the 1999-2000 applicants were accepted. The SAT I scores for the 1999-2000 freshman class were: Verbal--1% below 500, 8% between 500 and 599, 57% between 600 and 700, and 33% above 700; Math--1% below 500, 7% between 500 and 599, 51% between 600 and 700, and 42% above 700. The

ACT scores were 15% between 24 and 26, 37% between 27 and 28, and 48% above 28. 91% of the current freshmen were in the top fifth of their class; 99% were in the top two fifths. There were 33 National Merit finalists or semifinalists. 56 freshmen graduated first or second in their class.

Requirements: The SAT I or ACT is required, as well as 3 SAT II: Subject tests. Applicants must graduate from an accredited secondary school. They must earn 16 units, including 4 units in English, 3 in math, 2 in a foreign language, and 1 each in history and natural science. Course work in social sciences is also required. Essays are required, and interviews are recommended. Applications are accepted on-line. AP credits are accepted. Important factors in the admissions decision are advanced placement or honor courses, leadership record, and recommendations by school officials.

Procedure: Freshmen are admitted in the fall. Entrance exams should be taken between March of the junior year and January of the senior year. There are early decision and deferred admissions plans. Early decision applications should be filed by December 1; regular applications, by January 15 for fall entry, along with a $40 fee. Notification of early decision is sent December 20; regular decision, April 1. 192 early decision candidates were accepted for the 1999-2000 class. 20% of all applicants are on a waiting list.

Financial Aid: In 1998-99, 31% of all freshmen and 27% of continuing students received some form of financial aid. 23% of freshmen and 27% of continuing students received need-based aid. The average freshman award was $14,465. Of that total, scholarships or need-based grants averaged $11,930 ($25,000 maximum); loans averaged $1750 ($8000 maximum); and work contracts averaged $785 ($800 maximum). 46% of undergraduates work part time. Average annual earnings from campus work are $785. The average financial indebtedness of the 1998 graduate was $14,755. Washington and Lee is a member of CSS. The CSS/Profile or FAFSA and the noncustodial parent's statement, and business/farm supplement are required. The fall application deadline is February 1.

Computers: The mainframe is an HP 9000 series. There are about 200 PCs in 12 locations throughout academic buildings. All terminals and PCs are networked, providing access to the mainframe. Students who live off campus have dial-up access to the mainframe. All students may access the system 24 hours a day, 7 days a week, while classes are in session. There are no time limits and no fees.

WASHINGTON COLLEGE
Chestertown, MD 21620-1197

(410) 778-7700
(800) 422-1782; Fax: (410) 778-7287

Full-time: 431 men, 635 women	**Faculty:** 68; IIB, +$
Part-time: 14 men, 37 women	**Ph.D.s:** 95%
Graduate: 28 men, 49 women	**Student/Faculty:** 16 to 1
Year: semesters	**Tuition:** $20,200
Application Deadline: February 15	**Room & Board:** $5740
Freshman Class: 1479 applied, 1264 accepted, 281 enrolled	
SAT I Verbal/Math: 562/545	**VERY COMPETITIVE**

Washington College, founded in 1782, is an independent college offering programs in the liberal arts and sciences, business management, and teacher preparation. There is 1 graduate school. The library contains 217,000 volumes, 159,270 microform items, and 4158 audiovisual forms/CDs, and subscribes to 801 periodicals. Computerized library services include the card catalog, interlibrary loans, and database searching. Special learning facilities include a learning resource center. The 112-acre campus is in a small town 75 miles from Baltimore, Philadelphia, and Washington, D.C. Including residence halls, there are 39 buildings.

Programs of Study: WC confers B.A. and B.S. degrees. Master's degrees are also awarded. Bachelor's degrees are awarded in BIOLOGICAL SCIENCE (biology/biological science), BUSINESS (business administration and management), COMMUNICATIONS AND THE ARTS (art, dramatic arts, English, fine arts, French, German, music, and Spanish), COMPUTER AND PHYSICAL SCIENCE (chemistry, mathematics, and physics), ENGINEERING AND ENVIRONMENTAL DESIGN (environmental science), SOCIAL SCIENCE (American studies, economics, history, humanities, international studies, philosophy, political science/government, psychology, and sociology). Psychology, English, and chemistry are the strongest academically. Business management, English, and psychology are the largest.

Special: Internships are available in all majors. There is study abroad in 6 countries and a Washington semester at American University. The college offers a 3-2 engineering degree with the University of Maryland at College Park, as well as a 3-2 nursing program with John Hopkins University, credit by exam, and pass/fail options. There are 6 national honor societies.

Admissions: 85% of the 1999-2000 applicants were accepted. The SAT I scores for the 1999-2000 freshman class were: Verbal--22% below 500, 50% between 500 and 599, 22% between 600 and 700, and 6% above 700; Math--26% below 500, 45% between 500 and 599, 26% between 600 and 700, and 3% above 700. 65% of the current freshmen were in the top fifth of their class; 87% were in the top two fifths.

Requirements: The SAT I or ACT is required. A GPA of 2.5 is required. Applicants must be graduates of an accredited secondary school or have a GED. 16 Carnegie units are required. Applicants should take high school courses in English, foreign language, history, math, science, and social studies. An essay is required, and an interview is recommended. Applications are accepted on disk or on-line at the school's web site. AP and CLEP credits are accepted. Important factors in the admissions decision are advanced placement or honor courses, recommendations by school officials, and leadership record.

Procedure: Freshmen are admitted fall and spring. Entrance exams should be taken in the spring of the junior year or fall of the senior year. There are early decision and early admissions plans. Early decision applications should be filed by December 1; regular applications, by February 15 for fall entry and December 1 for spring entry, along with a $35 fee. Notification of early decision is sent December 15; regular decision, March 1. A waiting list is an active part of the admissions procedure.

Financial Aid: In a recent year, 88% of all freshmen and 85% of continuing students received some form of financial aid. 70% of undergraduates work part time. Average annual earnings from campus work are $1100. The average financial indebtedness of the recent graduate was $12,000. WC is a member of CSS. The CSS/Profile or FAFSA and the parents' and student's federal income tax returns are required. The fall application deadline is February 15.

Computers: The mainframe is a Data General Aviion 5500. Students may access the mainframe, the library collection, and the Internet via a campus network of more than 130 Macs in the library, academic buildings, and dormitories. All students may access the system. There are no time limits and no fees. It is strongly recommended that all students have personal computers, The preferred make is a Mac or a PowerBook.

WASHINGTON UNIVERSITY IN ST. LOUIS
St. Louis, MO 63130-4899
(314) 935-6000
(800) 638-0700; Fax: (314) 935-4290

Full-time: 2834 men, 2855 women	**Faculty:** 662; I, ++$
Part-time: 339 men, 481 women	**Ph.D.s:** 98%
Graduate: 2875 men, 2704 women	**Student/Faculty:** 9 to 1
Year: semesters, summer session	**Tuition:** $23,634
Application Deadline: January 15	**Room & Board:** $7313
Freshman Class: 17,109 applied, 5806 accepted, 1384 enrolled	
SAT I or ACT: required	**MOST COMPETITIVE**

Washington University, founded in 1853, is a private, independent institution offering undergraduate and graduate programs in arts and sciences, business, architecture, engineering, and art, and professional programs in law, medicine, and social work. There are 5 undergraduate and 8 graduate schools. In addition to regional accreditation, Washington has baccalaureate program accreditation with AACSB, ABET, and NASAD. The 14 libraries contain 3,350,122 volumes, 3,042,664 microform items, and 42,799 audiovisual forms/ CDs, and subscribe to 18,704 periodicals. Computerized library services include the card catalog, interlibrary loans, and database searching. Special learning facilities include a learning resource center, art gallery, radio station, TV station, dance studio, professional theater, observatory, and studio theater. The 169-acre campus is in a suburban area 7 miles west of downtown St. Louis. Including residence halls, there are 101 buildings.

Programs of Study: Washington confers B.A., B.S., B.F.A., B.M., B.S.B.A, B.S.B.M.E., B.S.C.E., B.S.Ch.E., B.S.C.S., B.S.Co.E., B.S.E.E., B.S.I.M., B.S.M.E., and B.S.S.S.E. degrees. Master's and doctoral degrees are also awarded. Bachelor's degrees are awarded in BIOLOGICAL SCIENCE (biochemistry, biology/biological science, biophysics, and neurosciences), BUSINESS (accounting, banking and finance, business administration and management, business economics, human resources, international business management, international economics, marketing/retailing/merchandising, and trade and industrial supervision and management), COMMUNICATIONS AND THE ARTS (advertising, American literature, Arabic, art history and appreciation, ceramic art and design, Chinese, classics, comparative literature, creative writing, dance, design, dramatic arts, drawing, East Asian languages and literature, English, English literature, fine arts, French, German, graphic design, Greek (classical), Hebrew, Italian, Japanese, languages, Latin, literature, music, music theory and composition, painting, performing arts, photography, printmaking, Russian, sculpture, Spanish, studio art, and visual and performing arts), COMPUTER AND PHYSICAL SCIENCE (applied mathematics, chemistry, computer science, earth science, information sciences and systems, mathematics, physical sciences, physics, and statistics), EDUCATION (art, education, elementary, foreign languages, mathematics, middle school, science, secondary, social science, and social studies), ENGINEERING AND ENVIRONMENTAL DESIGN (architecture, bioengineering, biomedical engineering, chemical engineering, civil engineering, commercial art, computer engineering, electrical/electronics engineering, engineering, engineering mechanics, engineering physics, environmental science, geological engineering, mechanical engineering, systems engineering, and technology and public affairs), HEALTH PROFESSIONS (predentistry, premedicine, prepharmacy, and preveterinary science), SOCIAL SCIENCE (African American studies, African studies, American studies, anthropology, archeology, Asian/Oriental studies, biopsychology, East Asian studies, economics, ethnic studies, European studies, fashion design and technology, history, humanities, international studies, Islamic studies, Judaic studies, Latin American studies, medieval studies, Middle Eastern studies, philosophy, political science/government, psychology, religion, Russian and Slavic studies, social science, systems science, urban studies, Western European studies, and women's studies). Natural sciences and engineering are the strongest academically. Natural sciences, engineering, business, and social sciences are the largest.

Special: Opportunities are provided for cooperative programs with other schools, internships, work-study programs, study abroad, a Washington (D.C.) semester, accelerated degree programs, a B.A.-B.S. engineering degree, credit by examination, nondegree study, pass/fail options, and dual and student-designed majors. There are 18 national honor societies, including Phi Beta Kappa.

Admissions: 34% of the 1999-2000 applicants were accepted. The SAT I scores for the 1999-2000 freshman class were: Verbal--2% below 500, 12% between 500 and 599, 53% between 600 and 700, and 33% above 700; Math--6% between 500 and 599, 45% between 600 and 700, and 49% above 700. The ACT scores were 3% between 21 and 23, 10% between 24 and 26, 20% between 27 and 28, and 67% above 28. 94% of the current freshmen were in the top fifth of their class; 99% were in the top two fifths. There were 157 National Merit finalists. 138 freshmen graduated first in their class.

Requirements: The SAT I or ACT is required. An essay is required from all applicants. Fine arts students may submit portfolios. 4 years of English, 3 each of math, science, and social science/history, and 2 of a foreign language are recommended. Also required are recommendations from a teacher and a counselor. Students may apply on computer disk via CollegeLink, ACT College Connector, or Apply, but a paper copy is also required. The Common Application is accepted. AP credits are accepted. Important factors in the admissions decision are advanced placement or honor courses, evidence of special talent, and extracurricular activities record.

Procedure: Freshmen are admitted in the fall. Entrance exams should be taken by December of the senior year. There are early decision and deferred admissions plans. Early decision applications should be filed by November 15 or January 1; regular applications, by January 15 for fall entry, along with a $55 fee. Notification of early decision is sent December 15 or January 15; regular decision, April 1. 284 early decision candidates were accepted for the 1999-2000 class. A waiting list is an active part of the admissions procedure.

Financial Aid: In 1999-2000, approximately 60% of all students received some form of financial aid. 45% of freshmen and 47% of continuing students received need-based aid. The average freshman award was $18,301. Of that total, scholarships or need-based grants averaged $15,000 ($20,500 maximum); loans averaged $5600; and work contracts averaged $2000 (maximum). 50% of undergraduates work part time. Average annual earnings from campus work are $2000. Washington is a member of CSS. The CSS/Profile or FAFSA is required. The fall application deadline is February 15.

Computers: The mainframe is an IBM 9121-511. Specialized computing resources are available to students. The Center for Engineering Computing has more than 200 workstations consisting of graphics terminals, PCs, and design workstations. The School of Business supports 2 interactive systems and provides a student lab with 50 PC workstations. In addition, University Academic Computing and Networking maintains 10 student labs, including 5 in residential areas, with PCs and laser printers. There is a Windows cluster in the main library. All dormitory rooms have direct Internet connections. All students may access the system 24 hours per day, 7 days per week. There are no time limits and no fees.

WAYNE STATE UNIVERSITY
Detroit, MI 48202
(313) 577-3577; Fax: (313) 577-7536

Full-time: 3635 men, 5380 women	**Faculty:** 1583; I, -$
Part-time: 3622 men, 5756 women	**Ph.D.s:** 85%
Graduate: 35,935 men, 6757 women	**Student/Faculty:** 6 to 1
Year: semesters, summer session	**Tuition:** $3818 ($8249)
Application Deadline: August 1	**Room & Board:** $2350 ($6350)
Freshman Class: 5230 applied, 4310 accepted, 2014 enrolled	
ACT: 20	**LESS COMPETITIVE**

Wayne State University, founded in 1868, is a state-supported, nonprofit institution. Primarily a commuter college, it offers a variety of academic and professional programs. There are 11 undergraduate and 14 graduate schools. In addition to regional accreditation, Wayne State has baccalaureate program accreditation with AACSB, ABET, ABFSE, ACPE, ADA, APTA, CAHEA, CSWE, NASM, NCATE, and NLN. The 6 libraries contain 3,045,681 volumes, 3,462,433 microform items, and 57,399 audiovisual forms/CDs, and subscribe to 24,200 periodicals. Computerized library services include the card catalog and database searching. Special learning facilities include a learning resource center, art gallery, natural history museum, planetarium, radio station, and tv station. The 203-acre campus is in an urban area 2 miles north of downtown Detroit in the New Center area. There are 95 buildings.

Programs of Study: Wayne State confers B.A., B.S., B.A.S., B.F.A., B.I.S., B. Mus., B.P.A., B.S.A.H.S., B.S.C.T., B.S.E.T., B.S.M.S., B.S.N., B.S.W., and B. T.I.S. degrees. Master's and doctoral degrees are also awarded. Bachelor's degrees are awarded in BIOLOGICAL SCIENCE (biology/biological science), BUSINESS (accounting, banking and finance, business economics, funeral home services, labor studies, management information systems, management science, and marketing/retailing/merchandising), COMMUNICATIONS AND THE ARTS (Arabic, art, art history and appreciation, broadcasting, classics, communications, dance, design, dramatic arts, English, film arts, fine arts, French, German, Greek, Hebrew, Italian, journalism, Latin, linguistics, music, music business management, music performance, music theory and composition, Polish, public relations, Russian, Slavic languages, Spanish, and speech/debate/rhetoric), COMPUTER AND PHYSICAL SCIENCE (chemistry, computer science, data processing, geology, information sciences and systems, mathematics, physics, and radiological technology), EDUCATION (art, bilingual/bicultural, business, early childhood, elementary, foreign languages, health, industrial arts, mathematics, music, physical, science, secondary, special, and technical), ENGINEERING AND ENVIRONMENTAL DESIGN (chemical engineering, civil engineering, computer technology, electrical/electronics engineering, engineering technology, industrial engineering technology, manufacturing engineering, manufacturing technology, materials engineering, materials science, mechanical engineering, mechanical engineering technology, and metallurgical engineering), HEALTH PROFESSIONS (cytotechnology, medical laboratory technology, music therapy, nursing, occupational therapy, pharmacy, physical therapy, radiation therapy, and speech pathology/audiology), SOCIAL SCIENCE (African American studies, African studies, American studies, anthropology, classical/ancient civilization, criminal justice, dietetics, economics, food science, geography, history, human development, humanities, international studies, liberal arts/general studies, Mexican-American/Chicano studies, Near Eastern studies, parks and recreation management, peace studies, philosophy, political science/government, psychology, public affairs, social studies, social work, sociology, urban studies, and women's studies). Chemistry, biology, and pharmacy are the strongest academically. Elementary education, art, and psychology are the largest.

Special: Special academic programs include cross-registration with Macomb University Center, the University of Michigan, and the University of Windsor; internships in business, industry, or communications; study abroad in Germany, Japan, or England; on-campus work-study programs; a general studies degree; co-op programs; nondegree study; and limited pass/fail options. The College of Lifelong Learning offers televised, weekend, and evening courses. There is 1 national honor society, Phi Beta Kappa, a freshman honors program, and 64 departmental honors programs.

Admissions: 82% of the 1999-2000 applicants were accepted. The ACT scores for the 1999-2000 freshman class were: 52% below 21, 22% between 21 and 23, 16% between 24 and 26, 6% between 27 and 28, and 4% above 28. 40% of the current freshmen were in the top fifth of their class.

Requirements: The ACT is recommended. A GPA of 2.8 is required. Admissions requirements include graduation from an accredited secondary school; the GED with an acceptable SAT I or ACT score is also allowable. If the GPA is below 2.75, the applicant must have composite SAT I scores totaling at least 990 and/or an ACT score of 21. AP and CLEP credits are accepted.

Procedure: Freshmen are admitted to all sessions. If necessary, the ACT should be taken in the junior year or the SAT I in the senior year. There is a deferred admissions plan. Applications should be filed by August 1 for fall entry, December 1 for winter entry, and April 1 for summer or spring entry, along with a $20 fee. Notification is sent on a rolling basis.

Financial Aid: In 1999-2000, 41% of all freshmen and 37% of continuing students received some form of financial aid. 29% of freshmen and 25% of continuing students received need-based aid. The average freshman award was $4499. Of that total, scholarships or need-based grants averaged $3000 ($5000 maximum); loans averaged $2600 ($5500 maximum); and work contracts averaged $3696 ($4000 maximum). 7% of undergraduates work part time. Average annual earnings from campus work are $2382. Wayne State is a member of CSS. The FAFSA and the college's own financial statement are required. The fall application deadline is May 1.

Computers: The mainframes are a CRAY J-916, an IBM 9672 R24, an RS/6000 Model 595, and an IBM 9121-411. There are 1000 Macs, IBM, and Zenith PCs available in the libraries, the student union, and academic departments. All students may access the system 24 hours a day. There are no time limits and no fees.

WEBB INSTITUTE
Glen Cove, NY 11542 (516) 671-2213; Fax: (516) 674-9838

Full-time: 67 men, 14 women	**Faculty:** 8
Part-time: none	**Ph.D.s:** 50%
Graduate: none	**Student/Faculty:** 10 to 1
Year: semesters	**Tuition:** see profile
Application Deadline: February 15	**Room & Board:** $6250
Freshman Class: 70 applied, 32 accepted, 23 enrolled	
SAT I Verbal/Math: 665/710	**MOST COMPETITIVE**

Webb Institute, founded in 1889, is a private engineering school devoted to professional knowledge of ship construction, design, and motive power. In addition to regional accreditation, Webb has baccalaureate program accreditation with ABET. The library contains 41,680 volumes, 1180 microform items, and 1230 audiovisual forms/CDs, and subscribes to 257 periodicals. Computerized library services include the card catalog, interlibrary loans, and database searching. Special learning facilities include a marine engineering lab and a ship model testing/towing tank. The 26-acre campus is in a suburban area 24 miles east of New York City. Including residence halls, there are 11 buildings.

Programs of Study: Webb confers the B.S. degree. Bachelor's degrees are awarded in ENGINEERING AND ENVIRONMENTAL DESIGN (naval architecture and marine engineering).

Special: All students are employed 2 months each year through co-op programs.

Admissions: 46% of the 1999-2000 applicants were accepted. The SAT I scores for the 1999-2000 freshman class were: Verbal--4% between 500 and 599, 65% between 600 and 700, and 30% above 700; Math--35% between 600 and 700 and 65% above 700. All current freshmen were in the top fifth of their class. There was 1 National Merit finalist. 2 freshmen graduated first in their class.

Requirements: The SAT I is required, with minimum scores of 500 verbal and 660 math. Webb requires applicants to be in the upper 20% of their class, with a GPA of 3.2. Applicants should be graduates of an accredited secondary school with 16 academic credits completed, including 4 each in English and math, 2 each in history and science, 1 in foreign language, and 3 in electives. 3 SAT II: Subject tests in writing, mathematics level I or II, and physics or chemistry are required, as is an interview. Candidates must be U.S. citizens. Important factors in the admissions decision are advanced placement or honor courses, evidence of special talent, and personality/intangible qualities.

Procedure: Freshmen are admitted in the fall. Entrance exams should be taken by January of the senior year. There is an early decision plan. Early decision applications should be filed by October 15; regular applications, by February 15 for fall entry, along with a $25 fee. Notification of early decision is sent December 10; regular decision, April 15. 2 early decision candidates were accepted for the 1999-2000 class.

Financial Aid: All students receive 4-year, full-tuition scholarships. The aid reported here, from external sources, assists with room and board. In 1999-2000, 29% of all freshmen and 14% of continuing students received some form of financial aid. 8% of freshmen and 7% of continuing students received need-based aid. The average freshman award was $5125. Of that total, scholarships or need-based grants averaged $1600 ($2500 maximum) and loans averaged $5125 ($6250 maximum). The average financial indebtedness of the 1999 graduate was $10,000. Webb is a member of CSS. The CSS/Profile and the institute's own financial statement are required. The fall application deadline is July 1.

Computers: There are 28 PCs available on campus. All students are issued a laptop, which connects to the network for access to E-mail and the Internet. Students can connect to the network from dormitory rooms, classrooms, labs, the library, and other public areas. All students may access the system 24 hours per day. There are no time limits and no fees.

Webster University, founded in 1915, is an independent institution with programs in fine and performing arts, liberal arts and sciences, education, nursing, and business. There are 4 undergraduate and 5 graduate schools. In addition to regional accreditation, Webster has baccalaureate program accreditation with AACSB, ACBSP, NASM, and NLN. The library contains 248,500 volumes, 135,000 microform items, and 9196 audiovisual forms/CDs, and subscribes to 1355 periodicals. Computerized library services include the card catalog, interlibrary loans, and database searching. Special learning facilities include a learning resource center, art gallery, radio station, media center, writing center, and theater. The 47-acre campus is in a suburban area 12 miles southwest of St. Louis. Including residence halls, there are 54 buildings.

Programs of Study: Webster confers B.A., B.S., B.B.A., B.F.A., B.S.N., B.M., and B.M.Ed. degrees. Master's and doctoral degrees are also awarded. Bachelor's degrees are awarded in BIOLOGICAL SCIENCE (biology/biological science), BUSINESS (accounting, business administration and management, and management science), COMMUNICATIONS AND THE ARTS (advertising, art, audio technology, broadcasting, communications, dance, dramatic arts, English, film arts, French, German, journalism, literature, media arts, music, musical theater, photography, public relations, Spanish, theater design, and video), COMPUTER AND PHYSICAL SCIENCE (computer science, information sciences and systems, and mathematics), EDUCATION (education and music), ENGINEERING AND ENVIRONMENTAL DESIGN (environmental science), HEALTH PROFESSIONS (nursing), SOCIAL SCIENCE (anthropology, economics, history, international relations, law, philosophy, political science/government, psychology, religion, social science, and sociology). Liberal arts is the strongest academically. Business and communications are the largest.

Special: Students may cross-register with Washington University and the University of Missouri/Columbia, and with Fontbonne, Maryville, Lindenwood, and Missouri Baptist Colleges and Eden Seminary. The university offers co-op programs, work-study programs, internships, dual majors, student-designed majors, B.A.-B.S. degrees, a 3-2 engineering degree with the University of Missouri/Columbia and Washington University, and a 3-4 architecture program with Washington University. Study abroad, nondegree study, pass/fail options, and credit for life, military, and work experience are available. There is 1 national honor society.

Admissions: 63% of the 1999-2000 applicants were accepted. The SAT I scores for the 1999-2000 freshman class were: Verbal--13% below 500, 39% between 500 and 599, 37% between 600 and 700, and 11% above 700; Math--24% below 500, 44% between 500 and 599, 29% between 600 and 700, and 3% above 700. The ACT scores were 20% below 21, 24% between 21 and 23, 28% between 24 and 26, 14% between 27 and 28, and 14% above 28. 50% of the current freshmen were in the top fifth of their class; 77% were in the top two fifths. There was 1

National Merit finalist and 3 semifinalists. 10 freshmen graduated first in their class.

Requirements: The SAT I or ACT is required. Webster requires applicants to be in the upper 50% of their class. A GPA of 2.5 is required. Applicants must be graduates of an accredited secondary school. The GED is accepted. Webster recommends that students complete 16 high school academic units, including 4 units of English, 3 each of social studies/history and math, and 2 each of foreign language, science, and electives. An essay is required of all students, and a portfolio or audition is required for art, dance, music, musical theater, and theater applicants. Applications are accepted on-line. AP and CLEP credits are accepted. Important factors in the admissions decision are advanced placement or honor courses, leadership record, and recommendations by school officials.

Procedure: Freshmen are admitted fall and spring. Entrance exams should be taken in the spring of the junior year. There are early admissions and deferred admissions plans. Applications should be filed by March 1 for fall entry and December 15 for spring entry, along with a $25 fee. Notification is sent on a rolling basis.

Financial Aid: In 1999-2000, 95% of all freshmen and 48% of continuing students received some form of financial aid. 69% of freshmen and 39% of continuing students received need-based aid. The average freshman award was $11,093. Of that total, scholarships or need-based grants averaged $5998 ($12,150 maximum); loans averaged $3109 ($6625 maximum); and work contracts averaged $1986 ($2500 maximum). 13% of undergraduates work part time. Average annual earnings from campus work are $2305. Webster is a member of CSS. The FAFSA and the university's own financial statement are required. The fall application deadline is April 1.

Computers: Student dormitories use the HP 9000 mainframe. In addition, there are 300 Pentium PCs and Macs available in the central labs, student lounges, and distributed departments. 10 E-mail stations are located in dormitories and classroom buildings. All computers access the Internet and Web. There are no time limits. The fee is $200.

WELLESLEY COLLEGE
Wellesley, MA 02481   (781) 283-2270; Fax: (781) 283-3678

Full-time: 2240 women	**Faculty:** 237; IIB, ++$
Part-time: 93 women	**Ph.D.s:** 97%
Graduate: none	**Student/Faculty:** 9 to 1
Year: semesters	**Tuition:** $23,320
Application Deadline: January 15	**Room & Board:** $7234
Freshman Class: 2903 applied, 1311 accepted, 605 enrolled	
SAT I Verbal/Math: 678/671	**ACT:** 29 **MOST COMPETITIVE**

Wellesley College, established in 1870, is a small, private, diverse liberal arts and sciences college for women. The 5 libraries contain 1 million volumes, 389,742 microform items, and 14,847 audiovisual forms/CDs, and subscribe to 4488 periodicals. Computerized library services include the card catalog, interlibrary loans, and database searching. Special learning facilities include a learning resource center, art gallery, radio station, science center, botanic greenhouse, observatory, center for developmental studies and services, centers for research on women and child study, and media and technology center. The 500-acre campus is in a suburban area 12 miles west of Boston. Including residence halls, there are 64 buildings.

Programs of Study: Wellesley confers the B.A. degree. Bachelor's degrees are awarded in BIOLOGICAL SCIENCE (biochemistry, biology/biological science, and biophysics), COMMUNICATIONS AND THE ARTS (art history and appreciation, Chinese, comparative literature, English, fine arts, French, German, Greek, Italian, Japanese, languages, Latin, music, Russian, Spanish, and studio art), COMPUTER AND PHYSICAL SCIENCE (astronomy, chemistry, computer science, geology, mathematics, and physics), EDUCATION (elementary and secondary), ENGINEERING AND ENVIRONMENTAL DESIGN (architecture), SOCIAL SCIENCE (African American studies, American studies, anthropology, Asian/Oriental studies, classical/ancient civilization, cognitive science, economics, European studies, history, international relations, Judaic studies, Latin American studies, medieval studies, peace studies, philosophy, political science/government, psychobiology, psychology, religion, sociology, and women's studies). Psychology, English, and economics are the largest.

Special: Students may cross-register at MIT, Brandeis University, or Babson College. Exchange programs are available with Spelman College in Georgia and Mills College in California, with members of the 12-College Exchange, with Williams College in Maritime Studies, and with the National Theatre Institute. Study abroad is possible in Wellesley-administered programs in various countries, in exchange programs in Russia and Japan, and at Cambridge and Oxford in England. There are summer internship programs in Boston and Washington, D.C. Dual majors, student-designed majors, nondegree study, and pass/fail options are possible. A 3-2 program with MIT awards a B.A.-B.S. degree. There are 2 national honor societies, including Phi Beta Kappa, and 10 departmental honors programs.

Admissions: 45% of the 1999-2000 applicants were accepted. The SAT I scores for the 1999-2000 freshman class were: Verbal--1% below 500, 13% between 500 and 599, 50% between 600 and 700, and 36% above 700; Math--2% below 500, 16% between 500 and 599, 52% between 600 and 700, and 29% above 700. The ACT scores were 40% above 28. 93% of the current freshmen were in the top fifth of their class; All were in the top two fifths.

Requirements: The SAT I or ACT is required. Wellesley College does not require a fixed plan of secondary school course preparation. Entering students normally have completed 4 years of college preparatory studies in secondary school that includes training in clear and coherent writing and interpreting literature; history; principles of math (typically 4 years); competence in at least 1 foreign language, ancient or modern (usually 4 years of study); and experience in at least 2 lab sciences. An essay is required, and an interview is recommended. The SAT I and 3 SAT IIs (including the writing test) or the ACT are required. AP credits are accepted. Applications are accepted on-line via Embark and CollegeLink. Important factors in the admissions decision are advanced placement or honor courses and extracurricular activities record.

Procedure: Freshmen are admitted in the fall. Entrance exams should be taken during the spring of the junior year or fall of the senior year (no later than December). There are early decision and deferred admissions plans. Early decision applications should be filed by November 1; regular applications, by January 15 for fall entry, along with a $50 fee. Notification of early decision is sent December 15; regular decision, April 1. 106 early decision candidates were accepted for the 1999-2000 class. 18% of all applicants are on a waiting list.

Financial Aid: In 1999-2000, 51% of all freshmen and 52% of continuing students received some form of financial aid, including need-based aid. The average freshman award was $18,100. Average annual earnings from campus work are $1800. The average financial indebtedness of the 1999 graduate was $15,500. Wellesley is a member of CSS. The CSS/Profile, FAFSA, the college's own financial statement, and the most recent income tax returns of parents and student are required. The fall application deadline is February 1.

Computers: The mainframes are composed of a DEC VAX 8550 and a Digital AXP. Students may access the mainframe through more than 200 PCs located in the science center, library, and dormitories. All students may access the system. There are no time limits and no fees.

WELLS COLLEGE
Aurora, NY 13026

(315) 364-3264
(800) 952-9355; Fax: (315) 364-3227

Full-time: 383 women	**Faculty:** 42; IIB, av$
Part-time: 3 men, 18 women	**Ph.D.s:** 100%
Graduate: none	**Student/Faculty:** 9 to 1
Year: semesters	**Tuition:** $12,300
Application Deadline: March 1	**Room & Board:** $6100
Freshman Class: 410 applied, 368 accepted, 135 enrolled	
SAT I Verbal/Math: 580/540	**ACT:** 25 **VERY COMPETITIVE**

Wells College, founded in 1868, is a private liberal arts institution for women. The library contains 248,130 volumes, 13,383 microform items, and 782 audiovisual forms/CDs, and subscribes to 412 periodicals. Computerized library services include interlibrary loans and database searching. Special learning facilities include an art gallery and and the Book Arts Center. The 365-acre campus is in a small town on Cayuga Lake, 25 miles north of Ithaca. Including residence halls, there are 22 buildings.

Programs of Study: Wells confers the B.A. degree. Bachelor's degrees are awarded in BIOLOGICAL SCIENCE (biochemistry, biology/biological science, and molecular biology), BUSINESS (business administration and management), COMMUNICATIONS AND THE ARTS (dance, dramatic arts, English, fine arts, French, German, language arts, music, Spanish, and visual and performing arts), COMPUTER AND PHYSICAL SCIENCE (chemistry, computer science, mathematics, and physics), EDUCATION (elementary), ENGINEERING AND ENVIRONMENTAL DESIGN (environmental science), SOCIAL SCIENCE (American studies, anthropology, economics, ethics, politics, and social policy, history, international studies, philosophy, political science/government, psychology, public affairs, religion, sociology, and women's studies). Biological sciences, chemistry, and English are the strongest academically. Psychology, English, and mathematical and physical sciences are the largest.

Special: Wells offers cross-registration with Cornell University and Ithaca College, a Washington semester with American University, internships, and accelerated degree programs in all majors. Study abroad in 12 countries is permitted. A 3-2 engineering degree is available with Washington University in St. Louis and Columbia, Clarkson, Case Western Reserve, and Cornell universities. Students may also earn 3-2 degrees in business and community health with the University of Rochester and a 3-4 degree in veterinary medicine with Cornell University. Student-designed majors and pass-fail options are available. There are 2 national honor societies, including Phi Beta Kappa.

Admissions: 90% of the 1999-2000 applicants were accepted. The SAT I scores for the 1999-2000 freshman class were: Verbal--17% below 500, 40% between 500 and 599, 39% between 600 and 700, and 4% above 700; Math--29% below 500, 46% between 500 and 599, 23% between 600 and 700, and 2% above 700. The ACT scores were 16% below 21, 20% between 21 and 23, 38% between 24 and 26, 16% between 27 and 28, and 9% above 28. 58% of the current freshmen were in the top fifth of their class; 87% were in the top two fifths. 3 freshmen graduated first in their class.

Requirements: The SAT I or ACT is required. Graduation from an accredited secondary school should include 20 academic credits or Carnegie units. High school courses must include 4 years of English, 3 each of a foreign language and math, and 2 each of history and lab science. 2 teacher recommendations and an essay/personal statement are required, and an interview is strongly recommended. Applications are accepted on-line via Common App. AP and CLEP credits are accepted. Important factors in the admissions decision are advanced placement or honor courses, geographic diversity, and extracurricular activities record.

Procedure: Freshmen are admitted in the fall. Entrance exams should be taken prior to application. There are early decision, early admissions, and deferred admissions plans. Early decision applications should be filed by December 15; regular applications, by March 1 for fall entry, along with a $40 fee. Notification of early decision is sent January 15; regular decision, April 1. 35 early decision candidates were accepted for the 1999-2000 class.

Financial Aid: In 1999-2000, 87% of all freshmen and 92% of continuing students received some form of financial aid. 81% of freshmen and 82% of continuing students received need-based aid. The average freshman award was $13,682. Of that total, scholarships or need-based grants averaged $9307 ($13,000 maximum); loans averaged $3175 ($4125 maximum); and work contracts averaged $1200 (maximum). 90% of undergraduates work part time. Average annual earnings from campus work are $1200. The average financial indebtedness of the 1999 graduate was $17,125. Wells is a member of CSS. The FAFSA is required, and early decision applicants must submit the CSS/profile. The fall application deadline is May 1.

Computers: The mainframe is an IBM AS/400 Model 720. There are 35 Macs (Power Macs and G3s) and 61 Pentium-level PCs available in academic buildings and residence halls. The computer-to-student ratio is 4 to 1. Students have access to the Internet and the World Wide Web. All students may access the system. There are no time limits and no fees.

WESLEYAN COLLEGE
Macon, GA 31210

(912) 757-5206
(800) 447-6610; Fax: (912) 757-4030

Full-time: 448 women	**Faculty:** 44
Part-time: 137 women	**Ph.D.s:** 100%
Graduate: 22 women	**Student/Faculty:** 10 to 1
Year: semesters, summer session	**Tuition:** $16,300
Application Deadline: March 1	**Room & Board:** $6600
Freshman Class: 338 applied, 296 accepted, 132 enrolled	
SAT I or ACT: required	**VERY COMPETITIVE**

Wesleyan College, founded in 1836, is a private liberal arts college for women, affiliated with the United Methodist Church. It is the world's first college chartered to grant degrees to women. In addition to regional accreditation, Wesleyan has baccalaureate program accreditation with NASM. The library contains 140, 923 volumes, 30,110 microform items, and 6553 audiovisual forms/CDs, and subscribes to 603 periodicals. Computerized library services include the card catalog, interlibrary loans, and database searching. Special learning facilities include an art gallery, a computerized teaching classroom, language and math labs, collaborative research science labs, and an arboretum. The 200-acre campus is in a suburban area 90 miles south of Atlanta. Including residence halls, there are 18 buildings.

Programs of Study: Wesleyan confers the A.B. degree. Master's degrees are also awarded. Bachelor's degrees are awarded in BIOLOGICAL SCIENCE (biology/biological science), BUSINESS (business administration and management and international business management), COMMUNICATIONS AND THE ARTS (art history and appreciation, communications, English, music, music history and appreciation, music performance, Spanish, and studio art), COMPUTER AND PHYSICAL SCIENCE (chemistry and mathematics), EDUCATION (early childhood, middle school, and secondary), SOCIAL SCIENCE (American studies, history, interdisciplinary studies, international relations, philosophy, political science/government, psychology, religion, and sociology). Art, biology, and business are the strongest academically. Biology, business, and education are the largest.

Special: Wesleyan offers cross-registration with Mercer University and a 3-2 engineering degree with Georgia Institute of Technology and Auburn and Mercer universities. More than 150 internships are available, as are interdisciplinary, student-designed, and dual majors, study abroad, a Washington semester, work-study programs, credit for life experience, nondegree study, and pass/fail options. There are 12 national honor societies and a freshman honors program. All departments have honors programs.

Admissions: 88% of the 1999-2000 applicants were accepted. The SAT I scores for the 1999-2000 freshman class were: Verbal--16% below 500, 39% between 500 and 599, 35% between 600 and 700, and 10% above 700; Math--32% below 500, 35% between 500 and 599, 31% between 600 and 700, and 2% above 700. The ACT scores were 23% below 21, 17% between 21 and 23, 38% between 24 and 26, 10% between 27 and 28, and 12% above 28. 65% of the current freshmen were in the top fifth of their class; 87% were in the top two fifths. There were 5 National Merit finalists. 5 freshmen graduated first in their class.

Requirements: The SAT I or ACT is required. The college uses a formula to predict the student's college GPA based on the high school GPA and standardized test scores for acceptance decisions. Applicants must be graduates of an accredited secondary school or have a GED certificate. They should have completed 16 Carnegie units, including 4 units each of English and electives, 3 units each of math and social science, and 2 units of natural science. An essay is required and an interview is recommended. A portfolio or an audition is required for art and music students. AP and CLEP credits are accepted. Important factors in the admissions decision are recommendations by school officials, leadership record, and extracurricular activities record.

Procedure: Freshmen are admitted fall and spring. Entrance exams should be taken by the fall of the senior year. There are early decision, early admissions, and deferred admissions plans. Early decision applications should be filed by November 1; regular applications, by March 1 for fall entry and November 15 for spring entry, along with a $30 fee. Notification of early decision is sent December 1; regular decision, April 1. 15 early decision candidates were accepted for the 1999-2000 class.

Financial Aid: In 1999-2000, all freshmen and 75% of continuing students received some form of financial aid. 76% of freshmen and 74% of continuing students received need-based aid. The average freshman award was $21,239. Of that total, scholarships or need-based grants averaged $17,327 ($22,900 maximum); loans averaged $3548 ($17,325 maximum); and work contracts averaged $1200 ($3200 maximum). 72% of undergraduates work part time. Average annual earnings from campus work are $1000. The average financial indebtedness of the 1999 graduate was $16,250. Wesleyan is a member of CSS. The FAFSA and the college's own financial statement are required. The fall application deadline is May 1.

Computers: The campus is fully networked and connected to the Internet. Students have E-mail access. All students may access the system. There are no time limits and no fees. All students are required to have a Compaq 1500c notebook.

WESLEYAN UNIVERSITY
Middletown, CT 06459   **(860) 685-3000; Fax: (860) 685-3001**

Full-time: 1322 men, 1431 women	**Faculty:** 241; IIA, ++$
Part-time: 4 men, 1 woman	**Ph.D.s:** 93%
Graduate: 181 men, 261 women	**Student/Faculty:** 11 to 1
Year: semesters	**Tuition:** $25,120
Application Deadline: January 1	**Room & Board:** $6510
Freshman Class: 6402 applied, 1856 accepted, 732 enrolled	
SAT I Verbal/Math: 690/680	**ACT:** 29 **MOST COMPETITIVE**

Wesleyan University, founded in 1831, is an independent institution offering programs in the liberal arts and sciences. There is 1 graduate school. The 4 libraries contain 1,161,832 volumes, 251,243 microform items, and 18,655 audiovisual forms/CDs, and subscribe to 3167 periodicals. Computerized library services include the card catalog, interlibrary loans, and database searching. Special learning facilities include a learning resource center, art gallery, radio station, and observatory. The 120-acre campus is in a suburban area 15 miles south of Hartford, and 2 hours from both Boston and New York City. Including residence halls, there are 90 buildings.

Programs of Study: Wesleyan confers the B.A. degree. Master's and doctoral degrees are also awarded. Bachelor's degrees are awarded in BIOLOGICAL SCIENCE (biochemistry, biology/biological science, molecular biology, and neurosciences), COMMUNICATIONS AND THE ARTS (art history and appreciation, classics, dance, dramatic arts, English, film arts, French, German, Italian, music, romance languages and literature, Russian, Spanish, and studio art), COMPUTER AND PHYSICAL SCIENCE (astronomy, chemistry, computer science, earth science, mathematics, physics, and science technology), SOCIAL SCIENCE (African American studies, American studies, anthropology, archeology, Asian/Oriental studies, classical/ancient civilization, economics, French studies, history, Latin American studies, medieval studies, philosophy, political science/government, psychology, religion, Russian and Slavic studies, sociology, and women's studies). Sciences, economics, and history are the strongest academically. English, government, and history are the largest.

Special: Wesleyan offers exchange programs with 11 northeastern colleges, cross-registration with 2 area colleges, study abroad in 41 countries on 6 continents, internships, a Washington semester, dual and student-designed majors, and pass/fail options. 3-2 engineering programs with Cal Tech and Columbia University are also available. There are 2 national honor societies, including Phi Beta Kappa, and 40 departmental honors programs.

Admissions: 29% of the 1999-2000 applicants were accepted. The SAT I scores for the 1999-2000 freshman class were: Verbal--1% below 500, 13% between 500 and 599, 38% between 600 and 690, and 48% above 700; Math--1% below 500, 12% between 500 and 599, 46% between 600 and 690, and 41% above 700. The ACT scores were 50% above 28. 86% of the current freshmen were in the top fifth of their class; 97% were in the top two fifths. There were 67 National Merit semifinalists. 44 freshmen graduated first in their class.

Requirements: The SAT I or ACT is required, as are SAT II: Subject tests in writing and 2 other subjects. In addition, applicants should have 20 academic credits, including 4 years each of English, foreign language, math, science, and

712

social studies. An essay is necessary. Applications are accepted on-line via Commonapp.org, Next Stop College, Embark.com, Apply!, or CollegeLink. AP credits are accepted. Important factors in the admissions decision are advanced placement or honor courses, recommendations by school officials, and leadership record.

Procedure: Freshmen are admitted in the fall. Entrance exams should be taken in the spring of the junior year and fall of the senior year. There are early decision and deferred admissions plans. Early decision applications should be filed by November 15; regular applications, by January 1 for fall entry, along with a $55 fee. Notification of early decision is sent December 15; regular decision, April 7. 293 early decision candidates were accepted for the 1999-2000 class. A waiting list is an active part of the admissions procedure.

Financial Aid: In 1999-2000, 45% of all freshmen and 47% of continuing students received some form of financial aid. 48% of freshmen and 41% of continuing students received need-based aid. The average freshman award was $21,136. Of that total, scholarships or need-based grants averaged $13,312; loans averaged $6502; and work contracts averaged $1322. 75% of undergraduates work part time. Average annual earnings from campus work are $1400. The average financial indebtedness of the 1999 graduate was $25,342. Wesleyan is a member of CSS. The CSS/Profile and FAFSA are required. The fall application deadline is February 1.

Computers: The mainframes are a DEC ALPHA and a Sun Ultra-SPARC. More than 150 PCs and Macs are connected to the mainframe at various campus locations. Students use a variety of public servers for E-mail, web access, and other applications. Software for word processing and statistical analysis is also available. All students may access the system. There are no time limits and no fees. It is strongly recommended that all students have personal computers.

WESTERN MARYLAND COLLEGE
Westminster, MD 21157-4390

(410) 857-2230
(800) 638-5005; Fax: (410) 857-2757

Full-time: 717 men, 847 women	**Faculty:** 85; IIB, ++$
Part-time: 24 men, 48 women	**Ph.D.s:** 97%
Graduate: 370 men, 1322 women	**Student/Faculty:** 18 to 1
Year: 4-1-4	**Tuition:** $18,650
Application Deadline: March 15	**Room & Board:** $5350
Freshman Class: 1576 applied, 1285 accepted, 413 enrolled	
SAT I Verbal/Math: 561/560	**VERY COMPETITIVE**

Western Maryland College, founded in 1867, is a private college offering programs in the liberal arts. There is 1 graduate school. In addition to regional accreditation, Western Maryland has baccalaureate program accreditation with CSWE and NASM. The library contains 201,804 volumes, 621,702 microform items, and 7883 audiovisual forms/CDs, and subscribes to 1603 periodicals. Computerized library services include the card catalog, interlibrary loans, and database searching. Special learning facilities include an art gallery, radio station, TV station, and physics observatory. The 160-acre campus is in a small town 30 miles northwest of Baltimore. Including residence halls, there are 60 buildings.

Programs of Study: Western Maryland confers the B.A. degree. Master's degrees are also awarded. Bachelor's degrees are awarded in BIOLOGICAL SCIENCE (biology/biological science), BUSINESS (business administration and management), COMMUNICATIONS AND THE ARTS (communications, English, fine arts, French, German, music, Spanish, and theater design), COMPUT-

ER AND PHYSICAL SCIENCE (chemistry, mathematics, and physics), EDU-CATION (physical), SOCIAL SCIENCE (economics, history, philosophy, political science/government, psychology, religion, social work, and sociology). Physics, English, and social work are the strongest academically. Biology, English, and foreign languages are the largest.

Special: Internships are available in all majors. Study abroad is available around the world. There is a Washington semester in conjunction with American University and 3-2 engineering programs with Washington University and the University of Maryland. The college offers work-study programs, dual and student-designed majors, credit by exam (in foreign languages), and pass/fail options. Western Maryland has a 5-year deaf education program and offers certification in elementary and secondary education. The college also offers advanced standing for international baccalaureate recipients. There are 12 national honor societies, including Phi Beta Kappa, a freshman honors program, and 19 departmental honors programs.

Admissions: 82% of the 1999-2000 applicants were accepted. The SAT I scores for the 1999-2000 freshman class were: Verbal--18% below 500, 49% between 500 and 599, 27% between 600 and 700, and 6% above 700; Math--26% below 500, 44% between 500 and 599, 25% between 600 and 700, and 5% above 700. 66% of the current freshmen were in the top fifth of their class; 89% were in the top two fifths. There were 3 National Merit finalists. 28 freshmen graduated first in their class.

Requirements: The SAT I is required with a minimum composite score of 900. Western Maryland requires applicants to be in the upper 50% of their class. A GPA of 2.5 is required. Applicants must be graduates of an accredited secondary school or have a GED. 16 academic credits are required, including 4 years of English, 3 each of foreign language, math, and social studies, and 2 of a lab science. SAT II: Subject tests and an interview are recommended. An essay is required. Applications are accepted on computer disk and on-line via CollegeLink and Common App. AP and CLEP credits are accepted. Important factors in the admissions decision are advanced placement or honor courses, leadership record, and evidence of special talent.

Procedure: Freshmen are admitted fall and spring. Entrance exams should be taken at the end of the junior year. There are early admissions and deferred admissions plans. Early action applications should be filed by December 1; regular applications, by March 15 for fall entry and January 15 for spring entry, along with a $40 fee. Notification is sent April 1.

Financial Aid: In 1999-2000, 89% of all students received some form of financial aid. 62% of freshmen and 59% of continuing students received need-based aid. The average freshman award was $14,142. Of that total, scholarships or need-based grants averaged $9387 ($24,000 maximum); loans averaged $3363 ($7825 maximum); and work contracts averaged $1392 ($1600 maximum). 21% of undergraduates work part time. Average annual earnings from campus work are $663. The average financial indebtedness of the 1999 graduate was $9687. Western Maryland is a member of CSS. The CSS/Profile, FAFSA, FFS or SFS and the college's own financial statement are required. The fall application deadline is March 1.

Computers: The mainframe is an IBM RISC 6000. 7 labs provide access to 132 PCs, all with acccess to the Internet and the World Wide Web. All students may access the system One lab is open 24 hours per day; other labs are open 8:30 a.m. to midnight daily. The network is available 24 hours per day. There are no time limits and no fees.

WESTERN MICHIGAN UNIVERSITY

Kalamazoo, MI 49008　　　　　(616) 387-2000; Fax: (616) 387-2096

Full-time: 8362 men, 9555 women	**Faculty:** 750; I, --$
Part-time: 1727 men, 2185 women	**Ph.D.s:** 92%
Graduate: 2373 men, 3542 women	**Student/Faculty:** 24 to 1
Year: semesters, summer session	**Tuition:** $4055 ($9177)
Application Deadline: open	**Room & Board:** $4831
Freshman Class: 12,929 applied, 11,000 accepted, 4426 enrolled	
ACT: 22	**COMPETITIVE**

Western Michigan University, founded in 1903, is a public institution offering degree programs in the liberal arts and sciences, aviation, business, education, engineering, fine arts, health and human services, and preprofessional studies. There are 7 undergraduate schools and 1 graduate school. In addition to regional accreditation, WMU has baccalaureate program accreditation with AACSB, ABET, AHEA, ASLA, CSAB, CSWE, NASAD, NASM, NCATE, and NLN. The 5 libraries contain 3,920,534 volumes, 1,748,351 microform items, and 25,937 audiovisual forms CDs, and subscribe to 6973 periodicals. Computerized library services include the card catalog, interlibrary loans, and database searching. Special learning facilities include a learning resource center, art gallery, radio station, and nuclear accelerator. The 504-acre campus is in an urban area 140 miles west of Detroit. Including residence halls, there are 130 buildings.

Programs of Study: WMU confers B.A., B.S., B.B.A., B.F.A., B.Mus., B.S., B.S.E., B.S.N., and B.S.W. degrees. Master's and doctoral degrees are also awarded. Bachelor's degrees are awarded in BIOLOGICAL SCIENCE (biochemistry and biology/biological science), BUSINESS (accounting, banking and finance, business administration and management, business economics, business statistics, insurance, management information systems, marketing/retailing/merchandising, purchasing/inventory management, real estate, recreation and leisure services, retailing, tourism, and transportation management), COMMUNICATIONS AND THE ARTS (advertising, applied music, art, art history and appreciation, broadcasting, ceramic art and design, communications, creative writing, dance, dramatic arts, English, English literature, French, German, graphic design, historic preservation, industrial design, jazz, journalism, Latin, linguistics, media arts, modern language, music, music history and appreciation, music theory and composition, painting, photography, public relations, sculpture, Spanish, telecommunications, and theater design), COMPUTER AND PHYSICAL SCIENCE (applied mathematics, chemistry, computer science, earth science, geology, geophysics and seismology, hydrology, information sciences and systems, mathematics, natural sciences, physical sciences, physics, and statistics), EDUCATION (art, business, education, elementary, health, home economics, marketing and distribution, middle school, music, physical, science, secondary, special, technical, and vocational), ENGINEERING AND ENVIRONMENTAL DESIGN (aeronautical engineering, aeronautical science, aeronautical technology, aircraft mechanics, architectural engineering, architecture, automotive technology, aviation administration/management, chemical engineering, computer engineering, construction engineering, construction management, drafting and design, electrical/electronics engineering, engineering, engineering management, environmental engineering, environmental science, graphic and printing production, graphic arts technology, industrial engineering, interior design, manufacturing technology, materials engineering, mechanical engineering, metallurgical engineering, paper and pulp science, paper engineering, petroleum/natural gas engineering, and transportation technology), HEALTH PROFESSIONS (biomedical science, community health work, exercise science, health science, music therapy, nursing, occupational therapy, predentistry, premedicine, and speech pathology/audiology), SOCIAL SCIENCE (African American studies, African studies, American studies, anthropology, Asian/Oriental studies, behavioral science, criminal justice, dietetics, economics, European studies, family/consumer studies, fashion design and technology, food production/management/services, food science, geography, history, home economics, humanities, interdisciplinary studies, Latin American studies, liberal arts/general studies, medieval studies, philosophy, political science/government, prelaw, psychology, public administration, religion, social science, social work, sociology, textiles and clothing, water resources, and women's studies). Marketing, finance and commercial law, and teaching are the largest.

Special: Cross-registration is available through the Kalamazoo Consortium. Opportunities are provided for internships in occupational and music therapy, work-study programs, student-designed majors, pass/fail options, and credit by exam. Students may study abroad in more than 20 countries on 4 continents. There are 25 national honor societies, including Phi Beta Kappa, a freshman honors program, and 6 departmental honors programs.

Admissions: 85% of the 1999-2000 applicants were accepted. The ACT scores for the 1999-2000 freshman class were: 35% below 21, 30% between 21 and 23, 22% between 24 and 26, 8% between 27 and 28, and 5% above 28. 40% of the current freshmen were in the top fifth of their class; 73% were in the top two fifths.

Requirements: The ACT is required. A GPA of 2.0 is required. Applicants must submit an official high school transcript. An audition is required for music majors. An interview may be recommended. Applications are accepted on-line via the WMU web site. AP and CLEP credits are accepted. Important factors in the admissions decision are advanced placement or honor courses, extracurricular activities record, and recommendations by school officials.

Procedure: Freshmen are admitted to all sessions. Entrance exams should be taken late in the junior year or early in the senior year. There is a deferred admissions plan. Application deadlines are open. The application fee is $25. Notification is sent on a rolling basis.

Financial Aid: In a recent year, 47% of all freshmen and 62% of continuing students received some form of financial aid. 45% of freshmen and 59% of continuing students received need-based aid. The average freshman award was $5427. Of that total, scholarships or need-based grants averaged $1286 ($3500 maximum); loans averaged $2604 ($4425 maximum); and work contracts averaged $1537 ($2300 maximum). 51% of undergraduates work part time. Average annual earnings from campus work are $1350. The average financial indebtedness of aa recent graduate was $16,042. WMU is a member of CSS. The FAFSA is required. The fall application deadline is April 1.

Computers: The mainframes are a DEC VAX 7620 and an IBM 3090/300J. The mainframe is used for institutional and research purposes as well as for course work. About 2000 workstations are available in classroom buildings, dormitories, and the student center. A Sun operating system is networked in labs for student use. All students may access the system 24 hours a day. Time limits are set individually by faculty and by class. There are no fees.

WESTERN WASHINGTON UNIVERSITY

Bellingham, WA 98225-5996

(360) 650-3440
Fax: (360) 650-7369

Full-time: 4611 men, 5901 women	**Faculty:** 443; IIA, av$
Part-time: 254 men, 276 women	**Ph.D.s:** 87%
Graduate: 283 men, 375 women	**Student/Faculty:** 24 to 1
Year: quarters, summer session	**Tuition:** $2991 ($9993)
Application Deadline: March 1	**Room & Board:** $4737
Freshman Class: 6431 applied, 5368 accepted, 2180 enrolled	
SAT I Verbal/Math: 550/550	**ACT:** 24 **VERY COMPETITIVE**

Western Washington University, founded in 1893, is a nonprofit, public, comprehensive institution whose emphasis is on the liberal arts and sciences, business and business administration and economics, art, fine arts, and performing arts, music, teacher preparation, interdisciplinary learning, and environmental studies. There are 6 undergraduate and 1 graduate school. In addition to regional accreditation, WWU has baccalaureate program accreditation with AACSB, ABET, ASLA, NASM, NCATE, and NRPA. The library contains 785,000 volumes, 3.4 million microform items, and 37,000 audiovisual forms/CDs, and subscribes to 4800 periodicals. Computerized library services include the card catalog, interlibrary loans, and database searching. Special learning facilities include a learning resource center, art gallery, planetarium, radio station, marine lab, neutron generator lab, motor vehicle research lab, wind tunnel, air pollution lab, electronic music studio, and performing arts center. The 195-acre campus is in a small town 60 miles south of Vancouver, British Columbia, and 90 miles north of Seattle. Including residence halls, there are 80 buildings.

Programs of Study: WWU confers B.A., B.S., B.A.E., B.F.A., and B.M. degrees. Master's degrees are also awarded. Bachelor's degrees are awarded in BIOLOGICAL SCIENCE (biochemistry and biology/biological science), BUSINESS (accounting, business administration and management, international business management, management science, and marketing/retailing/merchandising), COMMUNICATIONS AND THE ARTS (art, communications, dramatic arts, English, fine arts, French, German, journalism, linguistics, music, and Spanish), COMPUTER AND PHYSICAL SCIENCE (chemistry, computer science, geology, mathematics, and physics), EDUCATION (art, early childhood, elementary, foreign languages, health, music, science, and secondary), ENGINEERING AND ENVIRONMENTAL DESIGN (electrical/electronics engineering technology, engineering technology, environmental science, and manufacturing technology), HEALTH PROFESSIONS (predentistry, premedicine, preveterinary science, and speech pathology/audiology), SOCIAL SCIENCE (anthropology, Canadian studies, East Asian studies, economics, geography, history, human services, parks and recreation management, philosophy, political science/government, prelaw, psychology, sociology, and urban studies). Computer science, business, and technology are the strongest academically. Psychology, environmental studies, and education are the largest.

Special: Special academic programs include internships through various academic departments and study abroad in 75 countries. Dual majors are available through various departments, and there is a general studies degree, a B.A. in humanities. A 3-2 engineering degree is possible with the University of Washington. Student-designed majors are offered through the liberal studies department in the College of Arts and Sciences and through Fairhaven College, which affords students an unusual degree of involvement in the structure and content of their own programs and which uses faculty narrative for students' academic evaluations. In addition, Huxley College of Environmental Studies provides specialized education and research. Up to 30 credits of electives may be granted for military service, and nondegree study and pass/fail options are possible. There is 1 national honor society, and a freshman honors program.

Admissions: 83% of the 1999-2000 applicants were accepted. The SAT I scores for the 1999-2000 freshman class were: Verbal--26% below 500, 47% between 500 and 599, 23% between 600 and 700, and 4% above 700; Math--27% below 500, 47% between 500 and 599, 23% between 600 and 700, and 3% above 700. The ACT scores were 24% below 21, 28% between 21 and 23, 26% between 24 and 26, 12% between 27 and 28, and 10% above 28. 46% of the current freshmen were in the top fifth of their class; 83% were in the top two fifths. There were 10 National Merit finalists. 51 freshmen graduated first in their class.

Requirements: The SAT I or ACT is required. A GPA of 2.7 is required. Other admissions requirements include completion of 15 academic units, comprised of 4 years of college preparatory English composition and literature courses; 3 years of college preparatory math, including 2 years of algebra; 3 years of social studies/history; 2 years of science, including 1 year of a chemistry or physics with an algebra prerequisite; 2 years of the same foreign language; 1 semester of fine and performing arts; and 1 semester in another academic field. Freshman applicants meeting minimum GPA and subject requirements are ranked by an index combining the GPA and a standardized test score. The GED is also accepted. Other factors taken into consideration include curricular rigor (level of difficulty of courses), grade trends, leadership, community involvement, special talent, multicultural experience, and personal hardship or circumstances. Applications are accepted on computer disk or on-line at the school's web site. AP credits are accepted. Important factors in the admissions decision are advanced placement or honor courses, leadership record, and extracurricular activities record.

Procedure: Freshmen are admitted to all sessions. Entrance exams should be taken by fall of the senior year. Applications should be filed by March 1 for fall entry, October 15 for winter entry, January 15 for spring entry, and March 1 for summer entry, along with a $35 fee. Notification is sent March 15. 3% of all applicants are on a waiting list.

Financial Aid: In a recent year, 46% of all freshmen and 54% of continuing students received some form of financial aid. 46% of freshmen and 40% of continuing students received need-based aid. The average freshman award was $5925. Of that total, scholarships or need-based grants averaged $1686 ($3331 maximum); loans averaged $3824 ($4995 maximum); and work contracts averaged $415 ($1725 maximum). 41% of undergraduates work part time. Average annual earnings from campus work are $1502. The average financial indebtedness of a recent graduate was $5332. WWU is a member of CSS. The FAFSA is required. The fall application deadline is February 15.

Computers: The mainframe is a Sun E4000. There are more than 1000 PCs and Macs available in the student labs and residence halls. Students also have access to the Internet and the World Wide Web. All students may access the system. There are no time limits and no fees.

WESTMINSTER CHOIR COLLEGE OF RIDER UNIVERSITY
Princeton, NJ, USA 08540-3899   (609) 921-7144
(800) 96-CHOIR; Fax: (609) 921-2538

Full-time: 121 men, 188 women	**Faculty:** 37
Part-time: none	**Ph.D.s:** 80%
Graduate: 52 men, 105 women	**Student/Faculty:** 7 to 1
Year: semesters, summer session	**Tuition:** $17,180
Application Deadline: open	**Room & Board:** $7380
Freshman Class: 349 applied, 274 accepted, 165 enrolled	
SAT I Verbal/Math: 551/528	**ACT:** 24 **SPECIAL**

Westminster Choir College, founded in 1926, is a private school of music within Rider University, that focuses on undergraduate and graduate students seeking positions of music leadership in churches, schools, and communities. Some of the information in this profile is approximate. There is 1 graduate school. In addition to regional accreditation, Westminster Choir College has baccalaureate program accreditation with NASM. The library contains 56,000 volumes, 400 microform items, and 9000 audiovisual forms/CDs, and subscribes to 160 periodicals. Computerized library services include the card catalog, interlibrary loans, and database searching. Special learning facilities include a learning resource center, a music computer lab, and a vocal lab. The 23-acre campus is in a suburban area 50 miles south of New York City. Including residence halls, there are 12 buildings.

Programs of Study: Westminster Choir College confers B.A. and B.M. degrees. Master's degrees are also awarded. Bachelor's degrees are awarded in COMMUNICATIONS AND THE ARTS (music, music performance, music theory and composition, piano/organ, and voice), EDUCATION (music), SOCIAL SCIENCE (religious music). Music education is the largest.

Special: Cross-registration with Drew University, Princeton University, Rider University, and Princeton Theological Seminary, internships in the arts, church, box office management, and arts administration, work-study programs, dual majors in any combination of 7 majors in music, and pass/fail options are all available. In addition, individualized programs of study in Europe may be pursued. There is 1 national honor society.

Admissions: 79% of the 1999-2000 applicants were accepted.

Requirements: The SAT I or ACT is required. SAT I minimum scores should be 800 composite, 400 verbal and 400 math. A GPA of 2.0 is required. Applicants must present 4 years of credits in English, 3 in history, 2 in math, and 1 in science. An essay and music audition are required, whereas an interview is recommended. The GED is accepted. AP credits are accepted. Important factors in the admissions decision are evidence of special talent, recommendations by alumni, and recommendations by school officials.

Procedure: Freshmen are admitted fall and spring. Entrance exams should be taken at the time of the audition. There are early decision, early admissions, and deferred admissions plans. Application deadlines are open, and there is a $40 fee ($50 for international students). Notification is sent on a rolling basis.

Financial Aid: In 1999-2000, 88% of all freshmen and 80% of continuing students received some form of financial aid. 67% of freshmen and 79% of continuing students received need-based aid. The average freshman award was $14,724. The average financial indebtedness of the 1999 graduate was $12,500. Westminster Choir College is a member of CSS. The FAFSA is required. The fall application deadline is March 15.

Computers: PCs are available for academic use in the Music, Arts and Sciences, and Learning Center computer labs. All students may access the system. There are no time limits and no fees.

WESTMINSTER COLLEGE
Salt Lake City, UT 84105

(801) 832-2200
(800) 748-4753; Fax: (801) 484-3252

Full-time: 511 men, 901 women	**Faculty:** 109; IIB, av$
Part-time: 163 men, 207 women	**Ph.D.s:** 84%
Graduate: 288 men, 228 women	**Student/Faculty:** 13 to 1
Year: 4-4-1, summer session	**Tuition:** $12,726
Application Deadline: open	**Room & Board:** $4500
Freshman Class: 876 applied, 756 accepted, 330 enrolled	
SAT I Verbal/Math: 563/533	**ACT:** 23 **VERY COMPETITIVE**

Westminster College (formerly Westminster College of Salt Lake City), founded in 1875, is a private institution offering undergraduate programs in business, nursing and health sciences, arts and sciences, and education. There are 4 undergraduate and 4 graduate schools. In addition to regional accreditation, Westminster College has baccalaureate program accreditation with ACBSP and NLN. The library contains 88,086 volumes, 114,183 microform items, and 3819 audiovisual forms/CDs, and subscribes to 348 periodicals. Computerized library services include the card catalog, interlibrary loans, and database searching. Special learning facilities include a multipurpose theater. The 27-acre campus is in a suburban area 6 miles southeast of downtown Salt Lake City. Including residence halls, there are 20 buildings.

Programs of Study: Westminster College confers B.A. and B.S. degrees. Master's degrees are also awarded. Bachelor's degrees are awarded in BIOLOGICAL SCIENCE (biology/biological science), BUSINESS (accounting, business administration and management, and marketing/retailing/merchandising), COMMUNICATIONS AND THE ARTS (communications, English, and fine arts), COMPUTER AND PHYSICAL SCIENCE (chemistry, computer science, mathematics, and physics), EDUCATION (early childhood, elementary, and secondary), ENGINEERING AND ENVIRONMENTAL DESIGN (aviation administration/management), HEALTH PROFESSIONS (nursing), SOCIAL SCIENCE (economics, history, human development, philosophy, psychology, social science, and sociology). Nursing, biology, and English are the strongest academically. Business, biology, and nursing are the largest.

Special: The college offers internships in every major, study abroad in England, Spain, and Mexico, B.A.-B.S. degrees, dual and student-designed majors, a 3-2 engineering degree at USC at Los Angeles or Washington University in St. Louis, and freshman seminar courses. There is 1 national honor society, Phi Beta Kappa, a freshman honors program, and 1 departmental honors program.

Admissions: 86% of the 1999-2000 applicants were accepted. The SAT I scores for the 1999-2000 freshman class were: Verbal--29% below 500, 38% between 500 and 599, 23% between 600 and 700, and 10% above 700; Math--29% below 500, 48% between 500 and 599, 17% between 600 and 700, and 6% above 700. The ACT scores were 21% below 21, 27% between 21 and 23, 31% between 24 and 26, 13% between 27 and 28, and 8% above 28. 50% of the current freshmen were in the top fifth of their class; 83% were in the top two fifths. There was 1 National Merit finalist. 6 freshmen graduated first in their class.

Requirements: The SAT I or ACT is required. A GPA of 2.5 is required. In addition, applicants must be graduates of an accredited secondary school or have a

720

GED certificate. An interview is recommended. Applications are accepted on-line and on computer disk. AP and CLEP credits are accepted. Important factors in the admissions decision are evidence of special talent, extracurricular activities record, and advanced placement or honor courses.

Procedure: Freshmen are admitted to all sessions. Entrance exams should be taken in the junior or senior year. There are early admissions and deferred admissions plans. Application deadlines are open. There is a $25 fee. Notification is sent on a rolling basis.

Financial Aid: In 1999-2000, 98% of all freshmen and 78% of continuing students received some form of financial aid. 72% of freshmen and 52% of continuing students received need-based aid. The average freshman award was $9615. Of that total, scholarships or need-based grants averaged $6725 ($15,581 maximum); loans averaged $2620 ($7925 maximum); and work contracts averaged $2717 ($3100 maximum). 56% of undergraduates work part time. Average annual earnings from campus work are $2400. Westminster College is a member of CSS. The FAFSA is required.

Computers: The mainframe is an HP 9000. There are 238 networked PCs plus computer availability and hookups in the residence halls and library. All students may access the system from 7 a.m. to 11 p.m. There are no time limits and no fees. It is recommended that all students have personal computers.

WESTMONT COLLEGE
Santa Barbara, CA 93108

(805) 565-6200
(800) 777-9011; Fax: (805) 565-6234

Full-time: 529 men, 852 women	**Faculty:** 85; IIB, +$
Part-time: 3 men, 7 women	**Ph.D.s:** 88%
Graduate: none	**Student/Faculty:** 16 to 1
Year: semesters, summer session	**Tuition:** $19,746
Application Deadline: March 1	**Room & Board:** $6668
Freshman Class: 1292 applied, 918 accepted, 318 enrolled	
SAT I Verbal/Math: 600/590	**ACT:** 26 **VERY COMPETITIVE**

Westmont College, founded in 1937, is a private, interdenominational Christian institution offering a liberal arts and sciences program in a residential campus community. The library contains 158,096 volumes, 25,000 microform items, and 8180 audiovisual forms/CDs, and subscribes to 2500 periodicals. Computerized library services include the card catalog, interlibrary loans, and database searching. Special learning facilities include a learning resource center, art gallery, radio station, observatory, and science center with a premedical center. The 133-acre campus is in a suburban area 90 miles north of Los Angeles. Including residence halls, there are 30 buildings.

Programs of Study: Westmont confers B.A. and B.S. degrees. Bachelor's degrees are awarded in BIOLOGICAL SCIENCE (biology/biological science and neurosciences), BUSINESS (business economics), COMMUNICATIONS AND THE ARTS (art, communications, dramatic arts, English, fine arts, French, modern language, music, and Spanish), COMPUTER AND PHYSICAL SCIENCE (chemistry, computer science, mathematics, natural sciences, and physics), EDUCATION (art, English, mathematics, music, physical, and social science), ENGINEERING AND ENVIRONMENTAL DESIGN (engineering physics), SOCIAL SCIENCE (history, liberal arts/general studies, philosophy, physical fitness/movement, political science/government, psychology, religion, social science, and sociology). Biology, English, and economics/business are the largest.

Special: Westmont offers cross-registration with 12 Christian colleges, internships in local businesses and social agencies, study abroad in 11 countries, and semesters in Washington, D.C., San Francisco, and Los Angeles. B.A.-B.S. degrees, student-designed majors, work-study programs, a 3-2 engineering program with several California universities, the University of Washington, and Boston University, and pass/fail options also are available. There are also preprofessional programs in dentistry, law, medicine, ministry/missions, optometry, pharmacology, physical therapy, and veterinary medicine. There are 3 national honor societies, a freshman honors program, and 9 departmental honors programs.

Admissions: 71% of the 1999-2000 applicants were accepted. The SAT I scores for the 1999-2000 freshman class were: Verbal--8% below 500, 42% between 500 and 599, 38% between 600 and 700, and 12% above 700; Math--10% below 500, 42% between 500 and 599, 40% between 600 and 700, and 8% above 700. The ACT scores were 5% below 21, 21% between 21 and 23, 32% between 24 and 26, 19% between 27 and 28, and 23% above 28. 65% of the current freshmen were in the top fifth of their class; 90% were in the top two fifths. There were 7 National Merit finalists and 3 semifinalists.

Requirements: The SAT I or ACT is required. Westmont requires applicants to be in the upper 50% of their class. A GPA of 3.0 is required. SAT I scores of 500 verbal and 500 math or an ACT composite score of 25 is recommended. Applicants need 16 academic credits, including 4 years of high school English, 3 of math, 2 each of a foreign language, social science, and physical science, and 1 each of history and biological science. Interviews are recommended. Essays are required. The GED is accepted. Applications are accepted on computer disk, and on-line via Collegeline, XAP, and Westmont's web page. AP and CLEP credits are accepted. Important factors in the admissions decision are advanced placement or honor courses, leadership record, and extracurricular activities record.

Procedure: Freshmen are admitted fall and spring. Entrance exams should be taken during the spring of the junior year or the beginning of the senior year. There is a deferred admissions plan. Applications should be filed by March 1 for fall entry and November 1 for spring entry, along with a $40 fee. Notification is sent March 15. 191 early decision candidates were accepted for the 1999-2000 class.

Financial Aid: In 1999-2000, 74% of all freshmen and 93% of continuing students received some form of financial aid. 63% of freshmen and 59% of continuing students received need-based aid. The average freshman award was $13,798. Of that total, scholarships or need-based grants averaged $9924 ($22,045 maximum); loans averaged $3074 ($4625 maximum); and work contracts averaged $762 ($2000 maximum). 36% of undergraduates work part time. Average annual earnings from campus work are $1652. The average financial indebtedness of the 1999 graduate was $18,319. The FAFSA is required. The fall application deadline is March 2.

Computers: The mainframes are 3 IBM RS/6000s. There are 11 PCs and 47 Macs available in the library. There are Ethernet connections in every office, every dorm room, and many classrooms. The complete network has access to the Internet. All students may access the system. There are no time limits and no fees. It is strongly recommended that all students have personal computers.

WHEATON COLLEGE
Wheaton, IL 60187-5593

(630) 752-5005
(800) 222-2419; Fax: (630) 752-5285

Full-time: 1091 men, 1201 women	**Faculty:** 155; IIA, +$
Part-time: 20 men, 26 women	**Ph.D.s:** 89%
Graduate: 192 men, 202 women	**Student/Faculty:** 15 to 1
Year: semesters, summer session	**Tuition:** $14,930
Application Deadline: January 15	**Room & Board:** $5080
Freshman Class: 1964 applied, 1062 accepted, 583 enrolled	
SAT I or ACT: required	**HIGHLY COMPETITIVE**

Wheaton College, founded in 1860, is a nonprofit, private, nondenominational institution committed to providing students with a Christian education. Basically a liberal arts school, it offers undergraduate programs in business, the arts and fine arts, music, teacher preparation, and religious and Bible studies. There is 1 graduate school. In addition to regional accreditation, Wheaton has baccalaureate program accreditation with NASM and NCATE. The 2 libraries contain 355,971 volumes, 522,965 microform items, and 22,575 audiovisual forms/ CDs, and subscribe to 1702 periodicals. Computerized library services include the card catalog, interlibrary loans, and database searching. Special learning facilities include a radio station, a communications resource center with TV and audio studios, a special collection of British authors' books and papers, an evangelical museum with document archives, and the Center for Applied Christian Ethics. The 80-acre campus is in a suburban area 25 miles west of Chicago. Including residence halls, there are 35 buildings.

Programs of Study: Wheaton confers B.A., B.S., B.M., and B.M.E. degrees. Master's and doctoral degrees are also awarded. Bachelor's degrees are awarded in BIOLOGICAL SCIENCE (biology/biological science), BUSINESS (business economics), COMMUNICATIONS AND THE ARTS (art, classical languages, communications, English, French, German, music, and Spanish), COMPUTER AND PHYSICAL SCIENCE (chemistry, computer science, geology, mathematics, physical sciences, and physics), EDUCATION (elementary, music, science, and secondary), ENGINEERING AND ENVIRONMENTAL DESIGN (environmental science), SOCIAL SCIENCE (anthropology, archeology, biblical studies, economics, history, interdisciplinary studies, philosophy, physical fitness/movement, political science/government, psychology, religion, social science, and sociology). English, elementary education, and business economics are the largest.

Special: Special academic programs include internships, study abroad in 8 countries, an urban semester in Chicago, and a Washington semester. Dual majors are available in all areas, as are student-designed majors. A 3-2 engineering degree is offered with the Illinois Institute of Technology, University of Illinois, Case Western Reserve University School of Engineering, and Washington University School of Engineering and Applied Science; transfer to other engineering schools is also possible. A 3-2 nursing degree is offered with Emory University, Goshen Nursing School, University of Rochester, and Rush University. Pass/fail options are available. There are 10 national honor societies and 11 departmental honors programs.

Admissions: 54% of the 1999-2000 applicants were accepted. The SAT I scores for the 1999-2000 freshman class were: Verbal--2% below 500, 20% between 500 and 599, 45% between 600 and 700, and 33% above 700; Math--3% below 500, 20% between 500 and 599, 50% between 600 and 700, and 27% above 700. The ACT scores were 10% between 18 and 23, 52% between 24 and 29, and 43%

above 29. 86% of the current freshmen were in the top fourth of their class; 98% were in the top half. There were 59 National Merit finalists. 64 freshmen graduated first in their class.

Requirements: The SAT I or ACT is required. A high school diploma is required and the GED is accepted. Wheaton requires a general college-preparatory program of 18 units, including 4 of English, 3 to 4 of math, science, and social studies, and 2 to 3 of a foreign language. AP and CLEP credits are accepted. Personality/intangible qualities is an important factor in the admissions decision.

Procedure: Freshmen are admitted in the fall. Entrance exams should be taken by November of the senior year. There is a deferred admissions plan. Applications should be filed by January 15 for fall entry, along with a $35 fee. Notification is sent April 1. 17% of all applicants are on a waiting list.

Financial Aid: In 1999-2000, 73% of all freshmen and 64% of continuing students received some form of financial aid. 50% of freshmen and 51% of continuing students received need-based aid. The average freshman award was $11,000. Of that total, scholarships or need-based grants averaged $7462 ($20,405 maximum); loans averaged $3623 ($8325 maximum); and work contracts averaged $1168 ($2010 maximum). 48% of undergraduates work part time. Average annual earnings from campus work are $755. The average financial indebtedness of the 1999 graduate was $14,496. Wheaton is a member of CSS. The CSS/Profile or FAFSA and the college's own financial statement are required. The fall application deadline is February 15.

Computers: The mainframes are DEC ALPHA and RISC/Ultrix minicomputers. Also available are 95 PCs and Macs located in 5 student labs with networked print services and file servers, all of which have network access, plus 8 dial-up modem lines. There are 31 PCs and 5 printers located in 5 dormitory labs. Students also may access the campus network using their own computers in their dorm rooms. All students may access the system 24 hours a day. Students may access the system only 2 hours at one sitting if there is a waiting list; otherwise, there is no limit. There are no fees.

WHEATON COLLEGE
Norton, MA 02766
(508) 286-8251
(800) 394-6003; Fax: (508) 286-8271

Full-time: 508 men, 970 women	**Faculty:** 96; IIB, ++$
Part-time: 9 men, 13 women	**Ph.D.s:** 97%
Graduate: none	**Student/Faculty:** 14 to 1
Year: semesters	**Tuition:** $23,150
Application Deadline: February 1	**Room & Board:** $6730
Freshman Class: 2463 applied, 1759 accepted, 427 enrolled	
SAT I Verbal/Math: 610/590	**ACT:** 26 **VERY COMPETITIVE**

Wheaton College, established in 1834, is an independent liberal arts institution. The library contains 371,071 volumes, 72,277 microform items, and 8093 audio-visual forms/CDs, and subscribes to 2252 periodicals. Computerized library services include the card catalog, interlibrary loans, and database searching. Special learning facilities include an art gallery, planetarium, radio station, and TV station. The 385-acre campus is in a suburban area 35 miles southeast of Boston and 15 miles north of Providence. Including residence halls, there are 84 buildings.

Programs of Study: Wheaton confers the A.B. degree. Bachelor's degrees are awarded in BIOLOGICAL SCIENCE (biochemistry and biology/biological science), COMMUNICATIONS AND THE ARTS (art history and appreciation, classics, creative writing, English, fine arts, French, German, literature, music, and Russian), COMPUTER AND PHYSICAL SCIENCE (astronomy, chemistry, computer mathematics, computer science, mathematics, and physics), ENGINEERING AND ENVIRONMENTAL DESIGN (environmental science), SOCIAL SCIENCE (American studies, anthropology, Asian/Oriental studies, classical/ancient civilization, economics, Hispanic American studies, history, international relations, Italian studies, philosophy, political science/government, psychology, religion, Russian and Slavic studies, social psychology, sociology, and women's studies). Arts and sciences are the strongest academically. Psychology, economics, and sociology are the largest.

Special: Students at Brown University may cross-register with Colleges in the Southeastern Association for Cooperation in Higher Education in Massachusetts, and 12 other New England colleges. Wheaton offers study abroad in 23 countries, internship programs, nondegree study, dual majors, student-designed majors, a Washington semester at American University, and interdisciplinary majors, including math and economics, math and computer science, physics and astronomy, and theater and English dramatic literature. A 3-2 engineering degree is offered with George Washington University, Dartmouth College, and Worcester Polytechnic Institute. Pass/fail options are possible. There are 8 national honor societies, including Phi Beta Kappa, and a freshman honors program.

Admissions: 71% of the 1999-2000 applicants were accepted. The SAT I scores for the 1999-2000 freshman class were: Verbal--5% below 500, 36% between 500 and 599, 53% between 600 and 700, and 6% above 700; Math--4% below 500, 47% between 500 and 599, 43% between 600 and 700, and 6% above 700. The ACT scores were 48% between 21 and 23, 17% between 24 and 26, 33% between 27 and 28, and 2% above 28. 47% of the current freshmen were in the top fifth of their class; 82% were in the top two fifths. There were 10 National Merit semifinalists. 3 freshmen graduated first in their class.

Requirements: Submission of SAT I or ACT scores is optional. Upon enrollment, all students are required to submit results of SAT II: Applicants must be graduates of an accredited secondary school. Recommended courses include English with emphasis on composition skills, 4 years; foreign language and math, 3 to 4 years each; social studies, 3 years; and lab science, 2 to 3 years. The GED is accepted. Wheaton requires an essay and strongly recommends an interview. Applications can be submitted on-line or computer disk via Apply or CollegeLink. AP credits are accepted. Important factors in the admissions decision are advanced placement or honor courses, extracurricular activities record, and leadership record.

Procedure: Freshmen are admitted to all sessions. Entrance exams should be taken in October and/or November. There are early decision, early admissions, and deferred admissions plans. Early decision applications should be filed by November 15; regular applications, by February 1 for fall entry and November 15 for spring entry, along with a $50 fee. Notification of early decision is sent December 15; regular decision, April 1. 30 early decision candidates were accepted for the 1999-2000 class. 11% of all applicants are on a waiting list.

Financial Aid: In 1999-2000, 65% of all freshmen and 66% of continuing students received some form of financial aid. 56% of freshmen and 59% of continuing students received need-based aid. The average freshman award was $16,230. Of that total, scholarships or need-based grants averaged $11,970 ($22,000 maximum); loans averaged $3020 ($4625 maximum); and work contracts averaged $1240 ($1400 maximum). 72% of undergraduates work part time. Average annual earnings from campus work are $855. The average financial indebtedness of the 1999 graduate was $16,185. Wheaton is a member of CSS. The CSS/Profile or FAFSA and, if applicable, noncustodial parents statement and business 1 farm supplement, are required. The fall application deadline is February 1.

Computers: 100 public access PCs are available on campus. All buildings and residence halls are networked, and arriving students are given access to E-mail, the Web, the Internet, and the campus network. All students may access the system 24 hours a day, 7 days a week. There are no time limits and no fees. It is recommended that all students have personal computers.

WHITMAN COLLEGE
Walla Walla, WA 99362　　　　**(509) 527-5176; Fax: (509) 527-4967**

Full-time: 581 men, 773 women	**Faculty:** 107; IIB, +$
Part-time: 16 men, 30 women	**Ph.D.s:** 94%
Graduate: none	**Student/Faculty:** 13 to 1
Year: semesters	**Tuition:** $20,906
Application Deadline: February 1	**Room & Board:** $5900
Freshman Class: 2151 applied, 1072 accepted, 368 enrolled	
SAT I Verbal/Math: 660/650	**HIGHLY COMPETITIVE**

Whitman College, founded in 1859, is a nonprofit, private, independent residential liberal arts and sciences college. The library contains 355,911 volumes, 14,000 microform items, and 1776 audiovisual forms/CDs, and subscribes to 1800 periodicals. Computerized library services include the card catalog, interlibrary loans, and database searching. Special learning facilities include a learning resource center, an art gallery, a natural history museum, a planetarium, a radio station, an electron microscope lab, an observatory, an Asian art collection, a videoconferencing center, and an outdoor sculpture walk. The 55-acre campus is in a small town 150 miles south of Spokane, 260 miles southeast of Seattle, and 235 miles east of Portland. Including residence halls, there are 41 buildings.

Programs of Study: Whitman College confers the B.A. degree. Bachelor's degrees are awarded in BIOLOGICAL SCIENCE (biology/biological science), COMMUNICATIONS AND THE ARTS (art history and appreciation, dramatic arts, English, fine arts, French, German, music, Spanish, and studio art), COMPUTER AND PHYSICAL SCIENCE (chemistry, geology, mathematics, and physics), ENGINEERING AND ENVIRONMENTAL DESIGN (environmental science), SOCIAL SCIENCE (anthropology, Asian/Oriental studies, economics, history, philosophy, political science/government, psychology, and sociology). Politics, geology, and biology are the strongest academically. Biology, politics, and English are the largest.

Special: Special academic programs include more than 500 internships, study abroad in 43 countries, a Washington semester, and study programs in Chicago and Philadelphia. Dual majors are available in any area, and student-designed majors are offered. There is a 3-2 environmental management and forestry program with Duke University, a 3-2 engineering program with Washington University in St. Louis, California Institute of Technology, and Columbia and Duke universities, and a 3-3 law program is offered through Columbia University. A 4-1 education program is available through Bank Street College of Education. Certification is offered for elementary and secondary education. A pass-D-fail option is available. A special feature of the curriculum is the integrated general studies program for freshmen. There are 5 national honor societies, including Phi Beta Kappa, a freshman honors program, and 36 departmental honors programs.

Admissions: 50% of the 1999-2000 applicants were accepted. The SAT I scores for the 1999-2000 freshman class were: Verbal--2% below 500, 18% between 500 and 599, 50% between 600 and 700, and 30% above 700; Math--1% below 500, 20% between 500 and 599, 56% between 600 and 700, and 23% above 700. The ACT scores were 3% below 21, 2% between 21 and 23, 8% between 24 and 26, 29% between 27 and 28, and 58% above 28. 87% of the current freshmen

were in the top fifth of their class; 99% were in the top two fifths. There were 22 National Merit finalists. 42 freshmen graduated first in their class.

Requirements: The SAT I or ACT is required. The GED is accepted. 3 essays must be submitted, and an interview is recommended. Credit by challenge examination is accepted. The Whitman application is accepted on computer disk and on-line at the school's web site. AP credits are accepted. Important factors in the admissions decision are advanced placement or honor courses, evidence of special talent, and extracurricular activities record.

Procedure: Freshmen are admitted fall and spring. Entrance exams should be taken by February of the senior year. There are early decision, early admissions, and deferred admissions plans. Early decision applications should be filed by November 15 or January 1; regular applications, by February 1 for fall entry and December 1 for spring entry, along with a $45 fee. Notification of early decision is sent December 15 or January 25; regular decision, April 1. 123 early decision candidates were accepted for the 1999-2000 class. 7% of all applicants are on a waiting list.

Financial Aid: In 1999-2000, 92% of all students received some form of financial aid. 49% of freshmen and 51% of continuing students received need-based aid. The average freshman award was $11,349. Of that total, scholarships or need-based grants averaged $7348 ($20,875 maximum); loans averaged $3467 ($5000 maximum); work contracts averaged $1654 ($2000 maximum); and federal and state grants averaged $2284 ($7779 maximum). 70% of undergraduates work part time. Average annual earnings from campus work are $571. The average financial indebtedness of the 1999 graduate was $12,431. Whitman College is a member of CSS. The FAFSA and CSS Profile Application are required. The fall application deadline is February 1.

Computers: The mainframes are an HP 3000/968, an HP 3000/918, a Sun SPARC Station 20, a Sun SPARC Station 5, and an HP 9000/800. Students have unlimited network access from all student PCs on campus, including in residence halls. All students have E-mail accounts. There are 4 main computer labs and various departmental labs available to students, some portions open 24 hours a day. There are about 200 public access PCs available for student use. The labs include Mac, Windows, and UNIX stations. All students may access the system 24 hours a day. There are no time limits and no fees.

WILLAMETTE UNIVERSITY
Salem, OR 97301

(503) 370-6303
(877) 542-2787; Fax: (503) 375-5363

Full-time: 706 men, 863 women	**Faculty:** 131; IIB, ++$
Part-time: 60 men, 91 women	**Ph.D.s:** 93%
Graduate: 372 men, 312 women	**Student/Faculty:** 10 to 1
Year: semesters	**Tuition:** $21,700
Application Deadline: February 1	**Room & Board:** $5700
Freshman Class: 1541 applied, 1388 accepted, 368 enrolled	
SAT I Verbal/Math: 600/610	**ACT:** 26 **VERY COMPETITIVE**

Willamette University, founded in 1842, is an independent liberal arts institution. There are 3 graduate schools. In addition to regional accreditation, Willamette has baccalaureate program accreditation with NASM. The 2 libraries contain 280,000 volumes, 280,809 microform items, and 8456 audiovisual forms CDs, and subscribe to 1569 periodicals. Computerized library services include the card catalog, interlibrary loans, and database searching. Special learning facilities include a learning resource center, art gallery, natural history museum, radio station, botanical and Japanese gardens, multimedia center, and "smart" classrooms. The 72-acre campus is in an urban area 50 minutes south of Portland. Including residence halls, there are 44 buildings.

Programs of Study: Willamette confers B.A. and B.M. degrees. Master's and doctoral degrees are also awarded. Bachelor's degrees are awarded in BIOLOGICAL SCIENCE (biology/biological science), COMMUNICATIONS AND THE ARTS (comparative literature, dramatic arts, English, fine arts, French, German, music, music performance, music theory and composition, Spanish, and speech/debate/rhetoric), COMPUTER AND PHYSICAL SCIENCE (chemistry, computer science, mathematics, and physics), EDUCATION (music), ENGINEERING AND ENVIRONMENTAL DESIGN (environmental science), HEALTH PROFESSIONS (music therapy), SOCIAL SCIENCE (American studies, anthropology, classical/ancient civilization, economics, history, humanities, international studies, Japanese studies, Latin American studies, philosophy, physical fitness/movement, political science/government, psychology, religion, and sociology). Social sciences, natural science, and humanities are the strongest academically. Social sciences, humanities, and fine arts are the largest.

Special: Williamette offers internships with the state and city governments, a Chicago semester, a Washington semester, and a 3-2 engineering degree with Washington University, University of Southern California, and Columbia University. Nondegree study, B.A.-B.S. degrees, dual majors, work-study programs with numerous employers in the Salem area and at the University, and credit/no-credit options are also available. Study abroad programs are available in 14 countries. There are 3-2 degrees in management, forestry, and computer science. There are 11 national honor societies, including Phi Beta Kappa.

Admissions: 90% of the 1999-2000 applicants were accepted. The SAT I scores for the 1999-2000 freshman class were: Verbal--12% below 500, 36% between 500 and 599, 39% between 600 and 700, and 13% above 700; Math--11% below 500, 39% between 500 and 599, 40% between 600 and 700, and 10% above 700. The ACT scores were 8% below 21, 14% between 21 and 23, 28% between 24 and 26, 24% between 27 and 28, and 25% above 28. 79% of the current freshmen were in the top fifth of their class; 93% were in the top two fifths. There were 3 National Merit finalists and 5 semifinalists. 26 freshmen graduated first in their class.

Requirements: The SAT I or ACT is required. Willamette requires applicants to be in the upper 50% of their class. A GPA of 2.0 is required. Graduation from an accredited secondary school or satisfactory scores on the GED are required. Institutional preferences include 4 years each of English, math, social studies, or history, and 3 years of a foreign language. 2 essays are required and an interview is recommended. Portfolios or auditions are recommended for art and music students. Applications are accepted on computer disk and on-line via Common App, CollegeNET, and Embark. AP credits are accepted. Important factors in the admissions decision are advanced placement or honor courses, recommendations by school officials, and leadership record.

Procedure: Freshmen are admitted fall and spring. Entrance exams should be taken in November. There are early action, early admissions, and deferred admissions plans. Early action applications should be filed by December 1; regular applications, by February 1 for fall entry and November 1 for spring entry, along with a $35 fee. Notification of early action is sent January 15; regular decision, April 1. 67 early action candidates were accepted for the 1999-2000 class. 3% of all applicants are on a waiting list.

Financial Aid: In 1999-2000, 85% of all freshmen and 83% of continuing students received some form of financial aid. 68% of freshmen and 63% of continuing students received need-based aid. Scholarships or need-based grants averaged

$11,075 ($21,700 maximum); loans averaged $4430 ($5625 maximum); and work contracts averaged $1625 ($2000 maximum). 55% of undergraduates work part time. Average annual earnings from campus work are $1400. The average financial indebtedness of the 1999 graduate was $16,800. Willamette is a member of CSS. The CSS/Profile or FAFSA is required. The fall application deadline is February 1.

Computers: The mainframe is a Sun Enterprise 2. More than 250 IBM PCs and Macs are available for student use in the computer lab, library, and science building. Students may access the mainframe from their residence hall rooms through a network hookup. All students may access the system 24 hours per day. There are no time limits and no fees.

WILLIAMS COLLEGE
Williamstown, MA 01267
(413) 597-2211

Full-time: 1058 men, 1016 women	**Faculty:** 211; IIB, ++$
Part-time: 19 men, 20 women	**Ph.D.s:** 97%
Graduate: 20 men, 29 women	**Student/Faculty:** 10 to 1
Year: 4-1-4	**Tuition:** $24,790
Application Deadline: January 1	**Room & Board:** $6730
Freshman Class: 5007 applied, 1157 accepted, 544 enrolled	
SAT I Verbal/Math: 710/710	**MOST COMPETITIVE**

Williams College, founded in 1793, is a private institution offering undergraduate degrees in liberal arts and graduate degrees in art history and development economics. There are 2 graduate schools. The 11 libraries contain 834,755 volumes, 484,405 microform items, and 32,729 audiovisual forms/CDs, and subscribe to 2865 periodicals. Computerized library services include the card catalog, interlibrary loans, and database searching. Special learning facilities include a learning resource center, an art gallery, a planetarium, a radio station, a 2500-acre experimental forest, an environmental studies center, a center for foreign languages, literatures, and cultures, a rare book library, and a studio art center. The 450-acre campus is in a small town 150 miles north of New York City and west of Boston. Including residence halls, there are 97 buildings.

Programs of Study: Williams confers the B.A. degree. Master's degrees are also awarded. Bachelor's degrees are awarded in BIOLOGICAL SCIENCE (biology/biological science), COMMUNICATIONS AND THE ARTS (art, art history and appreciation, classics, dramatic arts, English, fine arts, French, German, literature, music, Russian, and Spanish), COMPUTER AND PHYSICAL SCIENCE (astronomy, astrophysics, chemistry, computer science, geology, mathematics, and physics), SOCIAL SCIENCE (American studies, anthropology, Asian/Oriental studies, economics, history, philosophy, political science/government, psychology, religion, and sociology). English, psychology, and economics are the largest.

Special: Students may cross-register at Bennington or Massachusetts College of Liberal Arts and study abroad in Madrid, Oxford, Cairo, Beijing, and Kyoto, or any approved program with another college or university. Teaching and medical field experiences, dual and student-designed majors, internships, and a 3-2 engineering program with Columbia and Washington universities are offered. There are pass/fail options during the winter term. Each department offers at least one Oxford-model tutorial every year. There are 2 national honor societies, including Phi Beta Kappa.

Admissions: 23% of the 1999-2000 applicants were accepted. The SAT I scores for the 1999-2000 freshman class were: Verbal--1% below 500, 9% between 500 and 599, 38% between 600 and 700, and 52% above 700; Math--1% below 500, 9% between 500 and 599, 37% between 600 and 700, and 54% above 700. 93% of the current freshmen were in the top fifth of their class; 99% were in the top two fifths.

Requirements: The SAT I or ACT is required. SAT II: Subject tests in 3 subjects are required. Secondary preparation should include 4 years each of English and math, 3 to 4 years of foreign language, and at least 2 years each of science and social studies. A personal essay must be submitted. Williams accepts the Common Application and applications via ExPAN, Apply, and College Link. AP credits are accepted. Important factors in the admissions decision are advanced placement or honor courses, recommendations by school officials, and evidence of special talent.

Procedure: Freshmen are admitted in the fall. There are early decision and deferred admissions plans. Early decision applications should be filed by November 15; regular applications, by January 1 for fall entry, along with a $50 fee. Notification of early decision is sent December 20; regular decision, April 1. 199 early decision candidates were accepted for the 1999-2000 class. A waiting list is an active part of the admissions procedure.

Financial Aid: In 1999-2000, 44% of all freshmen and 40% of continuing students received some form of financial aid. 44% of freshmen and 40% of continuing students received need-based aid. The average freshman award was $22,216. Of that total, scholarships or need-based grants averaged $19,901; loans averaged $2186; and work contracts averaged $1462. 60% of undergraduates work part time. Average annual earnings from campus work are $800. The average financial indebtedness of the 1999 graduate was $15,625. Williams is a member of CSS. The CSS/Profile or FAFSA and the college's own financial statement are required. The fall application deadline is February 1.

Computers: The mainframe is a DEC VAX 11/785. The Computer Center houses the mainframe, which has 40 ports, as well as 7 Sun Microsystems workstations and 100 assorted PCs, Macs, and graphics terminals. Additional PCs are located in the library and other academic buildings. All public-access DEC terminals and PCs are networked. All students may access the system. There are no time limits and no fees.

WISCONSIN LUTHERAN COLLEGE
Milwaukee, WI 53226 (414) 443-8811
(800) (888) 947-5884; Fax: (414) 443-8514

Full-time: 219 men, 300 women	**Faculty:** 40
Part-time: 10 men, 22 women	**Ph.D.s:** 76%
Graduate: none	**Student/Faculty:** 13 to 1
Year: semesters, summer session	**Tuition:** $12,586
Application Deadline: September 1	**Room & Board:** $4600
Freshman Class: 352 applied, 318 accepted, 164 enrolled	
ACT: 25	**VERY COMPETITIVE**

Wisconsin Lutheran College, founded in 1973 in affiliation with the Wisconsin Evangelical Lutheran Synod, offers higher education in the arts and sciences within a conservative Christian environment. The library contains 75,000 volumes, 9211 microform items, and 4000 audiovisual forms/CDs, and subscribes to 685 periodicals. Computerized library services include the card catalog, interlibrary loans, and database searching. Special learning facilities include a learning resource center, art gallery, sound studio, and electronic music lab. The 16-acre campus is in a suburban area on the western edge of Milwaukee. Including residence halls, there are 15 buildings.

Programs of Study: Wisconsin Lutheran confers B.A., B.S., and B.B.A. degrees. Bachelor's degrees are awarded in BIOLOGICAL SCIENCE (biology/biological science), BUSINESS (business administration and management), COMMUNICATIONS AND THE ARTS (art, communications, English, media arts, music, and Spanish), COMPUTER AND PHYSICAL SCIENCE (chemistry and mathematics), EDUCATION (elementary), SOCIAL SCIENCE (history, psychology, social studies, and theological studies). Math and education are the strongest academically. Business, psychology, and communication are the largest.

Special: Student-designed majors, work-study, and study abroad are offered. Internships are available in most departments.

Admissions: 90% of the 1999-2000 applicants were accepted. The ACT scores for the 1999-2000 freshman class were: 8% below 21, 25% between 21 and 23, 27% between 24 and 26, 25% between 27 and 28, and 16% above 28. 47% of the current freshmen were in the top fifth of their class; 74% were in the top two fifths. There were 2 National Merit semifinalists. 7 freshmen graduated first in their class.

Requirements: The ACT is required, with a minimum composite score of 945 on the SAT I or 20 on the ACT. Wisconsin Lutheran requires applicants to be in the upper 50% of their class. A GPA of 2.5 is required. Students should be graduates of an accredited high school or its equivalent with a minimum of 16 high school units, including 4 in English, 3 in academic electives, 3 in math, and 2 each in science, foreign language, and social studies/history. The Academic Recommendation Form must be submitted. A portfolio for art grants and an audition for music and drama grants are required. Applications may be made on-line at the Wisconsin Lutheran web site. AP and CLEP credits are accepted. Important factors in the admissions decision are leadership record and advanced placement or honor courses.

Procedure: Freshmen are admitted to all sessions. Entrance exams should be taken in the spring of the junior year. Applications should be filed by September 1 for fall entry and June 1 for summer entry, along with a $20 fee. Notification is sent on a rolling basis.

Financial Aid: In 1999-2000, of all students received some form of financial aid. 76% of freshmen and 77% of continuing students received need-based aid. The average freshman award was $12,092. Of that total, scholarships or need-based grants averaged $8064 ($17,075 maximum); loans averaged $2749 ($11,125 maximum); and work contracts averaged $1593 ($1600 maximum). 49% of undergraduates work part time. Average annual earnings from campus work are $1635. The average financial indebtedness of the 1999 graduate was $13,830. The FAFSA and the college's own financial statement are required. The fall application deadline is March 1.

Computers: The mainframe comprises 3 Compaq Proliant 2500 NT servers. 60 Pentium PCs with laser printers and 9 Mac Power PCs are available in various campus labs and the library. 22 Notebook computers are available on a checkout basis. Students may access the central network and the Internet from any computer lab or residence hall. All students may access the system. There are no time limits and no fees. The school strongly recommends that student have their own personal computer.

WITTENBERG UNIVERSITY
Springfield, OH 45501

(937) 327-6314
(800) 677-7558; Fax: (937) 327-6379

Full-time: 960 men, 1055 women	**Faculty:** 141; IIB, +$
Part-time: 30 men, 48 women	**Ph.D.s:** 97%
Graduate: none	**Student/Faculty:** 14 to 1
Year: semesters, summer session	**Tuition:** $20,906
Application Deadline: March 15	**Room & Board:** $5206
Freshman Class: 2390 applied, 2142 accepted, 625 enrolled	
SAT I Verbal/Math: 580/585	**ACT:** 25 **VERY COMPETITIVE**

Wittenberg University, founded in 1845, is a private liberal arts and sciences institution affiliated with the Evangelical Lutheran Church in America. The library contains 370,000 volumes, 90,000 microform items, and 26,000 audiovisual forms/CDs, and subscribes to 1200 periodicals. Computerized library services include the card catalog, interlibrary loans, and database searching. Special learning facilities include a learning resource center, art gallery, radio station, geology museum, and observatory. The 71-acre campus is in a suburban area 25 miles east of Dayton, 40 miles west of Columbus, and 75 miles from Cincinatti. Including residence halls, there are 35 buildings.

Programs of Study: Wittenberg confers B.A., B.F.A., B.M., and B.M.E. degrees. Bachelor's degrees are awarded in BIOLOGICAL SCIENCE (biology/biological science), BUSINESS (business administration and management), COMMUNICATIONS AND THE ARTS (communications, dramatic arts, English, fine arts, French, German, music, Russian, and Spanish), COMPUTER AND PHYSICAL SCIENCE (chemistry, computer science, earth science, geology, mathematics, and physics), EDUCATION (art, business, elementary, foreign languages, middle school, music, science, secondary, and special), HEALTH PROFESSIONS (predentistry and premedicine), SOCIAL SCIENCE (American studies, East Asian studies, economics, geography, history, international relations, philosophy, political science/government, prelaw, psychology, religion, and sociology). Education, biology, English, and political science are the strongest academically and have the largest enrollments.

Special: Special academic programs include internships, cross-registration through the Southwest Ohio Consortium, a Washington semester, work-study programs, study-abroad opportunities in many countries, accelerated degree programs, dual and student-designed majors, nondegree study, and pass/fail options. A 3-2 engineering degree is offered through Washington, Columbia, and Case Western Reserve Universities and Georgia Institute of Technology. There is also a 3-2 nursing program with Johns Hopkins University and an occupational therapy program with Washington University. There are 5 national honor societies, including Phi Beta Kappa, a freshman honors program, and 10 departmental honors programs.

Admissions: 90% of the 1999-2000 applicants were accepted. The SAT I scores for the 1999-2000 freshman class were: Verbal--13% below 500, 45% between 500 and 599, 35% between 600 and 700, and 7% above 700; Math--12% below 500, 46% between 500 and 599, 36% between 600 and 700, and 6% above 700. The ACT scores were 12% below 21, 24% between 21 and 23, 32% between 24 and 26, 21% between 27 and 28, and 12% above 28. 66% of the current freshmen were in the top fifth of their class; 95% were in the top two fifths. There were 4 National Merit finalists. 29 freshmen graduated first in their class.

Requirements: The SAT I or ACT is required. Students should have graduated from an accredited secondary school with 16 academic credits, including 4 units of English and 3 each of a foreign language, math, science, and social studies, which includes history. The SAT II: Writing test is recommended. An essay is required and an interview advised. Art students must present a portfolio, and music students must audition. Wittenberg will accept applications on-line via CollegeLink, Apply, or similar on-line applications; the school has its own application web site. AP credits are accepted. Important factors in the admissions decision are advanced placement or honor courses, recommendations by school officials, and leadership record.

Procedure: Freshmen are admitted to all sessions. Entrance exams should be taken by the fall of the senior year, but as early as possible. There are early decision, early admissions, and deferred admissions plans. Early decision applications should be filed by November 15; early action, by; December 1; regular applications, by March 15 for fall entry, December 1 for winter entry, and May 1 for summer entry, along with a $40 fee. Notification of early decision is sent January 1; regular decision, on a rolling basis after December 1. 35 early decision candidates were accepted for the 1999-2000 class. 2% of all applicants are on a waiting list.

Financial Aid: In 1999-2000, 74% of all freshmen and 72% of continuing students received need-based aid or some form of financial aid. The average freshman award was $14,500. Of that total, scholarships or need-based grants averaged $11,500 ($19,000 maximum); loans averaged $3500 ($4500 maximum); work contracts averaged $1500; and Choice Awards for studetns from Ohio attending Ohio private colleges, $950 per year. 55% of undergraduates work part time. Average annual earnings from campus work are $1500. The average financial indebtedness of the 1999 graduate was $10,000. Wittenberg is a member of CSS. The FAFSA is required. The fall application deadline is March 15.

Computers: The mainframe is a DEC VAX 11/750. There are 500 terminals and PCs located in residence halls and all academic buildings and libraries. All students may access the system 24 hours a day. There are no time limits and no fees. The school stronly recommends that all students have personal computers, specifically Pentium computers.

WOFFORD COLLEGE
Spartanburg, SC 29303-3663

(864) 597-4130
Fax: (864) 597-4149

Full-time: 576 men, 506 women	**Faculty:** 75; IIB, ++$
Part-time: 11 men, 7 women	**Ph.D.s:** 92%
Graduate: none	**Student/Faculty:** 14 to 1
Year: 4-1-4, summer session	**Tuition:** $16,975
Application Deadline: February 1	**Room & Board:** $5015
Freshman Class: 1279 applied, 1085 accepted, 307 enrolled	
SAT I Verbal/Math: 590/600	**ACT:** 24 **VERY COMPETITIVE**

Wofford College, founded in 1854, is a private institution affiliated with the United Methodist Church, offering programs in liberal arts and preprofessional studies. In addition to regional accreditation, Wofford has baccalaureate program accreditation with NASDTEC. The library contains 159,467 volumes, 67,336 microform items, and 2528 audiovisual forms/CDs, and subscribes to 585 periodicals. Computerized library services include the card catalog, interlibrary loans, and database searching. Special learning facilities include a learning resource center, art gallery, foreign language center, satellite earth station, and international studies center with simultaneous translation capabilities. The 140-acre campus is in an urban area 65 miles southeast of Charlotte. Including residence halls, there are 32 buildings.

Programs of Study: Wofford confers B.A. and B.S. degrees. Bachelor's degrees are awarded in BIOLOGICAL SCIENCE (biology/biological science), BUSINESS (accounting, banking and finance, and business economics), COMMUNICATIONS AND THE ARTS (art history and appreciation, English, French, German, and Spanish), COMPUTER AND PHYSICAL SCIENCE (chemistry, computer science, mathematics, and physics), SOCIAL SCIENCE (crosscultural studies, economics, history, humanities, philosophy, political science/government, psychology, religion, and sociology). Biology, foreign languages, and finance/accounting are the strongest academically. Business/economics, biology, and English are the largest.

Special: Special academic programs include limited cross-registration with Converse College and USC/Spartanburg, study abroad in more than 30 countries, and a concentration in Latin American and Caribbean studies. In addition, students can major in 2 fields or complete interdisciplinary, humanities, or intercultural studies majors. Wofford participates in 3-2 programs in engineering with Clemson and Columbia Universities. The January interim allows students to concentrate on a single study project, internship, or travel experience. There are 9 national honor societies, including Phi Beta Kappa.

Admissions: 85% of the 1999-2000 applicants were accepted. The SAT I scores for the 1999-2000 freshman class were: Verbal--13% below 500, 39% between 500 and 599, 42% between 600 and 700, and 7% above 700; Math--12% below 500, 38% between 500 and 599, 40% between 600 and 700, and 11% above 700. The ACT scores were 18% below 21, 32% between 21 and 23, 32% between 24 and 26, 13% between 27 and 28, and 5% above 28. 73% of the current freshmen were in the top fifth of their class; 95% were in the top two fifths. There were 4 National Merit finalists. 11 freshmen graduated first in their class.

Requirements: The SAT I or ACT is required, and SAT II: Subject tests are recommended. Applicants must be graduates of an accredited secondary school. The GED is accepted. Students should have completed 4 years each of high school English and math, 3 of lab science, and 2 each of a foreign language and social studies. An essay is required and an interview is strongly recommended. Applications are accepted on-line via Apply, Common Application, and CollegeLink. AP and CLEP credits are accepted. Important factors in the admissions decision are advanced placement or honor courses, leadership record, and personality/intangible qualities.

Procedure: Freshmen are admitted to all sessions. Entrance exams should be taken in the spring of the junior year or fall of the senior year. There are early decision, early admissions, and deferred admissions plans. Early decision applications should be filed by November 15; regular applications, by February 1 for fall entry, along with a $35 fee. Notification of early decision is sent December 1; regular decision, March 15. 137 early decision candidates were accepted for the 1999-2000 class.

Financial Aid: In 1999-2000, 83% of continuing students received some form of financial aid. 54% of freshmen and 55% of continuing students received need-based aid. The average financial aid package was $14,660. 35% of undergraduates work part time. Average annual earnings from campus work are $1200. The average financial indebtedness of the 1999 graduate was $12,260. Wofford is a member of CSS. The CSS/Profile, FAFSA, and the college's own financial statement are required. The fall application deadline is March 15.

Computers: The mainframes are a DEC VAX cluster with a DEC MicroVAX 3800 and 3100. The Wofford computer center is open 80 1/2 hours per week. Student PC labs are located in several academic buildings. Wofford's high-speed, fiber-optic campus technology network provides a multimedia intranet and voice telephone system as well as direct access to off-campus television programming,

E-mail, and the World Wide Web. All students may access the system 24 hours per day. There are no time limits and no fees.

WORCESTER POLYTECHNIC INSTITUTE
Worcester, MA 01609-2280   (508) 831-5286; Fax: (508) 831-5875

Full-time: 2067 men, 608 women	**Faculty:** 212; IIA, -$
Part-time: 61 men, 13 women	**Ph.D.s:** 95%
Graduate: 824 men, 267 women	**Student/Faculty:** 13 to 1
Year: 4 7-week terms, summer session	**Tuition:** $22,108
Application Deadline: February 1	**Room & Board:** $6912
Freshman Class: 3244 applied, 2562 accepted, 662 enrolled	
SAT I Verbal/Math: 620/660	**HIGHLY COMPETITIVE**

Worcester Polytechnic Institute, founded in 1865, is a private institution with a unique, project-oriented program of study primarily in engineering and other technical fields. In addition to regional accreditation, WPI has baccalaureate program accreditation with ABET. The library contains 350,000 volumes, 785,000 microform items, and 3342 audiovisual forms/CDs, and subscribes to 1200 periodicals. Computerized library services include the card catalog, interlibrary loans, and database searching. Special learning facilities include a learning resource center, radio station, tv station, a nuclear reactor, a robotics lab, a wind tunnel, and a greenhouse. The 80-acre campus is in a suburban area 40 miles west of Boston. Including residence halls, there are 30 buildings.

Programs of Study: WPI confers the B.S. degree. Master's and doctoral degrees are also awarded. Bachelor's degrees are awarded in BIOLOGICAL SCIENCE (biochemistry, biology/biological science, and biotechnology), BUSINESS (management engineering, management information systems, management science, and operations research), COMMUNICATIONS AND THE ARTS (English), COMPUTER AND PHYSICAL SCIENCE (actuarial science, chemistry, computer science, mathematics, and physics), ENGINEERING AND ENVIRONMENTAL DESIGN (aeronautical engineering, biomedical engineering, chemical engineering, civil engineering, computer engineering, construction management, electrical/electronics engineering, engineering, engineering physics, environmental science, fire protection engineering, industrial engineering, manufacturing engineering, materials engineering, mechanical engineering, and nuclear engineering), HEALTH PROFESSIONS (biomedical science, predentistry, premedicine, and preveterinary science), SOCIAL SCIENCE (economics, history, humanities, interdisciplinary studies, philosophy, and social science). Engineering is the largest.

Special: Students may cross-register with 9 other colleges in the Colleges of Worcester Consortium. Co-op programs in all majors, internships, work-study programs, dual majors in every subject, student-designed majors, 3-2 engineering degrees, nondegree study, and pass/fail options are all available. There is a 7-year veterinary medicine program with Tufts Veterinary School and an accelerated degree program in fire protection engineering. There are special project centers in Europe, Latin America, Asia, Australia, and Africa, as well as the U.S. There are 10 national honor societies.

Admissions: 79% of the 1999-2000 applicants were accepted. The SAT I scores for the 1999-2000 freshman class were: Verbal--8% below 500, 34% between 500 and 599, 44% between 600 and 700, and 14% above 700; Math--4% below 500, 17% between 500 and 599, 54% between 600 and 700, and 28% above 700. 69% of the current freshmen were in the top fifth of their class; 95% were in the top two fifths. There were 30 National Merit finalists in a recent year. 20 freshmen graduated first in their class.

Requirements: The SAT I or ACT is required. SAT II: Subject tests in writing, math I or II, and a science are also required. Applicants must have completed 4 years of math through precalculus and 2 lab sciences. An essay is optional. Students may apply at the school's web site or through Expan or CollegeLink. AP credits are accepted. Important factors in the admissions decision are advanced placement or honor courses, recommendations by school officials, and extracurricular activities record.

Procedure: Freshmen are admitted fall and spring. Entrance exams should be taken between April and December. There are early decision and deferred admissions plans. Early decision applications should be filed by November 15; regular applications, by February 1 for fall entry and November 15 for spring entry, along with a $60 fee. The web application is free. Notification of early decision is sent December 15; regular decision, April 1. 203 early decision candidates were accepted for the 1999-2000 class. A waiting list is an active part of the admissions procedure.

Financial Aid: In a recent year, 83% of all students received some form of financial aid. 73% of freshmen and 74% of continuing students received need-based aid. The average freshman award was $15,400. Of that total, scholarships or need-based grants averaged $9320 ($18,710 maximum); loans averaged $3320 ($5375 maximum); work contracts averaged $1050 ($1400 maximum); and outside scholarships averaged $730 ($20,000 maximum). 55% of undergraduates work part time. Average annual earnings from campus work are $850. The average financial indebtedness of the 1999 graduate was $16,000. WPI is a member of CSS. The CSS/Profile and FAFSA are required. The fall application deadline is March 1.

Computers: The UNIX-based mainframe is accessible via 8 parallel processors and a campuswide data network available in many locations, including the College Computer Center. The center also features 56 X terminals. More than 1000 IBM PC-6300 computers are available throughout the campus in general-access and specialized labs and computer classrooms. There is also a 32-PC documentation preparation lab for typesetting and desktop publishing applications. All residence halls provide access to the campus network for students bringing a computer. All students may access the system 24 hours daily. There are no time limits and no fees.

YALE UNIVERSITY
New Haven, CT 06520-8234

(203) 432-9316
Fax: (203) 432-9370

Full-time: 2656 men, 2601 women   **Faculty:** 1792; I, ++$
Part-time: none   **Ph.D.s:** 96%
Graduate: 3029 men, 2704 women   **Student/Faculty:** 3 to 1
Year: semesters, summer session   **Tuition:** $24,500
Application Deadline: December 31   **Room & Board:** $7440
Freshman Class: 13,300 applied, 2100 accepted, 1375 enrolled
SAT I Verbal/Math: 730/740   **ACT:** 31   **MOST COMPETITIVE**

Yale University, founded in 1701, is a private liberal arts institution. Some of the information in this profile is approximate. There are 11 graduate schools. In addition to regional accreditation, Yale has baccalaureate program accreditation with ABET, CAHEA, NAAB, NASM, NLN, and SAF. The 43 libraries contain 182, 263 audiovisual forms/CDs, and subscribe to 57,377 periodicals. Computerized library services include the card catalog, interlibrary loans, and database searching. Special learning facilities include an art gallery, natural history museum,

planetarium, radio station, Beinecke Rare Books and Manuscript Library, Marsh Botanical Gardens and Yale Natural Preserves, and several research centers. The 200-acre campus is in an urban area 75 miles northeast of New York City. Including residence halls, there are 200 buildings.

Programs of Study: Yale confers B.A., B.S., and B.L.S. degrees. Master's and doctoral degrees are also awarded. Bachelor's degrees are awarded in BIOLOGICAL SCIENCE (biochemistry, biology/biological science, and biophysics), COMMUNICATIONS AND THE ARTS (art, art history and appreciation, Chinese, classics, comparative literature, dramatic arts, English, film arts, French, German, Italian, Japanese, linguistics, literature, music, Portuguese, Russian, Spanish, and theater management), COMPUTER AND PHYSICAL SCIENCE (applied mathematics, astronomy, chemistry, computer science, geology, mathematics, and physics), ENGINEERING AND ENVIRONMENTAL DESIGN (architecture, biomedical engineering, chemical engineering, electrical/electronics engineering, engineering and applied science, and mechanical engineering), SOCIAL SCIENCE (African American studies, American studies, anthropology, archeology, classical/ancient civilization, East Asian studies, Eastern European studies, economics, ethics, politics, and social policy, ethnic studies, German area studies, history, history of science, humanities, Judaic studies, Latin American studies, Near Eastern studies, philosophy, political science/government, psychology, religion, sociology, and women's studies). History, biology, and English are the largest.

Special: The university offers study abroad in several countries including England, Russia, Germany, and Japan, an accelerated degree program, B.A.-B.S. degrees, dual majors, and student-designed majors. Directed Studies, a special freshman program in the humanities, offers outstanding students the opportunity to survey the Western cultural tradition. Programs in the residential colleges allow students with special interests to pursue them in a more informal atmosphere. There is a chapter of Phi Beta Kappa.

Admissions: 16% of the 1999-2000 applicants were accepted. 95% of the current freshmen were in the top fifth of their class; 99% were in the top two fifths.

Requirements: The SAT I or ACT is required. Only those applicants submitting SAT I scores must also take any 3 SAT II: Subject tests. Most successful applicants rank in the top 10% of their high school class. All students must have completed a rigorous high school program encompassing all academic disciplines. 2 essays are required and an interview is recommended. Applications are accepted on-line through the College Board's ExPAN program only. AP credits are accepted. Important factors in the admissions decision are advanced placement or honor courses, leadership record, and extracurricular activities record.

Procedure: Freshmen are admitted in the fall. Entrance exams should be taken any time up to and including the January test date in the year of application. There are early decision, early admissions, and deferred admissions plans. Early decision applications should be filed by November 1; regular applications, by December 31 for fall entry, along with a $65 fee. Notification of early decision is sent mid-December; regular decision, mid-April. 7% of all applicants are on a waiting list.

Financial Aid: In 1999-2000, 55% of all students received some form of financial aid. 38% of all students received need-based aid. The average freshman award was $16,000. Of that total, scholarships or need-based grants averaged $16,883; loans averaged $2870; and work contracts averaged $2000. Yale is a member of CSS. The CSS/Profile or FAFSA and student and parent tax returns, as well as the CSS Divorced/Separated Parents Statement and Business/Farm Supplement if applicable, are required. The fall application deadline is February 1.

Computers: The mainframes are 2 IBM 4341s, 5 DEC 11/750s, and a DEC VAX 8600. There are also IBM PCs and Macs available in dormitories, libraries, classrooms, and the computer center. All students may access the system 24 hours a day. There are no time limits and no fees.

YORK COLLEGE OF PENNSYLVANIA
York, PA 17405-7199 (717) 849-1600
(800) 455-8018; Fax: (717) 849-1607

Full-time: 1658 men, 2158 women	**Faculty:** 137; IIB, +$
Part-time: 439 men, 754 women	**Ph.D.s:** 75%
Graduate: 116 men, 79 women	**Student/Faculty:** 28 to 1
Year: semesters, summer session	**Tuition:** $6630
Application Deadline: open	**Room & Board:** $4670
Freshman Class: 3669 applied, 2612 accepted, 916 enrolled	
SAT I Verbal/Math: 549/540	**VERY COMPETITIVE**

York College of Pennsylvania, founded in 1787, is a private institution offering undergraduate programs in the liberal arts and sciences, as well as professional programs. There are 9 undergraduate schools and 1 graduate school. In addition to regional accreditation, YCP has baccalaureate program accreditation with NLN. The library contains 300,000 volumes, 500,000 microform items, and 11,000 audiovisual forms/CDs, and subscribes to 1500 periodicals. Computerized library services include interlibrary loans and database searching. Special learning facilities include a learning resource center, art gallery, radio station, TV station, a telecommunications center, Abraham Lincoln artifacts collection, rare books collection, oral history room, and a nursing education center. The 110-acre campus is in a suburban area 45 miles north of Baltimore. Including residence halls, there are 30 buildings.

Programs of Study: YCP confers B.A. and B.S. degrees. Associate and master's degrees are also awarded. Bachelor's degrees are awarded in BIOLOGICAL SCIENCE (biology/biological science), BUSINESS (accounting, banking and finance, business administration and management, international business management, management science, marketing/retailing/merchandising, office supervision and management, and sports management), COMMUNICATIONS AND THE ARTS (broadcasting, communications, English, fine arts, graphic design, music, and speech/debate/rhetoric), COMPUTER AND PHYSICAL SCIENCE (chemistry, computer programming, information sciences and systems, mathematics, and physical sciences), EDUCATION (business, elementary, science, and secondary), ENGINEERING AND ENVIRONMENTAL DESIGN (engineering management and mechanical engineering), HEALTH PROFESSIONS (medical laboratory technology, medical records administration/services, nuclear medical technology, nursing, premedicine, and respiratory therapy), SOCIAL SCIENCE (behavioral science, criminal justice, history, humanities, parks and recreation management, political science/government, prelaw, psychology, and sociology). Mechanical engineering, nursing, and education are the strongest academically. Education, nursing, and business are the largest.

Special: YCP offers internships for upper-division students and co-op programs in mechanical engineering. Exchange programs are offered with the University of Ripon and York St. John in York, England; Honam University in Kwanju, South Korea; and Pontificia Universidad Catolica del Equador in Quito, Equador. Dual majors in any combination, nondegree study, and pass/fail options are available. There are 2 national honor societies.

Admissions: 71% of the 1999-2000 applicants were accepted. The SAT I scores for the 1999-2000 freshman class were: Verbal--17% below 500, 55% between

500 and 599, 23% between 600 and 700, and 5% above 700; Math--18% below 500, 59% between 500 and 599, 20% between 600 and 700, and 3% above 700. 39% of the current freshmen were in the top fifth of their class; 76% were in the top two fifths. 4 freshmen graduated first in their class.

Requirements: The SAT I or ACT is required. YCP requires applicants to be in the upper 60% of their class. A GPA of 2.5 is required. In addition, applicants must be graduates of an accredited secondary school or have a GED certificate. 15 academic credits are required, including 4 units in English, 3 or 4 in math, 2 or 3 in science, 2 in history, and 1 in social studies. Music students must audition. Applications can be downloaded or sent on-line via the York College home page: www.yep.edu. AP and CLEP credits are accepted. Important factors in the admissions decision are advanced placement or honor courses, leadership record, and extracurricular activities record.

Procedure: Freshmen are admitted fall and spring. Entrance exams should be taken in the spring of the junior year or the fall of the senior year. There is a deferred admissions plan. Application deadlines are open; there is a $20 application fee. Notification is sent on a rolling basis.

Financial Aid: In 1999-2000, 75% of all freshmen and 81% of continuing students received some form of financial aid. 45% of freshmen and 56% of continuing students received need-based aid. The average freshman award was $5734. Of that total, scholarships or need-based grants averaged $3130 ($10,924 maximum); loans averaged $2834 ($6625 maximum); and work contracts averaged $1410 ($1600 maximum). 20% of undergraduates work part time. Average annual earnings from campus work are $1500. The average financial indebtedness of the 1999 graduate was $14,354. YCP is a member of CSS. The FAFSA, the college's own financial statement and the the PHEAA are required. The fall application deadline is April 15.

Computers: The mainframes are a Sun Enterprise 450s and a Sun Ultra SPARCS. All classrooms, offices, and student residence rooms are directly connected to the network, providing access to E-mail, the Internet, and the College's own intranet. 11 computer labs and 240 PCs are available for student use. 700 software packages are available on the campus network. All students may access the system. There are no time limits and no fees.

ALPHABETICAL INDEX